Accommodation

These are not hotels, but historic properties in which accommodation can be arranged. The standard ranges from basic comfort to ultimate luxury.

See page 27

Civil Weddings

Places with a marriage licence where the ceremony itself can take place. Many will also be able to provide facilities for receptions.

See page 29

Corporate Hospitality

Properties which are able to accommodate corporate functions, wedding receptions and events. Individual entries will give greater detail.

See pages 30 - 32

Special Events

Special Events, historical re-enactments, gardening festivals, country and craft fairs, concerts and fireworks, car and steam rallies are now an established part of the summer season and throughout the year.

Don't miss our Movie Map on page 53

See pages 33 - 37

WWW Websites

Many properties have their own website with more extensive information. If you want to make life easy, without having to type in each address, all you have to do is go to www.hudsons.co.uk and click on the direct link to any of these sites. Make your first stop

www.hudsons.co.uk

See page 38 - 45

Plant Sales

Many historic properties and gardens offer collections of rare and unusual plants not generally available.

See page 46 - 47

Open All Year

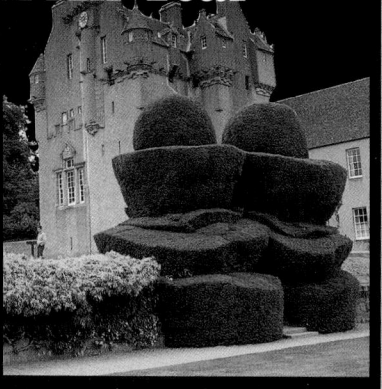

Properties and/or their grounds included in this list are open all or most of the year.

See pages 49 - 52

Access to Grant Aided Properties

English Heritage, as well as managing and opening properties in its care, has other equally important roles. It gives grants towards the cost of repairing outstanding buildings in private, National Trust and other ownerships. These grants are given subject to appropriate public access being given, details of which are incorporated in this section.

See pages 541

HUDSON'S

Gardens are the focus of much attention this year. They form the centrepiece of a worldwide campaign by the British Tourist Authority. The National Trust is also placing special emphasis on promoting the many gardens in their care.

A preoccupation with gardens and gardening, coupled with a climate favourable to a wide variety of plant species have produced in the British Isles some of the finest gardens in the world. They span many centuries in age and style. The process has not stopped. Private owners in particular continue to further enhance existing gardens and create new ones.

Garden visiting is a pastime for all seasons – providing you visit the right garden at the right time of year. In Spring, Summer and Autumn the choice is enormous.

Regular readers of *Hudson's* will also notice changes in region and county placements. In England we have listed properties within counties but otherwise, in co-ordination with The National Trust and English Heritage, have placed them in regions whose boundaries are aligned with the Regional Development Authorities. In Scotland, we have followed the boundaries of the Area Tourist Boards. Prefacing each section is a feature on a garden within the region.

Norman Hudson
Editor

Hudson's Historic Houses & Gardens

Editor .... Norman Hudson

Editorial/Production .... Edwina Brash

Administration .... Jennie Carwithen

Graphic Design .... KC Graphics

Page Layout & Maps .... Taurus Graphics

Scanning & Pre-press .... Spot-On Reprographics

Sales .... Fiona Rolt

Consultant/Maps .... Patrick Lane

Printed by .... E T Heron & Co Ltd

Distribution -
UK & Europe: .... Portfolio, tel: 020 8997 9000
USA:.......... The Globe Pequot Press, tel: 001 203 458 4505

Cover picture:
UK: Charlecote Park, Warwickshire.
© National Trust Photographic Library/Matthew Antrobus

USA: Newby Hall, Yorkshire
© R Compton

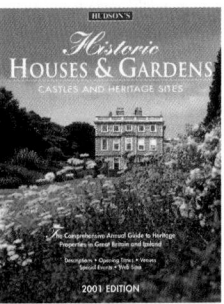

UK   USA

Published by:
Norman Hudson & Company,
High Wardington House, Upper Wardington,
Banbury, Oxfordshire OX17 1SP, UK
Tel: 01295 750750   Fax: 01295 750800
e-mail: enquiries@hudsons.co.uk
website: www.hudsons.co.uk

ISBN: 0-9531426-5-5

Co-published in the USA by:
The Globe Pequot Press,
246 Goose Lane, Guilford, Connecticut 06437, USA

**Library of Congress Cataloging-in-Publication
data is available.**
ISBN: 0-7627-0881-6

Foreword

BRITISH TOURIST AUTHORITY

by David Quarmby

Chairman, British Tourist Authority

There is no question that our heritage and its history are at the heart of Britain's attraction to overseas visitors. Whether visiting historic houses, gardens and castles or seeing some of our wonderful museums, galleries and theatre, experiencing our heritage remains the number one reason for visiting our shores. *Hudson's* provides a definitive guide to the best that Britain has to offer.

Britain's history and tradition is our unique selling point – no other country rivals us in the quality and breadth of what we have to offer. As we in the British Tourist Authority plan our promotional programmes in 27 countries round the world, we recognise the vital importance of sustaining this interest whilst also promoting our rich contemporary culture.

'The garden' is one of the BTA's themes for the year 2001. In Britain we have the best and most interesting choice of gardens anywhere in the world. Many are featured in this splendid guide and will, I'm quite sure, provide a source of delight and inspiration to our visitors – whatever the time of year. I shall be among them myself!

David Quarmby

Exbury Gardens, Hampshire.

Cottesbrooke Hall Gardens, Northamptonshire.

"The HHA Friends scheme provides amazing value for the interested house and gardens visitor..."

Bodrhyddan, Wales.

The HHA is a group of highly individualistic and diverse properties most of which are still lived-in family houses. They range from the great palaces to small manor houses.

Many HHA member properties are open to the public and offer free admission to Friends of the HHA.

Blenheim Palace, Oxfordshire.

Dalemain, Cumbria.

Somerleyton Hall, Suffolk.

Borde Hill Garden, Sussex.

Coton Manor Garden, Northamptonshire.

Tresco Abbey Gardens, Cornwall.

Benington Lordship Gardens, Hertfordshire.

Forde Abbey, Dorset.

Hestercombe Gardens, Somerset.

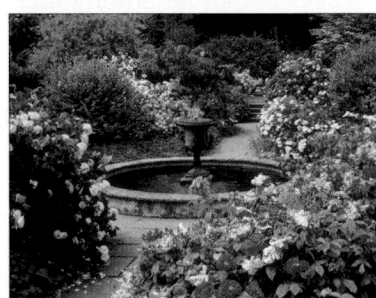

Newby Hall & Gardens, Yorkshire.

HISTORIC HOUSES ASSOCIATION

Become a Friend of the HHA and visit nearly 300 privately owned houses and gardens for FREE.

Other benefits:

- Receive the quarterly magazine of the HHA which gives news and features about the Association, its members and our heritage
- Take advantage of organised tours in the UK and overseas
- Join the specially arranged visits to houses, some of which are not usually open to the public

KINGSTON BAGPUIZE HOUSE, OXFORDSHIRE

LEVENS HALL GARDENS, CUMBRIA

Richard Wilkin, Director General of the HHA, explains . . .

"It is not generally realised that two-thirds of Britain's built heritage remains in private ownership. There are more privately-owned houses, castles and gardens open to the public than are opened by the National Trust, English Heritage and their equivalents in Scotland and Wales put together.

Successive Governments have recognised the private owner as the most economic and effective guardian of this heritage. But the cost of maintaining these properties is colossal, and the task is daunting. The owners work enormously hard and take a pride in preserving and presenting this element of Britain's heritage.

The HHA helps them do this by:

- *representing their interests in Government*
- *providing an advisory service for houses – taxation, conservation, security, regulations, etc.*
- *running charities assisting disabled visitors, conserving works of art and helping promote educational facilities*

There is a fascinating diversity of properties to visit free with a Friends of the HHA card – from the great treasure houses such as Blenheim and Castle Howard through to small manor houses. What makes these places so special is their individuality and the fact that they are generally still lived in – often by the same family that has owned them through centuries of British history. As well as the stunning gardens which surround the houses, there are over 60 additional wonderful gardens to visit.

We have held the subscription rate again this year, so it remains outstanding value for money at £28.00 for an individual or £40.00 for two people at the same address. If you do wish to become a Friend of the HHA, and I very much hope you will, then you can join, using your credit/debit card by calling 01462 896688 or simply fill in the form below."

HOLKHAM HALL, NORFOLK

Membership: Single £28, Double £40, £10 additional Friend at same address. Members of NADFAS, CLA and NACF are offered special rates of £25 Individual and £37 Double (at same address).

FRIENDS APPLICATION FORM HHHG/01

PLEASE USE BLOCK CAPITALS *DELETE AS APPROPRIATE

MR/MRS/MS or MR & MRS* INITIALS _____

SURNAME _____

ADDRESS _____

_____

_____ POST CODE _____

ADDITIONAL FRIENDS AT SAME ADDRESS

_____

I/We* are members of NADFAS/NACF/CLA (please circle name of organisation to which you belong) our membership number is: _____

☐ I/We* enclose remittance of £_____ payable to the Historic Houses Association.

☐ I/We* have completed the direct debit adjacent.

Please return to: Historic Houses Association, Friends Membership Department, Heritage House, PO Box 21, Baldock, Hertfordshire SG7 5SH. **Tel: (01462) 896688**

PHOTOCOPIES OF THIS FORM ARE ACCEPTABLE

INSTRUCTION TO YOUR BANK TO PAY DIRECT DEBITS

Please complete Parts 1 to 5 to instruct your Bank to make payments directly from your account. Then return the form to: Historic Houses Association, Membership Department, Heritage House, PO Box 21, Baldock, Herts, SG7 5SH.

1. Name and full postal address of your Bank

_____

_____

_____

Your Bank may decline to accept instructions to pay Direct Debits from some types of accounts.

2. Name of account holder _____

3. Account number ☐☐☐☐☐☐☐☐

4. Bank sort code ☐☐ ☐☐ ☐☐

Originator's identification number 9 3 0 5 8 7

Originator's reference (office use only) _____

5. Your instructions to the Bank and signature.

- I instruct you to pay Direct Debits for my annual subscription from my account at the request of the Historic Houses Association.
- The amounts are variable and may be debited on various dates.
- I understand that the Historic Houses Association may change the amounts and dates only after giving me prior notice of not less than 21 days.
- Please cancel all previous Standing Order and Direct Debiting instructions in favour of the Historic Houses Association.
- I will inform the Bank in writing if I wish to cancel this instruction.
- I understand that if any Direct Debit is paid which breaks the terms of the instruction, the Bank will make a refund.

Signature(s) _____

_____

_____

_____ Date _____

DIRECT Debit Completion of the form above ensures that your subscription will be paid automatically on the date that it is due. You may cancel the order at any time. The Association guarantees that it will only use this authority to deduct annually from your account an amount equal to the annual subscription then current for your class of membership.

IF COMPLETING THE DIRECT DEBIT FORM, YOU MUST ALSO COMPLETE THE APPLICATION FORM.

Tintinhull House Garden ~ view of the lily pool.

Rooted in history, growing forever

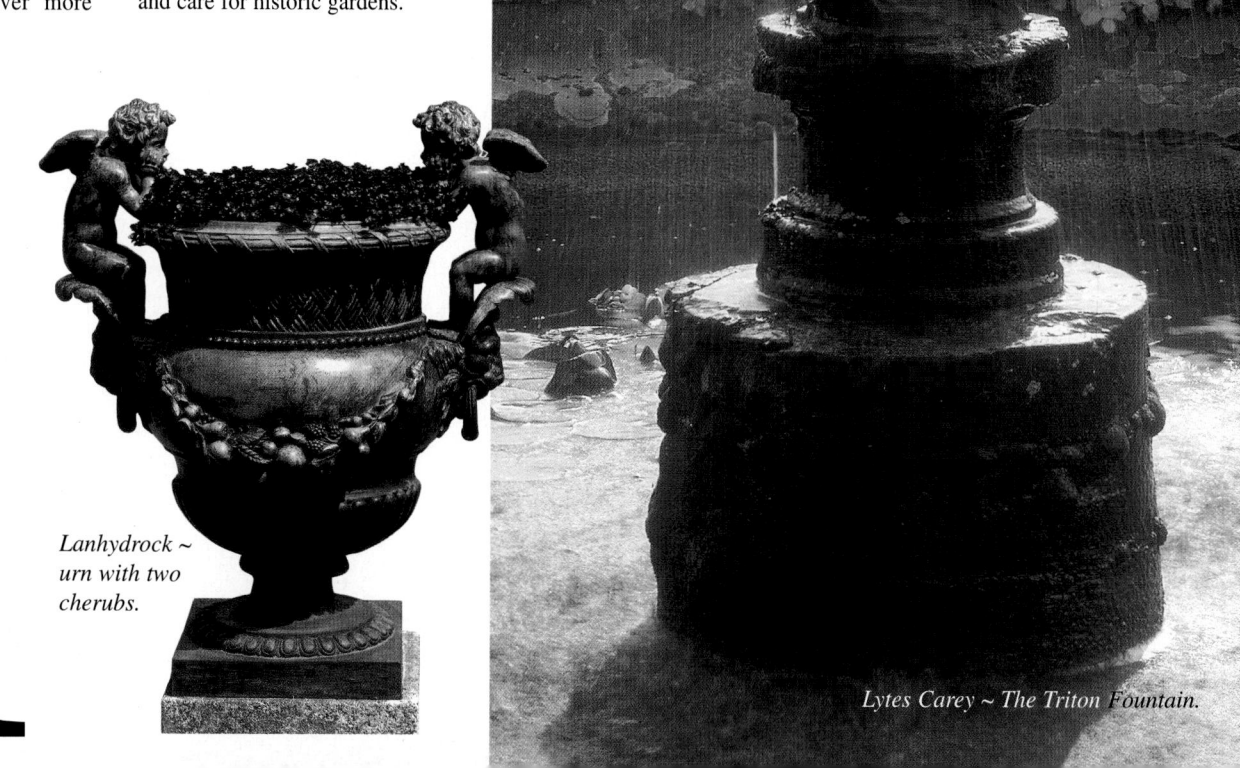

The National Trust looks after the largest and most important collection of historic gardens and cultivated plants in the world. Throughout 2001 the Trust will be celebrating its role as the world's leading garden conservation organisation, highlighting the work involved in caring for this living part of our cultural heritage and the need to consider the future of historic gardens at the beginning of a new millennium.

A major international gardens conference, a season of special nationwide garden events, an exhibition of contemporary art and craft inspired by historic gardens and a programme of lectures will focus on the Trust's collection of over 200 gardens and landscape parks.

National Trust 'Gardens Year 2001' has something to offer everyone who loves gardening and gardens from the horticultural professional to the millions who are passionate amatuer gardeners. It provides an opportunity for visitors to see what lies behind the Trust's garden gates, to share their own knowledge and passion for gardening and discover more

about the Trust's collection of gardens, from those of internationally repute to less well-known garden treasures.

As part of Gardens Year celebrations, visitors can enjoy hundreds of different garden events taking place nationwide throughout the season. From Spring Plant Fairs to Paint the Garden and Tree Dressing days, the 2001 programme of activities explores the multifaceted nature of National Trust gardens, offering visitors the opportunity to discover more about their history, design and plant collections as well as the special gardening skills and behind the scenes work needed to maintain and care for historic gardens.

Lanhydrock ~ urn with two cherubs.

Lytes Carey ~ The Triton Fountain.

Wallington ~ the Walled Garden.

Colby ~ Woodland Garden.

Beningbrough Hall ~ the Walled Garden.

Blickling Hall ~ the Parterre.

The National Trust is also planning an exciting new exhibition of contemporary art and craft, inspired by and located within several Trust gardens. 'VISTA' aims to bring together some of the country's leading artists, commissioned by the Trust to create new work celebrating the legacy of craftmanship to be found within gardens in the charity's care.

Prior Park ~ the Palladian Bridge.

Ham House ~ the Knot Garden.

Some National Trust Garden Facts and Figures:

- The National Trust looks after the largest and most important collection of historic gardens and cultivated plants in the world.

- Over 200 gardens and landscape parks are open to the public throughout England, Wales and Northern Ireland.

- Seven out of the top ten visited National Trust properties are those with gardens or landscape parks.

- The National Trust employs over 450 skilled gardeners and hundreds more garden volunteers.

- National Trust gardens encompass over 400 years of history.

- The National Trust is the world's leading conservation charity concerned for the long-term future of our garden heritage.

Visitors can find more information about National Trust gardens and 'Gardens Year 2001' by telephoning: 020 8315 1111.

Dunham Massey ~ Azaleas and Foxgloves.

Powis Castle ~ view from the Top Terrace.

CADW
WELSH HISTORIC MONUMENTS

The National Assembly for Wales
Cathays Park
Cardiff CF10 3NQ
Telephone: 029 2050 0200   Fax: 029 2082 6375
E-mail: cadw@wales.gsi.gov.uk

Cadw is the executive agency within the **National Assembly for Wales** that carries out the Assembly's statutory responsibilities to protect, conserve and promote an appreciation of the built heritage of Wales.

Cadw gives grant aid for the repair or restoration of outstanding historic buildings. Usually it is a condition of grant that the owner or occupier should allow some degree of public access to the property. Conditions of grant remain in force for ten years.

Details of properties grant aided by Cadw and to which the public currently enjoys a right of access can be found on Cadw's website: **www.cadw.wales.gov.uk**

Cadw's website contains a wide range of information, including details of buildings and monuments in its care and, where appropriate, related public access.

Cadw encourages you to visit these properties, as well as buildings and monuments in its care.

THE CHURCHES
CONSERVATION TRUST

Caring for historic churches throughout England

St Mary's, Lead,
North Yorkshire

St Mary's is just one of the 50 exceptional churches chosen by The Churches Conservation Trust to illustrate the gems it has in its care. *Your Starter for 50* churches all have something specially interesting or beautiful about them – and can be visited *free* throughout the year. Our map shows where they all are.

The job of The Churches Conservation Trust is to repair and preserve churches throughout England of outstanding architectural and historic interest when they are no longer needed for regular parish use. In many, you can see the results of conservation work we have undertaken to protect crumbling stone, or ancient stained glass or even mediaeval wall paintings.

We welcome visitors to all our churches; some are opened daily, others have more limited opening times and still others have nearby keyholders. Opening arrangements for the featured churches are included overleaf.

We have over 300 churches but why not begin your exploration by sampling the glories of our selected *Starter for 50*?

11

BRISTOL

Bristol, St John ▼

St John's is the sole survivor of four Bristol churches built on the city wall in the 12th century and its picturesque tower and spire surmount the old North Gate. Above an earlier 14th century vaulted crypt, the present Perpendicular church was founded by Walter Frampton (d 1388) whose tomb and fine effigy are in the north wall of the chancel. The small, but impressively tall interior has interesting and lovely fittings, mostly 17th century, and an air of mercantile splendour.

Bottom of Broad Street at intersection with Nelson Street, ST587732.
Open Tues-Fri 11-4.
or 07931 578 068.

CORNWALL

St Anthony-in-Roseland, St Anthony ▶

St Anthony's stands behind Place, looking across the creek to St Mawes, and is unusual in surviving in its 13th century form without later additions. Pevsner thought it 'the best example in the county of what a parish church was like in the 12th and 13th centuries.' The ingenious 1850 restoration was carried out by Revd C W Carlyon, an amateur architect, and a cousin of the Sprys of Place whose monuments are in the church. There is a fine Norman doorway which may have come from Plympton Priory nearby.

20m SW of St Austell off A3078 and opp. St Mawes, SW855320.
Open daily.

Boris Baggs

Boris Baggs

Boris Baggs

CUMBRIA

◀ Brougham, St Ninian

Known locally as Ninekirks, this lovely church is reached down a long track off the A66, and stands in fields above a bend in the River Eamont. In 1660 Lady Anne Clifford completely rebuilt the Norman church and it remains a fascinating example of what is known as Gothic Survival style, with furniture and fittings almost untouched. The simple whitewashed interior has clear glass in most windows and a stone-flagged floor. The family pews, complete with canopies, the box pews and benches, communion rails and screen, and the three-decker pulpit are all of late 17th century oak and of excellent quality.

3m E of Penrith off A66, NY559299. Open daily.

DORSET

▼ Winterborne Tomson, St Andrew

In a gentle farmyard setting, built of grey stone and flint with a bell-turret of board and tile, this small 11th century village church is a delight. It enchants on sight and is all one could hope for inside. Archbishop Wake of Canterbury presented the box pews, pulpit and other furnishings early in the 18th century and most are still there, under a barrel-roof whose arches continue over the apse. They are all of oak, bleached through the years to a magical silvery grey. The church was gently repaired in 1931 using money raised from the sale of Thomas Hardy manuscripts.

8m W of Wimborne Minster off A31, SY885974.
Open daily.

Christopher Dalton

KENT

Sandwich, St Peter ▶

The tower and Flemish cupola of this great town centre church, as well as the gable of its southeastern vestry, all show the influence of 16th and 17th century refugees from the Low Countries. But other parts of this church have stood for 900 years, so much of what we see was fashioned in the 1200s and 1300s. Mediaeval roofs, exquisite 14th century tombs under arches and a host of treasures, ancient and modern, may be enjoyed in this lofty, light and airy church, where we learn much about the history and life of the town and Cinque Port. St Peter's has a busy programme of events throughout the year.

In town centre, TR331580.
Usually open daily, or key available next door.

LINCOLNSHIRE

◀ Kingerby, St Peter

Set by fields in leafy countryside, this is a beautiful and unspoilt church. Its solid rustic tower may date from the 12th century or even earlier and the rest is mainly from the 13th and 14th. The nave roof timbers date from the 17th century. Three splendid 14th century monuments to the Disney family survive, two in the south aisle and one in the chancel. The church also had a north aisle, now long demolished. The church escaped Victorian restorers and the appealing simplicity of the interior remains.

5m NW of Market Rasen, TF057929.
Open daily.

NORFOLK

Hales, St Margaret ▼

Known far and wide for its thatched roofs and round tower, Hales is Norfolk's best example of a 12th century Norman church essentially in its original form, with fascinating arcading around the apse, a magnificent north doorway of somewhat later date and a very good one to the south too. There are wall paintings including a St Christopher, the remains of a 15th century screen and a beautiful 15th century font. Despite its solitary position, remote from its village, it remains a place of pilgrimage for architectural students and church crawlers alike.

12m SE of Norwich and W of A146, TM384962.
Usually open daily April-Sept,
or keyholder nearby.

Christopher Dalton   *Christopher Dalton*

NORFOLK

King's Lynn, St Nicholas Chapel ▲

This striking building, splendidly light and spacious within, was built as a chapel of ease to St Margaret's. The fine tower is Early English, with a spire added by Sir George Gilbert Scott in 1869, but most of the church you see was finished in 1419. Its glories include a superb two-storied south porch, vaulted and richly ornamented, huge east and west windows and a very beautiful angel roof. There are fine fittings and interesting monuments, many commemorating Lynn merchants through the centuries.

St Anne's St, TF618205.
Key at True's Yard, call Andrew Lane
01553 770 479.

SUSSEX

▲ Warminghurst, The Holy Sepulchre

Up a narrow lane and on a walled bank with fine views to the south, Warminghurst church is one of the delights of Sussex. A simple mainly 13th century sandstone building, its 18th century interior is magical and unforgettable. A triple-arched screen, under a tympanum carrying a splendid Royal Arms robed in crimson drapery, separates nave from chancel; a complete set of box pews and a clerk's pew and pulpit fill the nave; there are hatchments and monuments from the 18th century and earlier; and the natural wood furnishings and uneven floor are all lit through clear glass.

10m N of Worthing off A24, TQ117169.
Keyholder nearby 01903 892 353.

WEST YORKSHIRE

Harewood, All Saints ▼

All Saints stands in the park of Harewood House and was built around 1410. Sir George Gilbert Scott's restoration in 1862–63 reordered the interior considerably to accord with the Victorians' idea of a mediaeval church. Inside, the building is severe and the lack of decorative carving contrasts strongly with its greatest treasures: the six superb alabaster tombs and pairs of effigies of the owners of Harewood and nearby Gawthorpe, dating from 1419 to 1510. These provide a unique display of costume, armour and funerary design during those years. There is good Victorian glass by Kempe and others.

6m N of Leeds off A61, SE314451
Open 10-6 April-October, 7 days a week. At other times call 0113 288 6331

Boris Baggs

Boris Baggs   *Christopher Dalton*

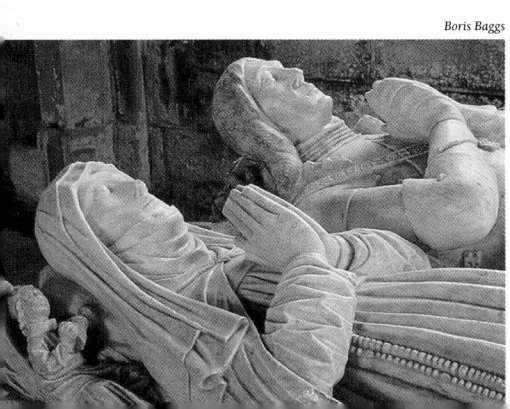

NORTH YORKSHIRE

Lead, St Mary ▲

Known as the Ramblers' Church this peaceful and well-visited place lies close to the battlefield of Towton where the wearisome Wars of the Roses ended. The field around is full of low earthworks, indicating the site of a manor house for which this was surely the chapel. It is tiny and rustic and the 14th century single cell building with a bell-cote is fitted with 18th century woodwork and earlier open benches. The floor includes mediaeval coffin lids and the font may be from an earlier church.

10m SE of Wetherby off B1217, SE464369.
Open daily.

WORCESTERSHIRE

Lower Sapey, St Bartholomew Old Church ▲

This humble two cell building is a rare survival: a rustic Norman or late Saxon church, memorably set in beautiful and remote country next to a 17th century farmhouse and close to the site of a Saxon settlement. Some alterations were made in the 14th century, others in the 18th, but the importance and charm of this church is that little has changed from its early times. Years of neglect followed the building of a new church in the 1870s, but the efforts of local people and its vesting in the Trust in 1994 secured its future.

13m NW of Worcester off B4204, SO699602.
Open daily.

Your Starter for 50 churches in the care of The Churches Conservation Trust

All churches on the map are opened regularly or have keyholders nearby*. Further details may be obtained by ordering the leaflets below.

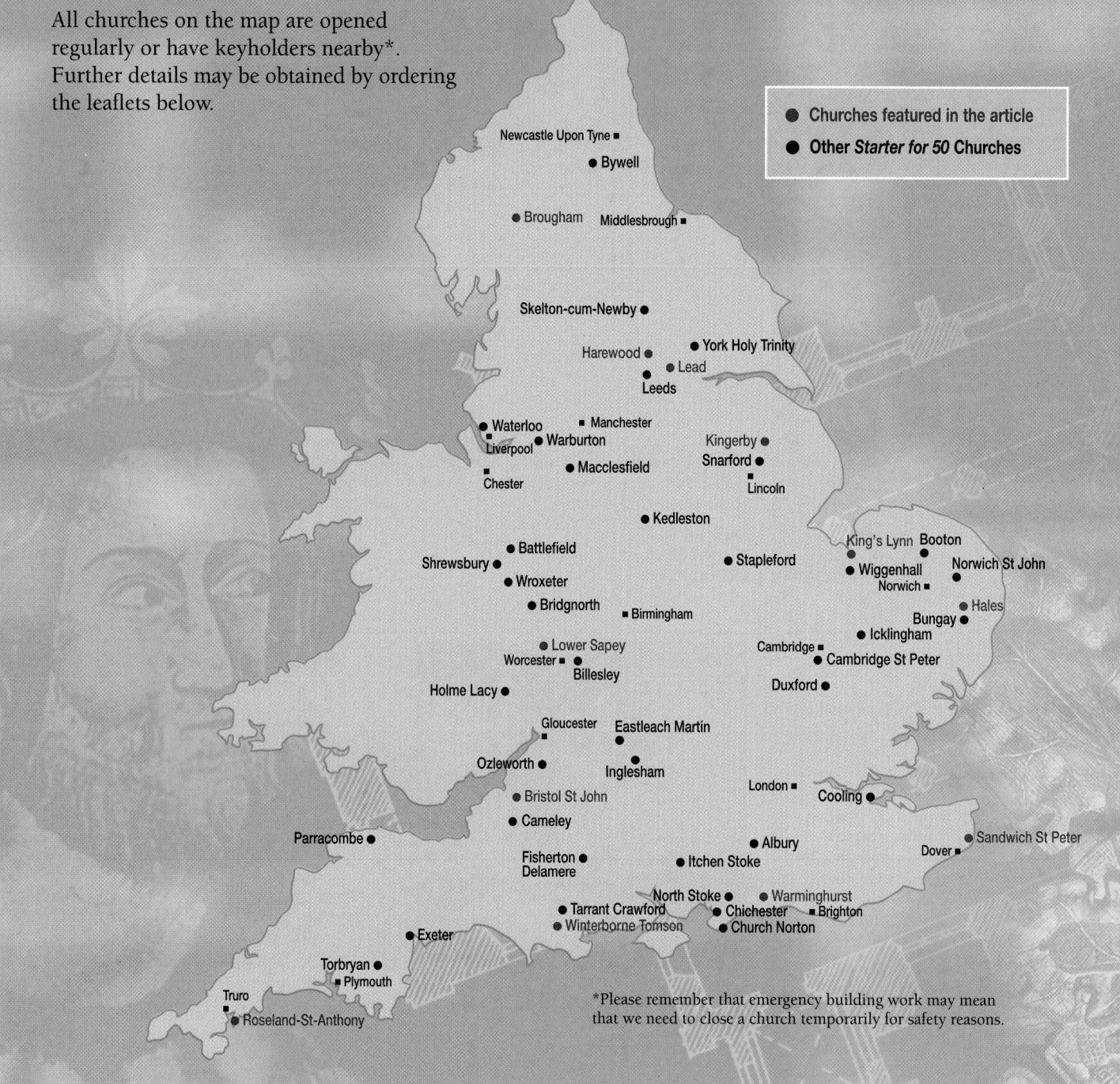

● Churches featured in the article
● Other *Starter for 50* Churches

Newcastle Upon Tyne
Bywell
Brougham
Middlesbrough
Skelton-cum-Newby
Harewood
York Holy Trinity
Lead
Leeds
Waterloo
Manchester
Liverpool
Warburton
Kingerby
Snarford
Chester
Macclesfield
Lincoln
Kedleston
Battlefield
Shrewsbury
King's Lynn
Booton
Wroxeter
Stapleford
Wiggenhall
Norwich St John
Norwich
Bridgnorth
Birmingham
Hales
Bungay
Lower Sapey
Icklingham
Worcester
Cambridge
Billesley
Cambridge St Peter
Holme Lacy
Duxford
Gloucester
Eastleach Martin
Ozleworth
Inglesham
London
Bristol St John
Cooling
Cameley
Parracombe
Sandwich St Peter
Albury
Dover
Fisherton Delamere
Itchen Stoke
North Stoke
Warminghurst
Tarrant Crawford
Chichester
Brighton
Exeter
Winterborne Tomson
Church Norton
Torbryan
Plymouth
Truro
Roseland-St-Anthony

*Please remember that emergency building work may mean that we need to close a church temporarily for safety reasons.

Complete and send to The Churches Conservation Trust, 89 Fleet Street, London, EC4Y 1DH

Name .... Title ....

Address .... Postcode ....

Please send me: *Your Starter for 50* leaflet(s). Please tick beside the area(s) you are interested in

North ☐   South West ☐   South East ☐   Central ☐   East ☐

Full List of Churches in the care of The Churches Conservation Trust ☐

County leaflets, please specify county(ies) ....

HHH2

The Maze at Chatsworth in Derbyshire.

MAZES
and labyrinths

The maze is a device of great antiquity. The labyrinth symbol is found in many parts of the world. Although spread across different civilisations and cultures and during different periods of history, it is remarkable that an archetypal labyrinth design seems to have prevailed. Some of the earliest turf and stone labyrinths found in Scandinavia are thought to be 3,000 years old. How does a labyrinth differ from a maze? True labyrinths have a single, meandering pathway leading from the entrance to the centre and sometimes back out again. One pathway 'unicursal' was the only form used for thousands of years and it was only after the Middle Ages that 'multi-cursal' or puzzle mazes with dead ends, false paths and choices to confuse, became familiar.

We can readily understand the appeal and intrigue of a hedge puzzle maze but what was the purpose of a 'unicursal' labyrinth that does not hide the goal from view and is merely marked on the ground by stones or turf? Its origin remains a mystery. While as

■ *The Maze at Leeds Castle, Kent.*

a symbol and concept often connected with the Minoan Temple at Knossos c1500 BC, and later popular with the Romans, there is evidence of labyrinths from much earlier time carved on rock faces in Africa and among remote jungle-dwelling tribes in Sumatra.

They had a religious significance also. Early Christians adopted the maze as they did other pagan symbols. In their symbolism the puzzle or labyrinth probably represented the vicissitudes of life before the goal of Heaven could be obtained.

Mazes have been associated with British historic houses since Tudor times when they often had Royal connections. In the 19th century there was a resurgence of interest and there has been a remarkable revival since 1970. Britain has led the field and has the world's greatest concentration and variety of mazes and labyrinths. They take various forms: the traditional hedge maze, modern path and grass mazes, pavement mazes, colour mazes and mirror mazes. The Marquess of Bath at Longleat is a great enthusiast but by far the leading protagonist and most experience modern maze designer and builder is Adrian Fisher who has been responsible for many of the great diversity of contemporary British mazes, pioneering new forms of construction.

The best and simplest way to experience the compelling mystery is to walk or run through the various mazes and labyrinths open to the public.

■ *Aerial view of the Sun Maze and Lunar Labyrinth at Longleat in Wiltshire.*

MAZES

■ *The Love Labyrinth at Longleat, Wiltshire.*

■ *Enjoying the maze at Leeds Castle, Kent.*

Mazes associated with historic houses and gardens which can be found in *Hudson's* are:

Buckinghamshire	Chenies Manor	turf and hedge
Cambridgeshire	Ely Cathedral	pavement
Cheshire	Tatton Park	hedge
Cornwall	Glendurgan	hedge
North Wales	Bodelwyddan	hedge
Derbyshire	Chatsworth	hedge
Herefordshire	Burford House	hedge
Hertfordshire	Hatfield House	low box
Kent	Hever Castle	hedge
Kent	Leeds Castle	hedge
Lancashire	Leighton Hall	turf
Lincolnshire	Doddington Hall	turf
London	Capel Manor	hedge
Highlands & Skye	Cawdor Castle	hedge
North Humberside	Burton Agnes Hall	hedge
Oxfordshire	Blenheim Palace	colour
Oxfordshire	Blenheim Palace	hedge
Oxfordshire	Greys Court	turf
Borders	Traquair House	hedge
Perthshire	Scone Palace	hedge
Suffolk	Kentwell Hall	courtyard
Suffolk	Somerleyton Hall	hedge
Surrey	Hampton Court Palace	hedge
Sussex	Parham Park	turf
Warwickshire	Ragley Hall	breezeblock
Wiltshire	Longleat	hedge

At Kentwell Hall, Suffolk, the maze is in the form of a brick-paved mosaic Tudor Rose. The owner, Patrick Phillips, takes the view that the concept of a 'goal' at the centre seems somewhat sterile as few mazes have a centre which is worth the effort when you get there, so the Kentwell maze has a start at the house and 'leads' eventually to the gardens. The maze is sited in the Courtyard, to pave that area in an interesting way, and to adapt the Tudor concept of a Knot Garden. Visitors have to 'submit' to the discipline of the maze which can be achieved merely by the path being clearly defined. Most obey the rules if they are interested. Where early mazes were largely two-dimensional, this differs by the introduction of junctions which notionally make it three-dimensional in that one path is deemed to pass 'over' or 'under' another.

The yew maze planted in 1906 by William Waldorf Astor at Hever Castle, Kent was a typical Victorian revival of a Renaissance tradition. It is situated at the edge of the Castle Courtyard, measuring 80' x 80' with almost a 1/4 mile of pathways inside. A very recent and exciting addition at Hever is the water maze, opened in 1997. This unique water maze with its 27m diameter pond and 4m high central folly and cascade is planted with a large collection of aquatic plants and ferns and complements the yew maze. Children and adults alike are challenged to avoid various water barriers and to reach the folly without getting wet. The stepping-stone path leads to water obstacles formed by jets of water, making the visitor divert to find an alternative way to the centre. Having reached the centre of the folly, visitors are greeted with a special water feature – a spiral staircase takes visitors to the top for an elevated view of the maze.

■ *The brick-paved mosaic Tudor Rose Maze at Kentwell Hall, Suffolk.*

■ *The Maze at Chatsworth, Derbyshire.*

■ *Aerial view of the Maze at Leeds Castle.*

At Chatsworth, Derbyshire the garden which has been made within the foundation walls of the old conservatory has in part been created as a maze. Planted in 1962 with 1,209 yew trees, its setting is sensational. The North part of the garden is devoted to Autumn flowers, dahlias and Michaelmas daisies and the South end is all lupins. Peonies are planted round the outside of the foundation walls, the whole overlooked by towering Wellingtonias. The hedge maze at Leeds Castle, Kent (designed by Adrian Fisher) was opened in 1998 by Princess Alexandra. It is a topiary castle with castellated yew hedges, an entrance bridge and a central tower. Inside it is challenging and teasing in several ways. From its central raised goal, the view from its stone parapet rewards the visitor with images of a Queen's crown and chalice, both laid out in the rows of the hedges. Looking down, visitors see splashing water and light 20' below them. Beneath the stone tower they discover the entrance to an underground grotto decorated with thousands of seashells, with statues in niches, and water cascading over a grotesque face. Still deeper, a 90' underground passage beneath the hedges of the maze leads through a dramatic vortex confronting visitors with a flooded cave, seat of the nymph of the grotto, before they ascend to the outside world. As Leeds Castle prepares to celebrate its Silver Jubilee as a charitable trust, they have developed the theme of mazes into a special event for May half-term. They will be holding a bonanza of 25 different mazes throughout the grounds on 26 May – 3 June 2001.

At Greys Court, Oxfordshire the Archbishop's maze is inspired by a dream of Dr Robert Runcie, formerly Archbishop of Canterbury. The turf maze abounds in Christian symbolism.

■ *The Archbishop's Maze, Greys Court, Oxfordshire.*

■ *The Maze at Blenheim Palace.*

■ *Below: The Hedge Maze at Longleat, Wiltshire.*

The inspiration for the Marlborough maze at Blenheim Palace, Oxfordshire came from stone sculptures depicting the Panoply of Victory carving by Grinling Gibbons from the roof of Blenheim Palace. Seen from above the lines of the yew hedges portray pyramids of cannonballs, a canon firing, and the air filled with banners, flags and the sound of trumpets. Two wooden bridges create a three-dimensional puzzle as well as giving tantalising views across parts of the world's largest symbolic hedge maze (designed by Adrian Fisher and Randoll Coat 1991).

The largest collection of mazes and labyrinths in Britain can be found at Longleat, Wiltshire. The 7th Marquess of Bath has an informed love of the ancient artefact. He has assigned a space for not one but two mazes immediately below his private apartments which look out on to a splendid vista of lawn, lake and rising parkland beyond. His challenge was to produce something which could measure up to the magnificence of its setting. His answer was to design a maze and join it to a labyrinth – perhaps a unique juxtaposition, each true to its definition and both highly symbolic in classical content and in their celestial shape. The two systems enable the visitor to savour their essential difference: the linear purity of the labyrinth with its unending unicursal corridor, and the dizzy gyrations of the maze with its multiple roots and wrong-turnings in the pursuit of an ultimate goal.

Longleat is now home to no less than five spectacular mazes. The latest maze, opened in 1998, is King Arthur's mirror maze. Visitors are invited to imagine they are knights who have set off from the Round Table to form a quest. On their journey they encounter mysterious sights, half-hidden faces, wild sounds, swirling fog and even seem to trigger off lightning and thunder. King Arthur's mirror maze, designed by Adrian Fisher, is a breakthrough in mirror maze design.

■ *Above: The Water Maze at Hever Castle in Kent.*

■ *Below: The World's longest Hedge Maze at Longleat, Wiltshire.*

■ *Veronica's Maze at Parham in Sussex.*

Parham Park, Sussex is one of the loveliest Tudor houses in England, lying below the South Downs. The design for Veronica's maze was inspired by the embroidery over the 'Great Bed' in the principal bedroom of the house. This is an unusual one-way puzzle maze. The goal is the centre but once you start you have to keep going forward. When you reach forks in the path you choose which way to go. You cannot double-back when joined by other paths, nor make right-angled turns where paths cross over each other (designed by Adrian Fisher 1991).

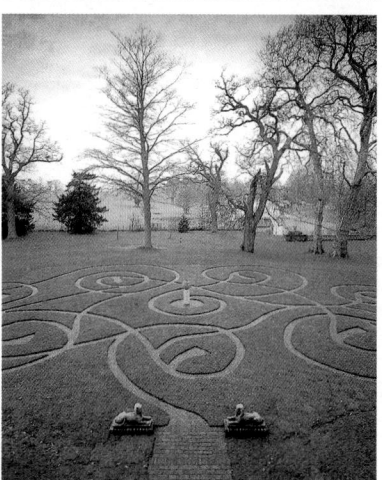

Further reading:

The Art of the Maze by Adrian Fisher and Georg Gerster, 1990
(available from Adrian Fisher Maze Design, Victoria Lodge, 5 Victoria Grove, Portsmouth, Hampshire PO5 1NE,
tel: +44 (0) 2392 355500   website: www.mazemaker.com)

The British Maze Guide by Adrian Fisher and Jeff Saward (also available from Adrian Fisher)

Mazes - Adrian Fisher and Diana Kingham, Shire Publications, 1991 (revised 1997)

Secrets of the Maze - an interactive guide to the world's most amazing mazes by Adrian Fisher and Howard Loxton (Thames and Hudson)

HISTORIC TRUST CHAPELS

The Historic Chapels Trust has been established to take into ownership redundant chapels and other places of worship in England of outstanding architectural and historic interest. Our object is to secure for public benefit the preservation, repair and maintenance of our buildings including their contents, burial grounds and curtilages.

The trust now has twelve chapels in its care which can be visited on application to the keyholder:-

Biddlestone RC Chapel .... 01665 574420 Northumberland	
Coanwood Friends Meeting House .... 01434 320256 Northumberland	
Cote Baptist Chapel .... 01993 850421 Oxfordshire	
Farfield Friends Meeting House .... 01756 710225 West Yorkshire	
The Dissenters' Chapel.. 020 7402 2749 Kensal Green Cemetery, London	
Salem Chapel, East Budleigh .... 01395 445236 Devon	
St Benet's Chapel and Presbytery .... 0151 520 2600 Netherton, Merseyside	
St George's German Lutheran Church .... 020 8302 3437 Tower Hamlets, London	
Todmorden Unitarian Church .... 01706 815648 West Yorkshire	
Umbersland Baptist Church .... 01564 783362 West Yorkshire	
Wallasey Unitarian Church .... 0151 639 5137 Merseyside	
Walpole Old Chapel .... 01986 798308 Suffolk	

For further information please ring the Director at the office address.

▲ **Walpole Old Chapel ~ Suffolk**

▲ **Dissenters' Chapel, Kensal Green Cemetery ~ London**

▲ **Farfield Friends Meeting House ~ West Yorkshire**

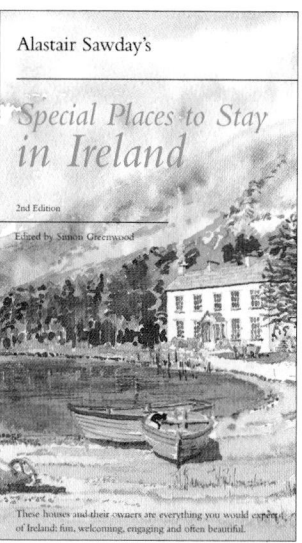

The Landmark Trust

The Landmark Trust is a preservation charity which rescues and restores historic and architecturally important buildings at risk and lets them for holidays. There are 168 Landmarks where you can become, for a short time, the owner of such a building, including follies, forts, castles, gatehouses and towers. The Landmark Handbook illustrates every building with 184 pages of plans, location maps and black and white photographs. The price, including post and packing, is refundable against a booking.

Warden Abbey
Near Biggleswade, Bedfordshire

Landmarks are chosen for their historic interest or architectural importance, and also because many are in surroundings which give unexpected pleasure. Warden Abbey is a fragment of a great Cistercian Abbey and a Tudor House, set in fruitful countryside, once farmed by monks.

Lundy: Old Light
Lundy Island, Bristol Channel

The beauty of the Landmark solution is not only that a building is saved and put to good use, but also that the restoration respects its original design. For a short time it is possible to live in surprising places. One of the light houses on Lundy Island, off the north coast of Devon, now provides unusual holiday accommodation.

Langley Gatehouse
Acton Burnell, Shropshire

Landmarks often lie off the beaten track. Langley is no exception, set in a remote valley with a view to the Wrekin. In our restorations, we prefer to repair the old, and avoid renewal, to preserve the building's texture. When the building is timber framed, this can be like trying to patch a cobweb!

Saddell
Kintyre, Argyll

Some Landmarks, like this one, are connected with great families. Saddell Castle, a fine tower house with battlements, was in the hands of the Campbells for 400 years. Today the Castle cottages, and the long white strand of Saddell Bay are available for holidays.

The historic properties listed below are not hotels. Their inclusion indicates that accommodation can be arranged, often for groups only. The type and standard of rooms offered vary widely from the luxurious to the utilitarian. Full details can be obtained from each individual property.

Eastnor Castle, Herefordshire.

SCOTLAND

WALES

IRELAND

ENGLAND

HERITAGE VENUES

HERITAGE VENUES is the company that has access to some of the finest properties in the United Kingdom. All of them have intrinsic historical or architectural interest, most have beautiful gardens and parks but some have never been opened to the general public – they don't even appear in Hudson's!

For the finest properties Heritage Venues provides the most professional service, the best entertainment and delicious food and wine.

Heritage Venues is the sensible answer for the discerning corporate or private client who wants the top event or function, with the minimum of fuss in a unique setting.

Head Office
HERITAGE VENUES
Bagendon, Cirencester, Gloucestershire GL7 7DU
Tel/Fax: 01285 831417
e-mail: heritage.venues@virgin.net
www.heritagevenues.co.uk

Bed & Breakfast
for Garden Lovers

The original garden B&B guide founded in 1994

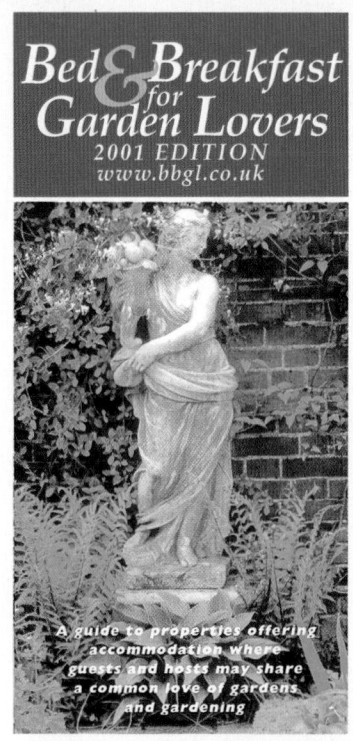

Quality accommodation in beautiful locations.

*103 quietly situated private homes
at various prices*

*Keen gardening hosts personally chosen for their
kindness, courtesy and helpfulness and
good local knowledge of horticultural matters*

Useful tips to help plan garden visits

*Excellent reputation for
personal service built up over 7 years*

TO OBTAIN BROCHURES:
From the UK: Send six loose first class stamps
per copy required, with a 11 x 22cm sae
From abroad: Send four international reply-paid coupons
per copy required, with a 11 x 22cm sae
*To: BBGL/HD, Handywater Farm, Sibford Gower
Banbury, Oxfordshire OX15 5AE*

Places at which the marriage ceremony itself can take place although many will also be able to provide facilities for wedding receptions.

Full details about each property are available in the regional listings. There are numerous other properties included within Hudson's which do not have a Civil Wedding Licence but which can accommodate wedding receptions. The Marriage Act 1995, which has resulted in many more wedding venues in England, has not changed the situation in Scotland. In Scotland religious wedding ceremonies can take place anywhere subject to the Minister being prepared to perform them. Civil Weddings, however, are still confined to Registry Offices.

All Wedding Photographs
© Sarah Ward-Hendry
tel: 01295 811092 or 0385 901522
e-mail: ward-hendry@msn.com
website: www.ward-hendry.com

This list is merely intended to draw attention to properties which can host Civil Weddings, it is intended only as a guide.

29

Highclere Castle, Hampshire.

ENGLAND

Properties which are able to accommodate corporate functions, wedding receptions and events.

Some properties specialise in corporate hospitality and are open only rarely, if ever, to day visitors. Others do both. See entry for details

The Banqueting House, London.

© Sarah Ward-Hendry.

2001

1
Leeds Castle, Kent
Treasure Trail.

1 – 6
Fairfax House, Yorkshire
Annual Exhibition on the 'Keeping of Christmas'.

1 – 31
Museum of Costume & Assembly Rooms, Somerset
'Fashion in the Fifties' traces the flowering of fashion talent in the glamorous decade following the War.

5
Harewood House, Yorkshire
Music at Harewood – Gallery Concert.

22 – 31
The Wallace Collection, London
"Thomas Sully and Queen Victoria" – marking the centenary of Queen Victoria's death, this exhibition will study Sully's portraits of the Queen and the objects associated with them.

FEBRUARY

1 – 28
Museum of Costume & Assembly Rooms, Somerset
'Fashion in the Fifties' traces the flowering of fashion talent in the glamorous decade following the War.

1 – 28
The Wallace Collection, London
"Thomas Sully and Queen Victoria" – marking the centenary of Queen Victoria's death, this exhibition will study Sully's portraits of the Queen and the objects associated with them.

3 – 4
Goodwood House, Sussex
Antiques Fair.

8 – 28
Abbot Hall Art Gallery, Cumbria
Andy Goldsworth – Photographic Works.

14
Baddesley Clinton, Warwickshire
Pruning Wall Climbers 'Wisteria', 10am.

19 – 23
Leeds Castle, Kent
Half Term Story-Telling.

23 – 25
Loseley Park, Surrey
Home Design Exhibition.

MARCH

1 – 18
Abbot Hall Art Gallery, Cumbria
Andy Goldsworth – Photographic Work.

1 – 31
Fairfax House, Yorkshire
Obsession – the collector and their collections.

1 – 31
Museum of Costume & Assembly Rooms, Somerset
'Fashion in the Fifties' traces the flowering of fashion talent in the glamorous decade following the War.

1 – 31
The Wallace Collection, London
"Thomas Sully and Queen Victoria" – marking the centenary of Queen Victoria's death, this exhibition will study Sully's portraits of the Queen and the objects associated with them.

2 – 4
Wilton House, Wiltshire
24th Annual Antiques Fair.

9 – 11
Hopetoun House, Edinburgh City, Coast & Countryside, Scotland
Antiques Fair.

10 – 11
Powderham Castle, Devon
Historic Devon Motor Rally.

12 – 18
Hever Castle, Kent
Spring Flower Week.

17 – 18
Ragley Hall, Warwickshire
Craft Fair.

22
Harewood House, Yorkshire
Music at Harewood – Gallery Concert.

23 – 25
Loseley Park, Surrey
Antique Fair.

25
Cobham Hall, Kent
National Garden Scheme.

25
Harewood House, Yorkshire
Mothers' Day.

26 – 29
Powderham Castle, Devon
Phillips Fine Art Sale.

27 – 31
Abbot Hall Art Gallery, Cumbria
Li Yuan-chia.

28
Holme Pierrepont Hall, Nottinghamshire
Old Photographs of Holme Pierrepont, coffee morning from 10 am - 1pm, fo raise funds for St Edmund's Church.

31
Leeds Castle, Kent
Gardeners' Weekend.

31
Nunnington Hall, Yorkshire
"Waltz of the Flowers" Art Exhibition by Angela McCall (normal opening times and prices apply).

APRIL

1
Leeds Castle, Kent
Gardeners' Weekend.

1 – 29
Nunnington Hall, Yorkshire
"Waltz of the Flowers" Art Exhibition by Angela McCall (normal opening times and prices apply).

1 – 29
The Wallace Collection, London
"Thomas Sully and Queen Victoria" – marking the centenary of Queen Victoria's death, this exhibition will study Sully's portraits of the Queen and the objects associated with them.

1 – 31
Abbot Hall Art Gallery, Cumbria
Li Yuan-chia.

1 – 30
Fairfax House, Yorkshire
Obsession – the collector and their collections.

1 – 30
Museum of Costume & Assembly Rooms, Somerset
'Fashion in the Fifties' traces the flowering of fashion talent in the glamorous decade following the War.

5 – 8
Ripley Castle, Yorkshire
Galloway Antiques Fair.

7 – 8
Capesthorne Hall, Cheshire
Rainbow Craft Fair.

7 – 12
Hopetoun House, Edinburgh City, Coast & Countryside, Scotland
Sotheby's Spring Sale.

8
Beaulieu, Hampshire
Boat Jumble.

10
Picton Castle, South Wales
RHS Lecture: Picton Castle Gardens in Early Spring.

13
Plas Newydd, North Wales
National Gardens Scheme Open Day.

13 – 16
Cobham Hall, Kent
Medway Craft Show.

13 – 16
Kentwell Hall, Suffolk
Re-creation: Easter.

13 – 16
Harewood House, Yorkshire
Easter Weekend.

13 – 16
Hever Castle, Kent
Easter Egg Trail and Brass Bands.

14 – 16
Leeds Castle, Kent
An Easter Celebration.

15
Plas Newydd, North Wales
Easter Eggstravaganza!

15
Lulworth Castle, Dorset
Easter Bunny Hunt.

15
Traquair, Borders, Scotland
Easter Egg Extravaganza.

15 – 16
Nunnington Hall, Yorkshire
Easter Egg Trail, 12.30-4.30pm (£1 per person, normal admission prices apply).

15 – 16
Rievaulx Terrace and Temples, Yorkshire
Easter Egg Trail, £1 per person (normal admission prices apply).

16
Ludlow Castle, Shropshire
Easter Egg Hunt.

20 – 22
Blair Castle, Perthshire, Scotland
Needlework & Lace Exhibition (contact: Lyndsey Dolliver on 01796 481207).

21 – 22
Goodwood House, Sussex
Home Design Interiors.

21 – 22
Shugborough, Staffordshire
Gamekeepers' Fair.

29
Wartnaby Gardens, Leicestershire
Plants for sale.

MAY

1 – 31
Abbot Hall Art Gallery, Cumbria
Li Yuan-chia.

1 – 31
Fairfax House, Yorkshire
Obsession – the collector and their collections.

1 – 31
Museum of Costume & Assembly Rooms, Somerset
'Fashion in the Fifties' traces the flowering of fashion talent in the glamorous decade following the War.

2 – 28
Nunnington Hall, Yorkshire
"Yorkshire Gems" Art Exhibition by G D Hemingway, a member of the British Watercolour Society (normal opening times and prices apply).

5 – 6
Kentwell Hall, Suffolk
Re-creation: May Day.

5 – 7
Hever Castle, Kent
May Day Music & Dance.

5 – 7
Leonardslee Gardens, Sussex
Bonsai Weekend.

6
Plas Newydd, North Wales
Spring Safari Family Fun Day.

6
Westbury Court Garden, Gloucestershire
Annual Plant Fair.

6 – 7
Catton Hall, Derbyshire
Classic Car Show.

6 – 7
Constable Burton Hall Gardens, Yorkshire
Tulip Festival.

6 – 7
Eastnor Castle, Herefordshire
Spring Country Crafts Fair.

8
Plas Newydd, North Wales
Walk with the Gardener, 2pm.

Special Events Index

9
Rievaulx Terrace and Temples, Yorkshire
History and Horticulture of Rievaulx Terrace – explore this important 18th century landscape garden, 2pm, £5 per person (normal admission applies – booking essential 01439 798340).

10 – 13
Hatfield House & Gardens, Hertfordshire
Living Crafts.

12 – 13
Beaulieu, Hampshire
Spring Autojumble.

12 – 13
Chatsworth, Derbyshire
International Horse Trials.

12 – 13
Goodwood House, Sussex
Antiques Fair.

12 – 13
Leeds Castle, Kent
Festival of English Food & Wine.

12 – 13
Lulworth Castle, Dorset
Country Gardening & Food Fair.

12 – 31
Warwick Castle, Warwickshire
Mediaeval Festival.

13
Baddesley Clinton, Warwickshire
Wild Flower Identification Tour, 10am.

13
Hanbury Hall, Worcestershire
Annual Plant Fair.

13
Ludlow Castle, Shropshire
Vintage Vehicle Display.

13
Newby Hall & Gardens, Yorkshire
Spring Plant Fair.

13
Packwood House, Warwickshire
Annual Plant Fair.

13
Picton Castle, South Wales
National Gardens Scheme.

14
Plas Newydd, North Wales
Spring Plant Fair.

16
Rievaulx Terrace and Temples, Yorkshire
History and Horticulture of Rievaulx Terrace – explore this important 18th century landscape garden, 2pm, £5 per person (normal admission applies – booking essential 01439 798340).

16
Westbury Court Garden, Gloucestershire
Meet the Gardener Evening Garden Tour.

17
Baddesley Clinton, Warwickshire
A Guided Tour of the Grounds, 10am.

19
Picton Castle, South Wales
Spring Plant Sale.

19
Ragley Hall, Warwickshire
Miniature Yacht Meet by the lake (free admission for Season Ticket Holders).

19 – 20
Chatsworth, Derbyshire
Angling Fair.

19 – 20
Kentwell Hall, Suffolk
Re-creation: Land Girls.

19 – 20
Parham House & Gardens, Sussex
Needlework Event.

20
Harewood House, Yorkshire
Teddy Bears Picnic (inc National Kidney Research Fund Sponsored Walk).

20
Wartnaby Gardens, Leicestershire
Plants for sale.

21 - 25
Chelsea Physic Garden, London
Chelsea Show Week, 12 noon - 5 pm with lunches.

24 – 28
Charleston, Sussex
Charleston Festival.

26
Blair Castle, Perthshire, Scotland
Atholl Highlanders' Parade (contact: Geoff Crerar on 01796 481207).

26
Nunnington Hall, Yorkshire
"Create your own Wild Flower Garden" Workshop, 1.30-5pm, £20 including a Cream Tea (booking essential).

26 – 27
Traquair, Borders, Scotland
Scottish Beer Festival.

26 – 28
Harewood House, Yorkshire
Live Crafts – May Bank Holiday Weekend.

26 – 28
Hever Castle, Kent
Merrie England Weekend.

26 – 28
Kentwell Hall, Suffolk
Re-creation: Whitsun.

26 – 28
Ludlow Castle, Shropshire
Festival of Crafts.

26 – 31
Leeds Castle, Kent
Amazing Mazes Week.

26 – 28
Shugborough, Staffordshire
Spring Craft Fair.

26 – 28
Skipton Castle, Yorkshire
Red Wyvern Society re-enactment of life in Skipton Castle in the 15th century.

27
Blair Castle, Perthshire, Scotland
Atholl Gathering & Highland Games (contact: Mr J Milliganr on 01796 481355).

27
Nunnington Hall, Yorkshire
Ryedale Centre Spring Fair, 12.30-5pm, £2 including NT Members (normal admission for house – proceeds for conservation work).

27
Plas Newydd, North Wales
Dragon Day Treasure Trail Family Fun Day.

27
Powderham Castle, Devon
The Great Farm Shop Open Day.

27 – 28
Finchcocks, Kent
Spring Garden Fair & Flower Festival.

28
Eastnor Castle, Herefordshire
Steam Fair & Country Show with Fred Dibnah.

28
Mottisfont Abbey Garden, Hampshire
Spring Holiday Plant Fayre, 12 noon-6pm.

29
Picton Castle, South Wales
RHS Lecture: Rare Conifers at Picton Castle.

30
Nunnington Hall, Yorkshire
"Light and Shade" Art Exhibition by Jim Wright (normal opening times and prices apply).

JUNE

1 – 2
Hopetoun House, Edinburgh City, Coast & Countryside, Scotland
Hopetoun Carriage Driving Event.

1 – 3
Abbot Hall Art Gallery, Cumbria
Li Yuan-chia.

1 – 3
Holker Hall & Gardens, Cumbria
Holker Garden Festival.

1 – 3
Leeds Castle, Kent
Amazing Mazes Week.

1 – 3
Longleat, Wiltshire
Longleat Horse Trials.

1 – 3
Loseley Park, Surrey
Craft Fair.

1 – 30
Museum of Costume & Assembly Rooms, Somerset
'Fashion in the Fifties' traces the flowering of fashion talent in the glamorous decade following the War.

1 – 30
Nunnington Hall, Yorkshire
"Light and Shade" Art Exhibition by Jim Wright (normal opening times and prices apply).

1 – 31
Warwick Castle, Warwickshire
Mediaeval Festival.

2 – 3
Cawdor Castle, Highlands & Skye, Scotland
Special Gardens Weekend: guided tours of gardens and Cawdor Big Wood.

3
Hopetoun House, Edinburgh City, Coast & Countryside, Scotland
Dolls House & Miniatures Fair.

3
Sutton Park, Yorkshire
Specialist Plant Fair.

6
Plas Newydd, North Wales
Antiques Valuation Day with Sotheby's, 10am-3pm.

7 – 10
Bramham Park, Yorkshire
Bramham International Horse Trials & Yorkshire Country Fair.

7 – 10
Ripley Castle, Yorkshire
Grand Summer Sale.

8 – 10
Newby Hall & Gardens, Yorkshire
Rainbow Craft Fair.

10
Burton Constable Hall, Yorkshire
Burton Constable Country Fair.

10
Harewood House, Yorkshire
Porsche Club – Yorkshire Region Annual Concours.

10
Nunnington Hall, Yorkshire
Open Air Concert by local choral group "Voicebox", 2pm (normal opening times and prices apply).

12
Plas Newydd, North Wales
Walk with the Gardener, 2pm.

12 – 30
Abbot Hall Art Gallery, Cumbria
Paula Rego.

13
Hanbury Hall, Worcestershire
Concert.

13
Westbury Court Garden, Gloucestershire
Meet the Gardener Evening Garden Tour.

16
Nunnington Hall, Yorkshire
Oddsocks – Shakespeare, outdoor concert – bring a picnic, £12.50, 7pm (tickets available from Nunnington Hall 01439 748283 or Fountains Abbey booking office 01765 609999).

16
Gilbert White's House & The Oates Museum, Hampshire
Picnic to 'Jazz in June'.

16 – 17
Parham House & Gardens, Sussex
Steam Rally in Park.

16 - 17
Gilbert White's House & The Oates Museum, Hampshire
Unusual Plants Fair.

17
Harewood House, Yorkshire
Vintage & Classic Car Rally.

17
Plas Newydd, North Wales
Fathers' Day Frolics.

17 – 30
Kentwell Hall, Suffolk
The Great Annual Re-creation (Sats & Suns only, 11am-5pm).

19
Picton Castle, South Wales
RHS Regional Lecture: Borders and Beyond (Lecturer: Stephen Lacey).

21
Baddesley Clinton, Warwickshire
Evening Garden Tour, 6pm.

22 – 28
Hever Castle, Kent
Rose Week.

23 - 24
Arley Hall, Cheshire
Arley Garden Festival.

23 – 24
Hatfield House & Gardens, Hertfordshire
Festival of Gardening.

23 – 24
Leonardslee Gardens, Sussex
West Sussex Country Craft Fair.

23 – 30
Ludlow Castle, Shropshire
Ludlow Festival.

24
Longleat, Wiltshire
Radio Rally & Computer Fair.

24
Nunnington Hall, Yorkshire
Specialist Plant Fair, 11am-5pm (normal admission).

24
Saint Hill Manor, Sussex
Open air production of Sheridan's "School for Scandal" by "Rain or Shine Theatre", 4pm.

24
Wartnaby Gardens, Leicestershire
Plant Fair with 20 Nurserymen. Sketching Club Exhibition.

🎭 **25 – 28**
Powderham Castle, Devon
Phillips Fine Art Sale.

🎭 **27**
Packwood House, Warwickshire
Evening Garden Tour, 7pm.

🎭 **29 – 30**
Powderham Castle, Devon
British Touring Shakespeare (open air).

🎭 **30**
Leeds Castle, Kent
Open Air Concert.

🎭 **30**
Shugborough, Staffordshire
Gardeners' Weekend.

JULY

🎭 **1**
Eastnor Castle, Herefordshire
Wood Festival.

🎭 **1**
Nunnington Hall, Yorkshire
"Light and Shade" Art Exhibition by Jim Wright (normal opening times and prices apply).

🎭 **1**
Powderham Castle, Devon
British Touring Shakespeare (open air).

🎭 **1**
Ragley Hall, Warwickshire
Caspian Horse Society (free admission for Season Ticket Holders).

🎭 **1**
Shugborough, Staffordshire
Gardeners' Weekend.

🎭 **1 – 8**
Kentwell Hall, Suffolk
The Great Annual Re-creation (Sats & Suns only, and Fri 6 July, 11am-5pm).

🎭 **1 – 8**
Ludlow Castle, Shropshire
Ludlow Festival.

🎭 **1 – 31**
Abbot Hall Art Gallery, Cumbria
Paula Rego.

🎭 **1 – 31**
Museum of Costume & Assembly Rooms, Somerset
'Fashion in the Fifties' traces the flowering of fashion talent in the glamorous decade following the War.

🎭 **1 – 31**
Warwick Castle, Warwickshire
Mediaeval Festival.

🎭 **3**
Plas Newydd, North Wales
Traditional Pole-lathe Turning, 11am-3pm.

🎭 **3 – 29**
Nunnington Hall, Yorkshire
"Nature on a Plate" Art Exhibition by Catherine Bell (normal opening times and prices apply).

🎭 **4**
Leeds Castle, Kent
Children's Promenade Concert.

🎭 **5**
Blair Castle, Perthshire, Scotland
Charity Day in Aid of McMillan Cancer Research (contact: Lyndsey Dolliver on 01796 481207).

🎭 **6**
Leighton Hall, Lancashire
Concert & Fireworks: 'Last Night of the Proms'.

🎭 **6 – 8**
Goodwood, Sussex
Goodwood Festival of Speed.

🎭 **6 – 31**
Blackwell – The Artistic House, Cumbria
Magdalene Odundo – Ceramic Vessels.

🎭 **7**
Nunnington Hall, Yorkshire
"Get Fruity with the Gardener" Workshop – how to look after your fruit trees. 1.30-5pm, £20 including a Cream Tea (booking essential).

🎭 **7**
Leeds Castle, Kent
Open Air Concert.

🎭 **7**
Ragley Hall, Warwickshire
"Battle Proms Concert" outdoor concert.

🎭 **7 – 8**
Powderham Castle, Devon
Historic Vehicle Gathering.

🎭 **7 – 8**
Scone Palace, Perthshire/Fife, Scotland
Game Conservancy Scottish Fair.

🎭 **8**
Harewood House, Yorkshire
Jaguar Rally.

🎭 **8**
Plas Newydd, North Wales
Guided Archaeological Walk, 2pm.

🎭 **8**
Rievaulx Terrace and Temples, Yorkshire
Open Air Concert by local choral group 'Voicebox', 2-4pm (normal opening times and prices apply).

🎭 **10**
Harewood House, Yorkshire
York Early Music Festival Concert.

🎭 **10**
Picton Castle, South Wales
RHS Lecture: Propagating Shrubs.

🎭 **10**
Plas Newydd, North Wales
An Evening Walk with the Gardener, 7pm.

🎭 **12**
Westbury Court Garden, Gloucestershire
Meet the Gardener Evening Garden Tour.

🎭 **12 – 15**
Ripley Castle, Yorkshire
Galloway Antiques Fair.

🎭 **14**
Nunnington Hall, Yorkshire
"Northanger Abbey" – outdoor concert – North Country Theatre, £12.50, 7pm – bring a picnic.

🎭 **14**
Wilton House, Wiltshire
Classical Firework Proms Night.

🎭 **14 – 15**
Eastnor Castle, Herefordshire
Medieval Jousting & Hot Air Balloon Festival.

🎭 **14 – 15**
Leonardslee Gardens, Sussex
Model Boat Regatta.

🎭 **14 – 15**
Parham House & Gardens, Sussex
Garden Weekend.

🎭 **15**
Cobham Hall, Kent
National Garden Scheme.

🎭 **15**
Newby Hall & Gardens, Yorkshire
Historic Vehicle Rally.

🎭 **15 - 31**
Chelsea Physic Garden, London
Summer Exhibition: "Myth and Magic".

🎭 **16 – 22**
Blair Castle, Perthshire, Scotland
Contemporary Textile Art Exhibition by Northern Fringes (tel: Lyndsey Dolliver on 01796 481207).

🎭 **17**
Plas Newydd, North Wales
Teddy Bear Family Fun Day.

🎭 **19 – 22**
Leeds Castle, Kent
A Festival of Summer Floral Art.

🎭 **20 – 22**
Loseley Park, Surrey
Garden Show.

🎭 **21**
Hever Castle, Kent
Jousting Tournament performed by 'The Knights of Royal England'.

🎭 **21**
Longleat, Wiltshire
Longleat Balloon Festival & Nightfire.

🎭 **21**
Ragley Hall, Warwickshire
Outdoor Concert.

🎭 **21 – 22**
Dalemain, Cumbria
Dalemain Rainbow Craft Fair.

🎭 **21 – 22**
Holkham Hall, Norfolk
Holkham Country Fair.

🎭 **22**
Chenies Manor House, Hertfordshire
Plant and Garden Fair.

🎭 **22**
Hever Castle, Kent
Medieval Archery demonstrated by the 'Company of 1415'.

🎭 **22**
Leighton Hall, Lancashire
Classic Car Rally.

🎭 **22**
Longleat, Wiltshire
Longleat Balloon Festival.

🎭 **22**
Picton Castle, South Wales
National Gardens Scheme.

🎭 **22**
Plas Newydd, North Wales
Military Re-enactment – Napoleonic Alliance.

🎭 **22**
Westbury Court Garden, Gloucestershire
Pillowell Silver Band.

🎭 **24**
Plas Newydd, North Wales
All the Fun of the Annual Summer Fair!

🎭 **26**
Packwood House, Warwickshire
Evening Garden Tour, 7pm.

🎭 **27**
Rievaulx Terrace and Temples, Yorkshire
Bat Walk, 8.30pm, £2 per adult, £1 per child including NT Members (booking essential).

🎭 **28**
Hever Castle, Kent
Jousting Tournament performed by 'The Knights of Royal England'.

🎭 **28**
Ragley Hall, Warwickshire
Newfoundland Dog Trails (free admission for Season Ticket Holders).

🎭 **28 – 29**
Lulworth Castle, Dorset
Lulworth Horse Trials & Country Fair.

🎭 **28 – 30**
Harewood House, Yorkshire
Leeds Championship Dog Show.

🎭 **29**
Hever Castle, Kent
Medieval Archery demonstrated by the 'Company of 1415'.

🎭 **29**
Plas Newydd, North Wales
Seaside Family Fun Day.

🎭 **31**
Goodwood House, Sussex
Race Week.

🎭 **31**
Nunnington Hall, Yorkshire
Art Exhibition by Stephanie Holmes (normal opening times and prices will apply).

AUGUST

🎭 **1 – 4**
Goodwood House, Sussex
Race Week.

🎭 **1 – 8**
Rievaulx Terrace and Temples, Yorkshire
History and Horticulture of Rievaulx Terrace – explore this important 18th century landscape garden, 2pm, £5 per person (normal admission applies – booking essential 01439 798340).

This list is merely intended to draw attention to properties who host Special Events, it is advisable to contact the property to confirm dates and times.

35

1 – 31
Abbot Hall Art Gallery, Cumbria
Paula Rego.

1 – 31
Blackwell – The Artistic House, Cumbria
Magdalene Odundo – Ceramic Vessels.

1 – 31
Chelsea Physic Garden, London
Summer Exhibition: "Myth and Magic".

1 – 31
Museum of Costume & Assembly Rooms,
Somerset
'Fashion in the Fifties' traces the flowering of
fashion talent in the glamorous decade following
the War.

1 – 31
Nunnington Hall, Yorkshire
Art Exhibition by Stephanie Holmes (normal
opening times and prices apply).

1 – 31
Warwick Castle, Warwickshire
Mediaeval Festival.

3
Nunnington Hall, Yorkshire
Bat Walk, 8.30pm, £2 per adult, £1 per child,
including NT Members (booking essential).

3
Powderham Castle, Devon
Bournemouth Symphony Orchester 'Last Night
of the Powederham Proms'.

3 – 4
Leighton Hall, Lancashire
Shakespeare in the Garden: 'Henry V'.

3 – 4
Scone Palace, Perthshire/Fife, Scotland
Perth Agricultural Show.

3 – 5
Hatfield House & Gardens, Hertfordshire
Art in Clay – Pottery & Ceramics Festival.

4
Powderham Castle, Devon
Open Air Rock Concert.

4
Ragley Hall, Warwickshire
"Fireworks & Laser Symphony"
outdoor concert.

4 – 5
Hever Castle, Kent
Jousting Tournament performed by 'The Knights
of Royal England'.

4 – 5
Kentwell Hall, Suffolk
Re-creation: World War II.

4 – 5
Traquair, Borders, Scotland
Traquair Fair.

5
Drummond Castle Gardens, Perthshire/Fife,
Scotland
Open Day – entertainments, teas, raffle.

5
Harewood House, Yorkshire
BMW Car Club 20th Annual Concours of the North.

5
Plas Newydd, North Wales
Clown Around with James the Juggler.

5
Shugborough, Staffordshire
Victorian Street Market.

8
Plas Newydd, North Wales
Evening Walk with the Gardener, 7pm.

11
Plas Newydd, North Wales
Worked Tapestry Pieces, 12 noon.

11 – 12
Hever Castle, Kent
Jousting Tournament performed by 'The Knights
of Royal England'.

12
Harewood House, Yorkshire
Rolls Royce Rally 21st Anniversary at
Harewood.

12
Loseley Park, Surrey
Outdoor Concert.

12
Plas Newydd, North Wales
Guided Archaeological Walk, 2pm.

13 – 17
Eastnor Castle, Herefordshire
Children's Fun Week.

16
Westbury Court Garden, Gloucestershire
Meet the Gardener Evening Garden Tour.

17 – 19
Parham House & Gardens, Sussex
Live Crafts in Park.

18
Chartwell, Kent
Opera Brava – an evening of Gilbert & Sullivan.

18
Nunnington Hall, Yorkshire
"The Art of Propagation" Workshop, 1.30-5pm,
£20 including a Cream Tea
(booking essential).

18
Plas Newydd, North Wales
Open Air Jazz Concert with Firework Finale, 7pm.

18 – 19
Bosworth Battlefield, Leicestershire & Rutland
Medieval Spectacular.

18 – 19
Hever Castle, Kent
Jousting Tournament performed by 'The Knights
of Royal England'.

18 – 19
Ragley Hall, Warwickshire
Warwickshire & West Midlands Game Fair
(Season Tickets do not apply this weekend).

18 – 19
Skipton Castle, Yorkshire
Feudal Archers: demonstration of arms, armour
and domestic life (1135 – 1216).

19
Chartwell, Kent
Opera Brava – "Tosca".

19
Harewood House, Yorkshire
Harewood Show.

19
Plas Newydd, North Wales
'Fleece to Garment.'

23
Baddesley Clinton, Warwickshire
A Guided Tour of the Grounds, 10am.

23 – 26
Blair Castle, Perthshire, Scotland
Bowmore Blair Castle International Horse Trials
& Country Fair (contact: The Horse Trials Office
on 01796 481543).

24 – 27
Kentwell Hall, Suffolk
Re-creation: High Summer.

24 – 27
Newby Hall & Gardens, Yorkshire
Rainbow Craft Fair.

25
Hever Castle, Kent
Jousting Tournament performed by 'The
Knights of Royal England'.

25
Rievaulx Terrace and Temples, Yorkshire
Peacocks & Dragons Workshop, starts at 12
noon, Art and Craft, £2 per person (normal
opening times and prices apply).

25 – 26
Plas Newydd, North Wales
Knights of Longshanks Combat Displays.

25 – 27
Harewood House, Yorkshire
Harewood Steam Rally.

25 – 27
Shugborough, Staffordshire
Summer Craft Fair.

26
Floors Castle, Borders, Scotland
Family Day with Massed Pipe Bands.

26 – 27
Eastnor Castle, Herefordshire
Berkeley Household: Living History in the 15th
century.

26 – 27
Finchcocks, Kent
Jane Austen Gala.

26 – 27
Hever Castle, Kent
Medieval Archery demonstrated by the
'Company of 1415'.

28
Picton Castle, South Wales
RHS Lecture: Herbaceous Plants at Picton
Castle.

31
Ragley Hall, Warwickshire
"Last Night of the Ragley Proms" outdoor
concert.

30
Rievaulx Terrace and Temples, Yorkshire
Tribal Rhythms Workshop, starts at 12 noon,
Music and Dance, £2 per person (normal
opening times and prices apply).

SEPTEMBER

1
Hever Castle, Kent
Jousting Tournament performed by 'The
Knights of Royal England'.

1 – 2
Catton Hall, Derbyshire
National Carriage Driving Trials.

1 – 2
Chatsworth, Derbyshire
Country Fair.

1 – 2
Nunnington Hall, Yorkshire
Art Exhibition by Stephanie Holmes (normal
opening times and prices apply).

1 – 2
Parham House & Gardens, Sussex
Autumn Flowers at Parham House.

1 – 9
Chelsea Physic Garden, London
Summer Exhibition: "Myth and Magic".

1 – 9
Warwick Castle, Warwickshire
Mediaeval Festival.

1 – 23
Blackwell – The Artistic House, Cumbria
Magdalene Odundo – Ceramic Vessels.

1 – 30
Abbot Hall Art Gallery, Cumbria
Paula Rego.

1 – 30
Fairfax House, Yorkshire
Cutting Edge – the evolution of cutlery and
place settings.

1 – 30
Museum of Costume & Assembly Rooms,
Somerset
'Fashion in the Fifties' traces the flowering of
fashion talent in the glamorous decade
following the War.

2
Hever Castle, Kent
Medieval Archery demonstrated by the
'Company of 1415'.

2
Plas Newydd, North Wales
Guided Fungus Foray Family Fun Day.

5 – 30
Nunnington Hall, Yorkshire
"Flower Power" Art Exhibition by Jeam Tilley
(normal opening times and prices apply).

7 – 9
Hatfield House & Gardens, Hertfordshire
Country Homes & Gardens Show.

7 – 9
Longleat, Wiltshire
Dog Agility Stakes.

7 – 9
Ludlow Castle, Shropshire
Food & Drink Fair.

8
Picton Castle, South Wales
Autumn Plant Sale.

8 – 9
Beaulieu, Hampshire
Autojumble.

8 – 9
Leeds Castle, Kent
Balloon & Vintage Car Weekend.

8 – 9
Leighton Hall, Lancashire
Rainbow Craft Fair.

8 – 9
Parham House & Gardens, Sussex
Country Show in Park.

8 – 9
Ragley Hall, Warwickshire
Garden Fair (Season Tickets holder free on Saturday only).

9
Plas Newydd, North Wales
Guided Archaeological Walk, 2pm.

9
Shugborough, Staffordshire
Heavy Horse & Harvest.

11
Plas Newydd, North Wales
Walk with the Gardener, 2pm.

14 – 16
Goodwood House, Sussex
Motor Circuit Event.

14 – 16
Hever Castle, Kent
Patchwork & Quilting Exhibition.

14 – 16
Lulworth Castle, Dorset
International Floral Design Show & Competition.

15 - 16
Capesthorne Hall, Cheshire
Rainbow Craft Fair.

22 – 23
Kentwell Hall, Suffolk
Re-creation: Michaelmas.

22 – 23
Longleat, Wiltshire
Tipadel Hill Climb.

O C T O B E R

1 – 7
Abbot Hall Art Gallery, Cumbria
Paula Rego.

1 – 31
Fairfax House, Yorkshire
Cutting Edge – the evolution of cutlery and place settings.

1 – 31
Museum of Costume & Assembly Rooms, Somerset
'Fashion in the Fifties' traces the flowering of fashion talent in the glamorous decade following the War.

3 – 31
Nunnington Hall, Yorkshire
"Aspects of Ryedale and the North York Moors" Art Exhibition by Heather Watson (normal opening times and prices apply).

4 – 31
Blackwell – The Artistic House, Cumbria
Kokten Korgei – Contemporary Crafts from Japan.

6 – 7
Eastnor Castle, Herefordshire
Festival of Fine Food and Drink.

8 – 14
Hever Castle, Kent
Autumn Colour Week.

9
Plas Newydd, North Wales
Walk with the Gardener, 2pm.

10 – 14
Leeds Castle, Kent
Autumn Gold – A Celebration of Flowers & Produce.

12 – 14
Finchcocks, Kent
Autumn Fair.

12 – 14
Hopetoun House, Edinburgh City, Coast & Countryside, Scotland
Antiques Fair.

13
Leighton Hall, Lancashire
Teddy Bear Fair.

13 – 14
Ragley Hall, Warwickshire
Craft Fair.

13 – 14
(Stop Press: this event will now take place on 27 – 28 Oct)
Kentwell Hall, Suffolk
Re-creation: World War II.

14
Leighton Hall, Lancashire
Dolls House & Miniaturist Fair.

16 – 31
Abbot Hall Art Gallery, Cumbria
Hughie O'Donoghue – Carborundum Prints: Process and Content.

17 – 21
Nunnington Hall, Yorkshire
Apple Week – display of apples and appletising recipes in the Tea Room (normal opening times and prices apply).

19 – 21
Loseley Park, Surrey
Antique Fair.

20 – 21
Cobham Hall, Kent
Medway Craft Fair.

20 – 28
Rievaulx Terrace and Temples, Yorkshire
Sammy Squirrel's Survival Trail, £1 per Trail (normal admission applies). Forage in the wood for acorns to help you make it through the winter.

21
Plas Newydd, North Wales
Marvellous Shows of Magic.

21
Westbury Court Garden, Gloucestershire
Apple Day.

22 – 25
Powderham Castle, Devon
Phillips Fine Art Sale.

22 – 26
Leeds Castle, Kent
Half Term Halloween Event.

23
Plas Newydd, North Wales
Clowns & Kites Workshop.

27
Blair Castle, Perthshire, Scotland
Glenfiddich Piping Championships (contact: Mrs L Maxwell on 01698 843843).

27 – 28
Kentwell Hall, Suffolk
Re-creation: World War II.

27 – 28
Stowe House, Buckinghamshire
Craft Fair.

28
Blair Castle, Perthshire, Scotland
Glenfiddich Fiddling Championships (contact: Mrs L Maxwell on 01698 843843).

28
Plas Newydd, North Wales
Tricks & Treats.

30 – 31
Holme Pierrepont Hall, Nottinghamshire
Needlework: Ancient & Modern, open from 2 - 5.30pm, to raise funds for St Edmund's Church.

N O V E M B E R

1
Holme Pierrepont Hall, Nottinghamshire
Needlework: Ancient & Modern, open from 2 - 5.30pm, to raise funds for St Edmund's Church.

1 – 4
Museum of Costume & Assembly Rooms, Somerset
'Fashion in the Fifties' traces the flowering of fashion talent in the glamorous decade following the War.

1 – 4
Nunnington Hall, Yorkshire
"Aspects of Ryedale and the North York Moors" Art Exhibition by Heather Watson (normal opening times and prices apply)

1 – 20
Fairfax House, Yorkshire
Cutting Edge – the evolution of cutlery and place settings.

1 – 30
Abbot Hall Art Gallery, Cumbria
Hughie O'Donoghue – Carborundum Prints: Process and Content.

1 – 30
Blackwell – The Artistic House, Cumbria
Kokten Korgei – Contemporary Crafts from Japan.

3
Leeds Castle, Kent
Grand Firework Spectacular.

3 – 4
Plas Newydd, North Wales
Autumn Book Fair.

10
Nunnington Hall, Yorkshire
"Putting the House to Bed", 10-12 noon, £5 adult, £2.50 child – coffee and biscuits (booking essential).

10 – 11
Plas Newydd, North Wales
Patchwork Display & Workshop.

17
Plas Newydd, North Wales
Display of Worked Tapestry Pieces.

18
Plas Newydd, North Wales
Make a Seasonal Decorated Swag, 1.30-3.30pm (booking essential).

17 – 18
Goodwood House, Sussex
Goodwood Antiques Fair.

23 – 25
Hopetoun House, Edinburgh City, Coast & Countryside, Scotland
Hopetoun's Present Event Shopping Fair.

24
Plas Newydd, North Wales
Sugarcraft Demonstration, 10am-12 noon, 1 - 3pm (booking essential).

24 – 25
Ludlow Castle, Shropshire
Medieval Christmas Fayre.

24 – 25
Nunnington Hall, Yorkshire
Ryedale Craft Weekend, 10.30am-3.30pm, £1.50, Tea Room and Shop open, House closed.

24 – 25
Ragley Hall, Warwickshire
Yuletide Craft Fair.

25
Gilbert White's House & Oates Museum, Hants
Annual Mulled Wine & Christmas Shopping Day.

25
Plas Newydd, North Wales
Make a Foliage Welcome Ring, 1.30-3.30pm (booking essential).

D E C E M B E R

1
Plas Newydd, North Wales
National Tree Dressing Day.

1 – 21
Abbot Hall Art Gallery, Cumbria
Hughie O'Donoghue – Carborundum Prints: Process and Content.

1 – 21
Blackwell – The Artistic House, Cumbria
Kokten Korgei – Contemporary Crafts from Japan.

1, 2, 8, 9, 15 & 16
Plas Newydd, North Wales
Father Christmas comes to Plas Newydd, 1-3pm.

2
Plas Newydd, North Wales
Make a Gorgeous Garland, 1.30-3.30pm (booking essential).

3 – 31
Fairfax House, Yorkshire
Annual Exhibition on the 'Keeping of Christmas'.

4 – 7
Shugborough, Staffordshire
Shuborough Victorian Christmas Evening.

5
Baddesley Clinton, Warwickshire
Pruning Fruit & Nut Trees, 10am.

8
Nunnington Hall, Yorkshire
The Leeds Waites – Christmas Concert, 7pm – Mulled Wine & Mince Pies, £10.

8
Plas Newydd, North Wales
Anglesey Farmhouse Chocolates, 1-4pm.

9
Plas Newydd, North Wales
Make a Christmas Arrangement, 1.30-3.30pm (booking essential).

10
Plas Newydd, North Wales
Christmas Concert in the Music Room, 7.30pm.

10 – 24
Leeds Castle, Kent
Christmas at the Castle.

This list is merely intended to draw attention to properties who host Special Events, it is advisable to contact the property to confirm dates and times.

37

www.hudsons.co.uk – your gateway to heritage sites

Useful Web Addresses

Hudson's	www.hudsons.co.uk
Historic Houses Association	www.hha.org.uk
National Trust	www.nationaltrust.org.uk
English Heritage	www.english-heritage.org.uk
National Trust For Scotland	www.nts.org.uk
Historic Scotland	www.historic-scotland.gov.uk
CADW	www.cadw.wales.gov.uk
Dúchas	www.heritageireland.ie
Historic Royal Palaces	www.hrp.org.uk
The Royal Collection	www.the-royal-collection.org.uk
National Gardens Scheme	www.ngs.org.uk
British Tourist Authority	www.visitbritain.com
Wordsworth's Lake District	www.wordsworthlakes.co.uk
Heritage Venues	www.heritagevenues.co.uk

PLACES TO STAY

Landmark Trust	www.landmarktrust.co.uk
Alastair Sawday Publishing	www.sawdays.co.uk
Bed & Breakfast for Gardens Lovers	www.bbgl.co.uk

www.hudsons.co.uk

Make your life easier. Go to www.hudsons.co.uk and you can click on direct links to all the properties in this index. No need to type in each address. More are being added all

PROPERTY	COUNTY	WEB ADDRESS
1 Royal Crescent	Somerset	www.bath-preservation-trust.org.uk
Abbey Pumping Station	Leicestershire	www.leicestermuseums.ac.uk
Abbot Hall Art Gallery	Cumbria	www.abbothall.org.uk
Aberglasney Gardens	South Wales	www.aberglasney.org
Adlington Hall	Cheshire	www.adlingtonhall.com
Alnwick Castle	Northumberland	www.alnwickcastle.com
Althorp	Northamptonshire	www.althorp.com
Ancient House	Suffolk	www.landmarktrust.co.uk
Angus Folk Museum	Scotland	www.nts.org.uk/angus.html
Anne of Cleves House	Sussex	www.sussexpast.co.uk
Apsley House	London	www.vam.ac.uk/Infodome
Arbuthnott House	Scotland	www.arbuthnott.co.uk
Archaeological Resource Centre	Yorkshire	www.jorvik-viking-centre.co.uk/arc.html
Ardington House	Oxfordshire	www.ardingtonhouse.com
Arduaine Garden	Scotland	www.nts.org.uk/arduaine.html
Arley Hall	Cheshire	www.arleyestate.zuunet.co.uk
Armadale Castle Garden & Musuem of the Isles	Scotland	www.cland.demon.co.uk
Arniston House	Scotland	www.arniston-house.co.uk
Arundel Castle	Sussex	www.arundelcastle.org
Astley Hall	Lancashire	www.astleyhall.co.uk
Athelhampton House & Gardens	Dorset	www.athelhampton.co.uk
Auckland Castle	Co Durham	www.auckland-castle.co.uk
Avington Park	Hampshire	www.avingtonpark.co.uk
Bachelors' Club	Scotland	www.nts.org.uk/bachelor.html
Baddesley Clinton	Warwickshire	www.ntrustsevern.org.uk/baddesle.htm
Ballindalloch Castle	Scotland	www.ballindallochcastle.co.uk
Ballindoolin House & Garden	Ireland	www.ballindoolin.com
Ballywalter Park	Ireland	www.dunleath-estates.co.uk
Bamburgh Castle	Northumberland	www.bamburghcastle.com
Bannockburn Heritage Centre	Scotland	www.nts.org.uk/bannockburn.html
Banqueting House	London	www.hrp.org.uk/bh/indexbh.htm
Bantry House & Garden	Ireland	www.cork-guide.ie/bnry_hse.htm
Barnsley House	Gloucestershire	www.barnsleyhouse.com
J M Barrie's Birthplace	Scotland	www.nts.org.uk/barrie.html
Barry Mill	Scotland	www.nts.org.uk/barry.html
Beaulieu	Hampshire	www.beaulieu.co.uk
Beaumaris Castle	North Wales	www.cadw.wales.gov.uk
Belchamp Hall	Suffolk	www.belchamphall.com
Belmont	Kent	www.swale.gov.uk/sbctourism/sta/belmont.htm
Belvoir Castle	Leicestershire & Rutland	www.belvoircastle.com
Benington Lordship	Hertfordshire	www.beningtonlordship.co.uk
Berrington Hall	Herefordshire	www.ntrustsevern.org.uk/berringt.htm
Birmingham Botanical Gardens	West Midlands	www.bham-bot-gdns.demon.co.uk
Birr CastleDemesne	Ireland	www.birrcastle.com
Blackwell – The Artistic House	Cumbria	www.blackwell.org.uk
Blaenavon Ironworks	South Wales	www.cadw.wales.gov.uk
Blairquhan Castle	Scotland	www.blairquhan.co.uk
Blenheim Palace	Oxfordshire	www.blenheimpalace.com
Bluecoat Arts Centre	Merseyside	www.bluecoatartscentre.com
Bodnant Garden	North Wales	www.sissons.demon.co.uk/bodnant.htm
Bolton Abbey	Yorkshire	www.boltonabbey.com
Bolton Castle	Yorkshire	www.boltoncastle.co.uk
Borde Hill Garden	Sussex	www.bordehill.co.uk
Bosworth Battlefield	Leicestershire & Rutland	www.leics.gov.uk
Boughton House	Northamptonshire	www.boughtonhouse.org.uk
Boughton Monchelsea	Kent	www.boughtonmonchelseaplace.co.uk
Bowood House	Wiltshire	www.bowood-estate.co.uk
Branklyn Garden	Scotland	www.nts.org.uk/branklyn.html

PROPERTY	COUNTY	WEB ADDRESS
Brodick Castle & Country Park	Scotland	www.nts.org.uk/brodick.html
Brodie Castle	Scotland	www.nts.org.uk/brodie.html
Broughton Castle	Oxfordshire	www.broughtoncastle.demon.co.uk
Broughton House & Garden	Scotland	www.nts.org.uk/broughton.html
Buckingham Palace	London	www.the-royal-collection.org.uk
Burghley House	Lincolnshire	www.burghley.co.uk
Burncoose Nurseries	Cornwall	www.burncoose.co.uk
Buscot Park	Oxfordshire	www.faringdon-coll.com
Cabinet War Rooms	London	www.iwm.org.uk
Cadhay	Devon	www.eastdevon.net/cadhay
Caerhays Castle	Cornwall	www.eclipse.co.uk/caerhays
Caerleon Roman Baths & Amphitheatre	South Wales	www.cadw.wales.gov.uk
Caerphilly Castle	South Wales	www.cadw.wales.gov.uk
Caernarfon Castle	North Wales	www.cadw.wales.gov.uk
Cambo Gardens	Scotland	www.camboestate.com
Canterbury Cathedral	Kent	www.canterbury-cathedral.org
Thomas Carlyle's Birthplace	Scotland	www.nts.org.uk/carlyles.html
Carreg Cennen Castle	South Wales	www.cadw.wales.gov.uk
Castell Coch	South Wales	www.cadw.wales.gov.uk
Castle Bromwich Hall Gardens	West Midlands	www.cbhgt.swinternet.co.uk
Castle Fraser & Garden	Scotland	www.nts.org.uk/fraser.html
Castle Howard	Yorkshire	www.castlehoward.co.uk
Cathedral Church of St Nicholas	Tyne & Wear	www.newcastle-ang-cathedral-stnicholas.org.uk
Catton Hall	Derbyshire	www.catton-hall.com
Cawdor Castle	Scotland	www.cawdorcastle.com
Charlecote Park	Warwickshire	www.ntrustsevern.org.uk/charleco.htm
Charleston	Sussex	www.charleston.org.uk
Chatsworth	Derbyshire	www.chatsworth-house.co.uk
Chavenage	Gloucestershire	www.chavenage.com
Chedworth Roman Villa	Gloucestershire	www.ntrustsevern.org.uk/chedwort.htm
Chepstow Castle	South Wales	www.cadw.wales.gov.uk
Chillingham Castle	Northumberland	www.chillingham-castle.com
Chillington Hall	Staffordshire	www.chillingtonhall.co.uk
Cilgerran Castle	South Wales	www.cadw.wales.gov.uk
Claverton Manor	Somerset	www.americanmuseum.org
Clifton Park Museum	Yorkshire	www.rma.org.uk
Cobham Hall	Kent	www.cobhamhall.com
Combermere Abbey	Shropshire	www.combermereabbey.co.uk
Conwy Castle	North Wales	www.cadw.wales.gov.uk
Corsham Court	Wiltshire	www.touristnetuk.com/S0/corsham/index.htm
Coton Manor Garden	Northamptonshire	www.cotonmanor.co.uk
Cottesbrooke Hall & Gardens	Northamptonshire	www.cottesbrookehall.co.uk
Coughton Court	Warwickshire	www.coughtoncourt.co.uk
Courtauld Gallery	London	www.courtauld.ac.uk
Coventry Cathedral	West Midlands	www.coventrycathedral.org
Cowper & Newton Museum	Buckinghamshire	www.mkheritage.co.uk/cnm
Cragside	Northumberland	www.ntnorth.demon.co.uk
Cranborne Manor Garden	Dorset	www.cranborne.co.uk
Crathes Castle & Garden	Scotland	www.nts.org.uk/crathes.html
Criccieth Castle	North Wales	www.cadw.wales.gov.uk
Croft Castle	Herefordshire	www.ntrustsevern.org.uk/croft.htm
Croome Park	Worcestershire	www.ntrustsevern.org.uk
Croxteth Hall & Country Park	Merseyside	www.croxteth.co.uk
Culloden	Scotland	www.nts.org.uk/culloden.html
Culross Palace	Scotland	www.nts.org.uk/culross.html
Culzean Castle & Country Park	Scotland	www.nts.org.uk/culzean.html
Cymer Abbey	North Wales	www.cadw.wales.gov.uk
Dalemain	Cumbria	www.dalemain.com
Dalmeny House	Scotland	www.dalmeny.co.uk

PROPERTY	COUNTY	WEB ADDRESS
Dapdune Wharf	Surrey	www.nationaltrust.org.uk/southern
Denbigh Castle	North Wales	www.cadw.wales.gov.uk
Dickens House Museusm	London	www.dickensmuseum.com
Dimbola Lodge	Isle of Wight	www.dimbola.co.uk
Docton Mill & Garden	Devon	www.doctonmill.co.uk
Doddington Hall	Lincolnshire	www.doddingtonhall.free-online.co.uk
Dolwyddelan Castle	North Wales	www.cadw.wales.gov.uk
Dorney Court	Berkshire	www.dorneycourt.co.uk
Dorset County Museum	Dorset	www.dorset.museum.clara.net
Dove Cottage & Wordsworth Museum	Cumbria	www.wordsworthlakes.co.uk
Drum Castle	Scotland	www.nts.org.uk/drum.html
Drumlanrig Castle	Scotland	www.drumlanrigcastle.org.uk
Duart Castle	Scotland	www.holidaymull.org/members/duart.html
Duncombe Park	Yorkshire	www.duncombepark.com
Duns Castle	Scotland	www.dunscastle.co.uk
Dunvegan Castle	Scotland	www.dunvegancastle.com
East Lambrook Manor Gardens	Somerset	www.margeryfish.com
Eastnor Castle	Herefordshire	www.eastnorcastle.com
Elgar Birthplace Museum	Worcestershire	www.elgar.org
Elsham Hall Country & Wildlife Park and Barn Theatre	Lincolnshire	www.brigg.com/elsham.htm
Englefield House	Berkshire	www.englefield-est.demon.co.uk
Essex Secret Bunker	Essex	www.essexsecretbunker.com
Escot Country Park & Gardens	Devon	www.escot-devon.co.uk
Exbury Gardens	Hampshire	www.exbury.co.uk
Eyam Hall	Derbyshire	www.eyamhall.co.uk
Fairfax House	Yorkshire	www.fairfaxhouse.co.uk
Falkland Palace	Scotland	www.nts.org.uk/falkland.html
Finchcocks	Kent	www.argonet.co.uk/finchcocks
Fishbourne Roman Palace	Sussex	www.sussexpast.co.uk
Ford Green Hall	Staffordshire	www.stoke.gov.uk/museums/fordgreen/
Forde Abbey	Dorset	www.fordeabbey.co.uk
Fountains Abbey	Yorkshire	www.fountainsabbey.org.uk
Freud Museum	London	www.freud.org.uk
Fursdon	Devon	www.fursdon.co.uk
Fyvie Castle	Scotland	www.nts.org.uk/fyvie.html
Gainsborough's House	Suffolk	www.gainsborough.org
Gardens of Easton Lodge	Essex	www.eastonlodge.co.uk
Gardens of the Rose	Hertfordshire	www.roses.co.uk/harkness/rnrs/gardens.htm
Gawsworth Hall	Cheshire	www.gawsworthhall.com
Georgian House	Scotland	www.nts.org.uk/georgian.html
Gilbert Collection	London	www.gilbert-collection.org.uk
Gladstone's Land	Scotland	www.nts.org.uk/gladstone.html
Glamis Castle	Scotland	www.great-houses-scotland.co.uk/glamis
Glastonbury Abbey	Somerset	www.glastonburyabbey.com
Glencoe	Scotland	www.nts.org.uk/glencoe.html
Glenfinnan Monument	Scotland	www.nts.org.uk/glenfinnan.html
Gloucester Cathedral	Gloucestershire	www.gloucestercathedral.uk.com
Goddards	Surrey	www.landmarktrust.co.uk
Goodwood House	Sussex	www.goodwood.co.uk
Great Comp	Kent	www.greatcomp.co.uk
Greenbank Garden	Scotland	www.nts.org.uk/greenbank.html
The Greyfriars	Worcestershire	www.ntrustsevern.org.uk/greyfria.htm
Greywalls	Scotland	www.greywalls.co.uk
Grimsthorpe Castle	Lincolnshire	www.grimsthorpe.co.uk
The Guildhall	Leicestershire	www.leicestermuseums.ac.uk
Guildhall Gallery	Hampshire	www.winchester.gov.uk/heritage/home.htm
Gwydir Castle	North Wales	www.gwydir-castle.co.uk
Haddo House	Scotland	www.nts.org.uk/haddo.html
Haddon Hall	Derbyshire	www.haddonhall.co.uk
Haddonstone Show Garden	Northamptonshire	www.haddonstone.co.uk

PROPERTY	COUNTY	WEB ADDRESS
∥ Haldon Belvedere/ Lawrence Castle	Devon	www.haldonbelvedere.co.uk
∥ Hall Place	Kent	www.bexley.gov.uk
∥ Ham House	London	www.nationaltrust.org.uk/southern
∥ Hammerwood Park	Sussex	www.name.is/hammerwood
∥ Hampton Court	Herefordshire	www.hamptoncourt.org.uk
∥ Hampton Court Palace	Surrey	www.hrp.org.uk/hcp/indexhcp.htm
∥ Hanbury Hall	Worcestershire	www.ntrustsevern.org.uk/hanbury.htm
∥ Harburn House	Scotland	www.harburnhouse.com
∥ Harewood House	Yorkshire	www.harewood.org
∥ Harlech Castle	North Wales	www.cadw.wales.gov.uk
∥ Harmony Garden	Scotland	www.nts.org.uk/harmony.html
∥ Hartland Abbey	Devon	www.hartlandabbey.com
∥ Harvington Hall	Worcestershire	www.harvingtonhall.org.uk
∥ Harwich Maritime & Lifeboat Museums	Essex	www.micrologic-ltd.co.uk/harwich/maritime.htm
∥ Harwich Redoubt Fort	Essex	www.micrologic-ltd.co.uk/harwich/redoubt.htm
∥ Hatchlands/Clandon Park	Surrey	www.nationaltrust.org.uk
∥ Helmingham Hall Gardens	Suffolk	www.helmingham.com
∥ Hengrave Hall Centre	Suffolk	www.hengravehallcentre.org.uk
∥ Hergest Croft Gardens	Herefordshire	www.hergest.co.uk
∥ Herstmonceux Castle Gardens	Sussex	www.seetb.org.uk/herstmonceux
∥ Hestercombe Gardens	Somerset	www.hestercombegardens.com
∥ Hever Castle	Kent	www.hevercastle.co.uk
∥ Hidcote Manor Garden	Gloucestershire	www.ntrustsevern.org.uk/hidcote.htm
∥ High Beeches Gardens	Sussex	www.highbeeches.com
∥ Higham Park	Kent	www.higham-park.co.uk
∥ Highclere Castle	Hampshire	www.highclerecastle.co.uk
∥ Highcliffe Castle	Dorset	www.christchurch.gov.uk/highcliffecastle
∥ Hill House	Scotland	www.nts.org.uk/hillhouse.html
∥ Hill of Tarvit Mansionhouse	Scotland	www.nts.org.uk/hill.html
∥ The Sir Harold Hillier Gardens & Arboretum	Hampshire	www.hillier.hants.gov.uk/
∥ Holker Hall & Gardens	Cumbria	www.furness.co.uk/on-line/holker.htm
∥ Holkham Hall	Norfolk	www.holkham.co.uk
∥ Holme Pierrepont Hall	Nottinghamshire	www.holmepierreponthall.com
∥ Holmwood House	Scotland	www.nts.org.uk/holmwood.html
∥ Holst Birthplace Museum	Gloucestershire	www.holstmuseum.org.uk
∥ Honeywood Heritage Centre	Surrey	www.sutton.gov.uk
∥ Hopetoun House	Scotland	www.hopetounhouse.com
∥ Houghton Lodge	Hampshire	www.hydroponicum.co.uk
∥ House of Dun	Scotland	www.nts.org.uk/dun.html
∥ House of the Binns	Scotland	www.nts.org.uk/binns.html
∥ Hugh Miller's Cottage	Scotland	www.nts.org.uk/hugh.html
∥ Hutchesons' Hall	Scotland	www.nts.org.uk/hutchesons.html
∥ Hylands House	Essex	www.chelmsfordbc.gov.uk
∥ Inverarary Castle	Scotland	www.inveraray-castle.com
∥ Inveresk Lodge Garden	Scotland	www.nts.org.uk/inversk.html
∥ Inverewe Garden	Scotland	www.nts.org.uk/inverewe.html
∥ Iona Abbey & Nunnery	Scotland	www.historic-scotland.gov.uk
∥ Irish Museum of Modern Art	Ireland	www.modernart.ie
∥ Ironbridge Gorge Museums	Shropshire	www.ironbridge.org.uk
∥ Judge's Lodging	South Wales	www.judgeslodging.org.uk
∥ Keats House	London	www.keatshouse.org.uk
∥ Kellie Castle & Garden	Scotland	www.nts.org.uk/kellie.html
∥ Kelmscott Manor	Gloucestershire	www.kelmscottmanor.co.uk
∥ Kensington Palace	London	www.hrp.org.uk/ken/indexken.htm
∥ Kentwell Hall	Suffolk	www.kentwell.co.uk
∥ Kidwelly Castle	South Wales	www.cadw.wales.gov.uk
∥ King's College	Cambridge	www.kings.cam.ac.uk
∥ Kinnersley Castle	Herefordshire	www.kinnersley.com/castle

PROPERTY	COUNTY	WEB ADDRESS
Knebworth House	Hertfordshire	www.knebworthhouse.com
Kylemore Abbey	Ireland	www.kylemoreabbey.com
Lamphey Bishop's Palace	South Wales	www.cadw.wales.gov.uk
Laugharne Castle	South Wales	www.cadw.wales.gov.uk
Layer Marney Tower	Essex	www.layermarneytower.co.uk
Leeds Castle	Kent	www.leeds-castle.co.uk
Leighton Hall	Lancashire	www.leightonhall.co.uk
Leighton House Art Gallery & Museum	London	www.rbkc.gov.uk/kcservices/libraries/leighton.htm
Leith Hall	Scotland	www.nts.org.uk/leith.htm
Lennoxlove House	Scotland	www.lennoxlove.org
Leonardslee Gardens	Sussex	www.leonardslee.com
Levens Hall	Cumbria	www.levenshall.co.uk
Lewes Castle & Barbican House Museum	Sussex	www.sussexpast.co.uk
Lichfield Cathedral	Staffordshire	www.lichfield-cathedral.org
Little Holland House	Surrey	www.sutton.gov.uk
David Livingstone Centre	Scotland	www.nts.org.uk
Lodge Park	Gloucestershire	www.ntrustsevern.org.uk
Lodge Park Walled Gardens & Steam Museum	Ireland	www.steam-museum.ie
Longleat House	Wiltshire	www.longleat.co.uk
Loseley Park	Surrey	www.loseley-park.com
Lost Gardens of Heligan	Cornwall	www.heligan.com
Lulworth Castle	Dorset	www.lulworth.com
Lydiard Park	Wiltshire	www.swindon.gov.uk/sbc.asp?s=CLMU
Macclesfield Museums	Cheshire	www.silk-macclesfield.org
Manderston	Scotland	www.manderston.co.uk
Mapledurham House & Watermill	Oxfordshire	www.mapledurham.co.uk
Mapperton	Dorset	www.mapperton.com
Marlipins Museum	Sussex	www.sussexpast.co.uk
Maunsel House	Somerset	www.sirbenslade.co.uk
Mawley Hall	Shropshire	www.mawley.com
Mellerstain House	Scotland	http://muses.calligrafix.co.uk/mellerstain
Merchant Adventurers' Hall	Yorkshire	www.theyorkcompany.sagenet.co.uk
Merriments Gardens	Sussex	www.merriments.co.uk
Michelham Priory	Sussex	www.sussexpast.co.uk
Milton's Cottage, John	Buckinghamshire	http:/home.clara.net/pbirger
Mount Stuart House & Gardens	Scotland	www.mountstuart.com
Muncaster Castle	Cumbria	www.muncastercastle.co.uk
Museum of Costume & Assembly Rooms	Somerset	www.museumofcostume.co.uk
Museum of Garden History	London	www.museumgardenhistory.org
Museum of Welsh Life	Wales	www.nmgw.ac.uk
New Lanark	Scotland	www.newlanark.org
Newby Hall	Yorkshire	www.newbyhall.co.uk
Normanby Hall	Yorkshire	www.northlincs.gov.uk
Norwood Park	Nottinghamshire	www.norwoodpark.org.uk
Nostell Priory	Yorkshire	www.nationaltrust.org.uk
Nymans Garden	Sussex	www.nationaltrust.org.uk/southern
Oakham Castle	Leicestershire & Rutland	www.rutnet.co.uk
Otley Hall	Suffolk	www.otleyhall.co.uk
Owlpen Manor	Gloucestershire	www.owlpen.com
Oxwich Castle	South Wales	www.cadw.wales.gov.uk
Packwood House	Warwickshire	www.ntrustsevern.org.uk/packwood.htm
Painshill Landscape Garden	Surrey	www.brainsys.com/cobham/painshill
Painswick Rococo Garden	Gloucestershire	www.rococogarden.co.uk
Palace of Holyroodhouse	Scotland	www.the-royal-collection.org.uk
Palace of Westminster	London	www.parliament.uk
Parham	Sussex	www.parhaminsussex.co.uk
Paxton House & Country Park	Scotland	www.paxtonhouse.com
Pencarrow	Cornwall	www.pencarrow.co.uk
Penhow Castle	South Wales	www.penhowcastle.com
Penshurst Place	Kent	www.penshurstplace.com

PROPERTY	COUNTY	WEB ADDRESS
Peto Garden at Iford Manor	Wiltshire	www.ifordmanor.co.uk
Petworth House	Sussex	www.nationaltrust.org.uk/southern
Picton Castle	South Wales	www.pictoncastle.co.uk
Pitmedden Garden	Scotland	www.nts.org.uk/pitmedden.html
Pitshanger Manor & Gallery	London	www.ealing.gov.uk/pitshanger
Plantation Garden	Norfolk	www.plantationgarden.co.uk
Plas Mawr	North Wales	www.cadw.wales.gov.uk
Polesden Lacey	Surrey	www.nationaltrust.org.uk/southern
Pollok House	Scotland	www.nts.org.uk/pollok.html
Portmeirion	North Wales	www.portmeirion.wales.com
Powderham Castle	Devon	www.powderham.co.uk
Powerscourt Estate	Ireland	www.powerscourt.ie
Prebendal Manor House	Northamptonshire	www.prebendal-manor.demon.co.uk
Preston Manor	Sussex	www.museums.brighton-hove.gov.uk
Preston Mill	Scotland	www.nts.org.uk/preston.html
The Priest House	Sussex	www.sussexpast.co.uk
Priorwood Garden & Dried Flower Shop	Scotland	www.nts.org.uk/priorwood.html
Provost Skene's House	Scotland	www.aagm.co.uk
Quaker Tapestry Exhibition Centre	Cumbria	www.quaker-tapestry.co.uk
Queen's Gallery	London	www.the-royal-collection.org.uk
RHS Garden Hyde Hall	Essex	www.rhs.org.uk
Raby Castle	Co Durham	www.rabycastle.com
Raglan Castle	South Wales	www.cadw.wales.gov.uk
Renishaw Hall	Derbyshire	www.sitwell.co.uk
Rhuddlan Castle	North Wales	www.cadw.wales.gov.uk
Ripley Castle	Yorkshire	www.ripleycastle.co.uk
Rochester Cathedral	Kent	www.rochester.anglican.org
Rockingham Castle	Northamptonshire	www.rockinghamcastle.com
Roman Baths & Pump Room	Somerset	www.romanbaths.co.uk
Rosslyn Chapel	Scotland	www.rosslynchapel.org.uk
Rousham House	Oxfordshire	www.information-britain.co.uk
Royal Mews	London	www.the-royal-collection.org.uk
Royal Observatory & Queen's House	London	www.rog.nmm.ac.uk
Royal Pavilion	Sussex	www.royalpavilion.brighton.co.uk
Royal Society of Arts	London	www.rsa.org.uk
Rug Chapel & Llangar Church	North Wales	www.cadw.wales.gov.uk
Rydal Mount	Cumbria	www.wordsworthlakes.co.uk
St Davids Bishop's Palace	South Wales	www.cadw.wales.gov.uk
St Edmundsbury Cathedral	Suffolk	www.stedmundsbury.anglican.org
St John's Gate	London	www.sja.org.uk/history
St Paul's Cathedral	London	www.stpauls.co.uk
Salisbury Cathedral	Wiltshire	www.salisburycathedral.org.uk
Sand	Devon	www.eastdevon.net/sand
Sandham MemorialChapel	Hampshire	www.nationaltrust.org.uk/southern
Sandon Hall	Staffordshire	www.sandonhall.co.uk
Sandringham	Norfolk	www.sandringhamestate.co.uk
Savill Garden	Berkshire	www.savillgarden.co.uk
Scampston Hall	Yorkshire	www.scampston.co.uk
Scone Palace	Scotland	www.scone-palace.co.uk
Shakespeare Houses	Warwickshire	www.shakespeare.org.uk
Sherborne Castle	Dorset	www.sherbornecastle.com
Sheffield Park Garden	Sussex	www.nationaltrust.org.uk/regionkentesussex
Shugborough	Staffordshire	www.staffordshire.gov.uk/shugboro/shugpark.htm
Sion Hill Hall	Yorkshire	www.sionhillhall.co.uk
Skipton Castle	Yorkshire	www.skiptoncastle.co.uk
Robert Smail's Printing Works	Scotland	www.nts.org.uk/robertsmail.html
Snowshill Manor	Gloucestershire	www.ntrustsevern.org.uk/snowshil.htm
Somerley	Hampshire	www.somerley.com
Somerleyton Hall	Suffolk	www.somerleyton.co.uk

PROPERTY	COUNTY	WEB ADDRESS
Somerset House	London	www.somerset-house.org.uk
Souter Johnnie's Cottage	Scotland	www.nts.org.uk
South Elmham Hall	Suffolk	www.southelmham.co.uk
Southwark Cathedral	London	www.dswark.org
Spencer House	London	www.spencerhouse.co.uk
Standen	Sussex	www.nationaltrust.org.uk/southern
Stansted Park	Sussex	www.stanstedpark.co.uk
Stoneleigh Abbey	Warwickshire	www.stoneleighabbey.org
Stonor	Oxfordshire	www.stonor.com
Stowe Gardens & Park	Buckinghamshire	www.nationaltrust.org.uk
Stowe House	Buckinghamshire	www.stowe.co.uk
Strata Florida Abbey	South Wales	www.cadw.wales.gov.uk
Sudeley Castle	Gloucestershire	www.stratford.co.uk/sudeley
Sulgrave Manor	Northamptonshire	www.stratford.co.uk/sulgrave
Sutton Park	Yorkshire	www.statelyhome.co.uk
Syon Park	London	www.syonpark.co.uk
Tate St Ives	Cornwall	www.tate.org.uk
Tatton Park	Cheshire	www.tatton.park.org.uk
Tenement House	Scotland	www.nts.org.uk/tenement.html
Thirlestane Castle	Scotland	www.thirlestanecastle.co.uk
Thorp Perrow Arboretum & The Falcons of Thorp Perrow	Yorkshire	www.thorpperrow.com
Threave Garden & Estate	Scotland	www.nts.org.uk/threave.html
Tintern Abbey	South Wales	www.cadw.wales.gov.uk
Tissington Hall	Derbyshire	www.tissington-hall.com
Titsey Place	Surrey	www.titsey.com
Torosay Castle & Gardens	Scotland	www.zynet.co.uk/mull/members/torosay.html
Tower of Hallbar	Scotland	www.vivat.org.uk
Tower of London	London	www.hrp.org.uk/tol/indextol.htm
Towneley Hall Art Gallery & Museums	Lancashire	www.burnley.gov.uk/towneley
Traquair	Scotland	www.traquair.co.uk
Trebah Garden	Cornwall	www.trebah-garden.co.uk
Treowen	South Wales	http://freespace.virginnet.co.uk/treowen.com
Tretower Court & Castle	South Wales	www.cadw.wales.gov.uk
Trewithen	Cornwall	www.trewithengardens.co.uk
Uppark	Sussex	www.nationaltrust.org.uk/southern
Upton House	Warwickshire	www.ntrustsevern.org.uk/upton.htm
Usk Castle	South Wales	www.castlewales.com/usk.html
Valle Crucis Abbey	North Wales	www.cadw.wales.gov.uk
The Vyne	Hampshire	www.nationaltrust.org.uk/southern
Waddesdon Manor	Buckinghamshire	www.waddesdon.org.uk
Wallace Collection	London	www.the-wallace-collection.org.uk
Waterperry Gardens	Oxfordshire	www.waterperrygardens.co.uk
Weaver's Cottage	Scotland	www.nts.org.uk/weaver.html
Weobley Castle	South Wales	www.cadw.wales.gov.uk
West Dean Gardens	Sussex	www.westdean.org.uk/gardens
Westbury Court Garden	Gloucestershire	www.ntrustsevern.org.uk/westbury.htm
Westminster Cathedral	London	www.westmintercathedral.org.uk
Weston Park	Shropshire	www.weston-park.com
White Castle	South Wales	www.cadw.wales.gov.uk
White Scar Cave	Yorkshire	www.wscave.co.uk
Whitehall	Surrey	www.sutton.gov.uk
Wilmington Priory	Sussex	www.landmarktrust.co.uk
Wilton House	Wiltshire	www.wiltonhouse.com
Wimpole Hall & Wimpole Home Farm	Cambridgeshire	www.wimpole.org
Winchester College	Hampshire	www.wincoll.ac.uk
Windsor Castle	Berkshire	www.the-royal-collection.org.uk
Winkworth Arboretum	Surrey	www.cornuswwweb.co.uk
Winton House	Scotland	www.wintonhouse.co.uk
Woburn Abbey	Bedfordshire	www.woburnabbey.co.uk
Wordsworth House	Cumbria	www.wordsworthlakes.co.uk

Arley Hall, Cheshire

ENGLAND

Plant Sales Index

Properties where plants are offered for sale

Newby Hall, Yorkshire.

The National Gardens Scheme
Gardens Open For Charity

Garden gates swing open to the public every year for charity, allowing visitors in to see what is behind the hedges of some of the finest private gardens in England and Wales.

Innovative or classic, the NGS embraces them all, from intimate city courtyards and cottage plots to 18th Century landscapes. Find novel solutions to all kinds of garden problems and enjoy privileged insight into inventive planting schemes. Interesting and unusual plants are often available, along with expert tips from the people in the know.

Gardens of England and Wales Open For Charity, the best-selling annual guide published by the NGS, lists all open days with short descriptions of the gardens. The 'Yellow Book', as it is familiarly known, is available at all major booksellers, and is also available on the NGS website.

Garden Finder, a search and mapping facility on the NGS website provides even more information about the gardens, often including photographs. Plan your itinerary using the latest opening information, including some garden openings exclusively announced on the NGS website **www.ngs.org.uk**

If you would like more information, or are interested in finding out about opening your own garden for the Scheme please contact:

Catherine Stepney, Public Relations Administrator
The National Gardens Scheme, Hatchlands Park, East Clandon, Surrey GU4 7RT

T 01483 211535   F 01483 211537   E ngs@ngs.org.uk

Properties included in this list are open to some extent for all or most of the year. See entry for details.

ENGLAND

LONDON

SOUTH EAST

SOUTH WEST

Borde Hill, Sussex.

This list is merely intended to draw attention to properties which are open for most of the year, it is intended only as a guide.

EASTERN REGION

Linlithgow Palace. Historic Scotland.

Stokesay Castle, Shropshire English Heritage

This list is merely intended to draw attention to properties which are open for most of the year, it is intended only as a guide.

5

Crathes Castle. National Trust for Scotland.

SCOTLAND

WALES

IRELAND

MOVIES...

Pictured left to right:
Shakespeare in Love,
Sense and Sensibility.,
Mrs Brown,
The Aristocrats,
The Buccaneers.

Glencoe

Castle Stalker

Megginch Castle

Dunnottar Castle

Drummond Castle

Doune Castle

Blackness Castle

Duns Castle

Manderston

Blairquhan Castle

Alnwick Castle

Warkworth Castle

Aydon Castle

Castle Howard

Hoghton Tower

Lyme Park

Tatton Park

Haddon Hall

Little Moreton Hall

Belton House

Sudbury Hall

Grimsthorpe Castle

Holkham

Portmeirion

Burghley

Wingfield Old College

Peckover House

Somerleyton Hall

Helmingham Hall

Honington Hall

Broughton Castle

Belchamp Hall

Waddesdon Manor

Knebworth

Chavenage

Luton Hoo

Dyrham

Hatfield House

Corsham

Dorney Court

Wilton

Old Wardour Castle

Mompesson House

Montacute House

Houghton Lodge

Mapperton

Arundel Castle

Prideaux Place

Osborne House

Cothele

Powderham Castle

Lanhydrock

Trerice

Saltram

St Michael's Mount

Hampton Court

Marble Hill House

Somerset House

Syon House

Tower of London

Discover the house locations used for some of your favourite films and TV programmes

Some people treat it as a game – trying to recognise the houses and places they see in films and on television. Looking at *Hudson's* can help. Many of the houses featured have been used as film and photographic locations, but that is hardly surprising. Film location managers, seeking historic houses, invariably turn to *Hudson's* as one of their first sources of reference.

Filming on location provides an authenticity that cannot be achieved with studio sets. Actors often find it easier. They can imbibe the atmosphere of a place which not only helps them to be totally natural, but is also conducive to their performance. They don't have to imagine that a building actually extends beyond the studio flat wall. That is why stately homes, manor houses, historic interiors, their landscaped parks and gardens, are regularly in demand by commercial film-makers for use as locations.

But for the house owner it can be alarming. Some have likened the arrival of a film crew to that of a circus coming to town. Space has to be found for mobile canteens, make-up and hairdressing caravans, props, generators, wardrobes and artists' trailers and a production office. Those who are unfamiliar with the filming of a full-scale drama for the cinema or TV will have no idea of how demanding and destructive to normal life location work can be. Nevertheless there is a financial incentive and it can be fun. Moreover, if the house is open and the film is a success, it adds further interest for the visitor.

Some properties are found to be particularly convenient as locations because they are close to London or major television studios such as at Bristol. **Knebworth House**, Hertfordshire (see p267), is used a great deal (*The Canterville Ghost*, 1997; *Wilde*, 1997) while nearby **Luton Hoo** (no longer open to the public) is also used a great deal (*Four Weddings and a Funeral*; *Mrs Brown*, 1997; *A Dance to the Music of Time*, 1997). The warm brick-and-timber façade of **Dorney Court** near Windsor (see p95), with its splendid Great Hall, is sufficiently close to London to feature in a wide variety of film and television productions. **Chavenage** (see p219) which is not far from Bristol, is regularly used, including for BBC's *Casualty* and *Cider with Rosie*, 1998.

...on location

ELIZABETH
1998 starring Cate Blanchett and Joseph Fiennes

Alnwick Castle

The young Queen Elizabeth inherits a country wracked by internal religious conflict through the rule of her father, Henry VIII and the intervention of her Catholic half-sister, Mary. In a few short years she overcomes all odds to become a powerful monarch. Shot around the UK at locations which included **Alnwick Castle** (see p431) and Bamburgh beach, **Aydon Castle** (see p434) and **Warkworth Castle** in Northumberland (see p438); **Haddon Hall**, Derbyshire (see p289) and the **Tower of London** (see p74).

HAMLET

1990 starring Mel Gibson and Glenn Close

Impressive version of Shakespeare's dark tale of Hamlet's vengeance for the murder of his father with the setting of the menacing Castle Elsinore as much a character in the story as the rest of the cast. Shot on location in Scotland using the imposing medieval **Blackness Castle** in Falkirk (see p466) and **Dunnottar Castle** near Stonehaven, Grampian (see p491).

THE MADNESS OF KING GEORGE
1994 starring Nigel Hawthorne and Helen Mirren

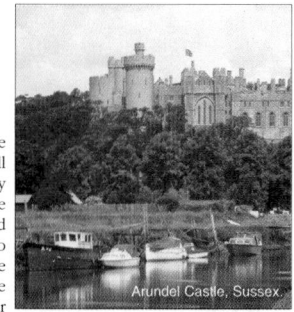
Arundel Castle, Sussex.

In the late 18th century the kindly King George is taken ill and his mental instability makes room for intrigue in the Court as his son and Parliament tussle to see who will take control. The Windsor Castle interiors were shot at **Wilton House** near Salisbury in Wiltshire (see p241) while also used were **Syon House** at Brentford (see p73), **Arundel Castle** in Sussex (see p159) and the impressive moated **Broughton Castle** near Banbury in Oxfordshire (see p144). Further scenes were shot in the Painted Hall of the Royal Naval College Greenwich and St Paul's Cathedral.

MRS BROWN (aka Her Majesty Mrs Brown),
1997 starring Judi Dench, Billy Connolly and Geoffrey Palmer

Much acclaimed and meticulously crafted drama about the extraordinary relationship between Queen Victoria, then the world's most powerful woman and John Brown, a simple but loyal Scottish Highlander. Filmed in **Osborne House**, Isle of Wight (see p181) (Victoria's elaborate holiday home), **Wilton House** near Salisbury (see p241) (doubling as Windsor Castle), **Duns Castle** west of Berwick-upon-Tweed in the Scottish Borders (see p452), and Lincoln's Inn Fields, London.

THE REMAINS OF THE DAY
1993 starring Anthony Hopkins and Emma Thompson

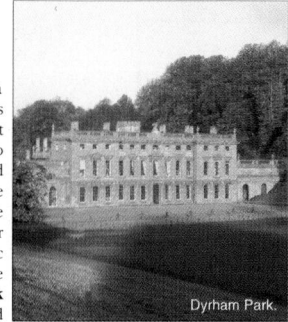
Dyrham Park.

Anthony Hopkins plays Mr Stephens the perfectionist butler at Darlington Hall, who watches over the ruling and serving classes during the 1930s and 40s but refuses to be emotionally drawn to events or even people. Four historic houses were used to create Darlington Hall. **Dyrham Park** near Bath (see p222) was used for exterior shots; **Corsham Court** near Chippenham (see p239) was used for the Library and Dining Room scenes; the Staircase Hall scenes were filmed at **Powderham Castle** near Exeter (see p201) and Badminton House, Gloucestershire (not open) was used for scenes of the servants' quarters.

ROB ROY
1995 starring Liam Neeson and Jessica Lange

Stirring adventure and fine retelling of the legend of the 18th century Scottish Highlander Rob Roy and his battles with the English. Shot around the west coast of Scotland and in Perthshire at **Megginch Castle** (see p481) and at **Drummond Castle** (see p479).

ROBIN HOOD PRINCE OF THIEVES
1991 starring Kevin Costner, Morgan Freeman and Alan Rickman

Shot almost everywhere except Sherwood Forest. Robin finds Marian at Hulme Priory, in the Park at **Alnwick Castle** in Northumberland (see p431); Locksley Castle is actually **Old Wardour Castle**, Wiltshire (see p245).

SENSE AND SENSIBILITY
1995 starring Emma Thompson, Kate Winslet and Alan Rickman

An Oscar winning adaptation of Jane Austen's classic novel about two sisters, one with good sense and the other with a wonderful excess of romantic sensibility. An elegant and witty film. Shot in part at **Montacute House,** Somerset (see p235); at **Saltram House** near Plymouth (see p208); at **Wilton** in Wiltshire (see p241) and at **Mompesson House** in Cathedral Close, Salisbury, Wiltshire (see p244).

SHAKESPEARE IN LOVE
1998 starring Gwyneth Paltrow, Joseph Fiennes, Judi Dench and Geoffrey Rush

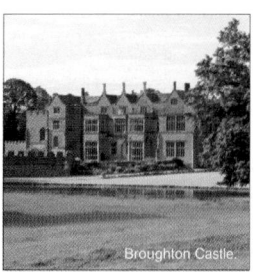
Broughton Castle.

Winner of 7 Oscars including Best Picture, this is a thoroughly enjoyable tale of a young Shakespeare (Fiennes) suffering from writer's block while setting out to write his new play, "Romeo and Ethel, the pirate's daughter". He falls for the beautiful Viola De Lesseps (Paltrow) who, in turn, disguises herself as a man to take part in his new play. Many sites were used including **Broughton Castle**, Oxfordshire (see p144) (stand-in for Viola's stately home); **Hatfield House**, Hertfordshire (see p266) doubled as Greenwich Palace, and the Great Hall at Middle Temple acted as the Banqueting Hall at Whitehall Palace (see p64). Other locations in London included **Marble Hill House** (see p82) and Spitalfields. The final scenes were shot at **Holkham** beach in Norfolk (see p270).

WILDE
1997 starring Stephen Fry and Jude Law

Impressive drama about the life of the playwright and *bon vivant* Oscar Wilde (wonderfully played by Fry), tracing his fame, family life and then fall from grace through his affair with Lord Alfred "Bosie" Douglas (Law). The film-makers made elegant use of locations which included Magdalen College, Oxford; Lulworth and Studland beaches and Swanage Pier in Dorset; **Houghton Lodge**, Hampshire (see p111); Luton Hoo near Luton; and **Somerset House** in London (see p71).

A MAN FOR ALL SEASONS
1966 starring Paul Schofield, Robert Shaw and Orson Welles

This Oscar winning adaptation of Robert Bolt's play about the politico-religious conflict between adulterous King Henry VIII and fervent Catholic Sir Thomas More, is an all-time classic. It was shot on location at **Hampton Court**, Surrey (see p152), the stunning 16th century Tudor Palace on the banks of the Thames.

MONTY PYTHON AND THE HOLY GRAIL
1975 starring John Cleese, Graham Chapman, Terry Jones, Terry Gilliam, Eric Idle and Michael Palin

This hilarious Python team send-up of Arthurian legend, the team of bungling knights encounter characters such as the Knights who say "Ni", flying cows, exploding rabbits, and a Knight who still fights with all his limbs cut off. Though dealing with English legend, most of the film was shot in Scotland, including **Doune Castle** near Stirling (see p485), **Glencoe** (see p485) (where the knights must answer questions to cross the stunning 'Bridge of Death' at the Meeting of Three Waters) and **Castle Stalker** near Oban (see p484) (where the Grail is found).

TWELFTH NIGHT
1996 starring Nigel Hawthorne, Helena Bonham-Carter, Ben Kingsley, Imelda Staunton and Richard E Grant

Prideaux Place.

Shot primarily in Cornwall including at **Prideaux Place**, Padstow (see p196); **Lanhydrock** (see p192) (Olivia's house, garden and estate); **Cotehele** (see p191) (quayside tavern and interior of Orsini's castle), **St Michael's Mount** (see p197) (Orsini's castle) and **Trerice** (see p199) (Olivia's estate – orchard). **Prideaux Place**, which was used extensively, was much altered for the film, but possibly the *piece de resistance* was one of the least expensive in terms of materials: an intricate ornamental grotto to form part of the Italian Garden contained thousands of shells coming from nearby beaches, local fishermen and Rick Stein's restaurant in Padstow.

BRIDESHEAD REVISITED

1982 starring Jeremy Irons and Anthony Andrews

An epic ITV adaptation of Evelyn Waugh's novel has been a hit around the world, with a story of love, loyalty and passion amongst the upper classes during the inter-war years. **Castle Howard** near York (see p369) played the home of the Marchmain family but some interiors were also shot at **Tatton Park** in Cheshire (see p400).

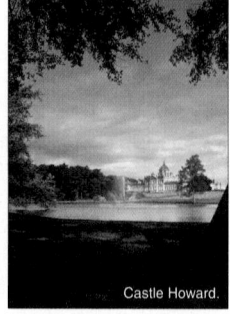
Castle Howard.

MIDDLEMARCH

1994 starring Juliet Aubrey, Patrick Malahide, Douglas Hodge and Rufus Sewell

This acclaimed and popular television version of George Eliot's classic novel tells of love and disillusionment against a backdrop of the 19th century Industrial Revolution. Filmed mainly in the historical Lincolnshire town of Stamford, using also nearby **Grimsthorpe Castle** (see p303) and **Burghley House** (see p301).

Grimsthorpe Castle.

PRIDE AND PREJUDICE

1995 starring Jennifer Ehle, Colin Firth and Alison Steadman

This very popular adaptation of Jane Austen's wonderful love story is about a young woman, Elizabeth Bennet (Ehle), her feminist views and her relationship with the dashing

Lyme Park.

Mr Darcy (Firth). Shot at various locations including the National Trust village of Lacock in Wiltshire; the exteriors of Pemberley are **Lyme Park** in Cheshire (see p403); **Sudbury Hall,** Derbyshire (see p295); **Belton House** near Grantham (see p302); and the Cathedral Close in Salisbury.

THE PRISONER

1966-68 starring Patrick McGoohan

A cult series from the 60s. Patrick McGoohan, as a former secret service agent, is kidnapped and transplanted to a surreal village from which he constantly tries to escape. Filmed at the privately owned Mediterranean-style village of **Portmeirion** in North Wales (see p517). The village was the inspiration of architect Sir Clough Williams-Ellis who fell in love with the Italian fishing village of Portofino and was determined to recreate it in Britain.

AN IDEAL HUSBAND

1999 starring Rupert Everett and Cate Blanchett

Part of the exterior scenes featuring characters and horse riders used in this filmed version of Wilde's play, were filmed at **Waddesdon Manor**, Buckinghamshire (see p98) and were supposed to portray Rotten Row in Hyde Park.

MARTIN CHUZZLEWIT

1994

The BBC version of this Dickens novel starring Paul Schofield, John Mills and Peter Postlethwaite, used as locations **Honington Hall**, Warwickshire (see p352) and **Peckover House**, Cambridgeshire (see p260).

LOVEJOY

1980s

This popular television series about a roguish antiques dealer was shot primarily in East Anglia, where one of the principal locations was **Belchamp Hall**, Suffolk (see p277) as Lady Jane's house. Other house locations for this series were **Helmingham Hall** (see p278), **Wingfield Old College** (see p281) and **Somerleyton Hall** (see p280).

MOLL FLANDERS

1996 starring Alex Kingston, Daniel Craig and Diana Rigg

Wonderful adaptation of Daniel Defoe's widely-read novel with the story romping through the bedrooms and boudoirs of 18th century England. Filmed at **Hoghton Tower**, Preston (see p418); **Grimsthorpe Castle**, Lincolnshire (see p303) and **Little Moreton Hall**, Cheshire (see p403).

TOM JONES

1997

BBC1 television version of Fielding's novel. **Mapperton** in Dorset (see p215) and **Belton**, Lincolnshire (see p302).

CHARLES AND DIANA – UNHAPPY EVER AFTER

1994. A production for ABC starring Catherine Oxenburg

Shot primarily at **Manderston**, Berwickshire (see p450) where different aspects of the house could be portrayed variously as Buckingham Palace, Kensington Palace, Highgrove and Sandringham.

THE BUCCANEERS

1994.

The television adaptation of Edith Wharton's novel "The Buccaneers" included locations at **Castle Howard**, Yorkshire (see p369) and at **Houghton Lodge**, Hampshire (see p111).

Houghton Lodge.

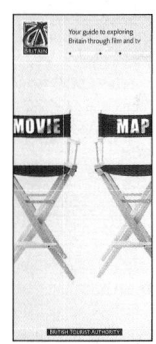

THE COUNTIES OF

ENGLAND

E N G L A N D

E N G L A N D

The Tower of London ·

London

The Tower of London

For nearly as long as the millennium itself, the Tower of London has stood guard over the capital city, its vast stone keep testament to the power of William the Conqueror. Over the centuries it has served as a fortress, royal palace, treasury, mint, state prison and even a zoo. Awarded London Tourist Board Visitor Attraction of the Year 2000, it is renowned as home to the Crown Jewels and world-famous Beefeaters.

Since at least 1661, the Crown Jewels have been on display to the public and having moved from various locations in the Tower they now take pride of place in the new Jewel House, opened by Her Majesty the Queen in 1994. The items on show are priceless, representing far more than just precious stones and gold; they symbolise hundreds of years of the British Monarchy and the history that surrounds it.

No visit to the Tower is complete without taking a Yeoman Warder guided tour. Better known as Beefeaters, these former Warrant Officers regale visitors with tales of Kings, Queens, history and intrigue. What better way to discover 900 years of Britain's royal past in 60 minutes?

The great White Tower in the centre of the complex is the heart around which the rest of the fortress grew. Today it houses the Royal Armouries' displays of arms and armour, including two complete suits belonging to Henry VIII. Used throughout the Middle Ages by the sovereign and his court, it was the setting for some of the greatest events in British royal history.

Patrolling the Tower's lawns, the legendary ravens have played their role in Tower life since at least the reign of Charles II. It is said that should they ever leave, the White Tower will crumble and a great disaster befall England. Unwilling to take that chance, a complement of six of the huge black birds and one spare, are kept and tended by the Raven Master.

Home to some of Britain's most spectacular pomp and pageantry, the Tower hosts a series of special events throughout the year to bring history and tradition to life. Please telephone in advance for details.

For further details about *The Tower of London* see entry in London region.

THE DOG-FACED BABOON.

London England

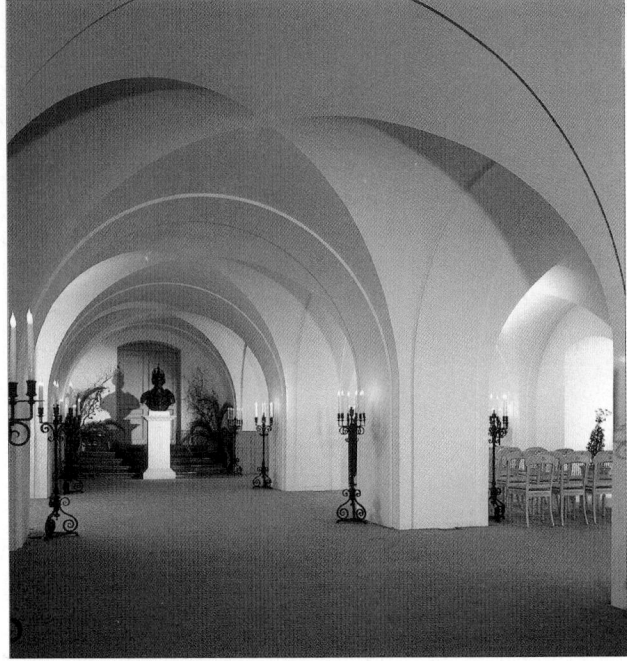

THE BANQUETING HOUSE
Whitehall

Owner:
Historic Royal Palaces

CONTACT

Irma Hay (day visitors)
Fiona Thompson
(functions)
The Banqueting House
Whitehall
London
SW1A 2ER

Tel: 020 7930 4179
or 020 7839 7569

Fax: 020 7930 8268

LOCATION

OS Ref. TQ302 801

Tube Stations:
Westminster,
Embankment
and Charing Cross.

Rail: Charing Cross.

The magnificent Banqueting House is all that survives of the great Palace of Whitehall which was destroyed by fire in 1698. It was completed in 1622, commissioned by King James I, and designed by Inigo Jones, the noted classical architect. In 1635 the main hall was further enhanced with the installation of 9 magnificent ceiling paintings by Sir Peter Paul Rubens, which survive to this day. The Banqueting House was also the site of the only royal execution in England's history, with the beheading of Charles I in 1649.

The Banqueting House is open to visitors, as well as playing host to many of society's most glittering occasions.

OPENING TIMES

All year
Mon - Sat
10am - 5pm
Last admission 4.30pm.

Closed
24 December - 1 January,
Good Friday and other
public holidays.

NB. Liable to close at short
notice for Government
functions.

ADMISSION

Adult £3.90
Child (5-15yrs)..........£2.30
Student...................£3.10
OAP/Conc...............£3.10
Under 5s ....Free

Groups...please telephone:
020 7839 7569 for details.

 Concerts.
No photography in house.

Banquets.

Undercroft suitable.

Video and audio guide.

No parking.

Welcome.

CONFERENCE/FUNCTION		
ROOM	SIZE	MAX CAPACITY
Main Hall	110' x 55'	400
Undercroft	64' x 55'	350

© HM Queen Elizabeth II

© HM Queen Elizabeth II

BUCKINGHAM PALACE
London

BUCKINGHAM PALACE, Windsor Castle and the Palace of Holyroodhouse are the Official residences of the Sovereign and are used by The Queen as both a home and office. The Queen's personal standard flies when Her Majesty is in residence. Furnished with works of art from the Royal Collection, these buildings are used extensively by The Queen for State ceremonies and Official entertaining. They are opened to the public as much as these commitments allow.

The Royal Mews is one of the finest working stables in existence. It provides a unique opportunity for visitors to see a working department of the Royal Household. The Monarch's magnificent Carriages and Coaches including the Gold State Coach are housed here, together with their horses and State liveries.

❖

Owner:
HM The Queen

CONTACT

The Visitor Office
Buckingham Palace
London
SW1A 1AA

Tel: 020 7839 1377

Fax: 020 7930 9625

e-mail: information@
royalcollection.org.uk

(W)

LOCATION

OS Ref. TQ291 796

Nearest underground stations: Green Park, Victoria, St James's Park.

Rail: Victoria.

Air: Heathrow.

Sightseeing tours

A number of tour companies include a visit to the State Rooms in their sightseeing tours. Ask your concierge or hotel porter for details.

© HM Queen Elizabeth II

OPENING TIMES

Opening arrangements may change at short notice.

The State Rooms

6 August - 30 September*
Daily: 9.30am - 4.30pm.

Tickets available during Aug & Sept from the Ticket Office in Green Park.
To pre-book your tickets telephone the Visitor Office 020 7321 2233.

The Queen's Gallery

The Queen's Gallery is closed for refurbishment and will reopen in 2002, the year of The Queen's Golden Jubilee.

The Royal Mews

All year: Monday - Thursday
12 noon - 4pm
Last adm. 3.30pm.
Extra hours are added during the summer months.

* Further days may be added.

ADMISSION

The State Rooms

Adult	£11.00
Child (up to 17yrs)	£5.50
OAP	£9.00
Family (2+2)	£27.50

Groups (15+)	
Per person	£10.00

  No photography inside.

 No guided tours.

Wheelchair users are required to pre-book for the summer opening. The Royal Mews is fully accessible.

No parking. Guide dogs only.

London
England

English Heritage Photo Library

Owner:
English Heritage

CONTACT

Visits:
House Manager
Chiswick House
Burlington Lane
London
W4 2RP

Tel: 020 8995 0508

English Heritage Hospitality:
The Hospitality Manager
Chiswick House
Burlington Lane
London
W4 2RP

Tel: 020 8742 1978

LOCATION

OS Ref: TQ210 775

Burlington Lane
London W4.

Rail: 1/4m NE of
Chiswick Station.

Bus: LT190, 290
(Hammersmith -
Richmond).

CHISWICK HOUSE
Chiswick

CHISWICK HOUSE is internationally renowned as one of the first and finest English Palladian villas. Lord Burlington, who built the villa from 1725 - 1729, was inspired by the architecture and gardens of ancient Rome and this house is his masterpiece. His aim was to create a fit setting to show his friends his fine collection of art and his library. The opulent interior features gilded decoration, velvet walls and painted ceilings. The important 18th century gardens surrounding Chiswick House have, at every turn, something to surprise and delight the visitor from the magnificent cedar trees to the beautiful Italianate gardens with their cascade, statues, temples, urns and obelisks.

English Heritage Hospitality
English Heritage Hospitality offers exclusive use of Chiswick House in the evenings for dinners, concerts, receptions and weddings.

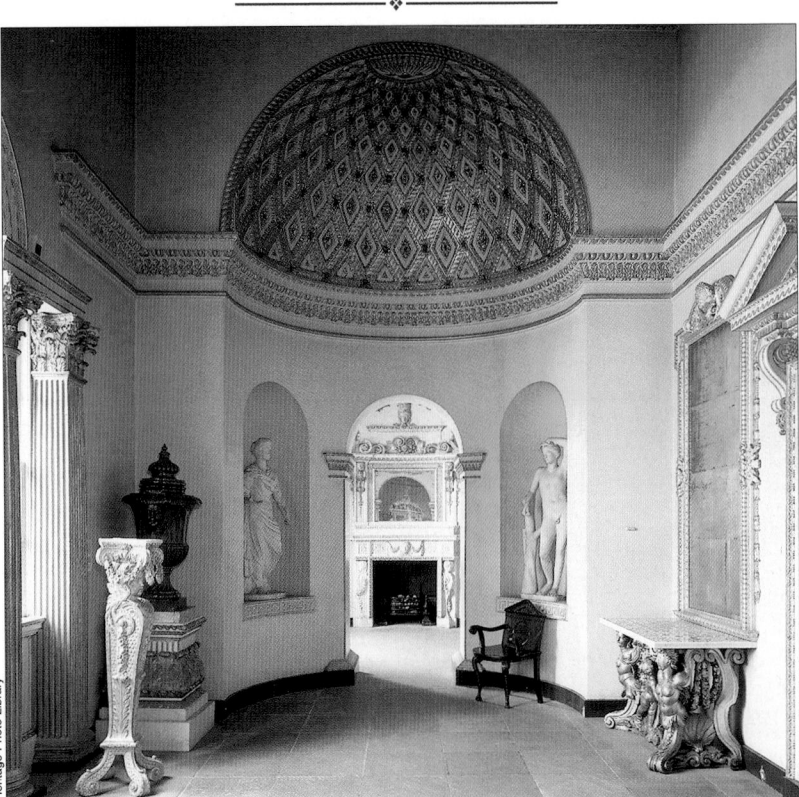

English Heritage Photo Library

CONFERENCE/FUNCTION

ROOM	MAX CAPACITY
Domed Saloon	100 standing 48 dining
Red Velvet Room	24 dining
Green Velvet Room	24 dining
Whole House	150 standing 80 dining

OPENING TIMES

SUMMER
1 April - 30 September
Daily, 10am - 6pm.

AUTUMN
1 - 28 October
Daily, 10am - 5pm.
29 - 31 October:
Daily, 10am - 4.30pm.

WINTER
1 Nov - 31 March
Wed - Sun, 10am - 4pm.

Note: opening times may change in April 2001, please telephone for details before you visit.

ADMISSION

Adult £3.30
Child (5-15yrs) £1.70
Conc £2.50

Groups (11+)
.... 15% discount

Tour leader and coach driver have free entry. 1 extra place for every 20 additional people.

Filming, plays, photographic shoots.

Exclusive private & corporate hospitality.

Access to ground floor.

Personal guided tours must be booked in advance. Colour guide book £2.25.

Free audio tours in English, French & German.

Free if booked in advance. Tel: 020 7973 3485.

Guide dogs in grounds.

Civil Wedding Licence.

Telephone for details.

English Heritage Photo Library/Jonathan Bailey

ELTHAM PALACE
Eltham

Owner: English Heritage

CONTACT

English Heritage Hospitality:
Hospitality Manager
Eltham Palace
Court Yard
Eltham
SE9 5QE

Tel: 020 8294 2577

Visits:
Property Secretary
Eltham Palace
Court Yard
Eltham
SE9 5QE

Tel: 020 8294 2548

LOCATION

OS Ref. TQ425 740

M25/J3, then A20 towards Eltham. The Palace is signposted from A20 and from Eltham High Street.

Rail: Eltham or Mottingham.

The epitome of 1930s chic, Eltham Palace dramatically demonstrates the glamour and allure of the period.

Bathe in the light flooding from a spectacular glazed dome in the Entrance Hall as it highlights beautiful blackbeam veneer and figurative marquetry. It is a *tour de force* only rivalled by the adjacent Dining Room - where an Art Deco aluminium-leafed ceiling is a perfect complement to the bird's-eye maple walls. Step into Virginia's magnificent gold-leaf and onyx bathroom and throughout the house discover lacquered, 'ocean liner' style veneered walls and built-in furniture. A Chinese sliding screen is all

that separates chic '30s Art Deco from the medieval Great Hall. You will find concealed electric lighting, centralised vacuum cleaning and a loud-speaker system that allowed music to waft around the house. Authentic interiors have been recreated by the finest contemporary craftsmen. Their appearance was painstakingly researched from archive photographs, documents and interviews with friends and relatives of the Courtaulds.

Outside you will find a delightful mixture of formal and informal gardens including a rose garden, pergola and loggia, all nestled around the extensive remains of the medieval palace.

❖

English Heritage Photo Library/Jonathan Bailey

CONFERENCE/FUNCTION

ROOM	MAX CAPACITY
Great Hall	400 standing 200 dining
Entrance Hall	100 seated
Drawing Room	120 standing 80 theatre-style
Dining Room	50 dining

OPENING TIMES

1 Apr - 30 September:
Wed - Fri & Sun
10am - 6pm.
1 - 31 October: Wed - Fri & Sun, 10am - 5pm.
1 November - 31 March:
Wed - Fri & Sun,
10am - 4pm.
Open BH Mons throughout the year.
Closed 24 - 26 December & 1 January 2001.
Groups visits must be booked two weeks in advance.

English Heritage Hospitality
English Heritage Hospitality offers exclusive use of the Palace on Mons, Tues or Sats for daytime conferences, meetings and weddings and in the evenings for dinners, concerts and receptions.

ADMISSION

House and Grounds
Adult £5.90
Child......................£3.00
OAP.......................£4.40

Grounds only
Adult £3.50
Child......................£1.80
OAP.......................£2.60

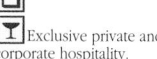 Filming, plays and photographic shoots.

 Exclusive private and corporate hospitality.

 Free.

 Coaches must book.

London England

Crown Copyright: Historic Royal Palaces

Crown Copyright: Historic Royal Palaces

Managed by:
Historic Royal Palaces

CONTACT

Kensington Palace
State Apartments
London
W8 4PX

Tel: 020 7937 9561

WW

LOCATION

OS Ref. TQ258 801

In Kensington Gardens.

Tube Station: Queensway
on Central Line,
High Street Kensington on
Circle & District Line.

KENSINGTON PALACE STATE APARTMENTS
Kensington

The history of Kensington Palace dates back to 1689 when the newly crowned William III and Mary II commissioned Sir Christopher Wren to convert the then Nottingham House into a Royal Palace. The Palace was again altered when George I had the artist William Kent paint the magnificent *trompe l'oeil* ceilings and staircases which can still be enjoyed at this most private of Palaces.

This beautiful historic building has seen such momentous events as the death of George II and the birth of Queen Victoria who began her long reign as Queen in 1837, with a meeting of her Privy Council in the Red Saloon.

Multi-language sound guides are available to lead visitors round the magnificent State Apartments. Highlights include the splendid Cupola Room, the most lavishly decorated state room in the Palace and where Queen Victoria was baptised, and the beautifully restored King's Gallery which is home to several Old Masters from the collection of HM the Queen.

Kensington Palace is also home to 'Dressing for Royalty' – a stunning presentation of Royal Court and Ceremonial Dress dating from the 18th century, which allows visitors to participate in the excitement of dressing for Court – from invitation to presentation. There is also a dazzling selection of 16 dresses owned and worn by HM Queen Elizabeth II.

❖

OPENING TIMES

2000/2001
Mid-October - mid-March:
Daily, 10am,
last entry at 4pm.

(Closed 24 - 26 December)

Mid-March - mid-October:
Daily, 10am -
last entry at 5pm.

ADMISSION

Adult	£8.50
Child* (5-15yrs)	£6.10
Conc.	£6.70
Family	£26.10

* Under 5yrs Free.

Groups:
Tel: 020 7937 7079

Crown Copyright: Historic Royal Palaces

  No photography indoors.

The Orangery serves light refreshments.

 Partially suitable.

Sound guides for Dress Collection and State Apartments.

P Nearby.

 Welcome, please book.

 In grounds, on leads. Guide dogs only in Palace.

❄

FUNCTIONS

ROOM	SIZE	MAX CAPACITY
Orangery	7.1 x 34m	250 receptions 150 dinners

English Heritage Photo Library

KENWOOD HOUSE
Hampstead

KENWOOD, one of the treasures of London, is an idyllic country retreat close to the popular villages of Hampstead and Highgate.

The house was remodelled in the 1760s by Robert Adam, the fashionable neo-classical architect. The breathtaking library or 'Great Room' is one of his finest achievements.

Kenwood is famous for the internationally important collection of paintings bequeathed to the nation by Edward Guinness, 1st Earl of Iveagh. Some of the world's finest artists are represented by works such as a Rembrandt *Self Portrait*, Vermeer's *The Guitar Player; Mary,*

Countess Howe by Gainsborough and paintings by Turner, Reynolds and many others.

As if the house and its contents were not riches enough, Kenwood stands in 112 acres of landscaped grounds on the edge of Hampstead Heath, commanding a fine prospect towards central London. The meadow walks and ornamental lake of the park, designed by Humphry Repton, contrast with the wilder Heath below. The open air concerts held in the summer at Kenwood have become part of London life, combining the charms of music with the serenity of the lakeside setting.

❖

Owner:
English Heritage

CONTACT

Visits:
The House Manager
Kenwood House
Hampstead Lane
London
NW3 7JR

Tel: 020 8348 1286

English Heritage Hospitality:
The Hospitality Manager
Kenwood House
Hampstead Lane
London
NW3 7JR

Tel: 020 7973 3507

LOCATION

OS Ref. TQ271 874

Hampstead Lane, NW3.

Bus: London Transport 210.

Rail: Hampstead Heath.

Underground: Archway or Golders Green Northern Line then bus 210.

English Heritage Photo Library

English Heritage Photo Library

OPENING TIMES

SUMMER
1 April - 30 September
Daily: 10am - 6pm.

1 - 31 October
Daily: 10am - 5pm.

WINTER
1 November - 31 March
Daily: 10am - 4pm.

Closed 24 & 25 December.

Open 1 January 2001.

English Heritage Hospitality offers exclusive use of Kenwood House in the evenings for dinners, concerts and receptions, and the lecture room for daytime events.

ADMISSION

House & Grounds:
Free. Donations welcome.

The 45 minute tour must be booked in advance. Please ask for details on tours available in different languages.

CONFERENCE/FUNCTION	
ROOM	MAX CAPACITY
Orangery	80 dining
Music Room	40 dining
Dining Room	50 dining
Lecture Room	80 theatre-style 300 dining
Whole House	150 dining

ℹ️ Concerts, exhibitions, filming. No photography in house.

🍽️ Exclusive private and corporate hospitality.

♿ Ground floor access.

☕ Available in the Brew House.

Foreign language tours by prior arrangement.

🎧 Personal stereo tours.

🅿️ West Lodge car park on Hampstead Lane. Parking for the disabled.

Free when booked in advance on 020 7973 3485.

Dennis Gilbert

ST PAUL'S CATHEDRAL
London

Owner: Dean & Chapter of St Paul's Cathedral

CONTACT

Mark McVay
The Chapter House
St Paul's Churchyard
London
EC4M 8AD

Tel: 020 7246 8346
020 7246 8348

Fax: 020 7248 3104

e-mail: chapterhouse@
stpaulscathedral.org.uk

LOCATION

OS Ref. TQ321 812

Central London.
Nearest Underground:
St Paul's, Mansion House,
Blackfriars, Bank.

Rail: Blackfriars,
City Thameslink.

Air: London Airports.

A Cathedral dedicated to St Paul has stood at the heart of the City of London for 1400 years, a constant reminder of the spiritual life in this busy commercial centre.

The present St Paul's, the fourth to occupy the site, was built between 1675 - 1710. Sir Christopher Wren's masterpiece rose from the ashes of the previous Cathedral, which had been destroyed in the Great Fire of London.

Over the centuries, the Cathedral has been the setting for royal weddings, state funerals and thanksgivings. Admiral Nelson and the Duke of Wellington are buried here, Queen Victoria celebrated her gold and diamond jubilees and Charles, Prince of Wales married Lady Diana Spencer. Most recently, St Paul's hosted the thanksgiving service for the 100th birthday of HM Queen Elisabeth the Queen Mother.

Hundreds of memorials pay tribute to famous statesmen, soldiers, artists, doctors and writers and mark the valuable contributions to national life made by many ordinary men and women.

The soaring dome, one of the largest in the world, offers panoramic views across London from the exterior galleries. Inside, a whisper in the Whispering Gallery can be heard on the opposite side.

Far more than a beautiful landmark, St Paul's Cathedral is a living symbol of the city and nation it serves.

  No photography, video or mobile phones.

Partially suitable.

 Licensed.

P No parking for cars, limited for coaches.

Guide dogs only.

Dennis Gilbert

CONFERENCE/FUNCTION		
ROOM	SIZE	MAX CAPACITY
Conference Suite		100 (standing)

OPENING TIMES

Mon - Sat, 8.30am - 4.30pm, last admission 4pm.

Guided tours: daily, 11.30am, 1.30pm and 2pm.

Tours of the Triforium: Mons & Thurs, 11.30am & 2.30pm.

Cathedral Shop & Café: 9am - 5.30pm, Suns, 10.30am - 5pm.

Restaurant: 11am - 3.30pm.

Service Times
Mon - Sat
7.30am Mattins (Sat 8.30am)
8am Holy Communion (said)
12.30pm Holy Communion (said)
5pm Choral Evensong

Suns: 8am Holy Communion (said)
10.15am Choral Mattins & sermon
11.30am Choral Eucharist & sermon
3.15pm Choral Evensong & sermon
6pm Evening service

The Cathedral may be closed to tourists on certain days of the year. It is advisable to phone or check our website for up-to-date information.

ADMISSION

Adult £5.00
Child.....................£2.50
Student...................£4.00
OAP......................£4.00

Groups (min 10)
Adult £4.50
Child.....................£2.25
Student...................£3.75
OAP......................£3.75

(2000 prices)

SOMERSET HOUSE
London
including Courtauld Gallery, Gilbert Collection and Hermitage Rooms

SOMERSET HOUSE, Sir William Chambers' 18th century architectural masterpiece, is open to the public for the first time. Situated between Covent Garden and the South Bank, it takes its place as one of Europe's great centres for art and culture, and the enjoyment of long-hidden classical interiors and architectural vistas.

The COURTAULD GALLERY has one of the greatest small collections of paintings in the world, including the finest Impressionist paintings in Britain.

The GILBERT COLLECTION is London's newest museum of the decorative arts. Given to the nation by Sir Arthur Gilbert, the magnificent collections of European silver, gold snuff boxes and Italian mosaics are pre-eminent in the world. Other displays include furniture, Russian Church art and portrait miniatures. The vaulted spaces of Somerset House provide an inspirational setting for these works of great historical and artistic importance.

The HERMITAGE ROOMS at Somerset House recreate, in miniature, the imperial splendour of the Winter Palace and its various wings, which now make up The State Hermitage Museum in St Petersburg. The inaugural exhibition 'Treasures of Catherine the Great' presents a dazzling mix of jewels, silver, antiquities and paintings.

❖

CONTACT

Somerset House
Owner: Somerset House Trust
Strand, London
WC2R 1LA
Contact: Edward Schofield

Tel: 020 7845 4600
Fax: 020 7836 7613
e-mail: info@ somerset-house.org.uk

(W)

Courtauld Gallery,
Courtauld Institute of Art
Tel: 020 7848 2526
e-mail: galleryinfo@ courtauld.ac.uk

(W)

Gilbert Collection
Tel: 020 7420 9400
e-mail: info@ gilbert-collection.org.uk

(W)

Hermitage Rooms
Tel: 020 7845 4630

(W)

LOCATION

OS Ref. TQ308 809

Entrances Victoria Embankment or Strand.
Rail: Underground: Temple or Covent Garden.
Air: London airports.

OPENING TIMES

Courtauld Gallery, Gilbert Collection & Hermitage Rooms
Mon - Sat except BHs, 10am - 6pm.
Suns & BHs, 12 noon - 6pm.
Last admission 5.15pm.

Closed 24 - 26 Dec & 1 Jan.

ADMISSION

Somerset House
Free except special exhibitions.

Courtauld Gallery & Gilbert Collection
Adult £4.00
Child (under 18) ......Free
Student (UK full)......Free
OAP.........................£3.00
Joint Ticket £7.00

Pre-booked Groups
Adult £3.00
Disabled & Helper.............
...........................£2.00pp

Courtauld Gallery
Mons, 10am - 2pm .....Free

Hermitage Rooms
Adult £6.00
Child (under 5) ....Free
Conc........................£4.00
Pre-booked Groups
Adult £4.00

Advance booking advised for Hermitage Rooms:
Ticketmaster 020 7413 3398

Peter Durant

🛍 ℹ Apply at desk for permission for photography/filming.

🍸

🍽 Licensed.

♿

🚶 By arrangement.

🎧 Gilbert Collection and Hermitage Rooms.

🏛 🅿 No parking.

🐕 Guide dogs only. ❄

FUNCTION/RECEPTION	
ROOM	MAX CAPACITY
Silver Gallery	350
Fine Rooms	250
Great Room	200
Fine & Gt Rm.	400
Seamen's Hall	200
Courtyard	2,700

Mark Fiennes

Mark Fiennes

SPENCER HOUSE
St James's Place

SPENCER HOUSE, built 1756 - 66 for the 1st Earl Spencer, an ancestor of Diana, Princess of Wales (1961-97), is London's finest surviving 18th century town house. The magnificent private palace has regained the full splendour of its late 18th century appearance, after a painstaking ten-year restoration programme.

Designed by John Vardy and James 'Athenian' Stuart, the nine state rooms are amongst the first neo-classical interiors in Europe. Vardy's Palm Room, with its spectacular screen of gilded palm trees and arched fronds, is a unique Palladian setpiece, while the elegant mural decorations of Stuart's Painted Room reflect the

18th century passion for classical Greece and Rome. Stuart's superb gilded furniture has been returned to its original location in the Painted Room by courtesy of the V&A and English Heritage. Visitors can also see a fine collection of 18th century paintings and furniture, specially assembled for the house, including five major Benjamin West paintings, graciously lent by Her Majesty The Queen.

The state rooms are open to the public for viewing on Sundays. They are also available on a limited number of occasions each year for private and corporate entertaining during the rest of the week.

❖

CONTACT

Jane Rick
Director
Spencer House
27 St James's Place
London
SW1A 1NR

Tel: 020 7514 1964

Fax: 020 7409 2952

Info Line: 020 7499 8620

LOCATION

OS Ref. TQ293 803

Central London:
off St James's Street,
overlooking Green Park.

Underground:
Green Park.

Mark Fiennes

CONFERENCE/FUNCTION

ROOM	SIZE	MAX CAPACITY
Receptions		400
Lunches & Dinners		130
Board Meetings		40
Theatre Style meetings		100

OPENING TIMES

ALL YEAR
All year
(except January & August)
Suns, 10.30am - 5.30pm.

Last tour 4.45pm.

Tours begin approximately every 20 mins and last 1hr 10 mins. Maximum number on each tour is 20.

Mon mornings for pre-booked groups only.

Open for corporate hospitality except during January & August.

ADMISSION

Adult £6.00
Conc.* £5.00

* Students, Friends of V&A, Tate Gallery and Royal Academy (all with cards), children under 16 (no under 10s admitted).

Prices include guided tour.

ℹ️ No photography inside House.

Ramps and lifts. WC.

Obligatory. Comprehensive colour guide-book £3.50.

P No parking facilities. Coaches can drop off at door.

 SPECIAL EVENTS

• **SPECIFIC SUNDAYS:**
The authentically restored garden of this 18th century London palace will be open to the public on specific Sundays during Spring and Summer. For updated information telephone 020 7499 8620 or see our website: www.spencerhouse.co.uk

Owner: The Duke of Northumberland

CONTACT

Louise Page-Bailey
Syon House
Syon Park
Brentford
TW8 8JF

Tel: 020 8560 0881

Fax: 020 8568 0936

e-mail: louise@
syonpark.co.uk

LOCATION

OS Ref. TQ173 767

Between Brentford and
Twickenham, off the A4,
A310 in SW London.

Rail: Kew Bridge or
Gunnersbury
Underground then
Bus 237 or 267.

Air: Heathrow 8m.

SYON PARK
Brentford

Described by John Betjeman as 'the Grand Architectural Walk', Syon House and its 200 acre park is the London home of the Duke of Northumberland, whose family, the Percys, have lived here since the late 16th century.

Originally the site of a late medieval monastery, Syon Park has a fascinating history. The present house has Tudor origins but contains some of Robert Adam's finest interiors, which were commissioned by the 1st Duke in the 1760s.

Within the 'Capability' Brown landscaped park are 40 acres of gardens which contain the spectacular Great Conservatory designed by Charles Fowler in the 1820s. The House and Great Conservatory are available for corporate and private hire.

Syon House is an excellent venue for small meetings, lunches and dinners in the Duke's private dining room (max 22). The State Apartments make a sumptuous setting for dinners, concerts, receptions, launches and wedding ceremonies (max 120). Marquees can be erected on the lawn adjacent to the house for balls and corporate events. The Great Conservatory is available for summer parties, launches and wedding receptions.

OPENING TIMES

House
14 March - 31 October only
Weds, Thurs, Suns & BHs
11am - 5pm
(open Good Fri &
Easter Sat).
Other times by
appointment for groups.

Gardens
Daily (except 25 & 26 Dec)
10am - 5.30pm or dusk if
earlier.

ADMISSION

House and Gardens
Adult £6.25
Child/Conc..............£5.25
Family (2+2) £15.00

Gardens only
Adult £3.00
Child/Conc..............£2.50
Family (2+2) £7.00

Groups (min 15, max 50)

House and Gardens
Adult £5.75
Child/Conc..............£4.75

Gardens only
Adult £3.00
Child/Conc..............£2.50

 No photography in house. Indoor adventure playground.

 Garden centre.

 Partially suitable.
Licensed.
By arrangement.

 Guide dogs only.

CONFERENCE/FUNCTION		
ROOM	SIZE	MAX CAPACITY
Great Hall	50' x 30'	120
Great Conservatory	60' x 40'	150
Marquee		1000

London England

Crown Copyright: Historic Royal Palaces

ENTRY TO THE TRAITORS GATE

Managed by:
Historic Royal Palaces

CONTACT

The Tower of London
London
EC3N 4AB

Tel: 020 7709 0765

LOCATION

OS Ref. TQ336 806

Tube Station: Tower Hill
on Circle/District Line.
Monument on
Northern Line.

**Docklands Light
Railway:**
Tower Gateway Station.

Rail: Fenchurch Street
Station and
London Bridge Station.

Bus: 15, 25, 42,
78, 100, D1.

Riverboat: From Charing
Cross, Westminster or
Greenwich to Tower Pier.

THE TOWER OF LONDON
London

William the Conqueror began building the Tower of London in 1078 as a royal residence and to control the volatile City of London. Over the ensuing 900 years the Tower has served as a royal fortress, mint, armoury and more infamously as a prison and place of execution.

The Tower of London has been home to the Crown Jewels for the last 600 years and today visitors can see them in all their glory in the magnificent new Jewel House. They are still used by HM The Queen for ceremonies such as the State Opening of Parliament and the 'Crowns and Diamonds' exhibition details the jewels' history, alongside a pile of 2,314 diamonds lent by De Beers.

Visit the White Tower, the original Tower of London, which features new displays by the

Royal Armouries including the Block and Axe, Tudor arms and armour and the Instruments of Torture.

Once inside, the Yeoman Warder 'Beefeaters' give free guided tours providing an unrivalled insight into the darker secrets of over 900 years of royal history. Above the notorious Traitors' Gate, costumed guides evoke life at the court of King Edward I in the recently restored rooms of his Medieval Palace.

See the execution site where many famous prisoners such as two of Henry VIII's wives were put to death and visit the Chapel Royal where they are buried. Special events take place throughout the year, including events during every school holiday, with costumed interpreters.

Crown Copyright: Historic Royal Palaces

Crown Copyright: Historic Royal Palaces 2000

OPENING TIMES

SUMMER
1 March - 31 October
Daily
Mon - Sat: 9am - 5pm
(last admission)
Suns: 10am - 5pm.

WINTER
1 November - 28 February
Tues - Sat: 9am - 5pm
(last admission)
Mons & Suns: 10am - 4pm.

Closed 24 - 26 December
and 1 January.

Buildings close 30 minutes
after last admission.
Tower closes 1 hour after
last admission.

ADMISSION

Telephone Info Line for
admission prices:
020 7709 0765.

**Groups are advised to book,
telephone: 020 7488 5681.**

 No photography
in Jewel House.

020 7488 5762.

Partially suitable. WC.

Available on the wharf.

Open from Feb 2001.

Obligatory. Yeoman
Warder tours are free and
leave front entrance every
1/2 hr.

No parking.

Welcome. Group rates
on request.

Telephone for details.

THE WALLACE COLLECTION
Manchester Square

Hertford House is home to the internationally renowned Wallace Collection, a national museum of fine and decorative arts principally from the 16th - 19th centuries. Originally built for the 4th Duke of Manchester between 1776 - 88, it was leased in 1797 by the 2nd Marquess of Hertford, so beginning 200 years of association between house and family. Today it still serves to display the family's treasures, which were accumulated over five generations, and then bequeathed to the nation by Sir Richard Wallace's widow in 1897.

The 5,470 works of art include some of the world's best-known paintings (among them Frans Hals's *The Laughing Cavalier*), over a thousand items of French 18th century furniture,

sculpture and porcelain and the finest collection of princely arms and armour in this country. Masterpieces by Rubens, Rembrandt, Velázquez, Watteau and Boucher hang above furniture made for the kings and queens of France.

The rich interiors of the ground and first floors continue to evoke something of the domestic splendor and atmosphere of a grandiose 19th century home. This 19th century aesthetic is complemented by the internal courtyard and lower ground floor, which were redeveloped in 2000. Designed by award-winning Rick Mather, the elegant contemporary design extensively features glass, steel and oak, as illustrated by the Sculpture Garden that is crowned by a spectacular glass roof.

CONTACT

Press & Marketing Office
The Wallace Collection
Hertford House
Manchester Square
London
W1U 3BN

Tel: 020 7563 9500

Fax: 020 7224 2155

LOCATION

OS Ref. TQ283 813

Central London behind Selfridges department store.

Tube Station:
Bond Street.

CONFERENCE/FUNCTION		
ROOM	SIZE	MAX CAPACITY
Great Gallery	35.8x10.5m	120
Sculpture Garden	23.1x15.3m	100/250
State & Dining Rms		40
Galleries		300
Lecture Theatre		150
Meeting Rm		50

OPENING TIMES

ALL YEAR

Mon - Sat: 10am - 5pm
Sunday: 12 noon - 5pm

Closed
Good Friday, May Day,
24 - 26 & 31 December
and 1 & 2 January.

ADMISSION

Free.

i No photography in house.

Full range of merchandise including catalogues, postcards, books & gifts.

Rooms are available for a range of events including formal dinners, receptions, seminars and conferences. Tel. Development Office 020 7563 9545.

Ramp access is to the right of the main entrance. A parking space may be booked in advance. Lift to all floors. For full details tel. Access Co-ordinator 020 7563 9515.

Café Bagatelle: morning coffee, lunch & afternoon tea.

Free lectures on the collection are given every day. Private tours can also be arranged. Please tel. Education Department on 020 7563 9551.

P Coaches may set down at Hertford House, parking is at Bayswater Road, W8. Meters in Manchester Square.

A free programme of teaching sessions is available. Please tel. the Education Department on 020 7563 9551.

Open all year.

Tel. for details.

London
England

2 WILLOW ROAD

HAMPSTEAD, LONDON NW3 1TH

Owner: *The National Trust*   **Contact:** *The Custodian*

Tel: 020 7435 6166   **e-mail:** twlgen@smtp.ntrust.org.uk

The former home of Erno Goldfinger, designed and built by him in 1939. A three-storey brick and concrete rectangle, it is one of Britain's most important examples of modernist architecture and is filled with furniture also designed by Goldfinger. The interesting art collection includes works by Henry Moore and Max Ernst.

Location: OS Ref. TQ270 858. Hampstead, London.

Opening Times: 4 - 24 Mar: Sats only, 12 - 5pm, free-flow with tours at 12.30 & 3.30pm; 30 Mar - 3 Nov: Thur - Sat, 12 - 5pm. Last admission 4pm. Guided tours every 45 mins.

Admission: Adult £4.30, Child £2.15. Joint ticket with Fenton House £6.30.

♿Small ground floor area accessible, filmed tour of whole house available.
🐕Obligatory.

APSLEY HOUSE

HYDE PARK CORNER, LONDON W1J 7NT

Owner: *V & A Museum & Dept. for Culture, Media & Sport* **Contact:** *The Administrator*

Tel: 020 7499 5676/495 8525   **Fax:** 020 7493 6576

Apsley House (No. 1, London) was originally designed by Robert Adam in 1771-8. In 1817 it was bought by the Duke of Wellington and enlarged. His London 'Palace' houses his magnificent collection: paintings by Velazquez, Goya, Rubens, Lawrence, Wilkie, Steen, de Hooch and other masters; sculpture, silver, porcelain, furniture, caricatures, medals and memorabilia.

Location: OS Ref. TQ284 799. N side of Hyde Park Corner. Nearest tube station: Hyde Park Corner exit 1 Piccadilly Line.

Opening Times: Tue - Sun, 11am - 5pm, last admission 4.30pm. Closed Mons, (except BHs), Good Fri, May Day BH, 24 - 26 Dec and New Year's Day.

Admission: Adult £4.50, Conc. £3 (both include Soundguide), Child (under 18yrs) Free. Pre-arranged groups (10+): £2.50. Over 60s Free.

📷 ℹ️No photography in house. 🍴 ♿Partially suitable.
🐕By arrangement. 🅿️ In Park Lane. 🐾 Guide dogs only. ✳️ (IW)

ALBERT MEMORIAL   **Tel:** 020 7495 0916 (Booking Agency)

Princes Gate, Kensington Gore SW7

Contact: The Royal Parks Agency (management agency).

An elaborate memorial by George Gilbert Scott to commemorate the Prince Consort.

Location: OS Ref. TQ266 798. Victoria Station 1¹/₂ m, South Kensington Tube ¹/₂ m.

Opening Times: All visits by booked guided tours.

Admission: Adult £3, Child £2.50.

NT Photographic Library/Geoffrey Frosh

Sutton House.

THE BANQUETING HOUSE   **See page 64 for full page entry.**

BLEWCOAT SCHOOL 🌿   **Tel:** 020 7222 2877

23 Caxton Street, Westminster, London SW1H 0PY

Owner: The National Trust   **Contact:** The Administrator

Built in 1709 at the expense of William Green, a local brewer, to provide an education for poor children. The building was used as a school until 1926, and is now the NT London Gift Shop and Information Centre.

Location: OS Ref. TQ295 794. Near the junction with Buckingham Gate.

Opening Times: All year: Mon - Fri, 10am - 5.30pm (Thurs 7pm). Also Sats 18 & 25 Nov & 2/9/16/23 Dec. Closed Bank Holidays.

BOSTON MANOR HOUSE   **Tel:** 020 8560 5441

Boston Manor Road, Brentford TW8 9JX

Owner: Hounslow Cultural & Community Services   **Contact:** Jerome Farrell

A fine Jacobean house built in 1623. The rooms that can be viewed include the State Drawing Room with a magnificent ceiling and fireplace designed in 1623.

Location: OS Ref. TQ168 784. 10 mins walk S of Boston Manor Station (Piccadilly Line) and 250yds N of Boston Manor Road junction with A4 - Great West Road, Brentford.

Opening Times: 1 Apr - 29 Oct: Sats, Suns & BHs, 2.30 - 5pm. Park open daily.

Admission: Free.

BRUCE CASTLE   **Tel:** 020 8808 8772

Haringey Museum & Archive Service, Lordship Lane, London N17 8NU

Owner: London Borough of Haringey

A Tudor building. Sir Rowland Hill (inventor of the Penny Post) ran a progressive school at Bruce Castle from 1827.

Location: OS Ref. TQ335 906. Corner of Bruce Grove (A10) and Lordship Lane, 600yds NW of Bruce Grove Station.

Opening Times: All year: Wed - Sun & Summer BHs, 1 - 5pm. Organised groups by appointment.

Admission: Free.

BUCKINGHAM PALACE

See page 65 for full page entry.

BURGH HOUSE   Tel: 020 7431 0144 Buttery: 020 7431 2516 **Fax:** 020 7435 8817

New End Square, Hampstead, London NW3 1LT

Owner: London Borough of Camden   **Contact:** Ms Helen Wilton

A Grade I listed building of 1703 in the heart of old Hampstead with original panelled rooms, "barley sugar" staircase bannisters and a music room. Home of the Hampstead Museum, permanent and changing exhibitions. Prize-winning terraced garden. Regular programme of concerts, art exhibitions, and meetings. Receptions, seminars and conferences. Rooms for hire. Special facilities for schools visits. Wedding receptions.

Location: OS Ref. TQ266 859. New End Square, E of Hampstead underground station.

Opening Times: All year: Wed - Sun, 12 noon - 5pm. Sats by appointment only. BH Mons, 2 - 5pm. Closed Christmas fortnight, Good Fri & Easter Mon. Groups by arrangement. Buttery: Wed - Sun, 11am - 5.30pm. BHs, 1 - 5.00pm.

Admission: Free.

⬜ ♿ Ground floor & grounds suitable. WC. ⬛ Licensed buttery.
🅿 No parking. 🐕 Guide dogs only. 🔔 ❄

CABINET WAR ROOMS

See right for half page entry.

CAPEL MANOR GARDENS

BULLSMOOR LANE, ENFIELD EN1 4RQ

Owner: Capel Manor Charitable Organisation   *Contact: Miss Julie Ryan*

Tel: 020 8366 4442 **Fax:** 01992 717544

These extensive, richly planted gardens are delightful throughout the year offering inspiration, information and relaxation. The gardens include various themes - historical, modern, walled, rock, water, sensory and disabled and an Italianate Maze, Japanese Garden and 'Gardening Which?' demonstration and model gardens. Capel Manor is a College of Horticulture and runs a training scheme for professional gardeners originally devised in conjunction with the Historic Houses Association.

Location: OS Ref. TQ344 997. Minutes from M25/J25. Tourist Board signs posted.

Opening Times: Daily in summer: 10am - 5.30pm. Last ticket 4.30pm. Check for winter times.

Admission: Adult £4, Conc. £3.50, Child £2, Family £10. Charges alter for special show weekends and winter months.

⬜ ♿ Grounds suitable. WC. ⬛ 🐕 In grounds, on leads. ❄
🛡 Tel. for details.

CABINET WAR ROOMS

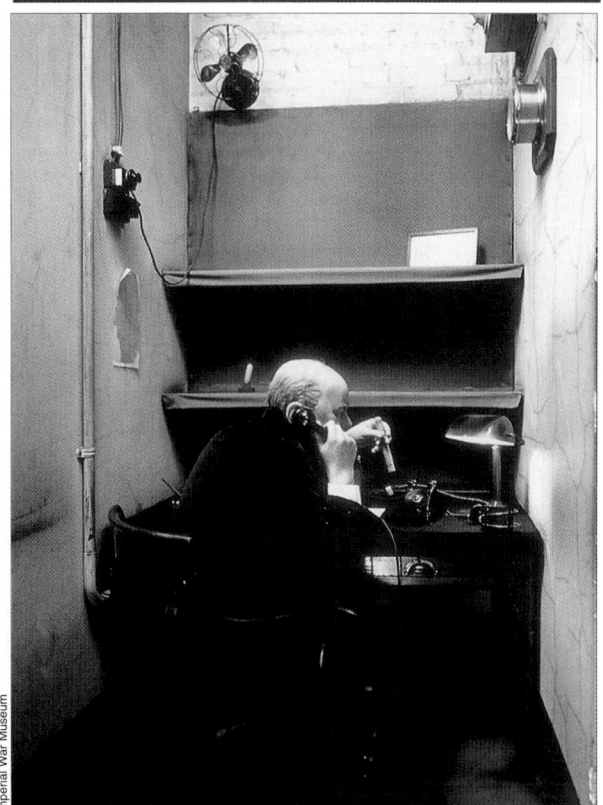

Imperial War Museum

CLIVE STEPS, KING CHARLES STREET, LONDON SW1A 2AQ

Director: Phil Reed   *Contact: Vanessa Rayner*

Tel: 020 7930 6961 **Fax:** 020 7839 5897   **e-mail:** cwr@iwm.org.uk

Visit the hidden world of Churchill's secret underground wartime headquarters and catch a glimpse of the spartan conditions in which he and his Cabinet worked and lived during the Blitz. A former storage basement, the bunker was hurriedly converted in 1939 to become the very nerve centre of the British war effort, operating around the clock, undisturbed by the heavy bombing raids above ground. Step back in time and view the original complex just as it was left at the end of six years of war, when the lights were finally extinguished. Free personal sound guides are provided for every visitor.

Location: OS Ref. TQ301 799. Buses: 3, 11, 12, 24, 53, 77a, 88, 159, 211. Westminster Underground.

Opening Times: All year: daily, 9.30am (1 Oct - 31 Mar: 10am) - 6pm. Last admission 5.15pm. Closed 24/25/26 Dec.

Admission: Adult £5, Child Free, Conc. £3.60. Booked groups (min 10): Adult £3.60, Child Free, Conc. £3.

⬜ ♿ By arrangement.   🅿 None. ❄

London
England

CARLYLE'S HOUSE

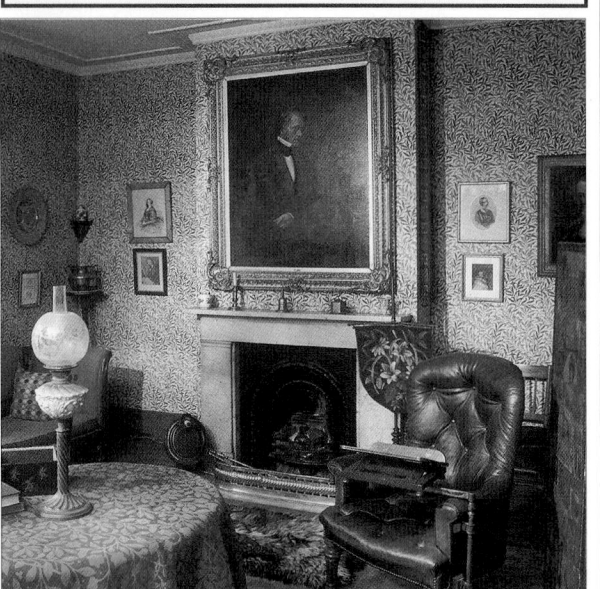

24 CHEYNE ROW, CHELSEA, LONDON SW3 5HL

Owner: The National Trust　　*Contact: The Custodian*

Tel: 020 7352 7087　**Info Line:** 01494 755559

In a quiet and beautiful residential area of London, this Queen Anne house was the home of Thomas Carlyle, the 'Sage of Chelsea', for some 47 years until his death in 1881. The skilful Scottish home-making of his wife Jane is much in evidence: the Victorian period décor, the furniture, pictures, portraits and books are all still in place. As an historian, social writer, ethical thinker and powerful public speaker, Thomas is honoured in the house, while Jane's strong belief in his genius and her own brilliant wit and gift for writing are recognised in the many existing letters. Their academic and domestic lives can be experienced today in the evocative atmosphere of the house.

NT Photographic Library: Michael Boys

Location: OS Ref. TQ272 777. Off Cheyne Walk, between Battersea and Albert Bridges on Chelsea Embankment, or off the King's Road and Oakley Street.

Opening Times: 31 Mar - 4 Nov: Wed - Sun & BH Mons, 11am - 5pm. Last admission 4.30pm. Closed Good Fri.

Admission: Adult £3.50, Child £1.75.

By arrangement for groups.　　Send SAE for details.

CHAPTER HOUSE, PYX CHAMBER & ABBEY MUSEUM

East Cloisters, Westminster Abbey, London SW1P 3PE　　**Tel:** 020 7222 5897

Owner: English Heritage　　　　**Contact:** Head Custodian

The Chapter House, built by the Royal masons in 1250 and faithfully restored in the 19th century, contains some of the finest examples of medieval English sculpture to be seen. The building is octagonal, with a central column, and still has its original floor of glazed tiles, which have been newly conserved. Its uses have varied and in the 14th century it was used as a meeting place for the Benedictine monks of the Abbey and as well as for Members of Parliament. The 11th century Pyx Chamber now houses the Abbey treasures, reflecting its use as the strongroom of the exchequer from the 14th to 19th centuries. The Abbey museum contains medieval Royal effigies.

Location: OS Ref. TQ301 795. Approach either through the Abbey or through Dean's Yard and the cloister.

Opening Times: 1 Apr - 30 Sept: daily, 9.30am - 5.30pm. 1 Oct - 31 Oct: daily 10am - 5pm. 1 Nov - 31 Mar: daily, 10am - 4pm. Liable to be closed at short notice on state occasions.

Admission: Adult £2.50, Child £1.30, Conc. £1.90.

Small charge.　Tel. for details.

CHELSEA PHYSIC GARDEN

66 ROYAL HOSPITAL ROAD, LONDON SW3 4HS

Owner: Chelsea Physic Garden Company　　*Contact: Sue Minter*

Tel: 020 7352 5646　**Fax:** 020 7376 3910

The second oldest botanic garden in Britain, founded in 1673. For many years these 4 acres of peace and quiet with many rare and unusual plants were known only to a few. Specialists in medicinal plants, tender species and the history of plant introductions.

Location: OS Ref. TQ277 778. Off Embankment, between Chelsea & Albert Bridges. Entrance - Swan Walk.

Opening Times: 1 Apr - 28 Oct: Weds, 12 noon - 5pm & Suns, 2 - 6pm. Snowdrop opening & winter festival: 4 & 11 Feb: 11am - 3pm.

Admission: Adult £4, Child £2, OAP £4, Conc. £2. Carers for disabled: Free.

SPECIAL EVENTS

MAY 21 - 25: Chelsea Show Week., 12 noon - 5pm with lunches.

JUL 15 - SEPT 9: Summer Exhibition: 'Myth and Magic'.

CHISWICK HOUSE　　　　**See page 66 for full page entry.**

COLLEGE OF ARMS　　**Tel:** 020 7248 2762　**Fax:** 020 7248 6448

Queen Victoria Street, London EC4V 4BT

Owner: Corp. of the Kings, Heralds & Pursuivants of Arms　**Contact:** The Officer in Waiting

Mansion built in 1670s to house the English Officers of Arms and their records.

Location: OS Ref. TQ320 810. On N side of Queen Victoria Street, S of St Paul's Cathedral.

Opening Times: Earl Marshal's Court only; open all year (except BHs, State and special occasions) Mon - Fri, 10am - 4pm. Group visits (up to 10) by arrangement only. Record Room: open for tours (groups of up to 20) by special arrangement in advance with the Officer in Waiting.

Admission: Free (groups by negotiation).

COURTAULD GALLERY　　　　**See page 71 for full page entry.**

THE DE MORGAN FOUNDATION

OLD BATTERSEA HOUSE, 30 VICARAGE CRESCENT, LONDON SW11 3LD

Contact: Susan Seagrave

Tel: 020 7371 8385

A substantial part of the De Morgan Foundation collection of ceramics by William De Morgan, and paintings by Evelyn De Morgan (née Pickering) are displayed on the ground floor of elegantly restored Old Battersea House - a Wren period building which is privately occupied.

Location: OS Ref. TQ267 767. Close to S shore of River Thames, 1/2 m SW of S end of Battersea Bridge, via Battersea Church Road and Vicarage Crescent.

Opening Times: Weds by appointment.

Admission: Groups (4-15 persons) £2.50.

ℹ️ No photography in house. ♿ Partially suitable. 🎫 Obligatory. 🅿️ Cars limited, no coach parking. 🍴 ❄️

THE DICKENS HOUSE MUSEUM

Courtesy of Dickens Museum

48 DOUGHTY STREET, LONDON WC1N 2LF

Owner: Dickens House Museum Trust *Contact:* Mr Andrew Xavier – Curator

Tel: 020 7405 2127 **Fax:** 020 7831 5175 **e-mail:** dhmuseum@rmplc.co.uk

House occupied by Charles Dickens and his family from 1837 - 1839 where he produced *Pickwick Papers, Oliver Twist, Nicholas Nickleby* and *Barnaby Rudge*. Contains the most comprehensive Dickens library in the world as well as portraits, illustrations and rooms laid out exactly as they were in Dickens' time. The house is one of the few venues open over Christmas itself.

Location: OS Ref. TQ308 822. W of Grays Inn Road.

Opening Times: All year: Mon - Sat, 10am - 5pm (last admission 4.30pm).

Admission: Adult £4, Child £2, Conc. £3, Family £9. Booked groups (min 10): Adult £3, Child £2.

📷 🍴 🎫 By arrangement. 🅿️ Limited. No coaches. ▦ 🐕 Guide dogs only. ❄️ 🎧 Telephone for details. (RW)

EASTBURY MANOR HOUSE 🌿 **Tel:** 020 8507 0119 **Fax:** 020 8507 0118

Barking IG11 9SN

Owner: The National Trust **Contact:** The Administrator

Eastbury is a rare example of a medium-sized Elizabethan manor house. Leased to the Borough of Barking and Dagenham and used for a variety of arts and heritage activities.

Location: OS177, Ref. TQ457 838. In Eastbury Square, 10 mins walk S from Upney Station.

Opening Times: Mar - Dec: first Sat every month (except Aug), 10am - 4pm. Telephone for details.

Admission: Adult £1.80, Child 60p, Conc. £1, Family £4.20. Group visits by arrangement. Rates on application. Evening tours also available.

♿ Ground floor suitable. 🎧 Visitor days. 🅿️ No parking. 🐕 Garden only. 🔔

ELTHAM PALACE ⊞ See page 67 for full page entry.

Civil Wedding Index ◀◀◀ page 29

Westminster Cathedral.

FENTON HOUSE

WINDMILL HILL, HAMPSTEAD, LONDON NW3 6RT

Owner: *The National Trust*   **Contact:** *The Custodian*

Tel: 020 7435 3471   **e-mail:** tfehse@smtp.ntrust.org.uk

A delightful late 17th century merchant's house, set among the winding streets of Old Hampstead. The charming interior contains an outstanding collection of Oriental and European porcelain, needlework and furniture. The Benton Fletcher Collection of beautiful early keyboard instruments is also housed at Fenton and the instruments are sometimes played by music scholars during opening hours. The walled garden has a formal lawn and walks, an orchard and vegetable garden and fine wrought-iron gates.

Location: OS Ref. TQ262 862. Visitors' entrance on W side of Hampstead Grove.

Hampstead underground station 300 yds.

Opening Times: 3 - 25 Mar: Sats & Suns, 2 - 5pm. 31 Mar - 4 Nov: daily except Mons & Tues (open BH Mons, closed Good Fri). Times: weekdays, 2 - 5pm. Weekends & BH Mons, 11am - 5pm. Groups at other times by appointment.

Admission: Adult £4.30, Child £2.15, Family £10.50. Joint ticket with 2 Willow Road, £6.30. No reduction for pre-booked groups. No picnics in grounds.

 Ground floor accessible.   **P** No parking.

---

18 FOLEGATE STREET

Tel: 020 7247 4013

Spitalfields, East London E1 6BX

Owner: Spitalfields Historic Buildings Trust   **Contact:** Mick Pedroli

A time capsule furnished and decorated to tell the story of the Jarvis family, Huguenot silk weavers from 1725 - 1919.

Location: OS Ref. TQ335 820. ¹/₂ m NE of Liverpool St. Station. E of Bishopsgate (A10), just N of Spitalfields Market.

Opening Times: First Sunday each month, 2 - 5pm. First Mon following the first Sun by candlelight "Silent Night". Times vary with the light of the seasons and booking is required. Group visits can be arranged by appointment.

Admission: Non negotiable contribution £7.00 for the houses upkeep. "Silent Night" £10.

The Kitchen, 18 Folegate Street.

FREUD MUSEUM

20 MARESFIELD GARDENS, LONDON NW3 5SX

Contact: *Ms E Davies*

Tel: 020 7435 2002 **Fax:** 020 7431 5452 **e-mail:** freud@gn.apc.org

The Freud Museum was the home of Sigmund Freud after he escaped the Nazi annexation of Austria. The house retains its domestic atmosphere and has the character of turn of the century Vienna. The centrepiece is Freud's study which has been preserved intact, containing his remarkable collection of antiquities: Egyptian, Greek, Roman, Oriental and his large library. The Freuds brought all their furniture and household effects to London; fine Biedermeier and 19th century Austrian painted furniture. The most famous item is Freud's psychoanalytic couch, where his patients reclined. Fine Oriental rugs cover the floor and tables. Videos are shown of the Freud family in Vienna, Paris and London.

Location: OS Ref. TQ265 850. Between Swiss Cottage and Hampstead.

Opening Times: Wed - Sun (inc) 12 noon - 5pm.

Admission: Adult £4, Child under 12 free, Conc. £2. Coach parties by appointment.

  Ground floor suitable.   **P** Limited.   Guide dogs only.

FULHAM PALACE & MUSEUM

BISHOPS AVENUE, FULHAM, LONDON SW6 6EA

Owner: London Borough of Hammersmith & Fulham & Fulham Palace Trust

Tel: 020 7736 5821 **Museum:** 020 7736 3233

Former home of the Bishops of London (Tudor with Georgian additions and Victorian Chapel). The gardens, famous in the 17th century, now contain specimen trees and a knot garden of herbs. The museum tells the story of this nationally important site. Education service available. Rooms and grounds are available for private functions.

Location: OS Ref. TQ240 761.

Opening Times: Gardens: open daylight hours. Museum: Mar - Oct: Wed - Sun, 2 - 5pm. Nov - Feb: Thur - Sun, 1 - 4pm. Tours of principal rooms and gardens every 2nd Sun - contact Museum; selected other Suns contact Fulham Archaeological Rescue Group 020 7385 3723, £2. Private tours £5 each by arrangement with either organisation. Private tours with teas (50 max.).

Admission: Gardens: Free. Museum: Adult £1, Conc. 50p.

Private & wedding receptions.   Partially suitable.   Obligatory.   No parking.   Guide dogs only.

Reg. Charity No. 1020063

HAM HOUSE

NT Photographic Library - Bill Batten

HAM, RICHMOND, SURREY TW10 7RS

Owner: The National Trust   *Contact: The Property Manager*

Tel: 020 8940 1950 **Fax:** 020 8332 6903 **e-mail:** shhgen@smtp.ntrust.org.uk

Ham House, on the banks of the River Thames, is perhaps the most remarkable Stuart house in the country. Apart from the fact that its architectural fabric has survived virtually unchanged since the 1670s, it still retains many of the furnishings from that period. Ham is presented today principally as the late 17th century Lauderdale residence with overlays of the 18th and 19th centuries. Visitors view the rooms in the sequence intended at the time, progressing through a hierarchy of apartments towards the Queen's Closet - the culmination of the sequence. The gardens are being restored using plans and images which were found in the house and were laid out in compartments, reflecting the ordered symmetry of the house and together they present the modern visitor with a complete picture of 17th century aristocratic life.

Location: OS Ref. TQ172 732. 1$^{1}/_{2}$ m from Richmond and 2m from Kingston. On the S bank of the River Thames, W of A307 at Petersham.

Opening times: 31 Mar - 1 Nov: daily except Thurs & Fris. House: 1 - 5pm, last adm. 4.30pm. Gardens: 11am - 6pm/dusk if earlier. Closed 25 - 26 Dec & 1 Jan.

Admission: House & Garden: Adult £6, Child £3, Family £15. Garden, Icehouse & Dairy: Adult £2, Child £1, Family £5. Pre-booked groups (min 15): Adult £5, Child £2.50.

Partially suitable. WC.   Guide dogs.

THE GEFFRYE MUSEUM

Tel: 020 7739 9893 **Fax:** 020 7729 5647

Kingsland Road, London E2 8EA   **e-mail:** info@geffrye-museum.org.uk

Owner: Independent Charitable Trust   **Contact:** Ms Nancy Loader

The Geffrye presents the changing styles of English domestic interiors through a series of period rooms from 1600 to present day.

Location: OS Ref. TQ335 833. 1m N of Liverpool St. Buses: 242, 149, 243, 67. Underground: Liverpool St. or Old St.

Opening Times: Museum: Tue - Sat, 10am - 5pm. Suns & BH Mons, 12 noon - 5pm. Closed Mons (except BHs) Good Fri, Christmas Eve, Christmas Day, Boxing Day & New Year's Day. Gardens: Apr - Oct.

Admission: Free.

GILBERT COLLECTION

See page 71 for full page entry.

GUNNERSBURY PARK MUSEUM

Tel: 020 8992 1612 **Fax:** 020 8752 0686

Gunnersbury Park, London W3 8LQ   **e-mail:** gp-museum@cip.org.uk

Owner: Hounslow and Ealing Councils   **Contact:** Vanda Foster

Built in 1802 and refurbished by Sydney Smirke for the Rothschild family.

Location: OS Ref. TQ190 792. Acton Town underground station. $^{1}/_{4}$ m N of the junction of A4, M4 North Circular.

Opening Times: Apr - Oct: daily: 1 - 5pm. (6pm weekends & BHs). Nov - Mar: daily: 1 - 4pm. Victorian kitchens summer weekends only. Closed Christmas Day and Boxing Day. Park: open dawn - dusk.

Admission: Free. Donations welcome.

HERMITAGE ROOMS

See page 71 for full page entry.

HOGARTH'S HOUSE

Tel: 020 8994 6757

Hogarth Lane, Great West Road, Chiswick, London W4 2QN

Owner: Hogarth House Foundation   **Contact:** Jerome Farrell

This late 17th century house was the country home of William Hogarth, the famous painter, engraver, satirist and social reformer between 1749 and his death in 1764.

Location: OS Ref. TQ213 778. 100 yds W of Hogarth roundabout on the Great West Road - junction of Burlington Lane. Car park in named spaces in Axis Business Centre behind house and Chiswick House grounds.

Opening Times: Apr - Oct: Tue - Fri, 1 - 5pm, Sats & Suns, 1 - 6pm. Nov - Mar: Tue - Fri, 1 - 4pm, Sats & Suns, 1 - 5pm. Closed Jan, Good Fri, 25 & 26 Dec. Closed Mons except BHs.

Admission: Free.

JEWEL TOWER

Tel: 020 7222 2219

Abingdon Street, Westminster, London SW1P 3JY

Owner: English Heritage   **Contact:** Head Custodian

Built c1365 to house the personal treasure of Edward III and one of two surviving parts of the Palace of Westminster.

Location: OS Ref. TQ302 794. Opposite S end of Houses of Parliament (Victoria Tower).

Opening Times: 1 Apr - 31 Mar: daily, 10am - 6pm (closes 5pm in Oct, & 4pm Nov - Mar).

Admission: Adult £1.60, Child 80p, Conc. £1.20.

DR JOHNSON'S HOUSE

Tel: 020 7353 3745

17 Gough Square, London EC4A 3DE   **e-mail:** curator@drjh.dircon.co.uk

Owner: The Trustees

Fine 18th century house, once home to Dr Samuel Johnson, the celebrated literary figure, famous for his English dictionary.

Location: OS Ref. TQ314 813. N of Fleet Street.

Opening Times: Oct - Apr: Mon - Sat, 11am - 5pm. May - Sept: Mon - Sat, 11am - 5.30pm.

Admission: Adult £4, Child £1 (under 10yrs Free), Conc. £3. Family Ticket £9.00. Groups: £3.

KEATS HOUSE

Tel: 020 7435 2062 **Fax:** 020 7431 9293
e-mail: keatshouse@corpoflondon.gov.uk

Keats Grove, Hampstead, London NW3 2RR
Owner: Corporation of London   **Contact:** C De' Freitas
Regency home of the poet John Keats (1795 - 1821).
Location: OS Ref. TQ272 856. Hampstead, NW3. Nearest Underground: Belsize Park & Hampstead.
Opening Times: Summer: May - end Oct: General opening: Tue - Sun & BHs, 12 noon - 5pm. Visits by appointment: Tues - Sat, 10am - 12 noon. Winter: Nov - Dec: General opening: Tues - Sun, 12 noon - 4pm. Visits by appointment, Tues - Sat, 10am - 12 noon. Due to ongoing building works from December 2001, please contact the house for opening times.
Admission: Adult £3, Under 16s Free, Conc. £1.50.

⬜ ♿ Ground floor & garden accessible 🅿 No parking. 🐕 Guide dogs only.
❄ 🚻

KENSINGTON PALACE STATE APARTMENTS

See page 68 for full page entry.

KENWOOD HOUSE ⌘

See page 69 for full page entry.

LEIGHTON HOUSE ART GALLERY & MUSEUM

12 HOLLAND PARK ROAD, KENSINGTON, LONDON W14 8LZ
Owner: Royal Borough of Kensington & Chelsea   *Contact: Curator*
Tel: 020 7602 3316 **Fax:** 020 7371 2467
Leighton House was the home of Frederic, Lord Leighton 1830 - 1896, painter and President of the Royal Academy, built between 1864 - 1879. It was a palace of art designed for entertaining and to provide a magnificent working space in the studio, with great north windows and a gilded apse. The Arab Hall is the centrepiece of the house, containing Leighton's collection of Persian tiles, a gilt mosaic frieze and a fountain. Victorian paintings by Leighton, Millais and Burne-Jones are on display.
Location: OS Ref. TQ247 793. N of High Street Kensington, off Melbury Rd, close to Commonwealth Institute.
Opening Times: Daily, except Tues. Spring & Summer BHs, 11am - 5.30pm.
Admission: Free. £3 per head for pre-booked tours.

⬜ 🍴 🚶 🎧 📖 ✂ ❄ 🚹 Please telephone for details. 🚻

LINDSEY HOUSE 🦋

Tel: 01494 528051

99 -100 Cheyne Walk, London SW10 0DQ
Owner: The National Trust   **Contact:** NT Regional Office
Part of Lindsey House was built in 1674 on the site of Sir Thomas More's garden, overlooking the River Thames. It has one of the finest 17th century exteriors in London.
Location: OS Ref. TQ268 775. On Cheyne Walk, W of Battersea Bridge near junction with Milman's Street on Chelsea Embankment.
Opening Times: By written appointment only. 17 May, 13 Jun, 12 Sept & 10 Oct: 2 - 4pm. Please write to (enc. SAE): The Secretary, 100 Cheyne Walk, London SW10 0DQ.

LINLEY SAMBOURNE HOUSE

Recorded Message: 020 7937 0663
Info: 020 7602 3316 **Fax:** 020 7371 2467

18 Stafford Terrace, London W8 7BH
Owner: The Royal Borough of Kensington & Chelsea   **Contact:** Assistant Curator
The home of Linley Sambourne (1844 - 1910) chief political cartoonist at Punch. A unique example of a late Victorian town house.
Location: OS Ref. TQ252 794. Bus: 9, 10, 27, 28, 31, 49, 52, 70 & C1. Tube: Kensington High Street. Parking on Sun in nearby streets.
Opening Times: Closed for conservation work, expected to re-open Autumn 2002.

MARBLE HILL HOUSE ⌘

Tel: 020 8892 5115

Richmond Road, Twickenham TW1 2NL
Owner: English Heritage   **Contact:** House Manager
This beautiful villa beside the Thames was built in 1724 - 29 for Henrietta Howard, mistress of George II. Here she entertained many of the poets and wits of the Augustan age including Alexander Pope and later Horace Walpole. The perfect proportions of the villa were inspired by the work of the 16th century Italian architect, Palladio. Today this beautifully presented house contains an important collection of paintings and furniture, including some pieces commissioned for the villa when it was built.
Location: OS Ref. TQ174 736. A305, 600yds E of Orleans House.
Opening Times: 1 Apr - 30 Sept: daily, 10am - 6pm. 1 Oct - 31 Oct: daily, 10am - 5pm. 1 Nov - 31 Mar, Wed - Sun, 10am - 4pm.
Admission: Adult £3.30, Child £1.70, Conc. £2.50.

⬜ ♿ Ground floor & grounds suitable. WC. 💼 ❄ 🚻 Tel. for details.

WILLIAM MORRIS GALLERY

Tel: 020 8527 3782 **Fax:** 020 8527 7070

Lloyd Park, Forest Road, Walthamstow, London E17 4PP
Owner: London Borough of Waltham Forest   **Contact:** Ms Nora Gillow
Location: OS Ref. SQ372 899. 15 mins walk from Walthamstow tube (Victoria line). 5 - 10 mins from M11/A406.
Opening Times: Tue - Sat and first Sun each month, 10am - 1pm and 2 - 5pm.
Admission: Free for all visitors but a charge is made for guided tours which must be booked in advance.

MUSEUM OF GARDEN HISTORY

LAMBETH PALACE ROAD, LONDON SE1 7LB
Owner: The Tradescant Trust
Tel: 020 7401 8865 **Fax:** 020 7401 8869 **e-mail:** info@museumgardenhistory.org
Fascinating permanent exhibition of the history of gardens, collection of ancient tools and recreated 17th century garden displaying flowers and shrubs of the period – seeds of which may be purchased in the garden shop. Visit the tombs of the Tradescants and Captain Bligh of the Bounty. They have knowledgeable staff and lectures, concerts, courses and art exhibitions are held regularly. The Knot Garden, part of the churchyard, is shown above.
Location: OS Ref. TQ306 791. At Lambeth Parish Church, next to Lambeth Palace, at E end of Lambeth Bridge. Buses: 3, 77, 344, C10. Tube: Westminster or Waterloo.
Opening Times: 1st Sun in Feb - late Dec: Daily, 10.30am - 5pm.
Admission: Adult £2, Conc. £1.50

⬜ 🍴 ♿ Partially suitable. 💼 🅿 No parking. 📖 ✂ ❄ 🚻

MYDDELTON HOUSE GARDENS

Tel: 01992 702200 **Fax:** 01992 702280

Bulls Cross, Enfield, Middlesex EN2 9HG

Owner: Lee Valley Regional Park Authority

Created by the famous plantsman E A Bowles.

Location: OS Ref. TQ342 992. $^1/_4$ m W of A10 via Turkey St. $^3/_4$ m S M25/J25.

Opening Times: Mon - Fri (except Christmas), 10am - 4.30pm. Easter - Oct: Suns & BHs, 2 - 5pm.

Admission: Adult £1.90, Conc. £1.30.

THE OCTAGON, ORLEANS HOUSE GALLERY

Tel: 020 8892 0221

Fax: 020 8744 0501

Riverside, Twickenham, Middlesex TW1 3DJ

Owner: London Borough of Richmond-upon-Thames **Contact:** Rachel Tranter

Outstanding example of baroque architecture built by James Gibbs c1720. Adjacent wing now converted to an art gallery.

Location: OS Ref. TQ168 734. On N side of Riverside, 700yds E of Twickenham town centre, 400yds S of Richmond Road, A305 via Lebanon Park Road and 500yds W of Marble Hill House.

Opening Times: Tue - Sat, 1 - 5.30pm (Oct - Mar closes 4.30pm). Sun & BHs, 2 - 5.30pm. Closed Mons. Garden: open daily, 9am - sunset.

Admission: Free.

OSTERLEY PARK

See right for half page entry.

PALACE OF WESTMINSTER

Tel: 020 7219 3000 **Ticketmaster:** 0207344 9966

London SW1A 0AA

Recorded Info: 0207219 5532

Contact: Information Office

The first Palace of Westminster was erected on this site by Edward the Confessor in 1042 and the building was a royal residence until a devastating fire in 1512. After this, the palace became the two-chamber Parliament for government - the House of Lords (largely hereditary until the reforms of the present Government) and the elected House of Commons. Following a further fire in 1834, the palace was rebuilt by Sir Charles Barry and decorated by A W Pugin.

Location: OS Ref. TQ303 795. Central London, W bank of River Thames. 1km S of Trafalgar Square. Underground: Westminster.

Opening Times: Summer opening until 16 Sept: timed tours including both Houses of Parliament, can be booked through the Ticketmaster or website. Palace closed Suns, BHs and some mornings. **Strangers' Gallery**, **House of Commons**: open when the House is sitting: Mon - Wed, 2.30pm; Thurs, 11.30am and (occasionally) Fris, 9.30am (check recorded info line). UK residents can apply in advance to their MP for tickets but requests for specific days cannot be guaranteed. Otherwise join public queue outside St Stephen's Entrance, may take an hour or two before popular periods such as Prime Mininster's Questions (Wed, 3pm). Places usually available after 6pm. **Strangers' Gallery, House of Lords**: Open when House is sitting (see above), separate queue at St Stephen's Entrance. **The 'line of route' tour**: weekday group tours during recess. When the Houses are sitting, official tours, (1 hour), are restricted to before noon and Fri afternoons. Groups (max 16) must be sponsored by an MP. **Big Ben**: group tours (max 12): Mon - Fri, 10.30am, 11.30am & 2.30pm, must contact your MP for a booking. **Lord Chancellor's Apartments**: 2 tours per week (max 25): Tues & Thurs am. Fully booked until end 2001 (cancellation list: 020 7219 2184). **Westminster Hall**: Mon - Sat, (until 15 Sept), 9.30am - 5pm.

Admission: Ticketmaster admin charge £3.50. The 'line of route' tour: gratuity of £20 - £25 per group. Big Ben: Free.

PITSHANGER MANOR & GALLERY

Tel: 020 8567 1227 **Fax:** 020 8567 0595

Walpole Park, Mattock Lane, Ealing W5 5EQ

e-mail: pitshanger@ealing.gov.uk

Owner: London Borough of Ealing **Contact:** Neena Sohal

Set in Walpole Park, once owned by the architect Sir John Soane (1753 - 1837). He rebuilt most of the house to create a Regency villa. The later addition of a Victorian wing now houses a collection of Martinware pottery. Adjoining the Manor is Pitshanger Manor Gallery, the largest space for contemporary art in West London.

Location: OS Ref. TQ176 805. Ealing, London.

Opening Times: Tue - Sat, 10am - 5pm. Closed Suns & Mons. Also closed Christmas, Easter and New Year.

Admission: Free. Adult group tours (10+): £3.

  By arrangement. Limited. In grounds, on leads.

THE QUEEN'S GALLERY

Tel: 020 7839 1377

Buckingham Palace, London SW1A 1AA

Owner: HM The Queen **Contact:** The Visitor Office

Location: OS Ref. TQ290 795. Buckingham Palace.

Opening Times: The Queen's Gallery is closed for major remodelling and extension and will re-open in 2002, the year of The Queen's Golden Jubilee.

OSTERLEY PARK

NT Photographic Library

ISLEWORTH TW7 4RB

Owner: The National Trust *Contact: The Property Manager*

Tel/Fax: 020 8568 7714

Osterley's four turrets look out across one of the last great landscaped parks in suburban London, its trees and lakes an unexpected haven of green. Originally built in 1575, the mansion was transformed in the 18th century into an elegant villa by architect Robert Adam. The classical interior, designed for entertaining on a grand scale, still impresses with its specially made tapestries, furniture and plasterwork.

NT Photographic Library: Dennis Gilbert

Location: OS Ref. TQ146 780. Access via Thornbury Road on N side of A4.

Opening Times: House: 31 Mar - 4 Nov: daily except Mons & Tues, 1 - 4.30pm. Closed Good Fri, open BH Mons. Last admission: 4pm. Grand Stable: Sun afternoon in summer. Park & Pleasure Grounds: All year, 9am - 7.30pm or sunset if earlier. Park will be closed early during major events. Car park closed Good Fri, 25 & 26 Dec. Jersey Galleries: as house.

Admission: Adult £4.30, Child £2.15, Family £10.50. Group: Wed - Sat £3.50, pre-booking required. Car Park: £2.50.

 Suitable, phone for details. On leads in park.

London England

THE RANGER'S HOUSE ⌗
Tel: 020 8853 0035

Chesterfield Walk, Blackheath, London SE10 8QX

Owner: English Heritage   **Contact:** House Manager

A handsome, red-brick house which lies between two of London's great open spaces, Greenwich Park and Blackheath. The house was built for a successful seafarer, Admiral Francis Hosier around 1700 who sited the house within view of the Thames estuary. A later owner Lord Chesterfield, used to boast that the grand bow-windowed gallery commanded the three finest views in the world. Today Ranger's House is home to the Suffolk collection of paintings including elegant full-length Jacobean portraits. The first floor of the house contains an exhibition space. There is also an Architectural Study Collection, with features from 17th, 18th and 19th century dwellings. The first floor houses an exciting programme of contemporary exhibitions.

Location: OS Ref. TQ388 768. N of Shooters Hill Road.

Opening Times: 1 Apr - 30 Sept: daily, 10am - 6pm. 1 - 31 Oct: daily 10am - 5pm. 1 Nov - 31 Mar: Wed - Sun, 10am - 4pm. Ranger's House may close in winter 2000 for major refurbishment. Please call the house before you visit.

Admission: Adult £2.80, Child £1.40, Conc. £2.10.

 Limited, lift available. Guide dogs only. Tel. for details.

THE ROYAL MEWS
Tel: 020 7839 1377

Buckingham Palace, London SW1A 1AA

Owner: HM The Queen   **Contact:** The Visitor Officer

Location: OS Ref. TQ289 794. Entrance in Buckingham Palace Road, W of The Queen's Gallery.

Opening Times: Oct - Jul: Mon - Thur, 12 noon - 4pm. Aug & Sept: Mon - Thur, 10.30am - 4.30pm. Last admission 30mins before closing.

Admission: Adult £4.60, Child (under 17yrs) £2.60, OAP £3.60. Family ticket (2+2) £11.80.

ROYAL SOCIETY OF ARTS

8 JOHN ADAM STREET, LONDON WC2N 6EZ

Owner: RSA   *Contact: Ms Nicki Kyle*

Tel: 020 7839 5049   **Fax:** 020 7321 0271

e-mail: conference@rsa-uk.demon.co.uk

The house of the Royal Society of Arts was designed by Robert Adam specially for the Society in the early 1770s. One of the few remaining buildings from the original Adelphi development, its Georgian façade conceals many unexpected delights of both traditional and contemporary architecture. Designed as one of London's earliest debating chambers, the Great Room is one of the most spectacular theatres in the city. The Benjamin Franklin Room is spacious and elegant, featuring an antique chandelier and two Adam fireplaces. The Vaults were originally designed as river front warehouses. Now fully restored they offer a striking contrast to the splendour of the rooms above. All rooms may be hired for meetings, receptions and weddings.

Location: OS Ref. TQ305 806. Near to Charing Cross and Waterloo.

Opening Times: All year: 8am - 8pm. Closed last 2 weeks of Aug, 24 Dec & 2 Jan.

Admission: For room hire prices, contact the RSA Conference Officer.

 Licensed. By arrangement. None.

ROYAL OBSERVATORY GREENWICH & QUEEN'S HOUSE

GREENWICH PARK, GREENWICH, LONDON SE10 9NF

Owner: National Maritime Museum   *Contact: Robin Scates*

Tel: 020 8858 4422   **Fax:** 020 8312 6632

24-hour info: 020 8312 6565   **e-mail:** bookings@nmm.ac.uk

The Maritime Greenwich World Heritage Site encompasses Wren's imposing Royal Observatory (1675), the National Maritime Museum and the Queen's House (Inigo Jones c.1635). The Royal Observatory defines the Prime Meridian of the world – Longitude 0°. Visit the Astronomer Royal's apartments, see the 1833 time ball and admire Harrison's intricate marine timekeepers. The National Maritime Museum's 20 modern galleries chart Britain's history of seafaring and Empire ranging from Nelson's navy to recent environmental protection. The Queen's House (open from Easter 2001 onwards) contains a new exhibition of the rich history of Greenwich and also the magnificent portrait collection of the Museum.

Location: OS Ref. TQ388 773. On the South Bank of the Thames at Greenwich.

Opening Times: All year: daily, 10am - 5pm. Closed 24 - 26 Dec (Queen's House closed until Easter 2001).

Admission: Each site from £6 - £7.50, Child/Seniors (60+) Free. Disabled, student and unemployed 20% discount. Other concessions and group discounts available.

No indoor photography. Partially suitable. WC. Phone for details. Nearby. By arrangement. Coaches nearby.

ST GEORGE'S CATHEDRAL, SOUTHWARK

Tel: 020 7928 5256
Fax: 020 7787 8923

Westminster Bridge Road, London SE1 7HY   **Contact:** Canon James Cronin
Neo-Gothic rebuilt Pugin Cathedral bombed during the last war and rebuilt by Romily Craze in 1958.
Location: OS Ref. TQ315 794. Near Imperial War Museum. 1/2 m SE of Waterloo Stn.
Opening Times: 8am - 8pm, every day, except BHs.
Admission: Free.

ST JOHN'S GATE
THE MUSEUM OF THE ORDER OF ST JOHN

ST. JOHN'S GATE, LONDON EC1M 4DA
Owner: The Order of St. John   Contact: Pamela Willis

Tel: 020 7253 6644 **Fax:** 020 7336 0587

Discover the rich history of the Knights Hospitaller, a monastic order dedicated to serving the sick and defending the faith, dating back to the Crusades. The Museum is in a Tudor Gatehouse, once the entrance to their English Priory and visitors can also see the 16th century church with remarkable 12th century crypt. After the Dissolution, the Gate was Hogarth's home and Dr Johnson's workplace. In Victorian times, St John Ambulance was founded here and a new interactive gallery tells its story.
Location: OS Ref. TQ317 821. St. John's Lane, Clerkenwell. Nearest underground: Farringdon, Barbican.
Opening Times: Mon - Fri: 10am - 5pm. Sats: 10am - 4pm. Closed BHs & Sat of BH weekend. Tours: Tues, Fris & Sats at 11am & 2.30pm. Reference Library: Open by appointment.
Admission: Museum Free. Tours of the building: £4, OAP £3 (donation).

 Ground floor suitable. WC. Guide dogs only.

ST PAUL'S CATHEDRAL

See page 70 for full page entry.

SIR JOHN SOANE'S MUSEUM

Tel: 020 7405 2107 **Fax:** 020 7831 3957

13 Lincoln's Inn Fields, London WC2A 3BP
Owner: Trustees of Sir John Soane's Museum   **Contact:** Ms S Palmer
The celebrated architect Sir John Soane built this in 1812 as his own house. It now contains his collection of antiquities, sculpture and paintings.
Location: OS Ref. TQ308 816. E of Kingsway, S of High Holborn.
Opening Times: Tue - Sat, 10am - 5pm. 6 - 9pm, first Tue of the month. Closed BHs & 24 Dec.
Admission: Free. Groups must book.

SOMERSET HOUSE INCLUDING COURTAULD GALLERY, GILBERT COLLECTION & HERMITAGE ROOMS

See page 71 for full page entry.

SOUTHSIDE HOUSE

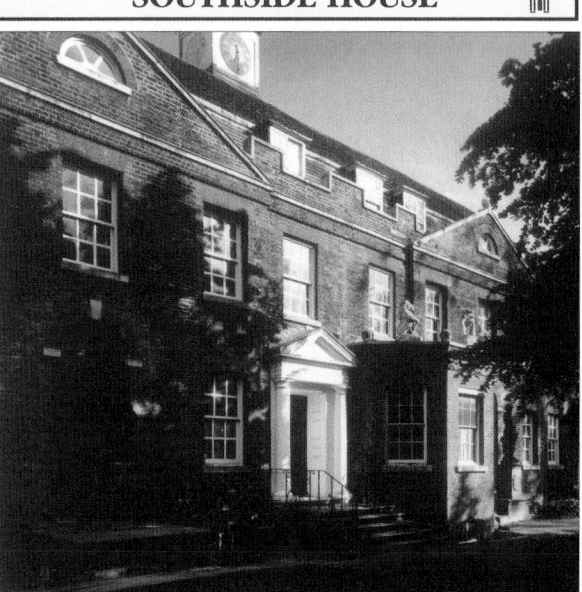

3 WOODHAYES ROAD, WIMBLEDON, LONDON SW19 4RJ
Owner: The Pennington-Mellor-Munthe Charity Trust   Contact: The Administrator

Tel: 020 8946 7643

Built by Robert Pennington in 1665, the family befriended or were related to many distinguished names - among others Ann Boleyn's descendents, Nelson, Hamilton, the 'Hell Fire Duke of Wharton' and Natalie, Queen of Serbia. Family portraits and possessions on show. Bedroom prepared for Prince of Wales in 1750. In 1907 the heiress, Hilda Pennington Mellor married Axel Munthe the Swedish doctor and philanthropist. After 1945 Hilda and her sons restored the house. Malcolm, who had lived extraordinary adventures during the war, determined to make a cultural art of the family inheritance. Guided tours give reality and excitement to the old family histories.

Location: OS Ref. TQ234 706. On S side of Wimbledon Common (B281), opposite Crooked Billet Inn.
Opening Times: 2 Jan - 24 Jun: Weds, Sats, Suns & BH Mons. Guided tours on the hour, 2 - 5pm (last tour 5pm). Also open for private parties by arrangement from 1 Dec - 24 Jun.
Admission: Adult £5, Child £3 (must be accompanied by an adult).

 Not suitable. Obligatory. **P** Limited.

SOUTHWARK CATHEDRAL
Tel: 020 7367 6700 **Fax:** 020 7367 6725
Welcome Desk: 020 7367 6734 **e-mail:** cathedral@dswark.org.uk
Montague Close, Southwark, London SE1 9DA
Owner: Church of England   **Contact:** Welcome Desk
London's oldest gothic building and a place of worship for over 1,000 years, St Mary Overie Priory became St Saviour's Parish Church at the Dissolution. In 1905 it became an Anglican Cathedral. It has literary connections: Gower, Chaucer, Shakespeare and Dickens, and associations with Harvard, founder of the American university. Interesting links with the Royal family over the centuries.
Location: OS Ref. TQ327 803. South side of London Bridge, near Shakespeare's Globe and Tate Modern.
Opening Times: Daily: 8.30am - 6pm. Weekday services: 8am, 12.30pm and 5.30pm. Sat services, 9am and 4pm. Sun services: 9am, 11am and 3pm.
Admission: Recommended donation of £2.50 per person. Booked groups (min 15): Adult £2.50, Child £1, Conc. £2.

ℹ️Indoor photography & video recording with permit. Exhibition centre (additional charge). 📷 🍴 ♿Partially suitable. WCs. 🍴 🍴Licensed. 🎟️By arrangement. 🎧 🅿️ No parking. 🚫 🐕Guide dogs only. ❄️ 🔵

SPENCER HOUSE
See page 72 for full page entry.

STRAWBERRY HILL

ST MARY'S, STRAWBERRY HILL, WALDEGRAVE ROAD, TWICKENHAM TW1 4SX
Contact: The Conference Office

Tel: 020 8240 4114/020 8240 4311/020 8240 4044
Horace Walpole converted a modest house at Strawberry Hill into his own version of a gothic fantasy. It is widely regarded as the first substantial building of the Gothic Revival and as such is internationally known and admired. A century later Lady Frances Waldegrave added a magnificent wing to Walpole's original structure. Lady Waldegrave's suite of rooms can be hired for weddings, corporate functions and conferences. Please telephone for details.
Location: OS Ref. TQ158 722. Off A310 between Twickenham & Teddington.
Opening Times: Easter - Oct: Suns. Please tel: 020 8240 4224 for opening times or to make an appointment 020 8240 4114.
Admission: Adult £5, OAP £4.25. Group bookings: £4.25.
ℹ️Conferences. 📷   🔵

SUTTON HOUSE

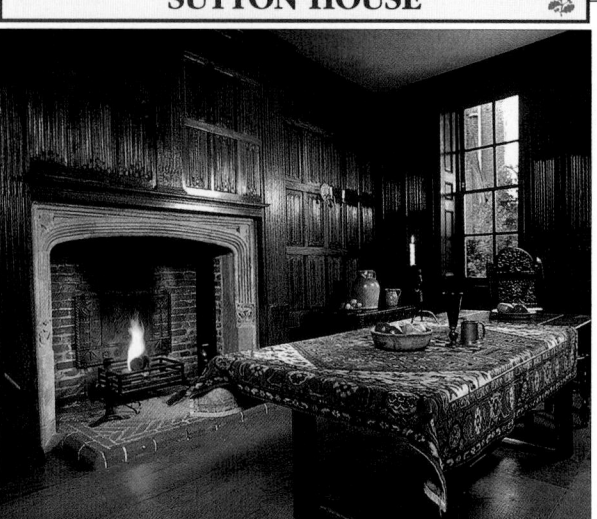

NT Photographic Library: Geoffrey Frosh

2 & 4 HOMERTON HIGH STREET, HACKNEY, LONDON E9 6JQ
Owner: The National Trust Contact: The Property Manager

Tel: 020 8986 2264
A rare example of a Tudor red-brick house, built in 1535 by Sir Rafe Sadleir, Principal Secretary of State for Henry VIII, with 18th century alterations and later additions. Restoration revealed many 16th century details, even in rooms of later periods. Notable features include original linenfold panelling and 17th century wall paintings.
Location: OS Ref. TQ352 851. At the corner of Isabella Road and Homerton High St.
Opening Times: 7 Feb - 28 Nov & from 6 Feb 2002: Weds, Suns & BH Mons only, 11.30am - 5pm. Café Bar: All year: Wed - Sun & BH Mons, 11.30am - 5pm. Closed 21 Dec - 8 Jan 2002.
Admission: £2.10, Child 50p, Family £4.70. Group visits by prior arrangement.
📷 ♿Ground floor only. WC. 🍴 🅿️ No parking. 🔔 🔵 Tel. for details.

SYON PARK
See page 73 for full page entry.

THE TOWER BRIDGE EXPERIENCE
Tel: 020 7378 1928 **Fax:** 020 7357 7935
Tower Bridge, London SE1 2UP
Owner: Corporation of London   **Contact:** Jo Skinner
One of London's most unusual and exciting exhibitions is situated inside Tower Bridge. Animatronic characters from the Bridge's past guide you through a series of audio-visual presentations.
Location: OS Ref. TQ337 804. Adjacent to Tower of London, nearest Tube: Tower Hill.
Opening Times: Nov - Mar: 9.30am - 6pm. Apr - Oct: 10am - 6.30pm (last entry 1¼ hrs before closing). Closed 24 - 25 Dec and 17 Jan 2001.
Admission: Adult £6.25, Child (5-15)/ Conc. £4.25, Family (2+2) £18.25 (subject to a small increase in Apr).

THE TOWER OF LONDON
See page 74 for full page entry.

THE WALLACE COLLECTION
See page 75 for full page entry.

✳️ **Plant Sales Index** ◀◀◀ **page 47**

WESTMINSTER ABBEY

Tel: 020 7222 5152 **Fax:** 020 7233 2072

London SW1P 3PA **e-mail:** press@westminster-abbey.org **Contact:** Press Officer

Westminster Abbey is a living church that enshrines the History of the British nation.

Location: OS Ref. TQ301 795. Westminster.

Opening Times: Mon - Fri, 9am - 4.45pm (last admission 3.45pm), Sats, 9am - 2.45pm (last admission 1.45pm).

Admission: Adult £6, Child under 11yrs Free, Under 16yrs/Student/OAP £3, Family (2+2) £12 (prices from Feb 2001).

WESTMINSTER CATHEDRAL

Tel: 020 7798 9055 **Fax:** 020 7798 9090

Victoria, London SW1P 1QW

Owner: Diocese of Westminster **Contact:** Rev Mgr George Stack

The Roman Catholic Cathedral of the Archbishop of Westminster. Spectacular building in the Byzantine style, designed by J F Bentley, opened in 1903, famous for its mosaics, marble and music. Westminster Cathedral celebrated the Centenary of its foundation in 1995.

Location: OS Ref. TQ293 791. On Victoria Street, between Victoria Station and Westminster Abbey.

Opening Times: All year: 7am - 7pm. Please telephone for times at Easter & Christmas.

Admission: Free. Lift charge: Adult £2. Child £1. Family (2+4) £5.

Ground floor suitable. Prior booking required. No parking. Worksheets & tours. Guide dogs only.

Syon Park, London.

Kingston Bagpuize, Oxfordshire

South East

Kingston Bagpuize

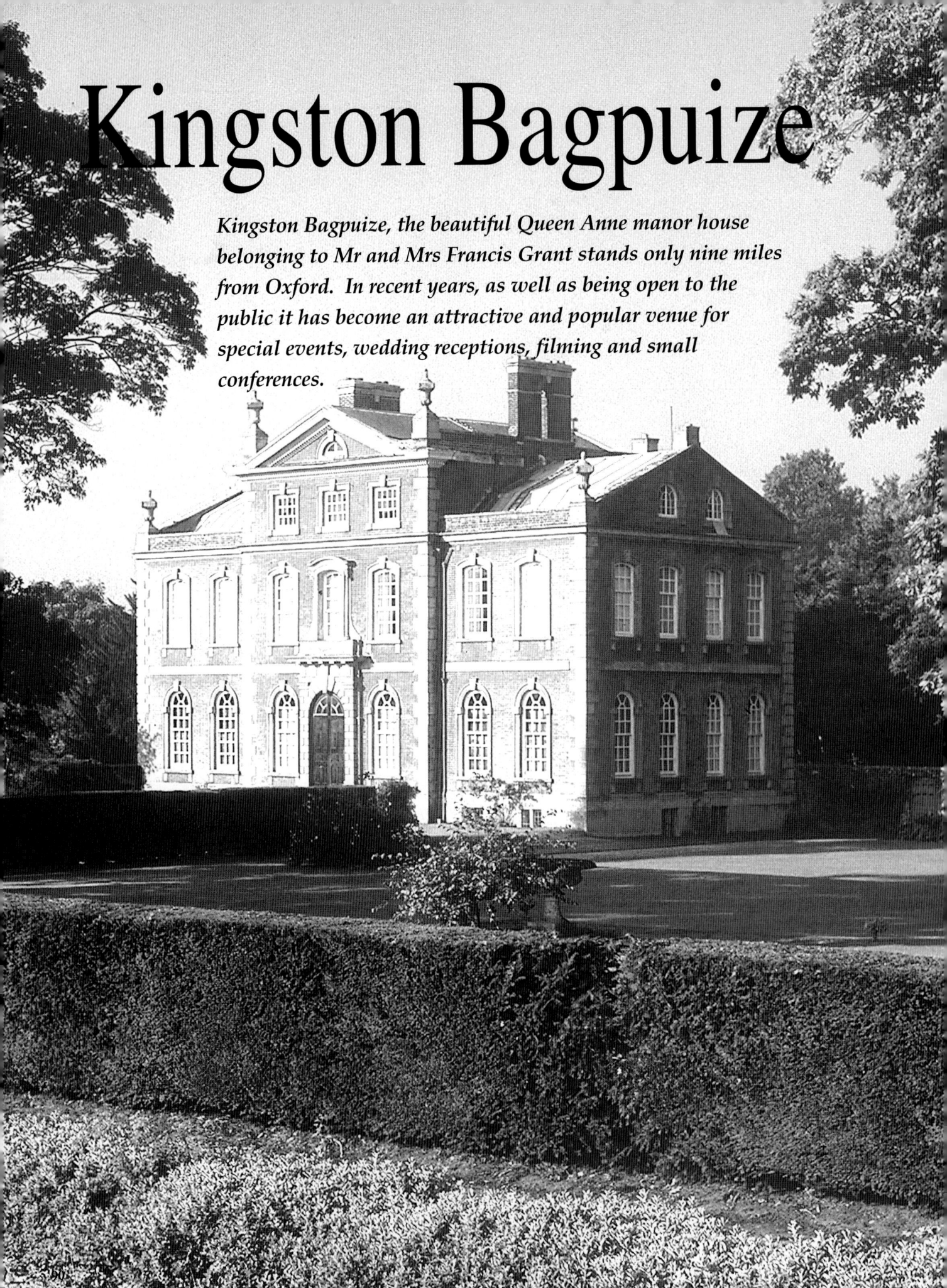

Kingston Bagpuize, the beautiful Queen Anne manor house belonging to Mr and Mrs Francis Grant stands only nine miles from Oxford. In recent years, as well as being open to the public it has become an attractive and popular venue for special events, wedding receptions, filming and small conferences.

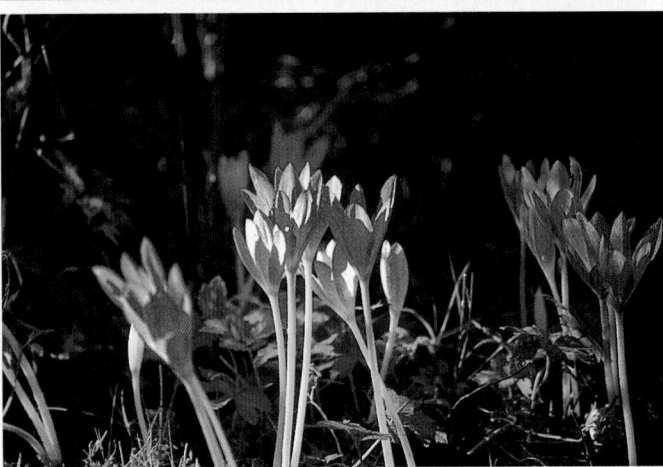

Set in mature parkland, the early origins of the house are unclear. A document of sale shows this present house to have been in existence since the 1660s, but it seems probable that it was substantially remodelled from the ground floor up in the 1720s. Townsend, a leading Oxford builder who worked under Nicholas Hawksmoor and others at Queen's College and elsewhere, may have been responsible for the alterations.

Despite the formal symmetry of the house, the interiors at Kingston Bagpuize feel immensely comfortable – the lightly coloured panelled main reception rooms creating a wonderful warm atmosphere. Dominating the Entrance Hall is the pine and oak cantilevered staircase and gallery. Thought to date from the 1720s, the staircase and gallery have no supporting columns, their weight being borne by the 3' thick walls.

Walking through the main reception rooms of the house, the visitor can see not only good Queen Anne and Georgian furniture but also in the Drawing Room beautiful French pieces from the 18th and 19th centuries. The house also has some fine paintings by Romney, Hoppner and Gainsborough.

In the Dining Room, over the fireplace, is a portrait of Marlie Raphael aged three, painted by Mrs Waller. Great Aunt of the current owner, it is to her that is owed much of the beauty of the formal and woodland gardens that surround the house today.

Marlie Raphael began adding to the existing formal gardens in the 1950s and, having removed the wartime Nissen huts from some areas of the estate, she planted the beech avenue and many specimen trees. Harold Hillier was one of the notable plantsmen who gave advice. The resulting collection contains many unusual species including *Albizia julibrissin*, *Ilex macrocarpa*, *Magnolia campbellii*, *Quercus pontica* and *Xanthoceras sorbifolium* as well as a wide variety of perennials and bulbs. These mature trees and shrubs today form a wonderful backdrop to the house.

The English, as a nation, have a passion for gardening. Gardens can be all things to all people and are never static. Francis and Virginia Grant, themselves keen and knowledgable gardeners, have over the last five years restored other areas of the garden and planted more specimen trees and shrubs to complement those already growing.

For further details about *Kingston Bagpuize* see entry in South East Region → Oxfordshire.

South East England

Paul Procter, Chorley Handford.

Owner: HM The Queen

CONTACT

The Visitor Office
Windsor Castle
Windsor
Berkshire
SL4 1NJ

Tel: 01753 869898
01753 831118

Fax: 01753 832290

e-mail: windsorcastle@
royalcollection.org.uk

LOCATION

OS Ref. SU969 770

M4/J6, M3/J3.
20m from central London.

Rail: Regular service from
London Waterloo.

Air: London Airport
(Heathrow) 15m.

Coach: Victoria Coach
Station - regular service.

Sightseeing tours:
Tour companies operate a
daily service with collection from many London
Hotels. Ask your hotel
concierge or porter for
information.

WINDSOR CASTLE
Windsor

WINDSOR CASTLE, Buckingham Palace, and the Palace of Holyroodhouse are the Official residences of the Sovereign and are used by The Queen as both a home and office. The Queen's personal standard flies when Her Majesty is in residence. Furnished with works of art from the Royal Collection, these buildings are used extensively by The Queen for State ceremonies and Official entertaining. They are opened to the public as much as these commitments will allow.

A significant proportion of Windsor Castle is opened to visitors on a regular basis including the Upper and Lower Wards, the North Terrace with its famous views towards Eton, Queen Mary's Dolls' House, the State Apartments including St. George's Hall and other newly restored rooms.

HM Queen Elizabeth II

March - October:
Daily except 13 April
& 18 June
9.45am - 5.15pm
(last admission 4pm)

November - February:
Daily except 25/26 Dec
9.45am - 4.15pm
(last admission 3pm).

St George's Chapel is closed to visitors on Sundays as services are held throughout the day. Worshippers are welcome.

The State Rooms
are closed during
Royal and State visits.

**Opening arrangements
may change at
short notice.**

ADMISSION

Adult £11.00
Child (up to 17yrs)....£5.50
OAP.........................£9.00
Family (2+2) £27.50

Groups (15+)
Discounts available.

 SPECIAL EVENTS

With the exception of Sundays, the Changing of the Guard takes place at 11am daily from April to the end of June and on alternate days at other times of the year.

 No photography.   No parking.   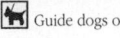 Guide dogs only.   ❄

BASILDON PARK

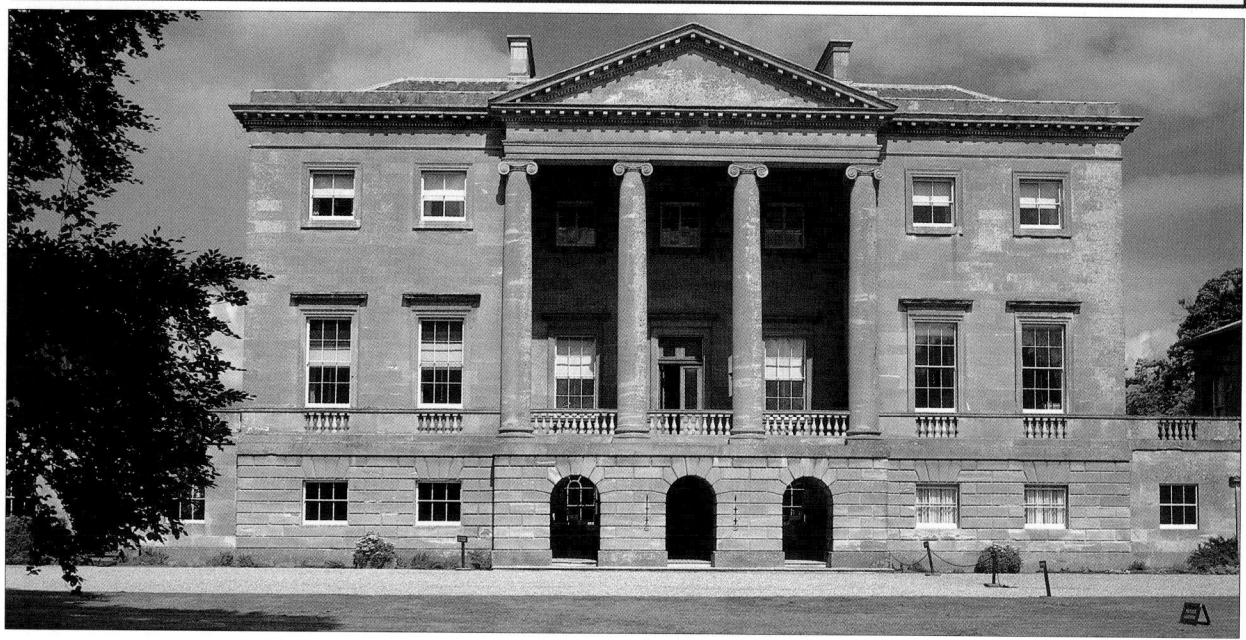

LOWER BASILDON, READING RG8 9NR

Owner: *The National Trust*   **Contact:** *The Property Manager*

Tel: 0118 984 3040 **Fax:** 0118 984 1267
e-mail: tbdgen@smtp.ntrust.org.uk

An elegant, classical house designed in the 18th century by Carr of York and set in rolling parkland in the Thames Valley. The house has rich interiors with fine plasterwork, pictures and furniture, and includes an unusual Octagon Room and a decorative Shell Room. Basildon Park has connections with the East through its builder and was the home of a wealthy industrialist in the 19th century. It was rescued from dereliction in the mid 20th century. Small flower garden, pleasure grounds and woodland walk.

Location: OS Ref. SU611 782. $2^1/_2$ m NW of Pangbourne on the west side of the A329, 7m from M4/J12.

Opening Times: House: 31 Mar - 4 Nov: daily except Mon & Tue (closed Good Fri, open BH Mons), 1 - 5.30. Park, Garden & Woodland Walk: as house 12 noon - 5.30pm. Property closes at 5pm on 17/18 Aug for concerts.

Admission: House, Park & Garden: Adult £4.30, Child £2.15, Family £10.50. Park & Garden only: Adult £1.80, Child 90p. Family £4.50. Groups of 15+ by appointment.

  P In grounds.   On leads, in grounds only.

DONNINGTON CASTLE

Tel: 02392 581059

Newbury, Berkshire

Owner: English Heritage   **Contact:** Area Manager

Built in the late 14th century, the twin towered gatehouse of this heroic castle survives amidst some impressive earthworks.

Location: OS Ref. SU463 691. 1m NW of Newbury off B4494.

Opening Times: Any reasonable time.

Admission: Free.

Patrick Lane.

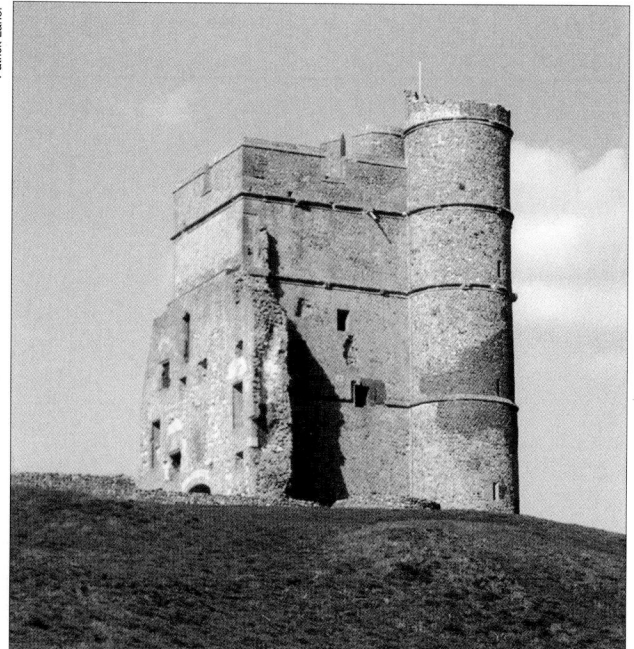

Donnington Castle, Berkshire.

DORNEY COURT

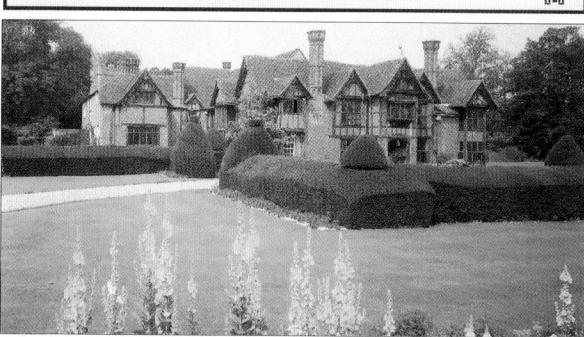

WINDSOR, BERKSHIRE SL4 6QP

Owner/Contact: Mrs P P D Peregrine Palmer

Tel: 01628 604638 **Fax:** 01628 665772 **e-mail:** palmer@dorneycourt.co.uk

Just a few miles from the heart of bustling Windsor lies "one of the finest Tudor Manor Houses in England", *Country Life.* Grade I listed with the added accolade of being of outstanding architectural and historical importance, the visitor can get a rare insight into the lifestyle of the squirearchy through 550 years, with the Palmer family, who still live there today, owning the house for 450 of these years. The house boasts a magnificent Great Hall, family portraits, oak and lacquer furniture, needlework and panelled rooms. A private tour on a 'non-open day' takes around $1^1/_2$ hours, but when open to the public this is reduced to around 40 mins. The adjacent 13th century Church of St James, with Norman font and Tudor tower can also be visited, as well as the adjoining Blooms of Bressingham Plant Centre in our walled garden where light lunches and full English cream teas are served in a tranquil setting throughout the day.

Location: OS Ref. SU926 791. 5 mins off M4/J7, 10mins from Windsor, 2m W of Eton.

Opening Times: May: BH Suns & Mons, 1.30 - 4.30pm. Aug: daily except Sats, 1.30 - 4.30pm. Last admission 4pm.

Admission: Adult: £5, Child (10yrs +) £3. Groups: By arrangement throughout the year.

i No photography in house. Film & photographic shoots. Pick your own: Jun - Aug.

Garden centre.   Garden centre suitable.   P

Guide dogs only.

ENGLEFIELD HOUSE 🏛

Tel: 01189 302221 **Fax:** 01189 303226

Englefield, Theale, Reading, Berkshire RG7 5EN **e-mail:** benyon@netcomuk.co.uk

Owner: Sir William & Lady Benyon   **Contact:** Mrs Gloria Sleep

Seven acres of woodland and water garden. Stone balustrades and staircases descending to terraces, herbaceous and rose borders. All set in a deer park. Elizabethan house is open by appointment.

Location: OS Ref. SU622 720. 6m W of Reading on A340. Theale 1m.

Opening Times: Garden only: All year: Mons, 10am - 6pm. Apr - Oct: Mon - Thur incl. 10am - 6pm.

Admission: £2.

ⓘ No photography in house. 👆 🍴 ♿ Partially suitable. WC.

🎦 By arrangement. 🅿 Ample for cars, limited for coaches. 🏪 🐕 ❄ (WH)

ETON COLLEGE

Tel: 01753 671177 **Fax:** 01753 671265

Windsor, Berkshire SL4 6DW   **e-mail:** visits@etoncollege.org.uk

Owner: Eton College   **Contact:** Rebecca Hunkin

Eton College, founded in 1440 by Henry VI, is one of the oldest and best known schools in the country. The original and subsequent historic buildings of the Foundation are a part of the heritage of the British Isles and visitors are invited to experience and share the beauty of the ancient precinct which includes the magnificent College Chapel, a masterpiece of the perpendicular style.

Location: OS Ref. SU967 779. Off M4/J5. Access from Windsor by footbridge only. Vehicle access from Slough 2m N.

Opening Times: Mar - early Oct: Times vary, best to check with the Visits Office.

Admission: Ordinary admissions and daily guided tours. Groups by appointment only. Rates vary according to type of tour.

📷 🍴 ♿ Ground floor suitable. WC. 🎦 🅿 Limited. 🐕 Guide dogs only.

ST GEORGE'S CHAPEL WINDSOR

Tel: 01753 868286

Fine example of perpendicular architecture. Open only in conjunction with Windsor Castle.

Location: OS Ref. SU968 770.

Opening Times: As Windsor Castle, but opening times subject to change at short notice.

Admission: Admission as part of Windsor Castle ticket.

TAPLOW COURT 🏛

BERRY HILL, TAPLOW, Nr MAIDENHEAD, BERKS SL6 0ER

Owner: SGI-UK   *Contact: Robert Samuels*

Tel: 01628 591215 **Fax:** 01628 773055

Set high above the Thames, affording spectacular views. Remodelled mid-19th century by William Burn. Earlier neo-Norman Hall. 18th century home of Earls of Orkney and more recently of Lord and Lady Désborough who entertained 'The Souls' here. Tranquil gardens & grounds. Anglo-Saxon burial mound. Permanent and temporary exhibitions.

Location: OS Ref. SU907 822. M4/J7 off Bath Road towards Maidenhead. 6m off M40/J2.

Opening Times: House & Grounds: Easter Sun & Mon, Suns & BH Mons up to the end of Jul: 2 - 6pm.

Admission: No charge. Free parking.

📷 ♿ 🎦 🏪 🅿 🐕 Guide dogs only.

SAVILL GARDEN

WINDSOR GREAT PARK, BERKSHIRE SL4 2HT

Owner: Crown Estate Commissioners   *Contact: Jan Bartholomew*

Tel: 01753 847518 **Fax:** 01753 847536 **e-mail:** savillgarden@crownestate.org.uk

World-renowned 35 acre woodland garden, providing a wealth of beauty and interest in all seasons. Spring is heralded by hosts of daffodils, masses of rhododendrons, azaleas, camellias, magnolias and much more. Roses, herbaceous borders and countless alpines are the great features of summer, and the leaf colours and fruits of autumn rival the other seasons with a great display.

Location: OS Ref. SU977 706. Wick Lane, Englefield Green. Clearly signposted from Ascot, Bagshot, Egham and Windsor. Nearest station: Egham.

Opening Times: Mar - Oct: 10am - 6pm. Nov - Feb: 10am - 4pm.

Admission: Apr - May: Adult £5, Child (6-16) £2, Conc. £4.50. Jun - Oct: Adult £4, Child (6-16) £1, Conc. £3.50. Nov - Mar: Adult £3, Child (6-16) £1, Conc. £2.50. Child under 6 Free. Prices subject to chnge from 1 Apr 2001.

🍴 Plant centre. ♿ Grounds suitable. WC. 🍴 Licensed. 🎦 🐕 Guide dogs only. ❄ (WH)

WELFORD PARK

Tel: 01488 608203

Newbury, Berkshire RG20 8HU

Owner/Contact: Mr J Puxley

A Queen Anne house, with attractive gardens and grounds. Riverside walks.

Location: OS Ref. SU409 731. On Lambourn Valley Road. 6m NW of Newbury.

Opening Times: 28 May, 1 - 26 Jun, 27 Aug: 11am - 5pm.

Admission: House by prior arrangement. Adult £3.50, Child Free, Conc. £2. Grounds Free.

♿ Grounds suitable. 🐕 On leads, in grounds.

WINDSOR CASTLE

See page 94 for full page entry.

❄ **Open All Year Index page 49** ◀◀◀

STOWE HOUSE
Buckingham

STOWE owes its pre-eminence to the vision and wealth of two owners. From 1715 to 1749 Viscount Cobham, one of Marlborough's Generals, continuously improved his estate, calling in the leading designers of the day to lay out the gardens, and commissioning several leading architects – Vanbrugh, Gibbs, Kent and Leoni – to decorate them with garden temples. From 1750 to 1779 Earl Temple, his nephew and successor continued to expand and embellish both Gardens and House. The House is now a major public school. Restoration of North Front and Colonnades will take place from August 2000 - October 2002.

Around the mansion is one of Britain's most magnificent landscape gardens now in the ownership of the National Trust. Covering 325 acres and containing no fewer than 6 lakes and 32 garden temples, it is of the greatest historic importance. During the 1730s William Kent laid out in the Elysian Fields at Stowe, one of the first 'natural' landscapes and initiated the style known as 'the English Garden'. 'Capability' Brown worked there for 10 years, not as a consultant but as head gardener, and in 1744 was married in the little church hidden between the trees.

❖

Owner: Stowe House Preservation Trust

CONTACT

The Commercial Director
Stowe School
Buckingham
MK18 5EH

Tel: 01280 818282
House only
or 01280 822850
Gardens

Fax: 01280 818186

e-mail: sses@stowe.co.uk

LOCATION

OS Ref. SP666 366

From London, M1 to Milton Keynes, 1½ hrs or Banbury 1¼ hrs, 3m NW of Buckingham.

Bus: from Buckingham 3m.
Rail: Milton Keynes 15m.
Air: Heathrow 50m.

CONFERENCE/FUNCTION		
ROOM	SIZE	MAX CAPACITY
Roxburgh Hall	–	460
Music Room	–	120
Marble Hall	–	150
State Dining Rm	–	160
Garter Room	–	180
Memorial Theatre	–	120

ℹ️ Indoor swimming pool, sports hall, tennis court, squash courts, parkland, cricket pitches and golf course. No photography in house.

🛍️ Call for opening times.

🍽️ International conferences, private functions, weddings, and prestige exhibitions. Catering on request.

♿ Visitors may alight at entrance. Allocated parking areas. WC in garden area. 'Batricars' available.

☕🍴 Morning coffee, lunch and afternoon tea available by pre-arrangement only, for up to 100.

🧑‍🏫 For parties of 30 at additional cost. Tour time: house and garden 2½ hrs, house only 45 mins.

🅿️ Ample.

🐕 In grounds on leads.

⛪ Civil Wedding Licence.

♿ Available. ❄️

National Trust Photographic Library: Flying Pictures

WADDESDON MANOR
Nr Aylesbury

WADDESDON MANOR was built (1874-89) for Baron Ferdinand de Rothschild to entertain his guests and display his vast collection of art treasures. It has won many awards including the Silver Award for Best Overall Property and the Europa Nostra Garden Award 1999.

This French Renaissance-style château houses one of the finest collections of French 18th century decorative arts in the world: Savonnerie carpets, Sèvres porcelain, Beauvais tapestries and furniture, as well as important portraits by Gainsborough and Reynolds and works by Dutch and Flemish Masters of the 17th century.

Waddesdon' has one of the finest Victorian gardens in Britain, renowned for its seasonal displays, colourful shrubs, mature trees and parterre. A children's garden has recently opened. Carpet bedding displays are newly created each year. In 2001 they will be created by the fashion designer, Oscar de la Renta. The rococo-style aviary houses a splendid collection of exotic birds, and thousands of bottles of vintage Rothschild wines are found in the wine cellars.

There is an award-winning gift shop, wine shop with a full selection of Rothschild wines and a licensed restaurant. Many events are organised throughout the year including special interest days, wine tastings and garden workshops.

CONTACT

Waddesdon
Nr Aylesbury
Buckinghamshire
HP18 0JH

Tel: 01296 653211

Booking: 01296 653226

Fax: 01296 653208

e-mail: twmsep
@smtp.ntrust.org.uk

LOCATION

OS Ref. SP740 169

Between Aylesbury & Bicester, off A41.

Rail: Aylesbury 6m.

National Trust Photographic Library: Andrew Peppard

OPENING TIMES

House
(including wine cellars)
28 Mar - 4 Nov: Wed - Sun,
also BH Mons, 11am - 4pm.
Last recommended
admission 2.30pm.
Bachelors' Wing
Wed - Fri, 11am - 4pm
(space is limited and entry
cannot therefore be
guaranteed).

Grounds
(including garden, aviary,
restaurant and shops)
28 Feb - 23 Dec: Wed - Sun
& BH Mons, 10am - 5pm.

ADMISSION

House & Grounds
Adult £10.00
Child (5-16 yrs) £7.50
Groups (15+)
Adult £8.00
Child £6.00

Grounds only
Adult £3.00
Child (5-16 yrs) £1.50
1 Nov - 24 Dec.........Free
Groups (15+)
Adult £2.40
Child £1.20
Bachelors' Wing.........£1.00
NT members free.HHA
Members free entry to grounds.
Timed tickets to the house
can be purchased on site or
reserved in advance by phoning
01296 653226 Mon - Fri, 10am -
4pm. Advance booking fee:
£3 per transaction.
Children under 5yrs are not
allowed in the house. Babies
must be carried in a front-sling
carrier.

SPECIAL EVENTS

Wine Tasting, Study Days,
Garden Workshops and tours,
Family Events, Floodlit Evenings:
please telephone 01295 653226
for details.

i No photography in house.		**✗** By arrangement.	
		∩	
⊤ Conferences, corporate hospitality.		**P** Ample for coaches and cars.	
♿ Suitable. WCs.		**🐕** Guide dogs only.	
☕ ⊺⊺ Licensed.		**⚭** Civil Wedding Licence.	

ASCOTT

Wing, Leighton Buzzard, Bucks LU7 0PS
Tel: 01296 688242 **Fax:** 01296 681904
e-mail: tacgen@smtp.ntrust.org.uk
Owner: The National Trust **Contact:** The Administrator

Originally a half-timbered Jacobean farmhouse, Ascott was bought in 1876 by the de Rothschild family and considerably transformed and enlarged. It now houses a quite exceptional collection of fine paintings, Oriental porcelain and English and French furniture. The extensive gardens are a mixture of the formal and natural, containing specimen trees and shrubs, as well as an herbaceous walk, lily pond, Dutch garden and remarkable topiary sundial.

Location: OS Ref. SP891 230. ¹/₂ m E of Wing, 2m SW of Leighton Buzzard, on A418.

Opening Times: House & Garden: 1 - 29 Apr & 7 Aug - 14 Sept: daily except Mons, 2 - 6pm, last admission 5pm. Garden only: 1 May - 1 Aug: every Wed & last Sun in each month, also 19 & 26 Sept, 2 - 6pm, last admission 5pm.

Admission: House & Garden: £5.60. Garden: £4. Child half price. No reduction for groups which must book.

Ground floor & grounds. 3 wheelchairs available. WCs. **P** 220 metres.
In car park only, on leads.

BLETCHLEY PARK

Tel: 01908 640404 **Fax:** 01908 274381
e-mail: majenkins@bletchleypark.org.uk
The Mansion, Wilton Avenue, Bletchley, Milton Keynes MK3 6EB
Owner: Bletchley Park Trust **Contact:** Merrill Jenkins

Centre of World War II Enigma code breaking operations.

Location: OS Ref. SP858 340. 200yds from Bletchley railway station. Just off the B4034 Bletchley to Buckingham road.

Opening Times: Every other weekend: 10.30am - 5pm, last admission 3.30pm. Last tour begins at 3pm.

Admission: Adult £5, Child & Conc. £4. Accompanied Child (under 8yrs) Free.

BOARSTALL DUCK DECOY

Tel: 01844 237488
Boarstall, Aylesbury, Buckinghamshire HP18 9UX
Owner: The National Trust **Contact:** The Administrator

A rare survival of a 17th century decoy in working order, set on a tree-fringed lake, with nature trail and exhibition hall.

Location: OS Ref. SP624 151. Midway between Bicester and Thame, 2m W of Brill.

Opening Times: 24 Mar - 26 Aug: Weds, 5 - 8pm, Sats, Suns & BH Mons, 10am - 5pm. Talk/demonstration: Sats, Suns & BH Mons if Warden available, tel. for details.

Admission: Adult £2.10, Family £5. Groups (6+) must book: £1.

Partially suitable. By arrangement. In car park only, on leads.

BOARSTALL TOWER

Boarstall, Aylesbury, Buckinghamshire HP18 90X
Owner: The National Trust **Contact:** The Tenant

The stone gatehouse of a fortified house long since demolished. It dates from the 14th century, and was altered in the 16th and 17th centuries, but retains its crossloops for bows. The gardens are surrounded by a moat on three sides.

Location: OS Ref. SP624 141. Midway between Bicester and Thame, 2m W of Brill.

Opening Times: 1 Apr - 31 Oct: Wed & BH Mons, 2 - 6pm. Also Sats by prior arrangement with tenant.

Admission: Adult £2.10, Child £1.05.

No WC. Ground floor & garden. In car park only.

BUCKINGHAM CHANTRY CHAPEL

Tel: 01280 823020
Market Hill, Buckingham, Buckinghamshire
Tel: 01494 528051
Owner: The National Trust **Contact:** Buckingham Heritage Trust

Rebuilt in 1475 and retaining a fine Norman doorway. The chapel was restored by Gilbert Scott in 1875, at which time it was used as a Latin or Grammar School.

Location: OS Ref. SP693 340. In narrow lane, NW of Market Hill.

Opening Times: Daily by written appointment with the Buckingham Heritage Trust, c/o Old Gaol Museum, Market Hill, Buckingham MK18 1JX.

Admission: Free.

Chicheley Hall.

Patrick Lane.

CHENIES MANOR HOUSE

CHENIES, RICKMANSWORTH, HERTS WD3 6ER

Owner: *Lt Col & Mrs MacLeod Matthews* **Contact:** *Lt Col & Mrs MacLeod Matthews or Sue Brock*

Tel/Fax: 01494 762888

15th & 16th century Manor House with fortified tower. Original home of the Earls of Bedford, visited by Henry VIII and Elizabeth I. Home of the MacLeod Matthews family. Contains contemporary tapestries and furniture, hiding places, collection of antique dolls, medieval undercroft and well. Surrounded by beautiful gardens which have featured in many publications and on TV, a Tudor sunken garden, a white garden, herbaceous borders, a fountain court, a physic garden containing a very wide selection of medicinal and culinary herbs, a parterre and two mazes. The kitchen garden is in the Victorian style with unusual vegetables and fruit. Special exhibitions, flower drying and arrangements. Many specialist and rare plants in a charming setting.

Location: OS Ref. TQ016 984. N of A404 between Amersham & Rickmansworth. M25/J18, 3m.

Opening Times: 1 Apr - 28 Oct: Wed & Thur & BH Mons, 2 - 5pm. Last entry to house 4.15pm. Groups by arrangement at other times.

Admission: House & Garden: Adult £5, Child £3. Garden only: Adult £3, Child £1.

Unusual plants for sale. Grounds suitable. **P** Free nearby.

CHICHELEY HALL

Tel: 01234 391252 **Fax:** 01234 391388
Newport Pagnell, Buckinghamshire MK16 9JJ
Owner: The Hon Nicholas Beatty **Contact:** Mrs V Child

Fine 18th century house. Naval museum, English sea paintings and furniture. Suitable for residential conferences up to 15 delegates.

Location: OS Ref. SP906 458. 2m from Milton Keynes, 5 mins from M1/J14. 10m W of Bedford.

Opening Times: All year: By appointment only

Admission: Groups (20+): Adult £5. Groups under 20: Adult £6, Child £2.

Conferences. By arrangement. Not suitable. Obligatory.

CHILTERN OPEN AIR MUSEUM

Tel: 01494 871117 **Fax:** 01494 872774
Newland Park, Gorelands Lane, Chalfont St Giles, Buckinghamshire HB8 4AB
Owner: Chiltern Open Air Museum Ltd **Contact:** Dr J Moir

A museum of historic buildings showing their original uses including a blacksmith's forge, stables, barns etc.

Location: OS Ref. TQ011 938. At Newland Park 1¹/₂ m E of Chalfont St Giles, 4¹/₂ m from Amersham. 3m from M25/J17.

Opening Times: Sat 31 Mar - end of Oct: daily, 10am - 5pm.

Admission: Adult £5.50, Child under 5yrs Free, Child (5-16yrs) £3, Over 60s £4.50, Family £15. 10% discount for groups (10+).

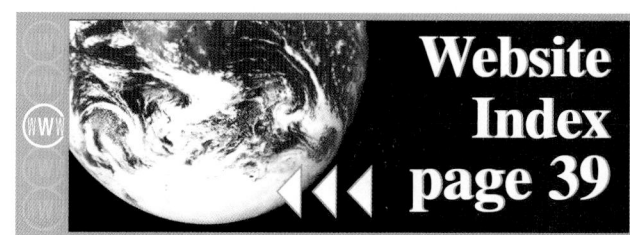

Website Index page 39

CLAYDON HOUSE

MIDDLE CLAYDON, Nr BUCKINGHAM MK18 2EY

Owner: *The National Trust*   **Contact:** *The Custodian*

Tel: 01296 730349 **Fax:** 01296 738511 **e-mail:** tcdgen@smtp.ntrust.org.uk

A fine 18th century house with some of the most perfect rococo decoration in England. A series of great rooms have wood carvings in Chinese and Gothic styles, and tall windows look out over parkland and a lake. The house has relics of the exploits of the Verney family in the English Civil War and also on show is the bedroom of Florence Nightingale, a relative of the Verneys and a regular visitor to this tranquil place.

Location: OS Ref. SP720 253. In Middle Claydon, 13m NW of Aylesbury, signposted from A413, A421 and A41. 3¹/₂ m SW of Winslow.

Opening Times: 31 Mar - 4 Nov: daily except Thur & Fri, 1 - 5pm. House closes 1hr early on event days. Gardens, church & tearoom open at 12 noon.

Admission: Adult £4.30, Family £10.50. Groups 15+ (must book): Mon - Wed & Sat. £3.60. Garden only: £1.

Ground floor & grounds. Braille guide. WC. In park, on leads.
Telephone for details.

CLIVEDEN

TAPLOW, MAIDENHEAD SL6 0JA

Owner: *The National Trust*   **Contact:** *Property Manager*

Tel: 01628 605069 **Fax:** 01628 669461

152 hectares of gardens and woodland. A water garden, 'secret' garden, herbaceous borders, topiary, a great formal parterre, and informal vistas provide endless variety. The garden statuary is one of the most important collections in the care of The National Trust and includes many Roman antiquities collected by 1st Viscount Astor. The Octagonal Temple (Chapel) with its rich mosaic interior is open on certain days, as are three of the principal rooms of the house (see below).

Location: OS Ref. SU915 851. 3m N of Maidenhead, M4/J7 onto A4 or M40/J4 onto A404 to Marlow and follow signs. From London by train take Thames Train service from Paddington to Burnham (taxi rank and office adjacent to station).

Opening Times: Estate & Garden: 14 Mar - 31 Dec, daily, 11am - 6pm (closes at 4pm from 1 Nov). House (3 rooms): Apr - Oct: Thurs & Sun, 3 - 6pm. Entry by times ticket from information kiosk. Otagonal Temple: as house. Woodlands car park: all year: daily, 11am - 5.30pm (closed at 4pm Nov - Mar).

Admission: Grounds: Adult £5, Child £2.50, Family £12.50. House: £1 extra, Child 50p. Groups (must book): Adult £4.50, Child £2.25. Woodlands car park: Adult £3, Child £1.50, Family £7.50. Note: Mooring charge on Cliveden Reach.

Partially suitable. WC. Licensed. Specified woodlands only.
Telephone for details.

South East England

COWPER & NEWTON MUSEUM Tel: 01234 711516 e-mail: cnm@mkheritage.co.uk

Home of Olney's Heritage, Orchard Side, Market Place, Olney MK46 4AJ

Owner: Board of Trustees   **Contact:** Mrs J McKillop

Once the home of 18th century poet and letter writer William Cowper and now containing furniture, paintings and belongings of both Cowper and his ex-slave trader friend, Rev John Newton (author of "Amazing Grace"). Attractions include re-creations of a Victorian country kitchen and wash-house, two peaceful gardens and Cowper's restored summerhouse. Costume gallery, important collections of dinosaur bones and bobbin lace, and local history displays.

Location: OS Ref. SP890 512. On A509, 6m N of Newport Pagnell, M1/J14.

Opening Times: 1 Mar - 23 Dec: Tue - Sat & BH Mons, 10am - 1pm & 2 - 5pm. Closed on Good Fri. Open on Sundays in June, July & August, 2 - 5pm.

Admission: Adult £3, Conc. £2, Child & Students (with card) £1.50, Family £7.50.

[i] No photography.   [icon] [icon] Gardens suitable.   [icon] By arrangement. [icon] Guide dogs only. [icon]

DORNEYWOOD GARDEN [icon]   Tel: 01494 528051 (NT Regional Office)

Dorneywood, Burnham, Buckinghamshire SL1 8PY

Owner: The National Trust   **Contact:** The Secretary

The house was given to the National Trust as an official residence for either a Secretary of State or Minister of the Crown. Garden only open.

Location: OS Ref. SU938 848. SW of Burnham Beeches. 2m E of Cliveden.

Opening Times: By written appointment only - one week in advance – 27 June, 18 July & 4 August: 2 - 5pm. Write to The Secretary, Dorneywood Trust at above address.

Admission: £3.

FORD END WATERMILL   Tel: 01582 600391

Station Road, Ivinghoe, Buckinghamshire   Contact: David Lindsey

The Watermill, a listed building, was recorded in 1767 but is probably much older.

Location: OS Ref. SP941 166. 600 metres from Ivinghoe Church along B488 (Station Road) to Leighton Buzzard.

Opening Times: Please telephone for opening dates and milling times.

Admission: Adult £1, Child 30p. School Groups: 50p each adult and child.

JOHN MILTON'S COTTAGE   Tel: 01494 872313   e-mail: pbirger@clara.net

21 Deanway, Chalfont St. Giles, Buckinghamshire HP8 4JH

Owner: Milton Cottage Trust   **Contact:** Mr E A Dawson

Grade I listed 16th century cottage where John Milton lived and completed 'Paradise Lost' and started 'Paradise Regained'. Three ground floor museum rooms contain important 1st editions of John Milton's 17th century poetry and prose works. Amongst many unique items on display is the portrait of John Milton by Sir Godfrey Kneller. Well stocked, attractive cottage garden, listed by English Heritage.

Location: OS Ref. SU987 933. $\frac{1}{2}$ m W of A413. 3m N of M40/J2. S side of street.

Opening Times: 1 Mar - 31 Oct: Tue - Sun, 10am - 1pm & 2 - 6pm. Closed Mons (open BH Mons). Coach parking by prior arrangement only.

Admission: Adult £2.50, under 15s £1, Groups (20+) £2.

[icon] [icon] Ground floor suitable.   [icon] Talk followed by free tour.   [P] [icon] [icon]

NETHER WINCHENDON HOUSE [icon]   Tel: 01844 290199

Aylesbury, Buckinghamshire HP18 0DY

Owner/Contact: Mr Robert Spencer Bernard

Medieval and Tudor manor house. There is a fine 16th century frieze, ceiling and original linenfold panelling. Altered in late 18th Century in the Strawberry Hill Gothick style. Fine furniture and family portraits. Continuous family occupation since mid-16th century. Home of the last British Governor of Massachussetts Bay, 1760. Interesting garden and specimen trees.

Location: OS Ref. SP734 121. 2m N of A418 equidistant between Thame & Aylesbury.

Opening Times: 1 - 28 May & 26/27 Aug: 2.30 - 5.30pm (last party at about 4.45pm).

Admission: Adult £4 (HHA members free), Child (under 12) & OAP £2 (not weekends or BHs). Groups: any time by written appointment, min charge £40.

[icon] [icon] By arrangement.   [icon]

HUGHENDEN MANOR [icon]

National Trust Photographic Library: Matthew Antrobus.

HIGH WYCOMBE HP14 4LA

Owner: *The National Trust*   **Contact:** *The Property Manager*

Tel: 01494 755573

Home of Prime Minister Benjamin Disraeli from 1847 - 1881, Hughenden has a red brick, 'gothic' exterior. The interior is a comfortable Victorian home and still holds many of Disraeli's pictures, books and furniture, as well as other fascinating mementoes of the life of the great statesman and writer. The surrounding park and woodland have lovely walks, and the formal garden has been recreated in the spirit of Mary Anne Disraeli's colourful designs.

Location: OS165 Ref. SU866 955. 1$\frac{1}{2}$ m N of High Wycombe on the W side of the A4128.

Opening Times: House: 3 - 31 Mar: Sats & Suns. 1 Apr - 4 Nov: Wed - Sun & BH Mons, 1 - 5pm (last admission 4.30pm). Closed Good Fri. On BHs and busy days entry is by timed ticket. Gardens open same days as house, 12 noon - 5pm. Park & Woodland: All year.

Admission: House & Garden: Adult £4.30, Child £2.15, Family £10.50. Garden only: Adult £1.50, Child 75p. Park & Woodland Free. Groups must book, no groups on Sat, Sun or BH Mons.

[i] Exhibition area.   [icon] [icon] Limited. WC.   [icon] [icon] In grounds, on leads. Guide dogs in house & formal gardens.   [icon] [icon] Telephone for details.

Stowe Gardens & Park.

PITSTONE WINDMILL

Ivinghoe, Buckinghamshire

Owner: The National Trust   **Contact:** The Administrator

One of the oldest post mills in Britain; in view from Ivinghoe Beacon.

Location: OS Ref. SP946 158. $^1/_2$ m S of Ivinghoe, 3m NE of Tring. Just W of B488.

Opening Times: Jun - end Aug: Sun & BHs, 2.30 - 6pm.

Admission: Adult £1, Child 30p.

PRINCES RISBOROUGH MANOR HOUSE   **Tel:** 01494 528051

Princes Risborough, Aylesbury, Buckinghamshire HP17 9AW

Owner: The National Trust   **Contact:** The Owner

A 17th century red-brick house with Jacobean oak staircase.

Location: OS Ref. SP806 035. Opposite church, off market square.

Opening Times: House (hall, drawing room & staircase) and front garden by written appointment only with the owner. Apr - Oct: Weds, 2.30 - 4.30pm.

Admission: £1.20.

STOWE GARDENS & PARK

Nr BUCKINGHAM MK18 5EH

Owner: *The National Trust*   **Contact:** *The Property Manager*

Tel: 01280 822850   **Infoline:** 01494 755568   **Fax:** 01280 822437

One of the finest Georgian landscape gardens, made up of valleys and vistas, narrow lakes and rivers, with more than 30 temples and monuments designed by many of the leading architects of the 18th century. At the centre is Stowe House, occupied by Stowe School, and all around is Stowe Gardens & Park.

The creation of the Temple family, Stowe has been described as a 'work to wonder at' in its size, splendour and variety. Many of the garden buildings have now been conserved, and thousands of new trees and shrubs have been planted in recent years. Work continues on this as well as on the Mansion itself. What's new in 2001: Four newly restored monuments: the Fane of Pastoral Poetry and Lord Cobham's Monument in the garden, and the Conduit House and Wolfe's Obelisk in the Park.

Location: OS Ref. SP665 366. Off A422 Buckingham - Banbury Rd. 3m NW of Buckingham.

Opening Times: Gardens: 3 Mar - 28 Oct (closed 26 May) & 1 - 23 Dec: Wed - Sun (open BH Mons), 10am - 5.30pm, last admission 4pm. Dec: 10am - 4pm, last admission 3pm. Gardens may close in bad weather.

Admission: Gardens: £4.60. Family £11.50. House: Adult £2. Groups by arrangement.

Pre-booked self-drive powered chairs available. WC. Licensed. By arrangement. In grounds, on leads. Send SAE for details.

STOWE HOUSE   See page 97 for full page entry.

WADDESDON MANOR   See page 98 for full page entry.

WEST WYCOMBE PARK   **Tel:** 01494 513569

West Wycombe, High Wycombe, Buckinghamshire HP14 3AJ

Owner: The National Trust   **Contact:** The Head Guide

A perfectly preserved rococo landscape garden, created in the mid-18th century by Sir Francis Dashwood, founder of the Dilettanti Society and the Hellfire Club. The house is among the most theatrical and Italiante in England, its façades formed as classical temples. The interior has Palmyrene ceilings and decoration, with pictures, furniture and sculpture dating from the time of Sir Francis.

Location: OS Ref. SU828 947. At W end of West Wycombe S of the A40.

Opening Times: Grounds only: 1 Apr - end May: Suns, Weds & BHs, 2 - 6pm. House & Grounds: Jun, Jul & Aug: daily except Fris & Sats, 2 - 6pm. Weekday entry by timed tour. Last admission 5.15pm.

Admission: House & Grounds: Adult £4.60, Child £2.30, Family £11.50. Grounds only: £2.60. Note: The West Wycombe Caves and adjacent café are privately owned and NT members must pay admission fees. Groups by arrangement.

Grounds partly suitable. In car park only, on leads.

Special Events Index ◀◀◀ **page 33**

WINSLOW HALL

Tel: 01296 712323

Winslow, Buckinghamshire MK18 3HL

Owner/Contact: Sir Edward Tomkins

William and Mary house generally attributed to Wren. Virtually unchanged structurally and mostly original interiors. Attractive garden with unusual trees and shrubs.

Location: OS Ref. SP772 275. In the town of Winslow on N side of the A413.

Opening Times: By appointment.

Admission: Please contact for details.

WYCOMBE MUSEUM

Tel: 01494 421895 **Fax:** 01494 421897

e-mail: enquiries@wycombemuseum.demon.co.uk

Priory Avenue, High Wycombe, Buckinghamshire HP13 6PX

Owner: Wycombe District Council   **Contact:** Vicki Wood (Museums Officer)

Set in historic Castle Hill House and surrounded by peaceful and attractive gardens, the Wycombe Museum explores the history of the Wycombe district.

Location: OS Ref. SU867 933. Signposted off the A404 High Wycombe/Amersham road. The Museum is about 5mins walk from the town centre and railway station.

Opening Times: Mon - Sat, 10am - 5pm. Open Suns, 2 - 5pm.

Admission: Free.

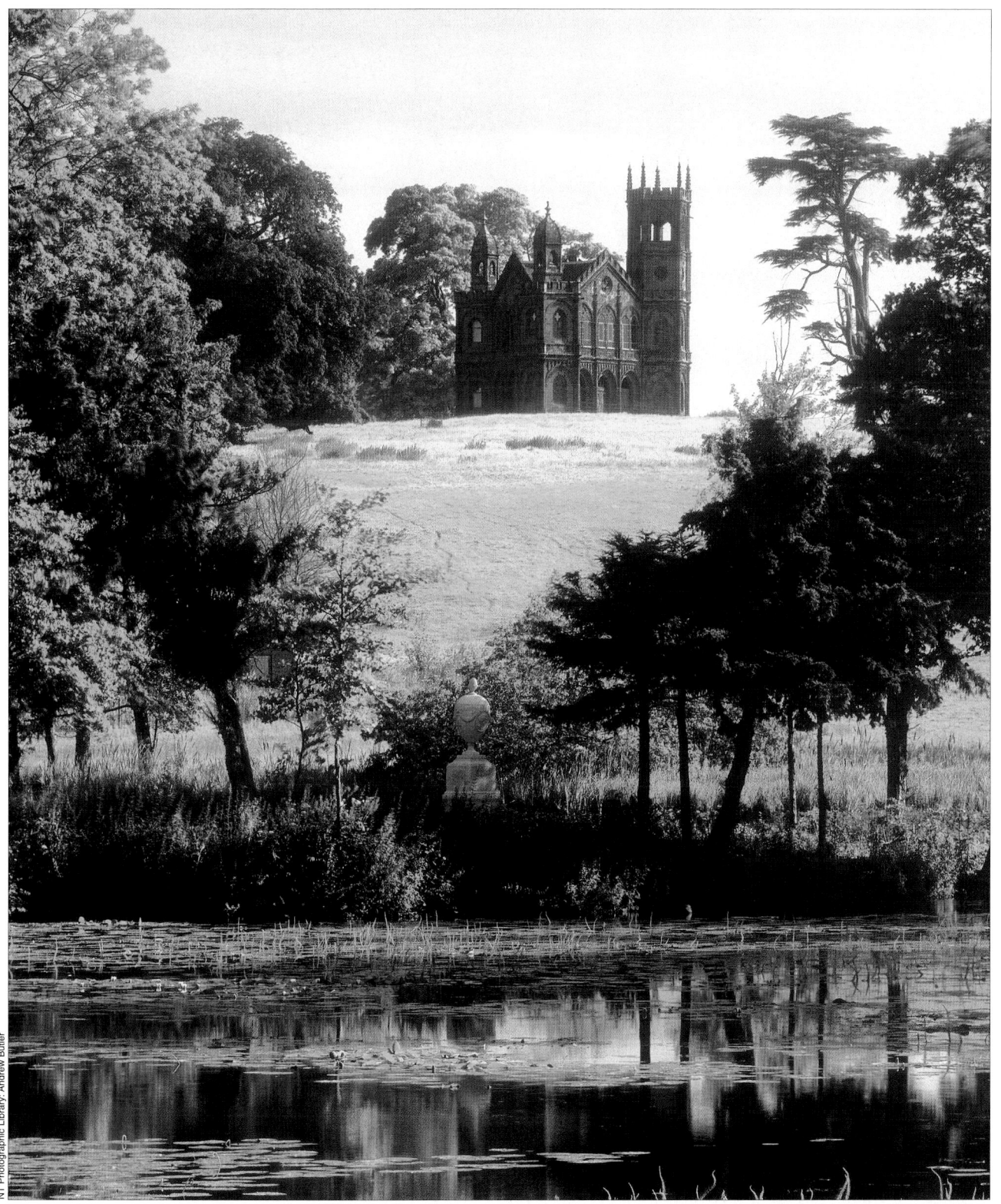

NT Photographic Library; Andrew Butler

Stowe Gardens & Park, Buckinghamshire

South East England

BEAULIEU
Beaulieu

Owner: Lord Montagu

CONTACT

Conference Office
John Montagu Building
Beaulieu
Brockenhurst
Hampshire
SO42 7ZN

Tel: 01590 614604

Fax: 01590 612624

e-mail: conference@
beaulieu.co.uk

LOCATION

OS Ref. SU387 025

From London, M3,
M27 W to J2,
A326, B3054 follow
brown signs.

Bus: Bus stops
within complex.

Rail: Stations at
Brockenhurst and
Beaulieu Rd
both 7m away.

BEAULIEU is set in the heart of the New Forest and is a place that gives enormous pleasure to people with an interest in seeing history of all kinds.

Overlooking the Beaulieu River, Palace House has been the ancestral home of the Montagus since 1538. The House was once the Great Gatehouse of Beaulieu Abbey and its monastic origins are reflected in such features as the fan vaulted ceilings. Many treasures, which are reminders of travels all round the world by past generations of the Montagu family, can also be seen. Walks amongst the gardens and by the Beaulieu River can also be enjoyed.

Beaulieu Abbey was founded in 1204 and although most of the buildings have now been destroyed, much of the beauty and interest remains. The former Monks' Refectory is now the local Parish Church. The Domus, which houses an exhibition of monastic life, is home to beautiful wall hangings and 15th century beamed ceilings.

Beaulieu also houses the world famous National Motor Museum which traces the story of motoring from 1894 to the present day. 250 vehicles are on display including legendary world record breakers plus veteran, vintage and classic cars and motorcycles.

The modern Beaulieu is very much a family destination where there are various free and unlimited rides and drives on a transportation theme to be enjoyed by everyone, including a mile long monorail and replica 1912 London open-topped bus.

OPENING TIMES

SUMMER
May - September
Daily, 10am - 6pm.

WINTER
October - April
Daily, 10am - 5pm.

Closed Christmas Day.

ADMISSION

ALL YEAR

Individual rates upon application.

Groups (15+)
Rates upon application.

◆ SPECIAL EVENTS

- **APR 8:**
  Boat Jumble.
- **MAY 12/13:**
  Spring Autojumble
- **SEPT 8/9:**
  Autojumble.

All enquiries should be made to our Special Events Booking Office where advance tickets can be purchased. The contact telephone is 01590 614645.

Other Event dates yet to be confirmed to include Motorcycle World, Palace House Prom, Fireworks Fair.

CONFERENCE/FUNCTION		
ROOM	SIZE	MAX CAPACITY
Brabazon (x3)	40'x40'	120 (x3)
Domus	69'x27'	140
Theatre		200
Hartford Suite	39'x17'	50
Palace House		60
Motor Museum		300

BEAULIEU

Catering and Functions

Beaulieu also offers a comprehensive range of facilities for conferences, company days out, product launches, management training, corporate hospitality, promotions, film locations, exhibitions and outdoor events.

The National Motor Museum is a unique venue for drinks receptions and dinners or the perfect complement to a conference as a relaxing visit.

The charming 13th century Domus banqueting hall with its beautiful wooden beams, stone walls and magnificent wall hangings, is the perfect setting for dinners, buffets or themed evenings – 17th century Royal Feasts with period entertainment are a speciality.

Palace House, the ancestral home of Lord Montagu is an exclusive setting for smaller dinners, buffets and receptions. With a welcoming log fire in the winter and the coolness of the courtyard fountain in the summer, it offers a relaxing yet truly 'stately' atmosphere to ensure a memorable experience for your guests whatever the time of year

A purpose-built theatre, with tiered seating, can accommodate 220 people whilst additional meeting and syndicate rooms can accommodate from 5 to 200 delegates. With the nearby Beaulieu River offering waterborne activities and the Beaulieu Estate giving you the opportunity of indulging in a variety of country pursuits and outdoor management training, Beaulieu provides a unique venue for your conference and corporate hospitality needs.

i Allow 3 hrs or more for visits. Last adm. 40 mins before closing. Helicopter landing point. When visiting Beaulieu arrangements can be made to view the Estate's vineyards. Visits, which can be arranged between Apr - Oct, must be pre-booked at least one week in advance with Beaulieu Estate Office.

Palace House Shop and Kitchen Shop plus Main Reception Shop.

Y

Disabled visitors may be dropped off outside Visitor Reception before parking. WC. Wheelchairs can be provided free of charge in Visitor Reception by prior booking.

The self-service Brabazon restaurant seats 300. Prices range to £7 for lunch. Groups can book in advance. Further details and menus from Catering Manager 01590 612345.

Attendants on duty. Guided tours by prior arrangement for groups.

P 1,500 cars and 30 coaches. During the season the busy period is from 11.30am to 1.30pm. Coach drivers should sign in at Information Desk. Free admission for coach drivers plus voucher which can be exchanged for food, drink and souvenirs.

Professional staff available to assist in planning of visits. Services include introductory talks, films, guided tours, rôle play and extended projects. In general, educational services incur no additional charges and publications are sold at cost. Starter sets available free of charge to pre-booked parties. Information pack available from Education at Beaulieu, John Montagu Building, Beaulieu, Hants SO42 7ZN.

In grounds, on leads only.

South East England

Owner:
The Earl of Carnarvon

CONTACT

Adrian Wiley
Highclere Castle
Newbury
Berkshire
RG20 9RN

Tel: 01635 253210

Fax: 01635 255315

e-mail: theoffice@
highclerecastle.co.uk

LOCATION

OS Ref. SU445 587

Approx 7m out
of Newbury on A34
towards Winchester.
From London: M4/J13,
A34 Bypass Newbury-
Winchester 20 mins.
M3/J5 approx 15m.

Air: Heathrow M4 45 mins.

Rail: Paddington -
Newbury 45 mins.

Taxi: 4^{1}/2 m
01635 40829.

CONFERENCE/FUNCTION		
ROOM	SIZE	MAX CAPACITY
Library	43' x 21'	120
Saloon	42' x 29'	150
Dining Rm	37' x 18'	70
Library, Saloon, Drawing Rm, Music Rm, Smoking Rm		400

HIGHCLERE CASTLE & GARDENS 🏛
Newbury

Designed by Charles Barry in the 1830s at the same time as he was building the Houses of Parliament, this soaring pinnacled mansion provided a perfect setting for the 3rd Earl of Carnarvon, one of the great hosts of Queen Victoria's reign. The extravagant interiors range from church Gothic through Moorish flamboyance and rococo revival to the solid masculinity in the long Library. Old master paintings mix with portraits by Van Dyck and 18th century painters. Napoleon's desk and chair rescued from St. Helena sits with other 18th and 19th century furniture.

The 5th Earl of Carnarvon discovered the Tomb of Tutankhamun with Howard Carter. The castle houses a unique exhibition of some of his discoveries which were only rediscovered in the castle in 1988. The current Earl is the Queen's Horseracing Manager. In 1993 to celebrate his 50th year as a leading owner and breeder 'The Lord Carnarvon Racing Exhibition' was opened to the public, and offers a fascinating insight into a racing history that dates back three generations.

GARDENS

The magnificent parkland with its massive cedars was designed by 'Capability' Brown. The walled gardens also date from an earlier house at Highclere but the dark yew walks are entirely Victorian in character. The glass Orangery and Fernery add an exotic flavour. The Secret Garden has a romance of its own with a beautiful curving lawn surrounded by densely planted herbaceous gardens. A place for poets and romantics.

❖

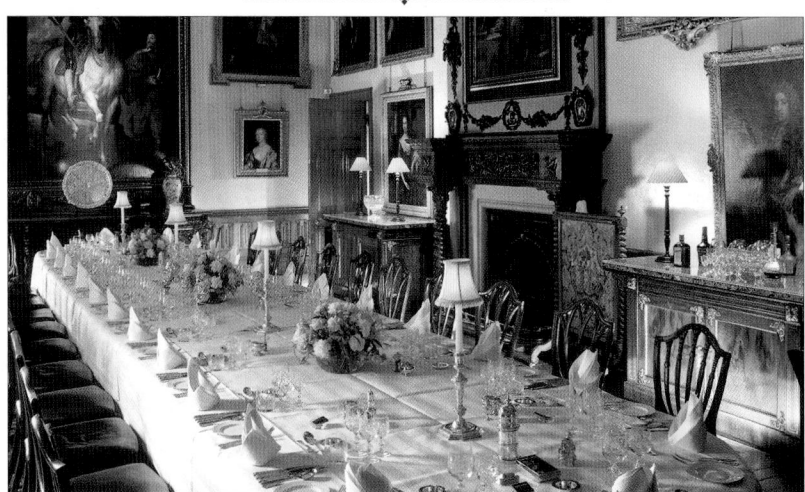

🛍 ℹ️ Conferences, exhibitions, filming, fairs, and concerts (cap. 8000). No photography in the house.

🍽 Receptions, dinners, corporate hospitality.

♿ Visitors may alight at the entrance. WC.

☕ Tearooms, licensed. Lunches for 20+ can be booked.

🅿 Ample.

Egyptian Exhibition: £3 per child. 1 adult free per every 10 children – includes playgroups, Brownie packs, Guides etc. Nature walks, beautiful old follies, Secret Garden.

🐕 In grounds, on leads. 🔔 Civil Wedding Licence.

OPENING TIMES

1 July - 30 August
Daily: 11am - 5pm.
Sats: 11am - 3.30pm. Last adm. 1 hour before closing.
The house is occasionally closed during this period - please call our information line.
Closed 21/22 July.

ADMISSION

Adult £6.50
Child (4-15yrs)........£3.00
Student/OAP...........£5.00
Wheelchair Pusher ..FOC

Grounds & Gardens only
Adult £3.00
Child (5-15yrs)........£1.50
Groups (20+)
Adult £5.00
Child (4-15yrs)........£3.00
Private guided tour by arrangement £10pp (min. £500 +VAT).

School Groups (to visit Egyptian Exhibition only)
Child £3.50
1 adult Free for every 10 children

VIP Season Ticket*
(2+3) £25.00
*Runs for one year from date of joining, Free admission for 2 adults & 3 children to the House, Exhibitions & Gardens: 1 Jul - 2 Sept & when special events are taking place. 10% off shop, tearooms, free admission to daytime events. Discounted rate for evening concerts, free admission to 'Shakespeare in the Park', £2 off Newbury Racecourse Members' Enclosure badges when pre-booked, Newbury Hilton - Fri, Sat, Sun evenings - dinner for two for the price of one from chef's hot or cold table, 10% off the price of lunch or dinner at Sharland's Restaurant, Newbury Manor Hotel.

📅 **SPECIAL EVENTS**

Please telephone
01635 253204 for details.

NT Photographic Library: Nick Carter

Owner: The National Trust

CONTACT

The Property Manager
Hinton Ampner Garden
Bramdean
Alresford
Hampshire
SO24 0LA

Tel: 01962 771305

Fax: 01962 793101

e-mail: shigen@
smtp.ntrust.org.uk

LOCATION

OS Ref. SU597 275

On A272, 1m W of
Bramdean village, 8m E of
Winchester.

HINTON AMPNER GARDEN
Bramdean

'I have learned during the past years what above all I want from a garden: this is tranquillity'. so said Ralph Dutton, 8th and last Lord Sherborne, of his garden at Hinton Ampner. He created one of the great gardens of the 20th century, a masterpiece of design based upon the bones of a Victorian garden, in which he united a formal layout with varied and informal planting in pastel shades. It is a garden of all year round interest with scented plants and magnificent vistas over the park and surrounding countryside.

The garden forms the link between the woodland and parkland planting, which he began in 1930, and the house, which he remodelled into a small neo-Georgian manor house in 1936. He made further alterations when the house was reconstructed after a fire in 1960. Today it contains his very fine collection of English furniture, Italian paintings and hard-stones. Both his collection and every aspect of the decoration at Hinton Ampner reflects Ralph Dutton's sure eye and fine aesthetic judgement.

He placed the whole within the rolling Hampshire landscape that he loved and understood so well.

❖

NT Photographic Library: Stephen Robson

OPENING TIMES

House
3 Apr - end Sept: Tues & Weds,
also Sats & Suns in Aug,
1.30 - 5pm.

Garden
18 & 25 Mar,
1 Apr - end Sept:
Tues, Weds, Sats, Suns & BH Mons, 1.30 - 5pm.

ADMISSION

House and Garden
Adult £5.00
Child (5-16).............£2.50

Garden only
Adult £4.00
Child (5-16).............£2.00
Children under 5yrs Free
Groups (min 15, max 60)
Adult £4.50
Child........................£2.25

NT Members free.

Limited for coaches.

South East England

SOMERLEY
Ringwood

Sitting on the edge of the New Forest in the heart of Hampshire, Somerley, home of the 6th Earl of Normanton and his three children, is situated in 7,000 acres of meadows, woods and rolling parkland. Designed by Samuel Wyatt in the mid 1700s, the house became the property of the Normanton family in 1825 and has remained in the same family through the years. Housing a magnificent art and porcelain collection, the house itself, albeit impressively splendid, still retains the warmth and character of a family home.

Although never open to the public, Somerley is available for corporate events and its location, along with its seclusion and privacy, provide the perfect environment for conferences and meetings, product launches, lunches and dinners, activity and team building days (the estate boasts a hugely challenging off-road driving course) and film and photographic work.

Somerley only ever hosts one event at a time so exclusivity in an outstanding setting is always guaranteed. From groups as small as eight to perhaps a large dinner for 120, the style of attention and personal service go hand in hand with the splendour of the house and the estate itself.

Owner:
The Earl of Normanton

CONTACT

Richard Horridge
Somerley
Ringwood
Hampshire
BH24 3PL

Tel: 01425 480819

Fax: 01425 478613

e-mail: info@somerley.com

LOCATION

OS Ref. SU134 080

Off the A31 to Bournemouth 2m. London 1³/₄ hrs via M3, M27, A31. 2m NW of Ringwood.

Air: Bournemouth International Airport 5m.

Rail: Bournemouth Station 12m.

Taxi: A car can be arranged from the House if applicable.

CONFERENCE/FUNCTION		
ROOM	SIZE	MAX CAPACITY
Picture Gall.	80' x 30'	200
Drawing Rm	38' x 30'	50
Dining Rm	39' x 19'	50
East Library	26' x 21'	30

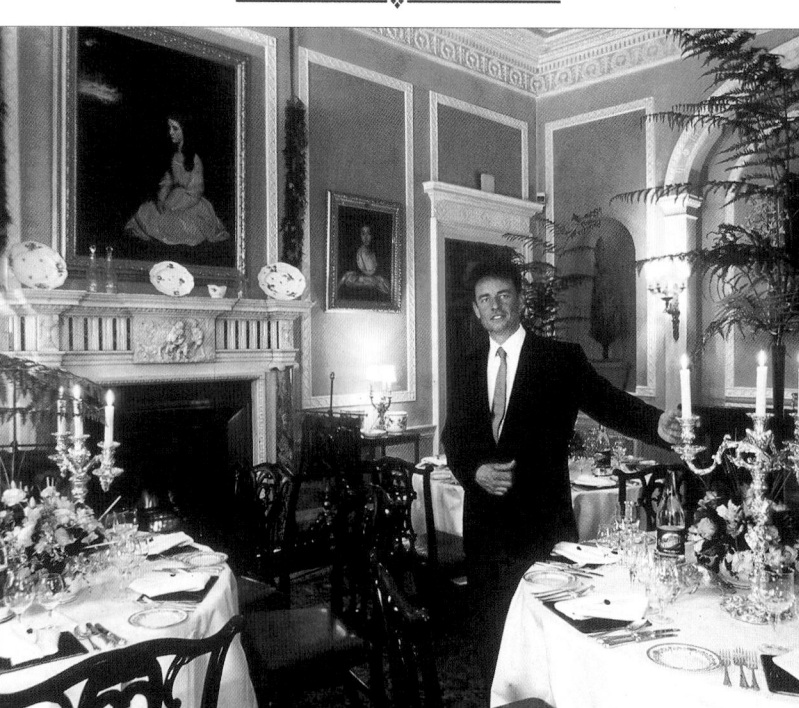

OPENING TIMES

Privately booked functions only.

ADMISSION

Privately booked functions only.

ℹ️ No individual visits, ideal for all corporate events, activity days and filmwork.

🍽️ Dining Room and picture gallery available for private parties.

🅿️ Unlimited.

🛏️ 4 twin & 4 double rooms.

JANE AUSTEN'S HOUSE

CHAWTON, ALTON, HAMPSHIRE GU34 1SD

Owner: Jane Austen Memorial Trust   *Contact: The Curator*

Tel/Fax: 01420 83262

17th century house where Jane Austen wrote or revised her six great novels. Contains many items associated with her and her family, documents and letters, first editions of the novels, pictures, portraits and furniture. Pleasant garden, suitable for picnics, bakehouse with brick oven and wash tub, houses Jane's donkey carriage.

Location: OS Ref. SU708 376. Just S of A31, 1m SW of Alton, signposted Chawton.

Opening times: 1 Mar - 1 Jan: daily, 11am - 4.30pm. Jan & Feb: Sats & Suns and half term in Feb (ring for dates). Closed 25 & 26 Dec.

Admission: Adult £3, Conc. £2.50. Groups (15+) £2.50, Child (8-18yrs) 50p.

Bookshop.   Ground floor & grounds suitable. WC.   Opposite house.   Opposite house.   Guide dogs only.

AVINGTON PARK

WINCHESTER, HAMPSHIRE SO21 1DB

Owner/Contact: Mrs S L Bullen

Tel: 01962 779260   **Fax:** 01962 779864   **e-mail:** sarah@avingtonpark.co.uk

Avington Park, where Charles II and George IV both stayed at various times, dates back to the 11th century. The house was enlarged in 1670 by the addition of two wings and a classical Portico surmounted by three statues. The State rooms are magnificently painted and lead onto the unique pair of conservatories flanking the South Lawn. The Georgian church, St. Mary's, is in the grounds.

Location: OS Ref. SU534 324. 4m NE of Winchester ½ m S of the B3047 in Itchen Abbas.

Opening Times: May - Sept: Suns & BH Mons, 2.30 - 5.30pm. Last tour 5pm. Other times by arrangement, coach parties welcome by appointment all year.

Admission: Adult £3.50, Child £2.

Conferences.   Partially suitable. WC.   Obligatory.   In grounds, on leads. Guide dogs only in house.

BASING HOUSE

Tel: 01256 467294

Redbridge Lane, Basing, Basingstoke RG24 7HB

Owner: Hampshire County Council   **Contact:** Alan Turton

Ruins, covering 10 acres, of huge Tudor palace. Recent recreation of Tudor formal garden.

Location: OS Ref. SU665 526. 2m E from Basingstoke town centre. Signposted car parks are about 5 or 10 mins walk from entrance.

Opening Times: 1 Apr - 30 Sept: Wed - Sun & BHs, 2 - 6pm.

Admission: Adult £1.50, Child 70p.

BEAULIEU

See pages 104/105 for double page entry.

BISHOP'S WALTHAM PALACE

Tel: 01489 892460

Bishop's Waltham, Hampshire SO32 1DH

Owner: English Heritage   **Contact:** The Custodian

This medieval seat of the Bishops of Winchester once stood in an enormous park. There are still wooded grounds and the remains of the Great Hall and the three storey tower can still be seen. Dower House furnished as a 19th century farmhouse.

Location: OS Ref. SU552 173. In Bishop's Waltham, 5m NE from M27/J8.

Opening Times: 1 Apr - 30 Sept: daily, 10am - 6pm. 1 Oct - 31 Oct: 10am - 5pm.

Admission: Adult £2.10, Child £1.10, Conc. £1.60.

Exhibition.   Grounds suitable.   Grounds only, on leads.   Tel. for details.

BOHUNT MANOR GARDENS

Tel: 01428 722208   **Fax:** 01428 727936

Liphook, Hampshire GU30 7DL

Owner/Contact: Lady Holman

Woodland gardens with lakeside walk, collection of ornamental waterfowl, herbaceous borders and unusual trees and shrubs.

Location: OS Ref. SU839 310. W side of B2070 at S end of village.

Opening Times: All year: daily, 10am - 6pm.

Admission: Adult £1.50, Child under 14 Free, Conc. £1. Group: 10% off.

BREAMORE HOUSE & MUSEUM

BREAMORE, FORDINGBRIDGE, HAMPSHIRE SP6 2DF

Owner/Contact: Sir Edward Hulse Bt

Tel: 01725 512233   **Fax:** 01725 512858   **e-mail:** breamore@estate.fsnet.co.uk

Elizabethan manor with fine collections of pictures and furniture. Countryside Museum takes visitors back to the time when a village was self-sufficient.

Location: OS Ref. SU152 191. W Off the A338, between Salisbury and Ringwood.

Opening Times: Apr: Easter Holiday, Tue, Wed & Sun. May, Jun, Jul & Sept: Tue, Wed, Thur, Sat & Sun & all hols. Aug: daily. House: 2 - 5.30pm. Countryside Museum: 1 - 5.30pm.

Admission: Combined ticket for house and museum: Adult £5, Child £3.50.

Ground floor & grounds suitable. WC.

South East
England

BROADLANDS

© Lord Romsey

ROMSEY, HAMPSHIRE SO51 9ZD

Owner: Lord & Lady Romsey   *Contact: Mrs S Armitage*

Tel: 01794 505010 **Event Enquiry Line:** 01794 505020

Famous as the home of the late Lord Mountbatten, and equally well known as the country residence of Lord Palmerston, the Great Victorian Prime Minister. Broadlands is an elegant Palladian mansion in a beautiful landscaped setting on the banks of the River Test. Visitors may view the House with its art treasures and mementoes of the famous, enjoy the superb views from the Riverside Lawns or relive Lord Mountbatten's life and times in the Mountbatten Exhibition and spectacular Mountbatten audio-visual presentation.

Location: OS Ref. SU355 204. On A31 at Romsey.

Opening Times: 11 Jun - 2 Sept: daily, 12 noon - 5.30pm. Last admission 4pm.

Admission: Adult £5.95, Child (12-16) £3.95, Conc. £4.95. Groups (10+): Adult £4.95, Child (12-16) £3.85, Conc. £4.65. All inclusive admission charges. Accompanied child under 12, Free.

⬚ 🌂 ⬚Ground floor & grounds suitable.WC. 💬 ⬚Obligatory. 🐕Guide dogs only.

CALSHOT CASTLE ⬚   **Tel:** 023 8089 2023

Calshot, Fawley, Hampshire SO45 1BR

Owner: English Heritage   **Contact:** Hampshire County Council

Henry VIII built this coastal fort in an excellent position, commanding the sea passage to Southampton. The fort houses an exhibition and recreated pre-World War I barrack room.

Location: OS Ref. SU488 025. On spit 2m SE of Fawley off B3053.

Opening Times: 1 Apr - 30 Sept: daily, 10am - 6pm. 1 Oct - 31 Oct: 10am - 5pm.

Admission: Adult £2, Child £1.

ELING TIDE MILL   **Tel:** 023 8086 9575

The Toll Bridge, Eling, Totton, Southampton, Hampshire SO40 9HF

Contact: Mr David Blackwell-Eaton   **e-mail:** eling.tidemill@argonet.co.uk

Owner: Eling Tide Mill Trust Ltd & New Forest District Council

Location: OS Ref. SU365 126. 4m W of Southampton. 1/2 m S of the A35.

Opening Times: Wed - Sun and BH Mons, 10am - 4pm.

Admission: Adult £1.65, Child 90p, OAP £1.25, Family £4.60. Discounts for groups and joint entry with Totton and Eling Heritage Centre. (Prices will probably change 1 Jan 2001, phone to confirm details).

EXBURY GARDENS 🏛   **Tel:** 023 8089 1203 **Fax:** 023 8089 9940

Exbury, Southampton, Hampshire SO45 1AZ

Owner: Edmund de Rothschild Esq   **Contact:** Gardens Office

Extensive landscaped woodland gardens overlooking the Beaulieu River. World famous Rothschild plant collection (rhododendrons, azaleas etc.) as well as many rare and wonderful trees: Rock Garden, Cascades, Ponds, River Walk, Rose Garden, Water Garden, Heather Gardens, seasonal trails and themed walks. Ample seating throughout. Gardens spectacular in Spring and Autumn.

Location: OS Ref. SU425 005. 11m SE of Totton (A35) via A326 & B3054 & minor road.

Opening Times: 24 Feb - 25 Nov: daily, 10am - 5.30pm or dusk if earlier.

Admission: Please telephone for details.

⬚ ⬚ Grounds suitable. WC. 💬 🍴 ⬚ In grounds, on leads. Telephone for details. ⓦ

FORT BROCKHURST ⬚   **Tel:** 023 9258 1059

Gunner's Way, Gosport, Hampshire PO12 4DS

Owner: English Heritage   **Contact:** The Head Custodian

This 19th century fort was built to protect Portsmouth, today its parade ground, moated keep and sergeants' mess are available to hire as an exciting setting for functions and events of all types. The fort is also open to visitors at weekends when tours will explain the exciting history of the site and the legend behind the ghostly activity in cell no. 3.

Location: OS196, Ref. SU596 020. Off A32, in Gunner's Way, Elson on N side of Gosport.

Opening Times: 1 Apr - 30 Sept: 10am - 6pm. 1 Oct - 31 Oct: 10am - 5pm. Weekends only.

Admission: Adult £2.10, Child £1.10, Conc. £1.60.

FURZEY GARDENS   **Tel:** 023 8081 2464 **Fax:** 023 8081 2297

Minstead, Lyndhurst, Hampshire SO43 7GL

Owner: Furzey Gardens Charitable Trust   **Contact:** Maureen Cole

Location: OS Ref. SU273 114. Minstead village 1/2 m N of M27/A31 junction off A337 to Lyndhurst.

Opening Times: Please contact property for details.

GREAT HALL & QUEEN ELEANOR'S GARDEN   **Tel:** 01962 846476
Fax: for bookings 01962 841326

Winchester Castle, Winchester, Hampshire SO23 8PJ

Owner: Hampshire County Council   **Contact:** Mrs Harris

The only surviving part of Henry III's medieval castle at Winchester, this 13th century hall was the centre of court and government life. The Round Table closely associated with the legend of King Arthur has hung here for over 700 years. Queen Eleanor's garden is a faithful representation of the medieval garden visited by Kings and Queens of England.

Location: OS Ref. SU477 295. Central Winchester. SE of Westgate archway.

Opening Times: All year: daily, 10am - 5pm (except weekends Nov - Feb, 10am - 4pm). Closed Christmas Day and Boxing Day.

Admission: Free .

⬚ By arrangement. ❋

GUILDHALL GALLERY   **Tel:** 01962 848289 (gallery) 01962 848269 (office)

The Broadway, Winchester SO23 9LJ   **Fax:** 01962 848299
e-mail: museums@winchester.gov.uk

Owner: Winchester City Council   **Contact:** Mr C Wardman Bradbury

A constantly changing programme of contemporary exhibitions including painting, sculpture, craft, photography and ceramics.

Location: OS Ref. SU485 293. Winchester - city centre. Situated above the Tourist Office in Winchester's 19th century Guildhall.

Opening Times: Apr - Oct: Mon - Sat, 10am - 5pm. Sun, 2 - 5pm. Nov - Mar: Tue - Sat, 10am - 4pm, Sun, 2 - 4pm.

Admission: Free.

♿ ❋ ⓦ

HIGHCLERE CASTLE & GARDENS 🏛   See page 106 for full page entry.

HINTON AMPNER GARDEN ✿   See page 107 for full page entry.

Lane Roberts.

The Sir Harold Hillier Gardens ~ Autumn colour in liquid amber.

South East England

THE SIR HAROLD HILLIER GARDENS & ARBORETUM

Justyn Willsmore

JERMYNS LANE, AMPFIELD, ROMSEY SO51 0QA

Managed by: *Hampshire County Council*
Contact: *Administration - Judith Drysdale   Marketing - Tim Brooks*

Tel: 01794 368787 **Fax:** 01794 368027

Set in the rolling Hampshire countryside between Winchester and the market town of Romsey, The Sir Harold Hillier Gardens & Arboretum comprises the greatest collection of hardy trees and shrubs in the world. Established in 1953, by the late Sir Harold Hillier, the 180-acre garden provides a stunning range of seasonal colour and interest and features 11 National Plant Collections, the Gurkha Memorial Gardens and the largest Winter Garden in Europe. A garden for all seasons.

Location: OS Ref. SU380 236. 3m NE of Romsey. Follow brown tourist signs from the town centre on A3090 (formerly A31) towards Winchester.
Opening times: Daily, 10.30am - 6pm or dusk if earlier. Closed Christmas BH.
Admission: Adult £4.25, Conc. £3.75, under 16s Free.

🏠 🍴 ♿ Partially suitable. WC. 🛍️ 🍴Licensed. 🎨 By arrangement.
🅿️ 🪑 🐕Guide dogs only. ❄️ 🎫 Tel for details. 🆔

HOUGHTON LODGE

STOCKBRIDGE, HAMPSHIRE, SO20 6LQ

Owner/Contact: *Captain M W Busk*

Tel: 01264 810502/810912 **Fax:** 01264 810177
e-mail: info@hydroponicum.co.uk

Enjoy this haven of peace beside the tranquil beauty of the River Test. 5 acres of informal landscape (Grade II*) with fine trees surrounds an 18th century Cottage Ornée. Walled garden, ancient espaliers, greenhouses and herb garden. Formal topiary 'Peacock Garden'. Wild flowers; Children's puffing topiary dragon. Popular TV/film location. Indoor hydroponicum: learn how to garden without soil or toil and control greenhouse pests with natural predators.

Location: OS Ref. SU344 332. 1¹/₂ m S of Stockbridge (A30) on minor road to Houghton village.
Opening times: Garden: 1 Mar - 30 Sept: Sat, Sun & BHs, 10am - 5pm also Mon, Tue, Thur & Fri, 2 - 5pm. House: by arrangement.
Admission: Adult £5 (Child Free).

🏠 ♿ 🛍️Free tea or coffee. 🎨 By arrangement. 🅿️
🐕In grounds, on leads. 🆔

HURST CASTLE ⚏   **Tel:** 01590 642344

Keyhaven, Lymington, Hampshire PO41 0PB
Owner: English Heritage   **Contact:** (Managed by) Hurst Castle Services

This was one of the most sophisticated fortresses built by Henry VIII, and later strengthened in the 19th and 20th centuries, to command the narrow entrance to the Solent. There is an exhibition in the Castle, and two huge 38-ton guns form the fort's armaments.

Location: OS196 Ref. SZ319 898. On Pebble Spit S of Keyhaven. Best approach by ferry from Keyhaven. 4m SW of Lymington.
Opening times: 1 Apr - 31 Oct: daily, 10am - 5.30pm. Café: open Apr - May weekends & Jun - Sept: daily.
Admission: Adult £2.50, Child £1.50, Conc. £2.

🏠 ♿ Not suitable. 🛍️

MEDIEVAL MERCHANTS HOUSE ⚏   **Tel:** 023 8022 4854

58 French Street, Southampton, Hampshire SO1 0AT
Owner: English Heritage   **Contact:** The Custodian

The life of the prosperous merchant in the Middle Ages is vividly evoked in this recreated, faithfully restored 13th century townhouse.

Location: OS Ref. SU419 112. 58 French Street. ¹/₄ m S of Bargate off Castle Way. 150yds SE of Tudor House.
Opening Times: 1 Apr - 30 Sept: daily, 10am - 6pm. 1 - 31 Oct: daily, 10am - 5pm.
Admission: Adult £2.20, Child £1.10, Conc. £1.60.

MOTTISFONT ABBEY GARDEN, HOUSE & ESTATE

NT Photographic Library: Stephen Robson

MOTTISFONT, Nr ROMSEY, HAMPSHIRE SO51 0LP

Owner: *The National Trust*   **Contact:** *The Property Manager*

Tel: 01794 340757 **Fax:** 01794 341492 **Recorded Message:** 01794 341220

The Abbey and Garden form the central point of an 809 ha estate including most of the village of Mottisfont, farmland and woods. A tributary of the River Test flows through the garden forming a superb and tranquil setting for a 12th century Augustinian priory which, after the Dissolution, became a house. It contains the spring or "font" from which the place name is derived. The magnificent trees, walled gardens and the National Collection of Old-fashioned Roses combine to provide interest throughout the seasons. The Abbey contains a drawing room decorated by Rex Whistler and the cellarium of the old Priory. In 1996 the Trust acquired Derek Hill's 20th century picture collection.

Location: OS Ref. SU327 270. 4¹/₂ m NW of Romsey, 1m W of A3057.
Opening times: Garden, Grounds & House: 17 Mar - 4 Nov: Sat - Wed (open Good Fri), 11am - 6pm (or dusk if earlier). During peak rose season 9 - 24 Jun: (check recorded message for state of roses) open daily, 11am - 8.30pm. Last admission to grounds 1 hr before closing. House: 1 - 5pm. (Whistler Room & Cellarium: as garden). The Derek Hill picture collection: Sun, Mon & Tues, 1 - 5pm.
Admission: Adult £6, Child (5-18yrs) £3, Family £15. No reduction for groups. Coaches must book.

🏠 🛍️ 🐕 Guide dogs only. 🔔 🎫 Tel. 01372 451596 for details.

Mottisfont Abbey Garden, Hampshire.

South East England

NETLEY ABBEY ⌗   Tel: 023 9258 1059

Netley, Southampton, Hampshire
Owner: English Heritage   **Contact:** Area Manager
A peaceful and beautiful setting for the extensive ruins of this 13th century Cistercian abbey converted in Tudor times for use as a house.
Location: OS Ref. SU453 089. In Netley, 4m SE of Southampton, facing Southampton Water.
Opening Times: Any reasonable time.
Admission: Free.

OLD PORTSMOUTH CATHEDRAL   Tel: 023 9282 3300   Fax: 023 9229 5480

Portsmouth, Hampshire PO1 2HH   **Contact:** Rosemary Fairfax
Maritime Cathedral founded in 12th century and finally completed in 1991. A member of the ship's crew of Henry VIII's flagship *Mary Rose* is buried in Navy Aisle.
Location: OS Ref. SZ633 994. 1½ m from end of M275. Follow signs to Historic Ship and Old Portsmouth.
Opening Times: 7.45am - 6pm all year. Sun service: 8am, 9.30am, 11am, 6pm. Weekday: 6pm (Choral on Tues and Fris in term time).
Admission: Donation appreciated.

PORTCHESTER CASTLE ⌗   Tel: 023 9237 8291   Fax: 023 9237 8291

Portsmouth, Hampshire PO16 9QW
Owner: English Heritage   **Contact:** The Custodian
The rallying point of Henry V's expedition to Agincourt and the ruined palace of King Richard II. This grand castle has a history going back nearly 2,000 years including the most complete Roman walls in Europe. Don't miss the interactive exhibition telling the story of the castle and see the newly conserved wallpaintings from the Viewing Gallery in the Keep.
Location: OS196, Ref. SU625 046. On S side of Portchester off A27, M27/J11.
Open: 1 Apr - 30 Sept: daily, 10am - 6pm. 1 - 31 Oct: 10am - 5pm. 1 Nov - 31 Mar: daily, 10am - 4pm. Closed 24 - 26 Dec & 1 Jan.
Admission: Adult £3, Child £1.50, Conc. £2.20. 15% discount for groups (11+). One extra place free for every additional 20.

ℹ️ Exhibition. 📷 ♿ Grounds & lower levels suitable. 🐕 In grounds, on leads. ❄️ 📠 Telephone for details.

SOMERLEY   See page 108 for full page entry.

STRATFIELD SAYE HOUSE 🏛   Tel: 01256 882882

Stratfield Saye, Basingstoke RG7 0AS
Owner: The Duke of Wellington   **Contact:** The Administrator
Family home of the Dukes of Wellington since 1817.
Location: OS Ref. SU700 615. Equidistant from Reading (M4/J11) & Basingstoke (M3/J6) 1½ m W of the A33.
Opening times: Jun - Aug: Wed - Sun. Groups by arrangement – Mons & Tues in Jun, Jul & Aug. and Mon - Fri in Sept. Grounds & Exhibition: 11.30am - 5pm. House 12 noon - 3pm (last admission).
Admission: Adult £5.50, Child £2.50, OAP £5.

TITCHFIELD ABBEY ⌗   Tel: 01329 842133

Titchfield, Southampton, Hampshire
Owner: English Heritage   **Contact:** Mr K E Groves
Remains of a 13th century abbey overshadowed by the grand Tudor gatehouse. Reputedly some of Shakespeare's plays were performed here for the first time. Under local management of Titchfield Abbey Society.
Location: OS Ref. SU544 067. ½ m N of Titchfield off A27.
Opening Times: 1 Apr - 30 Sept: daily, 10am - 6pm. 1 - 31 Oct: daily, 10am - 5pm. 1 Nov - 31 Mar: daily, 10am - 4pm.
Admission: Free.

TUDOR HOUSE MUSEUM   Tel: 023 8063 5904   Fax: 023 8033 9601

Bugle Street, Southampton, Hampshire
Owner: Southampton City Council   **Contact:** Caroline Blott
Late 15th century half timbered house. Unique Tudor knot garden.
Location: OS Ref. SU418 113. Follow signs to Old Town and waterfront from M27/M3. 150yds NW of Merchants House.
Opening Times: From end of Oct 2000 - end of Mar 2001: Tues - Fri, 10am - 4pm. Sats, 10am - 12 noon. Suns, 1 - 4pm. Closed Mons. From end of Mar 2001 - end of Oct 2001: Tues - Fri, 10am - 5pm. Sats, 10am - 4pm. Suns, 2 - 5pm. Closed Mons. Closed for lunch 1 - 2pm.
Admission: Free.

SANDHAM MEMORIAL CHAPEL 🌿

BURGHCLERE, Nr NEWBURY, HAMPSHIRE RG20 9JT
Owner: *The National Trust*   ***Contact:*** *Sarah Hook*

Tel/Fax: 01635 278394
Stanley Spencer's murals, which entirely cover the interior walls of this 1920s chapel, commemorate the First World War and constitute one of the greatest achievements of 20th century painting. The murals chronicle with minute accuracy the every day life of the soldier. Inspired by Giotto's Arena Chapel in Padua, this impressive project took Spencer five years to complete.
Location: OS Ref. SU463 608. 4m S of Newbury, ½ m E of A34, W end of Burghclere.
Opening times: Mar & Nov: Sats & Suns, Apr - end Oct: daily except Mons & Tues (open BH Mons): Dec - Feb 2002: by appointment only. Times: Mar & Nov: 11.30am - 4pm, Apr - end Oct: 11.30am - 5pm.
Admission: Adult £2.50, Child £1.25. Groups by prior arrangement, no reduction.

♿ Ramped steps. 🐕 In grounds, on leads. ❄️

Tall Chimneys at Houghton Lodge.

THE VYNE

NT Photographic Library: Andrea Jones

SHERBORNE ST JOHN, BASINGSTOKE RG24 9HL

Owner: *The National Trust* **Contact:** *The Property Manager*

Tel: 01256 881337 **Fax:** 01256 881720 **e-mail:** svygen@smtp.ntrust.org.uk

Built in the early 16th century for Lord Sandys, Henry VIII's Lord Chamberlain, the house acquired a classical portico in the mid-17th century (the first of its kind in England) and contains a fascinating Tudor chapel with Renaissance glass, a Palladian staircase and a wealth of old panelling and fine furniture. The attractive grounds feature herbaceous borders and a wild garden, with lawns, lakes and woodland walks.

Location: OS Ref. SU637 566. 4m N of Basingstoke between Bramley and Sherborne St John.

Opening times: House: 31 Mar - 4 Nov: daily except Thurs & Fris, 1 - 5pm (open Good Fri & BH Mons). Grounds: weekends in Feb & Mar, 11am - 4.30pm. 31 Mar - 4 Nov: daily except Thurs & Fris, 11am - 6pm (open Good Fri & BH Mons).

Admission: House & Grounds: Adult £5.50, Child £2.75, Family £13.75. Grounds only: Adult £3, Child £1.50. Groups: £4.50 (Mon - Wed only).

[i] No photography in house. By arrangement.
[P] Limited for coaches. Telephone for details.

GILBERT WHITE'S HOUSE & THE OATES MUSEUM

THE WAKES, HIGH STREET, SELBORNE, ALTON GU34 3JH

Owner: *Oates Memorial Trust* **Contact:** *Mrs Anna Jackson*

Tel: 01420 511275

Charming 18th century house in heart of old Selborne, home of Rev Gilbert White, author of *The Natural History of Selborne*. Lovely garden with many plants of the 18th century. Museum devoted to Captain Oates of Antarctic fame. Tea parlour with 18th century fare.

Location: OS Ref. SU741 336. On W side of B3006, in village of Selborne 4m NW of the A3.

Opening Times: 1 Jan - 24 Dec: daily, 11am - 5pm. Evenings also for groups.

Admission: Adult £4, Child £1, OAP £3.50.

[i] No photography in house. Partially suitable.
[K] By arrangement. [P] Guide dogs only.

SPECIAL EVENTS

JUN 16: Picnic to 'Jazz in June' **JUN 16/17:** Unusual Plants Fair.
NOV 25: Annual Mulled Wine & Christmas shopping day.

WINCHESTER CATHEDRAL

Tel: 01962 857200 **Fax:** 01962 857201

Winchester, Hants SO23 9LS **e-mail:** judy.george@winchester-cathedral.org.uk

The Cathedral was founded in 1079. **Contact:** Mrs J George

Location: OS Ref. SU483 293. Winchester city centre.

Opening Times: 8.30am - 5pm. East end closes 5pm. Access may be restricted during services. Weekday services:7.40am, 8am, 5.30pm. Sun services: 8am, 10am, 11.15am, 3.30pm.

Admission: Recommended donations may increase: Adult £3, Child 50p, Conc. £2, Family £6, charges apply for Triforium gallery & Library - £1. Tower & Roof Tours £1.50. Group tours £3.50 should be booked through the Education centre. (Tel: 01962 857225 between 9am - 1pm).

WINCHESTER COLLEGE

Tel: 01962 621209 **Fax:** 01962 621215
e-mail: enterprise@bursary.wincoll.ac.uk

College Street, Winchester, Hampshire SO23 9NA

Owner: Winchester College **Contact:** Marcus Van Hagen

Founded in 1382 with cobbled courtyards and vaulted ceilings to beautiful medieval stained glass windows.

Location: OS Ref. SU483 290. S of the Cathedral.

Opening Times: 1 Sept - 31 May: Mon - Sat, 11am, 12 noon, 2.15pm, 3.15pm. Sun, 2.15pm, 3.15pm. 1 Jun - 31 Aug: Mon - Sat, 10am, 11am, 12 noon, 2.15pm, 3.15pm. Sun, 2.15pm, 3.15pm. No tours Tues & Thurs afternoons all year.

Admission: Adult £1.50, Child/Conc. £1. Guided tours may be booked for groups (10+): Adult £2.50, Child/Conc. £2.

Ground floor & grounds suitable. Guide dogs only.

WOLVESEY CASTLE

Tel: 01962 854766

College Street, Wolvesey, Winchester, Hampshire SO23 8NB

Owner: English Heritage **Contact:** The Custodian

The fortified palace of Wolvesey was the chief residence of the Bishops of Winchester and one of the greatest of all medieval buildings in England. Its extensive ruins still reflect the importance and immense wealth of the Bishops of Winchester, occupants of the richest seat in medieval England. Wolvesey was frequently visited by medieval and Tudor monarchs and was the scene of the wedding feast of Philip of Spain and Mary Tudor in 1554.

Location: OS Ref. SU484 291. 3/4 m SE of Winchester Cathedral, next to the Bishop's Palace; access from College Street.

Opening Times: 1 Apr - 30 Sept: 10am - 6pm. 1 - 31 Oct: 10am - 5pm.

Admission: Adult £1.90, Child £1, Conc. £1.40.

Grounds suitable. In grounds, on leads.

South East England

BOUGHTON MONCHELSEA PLACE
Nr Maidstone

Owner:
Mr & Mrs D Kendrick

CONTACT

Mrs M Kendrick
Boughton Monchelsea Place
Boughton Monchelsea
Nr Maidstone
Kent
ME17 4BU

Tel: 01622 743120

Fax: 01622 741168

e-mail:
mk@boughtonmonchelsea
place.co.uk

LOCATION

OS Ref. TQ772 499

On B2163, $5^{1}/_{2}$ m from
M20/J8 or $4^{1}/_{2}$ m from
Maidstone via A229.

BOUGHTON MONCHELSEA PLACE is a battlemented manor house dating from the 16th century, set in its own country estate just outside Maidstone, within easy reach of London and the channel ports. This Grade I listed building has always been privately owned and is still lived in as a family home.

From the lawns surrounding the property there are spectacular views over unspoilt Kent countryside, with the historic deer park in the foreground. These views are shared by the 20 acre activity site set back a little way from the house. A wicket gate leads from the grounds to the medieval church of St Peter, with its rose garden and ancient lych gate. At the rear of the house are to be found a pretty courtyard and walled gardens, together with an extensive range of Tudor barns and outbuildings. Inside the house, rooms vary in character from Tudor through to Georgian Gothic; worthy of note are the fine Jacobean staircase and sundry examples of heraldic stained glass. Furnishings and paintings are mainly Victorian, with a few earlier pieces; the atmosphere is friendly and welcoming throughout.

The premises are licensed for Civil marriage ceremonies, although wedding receptions may only be held on weekdays. In addition we welcome conferences, group visits, location work and all types of corporate, private and public functions, but please note times of availability. Use outside these hours is sometimes possible, subject to negotiation. All clients are guaranteed exclusive use of this prestigious venue.

❖

OPENING TIMES

By prior arrangement only.

House & Garden

Not open to
individual visitors.

Private functions:
Mon - Fri, 9am - 8pm.

Group visits/ house tours:
(15-50 pax), Mon - Thur,
9am - 4pm.

Activity Site

365 days a year:
8am - 11.30pm.

ADMISSION

**Gardens &
Guided House Tour**
   Adult £4.50

Gardens only
   Adult £2.75

Venue Hire
   Prices on application.

 By arrangement.

 By arrangement.

 By arrangement.

CONFERENCE/FUNCTION		
ROOM	SIZE	MAX CAPACITY
Entrance Hall	25' x 19'	50 Theatre
Dining Room	31' x 19'	50 Dining
Drawing Room	28' x 19'	40 Reception
Courtyard Room	37' x 13'	70 Theatre

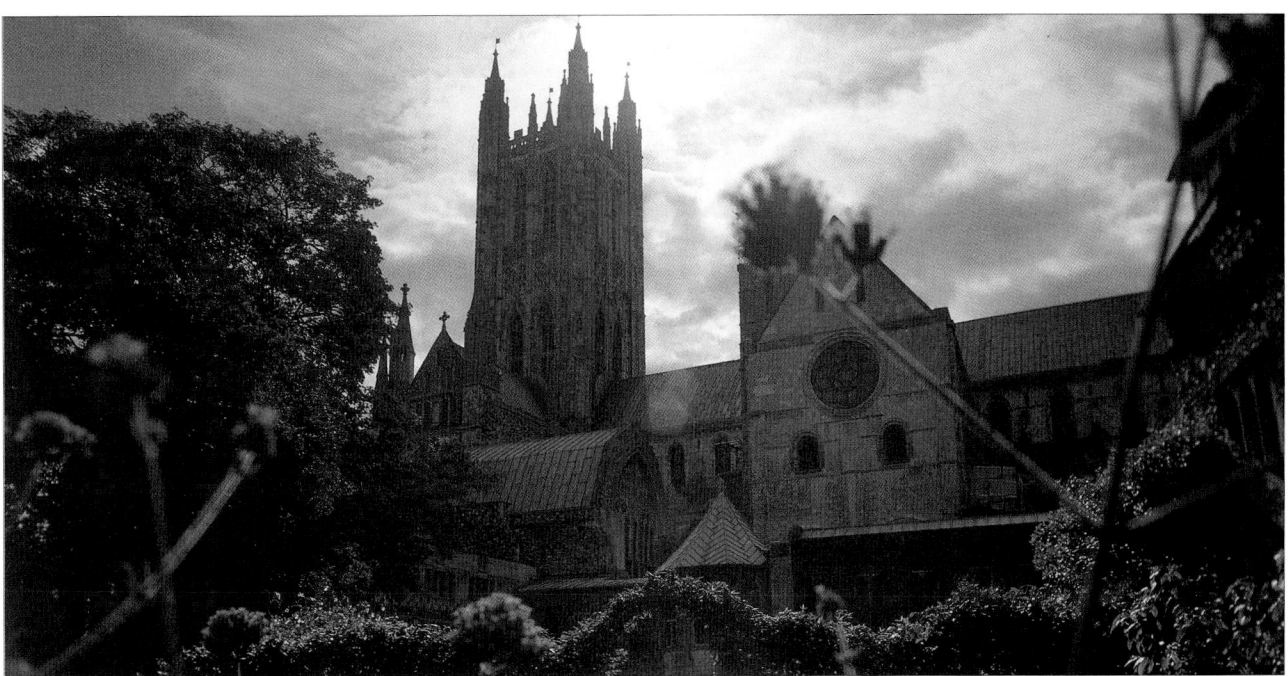

CANTERBURY CATHEDRAL
Canterbury

CONTACT

Visits Office
Canterbury Cathedral
The Precincts
Canterbury
CT1 2EH

Tel: 01227 762862

Fax: 01227 865222/865250

e-mail: visits@
canterbury-cathedral.org

LOCATION

OS Ref. TR151 579

Canterbury city centre.
M2/M20, then A2.

Bus: Victoria Station coach
– regular service.

Rail: London
Victoria/Dover Priory to
Canterbury East, London
Charing Cross to
Canterbury West.

Sightseeing Tours: Tour
operators operate a daily
service with collection from
most London hotels. Ask
your hotel concierge or
porter for information.

Canterbury Cathedral has a tradition of visitor welcome that reaches back to the days of medieval pilgrimages. A warm welcome is extended to all visitors and it is hoped that they will enjoy sharing the experience of one of the great holy places of Christendom.

St Augustine, sent by Pope Gregory the Great, arrived in 597 AD and became the first Archbishop, establishing his seat (or 'Cathedra') in Canterbury. In 1170 Archbishop Thomas Becket was murdered in the Cathedral and ever since, the Cathedral has attracted thousands of pilgrims.

The Cathedral is noteworthy for its medieval tombs of royal personages, such as King Henry IV and Edward the Black Prince, as well as numerous archbishops. To the later Middle Ages belong the great 14th century Nave and the famous central 'Bell Harry Tower'. The Quire dates back to the 12th century and the Crypt, the largest of its kind in the country, to the 11th century.

The Cathedral stands in spacious precincts amid the remains of the monastery – cloister, chapter house, and Norman water tower which have survived intact, from the Dissolution in the time of King Henry VIII to the present day.

Thomas Becket's shrine was destroyed by the Tudor King, but the site of that tomb is in the Trinity Chapel, near the High Altar. The saint is said to have worked miracles, and the Cathedral contains some rare stained glass depicting those events.

❖

ADMISSION

Adult	£3.00
Conc.	£2.00
Pre-booked school groups	£1.50

(2000 prices)

CONFERENCE/FUNCTION

ROOM	SIZE	MAX CAPACITY
Clagett Auditorium	10.5 x 15m	250
'The Barn'	14 x 5m	92
Lecture Theatre (x2)	7 x 7m	60
Seminar rms	vary	12 - 50

By arrangement.

Walmer Castle, Kent.

National Trust Photographic Library.

CHARTWELL
Westerham

Owner: The National Trust

CONTACT

The Property Manager
Chartwell
Westerham
Kent
TN16 1PS

Tel: 01732 866368
01732 868381

Fax: 01732 868193

e-mail: kchxxx@
smtp.ntrust.org.uk

The family home of Sir Winston Churchill from 1924 until the end of his life. He said of Chartwell, simply *'I love the place - a day away from Chartwell is a day wasted'*. With magnificent views over the Weald of Kent it is not difficult to see why.

The rooms are left as they were in Sir Winston & Lady Churchill's lifetime with daily papers, fresh flowers grown from the garden and his famous cigars. Photographs and books evoke his career and interests, as well as happy family life. Museum and exhibition rooms contain displays and sound recordings, superb collections of memorabilia from his political career, including uniforms and a 'siren-suit'.

The garden studio contains Sir Winston's easel and paintbox, as well as many of his paintings. Terraced and water gardens descend to the lake, the gardens also include a golden rose walk, planted by Sir Winston and Lady Churchill's children on the occasion of their golden wedding anniversary, and the Marlborough Pavilion decorated with frescoes depicting the battle of Blenheim. Visitors can see the garden walls that Churchill built with his own hands, the pond stocked with the golden orfe he loved.

The Mulberry Room and/or Cabinet Room at the restaurant can be booked for meetings, conferences, lunches and dinners. Please telephone for details.

LOCATION

OS Ref. TQ455 515

2m S of Westerham, forking left off B2026.

Bus: Chartwell Explorer 'green transport' bus link with Sevenoaks & Westerham. For more information contact: 01732 866368

OPENING TIMES

31 March - 4 November
Wed - Sun & BH Mons
11am - 5pm.

July & August only
Tue - Sun & BH Mon
11am - 5pm.

Last admission 4.15pm.

ADMISSION

Adult £5.60
Child......................£2.80
Family £14.00

National Trust Photographic Library; Andreas von Einsiedel.

SPECIAL EVENTS

- **AUG 18**
  Opera Brava presents 'An evening of Gilbert & Sullivan'.

- **AUG 19**
  Opera Brava presents 'Tosca'.

ℹ️ Conference facilities.   ♿ Partially suitable. WC. Please telephone before visit.   🍴 Licensed.

🚶 By arrangement.   🅿️   🐕 In grounds, on leads.

South East England

CHIDDINGSTONE CASTLE
Edenbridge

Owner: Denys Eyre Bower Bequest Reg. Charity Trust

CONTACT

Mrs R Vernon
Chiddingstone Castle
Edenbridge
Kent
TN8 7AD

Tel: 01892 870347

LOCATION

OS Ref. TQ497 452

B2027, turn to Chiddingstone at Bough Beech, 1m further on to crossroads, then straight to castle.
10m from Tonbridge, Tunbridge Wells and Sevenoaks.
4m Edenbridge.
Accessible from A21 and M25/J5.
London 35m.

Bus: Enquiries: Tunbridge Wells TIC 01892 515675.

Rail: Tonbridge, Tunbridge Wells, Edenbridge then taxi. Penshurst then 2m walk.

Air: Gatwick 15m.

CHIDDINGSTONE CASTLE has never seen battle. Even the Civil War left it unscathed, though the village was Royalist amid Parliamentary territory. Tudor in origin, it was twice fundamentally altered by the Streatfeilds, whose family seat it was. But they never entirely erased its ancient foundation.

The final remodelling, c1805, was by William Atkinson, Master of the Picturesque, an effect, he commented, difficult to achieve intentionally, being generally due to accidents of time - in which Chiddingstone abounds. The romantic result aroused the contempt of the architectural establishment. It was saved from dereliction by the fierce championship of

Denys Bower, wayward connoisseur and collector, who in 1955 defied the trend and bought it as his home. When he died in 1977 he left it to the Nation, so that, as his Will said, 'future generations may enjoy it as I do now'.

It is now lovingly administered by a charitable trust, a fascinating place with contents to enthrall everyone. Superb Japanese lacquer and swords, Egyptian antiquities, Royal Stuart history, furnishings and pictures. The grounds, one of the listed gardens of Kent, are being developed as a haven for wildlife. An afternoon is all too short to explore this tranquil corner of a vanishing England.

❖

Great Hall

OPENING TIMES

SUMMER
Easter Hol, Spring BH.

June - September
Wed - Fri & Sun
Weekdays: 2 - 5.30pm
Sun & BHs
11.30am - 5.30pm
Last admission 5pm.

WINTER
Open only for specially booked groups (20+).

ADMISSION

Adult...........................£4.00
 Child*.....................£2.00

Groups** (pre-booked 20+)
 Adult.....................£3.50
 Child*....................£2.00

Fishing..........£8.00 per day
Onlooker...................£3.50
(1 onlooker per fisherman, no children.)

* Child under 16yrs accompanied by adult. Under 5 yrs Free.

** Usual hours, other times by appointment. School groups only by appointment.

Chiddingstone may be closed without notice for Special Events.

CONFERENCE/FUNCTION		
ROOM	SIZE	MAX CAPACITY
Assembly Rm	14' x 35'	50
Seminar Rms	15' x 15'	
Stable Block	36' x 29'	

Conferences, receptions, concerts. No photography in house, no smoking, no prams.

Available for special events. Wedding receptions

Partially suitable. WC.

Licensed. By arrangement.

By arrangement.

Ample hardcore parking. Coaches, please book.

Teachers' pack. Educational programme.

In grounds, on leads.

CHIDDINGSTONE CASTLE

Grounds (above), The restored Stable Block (below) & The Assembly Room, Conference Centre (bottom right).

SMALL CONFERENCES AND FUNCTIONS: the old domestic quarters, grouped around the courtyard, have been converted into a unique and elegant centre for various events. The self-contained Goodhugh Wing offers Assembly Room (capacity 50), three seminar rooms, and tea-kitchen. Meals can be provided in the refectory by our approved caterers. Additional lecture/meeting accommodation in the adjoining stable block, recently restored.

CIVIL MARRIAGES: The Great Hall is licensed by Kent County Council, and is specially attractive to those who desire the dignity of a church ceremony without the religious aspect. We offer all features of wedding celebrations, including reception of guests and refreshments.

EDUCATION: We welcome visits from schools who wish to use the collections in connection with classroom work. No anxiety for the teachers (admitted free). The children are safe here, can picnic and play in the grounds. We may have some exciting developments with adult education in the restored stable block. Please enquire.

Jarrold Publishing.

South East England

COBHAM HALL
Cobham

'One of the largest, finest and most important houses in Kent', Cobham Hall is an outstandingly beautiful, red brick mansion in Elizabethan, Jacobean, Carolean and 18th century styles.

It yields much of interest to the student of art, architecture and history. The Elizabethan wings were begun in 1584 whilst the central section contains the Gilt Hall, wonderfully decorated by John Webb, Inigo Jones' most celebrated pupil, 1654. Further rooms were decorated by James Wyatt in the 18th century.

Cobham Hall, now a girls' school, has been visited by several of the English monarchs from Elizabeth I to Edward VIII, later Duke of Windsor. Charles Dickens used to walk through the grounds from his house in Higham to the Leather Bottle pub in Cobham Village. In 1883, the Hon Ivo Bligh, later the 8th Earl of Darnley, led the victorious English cricket team against Australia bringing home the 'Ashes' to Cobham.

GARDENS

The gardens, landscaped for the 4th Earl by Humphry Repton, are gradually being restored by the Cobham Hall Heritage Trust. Extensive tree planting and clearing have taken place since the hurricanes of the 1980s. The Gothic Dairy and some of the classical garden buildings are being renovated. The gardens are particularly delightful in Spring, when they are resplendent with daffodils and a myriad of rare bulbs.

Owner: Cobham Hall Heritage Trust

CONTACT

Mr N Powell
Bursar
Cobham Hall, Cobham
Kent DA12 3BL

Tel: 01474 823371

Fax: 01474 825906
or 01474 825904

e-mail: cobhamhall@aol.com

LOCATION

OS Ref. TQ683 689

Situated adjacent to the A2/M2. $\frac{1}{2}$ m S of A2 4m W of Strood. 8m E of M25/J2 between Gravesend & Rochester.

London 25m
Rochester 5m
Canterbury 30m

Rail: Meopham 3m
Gravesend 5m
Taxis at both stations.

Air: Gatwick 45 mins.
Heathrow 60 mins,
Stansted 50 mins.

CONFERENCE/FUNCTION

ROOM	SIZE	MAX CAPACITY
Gilt Hall	41' x 34'	180
Wyatt Dining Rm	49' x 23'	135
Clifton Dining Rm	24' x 23'	75
Activities Centre	119' x 106'	300

ℹ️ Conferences, business or social functions, 150 acres of parkland for sports, corporate events, open air concerts, sports centre, indoor swimming pool, art studios, music wing, tennis courts, helicopter landing area. Filming and photography. No smoking.

🍽️ In-house catering team for private, corporate hospitality and wedding receptions. (cap. 200).

♿ House tour involves 2 staircases, ground floor access for w/chairs.

☕ Afternoon teas, other meals by arrangement.

🚶 Obligatory guided tours; tour time 1$\frac{1}{2}$ hrs. Garden tours arranged outside standard opening times.

🅿️ Ample. Pre-booked coach groups are welcome any time.

📖 Guide provided, Adult £3.50, Child / OAP £2.50.

🐕 In grounds, on leads.

🛏️ 18 single and 18 double with bathroom. 22 single and 22 double without bathroom. Dormitory. Groups only.

🔔

English Heritage Photo Library

Owner: English Heritage

CONTACT

Mr K Scott
Dover Castle
Dover
Kent
CT16 1HU

Tel: 01304 211067

Info Line: 01304 201628

LOCATION

OS Ref. TR326 416

Easy access from A2 and M20. Well signed from Dover centre and east side of Dover. 2 hrs from central London.

Rail: London Charing Cross or Victoria 1¹/₂ hrs.

Bus: Freephone 0800 696996.

DOVER CASTLE & THE SECRET WARTIME TUNNELS
Dover

Journey deep into the White Cliffs of Dover and discover the top secret World War II tunnels. Through sight, sound and smells relive the wartime drama of the underground hospital as a wounded Battle of Britain pilot is taken to the operating theatre in a bid to save his life. Discover how life would have been during the planning days of the Dunkirk evacuation and Operation Dynamo as you are led around the network of tunnels and casements housing the communications centre.

Above ground you can explore the magnificent mediaeval keep and inner bailey of King Henry II. Visit the evocative Princess of Wales' Royal Regiment Museum. There is also the Roman Lighthouse and Anglo-Saxon church to see or take an audio tour of the intriguing 13th century underground fortifications and medieval battlements. Enjoy magnificent views of the White Cliffs from Admiralty lookout.

See the exciting 'Life Under Siege' exhibition, and discover, through a dramatic light and sound presentation, how it must have felt to be a garrison soldier defending Dover Castle against the French King in 1216. In the Keep, see a reconstruction of the Castle in preparation for a visit from Henry VIII and visit the hands-on exhibition explaining the travelling Tudor court. The land train will help you around this huge site.

Throughout the summer there are many fun events taking place, bringing the Castle alive through colourful enactments and living history.

❖ Two.

🍴 Functions catered for including themed evenings within the Keep. For private functions tel: 01304 205830.

♿ Lift for access to tunnels. Courtyard and grounds, some very steep slopes.

🍴🍴 2 restaurants, hot and cold food and drinks.

🚶 Tour of tunnels approx. every 20 mins, more at peak times when a 30 min. wait can occur.

🅿 Ample. Groups welcome, discounts available. Free entry for drivers. One extra place for each additional group of 20.

🖼 Free visits available for schools. Education centre. Pre-booking essential.

❄

English Heritage Photo Library

OPENING TIMES

SUMMER
1 Apr - 30 Sept
Daily: 10am - 6pm.

1 - 31 Oct:
Daily: 10am - 5pm.

WINTER
1 November - 31 March
Daily: 10am - 4pm.

Closed 24 - 26 Dec & 1 Jan.

ADMISSION

Adult	£7.00
Child	£3.50
OAP	£5.20
Family (2+3)	£17.50

Groups
15% discount for groups (11+).

SPECIAL EVENTS

Please telephone for details.

South East England

English Heritage Photo Library / Jonathan Bailey

Owner: English Heritage

CONTACT

The House Manager
Down House
Luxted Road
Downe
Kent
BR6 7JT

Tel: 01689 859119

DOWN HOUSE
Downe

A visit to Down House is a fascinating journey of discovery for all the family. This was the family home of Charles Darwin for over 40 years and now you can explore it to the full.

See the actual armchair in which Darwin wrote 'On the Origin of Species', which shocked and then revolutionised the way we think about the origins of mankind. His study is much the same as it was in his lifetime and is filled with belongings that give you an intimate glimpse into both his studies and everyday life.

At Down House you will discover both sides of Darwin - the great thinker and the family man.

Explore the family rooms where the furnishings have been painstakingly restored. An audio tour narrated by Sir David Attenborough will bring the house to life and increase your understanding of Darwin's revolutionary theory. Upstairs you will find state-of-the-art interpretation of the scientific significance of the house - especially designed to inspire a younger audience.

Outside, take the Sandwalk which he paced daily in search of inspiration, then stroll in lovely gardens. Complete your day by sampling the delicious selection of home-made cakes in the tea room.

OPENING TIMES

10 Apr - 31 Oct:
Wed - Sun, 10am - 6pm.

1 Nov - 23 Dec:
Wed - Sun, 10am - 4pm.

7 Feb - 31 Mar:
Wed - Sun, 10am - 4pm.

Closed 24 Dec - 6 Feb 2001.

On BHs and throughout August visits to Down House must be booked in advance. It is not necessary to book if you travel by public transport.

LOCATION

OS Ref, TQ431 611

In Luxted Road, Downe, off A21 near Biggin Hill.

Rail: From London Victoria or Charing Cross.

Bus: Orpington (& Bus R2) or Bromley South (& Bus 146). Buses R2 & 146 do not run on Sunday.

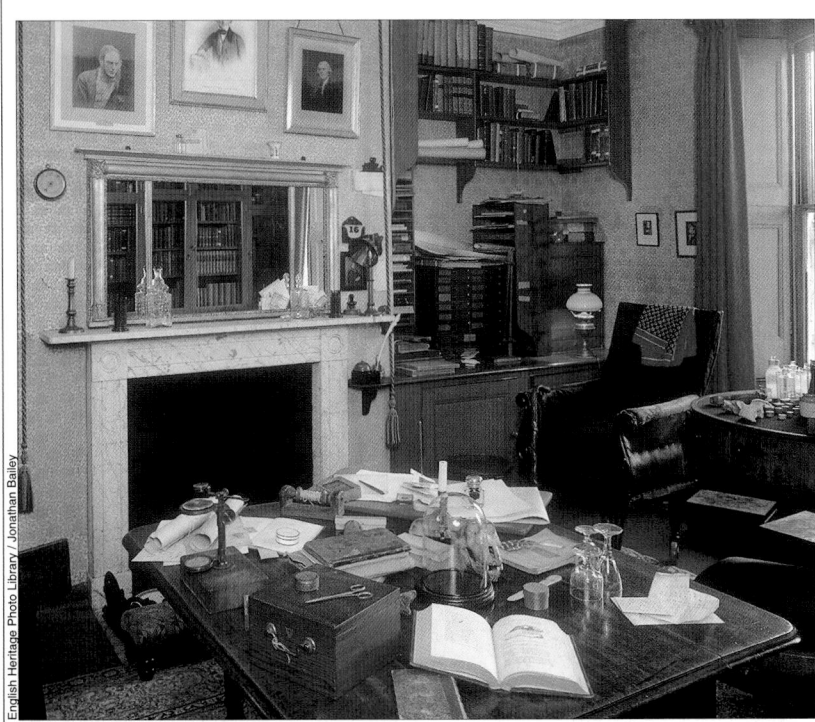

English Heritage Photo Library / Jonathan Bailey

ADMISSION

Timed ticketing: available on day or pre-booked on 01689 859119.

Adult £5.50
Child........................£2.80
Conc.......................£4.10

 Inclusive.
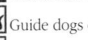 Limited for coaches.
Guide dogs only.

In 1970 Finchcocks was acquired by Richard Burnett, leading exponent of the early piano, and it now contains his magnificent collection of some eighty historical keyboard instruments: chamber organs, harpsichords, virginals, spinets and early pianos. About half of these are restored to full concert condition and are played whenever the house is open to the public. The house, with its high ceilings and oak panelling, provides the perfect setting for music performed on period instruments, and Finchcocks is now a music centre of international repute. Many musical events take place here.

There is also a fascinating collection of pictures and prints, mainly on musical themes, and there is a special exhibition on display on the theme of the 18th century pleasure gardens, such as Vauxhall and Ranelagh, which includes costumes and tableaux.

Finchcocks is a fine Georgian baroque manor noted for its outstanding brickwork, with a dramatic front elevation attributed to Thomas Archer. Named after the family who lived on the site in the 13th century, the present house was built in 1725 for barrister Edward Bathurst, kinsman to Earl Bathurst. Despite having changed hands many times, it has undergone remarkably little alteration and retains most of its original features. The beautiful grounds, with their extensive views over parkland and hop gardens, include the newly restored walled garden, which provides a dramatic setting for special events.

Owner:
Mr Richard Burnett

CONTACT

Mrs Katrina Burnett
Finchcocks
Goudhurst
Kent
TN17 1HH

Tel: 01580 211702

Fax: 01580 211007

e-mail: katrina@
finchcocks.co.uk

LOCATION

OS Ref. TQ700 365

1m S of A262, 2m W of village of Goudhurst. 5m from Cranbrook, 10m from Tunbridge Wells, 45m from London (1½ hrs)

Rail: Marden 6m (no taxi), Paddock Wood 8m (taxi), Tunbridge Wells 10m (taxi).

Air: Gatwick 1 hr.

Music events, conferences, seminars, promotions, archery, ballooning, filming, television. Keyboard instruments and musical furniture for hire, marquees erected for large functions. No videos in house, photography by permission only.

Private and corporate entertaining, weddings. Full catering by arrangement. Fully licensed.

Limited. WC. Suitable for visually handicapped.

Licensed. Teas and light refreshments. Picnics permitted in grounds.

Musical tours / recitals on instruments whenever required. Tour time: 2½ - 4 hrs.

Ample. Pre-booked groups (25 - 100) welcome from Apr - Oct. Free meals for couriers and drivers.

Opportunity to play instruments. Can be linked to special projects and National Curriculum syllabus.

Music a speciality, and musicians can be provided.

OPENING TIMES

SUMMER

Easter Sun - end Sept Sun & BH Mons, plus Wed & Thur in August, 2 - 6pm.

Pre-booked groups and individuals welcome most days April to October mornings, afternoons and evenings and in some circumstances up to Christmas.

WINTER

Closed
January - mid-March
Available for private functions October, November & December.

ADMISSION

Open Days
House, Garden & Music
Adult £7.00
Child £4.00
Student..................£5.00

Garden Only
Adult £2.50
Child £0.50

Groups*
Adult £7.00
Child £4.00
Student..................£5.00

* Min. of 25 to open house.

SPECIAL EVENTS

- **MAY 27/28:**
Spring Garden Fair & Flower Festival

- **AUG 26/27:**
Jane Austen Gala

- **SEPT WEEKENDS:**
Music Festival

- **OCT 12 - 14:**
Autumn Fair

HEVER CASTLE
Edenbridge

Owner:
Hever Castle Ltd

CONTACT

Anne-Marie
Critchley-Salmonson
Hever Castle
Hever, Edenbridge
Kent TN8 7NG

Infoline: 01732 865224
Fax: 01732 866796
e-mail: mail@HeverCastle.co.uk

HEVER CASTLE dates back to 1270, when the gatehouse, outer walls and the inner moat were first built. 200 years later the Bullen (or Boleyn) family added the comfortable Tudor manor house constructed within the walls. This was the childhood home of Anne Boleyn, Henry VIII's second wife and mother of Elizabeth I. There are many items relating to the Tudors, including two books of hours (prayer books) signed and inscribed by Anne Boleyn. The Castle was later given to Henry VIII's fourth wife, Anne of Cleves.

In 1903, the estate was bought by the American millionaire William Waldorf Astor, who became a British subject and the first Lord Astor of Hever. He invested an immense amount of time, money and imagination in restoring the castle and grounds. Master craftsmen were employed and the castle was filled with a magnificent collection of furniture, tapestries and other works of art. 'From Castles to Country Houses' the Miniature Model Houses exhibition, a collection of $^1/_{12}$ scale model houses, room views and gardens, depicts life in English Country Houses.

GARDENS

Between 1904-8 over 30 acres of formal gardens were laid out and planted, these have now matured into one of the most beautiful gardens in England. The unique Italian garden is a four acre walled garden containing a superb collection of statuary and sculpture. The award-winning gardens include the Rose garden and Tudor garden, a traditional yew maze and a 110 metre herbaceous border. A water maze has been added to the other water features in the gardens.

OPENING TIMES

SUMMER
1 March - 30 November
Daily:
Grounds: 11am - 6pm.
Castle: 12 noon - 6pm.
Last admission 5pm.

WINTER
March & November
Grounds: 11am - 4pm.

Castle: 12 noon - 4pm.

ADMISSION

Castle & Gardens
Adult £8.00
Child (5-16 yrs)........ £4.40
OAP £6.80
Family (2+2) £20.40
Please ring for group* prices.

Gardens only
Adult £6.30
Child (5-16 yrs)........ £4.20
OAP...................... £5.40
Family (2+2)........... £16.80
Please ring for group* prices.

*Min 15.

Pre-booked private guided tours are available before opening, during season.

LOCATION

OS Ref. TQ476 450

Exit M25/J5 & J6
M23/J10,
1¹/₂ m S of B2027 at
Bough Beech,
3m SE of Edenbridge.

Rail: Hever Station
1m (no taxis),
Edenbridge Town
3m (taxis).

ℹ 🎬 Suitable for filming, conferences, corporate hospitality, product launches. Outdoor heated pool, tennis court and billiard room. No photography in house.

🛍 Gift, garden and book.

🍴 250 seat restaurant available for functions wedding receptions, etc.

♿ Access to gardens, ground floor only (no ramps into castle), restaurants, gift shop, book shop and water maze. Wheelchairs. WC.

🍽 Two licensed restaurants. Supper provided during open air theatre season. Pre-booked lunches and teas for groups.

🚶 Pre-booked tours in mornings. 1 Mar - 30 Nov. Tour time 1 hr. Tours in French, German, Dutch, Italian and Spanish (min 20). Garden tours in English only (min 15).

P Free admission and refreshment voucher for driver and courier. Please book, group rates for 15+.

🎒 Welcome (min 5). Guide provided for groups of 20. 1:10 ratio. Free preparatory visits for teachers during opening hours. Please book.

🐕 In grounds, on leads.

CONFERENCE/FUNCTION

ROOM	SIZE	MAX CAPACITY
Dining Hall	35' x 20'	70
Breakfast Rm	22' x 15'	12
Sitting Rm	24' x 20'	20
Pavilion	96' x 40'	250
Moat Restaurant	25 'x 60'	75

HEVER CASTLE

Hever Castle Tudor Village was built in 1903 for William Waldorf Astor in the style of the Tudor period, to include every modern day comfort.

There are twenty individually designed rooms all with private bathroom, direct dial telephone, colour television, hair dryer, and tea and coffee making facilities. The billiard room, outdoor heated swimming pool, tennis court and croquet lawn are all available for guests to use. Hever Castle Estate includes Stables House, an imposing property with five bedrooms, overlooking the river Eden, providing additional accommodation.

The Tudor Village is a unique and unusual venue available only on an 'exclusive use' basis all year round for groups of 10 or more requiring the very highest standards of accommodation, dining and meeting facilities. There are three interconnecting reception rooms all available for private dining, receptions, product launches, private meetings or corporate hospitality.

The magnificent private dining rooms are able to seat up to 70 people for Tudor Banquets, lunches and dinners. Guests are able to enjoy a private guided tour of the Castle followed by a Tudor Banquet with Minstrels playing Tudor Music.

The Dining Hall, Sitting Room and Breakfast Room (which together form the Tudor Suite) provide formal meeting facilities for up to 30 people and 70 people 'theatre style'. Overhead projector, screen and flip charts can be provided and specialist audiovisual equipment hired. Additional arrangements can be made for laser clay pigeon shooting, archery, fishing, riding, golf and other pursuits on or near by the estate.

Hever Castle Tudor Village offers the following accommodation

- 4 single, 12 double, 4 twin bedded rooms in Tudor Village
- 4 twin, 1 double in Stables House

SPECIAL EVENTS

- **MAR 12 - 18**
  Spring Flower Week
- **APR 13 - 16**
  Easter Weekend
- **MAY 5 - 7**
  May Day Music & Dance
- **MAY 26 - 28**
  Merrie England Weekend
- **JUN 22 - 28**
  Rose Week

- **JUL 21, 28, AUG 4, 5, 11, 12, 18, 19, 25, SEPT 1.**
  Jousting Tournaments
- **JUL 22, 29. AUG 26, 27. SEPT 2.**
  Medieval Archery
- **SEPT 14 - 16**
  Patchwork Quilting Exhibition
- **OCT 8 - 14**
  Autumn Colour Week

Tulip Bedroom in Tudor Village.

Tudor Suite Dining Room in Tudor Village.

Panelled Bedroom.

South East England

© National Trust.

IGHTHAM MOTE
Sevenoaks

Beautiful moated manor house covering 650 years of history from medieval times to the 1960s. Extended visitor route now includes the newly refurbished North-West quarter with Tudor Chapel, Billiards Room and Drawing Room on view. Access in 2001 through the South West wing of the house for the first time ever. Ongoing conservation programme focusing on the Great Hall and Jacobean Staircase. Interpretation displays and special exhibition featuring Conservation in Action. Lovely gardens with lakes and woodland. Surrounding estate provides many country walks. Free introductory talks and garden tours.

Owner:
The National Trust

CONTACT

The Property Manager
Ightham Mote
Ivy Hatch
Sevenoaks
Kent
TN15 0NT

Tel: 01732 810378

Info: 01732 811145

Fax: 01732 811029

e-mail: kimxxx@
smtp.ntrust.org.uk

LOCATION

OS Ref. TQ584 535

6m E of Sevenoaks off A25. 2½ m S of Ightham off A227

OPENING TIMES

1 April - 4 November: daily except Tues & Sats, 11am - 5.30pm.
Last admission 1 hr before close.

ADMISSION

Adult	£5.00
Child	£2.50
Family	£12.50

Groups (pre-booked)
Adult	£4.25

© National Trust.

Ground floor. WC.

Tea Pavilion.

On leads, Estate only.

KNOLE
Sevenoaks

Set in an extensive deer park owned by Lord Sackville, Knole is one of the great 'treasure houses' of England. It has been the home of the Sackville family since 1603, including four Dukes of Dorset, and houses an extensive collection of furnishings and paintings, many in the house since the 17th century.

The largest private house in England, Knole is a spectacular example of late medieval architecture overlaid with extensive Jacobean embellishments, including remarkable carving and plasterwork. The Sackville family crest of the leopard rampant recurs throughout.

An internationally renowned collection of Royal Stuart furnishings, including three state beds, celebrated silver furniture, and the prototype of the 'Knole' settee. Thirteen years were spent restoring the fabrics on the bed in the Kings' room.

The 6th Earl of Dorset played host to poets Pope and Dryden. Knole was the birthplace of the writer, Vita Sackville-West, and the setting for Virginia Woolf's novel *Orlando*.

Important collection of paintings, including works by Van Dyck, Lely, Kneller,Gainsborough, Hoppner, Wootton, and a room devoted to the works of Sir Joshua Reynolds, commissioned for the house by the 3rd Duke of Dorset, including portraits of Dr Johnson, David Garrick and Oliver Goldsmith.

The experience of visiting the house, which has been little altered since the 18th century, is like stepping back in time.

Owner:
The National Trust

CONTACT

Property Manager
Knole
Sevenoaks
Kent TN15 0RP

Tel: 01732 462100

Info: 01732 450608

Fax: 01732 465528

e-mail: kknxxx@
smtp.ntrust.org.uk

LOCATION

OS Ref. TQ532 543

25m SE of London.
Just off A225 at S end of
High Street, Sevenoaks.

Rail: 1/2 hr from London
Charing Cross to
Sevenoaks.

Bus: Chartwell Explorer
'green transport' bus link
with Sevenoaks.
Tel: 01732 462100

OPENING TIMES

House

31 March - 4 November:
Wed - Sat, 12 noon - 4pm.

Last admission 3.30pm.

Sun, BH Mon & Good Fri
11am - 5pm.

Last admission 4pm.

Garden
May - September
1st Wed of month only
12 noon - 4pm.

Last admission 3pm.

Shop & Tearoom
1 April - 31 October:
11am - 4.30pm

ADMISSION

House & Garden

Adult £5.00
Child £2.50
Family £12.50

Groups (pre-booked)
Adult £4.25

Parking.....................£2.50

Garden only £1.00

NT members Free.

	Full range of NT goods and souvenirs of Knole.
	Wheelchair access to Green Court, Stone Court and Great Hall.
	Brewhouse Restaurant serving morning coffee, lunch and teas. Also ice-creams and snacks in courtyard.
	Guided tours for pre-booked groups: Thur mornings.
	Ample.
	Welcome. Contact Education Officer.

South East England

LEEDS CASTLE & GARDENS
Maidstone

This "loveliest castle in the world", surrounded by 500 acres of magnificent parkland and gardens and set in the middle of a natural lake, is one of the country's finest historic properties. Leeds is also proud to be one of the Treasure Houses of England.

The site of a Saxon royal manor, a Norman fortress and a royal palace to the Kings and Queens of England, the chequered history of Leeds Castle continues well into the 20th century. The last private owner, the Honourable Olive, Lady Baillie, purchased the Castle in 1926. Her inheritance helped to restore the Castle and, prior to her death, she established the Leeds Castle Foundation which now preserves the Castle for the nation, hosts important international conferences and supports the arts.

The Castle has a fine collection of paintings, tapestries and furnishings and is also home to a unique collection of antique dog collars. The Park and Grounds include the colourful and quintessentially English Culpeper Garden, the delightful Wood Garden, and the terraced Lady Baillie Garden with its views over the tranquil Great Water. An Aviary houses rare and endangered species from around the world and, next to the traditional Greenhouses can be found a Maze with its secret underground grotto.

A highly popular and successful programme of Special Events is arranged throughout the year, details of which can be found opposite.

❖

Owner:
Leeds Castle Foundation

CONTACT

Sandra Barrett
Leeds Castle
Maidstone
Kent
ME17 1PL

Tel: 01622 765400

Fax: 01622 735616

LOCATION

OS Ref. TQ835 533

From London to A20/M20/J8, 40m, 1 hr. 6m E of Maidstone, ¼ m S of A20.

Rail: BR Connex train and admission. London - Bearsted.

Coach: Nat Express/ Invictaway coach and admission from Victoria.

Air: Gatwick 45m. Heathrow 65m.

Channel Tunnel: 25m.

Channel ports: 38m.

CONFERENCE/FUNCTION

ROOM	SIZE	MAX CAPACITY
Fairfax Hall	19.8 x 1m	200
Gate Tower	9.8 x 5.2m	50
Culpeper	7.65 x 7.34m	40
Terrace	8.9 x 15.4m	80

Culpeper Garden

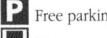 Residential conferences, exhibitions, sporting days, clay shooting, falconry, field archery, golf, croquet and heli-pad. Talks can be arranged for horticultural, viticultural, historical and cultural groups. No radios.

Corporate hospitality, large scale marquee events, wedding receptions, buffets and dinners.

Shuttle for elderly/disabled, wheelchairs, wheelchair lift, special rates. WC.

Two restaurants and a tearoom, group lunch menus. Refreshment kiosks.

Guides in rooms. French, Spanish, Dutch, German, Italian and Russian speaking guides.

Free parking.

Welcome, outside normal opening hours, private tours. Teacher's resource pack.

OPENING TIMES

OPEN ALL YEAR

SUMMER
1 March - 31 October
Daily:
10am - 5pm (last adm).

WINTER
1 November - 28 February
Daily:
10am - 3pm (last adm.).
(closed Christmas Day).

Also special private tours for pre-booked groups at any other time by appointment.

Castle & Grounds closed 30 Jun & 7 July prior to the Open Air Concerts.

ADMISSION

Rates from 1 March 2001.

Castle, Park & Gardens
Adult £10.00
Child (5 -15yrs).........£6.50
OAP/Student............£8.50
Family (2+3)...........£29.00
Disabled Visitors
Adult £5.50
Child (5 -15yrs).........£4.50
Groups (15+)
Adult £8.00
Child (5 -15yrs).........£6.00
OAP/Student............£7.00

Park & Gardens
Adult £8.50
Child (5 -15yrs).........£5.20
OAP/Student............£7.00
Family (2+3) £24.00
Disabled Visitors
Adult £4.50
Child (5 -15yrs).........£3.00
Groups (15+)
Adult £7.00
Child (5 -15yrs).........£5.00
OAP/Student............£6.00

A guidebook is published in English, French, German, Dutch, Spanish, Italian and Japanese.

LEEDS CASTLE

Open Air Concerts

Half Term Story Telling

Festival of Summer Floral Art

Autumn Gold

Grand Firework Spectacular

Festival of English Food & Wine

Christmas at the Castle

Balloon & Vintage Car Weekend

SPECIAL EVENTS

- **DEC 30/31 & JAN 1:**
  Treasure Trail
- **FEB 19 - 23:**
  Half Term Story-Telling
- **MAR 31 & APR 1:**
  Gardeners' Weekend
- **APR 14/15/16:**
  An Easter Celebration
- **MAY 12/13**
  Festival of English Food & Wine
- **MAY 26 - JUN 3**
  Amazing Mazes Week
- **JUN 30 & JUL 7:**
  Open Air Concerts
- **JUL 4:**
  Children's Promenade Concert
- **JUL 19 - 22:**
  A Festival of Summer Floral Art
- **SEPT 8/9:**
  Balloon & Vintage Car Weekend
- **OCT 10 - 14:**
  Autumn Gold - A Celebration of Flowers
  and Produce
- **OCT 22 - 26:**
  Half Term Halloween Event
- **NOV 3:**
  Grand Firework Spectacular
- **DEC 10 - 24:**
  Christmas at the Castle

Gardeners' Weekend

An Easter Celebration

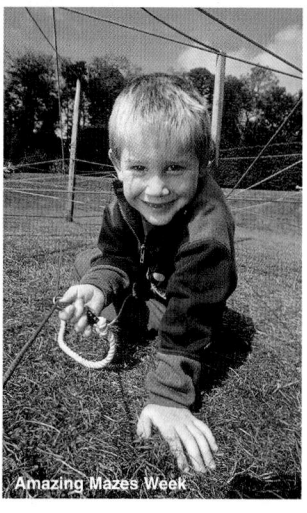
Amazing Mazes Week

South East England

PENSHURST PLACE & GDNS
Nr Tonbridge

PENSHURST PLACE is one of England's greatest family-owned stately homes with a history going back six and a half centuries.

In some ways time has stood still at Penshurst; the great House is still very much a medieval building with improvements and additions made over the centuries but without any substantial rebuilding. Its highlight is undoubtedly the medieval Barons' Hall, built in 1341, with its impressive 60ft-high chestnut-beamed roof.

A marvellous mix of paintings, tapestries and furniture from the 15th, 16th and 17th centuries can be seen throughout the House, including the helm carried in the state funeral procession to St. Paul's Cathedral for the Elizabethan courtier and poet, Sir Philip Sidney, in 1587. This is now the family crest.

GARDENS

The Gardens, first laid out in the 14th century, have been developed over successive years by the Sidney family who first came to Penshurst in 1552. A twenty-year restoration and re-planting programme undertaken by the late Viscount De L'Isle has ensured that they retain their historic splendour. He is commemorated with a new Arboretum, planted in 1991. The gardens are divided by a mile of yew hedges into "rooms", each planted to give a succession of colour as the seasons change. There is also an Adventure Playground, Woodland Trail and Toy Museum for children and an exhibition "Celebrating Seven Centuries of Gardening at Penshurst Place".

Owner:
Viscount De L'Isle

CONTACT

Bonnie Vernon
Penshurst Place
Penshurst
Nr Tonbridge
Kent
TN11 8DG

Tel: 01892 870307
Fax: 01892 870866

e-mail: enquiries
@penshurstplace.com

LOCATION

OS Ref. TQ527 438

From London M25/J5 then A21 to Hildenborough, B2027 via Leigh; from Tunbridge Wells A26, B2176.

Visitors entrance at SE end of village, S of the church.

Bus: Maidstone & District 231, 232, 233 from Tunbridge Wells.

Rail: Charing Cross/ Waterloo - Hildenborough, Tonbridge or Tunbridge Wells; then taxi.

CONFERENCE/FUNCTION		
ROOM	SIZE	MAX CAPACITY
Sunderland Room	45' x 18'	100
Barons' Hall	64' x 39'	250
Buttery	20' x 23'	50

🛍🌸ℹ Product launches, garden parties, photography, filming, fashion shows, receptions, archery, clay pigeon shooting, falconry, parkland for hire, lectures on property, its contents and history. Conference facilities. Adventure playground & parkland & riverside walks. No photography in house.

▼ Private banqueting, wedding receptions.

♿ Limited, disabled and elderly may alight at entrance. WC.

⎓ Licensed tearoom (waitress service can be booked by groups of 20+).

🚶 Mornings only by arrangement, lunch/dinner can be arranged. Out of season tours by appointment. Guided tours of the gardens.

🅿 Ample. Double decker buses to park from village.

▦ All year by appointment, discount rates, education room and packs.

🐕 Guide dogs only

OPENING TIMES

SUMMER
From 3 March weekends only.
31 March - 31 October

House
Daily, 12 noon - 5.30pm.
Last entry 5pm.

Grounds
Daily, 10.30am - 6pm.

Shop & Plant Centre
10.30am - 6pm.

WINTER
Open to Groups by appointment only
(see Guided Tours).

ADMISSION

House & Grounds
Adult £6.00
Child* £4.00
OAP........................£5.50
Family (2+2) £16.00
Groups**
Adult £5.30
Child £3.20

Garden only
Adult £4.50
Child* £3.50
OAP........................£4.00
Family (2+2) £13.00

Garden Season Ticket
..............................£25.00

House Tours (pre-booked)
Adult......................£6.00
Child......................£3.20

Garden Tours (pre-booked)
Adult......................£6.50
Child £4.00

House & Garden........£8.00

* Aged 5-15yrs; under 5s Free.
** Min 20 people, afternoons only. Special rates for morning Guided Tours.

SQUERRYES COURT & GDNS
Westerham

SQUERRYES COURT is a beautiful 17th century manor house which has been the Warde family home since 1731. It is surrounded by 10 acres of attractive and historic gardens which include a lake, restored parterres and an 18th century dovecote. Squerryes is 22 miles from London and easily accessible from the M25. There are lovely views and peaceful surroundings. Visitors from far and wide come to enjoy the atmosphere of a house which is still lived in as a family home.

There is a fine collection of Old Master paintings from the Italian, 17th century Dutch and 18th century English schools, furniture, porcelain and tapestries all acquired or commissioned by the family in the 18th century. General Wolfe of Quebec was a friend of the family and there are items connected with him in the Wolfe Room.

GARDENS
These were laid out in the formal style but were re-landscaped in the mid 18th century. Some of the original features in the 1719 Badeslade print survive. The family have restored the formal garden using this print as a guide. The garden is lovely all year round with bulbs, wild flowers and woodland walks, azaleas, summer flowering herbaceous borders and roses.

CONTACT

Mrs Vale or Mrs Warde
Squerryes Court
Westerham
Kent
TN16 1SJ

Tel: 01959 562345
or 01959 563118

Fax: 01959 565949

e-mail: squerryescourt
@pavilion.co.uk

LOCATION

OS Ref. TQ440 535

Off the M25/J6, 6m,
E along A25 $\frac{1}{2}$ m SW of
Westerham

London 1-1$\frac{1}{2}$ hrs.

Rail: Oxted Station 4m.
Sevenoaks 6m.

Air: Gatwick,
30 mins.

OPENING TIMES

SUMMER

1 April - 30 September
Wed, Sat, Sun & BH Mon.

Closed: Mon (except BH Mon), Tue, Thur & Fri.

Grounds: 12 noon - 5.30pm
House: 1.30 - 5.30pm
Last admission 5pm.

NB. Pre-booked groups welcome any day.

WINTER

October - 1 April
Closed.

ADMISSION

House & Garden
Adult £4.20
Child (under 14).....£2.50
OAP.......................£3.80
Groups (20+)
Adult £3.60
Child (under 14).....£1.80
OAP.......................£3.60

House only
Adult £4.20
Child (under 14).....£2.50
OAP.......................£3.80
Groups (20+)
Adult £3.60
Child (under 14).....£1.80
OAP.......................£3.60

Garden only
Adult £2.50
Child (under 14).....£1.50
OAP.......................£2.20
Groups (20+, booked)
Adult £2.20
Child (under 14).....£1.10
OAP.......................£2.20

CONFERENCE/FUNCTION		
ROOM	SIZE	MAX CAPACITY
Hall	32' x 32'	60
Old Library	20' x 25' 6"	40

Suitable for conferences, product launches, filming, photography, archery, clay pigeon shooting, garden parties. No photography in house.

Exclusive entertaining & wedding receptions (marquee).

Limited access in house and garden, please telephone before visiting. WC.

Home-made teas on open days. Groups must book for lunch or tea. Menus upon request.

For pre-booked groups (max 55), small additional charge. Owner will meet groups by prior arrangement. Tour time 1 hr.

Ample. Free teas for drivers and couriers.

Welcome, cost £1.50 per child, guide provided. Areas of interest: nature walk, ducks and geese.

On leads, in grounds.

THE ARCHBISHOPS' PALACE
Tel: 01622 663006 **Fax:** 01622 682451

Mill Street, Maidstone, Kent ME15 6YE
Owner: Maidstone Borough Council   **Contact:** Operations Manager
Recently refurbished 14th century Palace used as a resting place for Archbishops travelling from London to Canterbury.
Location: OS Ref. TQ760 555. On the banks of River Medway SW of the centre of Maidstone.
Opening Times: Daily: 10am - 4.30pm.
Admission: Entrance to 1st floor rooms is free.

BEDGEBURY NATIONAL PINETUM
Tel: 01580 211044   **Fax:** 01580 212423

Goudhurst, Cranbrook, Kent TN17 2SL   **e-mail:** bedgebury@forestry.gsi.gov.uk
Owner: Forestry Commission   **Contact:** Mr Colin Morgan
Location: OS Ref. TQ714 337 (gate on B2079). 7m E of Tunbridge Wells on A21, turn N on B2079 for 1m.
Opening Times: All year: daily, 10am - dusk or 7pm.
Admission: Adult £3, Child £1.50, OAP £2.50.

BEECH COURT GARDENS

CANTERBURY ROAD, CHALLOCK, Nr ASHFORD, KENT TN25 4DJ
Owner: Mr V Harmsworth   *Contact: Mrs Miller-Thomas*

Tel: 01233 740735   **Fax:** 01233 740842
Surrounding a medieval farm house the ten acre woodland garden has a fine collection of trees including many acers. Rhododendrons, azaleas, cascading roses, island beds and vivid blue hydrangeas with a finale of autumn colour makes this a true garden for all seasons. Tranquil atmosphere, bird song and surprising vistas.
Location: OS Ref. TQ999 501. Off A252 Charing side of Challock roundabout.
Opening Times: 31 Mar - 4 Nov: (Closed Good Fri) Mon - Thur, 10am - 5.30pm, Fri - Sun, 12 noon - 6pm.
Admission: Adult £3, Child £1, Conc. £2.50. Groups (12+): Adult £2.30, Child 50p, Conc. £2.

ℹ️ Map available.   📷   🌱   🍴   ♿   🚪   🔑 By arrangement.
P Ample for cars, coaches limited.   🛏️   🐕 Guide dogs only.

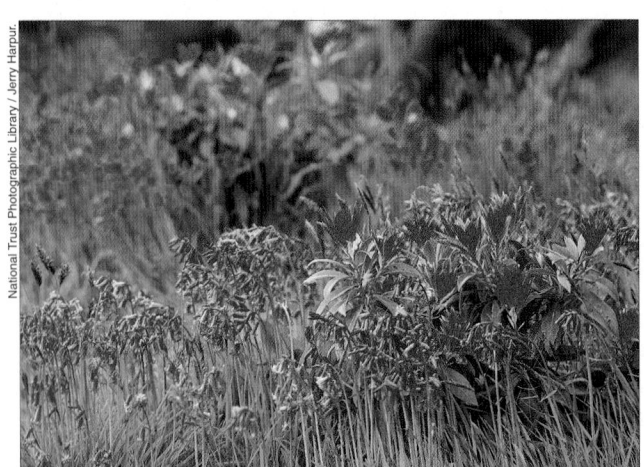

Emmetts Gardens, Kent.

BELMONT

BELMONT PARK, THROWLEY, FAVERSHAM ME13 0HH
Owner: Harris (Belmont) Charity   *Contact: Lt Col F E Grant*

Tel: 01795 890202   **Fax:** 01795 890042
Belmont is a charming late 18th century country mansion by Samuel Wyatt, set in delightful grounds. The seat of the Harris family since 1801 it is beautifully furnished and contains interesting items from India and Trinidad as well as the unique clock collection formed by the 5th Lord.
Location: OS Ref. TQ986 564. $4^1/2$ m SSW of Faversham, off A251.
Opening Times: 1 Apr - 30 Sept: Sats, Suns & BHs, 2 - 5pm. Last admission to house 4.30pm. Groups (20+) on other days by appointment.
Admission: House & Garden: Adult £5.25, Child £2.50, Conc. £4.75. Groups (20+): Adult £4.75, Child £2.50. Garden: Adult £2.75, Child £1. No discount for groups.

ℹ️ No photography in house.   📷   🌱   ♿ Partially suitable. WC.   🚪
🔑 Obligatory.   P   ✖️   (IW)

Open All Year
Index
◀◀◀ **page 49**

DEAL CASTLE

English Heritage Photo Library: Skyscan Balloon Photography.

VICTORIA ROAD, DEAL, KENT CT14 7BA
Owner: English Heritage *Contact:* The Custodian

Tel: 01304 372762

Crouching low and menacing, the huge, rounded bastions of this austere fort, built by Henry VIII, once carried 119 guns. A fascinating castle to explore, with long, dark passages, battlements and a huge basement. The interactive displays and exhibition give a fascinating insight into the Castle's history.

Location: OS Ref. TR378 521. SE of Deal town centre.

Opening Times: 1 Apr - 30 Sept: daily, 10am - 6pm. 1 - 31 Oct: 10am - 5pm. 1 Nov - 31 Mar: Wed - Sun only, 10am - 4pm. Closed 24 - 26 Dec & 1 Jan.

Admission: Adult £3.10, Child £1.60, Conc. £2.30.

Restricted. Coach parking on main road. Guide dogs only. Tel. for details.

DICKENS CENTRE - EASTGATE HOUSE
Tel: 01634 844176

High Street, Rochester, Medway ME1 1EW

Owner: Medway Council **Contact:** Head Custodian

Much altered late 16th century brick house, now containing the Dickens Centre, with exhibits of his life and works, including his best known characters. At the rear is Dickens' prefabricated chalet, brought from Switzerland.

Location: OS Ref. TQ746 683. N side of Rochester High Street, close to the Eastern Road. 400yds SE of the Cathedral.

Opening Times: Daily, 10am - 4.45pm (last admission).

Admission: Adult £3.60, Child £2.50, Family £9.70 (2000 prices).

DODDINGTON PLACE GARDENS
Tel: 01795 886101

Doddington, Sittingbourne, Kent ME9 0BB

Owner: Mr & Mrs Richard Oldfield **Contact:** Mrs Richard Oldfield

10 acres of landscaped gardens in an area of outstanding natural beauty.

Location: OS Ref. TQ944 575. 4m N from A20 at Lenham or 5m SW from A2 at Ospringe, W of Faversham. Signposted.

Opening Times: From Easter - Sept: Sun 2 - 6pm. Tues, Wed, Thurs & BHs 11am - 6pm. Groups at other times by appointment.

Admission: Adult £3, Child 50p. Groups: £2.50. Coaches by prior arrangement.

DOVER CASTLE & THE SECRET WARTIME TUNNELS
See page 121 for full page entry.

DOWN HOUSE
See page 122 for full page entry.

DYMCHURCH MARTELLO TOWER
Tel: 01304 211067

Dymchurch, Kent

Owner: English Heritage **Contact:** Area Manager

Built as one of 74 such towers to counter the threat of invasion by Napoleon, Dymchurch is perhaps the best example in the country. Fully restored. You can climb to the roof which is dominated by an original 24-pounder gun complete with traversing carriage.

Location: OS189, Ref. TR102 294. In Dymchurch, access from High Street.

Opening Times: Please telephone 01304 211067 for details.

Admission: Adult £1, Child 50p, Conc. 80p.

EASTBRIDGE HOSPITAL OF ST THOMAS
Tel: 01227 471688

High Street, Canterbury, Kent CT1 2BD

Contact: Louise Fittall

Medieval pilgrims' hospital with 12th century undercroft, refectory and chapel.

Location: OS189, Ref. TR148 579. S side of Canterbury High Street.

Opening Times: Mon - Sat, 10am - 4.45pm.

Admission: Adult £1, Child 50p, Conc. 75p (1999 prices).

Doddington Place Gardens, Kent.

National Trust Photographic Library.

Ightham Mote, Kent.

EMMETTS GARDEN

NT Photographic Library

IDE HILL, SEVENOAKS, KENT TN14 6AY

Owner: *The National Trust* **Contact:** *The Property Manager (Chartwell & Emmetts Garden, Mapleton Road, Westerham, Kent TN16 1PS)*

Tel: 01732 868381 (office)   **e-mail:** kchxxx@smtp.ntrust.org.uk
infoline: 01732 866368

Influenced by William Robinson, this charming and informal garden was laid out in the late 19th century, with many exotic and rare trees and shrubs from across the world. Wonderful views across the Weald of Kent – with the highest treetop in Kent. There are glorious shows of daffodils, carpets of bluebells, azaleas and rhododendrons, then acers and cornus in autumn, also a rose garden and rock garden.

Location: OS Ref. TQ477 524. $1^1/_2$ m N of Ide Hill off B2042. M25/J5, then 4m.
Opening Times: 31 Mar - 3 Jun: Wed - Sun, Good Fri & BH Mons. 6 Jun - 4 Nov: Sats, Suns & Weds, 11am - 5.30pm. Last admission 1 hr before close.
Admission: Adult £3.40, Child £1.70, Family £8.50.

⬚   ♿Steep in places. WC.   ▣   ⛩In grounds, on leads.   ♘Tel: 01892 891001.

FINCHCOCKS

See page 123 for full page entry.

THE FRIARS - RETREAT HOUSE   **Tel:** 01622 717272 **Fax:** 01622 715575

Aylesford Priory, Aylesford, Kent ME20 7BX

Owner: Carmelite Friars   **Contact:** Margaret Larcombe

A peaceful, tranquil retreat house with 100 beds, set in 42 acres of lovingly tended grounds. Outstanding ceramic works of art by Adam Kossowski. Visitors are invited to picnic in the grounds, visit the tearooms situated in the restored 17th century Barn, which also houses the gift and bookshops. While you are there do call into the pottery and the upholsterers' workshops.

Location: OS Ref. TQ724 588. W end of Aylesford village. 3m NW of Maidstone.
Opening Times: Grounds open Summer & Winter, 24 hrs, 365 days.
Admission: No charge.

⬚   Ⓣ   ♿Partially suitable.   ▣   Ⓧ By arrangement.   Ⓟ   ▥
⛩ Guide dogs only.   ▤   ✼

GAD'S HILL PLACE 🏛   **Tel:** 01474 822366 **Fax:** 01474 822977

Gad's Hill School, Higham, Rochester, Kent ME3 7PA

Owner: Gad's Hill School   **Contact:** Miss Anne Carter

This Grade I listed building dates from 1780. Charles Dickens lived here with his family from 1857 until his death in 1870, and wrote his last four novels here. Visitors can see his study, the newly restored conservatory, other rooms, the gardens and the grounds. Rooms can be hired for parties and weddings etc.

Location: OS Ref. TQ710 708. On A226, 3m from Rochester, 4m from Gravesend.
Opening Times: Apr - Oct: 1st Sun in month and BH Suns (inc Easter), 2 - 5pm. During Rochester Dickens Festivals (May/June & Dec), 11am - 4.30pm. At other times by appointment. Groups welcome.
Admission: Adult £2.50, Child £1.50, OAP £2.50, Student £1.50. Groups by arrangement.

⬚   Ⓣ   ♿Partially suitable.   ▣   ⓍObligatory.   ⛩Guide dogs only.   🔔

GODINTON HOUSE & GARDENS

GODINTON PARK, ASHFORD, KENT TN23 3BP

Owner: *Godinton House Preservation Trust*   **Contact:** *Mr D Bickle*

Tel: 01233 620773   **Fax:** 01233 632652   **e-mail:** ghpt@godinton.fsnet.co.uk

Jacobean House incorporating medieval hall, Tudor staircase and later additions, the carving, furniture, porcelain and contrasting decoration reflect its fascinating history. Topiary, terraces, ponds, herbaceous borders, new greenhouse; delphinium border, clematis collection, massed daffodils, wildflowers, fine trees, Italian, walled and formal gardens are surrounded by the famous yew hedge.

Location: OS Ref. TQ981 438. Godinton Lane, 2m NW of Ashford, off A20 (opposite Hare & Hounds public house).
Opening Times: Gardens: 17 Mar - 7 Oct: Thur - Mon, 2 - 5.30pm. House: 13 Apr - 7 Oct: Fris, Sats & Suns, 2 - 5.30pm. Last tour of house 4.30pm.
Admission: House & Gardens: Adult £5, Child £2. Garden only: Adult £2, Child £1.

ⓘNo photography in house. Groups must book.   ♿Partially suitable. WC.
▣For booked groups.   ⓍObligatory (house only).   ⓅLimited for coaches.
▥   ⛩Guide dogs only.

South East England

GOODNESTONE PARK GARDENS 🏛

GOODNESTONE PARK, Nr WINGHAM, CANTERBURY, KENT CT3 1PL

Owner: The Lord & Lady FitzWalter   *Contact:* Lady FitzWalter

Tel/Fax: 01304 840107

The garden is approximately 14 acres, set in 18th century parkland. There are many fine trees, a woodland area and a large walled garden with a collection of old-fashioned roses, clematis and herbaceous plants. Jane Austen was a frequent visitor, her brother Edward having married a daughter of the house.

Location: OS Ref. TR254 544. 8m ESE of Canterbury, 1$\frac{1}{2}$ m E of B2046, at S end of village. The B2046 runs from the A2 to Wingham, the gardens are signposted from this road.

Opening Times: 26 Mar - 26 Oct: Suns, 12 noon - 6pm. Mons, Wed - Fri, 11am - 5pm. Closed Tues & Sats. House open by appointment, at any time, to groups of 20 at £1.80.

Admission: Adult £3, Child (under 12yrs) 30p, OAP £2.50, Student £1.50. Groups (20+): Adult £2.50. Wheelchair users £1, Guided groups (20+) £3.50. House by appointment £1.80.

🏺 ♿ ☕ 🐕

GREAT COMP GARDEN

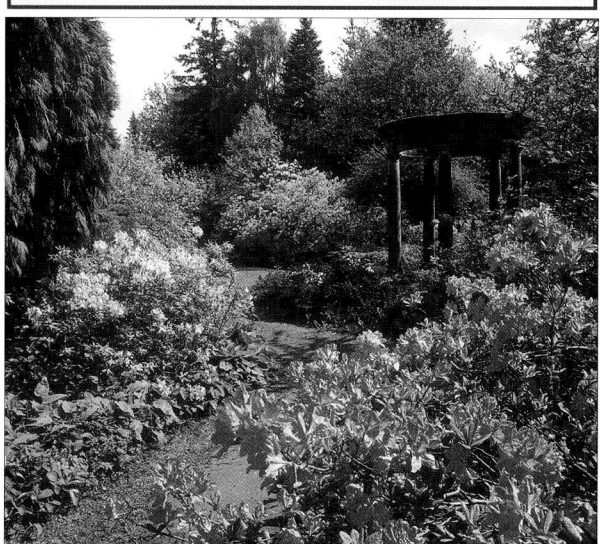

COMP LANE, PLATT, BOROUGH GREEN, KENT TN15 8QS

Owner: R Cameron Esq   *Contact:* Mr W Dyson

Tel: 01732 886154

One of the finest gardens in the country, comprising ruins, terraces, tranquil woodland walks and sweeping lawns with a breathtaking collection of trees, shrubs, heathers and perennials, many rarely seen elsewhere. The truly unique atmosphere of Great Comp is further complemented by its Festival of Chamber Music held in July/September.

Location: OS Ref. TQ635 567. 2m E of Borough Green, B2016 off A20. First right at Comp crossroads. $\frac{1}{2}$ m on left.

Opening Times: 1 Apr - 31 Oct: daily, 11am - 6pm.

Admission: Adult £3.50, Child £1. Groups (20+) £3, Annual ticket: Adult £10, OAP £7.

🏺 ♿ ☕ Teas daily. 🐕 Guide dogs only. Ⓦ

HALL PLACE   **Tel:** 01322 526574   **Fax:** 01322 522921

Bourne Road, Bexley, Kent DA5 1PQ

Owner: Bexley Council   **Contact:** Rosemary Evans

A fine Grade I listed country house built in 1540 for Sir John Champneis, a Lord Mayor of London. The house is set in beautiful formal gardens on the banks of the River Cray. Much of the house is open to the public, including the magnificent great hall.

Location: OS Ref. TQ502 743. Near the A2 less than 5m (London bound) from the M25/J2.

Opening Times: Mon - Sat, 10am - 5pm (4.15pm in winter), Sun & BHs, 2 - 6pm (BST only). Opening times may change from 2001, please phone to confirm times.

Admission: Free. Pre-arranged groups: £3.50.

📷 ♿ House suitable, lift & WC. 🖥 🍽 Licensed. 𝕏 By arrangement. 🅿 Ample for cars, limited for coaches. 🐕 Guide dogs only. 🔔 ❄ Ⓦ

HEVER CASTLE 🏛   See pages 124/125 for double page entry.

HIGHAM PARK, HOUSE & GARDENS

BRIDGE, CANTERBURY, KENT CT4 5BE

Owner/Contact: Patricia P Gibb

Tel/Fax: 01227 830830   **e-mail:** highampark@aol.com

Delight in Higham's (c1320) magnificently restored staterooms. Once home to Countess Margaret Zberanska (née Astor) and her son Louis, creator of the famous Chitty Chitty Bang Bang racing cars. Set on Barham Downs in 24 acres, surrounded by footpaths. Gardina d'Italiano. Trees, shrubs, roses, herbaceous. Kent's oldest acers, massed spring bulbs.

Location: OS Ref. TR183 541. On the A2 at Bridge between Canterbury and the channel ports.

Opening Times: Apr - end Sept: Garden: Suns, 11am - 6pm. Mon - Thur, 11am - 5pm. Closed Fris & Sats. House: Tours at 12.30pm, 2.30pm, 4pm (times may vary). Groups by arrangement at other times.

Admission: Garden: Adult £3, Child £1, OAP £2.50. Groups (20+): Adult £2.50. Guided groups (20+): £3.50. House Tours: £2.

🏺 🍸 ♿ Partially suitable. WC. 🖥 Licensed. Light lunches. 𝕏 Obligatory. 🎦 🅿 🐕 In grounds, on leads. ❄ 🛡 Tel. for details. Ⓦ

HOLE PARK 🏛   **Tel:** 01580 241251   **Fax:** 01580 241882

Rolvenden, Cranbrook, Kent TN17 4JB

Owner/Contact: D G W Barham

A 15 acre garden with all year round interest, set in beautiful parkland with fine views.

Location: OS Ref. TQ830 325. 1m W of Rolvenden on B2086 Cranbrook road.

Opening Times: 8, 22, 29 Apr. 6, 20, 27 May. 17 June: HP Society Plant Fair. 14 & 21 Oct (Suns), for NGS. Also Weds, April, May, Jun & Oct. All 2 - 6pm. Groups and individuals by arrangement. Guided tours available for groups.

Admission: Adult £3, Child 50p.

IGHTHAM MOTE 🌿   See page 126 for full page entry.

KNOLE 🌿   See page 127 for full page entry.

South East
England

LADHAM HOUSE GARDENS

LADHAM LANE, GOUDHURST, KENT TN17 1DB

Owner: Mr & Mrs Alastair Jessel **Contact:** *Mrs Jessel*

Tel: 01580 212674/211203   **Fax:** 01580 212596

This Georgian house with additional French features has been in the family for over 120 years and the garden developed over that period. Mixed shrub borders with famous magnolias. Interesting bog garden replacing a leaking pond and arboretum replacing old kitchen garden. Rare trees and shrubs including cornus cousa, embothriums, American oaks, carpenteria californica and others. 10 acres of gardens set in magnificent Wealden countryside. Superb site for wedding receptions, ceremonies and private parties.

Location: OS Ref. TQ732 384. $^3/_4$ NE of Goudhurst off A262. 5m NW of Cranbrook.

Opening Times: For NGS Sun 22 April, Sun 20 May, 2.30 - 5pm. All other times by prior arrangement.

Admission: Adult £3, Child 50p, OAP/Student £2.50. Groups (min 10, max 100): Adult £2.50, Child 50p, OAP/Student £2.

⊞ ▣ ☂ ⅃ Partially suitable. 🎭 By arrangement. ▦
Ⓟ Limited for coaches. ✗ ♤ ✳

LULLINGSTONE ROMAN VILLA ⌗

English Heritage Photo Library.

LULLINGSTONE LANE, EYNSFORD, KENT DA4 0JA

Owner: English Heritage **Contact:** *The Custodian*

Tel: 01322 863467

Recognised as one of the most exciting archaeological finds of the century, the villa has splendid mosaic floors and one of the earliest private Christian chapels. Take the free audio tour and discover how the middle-class owners lived, worked and entertained themselves.

Location: OS Ref. TQ529 651. $^1/_2$ m SW of Eynsford off A225, M25/J3. Follow A20 towards Brands Hatch. 600yds N of Castle.

Opening Times: 1 Apr - 30 Sept: daily, 10am - 6pm. 1 - 31 Oct: 10am - 5pm. 1 Nov - 31 Mar: 10am - 4pm. Closed 24 - 26 Dec & 1 Jan.

Admission: Adult £2.60, Child £1.30, Conc. £1.90.

▢   ⅃ Ground floor & grounds suitable. WC. 🎧 ✳ ⛨ Tel. for details.

LEEDS CASTLE   See pages 128/129 for double page entry.

LESNES ABBEY   **Tel:** 020 8303 9052

Abbey Road, Abbey Wood, London DA17 5DL

Owner: Bexley Council   **Contact:** TIC Manager

The Abbey was founded in 1178 by Richard de Lucy as penance for his involvement in events leading to the murder of Thomas à Becket. Today only the ruins remain.

Location: OS Ref. TQ479 788. In public park on S side of Abbey Road (B213), 500yds E of Abbey Wood Station, $^3/_4$ m N of A206 Woolwich - Erith Road.

Opening Times: Any reasonable time.

Admission: Free.

LULLINGSTONE CASTLE 🏛   **Tel:** 01322 862114   **Fax:** 01322 862115

Lullingstone Castle, Eynsford, Kent DA4 0JA

Owner/Contact: Guy Hart Dyke Esq

Fine state rooms, family portraits and armour in beautiful grounds. The 15th century gatehouse was one of the first ever to be made of bricks.

Location: OS Ref. TQ530 644. 1m S Eynsford W side of A225. 600yds S of Roman Villa.

Opening Times: May - Aug: Sats, Suns & BHs, 2 - 6pm. Booked groups by arrangement.

Admission: Adult £4, Child £1.50, Conc. £3, Family £10. Groups (25+) 10% discount.

ⓘ No interior photography. ▢ ⊞ ⅃ Partially suitable.
▣ Teas at visitor centre, 1km. 🎭 By arrangement. Ⓟ Limited. ✗

MAISON DIEU ⌗   **Tel:** 01795 534542

Ospringe, Faversham, Kent

Owner: English Heritage   **Contact:** The Faversham Society

This forerunner of today's hospitals remains largely as it was in the 16th century with exposed beams and an overhanging upper storey.

Location: OS Ref. TR002 608. In Ospringe on A2, $^1/_2$ m W of Faversham.

Opening Times: 3 Apr - 31 Oct: Weekends & BHs, 2 - 5pm. Keykeeper in Winter.

Admission: Adult £1, Child/OAP 80p.

MILTON CHANTRY ⌗   **Tel:** 01474 321520

New Tavern Fort Gardens, Gravesend, Kent

Owner: English Heritage   **Contact:** Gravesend Borough Council

A small 14th century building which housed the chapel of the leper hospital and the chantry of the de Valence and Montechais families and later became a tavern and in 1780 part of a fort.

Location: OS Ref.TQ652 743. In New Tavern Fort Gardens $^1/_4$ m E of Gravesend off A226.

Opening Times: 1 Mar - 23 Dec: Wed - Sun & BH Mons, 10am - 4pm. Closed Jan & Feb.

Admission: Adult £1.50, Child 75p, Conc. 75p.

MOUNT EPHRAIM GARDENS 🏛   **Tel:** 01227 751496   **Fax:** 01227 750940

Hernhill, Faversham, Kent ME13 9TX

Owner: Mr & Mrs E S Dawes & Mrs M N Dawes   **Contact:** Mrs L Dawes

8 acres of superb gardens set in the heart of family run orchards.

Location: OS Ref.TR065 598. In Hernhill village, 1m from end of M2. Signed from A2 & A299.

Opening Times: Easter - end Sept: Mons, Weds, Thurs, Sats & Suns, 1 - 6pm. Groups at all times by arrangement. (Details apply to 2000 please confirm opening times).

Admission: Adult £3, Child £1. Groups: £2.50 (2000 prices).

OWL HOUSE GARDENS

Tel: 01892 890230 **Fax:** 01892 891222

Lamberhurst, Kent TN3 8LY

Contact: James & Angela Kelso

16.5 acres of romantic gardens surrounding a 16th century timber framed wool smuggler's cottage (not open to the public). Woodland walks with oaks, elm, birch and beech trees. Rhododendrons, azaleas and camellias surround sunken water gardens.

Location: OS Ref. TQ665 372. 8m SE of Tunbridge Wells; 1m from Lamberhurst off A21.

Opening Times: Gardens only: All year, daily, 11am - 6pm, except 25 Dec & 1 Jan.

Admission: Adult £4, Child £1. Coach parties welcome.

    P Free. On leads. ❄

PENSHURST PLACE & GARDENS

See page 130 for full page entry.

QUEBEC HOUSE

Tel: 01892 890651

Westerham, Kent TN16 1TD

Owner: The National Trust **Contact:** Regional Office

General Wolfe spent his early years in this gabled, red-brick 17th century house. Four rooms containing portraits, prints and memorabilia relating to Wolfe's family and career are on view. In the Tudor stable block is an exhibition about the Battle of Quebec (1759) and the parts played by Wolfe and his adversary, the Marquis de Montcalm.

Location: OS Ref. TQ449 541. At E end of village, on N side of A25, facing junction with B2026, Edenbridge Road.

Opening Times: 3 Apr - 30 Oct: Suns & Tues, 2 - 6pm, last admission 5.30pm.

Admission: Adult £2.60, Child £1.30, Family (2+3) £6.50. Groups £2.20.

QUEX HOUSE & GARDEN & POWELL COTTON MUSEUM

Quex Park, Birchington, Kent CT7 0BH

Tel: 01843 842168

e-mail: powell-cotton-museum@virgin.net

Owner: Trustees of Powell Cotton Museum **Contact:** John Harrison

Regency/Victorian country residence, walled gardens and Victorian explorers' museum.

Location: OS Ref. TR308 683. ½ m from Birchington Church via Park Lane.

Opening Times: Please contact Museum for details.

Admission: Summer: Adult £3.50, Child, OAP, Disabled & Carer £2.80, Student £2, Family (2+3) £11. Winter: Adult £2.50, Child, OAP, Disabled & Carer £1.80, Family (2+3) £7.50.

RECULVER TOWERS & ROMAN FORT

Tel: 01227 740676

Reculver, Herne Bay, Kent

Owner: English Heritage **Contact:** Reculver Country Park

This 12th century landmark of twin towers has guided sailors into the Thames estuary for seven centuries. Walls of a Roman fort, which were erected nearly 2,000 years ago.

Location: OS Ref. TR228 694. At Reculver 3m E of Herne Bay by the seashore.

Opening Times: Any reasonable time. External viewing only.

Admission: Free.

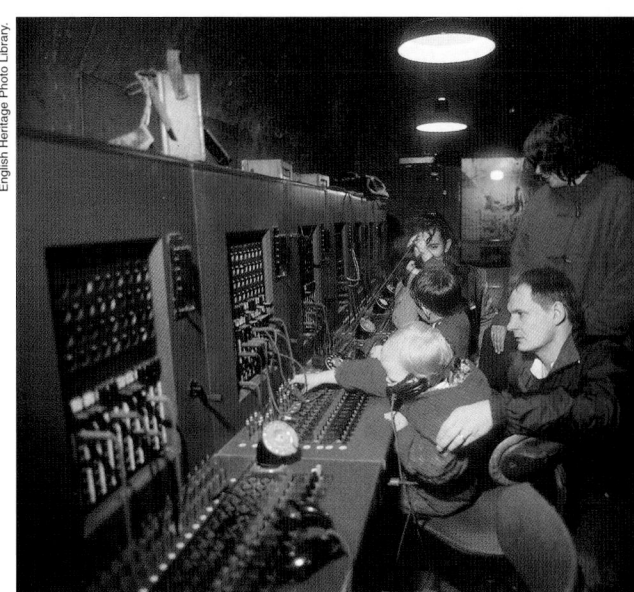

Dover Castle, Kent.

RESTORATION HOUSE

17 - 19 CROW LANE, ROCHESTER, KENT ME1 1RF

Owner: *Messrs R Tucker & J Wilmot* **Contact:** *Robert Tucker*

Tel: 01634 848520 **Fax:** 01634 880058

Historic city mansion with unique old atmosphere. Links to Charles II, Pepys, Dickens (Miss Havisham's House). Beautiful interiors with early paintwork, fine furniture and pictures (including Kneller, Dahl, Reynolds, Gainsborough). Charming interlinked walled gardens of ingenious plan in classic English style. A private gem.

Location: OS Ref. TQ744 683. Historic centre of Rochester, off High Street, opposite the Vines Park.

Opening Times: 3 May - 28 Sept: Thurs & Fris, 10am - 5pm.

Admission: Adult £4.50 includes 24 page illustrated guidebook), Child £2. Booked groups (12+): Adult £4, Child £2.

i No stiletto heels.

RICHBOROUGH ROMAN FORT

Tel: 01304 612013

Richborough, Sandwich, Kent CT13 9JW

Owner: English Heritage **Contact:** The Custodian

This fort and township date back to the Roman landing in AD43. The fortified walls and the massive foundations of a triumphal arch which stood 80 feet high still survive. The inclusive audio tour and the museum give an insight into life in Richborough's heyday as a busy township.

Location: OS Ref. TR324 602. 1½ m NW of Sandwich off A257.

Opening Times: 1 Apr - 30 Sept: daily, 10am - 6pm. 1 - 31 Oct: 10am - 5pm. 1 - 31 Nov: Wed - Sun only, 10am - 4pm. Weekends only in Dec, Jan & Feb, 10am - 4pm. 1 - 31 Mar: Wed - Sun, 10am - 4pm. Closed 24 - 26 Dec & 1 Jan.

Admission: Adult £2.70, Child £1.40, Conc. £2.

i Museum. Ground floor suitable. **P** Guide dogs only. ❄ Tel. for details.

RIVERHILL HOUSE

Tel: 01732 458802/452557 **Fax:** 01732 458802

Sevenoaks, Kent TN15 0RR

Owner: The Rogers Family **Contact:** Mrs Rogers

Small country house built in 1714, home of the Rogers family since 1840. Panelled rooms, portraits and interesting memorabilia. Historic hillside garden with extensive views, rare trees and shrubs. Sheltered terraces and rhododendrons and azaleas in a woodland setting. Bluebells.

Location: OS Ref. TQ541 522. 2m S of Sevenoaks on E side of A225.

Opening Times: Garden: Apr, May & Jun: Weds, Suns & BH weekends, 12 noon - 6pm. Coaches by arrangement. House: open only to pre-booked groups of adults (20+) on any day: Apr, May & Jun.

Admission: Adult £3, Child 50p. Pre-booked groups: £4.

i Conferences. Not suitable. By arrangement.

ROCHESTER CASTLE

Tel: 01634 402276

The Lodge, Rochester-upon-Medway, Medway ME1 1SX

Owner: English Heritage **Contact:** Head Custodian (Managed by Medway Council)

Built in the 11th century. The keep is over 100 feet high and with walls 12 feet thick. At the top you will be able to enjoy fine views over the river and surrounding city of Rochester.

Location: OS Ref. TQ743 685. By Rochester Bridge (A2), M2/J1 & M25/J2.

Opening Times: 1 Apr - 30 Sept: daily, 10am - 6pm. 1 - 31 Oct: daily, 10am - 5pm. 1 Nov - 31 Mar: daily, 10am - 4pm. Closed 24 - 26 Dec & 1 Jan.

Admission: Please telephone for details.

South East England

ROCHESTER CATHEDRAL

Tel: 01634 401301 Fax: 01634 401410

c/o 70a High Street, Rochester, Kent ME1 1JY   Contact: Mrs S Strong

Founded in 604AD, Rochester Cathedral has been a place of Christian worship for nearly 1,400 years. The present building is a blend of Norman and gothic architecture with a fine medieval crypt. In the cloister are the remains of the 12th century chapter house and priory. A focal point is the Doubleday statue.

Location: OS Ref. TQ742 686. Signposted from M20/J6 and on the A2/M2/J3. Best access from M2/J3.

Opening Times: All year: 8.30am - 5pm. Visiting may be restricted during services.

Admission: £2 donation. Groups: £2.50 guided. Groups must book on above number. Separate prices for schools.

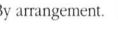 Photography permit £1. By arrangement. P

ROMAN PAINTED HOUSE

Tel: 01304 203279

New Street, Dover, Kent CT17 9AJ

Owner: Dover Roman Painted House Trust   Contact: Mr B Philip

Discovered in 1970. Built around 200AD as a hotel for official travellers. Impressive wall paintings, central heating systems and the Roman fort wall built through the house.

Location: OS Ref. TR318 414. Dover town centre. E of York St.

Opening Times: Apr - Sept: 10am - 5pm, except Mons.

Admission: Adult £2, Child/OAP 80p.

ROYDON HALL

Tel: 01622 812121 Fax: 01622 813959

Nr Tonbridge, Kent TN12 5NH   e-mail: roydonhall@btinternet.com

Owner: Maharishi Foundation   Contact: The Events Manager

Roydon Hall is a very fine Tudor manor house which was 'modified' by the Victorians.

Location: OS Ref. TQ664 518. M25 then M40 towards Paddock Wood. Follow signs for Paddock Wood into Seven Mile Lane. Sign for Roydon on right indicating turn to left on brow of hill about 4m down lane.

Opening Times: Available for film location work and corporate events. Bed and breakfast accommodation also.

ST AUGUSTINE'S ABBEY

Tel: 01227 767345

Longport, Canterbury, Kent CT1 1TF

Owner: English Heritage   Contact: The Custodian

The Abbey, founded by St Augustine in 598, is a World Heritage Site. Take the free interactive audio tour which gives a fascinating insight into the Abbey's history and visit the museum displaying artifacts uncovered during archaeological excavations of the site.

Location: OS Ref. TR154 578. In Canterbury ½m E of Cathedral Close.

Opening Times: 1 Apr - 30 Sept: daily, 10am - 6pm. 1 - 31 Oct: 10am - 5pm. 1 Nov - 31 Mar: daily, 10am - 4pm. Closed 24 - 26 Dec & 1 Jan.

Admission: Adult £2.60, Child £1.30, Conc. £1.90. 15% discount for groups (11+). One extra place for every additional 20.

Grounds suitable. WC. Free. Guide dogs only. Tel. for details.

ST JOHN'S COMMANDERY

Tel: 01304 211067

Densole, Swingfield, Kent

Owner: English Heritage   Contact: The South East Regional Office

A medieval chapel built by the Knights Hospitallers. It has a moulded plaster ceiling and a remarkable timber roof and was converted into a farmhouse in the 16th century.

Location: OS Ref. TR232 440. 2m NE of Densole on minor road off A260.

Opening Times: Any reasonable time for exterior viewing. Internal viewing by appointment only.

Admission: Free.

Website Index page 39

SCOTNEY CASTLE GARDEN

NT Photographic Library: Jenny Harpur.

NT Photographic Library: Stephen Robson.

LAMBERHURST, TUNBRIDGE WELLS, KENT TN3 8JN

Owner: The National Trust   *Contact:* Administrative Assistant

Tel: 01892 891081 Fax: 01892 890110 e-mail: kscxxx@smtp.ntrust.org.uk

One of England's most romantic gardens designed by Edward Hussey in the picturesque style. Dramatic vistas from the terrace of the new Scotney Castle, built in the 1830s, lead down to the ruins of a 14th century moated castle. Rhododendrons, kalmia, azaleas and wisteria flower in profusion. Roses and clematis scramble over the remains of the Old Castle, which is open for the summer. In autumn the garden's glowing colours merge with the surrounding woodlands where there are many country walks to be explored.

Location: OS Ref. TQ688 353. Signed off A21 1m S of Lamberhurst village.

Opening Times: 17 - 25 Mar: Sats & Suns, 12 noon - 4pm. 31 Mar - 4 Nov: Wed - Fri, 11am - 6pm, Sats & Suns, 2 - 6pm, BH Suns & Mons 12 noon - 6pm (closed Good Fri). Last adm. 1 hr before close. Car park: All year for estate walks.

Admission: Adult £4.40, Child £2.20, Family (2+3) £11. Pre-booked groups weekdays £3.80.

 Grounds (but steep parts). Outside garden only, on leads.

South East England

SMALLHYTHE PLACE

TENTERDEN, KENT TN30 7NG

Owner: *The National Trust* **Contact:** *The Custodian*

Tel: 01580 762334 **Fax:** 01580 762334 **e-mail:** ksmxxx@smtp.ntrust.org.uk

This early 16th century half-timbered house was home to Shakespearean actress Ellen Terry from 1899 to 1928. The house contains many personal and theatrical mementoes including many of her lavish costumes. The charming cottage grounds include her rose garden and the Barn Theatre, which is open most days by courtesy of the Barn Theatre Society.

Location: OS Ref. TQ893 300. 2m S of Tenterden on E side of the Rye road B2082.

Opening Times: 31 Mar - 31 Oct: daily except Thurs & Fris (open Good Fri), 1.30 - 6pm or dusk if earlier. Groups (max. 25) Tues morning only.

Admission: Adult £3.20, Child £1.60, Family £8.

ⓘ No photography in house. Not suitable. P Limited.

SOUTH FORELAND LIGHTHOUSE & GATEWAY TO THE WHITE CLIFFS

LANGDON CLIFFS, Nr DOVER, KENT CT16 1HJ

Owner: *The National Trust* **Contact:** *Countryside Manager*

Tel: 01304 202756 **Fax:** 01304 205295 **e-mail:** kwcxxx@smtp.ntrust.org.uk

The Gateway to the White Cliffs is a visitor centre with spectacular views across the English Channel. It introduces the visitor to its coast and countryside through imaginative displays and interpretation. High up on the cliffs is South Foreland Lighthouse, used by Marconi for his first ship-to-shore radio experiments.

Location: OS138 Ref. TR336 422. Follow White Cliffs brown signs from roundabout 1m NE of Dover at junction of A2/A258.

Opening Times: Gateway: 1 Mar - 31 Oct: daily 10am - 5pm. 1 Nov - 28 Feb: daily 11am - 4pm. Lighthouse: 1 Mar - 31 Oct: daily except Tues & Weds, 11am - 5.30pm (last admission 5pm).

Admission: Adult £1.80, Child 90p. Car Park £1.50. Groups £1.50.

Limited range.   Partially suitable. WC. By arrangement. P In grounds, on leads. Holiday cottage, 1dbl & 2 single.

SQUERRYES COURT & GARDENS   See page 131 for full page entry.

STONEACRE

Tel: 01622 862871 **Fax:** 01622 862157

Otham, Maidstone, Kent ME15 8RS

Owner: The National Trust **Contact:** The Tenant

A half-timbered mainly late 15th century yeoman's house, with great hall and crownpost, and restored cottage-style garden.

Location: OS Ref. TQ800 535. In narrow lane at N end of Otham village, 3m SE of Maidstone, 1m S of A20.

Opening Times: 4 Apr - 31 Oct: Weds & Sats, 2 - 6pm. Last admission 1hr before close.

Admission: Adult £2.60, Child £1.30, Family (2+3) £6.50. Groups £2.20.

TEMPLE MANOR

Tel: 01634 827980

Strood, Rochester, Kent

Owner: English Heritage **Contact:** Medway Council

The 13th century manor house of the Knights Templar which mainly provided accommodation for members of the order travelling between London and the Continent.

Location: OS Ref. TQ733 686. In Strood (Rochester) off A228.

Opening Times: 1 Apr - 30 Sept: weekends & BHs, 10am - 6pm.

Admission: Free.

THE THEATRE ROYAL, CHATHAM

Tel: 01634 306367

102 High Street, Chatham, Kent ME4 4BY

Owner: Chatham Theatre Royal Trust Ltd **Contact:** The Administrator

Built in 1899, it is Kent's finest surviving Victorian Theatre.

Location: OS Ref. TQ755 679. In Chatham High Street.

Opening Times: Mon - Sat, 10am - 3pm. Guided tours most weekdays. Groups welcome by appointment.

Admission: Donation.

TONBRIDGE CASTLE

Tel: 01732 770929

Castle Street, Tonbridge, Kent TN9 1BG

Owner: Tonbridge & Malling Borough Council **Contact:** The Administrator

Location: OS Ref. TQ588 466. 300 yds NW of the Medway Bridge at town centre.

Opening Times: All year: Mon - Sat, 9am - 4pm. Suns & BHs, 10.30am - 4pm.

Admission: Adult £3.60, Conc £1.80. Family £8.50. Admission includes audio tour.

UPNOR CASTLE

Tel: 01634 718742

Upnor, Kent

Owner: English Heritage **Contact:** Medway Council

Well-preserved 16th century gun fort built to protect Queen Elizabeth I's warships. However in 1667 it failed to prevent the Dutch Navy which stormed up the Medway destroying half the English fleet.

Location: OS Ref. TQ758 706. At Upnor, on unclassified road off A228. 2m NE of Strood.

Opening Times: 1 Apr - 30 Sept: daily, 10am - 6pm.

Admission: Please telephone for details.

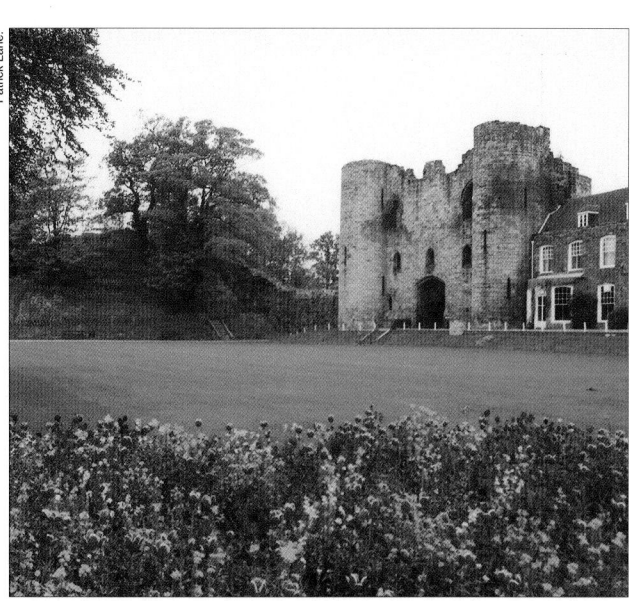

Tonbridge Castle, Kent.

WALMER CASTLE & GARDENS

WALMER, DEAL, KENT CT14 7LJ

Owner: English Heritage   *Contact:* The Custodian

Tel: 01304 364288

A Tudor fort transformed into an elegant stately home. The residence of the Lords Warden of the Cinque Ports and still used by HM The Queen Mother today. Take the new free audio tour and see the Duke of Wellington's rooms and even his famous boots. Beautiful gardens including the Queen Mother's Garden, The Broadwalk with its famous yew tree hedge, Kitchen Garden and Moat Garden. Lunches and cream teas available in the delightful Lord Warden's tearooms.

Location: OS Ref. TR378 501. S of Walmer on A258, M20/J13 or M2 to Deal.

Opening Times: 1 Apr - 30 Sept: daily, 10am - 6pm. 1 - 31 Oct: daily, 10am - 5pm. 1 Nov - 31 Dec & 1 - 31 Mar: Wed - Sun only, 10am - 4pm. Jan & Feb: Sats & Suns, 10am - 4pm. Closed 24 - 26 Dec & 1 Jan and when Lord Warden is in residence.

Admission: Adult £4.80, Child £2.40, OAP/Student £3.60. 15% discount for groups (11+). One extra place for each additional 20. EH members free.

Grounds suitable. Guide dogs only. Tel. for details.

WILLESBOROUGH WINDMILL   **Tel:** 01233 661866

Mill Lane, Willesborough, Ashford, Kent

125 year old restored smock mill.

Location: OS Ref. TR031 421. Off A292 close to M20/J10. At E end of Ashford.

Opening Times: Apr - Sept; Sats, Suns and BH Mons, 2 - 5pm or dusk if earlier.

Admission: Adult £1, Child/Conc. 50p. Groups 10% reduction by arrangement only.

YALDING ORGANIC GARDENS   **Tel:** 01622 814650 **Fax:** 01622 814 650

Benover Road, Yalding, Maidstone, Kent ME18 6EX

Owner: HDRA - the organic organisation   **Contact:** David Holdsworth

Fourteen newly created gardens reflecting mankind's experience of gardening over the centuries.

Location: OS Ref. TQ698 492. 6m SW of Maidstone, 1/2 m S of village at Yalding on B2162.

Opening Times: Apr - w/ends only, 10am - 5pm. May - Sept: Wed - Sun, 10am - 5pm. Oct: w/ends only.

Admission: Adult £3 (no concessions), accompanied Child (up to 16yrs) Free. Groups (14+) £2.50 plus 50p for guided tour.

Sir Winston Churchill and others at Chartwell, Kent, of which he said " I love the place – a day away from Chartwell is a day wasted".

*Broughton Castle,
Oxfordshire.*

141

South East England

Owner:
The Duke of Marlborough

CONTACT

Nicholas Day
Blenheim Palace
Woodstock
OX20 1PX

Tel: 01993 811091

Fax: 01993 813527

e-mail: administration
@blenheimpalace.com

LOCATION

OS Ref. SP441 161

From London, M40, A44
(1½ hrs), 8m NW of
Oxford. London 63m
Birmingham 54.

Air: Heathrow 60m.
Birmingham 54m.

Coach: From London
(Victoria) to Oxford.

Rail: Oxford Station.

Bus: Oxford (Cornmarket)
- Woodstock.

CONFERENCE/FUNCTION		
ROOM	SIZE	MAX CAPACITY
Orangery		200
Great Hall	70' x 40'	150
Saloon	50' x 30'	72
with Great Hall		450
with Great Hall & Library		750
Library	180' x 30'	300

BLENHEIM PALACE
Woodstock

BLENHEIM PALACE, home of the 11th Duke of Marlborough and birthplace of Sir Winston Churchill, was built between 1705-1722 for John Churchill, 1st Duke of Marlborough, in grateful recognition of his magnificent victory at the Battle of Blenheim in 1704. One of England's largest private houses, it was built in the baroque style by Sir John Vanbrugh and is considered his masterpiece. The land and £240,000 were given by Queen Anne and a grateful nation.

Blenheim's wonderful interior reveals striking contrasts – from the lofty Great Hall to gilded state rooms and the majestic Long Library. The superb collection includes fine paintings, furniture, bronzes and the famous Marlborough Victories tapestries. The five-room Churchill Exhibition includes his birth room.

GARDENS

The Palace grounds reflect the evolution of grand garden design. Of the original work by Queen Anne's gardener, Henry Wise, only the Walled Garden remains; but dominating all is the superb landscaping of 'Capability' Brown. Dating from 1764, his work includes the lake, park and gardens. Achille Duchêne, employed by the 9th Duke, subsequently recreated the Great Court and built the Italian Garden on the east and the Water Terraces on the west of the Palace. Recently the Pleasure Gardens complex has been developed. This includes the Marlborough Maze, Herb Garden, Adventure Playground, Butterfly House and Putting Greens.

OPENING TIMES

SUMMER
Palace
Mid March - 31 October
Daily: 10.30am-5.30pm
Last admission 4.45pm.

WINTER
Park only
1 November - Mid March
The Duke of Marlborough reserves the right to close the Palace or Park or to amend admission prices without notice.

ADMISSION

(Prices: 12.3.01 - 31.10.01)
- Palace Tour and Churchill Exhibition
- Park
- Garden
- Butterfly House
- Herb & Lavender Garden
- Train
- Car or coach parking
- Maze & Adventure Play Area and rowing boat hire optional extras

    Adult £9.30
    Child (5 - 15 yrs.)......£4.80
    Child (16 & 17 yrs.)...£7.30
    OAP.........................£7.30
    Family £23.00
Groups
    Adult £7.50
    OAP/Student...........£6.50
    Child (5 - 15 yrs.)......£4.00
    Child (16 & 17 yrs.)...£6.50

- Blenheim Park, Butterfly House, Train, Parking, (Maze & Adventure Play Area and rowing boat hire optional extras).

    Coaches* £30.00
    Cars*.......................£6.00
    Adult**....................£2.00
    Child**....................£1.00

- Private visits† £15.00

* Including occupants.
** Pedestrians.
† By appointment only.
Min. charge of £375 (mornings and £525 (evenings).

BLENHEIM PALACE

Five Shops. Filming, Equestrian Events, Craft Fairs. Will consider any proposals (contact Admin Office). Lake (Rowing Boats for hire), Golf Buggy rides, Train rides. Photography outside only.

Corporate hospitality, including dinners and receptions. The Orangery seats 200 for luncheon or dinner, throughout the year together with the Spencer Churchill Conference Room. For the Palace contact the Administrator, & for the Orangery contact Sodexho Prestige tel: 01993 813874/811274.

Visitors may alight at the Palace entrance then park in allocated area. WCs.

2 Restaurants, 2 Cafeterias. Group capacity 150. Groups can book for afternoon tea, buffets and luncheon. Menus on request. Contact Sodexho Prestige for further info: 01993 813874/811274.

 Included in the cost of entry. Private and language tours may be pre-booked.

Unlimited for cars and coaches. Advise Administrator's office for groups of over 100. Coaches/groups welcome, without pre-booking. Group organisers guide available by post.

Blenheim has held the Sandford Award for an outstanding contribution to Heritage Education since 1982. Operated by a very experienced headmaster, education groups may study virtually all subjects at all four stages of the National Curriculum as well as have general interest or leisure visits. Tourism Studies (all levels) available.

Dogs on leads in Park. Guide dogs for the blind & hearing dogs for the deaf only in house and garden.

The Water Terrace

South East England

Owner:
Lord Saye & Sele

CONTACT

Mrs J Moorhouse
Broughton Castle
Banbury
OX15 5EB

Tel/Fax: 01295 276070

Tel/Fax: 01295 722547

e-mail: admin@broughton
castle.demon.co.uk

LOCATION

OS Ref. SP418 382

Broughton Castle is
2^1/2m SW of Banbury Cross
on the B4035,
Shipston-on-Stour -
Banbury Road.
Easily accessible from
Stratford-on-Avon,
Warwick, Oxford, Burford
and the Cotswolds.
M40/J11.

Rail: From London/
Birmingham to Banbury.

BROUGHTON CASTLE
Banbury

BROUGHTON CASTLE is essentially a family home lived in by Lord and Lady Saye & Sele and their family.

The original medieval Manor House, of which much remains today, was built in about 1300 by Sir John de Broughton. It stands on an island site surrounded by a 3-acre moat. The Castle was greatly enlarged between 1550 and 1600, at which time it was embellished with magnificent plaster ceilings, splendid panelling and fine fireplaces.

In the 17th century William, 8th Lord Saye & Sele, played a leading role in national affairs. He opposed Charles I's efforts to rule without Parliament and Broughton became a secret meeting place for the King's opponents.

During the Civil War William raised a regiment and he and his four sons all fought at the nearby Battle of Edgehill. After the battle the Castle was besieged and captured.

Arms and armour for the Civil War and from other periods are displayed in the Great Hall. Visitors may also see the gatehouse, gardens and park together with the nearby 14th century Church of St Mary, in which there are many family tombs, memorials and hatchments.

GARDENS

The garden area consists of mixed herbaceous and shrub borders containing many old roses. In addition, there is a formal walled garden with beds of roses surrounded by box hedging and lined by more mixed borders.

SUMMER

20 May - 12 September
Weds & Suns
2 - 5pm.

Also Thurs in July and August and all Bank Holiday Suns and Bank Holiday Mons (including Easter) 2 - 5pm.

Groups welcome on any day and at any time throughout the year by appointment.

ADMISSION

Adult	£4.50
Child (5-15yrs)	£2.00
OAP/Student	£4.00
Groups*	
Adult	£4.00
Child (5-15yrs)	£1.75
Student	£3.00
OAP	£4.00

* Min payment: adults £80, children £50.

Filming, product launches, advertising features, corporate events in park. Photography permitted for personal use. Brief guidance notes available in French, Spanish, Dutch, Italian, Japanese, German, Polish, Greek & Russian.

Visitors allowed vehicle access to main entrance.

Tea/coffee for guided groups if pre-booked. Other meals by arrangement.

Available to pre-booked groups at no extra charge. Not available on open days.

P 300 yards from the castle.

Welcome.

No dogs inside House.

STONOR
Henley-on-Thames

Owner:
Lord & Lady Camoys

CONTACT

Lisa Absalom
The Administrator
Stonor Park
Henley-on-Thames
Oxfordshire
RG9 6HF

Tel/Fax: 01491 638587

e-mail: lisa@
stonorpark.demon.co.uk

LOCATION

OS Ref. SU743 893

1 hr from London,
M4/J8/9. A4130 to
Henley-on-Thames.
On B480 NW of Henley.
A4130/B480 to Stonor.

Bus: 3m along the
Oxford - London route.

Rail: Henley-on-Thames
Station 5m.

STONOR, family home of Lord and Lady Camoys and the Stonor family for over 800 years, is set in a valley in the beautiful woods of the Chiltern Hills and surrounded by an extensive deer park.

The earliest part of the house dates from the 12th century, whilst most of the house was built in the 14th century. Early use of brick in Tudor times resulted in a more uniform façade concealing the earlier buildings, and changes to the windows and the roof in the 18th century reflect the Georgian appearance still apparent today.

Inside, the house shows strong Gothic decoration, also from the 18th century, and contains many items of rare furniture, sculptures, bronzes, tapestries, paintings and portraits of the family from Britain, Europe and America.

The Catholic Chapel used continuously through the Reformation is sited close by a pagan stone circle. In 1581 Stonor served as a sanctuary for St Edmund Campion, and an exhibition at the house features his life and work.

John Steane says of Stonor – *'If I had to suggest to a visitor who had only one day to sample the beauties of Oxfordshire I would suggest a visit to Stonor and a walk through its delectable park'.*

GARDENS

Extensive gardens enclosed at the rear of the house face south and have fine views over the park. The springtime display of daffodils is particularly outstanding. Fine irises and roses.

OPENING TIMES

**Suns & Bank Holiday
Mons**: April - September,
2 - 5.30pm.

Weds: July & August only:
2 - 5.30pm.

Private groups by
arrangement:
April - September,
Tue - Thur.

ADMISSION

House, Garden & Chapel
Adult £4.50
Child (under 14yrs).....Free
Groups* (12+)............£4.00

Garden and Chapel
Adult £2.50

* Min. 12 persons by a single
payment. Private guided
tours £5pp, min. 20 persons
and by a single payment.

School groups £2.50 per
head, 1 teacher for every
10 children admitted free.

Filming, craft fairs, photo shoots, car displays, product promotion. Evening tours and buffet suppers by prior arrangement. Lectures can be given on the property, its contents and history. No smoking and no photography in house.

Visitors may alight at the entrance before parking. Ramp access to gardens, tearoom & shop. House not suitable.

Open as house. Lunches, teas & suppers by arrangement for groups (20+). Licensed.

Outside normal hours for 20 - 60 people per tour. Tour time: 1¼ hrs. Single payments for group bookings.

100 yds away.

In grounds, on leads.

Tel. for details.

26A EAST ST HELEN STREET

Tel: 01865 242918

Abingdon, Oxfordshire

Owner: Oxford Preservation Trust   **Contact:** Ms Debbie Dance

One of best preserved examples of a 15th century dwelling in the area. Originally a Merchant's Hall House with later alterations, features include a remarkable domestic wall painting, an early oak ceiling, traceried windows and fireplaces. The remains of a 17th century boy's doublet found in the roof during restoration works is on display.

Location: OS Ref. SU497 969. 300 yards SSW of the market place and Town Hall.

Opening Times: By prior appointment.

Admission: Free.

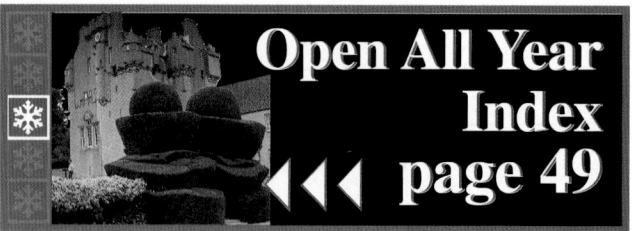

Open All Year
Index
◀◀◀ page 49

ARDINGTON HOUSE

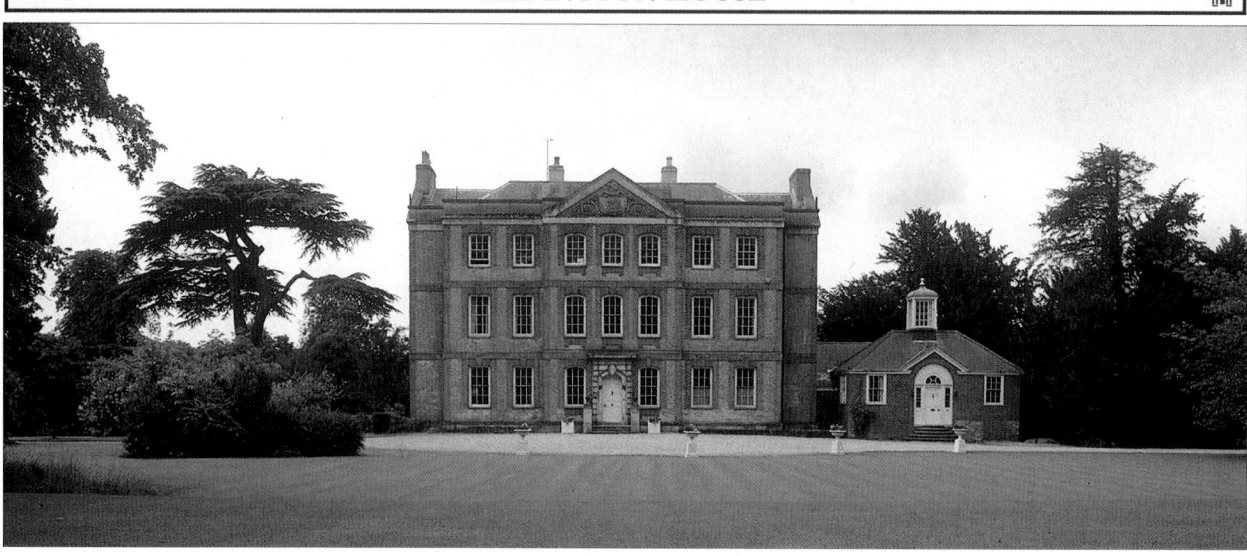

WANTAGE, OXFORDSHIRE OX12 8QA

Owner: *The Baring Family*   **Contact:** *Sharon Collerton*

Tel: 01235 821566   **Fax:** 01235 821151   **e-mail:** info@ardingtonhouse.com

Just a few miles south of Oxford stands the hauntingly beautiful, gracefully symmetric Ardington House. Surrounded by well-kept lawns, terraced gardens and peaceful paddocks this baroque house is still the private home of the Baring family. You'll find it in the village of Ardington in the lee of the Berkshire Downs close to the Ridgeway, the historic path that runs along the top of the Downs linking the Thames Valley to the Kennet. Its rooms to the south look across the garden and grazing horses to the river, well known to enthusiastic fly fisherman. To the front is an immaculately tended lawn, ideal for croquet and enjoyed by different generations of the Baring family as they grew up in this beautiful setting. Sir John Betjeman, one of the best loved poets of recent times, thought highly of this gracious home. But it doesn't end there because one of the greatest joys in this impressive home is the wood panelled dining room with its large oil painting of the father of the founder of this famous banking family.

The astonishing mixture of history, warmth and style you'll find at Ardington truly does place it in a class of its own.

Location: OS Ref. SU432 883. 12m S of Oxford, 12m N of Newbury, $2^{1}/_{2}$ m E of Wantage.

Opening Times: 1 - 4, 7 - 11, 14 - 16, 18, 21 May; 1 - 3, 6 - 7, 9 - 10, 13 - 16 Aug & BH Mons, 2.30 - 4.30pm.

Admission: House & Gardens: Adult £3.50.

ⓘ Conferences, product launches, films.   🍴   🍷 By arrangement. 🎟 By members of the family.   Ⓟ   🐕 Guide dogs only.   🔔   Ⓦ

ASHDOWN HOUSE 🌿

Tel: 01488 72584   **e-mail:** tadgen@smtp.ntrust.org.uk

Lambourn, Newbury RG16 7RE

Owner: The National Trust   **Contact:** Ashdown Estate Office

An extraordinary Dutch-style 17th century house, perched on the Berkshire Downs and famous for its association with Elizabeth of Bohemia (The Winter Queen), Charles I's sister, to whom the house was 'consecrated'. The interior has an impressive great staircase rising from hall to attic, and important paintings contemporary with the house. There are spectacular views from the roof over the formal parterre, lawns and surrounding countryside, as well as beautiful walks in neighbouring Ashdown Woods.

Location: OS Ref. SU282 820. $3^{1}/_{2}$ m N of Lambourn, on W side of B4000.

Opening Times: Hall, Stairway, Roof & Garden: Apr - end Oct: Weds & Sats. Guided tours of house only at 2.15pm, 3.15pm & 4.15pm from front door. Woodland: All year: daily except Fris, dawn - dusk.

Admission: Adult £2.10, Woodland Free. No reduction for groups which must book in writing.

ⓘ No WCs.   ♿ Garden suitable.   🎟 Obligatory.   Ⓟ 250 metres from house. 🐾 Woodland only, on leads.   ❄   Ⓦ

BLENHEIM PALACE 🏛

See pages 142/143 for double page entry.

BROOK COTTAGE

Tel: 01295 670303 / 670590

Well Lane, Alkerton, Nr Banbury OX15 6NL

Owner/Contact: Mrs David Hodges

4 acre hillside garden. Roses, clematis, water gardens, colour co-ordinated borders, trees, shrubs.

Location: OS Ref. SP378 428. 6m NW of Banbury, $1/_2$ m SW of A422 Banbury to Stratford-upon-Avon road.

Opening Times: 16 Apr - 26 Oct: Mon - Fri, 9am - 6pm. Evenings, weekends and all group visits by appointment.

Admission: Adult £3, OAP £2, Child Free. In aid of National Gardens Scheme.

BROUGHTON CASTLE 🏛

See page 144 for full page entry.

BUSCOT OLD PARSONAGE 🌿

Tel: 01793 762209

Buscot, Faringdon, Oxfordshire SN7 8DQ   **e-mail:** tbcjap@smtp.ntrust.org.uk

Owner: The National Trust   **Contact:** Coleshill Estate Office

An early 18th century house of Cotswold stone on the bank of the Thames with a small garden.

Location: OS Ref. SU231 973. 2m from Lechlade, 4m N of Faringdon on A417.

Opening Times: Apr - end Oct, Weds, 2 - 6pm by written appointment with tenant.

Admission: £1.20. Not suitable for groups.

BUSCOT PARK

Tel: 01367 240786 **Fax:** 01367 241794
e-mail: estbuscot@aol.com

Buscot, Faringdon, Oxfordshire SN7 8BU
Owner: The National Trust   **Contact:** Lord Faringdon
A late 18th century house with pleasure gardens, set within a park.
Location: OS Ref. SU239 973. Between Lechlade and Faringdon on A417.
Opening Times: House: 4 Apr - 28 Sept: Wed - Fri. Easter Sat & Sun, plus weekends of 28/29 Apr; 12/13, 26/27 May; 9/10, 23/24 Jun; 14/15, 28/29 Jul; 11/12, 25/26 Aug; 8/9, 22/23 Sept, last admission to house 5.30pm. Grounds: 2 Apr - 28 Sept: Mon - Fri (closed BH Mons) and same weekends as house, 2 - 6pm.
Admission: House & Grounds £4.40, Grounds only £3.30. Children half price. Groups must book in writing, or by fax or e-mail.

⌖ Not suitable. 🅿 (MW)

CHASTLETON HOUSE

Infoline/Fax: 01608 674355
e-mail: tchgen@smtp.ntrust.org.uk

Chastleton, Moreton-in-Marsh, Gloucestershire GL56 0SU
Owner: The National Trust   **Contact:** The Custodian
One of England's finest and most complete Jacobean houses, dating from 1612. It is filled with a mixture of rare and everyday objects and the atmosphere of four hundred years of continuous occupation by one family. The gardens have a Jacobean layout and the rules of modern croquet were codified here.
Location: OS Ref. SP248 291. 6m ENE of Stow-on-the-Wold. 1¹/₂ m NW of A436. Approach only from A436 between the A44 (W of Chipping Norton) and Stow.
Opening Times: 4 Apr - 29 Sept: Wed - Sat, 1 - 5pm, last admission 4pm. 3 Oct - 3 Nov: Wed - Sat, 1 - 4pm, last admission 3pm. Admission for all visitors (including NT members) by timed tickets booked in advance. Bookings can be made by telephone (01494 755585) on weekdays between 10am - 4pm.
Admission: Adult £5.20, Child £2.60. Family £13. Groups (11-25) by appointment.

⌖ Not suitable. 🅿 Coaches limited to 25 seat minibuses. 🐕 Guide dogs only.

CHRIST CHURCH CATHEDRAL

Tel: 01865 276154

The Sacristy, The Cathedral, Oxford OX1 1DP   **Contact:** Mr Jim Godfrey
12th century Norman Church, formerly an Augustinian monastery, given Cathedral status in 16th century by Henry VIII.
Location: OS Ref. SP515 059. Just S of city centre, off St Aldates. Entry via Meadow Gate visitors' entrance on S side of college.
Opening Times: Mon - Sat: 9am - 5pm. Suns: 1 - 5pm, closed Christmas Day. Services: weekdays 7.20am, 6pm. Suns: 8am, 10am, 11.15am & 6pm.
Admission: Adult £3, Child under 5 Free, Conc. £2, Family £6.

COGGES MANOR FARM MUSEUM

Tel: 01993 772602 **Fax:** 01993 703056

Church Lane, Witney, Oxfordshire OX8 6LA
Administered by: West Oxfordshire District Council   **Contact:** Carol Nightingale
The Manor House dates from the 13th century, rooms are furnished to show life at the end of the 19th century. Daily cooking on the Victorian range. On the first floor, samples of original wallpapers and finds from under the floorboards accompany the story of the history of the house. In one of the rooms, rare 17th century painted panelling survives. Farm buildings including two 18th century barns, stables and a thatched ox byre, display farm implements. Traditional breeds of farm animals, hand-milking demonstration each day. Seasonal produce from the walled kitchen garden sold in the museum shop.
Location: OS Ref. SP362 097. Just off A40 Oxford - Burford Road. Access by footbridge from centre of Witney, 600 yds. Vehicle access from S side of B4022 near E end of Witney.
Opening Times: Apr - end-Oct: Tue - Fri & BH Mons, 10.30am - 5.30pm; Sat & Sun, 12 - 5.30pm. Closed Good Fri. Early closing in Oct. Limited opening in Nov & Mar.
Admission: Adult £4, Child £2, Conc. £2.50 Family (2+2) £11.00

📷 ⌖ Ground floor suitable. WCs. 🅿 🐕 In grounds, on leads.

DEDDINGTON CASTLE ⌗

Tel: 023 9258 1059

Deddington, Oxfordshire
Owner: English Heritage   **Contact:** Area Manager
Extensive earthworks concealing the remains of a 12th century castle which was ruined as early as the 14th century.
Location: OS Ref. SP471 316. S of B4031 on E side of Deddington, 17m N of Oxford on A423. 5m S of Banbury.
Opening Times: Any reasonable time.
Admission: Free.

DITCHLEY PARK

Tel: 01608 677346

Enstone, Oxfordshire OX7 4ER
Owner: Ditchley Foundation   **Contact:** Brigadier Christopher Galloway
The most important house by James Gibbs with most distinguished interiors by Henry Flitcroft and William Kent.
Location: OS Ref. SP391 214. 2m NE from Charlbury. 13m NW of Oxford.
Opening Times: Visits only by prior arrangement with the Bursar.
Admission: £5 per person (minimum charge £40).

FAWLEY COURT

HISTORIC HOUSE & MUSEUM, HENLEY-ON-THAMES RG9 3AE
Owner: Marian Fathers   *Contact: The Secretary*

Tel: 01491 574917 **Fax:** 01491 411587
Designed by Christopher Wren, built in 1684 for Col W Freeman, decorated by Grinling Gibbons and by James Wyatt. The Museum consists of a library, various documents of the Polish Kings, a very well-preserved collection of historical sabres and many memorable military objects of the Polish army. Paintings, early books, numismatic collections, arms and armour.
Location: OS Ref. SU765 842. 1m N of Henley-on-Thames E to A4155 to Marlow.
Opening Times: May - Oct: Weds, Thurs & Suns, 2 - 5pm. Other dates by arrangement. Closed Whitsuntide and Nov - Apr inclusive.
Admission: House, Museum & Gardens: Adult £4, Child £1.50, Conc. £3. Groups (15+) £3.

📷 ⌖ Ground floor & grounds suitable. WC. 🅿 🐕 Guide dogs only.

GREAT COXWELL BARN

Tel: 01793 762209
e-mail: tbcjap@smtp.ntrust.org.uk

Great Coxwell, Faringdon, Oxfordshire
Owner: The National Trust   **Contact:** Coleshill Estate Office
A 13th century monastic barn, stone built with stone tiled roof, which has an interesting timber construction.
Location: OS Ref. SU269 940. 2m SW of Faringdon between A420 and B4019.
Opening Times: All year: daily at reasonable hours.
Admission: 50p.

Broughton Castle, Oxfordshire.

GREYS COURT

NT Photographic Library: Nick Meers

ROTHERFIELD GREYS, HENLEY-ON-THAMES, OXFORDSHIRE RG9 4PG

Owner: The National Trust   *Contact:* The Property Manager

Infoline: 01494 755564 **Tel:** 01491 628529

e-mail: tgrgen@smtp.ntrust.org.uk

Rebuilt in the 16th century and added to in the 17th, 18th and 19th centuries, the house is set amid the remains of the courtyard walls and towers of a 14th century fortified house. A Tudor donkey wheel, well-house and an ice house are still intact, and the garden contains Archbishop's Maze, inspired by Archbishop Runcie's enthronement speech in 1980.

Location: OS Ref. SU725 834. 3m W of Henley-on-Thames, E of B481.

Opening Times: 3 Apr - end Sept: House; Wed - Fri & BH Mons, 2 - 6pm (closed Good Fri) Garden: daily Tue - Sat & BH Mons 2 - 6pm (closed Good Fri) Last admission 5.30pm.

Admission: House & Garden: Adult £4.60, Child £2.30, Family £11.50. Garden only: £3.20, Family £8. Coach parties must book in advance.

Grounds partly suitable. WCs.   In car park only, on leads.

Contact Custodian.

University of Oxford Botanic Garden.

KINGSTON BAGPUIZE HOUSE

ABINGDON, OXFORDSHIRE OX13 5AX

Owner: Mr & Mrs Francis Grant   *Contact:* Mrs Francis Grant

Tel: 01865 820259 **Fax:** 01865 821659

A family home, this beautiful house originally built in the 1660s was remodelled in the early 1700s in red brick with stone facings. It has a cantilevered staircase and panelled rooms with some good furniture and pictures. Set in mature parkland, the gardens, including shrub border and woodland garden, contain a notable collection of trees, shrubs, perennials and bulbs planted for year round interest. A raised terrace walk leads to an 18th century panelled gazebo with views of the house and gardens, including a large herbaceous border and parkland. Available for special events, wedding receptions and filming. Facilities for small conferences.

Location: OS Ref. SU408 981. In Kingston Bagpuize village, off A415 Abingdon to Witney road S of A415/A420 intersection. Abingdon 5m, Oxford 9m.

Opening Times: Feb 18; Mar 4, 18; Apr 1, 14, 15, 16, 29; May 5, 6, 7, 26, 27, 28; Jun 10, 24; Jul 1, 21, 22; Aug 11, 12, 15, 25, 26, 27; Sept 8, 9, 12, 22, 23, 30; Oct 14; Nov 11. 2 - 5.30pm (tours of the house: 2.30 - 4.45pm). House: guided tours only. Last entry to garden 5pm.

Admission: House & Garden: Adult £3.50, Child £2.50, (children under 5yrs not admitted to house), OAP £3. Gardens: £1.50. (child under 5yrs Free). Groups (20-100) by appointment throughout the year, prices on request.

No photography.   Grounds suitable. WC.

Obligatory tours of house.

KINGSTONE LISLE PARK

Norman Hudson

KINGSTONE LISLE PARK, WANTAGE, OXON OX12 9QG

Owner: *Mr James Lonsdale*   ***Contact:*** *The Secretary*

Tel: 01367 820599   **Fax:** 01367 820749

A sensational Palladian house, set in 140 acres of parkland. Superb views up to the Lambourn Downs. Three lakes beside the house complete this very attractive landscape. The hall, in the style of Sir John Soane, gives a strong impression of entering an Italian palazzo with beautiful ornate plaster ceilings, columns and figurines. In complete contrast the inner hall becomes the classical English country house, the most exciting feature being the Flying Staircase winding its way up, totally unsupported. A fine collection of art, furniture, clocks, glass and needlework, together with the architecture, evoke admiration for the craftsmanship that has existed in Britain over the centuries. 12 acres of gardens. Suitable for films, wedding receptions, functions and 'fun days'.

Location: OS Ref. SU326 876. M4/J14.

Opening Times: Coach parties only, strictly by appointment.

Admission: Telephone for details.

In grounds, on leads.

MAPLEDURHAM HOUSE & WATERMILL

MAPLEDURHAM, READING RG4 7TR

Owner: *The Mapledurham Trust*   ***Contact:*** *Mrs Lola Andrews*

Tel: 01189 723350   **Fax:** 01189 724016   **e-mail:** mtrust1997@aol.com

Late 16th century Elizabethan home of the Blount family. Original plaster ceilings, great oak staircase, fine collection of paintings and a private chapel in Strawberry Hill Gothick added in 1797. Interesting literary connections with Alexander Pope, Galsworthy's *Forsyte Saga* and Kenneth Grahame's *Wind in the Willows*. 15th century watermill fully restored producing flour and bran which is sold in the giftshop.

Location: OS Ref. SU670 767. N of River Thames. 4m NW of Reading, 1¹/₂ m W of A4074.

Opening Times: Easter - Sept: Sats, Suns & BHs, 2 - 5.30. Last admission 5pm. Midweek parties by arrangement only (Tue - Thur).

Admission: Please call 01189 723350 for details.

Grounds suitable. WCs.   Guide dogs only.
11 holiday cottages available all year.

MILTON MANOR HOUSE

MILTON, ABINGDON, OXFORDSHIRE OX14 4EN

Owner: *Anthony Mockler-Barrett Esq*   ***Contact:*** *Gwendoline Marsh*

Tel: 01235 862321   **Fax:** 01235 831287

Dreamily beautiful mellow brick house, traditionally designed by Inigo Jones, with a celebrated Gothick library (pictured on right) and a startling Catholic chapel. Lived in by the family; pleasant, relaxed and informal atmosphere. Park with fine old trees, stables (pony rides usually available); swings, see-saw, small adventure playground. Walled garden, woodland walk, two lakes, variety of charming annuals and unusual ornaments. Plenty to see and enjoy for all ages.

Location: OS Ref. SU485 924. Just off A34, village and house signposted, 9m S of

Oxford, 15m N of Newbury. 3m from Abingdon and Didcot.

Opening Times: 1 - 15 May & 1 - 15 Aug: 2 - 5pm plus all BH weekends Easter - end Aug: Sat - Mon, 12 noon - 5pm. Guided tours of the house at 2pm, 3pm, 4pm.

Admission: House & Gardens: Adult £4, Child £2. House: Guided tours only. Grounds only: Adult £2.50, Child £1. Free parking. Groups by arrangement throughout the year. For group bookings only please write or phone 01235 831871.

Available.   Grounds suitable.   Guide dogs only.

MINSTER LOVELL HALL & DOVECOTE ⌗

Tel: 023 9258 1059

Witney, Oxfordshire

Owner: English Heritage　　　　**Contact:** Area Manager

The ruins of Lord Lovell's 15th century manor house stand in a lovely setting on the banks of the River Windrush.

Location: OS Ref. SP324 114. Adjacent to Minster Lovell Church, ½ m NE of village. 3m W of Witney off A40.

Opening Times: Any reasonable time.

Admission: Free.

NUFFIELD PLACE

Tel: 01491 641224

Huntercombe, Henley-on-Thames, Oxfordshire RG9 5RY

Owner: Nuffield College　　　　**Contact:** David Haenlein

The former home and gardens of Lord Nuffield founder of Morris Motors.

Location: OS Ref. SU679 879. Signposted off A4130 between Henley-on-Thames and Wallingford.

Opening Times: Apr - Sept: 2nd & 4th Suns in each month; 29 Apr, 13 & 27 May, 10 & 24 Jun, 8 & 22 Jul, 12 & 26 Aug, 9 & 23 Sept, 2 - 5pm.

Admission: Please contact for details.

PRIORY COTTAGES 🌿

Tel: 01793 762209　**e-mail:** tbcjap@smtp.ntrust.org.uk

1 Mill Street, Steventon, Abingdon, Oxfordshire OX13 6SP

Owner: The National Trust　　　**Contact:** Coleshill Estate Office

Former monastic buildings, converted into two houses. South Cottage contains the Great Hall of the original priory.

Location: OS Ref. SU466 914. 4m S of Abingdon, on B4017 off A34 at Abingdon West or Milton interchange on corner of The Causeway and Mill Street, entrance in Mill Street.

Opening Times: The Great Hall in South Cottage only: Apr - end Sept: Weds, 2 - 6pm by written appointment.

Admission: £1.

ROUSHAM HOUSE

Nr STEEPLE ASTON, BICESTER, OXFORDSHIRE OX6 3QX

Owner/Contact: Charles Cottrell-Dormer Esq

Tel: 01869 347110/0860 360407

Rousham represents the first stage of English landscape design and remains almost as William Kent (1685 - 1748) left it. One of the few gardens of this date to have escaped alteration. Includes Venus' Vale, Townesend's Building, seven-arched Praeneste, the Temple of the Mill and a sham ruin known as the 'Eyecatcher'. The house was built in 1635 by Sir Robert Dormer.

Location: OS Ref. SP477 242. E of A4260, 12m N of Oxford, S of B4030, 7m W of Bicester.

Opening Times: House: Apr - Sept: Wed, Sun and BH Mon 2 - 4.30pm. Garden: All year: daily, 10am - 4.30pm.

Admission: House: £3. Garden: Adult £3. No children under 15yrs.

♿ Partially suitable.　🎥 Obligatory.　

RYCOTE CHAPEL ⌗

Tel: 023 9258 1059

Rycote, Oxfordshire

Owner: English Heritage　　　　**Contact:** Area Manager

A 15th century chapel with exquisitely carved and painted woodwork. It has many intriguing features, including two roofed pews and a musicians' gallery.

Location: OS165 Ref. SP667 046. 3m SW of Thame, off A329. 1½ m NE of M40/J7.

Opening Times: 1 Apr - 30 Sept: Fri - Sun & BHs, 2 - 6pm.

Admission: Adult £1.70, Child 90p, Conc. £1.30. 15% discount for groups (11+).

STANTON HARCOURT MANOR 🏛

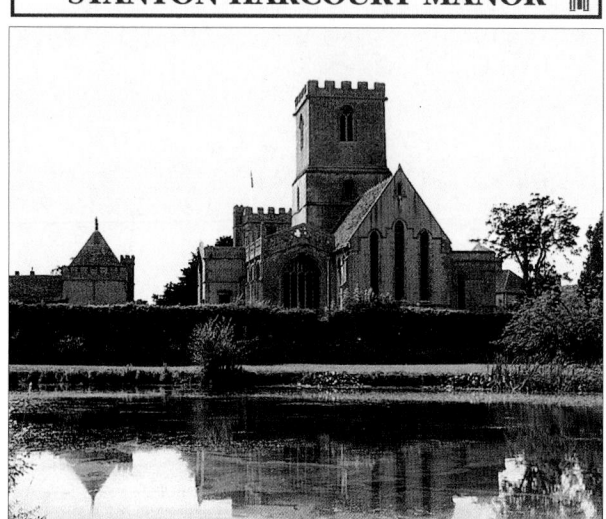

STANTON HARCOURT, Nr WITNEY, OXFORDSHIRE OX8 1RJ

Owner/Contact: The Hon Mrs Gascoigne

Tel: 01865 881928　**Answerphone / Fax:** 01865 880117

12 acres of garden with Great Fish Pond and Stew Ponds provide tranquil surroundings for the unique mediaeval buildings, Old Kitchen (Alexander) Pope's Tower and Domestic Chapel. The house, a fine example of a very early unfortified Manor House built to house the Harcourt family and its retainers, is still maintained as the family home.

Location: OS Ref. SP416 056. 9m W of Oxford, 5m SE of Witney off B4449 between Eynsham and Standlake.

Opening Times: 15, 16, 26, 29 Apr, 3, 6, 7, 17, 20, 24, 27, 28 May, 14, 17, 28 Jun, 1, 5, 8, 19, 22 Jul, 2, 5, 16, 19, 23, 26, 27 Aug, 6, 9, 20, 23 Sept: 2 - 6pm.

Admission: House & Garden: Adult £5, Child (under 12yrs)/OAP £3. Garden: Adult £3, Child (under 12yrs) /OAP £2. Group visits and access to the upper floors of Popes Tower by prior arrangement.

♿　🖼　🅿 Limited.　🐕 Guide dogs in grounds.

STONOR 🏛

See page 145 for full page entry.

See page 145 for full page entry.

SWALCLIFFE BARN

Tel: 01295 788278

Swalcliffe Village, Banbury, Oxfordshire　**Contact:** Jeffrey Demmar

15th century half cruck barn, houses agricultural and trade vehicles.

Location: OS Ref. SP378 378. 6m W of Banbury Cross on B4035.

Opening Times: Easter - end Oct: Suns & BHs, 2 - 5pm.

Admission: Free.

Website Index page 39

UNIVERSITY OF OXFORD BOTANIC GARDEN

ROSE LANE, OXFORD OX1 4AZ

Owner: *University of Oxford*   **Contact:** *Timothy Walker*

Tel/Fax: 01865 286690 **e-mail:** postmaster@botanic-garden.ox.ac.uk

Founded in 1621; oldest botanic garden in Britain; 8,000 plants from all over the world; original walled garden; many trees over 200 years old; herbaceous borders, recently renovated rock and bog gardens; national collection of euphorbias, tropical glasshouses including a 100 year old cacti and waterlillies; a peaceful oasis in the city centre.

Location: OS Ref. SP520 061. E end of High Street, on the banks of the River Cherwell.

Opening Times: Apr - Sept: 9am - 5pm (glasshouses: 10am - 4.30pm). Oct - Mar: 9am - 4.30pm (glasshouses: 10am - 4pm). Closed 25 Dec & Good Fri. Last admission 4.15pm.

Admission: Adult £2, Child (under 12ys) Free.

ℹ️ WCs for disabled only. ♿ 🎨 By arrangement. 🅿 No parking. 🏛

🐕 Guide dogs only. ❄

WATERPERRY GARDENS

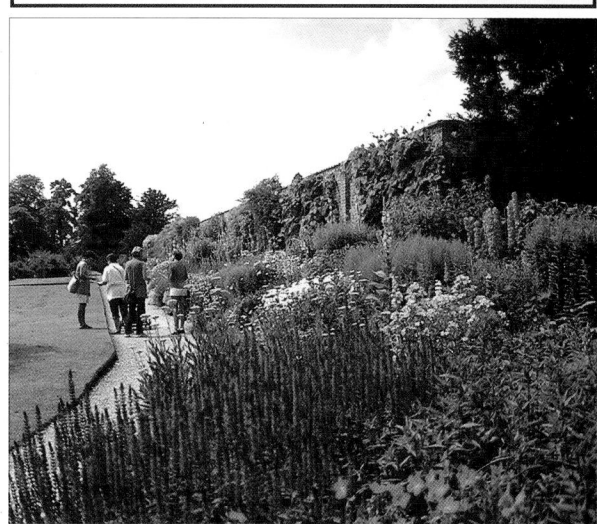

WATERPERRY, Nr WHEATLEY, OXFORDSHIRE OX33 1LB

Owner: *School of Economic Science*   **Contact:** *P Maxwell*

Tel: 01844 339226 **Fax:** 01844 339883

e-mail: office@waterperrygardens.f.s.net.co.uk

Here is the chance to enjoy the order of careful cultivation. See one of Britain's finest herbaceous borders which flowers continually from May to October. Rose garden; alpine gardens, formal garden, shrub borders, perennial borders and river walk.

Location: OS Ref. SP630 063. Oxford 9m, London 52m, Birmingham 42m. M40/J8. Well signposted locally.

Opening Times: Apr - Oct: 9am - 5.30pm. Nov - Mar: 9am - 5pm. Closed during Art in Action Festival.

Admission: Adult £3.40, Child £1.75, OAP £2.90. Groups (20+) £2.75, Child £1.50.

🏠 🚻 ♿ Partially suitable. ☕ 🎨 By arrangement.

🅿 Limited for coaches. 🏛 🐕 In grounds, on leads. ❄ 🏷

University of Oxford Botanic Garden.

Crown Copyright: Historic Royal Palaces

HAMPTON COURT PALACE
Surrey

Managed by:
Historic Royal Palaces

CONTACT

Hampton Court Palace
Surrey
KT8 9AU

For all enquiries
please telephone:

Tel: 020 8781 9500

LOCATION

OS Ref. TQ155 686

From M25/J15 and A312,
or M25/J12 and A308, or
M25/J10 and A307.

Rail: From London
Waterloo direct to
Hampton Court (32 mins).

The magnificent Hampton Court Palace has been a favoured home to some of our most famous Kings and Queens from Henry VIII to George II. Today it serves to intrigue and amaze thousands of visitors a year.

Cardinal Wolsey created it; Henry VIII, Hampton Court's most famous occupant and first royal owner, spent £62,000 enlarging it (£18 million in today's terms); Charles I was imprisoned in it; William III and Mary II commissioned Sir Christopher Wren to rebuild it; and Queen Victoria opened its doors to the public. Today the beauty of Wren's building is combined with the finest Tudor architecture in Britain.

Costumed guides bring the Palace to life, with informative tours of the sumptuous interiors of the State Apartments, giving a unique insight into the daily lives of the Kings and their courtiers, and entertaining with tales of the etiquette and gossip of court life throughout the centuries.

The Chapel Royal is a stunning example of the Palace's rich interiors, while the Great Hall is still decorated with Henry VIII's priceless Flemish tapestries. Hampton Court is also home to important Renaissance paintings from the collection of HM The Queen.

The Tudor Kitchens are the most extensive surviving 16th century kitchens in Europe. They once cooked for over a thousand people a day, and are laid out as if a feast was being prepared, with a roaring log fire and boiling cauldrons.

Hampton Court Palace is set in sixty acres of beautiful riverside Tudor, baroque and Victorian gardens, which feature the world famous maze, and the Great Vine, the oldest and largest grapevine in the world, believed to have been planted in 1768 by 'Capability' Brown.

With its five hundred years of royal history, Hampton Court Palace is a living tapestry portraying the life and times of Henry VIII to George II. It is both visually and historically interesting, and a visit here has something for everyone.

❖

SUMMER
Mid March - mid October
Tue - Sun:
9.30am - 6pm
Mon: 10.15am - 6pm.

WINTER
Mid October - mid March
Tue - Sun: 9.30am - 4.30pm
Mon: 10.15am - 4.30pm

Closed 24 - 26 December.

Last admission 45 mins
before closing.

ADMISSION

Adult	£10.50
Child (under 16yrs)	£7.00
Child (under 5yrs)	Free
OAP/Conc.	£8.00
Family (2+3)	£31.40

Crown Copyright: Historic Royal Palaces

ℹ️ Information Centre.
No photography indoors.

🍷 Available by arrangement.

♿ Motorised buggies available at main entrance. WCs.

🍴 Licensed.

P Ample for cars, coach parking nearby.

Rates on request.

🐕 In grounds, on leads. Guide dogs only in Palace.

❄️

SPECIAL EVENTS

For a full list of special events
please telephone for details.

CONFERENCE/FUNCTION

ROOM	SIZE	MAX CAPACITY
Great Hall	88'6" x 35'6"	280/400
Cartoon Gallery	22'6" x 116'	220/350
Gt Watching Chamber	66'6" x 25'	120
Painted Room	33'3" x 21'3"	60/100
Ante Room	22' x 21'6"	60/100
King's Award Chamber	60'3" x 36'4"	120/150
Public Dining Room	31'6" x 55'6"	80/150

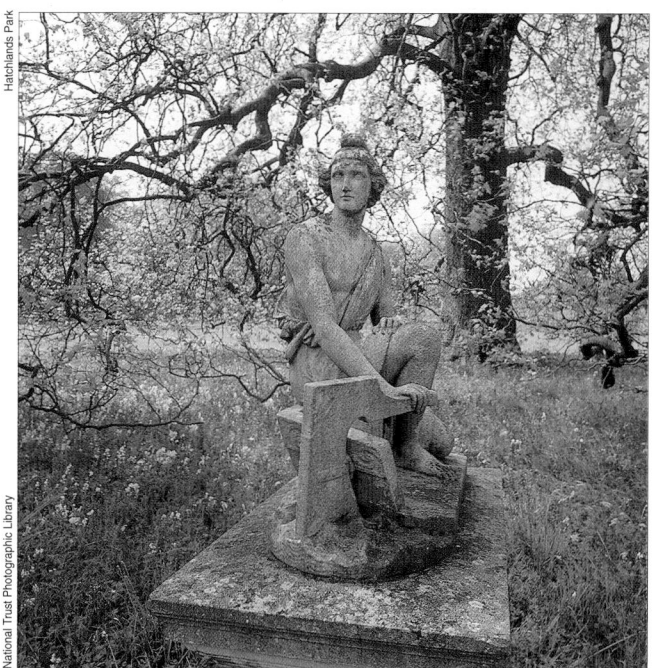

Hatchlands Park

National Trust Photographic Library

Clandon Park

National Trust Photographic Library

HATCHLANDS/CLANDON PARK
Guildford

Owner: The National Trust

CONTACT

The Property Manager
Hatchlands Park/
Clandon Park
East Clandon
Guildford
Surrey
GU4 7RT

Tel: 01483 222482

Fax: 01483 223176

e-mail: shagen@
smtp.ntrust.org.uk

LOCATION

HATCHLANDS
OS Ref. TQ063 516

E of East Clandon
on the A246 Guildford -
Leatherhead road.

Rail: Clandon BR
2¹/₂ m,
Horsley 3m.

CLANDON
OS Ref. TQ042 512

At West Clandon on
the A247, 3m E of
Guildford.

Rail: Clandon BR 1m.

HATCHLANDS PARK & CLANDON PARK were built during the 18th century and are set amidst beautiful grounds. They are two of England's most outstanding country houses and are only five minutes' drive apart.

Hatchlands Park was built in 1758 for Admiral Boscawen and is set in a beautiful Repton park offering a variety of park and woodland walks. Hatchlands contains splendid interiors by Robert Adam, decorated in appropriately nautical style. It houses the Cobbe Collection, the world's largest group of early keyboard instruments associated with famous composers, eg Purcell, J C Bach, Chopin, Mahler, Elgar and Marie Antoinette. There is also a small garden by Gertrude Jekyll

flowering from late May to early July.

Clandon Park is a grand Palladian mansion, built c1730 by the Venetian architect, Leoni and notable for its magnificent two-storey marble hall. The house is rightly acclaimed for its remarkable collection of 18th century porcelain, textiles and furniture, which includes the Ivo Forde Meissen collection of Italian comedy figures and a series of Mortlake tapestries. The attractive gardens feature a parterre, grotto, Dutch garden and a Maori house with a fascinating history. Clandon is also home to the Queen's Royal Surrey Regiment Museum. The excellent restaurant is renowned for its Sunday lunches - booking is advisable.

Clive Barda, London.

The Cobbe Collection of historic keyboard instruments can be seen at Hatchlands Park. Concerts and tours take place throughout the season. Both Beethoven and Schubert owned pianos made by Graf, the maker of the piano shown on the left, and many instruments in the collection were owned or played by great composers, including Chopin, Mahler and Elgar.

The Cobbe Collection Trust
Hatchlands Park, East Clandon
Guildford GU4 7RT
Tel: 01483 211474

Piano by Conrad Graf, Vienna, c.1820.

OPENING TIMES

HATCHLANDS
House
1 April - 31 October
Tue - Thur,
Suns & BH Mon,
Fris in August only.
2 - 5.30pm.

Park Walks
Daily (April - October)
11am - 6pm. Trail leaflets.

CLANDON
House
1 April - 4 November
Tue - Thur, Suns &
BH Mons, Good Fri
& Easter Sat
11am - 5pm.

Garden
As house: 9am - dusk.

Museum
1 April - 4 November
Tue - Thur & Suns,
BH Mons, Good Fri
& Easter Sat
12 noon - 5pm.

ADMISSION

Hatchlands
Adult £5.00
Park Walks £2.00
Child £2.50
Park Walks £1.00
Family £12.50
Groups (Tue - Thur only)
Adult £4.00

Clandon
Adult £5.00
Child £2.50
Family £12.50
Groups (Tue - Thur only)
Adult £4.00

Combined ticket
Hatchlands/Clandon .. £7.50
Family £18.00
Under 5s Free

CONFERENCE/FUNCTION		
ROOM	SIZE	MAX CAPACITY
Marble Hall Clandon Pk	40' x 40'	160 seated 200 standing

Clandon Park. Tel: 01483 222482. No photography.

For Clandon wedding receptions Tel: 01483 224912.

Hatchlands suitable. Clandon partially suitable. WCs.

Hatchlands: 01483 211120.

Licensed. Clandon: 01483 222502. H'lands: 01483 211120.

Clandon - by arrangement. Connoisseur Tours.

Hatchlands only.

Children's quizzes available.

Clandon only.

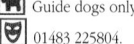

Guide dogs only.

01483 225804.

South East England

LOSELEY PARK
Guildford

LOSELEY PARK, built in 1562 by Sir William More, is a fine example of Elizabethan architecture, its mellow stone brought from the ruins of Waverley Abbey now over 850 years old. The house is set amid magnificent parkland grazed by the Loseley Jersey herd. Many visitors comment on the very friendly atmosphere of the house, it is a country house, the family home of descendants of the builder.

Furniture has been acquired by the family and includes an early 16th century Wrangelschrank beautifully inlaid with many different woods, a Queen Anne cabinet, Georgian armchairs and settee, a Hepplewhite four-poster bed and King George IV's coronation chair. The King's bedroom has Oudenarde tapestry and a carpet commemorating James I's visit.

The Christian pictures include the Henri Met de Bles triptych of the Nativity and modern mystical pictures of the living Christ, St Francis and St Bernadette. A Christian Cancer Help Centre meets twice monthly. Loseley House is available for dinners, functions and Civil weddings.

GARDEN

A magnificent Cedar of Lebanon presides over the front lawn. Parkland adjoins the lawn and a small lake adds to the beauty of Front Park. In the Walled Garden are mulberry trees, yew hedges, a grass terrace and a moat walk with herbaceous borders. Other features include an award-winning rose garden, a herb garden, flower garden, vegetable garden and idyllic fountain garden.

Owner:
Mr Michael More-Molyneux

CONTACT

Michelle Wheeler
Loseley Park
Guildford
Surrey
GU3 1HS

Tel: 01483 304440

Fax: 01483 302036

e-mail: enquiries@ loseley-park.com

LOCATION

OS Ref. SU975 471

30m S of London, leave A3 S of Guildford on to B3000. Signposted.

Bus: 1^1/4 m from House.

Rail: Farncombe 1^1/2m, Guildford 2m, Godalming 3m.

Air: Heathrow 30m, Gatwick 30m.

CONFERENCE/FUNCTION		
ROOM	SIZE	MAX CAPACITY
Tithe Barn	100' x 18'	200
Marquee		sites available
Great Hall	70' x 40'	100
Drawing Rm	40' x 30'	50
Walled Gdn	Marquee	sites

Chapel. New lakeside walk. Business launches & promotions. 10 - 12 acre field can be hired in addition to the lawns. Fashion shows, air displays, archery, garden parties, shows, rallies, filming, parkland, moat walk & terrace. Lectures can be arranged on the property, its contents, gardens & history. Loseley Christian Trust Exhibition, children's play area, picnic area, nature trail, home to Jersey herd since 1916; No unaccompanied children, no photography in house, no videos on estate. All group visits must be booked in advance.

Special functions, banquets and conference catering. Additional marquees for hire. Wedding receptions.

May alight at entrance to property. Access to all areas except house first floor. WCs.

Courtyard Tea Room.

Obligatory. Tour time for house, 40 mins.

150 cars, 6 coaches. Summer overflow car park.

Guide dogs only.

OPENING TIMES

SUMMER
Garden, Shop & Tea Room
May - September
Wed - Sun, 11am - 5pm.

House Tours
June - August
Wed - Sun, 1 - 5pm.

ALL YEAR
Tithe Barn, House and Grounds available for private/business functions, Civil weddings and receptions.

ADMISSION

House & Gardens
Adult	£6.00
Child (3-16yrs)	£3.00
Conc.	£5.00
Child (under 3yrs)	Free

Groups (15+)
Adult	£4.50
Child (3-16yrs)	£2.50
Conc.	£3.50

SPECIAL EVENTS

- **FEB 23 - 25:**
  Home Design Exhibition.
- **MAR 23 - 25:**
  Antique Fair.
- **JUN 1 - 3:**
  Craft Fair.
- **JUL 20 - 22:**
  Garden Show.
- **AUG 12:**
  Outdoor Concert.
- **OCT 19 - 21:**
  Antique Fair.

CARSHALTON HOUSE

Tel: 020 8770 4781 **Fax:** 020 8770 4777

Pound Street, Carshalton, Surrey SM5 3PN

Owner: St Philomena's Catholic High School for Girls   **Contact:** Ms V Murphy

A Queen Anne mansion built c1707, now in use as a school, with grounds originally laid out by Charles Bridgeman.

Location: OS Ref. TQ275 644. On A232 just S of junction with B278.

Opening Times: Please telephone for details.

Admission: Adult £3, Child under 16/Full-time students £1.50.

CLANDON/HATCHLANDS PARK   See page 153 for full page entry.

CLAREMONT LANDSCAPE GARDEN

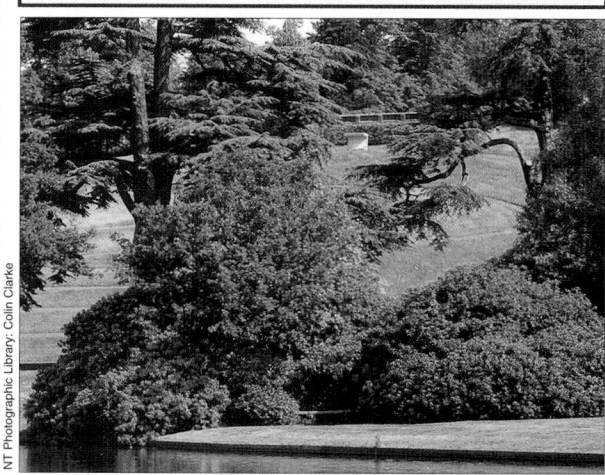

NT Photographic Library: Colin Clarke

PORTSMOUTH ROAD, ESHER, SURREY KT10 9JG

Owner: The National Trust *Contact:* The Property Manager

Tel: 01372 467806 **Fax:** 01372 464394 **e-mail:** sclgen@smtp.ntrust.org.uk

One of the earliest surviving English landscape gardens, restored to its former glory. Begun by Sir John Vanbrugh and Charles Bridgeman before 1720, the garden was extended and naturalised by William Kent. 'Capability' Brown also made improvements. Features include a lake, island with pavilion, grotto, turf amphitheatre, viewpoints and avenues.

Location: OS Ref. TQ128 632. On S edge of Esher, on E side of A307 (no access from Esher bypass).

Opening Times: Jan - end Mar, Nov - end Dec: daily except Mons: 10am - 5pm or sunset if earlier. Apr - end Oct: daily: Mon - Fri, 10am - 6pm, Sats, Suns & BHs, 10am - 7pm. NB: closed 10/11 Jul from 2pm, 12 - 15 Jul and all day 25 Dec & 1 Jan.

Admission: Adult £3.50, Child £1.75. Coach parties must book; no coach parties on Suns. Family (2+2) £8.75. Groups (15+), £3. 50p discount if using public transport.

Limited suitability. WC. No dogs (Apr - Oct). Telephone for details.

CROYDON PALACE

Tel: 020 8688 2027

Old Palace Road, Croydon, Surrey CR0 1AX

Owner/Contact: The Whitgift Foundation

A residence of the Archbishops of Canterbury between the 12th and 18th centuries. 15th century Banqueting Hall (one of the outstanding great medieval halls of London); Norman Undercroft; 15th century Guard Room and Chapel; Tudor Long Gallery; Elizabeth I's bedroom. West wing contains some of the earliest medieval brickwork in England.

Location: OS Ref. TQ320 654. 200 yds S of Croydon parish church, 400 yds W of Croydon High St.

Opening Times: 17 - 21 Apr, 28 May - 1 Jun, 16 - 21 Jul and 23 - 28 Jul.

Admission: Adult £4, Child/OAP £3.

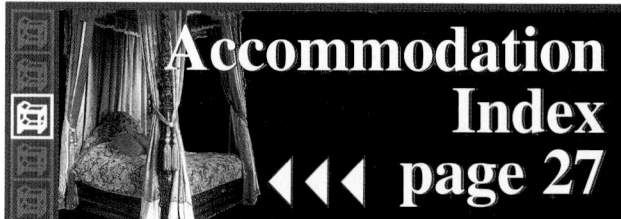

Accommodation Index ◀◀◀ ◀◀ page 27

DAPDUNE WHARF

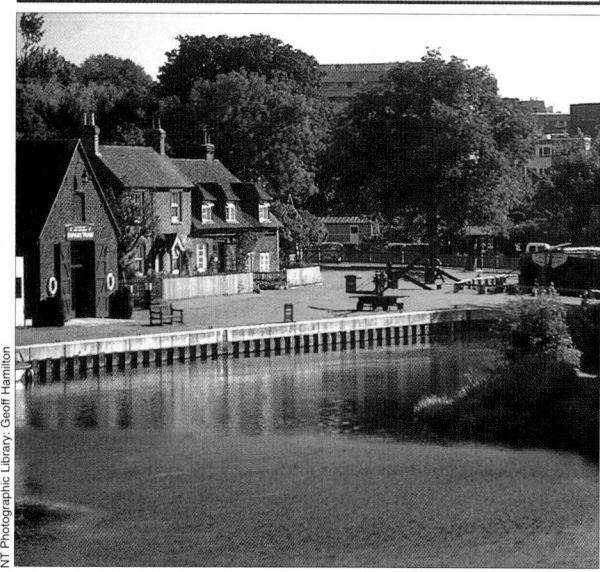

NT Photographic Library: Geoff Hamilton

RIVER WEY NAVIGATIONS, WHARF ROAD, GUILDFORD GU1 4RR

Owner: The National Trust *Contact:* Andrea Selley

Tel: 01483 561389 **Fax:** 01483 531667 **e-mail:** swybeb@smtp.ntrust.org.uk

Dapdune Wharf is the centrepiece of one of The National Trust's most unusual properties, the River Wey Navigations. Restored wharf buildings and a Wey barge can be seen. Interactive exhibits and displays tell the fascinating story of Surrey's secret waterway, one of the first British rivers to be made navigable.

Location: OS Ref. SU993 502. On Wharf Road to rear of Surrey County Cricket Ground, 1/2 m N of Guildford town centre off Woodbridge Road (A322).

Opening Times: 31 Mar - 4 Nov: Thurs, Sats, Suns & BHs, 11am - 5pm. River bus service 11am - 5pm

Admission: Adult £2.50, Child £1, Family £6. Groups (booked, min 15): Adult £2.

By arrangement. Limited. In grounds, on leads.

FARNHAM CASTLE

Tel: 01252 721194 **Fax:** 01252 711283

Farnham, Surrey GU9 0AG   **e-mail:** info@cibfarnham.com

Owner/Contact: The Church Commissioners

Bishop's Palace built in Norman times by Henry of Blois, with Tudor and Jacobean additions.

Location: OS Ref. SU839 474. 1/2 m N of Farnham town centre on A287.

Opening Times: Please telephone for details.

Admission: Adult £2, Child, £1, Conc. £1.50 (2000 prices).

FARNHAM CASTLE KEEP

Tel: 01252 713393

Castle Hill, Farnham, Surrey GU6 0AG

Owner: English Heritage   **Contact:** The Head Custodian

Used as a fortified manor by the medieval Bishops of Winchester, this motte and bailey castle has been in continuous occupation since the 12th century. You can visit the large shell-keep enclosing a mound in which are massive foundations of a Norman tower.

Location: OS Ref. SU839 474. 1/2 m N of Farnham town centre on A287.

Opening Times: 1 Apr - 30 Sept: 10am - 6pm. 1 - 31 Oct, 10am - 5pm.

Admission: Adult £2.10, Child, £1.10, Conc. £1.60.

Ground floor & grounds. Free. In grounds, on leads.

GODDARDS

Tel: 01628 825920 or 01628 825925 (bookings)

Abinger Common, Dorking, Surrey RH5 6TH

Owner: The Lutyens Trust, leased to The Landmark Trust   **Contact:** The Landmark Trust

Built by Sir Edwin Lutyens in 1898 - 1900 and enlarged by him in 1910. Garden by Gertrude Jekyll. Given to the Lutyens Trust in 1991 and now managed and maintained by the Landmark Trust, which let buildings for self-catering holidays. The whole house, apart from the library, is available for up to 12 people. Full details of Goddards and 170 other historic buildings available for holidays are featured in The Landmark Handbook (price £9.50 refundable against booking), from The Landmark Trust, Shottesbrooke, Maidenhead, Berkshire SL6 3SW.

Location: OS Ref. TQ120 450. 4 1/2 m SW of Dorking on the village green in Abinger Common. Signposted Abinger Common, Friday Street and Leith Hill from A25.

Opening Times: Strictly by appointment. Must be booked in advance, including parking, which is very limited. Visits booked for Weds afternoons from the Wed after Easter until the last Wed of Oct, between 2.30 - 5pm. Only those with pre-booked tickets will be admitted.

Admission: £3. Tickets available from Mrs Baker on 01306 730871, Mon - Fri, 9am & 6pm. Visitors will have access to part of the garden and house only.

HAMPTON COURT PALACE

See page 152 for full page entry.

HATCHLANDS/CLANDON PARK

See page 153 for full page entry.

HONEYWOOD HERITAGE CENTRE

Tel: 020 8770 4297 **Fax:** 020 8770 4777

e-mail: lbshoneywood@netscapeonline.co.uk

Honeywood Walk, Carshalton, Surrey SM5 3NX

Owner: London Borough of Sutton   **Contact:** The Curator

A 17th century listed building next to the picturesque Carshalton Ponds, containing displays on many aspects of the history of the London Borough of Sutton plus a changing programme of exhibitions and events on a wide range of subjects. Attractive garden at rear.

Location: OS Ref. TQ279 646. On A232 approximately 4m W of Croydon.

Opening Times: Wed - Fri, 10am - 5pm. Sat, Suns & BH Mons, 10am - 5.30pm. Tearooms open Tue - Sun, 10am - 5pm.

Admission: Adult £1.20, Child 50p, under 5 Free. Groups by arrangement.

Ground floor. WC. P Limited. Guide dogs only. Telephone for details.

KEW GARDENS

Tel: 020 8940 1171 **Fax:** 020 8332 5197

Kew, Richmond, Surrey TW9 3AB   **Contact:** Enquiry Unit

Kew's 300 acres offer many special attractions: including the 65ft high Palm House.

Location: OS Ref. TQ188 776. A307. Junction A307 and A205 (1m Chiswick roundabout M4).

Opening Times: 9.30am, daily except Christmas Day and New Year's Day. Closing time varies according to the season. Please telephone for further information.

Admission: Adult £5, Child £2.50, Conc. £3.50, Family £13. Groups 20% discount when pre-booked and paid. Prices subject to revision April 2001.

Loseley Park, Surrey.

LITTLE HOLLAND HOUSE

Tel: 020 8770 4781 **Fax:** 020 8770 4777

e-mail: valary.murphy@sutton.gov.uk

40 Beeches Avenue, Carshalton, Surrey SM5 3LW

Owner: London Borough of Sutton   **Contact:** Ms V Murphy

The home of Frank Dickinson (1874 - 1961) artist, designer and craftsman, who dreamt of a house that would follow the philosophy and theories of William Morris and John Ruskin. Dickinson designed, built and furnished the house himself from 1902 onwards. The Grade II* listed interior features handmade furniture, metal work, carvings and paintings produced by Dickinson in the Arts and Crafts style.

Location: OS Ref. TQ275 634. On B278 1m S of junction with A232.

Opening Times: First Sun of each month and BH Suns & Mons, 1.30 - 5.30pm.

Admission: Free. Groups by arrangement, £2 per person (includes talk and guided tour).

ℹ️ No photography in house. Ground floor only. By arrangement. P No parking. Guide dogs only.

LOSELEY PARK

See page 154 for full page entry.

OAKHURST COTTAGE

Tel: 01428 684090

Hambledon, Godalming, Surrey GU8 4HF

Owner: The National Trust   **Contact:** The Witley Centre

A small 16th century timber-framed cottage, painted by both Helen Allingham and Myles Birket Foster, containing furniture and artefacts reflecting two or more centuries of continuing occupation. There is a delightful cottage garden and a small barn containing agricultural implements.

Location: OS Ref. SU965 385. Hambledon, Surrey.

Opening Times: 31 Mar - 4 Nov: Weds, Thurs, Sats, Suns & BH Mons, 2 - 5pm. Strictly by appointment only.

Admission: Adult £2.50, Child £1.25 (including guided tour). No reduction for parties.

Not suitable. Obligatory, by arrangement. P Limited.

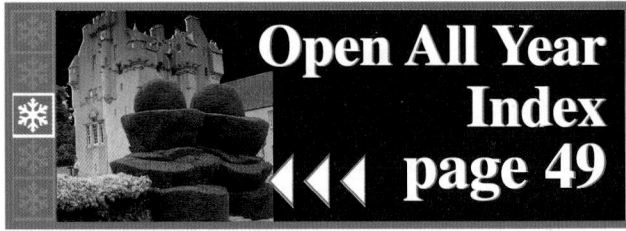
Open All Year
Index
page 49

PAINSHILL LANDSCAPE GARDEN

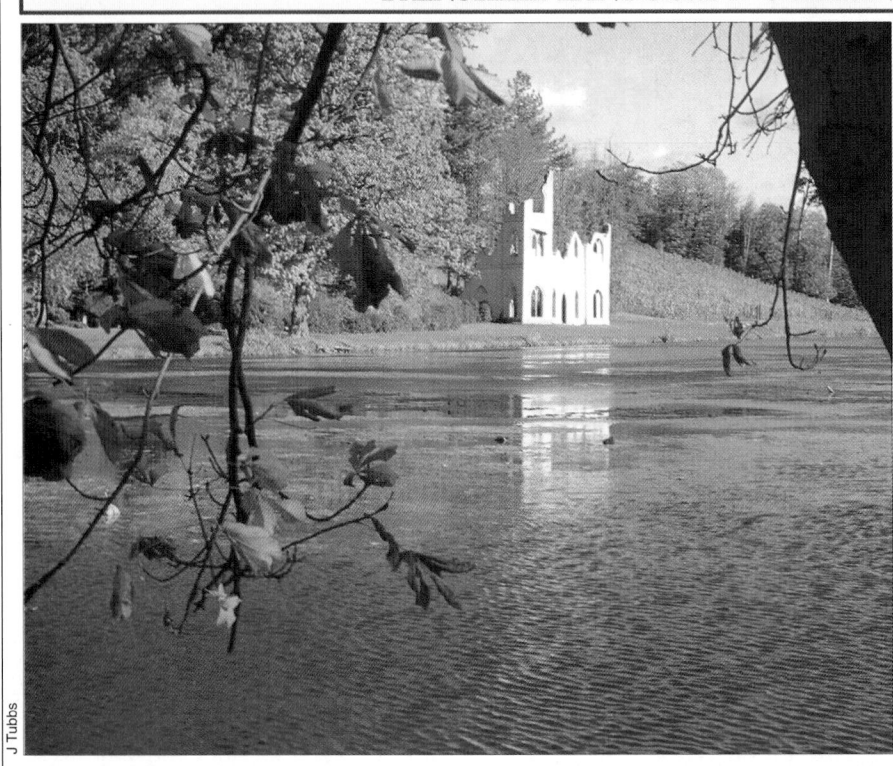

J Tubbs

PORTSMOUTH ROAD, COBHAM, SURREY KT11 1JE

Owner: Painshill Park Trust
Contact: Visitor Management

Tel: 01932 868113 **Fax:** 01932 868001

One of Europe's finest 18th century landscape gardens, contemporary with Stourhead and Stowe, created by the Hon Charles Hamilton between 1738 - 1773. Europa Nostra Medal winner for 'exemplary restoration'. Situated in 158 acres, visitors can take a circuit walk through a series of emerging scenes, each one more surprising than the last. A 14-acre lake fed by a massive waterwheel gives a breathtaking setting for a variety of spectacular features including a Gothic temple, ruined abbey, Turkish tent, crystal grotto, Chinese bridge, magnificent Cedars of Lebanon, replanted 18th century shrubberies and vineyard. Available for corporate and private hire, location filming, wedding receptions, etc.

Location: OS Ref. TQ099 605. M25/J10 to London. W of Cobham on A245. Entrance 200 yds E of A245/A307 roundabout.

Opening Times: Apr - Oct: Tue - Sun and BH Mons, 10.30am - 6pm (last admission 4.30pm). Gates close 6pm. Nov - Mar: daily except Mons & Fris (open BHs), 11am - 4pm or dusk if earlier (last admission 3pm). Closed Christmas and Boxing Day.

Admission: Adult £4.20, Child (5-16) £1.70, under 5 Free, Conc. £3.70. Groups (10+) £3.30.

Marquee site. P Guide dogs only.

POLESDEN LACEY

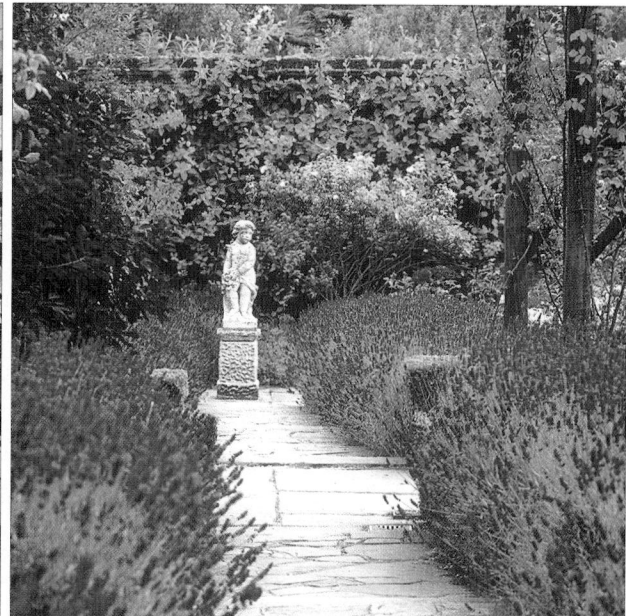

National Trust Photographic Library

GREAT BOOKHAM, Nr DORKING, SURREY RH5 6BD

Owner: The National Trust *Contact:* The Property Manager

Tel: 01372 452048 **Infoline:** 01372 458203
Fax: 01372 452023 **e-mail:** spljac@ smtp.ntrust.org.uk

Originally an elegant 1820s Regency villa in magnificent landscape setting. The house was remodelled after 1906 by the Hon Mrs Ronald Greville, a well-known Edwardian hostess. Her collection of fine paintings, furniture, porcelain and silver are still displayed in the reception rooms and galleries, which surround an inner courtyard. Extensive grounds, walled rose garden, lawns and landscaped walks. King George VI and Queen Elizabeth, The Queen Mother spent part of their honeymoon here.
Location: OS Ref. TQ136 522. 5m NW of Dorking, 2m S of Great Bookham, off A246.

Opening Times: House: 31 Mar - 4 Nov: Wed - Sun, 1 - 5pm also BH Mons starting with Easter, 11am - 5pm. Grounds: All year: daily, 11am - 6pm/dusk. Last admission to house ^{1}/$_2$ hr before closing.
Admission: Garden, grounds & landscape walks: Adult £4, Family £10. House: £3 extra. Family £7.50 extra. All year, booked groups £6 (house, garden & walks).

Licensed. Limited for coaches. In grounds on leads. Tel: 01372 452048 for info.

RHS GARDEN WISLEY

M C Sleigh

Nr WOKING, SURREY GU23 6QB

Owner/Contact: The Royal Horticultural Society

Tel: 01483 224234 **Fax:** 01483 211750

A world famous garden which extends to 240 acres and provides the chance to glean new ideas and inspiration. Highlights include the azaleas and rhododendrons in spring, the Glasshouses and the Model Gardens. The Giftshop and Plant Centre offer the world's finest collection of horticultural books and over 10,000 varieties of plants for sale.
Location: OS Ref. TQ066 583. NW side of A3 ^{1}/$_2$ m SW of M25/J10.
Opening Times: All year: Mon - Fri (except Christmas Day), 10am - sunset or 6pm during the summer; Sats, 9am - sunset or 6pm during summer. RHS members only on Suns.
Admission: Adult £5, Child (up to 6) Free, Child (6-16yrs) £2. Groups (10+) £4. Companion for disabled or blind visitors, Free.

Wheelchairs available tel: 01483 211113 & special map. Guide dogs only.

RAMSTER GARDENS

Tel: 01428 654167 **Fax:** 01428 658345

Ramster, Chiddingfold, Surrey GU8 4SN
Owner/Contact: Mrs M Gunn
20 acres of woodland and shrub garden.
Location: OS Ref. SU950 333. 1^1/$_2$ m S of Chiddingfold on A283.
Opening Times: 14 Apr - 1 Jul: 11am - 5pm.
Admission: £3, Child Free.

SHALFORD MILL

Tel: 01483 561617

Shalford, Guildford, Surrey GU4 8BS
Owner: The National Trust
18th century watermill on the Tillingbourne, given in 1932 by "Ferguson's Gang".
Location: OS Ref. TQ000 476. 1^1/$_2$ m S of Guildford on A281, opposite Sea Horse Inn.
Opening Times: Daily, 10am - 5pm.
Admission: Free. No unaccompanied children.

Patrick Lane

Claremont Landscape Garden, Surrey.

TITSEY PLACE

TITSEY, OXTED, SURREY RH8 0SD

Owner: Trustees of the Titsey Foundation **Contact:** *Kate Moisson*

Tel: 01273 407056 **Fax:** 01273 478995
e-mail: kate.moisson@struttandparker.co.uk
Stunning mansion house. Situated outside Limpsfield. Extensive formal and informal gardens containing Victorian walled garden, lakes, fountains and rose gardens. Outstanding features of this house include important paintings and *objets d'art*. Home of the Gresham and Leveson Gower family since the 15th century. Infinite capacity in this magnificent garden, numbers unavoidably restricted on house tours.
Location: OS Ref. TQ406 553. A25 Oxted - Westerham, through Limpsfield and into Bluehouse Lane and Water Lane, follow blue signs.
Opening Times: 15 May - 30 Sept: Weds & Suns, 1 - 5pm including BH Mons. Garden only: Easter Mon.
Admission: Adult £4.50, Child £2. Groups (20+): Adult £5.50.

ℹ️ No photography in house. No barbecues. ♿ Not suitable.
🎫 Obligatory. 🅿️ Limited for coaches. ✖️ (W)

WHITEHALL

Tel: 020 8643 1236 **Fax:** 020 8770 4777
e-mail: curators@whitehallcheam.fsnet.co.uk

1 Malden Road, Cheam, Surrey SM3 8QD

Owner: London Borough of Sutton **Contact:** The Curator
A Tudor timber-framed house, c1500 with later additions, in the heart of Cheam village conservation area. Twelve rooms open to view with displays on Nonsuch Palace, timber-framed buildings, Cheam pottery, Cheam school and William Gilpin. Changing exhibition programme and special event days throughout the year. Attractive rear garden features medieval well from c1400.
Location: OS Ref. TQ242 638. Approx. 2m S of A3 on A2043 just N of junction with A232.
Opening Times: 1 Oct - 31 Mar: Weds, Thurs, Suns, 2 - 5.30pm; Sats, 10am - 5.30pm. 1 Apr - 30 Sept: Tue - Fri, Sun, 2 - 5.30pm; Sats, 10am - 5.30pm; BH Mons, 2 - 5.30pm. Closed Christmas and New Year.
Admission: Adult £1.20, Child (under 16yrs) 50p, Child under 5yrs Free. Groups by arrangement.

📷 ♿ Ground floor only. 🍴 🎫 🎁 🐕 Guide dogs only.
✳️ 🅟 Tel. for details. (W)

Titsey Place, Surrey.

WINKWORTH ARBORETUM 🌳

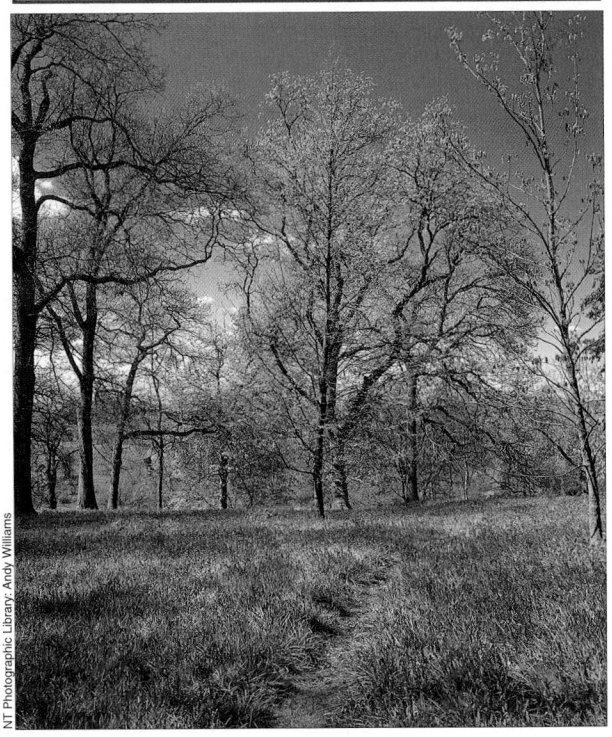

HASCOMBE ROAD, GODALMING, SURREY GU8 4AD

Owner: The National Trust **Contact:** *The Head of Arboretum*

Tel: 01483 208477 **Fax:** 01483 208252 **e-mail:** swagen@smtp.ntrust.org.uk
Hillside woodland with two lakes, many rare trees and shrubs and fine views. The most impressive displays are in spring for bluebells and azaleas, autumn for colour and wildlife. Delightful 100 year old boathouse on Rowes Flashe lake. Seasonal opening.

Location: OS Ref. SU990 412. Near Hascombe, 2m SE of Godalming on E side of B2130.
Opening times: All year: daily during daylight hours. May be closed due to high winds. Boathouse: 1 Apr - 31 Oct.
Admission: Adult £3.50, Child (5-16yrs) £1.75, Family (2+2) £8.75, additional family member £1.50. Discounts for 10 or more.

📷 ♿ Limited. WC. 🎁 🐕 In grounds, on leads. ✳️ (W)

ARUNDEL CASTLE
Arundel

This great castle, home of the Dukes of Norfolk, dates from the Norman Conquest. Containing a very fine collection of furniture and paintings, Arundel Castle is still a family home, reflecting the changes of nearly a thousand years.

In 1643, during the Civil War, the original castle was very badly damaged and it was later restored by the 8th, 11th and 15th Dukes in the 18th and 19th centuries. Amongst its treasures are personal possessions of Mary Queen of Scots and a selection of historical, religious and heraldic items from the Duke of Norfolk's collection.

The Duke of Norfolk is the Premier Duke, the title having been conferred on Sir John Howard in 1483 by his friend King Richard III. The Dukedom also carries with it the hereditary office of Earl Marshal of England. Among the historically famous members of the Howard family are Lord Howard of Effingham who, with Drake, repelled the Spanish Armada; the Earl of Surrey, the Tudor poet and courtier and the 3rd Duke of Norfolk, uncle of Anne Boleyn and Catherine Howard, both of whom became wives of King Henry VIII.

Owner:
Arundel Castle Trustees Ltd

CONTACT

The Comptroller
Arundel Castle
Arundel
West Sussex
BN18 9AB

Tel: 01903 883136
or 01903 882173

Fax: 01903 884581

e-mail: arundelcastle@
compuserve.com

LOCATION

OS Ref. TQ018 072

1m Arundel, N of A27
Brighton 40 mins,
Worthing 15 mins,
Chichester 15 mins.
From London A3 or A24,
1¹/₂ hrs.
M25 motorway, 30m.

Bus: Bus stop 100 yds.

Rail: Station ¹/₂ m.

Air: Gatwick 25m.

OPENING TIMES

SUMMER

1 April - 31 October
Daily (except Sats &
Good Fri)
12 noon - 5pm
Last admission 4pm.

WINTER

1 November - 31 March
Pre-booked groups only.

ADMISSION

SUMMER

Adult £7.50
Child (5-15).............£5.00
OAP £6.50
Family (2+2) £21.00

Groups (20+)
Adult £7.00
Child (5-15).............£4.50
OAP........................£6.00

WINTER

Pre-booked parties
Mornings................£9.00
(Min Fee ....£450.00)
Evenings, Sats &
Suns......................£10.00
(Min Fee ....£500.00)

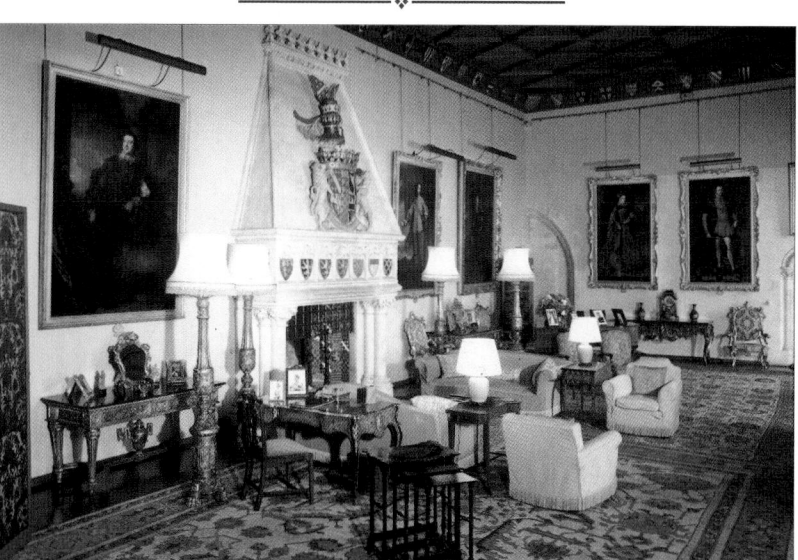

No unaccompanied children or photography inside the Castle.

Visitors may alight at the entrance, before parking in the allocated areas. WCs.

Restaurant seats 140. Special rates for booked groups. Self-service restaurant in Castle serves home-made food. Groups must book in advance for afternoon tea, lunch or dinner.

Pre-booked groups only, £9. Tour time 1¹/₂ hrs. Guide book translations in English, French and German.

P Ample. Coaches can park opposite the Castle entrance.

Items of particular interest include a Norman Keep and Armoury. Special rates for schoolchildren (aged 5-15) and teachers.

National Trust Photographic Library: M J O'Neill

Owner: The National Trust

CONTACT

The Property Manager
Burwash
Etchingham
East Sussex
TN19 7DS

Tel: 01435 882302

Fax: 01435 882811

e-mail: kbaxxx@
smtp.ntrust.org.uk

LOCATION

OS Ref. TQ671 238

1/2 m S of Burwash off A265.

Rail: Etchingham 3m, then bus (twice daily).

Air: Gatwick 40m.

BATEMAN'S
Burwash

Built in 1634 and home to Rudyard Kipling for over 30 years, Bateman's lies in the richly wooded landscape of the Sussex Weald. Visit this Sussex sandstone manor house, built by a local ironmaster, where the famous writer lived from 1902 to 1936. See the rooms as they were in Kipling's day, including the study where the view inspired him to write some of his well-loved works including *Puck of Pook's Hill* and *Rewards and Fairies*. Find the mementoes of Kipling's time in India and illustrations from his famous *Jungle Book* tales of *Mowgli*, *Baloo* and *Shere Khan*.

Wander through the delightful Rose Garden with its pond and statues, with Mulberry and Herb gardens and discover the wild garden, through which flows the River Dudwell. Through the wild garden, you will find the Mill where you can watch corn being ground on most Saturday afternoons and one of the world's first water-driven turbines installed by Kipling to generate electricity for the house. In the garage, see a 1928 Rolls Royce, one of several owned by Kipling who was a keen early motorist.

Savour the peace and tranquillity of this beautiful property which Kipling described as '*A good and peaceable place*' and of which he said '*we have loved it, ever since our first sight of it...*'.

There is a picnic glade next to the car park, or you can enjoy morning coffee, a delicious lunch or afternoon tea in the licensed tearoom where there is special emphasis on using local produce. The well-stocked gift shop offers the largest collection of Kipling books in the area.

OPENING TIMES

1 Apr - 1 Nov: Sat - Wed, Good Fri & BH Mons, 11am - 5.30pm. Last admission 4.30pm.

Wild Garden:
Open in March 2001.

ADMISSION

House and Garden

Adult £5.00
Child.......................£2.50
Family (2+3) £12.50
Groups £4.25

SPECIAL EVENTS

• **AUG:**
Last Night of the Proms & Sixties Concert.
Tel: 01892 891001 for details.

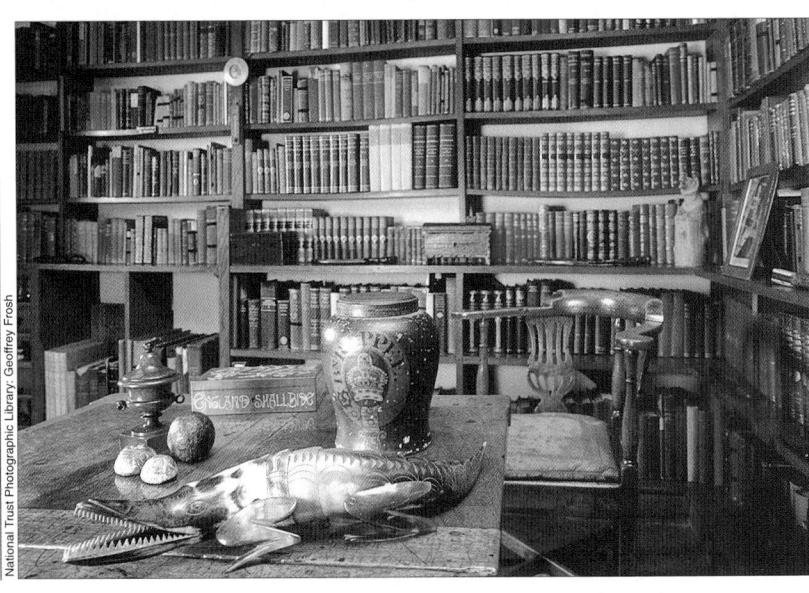

National Trust Photographic Library: Geoffrey Frosh

 Ground floor & grounds suitable. WC.

Licensed.

Verity Welstead, courtesy of Charleston Trust

CHARLESTON
Lewes

A mile or so from Firle village, near the end of a track leading to the foot of the Downs, lies Charleston. It was discovered in 1916 by Virginia and Leonard Woolf when Virginia's sister, the painter Vanessa Bell, was looking for a place in the country. Vanessa moved here with fellow artist Duncan Grant, the writer David Garnett, her two young sons and an assortment of animals. It was an unconventional and creative household which became the focal point for artists and intellectuals later to be known as the Bloomsbury set, among them Roger Fry, Lytton Strachey and Maynard Keynes.

Over the years the artists decorated the walls, furniture and ceramics with their own designs, influenced by Italian fresco painting and post-impressionist art. Creativity extended to the garden too. Mosaics were made in the piazza, sculpture was cleverly positioned to intrigue and subtle masses of colour were used in the planting.

After Duncan Grant's death in 1978, the Charleston Trust was formed to save and restore the house to its former glory. The task has been described as "one of the most difficult and imaginative feats of restoration current in Britain".

Owner:
The Charleston Trust

CONTACT

Emma Whelan
Charleston
Nr Firle
Lewes
East Sussex
BN8 6LL

Tel: 01323 811265
(Visitor information)
01323 811626 (Admin)

Fax: 01323 811628

e-mail: charles
@solutions-inc.co.uk

LOCATION

OS Ref. TQ490 069

6m E of Lewes on A27 between Firle & Selmeston. The lane to Charleston leads off the A27, 2m beyond the Firle turning.

London 60m. Brighton 15m. Monk's House, Rodmell (Leonard and Virginia Woolf's house) 11m.

Air: Gatwick 35m.

Rail: London (Victoria) hourly to Lewes (65 mins). Occasional train to Berwick.

Bus: Rider 125 Charleston Rambler Suns & BHs Route on A27.
Taxi: George & Graham, Lewes 473692.

Pls Tryde, courtesy of Charleston Trust

Filming and photo-graphy contact Shaun Romain: 01323 811626. Small lecture room available by special arrangement. No filming, video or photography in house.

Visitors may alight at entrance. Wheelchair visitors by prior arrange-ment. Ground floor only suitable. WCs.

Wed - Sun, 2 - 5pm.

Obligatory.

50 spaces. Mini coaches and cars only. Mini coaches may use the lane to the property. It is essential to arrange group visits (up to 50) in advance and out of public hours. All group visits to the house are guided. Large coaches may set down at the start of the lane, 10 mins walk.

Student pack and a teacher's guide suitable for KS I & II.

Guide dogs only.

OPENING TIMES

1 April - 31 October
Wed - Sun: 2 - 5pm.

Extra Summer Opening Times: July & August
Wed - Sat: 11.30am - 5pm
Sun: 2 - 5pm.

November - December Christmas shopping
Sat & Sun, 1 - 4pm.

Guided visits
Wed - Sat,
unguided on Suns.

House closed Mon & Tue except BH Mons.

Connoisseur Fridays
April - June, September and October, in-depth tour of the house, including Vanessa Bell's studio and the kitchen.

ADMISSION

House & Garden
Adult £5.50
Child (5+)/Conc*. £4.00
Child (under 5)...........Free
Disabled.................£4.00

Groups (min 10)
Adult £5.00
Child/Student..........£4.00
OAP.......................£5.00

Connoisseur Fridays
Adult £6.50

* OAPs, Students & UB40 Wed & Thur only throughout season. Organised tours should telephone for group rates.

SPECIAL EVENTS

• **MAY 24 - 28:**
Charleston Festival

For other events see
www.charleston.org.uk

GOODWOOD HOUSE
Chichester

Owner:
The Earl of March

CONTACT

Kathryn Bellamy
Goodwood House
Goodwood
Chichester
West Sussex
PO18 0PX

Tel: 01243 755048

Fax: 01243 755005

Recorded info:
01243 755040

e-mail: enquiries
@goodwood.co.uk

LOCATION

OS Ref. SU888 088

4m NE of Chichester. A3
from London then A286 or
A285. M27/A27 from
Portsmouth or Brighton.

Rail: Chichester 4m
Arundel 9m.

Air: Heathrow 1¹/₂ hrs
Gatwick ³/₄ hr.

It is now 200 years since the 3rd Duke of Richmond embarked upon an ambitious scheme to turn his small country house into a magnificent ducal residence. In keeping with the fashion, the two new Regency wings were added to afford the best possible views of the picturesque parkland and beyond, to Chichester and the sea. Today, Goodwood encapsulates the flamboyance, innovation and style that have been the signature of the Richmond family ever since the time of the 1st Duke. The natural son of King Charles II and his beautiful French mistress, Louise de Keroualle, he was renowned for his love of life

and brilliance at entertaining – a tradition which continues to this day. The French interest was pursued by the 3rd Duke who, as British Ambassador to Paris, collected important French furniture which now sets off the newly restored Tapestry Drawing Room, and Sèvres porcelain, which can still be seen. Still owned and lived in by the Earl and Countess of March, Goodwood effortlessly exudes the glamour of a ducal seat and is not only a beautiful house to visit, but has also established a worldwide reputation for excellence as the location for corporate, private and incentive entertainment.

Stephen Hayward

Goodwood Photo Collection

 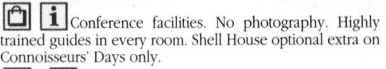 Conference facilities. No photography. Highly trained guides in every room. Shell House optional extra on Connoisseurs' Days only.

Suitable.

By appointment: open mornings & on Connoisseurs' Days.

Ample.

In grounds, on leads. Guide dogs only in house.

Civil Wedding Licence.

OPENING TIMES

SUMMER

1 Apr - 1 Oct:
Most Suns & Mons.

5 Aug - 6 Sept:
Sun - Thur,
1 - 5pm.

Closed on Special Event
Days (see list below):
and occasional others
including Sundays 6 & 27
May. To check please ring
Recorded Information on
01243 755040.

Connoisseurs' Days
Group visits with special
guided tours can be
booked.

ADMISSION

House

Adult	£6.50
Child*	£3.00
Conc.	£6.00

Groups (20 - 200)
Economy	£5.50
Connoisseur	£8.50

*12 - 18 yrs, under 12 yrs free

SPECIAL EVENTS

- **FEB 3/4**
Antiques Fair.

- **APR 21/22**
Home Design Interiors.

- **MAY 12/13**
Antiques Fair.

- **JUL 31 - AUG 4**
Race Week.

- **MID SEPTEMBER**
Motor Circuit Revival Meeting.

- **NOV 17/18**
Antiques Fair.

Festival of Speed between
mid-June & early July, please
telephone to confirm the dates.

CONFERENCE/FUNCTION

ROOM	SIZE	MAX CAPACITY
Ballroom	79' x 23'	200
11 other rooms also available		

LEONARDSLEE GARDENS
Horsham

Owner:
R Loder Esq

CONTACT

R Loder Esq
Leonardslee Gardens
Lower Beeding
Horsham
West Sussex
RH13 6PP

Tel: 01403 891212

Fax: 01403 891305

LOCATION

OS Ref. TQ222 260

M23 to Handcross then
B2110 (signposted
Cowfold) for 4m.
From London:
1 hr 15 mins.

Rail: Horsham
Station $4^1/_2$ m

Bus: No. 107 from
Horsham and Brighton

LEONARDSLEE GARDENS represent one of the largest and most spectacular woodland gardens in England with one of the finest collections of mature rhododendrons, azaleas, choice trees and shrubs to be seen anywhere. It is doubly fortunate in having one of the most magnificent settings, within easy reach of London, only a few miles from the M23. Laid out by Sir Edmund Loder since 1889, the gardens are still maintained by the Loder family today. The 240 acre (100 hectare) valley is world famous for its spring display of azaleas and rhododendrons around the 7 lakes, giving superb views and reflections.

The delightful Rock Garden, a photographer's paradise, is a kaleidoscope of colour in May. The superb exhibition of Bonsai in a walled courtyard shows the fascinating living art-form of Bonsai to perfection. The Alpine House has 400 different alpine plants growing in a natural rocky setting. Wallabies (used as mowing machines!) have lived wild in part of the garden for over 100 years, and deer (Sika, Fallow & Axis) may be seen in the parklands.

Many superb rhododendrons have been raised at Leonardslee. The most famous is *rhododendron loderi* raised by Sir Edmund Loder in 1901. The original plants can still be seen in the garden. In May the fragrance of their huge blooms pervades the air throughout the valley.

The Loder family collection of Victorian motorcars (1895 - 1900) provides a fascinating view of the different designs adopted on the first auto-mobile constructors.

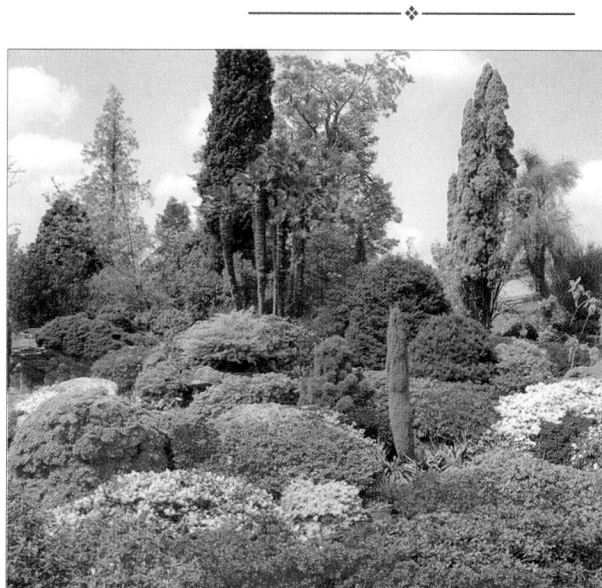

❖

OPENING TIMES

SUMMER
1 April - 31 October
Daily 9.30am - 6pm

WINTER
1 November - 31 March
Closed to the general
public.

Available for functions.

ADMISSION

April, June - October
    Adult £5.00

May (Mon - Fri)
    Adult £6.00

May (Sats, Suns & BH Mons)
    Adult £7.00
    Child (anytime).........£3.00

Groups
April, June - October
    Adult £4.00

May: (Mon - Fri).........£5.00
Sat, Sun &
BH Mons: £6.00
    Child (anytime).........£2.50

📷 🌱 ℹ️ Photography
- landscape and fashion, film
location.

🍽 Restaurant available for
private and corporate function in the evenings and out
of season.

♿ Not suitable.

☕ 🍴 Restaurant and
café. Morning coffee, lunch
and teas.

🅿️ Ample. Refreshments
free to coach drivers.
Average length of visit 2 - 4
hours.

🐕

SPECIAL EVENTS

- **MAY 5 - 7:**
  Bonsai Weekend.

- **JUN 23 - 24:**
  West Sussex Country Craft Fair.

- **JUL 14 - 15:**
  Model Boat Regatta.

CONFERENCE/FUNCTION		
ROOM	SIZE	MAX CAPACITY
Clock Tower		100

South East England

Oliver Benn

PETWORTH HOUSE
Petworth

PETWORTH HOUSE is one of the finest houses in the care of the National Trust and is home to an art collection that rivals many London galleries. Assembled by one family over 350 years, it includes works by Turner, Van Dyck, Titian, Claude, Gainsborough, Bosch, Reynolds and William Blake.

The state rooms contain sculpture, furniture and porcelain of the highest quality and are complemented by the opening of the old kitchens in the servants' block.

A continuing programme of repairs and restoration brings new interest for the visitor each year. Petworth House is also the home of Lord and Lady Egremont and extra family rooms are open on weekdays by kind permission (not Bank Holidays).

Petworth Park is a 700 acre park landscaped by 'Capability' Brown and is open to the public all year free of charge. Spring and autumn are particularly breathtaking and the summer sunsets over the lake are spectacular.

❖

Owner:
The National Trust

CONTACT

The Administration Office
Petworth House
Petworth
West Sussex
GU28 0AE

Tel: 01798 342207

Info Line: 01798 343929

Fax: 01798 342963

e-mail: spegen@
smtp.ntrust.org.uk

LOCATION

OS Ref. SU976 218

In the centre of Petworth town (approach roads A272/A283/A285) Car park signposted.

Rail: Pulborough BR 5¼ m.

Andreas Von Einsiedel

[i] Events throughout the year. Large musical concerts in the park. Baby feeding and changing facilities, highchairs. Pushchairs admitted in house but no prams, please. No photography in house.

[Y] Contact Retail & Catering Manager on 01798 344975.

[♿] Car park is 800 yards from house; there is a vehicle available to take less able visitors to house.

[⍯] Licensed. 12-5pm.

[🧍] By arrangement (Mon - Wed mornings) with the Administration Officer on variety of subjects, tailor-made to suit your group (additional charge).

[P] 800 yards from house. Coach parties alight at Church Lodge entrance, coaches then park in NT car park. Coaches **must** book in advance.

[👥] Welcome. Must pre-book. Teachers' pack available.

[🐕] Guide dogs only in house. Dogs in park only.

[❄]

[🎭] Tel. for details.

OPENING TIMES

**House &
Servants' Quarters**
31 March - 4 November
Daily except Thurs & Fris
but open Good Fri and
every following Fri in
July & August. 1 - 5.30pm.
Last admission to house &
servants' quarters 5pm.
Extra rooms shown on
Mons, Tues & Weds,
not BH Mons.

**Pleasure Ground
and Car Park**
17/18 & 24/25 March
for spring bulbs, 12 noon -
4pm. Dates as house
12 noon - 6pm. BH Mons,
July & August, 11am - 6pm.

Park
All year: Daily, 8am - sunset.
Closed 29, 30 Jun & 1 Jul
for concerts.

**Servants Quarters,
Pleasure Grounds, Shop
& Restaurant:**
14 Nov - 22 Dec, Wed - Sat,
10.30am - 3.30pm. Thurs
only: guided tour of house
to see work in progess.

ADMISSION

**House, Servants'
Quarters &
Pleasure Ground**
Adult £6.00
Child* (5-17yrs) £3.00
Family (2+2) £15.00
Park Only .... Free
Groups (pre-booked 15+)
Adult £5.50

Pleasure Ground
Adult £1.50
Park ....Free
NT Members Free.

* Under 5yrs Free

South East England

THE ROYAL PAVILION
Brighton

Owner:
Brighton & Hove Council

CONTACT

Visitor Services
The Royal Pavilion
Brighton
East Sussex
BN1 1EE

Tel: 01273 290900

Fax: 01273 292871

LOCATION

OS Ref. TQ313 043

The Royal Pavilion is in the centre of Brighton easily reached by road and rail. From London M25, M23, A23 - 1 hr 30 mins.

Rail: Victoria to Brighton station 50 mins. 15 mins walk from Brighton station.

Air: Gatwick 20 mins.

CONFERENCE/FUNCTION

ROOM	SIZE	MAX CAPACITY
Banqueting Room		200
Great Kitchen		90
Music Rm		180
Queen Adelaide Suite		100
Small Adelaide		40
William IV		80

Universally acclaimed as one of the most exotically beautiful buildings in the British Isles, the Royal Pavilion is the former seaside residence of King George IV.

Originally a simple farmhouse, in 1787 architect Henry Holland created a neo-classical villa on the site. It was later transformed into its current Indian style by John Nash between 1815 and 1822. With interiors decorated in the Chinese style and an astonishingly exotic exterior, this Regency Palace is quite breathtaking.

Magnificent decorations and fantastic furnishings have been re-created in the recent extensive restoration programme. From the opulence of the main state rooms to the charm of the first floor bedroom suites, the Royal Pavilion is filled with astonishing colours and superb craftsmanship.

Witness the magnificence of the Music Room with its domed ceiling of gilded scallop-shaped shells and hand-knotted carpet, and promenade through the Chinese bamboo grove of the Long Gallery.

Lavish menus were created in the Great Kitchen, with its cast iron palm trees and dazzling collection of copperware, and then served in the dramatic setting of the Banqueting Room, lit by a huge crystal chandelier held by a silvered dragon.

Set in restored Regency gardens replanted to John Nash's elegant 1820s design, the Royal Pavilion is an unforgettable experience.

Visitors can discover more about life behind the scenes at the Palace during the last 200 years with a new specially commissioned interactive multi-media presentation. Public guided tours take place daily at 11.30am and 2.30pm for a small additional charge.

[i] Location filming and photography, including feature films, fashion shoots and corporate videos.

[gift] Gift shop with souvenirs unique to the Royal Pavilion.

[dining] Spectacular rooms available for prestigious corporate and private entertaining and wedding receptions.

[access] Access to ground floor. Free admission. Guided tours, including tactile and signed tours, are free of charge to those with disabilities but must be booked in advance with Visitor Services Tel: 01273 292820/2.

[tea] Tearooms with a balcony providing sweeping views across the restored Regency gardens.

[tours] Tours in English, French and German by prior arrangement. General introduction and specialist tours provided.

[P] Close to NCP car parks, town centre voucher parking. Coach drop-off point in Church Street, parking in Madeira Drive. Free entry for coach drivers.

[education] Specialist tours relating to all levels of National Curriculum, must be booked in advance with Visitor Services. Special winter student rates. Slide lecture presentations by arrangement.

[bell] Civil Wedding Licence.

[❄]

OPENING TIMES

SUMMER
June - September
Daily: 10am - 6pm
Last admission at 6pm.

WINTER
October - May
Daily: 10am - 5pm
Last admission at 5pm.

Closed 25/26 December.

ADMISSION

Adult	£4.90
Child	£3.00
Conc	£3.55

Groups (20+)
Adult £4.10

Prices valid until 31.3.2001

SPECIAL EVENTS

- **SPRING & AUTUMN HALF TERM:** Children's Events.

- **OCT - MAR:** Winter programme of events – call for details.

South East England

SAINT HILL MANOR
East Grinstead

Owner: Church of Scientology

CONTACT

Mrs Liz Nyegaard
Saint Hill Manor
Saint Hill Road
East Grinstead
West Sussex
RH19 4JY

Tel: 01342 326711

Fax: 01342 317057

Built 1792 by Gibbs Crawfurd. One of the finest Sussex sandstone buildings in existence and situated near the breathtaking Ashdown Forest. Subsequent owners included Edgar March Crookshank and the Maharajah of Jaipur. In 1959, Saint Hill Manor's final owner, acclaimed author and humanitarian L Ron Hubbard, acquired the Manor, where he lived for many years with his family. As a result of the work carried out under Mr Hubbard's direction, the Manor has been restored to its original beauty, including the uncovering of fine oak wood panelling, marble fireplaces and plasterwork ceilings.

Other outstanding features of this lovely house include an impressive library of Mr Hubbard's works, elegant winter garden, and delightful Monkey Mural painted in 1945 by Winston Churchill's nephew John Spencer Churchill. This 100-foot mural depicts many famous personalities as monkeys, including Winston Churchill. Also open to the public are 59 acres of landscaped gardens, lake and woodlands. Ideal for corporate functions, wedding receptions and also available as a film location. Annual events include open-air theatre, arts festivals, classical and jazz concerts.

LOCATION

2m SW of East Grinstead. At Felbridge, turn off A22, down Imberhorne Lane and over crossroads into Saint Hill Road, 200yds on right.

Rail: East Grinstead station.

Air: 15 mins drive from Gatwick airport.

OPENING TIMES

All year: daily, 2 - 5pm, on the hour.
Groups welcome throughout the year.

ADMISSION

Free.

Ground floor suitable.
Teas available.
Obligatory.

SPECIAL EVENTS

- **JUN 24:**
  Open air production of Sheridan's 'School for Scandal'

Mark Fiennes

STANSTED PARK
Rowlands Castle

Owner: Trustees of Stansted Park Foundation

CONTACT

The House Manager
Stansted Park
Rowlands Castle
Hampshire
PO9 6DX

Tel: 023 9241 2265/
023 9241 3380

Fax: 023 9241 3773

e-mail: enquiries@
stanstedpark.co.uk

LOCATION

OS Ref. SU761 104

Follow brown heritage signs from A3 (Rowlands Castle) or A27 (Havant)

Rail: Rowlands Castle (London Waterloo 1½ hrs.

Air: Eastleigh, Southampton.

STANSTED is more than an elegant house. Set in 1750 acres of glorious park and woodland, rich in wildlife and famous for its tranquillity, it is a prime example of the Caroline revival. Not only is Stansted one of the South's most beautiful stately homes, it is also one of Sussex's best-kept secrets.

The contrast between the magnificent State Rooms and the purpose-built Servants' Quarters gives an insight into the social history of an English Country House in its heyday. The Bessborough family collection includes paintings of the famous Georgiana, Duchess of Devonshire and her sister Henrietta Frances, wife to the 3rd Earl and

mother of the equally famous Lady Caroline Lamb. The visionary stained glass windows in the exquisitely decorated Ancient Chapel inspired some of Keats' finest poetry.

The restored Dutch Garden, Circular Garden, Ivan Hicks' famous 'Garden in Mind' and the large, well-stocked Garden Centre within the unique Walled Gardens are a must for people who love plants.

Stansted's 12th century origins were related to hunting and hawking and Henry II visited often to enjoy the chase. The new Falconry revives this tradition and appeals to everyone, whatever their age.

❖

 A unique range of facilities for conferences and business meetings. A variety of activities for Corporate Hospitality, including clay shooting, off-road driving, team-building games, action-theme days, even murder mystery evenings. Excellent film location. Childrens' play area, picnic area, woodland walk, arboretum, Garden Centre & Falconry.

 Partially suitable. WC.

Licensed.

By arrangement.

 In woods, on leads.

A wide variety of facilities to suit parties of all sizes. A complete package with both ceremony and reception is just one of the options offered. Every function is tailored to individual requirements and we guarantee a special day.

❄ Please tel. for details.

CONFERENCE/FUNCTION

ROOM	SIZE	MAX CAPACITY
Mail Hall & Music Room		100 - 150

OPENING TIMES

House
1 April - 31 October:
Sun - Wed, 1 - 5pm.

Grounds, including Ivan Hicks' 'Garden in Mind' & Arboretum:
All year: daily, 1 - 5pm (closed Christmas & New Year BHs).

Falconry:
All year: daily except Thurs, 9am - 5pm. Flying times: 11am, 1pm & 3pm (weather permitting).

Garden Centre:
All year:
Mon - Sat, 9am - 5pm.
Suns, 10.30am - 4.30pm.

ADMISSION

House & Grounds
Adult £5.50
Child (5-17yrs)........£3.50
OAP/Student...........£2.70
Family (2+3) £14.50

Grounds
Adult £3.50
Child (5-17yrs)........£2.00
OAP/Student...........£3.00
Family (2+3) £9.00

Stansted Falconry
Adult £3.00
Child (5-17yrs)........£2.00
OAP/Student...........£2.50
Family (2+3) £8.00

Groups (30-50)
10% discount off the above prices.

NT Photographic Library: David Sellman

Owner: The National Trust

CONTACT

The Property Manager
Uppark
South Harting
Petersfield
GU31 5QR

Tel: 01730 825415

Info Line: 01730 825857

Fax: 01730 825873

e-mail: supgen@
smtp.ntrust.org.uk

LOCATION

OS Ref. 197 SU781 181

5m SE of Petersfield
on B2146, 1½ m S of
South Harting.

Bus: Stagecoach Sussex
Bus 54 (not Sun).

Rail: Petersfield 5½ m.

UPPARK
South Harting

A fine late 17th century house set high on the South Downs with magnificent sweeping views to the sea. An extensive, award-winning exhibition tells the dramatic story of the 1989 fire and restoration of the house and its collections.

The elegant Georgian interior houses a famous Grand Tour collection that includes paintings by Pompeo Batoni, Luca Giordano, and Joseph Vernet, with furniture and ceramics of superb quality. The famous 18th century dolls' house with original contents is one of the star items in the collection, and provides a rare insight into life in a great house 300 years ago.

The restaurant in the Georgian kitchen in the East Pavilion serves a Georgian themed menu using local produce. The West Pavilion houses the beautiful stables and the atmospheric and romantic Dairy. The complete servants' quarters in the basement are shown as they were in Victorian days when H G Wells' mother was housekeeper. From the basement visitors leave the house via the atmospheric subterranean passages.

The fine, peaceful, historic garden is now fully restored in the early 19th century 'Picturesque' style, with flowering shrubs and under-plantings of bulbs, perennials and herbaceous plants in a magical woodland and downland setting.

NT Photographic Library: Nadia MacKenzie

OPENING TIMES

1 April - 1 November:
Daily except Fris & Sats.

House: 1 - 5pm
(opens 12 noon on Suns
in Jul & Aug).

Last admission 4.15pm.

Print room open on 1st
Mon of each month.

Grounds, exhibition,
garden, shop & restaurant:
11.30am - 5pm.

ADMISSION

**House, Garden &
Exhibition**

Adult	£5.50
Child	£2.75
Family	£13.75

Groups (min 15, week-
days only, must book)
Apr, May & Oct.......£4.50

Booked group guided
tours: mornings by
arrangement.

Special group catering
arrangements: please
telephone for details.

NT members Free.

Pushchairs on weekdays only. No photography, large bags or sharp heeled shoes in the house.

Tel. for Xmas opening.

Partially suitable. WC. Wheelchairs available.

Licensed.

Coaches must pre-book.

On leads, in Car Park (no shade) & woodland only.

Please telephone for details.

CONFERENCE/FUNCTION		
ROOM	SIZE	MAX CAPACITY
Restaurant		50
Lower Servants Hall		50

ALFRISTON CLERGY HOUSE

THE TYE, ALFRISTON, POLEGATE, EAST SUSSEX BN26 5TL

Owner: The National Trust   *Contact:* The Property Manager

Tel: 01323 870001   **Fax:** 01323 871318   **e-mail:** ksdxxx@smtp.ntrust.org.uk

Step back into the Middle Ages with a visit to this 14th century thatched Wealden 'Hall House'. Trace the history of this magnificent building - the first to be acquired by the National Trust in 1896. Discover why the chalk floor is soaked in sour milk, and visit the excellent shop with its local crafts. Explore the delightful cottage garden, filled with traditional cottage favourites and savour the idyllic setting beside Alfriston's famous parish church, with stunning views across the meandering River Cuckmere. An intriguing variety of shops, pubs and restaurants in Alfriston village make this a wonderful day out.

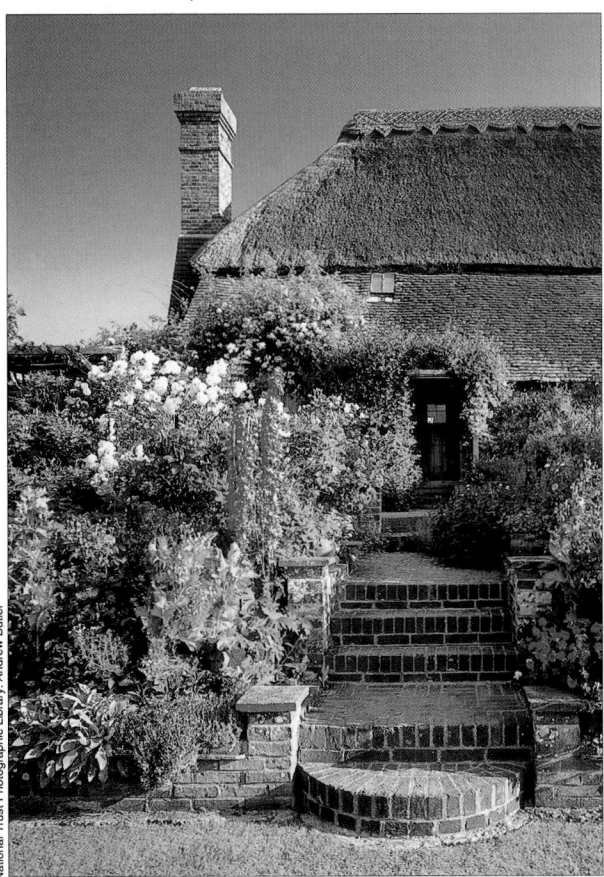

Location: OS Ref. TQ521 029. 4m NE of Seaford, just E of B2108.

Opening times: 3 - 25 Mar: Sats & Suns. 11am - 4pm. Last admission 3.30pm. 31 Mar - 4 Nov: daily except Tues & Fris, 10am - 5pm, last entry 4.30pm.

Admission: Adult £2.60, Child £1.30, Family (2+3) £6.50. Pre-booked groups £2.20 or £3.20 with guided tour.

⬜ ♿Not suitable. 🅿Parking in village car parks.

ANNE OF CLEVES HOUSE

Tel: 01273 474610 **Fax:** 01273 486990

52 Southover High Street, Lewes, Sussex BN7 1JA

Owner: Sussex Archaeological Society   **Contact:** Mr Stephen Watts

Anne of Cleves' house formed part of her divorce settlement from Henry VIII in 1541, although she never actually lived here. The 16th century timber-framed Wealden hall-house contains wide-ranging collections of Sussex interest. Furnished rooms give an impression of life in the 17th and 18th centuries. Artefacts from Lewes Priory, Sussex pottery and Wealden ironwork.

Location: OS198 Ref. TQ410 096. S of Lewes town centre, off A27/A275/A26.

Opening Times: 2 Jan - 17 Feb: Tues, Thurs & Sats, 10am - 5pm. 19 Feb - 4 Nov: Mon - Sat, 10am - 5pm; Sun, 12 noon - 5pm. 6 Nov - 23 Dec: Tue - Sat, 10am - 5pm; Sun, 12 noon - 5pm.

Admission: Adult £2.60, Child £1.30, Conc. £2.40, Family (2+2) £6.80 or (1+4) £5.20. Combined ticket with Lewes Castle is also available. Groups (15+): Adult £2.40, Child £1.10, Conc. £2.20.

⬜ ♿ Not suitable. 🖼 🐕 Guide dogs only. 🔔 ❄ 🅦

ARUNDEL CASTLE

See page 159 for full page entry.

ARUNDEL CATHEDRAL

Tel: 01903 882297 **Fax:** 01903 885335

Parsons Hill, Arundel, Sussex BN18 9AY   **e-mail:** aruncath1@aol.com
      Contact: Rev A Whale

French Gothic Cathedral, church of the RC Diocese of Arundel and Brighton built by Henry, 15th Duke of Norfolk and opened 1873. Carpet of Flowers and Floral Festival held annually on the Feast of Corpus Christi (60 days after Easter) and day preceding.

Location: OS Ref. TQ015 072. Above junction of A27 and A284.

Opening Times: Summer: 9am - 6pm. Winter: 9am - dusk. Mass at 10am each day. Sun Masses: 8am, 9.30am & 11am, Vigil Sat evening: 6.30pm. Shop opened after services and on special occasions and otherwise at request.

Admission: Free.

1066 BATTLE OF HASTINGS BATTLEFIELD & ABBEY

BATTLE, SUSSEX TN33 0AD

Owner: English Heritage   *Contact:* The Custodian

Tel: 01424 773792 **Fax:** 01424 775059

Visit the site of the 1066 Battle of Hastings. A free interactive audio tour will lead you around the battlefield and to the exact spot where Harold fell. Explore the magnificent Abbey ruins and see the fascinating exhibition in the gate house and '1066 Prelude to Battle' exhibition. Children's themed play area.

Location: OS Ref. TQ749 157. Top of Battle High Street. Turn off A2100 to Battle.

Opening Times: 1 Apr - 30 Sept: daily, 10am - 6pm. 1 - 31 Oct: 10am - 5pm. 1 Nov - 31 Mar: daily 10am - 4pm. Closed 24 - 26 Dec & 1 Jan.

Admission: Adult £4.30, Child £2.20, Conc. £3.20, Family £10.80. 15% discount for groups (11+). EH members Free.

⬜ ♿Ground floor & grounds. ⎔Free. 🐕In grounds, on leads. ❄
📺Tel. for details.

BATEMAN'S

See page 160 for full page entry.

BAYHAM OLD ABBEY

Tel/Fax: 01892 890381

Lamberhurst, Sussex

Owner: English Heritage   **Contact:** The Custodian

These riverside ruins are of a house of 'White' Canons, founded c1208 and preserved in the 18th century, when its surroundings were landscaped to create its delightful setting.

Location: OS Ref. TQ651 366. 1³/₄ m W of Lamberhurst off B2169.

Opening Times: 1 Apr - 30 Sept: daily, 10am - 6pm. 1 - 31 Oct: 10am - 5pm. 1 Nov - 31 Mar: w/ends only 10am - 4pm. Closed 24 - 26 Dec & 1 Jan.

Admission: Adult £2.20, Child £1.10, Conc. £1.60.

 Grounds suitable. WC. In grounds, on leads.

BENTLEY HOUSE & MOTOR MUSEUM

Tel: 01825 840573   **Fax:** 01825 841322

Halland, Lewes, East Sussex BN8 5AF   **e-mail:** barrysutherland@pavilion.co.uk

Owner: East Sussex County Council   **Contact:** Mr Barry Sutherland - Manager

Early 18th century farmhouse with a large reception room of Palladian proportions added on either end in the 1960s by the architect Raymond Erith, each lit by large Venetian windows. Furnished to form a grand 20th century evocation of a mid-Georgian house.

Location: OS Ref. TQ485 160. 7m NE from Lewes, signposted off A22, A26 & B2192.

Opening Times: Estate: 19 Mar - 31 Oct: daily, 10.30am - 4.30pm (last adm.). Nov, Feb - Mar: weekends only, 10.30am - 4pm (last adm.). House: 1 Apr - 31 Oct: daily 12 noon - 5pm. Estate closed Dec & Jan.

Admission: Adult £4.80 (£3.80 in winter), Child (4-15) £3, Conc.£3.80, Family (2+4) £13.50. Coach drivers free admission & refreshment ticket. 10% discount for groups of 11+. Special rates for the disabled. Call to verify prices (2000 rates).

Wedding receptions. Licensed. By arrangement. Guide dogs only.

Bodiam Castle, Sussex.

BODIAM CASTLE

BODIAM, Nr ROBERTSBRIDGE, EAST SUSSEX TN32 5UA

Owner: The National Trust   *Contact:* The Administrator

Tel: 01580 830436   **Fax:** 01580 830398   **e-mail:** kboxxx@smtp.ntrust.org.uk

Built in 1385 against a French invasion that never came and as a comfortable dwelling for a rich nobleman, Bodiam Castle is one of the finest examples of medieval architecture. The virtual completeness of its exterior makes it popular with adults, children and film crews alike. Inside, although a ruin, floors have been replaced in some of the towers and visitors can climb the spiral staircase to enjoy superb views from the battlements. Discover more of its intriguing past in the museum and video room, and wander in the romantic Castle grounds peacefully set on the banks of the River Rother.

Location: OS Ref. TQ782 256. 3m S of Hawkhurst, 2m E of A21 Hurst Green.

Opening Times: 6 Jan - 16 Feb: Sats & Suns, 11am - 4pm. 17 Feb - 31 Oct: daily, 10am - 6pm. 3 Nov - mid Feb 2002: Sats & Suns, 10am - 4pm. Last admission 1 hour before closing. Ring for information on Christmas Day and New Year holiday opening arrangements.

Admission: Adult £3.70, Child £1.85, Family ticket (2+3) £9.25. Groups £3.15. Car parking £1.50 per car.

Small museum. Ground floor & grounds suitable. Teacher and student packs and education base.

BORDE HILL GARDEN

HAYWARDS HEATH, WEST SUSSEX RH16 1XP

Owner: Mr & Mrs A P Stephenson Clarke   *Contact:* Sarah Brook

Visitor Attraction of the Year 1999 SEETB

Tel: 01444 450326   **Fax:** 01444 440427   **e-mail:** info@bordehill.co.uk

Winner of two prestigious awards. A haven of peace and tranquillity can be found at Borde Hill Garden, created in the 1890s, where botanical interest as well as garden design and renaissance play equally important roles. 'Linked' gardens, each with their own unique style, offer a rich variety of seasonal colours. Marvel at the splendour of flowering bulbs in early spring and award-winning collections of camellias, rhododendrons and azaleas in May and June. In summer, the exuberant herbaceous borders and fragrant English roses give way to a vivid blaze of autumnal colour. Borde Hill House, dating from 1593, is open to groups by appointment.

Location: OS Ref. TQ324 265. 1$^1/_2$ m N of Haywards Heath on Balcombe Road, 3m from A23. 45mins from Victoria Station.

Opening Times: All year: daily (including Christmas Day), 10am - 6pm (dusk if earlier).

Admission: Adult £5, Child £2.50, OAP £4.50, Family (2+3) £13. Pre-booked groups (20+): £4.25.

Licensed.   Licensed.   By arrangement.   P   In grounds, on leads.   Tel. for details.

BOXGROVE PRIORY

Tel: 01424 775705

Boxgrove, Chichester, Sussex

Owner: English Heritage   **Contact:** Area Manager

Remains of the Guest House, Chapter House and Church of this 12th century priory, which was the cell of a French abbey until Richard II confirmed its independence in 1383.

Location: OS Ref. SU909 076. N of Boxgrove, 4m E of Chichester on minor road N of A27.

Opening Times: Any reasonable time.

Admission: Free.

BRAMBER CASTLE

Tel: 01424 775705

Bramber, Sussex

Owner: English Heritage   **Contact:** Area Manager

The remains of a Norman castle gatehouse, walls and earthworks in a splendid setting overlooking the Adur valley.

Location: OS Ref. TQ187 107. On W side of Bramber village NE of A283.

Opening Times: Any reasonable time.

Admission: Free.

BRICKWALL HOUSE & GARDENS

Tel: 01797 253388   **Fax:** 01797 252567

Northiam, Rye, Sussex TN31 6NL

Owner: Frewen Educational Trust   **Contact:** The Curator

Impressive timber-framed house. 17th century drawing room with magnificent plaster ceilings and good portraits including by Lely, Kneller and Vereist. Topiary, chess garden.

Location: OS Ref. TQ831 241. S side of Northiam village at junction of A28 and B2088.

Opening Times: By appointment only.

Admission: £3.

CAMBER CASTLE

Tel: 01797 223862

Camber, Nr Rye, East Sussex

Owner: English Heritage   **Contact:** Rye Harbour Nature Reserve

A fine example of one of many coastal fortresses built by Henry VIII to counter the threat of invasion during the 16th century. Monthly guided walks of Rye Nature Reserve including Camber Castle, telephone for details.

Location: OS189, Ref. TQ922 185. Across fields off A259, 1m S of Rye off harbour road.

Opening Times: 1 Jul - 30 Sept: Sat & Sun, 2 - 5pm.

Admission: Adult £2, Child £1, Conc. £1.50.

Not suitable.   By arrangement.   P   No parking.   Guide dogs only.

CHARLESTON

See page 161 for full page entry.

CHICHESTER CATHEDRAL

Tel: 01243 782595   **Fax:** 01243 536190

Chichester, Sussex PO19 1PX   **Contact:** Mrs J Thom

In the heart of the city, this fine Cathedral has been a centre of Christian worship and community life for 900 years.

Location: OS Ref. SU860 047. West Street, Chichester.

Opening Times: Summer: 7.30am - 7pm, Winter: 7.30am - 5pm. Choral Evensong daily (except Weds) during term time.

Admission: Donation.

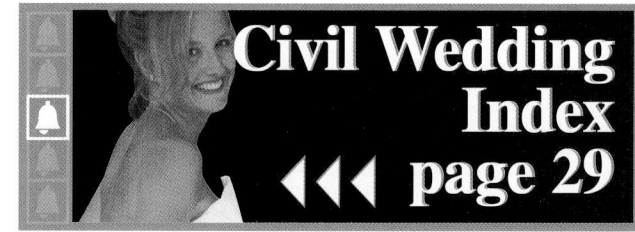

Civil Wedding Index ◀◀◀ page 29

FIRLE PLACE

FIRLE, Nr LEWES, EAST SUSSEX BN8 6LP

Owner: *The Rt Hon Viscount Gage*

Tel: 01273 858307 (enquiries) **Info:** 01273 858335 **Events:** 01273 858567
Fax: 01273 858188 **Restaurant:** 01273 858307 **e-mail:** gage@firleplace.co.uk

Firle Place is the home of the Gage family, and has been for over 500 years. Set at the foot of the Sussex Downs within its own parkland, this unique house originally Tudor, was built of Caen stone, possibly from a monastery dissolved by Sir John Gage, friend of Henry VIII. Remodelled in the 18th century it is similar in appearance to that of a French chateau. The house contains a magnificent collection of Old Master paintings, fine English and European furniture and an impressive collection of Sèvres porcelain collected mainly by the 3rd Earl Cowper from Panshanger House, Hertfordshire.

Events: The Great Tudor Hall can, on occasion, be used for private dinners, with drinks on the Terrace or in the Billiard Room. A private tour of the house can be arranged. The paddock area is an ideal site for a marquee. The park can be used for larger events, using the house as a backdrop.

Location: OS Ref. TQ473 071. 4m S of Lewes on A27 Brighton/Eastbourne Road.
Opening Times: 15/16 Apr & 6/7 May. 23 May - 27 Sept: Wed - Thur, Suns & BHs, 2 - 4.30pm. Guided tours.
Admission: Adult £4.50, Child £2, Conc. £4 Connoisseurs' Day (last Thurs each month, Jun - Sept) £5.

No photography in house.   Ground floor & restaurant suitable. Licensed. Tea Terrace.   In grounds on leads.

FISHBOURNE ROMAN PALACE

SALTHILL ROAD, FISHBOURNE, CHICHESTER, SUSSEX PO19 3QR

Owner: *Sussex Archaeological Society*   ***Contact:*** *David Rudkin*

Tel: 01243 785859   **Fax:** 01243 539266   **e-mail:** adminfish@sussexpast.co.uk

A Roman site built around AD75. A modern building houses part of the extensive remains including a large number of Britain's finest in-situ mosaics. The museum displays many objects discovered during excavations and an audio-visual programme tells Fishbourne's remarkable story. Roman gardens have been reconstructed and include a museum of Roman gardening.

Location: OS Ref. SU837 057. 1½ m W of Chichester in Fishbourne village off A27/A259.
Opening Times: 5 Feb - 14 Dec: daily. Feb, Nov - Dec: 10am - 4pm. Mar - Jul & Sept - Oct: 10am - 5pm. Aug: 10am - 6pm. 15 Dec - 4 Feb (excluding Christmas): Sats & Suns, 10am - 4pm.
Admission: Adult £4.50, Child £2.40, Conc. £3.90, Family (2+2): £11.70, Registered disabled £3.70. Groups (20+): Adult £3.90, Child £2.25, Conc. £3.70.

By arrangement.   Guide dogs only.   Tel. for details.

GLYNDE PLACE

GLYNDE, LEWES, SUSSEX BN8 6SX

Owners: *Viscount & Viscountess Hampden*   ***Contact:*** *Viscount Hampden*

Tel: 01273 858224   **Fax:** 01273 858224

Glynde Place is a magnificent example of Elizabethan architecture commanding exceptionally fine views of the South Downs. Amongst the collections of 400 years of family living can be seen a fine collection of 17th and 18th century portraits of the Trevors and a room dedicated to Sir Henry Brand, Speaker of the House of Commons 1872 - 1884 and an exhibition of 'Harbert Morley and the Great Rebellion 1638 - 1660' the story of the part played by the owner of Glynde Place in the Civil War. Plus a collection of 18th century Italian masterpieces.

Location: OS Ref. TQ457 093. In Glynde village 4m SE of Lewes on A27.
Opening Times: House & Garden: Jun & Sept: Weds & Suns. Jul & Aug: Weds, Thus & Suns, 2 - 5pm. Last adm. 4.45pm.
Admission: Adult £5, Child £2.50.

    Free.

South East England

GOODWOOD HOUSE   See page 162 for full page entry.

Goodwood House, Sussex.

GREAT DIXTER HOUSE & GARDENS

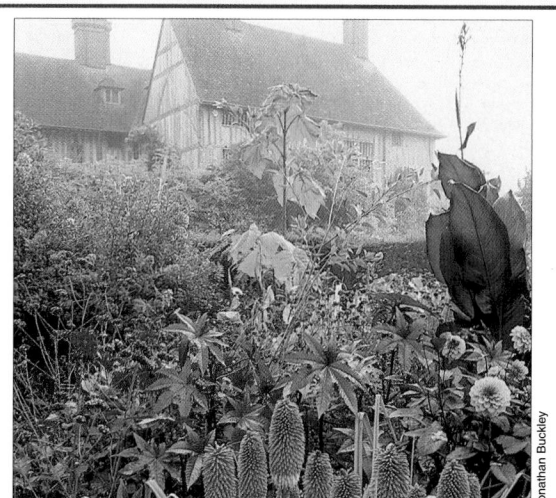

Jonathan Buckley

NORTHIAM, RYE, EAST SUSSEX TN31 6PH

Owner: Christopher Lloyd Contact: Elaine Francis, Business Manager

Tel: 01797 252878 **Fax:** 01797 252879 **e-mail:** greatdixter@compuserve.com
Great Dixter, birthplace and home of gardening writer Christopher Lloyd, was built c1450 and boasts one of the largest surviving timber-framed halls in the country. Lutyens was employed to restore both the house and gardens in 1910. The gardens are now the hallmark of Christopher Lloyd with an exciting combination of meadows, ponds, topiary and the famous Long Border and Exotic Garden.

Location: OS Ref. TQ817 251. Signposted off the A28 in Northiam.

Opening Times: 1 Apr - 28 Oct: Tue - Sun & BH Mons, 2 - 5.30pm (last admission 5pm). Gardens only open BH Suns & Mons, 11am - 5.30pm.

Admission: House & Garden: Adult £6, Child £1.50. Garden only: Adult £4.50, Child £1. Groups (25+) by appointment. House & garden: Adult £5, Child £1.50.

ⓘ No photography in House. 📷 ♿ 🅺 Obligatory.
🅿 Limited for coaches. 🐕 Guide dogs only.

HAMMERWOOD PARK

EAST GRINSTEAD, SUSSEX RH19 3QE

Owner/Contact: David Pinnegar

Tel: 01342 850594 **Fax:** 01342 850864 **e-mail:** latrobe@mistral.co.uk
Built in 1792 as an Apollo's hunting lodge by Benjamin Latrobe, architect of the Capitol and the White House, Washington DC. Owned by Led Zepplin in the 1970s, rescued from dereliction in 1982. Teas in the Organ Room; mural by French artists in the hall; and a derelict dining room still shocks the unwary. Guided tours (said by many to be the most interesting in Sussex) by the family.

Location: OS Ref. TQ442 390. 3¹/₂ m E of East Grinstead on A264 to Tunbridge Wells, 1m W of Holtye.

Opening Times: Easter Mon - end Sept: Wed, Sat & BH Mon, 2 - 5pm. Guided tour starts 2.05pm. Coaches strictly by appointment. Small groups any time throughout the year by appointment.

Admission: House & Park: Adult £5, Child £2. Private viewing by arrangement.

ⓘ Conferences. 🍽 🖥 🅺 Obligatory. 📷
🐕 In grounds. 🛏 B&B. ✳ ⛪ Please tel for details.

HERSTMONCEUX CASTLE GARDENS
Tel: 01323 833816   **Fax:** 01323 834499

Hailsham, Sussex BN27 1RN

e-mail: c_cullip@isc.queensu.ac.uk

Owner: Queen's University, Canada   **Contact:** C Cullip

This breathtaking 15th century moated Castle is within 500 acres of parkland and gardens (including Elizabethan Garden) and is ideal for picnics and woodland walks. At Herstmonceux there is something for all the family. For information on our attractions or forthcoming events tel: 01323 834457.

Location: OS Ref. TQ646 104. 2m S of Herstmonceux village (A271) by minor road. 10m WNW of Bexhill.

Opening Times: 13 Apr - 28 Oct: daily, 10am - 6pm (last adm. 5pm) Closes 5pm from Oct.

Admission: Grounds and Gardens: Adults £4, Child under 5 Free, Conc. £3. Castle Tour: Adult £2.50, Child £1 (under 5 Free). Group rates/bookings available.

[i] Visitor Centre.   [symbol] Suitable, limited for Castle Tour.   [symbols] [P]

[symbol] On leads.   [symbols] Tel. for details.

HIGH BEECHES GARDENS

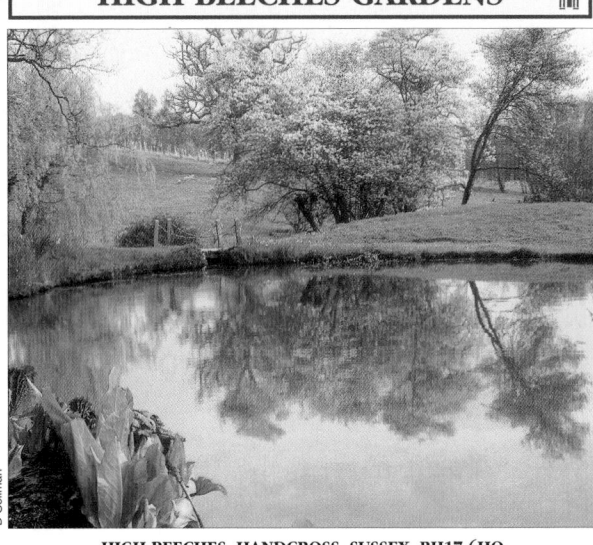

D Sellman

HIGH BEECHES, HANDCROSS, SUSSEX RH17 6HQ

Owner: *High Beeches Gardens Conservation Trust (Reg. Charity)*   **Contact:** *Sarah Bray*

Tel: 01444 400589   **Fax:** 01444 401543   **e-mail:** office@highbeeches.com

Help preserve these 20 acres of magically beautiful, peaceful woodland and water gardens. Daffodils, bluebells, azaleas, naturalised gentians, autumn colours. Rippling streams, enchanting vistas. Four acres of natural wildflower meadows. Rare plants. Tree trail. Recommended by Christopher Lloyd. Picnic area. Gardens may be booked for photographic sessions.

Location: OS Ref. TQ275 308. S side of B2110. 1m NE of Handcross.

Opening Times: 17 Mar - 30 Jun & 1 Sept - 31 Oct: Thur - Tue, 1 - 5pm (last admission). Jul & Aug: Sun - Tue, 1 - 5pm. Coaches and guided tours by appointment only.

Admission: Adult £4, Child (under 14) Free. Season ticket (admits 2): £20. Groups (30+) anytime by appointment: £3.50pp. Guided tours for groups £5pp.

[symbol] On Event Days.   [symbol] Not suitable.   [symbols] By appointment.   [P]   [symbol]
[symbol] Tel. for details.

HIGHDOWN GARDENS
Tel: 01903 501054

Littlehampton Road, Goring-by-Sea, Worthing, Sussex BN12 6PE

Owner: Worthing Borough Council   **Contact:** C Beardsley Esq

Unique gardens in disused chalk pit, begun in 1909.

Location: OS Ref. TQ098 040. 3m WNW of Worthing on N side of A259, just W of the Goring roundabout.

Opening Times: 1 Apr - 30 Sept: Mon - Fri, 10am - 6pm. W/ends & BHs, 10am - 6pm. 1 Oct - 30 Nov: Mon - Fri, 10am - 4.30pm. 1 Dec - 31 Jan: 10am - 4pm. 1 Feb - 31 Mar: Mon - Fri, 10am - 4.30pm.

Admission: Free.

LAMB HOUSE [symbol]
Tel: 01892 890651   **Fax:** 01892 890110

West Street, Rye, Sussex TN31 7ES

Owner: The National Trust   **Contact:** Regional Office

The home of the writer Henry James from 1898 to 1916 where he wrote the best novels of his later period.

Location: OS Ref. TQ920 202. In West Street, facing W end of church.

Opening Times: 4 Apr - 31 Oct: Weds & Sats only, 2 - 6pm. Last admission 5.30pm.

Admission: Adult £2.60, Child £1.30, Family (2+3) £6.50. Group: £2.20.

LEONARDSLEE GARDENS
See page 163 for full page entry.

LEWES CASTLE & BARBICAN HOUSE MUSEUM

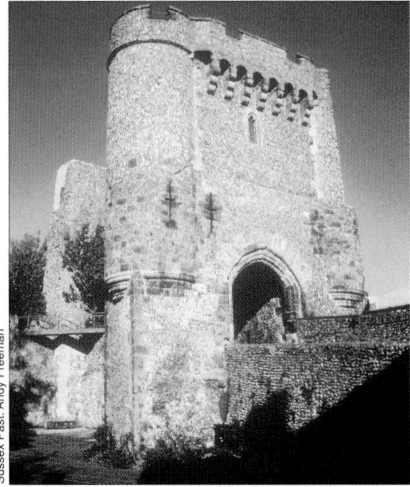

Sussex Past: Andy Freeman

169 HIGH STREET, LEWES, SUSSEX BN7 1YE

Owner: *Sussex Archaeological Society*   **Contact:** *Mrs Jill Allen*

Tel: 01273 486290   **Fax:** 01273 486990   **e-mail:** castle@sussexpast.co.uk

Lewes's imposing Norman castle offers magnificent views across the town and surrounding downland. Barbican House towered over by the Barbican Gate is home to the Museum of Sussex Archaeology; a superb scale model of Victorian Lewes provides the centrepiece of a 25 minute audio-visual presentation telling the story of the county town of Sussex.

Location: OS198 Ref. TQ412 101. Lewes town centre off A27/A26/A275.

Opening Times: Daily (except 8 Jan & 24 - 26 Dec). Mon - Sat: 10am - 5.30pm; Suns & BHs, 11am - 5.30pm. Castle closes at dusk in winter.

Admission: Adult £4, Child £2, Conc. £3.50 Family (2+2) £10.90 or (1+4) £8.00. Groups (15+): Adult £3.50, Child £1.60, Conc. £3. Combined ticket with Anne of Cleves House available.

[symbol]   [symbol] Not suitable.   [symbol] By arrangement.   [symbols] Tel. for details.

MARLIPINS MUSEUM
Tel: 01273 462994

High Street, Shoreham-by-Sea, Sussex BN43 5DA

Owner: Sussex Archaeological Society   **Contact:** Helen Poole

Shoreham's local and especially maritime history is explored at Marlipins, an important historic building of Norman origin.

Location: OS198 Ref. TQ214 051. Shoreham town centre on A259, W of Brighton.

Opening Times: Due to major rebuilding work Marlipins Museum's opening times during 2001 are uncertain. Please telephone 01273 487188 for details.

Admission: Adult £1.50, Child 75p (accompanied children, free), Conc. £1.

Patrick Lane.

Herstmonceux Castle Gardens, Sussex.

MERRIMENTS GARDENS

HAWKHURST ROAD, HURST GREEN, EAST SUSSEX TN19 7RA

Owner: Family owned   *Contact:* Mark Buchele

Tel: 01580 860666 **Fax:** 01580 860324 **e-mail:** info@merriments.co.uk

'A unique experiment in colour composition'.

Set in 4 acres of gently sloping Weald farmland, a naturalistic garden which never fails to delight. Deep curved borders richly planted and colour themed. An abundance of rare plants will startle the visitor with sheer originality.

The garden is planted according to prevailing conditions and only using plants suited for naturalising and colonising their environment. This natural approach to gardening harks back to the days of William Robinson and is growing in popularity, especially in Northern Europe. Alternatively many borders are colour themed and planted in the great tradition of English gardening. These borders use a rich mix of trees, shrubs, perennials and grasses and give an arresting display from spring to autumn.

Location: OS198, Ref. TQ412 101. Signposted off A21 London - Hastings road, at Hurst Green.

Opening Times: Apr - Sept: Mon - Sat, 10am - 5pm, Suns, 10.30am - 5pm.

Admission: Adult £3.50, Child £2. Groups (5+) by arrangement.

🏠 🥄 ♿ Partially suitable. 📷 Licensed. 🎋 By arrangement. 🅿
🐕 In grounds, on leads. (TW)

MICHELHAM PRIORY 🏛

Sussex Past: Andy Freeman

UPPER DICKER, HAILSHAM, SUSSEX BN27 3QS

Owner: Sussex Archaeological Society   *Contact:* Mr Simon Turner

Tel: 01323 844224   **Fax:** 01323 844030   **e-mail:** adminmich@sussexpast.co.uk

Set on a medieval moated island surrounded by superb gardens, the Priory was founded in 1229. The remains after the Dissolution were incorporated into a Tudor farm and country house that now contains a fascinating array of exhibits. Grounds include 14th century gatehouse, watermill, physic and cloister gardens and Elizabethan great barn.

Location: OS Ref. TQ557 093. 8m NW of Eastbourne off A22 / A27. 2m W of Hailsham.

Opening Times: 14 Mar - 28 Oct: Wed - Sun & BH Mons & daily in Aug. Mar & Oct: 10.30am - 4pm. Apr - Jul & Sept: 10.30am - 5pm. Aug: 10.30am - 5.30pm.

Admission: Adult £4.70, Child £2.30, Conc. £4, Family (2+2 or 1+4)) £11.50, Registered disabled & carer £2.35. Groups (15+): Adult/Conc. £3.80, Child £2.10.

🏠 🥄 ♿ 🍴 Licensed. 🎋 By arrangement. 🅿
🐕 Guide dogs only. 🔔 📱Tel. for details. (TW)

MONK'S HOUSE 🌿   **Tel:** 01892 890651 **Fax:** 01892 890110

Rodmell, Lewes BN7 3HF

Owner: The National Trust   **Contact:** Regional Office

A small weather-boarded house, the home of Leonard and Virginia Woolf until Leonard's death in 1969.

Location: OS Ref. TQ421 064. 4 m E of Lewes, off former A275 in Rodmell village, near church.

Opening Times: 4 Apr - 31 Oct: Weds & Sats, 2 - 5.30pm. Last admission 5pm.

Admission: Adult £2.60, Child £1.30, Family £6.50. Groups: Thurs only, 2 - 5.30pm, by arrangement with tenant.

MOORLANDS   **Tel:** 01892 652474

Friar's Gate, Crowborough, East Sussex TN6 1XF

Owner: Dr & Mrs Steven Smith   **Contact:** Dr Steven Smith

Four acre garden set in a lush valley adjoining Ashdown Forest. Primulas, azaleas and rhododendrons flourish by streams and a small lake. New river walk with views over garden. Many unusual trees and shrubs. Good autumn colour. Featured in Meridien TV programme.

Location: OS Ref. TQ498 329. 2m NW of Crowborough. From B2188 at Friar's Gate, take left fork signposted 'Crowborough Narrow Road', entrance 100yds on left. From Crowborough crossroads take St John's Road to Friar's Gate.

Opening Times: 1 Apr - 1 Oct: Weds, 11am - 5pm. 20 May & 15 Jul: Suns, 2 - 6pm. Other times by appointment only.

Admission: Adult £2.50, Child Free.

📷 ❄

Plant Sales Index page 47 ◀◀◀

NYMANS GARDEN

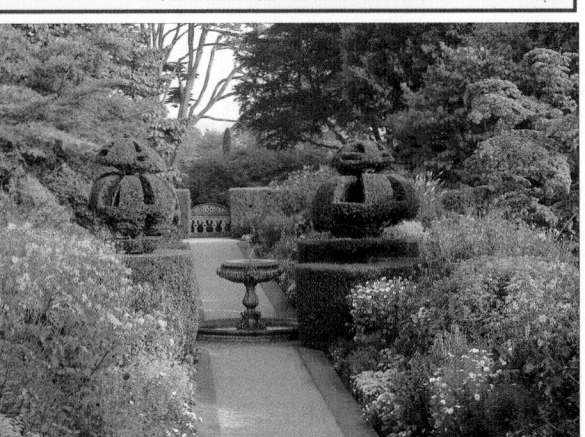

NT Photographic Library: Stephen Robson

HANDCROSS, HAYWARDS HEATH, SUSSEX RH17 6EB

Owners: *The National Trust*   **Contact:** *The Property Manager*

Tel: 01444 400321/400777 **Fax:** 01444 400253 **e-mail:** snygen@smtp.ntrust.org.uk

One of the great gardens of the Sussex Weald, with rare and beautiful plants, shrubs and trees from all over the world. Wall garden, hidden sunken garden, pinetum, laurel walk and romantic ruins. Lady Rosse's library, drawing room and forecourt garden also open. Woodland walks and Wild Garden.

Location: OS Ref. TQ265 294. On B2114 at Handcross, 4$^{1}/_{2}$ m S of Crawley, just off London - Brighton M23 / A23.

Opening Times: 1 Mar - 4 Nov: daily except Mon & Tue but open BHs, 11am - 6pm or sunset if earlier. House: 28 Mar - 4 Nov: same days as garden, closes at 4.30pm. Garden, tearoom & shop: Nov - Mar: Sats & Suns, 11am - 4pm. Closed 29 & 30 Dec 2001.

Admission: Adult £6, Child £3, Family £15. Pre-booked Groups £5. Joint group ticket which includes same day entry to Standen £9, available Wed - Fri only. Winter weekends: Adult £3, Child £1.50, Family £7.50. Booked groups: £2.50.

  Grounds suitable. WC. Licensed.

PALLANT HOUSE GALLERY   Tel: 01243 774557   Fax: 01243 536038

9 North Pallant, Chichester, West Sussex PO19 1TJ

Owner: Pallant House Gallery Trust   **Contact:** Mr Andrew Churchill

Lovingly restored Queen Anne townhouse with historic rooms in Georgian style, fine antique furniture and formal garden. Highly important collection of Bow porcelain and displays of modern British art (Nicholson, Nash, Moore, Sutherland, Piper etc). Georgian style walled garden.

Location: OS Ref. SU861 047. City centre, SE of the Cross.

Opening Times: All year: Tue - Sat ,10am - 5pm. Suns & BHs 12.30 - 5pm. Last admission 4.45pm. Closed Mons.

Admission: Adult £4, OAP. £3, Student/Unemployed £2.50. West Sussex students and child under 16 Free.

Peter Stiles.

Parham Park, Sussex.

PARHAM HOUSE & GARDENS

PARHAM PARK, Nr PULBOROUGH, WEST SUSSEX RH20 4HS

Owners: *Parham Park Trust*   **Contact:** *Patricia Kennedy*

Tel: 01903 744888/742021 **Fax:** 01903 746557 **e-mail:** Parham@dial.pipex.com

Friendly staff give a warm welcome to this stunning Elizabethan house with award-winning gardens, set in the heart of a medieval deer park below the South Downs. The light, panelled rooms, from Great Hall to magnificent Long Gallery house an important collection of contemporary paintings, furniture, working clocks and needlework, all complemented by informal arrangements of flowers, freshly cut twice a week from the four acre walled garden. Light lunches and cream teas are served in the 15th century Big Kitchen (licensed), and souvenirs and gifts can be purchased from the shop, with plants and herbs on sale from the garden shop.

STITCHES IN TIME
A needlework weekend 19 - 20 May 2001
Official opening by Kaffe Fassett

Parham is home to perhaps the finest and most important collection of 17th century embroidery to be found anywhere in the United Kingdom. During this weekend there will be a display of 18th and 19th century Samplers never before seen by visitors to Parham, demonstrations of needleworking techniques, lectures and sales tables.

John Bushell

Location: OS Ref. TQ060 143. Midway between Pulborough & Storrington on A283.

Opening Times: 1 Apr - 31 Oct: Weds, Thurs, Suns & BH Mons. Also Sats 19 May, 14 Jul & 1 Sept (special events). Private groups by arrangement at other times. Picnic area, Big Kitchen, and Gardens, 12 noon - 6pm. House: 2 - 6pm. Last entry 5pm.

Admission(2000 prices): House & Gardens: Adult £5, OAP £4, Child £1, Family (2+2) £10. Unguided booked groups (20+) £4. Garden only: Adult/OAP £3, Child 50p.

 No photography in house.   Partially suitable. Licensed.
In grounds, on leads.

South East England

PASHLEY MANOR GARDENS

TICEHURST, WADHURST, EAST SUSSEX TN5 7HE

Owner: James A Sellick   *Contact:* Caroline Foster

Tel: 01580 200888 **Fax:** 01580 200102 **e-mail:** pashleymanor@email.msn.com
HHA/Christie's Garden of the Year 1999. The gardens offer a sumptuous blend of romantic landscaping, imaginative plantings and fine old trees, fountains, springs and large ponds. This is a quintessentially English garden of a very individual character with exceptional views to the surrounding valleyed fields. Many eras of English history are reflected here, typifying the tradition of the English Country House and its garden.

Pashley prides itself on its delicious food. Home-made soups, ploughman's lunches with pickles and patés, fresh salad from the garden (whenever possible), home-made scones and delicious cakes, filter coffee, specialist teas, fine wines - served at the Terrace Restaurant or in the Old Stables Tearoom. The gift shop caters for every taste… from postcards and local honey to traditional hand-painted ceramics and

tapestry cushions. A wide selection of plants and shrubs, many of which grow at Pashley, are available for purchase.

Location: OS Ref. TQ 707 291. On B2099 between A21 and Ticehurst village.

Opening Times: 7 Apr - 29 Sept: Tues, Weds, Thurs, Sats and all BH Mons, 11am - 5pm. Garden only (restaurant & shop closed): 1 - 31 Oct: Mon - Fri, 11am - 4pm.

Admission: Adult £5, Child/OAP £4.50. Groups (min 20): £4.50. Coaches by appointment only.

⬜ 🌿 ♿Partially suitable. 🍽Licensed. 🍴By arrangement. 🅿
🐕Guide dogs only.

PETWORTH HOUSE 🌿   **See page 164 for full page entry.**

PEVENSEY CASTLE ⛩   **Tel:** 01323 762604

Pevensey, Sussex BN24 5LE

Owner: English Heritage   **Contact:** The Custodian

Originally a 4th century Roman Fort, Pevensey was the place where William the Conqueror landed in 1066 and established his first stronghold. The Norman castle included the remains of an unusual keep within the massive walls. Free audio tour tells the story of the Castle's 2,000 year history.

Location: OS Ref. TQ645 048. In Pevensey off A259.

Opening Times: 1 Apr - 30 Sept: daily, 10am - 6pm. 1 - 31 Oct: 10am - 5pm. 1 Nov - 31 Mar: Wed - Sun only, 10am - 4pm. Closed 24 - 26 Dec & 1 Jan.

Admission: Adult £2.50, Child £1.30, Conc. £1.90. 15% discount for groups of 11+.

♿Grounds suitable. 🍽 🎧Free. 🐕In grounds, on leads. ❋ 🎫Tel. for details.

PRESTON MANOR

PRESTON DROVE, BRIGHTON, EAST SUSSEX BN1 6SD

Owner: Brighton & Hove Council   *Contact:* David Beevers

Tel: 01273 292770 **Fax:** 01273 292771

A delightful Manor House which powerfully evokes the atmosphere of an Edwardian gentry home both 'upstairs' and 'downstairs'. Explore more than twenty rooms over four floors – from the servants' quarters, kitchens and butler's pantry in the basement to the attic bedrooms and nursery on the top floor. Plus charming walled gardens, pets' cemetery and 13th century parish church.

Location: OS Ref. TQ303 064. 2m N of Brighton on the A23 London road.

Opening Times: All year: Tue - Sat 10am - 5pm, Suns 2 - 5pm, Mons 1 - 5pm (BHs 10am - 5pm). Closed Good Fri, 25/26 Dec.

Admission: Adult £3.20, Child £2, Conc. £2.70. Groups (20+) £2.70. Prices valid until 31 Mar 2001.

ℹ️No photography. 🏪Gift kiosk. 🚽 ♿Not suitable.
🍴By arrangement. 🔲 🅿For coaches. 🐕 ❋ 🎫

Pashley Manor Gardens, Sussex.

THE PRIEST HOUSE

Tel: 01342 810479

North Lane, West Hoathly, Sussex RH19 4PP

Owner: Sussex Archaeological Society   **Contact:** Antony Smith

Standing in the beautiful surroundings of a traditional cottage garden on the edge of Ashdown Forest, the Priest House is an early 15th century timber-framed hall-house. In Elizabethan times it was modernised into a substantial yeoman's dwelling. Its furnished rooms contain 17th and 18th century furniture, kitchen equipment, needlework and household items. Formal herb garden.

Location: OS187 Ref. TQ362 325. In triangle formed by Crawley, East Grinstead and Haywards Heath, 4m off A22, 6m off M23.

Opening Times: 1 Mar - 31 Oct: Mon - Sat, 11am - 5.30pm, Suns, 2 - 5.30pm.

Admission: Adults £2.50, Child £1.20, Conc. £2.30. Groups (15+): Adult £2.30, Child £1.10.

⬚ ♿ Partially suitable. 🎨 By arrangement. 🅿 Limited. ▨
🐕 Guide dogs only. (W)

THE ROYAL PAVILION

See page 165 for full page entry.

Website Index page 39 ◀◀◀

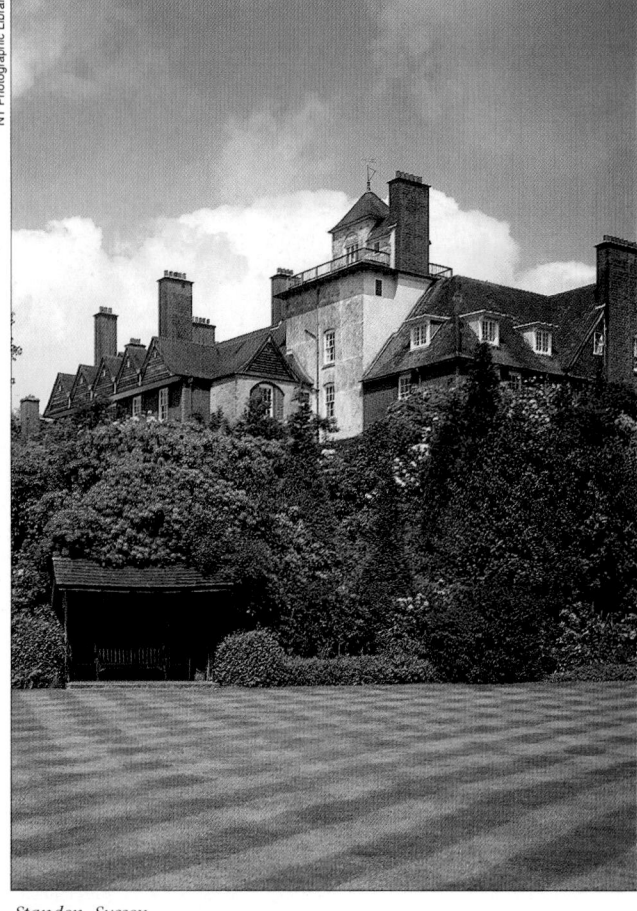

Standen, Sussex.

ST MARY'S HOUSE & GARDENS

BRAMBER, WEST SUSSEX BN44 3WE

Owner/Contact: Mr Peter Thorogood

Tel/Fax: 01903 816205 **e-mail:** stmaryshouse@btinternet.com

This enchanting, medieval timber-framed house is situated in the downland village of Bramber. The fine panelled interiors of St Mary's, which include the famous 'King's Room' associated with the escape of Charles II in 1651, and the unique Elizabethan 'Painted Room' with its intriguing *trompe l'oeil* murals, give an air of tranquillity and timelessness. Informative guided tours tell of fact and legend from earlier Knights Templar foundations to the present day. Once the home of the real Algernon and Gwendolen, brilliantly portrayed in Oscar Wilde's comedy, *The Importance of Being Earnest*, St Mary's was more than likely the setting for the Sherlock Holmes story, *The Musgrave Ritual*, and has served as a location for a number of television series including the world-famous *Dr Who*. The formal gardens with amusing animal topiary include an exceptional example of the 'Living Fossil' tree, *Gingko biloba*, and a mysterious ivy-clad 'Monk's Walk'. In the 'Secret Garden' can still be seen the Victorian original fruit-wall, potting shed, circular orchard, and woodland walk.

St Mary's is a house of fascination and mystery. Many thousands of visitors have admired its picturesque charm and enjoyed its atmosphere of friendliness and welcome, qualities which make it a visit to remember.

Location: OS Ref. TQ189 105. Bramber village off A283. From London 56m via M23/A23 or A24. Bus from Shorham to Steyning, alight St Mary's, Bramber.

Opening Times: Easter - Sept: Suns, Thurs & BH Mons, 2 - 6pm. Groups at other times by arrangement.

Admission: House & Garden: Adult £4, Child £2. Secret Garden: Adult £2, Child Free. Groups (25+) £3.80.

ℹ No photography in house. ⬚ ▮ ♿ Not suitable. ▨
🎨 Obligatory. Groups (max 60). Visit time $2^{1}/_{2}$hrs. 🅿 30 cars, 2 coaches. ▨
🐕 ▨ Tel. for details.

South East England

SHEFFIELD PARK GARDEN

SHEFFIELD PARK, EAST SUSSEX TN22 3QX

Owner: The National Trust   *Contact:* The Property Manager

Tel: 01825 790231 **Fax:** 01825 791264 **e-mail:** kshxxx@smtp.ntrust.org.uk

A magnificent tranquil 120 acre landscape garden, with 4 lakes, laid out in the 18th century by 'Capability' Brown. A garden for all seasons. Daffodils, snowdrops and bluebells in spring, its rhododendrons, azaleas and spring garden are spectacular in early summer. Cool tree-lined paths and lake reflections make it perfect for a stroll in high summer and the garden is ablaze with colour from its rare trees and shrubs in autumn. The mists and frosts in wintertime create a mystical mood and give the garden a unique atmosphere.

Location: OS Ref. TQ415 240. Midway between East Grinstead and Lewes, 5m NW

of Uckfield on E side of A275.

Opening Times: Jan & Feb: Sats & Suns only, 10.30am - 4pm. Mar - end Oct: Tue - Sun, BH Mons & Good Fri, 10.30am - 6pm, last admission 5pm or sunset if earlier. Nov & Dec: Tue - Sun, 10.30am - 4pm.

Admission: Adult £4.60, Child £2.30, Family (2+3) £11.50. Pre-booked groups £4.00. Joint ticket available with Bluebell Railway.

⬜ ♿ Grounds suitable. WC. ▣ Licensed (not NT).
🐕 Guide dogs only. ❄ ⓦ

STANDEN

NT Photographic Library, Jonathan Gibson.

EAST GRINSTEAD, WEST SUSSEX RH19 4NE

Owner: The National Trust   *Contact:* The Property Manager

Tel: 01342 323029 **Fax:** 01342 316424 **e-mail:** sstpro@smtp.ntrust.org.uk

Dating from the 1890s and containing original Morris & Co furnishings and decorations, Standen survives today as a remarkable testimony to the ideals of the Arts and Crafts movement. The property was built as a family home by the influential architect Phillip Webb and retains a warm, welcoming atmosphere. Details of Webb's designs can be found everywhere from the fireplaces to the original electric light fittings.

Location: OS Ref. TQ389 356. 2m S of East Grinstead, signposted from B2110.

Opening Times: 28 Mar - 4 Nov: Wed - Sun & BH Mons. House: 12.30 - 4pm (last admission). Garden: As house, 11am - 6pm. Garden only: 9 Nov - 16 Dec: Fri - Sun, 11am - 3pm.

Admission: House & Garden: £5.50, Family £13.75. Garden only: £3. Joint ticket with same day entry to Nymans Garden £9, available Wed - Fri. Groups: £4.50, Wed - Fri only, if booked in advance.

⬜ ♿ Partially suitable. WC. ▣ Licensed. 🚶 By arrangement. 🛏
🐕 In grounds on leads, not in garden. ⓦ

SAINT HILL MANOR

See page 166 for full page entry.

STANSTED PARK 🏠

See page 167 for full page entry.

UPPARK 🌿

See page 168 for full page entry.

WAKEHURST PLACE 🌿

Tel: 01444 894066

Ardingly, Haywards Heath, Sussex RH17 6TN

Owner: The National Trust (managed by Royal Botanic Gdns) **Contact:** The Administrator

A superb collection of exotic trees, shrubs and other plants, many displayed in a geographic manner. Extensive water gardens, a winter garden, a rock walk and many other features. The Loder Valley Nature Reserve can be visited by prior arrangement.

Location: OS Ref. TQ339 314. 1½ m N of Ardingly, on B2028.

Opening Times: Daily (not 25 Dec & 1 Jan). Feb & Oct: 10am - 5pm. Mar: 10am - 6pm. Apr - end Sept: 10am - 7pm. Nov - end Jan 2000: 10am - 4pm. Mansion closed 1hr before gardens.

Admission: Adult £5, Child (5-16) £2.50, Conc. £3.50, Family (2+4) £13. Reductions for pre-paid booked groups. (Prices valid until 31 March 2001).

⬜ ♿ Ground floor & grounds suitable. ▣ ▣ Tel. for details.

WEALD & DOWNLAND OPEN AIR MUSEUM

Tel: 01243 811363

Singleton, Chichester, Sussex PO18 0EU

40 original historic buildings. Interiors and gardens through the ages.

Location: OS Ref. SU876 127. 6m N of Chichester. SE side of A286. W of Singleton.

Opening Times: 1 Mar - 31 Oct: daily, 10.30am - 6pm. Nov - Feb: Weds & w/ends only. 10.30am - 4pm. 26 Dec - 3 Jan: 10.30am - 4pm.

Admission: Adult £7, Child/Student £4, OAP £6.50. Family (2+3) £17. Prices from 1 Mar 2001. Group rates on request.

WEST DEAN GARDENS

Carl Pendle

WEST DEAN, CHICHESTER, WEST SUSSEX PO18 0QZ

Owner: The Edward James Foundation   *Contact:* Jim Buckland, Gardens Manager

Tel: 01243 818210 **Fax:** 01243 811342 **e-mail:** westdean@pavilion.co.uk

Visiting the Gardens you are immersed in a classic 19th century designed landscape with its 2$^1/_2$ acre walled kitchen garden, 13 original glasshouses dating from the 1890s, 35 acres of ornamental grounds, 240 acre landscaped park and the 49 acre St Roche's arboretum, all linked by a scenic 2$^1/_4$ mile parkland walk. Features of the grounds are a lavishly planted 300ft long Edwardian pergola terminated by a flint and stone gazebo and sunken garden. The Visitor Centre (free entry) houses a licensed restaurant and an imaginative garden shop.

Location: OS Ref. SU863 128. SE side of A286 Midhurst Road, 6m N of Chichester.

Opening Times: 1 Mar - 31 October: daily. Mar, Apr & Oct: 11am - 5pm. May - Sept: 10.30am - 5pm.

Admission: Adult £4.50, Child £2, OAP £4. Groups (12+): Adult £4, Child £2.

ℹ No photography in house. 📷 ♿ 🍴 Licensed.
🅿 Limited for coaches. 🚶 By arrangement. 🐕 Guide dogs only.
Telephone for details.

WILMINGTON PRIORY

Tel: 01628 825920 or 825925 (bookings)

Wilmington, Nr Eastbourne, East Sussex BN26 5SW

Owner: Leased to the Landmark Trust by Sussex Archaeological Society

Contact: The Landmark Trust

Founded by the Benedictines in the 11th century, the surviving, much altered buildings date largely from the 14th century. Managed and maintained by the Landmark Trust, which lets buildings for self-catering holidays. Full details of Wilmington Priory and 170 other historic buildings available for holidays are featured in The Landmark Handbook (price £9.50 refundable against booking), from The Landmark Trust, Shottesbrooke, Maidenhead, Berkshire, SL6 3SW.

Location: OS Ref. TQ543 042. 600yds S of A27. 6m NW of Eastbourne.

Opening Times: Grounds, Ruins, Porch & Crypt: on 30 days between Apr - Oct. Whole property including interiors on 8 of these days, 22 - 25 May & 7 - 10 Sept 2001. Telephone for details. Accommodation is available for up to 6 people for self-catering holidays.

Admission: Please contact Landmark Trust for details.

Jim Buckland

West Dean Gardens, Sussex.

Merriments Garden, Sussex.

English Heritage Photo Library

OSBORNE HOUSE
East Cowes

Owner: English Heritage

CONTACT

The House Administrator
Osborne House
Royal Apartments
East Cowes
Isle of Wight
PO32 6JY

Tel: 01983 200022

Fax: 01983 297281

LOCATION

OS Ref. SZ516 948

1m SE of East Cowes.

Ferry: Isle of Wight
ferry terminals .

East Cowes 1¹/₂ m
Tel: 02380 334010.

Fishbourne 4m
Tel: 0870 58277441.

OSBORNE HOUSE was the peaceful, rural retreat of Queen Victoria, Prince Albert and their family; they spent some of their happiest times here.

Many of the apartments have a very intimate association with the Queen who died here in 1901 and have been preserved almost unaltered ever since. The nursery bedroom remains just as it was in the 1870s when Queen Victoria's first grandchildren came to stay. Children were a constant feature of life at Osborne (Victoria and Albert had nine). Don't miss the Swiss Cottage, a charming chalet in the grounds built for the Royal children to play and entertain their parents in.

Enjoy the beautiful gardens with their stunning views over the Solent and the newly opened fruit and flower Victorian walled garden. In commemoration of the 100th anniversary of Queen Victoria's death the Durbar Wing has been refurbished. In addition, for 2001 only, the Queen's bedroom will be re-displayed to recreate the historic and atmospheric arrangement of the room after her death on 22 January 1901

❖

English Heritage Photo Library

📷 ℹ️ Suitable for filming, concerts, drama. No photography in the House. Children's play area.

🍽️ Durbar Room available for functions.

♿ Wheelchairs available, access to house via ramp, ground floor access only. WC.

☕ Teas, coffees and light snacks. Waitress service in Swiss Cottage tearoom.

🅿️ Ample. Coach drivers and tour leaders free, one extra place for every additional 20. Group rates.

▪️ Visits free, please book. Education room available.

OPENING TIMES

House
1 April - 30 September
Daily: 10am - 6pm.

1 - 31 Oct
Daily: 10am - 5pm
Last admission 4pm.

May close earlier on concert days, please telephone for details.

Winter Tours:
1 Nov - 9 Dec 2001
Daily: 10am - 2.30pm
Sun, Mon, Wed & Thur.
Guided tours only, booking essential - please telephone 01983 200022.

Closed 10 Dec - 2 Feb 2002.

ADMISSION

House & Grounds
Adult	£7.20
Child* (5-15yrs)	£3.60
Conc.	£5.30
Family	£18.00

Grounds only
Adult	£3.80
Child* (5-15yrs)	£1.90
Conc.	£2.80

Winter & Spring Guided Tours
Adult	£6.00
Child	£3.30
Conc.	£4.40

Plus normal 15% discount for groups.

* Under 5yrs Free.

APPULDURCOMBE HOUSE ⌗

Tel: 01983 852484

Wroxall, Shanklin, Isle of Wight
Owner: English Heritage   **Contact:** Mr & Mrs Owen
The bleached shell of a fine 18th century Baroque style house standing in grounds landscaped by 'Capability' Brown. New Falconry Centre.
Location: OS Ref. SZ543 800. $^{1}/_{2}$ m W of Wroxall off B3327.
Opening Times: 1 Mar - 31 Mar: Sat & Sun, 10am - 4pm. 1 Apr - 30 Sept, daily, 10am - 6pm (last entry 5pm). 1 Oct - 31 Oct, daily, 10am - 4pm. 1 Nov - 19 Dec, Sat & Sun, 10am - 4pm.
Admission: Adult £2, Child £1, Conc. £1.50.

🖽   ♿   🅿 Limited.   🐕 In grounds, on leads.   ♥ Tel. for details.

BARTON MANOR GARDENS

Tel: 01983 292835 **Fax:** 01983 293923

Wippingham, East Cowes, Isle of Wight PO32 6LB
Owner: Robert Stigwood   **Contact:** Julia Richards
Location: OS Ref. SZ519 944. Wippingham, East Cowes, Isle of Wight.
Opening Times: Four Sundays in the year, please telephone 01983 528989 for details. Hospice contact Julia Clifton.
Admission: Please telephone for details.

BEMBRIDGE WINDMILL 🌿

Tel: 01983 873945

Enquiries to: NT Office, Strawberry Lane, Mottistone, Isle of Wight PO30 4EA
Owner: The National Trust   **Contact:** The Custodian
Dating from around 1700, this is the only windmill to survive on the Island. Much of its original wooden machinery is still intact and there are spectacular views from the top.
Location: OS Ref. SZ639 874. $^{1}/_{2}$ m W of Bembridge off B3395.
Opening Times: 1 Apr - end Jun, Sept - 26 Oct: Sun - Fri, but open Easter Sat. Jul & Aug: daily, 10am - 5pm (last admission 4.30pm).
Admission: Adult £1.60, Child 80p. Special charge for guided tours.

🖽   ♿ Not suitable.   🗝 By arrangement.   🐕

CARISBROOKE CASTLE ⌗

NEWPORT, ISLE OF WIGHT PO30 1XY
Owner: English Heritage   *Contact:* The Custodian

Tel: 01983 522107 **Fax:** 01983 528632
The Island's Royal fortress and prison of King Charles I before his execution in London in 1648. See the famous Carisbrooke donkeys treading the wheel in the Well House or meet them in the donkey centre. Don't miss the castle story in the gatehouse, the museum in the great hall and the interactive coach house museum. Costumed guided tours available in summer.
Location: OS196 Ref. SZ486 877. Off the B3401, 1$^{1}/_{4}$ m SW of Newport.
Opening times: 1 Apr - 30 Sept: daily, 10am - 6pm. 1 - 31 Oct: 10am - 5pm. 1 Nov - 31 Mar: daily, 10am - 4pm. Closed 24 - 26 Dec & 1 Jan.
Admission: Adult £4.50, Child £2.30, Conc. £3.40, Family (2+3) £11.30. 15% discount for groups (11+), extra place for additional groups of 20.

🖽   ♿   🍴   🐕 In grounds, on leads.   ❄   ♥ Tel. for details.

Photo credit (vertical): © English Heritage Photo Library © Skyscan Balloon Photography

DIMBOLA LODGE

TERRACE LANE, FRESHWATER BAY PO40 9QE
Owner: Julia Margaret Cameron Trust   *Contact:* The Administrator

Tel: 01983 756814 **Fax:** 01983 755578
e-mail: administrator@dimbola.co.uk
Historic house, former home of internationally known 19th century photographer Julia Margaret Cameron, with museum and galleries. Permanent display of Cameron images. Contemporary revolving photographic exhibitions, lectures, photographic courses, and musical performances. Available for hire, book launches, etc.
Location: OS Ref. SZ348 858. From Lymington to Yarmouth and Portsmouth to Fishbourne, Wight Link Ferries. Then A3054 to Totland and then A3055. From Southampton, Red Funnel Ferries to Cowes then A3021 to A3054.
Opening Times: All year: Tue - Sun inclusive & BH Mons, 10am - 5pm. Closed for 5 days at Christmas.
Admission: Adult £3, Child (under 16yrs) Free. Groups (5 - 45) 10% discount.

ℹ No photography in house.   🖽   🍸   ♿   🎁   🍴   🗝 By arrangement.   🅿 Limited.   🍴   🐕   ❄   (IW)

MORTON MANOR

Tel: 01983 406168

Brading, Isle of Wight PO36 0EP
Owner/Contact: Mr J B Trzebski
Refurbished in the Georgian period. Magnificent gardens and vineyard.
Location: OS Ref. SZ603 863 (approx.). $^{1}/_{4}$ m W of A3055 in Brading.
Opening Times: 8 Apr - end Oct: daily except Sats, 10am - 5.30pm.
Admission: Adult £4, Child £1.75, Conc. £3.50, Group £3. (Prices subject to review in 2001.)

MOTTISTONE MANOR GARDEN 🌿

Tel: 01983 741302

Mottistone, Isle of Wight
Owner: The National Trust   **Contact:** The Gardener
A haven of peace and tranquillity with colourful herbaceous borders and a backdrop of the sea making a perfect setting for the historic Manor House. An annual open air Jazz Concert is held in the grounds during July/August.
Location: OS Ref. SZ406 838. 2m W of Brightstone on B3399.
Opening Times: 25 Mar - 28 Oct: Suns, Weds & BH Mons, 2 - 5.30pm. House: Aug BH Mon only, 2 - 5.30pm.
Admission: Adult £2.50, Child £1.20.

♿ Not suitable.   🎁   🐕 In grounds, on leads.

NEEDLES OLD BATTERY

Tel: 01983 754772

West High Down, Isle of Wight PO39 0JH

Owner: The National Trust   **Contact:** The Administrator

High above the sea, the Old Battery was built in the 1860s against the threat of French invasion.

Location: OS Ref. SZ300 848. Needles Headland W of Freshwater Bay & Alum Bay (B3322).

Opening Times: 1 Apr - 28 Jun, 2 Sept - 1 Nov: Sun - Thur (open Easter weekend) & Jul & Aug: daily, 10.30am - 5pm (last admission 4.30pm).

Admission: Adult £3, Child £1.50, Family £6. Special charge for guided tours.

Grounds suitable.   In grounds, on leads.

NUNWELL HOUSE & GARDENS

Tel: 01983 407240

Brading, Isle of Wight PO36 0JQ

Owner: Col & Mrs J A Aylmer   **Contact:** Mrs J A Aylmer

A lived in family home with fine furniture, attractive gardens and historic connections with Charles I.

Location: OS Ref. SZ595 874. 1m NW of Brading. 3m S of Ryde signed off A3055.

Opening Times: 27/28 May, then Mon - Wed, 2 Jul - 5 Sept: 1 - 5pm.

Admission: Adult £4, Pair of Adults £7.50 (inc guide book), OAP/Student £3, Child (up to 10yrs) £1. Garden only: Adult £2.50.

OLD TOWN HALL

Tel: 01983 531785

Newtown, Isle of Wight

Owner: The National Trust   **Contact:** The Custodian

A charming small 18th century building that was once the focal point of the 'rotten borough' of Newtown.

Location: OS Ref. SZ424 905. Between Newport and Yarmouth, 1m N of A3054.

Opening Times: 28 Mar - end Jun, Sept - 31 Oct: Mons, Weds & Suns (open Good Fri & Easter Sat) & Jul & Aug: daily except Fri & Sat, 2 - 5pm last admission 4.30pm.

Admission: Adult £1.50, Child 75p. Special charge for guided tours (written application).

Not suitable.   **P** Limited.   Guide dogs only.

OSBORNE HOUSE

See page 181 for full page entry.

YARMOUTH CASTLE

Tel: 01983 760678

Quay Street, Yarmouth, Isle of Wight PO41 0PB

Owner: English Heritage   **Contact:** The Custodian

This last addition to Henry VIII's coastal defences was completed in 1547 and is, unusually for its kind, square with a fine example of an angle bastion. It was garrisoned well into the 19th century. It houses exhibitions of paintings of the Isle of Wight and photographs of old Yarmouth.

Location: OS Ref. SZ354 898. In Yarmouth adjacent to car ferry terminal.

Opening Times: 1 Apr - 30 Sept: daily, 10am - 6pm. 1 - 31 Oct: 10am - 5pm.

Admission: Adult £2.20, Child £1.10, Conc. £1.60.

Ground floor suitable.   **P** No parking.   In grounds, on leads.

The Needles, Isle of Wight.

Minterne Gardens, Dorset

South West

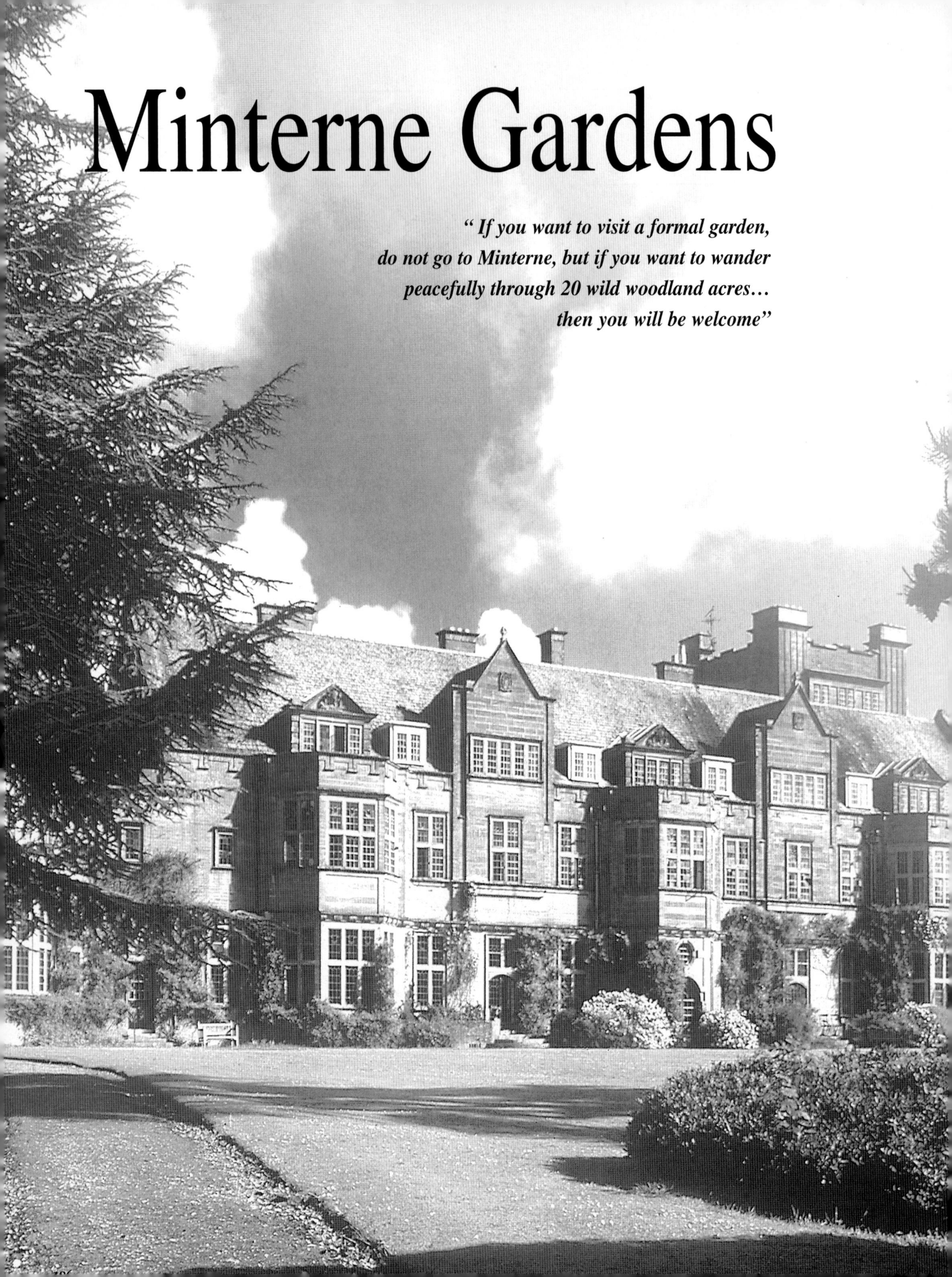

Minterne Gardens

*" If you want to visit a formal garden,
do not go to Minterne, but if you want to wander
peacefully through 20 wild woodland acres…
then you will be welcome"*

Once the home of the Churchill family, Minterne has been the property of the Digbys for the last 350 years. Admiral Robert Digby, on purchasing the estate in 1768, was to write, *"Visited my new estate, valley very bare, trees not thriving, house ill contrived and ill situated!"* – yet he obviously immediately saw the potential of this beautiful deep cut valley, as has every succeeding generation of the Digby family, all of whom are responsible for the interest found throughout the garden today.

The gardens are laid out in a horseshoe below Minterne House, with a chain of small lakes, streams and cascades. The house itself is not open to the general public but it is an integral part of the visit to the gardens. Built on the site of the original Churchill house, it is one of the great Edwardian houses of England. Designed by Leonard Stokes, a founder member of the Arts & Crafts movement and completed in 1906, built in soft apricot Ham Hill stone it shows an Elizabethan South Front and Gothic North Front.

The gardens are themselves composed of two quite different elements, an 18th century landscape, possibly influenced by 'Capability' Brown, and a 19th century woodland garden.

Admiral Robert Digby created the lakes, the cascades and Eleanor's bridge in 1785, together with the planting of the shelter belts of beech and pines along the tops of the hills and the park trees.

In the 1880s the family was to add rhododendrons from the Hooker expedition to the Himalayas and seedlings from the Wilson collection were brought back from China in 1903 and 1906.

Today, wandering along the paths and over the stepping stones and bridges, these two gardens seem to have meshed together imperceptibly, creating an atmosphere as rich as a Himalayan forest. At Minterne enjoy some of the most exciting varieties of azaleas, maples and magnolias, together with handkerchief trees, bamboos and swamp cypress – the result is a wonderfully lush and colourful visit.

The house, which contains magnificent Churchill tapestries and naval and other historical pictures, is open for special interest groups only, which may be arranged by prior appointment. Contact The Lord Digby on 01300 341370.

For further details about *Minterne Gardens* see entry in South West Region ➔ Dorset.

South West England

National Trust/Peter Cade.

ANTONY HOUSE & GDN.
& ANTONY WOODLAND GDN.
Torpoint

Antony House
Owner: The National Trust

**Antony Woodland
Garden
Owner:**
Carew Pole Garden Trust

CONTACT

Antony House
The Administrator
Antony House & Gdn
Torpoint
Cornwall
PL11 2QA

Tel: 01752 812191

**Antony Woodland
Garden**
Mrs Valerie Anderson
Antony
Torpoint
Cornwall
PL11 2QA

Tel: 01752 812364

LOCATION

OS Ref. SX418 564

**Antony House and
Antony Woodland
Garden**
5m W of Plymouth via
Torpoint car ferry,
2m NW of Torpoint.

ANTONY HOUSE AND GARDEN: A superb example of an early 18th century mansion. The main block is faced in lustrous silver-grey stone, flanked by mellow brick pavilions. The ancestral home of the Carew family for nearly 600 years, the house contains a wealth of paintings, tapestries, furniture and embroideries, many linking the great families of Cornwall – set in parkland and fine gardens (including the National Collection of day lilies), overlooking the Lynher river. An 18th century Bath House can be viewed by arrangement.

ANTONY WOODLAND GARDEN: The woodland garden was established in the late 18th century with the assistance of Humphrey Repton. It features numerous varieties of camellias, together with magnolias, rhododendrons, azaleas and other flowering shrubs, interspersed with many fine species of indigenous and exotic trees. A further 50 acres of natural woods bordering the tidal waters of the Lynher provide a number of delightful walks. The Woodland Garden is at its finest in the spring and autumn months.

❖

National Trust/ Dan Flunder.

📷 ♿ Braille guide. ☕ 🐕

OPENING TIMES

**Antony House
and Garden**
3 Apr - 31 May &
4 Sept - 1 Nov:
Tue - Thur & BH Mons.

Jun, Jul & Aug: daily
except Mons, Fris & Sats
(open BH Mons),
1.30 - 5.30pm.
Last admission 4.45pm.

The Bath Pond House
can be seen by written
application.

Guided tours at
less busy times.

**Antony Woodland
Garden**
1 March - 31 October
Daily except Mons & Fris
but open BHs
11am - 5.30pm.

National Trust Tearoom
On open days,
12.30 - 5.30pm.

ADMISSION

Antony House & Garden
Adult £4.20
Groups.................. £3.50
Family £10.50

NT Garden only:
.............................£2.00
Groups..................£1.80

**Antony Woodland
Garden:**
Adult £3.00

Joint Gardens-only ticket
to NT-owned garden and
Antony Woodland Garden
Adult £3.60
Child £1.50
Groups £3.00

NB. Entrance to the
Woodland Garden is free
to NT members on days
when the house is open.

National Trust/Andrew Besley.

Owner: The National Trust

CONTACT

Lewis Eynon
Property Manager
Cotehele
St Dominick
Saltash
Cornwall
PL12 6TA

Tel: 01579·351346

Fax: 01579 351222

e-mail:
cctlce@smtp.ntrust.org.uk

LOCATION

OS Ref. SX422 685

1m SW of Calstock by foot.
8m S of Tavistock,
4m E of Callington,
15m from Plymouth via the
Tamar bridge at Saltash

Trains: Limited service
from Plymouth to Calstock
($1^1/_4$ m uphill)

Boats: Limited (tidal)
service from Plymouth to
Calstock Quay (Plymouth
Boat Cruises)
Tel: 01752 822797

River taxi: Privately run
from Calstock to Cotehele
Quay. Tel: 01579 351346

Buses: Western National
(seasonal variations)
Tel: 01752 222666

COTEHELE
Saltash

COTEHELE, owned by the Edgcumbe family for nearly 600 years, is a fascinating and enchanting estate set on the steep wooded slopes of the River Tamar. Exploring Cotehele's many and various charms provides a full day out for the family and leaves everyone longing to return.

The steep valley garden contains exotic and tender plants which thrive in the mild climate. Remnants of an earlier age include a mediaeval stewpond and domed dovecote, a 15th century chapel and 18th century tower with fine views over the surrounding countryside. A series of more formal gardens, terraces, an orchard and a daffodil meadow surround Cotehele House.

One of the least altered medieval houses in the country, Cotehele is built in local granite, slate and sandstone. Inside the ancient rooms, unlit by electricity, is a fine collection of textiles, tapestries, armour and early dark oak furniture. The chapel contains the oldest working domestic clock in England, still in its original position.

A walk through the garden and along the river leads to the quay, a busy river port in Victorian times. The National Maritime Museum worked with the National Trust to set up a museum here which explains the vital role that the Tamar played in the local economy. As a living reminder, the restored Tamar sailing barge *Shamrock* (owned jointly by the Trust and the National Maritime Museum) is moored here.

A further walk through woodland along the Morden stream leads to the old estate corn mill which has been restored to working order.

This large estate with many footpaths offers a variety of woodland and countryside walks, opening up new views and hidden places. The Danescombe Valley, with its history of mining and milling, is of particular interest.

National Trust /Tymn Lintell.

[i] No photography in house. *NPI National Heritage Award winners 1996 & 1999.*

[icon] Cotehele Quay Gallery offers a wide range of local hand-made arts and crafts.

[icon] Available for up to 90 people.

[icon] 2 wheelchairs at Reception. Hall & kitchen accessible. Ramps at house, restaurant and shop. Most of garden is very steep with loose gravel. Riverside walks are flatter (from Cotehele Quay) & Edgcumbe Arms is accessible. WCs near house and at Quay. Parking near house & mill by arrangement.

[icon] In Barn restaurant (can be booked) daily (except Fri), Apr - Oct. At the Quay, Edgcumbe Arms offers lighter meals daily, Apr - Oct (plus weekends in March). Both licensed.

[P] Near house and garden and at Cotehele Quay. No parking at Mill.

[icon] Groups (15+) must book with Property Manager and receive a coach route (limited to two per day). No groups Sun & BH weekends. Visitors to house limited to 80 at any one time. Please arrive early and be prepared to queue. Avoid dull days early and late in the season. Allow a full day to see estate.

[icon] Under control welcome only on woodland walks. [icon]

OPENING TIMES

House & Restaurant
31 Mar - 4 Nov: Daily
except Fris (but open
Good Fri), 11am - 5pm
(Oct & Nov:
11am - 4.30pm).

Mill
31 Mar - 30 June &
1 Sept - 4 Nov: Daily
except Fris (but open
Good Fri). Jul & Aug: Daily
Jul & Aug: 1 - 6pm
Mar, Jun & Sept: 1 - 5.30pm
Oct & Nov: 1 - 4.30pm.

Garden
All year: daily,
10.30am - dusk.

Gallery & Tearoom on Quay
31 Mar - 4 Nov: Daily,
11am - 5pm.
Gallery: 12 noon - 5pm or
dusk. Nov & Dec:
Christmas openings,
telephone 01579 351494.

ADMISSION

House, Garden & Mill
Adult £6.20
Family Tickets.......£15.50

Pre-booked Groups
.................................£5.20

Garden & Mill only
Adult £3.40
Family £8.50

*Groups must book in
advance with the
Property Manager. No
groups Suns or BHs.

NT members free.
You may join here.

National Trust Photographic Library. R Truman.

Owner: The National Trust

CONTACT

Property Manager
Lanhydrock
Bodmin
Cornwall
PL30 5AD

Tel: 01208 73320

Fax: 01208 74084

e-mail:
clhlan@smtp.ntrust.org.uk

LOCATION

OS Ref. SX085 636

2½ m SE of Bodmin,
follow signposts from
either A30, A38 or B3268.

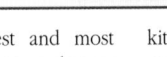

LANHYDROCK
Bodmin

LANHYDROCK is the grandest and most welcoming house in Cornwall, set in a glorious landscape of gardens, parkland and woods overlooking the valley of the River Fowey.

The house dates back to the 17th century but much of it had to be rebuilt after a disastrous fire in 1881 destroyed all but the entrance porch and the north wing, which includes the magnificent Long Gallery with its extraordinary plaster ceiling depicting scenes from the Old Testament. A total of 49 rooms are on show today and together they reflect the entire spectrum of life in a rich and splendid Victorian household, from the many servants' bedrooms and the fascinating complex of kitchens, sculleries and larders to the nursery suite where the Agar-Robartes children lived, learned and played, and the grandeur of the dining room with its table laid and ready.

Surrounding the house on all sides are gardens ranging from formal Victorian parterres to the wooded higher garden where magnificent displays of magnolias, rhododendrons and camellias climb the hillside to merge with the oak and beech woods all around. A famous avenue of ancient beech and sycamore trees, the original entrance drive to the house, runs from the pinnacled 17th century gatehouse down towards the medieval bridge across the Fowey at Respryn.

National Trust Photographic Library, Andreas von Einsiedel.

National Trust/Tony Kent.

 No photography in house.

By arrangement.

Suitable. Braille guide. WC.

Licensed restaurant

In park, on leads. Guide dogs only in house.

P Limited for coaches.

ANTONY HOUSE & GARDEN
ANTONY WOODLAND GARDEN

See page 190 for full page entry.

BOSVIGO

Tel/Fax: 01872 275774

Bosvigo Lane, Truro, Cornwall TR1 3NH   **e-mail:** bosvigo.plants@virgin.net

Owner: Michael & Wendy Perry   **Contact:** Michael Perry

A series of small, densely planted 'rooms', each with its own colour theme, surround the Georgian house (not open). The mainly herbaceous plantings give non-stop colour from June to the end of September. The Hot Garden will 'blow your socks off' in August. Small specialist nursery attached.

Location: OS Ref. SW815 452. ³/₄ m W of Truro city centre. Turn off A390 down Dobbs Lane just W of Sainsbury foodstore.

Opening Times: Mar - end Sept: Thur - Sat, 11am - 6pm.

Admission: Adult £3, Child (5-15yrs) £1. No group concessions.

[icons] Partially suitable. [P] Limited. [icon]

BURNCOOSE NURSERIES & GARDEN

Gwennap, Redruth, Cornwall TR16 6BJ   **Tel:** 01209 860316 **Fax:** 01209 860011

Owner/Contact: C H Williams   **e-mail:** burncoose@eclipse.co.uk

The Nurseries are set in the 30 acre woodland gardens of Burncoose.

Location: OS Ref. SW742 395. 2m SE of Redruth on main A393 Redruth to Falmouth road between the villages of Lanner and Ponsanooth.

Opening Times: Mon – Sat: 9am - 5pm, Suns, 11am - 5pm. Gardens and Tearooms open all year (except Christmas Day).

Admission: Nurseries: Free. Gardens: Adult/Conc. £2. Children Free. Group tours: £2.50 by arrangement.

[icons] Grounds suitable. WCs. [icon] In grounds, on leads. [icons]

CAERHAYS CASTLE & GARDEN

Tel: 01872 501310 **Fax:** 01872 501870

Caerhays, Gorran, St Austell, Cornwall PL26 6LY   **e-mail:** estateoffice@caerhays.co.uk

Owner: F J Williams Esq   **Contact:** Miss A B Mayes

One of the very few Nash built castles still left standing – situated within approximately 60 acres of informal woodland gardens created by J C Williams, who sponsored plant hunting expeditions to China at the turn of the century. Noted for its camellias, magnolias, rhododendrons and oaks. English Heritage listing - Grade I: Outstanding.

Location: OS Ref. SW972 415. S coast of Cornwall – between Mevagissey and Portloe. 9m SW of St Austell.

Opening Times: House: 19 Mar - 27 Apr: Mon - Fri (excluding BHs), 2 - 4pm, booking recommended. Gardens: 12 Mar - 18 May: Mon - Fri, 10am - 4pm. Charity openings (gardens only): 25 Mar, 15 Apr & 7 May: 10am - 4pm.

Admission: House: £3.50. Gardens: £3.50. House & Gardens: £6. Guided group tours by Head Gardener £4.50. These can be arranged outside normal opening times.

[icons] Not suitable. [icon] In grounds, on leads. [icon]

CHYSAUSTER ANCIENT VILLAGE

Tel: 07831 757934

Nr Newmill, Penzance, Cornwall TR20 8XA

Owner: English Heritage   **Contact:** The Custodian

On a windy hillside, overlooking the wild and spectacular coast, is this deserted Romano-Cornish village with a 'street' of eight well preserved houses, each comprising a number of rooms around an open court.

Location: OS203 Ref. SW473 350. 2¹/₂ m NW of Gulval off B3311.

Opening Times: 1 Apr - 31 Oct: daily, 10am - 6pm (5pm in Oct). Winter: closed.

Admission: Adult £1.70, Child 90p, Conc. £1.30. 15% discount for groups (11+).

[P] No coaches. [icon] On leads. [icon] Telephone for details.

CHYVERTON

Tel: 01872 540324 **Fax:** 01872 540648

Zelah, Truro, Cornwall TR4 9HD

Owner/Contact: Nigel Holman

The garden contains one of the finest collections of woody plants in private hands originating from all the temperate regions of the world, built up over the past 75 years by the Holman family. Exceptional magnolias. All growing in the setting of a Georgian landscape garden, creating 'The Magic Jungle of Chyverton' *(Tradescant - The Garden)*.

Location: OS Ref. SW797 512. A30, 20m W of Bodmin, 8m E of Redruth signed 1m W of Zelah.

Opening Times: 1 Mar - 30 Sept: by appointment.

Admission: Groups of 1-20 £4 and 21+ £3.50. Child under 16yrs Free.

[icon] Not suitable. [icon] Lunch in House (II*) by arrangement (20 max). [icon] Obligatory. [P] Limited for coaches. [icon] [icon] In grounds on leads.

COTEHELE

See page 191 for full page entry.

GLENDURGAN GARDEN

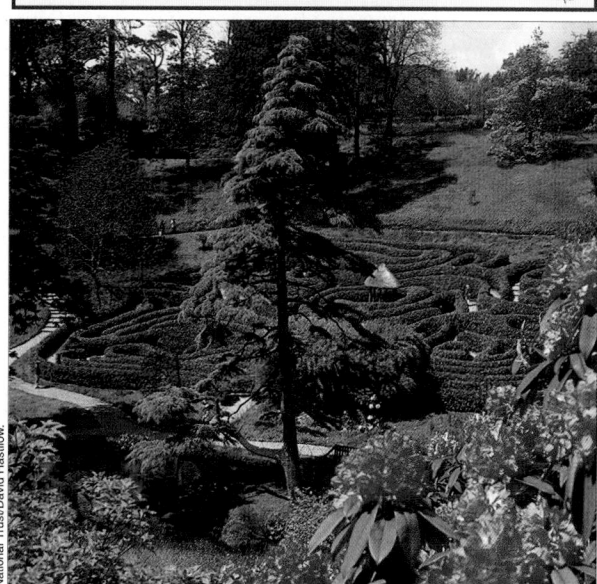

National Trust/David Hastilow

MAWNAN SMITH, FALMOUTH, CORNWALL TR11 5JZ

Owner: The National Trust   Contact: Reception

Tel: 01326 250906 (opening hours) or 01872 862090 **Fax:** 01872 865808

A valley garden of great beauty with fine trees, shrubs and water gardens. The laurel maze, recently restored, is an unusual and popular feature. The garden runs down to the tiny village of Durgan and its beach on the Helford River.

Location: OS Ref. SW772 277. 4m SW of Falmouth, ¹/₂ m SW of Mawnan Smith, on road to Helford Passage. 1m E of Trebah Garden.

Opening Times: 17 Feb - 3 Nov: Tue - Sat & BH Mons (closed Good Fri), 10.30am - 5.30pm. Last admission 4.30pm.

Admission: £3.60, Family £9. Pre-arranged groups: £3.

[icons] Braille guide. [icons]

GODOLPHIN

GODOLPHIN CROSS, HELSTON, CORNWALL TR13 9RE

Owner: Mrs L M P Schofield   Contact: Mrs Joanne Schofield

Tel/Fax: 01736 763194 **e-mail:** godo@euphony.net

A romantic Tudor and Stuart mansion, commenced in c1475. The development of the Godolphin family's courtly ambition and taste is beautifully expressed in the evolving architecture of the house. Exploitation of tin provided the wealth for this family of soldiers, entrepreneurs, poets and government officials. Birthplace of Queen Anne's Lord Treasurer. The large, compartmented Side Garden dates from the late 15th century also, though it grew out of an early 14th century Castle garden (still gardened). Good 16th and 17th century English Oak furniture. 1731 painting of the Godolphin Arabian by John Wotton and pictures by American impressionist Elmer Schofield. Godolphin is undergoing a programme of English Heritage funded repairs but works will cease from Easter to October 2001. Adjacent walks on the National Trust estate.

Location: OS Ref. SW602 318. Breage, Helston. On minor road from Breage to Townshend.

Opening Times: May - Jun: Thurs & Suns, 2 - 5pm. Jul, Aug & Sept: Thur & Fri & Suns, 2 - 5pm. Open BHs from Easter - end Sept: 2 - 5pm. Group bookings and tours by prior arrangement.

Admission: Adults £3, Child £1

[icons] Limited. [icon] [P] 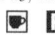 Guide dogs only.

THE JAPANESE GARDEN & BONSAI NURSERY

Tel: 01637 860116

e-mail: rob@thebonsainursery.com   **Fax:** 01637 860887

St Mawgan, Nr Newquay, Cornwall TR8 4ET   **Owner/Contact:** Mr & Mrs Hore

Authentic Japanese Garden set in 1¹/₂ acres.

Location: OS Ref. SW873 660. Follow road signs from A3059 & B3276.

Opening Times: Summer: Daily 10am - 6pm. WInter: 10am - 5.30pm. Closed Christmas Day - New Year's Day.

Admission: Adult £2.50, Child £1. Groups (10+): £2.

KEN CARO

Tel: 01579 362446

Bicton, Liskeard PL14 5RF   **Owner/Contact:** Mr and Mrs K R Willcock

4 acre plantsman's garden.

Location: OS Ref. SX313 692. 5m NE of of Liskeard.

Opening Times: 15 Apr - 30 Aug, Sun - Thur, 2 - 6pm.

Admission: Adult £2.50, Child £1.

LANHYDROCK 🌿

See page 192 for full page entry.

LAUNCESTON CASTLE ⛬

Tel: 01566 772365

Castle Lodge, Launceston, Cornwall PL15 7DR

Owner: English Heritage   **Contact:** The Custodian

Set on the motte of the original Norman castle and commanding the town and surrounding countryside. The shell keep and tower survive of this medieval castle which controlled the main route into Cornwall. An exhibition shows the early history.

Location: OS201 Ref. SX330 846. In Launceston.

Opening Times: 1 Apr - 31 Oct: daily, 10am - 6pm (5pm in Oct). Winter: Fri - Sun, 10am - 4pm. Closed 24 - 26 Dec & 1 Jan.

Admission: Adult £1.90, Child 90p, Conc. £1.50. 15% discount for groups (11+).

📷   ♿ Grounds suitable.   🚻   🅿 Limited.   🐕 In grounds, on leads.   🎫 Tel. for details.

MOUNT EDGCUMBE HOUSE & COUNTRY PARK

CREMYLL, TORPOINT, CORNWALL PL10 IHZ

Owner: *Cornwall County & Plymouth City Councils*   **Contact:** *Cynthia Gaskell Brown*

Tel: 01752 822236 **Fax:** 01752 822199

Tudor home of Earls of Mount Edgcumbe, set in historic 18th century gardens on the dramatic sea-girt Rame peninsula. Wild fallow deer, follies, forts; national camellia collection. One of the Great Gardens of Cornwall.

Location: OS Ref. SX452 527. 10m W of Plymouth via Torpoint.

Opening Times: House and Earls' Garden: 1 Apr - 30 Sept: Wed - Sun & BH Mons, 11am - 4.30pm. Country Park: All year, daily 8am - dusk.

Admission: Adult £4.50, Child (5-15) £2.25, Conc. £3.50, Family (2+2 or 1+3) £10, Season Ticket £7.50. Groups: £3.50. Park: Free.

📷   ♿   🍴 Licensed.   🅿   🐕 Grounds only.   ❄

THE LOST GARDENS OF HELIGAN

PENTEWAN, ST AUSTELL, CORNWALL PL26 6EN

Owner: *Mr T Smit*   **Contact:** *Mr C A Howlett*

Tel: 01726 845100   **Fax:** 01726 845101   **e-mail:** info@heligan.com

These award-winning Gardens are 80 acres of superb pleasure grounds together with a magnificent complex of four walled gardens and kitchen garden, all being restored to their former glory as a living museum of 19th century horticulture. An Italian Garden, Fern Ravine, Crystal Grotto, Summerhouses, Rides, Lawns and a 20 acre sub-tropical "Jungle Garden" are just some of the delights of this "Sleeping Beauty".

Location: OS Ref. SX000 465. 5m SW of St Austell. 2m NW of Mevagissey. Take the B3273 to Mevagissey – follow tourist signs.

Opening Times: Daily except 24 & 25 Dec: 10am - 6pm. Last adm. 4.30pm.

Admission: Adult: £5.50. Child (5-15) £2.50, OAP £5. Family £15. Groups: Adult £5, OAP £4.50. Children under 5 Free. Groups and tours by prior arrangement.

📷   ♿ 🅿 🐕 On leads only. ❄

PENCARROW 🏛

BODMIN, CORNWALL PL30 3AG

Owner: *Molesworth-St Aubyn family*   **Contact:** *The Administrator*

Tel/Fax: 01208 841369   **e-mail:** pencarrow@aol.com

Still owned and lived in by the family. Georgian house and listed gardens. Superb collection of pictures, furniture and porcelain. Marked walks through 50 acres of beautiful formal and woodland gardens, Victorian rockery, Italian garden, over 700 different varieties of rhododendrons, lake and ice house.

Location: OS Ref. SX040 711. Between Bodmin and Wadebridge. 4m NW of Bodmin off A389 & B3266 at Washaway.

Opening Times: 1 Apr - 14 Oct: Sun - Thur, 1.30 - 5pm. Spring BH through to Summer BH opens 11am.

Admission: House & Garden: Adult £5, Child £2.50. Garden only: Adult £2.50, Child Free. Groups (throughout year by arrangement): House & Garden: £4.

ℹ Craft centre, small childrens' play area, self-pick soft fruit.
🍴 By arrangement.   ♿   🍴 Licensed.   🐕 Grounds only.

PENDENNIS CASTLE

© English Heritage Photo Library. © Skyscan Balloon Photography.

FALMOUTH, CORNWALL TR11 4LP

Owner: *English Heritage*   ***Contact:*** *The Head Custodian*

Tel: 01326 316594

Pendennis and its neighbour, St Mawes Castle, face each other across the mouth of the estuary of the River Fal. Built by Henry VIII in 16th century as protection against threat of attack and invasion from France. Extended and adapted over the years to meet the changing threats to national security from the French and Spanish and continued right through to World War II. It withstood five months of siege during the Civil War before becoming the penultimate Royalist Garrison to surrender on the mainland. Pendennis today stands as a landmark, with fine sea views and excellent site facilities including exhibitions, a museum and guardhouse.

Location: OS204, Ref SW824 318. On Pendennis Head.

Opening Times: 1 Apr - 31 Oct: daily, 10am - 6pm or dusk if earlier. 1 Nov - 31 Mar: daily, 10am - 4pm. Closed 24 - 26 Dec.

Admission: Adult £3.80, Child £1.90, Conc. £2.90. 15% discount for groups of 11+.

Partially suitable. By arrangement. Ample. In grounds only. Tel. for details.

PINE LODGE GARDENS
Tel/Fax: 01726 73500

Cuddra, St Austell, Cornwall PL25 3RQ   **Owner/Contact:** Mr & Mrs R H J Clemo

30 acre estate with a wide range of 5,500 plants.

Location: OS Ref. SX044 527. Signposted on A390.

Opening Times: April - September: Wed - Sun & Bank Holidays, 10am - 5pm.

Admission: Adult £3.50, Child half price.

Patrick Lane.

Antony Woodland Garden, Cornwall.

PRIDEAUX PLACE

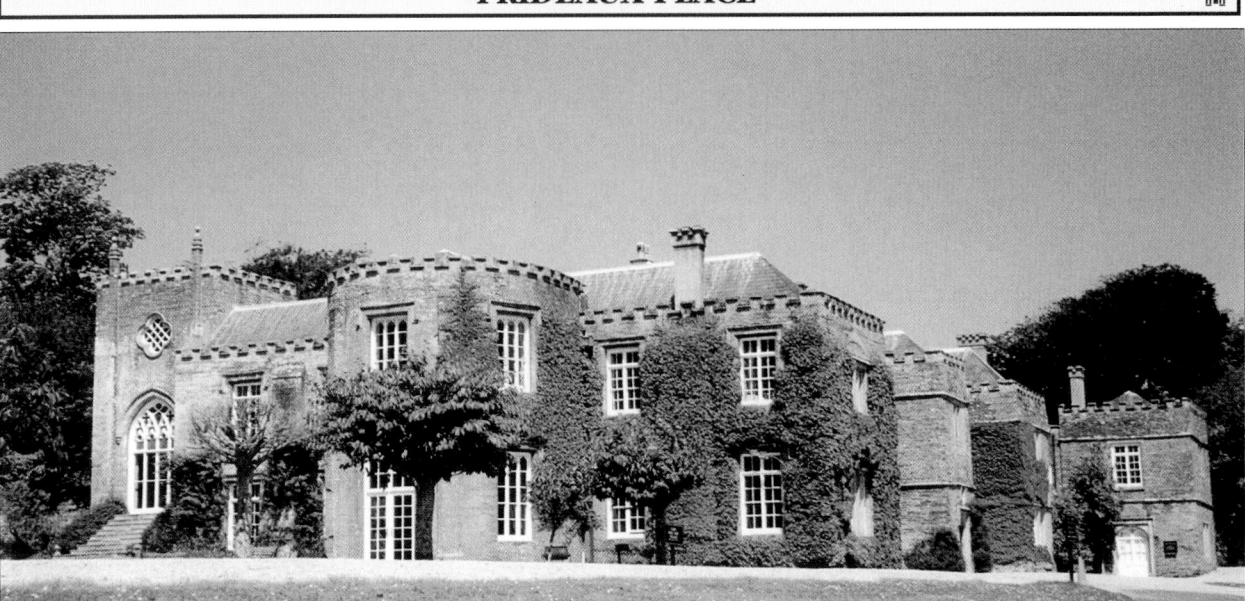

PADSTOW, CORNWALL PL28 8RP

Owner/Contact: Peter Prideaux-Brune Esq

Tel: 01841 532411 **Fax:** 01841 532945

Tucked away above the busy port of Padstow, the home of the Prideaux family for over 400 years, is surrounded by gardens and wooded grounds overlooking a deer park and the Camel estuary to the moors beyond. The house still retains its 'E' shape Elizabethan front and contains fine paintings and furniture as well as an exhibition reflecting its emergence as a major international film location. The impressive outbuildings have been restored in recent years and the 16th century plaster ceiling in the great chamber has been uncovered for the first time since 1760.

Location: OS Ref. SW913 756. 5m from A39 Newquay/Wadebridge link road. Signposted by Historic House signs.
Opening Times: Easter Sun 15 - 24 Apr & Sun 27 May - 4 Oct: Sun - Thur, 1.30 - 5pm. Open all year for groups 15+ by arrangement.
Admission: Adult £5, accompanied children £2. Grounds only: Adult £2 Child £1. Groups £4.

By arrangement.   Ground floor & grounds suitable.
By arrangement.   In grounds, on leads.

RESTORMEL CASTLE

Tel: 01208 872687

Lostwithiel, Cornwall PL22 0BD

Owner: English Heritage   **Contact:** The Custodian

Perched on a high mound, surrounded by a deep moat, the huge circular keep of this splendid Norman castle survives in remarkably good condition. It is still possible to make out the ruins of Restormel's Keep Gate, Great Hall and even the kitchens and private rooms.
Location: OS200 Ref. SX104 614. 1¹/₂ m N of Lostwithiel off A390.
Opening Times: 1 Apr - 31 Oct: daily, 10am - 6pm (5pm in Oct). Winter: closed.
Admission: Adult £1.80, Child 90p, Conc. £1.30. 15% discount for groups (11+).

Grounds suitable.   P Limited for coaches.   In grounds, on leads.
Telephone for details.

ST CATHERINE'S CASTLE

Tel: 0117 9750700

Fowey, Cornwall

Owner: English Heritage   **Contact:** The South West Regional Office

A small fort built by Henry VIII to defend Fowey harbour, with fine views of the coastline and river estuary.
Location: OS200 Ref. SX118 508. ³/₄ m SW of Fowey along footpath off A3082.
Opening Times: Any reasonable time.
Admission: Free.

Patrick Lane.

Cornish Engines.

ST MAWES CASTLE

ST MAWES, CORNWALL TR2 3AA

Owner: English Heritage   *Contact: The Head Custodian*

Tel: 01326 270526

The pretty fishing village of St Mawes is home to this castle. On the opposite headland to Pendennis Castle, St Mawes shares the task of watching over the mouth of the River Fal as it has done since Henry VIII built it as a defence against the French. With three huge circular bastions shaped like clover leaves, St Mawes was designed to cover every possible angle of approach. It is the finest example of Tudor military architecture. The castle offers views of St Mawes' little boat-filled harbour, the passenger ferry tracking across the Fal, and the splendid coastline which featured in the *Poldark* TV series. Also the start of some delightful walks along the coastal path.
Location: OS204 Ref. SW842 328. W of St Mawes on A3078.
Opening Times: 1 Apr - 31 Oct: daily, 10am - 6pm (5pm in Oct). Winter: 1 Nov - 31 Mar: Wed - Sun, 10am - 4pm. Closed 1 - 2pm & 24 - 26 Dec & 1 Jan.
Admission: Adult £2.70, Child £1.40, Conc. £2.20. 15% discount for groups (11+).

Grounds suitable. WC.   P Limited.   Guide dogs only.
Telephone for details.

ST MICHAEL'S MOUNT

MARAZION, Nr PENZANCE, CORNWALL TR17 0EF

Owner: The National Trust   *Contact:* The Manor Office

Tel: 01736 710507 (710265 tide & ferry information) **Fax:** 01736 711544

This magical island is the jewel in Cornwall's crown. The great granite crag which rises from the waters of Mount's Bay is surmounted by an embattled medieval castle, home of the St Aubyn family for over 300 years. The Mount's flanks are softened by lush sub-tropical vegetation and on the water's edge there is a harbourside community which features shops and restaurants.

Location: OS Ref. SW515 300. At Marazion there is access on foot over causeway at low tide. In summer months there is a ferry at high tide. 4m E of Penzance.

Opening Times: 2 Apr - 2 Nov: Mon - Fri, 10.30am - 5.30pm. Last admission 4.45pm. 3 Nov - end Mar: guided tours as tide, weather and circumstances permit. Please telephone. Shops & restaurant: 2 Apr - 2 Nov: daily (restaurant closed Sats in Oct). The castle & grounds are open most weekends during the season. These are special charity days when National Trust members are asked to pay admission.

Admission: Adult £4.50, Family £12. Pre-arranged groups £4.10.

 Braille and taped guides. 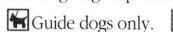 Guide dogs only.

TINTAGEL CASTLE

TINTAGEL, CORNWALL PL34 0HE

Owner: English Heritage   *Contact:* The Head Custodian

Tel: 01840 770328

The spectacular setting for the legendary castle of King Arthur is the wild and windswept Cornish coast. Clinging precariously to the edge of the cliff face are the extensive ruins of a medieval royal castle, built by Richard, Earl of Cornwall, younger brother of Henry III. Also used as a Cornish stronghold by subsequent Earls of Cornwall. Despite extensive excavations since the 1930s, Tintagel Castle remains one of the most spectacular and romantic spots in the entire British Isles. Destined to remain a place of mystery and romance, Tintagel will always jealously guard its marvellous secrets.

Location: OS200 Ref. SX048 891. On Tintagel Head, 1/2 m along uneven track from Tintagel.

Opening Times: 1 Apr - 31 Oct: daily, 11am - 6pm (5pm in Oct). 1 Nov - 31 Mar: daily, 10am - 4pm. Closed 24 - 26 Dec & 1 Jan.

Admission: Adult £3, Child £1.50, Conc. £2.20. 15% discount for groups (11+).

No vehicles. Telephone for details.

TATE ST IVES

Tel: 01736 796226   **Fax:** 01736 794480

Porthmeor Beach, St Ives, Cornwall TR26 1TG

Owner: Tate Gallery   **Contact:** Ina Cole

Changing displays from the Tate Gallery collection of British and modern art, focusing on the modern movement that St Ives is famous for. Also displays of new work by contemporary artists. Events programme, guided tours, gallery shop, rooftop café, with spectacular views over the beach. The Tate also manages the Barbara Hepworth Museum and Sculpture Garden in St Ives.

Location: OS Ref. SW515 407. Situated by Porthmeor Beach.

Opening Times: Tues - Sun, 10.30am - 5.30pm. Also open Mons in Jul/Aug & Bank Holidays.

Admission: Adult £3.95, Conc £2.50. Groups (10 - 30): Adult £2.50, Conc. £1.50.

  Licensed. Daily. 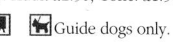 Nearby. Guide dogs only.
Telephone for details.

TINTAGEL OLD POST OFFICE

Tel: 01840 770024 or 01208 74281

Tintagel, Cornwall PL34 0DB

Owner: The National Trust   **Contact:** The Custodian

One of the most characterful buildings in Cornwall, and a house of great antiquity, this small 14th century manor is full of charm and interest.

Location: OS Ref. SX056 884. In the centre of Tintagel.

Opening Times: 31 Mar - 4 Nov: daily, 11am - 5.30pm (closes 4pm from Oct - 4 Nov).

Admission: Adult £2.30, Child £1.10. Family £5.70. Pre-arranged groups £1.80.

Caerhays Castle & Garden, Cornwall.

TREBAH GARDEN

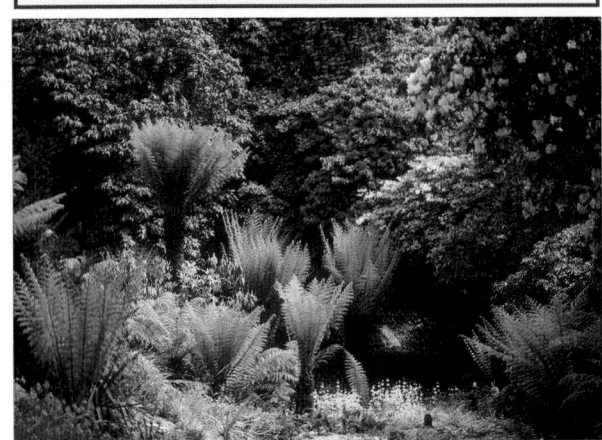

MAWNAN SMITH, Nr FALMOUTH, CORNWALL TR11 5JZ

Owner: Trebah Garden Trust   *Contact:* Vera Woodcroft

Tel: 01326 250448   **Fax:** 01326 250781   **e-mail:** mail@trebah-garden.co.uk

Steeply wooded 25 acre sub-tropical ravine garden falls 200 feet from 18th century house to private beach on Helford River. Stream cascading over waterfalls through ponds full of Koi Carp and exotic water plants winds through 2 acres of blue and white hydrangeas and spills out over beach. Huge Australian tree ferns and palms mingle with shrubs of ever-changing colours and scent beneath over-arching canopy of 100 year old rhododendrons and magnolias. A paradise for plantsmen, artists and families.

Location: OS Ref. SW768 275. 4m SW of Falmouth, 1m SW of Mawnan Smith. Follow brown and white tourism signs from Treliever Cross roundabout at A39/A394 junction through Mawnan Smith to Trebah.

Opening Times: All year: daily, 10.30am - 5pm (last admission).

Admission: Adult £3.75, Child (5-15yrs)/Disabled £2, OAP £3.50. Child under 5yrs Free, Groups (12 - 50): Adult £3.25, Child £1.75. RHS members have free entry all year, NT members have free entry 1 Nov - end Feb.

⬜ 👣 ♿Partially suitable. 🖦 🗝By arrangement. 🅿 🍴
🐾In grounds, on leads. ❄ 🆆

TRELISSICK GARDEN

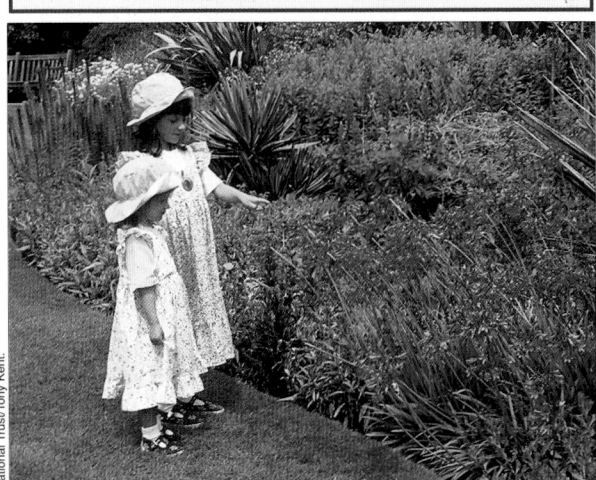

National Trust/Tony Kent.

FEOCK, TRURO, CORNWALL TR3 6QL

Owner: The National Trust   *Contact:* The Property Manager

Tel: 01872 862090 **Fax:** 01872 865808

A garden and estate of rare tranquil beauty with glorious maritime views over Carrick Roads to Falmouth Harbour. The tender and exotic shrubs make this garden attractive in all seasons. Extensive park and woodland walks beside the river. There is an Art and Craft Gallery.

Location: OS Ref. SW837 396. 4m S of Truro by road, on both sides of B3289 above King Harry Ferry.

Opening Times: 17 Feb - 4 Nov: daily. Apr - Sept: Mon - Sat, 10.30am - 5.30pm, Suns, 12.30 - 5.30pm. Feb, Mar, Oct & Nov: Mon - Sat, 10.30am - 5pm, Suns, 12.30 - 5pm. Restaurant: as above but opens 12 noon on Suns. Shop, Art & Craft Gallery & Plant Sales: 17 Feb - 23 Dec: daily.

Admission: Adult £4.40, Family £11. Pre-arranged group £3.70. £1.50 car park fee (refundable on admission).

⬜ 👣 🍵By arrangement. ♿ 🍴 🗝By arrangement.
🐾In park on leads; only guide dogs in garden. ❄

TRELOWARREN HOUSE & CHAPEL   **Tel:** 01326 221366

Mawgan-in-Meneage, Helston, Cornwall TR12 6AD

Owner: Sir Ferrers Vyvyan Bt   **Contact:** The Warden

Tudor and 17th century house. Chapel and main rooms of house are open to the public on a limited basis.

Location: OS Ref. SW721 238. 6m S of Helston, off B3293 to St Keverne.

Opening Times: Please telephone for details.

Admission: Please telephone for details.

TRENANCE HERITAGE COTTAGES   **Tel/Fax:** 01637 873922

Trenance Gardens, Newquay, Cornwall

Owner: Restormel Borough Council   **Contact:** Derek James Esq

The oldest cottages in Newquay now house an exhibition of life in the early 1900s, a traditional shop and photographic exhibition.

Location: OS Ref. SW815 612. In Newquay.

Opening Times: Mar - Oct: daily, 10am - 4pm. Closed on Sundays.

Admission: Adult £1, Child under 12yrs Free.

TRENGWAINTON GARDEN

NT Photographic Library / Giles Clotworthy.

PENZANCE, CORNWALL TR20 8RZ

Owner: The National Trust   *Contact:* The Property Manager

Tel/Fax: 01736 362297

This large shrub garden, with many plants brought back from 1920s' plant-gathering expeditions, is a beautiful place throughout the year and a plantsman's delight. Splendid views over Mount's Bay can be gained from summer-houses at either end of the restored terrace. The walled gardens have many tender plants which cannot be grown in the open anywhere else in England and restoration of the kitchen gardens is underway. The new tea-house serves a full range of snacks and meals.

Location: OS Ref. SW445 315. 2m NW of Penzance, ¹/₂m W of Heamoor on Penzance - Morvah road (B3312), ¹/₂m off St. Just road (A3071).

Opening Times: 18 Feb - 4 Nov: Sun - Thur & Good Fri, 10am - 5.30pm. NB: Closes 5pm in Feb, Mar, Oct & Nov. Last admission ¹/₂ hr before closing.

Admission: Adult £3.60. Family £9. Pre-booked groups: £2.90.

⬜ 👣 ♿Partially suitable. 🖦Tea-house. 🐾On leads.

TRERICE

National Trust/Marcus Way.

NEWQUAY, CORNWALL TR8 4PG

Owner: The National Trust **Contact:** The Property Manager

Tel: 01637 875404 **Fax:** 01637 879300

Trerice is an architectural gem and something of a rarity – a small Elizabethan manor house hidden away in a web of narrow lanes and still somehow caught in the spirit of its age. An old Arundell house, it contains much fine furniture, ceramics, glasses and a wonderful clock collection. A small barn museum traces the development of the lawn mower.

Location: OS Ref. SW841 585. 3m SE of Newquay via the A392 & A3058 (right at Kestle Mill).

Opening Times: 1 Apr - 16 Jul & 12 Sept - 4 Nov: daily except Tues & Sats. 17 Jul - 11 Sept: daily (except Sats), 11am - 5.30pm (closes 5pm in Oct & Nov).

Admission: £4.30, Family £10.75. Pre-arranged groups £3.60.

🖼 ♿ 🔗 Braille & taped guides. WC. 🎧 Licensed. 🐕 Guide dogs only.

TREVARNO ESTATE GARDENS & NATIONAL MUSEUM OF GARDENING

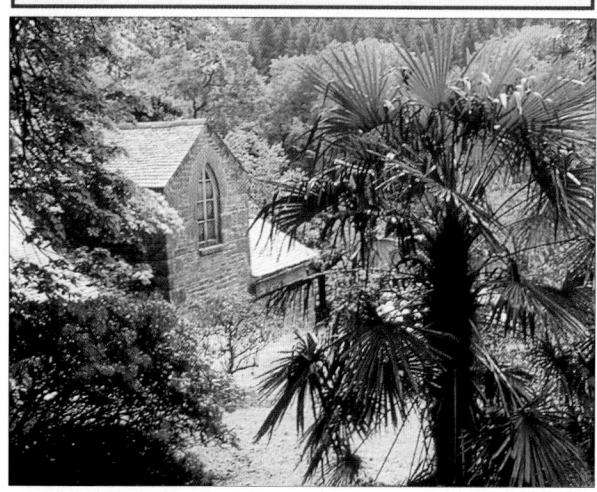

HELSTON, CORNWALL TR13 0RU

Contact: Kate Daughtery

Tel: 01326 574274 **Fax:** 01326 574282

An unforgettable gardening experience combining beautiful Victorian and Georgian gardens with the splendid fountain garden conservatory, unique range of craft workshops and the amazing National Museum of Gardening. Relax in the tranquil gardens and grounds, follow the progress of major restoration projects, visit the craft areas including handmade soap workshop and organic herbal workshop, explore Britain's largest and most comprehensive collection of antique tools, implements, memorabilia and ephemera creatively displayed to illustrate how gardens and gardening influence most peoples' lives.

Location: OS Ref. SW642 302. Leave Helston on Penzance road, signed from B3302 junction and N of Crowntown village.

Opening Times: All year, 10.30am - 5pm. Groups welcome by prior arrangement.

Admission: Adult £3.50, Child (5-14yrs) £1.25, Conc. £3.20.

🍽 ♿ Partially suitable. 🎧 🅿 🎦 🐕 On leads. 🔔 ❄

TRESCO ABBEY GARDENS

ISLES OF SCILLY, CORNWALL TR24 0QQ

Owner: Mr R A and Mrs L A Dorrien-Smith **Contact:** Mr M A Nelhams

Tel: 01720 424105 or **Tel/Fax:** 01720 422868 **e-mail:** mikenelhams@tresco.co.net

Tresco Abbey, built by Augustus Smith, has been the family home since 1834. The garden here flourishes on the small island. Nowhere else in the British Isles does such an exotic collection of plants grow in the open. Agaves, aloes, proteas and acacias from such places as Australia, South Africa, Mexico and the Mediterranean grow within the secure embrace of massive Holm Oak hedges. Valhalla Ships Figurehead Museum.

Location: OS Ref. SV895 143. Isles of Scilly. Isles of Scilly Steamship 0345 105555. BIH Helicopters 01736 363871. Details of day trips on application.

Opening Times: All year: 10am - 4pm.

Admission: Adult £6, (under 14yrs free). Weekly ticket £10. Guided group tours available.

🖼 ♿ Grounds suitable. 🎧 🍴 🐕 In grounds, on leads. ❄

❄ Open All Year Index ◀◀◀ page 49

NT Photographic Library.

Trengwainton Garden, Cornwall.

TREWITHEN

Hugh Palmer.

GRAMPOUND ROAD, TRURO, CORNWALL TR2 4DD

Owner: A M J Galsworthy　　*Contact:* The Estate Office

Tel: 01726 883647 **Fax:** 01726 882301
e-mail: gardens@trewithen-estate.demon.co.uk

Trewithen means 'house of the trees' and the name truly describes this fine early Georgian House in its splendid setting of wood and parkland. *Country Life* described the house as *'one of the outstanding West Country houses of the 18th century'*.

The gardens at Trewithen are outstanding and of international fame. Created since the beginning of the century by George Johnstone, they contain a wide and rare collection of flowering shrubs. Some of the magnolias and rhododendron species in the garden are known throughout the world. They are one of two attractions in this country awarded three stars by Michelin.

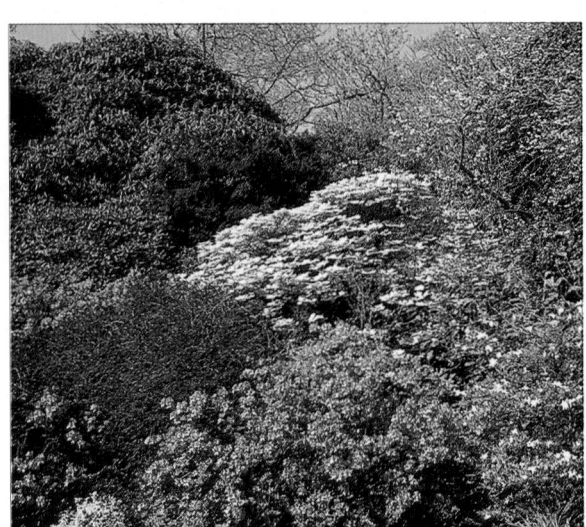

Location: OS Ref. SW914 476. S of A390 between Grampound and Probus villages. 7m WSW of St Austell.

Opening Times: Gardens: 1 Mar - 30 Sept: Mon - Sat, 10am - 4.30pm. Suns in Apr & May only. Walled Garden: Mons & Tues in June & 2/3 July only. House: Apr - Jul & Aug: BH Mons, Mons & Tues, 2 - 4pm.

Admission: Adult £3.75, Child £2. Pre booked groups (20+): Adult £3.50, Child £2. Combined gardens & house £6.

ℹ️No photography in house.　♿ &Partially suitable. WC.
🎦By arrangement. 🅿️ Limited for coaches. 🐕In grounds, on leads. 🏛️

TRURO CATHEDRAL　　　　　　**Tel:** 01872 276782 **Fax:** 01872 277788

Truro, Cornwall TR1 2AF　　　　　**Contact:** The Visitors Officer

It is a perfect example of a gothic Cathedral. The architect was J L Pearson. The Victorian stained glass is considered to be the finest in England.

Location: SW826 449. Truro city centre.

Opening Times: 7.30am - 6.30pm. Sun services: 8am, 9am, 10am and 6pm. Weekday services: 7.30am, 8am and 5.30pm.

Admission: Free.

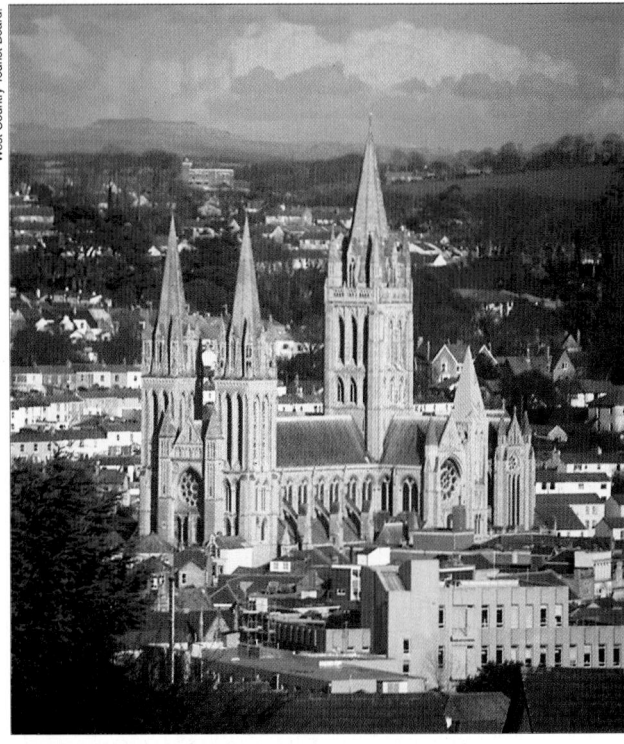

West Country Tourist Board.

Truro Cathedral, Cornwall.

Patrick Lane.

Godolphin, Cornwall.

POWDERHAM CASTLE
Exeter

Owner:
The Earl of Devon

CONTACT

Mr Tim Faulkner
The Estate Office
Powderham Castle
Kenton, Exeter
Devon
EX6 8JQ

Tel: 01626 890243

Fax: 01626 890729

e-mail:
castle@powderham.co.uk

LOCATION

OS Ref. SX965 832

6m SW of Exeter,
4m S M5/J30.
Access from A379 in
Kenton village.

Air: Exeter Airport 9m.

Rail: Starcross
Station 2m.

Bus: Devon General
No: 85, 85A, 85B to
Castle Gate.

Historic family home of the Earl of Devon, Powderham Castle was built between 1390 and 1420 by Sir Philip Courtenay. The present Earl is his direct descendant. The Castle was extensively damaged during the Civil War and fell to the Parliamentary Forces after a protracted siege. When the family returned to the Castle seventy years later they embarked on a series of rebuilding and restoration which continued into the 19th century.

The Castle contains a large collection of portraits by many famous artists, including Cosway, Reynolds, Kneller and Hudson as well as some charming paintings by gifted members of the family. The 14ft high Stumbels Clock and the magnificent rosewood and brass inlaid bookcases by John Channon are particularly fine. One of the most spectacular rooms on view is the Music Room, designed for the 3rd Viscount by James Wyatt. It contains an exceptional Axminster carpet upon which sits recently commissioned carved gilt wood furniture.

GARDENS

2001 will see the opening of 'The Powderham Castle Steam Railway' taking visitors to the woodland gardens and smithy. The Castle is set within an ancient deer park beside the Exe Estuary and the Gardens and grounds are informally laid out. The fine Victorian Rose Garden is the home of Timothy, a 150 year old tortoise; The Children's Secret Garden houses a collection of pets and animals behind its walls to delight children and visitors of all ages; and the newly restored Woodland Garden is open in Spring and early Summer when at its best. Visit the new Farm Shop at Powderham Castle, open 364 days. Featuring high quality West Country food, a Plant Centre, Craft Shops and Restaurant, this free attraction adds another reason for visiting Powderham Castle. The Knights of Powderham joust daily (except Saturdays) in the grounds in the summer holidays at 3pm (separate admission applies).

 Filming and car launches including 4WD vehicle rallies, open air concerts, etc. Grand piano in Music Room, 3800 acre estate, tennis court, cricket pitch, horse trials course. Deer park safari.

Conferences, dinners, corporate entertainment.

Limited facilities. Some ramps. WC.

Fully licensed restaurant and coach room access.

Fully inclusive. Tour time: 1 hr. Guide book available in French, Dutch & German.

P Unlimited free parking. Commission and complimentary drinks / meals for drivers. Advance warning of group bookings preferred but not essential.

 Welcome. Fascinating tour and useful insight into the life of one of England's Great Houses over the centuries. Victorian School Room and teacher pack.

In grounds, on leads.

Civil Wedding Licence.

CONFERENCE/FUNCTION

ROOM	SIZE	MAX CAPACITY
Music Room	56' x 25'	170
Dining Room	42' x 22'	100
Ante Room	28' x 18'	25
Library 1	32' x 18'	85
Library 2	31"x18'	85

OPENING TIMES

SUMMER

1 April - 28 October

Daily*: 10am - 5.30pm
*Except Sat: closed to
public, but available
for private hire.
Gardens only open Suns in
March.

Farm Shop: daily, 9am - 6pm,
Suns, 10am - 4pm.

WINTER

Available for hire for
conferences, receptions and
functions, tel. for details.

ADMISSION

Adult	£5.85
OAP	£5.35
Child	£2.95
Group Rates	
Adult	£5.15
OAP	£4.65
Child	£2.45
Family*	£14.65

*2 adults + 2 children or
1 adult + 3 children.

SPECIAL EVENTS

- **MAR 10 - 11**
  Historic Devon Motor Rally.

- **MAR 26 - 29**
  Phillips Fine Art Sale.

- **MAY 27**
  The Great Farm Shop Open Day.

- **JUN 25 - 28**
  Phillips Fine Art Sale.

- **JUN 29 - 1 JUL**
  British Touring Shakespeare (open air).

- **JUL 7 - 8**
  Historic Vehicle Gathering.

- **AUG 3**
  Bournemouth Symphony Orchestra 'Last Night of the Powderham Proms'.

- **AUG 4**
  Open Air Rock Concert

- **OCT 22 - 25**
  Phillips Fine Art Sale.

A LA RONDE

NT Photographic Library; David Garner.

SUMMER LANE, EXMOUTH, DEVON EX8 5BD

Owner: The National Trust   *Contact:* John Rolfe – Custodian

Tel: 01395 265514

A unique 16-sided house built on the instructions of two spinster cousins, Jane and Mary Parminter, on their return from a grand tour of Europe. Completed c1796, the house contains many 18th century contents and collections brought back by the Parminters. The fascinating interior decoration includes a feather frieze and shell-encrusted gallery which, due to its fragility, can only be viewed on closed circuit television.

Location: OS Ref. SY004 834. 2m N of Exmouth on A376.

Opening Times: 31 Mar - 4 Nov: daily except Fris & Sats, 11am - 5.30pm. Last admission ½ hr before closing.

Admission: Adult £3.30, Child £1.70. No reduction for groups.

ARLINGTON COURT

National Trust / Andreas Von Einsiedel.

Nr BARNSTAPLE, NORTH DEVON EX31 4LP

Owner: The National Trust   *Contact:* Susie Mercer - Property Manager

Tel: 01271 850296   **Fax:** 01271 850711

The house, built for the Chichesters in 1822 and still with much original furniture, is full of collections for every taste, including model ships, costume, pewter, shells and many other fascinating objects. Housed in the stables is the Trust's large collection of horse drawn carriages. Carriage rides through the 30 acres of peaceful informal gardens and past the formal terraced Victorian garden, start from the front of the house. Miles of walks through woods. Parks grazed by Shetland ponies and Jacob sheep.

Location: OS180 Ref. SS611 405. 7m NE of Barnstaple on A39.

Opening Times: 31 Mar - 4 Nov: daily except Tues, 11am - 5.30pm. Paths through park and woods open during daylight hours from Nov - Mar.

Admission: House & Garden: Adult £5.40, Child £2.70, Family £13.50. Booked groups (15+) £4.60, Child £2.30. Garden & Carriage Museum only: Adult £3.40, Child £1.70.

Ground floor & grounds suitable. WC.   Licensed.   P
Teachers' pack.   In grounds, on leads.

AVENUE COTTAGE GARDENS

Tel/Fax: 01803 732769

Ashprington, Totnes, Devon TQ9 7UT

Owner/Contact: R J Pitts Esq & R C H Soans Esq

A completely secluded and secret garden, yet one which has been in existence for over 200 years. For the last 10 years it has been undergoing restoration and recreation by the present owners. In this lovely valley site there is a large and fascinating collection of plants which is full of interest from spring until autumn.

Location: OS Ref. SX821 574. 3m SE of Totnes, from centre of village, up hill past church for 400 yds.

Opening Times: 1 Apr - 30 Sept, Tue - Sat, 11am - 5pm. Other times by appointment.

Admission: Adult £2, Child 25p. Entrance, guided tour & tea £3.50.

Wheelchairs in grounds.   By arrangement.   In grounds, on leads.

BAYARD'S COVE FORT

Tel: 01803 861234

Dartmouth, Devon

Owner: English Heritage   **Contact:** South Hams District Council

Set among the picturesque gabled houses of Dartmouth, on the waterfront at the end of the quay, this is a small artillery fort built 1509 - 10 to defend the harbour entrance.

Location: OS Ref. SX879 510. In Dartmouth, on riverfront 200 yds, S of South ferry.

Opening Times: Any reasonable time.

Admission: Free.

BERRY POMEROY CASTLE

Tel: 01803 866618

Totnes, Devon TQ9 6NJ

Owner: The Duke of Somerset   **Contact:** English Heritage

A romantic late medieval castle, dramatically sited half-way up a wooded hillside, looking out over a deep ravine and stream. It is unusual in combining the remains of a large castle with a flamboyant courtier's mansion. Reputed to be one of the most haunted castles in the country.

Location: OS202 Ref. SX839 623. 2½m E of Totnes off A385. Entrance gate ½m NE of Berry Pomeroy village, then ½m drive. Narrow approach, unsuitable for coaches.

Opening Times: 1 Apr - 31 Oct: daily, 10am - 6pm (5pm in Oct). Winter: closed.

Admission: Adult £2.20, Child £1.10, Conc £1.70. 15% discount for groups (11+).

Ground floor & grounds suitable.   Not EH.   P No access for coaches.
Telephone for details.

BICKLEIGH CASTLE

BICKLEIGH, Nr TIVERTON, DEVON EX16 8RP

Owner/Contact: M J Boxall Esq

Tel: 01884 855363

Royalist stronghold: 900 years of history and architecture. 11th century detached Chapel; 14th century Gatehouse – Armoury (Cromwellian), Guard Room – Tudor furniture and fine oil paintings, Great Hall – 52' long and 'Tudor' Bedroom, massive fourposter. 17th century Farmhouse: inglenook fireplaces, bread ovens, oak beams. The Spooky Tower, Great Hall and picturesque moated garden make Bickleigh a favoured venue for functions, particularly wedding receptions.

Location: OS Ref. SS936 068. Off the A396 Exeter-Tiverton road. Follow signs SW from Bickleigh Bridge 1m.

Opening Times: Easter Sun - Fri, then Weds, Suns & BHs until late May BH, then daily (except Sats) until 1st Sun in Oct, 2 - 5pm. Coaches & groups welcome at any time by appointment.

Admission: Adult £4, Child (5-15yrs) £2, Family £10.

Conferences.   Ground floor suitable.   Licensed.   Obligatory.

BICTON COLLEGE GARDEN & ARBORETUM

Tel: 01395 562400

East Budleigh, Budleigh Salterton, Devon EX9 7BY

Owner: Bicton College of Agriculture   **Contact:** Paul Champion

Grade I listed parkland, lake, monkey puzzle avenue, woodland garden.

Location: OS Ref. SY074 857. Off B3178 next door to Bicton Park, follow signs to plant centre.

Opening Times: Apr - Oct: daily 10am - 4.30pm. Nov - Mar: weekdays only 10am - 4.30pm.

Admission: Adult £2, Child (under 16yrs) Free.

BICTON PARK BOTANICAL GARDENS

Tel: 01395 568465   **Fax:** 01395 568374

Budleigh Salterton, Devon EX9 7DP

Owner: Mr & Mrs S E Lister   **Contact:** Mr Simon Lister

Over 60 acres of Parkland and Garden, Palm House and specialist greenhouses.

Location: OS Ref. SY074 856. 2m N of Budleigh Salterton on B3178.

Opening Times: Summer: 10am - 6pm. Winter: 10am - 5pm. Closed Christmas Day.

Admission: Adult £4.95, Child £2.95, Conc. £3.95.

BOWDEN HOUSE

Tel: 01803 863664

Totnes, Devon TQ9 7PW   **Owner/Contact:** Mrs Belinda Petersen

Elizabethan mansion with Queen Anne façade.

Location: OS Ref. SX800 600. Follow signs from Totnes. 1½ m S of Totnes, E of A381.

Opening Times: House: 2nd May BH - end Sept: Thur & Fri plus BH Suns. Museum opens 12 noon, Tours start at 2pm, or 1.30pm in high season, with ghost stories.

Admission: Adult £4.95, Child: (10-13yrs) £3.40, (6-9yrs) £2.20, (2-5yrs) £1. Tickets include Photo Museum and old film shows.

BRADLEY MANOR

Tel: 01626 354513

Newton Abbot, Devon TQ12 6BN

Owner: The National Trust   **Contact:** Mrs A H Woolner

A small medieval manor house set in woodland and meadows.

Location: OS Ref. SX848 709. On Totnes road A381. ¾ m SW of Newton Abbot.

Opening Times: Apr - end Sept: Weds & Thurs, 2 - 5 pm. Last admission 4.30pm.

Admission: £2.80, no reduction for groups.

BRANSCOMBE MANOR MILL, THE OLD BAKERY & FORGE

Tel: Manor Mill - 01392 881691   **Old Bakery** - 01297 680333   **Forge** - 01297 680481

Branscombe, Seaton, Devon EX12 3DB

Owner: The National Trust   **Contact:** NT Devon Regional Office

Manor Mill, still in working order and recently restored, is a water-powered mill which probably supplied the flour for the bakery, regular working demonstrations are held. The Old Bakery was, until 1987, the last traditional working bakery in Devon. The old baking equipment has been preserved in the baking room and the rest of the building is now a tearoom. Information display in the outbuildings. The Forge is open regularly and the blacksmith sells the ironwork he produces - please telephone to check opening times (01297 680481).

Location: OS Ref. SY198 887. In Branscombe ½ m S off A3052 by steep, narrow lane.

Opening Times: Manor Mill: 1 Apr - 4 Nov: Suns, 2 - 5pm; also Weds in Jul & Aug. The Old Bakery: Easter - Oct, daily, weekends in winter months, 11am - 5pm.

Admission: £1 Manor Mill only.

BUCKFAST ABBEY

Tel: 01364 645500   **Fax:** 01364 643891

Buckfastleigh, Devon TQ11 0EE

Owner: Buckfast Abbey Trust   **Contact:** The Warden

Medieval and modern Abbey.

Location: OS Ref. SX741 674. ½ m from A38 Plymouth - Exeter route.

Opening Times: Church & Grounds: All year: 5.30am - 7pm.

Admission: Free.

Branscombe Manor Mill, Devon.

BUCKLAND ABBEY

National Trust Photographic Library.

YELVERTON, DEVON PL20 6EY

Owner: *The National Trust*   **Contact:** *Michael Coxson - Property Manager*

Tel: 01822 853607   **Fax:** 01822 855448

The spirit of Sir Francis Drake is rekindled at his home with exhibitions of his courageous adventures and achievements throughout the world. One of the Trust's most interesting historical buildings and originally a 13th century monastery, the abbey was transformed into a family residence before Sir Francis bought it in 1581. Fascinating new decorated plaster ceiling in Tudor Drake Chamber. Outside there are monastic farm buildings, herb garden, craft workshops and country walks. Introductory video presentation. New Elizabethan garden under construction.

Location: OS201 Ref. SX487 667. 6m S of Tavistock; 11m N of Plymouth off A386.

Opening Times: 23 Mar - 4 Nov: daily except Thur, 10.30am - 5.30pm (last adm. 4.45pm). 5 Nov - 22 Mar 2002: Sat & Sun, 2 - 5pm, (last adm. 4.15pm). Closed 24 Dec - 15 Feb 2002. Other days for pre-booked groups.

Admission: Abbey & Grounds: Adult £4.60, Child £2.30, Family £11.50. Group: £3.80. Grounds only: Adult £2.40, Child £1.20. Winter: half price Abbey admission.

⬩ Ground floor & grounds suitable. Wheelchair stairclimber may be available. WC.
⬩ ⬩ Guide dogs only. ❄

CADHAY

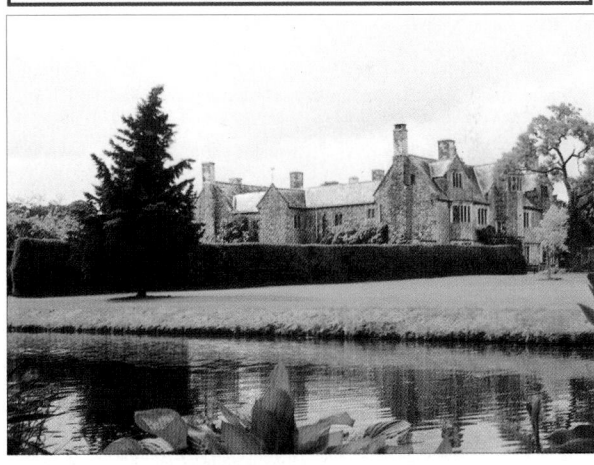

OTTERY ST MARY, DEVON EX11 1QT

Owner/Contact: *Mr O N W William-Powlett*

Tel/Fax: 01404 812432   **e-mail:** cadhay@eastdevon.net

Cadhay is approached by an avenue of lime-trees, and stands in a pleasant listed garden, with herbaceous borders and yew hedges, with excellent views over the original medieval fish ponds. The main part of the house was built about 1550 by John Haydon who had married the de Cadhay heiress. He retained the Great Hall of an earlier house, of which the fine timber roof (about 1420) can be seen. An Elizabethan Long Gallery was added by John's successor at the end of the 16th century, thereby forming a unique and lovely courtyard.

Location: OS Ref. SY090 962. 1m NW of Ottery St Mary. From W take A30 and exit at Pattersons Cross, follow signs for Fairmile and then Cadhay. From E, exit at the Iron Bridge and follow signs as above.

Opening Times: Jul & Aug: Tues, Weds & Thurs, also Suns & Mons in late Spring & Summer BHs, 2 - 5.30pm. Groups by appointment only.

Admission: Adult £4, Child £2.

⬩ Ground floor & grounds suitable. ⬩ Gardens available.
⬩ Guide dogs only. 🔔 RW

South West
England

CASTLE DROGO

David Cripps.

DREWSTEIGNTON, EXETER EX6 6PB

Owner: The National Trust　　*Contact: Peter Jennings, Property Manager*

Tel: 01647 433306　**Fax:** 01647 433186

Extraordinary granite and oak castle, designed by Sir Edwin Lutyens, which combines the comforts of the 20th century with the grandeur of a Baronial castle. Elegant dining and drawing rooms and fascinating kitchen and scullery. Terraced formal garden with colourful herbaceous borders and rose beds. Panoramic views over Dartmoor and delightful walks in the 300ft Teign Gorge.

Location: OS191 Ref. SX721 900. 5m S of A30 Exeter - Okehampton road.

Opening Times: Castle: 31 Mar - 4 Nov: daily except Fris (open Good Fri), 11am - 5.30pm (last admission 5pm). Sats & Suns in Mar: guided tours only (4 per day). Garden: All year: daily, 10.30am - dusk. Shop & tearoom open as Castle.

Admission: House & Garden: Adult £5.60, Child £2.80, Family £14. Group: £4.70. Garden only: Adult £2.80, Child £1.40.

⬜ ♿ Grounds floor & grounds suitable. WCs. 🍴 Licensed.
🚶 By arrangement.　🐕 Guide dogs only in certain areas.　❄

COLETON FISHACRE HOUSE & GDN

BROWNSTONE ROAD, KINGSWEAR, DARTMOUTH TQ6 0EQ

Owner: The National Trust　　*Contact: David Mason, Property Manager*

Tel/Fax: 01803 752466　**e-mail:** dcfdmx@smtp.ntrust.org.uk

A 9 hectare property set in a stream-fed valley within the spectacular scenery of the South Devon coast. The Lutyenesque style house with art deco interior was built in the 1920s for Rupert and Lady Dorothy D'Oyly Carte who created the delightful garden, planted with a wide range of rare and exotic plants giving year round interest.

Location: OS202 Ref. SX910 508. 3m E of Kingswear, follow brown tourist signs.

Opening Times: Garden: Mar: Suns only, 11am - 5pm. House & Garden: 31 Mar - 4 Nov: Wed - Sun & BH Mons. House: 11am - 4.30pm, Garden: 10.30am - 5.30pm.

Admission: Adult £4.80, Child £2.40. Family £12. Booked groups (15+) £4.10. Garden only: Adult £3.80, Child £1.90, Booked groups (15+) £3.10.

ℹ No photography in house.　⬜ 🌳 ♿ Limited access to grounds. WC.
📷 P Limited. Coaches must book.　🐕 Guide dogs only in garden.

COMPTON CASTLE 🌿

Tel: 01803 875740 (answerphone)

Marldon, Paignton TQ3 1TA

Owner: The National Trust　　**Contact:** The Administrator

A fortified manor house with curtain wall, built at three periods: 1340, 1450 and 1520 by the Gilbert family.

Location: OS Ref. SX865 648. At Compton, 3m W of Torquay.

Opening Times: 2 Apr - 31 Oct: Mons, Weds & Thurs, 10am - 12.15pm & 2 - 5pm. The courtyard, restored great hall, solar, chapel, rose garden and old kitchen are shown. Last admission ½ hr before closing.

Admission: £2.90, pre-arranged groups £2.30.

CROWNHILL FORT

CROWNHILL FORT ROAD, PLYMOUTH, DEVON PL6 5BX

Owner: Landmark Trust　　*Contact: James Breslin*

Tel: 01752 793754　**Fax:** 01752 770065　**e-mail:** ltcfort@aol.com

At Crownhill Fort you are free to explore the 16 acre site, honeycombed with tunnels, surrounded by massive ramparts, protected by a deep dry moat and guarded by many cannon. After a long restoration the Fort now stands proud as one of the largest and best preserved of Britain's great Victorian forts, and in particular boasts the Moncrieff Disappearing Gun, the only example in the world.

Location: OS Ref. SX487 593. 4m from Plymouth City Centre and less than 1m from A38, signposted from A386 Tavistock Road.

Opening Times: 8 Jan - 1 Apr: Groups by appointment only. 2 Apr - 28 Oct: daily, 10am - 5pm. Nov & Dec: Weekends, 10am - 5pm. Weekdays, groups by appointment only.

Admission: Adult £3.75, Child £2.25, OAP £3.50, Family (2+2) £10. Groups (15+) Adult £3.50, Child £2.

⬜ 🍴 ♿ Partially suitable. WC. ☕ 🚶 By arrangement.
P Ample for cars. Limited for coaches.　🏛 🐕 In grounds, on leads.　❄

DARTINGTON HALL GARDENS

Tel/Fax: 01803 862367

Dartington, Totnes, Devon TQ9 6EL　　**e-mail:** graham@dartingtonhall.org.uk

Owner: Dartington Hall Trust　　**Contact:** Mr G Gammin

28 acre gardens surrounds 14th century Hall.

Location: OS Ref. SX798 628. 30 mins from M5 at Exeter (off A38 at Buckfastleigh).

Opening Times: All year. Groups by appointment only. Guided tours by arrangement £4.

Admission: £2 donation welcome.

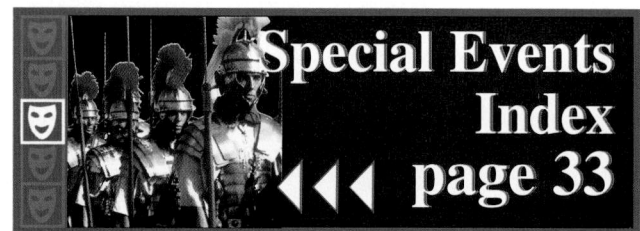

Special Events Index ◀◀◀ **page 33**

DARTMOUTH CASTLE

© English Heritage Photo Library.

CASTLE ROAD, DARTMOUTH, DEVON TQ6 0JH

Owner: *English Heritage*   **Contact:** *The Custodian*

Tel: 01803 833588

This brilliantly positioned defensive castle juts out into the narrow entrance to the Dart estuary, with the sea lapping at its foot. When begun in 1480s it was one of the most advanced fortifications in England, and was the first castle designed specifically with artillery in mind. For nearly 500 years it kept its defences up-to-date in preparation for war. Today the castle is in a remarkably good state of repair, along with excellent exhibitions, the history of the castle comes to life. A picnic spot of exceptional beauty.

Location: OS202 Ref. SX887 503. 1m SE of Dartmouth off B3205, narrow approach road.

Opening Times: 1 Apr - 31 Oct: daily, 10am - 6pm (5pm in Oct). 1 Nov - 31 Mar: Wed - Sun, 10am - 4pm. Closed 24 - 26 Dec & 1 Jan.

Admission: Adult £3.20, Child £1.60, Conc. £2.50. 15% discount for groups (11+).

Ground floor suitable.   P Limited.   Tel. for details.

DOCTON MILL & GARDEN   Tel/Fax: 01237 441369

Spekes Valley, Hartland, Devon EX39 6EA   **e-mail:** john@doctonmill.freeserve.co.uk

Owner/Contact: John Borrett

Garden for all seasons in 8 acres of sheltered wooded valley, plus working mill.

Location: OS Ref. SS235 226. 3m Hartland Quay. 15m N of Bude. 3m W of A39, 3m S of Hartland.

Opening Times: Mar - Oct: 10am - 6pm. Coaches by appointment.

Admission: Adult £3.25, OAP £3.00, Child (under 14 yrs) £1.

THE ELIZABETHAN GARDENS   Tel: 01752 301010   Fax: 01752 312430

Plymouth Barbican Assoc. Ltd, New St, The Barbican, Plymouth

Owner: Plymouth Barbican Association Limited   **Contact:** Tony Golding Esq

Very small series of four enclosed gardens laid out in Elizabethan style in 1970.

Location: OS Ref. SX477 544. 3 mins walk from Dartington Glass (a landmark building) on the Barbican.

Opening Times: Mon - Sat, 9am - 5pm. Closed Christmas.

Admission: Free.

ESCOT COUNTRY PARK & GDNS   Tel: 01404 822188   Fax: 01404 822903

Escot, Ottery St Mary, Devon EX11 1LU   **e-mail:** escot@eclipse.co.uk

Owner/Contact: Mr J-M Kennaway

Otters, wild boar, birds of prey, 2 acre walled Victorian rose garden, 25 acres of shrubbery, rhododendrons and azaleas. 'Capability' Brown parkland, national award-winning pet & aquatic centre, wetlands and waterfowl park, Coach House Restaurant (all home cooking). The Kennaway family estate for over 200 years.

Location: OS Ref. SY080 977 (gate). 9m E of Exeter on A30 at Fairmile.

Opening Times: Easter - 31 Oct: Gardens, Aquatic Centre & Restaurant, daily, 10am - 6pm. 1 Nov - Easter: Gardens closed except by prior arrangement. Aquatic Centre & Restaurant: daily, 10am - 5pm except 25, 26 Dec & Mons in Jan, Feb & Mar.

Admission: Adult £3.50, Child £3, Child (under 4yrs) Free, OAP £3, Family (2+2) £12.

Partially suitable.   Licensed.   By arrangement.   P
   In grounds on leads.   Tel. for details.

EXETER CATHEDRAL   Tel: 01392 255573   Fax: 01392 498769

Exeter, Devon EX1 1HS   **Contact:** Mrs Juliet Dymoke-Marr

Fine example of decorated gothic architecture. Longest unbroken stretch of gothic vaulting in the world.

Location: OS Ref. SX921 925. Central to the City - between High Street and Southernhay. Groups may be set down in South Street.

Opening Times: All year: Mon - Fri 7.30am - 6.30pm, Sats, 7.30am - 5pm, Suns, 8am - 7.30pm.

Admission: No formal charge – donation requested of £2.50 per person.

FURSDON HOUSE   Tel: 01392 860860   Fax: 01392 860126

Cadbury, Thorverton, Exeter, Devon EX5 5JS   **e-mail:** enquiries@fursdon.co.uk

Owner: E D Fursdon Esq   **Contact:** Mrs C Fursdon

The home of the Fursdon family is in beautiful hilly countryside above the Exe valley. The architecture reflects changes made throughout the centuries. Family memorabilia is displayed including scrap books, fine examples of 18th century costume and textiles and a letter from King Charles I during the Civil War.

Location: OS Ref. SS922 046. 1½m S of A3072 between Tiverton & Crediton, 9m N of Exeter. 2m N of Thorverton by narrow lane.

Opening Times: BHs Easter - August. Jun, Jul & Aug, Wed & Thurs. Gardens & Tearoom: 2 - 5pm. Guided house tours at 2.30pm & 3.30pm.

Admission: Adult £4, Child (11-16yrs) £2, (under 10yrs Free). Groups (20+) £3.50. Gardens only: £2.

Conferences.   Partially suitable.   Compulsory.   P   Self-catering

---

THE GARDEN HOUSE   Tel: 01822 854769   Fax: 01822 855358

Buckland Monachorum, Yelverton, Devon PL20 7LQ

Owner: Fortescue Garden Trust   **Contact:** Stuart Fraser

An 8 acre garden of interest throughout the year including a romantic terraced, walled garden around the ruins of a 16th century vicarage.

Location: OS Ref. SX490 682. Signposted W off A386 near Yelverton, 10m N of Plymouth.

Opening Times: 1 Mar - 31 Oct: daily, 10.30am - 5pm. Last admission 4.30pm.

Admission: Adult £4, Child £1, OAP £3.50, pre-booked groups (15+) £3 (if deposit paid).

HALDON BELVEDERE/LAWRENCE CASTLE   Tel/Fax: 01392 833668

e-mail: turner@haldonbelvedere.co.uk

Higher Ashton, Nr Dunchideock, Exeter, Devon EX6 7QY

Owner: Devon Historic Building Trust   **Contact:** Ian Turner

18th century Grade II* listed triangular tower with circular turrets on each corner. Built in memory of Major General Stringer Lawrence, founder of the Indian Army. Recently restored to illustrate the magnificence of its fine plasterwork, gothic windows, mahogany flooring and marble fireplaces. Breathtaking views of the surrounding Devon countryside.

Location: OS Ref. SX875 861. 7m SW of Exeter. Exit A38 at Exeter racecourse for 2½m.

Opening Times: Mar - Oct: Suns & BHs, 2 - 5pm.

Admission: Adult £1.50, Child 75p. No discount for groups (20-50).

Not suitable.   By arrangement.   P Limited.   In grounds, on leads.

NT Photographic Library: Nicholas Toyne.

Compton Castle, Devon.

South West England

HARTLAND ABBEY

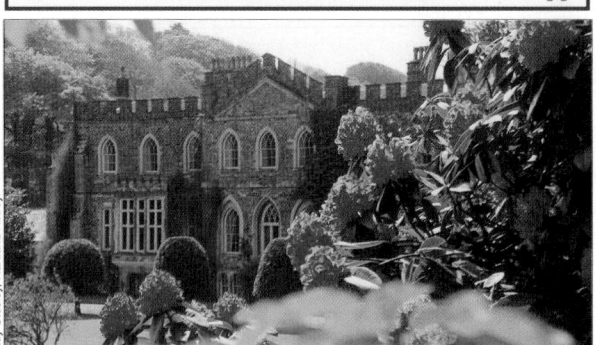

Lady Stucley, Hartland Abbey.

HARTLAND, BIDEFORD, DEVON EX39 6DT

Owner: Sir Hugh Stucley Bt *Contact:* The Administrator

Tel: 01237 441264/441234 **Fax:** 01237 441264/01884 861134

Founded as an Augustinian Monastery in 1157 in a beautiful valley only 1 mile's walk from a spectacular Atlantic Cove, the Abbey was given by Henry VIII in 1539 to the Sergeant of his Wine Cellar, whose descendants live here today. Remodelled in the 18th & 19th century, it contains spectacular architecture and murals. Important paintings, furniture, porcelain collected over generations. Documents from 1160. Victorian and Edwardian photographs. Museum. Dairy. Recently discovered Victorian fernery and paths by Jekyll. Extensive woodland gardens of camellias, rhododendrons etc. Bog Garden. 18th century Walled gardens of vegetables, summer borders, tender and rare plants including echium pininana. Peacocks, donkeys and Welsh Mountain sheep in the park. NPI Heritage Award winner 1998.

Location: OS Ref. SS240 249. 15m W of Bideford, 15m N of Bude off A39 between Hartland and Hartland Quay.

Opening Times: 1 Apr - end Sept: Wed, Thur, Sun & BHs, plus Tues in Jul & Aug, 2 - 5.30pm. Gardens: 1 Apr - end Oct: daily except Sats, 2 - 5.30pm.

Admission: House, Gardens & Grounds: Adult £5, Child (9-15ys) £1.50, OAP £4.50. Groups (20+): Adult £4, Child £1.50. Gardens & Grounds: Adult £3, Child 50p. Groups: £2.75.

[icons] Wedding receptions. Partially suitable. WC.
By arrangement. P In grounds, on leads.

KILLERTON HOUSE & GARDEN

National Trust / Chris Vile.

BROADCLYST, EXETER EX5 3LE

Owner: The National Trust *Contact:* Denise Melhuish - Property Manager

Tel: 01392 881345

The spectacular hillside garden is beautiful throughout the year with spring flowering bulbs and shrubs, colourful herbaceous borders and fine trees. The garden is surrounded by parkland and woods offering lovely walks. The house is furnished as a family home and includes a costume collection dating from the 18th century in a series of period rooms and a Victorian laundry.

Location: OS Ref. SS977 001. Off Exeter – Cullompton Rd (B3181). M5 N'bound J30, M5 S'bound J28.

Opening Times: House: 10 - 31 Mar & 1 Oct - 4 Nov, daily except Mons & Tues. 1 Apr - 31 Jul & Sept, daily except Tues. Aug: daily, 11am - 5.30pm (5pm during Oct) last entry 1/2 hr before closing.

Admission: House & Garden: Adult £5.20, Child £2.60, Family £13, Group £4.30. Garden only: Adult £3.70, Child £1.80. Reduced Nov - Feb.

[icons] Guide dogs only in house.

HEMERDON HOUSE

Tel: w/days 01752 841410 w/ends 01752 337350

Sparkwell, Plympton, Plymouth, Devon PL7 5BZ

Fax: 01752 331477

Owner: J H G Woollcombe Esq **Contact:** Paul Williams & Partners

Late 18th century family house, rich in local history.

Location: OS Ref. SX564 575. 3m E of Plympton off A38.

Opening Times: 1 May - 30 Sept: for only 30 days including May & Aug BHs, 2 - 5.30pm. Last admission 5pm. Please contact the Administrator for opening dates.

Admission: £3.

[icons] Ground floor suitable. Obligatory. P

HEMYOCK CASTLE

Tel: 01823 680745

Hemyock, Cullompton, Devon EX15 3RJ

Owner/Contact: Mrs Sheppard

Former medieval moated castle, displays show site's history as fortified manor house, castle and farm. Medieval, Civil war and Victorian tableaux, archaeological finds, cider press and cow parlour.

Location: OS Ref. ST135 134. M5/J26, Wellington then 5m S over the Blackdown Hills.

Opening Times: BH Mons 2 - 5pm. Other times by appointment. Groups and private parties welcome.

Admission: Adult £1, Child 50p. Group rates available.

HOUND TOR DESERTED MEDIEVAL VILLAGE

Tel: 01626 832093

Ashburton Road, Manaton, Dartmoor, Devon

Owner: English Heritage **Contact:** Dartmoor National Park Authority

The remains of the dwellings.

Location: OS191 Ref. SX746 788. 1 1/2 m S of Manaton off Ashburton road. 6m N of Ashburton.

Opening Times: Any reasonable time.

Admission: Free.

KNIGHTSHAYES

National Trust Photographic Library / Stephen Robson.

BOLHAM, TIVERTON, DEVON EX16 7RQ

Owner: The National Trust *Contact:* Penny Woollams - Property Manager

Tel: 01884 254665 **Fax:** 01884 243050

The striking Victorian gothic house is a rare survival of the work of William Burges with ornate patterns in many rooms. One of the finest gardens in Devon, mainly woodland and shrubs with something of interest throughout the seasons. Drifts of spring bulbs, summer flowering shrubs, pool garden and amusing animal topiary.

Location: OS Ref. SS960 151. 2m N of Tiverton (A396) at Bolham.

Opening Times: House: 24 Mar - 4 Nov: daily except Fris (but open Good Fri), 11am - 5.30pm (Oct: 11.30am - 4.30pm). Closed Thurs/Fris). Nov/Dec: Suns, 2 - 4pm, pre-booked groups only. Gardens: 27 Mar - 31 Oct: daily, 11am - 5.30pm.

Admission: House & Garden: Adult £5.40, Child £2.70, Family £13.50. Group £4.70. Garden only: Adult £3.80, Child £1.90.

[icons] Ground floor & grounds suitable. WC. Guide dogs in park.

LYDFORD CASTLES & SAXON TOWN ⌗

Tel: 01822 820320

Lydford, Okehampton, Devon

Owner: English Heritage   **Contact:** The National Trust

Standing above the lovely gorge of the River Lyd, this 12th century tower was notorious as a prison. The earthworks of the original Norman fort are to the south. A Saxon town once stood nearby and its layout is still discernible.

Location: OS191 Castle Ref. SX510 848, Fort Ref. SX509 847. In Lydford off A386 8m SW of Okehampton.

Opening Times: Any reasonable time.

Admission: Free.

MARKERS COTTAGE

Tel: 01392 461546

Broadclyst, Exeter, Devon EX5 3HR

Owner: The National Trust   **Contact:** The Custodian

Medieval cob house containing a cross-passage screen decorated with a painting of St Andrew and his attributes.

Location: OS Ref. SX985 973. 1/4 E of B3181 in village of Broadclyst.

Opening Times: 1 Apr - 30 Oct: Sun - Tue, 2 - 5pm.

Admission: £1.

MARWOOD HILL

Tel: 01271 342528

Barnstaple, Devon EX31 4EB   **Owner/Contact:** Dr J A Smart

20 acre garden with 3 small lakes. Extensive collection of camellias, bog garden. National collection of astilbes.

Location: OS Ref. SS545 375. 4m N of Barnstaple. 1/2 m W of B3230. Signs off A361 Barnstaple - Braunton road.

Opening Times: Dawn to dusk throughout the year.

Admission: Adult £3, Child (under 12yrs) Free.

MORWELLHAM QUAY

Tel: 01822 832766 **Fax:** 01822 833808

Morwellham, Tavistock, Devon PL19 8JL

Owner: The Morwellham & Tamar Valley Trust   **Contact:** Anne Emerson

Award-winning visitor centre at historic river port. Train ride into old mine workings. Shire horses and stables, staff in costume, costumes to try on. Museums, workshops, cottages, woodland walks in beautiful Tamar Valley. Average visit length 5 - 6 hours.

Location: OS Ref. SX446 697. Off A390 about 15 mins drive from Tavistock, Devon. 5m SW of Tavistock. 3m S of A390 at Gulworthy.

Opening Times: Summer: daily, 10am - 5.30pm, last adm. 3.30pm. Winter: daily, 10am - 4.30pm, last adm. 2.30pm.

Admission: Adult £8.80, Child £6. Family (2+2) £27. Group rate please apply for details. Usual concessions.

⬜ ♿ 🖥 🍴 Licensed. 🐕 In grounds, on leads. ❄

OKEHAMPTON CASTLE ⌗

Tel: 01837 52844

Okehampton, Devon EX20 1JB

Owner: English Heritage   **Contact:** The Custodian

The ruins of the largest castle in Devon stand above a river surrounded by splendid woodland. There is still plenty to see, including the Norman motte and the jagged remains of the Keep. There is a picnic area and lovely woodland walks.

Location: OS191 Ref. SX584 942. 1m SW of Okehampton town centre off A30 bypass.

Opening Times: 1 Apr - 31 Oct: daily, 10am - 6pm (5pm in Oct). Winter: Closed.

Admission: Adult £2.50, Child £1.30, Conc. £1.80. 15% discount for groups (11+).

⬜ ♿ Grounds suitable. WC. 🖥 🎧 🅿 🐕 In grounds, on leads. 🖥 Tel. for details.

OLDWAY MANSION

Tel: 01803 201201 **Fax:** 01803 292866

Paignton, Devon   **e-mail:** webmaster@torbay.gov.org

Owner: Torbay Council   **Contact:** Peter Carpenter

Built by sewing machine entrepreneur I M Singer in the 1870s. Popular Civil wedding venue.

Location: OS Ref. SX888 615. Off W side of A3022.

Opening Times: Easter - Oct: Suns, 2 - 5pm. Visitors should note that not all rooms will always be open, access depends on other activities.

Admission: Free.

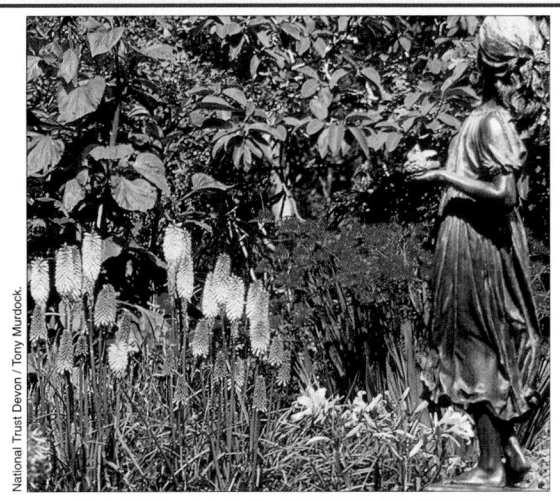

OVERBECKS MUSEUM & GDN 🌿

National Trust Devon / Tony Murdock

SHARPITOR, SALCOMBE, SOUTH DEVON TQ8 8LW

Owner: *The National Trust*   **Contact:** *Roy Chandler - Property Manager*

Tel: 01548 842893

A sub-tropical garden with rare and tender plants thriving in the mild climate and spectacular views over the Salcombe Estuary. In the Edwardian house are curios such as a polyphon and rejuvenating machine and displays on the maritime history and wildlife of the area. There is also a secret room for children, with dolls, tin soldiers, other toys and a ghost hunt.

Location: OS202 Ref. SX728 374. 1 1/2 m SW of Salcombe. Signposted from Salcombe (single track lanes).

Opening Times: Museum: 1 Apr - 31 July, Sept: Sun - Fri (open Easter Sat), 11am - 5.30pm. August, daily, 11am - 5.30pm. October, Sun - Thur, 11am - 5pm. Garden: All year: daily, 10am - 8pm.

Admission: House & Garden: Adult £4.10, Child £2. Garden only: Adult £2.90, Child £1.40.

ℹ No photography in house. ⬜ 🚻 ♿ Partially suitable. 🖥 🏃 By arrangement. 🅿 Limited. 📖 ❌ ❄

POWDERHAM CASTLE 🏛

See page 201 for full page entry.

PUSLINCH

Tel: 01752 880555 **Fax:** 01752 880909

Yealmpton, Plymouth, Devon PL8 2NN

Owner/Contact: Sebastian Fenwick

A perfect example of a medium sized early Georgian house in the Queen Anne tradition with fine contemporary interiors. Built in 1720 by the Yonge family and still in their ownership.

Location: OS Ref. SX570 509. 1m SW of Yealmpton on Newton Ferrers Road.

Opening Times: Groups only (8-60). All year except Christmas & Boxing Day by prior written appointment only.

Admission: Adult £5.

ℹ No photography. 🏃 Obligatory. 🅿 ❄ ❌

RHS GARDEN ROSEMOOR

Tel: 01805 624067 **Fax:** 01805 624717

Great Torrington, Devon   **Owner/Contact:** The Royal Horticultural Society

40 acres of gardens.

Location: OS Ref. SS500 183. 1m S of Great Torrington on A3124.

Opening Times: Apr - Sept: 10am - 6pm. Oct - Mar: 10am - 5pm.

Admission: Adult £4.50, Child (6 - 16yrs) £1, Child (under 6yrs) Free. Groups (10+) £3.50. Companion for disabled visitor Free.

ROYAL CITADEL ⌗

Tel: 01752 775841

Plymouth Hoe, Plymouth, Devon

Owner: English Heritage   **Contact:** Blue Badge Guides

A large, dramatic 17th century fortress, with walls up to 70 feet high, built to defend the coastline from the Dutch and still in use today.

Location: OS201 Ref. SX480 538. At E end of Plymouth Hoe. SE of city centre.

Opening Times: By guided tour only (1 1/2 hrs) at 2.30pm. 1 May - 30 Sept. Tickets at Plymouth Dome below Smeaton's Tower on the Hoe and TIC in Plymouth.

Admission: Adult £3, Child £2, OAP £2.50.

South West England

SALTRAM HOUSE

PLYMPTON, PLYMOUTH, DEVON PL7 1UH

Owner: The National Trust   *Contact: Kevan Timms - Property Manager*

Tel: 01752 336546 **Fax:** 01752 336474

A magnificent George II mansion set in beautiful gardens and surrounded by landscaped park overlooking the Plym estuary. Visitors can see the original contents including important work by Robert Adam, Chippendale, Wedgwood and Sir Joshua Reynolds. You can explore the garden follies including Fanny's Bower and the Castle, follow the tree trail in the garden and enjoy fascinating walks beside the river, through the parkland and in the woods. Saltram starred as Norland Park in the award winning film *Sense & Sensibility.*

Location: OS Ref. SX520 557. 3^{1}/2 m E of Plymouth city centre. ^{3}/4 m S of A38.

Opening Times: House & Great Kitchen: 1 Apr - 4 Nov: Sun - Thur & Good Fri, 12 noon - 5pm (from 1 Oct: 12 noon - 4pm). Art Gallery: open as house but from 10.30am. Garden: Feb & Mar: Sats & Suns only, 11am - 4pm; from 1 Apr - 4 Nov as house but from 10.30am - 5.30pm.

Admission: House & Garden: Adult £6, Child £3, Family £15. Groups £5.20. Garden only: Adult £3, Child £1.50.

ℹ️ Conferences.   📷   ♿ WC. Braille guide. Audio-visual tape.

🍴 Licensed.   🐕 In grounds, on leads. Guide dogs in house.

SAND 🏛️

SIDBURY, SIDMOUTH EX10 0QN

Owner/Contact: Lt Col P Huyshe

Tel: 01395 597230

Lived-in manor house owned by the Huyshe family since 1560 rebuilt 1592-4 lying in unspoilt valley. Mixed 4-acre garden with something for everyone. Screens passage, panelling, family documents and heraldry. Also Sand Lodge, roof structure of late 15th century hall house.

Location: OS Ref. SY146 925. ^{1}/4 m off A375, ^{1}/2 m N of Sidbury. Well signed.

Opening Times: House: 15/16 Apr; 6/7/27/28 May; 10/11 Jun; 1/2/15/16/29/30 Jul; 12/13/26/27 Aug. Garden only: Apr - end Sept: Sun - Tue. 2 - 6pm, last admission to house and garden 5pm.

Admission: House & Garden: Adult £4, Child/Student £1. Garden only: Adult £2.50, accompanied Child (under 16) Free.

ℹ️ No photography in house.   ♿ Partially suitable.   💷   🎟️ Obligatory.

🅿️ Limited for coaches.   🐕 In grounds, on leads.   🏠 Tel. for details.

SHOBROOKE PARK
Tel: 01363 775153 **Fax:** 01363 775153

Crediton, Devon EX17 1DG   **e-mail:** admin@shobrookepark.com

Owner: Dr J R Shelley   **Contact:** Clare Shelley

A classical English 180-acre park. The lime avenue dates from about 1800 and the cascade of four lakes was completed in the 1840s. Millennium amphitheatre built in the year 2000. The southern third of the Park is open to the public under the Countryside Commission Access Scheme. The 15 acre garden, created c1845 with Portland stone terraces, roses and rhododendrons is being restored.

Location: OS Ref. SS848 010. 1m E of Crediton. Access to park by kissing gate at SW end of park, just S of A3072. Garden access on A3072.

Opening Times: South Park: All daylight hours. Gardens: Sats, 19 May, 9 & 23 Jun, 2 - 5pm.

Admission: Park: No charge. Gardens: NGS £2, accompanied children under 14 Free.

♿ Limited, wheelchairs in garden only.   🐕 Guide dogs only in garden.   ❄️

SHUTE BARTON 🌿
Tel: 01297 34692

Shute, Axminster, Devon EX13 7PT

Owner: The National Trust

One of the most important surviving non-fortified manor houses of the Middle Ages.

Location: OS Ref. SY253 974. 3m SW of Axminster, 2m N of Colyton, 1m S of A35.

Opening Times: 4 Apr - 31 Oct: Weds & Sats, 2 - 5.30pm. Last admission 5pm.

Admission: £1.80, No group reductions.

TAPELEY PARK 🏛️
Tel: 01271 342558 **Fax** 01271 342371

Instow, Bideford, Devon EX39 4NT

Owner: Tapeley Park Trust

Much altered Queen Anne building with extensive gardens and park.

Location: OS Ref. SS478 291. Between Bideford and Barnstaple near Instow. Follow brown tourist signs from the A39 onto B3233.

Opening Times: Good Fri - end Oct: daily except Sats, 10am - 5pm.

Admission: Adult £3.50, Child £2, OAP £3. House only open to pre-booked groups, extra £2 admission.

TIVERTON CASTLE 🏛️
Tel: 01884 253200/255200 **Fax:** 01884 254200

Tiverton, Devon EX16 6RP   **e-mail:** tiverton.castle@ukf.net

Owner: Mr and Mrs A K Gordon   **Contact:** Mrs A Gordon

After nearly 900 years few buildings evoke such an immediate feeling of history as Tiverton Castle. Many ages of architecture can be seen, from medieval to modern. With continuing conservation there is always something new and interesting to see. Old walls, new gardens. Civil War Armoury – try some on.

Location: OS Ref. SS954 130. Just N of Tiverton town centre.

Opening Times: Easter - end of Jun, Sept: Sun, Thur, BH Mon, Jul & Aug, Sun - Thur, 2.30 - 5.30pm. Open to groups (12+) by prior arrangement at any time.

Admission: Adult £3.50, Child (7-16yrs) £2, Child under 7 Free. Groups (12+): Adult £4, Child £2.

📷   🌱 Plant centre. 🎫   ♿   🅿️ Ample for cars, limited for coaches.   🏠

🐕 In grounds, on leads.   🔔   🏠   ❄️

Markers Cottage, Devon.

TORRE ABBEY

THE KINGS DRIVE, TORQUAY, DEVON TQ2 5JE

Owner: Torbay Council   *Contact:* L Retallick

Tel: 01803 293593 **Fax:** 01803 215948 **e-mail:** torre-abbey@torbay.gov.uk

Torre Abbey was founded as a monastery in 1196. Later adapted as a country house and in 1741-3 remodelled by the Cary family. Bought by the Council in 1930 for an art gallery. Visitors can see monastic remains, historic rooms, family chapel, mementoes of Agatha Christie, Victorian paintings including Holman Hunt & Burne-Jones & Torquay terracotta. Torre Abbey overlooks the sea and is surrounded by parkland and gardens. Teas served in Victorian Kitchen.

Location: OS Ref. SX907 638. On Torquay sea front. Between station and town centre.

Opening Times: Apr - 1 Nov: daily, 9.30am - 6pm, last adm. 5pm. Free access to members of the National Art Collections Fund.

Admission: Adult £3, Child £1.50, Conc. £2.50, Family £7.25. Groups (pre-booked, 10+): Adult £2.25, Child £1.30.

Conferences.   Not suitable.   By arrangement.   Schools' programme, apply for details.   Guide dogs only.

TOTNES CASTLE   **Tel:** 01803 864406

Castle Street, Totnes, Devon TQ9 5NU

Owner: English Heritage   **Contact:** The Custodian

By the North Gate of the hill town of Totnes you will find a superb motte and bailey castle, with splendid views across the roof tops and down to the River Dart. It is a symbol of lordly feudal life and a fine example of Norman fortification.

Location: OS202 Ref. SX800 605. In Totnes, on hill overlooking the town. Access in Castle St off W end of High St.

Opening Times: 1 Apr - 31 Oct: daily 10am - 6pm (5pm in Oct). 1 Nov - 31 Mar: Wed - Sun, 10am - 4 pm. Closed: 24 - 26 Dec & 1 Jan.

Admission: Adult £1.60, Child 80p, Conc. £1.20. 15% discount for groups (11+).

Not suitable.   In grounds, on leads.   Tel. for details.

UGBROOKE PARK   **Tel:** 01626 852179

Chudleigh, Devon TQ13 0AD

Owner: Captain The Lord Clifford of Chudleigh   **Contact:** Mrs Martin

Location: OS Ref. SX875 000. $^3/_4$ m NW of A380, 1m SE of Chudleigh.

Opening Times: Please contact for details.

Admission: Adult £4.80, Child (5-16yrs) £2. Groups (20+) £4.50 (2000/01 prices).

YARDE MEDIEVAL FARMHOUSE   **Tel:** 01548 842367

Malborough, Kingsbridge, Devon TQ7 3BY

Owner/Contact: John R Ayre Esq

Location: OS Ref. SX718 400. 5m S of Kingsbridge $^1/_4$ m N of A381. $^1/_2$ m E of Malborough. $1^1/_2$ m W of Salcombe. Coaches only by appointment.

Opening Times: Easter - 30 Sept: Suns only, 2 - 5pm.

Admission: Adult £2.50, Child 50p, (under 5yrs Free). Groups by appointment only.

Fursdon House, Devon.

South West England

Owner:
Patrick Cooke Esq

CONTACT

Owen Davies
Athelhampton House
Dorchester
DT2 7LG

Tel: 01305 848363

Fax: 01305 848135

e-mail: pcooke@
athelhampton.co.uk

LOCATION

OS Ref. SY771 942

Off A35 (T) at Puddletown
Northbrook junction, 5m E
of Dorchester.

Rail: Dorchester.

ATHELHAMPTON HOUSE & GARDENS
Dorchester

Athelhampton is one of the finest 15th century manor houses and is surrounded by one of the great architectural gardens of England. The Great Hall was built by Sir William Martyn in 1485. The West wing is Elizabethan in period and contains the Great Chamber, Library and Wine Cellar. On the East side of the house are the Green Parlour, Dining Room and three bedrooms opening off the Landing. Athelhampton houses a fine collection of English furniture starting in the Jacobean period leading on to late Victorian. There is also a collection relating to A W Pugin and The Palace of Westminster.

The glorious Grade I gardens, dating from 1891, contain the world-famous topiary pyramids, fountains and the River Piddle. Collections of tulips, magnolias, roses, clematis and lilies can be seen in season. Located in the gardens are a number of small buildings each with their own unique history. The two garden pavilions were used as water towers for the original fountain system. The Toll house was a collection point for the Wimborne turnpike trust between 1842 and 1878 and has now been restored along with its garden. The dovecote is one of the earliest in Dorset and with a capacity for 1200 birds would have supported a large household.

The Coach House contains all the facilities required for the comfort of daily visitors with private rooms available for visiting groups. The House and Gardens can be opened by appointment for evening visits and dinners. Saturdays are reserved exclusively for wedding ceremonies and receptions.

OPENING TIMES

March - October:
Daily (closed Saturdays).

Open Saturdays at Easter &
August BH weekends.

November - February:
Sundays only,
10.30am - 5pm/dusk.

Coach House Restaurant open
as house & gardens. Carvery on
Suns. Please book.

All facilities at Athelhampton are
available for private hire outside
our normal opening hours.
We specialise in weddings on
Saturdays and dinners on any
evening. Please contact
Owen Davies, Manager.

ADMISSION

House and Gardens
Adult	£5.50
Child	Free
Student	£3.50
Disabled	£3.50
OAP	£5.20

Groups (12+)
Adult	£4.20

Gardens only
Adult	£3.95
Child	Free

By arrangement.
Partially suitable. WC.
Licensed.
Licensed.
By arrangement.
P
Guide dogs only.

CONFERENCE/FUNCTION		
ROOM	SIZE	MAX CAPACITY
Coach House		
Long Hall	11 x 9m	80
Conservatory	16 x 11m	130
Main House		
Great Hall	12 x 8m	70
Great Chamber	10 x 6m	40
All four rooms are licensed for Civil wedding ceremonies.		

Above: Great Hall.   *Right:* Conservatory.

LULWORTH CASTLE
Dorset

Owner: The Weld Estate

CONTACT

East Lulworth
Wareham
Dorset
BH20 5QS

Tel: 01929 400352

Fax: 01929 400563

LOCATION

OS194 Ref. SY853 822

In E Lulworth off B3070,
3m NE of Lulworth Cove.

A 17th century hunting lodge restored by English Heritage after the fire of 1929. Features include a gallery devoted to the Weld family, owners of the Castle and Estate since 1641. The kitchen and wine cellar have been furnished and the history of the building is brought to life through a video presentation. The Chapel of St Mary in the Castle grounds is reputed to be one of the finest pieces of architecture in Dorset. It is the first free standing Roman Catholic church to be built in England since the Reformation and contains an exhibition of 18th and 19th century vestments, church and recusant silver. A short walk from the Castle and Chapel is the Animal Farm, Play Area and Woodland Walk. The stables have been converted to house the licensed café serving morning coffee, light lunches and traditional cream teas. The Courtyard Shop offers a wide range of unusual gift items. Coach and car parking and access to the shop and café is free.

Lulworth Castle House

Modern house of the Weld family containing the Blundell collection of pictures and 18th century sculptures as well as portraits and furniture from Lulworth Castle. Walled garden and grounds.

❖

By kind permission of Dorset Life.

Lulworth Castle House

🛍 Corporate hospitality, conferences, receptions etc.

♿ Partially suitable. WC.

☕

🍴 Licensed.

🏃 By arrangement.

🅿

🐕 In grounds, on leads.

🏠 5 holiday cottages, tel: 01929 400100 (Mrs Weld).

🔔

❄

OPENING TIMES

Lulworth Castle

30 Oct - 26 Mar 2001:
10am - 4pm or dusk if earlier.
27 Mar - 26 Oct 2001:
10.30am - 6pm. 28 Oct -
24 Mar 2002: 10.30am - 4pm
or dusk if earlier.
Sun - Fri, plus Easter Sat.
Closed Sats and 24/25 Dec.
Lulworth Leisure reserve the
right to close the Castle
without notice.

Lulworth Castle House

30 May - 26 Sept: Weds,
2 - 5pm. Groups: Mon - Fri
by appointment only.

ADMISSION

Lulworth Castle

Adult	£5.50
Child (5-16)	£3.00
Conc.	£4.50
Family (2+3)	£14.00

Groups (10-200)

Adult	£4.95
Child (5-16)	£2.70
Conc.	£4.05

Lulworth Castle House

Adult	£4.00
Child (5-16)	£1.50
OAP	£3.50
Family (2+3)	£10.00

Joint Ticket with Lulworth
Castle

Adult	£7.50
Child (5-16)	£3.50
OAP	£6.00
Family	£16.00

Children under 5yrs Free.

🎭 SPECIAL EVENTS

• **APR 15/16**
Easter Bunny Hunt.

• **MAY 12/13**
Country Gardening & Food Fair.

• **JUL 28/29**
Lulworth Horse Trials
& Country Fair.

• **SEPT 14 - 16**
International Floral Design
Show & Competition.

ABBOTSBURY SUB-TROPICAL GARDENS

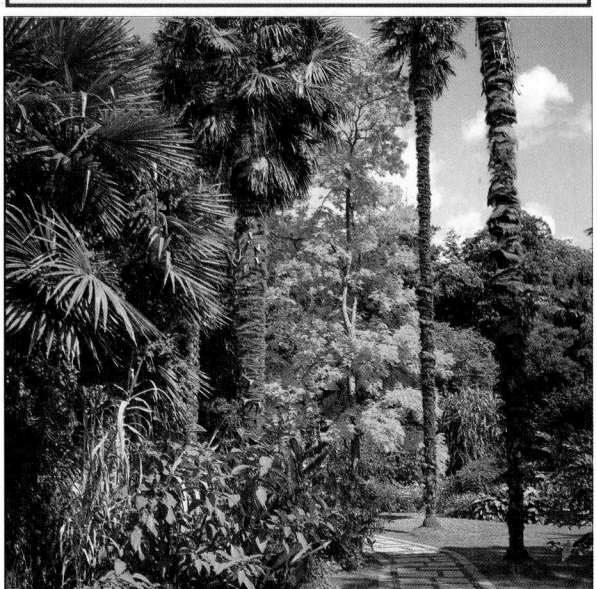

ABBOTSBURY, WEYMOUTH, DORSET DT3 4JT
Owner: The Hon Mrs Townshend DL   *Contact: Shop Manager*

Tel: 01305 871387
Over 20 acres of exotic and rare plants. Established in 1765. Superb colonial-style Teahouse. Extensively stocked plant centre. Quality gift shop.
Location: OS Ref. SY564 851. On B3157. Off the A35 between Weymouth & Bridport.
Opening Times: Mar - Nov, daily 10am - 6pm. Winter, daily 10am - 4pm. Last admission 1 hr before closing.
Admission: Adult £4.70, Child £3.20, OAP £4.50.

🖼️ 🚻 🍴 ♿Partially suitable. 📷Licensed. 🍴 👤By arrangement.
🅿️Free. 🎦 🐕In grounds, on leads. ❄️

ATHELHAMPTON HOUSE & GDNS 🏛️   See page 210 for full page entry.

BROWNSEA ISLAND 🌿   **Tel:** 01202 707744 **Fax:** 01202 701635

Poole Harbour, Dorset BH13 7EE
Owner: National Trust   **Contact:** The Property Manager
A wonderfully atmospheric island of heath and woodland. Privately owned until aquired by the Trust in 1962 and now a haven for a rich variety of wildlife, including red squirrels and many species of bird. Part of the island is leased as a nature reserve to the Dorset Wildlife Trust. There are many fine walks and spectacular views of Poole Harbour. Note: Boats run from Poole Quay, Bournemouth and Sandbanks. Visitors may land from own boats at Pottery Pier at West end of island, accessible at all stages of the tide. Please note that the island's paths are uneven in places.
Location: OS Ref. SZ032 878. In Poole Harbour. Boats run from Poole Quay, Bournemouth and Sandbanks. Visitors may land on the beach with a dinghy.
Opening Times: 31 Mar - 7 Oct: daily, 10am - 5pm. Jul & Aug: 10am - 6pm.
Admission: Landing fee £3.50, Child £1.50, Family (2+3) £8.50 (1+3) £5. Groups £3.20, Child £1.20 by written appointment with the Property Manager.

🖼️ ♿Partially suitable. 📷 👤 🎦 🛡️Tel. for details.

CHETTLE HOUSE   **Tel:** 01258 830209 **Fax:** 01258 830380

Chettle, Blandford Forum, Dorset DT11 8DB
Owner/Contact: Patrick Bourke Esq
A fine Queen Anne manor house designed by Thomas Archer and a fine example of English baroque architecture. The house features a basement with the typical north-south passage set just off centre with barrel-vaulted ceilings and a magnificent stone staircase. The house is set in 5 acres of peaceful gardens and there is a new rose garden.
Location: OS Ref. ST952 132. 6m NE of Blandford NW of A354.
Opening Times: Easter Sun - end Sept: Suns only. Groups: by appointment any day.
Admission: Adult £2.50, Child Free (under 16yrs).

♿Grounds suitable. 📷 ❄️

CHRISTCHURCH CASTLE & NORMAN HOUSE ⛬   **Tel:** 0117 9750700

Christchurch, Dorset
Owner: English Heritage   **Contact:** The South West Office
Early 12th century Norman keep and Constable's house, built c1160.
Location: OS195. Ref. SZ160 927. In Christchurch, near the Priory.
Opening Times: Any reasonable time.
Admission: Free.

CLOUDS HILL 🌿   **Tel:** 01929 405616

Wareham, Dorset BH20 7NQ
Owner: The National Trust   **Contact:** The Custodian
A tiny isolated brick and tile cottage, bought in 1925 by T E Lawrence (Lawrence of Arabia) as a retreat. The austere rooms inside are much as he left them and reflect his complex personality and close links with the Middle East.
Location: OS Ref. SY824 909. 9m E of Dorchester, $1^{1}/_{2}$ m E of Waddock crossroads B3390.
Opening Times: 1 Apr - 28 Oct: daily except, Mons, Tues, & Sats (open BH Mons), 12 noon - 5pm or dusk if earlier, (no electric light). Groups wishing to visit at other times must telephone in advance.
Admission: £2.60, no reduction for children or groups.

ℹ️No WC. ♿Braille guide. 🅿️No coaches.

CORFE CASTLE 🌿

Joe Cornish

WAREHAM, DORSET BH20 5EZ
Owner: The National Trust   *Contact: The Property Manager*

Tel: 01929 481294
One of Britain's most majestic ruins, the Castle controlled the gateway through the Purbeck Hills and had been an important stronghold since the time of William the Conqueror. Defended during the Civil War by the redoubtable Lady Bankes, the Castle fell to treachery from within and was heavily slighted afterwards by the Parliamentarians. Many fine Norman and early English features remain. Visitor Centre at Castle View.
Location: OS Ref. SY959 824. On A351 Wareham - Swanage Rd. NW of the village.
Opening Times: All year: daily. Mar: 10am - 5pm; Apr - Oct: 10am - 6pm; Nov - Feb 2002: 10am - 4pm, last admission $1/_2$ hr before closing. Closed 25/26 Dec & 2 days end Jan, tel for details.
Admission: Adult £4.20, Child £2.10, Family (2+3) £10.50/ (1+3) £6. Groups: Adult £3.60, Child £1.80.

🖼️ ♿Limited. WC. 📷 🎦 🐕On leads. ❄️

CRANBORNE MANOR GARDEN   **Tel:** 01725 517248 **Fax:** 01725 517862

Cranborne, Wimborne, Dorset BH21 5PP
Owner: The Viscount & Viscountess Cranborne   **Contact:** The Manor Garden Centre
The beautiful and historic gardens of yew hedges, walled, herb, mount and wild gardens originate from the 17th century – originally laid out by Mounten Jennings with John Tradescant supplying many of the plants. Spring time is particularly good with displays of spring bulbs and crab apple orchard in the wild garden.
Location: OS Ref. SU054 133. On B3078 N of Bournemouth (18m), S of Salisbury (16m).
Opening Times: Mar - Sept: Weds, 9am - 5pm. Occasional weekends, phone for details. Entrance, parking and tearoom via the Garden Centre.
Admission: Adult £3, Child 50p, OAP £2.50.

🖼️ 🌿Garden centre. ♿Partially suitable. 📷 👤By arrangement.
🅿️ ❄️ 🐾

DEANS COURT

Tel: 01202 886116

Wimborne, Dorset BH21 1EE

Owner: Sir Michael & Lady Hanham   **Contact:** Wimborne Tourist Information Centre

13 peaceful acres a few minutes walk south of the Minster. Specimen trees, lawns, borders, herb garden, kitchen garden with long serpentine wall and rose garden. Chemical-free produce usually for sale, also interesting herbaceous plants. Wholefood teas in garden or in Housekeeper's room (down steps).

Location: OS Ref. SZ010 997. 2 mins walk S from centre of Wimborne Minster.

Opening Times: 15 Apr, 6 & 27 May, 10 & 24 Jun, 22 Jul, 4/5 Aug: 2 - 6pm. 16 Apr, 7 & 28 May: 10am - 6pm. Organic Gardening Weekends: 26 Aug, 16 Sept: 2 - 6pm. 27 Aug: 10am - 6pm.

Admission: Adult £2, Child (5-15yrs) 50p, OAP £1.50. Groups by arrangement. Exhibition: Adult £3.50, Child (5-16yrs)/Student £1.50, Child (under 5yrs) Free, OAP £3. Family £6 (2+2).

Garden produce sales.   📷   🅿   Guide dogs only.

DORSET COUNTY MUSEUM

HIGH WEST STREET, DORCHESTER, DORSET DT1 1XA

Owner: The Dorset Natural History & Archaeological Society   *Contact: Richard De Peyer*

Tel: 01305 262735 **Fax:** 01305 257180

Sixteen exhibition rooms in a distinguished high Victorian museum building. New 'Dorset Writer's Gallery' includes a reconstruction of Thomas Hardy's study, displays on William Barnes, author of *Lyndon Lea* and many others. Evocative Victorian Hall paved with Roman mosaics; award-winning Archaeology Gallery, Geology, Natural History and local history displays; fine temporary exhibitions gallery. Interpret Britain commendation 1997. Best Social History Museum Award 1998.

Location: OS Ref. SY688 906. In the centre of Dorchester.

Opening Times: 1 Nov - 30 Apr: Mon - Sat, 10am - 5pm. May - Oct: daily, 10am - 5pm.

Admission: Adult £3.30, Child £1.60, Conc. £2.20, Family £8.20. Groups (15+): Adult £2.75.

📷   ♿ Partially suitable.   🅿 None - set down bay for coaches.   🏪   Guide dogs only.   ❄   (NW)

Brownsea Island, Dorset.

EDMONDSHAM HOUSE & GARDENS

Tel: 01725 517207

Cranborne, Wimborne, Dorset BH21 5RE

Owner/Contact: Mrs Julia E Smith

Charming blend of Tudor and Georgian architecture with interesting contents. Organic walled garden, dower house garden, 6 acre garden with unusual trees and spring bulbs. 12th century church nearby.

Location: OS Ref. SU062 116. Off B3081 between Cranborne and Verwood, NW from Ringwood 9m, Wimborne 9m.

Opening Times: House & Gardens: All BH Mons & Weds in Apr & Oct 2 - 5pm. Gardens: Apr - Oct, Suns & Weds 2 - 5pm.

Admission: House & Garden: Adult £3, Child £1 (under 5yrs Free). Garden only: Adult £1.50, Child 50p. Groups by arrangement, teas for groups.

👶   ♿   🍴 Available if booked, max 50 persons.   🍽 Obligatory.   🐕 Car park only.   🔔 (max 50).

FIDDLEFORD MANOR

Tel: 0117 9750700

Sturminster Newton, Dorset

Owner: English Heritage   **Contact:** The South West Regional Office

Part of a medieval manor house, with a remarkable interior. The splendid roof structures in the hall and upper living room are the best in Dorset.

Location: OS194 ST801 136. 1m E of Sturminster Newton off A357.

Opening Times: 1 Apr - 30 Sept: daily, 10am - 6pm. 1 Nov - 31 Mar: daily 10am - 4pm. Closed 24 - 26 Dec & 1 Jan.

Admission: Free.

FORDE ABBEY

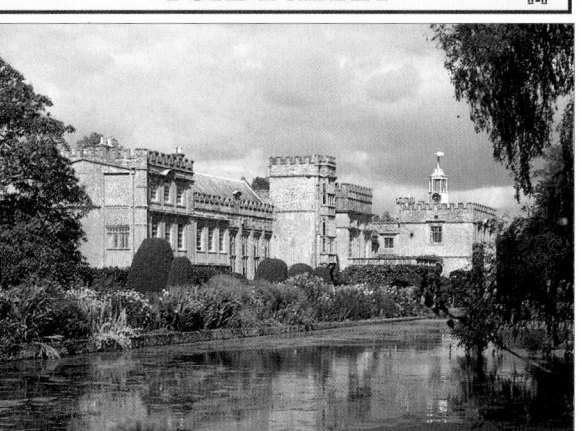

Nr CHARD, SOMERSET TA20 4LU

Owner/Contact: Mark Roper Esq

Tel: 01460 221290

One of the top ten gardens in England. 30 acres of timeless elegance, old walls, colourful borders, wide lawns, ponds, cascades, statuary, a walled working kitchen garden and huge mature trees surround a unique former Cistercian monastery that has been a private home since 1649. The medieval abbey was founded in 1140 and survives externally almost as the monks left it in 1539. Home to the Roper family and the world famous Mortlake tapestries and a host of outstanding pictures and furniture.

Location: OS Ref. ST358 041. Just off the B3167 4m S of Chard.

Opening Times: House: Apr - Oct, Suns, Tues - Thurs & BHs, 1 - 4.30pm. Gardens: All year: daily, 10am - 4.30pm.

Admission: House & Gardens: Adult £5.40, Child Free, OAP £5, Groups (20+) £4.50. Gardens: Adult £4.20, Child Free, OAP £3.95, Groups (20+) £3.75.

ℹ Conferences. No photography in house.   📷   👶   🍷 Wedding receptions.   ♿ Ground floor & gardens suitable. WC. Wheelchair available, please telephone.   🍽 Licensed.   🍴 By arrangement.   🅿   🐕 In grounds, on leads.   ❄   (NW)

Open All Year Index ◀◀◀ page 49

HARDY'S COTTAGE 🌿   **Tel:** 01305 262366

Higher Bockhampton, Dorchester, Dorset DT2 8QJ

Owner/Contact: The National Trust

A small thatched cottage where the novelist and poet Thomas Hardy was born in 1840, and from where he would walk to school every day in Dorchester, six miles away. It was built by his great-grandfather and is little altered since. The interior has been furnished by the Trust (see also Max Gate).

Location: OS Ref. SY728 925. 3m NE of Dorchester, ¹/₂ m S of A35. 10 mins walk through the woods from car park.

Opening Times: 1 Apr - 4 Nov: daily except Fris & Sats (open Good Fri), 11am - 5pm or dusk if earlier.

Admission: £2.60. No reduction for children or groups. School groups and coaches by arrangement only.

ℹ️ No WC. ♿ Garden suitable. 🅿️ No coach parking. 🐕

HIGHCLIFFE CASTLE 🏛️   See below for half page entry.

HIGHER MELCOMBE 🏛️   **Tel:** 01258 880251

Melcombe Bingham, Dorchester, Dorset DT2 7PB

Owner: Mr M C Woodhouse   **Contact:** Lt Col J M Woodhouse

Consists of the surviving wing of a 16th century house with its attached domestic chapel. A fine plaster ceiling and linenfold panelling. Conducted tours by owner.

Location: OS Ref. ST749 024. 1km W of Melcombe Bingham.

Opening Times: May - Sept by appointment.

Admission: Adult £2 (takings go to charity).

♿ Not suitable. 🕴️ By written appointment only. 🅿️ Limited. 🐕 Guide dogs only.

HORN PARK GARDENS   **Tel:** 01308 862212

Beaminster, Dorset DT8 3HB

Owner/Contact: John Kirkpatrick Esq

Large, beautiful garden; unique position, magnificent view to sea. Plantsman's Garden, unusual trees, shrubs and plants, in rock, water garden, terraces and herbaceous borders. Woodland Garden, Bluebell Woods. Wild Flower Meadow, with over 160 species, including orchids. Plants for sale. In "Twelve Beautiful Gardens" calendar for 1998 and "Twelve Gardens to Remember" for 1999.

Location: OS Ref. ST468 030. 1m NW of Beaminster, just S of the tunnel on the A3066.

Opening Times: 1 Apr - 31 Oct: Sun - Thur, 2 - 6pm.

Admission: Adult £3.50, Child (under 16yrs) Free. Groups £3.50.

🌿 🍽️ By arrangement. 🐕 Dogs on leads.

THE KEEP MILITARY MUSEUM OF DEVON & DORSET   **Tel:** 01305 264066

Bridport Rd, Dorchester, Dorset DT1 1RN   **Fax:** 01305 250373

Owner: Ministry of Defence (Museums Trustees)   **Contact:** The Curator

There are four floors to explore in this Grade II listed building. Uniforms, medals and weapons reside alongside touch pad technology. Feel the experience of how it really was in the re-created world war bunker. Climb to the roof to view the county town and Hardy country. Lift available.

Location: OS Ref. SY687 906. In Dorchester at the top of High West Street.

Opening Times: All year: Mon - Sat 9.30am - 5pm (last admission 4.15pm). Suns during Jul & Aug, 10am - 4pm.

Admission: Adult £3, Conc. £2. Groups (10-100): Adult £2, Conc. £1.

ℹ️ No flash photography. 📷 🍽️ ♿ 🕴️ By arrangement. 🅿️ Limited. 🐕 Guide dogs only. ✳️ 🛡️ Tel. for details.

HIGHCLIFFE CASTLE 🏛️

ROTHSAY DRIVE, HIGHCLIFFE-ON-SEA, CHRISTCHURCH BH23 4LE

Owner: Christchurch Borough Council   *Contact: Mike Allen, Manager*

Tel: 01425 278807 or 01202 495131 **Fax:** 01425 280423
e-mail: m.allen@christchurch.gov.uk

Built in 1830 in the Romantic and Picturesque style of architecture for Lord Stuart de Rothesay using his unique collection of French medieval stonework and stained glass. Recently repaired externally, it remains mostly unrepaired inside. Five rooms house a visitor centre, exhibitions, events and gift shop. Coastal grounds, village trail and nearby St Mark's church.

Location: OS Ref. SZ200 930. Off the A337 Lymington Road, between Christchurch and Highcliffe-on-Sea.

Opening Times: May - Oct (check exact dates): daily, 1 - 5pm. Grounds: All year.

Admission: Adult £1.50, Child Free. Group guided tour (min 12): Adult £2.50, Child £1. Grounds: Free.

📷 🍽️ ♿ Partially suitable. WC. 🍴 10am - 5pm. 🕴️ By arrangement. 🅿️ Limited. Parking charge. ▪️ By arrangement. 🐕 In grounds, on leads. 🔲 ✳️ 🛡️ Ⓦ

KINGSTON LACY

Rupert Truman

WIMBORNE MINSTER, DORSET BH21 4EA

Owner: The National Trust   *Contact:* The Property Manager

Tel: 01202 883402   **Infoline:** 01202 880413   **Fax:** 01202 882402

A 17th century house, designed by Sir Roger Pratt for Sir Ralph Bankes to replace his ruined family seat at Corfe Castle. Altered by Sir Charles Barry in the 19th century, the house contains the outstanding collection of paintings and other works of art accumulated by William Bankes. It is famous for its dramatic Spanish room, with walls hung in magnificent gilded leather. The house and garden are set in a wooded park with attractive waymarked walks and a fine herd of Red Devon cattle. The surrounding estate is crossed by many paths (leaflet available from shop) and dominated by the Iron Age hill fort of Badbury Rings. The botanically rich rings are managed by grazing and dogs are not permitted. Point-to-Point races are held 24 Feb, 24 Mar & 14 Apr and on these days a charge is made for car-parking.

Location: OS Ref. ST978 013. On B3082 - Blandford / Wimborne road, $1^{1}/_{2}$ m NW of Wimborne.

Opening Times: House: 31 Mar - 4 Nov: daily except Mons & Tues (open BH Mons, closed Good Fri), 12 noon - 5.30pm (last admission 4.30pm). Garden & Park: 3 Feb - 25 Mar: Sats & Suns only, 11am - 4pm. 31 Mar - 4 Nov: daily, 11am - 6pm; 9 Nov - 23 Dec: Fri - Sun, 11am - 4pm. Special Snowdrop Days early 2002, telephone infoline.

Admission: Adult £6.50, Child £3, Family £17. Park & garden only: Adult £3, Child £1.50. Pre-booked groups (15+): £5.

🗖 &Garden only. Braille guide. WC. 🍴 🏃By arrangement. 🅿 🏛
🐕In park only. 🛡Telephone for details.

KINGSTON MAURWARD GARDENS

DORCHESTER, DORSET DT2 8PY

Contact: Mike Hancock

Tel: 01305 215003   **Fax:** 01305 215001   **e-mail:** administration@kmc.ac.uk

Classical Georgian mansion set in 35 acres of 18th century gardens including 5 acre lake. Restored Edwardian gardens with dividing hedges, stone balustrading features. Walled demonstration garden, National collections of Penstemons and Salvias. Animal park, Nature and Tree Trails. Visitors' Centre and restaurant.

Location: OS Ref. SY713 911. 1m E of Dorchester. Roundabout off A35 by-pass.

Opening Times: 6 Jan - 23 Dec: daily, 10am - 5.30pm or dusk if earlier.

Admission: Adult £3.75, Child £2 (under 3yrs Free). Groups (10+): Adult £3.25. Guided tours (by arrangement) (12+): £3.75.

ℹConferences. 🗖 🏃 🎭Wedding receptions. 🍴 🏃By arrangement. 🅿 🏛 🐕Guide dogs only. 🖼

KNOLL GARDENS & NURSERY   **Tel:** 01202 873931 **Fax:** 01202 870842

Stapehill Road, Hampreston, Wimborne BH21 7ND

Owner: J & J Flude & N R Lucas   **Contact:** Mr John Flude

Award-winning 6 acre gardens, with 6000+ named plants from the world over.

Location: OS Ref. SU059 001. Between Wimborne & Ferndown. Exit A31 Canford Bottom roundabout, B3073 Hampreston. Signposted $1^{1}/_{2}$ m.

Opening Times: Mar: Wed - Sun, 10am - 4.30pm. Apr - Sept: daily 10am - 5pm. Oct & Nov: Wed - Sun, 10am - 4.30pm. Closed Dec - Feb inclusive.

Admission: Adult £4, Child (5-15yrs) £2, OAP £3.50, Student £3. Groups: Adult £3, Child £1.75, Student £2.50. Family (2+2) £9.75.

LULWORTH CASTLE ⛫ 🏛   See page 211 for full page entry.

MAPPERTON   🏛

George Wright

BEAMINSTER, DORSET DT8 3NR

Owner/Contact: The Earl & Countess of Sandwich

Tel: 01308 862645   **Fax:** 01308 863348   **e-mail:** office@mapperton.com

Jacobean 1660s manor with Tudor features and classical north front. Italianate upper garden with orangery, topiary and formal borders descending to fish ponds and shrub gardens. All Saints Church forms south wing opening to courtyard and stables. Area of outstanding natural beauty with fine views of Dorset hills and woodlands. House and Gardens featured in *Restoration, Emma* and *Tom Jones*.

Location: OS Ref. SY503 997. 1m S of B3163, 2m NE of B3066, 2m SE Beaminster, 5m NE Bridport.

Opening Times: Gardens: 1 Mar - 31 Oct: daily, 2 - 6pm. House: Open only to groups by appointment (times as for gardens, but not Sat or Sun).

Admission: Gardens: £3.50, House (tour) £3.50. Child (under 18yrs) £1.50, under 5 Free.

🗖 🏃 &Partially suitable. ☕ 🏃By arrangement. 🖼
🅿Limited for coaches. 🐕Guide dogs only. (W)

MAX GATE 🌺   **Tel:** 01305 262538 **Fax:** 01305 250978

Alington Avenue, Dorchester, Dorset DT1 2AA   **e-mail:** max.gate@btinternet.com

Owner: The National Trust   **Contact:** The Tenant

Poet and novelist Thomas Hardy designed and lived in the house from 1885 until his death in 1928. The house is leased to tenants and contains several pieces of Hardy's furniture.

Location: OS Ref. SY704 897. 1m E of Dorchester just N of the A352 to Wareham. From Dorchester follow A352 signs to the roundabout named Max Gate (at Jct. of A35 Dorchester bypass). Turn left and left again into cul-de-sac outside Max Gate.

Opening Times: 1 Apr - 30 Sept: Mons, Weds & Suns, 2 - 5pm. Only dining and drawing rooms open.

Admission: Adult £2.30, Child £1.20.

&Limited access to ground floor for wheelchairs. 🅿Limited. 🖼

MILTON ABBEY CHURCH   **Tel:** 01258 880489

Milton Abbas, Blandford, Dorset DT11 0BZ

Owner: Diocese of Salisbury   **Contact:** Chris Fookes

Abbey church dating from 14th century.

Location: OS117 ST798 024. $3^{1}/_{2}$ m N of A354. Between Dorchester/Blandford Road.

Opening Times: Abbey Church: daily 10am - 6pm. Groups by arrangement please.

Admission: By donation except Easter & mid-Jul - end Aug. Adult £1.75, Child Free.

MINTERNE GARDENS

Tel: 01300 341370   **Fax:** 01300 341747

Minterne Magna, Nr Dorchester, Dorset DT2 7AU

Owner/Contact: The Lord Digby

If you want to visit a formal garden, do not go to Minterne, but if you want to wander peacefully through 20 wild woodland acres, where magnolias, rhododendrons, eucryphias, hydrangeas, water plants and water lilies, provide a new vista at each turn and where ducks enhance the small lakes and cascades, then you will be welcome at Minterne, the home of the Churchill and Digby families for 350 years. The house which contains magnificent Churchill tapestries and naval and other historical pictures is open for Special Interest groups only which may be arranged by prior appointment.

Location: OS Ref. ST660 042. On A352 Dorchester/Sherborne Road, 2m N of Cerne Abbas.

Opening Times: 1 Mar - 10 Nov: daily, 10am - 7pm.

Admission: Adult £3, accompanied children Free.

Not suitable.   In grounds on leads.

PORTLAND CASTLE

Tel: 01305 820539

Castletown, Portland, Weymouth, Dorset DT5 1AZ

Owner: English Heritage   **Contact:** The Custodian

Discover one of Henry VIII's finest coastal fortresses. Perfectly preserved in a waterfront location overlooking Portland harbour, it is a marvellous place to visit for all the family whatever the weather. You can try on armour, explore the Tudor kitchen and gun platform, see ghostly sculptured figures from the past, enjoy the superb battlement views or picnic on the lawn in front of the newly re-opened Captain's House. An excellent new audio tour, included in the admission charge, brings the castle's history and characters to life.

Location: OS194 Ref. SY684 743. Overlooking Portland harbour.

Opening Times: 1 Apr - 31 Oct: daily, 10am - 6pm (5pm in Oct). Winter 2000 closed. From Nov 2001 - Mar 2002: Fri - Sun, 10am - 4pm. Closed 24/26 Dec & 1 Jan.

Admission: Adult £3, Child £1.50, Conc. £2.20. 15% discount for groups (11+).

Ground floor suitable. WCs.   Tel. for details.

PURSE CAUNDLE MANOR

Tel: 01963 250400

Purse Caundle, Sherborne, Dorset DT9 5DY

Owner/Contact: Michael de Pelet Esq

15th & 16th century manor house. Great Hall with minstrels gallery. Upstairs great chamber with barrel ceiling and oriel window. Family home.

Location: OS Ref. ST695 177. 4m E of Sherborne, just S of the A30.

Opening Times: 1 May - 30 Sept: Thurs by appointment, 2 - 5pm.

Admission: Adult £2.50, Child Free. Groups by appointment.

For groups.

ST CATHERINE'S CHAPEL

Tel: 0117 9750700

Abbotsbury, Dorset

Owner: English Heritage   **Contact:** The South West Regional Office

A small stone chapel, set on a hilltop, with an unusual roof and small turret used as a lighthouse.

Location: OS194 Ref. SY572 848. ½ m S of Abbotsbury by pedestrian track to the hilltop.

Opening Times: Any reasonable time.

Admission: Free at any reasonable daylight hour.

SANDFORD ORCAS MANOR HOUSE

Tel: 01963 220206

Sandford Orcas, Sherborne, Dorset DT9 4SB

Owner/Contact: Sir Mervyn Medlycott Bt

Tudor manor house with gatehouse, fine panelling, furniture, pictures. Terraced gardens with topiary and herb garden. Personal conducted tour by owner.

Location: OS Ref. ST623 210. 2½ m N of Sherborne, Dorset 4m S of A303 at Sparkford. Entrance next to church.

Opening Times: Easter Mon, 10am - 6pm. May - Sept: Suns, 2 - 6pm, Mons, 10am - 6pm.

Admission: Adult £3, Child £1.50. Groups (10+): Adult £2.50, Child £1.

Not suitable.   Obligatory.   In grounds, on leads.

Mapperton, Dorset.

SHERBORNE CASTLE

SHERBORNE, DORSET DT9 5NR

Owner: Mr & Mrs John Wingfield Digby   *Contact: Castle & Events Manager*

Tel: 01935 813182   **Fax:** 01935 816727   **e-mail:** enquiries@sherbornecastle.com
Built by Sir Walter Raleigh in 1594, Sherborne Castle has been the home of the Digby family since 1617. Prince William of Orange was entertained here in 1688, and George III visited in 1789. Splendid collections of art, furniture and porcelain are on view in the Castle. Lancelot 'Capability' Brown created the lake in 1753 and gave Sherborne the very latest in landscape gardening.

Location: OS Ref. ST649 164. $^3/_4$ m SE of Sherborne town centre. Follow brown signs from A30 or A352. $^1/_2$ m S of the Old Castle.

Opening Times: 1 Apr - 31 Oct: Castle: Tues, Thurs, Suns & BH Mons, 12.30 - 4.30pm, Sats, 2.30 - 4.30pm (last admission). Gardens: daily except Weds, 10am - 5pm (last admission). Tearoom & Shop: daily (except Weds), 12.30 - 5pm (last admission). Groups (15+) by arrangement during normal opening hours and on other days if possible.

Admission: Castle & Gardens: Adult £5.50, Child (5-16yrs) £2.75, OAP £5, Family (2+2) £13.75. Groups (15+): Adult £4.75, Child (5-16) £2.30. Private Views: Adult £8.50, Child £4.25 (min charge for 15 people). Gardens only: Adult £2.75, Child (5-16) £1.30. Children under 5 Free, no concessions or group rates.

Partially suitable.   By arrangement.
In grounds, on leads.   Telephone for details.

SHERBORNE OLD CASTLE

Tel: 01935 812730

Castleton, Sherborne, Dorset DT9 3SA

Owner: English Heritage   **Contact:** The Custodian
The ruins of this early 12th century Castle are a testament to the 16 days it took Cromwell to capture it during the Civil War, after which it was abandoned. A gatehouse, some graceful arcading and decorative windows survive.

Location: OS183 Ref ST647 167. $^1/_2$ m E of Sherborne off B3145. $^1/_2$ m N of the 1594 Castle.

Opening Times: 1 Apr - 31 Oct: daily, 10am - 6pm (5pm in Oct). 1 Nov - 31 Mar: Wed - Sun, 10am - 4pm. Closed 24 - 26 Dec & 1 Jan.

Admission: Adult £1.80, Child 90p, Conc. £1.30. 15% discount for groups of 11+.

Grounds suitable.   Limited for cars. No coach parking.

SMEDMORE HOUSE

Tel/Fax: 01929 480702

Smedmore, Kimmeridge, Wareham BH20 5BG

Owner: Dr Philip Mansel   **Contact:** Mr B Belsten
The home of the Mansel family for nearly 400 years nestles at the foot of the Purbeck hills looking across Kimmeridge Bay to Portland Bill.

Location: OS Ref. SY924 787. 15m SW of Poole.

Opening Times: 13 May & 9 Sept: 2 - 5pm.

Admission: Adult £3.50, under 16s Free.

WHITE MILL

Tel: 01258 858051

Sturminster Marshall, Nr Wimborne, Dorset

Owner: The National Trust   **Contact:** The Custodian
Rebuilt in 1776 on a site marked as a mill in the Domesday Book, this corn mill was extensively repaired in 1994 and still retains its original elm and applewood machinery (now too fragile to be operative). Peaceful setting with nearby riverside picnic area.

Location: OS Ref. ST958 007. On River Stour $^1/_2$ m NE of Sturminster Marshall from the B3082 Blandford to Wareham Rd, take road to SW signposted Sturminster Marshall. Mill is 1m on right. Car park nearby.

Opening Times: 31 Mar - 28 Oct: Weekends & BH Mons, 12 noon - 5pm.

Admission: Adult £2.50, Child £1.25.

Ground floor suitable. Large print guide.   Obligatory.

WOLFETON HOUSE

Tel: 01305 263500   **Fax:** 01305 265090

Nr Dorchester, Dorset DT2 9QN   e-mail:kthimbleby@wolfeton.freeserve.co.uk

Owner: Capt N T L L Thimbleby   **Contact:** The Steward
A fine mediaeval and Elizabethan manor house lying in the water-meadows near the confluence of the rivers Cerne and Frome. It was much embellished around 1580 and has splendid plaster ceilings, fireplaces and panelling of that date. To be seen are the Great Hall, Stairs and Chamber, Parlour, Dining Room, Chapel and Cyder House. The mediaeval Gatehouse has two unmatched and older towers. There are good pictures and furniture.

Location: OS Ref. SY678 921. 1$^1/_2$ m from Dorchester on the A37 towards Yeovil. Indicated by Historic House signs.

Opening Times: 15 Jul - 15 Sept: Mons, Weds & Thurs. 2 - 6pm. Groups by appointment throughout the year.

Admission: Adult £4, Child £2.

By arrangement.   Ground floor suitable.   By arrangement.
By arrangement.

Special Events Index ◄◄◄ **page 33**

South West England

BERKELEY CASTLE
Berkeley

Owner: Mr R J G Berkeley

CONTACT

The Custodian
Berkeley Castle
Gloucestershire
GL13 9BQ

Tel: 01453 810332

Not many can boast of having their private house celebrated by Shakespeare nor of having held it in the possession of their family for nearly 850 years, nor having a King of England murdered within its walls, nor of having welcomed at their table the local vicar and Castle Chaplain, John Trevisa (1342-1402), reputed as one of the earliest translators of the Bible, nor of having a breach battered by Oliver Cromwell, which to this day it is forbidden by law to repair even if it was wished to do so. But such is the story of Berkeley.

This beautiful and historic Castle, begun in 1117, still remains the home of the famous family who gave their name to numerous locations all over the world, notably Berkeley Square in London, Berkeley Hundred in Virginia and Berkeley University in California. Scene of the brutal murder of Edward II in 1327 (visitors can see his cell and nearby the dungeon) and besieged by Cromwell's troops in 1645, the Castle is steeped in history but twenty-four generations of Berkeleys have gradually transformed a Norman fortress into the lovely home it is today.

The State Apartments contain magnificent collections of furniture, rare paintings by primarily English and Dutch masters, and tapestries. Part of the world-famous Berkeley silver is on display in the Dining Room. Many other rooms are equally interesting including the Great Hall upon which site the Barons of the West Country met in 1215 before going to Runnymede to force King John to put his seal to the Magna Carta.

The Castle is surrounded by lovely terraced Elizabethan Gardens with a lily pond, Elizabeth I's bowling green, and sweeping lawns.

LOCATION

OS Ref. ST685 990

SE side of Berkeley village.
Midway between
Bristol & Gloucester,
2m W off the A38.

From motorway
M5/J14 (5m) or
J13 (9m).

Bus: No 308 from
Bristol & Gloucester.

 Fashion shows and filming. Butterfly farm. No photography inside the Castle.

Wedding receptions and corporate entertainment.

Visitors may alight in the Outer Bailey.

Licensed. Serving lunches and home-made teas.

Free. Max. 120 people. Tour time: One hour. Evening groups by arrangement. Group visits must be booked.

Cars 150 yds from Castle and up to 15 coaches 250 yds away.

Welcome. General and social history and architecture.

CONFERENCE/FUNCTION

ROOM	SIZE	MAX CAPACITY
Great Hall		200
Long Drawing Rm		100

OPENING TIMES

April & May
Tue - Sun, 2 - 5pm.

June & September
Tue - Sat, 11am - 5pm,
Suns, 2 - 5pm.

July & August
Mon - Sat, 11am - 5pm
Suns, 2 - 5pm

October
Suns only, 2 - 5pm

BH Mons, 11am - 5pm

NB. Groups must book.

ADMISSION

Castle and Garden
Adult £5.50
Child £3.00
OAP.........................£4.50
Family (2+2) £15.00

Groups (25+ pre-booked)
Adult £5.00
Child £2.70
OAP £4.20

Gardens only
Adult £2.00
Child £1.00

Butterfly Farm
Adult £2.00
Child/OAP £1.00
Family (2+2) £5.00
School Groups 80p

CHAVENAGE
Tetbury

Owner:
Mr David Lowsley-Williams

CONTACT

D Lowsley-Williams
Chavenage
Tetbury
Gloucestershire
GL8 8XP

Tel: 01666 502329

Fax: 01453 836778

e-mail: caroline@
chavenage.com

LOCATION

OS Ref. ST872 952

Less than 20m
from M4/J16/17 or 18.
1³/₄ m NW of Tetbury
between the B4104 &
A4135. Signed from
Tetbury. Less than 15m
from M5/J13 or 14.
Signed from A46
(Stroud -Bath road)

Rail: Kemble Station 7m.

Taxi: Pride Taxis:
01666 502555

Air: Bristol 35m.
Birmingham 70m.
Grass airstrip on farm.

CHAVENAGE is a wonderful Elizabethan house of mellow grey Cotswold stone and tiles which contains much of interest for the discerning visitor.

The approach aspect of Chavenage is virtually as it was left by Edward Stephens in 1576. Only two families have owned Chavenage; the present owners since 1891 and the Stephens family before them. A Colonel Nathaniel Stephens, MP for Gloucestershire during the Civil War was cursed for supporting Cromwell, giving rise to legends of weird happenings at Chavenage since that time.

Inside Chavenage there are many interesting rooms housing tapestries, fine furniture, pictures and many relics of the Cromwellian period. Of particular note are the Main Hall, where a contemporary screen forms a minstrels'

gallery and two tapestry rooms where it is said Cromwell was lodged.

Recently Chavenage has been used as a location for TV and film productions including a Hercule Poirot story *The Mysterious Affair at Styles*, many episodes of the sequel to *Are you Being Served* now called *Grace & Favour*, a *Gotcha* for *The Noel Edmonds' House Party*, episodes of *The House of Elliot* and *Casualty* and in 1997/98 *Berkeley Square* and *Cider with Rosie*.

Chavenage is especially suitable for those wishing an intimate, personal tour, usually conducted by the owner, or for groups wanting a change from large establishments. Meals for pre-arranged groups have proved hugely popular. It also provides a charming venue for small conferences and functions.

OPENING TIMES

SUMMER
May - September
Easter Sun, Mons
& BHs, 2 - 5pm.

Thurs & Suns
2 - 5pm.

NB. Will open at other times by prior arrangement for groups.

WINTER
October - March
By appointment only
for groups.

ADMISSION

Tours are inclusive
in the following prices.

SUMMER
Adult £4.00
Child (5 - 16 yrs).......£2.00

CONCESSIONS
By prior arrangement, concessions may be given to groups of 40+ and also to disabled and to exceptional cases.

WINTER
Groups only:
Rates by arrangement.

CONFERENCE/FUNCTION		
ROOM	SIZE	MAX CAPACITY
Ballroom	70' x 30'	120
Oak Room	25 'x 20'	30

i Clay pigeon shooting, archery, cross-bows, pistol shooting, ATV driving, small fashion shows, concerts, plays, seminars, filming, product launching, photography. No casual photography in house.

T Corporate entertaining. In-house catering for drinks parties, dinners, wedding receptions. Telephone for details.

♿ Partially suitable. WC.

☕ Lunches, teas, dinners and picnics by arrangement.

🚶 By owner. Large groups given a talk prior to viewing. Couriers and group leaders should arrange tour format prior to visit.

P Up to 100 cars and 2 - 3 coaches. Coaches only by appointment; stop at gates for parking instructions.

▪ Chairs can be arranged for lecturing. Tour of working farm, modern dairy and corn facilities can be arranged.

🐕 In grounds on leads. Guide dogs only in house. ❄

Derek Harris.

Owner: Lady Ashcombe

CONTACT

The Secretary
Sudeley Castle
Winchcombe
Nr Cheltenham
Gloucestershire
GL54 5JD

Tel: 01242 602308

Fax: 01242 602959

e-mail: marketing@
sudeley.org.uk

LOCATION

OS Ref. SP032 277

8m NE of Cheltenham,
at Winchcombe off B4632.

From Bristol or
Birmingham M5/J9.
Take A46 then B4077
towards Stow-on-the-Wold.

Bus: Castleways to
Winchcombe.

Rail: Cheltenham
Station 8m.

Air: Birmingham or
Bristol 45m.

CONFERENCE/FUNCTION		
ROOM	SIZE	MAX CAPACITY
Chandos Hall		80
North Hall		40
Library		80
Banquet Hall & Pavilion		150

SUDELEY CASTLE
Winchcombe

SUDELEY CASTLE, home of Lord and Lady Ashcombe, is one of England's great historic houses with royal connections stretching back 1000 years. Once the property of King Ethelred the Unready, Sudeley was later the magnificent palace of Queen Katherine Parr, Henry VIII's sixth wife, who is buried in St Mary's church, in the grounds. Henry VIII, Anne Boleyn, Lady Jane Grey and Elizabeth I all visited Sudeley. King Charles I stayed here and his nephew, Prince Rupert established it as his headquarters during the Civil War.

During the 19th century a programme of reconstruction, under the aegis of Sir Giles Gilbert Scott, restored Sudeley for its new owners, the Dent brothers. The interiors were largely furnished with pieces bought by the Dents at the famous Strawberry Hill sale, when the contents of Horace Walpole's house were sold.

Surrounding the Castle are the enchanting and award-winning gardens that have gained international recognition. Famous for its topiary and fine collection of old roses, the Queen's Garden is sited on the original Tudor parterre. The visitor must also see the Knot Garden, the Heritage Seed Library Garden and the recently replanted Secret Garden.

The Castle contains some interesting pieces of Civil War memorabilia, as well as pictures by Turner, Van Dyck and Rubens. The Emma Dent exhibition illustrates, at a personal level, the values and interests of the Victorian age. A licensed restaurant, gift shop and plant centre, specialising in old-fashioned roses, complete a perfect day.

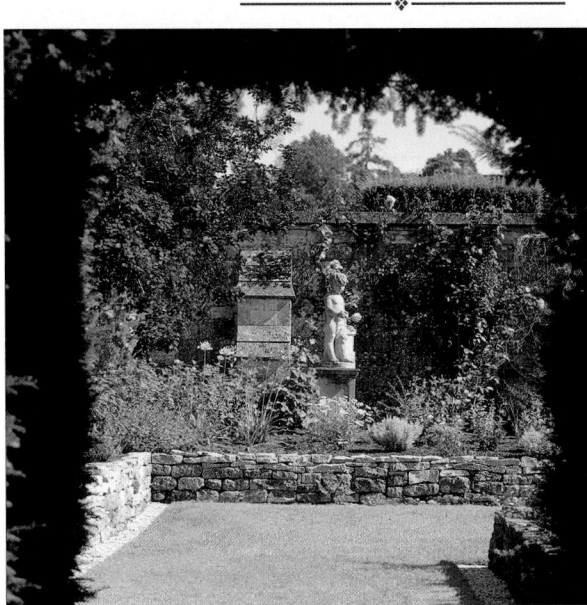

Photography and filming, concerts, corporate events and conferences. Product launches, garden parties, craft fairs and activity days. Sudeley reserves the right to close part or all of the castle, gardens and grounds and to amend information as necessary.

Private dining, banquets, and medieval dinners.

Not suitable.

 Licensed restaurant and tearooms. Groups should book.

Special interest tours can be arranged.

1,000 cars. Meal vouchers, free access for coach drivers.

 14 holiday cottages for 2 - 5 occupants.

OPENING TIMES

SUMMER
Gardens, Exhibition Centre, Shop & Plant Centre
3 March - 28 October
Daily: 10.30am - 5.30pm.

Castle Apartments & Church
31 March - 28 October
Daily: 11am - 5pm.

Restaurant
31 March - 28 October
Daily: 10.30am - 5pm.

WINTER
Groups (30+)
by appointment.

ADMISSION

Castle & Gardens
Adult £6.20
Child (5-15 yrs.)........£3.20
Conc........................£5.20
Family (2+2) £17.00

Groups (min. 20)
Adult £5.20
Child (5-15 yrs.)........£3.20
Conc........................£4.20

Gardens & Exhibitions
Adult £4.70
Child (5-15 yrs.)........£2.50
OAP.........................£3.70

Audio tour...............£2.00

Adventure Playground only (5-15 yrs.) £1.00

SPECIAL EVENTS

Please telephone for details.

ASHLEWORTH TITHE BARN

Tel: 01684 855300

Ashleworth, Gloucestershire

Owner: The National Trust   **Contact:** NT Regional Office

A c15th tithe barn with two projecting porch bays and fine roof timbers with queenposts.

Location: OS Ref. SO818 252. 6m NW of Gloucester, 1¼ m E of Hartpury A417.

Opening Times: 1 Apr - 31 Oct: daily, 9am - 6pm or sunset if earlier. Closed Good Fri (may be closed during part of 2001 for major repairs, please contact for details).

Admission: 60p.

BARNSLEY HOUSE GARDEN

Tel: 01285 740561 **Fax:** 01285 740628

Barnsley House, Cirencester GL7 5EE

Owner: Mr & Mrs Charles Verey   **Contact:** Charles Verey

Mature 4½ acre garden designed by Rosemary Verey. Bulbs, mixed borders, autumn colours, knot of herb garden, laburnum walk (late May, early June). Decorative vegetable garden, garden furniture by Charles Verey. Fountain and statues by Simon Verity. Two 18th century summer houses. Winner of the HHA/Christie's Garden of the Year award, 1988.

Location: OS Ref. SP076 049. In Barnsley village, 4m NE of Cirencester on B4425.

Opening Times: 1 Feb - mid Dec: Mons, Wed - Sat, 10am - 5.30pm.

Admission: Adult £3.75, Child under 16 Free, OAP £3. No charge for group tour leader.

📷 🚻 ♿ Partially suitable. 𝄇 By arrangement. 🅿 Ample for cars. Limited for coaches. 🐕 ❄ (wc)

BATSFORD ARBORETUM

Tel: 01386 701441 **Fax:** 01386 701829

Moreton-in-Marsh, Gloucestershire GL56 9QB

Owner: The Batsford Foundation   **Contact:** Admissions Centre

50 acres of arboretum.

Location: OS Ref. SP183 324. 1½ m NW of Moreton-in-Marsh, off A44 to Broadway.

Opening Times: Jan, Feb & Dec: weekends only. Mar - Nov: daily.

Admission: Adult £4, Child Free, OAP £3.

BERKELEY CASTLE

See page 218 for full page entry.

BLACKFRIARS

Tel: 0117 9750700

Ladybellegate Street, Gloucester

Owner: English Heritage   **Contact:** The South West Regional Office

A small Dominican priory church converted into a rich merchant's house at the Dissolution. Most of the original 13th century church remains, including a rare scissor-braced roof.

Location: OS Ref. SO830 186. In Ladybellegate St, Gloucester, off Southgate Street and Blackfriars Walk.

Opening Times: Please contact the South West Regional Office.

Admission: Free.

BOURTON HOUSE GARDEN

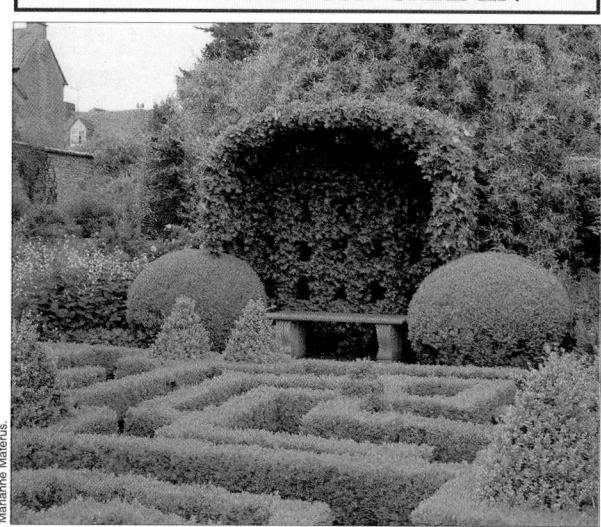

Marianne Majerus.

BOURTON-ON-THE-HILL GL56 9AE

Owner/Contact: Mr & Mrs Richard Paice

Tel: 01386 700121 **Fax:** 01386 701081

Exciting 3 acre garden surrounding a delightful 18th century Cotswold manor house and 16th century tithe barn. Featuring flamboyant borders, imaginative topiary, a unique shade house, a profusion of herbaceous and exotic plants and, not least, a myriad of magically planted pots. The mood is friendly and welcoming, the atmosphere tranquil yet inspiring. The garden... "positively fizzes with ideas".

Location: OS Ref. SP180 324. 1¾ m W of Moreton-in-Marsh on A44.

Opening Times: 24 May - 26 Oct: Thurs & Fris, 10am - 5pm. 27 - 28 May & 26 - 27 Aug: 10am - 5pm.

Admission: Adult £3.50, Child Free.

📷 🚻 ♿ Partially suitable. 🛍 𝄇 By arrangement. 🅿 Ample for cars. Limited for coaches. 🐕

CHAVENAGE

See page 219 for full page entry.

Sudeley Castle, Gloucestershire.

CHEDWORTH ROMAN VILLA

NT Photographic Library: Ian Shaw.

YANWORTH, CHELTENHAM, GLOS GL54 3LJ

Owner: The National Trust   *Contact:* The Property Manager

Tel: 01242 890256 **Fax:** 01242 890544 **e-mail:** chedworth@smtp.ntrust.org.uk

The remains of a Romano-British villa, excavated 1864. Set in beautiful wooded combe. Includes fine 4th century mosaics, two bath houses, spring with temple. A museum houses the smaller finds.

Location: OS163 Ref. SP053 135. 3m NW of Fossebridge on Cirencester - Northleach road A429. Coaches must avoid Withington.

Opening Times: 27 Feb - 30 Mar: 11am - 4pm. 31 Mar - 28 Oct: 10am - 5pm; 30 Oct - 18 Nov: 11am - 4pm; daily except Mons (open BH Mons)

Admission: Adult £3.70, Child £1.85, Family £9.30. (Increased charge on special event days, including NT members).

⬛ ⬛Grounds limited. WC. ⬛By arrangement. ⬛Limited. ⬛
⬛Tel. for details. · ⬛

DYRHAM PARK

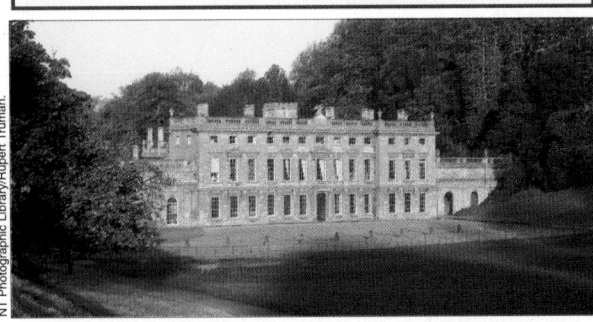

NT Photographic Library/Rupert Truman.

Nr CHIPPENHAM, WILTSHIRE SN14 8ER

Owner: The National Trust   *Contact:* The Property Manager

Tel/Fax: 0117 9372501

Crowned with a balustrade and with fine views over its ancient deer park, Dyrham was built between 1691 and 1702 for William Blathwayt, William III's Secretary at War and Secretary of State. The rooms have changed little since they were furnished by Blathwayt and their contents are recorded in his housekeeper's inventory. There are many fine textiles and paintings, as well as items of blue-and-white Delftware, reflecting the contemporary taste for Dutch fashions. Restored Victorian domestic rooms open (and for extended period, see below), including kitchen bells passage, bakehouse, larders, tenants' hall and Delft-tiled dairy. Car park has been relocated to the East Lodge and a free bus now takes visitors to and from the house, thereby restored to its original, car-free, setting. CD-ROM available for purchase.

Location: OS Ref. ST743 757. 8m N of Bath, 12m E of Bristol. Approached from Bath - Stroud road (A46), 2m S of Tormarton interchange with M4/J18.

Opening Times: House: 31 Mar - 4 Nov: Fri - Tue, 12 noon - 5.30pm, last admission 4.45pm. Garden: as house, 11am - 5.30pm or dusk if earlier. Park: daily (closed 25 Dec), 12 noon - 5.30pm or dusk if earlier (opens 11am if garden open). Winter opening for domestic rooms: 10 Nov - 16 Dec: Sats & Suns, 12 noon - 4pm. Note: property closed 6 - 9 Jul.

Admission: Adult £7.80, Child £3.90, Family £19. Grounds only: Adult £3, Child £1.50, Family £7. Park only (on days when house & garden closed): Adult £1.90, Child 90p. Winter: Park & Domestic Rooms: Adult £4, Child £2. Group rate weekdays only: contact the Property Manager.

⬛ ⬛Licensed. ⬛ ⬛ ⬛Tel. for details.

FRAMPTON COURT

Tel: 01452 740267 **Fax:** 01452 740698

Frampton-on-Severn, Gloucestershire GL2 7EU

Owner/Contact: Mrs Peter Clifford

Listed Grade I, by Vanburgh. 1732. Stately family home of the Cliffords who have lived at Frampton since granted land by William the Conqueror, 1066. Fine collection of original period furniture, tapestries, needlework and porcelain. Panelled throughout. The famous botanical paintings of *The Frampton Flora* are all on show. Fine views over parkland to extensive lake. A famous gothic orangery stands in the garden reflected in a Dutch ornamental canal.

Location: OS Ref. SO750 078. In Frampton, ¼ m SW of B4071, 3m NW of M5/J13.

Opening Times: By arrangement.

Admission: House & Garden: £4.50.

ⓘNo photography in house. ⬛Not suitable. ⬛ ⬛Obligatory.
⬛Limited for coaches. ⬛In grounds on leads. ⬛Ensuite. Tel for details. ⬛

FRAMPTON MANOR

Fax: 01452 740698

Frampton-on-Severn, Gloucestershire GL2 7EU

Owner: Mr & Mrs P R H Clifford   **Contact:** Mrs P R H Clifford

Medieval/Elizabethan timber-framed manor house with walled garden. Reputed 12th century birthplace of 'Fair Rosamund' Clifford, mistress of King Henry II. Wool barn c1500 and c1800 granary with dovecote.

Location: OS Ref. SO748 080. 3m M5/J13.

Opening Times: House & Garden: open throughout the year by written appointment. Garden: 1 May - 17 Jul: Mons, 2 - 5pm.

Admission: House & Garden: £3.50. Garden only: £2.

⬛

GLOUCESTER CATHEDRAL

Tel: 01452 528095 **Fax:** 01452 300469

Chapter Office, College Green, Gloucester GL1 2LR

Contact: Mrs L Henderson

Daily worship and rich musical tradition continue in this abbey church founded 1300 years ago. It has a Norman nave with massive cylindrical pillars, a magnificent east window with medieval glass and glorious fan-vaulted cloisters. You can also find the tombs of King Edward II and Robert of Normandy.

Location: OS Ref. SO832 188. Off Westgate Street in central Gloucester.

Opening Times: Daily, 8am until after Evensong. Groups must book via the Chapter Office.

Admission: £2.50 donation requested.

⬛ ⬛ ⬛Partially suitable. WC. ⬛Licensed. ⬛By arrangement. ⬛
⬛None. ⬛In grounds, on leads. ⬛

HAILES ABBEY

Tel: 01242 602398

Nr Winchcombe, Cheltenham, Gloucestershire GL54 5PB

Owner: English Heritage & The National Trust   **Contact:** The Custodian

Seventeen cloister arches and extensive excavated remains in lovely surroundings of an abbey founded by Richard, Earl of Cornwall, in 1246. There is a small museum and covered display area.

Location: OS150, Ref. SP050 300. 2m NE of Winchcombe off B4632. ½ m SE of B4632.

Opening Times: 1 Apr - 31 Oct: daily, 10am - 6pm (5pm in Oct). 1 Nov - 31 Mar: Sat - Sun, 10am - 4pm. Closed 24 - 26 Dec & 1 Jan.

Admission: Adult £2.60, Child £1.30, Conc. £2.

⬛ ⬛Partially suitable. WC. ⬛ ⬛In grounds, on leads. ⬛ ⬛Tel. for details.

HARDWICKE COURT

Tel: 01452 720212 **Fax:** 01452 724465

Gloucester GL2 4RS   **Owner/Contact:** C G M Lloyd Baker Esq

Early 19th century small country house designed by Robert Smirke.

Location: OS150, Ref. SO787 118. 6m S of Gloucester on A38.

Opening Times: Easter - end Sept: Mons, 2 - 4pm.

Admission: Please contact property for details.

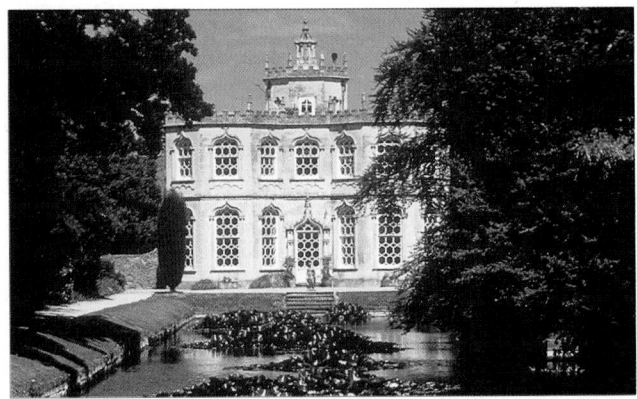

Frampton Court, Gloucestershire.

HIDCOTE MANOR GARDEN

NT Photographic Library: Nick Meers.

CHIPPING CAMPDEN, GLOUCESTERSHIRE GL55 6LR

Owner: The National Trust   *Contact:* The Property Manager

Tel: 01386 438333 **Fax:** 01386 438817 **e-mail:** hidcote_manor@smtp.ntrust.org.uk

One of the most delightful gardens in England, created this century by the great horticulturist Major Lawrence Johnston; a series of small gardens within the whole, separated by walls and hedges of different species; famous for rare shrubs, trees, herbaceous borders, 'old' roses and interesting plant species.

Location: OS151 Ref. SP176 429. 4m NE of Chipping Campden, 1m E of B4632 off B4081. At Mickleton 1/4m E of Kiftsgate Court.

Opening Times: 31 Mar - end May & Aug - 4 Nov: daily except Tues & Fris (open Good Fri). Jun & Jul: daily except Fris. Times: Apr - end Sept: 10.30am - 6.30pm; Oct: 10.30am - 5.30pm. Last admission 1 hour before closing or dusk if earlier.

Admission: Adult £5.70, Child £2.85, Family £14.

Grounds, but limited. WC. Licensed. Send SAE for details.

HOLST BIRTHPLACE MUSEUM

Woodley & Quick.

4 CLARENCE ROAD, PITTVILLE, CHELTENHAM GL52 2AY

Owner: Holst Birthplace Trust   *Contact:* Dr Joanna Archibald

Tel: 01242 524846 **e-mail:** holstmuseum@btconnect.com

Birthplace of Gustav Holst (1874 - 1934), composer of *The Planets*, containing his piano and personal memorabilia. (Holst's music is played.) The museum is also a fine period house showing the 'upstairs – downstairs' way of life in Regency and Victorian times, including a working kitchen, elegant drawing room and charming nursery.

Location: OS163 Ref. SO955 237. 5mins walk from town centre, opposite Pittville Gates.

Opening Times: All year: Tue - Sat, 10am - 4pm. Closed BHs. Guided tours for groups welcome by appointment.

Admission: Adult £2.50, Child/Conc. £1.25. Groups pay same prices unless having a guided tour (6-20): Adult £3.50, Conc. £2. Special rate for school groups: £75p.

Photography by prior permission only. Not suitable. By arrangement. No parking. Guide dogs only. Tel. for details.

HORTON COURT

Tel: 01249 730141

Horton, Nr Chipping Sodbury B17 6QR

Owner: The National Trust   **Contact:** Lacock Estate Office

A Cotswold manor house with 12th century Norman hall and early Renaissance features. Of particular interest is the late perpendicular ambulatory, detached from the house. Norman hall and ambulatory only shown.

Location: OS Ref. NT766 849. 3m NE of Chipping Sodbury, 3/4m N of Horton, 1m W of A46.

Opening Times: 4 Apr - 31 Oct: Weds & Sats, 2 - 6pm or dusk if earlier.

Admission: Adult £2, Child £1.

KELMSCOTT MANOR

Nigel Fisher.

KELMSCOTT, Nr LECHLADE, GLOUCESTERSHIRE GL7 3HJ

Owner: Society of Antiquaries   *Contact:* Helen Webb

Tel: 01367 252486 **Fax:** 01367 253754 **e-mail:** admin@kelmscottmanor.co.uk

The home of William Morris, poet, craftsman and socialist from 1871 until his death in 1896. The house contains a collection of the possessions and works of Morris and his associates including furniture, textiles, carpets and ceramics. An exhibition of 'William Morris at Kelmscott' is being held in one of the barns during normal opening times.

Location: OS Ref. SU252 988. At SE end of the village, 2m due E of Lechlade, off the Lechlade - Faringdon Road.

Opening Times: Apr - Sept: Weds, 11am - 5pm. 3rd Sat in Apr, May, Jun & Sept, also 1st & 3rd Sat in July & Aug, 2 - 5pm. Private visits for groups on Thurs & Fris. Please note house only closed on Weds, 1 - 2pm.

Admission: Adult £7, Child/Student £3.50.

Grounds suitable. WCs. Licensed. By arrangement. Limited for coaches.

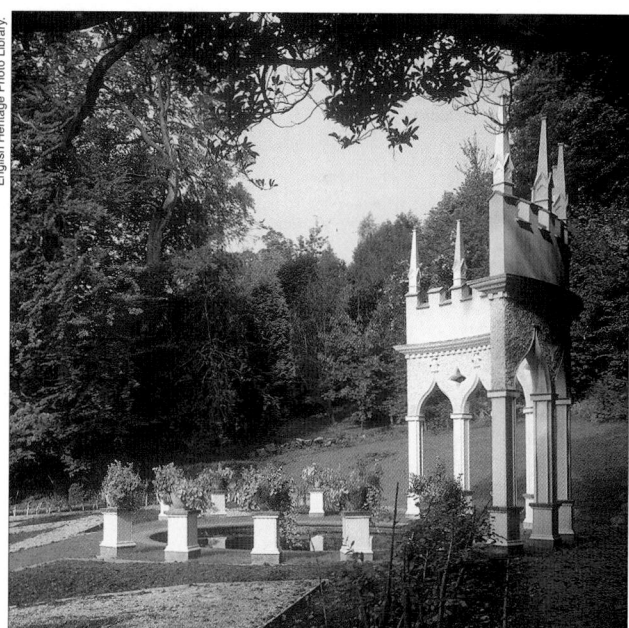

English Heritage Photo Library.

Painswick Rococo Garden, Gloucestershire.

KIFTSGATE COURT GARDENS

CHIPPING CAMPDEN, GLOUCESTERSHIRE GL55 6LW

Owner: Mr and Mrs J G Chambers   *Contact:* Mr J G Chambers

Tel/Fax: 01386 438777

Magnificently situated garden on the edge of the Cotswold escarpment with views towards the Malvern Hills. Many unusual shrubs and plants including tree peonies, abutilons, specie and old-fashioned roses.

Location: OS Ref. SP173 430. 4m NE of Chipping Campden. 1/4 m W of Hidcote Garden.

Opening Times: Apr, May, Aug, Sept: Weds, Thurs & Suns, 2 - 6pm. Jun & Jul: Weds, Thurs, Sats & Suns, 12 noon - 6pm. BH Mons, 2 - 6pm. Coaches by appointment.

Admission: Adult: £4, Child £1.

LODGE PARK

ALDSWORTH, Nr CHELTENHAM, GLOUCESTERSHIRE GL54 3PP

Owner: The National Trust   *Contact:* The Property Manager

Tel: 01451 844130   **Fax:** 01451 844794   **e-mail:** lodgepark@smtp.ntrust.org.uk

Situated on the picturesque Sherborne Estate in the Cotswolds, Lodge Park was created in 1634 by John 'Crump' Dutton. Inspired by his passion for gambling and banqueting, it is a unique survival of a Grandstand, Deer Course and Park.

Location: OS163 Ref. SP146 123. 3m E of Northleach, approach only from A40.

Opening Times: 1 Mar - 4 Nov: Fri - Mon, 11am - 4pm. Slide talks at regular intervals.

Admission: Adult £4, Child £2, Family £10.

LITTLEDEAN HALL   Tel: 01594 824 213

Littledean, Gloucestershire GL14 3NR

Owner/Contact: Mrs S Anthony

'*Reputedly England's oldest inhabited house*', Guinness Book of Records. Site of Roman temple.

Location: OS Ref. SO673 131. 2m E of Cinderford, 500 yds S of A4151.

Opening Times: 1 Apr - 31 Oct: daily, 11am - 5pm.

Admission: Adult £3.50, Child £1.50, OAP £2.50. Groups £2.25 (by appointment).

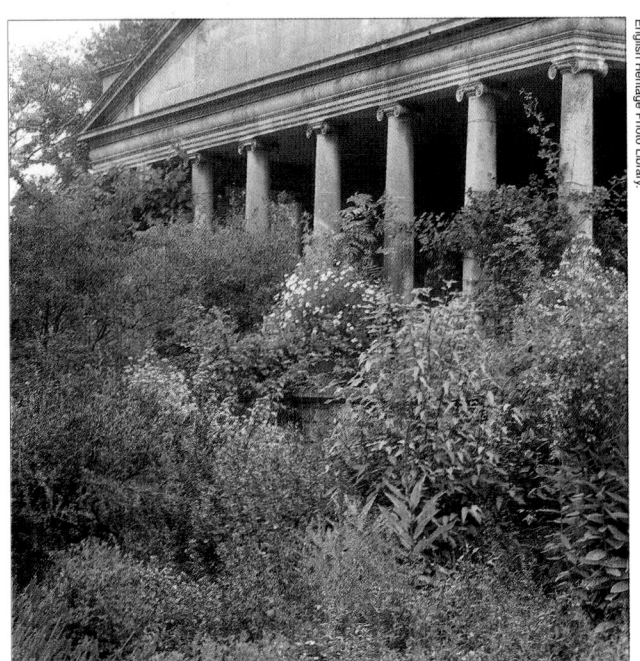

Kiftsgate Court Gardens, Gloucestershire.

LYDNEY PARK GARDENS & ROMAN TEMPLE SITE   Tel/Fax: 01594 842027

Lydney, Gloucestershire GL15 6BU

Owner: The Viscount Bledisloe   **Contact:** Mrs Sylvia Jones

Eight acres of extensive valley gardens with trees and lakes. Roman temple site and museum.

Location: OS Ref. SO620 022. On A48 between Lydney and Aylburton.

Opening Times: 26 Mar - 3 Jun: Suns, Weds & BH Mons. Easter week & 27 May - 1 Jun: daily.

Admission: Adult £3 (Wed £2), Child 50p. Groups of (25+) by arrangement.

MISARDEN PARK GARDENS   Tel: 01285 821303   Fax: 01285 821530

Stroud, Gloucestershire GL6 7JA

Owner/Contact: Major M T N H Wills

Noted in the spring for its bulbs and flowering trees and in mid-summer for the large double herbaceous borders. Fine topiary throughout and a new parterre of hebes, aliums and lavender within the rose garden. Outstanding position, standing high overlooking the 'Golden Valley'.

Location: OS Ref. SO940 089. 6m NW Cirencester. Follow signs westward from A417 from Gloucester or Cirencester or B4070 from Stroud.

Opening Times: 3 Apr - 27 Sept: Tue - Thur, 10am - 5pm.

Admission: Adult £3 (guided tours extra), Child Free. 10% reduction for pre-arranged groups (20+).

Nurseries: daily except Mons.   Grounds suitable.   Guide dogs only.

OWLPEN MANOR

Nr ULEY, GLOUCESTERSHIRE GL11 5BZ

Owner: Mr & Mrs Nicholas Mander   *Contact:* Julia Webb

Tel: 01453 860261   **Fax:** 01453 860819   **Restaurant:** 01453 860816
e-mail: sales@owlpen.com

Romantic Tudor manor house, 1450-1616, with Cotswold Arts & Crafts associations. Remote wooded valley setting, with 16th and 17th century formal terraced gardens and magnificent yews. Contains unique painted cloth wall hangings, family and Arts & Crafts collections. Mill (1726), Court House (1620); licensed restaurant in medieval Cyder House. Victorian church. *"Owlpen - ah, what a dream is there!"* - Vita Sackville-West.

Location: OS Ref. ST801 984. 3m E of Dursley, 1m E of Uley, off B4066, by Old Crown pub.

Opening Times: Apr - Sept: daily, Tue - Sun & BH Mons, 2 - 5pm. Restaurant 12 noon - 5pm.

Admission: Adult £4.75, Child (5-14yrs) £2, Family (2+4) £13. Gardens and Grounds: Adult £3.25, Child £1. Group rates available.

⊤   ♿Not suitable.   Licensed.   **P**   Holiday cottages, sleep 2 - 9.

PAINSWICK ROCOCO GARDENS

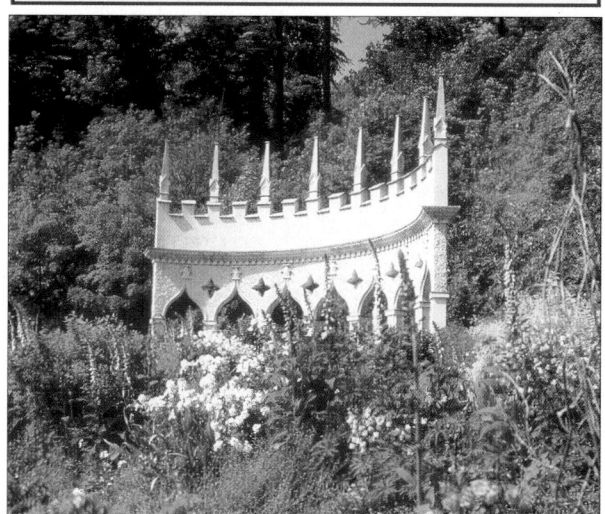

PAINSWICK, GLOUCESTERSHIRE GL6 6TH

Owner: Painswick Rococo Garden Trust   *Contact:* P R Moir

Tel: 01452 813204   **Fax:** 01452 814888   **e-mail:** paulmoir@rococogarden.co.uk

Unique 18th century garden restoration situated in a hidden 6 acre Cotswold combe. Charming contemporary buildings are juxtaposed with winding woodland walks and formal vistas. Famous for its early spring show of snowdrops. Newly planted maze.

Location: OS Ref. SO864 106. ¹/₂ m NW of village of Painswick on B4073.

Opening Times: Jan - Apr, Oct & Nov: Wed - Sun, 11am - 5pm. May - Sept: daily, 11am - 5pm.

Admission: Adult £3.30, Child £1.75, OAP £3. Family (2+2) £8.75. Free introductory talk.

❐   Partially suitable. WC.   Licensed.   🍽   **P**   In grounds, on leads.   Tel. for details.

THE PRIORY GARDENS   **Tel/Fax:** 01386 725258

The Priory, Kemerton, Nr Tewkesbury GL20 7JN
Owner/Contact: The Hon Mrs Healing

This 4 acre garden was replanned and planted by the present owner and her husband in 1965, though tree planting had been thoughtfully planned since they came to the garden in 1939, and some 70 new specimen trees were planted. On the south facing slopes of Bredon Hill, the garden has matured and features long herbaceous borders planted in colour groups, at their best from mid-July through September and includes a stream garden, sunken garden and sweeping lawns down to a part reserved for wild flowers. There is a well-stocked kitchen garden.

Location: OS Ref. SO950 378. In Kemerton. 5m NE of Tewkesbury via B4080 at Bredon.

Opening Times: Jul - Sept: Thurs & selected Suns, 2 - 6pm. Groups (25+): by appointment, Jun - Sept.

Admission: Adult: Jun: £2.50, Jul - Sept: £2. Groups (min 20): £2.50 on non-open days.

♿ Partially suitable. WC.   By arrangement.   **P** Limited for coaches. In grounds on leads.

RODMARTON MANOR

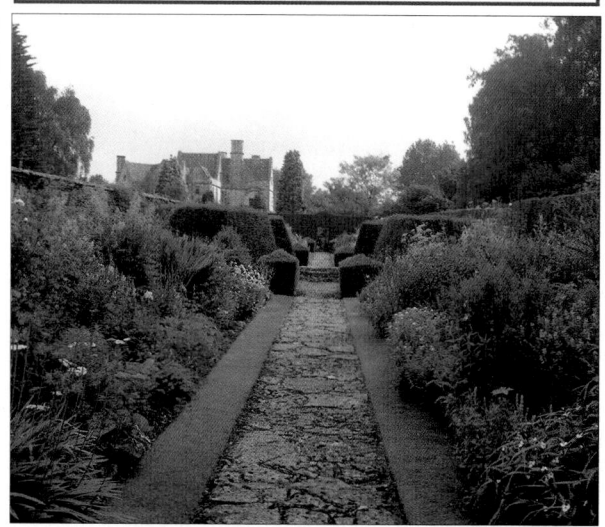

CIRENCESTER, GLOUCESTERSHIRE GL7 6PF

Owner: Mr & Mrs Simon Biddulph   *Contact:* Simon Biddulph

Tel: 01285 841253   **Fax:** 01285 841298

One of the last great country houses to be built in the traditional way and containing beautiful furniture, ironwork, china and needlework specially made for the house. The large garden complements the house and contains many areas of great beauty and character including the magnificent herbaceous borders, topiary, roses, rockery and kitchen garden.

Location: OS Ref. ST943 977. Off A433 between Cirencester & Tetbury.

Opening Times: House & Garden: 9 May - 29 Aug: Weds, Sats & BH Mons, 2 - 5pm. Groups please book. Guided house tours (20+) can be booked at other times by appointment. Guided tours of garden can also be booked.

Admission: House & Garden: £6, Child (under 14yrs) £3. Min. group charge £120. Garden only: £3, accompanied children Free.

By arrangement.

ST MARY'S CHURCH   **Tel:** 0117 9750700

Kempley, Gloucestershire
Owner: English Heritage   **Contact:** The South West Regional Office

A delightful Norman church with superb wall paintings from the 12th - 14th centuries which were only discovered beneath whitewash in 1871.

Location: OS149 SO670 313. On minor road. 1¹/₂ m SE of Much Marcle, A449.

Opening Times: 1 Apr - 30 Sept: 10am - 6pm, 1 Oct - 31 Mar: 10am - 4pm.

Admission: Free.

Accommodation Index ◀◀◀ page 27

South West England

SEZINCOTE

Moreton-in-Marsh, Gloucestershire GL56 9AW

Owner: Mr and Mrs D Peake   **Contact:** Mrs D Peake

Exotic oriental water garden by Repton and Daniell. Large semi-circular orangery. House by S P Cockerell in Indian style was the inspiration for Brighton Pavilion.

Location: OS Ref. SP183 324. 2¹/₂ m SW of Moreton-in-Marsh. Turn W along A44 to Broadway and left into gateway just before Bourton-on-the-Hill (opposite the gate to Batsford Park), then 1m drive.

Opening Times: Garden: Thurs, Fris & BH Mons, 2 - 6pm (dusk if earlier) throughout the year except Dec. House: May, Jun, Jul & Sept, Thurs & Fris, 2.30 - 6pm. Groups by written appointment.

Admission: House & Garden £5 (no children in house). Garden: Adult £3.50, Child £1 (under 5yrs Free).

♿ Not suitable. 🐕 Guide dogs only. ❄

STANWAY WATER GARDEN

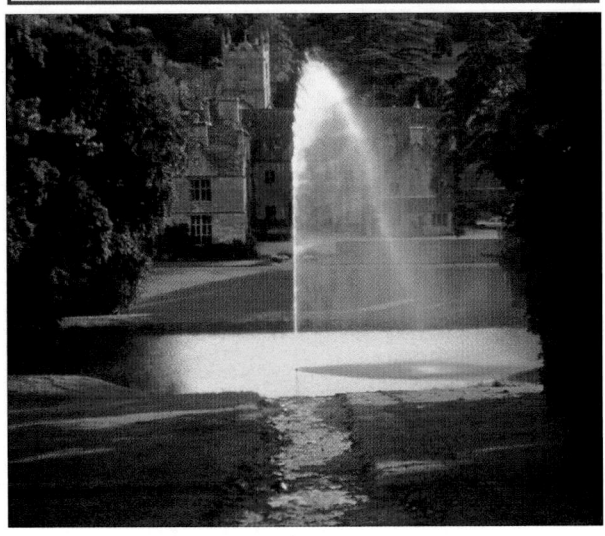

STANWAY, CHELTENHAM, GLOS GL54 5PQ

Owner: *Lord Neidpath*   **Contact:** *Lorna Poulton*

Tel: 01386 584469 **Fax:** 01386 584688

"*As perfect and pretty a Cotswold manor house as anyone is likely to see*" (Fodor's '*Great Britain '98* guidebook), Stanway's peaceful Jacobethan architecture and the beauty of its surrounding villages and parkland are now complemented by its magnificent, newly restored baroque water garden, with pyramid, cascade, upper pond, waterfall, grand canal and 70 ft high fountain.

Location: OS Ref. SP061 323. N of Winchcombe, just off B4077.

Opening Times: Gardens: Aug & Sept: Tues & Thurs, 2 - 5pm. Private tours by arrangement at other times.

Admission: Adult £3, Child £1, OAP £2.50.

ℹ Film & photographic location. 🎦 By arrangement. 🅿
🐕 In grounds on leads. ❄

SNOWSHILL MANOR

NT Photographic Library/Nick Meers.

SNOWSHILL, Nr BROADWAY WR12 7JU

Owner: *The National Trust*   **Contact:** *The Property Manager*

Tel/Fax: 01386 852410 **e-mail:** snowshill@smtp.ntrust.org.uk

A Tudor house with a c1700 façade, 21 rooms containing Charles Paget Wade's collection of craftsmanship, including musical instruments, clocks, toys, bicycles, weavers' and spinners' tools, Japanese armour, small formal garden and Charles Wade's cottage. The Manor is a 10 minute walk (500 yds) along an undulating countryside path.

Location: OS150 Ref. SP096 339. 3m SW of Broadway, turning off the A44, by Broadway Green.

Opening Times: 31 Mar - 4 Nov: daily except Mons & Tues, 12 noon - 5pm (open BH Mons) & Mons in Jul & Aug. Last entry to Manor 4.30pm, last entry to the property 5pm. Timed tickets issued for Manor. Grounds: as house, 11am - 5.30pm.

Admission: Adult £6, Child £3, Family £15. Grounds, shop & restaurant £3.

📷 🍽 🐕 ♿

SUDELEY CASTLE   **See page 220 for full page entry.**

NT Photographic Library/Andreas von Einsiedel.

Dyrham Park, Gloucestershire.

❄ **Open All Year Index** ◀◀◀ **page 49**

WESTBURY COURT GARDEN

NT Photographic Library: Stephen Robson

WESTBURY-ON-SEVERN, GLOUCESTERSHIRE GL14 1PD

Owner: *The National Trust*   **Contact:** *The Head Gardener*

Tel: 01452 760461 **e-mail:** westbury@smtp.ntrust.org.uk

A formal water garden with canals and yew hedges, laid out between 1696 and 1705; the earliest of its kind remaining in England. Restored in 1971 and planted with species dating from pre-1700 including apple, pear and plum trees.

Location: OS162 SO718 138. 9m SW of Gloucester on A48.

Opening Times: 1 Mar - 30 Jun: Wed - Sun, Good Fri & BH Mons, 10am - 6pm. 1 Jul - 31 Aug: daily, 10am - 6pm. 1 Sept - 28 Oct: Wed - Sun, 10am - 6pm.

Admission: Adult £2.90, Child £1.45.

Access to most parts of the garden. WC. Guide dogs only.

WESTONBIRT ARBORETUM
Tel: 01666 880220 **Fax:** 01666 880559

Tetbury, Gloucestershire GL8 8QS
Owner: The Forestry Commission   **Contact:** Mr A Russell
600 acres arboretum begun in 1829, now with 18,000 catalogued trees.
Location: OS Ref. ST856 896. 3m S of Tetbury on the A433.
Opening Times: 365 days a year, 10am - 8pm (or dusk if earlier).
Admission: Adult £4.50, Child £1, OAP £3.50.

WHITTINGTON COURT
Tel: 01242 820556 **Fax:** 01242 820218

Whittington, Cheltenham, Gloucestershire GL54 4HF
Owner: Mr & Mrs Jack Stringer   •   **Contact:** Mrs J Stringer
Elizabethan manor house. Family possessions.
Location: OS Ref. SP014 206. 4m E of Cheltenham on N side of A40.
Opening Times: 14 - 29 Apr & 11 - 27 Aug inclusive: 2 - 5pm.
Admission: Adult £3, Child £1, OAP £2.50.

WOODCHESTER PARK MANSION
Tel: 01453 750455 **Fax:** 01453 750457

Stroud, Gloucestershire GL5 1AP
Owner: Woodchester Mansion Trust   **Contact:** Matthew Haynes
Hidden in a wooded valley near Stroud is one of the most intriguing houses in the country. Woodchester Mansion was started in 1856 but abandoned incomplete in 1870. It offers a unique insight into traditional building techniques. The Trust's repair programme includes courses in stone masonry and building conservation.
Location: OS Ref. SO795 015 (gateway on B4066). 5m S of Stroud on B4066. NW of the village of Nympsfield, then 1m path E from gate.
Opening Times: Weekends throughout the summer. Please telephone for details.
Admission: Adult £4, Child (under 12yrs) £2, Student £2. Groups (min 10 people or £50): Adult £5.

[icons] Not suitable.   [icons]   Guide dogs only in Mansion.

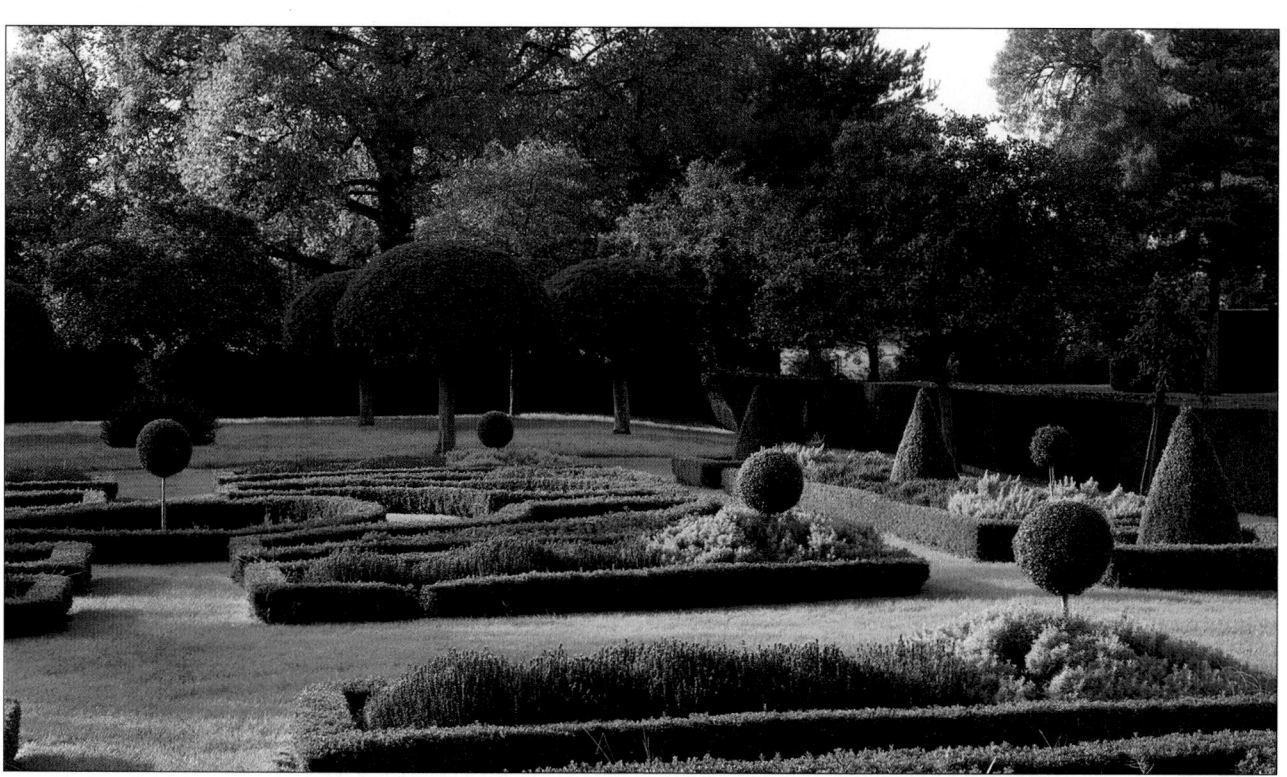

Westbury Court Garden, Gloucestershire.

South West England

NO. 1 ROYAL CRESCENT
Bath

NUMBER 1 was the first house to be built in the Royal Crescent, John Wood the Younger's fine example of Palladian architecture. The Crescent was begun in 1767 and completed by 1774.

The House was given to the Bath Preservation Trust in 1968 and both the exterior and interior have been accurately restored. Visitors can see a grand town-house of the late 18th century with authentic furniture, paintings and carpets.

On the ground floor are the Study and Dining Room and on the first floor a Lady's Bedroom and Drawing Room. A series of maps of Bath are on the second floor landing. In the Basement is a Kitchen and a Museum Shop.

Owner:
Bath Preservation Trust

CONTACT

Mrs Ann Hollas
Administrator
1 Royal Crescent
Bath
BA1 2LR

Tel: 01225 428126

Fax: 01225 481850

LOCATION

OS Ref. ST746 653

M4/J18,
then the A46 to Bath
2½ hrs from London
¼ m NW of city centre.

Rail: Bath Spa
Railway Station
(1hr, 20 mins
from London).

Taxi: Streamline.

OPENING TIMES

SUMMER

Mid February - End October
Daily except Mons
10.30am - 5pm
Closed Good Fri.
Open BHs and
Bath Festival Mon.

WINTER

November
Daily except Mons
10.30am - 4pm.

Last admission 30 mins before closing.

Special tours outside normal opening hours by arrangement with the administrator.

ADMISSION

ALL YEAR

Adult	£4.00
Child*	£3.50
Student	£3.50
OAP	£3.50
Family	£10.00

Groups
Adult	£2.50
School*	£2.50
Student	£2.50

* Aged 5 - 16yrs.

Not suitable. No restaurant or tearoom, but many facilities in Bath.

Guides in every room. Tours in French and Italian on request. Tour time 45 mins. Guide sheets available in French, German, Spanish, Italian, Japanese, Chinese, Danish, Dutch, Russian and Portuguese translations on request.

Be aware of restrictions in The Royal Crescent and parking regulations in the centre of Bath.

The cost per child is £2.50. School group rates on request. Guides can be provided.

National Trust Photographic Library. Andreas von Einsiedel.

Owner: The National Trust

CONTACT

For Room Hire:
Mr Tom Deller
Room Hire Manager
Stall Street
Bath
BA1 1LZ

Tel: 01225 477734

Fax: 01225 477476

e-mail: tom_deller@
bathnes.gov.uk

Museum Enquiries:
Tel: 01225 477785
Fax: 01225 477743

LOCATION

OS Ref. ST750 648

Near centre of Bath,
10m from M4/J18.

Rail: Great Western from
London Paddington
(regular service) 1 hour
17mins duration.

Air: Bristol airport 40 mins.

CONFERENCE/FUNCTION		
ROOM	SIZE	MAX CAPACITY
Ballroom	103' x 40'	450
Octagon	47' x 47'	200
Tea Room	58' x 40'	250
Card Room	59' x 18'	70

MUSEUM OF COSTUME & ASSEMBLY ROOMS
Bath

THE ASSEMBLY ROOMS in Bath are open to the public daily (free of charge) and are also popular for dinners, dances, concerts, conferences and civil weddings.

Originally known as the Upper Rooms, they were designed by John Wood the Younger and opened in 1771. The magnificent interior consists of a splendid Ball Room, Tea Room and Card Room, connected by two fine octagonal rooms. This plan was perfect for 'assemblies', evening entertainments popular in the 18th century, which included dancing, music, card-playing and tea drinking. They are now owned by The National Trust and managed by Bath & North East Somerset Council, which runs a full conference service.

The building also houses one of the largest and most comprehensive collections of fashionable dress in the country, the Museum of Costume. Its extensive displays cover the history of fashion from the late 16th century to the present day. Hand-held audioguides allow visitors to learn about the fashions on display while the lighting is kept to levels suitable for fragile garments. The 'Dress of the Year' collection traces significant moments in modern fashion history from 1963. 'Fashion in the Fifties', the special exhibition until 4 November 2001, traces the flowering of fashion talent in the glamorous decade following the war. For the serious student of fashion, the reference library and study facilities of the nearby Fashion Research Centre are available by appointment.

The museum shop sells publications and gifts associated with the history of costume and is open daily to all visitors.

Museum of Costume.

Museum of Costume.

OPENING TIMES

ALL YEAR
10am - 5pm

Closed 25 & 26 December

Last admission 30 mins before closing.

ADMISSION

Assembly Rooms:.....Free
Museum of Costume:
  Adult £4.00
  Child* £2.90
  OAP.........................£3.60
Groups (20+)
  Adult £3.80
  Child* (summer) £2.30
  Child* (winter)........£1.90
Combined ticket with
Roman Baths
  Adult £8.90
  Child* £5.30
  OAP.........................£8.00
  Family (2+4) £23.50
Groups (20+)
  Adult £6.80
  Child* (summer) £4.00
  Child* (winter)........£3.20

* Age 6 - 18yrs.
  Child under 6yrs Free

(2000 prices)

ℹ Conference facilities.

🛍 Extensive book & gift shop.

☂ Corporate hospitality.
Function facilities.

♿ Suitable. WC.

🚶 Hourly. Individual guided tours by arrangement.

🎧 English, French, German, Italian, Japanese, Spanish.

🅿 Nearby car park.

👥 Teachers' pack.

🐕 Guide dogs only.

🔔 Civil Weddings/Receptions.

❄

B & NES Council: Simon Mc Bride.

THE ROMAN BATHS & PUMP ROOM
Bath

The first stop for any visitor to Bath is the Roman Baths surrounding the hot springs where the city began and which are still its heart. Here you'll see one of the country's finest ancient monuments – the great Roman temple and bathing complex built almost 2000 years ago. Discover the everyday life of the Roman spa and see ancient treasures from the Temple of Sulis Minerva. A host of new interpretive methods bring these spectacular buildings vividly to life and help visitors to understand the extensive remains.

The Grand Pump Room, overlooking the Spring, is the social heart of Bath. The elegant interior of 1795 is something every visitor to Bath should see. You can enjoy a glass of spa water drawn from the fountain, perhaps as an appetiser to a traditional Pump Room tea, morning coffee or lunch. The Pump Room Trio and resident pianists provide live music daily. The Roman Baths shop sells publications and gifts related to the site.

In the evening, the Pump Room is available for banquets, dances and concerts. Nothing could be more magical than a meal on the terrace which overlooks the Great Bath, or a pre-dinner drinks reception by torchlight around the Great Bath itself.

◆

Owner:
Bath & North East
Somerset Council

CONTACT

For Room Hire:
Mr Tom Deller
Room Hire Manager
Stall Street
Bath BA1 1LZ
Tel: 01225 477734
Fax: 01225 477476
e-mail:
tom_deller@bathnes.gov.uk

For visits to Roman Baths:
Tel: 01225 477785
Fax: 01225 477743

LOCATION

OS Ref. ST750 648

Centre of Bath,
10m from M4/J18

Rail: Great Western from
London Paddington,
half hourly service,
1 hr 17 mins duration.
Good connection
to other UK cities.

CONFERENCE/FUNCTION		
ROOM	SIZE	MAX CAPACITY
Great Roman Bath		400 summer 200 winter
Pump Rm.	57' x 41'	180
Terrace overlooking Great Bath	83' x 11'	70
Concert Rm	56' x 44'	100
Smoking Rm & Drawing Rm	28' x 16'	40

B & NES Council: Simon Mc Bride.

🎁 Extensive gift shop. ℹ️ Award-winning guide book in English, French and German. The Historic Buildings of Bath include the Assembly Rooms, Guildhall, and Victoria Art Gallery.

🍽️ Comprehensive service for private and corporate entertainment. The Assembly Rooms, Guildhall, Victoria Art Gallery and Pump Room are all available for private hire, contact the Pump Room.

♿ Free access to terrace. Restricted access to the Museum, special visits for disabled groups by appointment. People with special needs welcome, teaching sessions available.

☕ Pump Room coffees, lunches and teas, no reservation needed. Music by Pump Room Trio or pianist.

🕐 Hourly. Private tours by appointment.

🗣️ English, French, German, Italian, Japanese, Spanish.

📖 Teaching sessions available. Pre-booking necessary.

🔔 Civil Weddings in two private rooms with photographs around the Great Bath.

NO. 1 ROYAL CRESCENT   See page 228 for full page entry.

BARRINGTON COURT

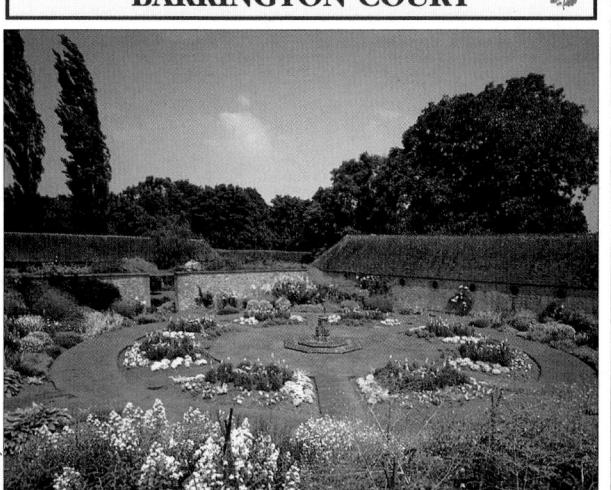

Rick Godley

BARRINGTON, ILMINSTER, SOMERSET TA19 0NQ

Owner: The National Trust   *Contact:* Visitor Reception Manager

Tel: 01460 241938

A beautiful garden influenced by Gertrude Jekyll and laid out in a series of walled rooms, including the white garden, the rose and iris garden and the lily garden. The working kitchen garden has apple, pear and plum trees trained along high stone walls. The Tudor Manor house was restored in the 1920s by the Lyle family. It is let to Stuart Interiors as showrooms with antique furniture for sale and is also open to NT visitors.

Location: OS Ref. ST395 181. In Barrington village, 5m NE of Ilminster, on B3168.

Opening Times: Mar & Oct - 4 Nov Thur - Sun: 11am - 4.30pm. 1 Apr - 30 Jun & Sept: daily except Fri, 11am - 5.30pm. Jul & Aug: daily (Fri: garden only), 11am - 5.30pm. Coach parties by appointment only.

Admission: Adult £5, Child £2.50, Family £12.50. Groups: Adult £4.50, Child £2.25.

▢ &Grounds suitable. WC. ▣Licensed.

BECKFORD'S TOWER   **Tel:** 01225 422212 **Fax:** 01225 481850

Lansdown Road, Bath BA1 9BH

Owner: Bath Preservation Trust   **Contact:** The Administrator

Built in 1827 for eccentric William Beckford. The tower is a striking feature of the Bath skyline.

Location: OS Ref. ST735 676. Lansdown Road, 2m NNW of city centre.

Opening Times: Easter weekend - end of October: Sats, Suns & BH Mons, 10.30am - 5pm.

Admission: Adult £2.50, Child/OAP £2, Family £6. BPT & NACF members: Free. Groups by arrangement – Tel: 01225 460705.

THE BISHOP'S PALACE 🏛   **Tel/Fax:** 01749 678691

Wells, Somerset BA5 2PD

Owner: Church Commissioners   **Contact:** Mrs K J Scarisbrick

Fortified and moated medieval palace which is today the private residence of the Bishop of Bath and Wells. Extensive grounds and arboretum. Available for functions.

Location: OS Ref. ST552 457. 20m S of Bristol and Bath on A39.

Opening Times: 1 Apr - 31 Oct: Tue - Fri & BHs & daily in Aug, 10.30am - 6pm. Suns: 2 - 6pm.

Admission: Adult £3, Child (12 - 18) £1, OAP £2, Conc. £1.50. Groups (10+) £2. Guided tour £30 plus £2 per person.

T Corporate hospitality. Wedding receptions.   &Partially suitable. ▣ ⓘⓘ

♿By arrangement.   🐕In grounds on leads.

THE BUILDING OF BATH MUSEUM   **Tel:** 01225 333895 **Tel:** 01225 445473

The Countess of Huntingdon's Chapel, The Vineyards, The Paragon, Bath BA1 5NA

Owner: Bath Preservation Trust   **Contact:** The Administrator

Discover the essence of life in Georgian Bath.

Location: OS Ref. ST751 655. 5 mins walk from city centre. Bath M4/J18.

Opening Times: 15 Feb - 30 Nov: Tue - Sun and BH Mons, 10.30am - 5pm.

Admission: Adult £3.50, Child £1.50, Conc. £2.50. Groups: Adult £2.50. Child £1.50.

CLAVERTON MANOR

THE AMERICAN MUSEUM, BATH, SOMERSET BA2 7BD

Owner: The Trustees of the American Museum in Britain   *Contact:* Miss S Carter

Tel: 01225 460503 **Fax:** 01225 480726 **e-mail:** amibbath@aol.com

The American Museum is housed in a Georgian mansion set in extensive grounds which include a replica of George Washington's garden and arboretum of North American trees and shrubs. The museum shows, in a series of period rooms, life from early New England Colonies to New Orleans on the eve of the Civil War. 2001 Exhibition: The Textile Tradition Then and Now.

Location: OS Ref. ST784 640. 2m SE of Bath. Well-signed from city centre.

Opening Times: 24 Mar - 4 Nov: Tue - Sun. Grounds: 1 - 6pm. Museum: 2 - 5pm (closed Mons). Christmas openings: 24 Nov - 16 Dec, 1 - 4pm.

Admission: Adult £5.50, Child £3, Conc. £5. Group concessions available.

▢ T &Ground floor suitable. WC. ▣ 🍴
🐕In grounds, on leads. ❄ 🛡 Tel for details. Ⓦ

CLEEVE ABBEY ⌗   **Tel:** 01984 640377

Washford, Nr Watchet, Somerset TA23 0PS

Owner: English Heritage   **Contact:** The Custodian

There are few monastic sites where you will see such a complete set of cloister buildings, including the refectory with its magnificent timber roof. Built in the 13th century, this Cistercian abbey was saved from destruction at the Dissolution by being turned into a house and then a farm.

Location: OS181 Ref. ST047 407. In Washford, 1/4 m S of A39.

Opening Times: 1 Apr - 31 Oct: daily 10am - 6pm (5pm in Oct). 1 Nov - 31 Mar: daily 10am - 4pm (closed lunch 1 - 2pm). Closed 24 - 26 Dec & 1 Jan.

Admission: Adult £2.60, Child £1.30, Conc. £2. 15% discount for groups (11+).

▢ &Partially suitable. ▣ P 🐕In grounds, on leads. ❄ 🛡 Tel. for details.

CLEVEDON COURT 🌿   **Tel:** 01275 872257

Tickenham Road, Clevedon, North Somerset BS21 6QU

Owner: The National Trust   **Contact:** The Administrator

Home of the Elton family since 1709, this 14th century manor house, once partly fortified, has a 12th century tower and 13th century hall. Collection of Nailsea glass and Eltonware. Beautiful terraced garden.

Location: OS Ref. ST423 716. 1 1/2 m E of Clevedon, on B3130, signposted from M5/J20.

Opening Times: 1 Apr - 30 Sept: Weds, Thurs, Suns & BH Mons, 2 - 5pm.

Admission: Adult £4.50, Child £2. Groups & coaches by arrangement.

&Ground floor suitable. ▣ PLimited. 🐕

COLERIDGE COTTAGE 🌿   **Tel:** 01278 732662

35 Lime Street, Nether Stowey, Bridgwater, Somerset TA5 1NQ

Owner: The National Trust   **Contact:** The Custodian

The home of Samuel Taylor Coleridge for three years from 1797, with mementoes of the poet on display. It was here that he wrote *The Rime of the Ancient Mariner*, part of *Christabel* and *Frost at Midnight*.

Location: OS Ref. ST191 399. At W end of Nether Stowey, on S side of A39, 8m W of Bridgwater.

Opening Times: 1 Apr - 30 Sept: Tue - Thur & Suns, 2 - 5pm.

Admission: Adult £3, Child £1.50, no reduction for groups, which must book.

🐕 ❄

COMBE SYDENHAM COUNTRY PARK

Tel: 01984 656284

Monksilver, Taunton, Somerset TA4 4JG
Owner: Theed Estates   **Contact:** Mr A Hudson
Built in 1580 on the site of a monastic settlement. Deer Park and woodland walks.
Location: OS Ref. ST075 366. Monksilver
Opening Times: Guided tours Mons, Weds, Thurs. Please telephone for details.
Admission: £3 per vehicle. Adult £5, Child £2.50 for guided tours. (2000 prices.)

COTHAY MANOR

Andrew Lawson.

GREENHAM, WELLINGTON, SOMERSET TA21 0JR

Owner/Contact: Mr & Mrs Alastair Robb

Tel: 01823 672283   **Fax:** 01823 672345

It has been said that Cothay Manor is the finest example of a small classic, medieval manor house in England. The manor has remained virtually untouched since it was built in 1480. The gardens, laid out in the 1920s have been completely re-designed and replanted within the original framework of yew hedges. A white garden, scarlet and purple garden, herbaceous borders and bog garden are but a few of the delights to be found in this magical place.

Location: OS Ref. ST721 214. From M5 W J/27, take A38 dir Wellington. 3$^{1}/_{2}$m left to Greenham. From N take A38 dir. Exeter. 3$^{1}/_{2}$m right to Greenham (1$^{1}/_{2}$m). On LH corner at bottom of hill turn right. Cothay 1$^{1}/_{2}$m left, always keeping left.
Opening Times: May - Sept: Weds, Thurs, Suns & BHs, 2 - 6pm.
Admission: Garden: Adult £3.50, Child (under 12yrs) Free. House: Groups (20+): by arrangement throughout the year, £4.50.

ℹ No photography in house. 🚻 ♿ 🛍 ⏰ By arrangement. 🅿 ✂ ❄

CROWE HALL

Tel: 01225 310322

Widcombe Hill, Bath, Somerset BA2 6AR
Owner/Contact: John Barratt Esq
Ten acres of romantic hillside gardens. Victorian grotto, classical Bath villa with good 18th century furniture and paintings.
Location: OS Ref. ST760 640. In Bath, 1m SE of city centre.
Opening Times: Gardens only open 18 Mar, 22 Apr, 13 May, 10 Jun, 15 Jul: 2 - 6pm. House and Gardens by appointment.
Admission: House & Gardens: Adult £4. Gardens only: Adult £2, Child £1.

DUNSTER CASTLE 🌿

Tel: 01643 821314   **Fax:** 01643 823000

Dunster, Nr Minehead, Somerset TA24 6SL
Owner: The National Trust   **Contact:** The Property Manager
From Norman motte-and-bailey to Jacobean mansion and Victorian eccentricity there is something for everyone. 600 years of Luttrell family residence has groomed and moulded the property from coastal fortress to a secluded country seat. The house and medieval ruins are magically framed with sub-tropical plants including the famous Dunster Lemon.
Location: OS Ref. SS992 436. In Dunster, 3m SE of Minehead.
Opening Times: Contact property for details.
Admission: Contact property for details.

📷 ♿ 🏪 🐕Guide dogs only.

DUNSTER WORKING WATERMILL 🌿

Tel: 01643 821759

Mill Lane, Dunster, Minehead, Somerset TA24 6SW
Owner: The National Trust   **Contact:** The Tenant
Built on the site of a mill mentioned in the Domesday Survey of 1086, the present mill dates from the 18th century and was restored to working order in 1979. Note: the mill is a private business and all visitors, including NT members are asked to pay the admission charge.
Location: OS Ref. SS991 434. On River Avill, beneath Castle Tor, approach via Mill Lane or Castle gardens on foot.
Opening Times: 1 Apr - 31 Oct: daily, 10.30am - 5pm.
Admission: £2.20. Family tickets available. Group rates by prior arrangement.

📷 ♿Ground floor suitable. 🛍 🅿

EAST LAMBROOK MANOR GARDENS

Tel: 01460 240328   **Fax:** 01460 242344

South Petherton, Somerset TA13 5HL   **e-mail:** ELambrook@aol.com
Owner: Mr & Mrs Robert Williams   **Contact:** Mark Stainer - Head Gardener
Grade I listed cottage-style garden, developed by the famous Margery Fish, containing many rare and unusual plants saved from extinction.
Location: OS177 Ref. ST431 189. 2m N of S Petherton off A303 (signed).
Opening Times: Gardens only: All year: daily, 10am - 5pm. For winter opening hours please telephone first.
Admission: Groups by prior arrangement.

ℹ Art gallery. NCCPG National Geranium collection. 📷 🏪 ♿ Not suitable.
🛍 ⏰By arrangement. 🅿Limited for coaches. 🏪 ✂ ❄ 🌳

ENGLISHCOMBE TITHE BARN

Tel: 01225 425073

Rectory Farmhouse, Englishcombe, Bath BA2 9DU   **e-mail:** tithebarn@ntlworld.com
Owner/Contact: Mrs Jennie Walker
An early 14th century cruck-framed Tithe Barn built by Bath Abbey.
Location: OS172 Ref. ST716 628. Adjacent to Englishcombe Village Church. 1m SW of Bath.
Opening Times: 15 - 20 Apr, 6 - 11 May, 27 May - 1 June, 25 - 29 June & 26 - 30 August, 3 - 6pm.
Admission: Free.

FARLEIGH HUNGERFORD CASTLE 🏰

Tel: 01225 754026

Farleigh Hungerford, Bath, Somerset BA3 6RS
Owner: English Heritage   **Contact:** The Custodian
Extensive ruins of 14th century castle with a splendid chapel containing wall paintings, stained glass and the fine tomb of Sir Thomas Hungerford, builder of the castle.
Location: OS173 Ref. ST801 577. In Farleigh Hungerford 3$^{1}/_{2}$m W of Trowbridge on A366.
Opening Times: Apr - Oct: daily 10am - 6pm (5pm in Oct). Nov - Mar: Wed - Sun, 10am - 4pm (closed for lunch 1 - 2 pm). Closed 24 - 26 Dec & 1 Jan.
Admission: Adult £2.30, Child £1.20, Conc. £1.70. 15% discount for groups of 11+.

📷 ♿Grounds suitable. 🛍 🅿 🎧 🐕Guide dogs only. ❄ 🛍 Tel. for details.

GANTS MILL

Tel: 01749 812393

Bruton, Somerset BA10 0DB
Owner/Contact: Brian and Alison Shingler
4-storey working watermill with beautiful colour-themed designer garden.
Location: OS Ref. ST674 342. Off A359 $^{1}/_{2}$m SW of Bruton.
Opening Times: Mill: Easter - end of May, Thur & BH Mons. Mill & Garden: June - end Sept, Thurs, Suns & BH Mons, 2 - 5pm.
Admission: Adult £3.50, Child £1. Groups by arrangement.

GATCOMBE COURT

Tel: 01275 393141   **Fax:** 01275 394274

Flax Bourton, Somerset BS48 3QT
Owner: Mr & Mrs Charles Clarke   **Contact:** Mr Charles Clarke
A Somerset manor house, dating from early 13th century, which has evolved over the centuries since. It is on the site of a large Roman village, traces of which are apparent.
Location: OS Ref. ST525 698. 5m W of Bristol, N of the A370, between the villages of Long Ashton and Flax Bourton.
Opening Times: By written appointment only.

♿Not suitable. ⏰By arrangement. 🅿 ✂ ❄

Special Events Index ◀◀◀ **page 33**

GAULDEN MANOR

Tel: 01984 667213

Tolland, Lydeard St Lawrence, Nr Taunton, Somerset TA4 3PN

Owner/Contact: James Le Gendre Starkie

Small historic manor of great charm. A real lived-in family home, guided tours by owner. Past seat of the Turberville family, immortalised by Thomas Hardy. Magnificent early plasterwork, fine furniture, many examples of embroidery by owner's wife. Interesting gardens include herb garden, old fashioned roses, bog garden and secret garden beyond monks fish pond.

Location: OS Ref. ST111 314. 9m NW of Taunton off A358 and B3224.

Opening Times: Garden: 3 Jun - 27 Aug. Thurs, Suns & BH Mons, 2 - 5pm. House & Garden: groups (15+): Jun, Jul & Aug: by written appointment at any time.

Admission: House & Garden: Adult £4.20, Child £1. Garden only: Adult £3, Child £1.

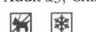 Ground floor & grounds suitable. Obligatory. P

THE GEORGIAN HOUSE

Tel: 0117 921 1262

7 Great George Street, Bristol, Somerset BS1 5RR

Owner: City of Bristol Museums & Art Gallery   **Contact:** Karin Walton

Location: OS172 ST582 730. Bristol.

Opening Times: 1 Apr - 31 Oct: Sat - Wed, 10am - 5pm. 1 Nov - 31 Mar: closed.

Admission: Free.

THE WILLIAM HERSCHEL MUSEUM

Tel: 01225 311342 **Fax:** 01225 446865

19 New King Street, Bath, Somerset BA1 2BL

Owner: The Herschel House Trust   **Contact:** The Curator

The astronomer and musician William Herschel lived here with his sister Caroline during the latter part of the 18th century. 'Star Vault' opening 2001.

Location: OS Ref. ST750 648. Bath, Somerset.

Opening Times: Mar - Oct: daily, 2 - 5pm. Weekends throughout the winter, 2 - 5pm.

Admission: Adult £2.50, Child £1. Organised educational events: £2.50. Free entry to Herschel Society members and Museums Association members.

GLASTONBURY TRIBUNAL

Tel: 01458 832954

Glastonbury High Street, Glastonbury, Somerset

Owner: English Heritage   **Contact:** The TIC Manager

A well preserved medieval town house, reputedly once used as the courthouse of Glastonbury Abbey. Now houses Glastonbury Tourist Information Centre.

Location: OS182 Ref. ST499 390. In Glastonbury High Street.

Opening Times: Apr - Sept: Sun - Thur 10am - 5pm (Fri & Sat to 5.30pm). Oct - Apr: Sun - Thur, 10am - 4pm (Fri & Sat, 4.30pm). Closed 25 - 26 Dec & 1 Jan.

Admission: TIC Free. Display areas: Adult £2, Child £1.

GLASTONBURY ABBEY

ABBEY GATEHOUSE, MAGDALENE STREET, GLASTONBURY BA6 9EL

Owner: Glastonbury Abbey Estate   Contact: F C Thyer - Deputy Custodian

Tel/Fax: 01458 832267   **e-mail:** glastonbury.abbey@dial.pipex.com

Magnificent Abbey ruins steeped in history and legend, situated in 36 acres of glorious Somerset parkland. Traditionally the first Christian sanctuary in Britain and legendary burial place of King Arthur. Award-winning museum with model of pre-Reformation Abbey and 16th century Othery Cope. See the Holy Thorn Tree. Picnics welcomed

Location: OS Ref. ST499 388. 50 yds from the Market Cross, in the centre of Glastonbury. M5/J23, then A39.

Opening Times: Daily (except Christmas Day), 9.30am - 6pm or dusk if earlier. Jun, Jul & Aug: opens 9am. Dec, Jan & Feb: opens 10am.

Admission: Adult £3, Child £1, Conc. £2.50. Groups (booked, 10+): Adult £2.50.

  Summer only. By arrangement. P In grounds, on leads. Tel. for details.

Tintinhull Garden, Somerset.

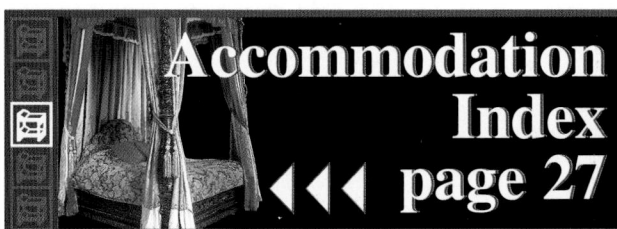

Accommodation Index
◀◀◀ page 27

South West England

HESTERCOMBE GARDENS

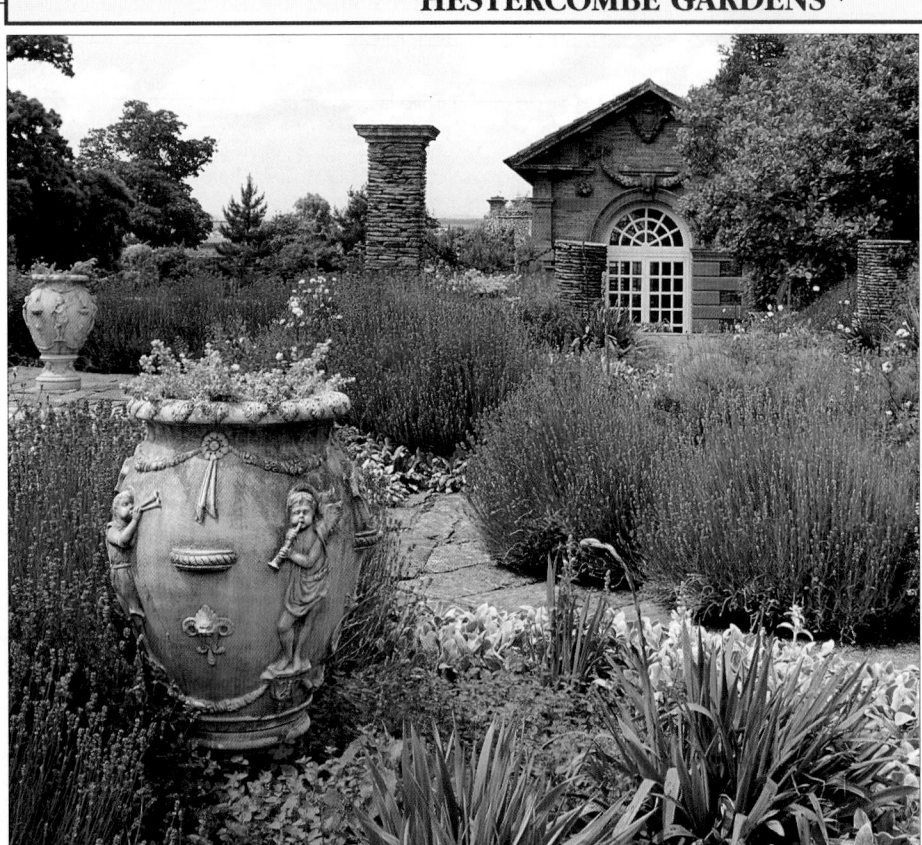

CHEDDON FITZPAINE, TAUNTON, SOMERSET TA2 8LG

Owner: Somerset County Council & Hestercombe Gardens Project

Contact: *Mr P White*

Tel: 01823 413923 **Fax:** 01823 413747

Hestercombe's 50 acres of gardens are listed Grade I on the English Heritage Register of Parks and Gardens and encompass over three centuries of garden history.

The formal gardens, designed by Sir Edwin Lutyens and planted by Gertrude Jekyll, were completed in 1906. With terraces, pools and an orangery, they are the supreme example of their famous partnership. These gardens are now reunited with Hestercombe's secret Landscape Garden, which opened in the Spring of 1997 for the first time in 125 years. Created by Coplestone Warre Bampfylde in the 1750s, these Georgian pleasure grounds comprise 40 acres of lakes, temples and delightful woodland walks. Our tearoom, shop and plant sales area are open daily from 10am to 5pm.

Location: OS Ref. ST241 287. 4m NE from Taunton, 1m NW of Cheddon Fitzpaine.

Opening Times: All year: daily, 10am - 6pm (last admission 5pm). Groups & coach parties by arrangement.

Admission: Adult £4. Child (5-15yrs) £1, Child under 5 Free, Conc. £3.80. Guided tour: £6.50 (min. charge £100).

◻ ⚤ ♿ Partially suitable. WC.

⬛ Licensed. ⍟ Licensed

𝄖 By arrangement.

P Limited for coaches.

🐕 On short leads. ❄ Ⓦ

KENTSFORD   **Tel:** 01984 631307

Washford, Watchet, Somerset TA23 0JD

Owner: Wyndham Estate   **Contact:** Mr R Dibble

Location: OS Ref. ST058 426.

Opening Times: House open only by written appointment with Mr R Dibble. Gardens: 6 Mar - 27 Aug: Tues & BHs.

Admission: House: £2, Gardens: Free.

♿ Gardens only. **P** Limited. 🐕 In grounds, on leads. ❄

KING JOHN'S HUNTING LODGE 🌿   **Tel:** 01934 732012

The Square, Axbridge, Somerset BS26 2AP

Owner/Contact: The National Trust

An early Tudor merchant's house, extensively restored in 1971. Note: the property is run as a local history museum by Sedgemoor District Council in co-operation with Somerset County Museum's Service and Axbridge Archaeological & Local History Society.

Location: OS Ref. ST431 545. In the Square, on corner of High Street, off A371.

Opening Times: Easter - end Sept: daily, 2 - 5pm.

Admission: Free. School groups by arrangement.

♿ Ground floor suitable. **P**

LOWER SEVERALLS   **Tel:** 01460 73234 **Fax:** 01460 76105

Crewkerne, Somerset TA18 7NX

Owner: Mr & Mrs Howard Pring   **Contact:** Mary Cooper

2½ acre garden, developed over the last 25 years including herb garden, mixed borders and island beds with innovative features, ie a giant living dogwood basket and a wadi.

Location: OS Ref. ST457 112. 1½ m NE of Crewkerne, between A30 & A356.

Opening Times: 2 Mar - 20 Oct: daily (except Thurs), 10am - 5pm (Suns, 2 - 5pm in May/June only).

Admission: Adult £2, Child (under 16yrs) Free.

LYTES CARY MANOR 🌿   **Tel:** 01985 843600

Nr Charlton Mackrell, Somerset TA11 7HU

Owner: The National Trust   **Contact:** The Regional Office

A charming manor house with a 14th century chapel and Tudor Great Hall, much added to in the 16th century. Once the home of Henry Lyte, translator of Niewe Herball (1578). Attractive hedged garden.

Location: OS Ref. ST534 265. 1m N of Ilchester bypass A303, signposted from roundabout at junction of A303. A37 take A372.

Opening Times: 2 Apr - 31 Oct: Mons, Weds & Sats, 2 - 6pm or dusk if earlier. Also Fris in Jun, Jul & Aug: 2 - 6pm. Last admission 5.30pm.

Admission: £4.50, Child £2.

♿ Grounds suitable. **P** Limited. 🐕

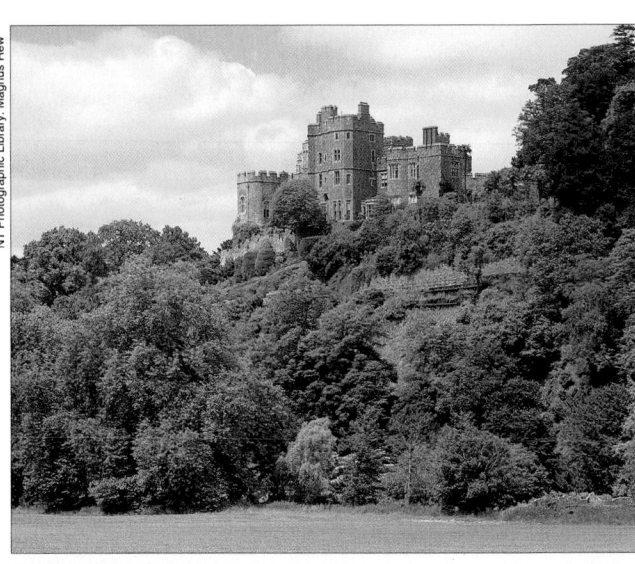

NT Photographic Library: Magnus Rew

Dunster Castle, Somerset.

MAUNSEL HOUSE

NORTH NEWTON, Nr BRIDGWATER, SOMERSET TA7 0BU

Owner: Sir Benjamin Slade **Contact:** *Olivia Boyle*

Tel: 0207 352 1132 **Fax:** 0207 352 5697

This imposing 13th century manor house offers the ideal location for wedding receptions, corporate events, private and garden parties, filming and family celebrations. The ancestral seat of the Slade family and home of the 7th baronet Sir Benjamin Slade; the house can boast such visitors as Geoffrey Chaucer, who wrote part of the *Canterbury Tales* whilst staying there. The beautiful grounds and spacious rooms provide both privacy and a unique atmosphere for any special event.

Location: OS Ref. ST302 303. Bridgwater 4m, Bristol 20m, Taunton 7m, M5/J24, turn left North Petherton. 2¹/₂ m SE of A38 at North Petherton.

Opening Times: Coach parties and groups welcome by appointment. Caravan rally field available.

⊤ Functions. ♿ Partially suitable. 🐕 In grounds, on leads. (TW)

MONTACUTE HOUSE

MONTACUTE, SOMERSET TA15 6XP

Owner: The National Trust **Contact:** *The Property Manager*

Tel/Fax: 01935 823289

A magnificent Elizabethan house, with an H-shaped ground plan and many Renaissance features, including contemporary plasterwork, chimneypieces and heraldic glass. The house contains fine 17th and 18th century furniture, an exhibition of samplers dating from the 17th century and Elizabethan and Jacobean portraits from the National Portrait Gallery displayed in the Long Gallery and adjoining rooms. The formal garden includes mixed borders and old roses, also a landscaped park. Montacute featured in the award-winning film *Sense & Sensibility*.

Location: OS Ref. ST499 172. In Montacute village, 4m W of Yeovil, on S side of A3088, 3m E of A303.

Opening Times: House: 31 Mar - 4 Nov: daily except Tues, 12 noon - 5.30pm. Garden & Park: 31 Mar - 4 Nov: daily except Tues, 11am - 5.30pm or dusk if earlier. 7 Nov - Mar 2002 daily except Mons & Tues, 11.30am - 4pm.

Admission: House, Park & Garden: Adult £6, Child £3, Family £15. Groups (15+) (must book): Adult £5.50, Child £2.80. Garden & Park only (31 Mar - 4 Nov): Adult £3.30, Child £1.50. 7 Nov - Mar 2002: Adult £2, Child £1.

📷 ♿ Grounds suitable. WC. ⊤ Licensed. 🅿 🐕 In park only.
🏛 ❄

MILTON LODGE GARDENS 🏛   **Tel:** 01749 672168

Wells, Somerset BA5 3AQ

Owner/Contact: D Tudway Quilter Esq

"The great glory of the gardens of Milton Lodge is their position high up on the slopes of the Mendip Hills to the north of Wells … with broad panoramas of Wells Cathedral and the Vale of Avalon", (Lanning Roper). Charming, mature, Grade II listed terraced garden dating from 1909. Replanned 1962 with mixed shrubs, herbaceous plants, old fashioned roses and ground cover; numerous climbers; old established yew hedges. Fine trees in garden and in 7-acre arboretum.

Location: OS Ref. ST549 470. ¹/₂ m N of Wells from A39. N up Old Bristol Road. Free car park first gate on left.

Opening Times: Garden & Arboretum: Easter - end Oct: Tues, Weds, Suns & BHs, 2 - 5pm Parties & coaches by prior arrangement.

Admission: Adult £2.50, Child (under 14yrs) Free. Open certain Suns in aid of National Gardens Scheme.

📷 🍴 ♿ Not suitable. 🅿 🐕

MUCHELNEY ABBEY ⛪   **Tel:** 01458 250664

Muchelney, Langport, Somerset TA10 0DQ

Owner: English Heritage   **Contact:** The Custodian

Well-preserved ruins of the cloisters, with windows carved in golden stone, and abbot's lodging of the Benedictine abbey, which survived by being used as a farmhouse after the Dissolution.

Location: OS193 Ref. ST428 248. In Muchelney 2m S of Langport.

Opening Times: 1 Apr - 31 Oct: daily 10am - 6pm (5pm in Oct). Winter: closed.

Admission: Adult £1.90, Child £1, Conc. £1.50. 15% discount for groups (11+).

📷 ♿ Ground floor & grounds suitable. 🅿 🐕 Tel. for details.

MUSEUM OF COSTUME & ASSEMBLY ROOMS

See page 229 for full page entry.

NUNNEY CASTLE ⛪   **Tel:** 0117 9750700

Nunney, Somerset

Owner: English Heritage   **Contact:** The South West Regional Office

A small 14th century moated castle with a distinctly French style. Its unusual design consists of a central block with large towers at the angles.

Location: OS183 Ref. ST737 457. In Nunney 3¹/₂ m SW of Frome, 1m N of the A361.

Opening Times: Any reasonable time.

Admission: Free.

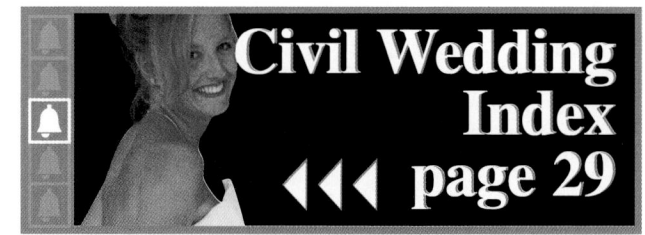
Civil Wedding Index ◀◀◀ page 29

Montacute House, Somerset.

South West England

ORCHARD WYNDHAM
Tel: 01984 632309 **Fax:** 01984 633526

Williton, Taunton, Somerset TA4 4HH

Owner: Wyndham Estate　　　　**Contact:** Wyndham Estate Office

English manor house. Family home for 700 years encapsulating continuous building and alteration from the 14th to the 20th century. Limited showing space within the house. To avoid disappointment book places on tour by telephone or fax. Access only suitable for cars.

Location: OS Ref. ST072 400. 1m from A39 at Williton.

Opening Times: Aug: Thurs & Fris, 2 - 5pm; BH, 11am - 5pm. Guided tours only. Last tour at 4pm.

Admission: Adult £5, Child (under 12) £1.

Obligatory & pre-booked.　Limited. No coach parking.　In grounds, on leads.

PRIEST'S HOUSE
Tel: 01458 252621

Muchelney, Langport, Somerset TA10 0DQ

Owner: The National Trust　　　**Contact:** The Administrator

A late medieval hall house with large gothic windows, originally the residence of priests serving the parish church across the road. Lived-in and recently repaired.

Location: OS Ref. ST429 250. 1m S of Langport.

Opening Times: 1 Apr - 30 Sept: Suns & Mons, 2.30 - 5.30pm, last admission 5.15pm.

Admission: £2, no reduction for groups or children.

PRIOR PARK LANDSCAPE GARDEN

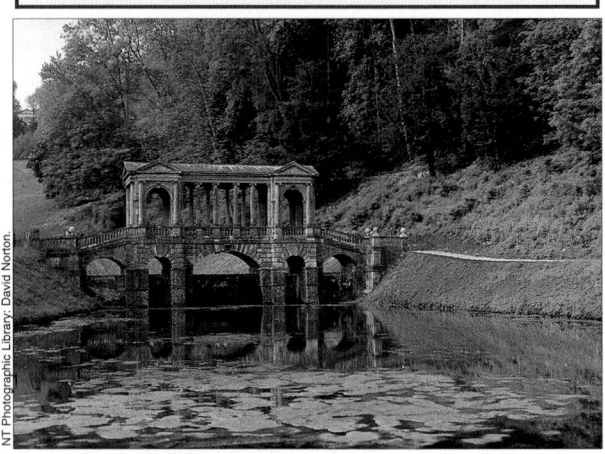

NT Photographic Library: David Norton.

RALPH ALLEN DRIVE, BATH BA2 5AH
Owner: *The National Trust*　　**Contact:** *Gardener-in-Charge*

Tel: 01225 833422

Beautiful and intimate 18th century landscape garden created by Bath entrepreneur Ralph Allen (1693 - 1764) with advice from the poet Alexander Pope and Lancelot 'Capability' Brown. Sweeping valley with magnificent views of the City of Bath Palladian bridge and lakes. Restoration of the garden continues. All visitors must use public transport as there is no car park. For further details 01225 833422 or 24 hour information line 09001 335242 (60p per minute). Prior Park College, a co-educational school, operates from the mansion (not NT).

Location: OS Ref. ST760 632. Frequent bus service from City Centre. Badgerline 2 & 4.

Opening Times: Feb - Nov & 1 - 28 Feb 2002: daily except Tues. Dec & Jan 2002: Fri - Sun (closed 25/26 Dec & 1 Jan 2002). Times: Feb - Good Fri 12 noon - 5.30pm or dusk if earlier. Easter Sat - 11 Sept: 11am - 5.30pm. Oct - Feb 12 noon - 5.30pm or dusk if earlier.

Admission: Adult: £4, Child £2. All visitors who produce a valid bus or train ticket will receive £1 off admission. NT members will receive a £1 voucher.

Grounds suitable. WC.　No parking.

THE ROMAN BATHS & PUMP ROOM
See page 230 for full page entry.

STEMBRIDGE TOWER MILL
Tel: 01458 250818

High Ham, Somerset TA10 9DJ

Owner: The National Trust　　　**Contact:** The Administrator

The last thatched windmill in England, dating from 1822 and in use until 1910.

Location: OS Ref. ST432 305. 2m N of Langport, ¹/₂ m E of High Ham.

Opening Times: 1 Apr - 30 Sept: Suns, Mons & Weds, 2 - 5pm.

Admission: Adult £2, Child £1. Special arrangements may be made for coach/school groups.

Limited.

STOKE-SUB-HAMDON PRIORY
Tel: 01985 843600

North Street, Stoke-sub-Hamdon Somerset TA4 6QP

Owner/Contact: The National Trust

A complex of buildings, begun in the 14th century for the priests of the chantry chapel of St Nicholas, which is now destroyed.

Location: OS Ref. ST473 174. ¹/₂ m S of A303. 2m W of Montacute between Yeovil and Ilminster.

Opening Times: 31 Mar - 4 Nov: daily, 10am - 6pm or dusk if earlier. Only Great Hall open.

Admission: Free.

No WC.　Limited.

TINTINHULL GARDEN

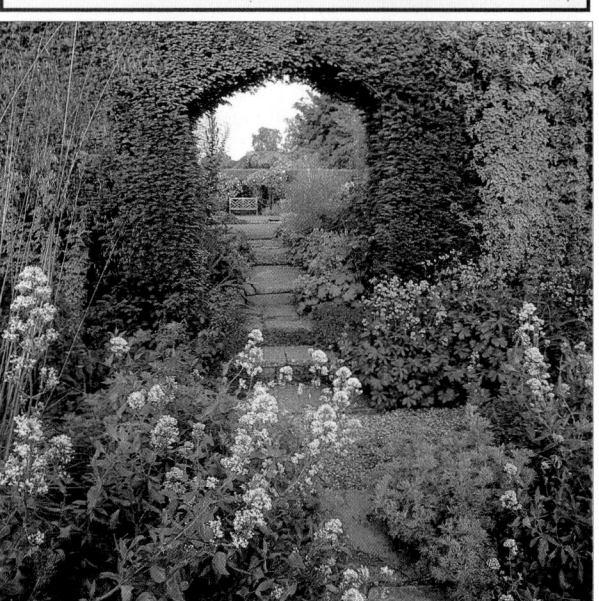

NT Photographic Library: Nick Meers.

FARM STREET, TINTINHULL, SOMERSET BA22 9PZ
Owner: *The National Trust*　　**Contact:** *The Head Gardener*

Tel: 01935 822545

A delightful formal garden, created in the 20th century around a 17th century manor house. Small pools, varied borders and secluded lawns are neatly enclosed within walls and clipped hedges and there is also an attractive kitchen garden.

Location: OS Ref. ST503 198. 5m NW of Yeovil, ¹/₂ m S of A303, on E outskirts of Tintinhull.

Opening Times: 1 Apr - 30 Sept: Wed - Sun, 12 noon - 6pm (open BH Mons).

Admission: Adult £3.80, Child £1.80. No reduction for groups.

Grounds suitable.　Limited.

Gants Mill, Somerset.

TREASURER'S HOUSE

Tel: 01935 825801

Martock, Somerset TA12 6JL

Owner/Contact: The National Trust

A small medieval house, recently refurbished by The Trust. The two-storey hall was completed in 1293 and the solar block is even earlier. There is also a kitchen, added later, and an interesting wall painting.

Location: OS Ref. ST462 191. 1m NW of A303 between Ilminster and Ilchester.

Opening Times: 1 Apr - 30 Sept: Sun - Tue, 2 - 5pm. Only medieval hall, wall paintings and kitchen are shown.

Admission: Adult £2 (no reduction for children). Groups by prior appointment.

P Limited for cars. None for coaches & trailer caravans.

WELLS CATHEDRAL

Tel: 01749 674483 **Fax:** 01749 677360

Cathedral Green, Wells, Somerset BA5 2UE

Owner: The Chapter of Wells **Contact:** Mr John Roberts

Fine medieval Cathedral. The West front with its splendid array of statuary, the Quire with colourful embroideries and stained glass, Chapter House and astronomical clock should not be missed.

Location: OS Ref. ST552 458. In Wells, 20m S from both Bath & Bristol.

Opening Times: Daily: 7.15am - 8.30pm (summer), or 7.15am - 6pm (winter).

Admission: No entry charge. Donations welcomed. Photo permit £1.

WESTBURY COLLEGE GATEHOUSE

Tel: 01985 843600

College Road, Westbury-on-Trym, Bristol

Owner: The National Trust **Contact:** Rev G M Collins

The 15th century gatehouse of the College of Priests (founded in the 13th century) of which John Wyclif was a prebend.

Location: OS Ref. ST572 775. 3m N of the centre of Bristol. Just E of main street.

Opening Times: Access by key only, to be collected by prior written or telephone appointment (0117 962 1536). Rev. G M Collins, The Vicarage, 44 Eastfield Road, Westbury-on-Trym, Bristol BS9 4AG.

Admission: Adult £1.10, Child 50p.

P Limited.

Costumes from the Museum of Costume and Assembly Rooms, Bath.

BOWOOD HOUSE & GARDENS
Calne

Owner:
The Marquis of Lansdowne

CONTACT

The Administrator
Bowood House and
Gardens
Calne
Wiltshire
SN11 0LZ

Tel: 01249 812102

Fax: 01249 821757

e-mail: houseandgardens@
bowood-estate.co.uk

LOCATION

OS Ref. ST974 700

From London M4/J17,
off the A4 between
Chippenham and Calne.
Swindon 17m,
Bristol 26m,
Bath 16m.

Bus: to the gate,
1¹/₂ m through
park to House.

Rail: Chippenham
Station 5m.

Taxi: AA Taxis,
Chippenham 657777.

BOWOOD is the family home of the Marquis and Marchioness of Lansdowne. Begun c1720 for the Bridgeman family, the house was purchased by the 2nd Earl of Shelburne in 1754 and completed soon afterwards. Part of the house was demolished in 1955, leaving a perfectly proportioned Georgian home, over half of which is open to visitors. Robert Adam's magnificent Diocletian wing contains a splendid library, the laboratory where Joseph Priestley discovered oxygen gas in 1774, the orangery, now a picture gallery, the Chapel and a sculpture gallery in which some of the famous Lansdowne Marbles are displayed.

Among the family treasures shown in the numerous exhibition rooms are Georgian costumes, including Lord Byron's Albanian dress; Victoriana; Indiana (the 5th Marquess was Viceroy 1888-94); and superb collections of watercolours, miniatures and jewellery.

The House is set in one of the most beautiful parks in England. Over 2,000 acres of gardens and grounds were landscaped by 'Capability' Brown between 1762 and 1768, and are embellished with a Doric temple, a cascade, a pinetum and an arboretum. The Rhododendron Gardens are open for six weeks from late April to early June. All the walks have seats.

OPENING TIMES

House & Garden

1 Apr - 28 Oct:
Daily
11am - 6pm or
dusk if earlier.

Rhododendron Walks
Late April to early June
(depending on flowering
season) for 6 weeks
11am - 6pm.

ADMISSION

House and Garden
Adult £5.90
Child (5-15yrs).........£3.70
OAP.......................£4.90
Groups (20+)
Adult £4.95
Child (5-15yrs).........£3.20
OAP.......................£4.20
(children under 5yrs Free)

Rhododendron Walks
Adult £3.25
Child (0-15yrs) ....Free
OAP.......................£3.25

The charge for
Rhododendron Walks is
£2.25 if combined on same
day with a visit to Bowood
House & Gardens.

Owner:
J Methuen-Campbell Esq

CONTACT

Corsham Court
Corsham
Wiltshire
SN13 0BZ

Tel/Fax: 01249 701610

LOCATION

OS Ref. ST874 706

Corsham Court
is signposted
from the A4, approx. 4m
W of Chippenham.
From Edinburgh, A1, M62,
M6, M5, M4, 8 hrs.
From London, M4, 2¼ hrs.
From Chester,
M6, M5, M4, 4 hrs.

Motorway: M4/J17 9m.

Rail: Chippenham
Station 6m.

Taxi: 01249 715959.

CORSHAM COURT
Corsham

CORSHAM COURT is an Elizabethan house of 1582 and was bought by Paul Methuen in the mid-18th century, to house a collection of 16th and 17th century Italian and Flemish master paintings and statuary. In the middle of the 19th century, the house was enlarged to receive a second collection, purchased in Florence, principally of fashionable Italian masters and stone-inlaid furniture.

Paul Methuen (1723-95) was a great-grandson of Paul Methuen of Bradford-on-Avon and cousin of John Methuen, ambassador and negotiator of the Methuen Treaty of 1703 with Portugal which permitted export of British woollens to Portugal and allowed a preferential 33⅓ percent duty discount on Portuguese wines, bringing about a major change in British drinking habits.

The architects involved in the alterations to the house and park were Lancelot 'Capability' Brown in the 1760s, John Nash in 1800 and Thomas Bellamy in 1845-9. Brown set the style by retaining the Elizabethan Stables and Riding School, but rebuilding the Gateway, retaining the gabled Elizabethan stone front and doubling the gabled wings at either end and inside, by designing the East Wing as Stateroom Picture Galleries. Nash's work has now largely disappeared, but Bellamy's stands fast, notably in the Hall and Staircase.

The State Rooms, including the Music Room and Dining Room, provide the setting for the outstanding collection of over 150 paintings, statuary, bronzes and furniture. The collection includes work by such names as Chippendale, the Adam brothers, Van Dyck, Reni, Rosa, Rubens, Lippi, Reynolds, Romney and a pianoforte by Clementi.

GARDENS

'Capability' Brown planned to include a lake, avenues and specimen trees such as the Oriental Plane now with a 200-yard perimeter. The gardens, designed not only by Brown but also by Repton, contain a ha-ha, herbaceous borders, secluded gardens, lawns, a rose garden, a lily pool, a stone bath house and the Bradford Porch.

ℹ️ Souvenir desk. No umbrellas, no photography.

♿ Visitors may alight at the entrance to the property, before parking in the allocated areas.

☕ Tearooms nearby.
Tel: Corsham 01249 713260.

🚶 For up to 55. If requested the owner may meet the group. Tour time 1½ hrs.

🅿️ 400 cars, 120 yards from the house. Coaches may park at the door to the house. Coach parties must book in advance.

Available: rate negotiable. A guide will be provided.

🐕 Must be kept on leads in the garden.

OPENING TIMES

SUMMER
20 March - 30 September
Daily except Mons but
including BH Mons
2 - 5.30pm
Last admission 5pm.

WINTER
1 October - 19 March
Weekends only
2 - 4.30pm
Last admission 4pm.

Closed December.

NB: Open throughout the year by appointment only for groups of 15+.

ADMISSION

House & Garden

Adult £5.00
Child (5-15yrs)........£2.50
OAP........................£4.50
Groups
(includes guided tour - 1 hr)
Adult £4.50

Garden only

Adult £2.00
Child (5-15yrs)........£1.00
OAP........................£1.50
Groups
Per person £4.50

LONGLEAT
Warminster

Longleat hit the headlines in 2000 enjoying national recognition as one of the top tourist attractions in the UK. The prestigious 'Which? Guide to Tourist Attractions' voted Longleat one of the 'Best Animal Attractions' in the UK whilst early July saw Longleat voted as the 'Visitor Attraction of the Year' in the Southern Tourist Board's England for Excellence Awards. Special mentions were made in both reports on the excellent value for money Passport Ticket which offers entrance to all 12 of the Longleat attractions.

Set within 900 acres of 'Capability' Brown designed parkland the magnificent Elizabethan property, Longleat House, is widely regarded as the best example of Elizabethan architecture in Britain and one of the most beautiful stately homes open to the public. Built by Sir John Thynne and substantially completed by 1580, Longleat House has been the home of the same family ever since. Many treasures are included within; paintings by Tintoretto and Wootton, exquisite Flemish tapestries, fine French

furniture and elaborate ceilings by John Dibblee Crace incorporating paintings from the 'School of Titian'. The Murals in the family apartments in the West Wing were painted by Alexander Thynn, the present Marquess, and are fascinating and remarkable additions to the collections.

Apart from the ancestral home, Longleat is also renowned for its Safari Park, the first of its kind outside Africa. Here, visitors have a remarkable opportunity to see hundreds of animals in a natural woodland and parkland setting. Amongst the most magnificent sights are the famous pride of lions, a white tiger, wolves, rhesus monkeys, elephants and giraffe..

Don't miss the other attractions which make Longleat a fun day out for all the family… get lost in the 'World's Longest Hedge Maze', let off steam in the Adventure Castle, travel on the Longleat Railway, get close to the creatures in Pets Corner and marvel at the sealions on the Safari Boats… your day at Longleat will never be long enough!

❖

Rooms in Longleat House can be hired for conferences, gala dinners and product launches. Extensive parkland for car launches, ride n' drives, company fun days, marquee based events, concerts, balloon festivals, equestrian events, caravan rallies & fishing. Film location.

Licensed.

Cellar Café (capacity 80). Groups must book. From 3 course meals to cream teas, sandwiches & snacks. Traditional Wiltshire Fare. Not open all year.

Groups (max 20, 15 in murals). Booking essential.

Ample.

Welcome with 1 teacher free entry per 8 children. GNVQ talks and packs available on request. Booking essential. Education sheets.

In grounds, on leads.

Orangery.

PASSPORT TICKETS - includes all the following attractions:
Safari Park, Longleat House, Safari Boats, World's Longest Hedge Maze, King Arthur's Mirror Maze, Pets' Corner & Parrot Show, Adventure Castle, Longleat Railway, VirtuaScope Motion Ride, Butterfly Garden, Postman Pat Village, Dr Who Exhibition, Grounds & Gardens.

Owner:
The Marquess of Bath

CONTACT

The Estate Office
Longleat
Warminster
Wiltshire
BA12 7NW

Tel: 01985 844400

Fax: 01985 844885

e-mail: marketing@
longleat.co.uk

LOCATION

OS Ref. ST809 430

Just off the A36 between Bath & Salisbury.(A362 Warminster - Frome). Just 2hrs from London following M3, A303, A36, A362 or M4/J18/A46-A36.

Rail: Mainline Paddington to Westbury (12m) or Warminster station on Bristol-Salisbury line. Lion-Link bus from Warminster station to Longleat (tel. for details).

Air: Bristol airport 30m.

Taxi: Starline Taxis
01985 212215.

CONFERENCE/FUNCTION		
ROOM	SIZE	MAX CAPACITY
Banqueting Suite	2 x (10m x 7m)	40
Great Hall	8m x 13m	150

OPENING TIMES

SUMMER
24 March - 4 November
House: Easter - Sept: 10am - 5.30pm. Rest of year, guided tours at set times between 11am - 4pm

Safari Park: 10am - 4pm (10am - 5pm on weekends, BHs & in school holidays).

Other attractions:
11am - 5.30pm.

WINTER
House & grounds only:
1 January - 23 March
Limited openings please telephone for details.

5 November - 31 December
Guided tours at set times between 11am - 4pm (closed Christmas Day).

ADMISSION

House & Grounds
Adult £9.00
Child (4 -14yrs).........£6.00
OAP.........................£6.00

Passport Ticket
(see left under photo)
Adult £14.00
Child (4 -14yrs).......£11.00
OAP.......................£11.00
Groups (50+)
Adult £9.30
Child (4 -16yrs).........£7.30
OAP.........................£7.30

Special discounted rates for groups of 12 - 49 & 50+.

WILTON HOUSE
Nr Salisbury

The 17th Earl of Pembroke and his family live in Wilton House which has been their ancestral home for 450 years. In 1544 Henry VIII gave the Abbey and lands of Wilton to Sir William Herbert who had married Anne Parr, sister of Katherine, sixth wife of King Henry.

The Clock Tower, in the centre of the east front, is reminiscent of this part of the Tudor building which survived a fire in 1647. Inigo Jones and John Webb were responsible for the rebuilding of the house in the Palladian style, whilst further alterations were made by James Wyatt from 1801.

The chief architectural features are the magnificent 17th century state apartments (including the famous Single and Double Cube rooms) and the 19th century cloisters.

The house contains one of the finest art collections in Europe, with over 230 original paintings on display, including works by Van Dyck, Rubens, Joshua Reynolds and Brueghel. Also on show are Greek and Italian statuary, a lock of Queen Elizabeth I's hair, Napoleon's despatch case, and Florence Nightingale's sash.

The visitor centre houses a dynamic introductory film (narrated by Anna Massey), the reconstructed Tudor kitchen and the Estate's Victorian laundry. The house is set in magnificent landscaped parkland, bordered by the River Nadder which is the setting for the majestic Palladian Bridge. The current Earl of Pembroke is a keen gardener who has created four new gardens since succeeding to the title in 1969 including the North Forecourt Garden, Old English Rose Garden, Water and Cloister Gardens.

Owner:
The Earl of Pembroke

CONTACT

Sally Salmon
The Estate Office
Wilton House
Wilton
Salisbury
SP2 0BJ

Tel: 01722 746720

Fax: 01722 744447

e-mail:
tourism@wiltonhouse.com

LOCATION

OS Ref. SU099 311

3m W of Salisbury
on the A30.

Rail: Salisbury
Station 3m.

Bus: Every 10 mins from
Salisbury, Mon - Sat.

Taxi: Sarum Taxi
01722 334477.

CONFERENCE/FUNCTION		
ROOM	SIZE	MAX CAPACITY
Double cube	60' x 30'	150
Exhibition Centre	50' x 40'	140
Film Theatre	34" x 20"	67

Film location, fashion shows, product launches, equestrian events, garden parties, antiques fairs, concerts, vehicle rallies. No photography in house. French, German, Spanish, Italian, Japanese and Dutch information.

Exclusive banquets.

Excellent access. Visitors may alight at the entrance. WCs.

Licensed. Self-service restaurant open 10.30am - 5pm. Groups must book. Hot lunches 12 noon - 2pm.

By arrangement.

200 cars and 12 coaches. Free coach parking. Group rates (min 15), meal vouchers, drivers' lounge.

Teachers' handbook for National Curriculum. EFL students welcome. Free preparatory visit for group leaders.

Guide dogs only.

OPENING TIMES

SUMMER
4 April - 28 October
Daily: 10.30am - 5.30pm.

Last admission 4.30pm.

WINTER
Closed, except for private parties by prior arrangement.

ADMISSION

SUMMER
House, Grounds & Exhibition

Adult	£7.25
Child*	£4.50
OAP/Student	£6.25
Family (2+2)	£20.00

Groups (15+)

Adult	£5.50
Child	£4.00

Grounds only

Adult	£3.75
Child	£2.75

Season Tickets

Family	£43.00
Individual	£22.00

WINTER
Prices on application.

* 5 - 15 yrs - under 5s Free.

SPECIAL EVENTS

- **MAR 2 - 4:**
  24th Annual Antiques Fair.

- **JUL 14:**
  Classical Firework Proms Night.

South West England

ALEXANDER KEILLER MUSEUM

Tel: 01672 539250

Avebury, Nr Marlborough, Wiltshire SN8 1RF

Owner: The National Trust   **Contact:** The Custodian

The investigation of Avebury Stone Circles was largely the work of Alexander Keiller in the 1930s. He put together one of the most important prehistoric archaeological collections in Britain which can be seen at the Alexander Keiller Museum.

Location: OS Ref. SU100 699. In Avebury 6m W of Marlborough.

Opening Times: 1 Apr - 31 Oct: daily, 10am - 6pm/dusk if earlier. 1 Nov - 31 Mar 2002: daily, 10am - 4pm. Closed 24 - 26 Dec & 1 Jan.

Admission: Adult £2, Child £1. English Heritage members Free (tel. 01672 539250).

AVEBURY MANOR & GARDEN

Tel: 01672 539250

Avebury, Nr Marlborough, Wiltshire SN8 1RF

Owner: The National Trust   **Contact:** The Custodian

A much altered house of monastic origin, the present buildings date from the early 16th century, with notable Queen Anne alterations and Edwardian renovation by Col Jenner. The topiary and flower gardens contain medieval walls, ancient box and numerous 'rooms'. Note: Manor house is occupied by tenants who open parts of it to visitors. Timed tickets may be in operation at busy times.

Location: OS Ref. SU101 701. 6m W of Marlborough, 1m N of the A4 on A4361 and B4003.

Opening Times: House: 1 Apr - 31 Oct: Tue - Wed, Suns & BH Mons, 2 - 5.30pm. Garden: 1 Apr - 31 Oct: daily except Mons & Thurs (open BH Mons), 11am - 5.30pm.

Admission: House & Garden: Adult £3.50, Child £1.70. Groups: Adult £3.20, Child £1.50. Garden only: Adult £2.50, Child £1.20. Groups: Adult £2.20, Child £1.

Gardens largely suitable.   No dogs in house. Guide dogs only in garden.

AVEBURY STONE CIRCLE

Tel: 01672 539250

Avebury, Nr Marlborough, Wiltshire SN8 1RF

Owner: The National Trust   **Contact:** The Property Manager

One of the most important Megalithic monuments in Europe, this 28½ acre site with stone circles enclosed by a ditch and external bank, is approached by an avenue of stones. The site includes the Alexander Keiller Museum and is managed and owned by the National Trust.

Location: OS Ref. SU102 699. 6m W of Marlborough, 1m N of the A4 on A4361 and B4003.

Opening Times: Stone Circle: daily.

BOWOOD HOUSE

See page 238 for full page entry.

BRADFORD-ON-AVON TITHE BARN

Tel: 0117 975 0700

Bradford-on-Avon, Wiltshire

Owner: English Heritage   **Contact:** South West Regional Office

A magnificent medieval stone-built barn with a slate roof and wooden beamed interior.

Location: OS173 Ref. ST824 604. ¼ m S of town centre, off B3109.

Opening Times: Daily, 10.30am - 4pm. Closed 25 Dec.

Admission: Free.

BROADLEAS GARDENS

Tel: 01380 722035

Devizes, Wiltshire SN10 5JQ

Owner: Broadleas Gardens Charitable Trust   **Contact:** Lady Anne Cowdray

10 acres full of interest, notably The Dell, where the sheltered site allows plantings of magnolias, camellias, rhododendrons and azaleas.

Location: OS Ref. SU001 601. Signposted SW from town centre at S end of housing estate, (coaches must use this entrance) or 1m S of Devizes on W side of A360.

Opening Times: Apr - Oct: Sun, Weds & Thurs, 2 - 6pm or by arrangement for groups.

Admission: Adult £3, Child (under 12yrs) £1, Groups (10+) £2.50.

CORSHAM COURT

See page 239 for full page entry.

Open All Year Index page 49 ◄◄◄

THE COURTS

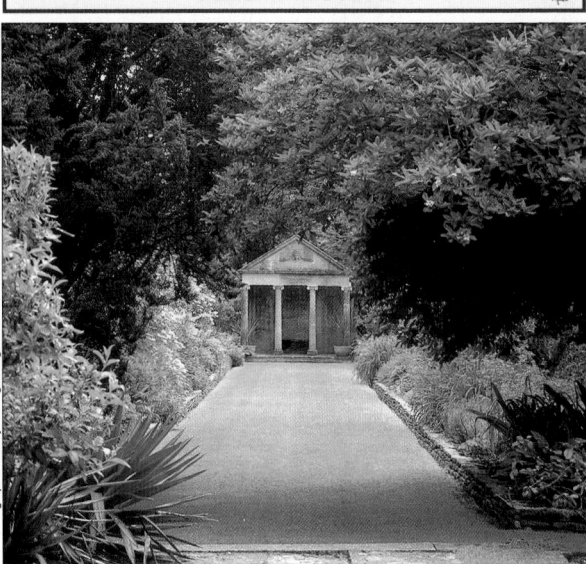

NT Photographic Library: George Wright.

HOLT, TROWBRIDGE, WILTSHIRE BA14 6RR

Owner: *The National Trust* **Contact:** *Head Gardener*

Tel: 01225 782340

One of Wiltshire's best-kept secrets, the English garden style at its best, full of charm and variety. There are many interesting plants and an imaginative use of colour surrounding water features, topiary and herbaceous borders. Complemented by an arboretum with natural planting of spring bulbs.

Location: OS Ref. ST861 618. 3m SW of Melksham, 3m N of Trowbridge, 2½ m E of Bradford-on-Avon, on S side of B3107.

Opening Times: 1 Apr - 14 Oct: daily except Sats, 1 - 5.30pm. Out of season by appointment only.

Admission: Adult £3.50, Child £1.50. Groups by arrangement with Head Gardener.

No WC.   Limited.

GREAT CHALFIELD MANOR

Tel: 01225 782239 **Fax:** 01225 783379

Melksham, Wiltshire SN12 8NJ

Owner: The National Trust   **Contact:** The Tenant

A charming manor house enhanced by a moat and gatehouse and with beautiful oriel windows and a great hall. Completed in 1480, the manor and gardens were restored earlier last century (c1905 - 1911) by Major R Fuller, whose family live here and manage the property. The garden, designed by Alfred Parson, to compliment the Manor, has been replanted.

Location: OS Ref. ST860 633. 3m SW of Melksham via Broughton Gifford Common.

Opening Times: 3 Apr - 1 Nov: Tue - Thur, guided tours only at 12.15, 2.15, 3, 3.45 & 4.30pm. The tours take 45 mins and numbers are limited to 25. Visitors arriving during a tour can visit the adjoining parish church and garden first. Note: Group visits are welcome on Fris & Sats (not BHs) by written arrangement with Mrs Robert Floyd. Organisers of coach parties should allow 2 hours because of limits on numbers in the house.

Admission: £3.80, no reductions for children and groups.

Grounds suitable.   Obligatory.   Limited.

Patrick Lane.

Newhouse, Wiltshire

HAMPTWORTH LODGE

HAMPTWORTH, LANDFORD, SALISBURY, WILTSHIRE SP5 2EA

Owner/Contact: *Mr N J M Anderson*

Tel: 01794 390215 **Fax:** 01794 390644

Rebuilt Jacobean manor house standing in woodlands on the edge of the New Forest. Grade II* family house with period furniture including clocks. The Great Hall has an unusual roof construction. There is a collection of prentice pieces and the Moffatt collection of contemporary copies. Garden also open.

Location: OS Ref. SU227 195. 10m SE of Salisbury on road linking Downton on Salisbury/ Bournemouth Road (A338) to Landford on A36, Salisbury - Southampton.

Opening Times: 30 Mar - 30 Apr: 2.15 - 5pm except Suns. Coaches, by appointment only, 1 Apr - 30 Oct except Suns.

Admission: £3.50, Child (under 11yrs) Free. Groups by arrangement.

♿ Ground floor & grounds suitable.

THE KING'S HOUSE
Tel: 01722 332151 **Fax:** 01722 325611

SALISBURY & SOUTH WILTSHIRE MUSEUM
e-mail: museum@salisburymuseum.freeserve.co.uk
65 The Close, Salisbury, Wiltshire SP1 2EN
Owner: Occupied by Salisbury & South Wiltshire Museum Trust **Contact:** P R Saunders
Location: OS Ref. SU141 295. In Salisbury Cathedral Close, W side, facing cathedral.
Opening Times: All year: Mon - Sat: 10am - 5pm. Suns in Jul & Aug: 2 - 5pm.
Admission: Adult £3, Child 75p, Conc. £2, Groups £2.

Salisbury Cathedral, Wiltshire

LACOCK ABBEY, FOX TALBOT MUSEUM & VILLAGE

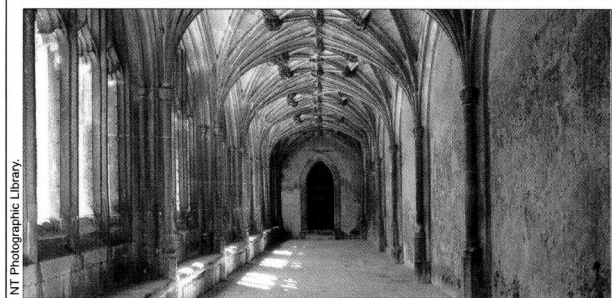

LACOCK, CHIPPENHAM, WILTSHIRE SN15 2LG

Owner: *The National Trust* **Contact:** *The Property Manager*

Tel: 01249 730227/730459

Founded in 1232 and converted into a country house c1540, the fine medieval cloisters, sacristy, chapter house and monastic rooms of the abbey have survived largely intact. The handsome 16th century stable courtyard has half-timbered gables, a clockhouse, brewery and bakehouse. The Victorian woodland garden boast a fine display of spring flowers, magnificent trees, an 18th century summer house, Victorian rose garden and ha-ha. The Museum of Photography commemorates the achievements of a former resident of the abbey, William Fox Talbot (1800-77), inventor of the modern photographic negative and whose descendants gave the abbey and village to the Trust in 1944. The village, which dates from the 13th century and has many limewashed half-timbered and stone houses, featured in the TV and film production of *Pride & Prejudice*, *Moll Flanders* and *Emma*.

Location: OS Ref. ST919 684. In the village of Lacock, 3m N of Melksham, 3m S of Chippenham just E of A350.

Opening Times: Museum, Cloisters & Garden: 3 Mar - 4 Nov: daily, 11am - 5.30pm (closed Good Fri). Abbey: 31 Mar - 4 Nov: daily except Tues & Good Fri, 1 - 5.30pm. Museum: open weekends in winter, closed 22 & 23 Dec - 30 Dec. Tel for details.

Admission: Abbey, Museum, Cloisters and Garden: Adult £6, Child £3.30, Family £16.30. Groups: Adult £5.50, Child £2.80. Garden, Cloisters & Museum only: Adult £3.80, Child £2.30, Family £10.90. Abbey & Garden only: Adult £4.80, Child £2.70, Family £12.30.

🏠 ♿ 📷 ✂ ❄ 🛡 Tel. for details.

LARMER TREE GARDENS

RUSHMORE ESTATE, TOLLARD ROYAL, SALISBURY, WILTSHIRE SP5 5PT

Owner: *Mr William Gronow Davis (Pitt-Rivers Trustees)* **Contact:** *Tracey Hartles*

Tel: 01725 516228 **Fax:** 01725 516449

Historical gardens of General Pitt Rivers, set high on the Cranborne Chase. One of the most unusual gardens in England containing an extraordinary collection of Colonial and Oriental buildings, a Roman Temple and Open air Theatre. Created in 1880, the gardens are recognised as one of national importance and hold a unique place in history. Regular concerts, festivals, exhibitions and meetings. Licensed wedding venue available for hire all year.

Location: OS Ref. ST943 169. Tollard Royal.

Opening Times: Easter Sun - end Oct. Closed Sats.

Admission: Adult £3.50, Child £1.50, OAP/Student £3. Booked groups (15+): Adult £3.25, Child £1.35, OAP/Student £2.75.

🏠 🚻 🍴 🍷 Licensed. Closed Mons & Tues. 🎥 By arrangement. 🅿
🍴 🐕 Guide dogs only. 🔔 🛡 Tel. for details.

LITTLE CLARENDON

Tel: 01985 843600

Dinton, Salisbury, Wiltshire SP3 5OZ

Owner: The National Trust **Contact:** The Regional Office

A Tudor house, but greatly altered in the 17th century. The principal rooms on the ground floor are open to visitors. There is also a 20th century Catholic chapel.

Location: OS Ref. SU015 316. ¼ m E of Dinton Church. 9m W of Salisbury.

Opening Times: 31 Mar - 29 Oct:, Sats, 10am - 1pm, Mons, 1 - 5pm.

Admission: £2, no reductions.

ⓘ No WC, no pushchairs or prams, no coaches. ♿ Unsuitable. Ⓟ At Dinton Post Office.

LONG HALL GARDENS

Tel: 01985 850424

Stockton, Warminster, Wiltshire BA12 0SE

Owner/Contact: N H Yeatman-Biggs Esq

4 acres of gardens. Long Hall Nursery is adjacent.

Location: OS Ref. ST982 381. Stockton 7m SE of Warminster, off A36, W of A303 Wylye interchange.

Opening Times: The gardens will be closed during 2001 except to groups by appointment, Mar - Aug.

Admission: Please contact for details.

LONGLEAT

See page 240 for full page entry.

LYDIARD PARK

LYDIARD TREGOZE, SWINDON, WILTSHIRE SN5 9PA

Owner: *Swindon Borough Council* **Contact:** *The Keeper*

Tel: 01793 770401 **Fax:** 01793 877909

Lydiard Park, ancestral home of the Bolingbrokes, is Swindon's treasure. Set in rolling lawns and woodland this beautifully restored Georgian mansion contains the family's furnishings and portraits, exceptional plasterwork, rare 17th century window and room devoted to 18th century society artist Lady Diana Spencer. Exceptional monuments such as the 'Golden Cavalier' in adjacent church.

Location: OS Ref. SU104 848. 4m W of Swindon, 1½ m N of M4/J16.

Opening Times: House: Mon - Fri, 10am - 1pm, 2 - 5pm, Sat & school summer holidays, 10am - 5pm, Sun, 2 - 5pm. Nov - Feb: early closing at 4pm. Grounds: all day, closing at dusk. Victorian Christmas decorations throughout December.

Admission: Adult £1.20, Child 60p (reviewed April 2000). Groups by appointment.

ⓘ No photography in house. 📷 ♿ 🖥 ⓧ By arrangement. 🎧
Ⓟ Limited for coaches. ▥ 🐕 In grounds on leads. ❄ 🍴 Tel. for details.
🌐

Website Index page 39 ◀◀◀

MOMPESSON HOUSE

NT Photographic Library.

THE CLOSE, SALISBURY, WILTSHIRE SP1 2EL

Owner: *The National Trust* **Contact:** *The Property Manager*

Tel: 01722 335659

Fine Queen Anne town house containing high quality 18th century furniture, ceramics and textiles. Also the renowned Turnbull Collection of 18th century drinking glasses. Tranquil walled garden with many perfumed plants. Garden tea room serves home-made cakes. Featured in *Sense and Sensibility*.

Location: OS Ref. SU142 295. On N side of Choristers' Green in Cathedral Close, near High Street Gate.

Opening Times: 31 Mar - 4 Nov: Sat - Wed, 12 noon - 5.30pm.

Admission: Adult £3.90, Child £1.95. Groups: £3.40. Garden only: 80p.

📷 ♿ Ground floor & grounds suitable. WC. 🖥 ✗

NEWHOUSE

REDLYNCH, SALISBURY, WILTSHIRE SP5 2NX

Owner: *George & June Jeffreys* **Contact:** *Mrs Jeffreys*

Tel: 01725 510055 **Fax:** 01725 510284

A brick, Jacobean 'Trinity' House, c1609, with two Georgian wings and a basically Georgian interior. Home of the Eyre family since 1633. Contents include costume, textiles and the Hare picture.

Location: OS184 Ref. SU218 214. 9m S of Salisbury between A36 & A338.

Opening Times: 2 Apr - 11 May: Mon - Fri, 2 - 5.30pm.

Admission: Adult £3.50, Child £2.50, Conc. £3.50. Groups (15+): Adult £3, Child £2.50, Conc. £3.

ⓘ No photography in house, except at weddings. 🍴 ♿ Not suitable.
ⓧ By arrangement. Ⓟ Limited for coaches. 🐕 Guide dogs only. 🔔

South West England

NORRINGTON MANOR

Tel: 01722 780367 **Fax:** 01722 780667

Alvediston, Salisbury, Wiltshire SP5 5LL

Owner/Contact: T Sykes

Built in 1377 it has been altered and added to in every century since, with the exception of the 18th century. Only the hall and the 'undercroft' remain of the original. It is currently a family home and the Sykes are only the third family to own it.

Location: OS Ref. ST966 237. Signposted to N of Berwick St John and Alvediston road (half way between the two villages)

Opening Times: By appointment in writing.

Admission: A donation to the local churches is asked for.

Not suitable. By arrangement. Limited for cars, none for coaches.

OLD SARUM

Tel: 01722 335398

Castle Road, Salisbury, Wiltshire SP1 3SD

Owner: English Heritage **Contact:** The Head Custodian

Built around 500BC by the iron age peoples, Old Sarum is the former site of the first cathedral and ancient city of Salisbury. A prehistoric hillfort in origin, Old Sarum was occupied by the Romans, the Saxons, and eventually the Normans who made it into one of their major strongholds, with a motte-and-bailey castle built at its centre. Old Sarum eventually grew into one of the most dramatic settlements in medieval England as castle, cathedral, bishop's palace and thriving township. When the new city we know as Salisbury was founded in the early 13th century the settlement faded away. With fine views of the surrounding countryside, Old Sarum is an excellent picnic spot.

Location: OS184 Ref. SU138 327. 2m N of Salisbury off A345.

Opening Times: 1 Apr - 31 Oct: daily, 10am - 6pm (5pm in Oct). 1 Nov - 31 Mar: daily 10am - 4pm. Closed 24 - 26 Dec & 1 Jan.

Admission: Adult £2, Child £1, Conc. £1.50. 15% discount for groups (11+).

Grounds suitable. In grounds, on leads. Tel. for details.

OLD WARDOUR CASTLE

Nr TISBURY, WILTSHIRE SP3 6RR

Owner: *English Heritage* **Contact:** *The Custodian*

Tel: 01747 870487

In a picture-book setting, the unusual hexagonal ruins of this 14th century castle stand on the edge of a beautiful lake, surrounded by landscaped grounds which include an elaborate rockwork grotto.

Location: OS184 Ref. ST939 263. Off A30 2m SW of Tisbury.

Open: 1 Apr - 31 Oct: daily, 10am - 6pm (5pm in Oct). 1 Nov - 31 Mar: Wed - Sun, 10am - 4pm. Closed for lunch 1 - 2pm. Closed 24 - 26 Dec & 1 Jan.

Admission: Adult £2.50, Child £1.30, Conc. £1.90. 15% discount for groups (11+).

Grounds suitable. In grounds, on leads. Tel. for details.

THE PETO GARDEN AT IFORD MANOR

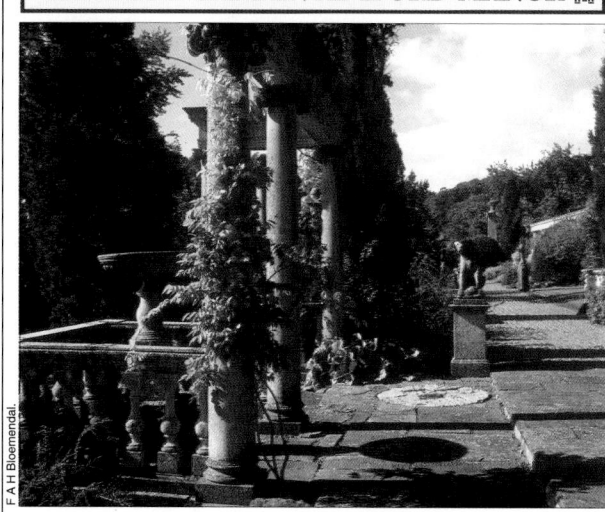

F A H Bloemendal.

BRADFORD-ON-AVON, WILTSHIRE BA14 2BA

Owner/Contact: *Mrs E A J Cartwright-Hignett*

Tel: 01225 863146 **Fax:** 01225 862364

This unique Grade I Italian-style garden is set on a romantic hillside beside the River Frome. Designed by the Edwardian architect Harold A Peto, who lived at Iford Manor from 1899 - 1933, the garden has terraces, a colonnade, cloister, casita, statuary, evergreen planting and magnificent rural views. Renowned for its tranquillity and peace, the Peto Garden won the 1998 HHA/Christie's Garden of the Year Award.

Location: OS Ref. ST800 589. 7m SE of Bath via A36, signposted Iford. 2m SW of Bradford-on-Avon via Westwood.

Opening Times: Apr & Oct: Suns only & Easter Mon, 2 - 5pm. May - Sept: Tue - Thur, Sats, Suns & BH Mons, 2 - 5pm. Coaches by appointment at other times. Children under 10yrs not admitted at weekends.

Admission: Adult £3, Child (10-16yrs)/OAP £2.50. Picnic area by River Frome.

Teas (May-Aug: Sats & Suns, 2 - 5pm). Coaches by appointment.

PHILIPPS HOUSE & DINTON PARK

Tel: 01985 843600

Dinton, Salisbury, Wiltshire SP3 5HJ

Owner: The National Trust **Contact:** The Regional Office

A neo-Grecian house by Jeffry Wyattville, completed in 1820. Principal rooms on ground floor are open and possess fine Regency furniture. Lovely walks in surrounding parkland.

Location: OS Ref. SU004 319. 9m W of Salisbury, N side of B3089, 1/2 m W of Little Clarendon. Car park off St Mary's Road next to church.

Opening Times: House: 31 Mar - 29 Oct: Mons, 1 - 5pm, Sats, 10am - 1pm. Park: All year: daily (may be closed for one day in Aug for music event).

Admission: House £3. Dinton Park Free.

No WC. House suitable, Park limited.

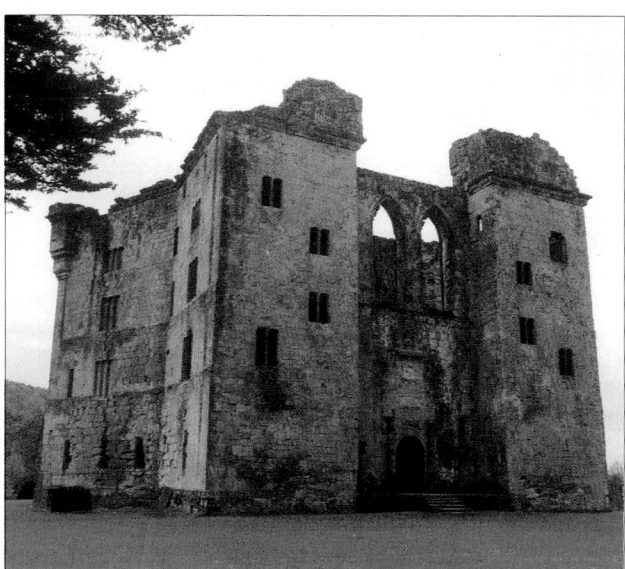

Patrick Lane.

Old Wardour Castle, Wiltshire

SALISBURY CATHEDRAL

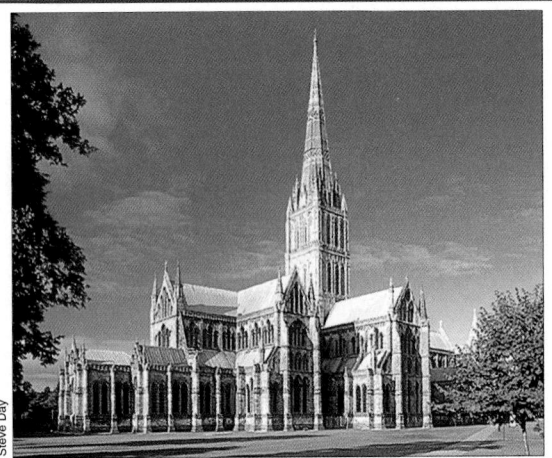

Steve Day

33 THE CLOSE, SALISBURY SP1 2EJ

Owner: The Dean & Chapter   *Contact: Visitor Services*

Tel: 01722 555120   **Fax:** 01722 555116   **e-mail:** visitors@salcath.co.uk

Salisbury Cathedral is a building of world importance. Set within the elegant splendour of the Cathedral Close it is probably the finest medieval building in Britain. Built in one phase from about 1220 to 1258 Britain's highest spire (123m/404ft) was added a generation later. Also, the best preserved Magna Carta, Europe's oldest working clock and a unique 13th century frieze of bible stories in the octagonal Chapter House. Boy and girl choristers sing daily services which follow a tradition of worship that goes back over 750 years. Join a tower tour climbing 332 steps to the base of the spire, and marvel at the medieval craftsmanship and the magnificent views.

Location: OS Ref. SU143 295. S of City. M3, A303, A30 from London or A36.

Open: All year: Every Sunday 7.15am - 6.15pm. Sept - May: Daily, 7.15am - 6.15pm. June - August: Daily, 7.15am - 8.15pm.

Admission: Donation: Adult £3.50, Child £2, Conc. £2.50, Family (2+2) £8.

🏠 🍵 ♿ 🍽 Licensed. 🍴 By arrangement. 🅿 In city centre. 🔲 In grounds, on leads. ❋ 🛡 Tel. for details. Ⓦ

STONEHENGE

© English Heritage Photo Library.

AMESBURY, WILTSHIRE SP4 7DE

Owner: English Heritage

Tel: 01980 624715 (Information Line)

The mystical and awe-inspiring stone circle at Stonehenge is one of the most famous prehistoric monuments in the world, designated by UNESCO as a World Heritage Site. Stonehenge's orientation on the rising and setting sun has always been one of its most remarkable features. Whether this was simply because the builders came from a sun-worshipping culture, or because – as some scholars have believed – the circle and its banks were part of a huge astronomical calendar, remains a mystery. Visitors to Stonehenge can discover the history and legends which surround this unique stone circle, which began over 5,000 years ago, with a complimentary three part audio tour available in 9 languages (subject to availability).

Location: OS Ref. SU123 422. 2m W of Amesbury on junction of A303 and A344/A360.

Opening Times: 16 - 23 Oct: 9.30am - 5pm, 24 Oct - 15 Mar: 9.30am - 4pm, 16 Mar - 31 May & 1 Sept - 15 Oct: 9.30am - 6pm. 1 Jun - 31 Aug: 9am - 7pm. Closed 24 - 26 Dec & 1 Jan. Last adm. is ¹/₂ hr before advertised closing times and the site will be closed promptly 20mins after the advertised closing times.

Admission: Adult £4.20, Child £2.20, Conc. £3.20. Family (2+3) £10.60. Groups (11+) 10% discount.

❋ 🛡 Tel. for details.

STOURHEAD

National Trust Photographic Library.

THE ESTATE OFFICE, STOURTON, Nr WARMINSTER BA12 6QD

Owner: The National Trust   *Contact: The Property Manager*

Tel: 01747 841152   **Fax:** 01747 841152 (office hours only)

An outstanding example of the English landscape style of garden. Designed by Henry Hoare II and laid out between 1741 and 1780. Classical temples, including the Pantheon and Temple of Apollo, are set around the central lake at the end of a series of vistas, which change as the visitor moves around the paths and through the magnificent mature woodland with its extensive collection of exotic trees. The house, begun in 1721 by Colen Campbell, contains furniture by the younger Chippendale and fine paintings. King Alfred's Tower, an intriguing red-brick folly built in 1772 by Henry Flitcroft, is almost 50m high and gives breathtaking views over the estate.

Location: OS183 Ref. ST778 341. At Stourton off the B3092, 3m N of A303 (Mere).

Opening Times: Garden: All year, daily, 9am - 7pm or sunset if earlier. House: 31 Mar - 4 Nov: daily (except Thur & Fri), 12 noon - 5.30pm or dusk. King Alfred's Tower: 31 Mar - 4 Nov: daily except Mon (open BH Mons). Times: Tue - Fri, 2 - 5.30pm; Sats, Suns & BH Mons: 11.30am - 5.30pm or dusk.

Admission: House & Garden: Adult £8.50, Child £4, Family £20. Booked groups (15+) by appointment: £8. House or Garden: Mar - Oct: Adult £4.80, Child £2.60, Family £12, Booked groups: £4.30. Garden only: Nov - end Feb: Adult £3.70, Child £1.80, Family £9. Booked groups: £3.50. King Alfred's Tower: Adult £1.60, Child 80p, Family £4.

ℹ Exhibition in Reception Building. 🏠 ♿ Wheelchair accessible. 🅿 🔲 🔲 ❋ 🛡 Tel. for details.

STOURTON HOUSE FLOWER GARDEN   **Tel:** 01747 840417

Zeals, Warminster, Wiltshire BA12 6QF

Owner/Contact: Mrs E Bullivant

Four acres of peaceful, romantic garden where grass paths lead through unique daffodils, spring flowers, camellias, azaleas, delphiniums, hydrangeas and hedged borders. Homemade refreshments.

Location: OS Ref. ST780 340. 2m NW of Mere next to Stourhead car park, A303. Follow blue signs.

Opening Times: Apr - end Nov: Weds, Thurs, Suns, and BH Mons, 11am - 6pm. Plants & dried flowers for sale during the winter on weekdays.

Admission: Please contact property for details. Group guided tours by appointment.

WESTWOOD MANOR   **Tel:** 01225 863374

Bradford-on-Avon, Wiltshire BA15 2AF

Owner: The National Trust   **Contact:** The Tenant

A 15th century stone manor house, altered in the early 17th century, with late gothic and Jacobean windows and fine plasterwork. There is a modern topiary garden. Note: Westwood Manor is administered for The National Trust by the tenant.

Location: OS Ref. ST813 589. 1¹/₂m SW of Bradford-on-Avon, in Westwood village, beside the church.

Opening Times: 1 Apr - 30 Sept: Suns, Tues & Weds, 2 - 5pm.

Admission: £3.80. No reduction for groups or children.

ℹ No WC. ♿ Not suitable. 🅿 Limited. 🔲

WILTON HOUSE   See page 241 for full page entry.

Longleat, Wiltshire.

Helmingham Hall Gardens, Suffolk

Eastern Region

Helmingham Hall

Helmingham 'both grand and lovable' – Sir Nikolaus Pevsner

The approach to Helmingham Hall is one of the loveliest in England. The drive winds across an ancient, oak studded, 400 acre deer park where large herds of red and fallow deer still graze.

Helmingham Hall and the Tollemache family have been together for nearly 500 years, but it was not until 1510 that the present redbrick house was built. Although subsequent generations have added to and altered the house and its garden over the centuries, both retain a strong Elizabethan character.

Helmingham's romantic moat, with two drawbridges that are pulled up every night as they have been since 1510, fine barley twist chimneys, gables and decorative finials, provide the visitor with a wonderful timeless and secure atmosphere. It is, though, mainly due to the present Lord and Lady Tollemache that we owe the exquisitely planted gardens which clothe this early Tudor house.

Moated, like the house, the main part of the garden is reached by crossing a bridge, but between this and the elegant gates of the original walled kitchen garden is lawn patterned with a parterre of box-edged beds. Redesigned in 1978, the permanent planting of box hedging is infilled with *santolina incana*. Beyond the parterre and surrounding it on three sides is a rose garden planted in 1965 by Dinah, Lady Tollemache, mother of the present Lord Tollemache. The rose garden billows with an immense collection of hybrid musk roses edged with Hidcote lavender and underplanted with London Pride.

The cruciform herbaceous borders are the highlight of the walled kitchen garden. After finding old plans for this garden, in 1986 the garden was again divided into eight sections. The visitor can now wander through cross-paths planted with runner beans, sweet peas and gourds. Behind the garden's deep borders are walls covered in a rich combination of climbing roses, interplanted with clematis, hoheria and everlasting pea, to span the flowering times of the roses.

Two bridges lead out of the walled garden: an ancient one that takes visitors to the Apple Walk and a new bridge leading into the wild flower garden and orchard. This area of the garden, with cut paths making a walkway through long grass filled with cowslips, ox-eye daisies and orchids, provides a soft gentle contrast to the highly cultivated, more formal areas of Helmingham.

In 1982 Lord and Lady Tollemache decided to create a new garden historically sympathetic to the house – the result, a herb and knot garden stands on the far side of the house. These beautiful box-edged knot patterns are filled with herbs and flowers which were introduced to Britain before 1750 and, as with every other area of the gardens at Helmingham, they are an example of the perfectionist's eye. Beyond a wall of *rosa mundi* lie beds of old roses set against a tall yew hedge where a statue of Flora serenely surveys the scene.

The parks and gardens at Helmingham Hall are truly a gem, and richly deserve the Grade I status awarded by English Heritage.

For further details about *Helmingham Hall Gardens* see entry in Eastern Region ➜ Suffolk.

WOBURN ABBEY
Woburn

Owner: Trustees of Bedford Estates

CONTACT

William Lash
Woburn Abbey
Woburn
Bedfordshire
MK17 9WA

Tel: 01525 290666

Fax: 01525 290271

e-mail: enquiries@ woburnabbey.co.uk

LOCATION

OS Ref. SP965 325

On A4012, midway between M1/J13, 3m, J14, 6m and the A5 (turn off at Hockliffe). London approx. 1hr by road (43m).

Rail: London Euston to Leighton Buzzard, Bletchley/Milton Keynes. Kings Cross Thameslink to Flitwick.

Air: Luton 14m. Heathrow 39m.

Set in a beautiful 3,000 acre deer park, Woburn Abbey has been the home of the Dukes of Bedford for nearly 400 years. It is now lived in by the present Duke's heir, the Marquess of Tavistock and his family. One of the most important private art collections in the world can be seen here, including paintings by Van Dyck, Cuyp, Gainsborough, Reynolds and Velazquez. In the Venetian Room there are 21 views of Venice by Canaletto. The collection also features French and English 18th century furniture and silver. The tour of the Abbey covers three floors, including vaults, where the fabulous Sèvres dinner service presented to the 4th Duke by Louis XV of France is on display.

The deer park has nine species of deer, roaming freely. One of these, the Père David, descended from the Imperial Herd of China, was saved from extinction at Woburn and is now the largest breeding herd of this species in the world. In 1985 22 Père David were given by the Family to the People's Republic of China and these are now successfully re-established in their natural habitat and number several hundred.

We carry out catering ourselves with banqueting, conferences, receptions and company days out our specialities in the beautiful setting of the Sculpture Gallery, overlooking the Private Gardens. It is also a popular choice for wedding receptions and we hold a Civil Wedding Licence.

There are extensive picnic areas. Events are held in the Park throughout the summer including the Woburn Garden Show, Craft Fair and the annual fly-in of the de Havilland Moth Club. The 40-shop Antique Centre is probably the most unusual such centre outside London.

❖

ℹ️ Suitable for fashion shows, product launches, filming & company 'days out'. Use of parkland and garden. No photography in House.

🛍️ Two shops.

🍽️ Conferences, exhibitions, banqueting, luncheons, dinners in the Sculpture Gallery, Lantern & Long Harness rooms.

♿ Wheelchairs in the Abbey by prior arrangement (max. 8 per group).

🍴 Licensed. 📷 Group bookings in Sculpture Gallery. Flying Duchess Pavilion Coffee Shop.

🎧🚶 By arrangement, max 15. Tours in French, German & Dutch at an additional charge of £10.00 per guide. Audio tape tour available – £1pp. Lectures on the property, its contents, gardens and history can be arranged.

🅿️ Ample. Free.

🏫 Welcome. Special programme on request. Cost: £2.50pp (group rate).

🐕 In park on leads, and guide dogs in house.

🔔 Civil Wedding Licence. ❄️

CONFERENCE/FUNCTION

ROOM	SIZE	MAX CAPACITY
Sculpture Gallery	130' x 25'	400 / 220 (sit-down)
Lantern Rm	24' x 21'	100

OPENING TIMES

1 January - 25 March
Abbey: weekends only 11am - 4pm*
Deer Park: Daily 10.30am - 3.45pm

26 March - 30 September
Abbey:
Mon - Sat: 11am - 4pm*
Sun & BHs: 11am - 5pm
Deer Park:
Mon - Sat: 10am - 4.30pm
Sun & BHs: 10am - 4.45pm

1 Oct - 28 Oct
Abbey: weekends only 11am - 5pm*
Deer Park:
10.30am - 4.45pm

Abbey closed:
29 Oct - end Dec

Antiques Centre:
All year, daily (except 24 - 26, 31 Dec 2000 & 1 Jan, 24 - 26 Dec 2001).

*last entry time

ADMISSION

Woburn Abbey
(Prices incl. Private Apts)
Adult £7.50
Child (12 - 16yrs) £2.50
OAP £6.50
Group rates & family tickets available.

Antiques Centre ..... Free

Grounds & Deer Park only
Car £5.00
Motorcycle £2.00
Coaches .... Free
Other £0.50
Visitors from Safari Park .... Free

Reduced rates apply when Private Apartments are in use by the family.

🛡️ SPECIAL EVENTS

Please telephone for details.

BROMHAM WATERMILL & ART GALLERY

Tel: 01234 824330

Bromham, Bedfordshire MK43 8LP

Owner: Bedfordshire County Council **Contact:** Sally Wileman

Working water mill on River Ouse. Flour milling.

Location: OS Ref. TL010 506. Location beside the River Ouse bridge on N side of the former A428, 2¹/₂ m W of Bedford.

Opening Times: Wed - Sat, 12 noon - 4pm. Suns, 10.30am - 5pm. Last entry 30 mins before closing.

Admission: Please telephone for admission prices.

BUSHMEAD PRIORY ⬥

Tel: 01234 376614

Colmworth, Bedford, Bedfordshire MK44 2LD **Regional Office:** 01223 582700

Owner: English Heritage **Contact:** The Custodian

A rare survival of the medieval refectory of an Augustinian priory, with its original timber-framed roof almost intact and containing interesting wall paintings and stained glass.

Location: OS Ref. TL115 607. On unclassified road near Colmworth; off B660, 2m S of Bolnhurst. 5m W of St. Neots (A1).

Opening Times: Jul - Aug weekends & BHs only: 10am - 6pm. Closed 1 - 2pm.

Admission: Adult £2, Child £1, Conc. £1.50.

🅿 ✖

CECIL HIGGINS ART GALLERY

CASTLE CLOSE, CASTLE LANE, BEDFORD MK40 3RP

Owner: Bedford Borough Council & Trustees of Gallery *Contact: The Gallery*

Tel: 01234 211222 **Fax:** 01234 327149 **e-mail:** chag@bedford.gov.uk

An unusual combination of recreated Victorian Mansion (originally the home of the Higgins family, wealthy Bedford brewers) and adjoining modern gallery housing internationally renowned collection of watercolours, prints and drawings, ceramics and glass. Room settings include many items from the Handley-Read Collection and furniture by Victorian architect William Burges. Situated in pleasant gardens near the river embankment.

Location: OS Ref. TL052 497. Centre of Bedford, just off The Embankment. E of High St.

Opening Times: Tue - Sat, 11am - 5pm (last admission 4.45pm). Sun & BH Mons, 2 - 5pm. Closed Mons, Good Fri & 25/26 Dec.

Admission: Adults £2, Conc. Free (includes visit to Bedford Museum).

ℹ️ Photography in house by arrangement. 📷 ☕ By arrangement.
♿ House & garden suitable. WC. ☕ By arrangement. 🎭 By arrangement.
🅿 No parking. 🍴 🐕 Guide dogs only. ❄ 🛡 Telephone for details.

DE GREY MAUSOLEUM ⬥

Tel: 01525 860094 (Key-keeper)

Flitton, Bedford, Bedfordshire

Owner: English Heritage **Contact:** Mrs Stimson

A remarkable treasure-house of sculpted tombs and monuments from the 16th to 19th centuries dedicated to the de Grey family of nearby Wrest Park.

Location: OS Ref. TL059 359. Attached to the church on unclassified road 1¹/₂ m W of A6 at Silsoe.

Opening Times: Weekends only. Key: Mrs Stimson, 3 Highfield Rd, Flitton.

Admission: Free.

HOUGHTON HOUSE ⬥

Tel: 01223 582700

Ampthill, Bedford, Bedfordshire

Owner: English Heritage **Contact:** The East of England Regional Office

Reputedly the inspiration for "House Beautiful" in Bunyan's "Pilgrim's Progress", the remains of this early 17th century mansion still convey elements which justify the description, including work attributed to Inigo Jones.

Location: OS Ref. TL039 394. 1m NE of Ampthill off A421, 8m S of Bedford, then by footpath to NE.

Opening Times: Any reasonable time.

Admission: Free.

LUTON MUSEUM & ART GALLERY

Tel: 01582 546739

Wardown Park, Luton, Bedfordshire

Owner: Luton Borough Council **Contact:** Lynette Burgess

Lively and varied collections housed in an impressive Victorian Mansion set in Wardown Park.

Location: OS Ref. TL089 230. 1¹/₄ m N of town centre between New and Old Bedford Rd.

Opening Times: Tue - Sat, 10am - 5pm, Suns, 1 - 5pm. Closed 25/26 Dec & New Year's Day.

Admission: Free.

MOOT HALL

Tel: 01234 266889

Elstow Green, Church View, Elstow, Bedford

Owner: Bedfordshire County Council

Timber framed market hall.

Location: OS Ref. TL048 475. 1m from Bedford, signposted from A6.

Opening Times: Apr - Oct: Tue, Wed, Thur, Sat, Sun & BHs: 2 - 5pm.

Admission: Adult £1, Conc. 50p.

STOCKWOOD PERIOD GARDENS

Tel: 01582 546739

Farley Hill, Luton, Bedfordshire

Owner: Luton Borough Council **Contact:** Lynette Burgess

Includes Knot, Medieval, Victorian and Italian gardens.

Location: OS Ref. TL085 200. 1¹/₄ m SW of Luton town centre by Farley Road B4546.

Opening Times: Apr - Oct: Tue - Sun & BHs, 10am - 5pm. Nov - Mar: Sat - Sun, 10am - 4pm.

Admission: Free.

SWISS GARDEN

Tel: 01767 627666 **Fax:** 01767 627443

Old Warden Park, Bedfordshire

Operated By: Bedfordshire County Council

Laid out in the early 1800s and steeped in the indulgent romanticism of the time, Swiss Garden combines all the elements of high fashion: formal walks and vistas, classical proportions, tiny thatched buildings, woodland glades and, hidden away, a fairytale grotto with a brilliant glazed fernery, magnificent trees and a network of ponds and bridges. Shuttleworth Mansion, home of the family that owned Swiss Garden, is open on a number of days during the year. Cream teas are served during the summer on the lawn beside the house.

Location: OS Ref. TL150 447. 1¹/₂ m W of Biggleswade A1 roundabout, signposted from A1 and A600. Approached from Shuttleworth Mansion, Old Warden Park.

Opening Times: Mar - Sept: Sun & BHs, 10am - 6pm. Weekdays & Sat: 1 - 6pm. Jan, Feb & Oct: Suns & New Year's Day, 11am - 3pm. Last admission ³/₄ hr before closing. Groups at any time on request.

Admission: Adult £3, Conc. £2, Family £8. Season ticket available. Special rates for groups and guided tours.

♿ ☕ Catering. Cream teas during summer. 🍴 ❄

WOBURN ABBEY

See page 254 for full page entry.

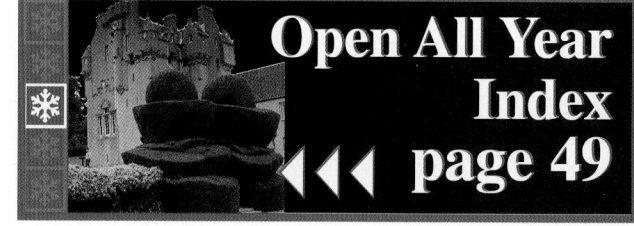

Open All Year
Index
◀◀◀ **page 49**

WREST PARK GARDENS

SILSOE, LUTON, BEDFORDSHIRE MK45 4HS

Owner: *English Heritage* **Contact:** *The Custodian*

Tel: 01525 860152

Over 90 acres of wonderful gardens originally laid out in the early 18th century, including the Great Garden. During the 18th and 19th centuries the formal parterre was introduced together with marble fountains, the Bath House and the vast Orangery, built by the Earl de Grey. The gardens form a delightful backdrop to the house, built in the style of an 18th century French chateau.

Location: OS153, Ref. TL093 356. ³/₄ m E of Silsoe off A6, 10m S of Bedford.

Opening Times: 1 Apr - 31 Oct: Weekends and BHs only, 10am - 6pm (5pm in Oct). Last admission 1hr before closing time.

Admission: Adult £3.50, Child £1.75, Conc. £2.65. 15% discount for groups (11+). Family Ticket £8.75.

♿ ☕ 🛡 Telephone for details.

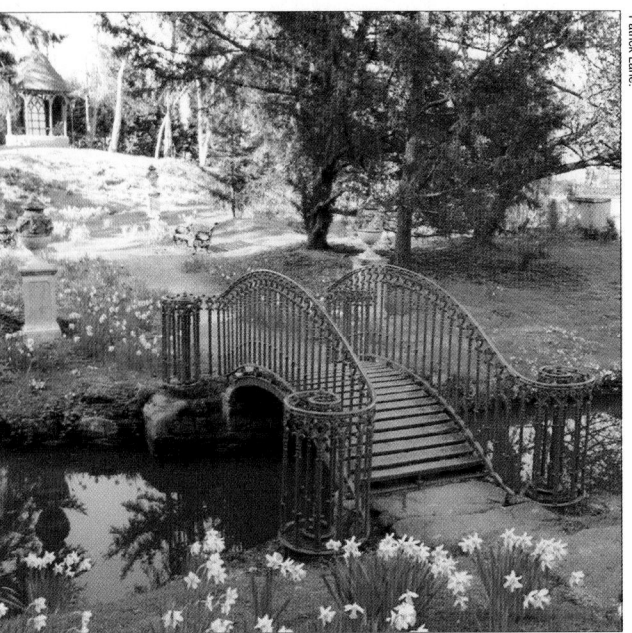

Swiss Garden, Bedfordshire.

Patrick Lane.

Website Index page 39 ◀◀◀

Woburn Abbey Grotto, Bedfordshire.

Woburn Abbey, Bedfordshire.

ANGLESEY ABBEY

LODE, CAMBRIDGE, CAMBRIDGESHIRE CB5 9EJ

Owner: The National Trust   Contact: The Property Manager

Tel/Fax: 01223 811200

Dating from 1600, the house, built on the site of an Augustinian priory, contains the famous Fairhaven collection of paintings and furniture. Surrounded by an outstanding 100 acre garden and arboretum, with a wonderful display of hyacinths in spring and magnificent herbaceous borders and a dahlia garden in summer. A watermill in full working order is demonstrated on the first Saturday in each month.

Location: OS Ref 154. TL533 622. In Lode village, 6m NE of Cambridge on B1102, signs from A14.

Opening Times: House: 28 Mar - 21 Oct: Wed - Sun & BH Mons, 1 - 5pm (Noon opening for pre-booked groups). Garden: 28 Mar - 1 Jul: Wed - Sun; 2 Jul - 9 Sept: daily; 12 Sept - 21 Oct: Wed - Sun, 10.30am - 5.30pm. Winter Season: 24 Oct - 23 Dec; 2 Jan - 24 Feb 2002: Wed - Sun, 10.30am - 4.30pm. Mar 2002 until 5.30pm. Lode Mill: As garden except 1 - 4.30pm. Winter season: Sats & Suns only, 11am - 4pm. Last admission to house & Mill 4.30pm (Mar - Oct). Timed entry to house on Suns & BH Mons. Closed Good Fri. Winter season part of gardens only.

Admission: House & garden: £6.25, Family discounts. Groups: £5. Garden & Mill only: £3.85 (groups £3.25). Group visit information pack (no groups Suns & BH Mons).

🖼 ♿Partially suitable. 🍴Licensed. 🐕In park, on leads. ❄
📺 Tel. for details.

CAMBRIDGE UNIVERSITY BOTANIC GARDEN

Bateman Street, Cambridge CB2 1JF

Owner: University of Cambridge   Contact: Mrs B Stacey, Administrative Secretary

Tel: 01223 336265 **Fax:** 01223 336278 **e-mail:** gardens@hermes.cam.ac.uk

40 acres of outstanding gardens with lake and glasshouses, near the centre of Cambridge, incorporating nine National collections, including Geranium and Fritillaria. Café and shop in the Gilmour building.

Location: OS Ref. TL453 573. 1m S of Cambridge city centre, off A1309 (Trumpington Rd).

Opening Times: Daily (except Christmas Day & Boxing Day), 10am - 6pm (Summer), 10am - 5pm (Spring & Autumn) 10am - 4pm (Winter). Glasshouses: daily, 10am - 3.45pm. Tours by arrangement.

Admission: Admission charged weekdays Mar - Oct inclusive, plus weekends & BHs all year.

🖼 ♿Grounds suitable. WCs. 📷 🅿 Street/Pay & Display.
🐕Guide dogs only. ❄

OLIVER CROMWELL'S HOUSE   **Tel:** 01353 662062 **Fax:** 01353 668518

29 St Mary's Street, Ely, Cambridgeshire CB7 4HF   e-mail: elytic@compuserve.com

Owner: East Cambridgeshire District Council   **Contact:** Mrs A Smith

The former home of the Lord Protector.

Location: OS Ref. TL538 803. N of Cambridge, ¼ m W of Ely Cathedral.

Opening Times: 1 Oct - 31 Mar, Mon - Sat, 10am - 5pm, Suns, 12 noon - 4pm. 1 Apr -30 Sept: daily, 10am - 5.30pm.

Admission: Adult £2.70, Conc. £2.20, Family £7. Joint Ticket (including Cathedral, Ely Museum and the Stained Glass Museum): Adult £8, Conc. £6. Group prices on application. (2000 prices - please confirm before visit).

DENNY ABBEY & THE FARMLAND MUSEUM ⌗

Ely Road, Chittering, Waterbeach, Cambridgeshire CB5 9TQ   Tel: 01223 860489

Owner: English Heritage/Managed by the Farmland Museum Trust **Contact:** The Custodian

What at first appears to be an attractive stone-built farmhouse is actually the remains of a 12th century Benedictine abbey which, at different times, also housed the Knights Templar and Franciscan nuns. Founded by the Countess of Pembroke.

Location: OS Ref. TL495 684. 6m N of Cambridge on the E side of the A10.

Opening Times: 1 Apr - 31 Oct: 12 noon - 5pm..

Admission: Adult £3.50, Child £1.30, Conc. £2.50, Family £8.30.

DOCWRA'S MANOR GARDEN 🏛   **Tel:** 01763 261473 **Fax:** 01763 260677

Shepreth, Royston, Hertfordshire SG8 6PS

Owner: Mrs Faith Raven   **Contact:** Peter Rocket

Extensive garden around building dating from the 18th century.

Location: OS Ref. TL393 479. In Shepreth via A10 from Royston.

Opening Times: All year: Weds & Fris, 10am - 4pm & 1st Sun in month from Apr - Oct: 2 - 5pm.

Admission: £3.

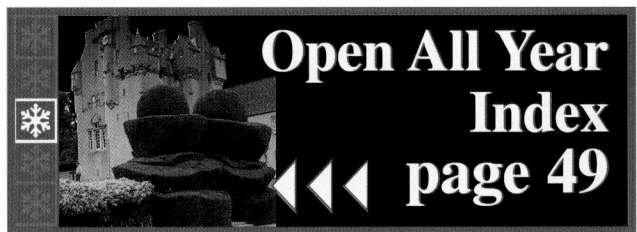

❄ **Open All Year**
Index
◄◄◄ **page 49**

Docwra's Manor, Cambridgeshire.

ELTON HALL

Nr PETERBOROUGH PE8 6SH

Owner: *Mr & Mrs W Proby*   **Contact:** *The Administrator*

Tel: 01832 280468 **Fax:** 01832 280584 **e-mail:** office@eltonhall.com

Elton Hall, the home of the Proby family for over 350 years is a fascinating mixture of styles. Every room contains treasures, magnificent furniture and fine paintings from the early 15th century. The library is one of the finest in private hands and includes Henry VIII's prayer book. The beautiful gardens have been carefully restored, with the addition of a new gothic Orangery to celebrate the Millennium.

Location: OS Ref. TL091 930. Close to A1 in the village of Elton, off A605 Peterborough - Oundle road.

Opening Times: 27/28 May. Jun: Weds. Jul & Aug: Wed, Thur & Sun. Plus Aug BH Mon. 2 - 5pm. Private groups by arrangement on weekdays Apr - Sept.

Admission: Hall & Gardens: Adult £5, Child (accompanied) Free. Gardens only: Adult £2.50, Child (accompanied) Free.

ⓘ No photography in house. Hall not suitable. Obligatory. Guide dogs in gardens only. Tel. for details.

ISLAND HALL

GODMANCHESTER, CAMBRIDGESHIRE PE29 2BA

Owner: *Mr Christopher & Lady Linda Vane Percy*   **Contact:** *Mr C Vane Percy*

Tel: 020 7491 3724 **Fax:** 020 7355 4006

An important mid 18th century mansion of great charm, owned and restored by an award-winning interior designer. This family home has lovely Georgian rooms, with fine period detail, and interesting possessions relating to the owners' ancestors since their first occupation of the house in 1800. A tranquil riverside setting with formal gardens and ornamental island forming part of the grounds in an area of Best Landscape. Octavia Hillwrote "*This is the loveliest, dearest old house, I never was in such a one before.*"

Location: OS Ref. TL244 706. Centre of Godmanchester, Post Street next to car park. 1m S of Huntingdon, 15m NW of Cambridge A14.

Opening Times: Groups only, by arrangement: May - Jul & Sept.

Admission: (30+) Adult £3.50, (15-30 persons) Adult £4. Under 15 persons, min charge £60 per group (sorry but no children under 13).

Not suitable. Home made teas.

KIMBOLTON CASTLE

Tel: 01480 860505 **Fax:** 01480 861763

Kimbolton, Huntingdon, Cambridgeshire PE28 0EA

Owner: Governors of Kimbolton School   **Contact:** Mr J Mcleod

A late Stuart house, an adaptation of a 13th century fortified manor house, with evidence of Tudor modifications. The seat of the Earls and Dukes of Manchester 1615 - 1950, now a school. Katharine of Aragon died in the Queen's Room - the setting for a scene in Shakespeare's *Henry VIII*. A minor example of the work of Vanbrugh and Hawksmoor; Gatehouse by Robert Adam; the Pellegrini mural paintings on the Staircase, in the Chapel and in the Boudoir are the best examples in England of this gifted Venetian decorator.

Location: OS Ref. TL101 676. 7m NW of St Neots on B645.

Opening Times: 15/16 Apr, 27/28 May, 29 Jul & 5, 12, 19, 26/27 Aug: 2 - 6pm.

Admission: Adult £2.50, Child/Conc. £1.50. Groups by arrangement.

Not suitable. By arrangement. On leads in grounds.

Kimbolton Castle, Cambridgeshire.

Patrick Lane.

KING'S COLLEGE

KING'S PARADE, CAMBRIDGE CB2 1ST

Owner: *Provost and Fellows*   **Contact:** *Mr D Buxton*

Tel/Fax: 01223 331212 **e-mail:** chapel.shop@kings.cam.ac.uk

Visitors are welcome, but remember that this is a working college. Please respect the privacy of those who work, live and study here. The Chapel is often used for services, recordings, broadcasts, etc, and ideally visitors should check before arriving. Recorded message for services, concerts and visiting times: 01223 331155.

Location: OS Ref. TL447 584.

Opening Times: Out of term: Mon - Sat, 9.30am - 4.30pm. Sun, 10am - 5pm. In term: Mon - Fri: 9.30am - 3.30pm. Sat: 9.30am - 3.15pm. Sun: 1.15 - 2.15pm, 5 - 5.30pm.

Admission: Adult £3.50, Child (12-17yrs)/Student (ID required) £2.50, OAP £3.50. Child (under 12 & accompanied) Free.

ⓘ No photography inside Chapel. Conferences. By arrangement. By arrangement. No parking. Guide dogs only.

LONGTHORPE TOWER

Tel: 01733 268482

Thorpe Rd, Longthorpe, Cambridgeshire PE1 1HA

Owner: English Heritage   **Contact:** The Custodian

The finest example of 14th century domestic wall paintings in northern Europe showing a variety of secular and sacred objects. The tower, with the Great Chamber that contains the paintings, is part of a fortified manor house. Special exhibitions are held on the upper floor.

Location: OS Ref. TL163 983. 2m W of Peterborough just off A47.

Opening Times: 1 Apr - 31 Oct: weekends & BHs only: 12 noon - 5pm.

Admission: Adult £1.60, Child 80p, Conc. £1.20.

THE MANOR, HEMINGFORD GREY

HUNTINGDON, CAMBRIDGESHIRE PE28 9BN

Owner: Mrs D S Boston   *Contact: Diana Boston*

Tel: 01480 463134 **Fax:** 01480 465026

Built about 1130 and made famous as 'Green Knowe' by the author Lucy Boston. Her patchworks are also shown. Four acre garden with topiary and old roses.

Location: OS Ref. TL290 706. Off A14, 3m SE of Huntingdon. 12m NW of Cambridge. Access is by a small gate on the riverside footpath.

Opening Times: House: All year (except Aug), by appointment only to individuals or groups. Aug: open access. Guided tours at 10am, 12 noon, 2pm & 4pm. Small house so tour size is limited. Advisable to book to avoid disappointment. Garden: All year, daily, 10am - 6pm (4pm in winter).

Admission: Adult £4, Child £1.50, OAP £3.50. Garden only: Adult £1, Child 50p.

ⓘ No photography in house. 　 🖭 🌱 🛍 Locally, by arrangement. 🎟 Obligatory. 　 🍴 🅿 Disabled only. 　 🐕 In garden, on leads. ❋

PECKOVER HOUSE & GARDEN 🍂

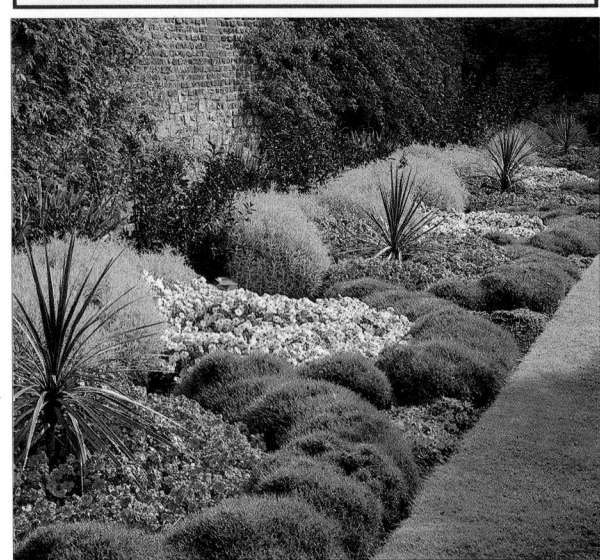

NORTH BRINK, WISBECH, CAMBRIDGESHIRE PE13 1JR

Owner: The National Trust   *Contact: The Property Manager*

Tel/Fax: 01945 583463 **e-mail:** aprigx@smtp.ntrust.org.uk

A town house, built c1722 and renowned for its very fine plaster and wood rococo decoration. The outstanding Victorian garden includes an orangery, summer-houses, roses, herbaceous borders, fernery, croquet lawn and reed barn.

Location: OS Ref. TF458 097. On N bank of River Nene, in Wisbech B1441.

Opening Times: House: 31 Mar - 30 Sept: Weds, Sats, Suns & BH Mons, 12.30 - 5.30pm. 3 Oct - 4 Nov: 12.30 - 4pm. Garden: 31 Mar - 4 Nov: Sat - Thur, 12.30 - 5.30pm. Groups welcome when house open and at other times by appointment.

Admission: Adult £3.80. Garden only: £2.50. Groups: £3.

🍴 🅳 Partially suitable. 　 🛍 🎟 By arrangement. 🅿 Signposted. 🎦 🔊 🛡 Tel. for details.

PETERBOROUGH CATHEDRAL   **Tel:** 01733 343342 **Fax:** 01733 552465

Peterborough, Cambridgeshire PE1 1XS   **Contact:** Visitors' Officer

One of the finest Norman buildings in Europe, with a magnificent early English West Front. The 13th century painted Nave ceiling is the largest in the world. Admire the exquisite fan vaulting. You may also visit the tomb of Katharine of Aragon, the first wife of Henry VIII, and see the former burial place of Mary, Queen of Scots. Tourist Information Centre is also in the Cathedral precincts.

Location: OS Ref. TL194 986. 4m E of A1, in City Centre.

Opening Times: All year: daily, 8.30am - 5.15pm. Sats, 8.30am - 5.45pm. Suns, 12 noon - 5.45pm.

Admission: Donations are requested.

ⓘ Visitors' Centre. 　 🖭 🅳 🛍 Mon - Sat. 🎟 By arrangement. 🅿 No parking. 🎦 🐕 Guide dogs only. ❋

RAMSEY ABBEY GATEHOUSE 🍂   **Tel:** 01263 733471 (Regional office)

Abbey School, Ramsey, Cambridgeshire PE17 1DH

Owner: The National Trust   **Contact:** The Curator (in writing)

Remains of a 15th century gatehouse of the Benedictine Abbey.

Location: OS Ref. TL291 851. At SE edge of Ramsey at point where Chatteris road leaves B1096, 10m SE of Peterborough.

Opening Times: 1 Apr - end Oct: daily, 10am - 5pm, other times by written application to curator.

Admission: Donation.

🅿 Limited. 　 🐕 Guide dogs only.

WIMPOLE HALL & HOME FARM 🍂

ARRINGTON, ROYSTON, CAMBRIDGESHIRE SG8 0BW

Owner: The National Trust   *Contact: The Property Manager*

Tel: 01223 207257 **Fax:** 01223 207838 **e-mail:** aweusr@smtp.ntrust.org.uk

Wimpole is a magnificent country house built in 18th century style with a colourful history of owners. The Hall is set in recently restored formal gardens including parterres and a rose garden. Home Farm is a working farm and is the largest rare breeds centre in East Anglia.

Location: OS154 Ref. TL336 510. 8m SW of Cambridge (A603), 6m N of Royston (A1198).

Opening Times: Hall: 17 Mar - 30 Jul & 2 Sept - 4 Nov: daily except Mons & Fris open Good Fri & BH Mons. Aug: Tue - Sun & BH Mons; 11, 18 & 25 Nov: Suns only. 1 - 5pm. BH Mons: 11am - 5pm. Closes 4pm after 28 Oct. Garden: As Farm. Park: dawn - dusk (closed 5pm on concert nights). Farm: 17 Mar - 2 Jul, 1 Sept - 4 Nov: daily except Mons & Fris (open Good Fri & BH Mons); Jul & Aug: Tue - Sun (open BH Mons), 10.30am - 5pm. Nov - Mar 2002: Sats & Suns (open Feb half-term week), 11am - 4pm.

Admission: Hall: Adult £5.90, Child £2.70. Joint ticket with Home Farm: Adult £8.50, Child £4.20, Family £21. Garden: £2.50. Group rates (not on Suns or BH Mons). Farm: Adult £4.70, Child (over 3yrs) £2.70. Discounts for NT members (not Suns or BH Mons).

🖭 🅳 Partially suitable. 　 🛍 🍴 Licensed. 🎟 By arrangement. 🅿 Limited. 　 🎦 🐕 In park only, on leads. 🛡 Tel. for details.

HUDSON'S

ESSEX

Eastern Region
England

English Heritage Photo Library.

AUDLEY END HOUSE & GDNS ⌗
Saffron Walden

AUDLEY END was a palace in all but name. Built by Thomas Howard, Earl of Suffolk, to entertain King James I. The King may have had his suspicions, for he never stayed there; in 1618 Howard was imprisoned and fined for embezzlement.

Charles II bought the property in 1668 for £50,000, but within a generation the house was gradually demolished, and by the 1750s it was about the size you see today. There are still over 30 rooms to see, each with period furnishings.

The house and its gardens, including a 19th century parterre and rose garden, are surrounded by an 18th century landscaped park laid out by 'Capability' Brown.

Visitors can now also visit the working organic walled garden and purchase produce from its shop. Extending to nearly 10 acres the garden includes a 170ft long, five-bay vine house, built in 1802.

❖

Owner:
English Heritage

CONTACT

The General Manager
Audley End House
Audley End
Saffron Walden
Essex
CB11 4JF

Tel: 01799 522842

Fax: 01799 521276

LOCATION

OS Ref. TL525 382

1m W of Saffron Walden
on B1383,
M11/J8 & 9 northbound
only & J10.

Rail: Audley End 1¼m.

English Heritage Photo Library

OPENING TIMES

House
1 April - 30 September
Wed - Sun and BHs
1 - 6pm.
Last admission 5pm.

Grounds
1 April - 30 September
Wed - Sun and BHs
11am - 6pm.
Last admission 5pm.

House & Grounds
1 - 31 October
Wed - Sun
10am - 3pm
(site closes at 4pm).

House by pre-booked
guided tour:
1 April - 30 Sept:
Wed - Fri,
10am - 12 noon (extra
charge).

ADMISSION

House & Grounds
Adult	£6.75
Child (5 - 15yrs) *	£3.40
Conc.	£5.10
Family (2+3)	£16.90

Grounds only
Adult	£4.00
Child (5 - 15yrs) *	£2.00
Concessions	£3.00
Family (2+3)	£10.00

* Under 5yrs Free.

Groups (11+)
15% discount.

ℹ️ Open air concerts and other events.

♿ Ground floor and grounds suitable.

🍴 Restaurant (max 50).

🚶 By arrangement for groups.

🅿️ Coaches to book in advance, £5 per coach. Free entry for coach drivers and tour guides. One additional place for every extra 20 people.

🎒 School visits free if booked in advance. Contact the Administrator or tel. 01223 582700 for bookings.

🐕 On leads only.

🛡️ **SPECIAL EVENTS**
Please telephone for details of special events.

Eastern Region England

AUDLEY END HOUSE & GARDENS See page 261 for full page entry.

BOURNE MILL

Tel: 01206 572422

Colchester, Essex CO2 8RT

Owner: The National Trust **Contact:** The Custodian

Originally a fishing lodge built in 1591. It was later converted into a mill with a 4 acre mill pond. Much of the machinery, including the waterwheel, is intact.

Location: OS Ref. TM006 238. 1m S of Colchester centre, in Bourne Road, off the Mersea Road B1025.

Opening Times: BH Suns & Mons only; also Suns & Tues in Jun, Jul & Aug, 2 - 5.30pm.

Admission: Adult £2. No reduction for groups.

Guide dogs only.

CHELMSFORD CATHEDRAL

Tel: 01245 294480

New Street, Chelmsford, Essex CM1 1AT **Contact:** Mrs Bobby Harrington

15th century building became a Cathedral in 1914. Extended in 1920s, major refurbishment in 1980s with contemporary works of distinction and splendid new organs in 1994 and 1996.

Location: OS Ref. TL708 070. In Chelmsford.

Opening Times: Daily: 8am - 5.30pm. Sun services: 8am, 9.30am, 11.15am and 6pm. Weekday services: 8.15am and 5.15pm. Tours by prior arrangement.

Admission: No charge but donation invited.

COLCHESTER CASTLE MUSEUM

Tel: 01206 282931/2 **Fax:** 01206 282925

14 Ryegate Road, Colchester, Essex CO1 1YG

Owner: Colchester Borough Council **Contact:** Museum Resource Centre

The largest Norman Castle Keep in Europe with fine archaeological collections on show.

Location: OS Ref. TL999 253. In Colchester town centre, off A12.

Opening Times: All year: Mon - Sat, 10am - 5pm, also Suns, 11am - 5pm.

Admission: Adult £3.80, Child/Conc. £2.50, Saver ticket £10.20. Booked groups (20+) £3.30. Prices will increase from 1 April 2001.

ESSEX SECRET BUNKER

Tel: 01206 392271 **Fax:** 01206 393847
e-mail: info@essexsecretbunker.com

Crown Building, Shrubland Road, Mistley, Manningtree, Essex CO11 1HS

Owner: The Bunker Preservation Trust **Contact:** The Curator

The huge concrete bunker half above and half below ground, gives a chilling insight into how 'Essex' stood ready for nuclear attack throughout the 40 years of the 'Cold War'. Cinemas, sound effects and historically accurate displays help you to explore the maze of passageways and rooms. Suitable for all the family.

Location: OS Ref. TM120 315. In Mistley near Manningtree on the B1352. Follow brown tourist signs from A120.

Opening Times: 1 Mar - 31 Oct: daily, 10.30am - 5pm (Aug 6pm). 1 Nov - 28 Feb: Sats & Suns, 10.30am - 4.30pm. Closed 20 Dec - 5 Jan.

Admission: Adult £4.95, Child £3.75, OAP £4.45, Student £2.50, Family £15.75. Groups (10-50): Adult £3.95, Child £2.75, OAP £3.45. Special evening tours throughout the year by appointment for groups: (10+) £6. Further discounts for groups of 30+.

Photography & video welcomed. Partially suitable. WC. By arrangement. Guide dogs only.

FEERINGBURY MANOR

Tel: 01376 561946

Coggeshall Road, Feering, Colchester, Essex CO5 9RB

Owner/Contact: Mrs Giles Coode-Adams

Location: OS Ref. TL864 215. 1½ m N of A12 at Feering, by B1024.

Opening Times: From 1st Tuesday in April to last Friday in July, Thurs & Fris only, 8am - 4pm.

Admission: £2 in aid of National Gardens Scheme.

COPPED HALL

CROWN HILL, EPPING, ESSEX CM16 5HH

Owner: Copped Hall Trust Contact: Alan Cox

Tel: 020 7267 1679 **Fax:** 020 7482 0557

Burnt-out 18th century Palladian mansion situated on ridge overlooking excellent landscaped park. Built adjacent to site of 16th century mansion where 'A Midsummer's Night Dream' was first performed. Former elaborate gardens gradually being rescued from abandonment. Victorian ancillary building including stables and small racquets court. Very large early 18th century walled garden.

Location: OS Ref. TL433 016. 4m SW of Epping, N of M25.

Opening Times: By appointment only.

Admission: Pre-arranged groups (20+) only: Adult £3, Child £1.

Partially suitable. Obligatory. In grounds on leads.

GARDENS OF EASTON LODGE

WARWICK HOUSE, EASTON LODGE, LITTLE EASTON, GT DUNMOW CM6 2BB

Owner/Contact: Mr Brian Creasey

Tel/Fax: 01371 876979 **e-mail:** enquiries@eastonlodge.co.uk

Beautiful gardens set in 25 acres. Horticultural associations from the 16th century to date. Visit the Italian gardens, currently undergoing restoration, designed by Harold Peto for 'Daisy' Countess of Warwick (Edward VII's mistress). In the dovecote, study the history of the house, garden and owners over 400 years. A peaceful and atmospheric haven! Millennium Project: Living yew and box sundial and Shakespeare border.

Location: OS Ref. TL593 240. 4m NW of Great Dunmow, off the B184 Dunmow to Thaxted road.

Opening Times: Feb/Mar (snowdrops): daily. Easter - 31 Oct: Fri - Sun & BHs, 12 noon - 6pm or dusk if earlier. Groups at other times by appointment.

Admission: Adult £3.80, Child (3-12yrs) £1.50, Conc. £3.50. Group (20+): £3.50. Schools (20+) £1.50 per child, 1 teacher free per 10 children.

Exhibition & Study Centre in Dovecote. Partially suitable. WC. Picnics. By arrangement. Limited for coaches. In grounds on leads.

GRANGE BARN, COGGESHALL
Tel: 01376 562226

Coggeshall, Colchester, Essex CO6 1RE

Owner: The National Trust   **Contact:** The Custodian

The oldest surviving timber framed barn in Europe, dating from around 1140, and originally part of a Cistercian Monastery. It was restored in the 1980s by the Coggeshall Grange Barn Trust, Braintree District Council and Essex County Council. Features a small collection of farm carts and wagons.

Location: OS Ref. TL848 223. Signposted off A120 Coggeshall bypass. West side of the road southwards to Kelvedon.

Opening Times: 1 Apr - 14 Oct: Tues, Thurs, Suns & BH Mons, 2 - 5pm.

Admission: £1.60. Joint ticket with Paycocke's £3.

♿ **P** Coaches must book. 🐕 Guide dogs only.

HARWICH MARITIME & LIFEBOAT MUSEUMS
Tel: 01255 503429

Harwich Green, Harwich, Essex

Owner: The Harwich Society   **Contact:** Mr Sheard

One housed in a disused lighthouse and the other in the nearby disused Victorian Lifeboat House, complete with full size lifeboat.

Location: OS Ref. TM262 822. On Harwich Green.

Opening Times: 1 May - 31 Aug: daily, 10am - 1pm & 2 - 5pm. Groups by appointment at any time.

Admission: Adult 50p, Child Free (no unaccompanied children).

❇ Ⓥ

HARWICH REDOUBT FORT
Tel: 01255 503429

Main Road, Harwich, Essex

Owner: The Harwich Society   **Contact:** Mr Sheard

180ft diameter circular fort built in 1808 to defend the port against Napoleonic invasion. Being restored by Harwich Society and part is a museum. Eleven guns on battlements.

Location: OS Ref. TM262 322. Rear of 29 Main Road.

Opening Times: 1 May - 31 Aug: daily, 10am - 5pm. Sept - Apr: Suns only. Groups by appointment at any time.

Admission: Adult £1, Child Free (no unaccompanied children).

❇ Ⓥ

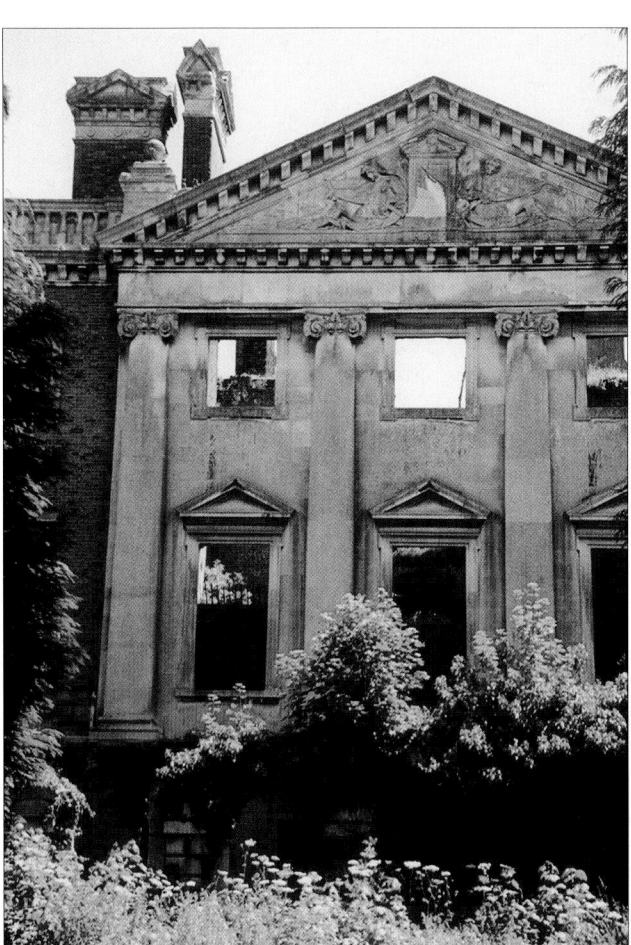
Copped Hall, Essex.

HEDINGHAM CASTLE

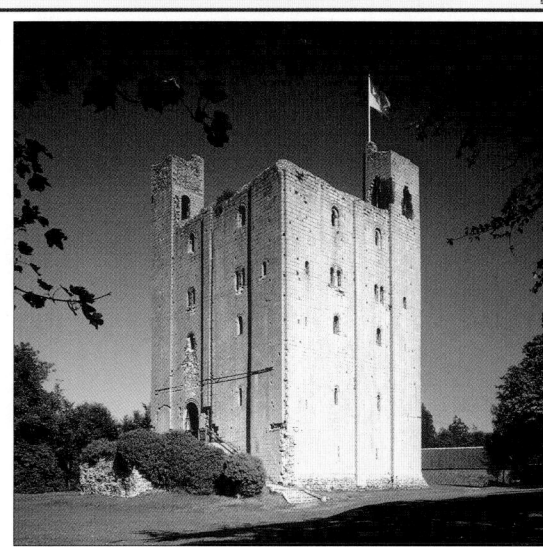

CASTLE HEDINGHAM, Nr HALSTEAD, ESSEX CO9 3DJ
Owner: The Hon Thomas Lindsay   *Contact: Mrs Diana Donoghue*

Tel: 01787 460261 **Fax:** 01787 461473 **e-mail:** hedinghamcastle@aspects.net

Splendid Norman keep built in 1140 by the famous de Veres, Earls of Oxford. Visited by Kings Henry VII and VIII and Queen Elizabeth I and besieged by King John. Magnificent banqueting hall with minstrel's gallery and finest Norman arch in England. Beautiful grounds, peaceful woodland and lakeside walks. Beside medieval village with fine Norman church.

Location: OS Ref. TL787 358. On B1058, 1m off A1017 between Cambridge and Colchester.

Opening Times: Week before Easter - 31 Oct: daily, 10am - 5pm.

Admission: Adult £4, Child £3, Conc. £3.50. Groups (20+): £3.50.

📷 🏬 ♿ Partially suitable. 🕸 🎩 By arrangement. **P** 🗲
🐾 In grounds, on leads. 🔔 🕶 Tel. for details.

HYLANDS HOUSE

HYLANDS PARK, LONDON ROAD, CHELMSFORD CM2 8WQ
Owner: Chelmsford Borough Council   *Contact: Ceri Lowen*

Tel: 01245 606812 **Fax:** 01245 606970

This beautiful villa, with its neo-classical exterior is surrounded by over 500 acres of parkland, including formal gardens. The house re-opened at Easter 1999 after a period of restoration work. The Library, Drawing Room and Saloon have been restored to their appearance in the early Victorian period. The Entrance Hall was restored to its Georgian origins in the 1995 restoration. It is possible to view the Banqueting Room and Victorian staircase, as yet unrestored. There is an exhibition detailing the restoration work and the history of the house.

Location: OS Ref. TL681 054. 2m SW of Chelmsford. Signposted on A1016 near Chelmsford.

Opening Times: All year: Suns, Mons & BHs, 11am - 6pm, except Christmas Day.

Admission: Adults £3, Child (12-16 yrs) £2, (under 12yrs) Free, Conc. £2. Groups: £3pp or £75 (whichever greater).

ℹ No photography in house. 📷 🏬 🕶 Sun only. 🎩 By arrangement. **P** Limited for coaches. 🗲 In grounds. Guide dogs only in house. 🔔 🕶 Please tel. for details. ❇ Ⓥ

Eastern Region
England

INGATESTONE HALL

HALL LANE, INGATESTONE, ESSEX CM4 9NR

Owner: The Lord Petre   *Contact:* The Administrator

Tel: 01277 353010   **Fax:** 01245 248979

16th century mansion, set in 11 acres of grounds (formal garden and wild walk), built by Sir William Petre, Secretary of State to four Tudor monarchs, which has remained in the hands of his family ever since. The two Priests' hiding places can be seen, as well as the furniture, portraits and family memorabilia accumulated over the centuries.

Location: OS Ref. TQ653 986. Off A12 between Brentwood & Chelmsford. Take Station Lane at London end of Ingatestone High Street, cross level-crossing and continue for $^1/_2$ m to SE.

Opening Times: 14 Apr - 30 Sept: Sats, Suns & BH Mons, plus 11 Jul - 7 Sept: Wed - Fri, 1 - 6pm.

Admission: Adult £3.50, Conc. £3, Child £2, Under 5yrs Free. 50p per head discount for groups (20+). Family Ticket (admits 5, up to 3 adults) £10.50.

ℹ️ No photography in house.   🏷️ 📷   ♿ Grounds suitable. WC. 🛍️
🎟️ By arrangement.   🅿️ 🚌   🐕 Guide dogs only.

LAYER MARNEY TOWER

Nr COLCHESTER, ESSEX CO5 9US

Owner/Contact: Mr Nicholas Charrington

Tel/Fax: 01206 330784

Built in the reign of Henry VIII, the tallest Tudor gatehouse in Great Britain. Lord Henry Marney clearly intended to rival Wolsey's building at Hampton Court, but he died before his masterpiece was finished. His son John died two years later, in 1525, and building work stopped. Layer Marney Tower has some of the finest terracotta work in the country, most probably executed by Flemish craftsmen trained by Italian masters. The terracotta is used on the battlements, windows, and most lavishly of all, on the tombs of Henry and John Marney. Visitors may climb the Tower, passing through the History Room, and enjoy the marvellous views of the Essex countryside. There are fine outbuildings, including the Long Gallery with its magnificent oak roof and the medieval barn which now houses some of the Home Farm's collection of Rare Breed farm animals. Function room available for receptions, etc.

Location: OS Ref. TL929 175. 5m SW of Colchester, signed off B1022.

Opening Times: 1 Apr - 7 Oct: Sun - Fri, 12 noon - 5pm. Group visits and guided tours throughout the year by arrangement.

Admission: Adult £3.50, Child £2, Family £10. Groups (15+): Adult £3.25, Child £1.75. Guided tours (pre-booked) £4.75, min. charge £120. Schools by arrangement.

📷 🏷️ 🍴 ♿ Partially suitable. WC. 🛍️ 🅿️ 🎟️ By arrangement. 🏛️
🐕 In grounds, on leads. 🛏️ 1 dble, 2 single. 🔔 ❄️ 📞 Tel. for details. (W)

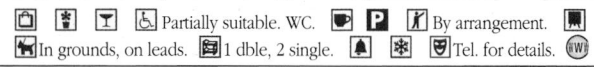

LOWER DAIRY HOUSE GARDEN   **Tel:** 01206 262220

Water Lane, Nayland, Colchester, Essex CO6 4JS

Owner/Contact: Mr & Mrs D J Burnett

Plantsman's garden, approx 1$^1/_2$ acres.

Location: OS Ref. TL966 330. 7m N of Colchester off A134. 1m SW of Nayland on E side of road to Little Horkesley.

Opening Times: Contact property for details. Groups by appointment only.

Admission: £2.

MISTLEY TOWERS ⛪   **Tel:** 01206 393884

Colchester, Essex

Owner: English Heritage   **Contact:** The Keykeeper (Mistley Quay Workshops)

The remains of one of only two churches designed by the great architect Robert Adam. Built in 1776. It was unusual in having towers at both the east and west ends.

Location: OS Ref. TM116 320. On B1352, 1$^1/_2$ m E of A137 at Lawford, 9m E of Colchester.

Opening Times: Telephone for opening times.

Admission: Key available from Mistley Quay workshops - 01206 393884.

SIR ALFRED MUNNINGS ART MUSEUM

CASTLE HOUSE, DEDHAM, ESSEX CO7 6AZ

Owner: Castle House Trust   *Contact:* Mrs C Woodage

Tel/Fax: 01206 322127

The home, studios and grounds where Sir Alfred Munnings, KCVO, 1878 – 1959 (PRA 1944 – 1949) lived and painted for 40 years. Castle House, part Tudor part Georgian, restored and with original Munnings' furniture, exhibits over 200 Munnings' works representing his life's work, is augmented by private loans each season. Annual Special Exhibition.

Location: OS Ref. TM060 328. $^3/_4$ m from Dedham centre. 8m from Colchester, 12m from Ipswich.

Opening Times: Easter Sun - first Sun in Oct: Weds, Suns & BH Mons, 2 - 5pm. Additionally Thurs & Sats in Aug, 2 - 5pm.

Admission: Adult £3, Child 50p, Conc. £2. Groups (25+): min. price £75, larger groups per admission prices.

ℹ️ No photography in house.   📷   ♿ Partially suitable.
🅿️ Ample for cars. Limited for coaches.   🐕 In grounds, on leads.

PAYCOCKE'S 🌿   **Tel:** 01376 561305

West Street, Coggeshall, Colchester, Essex CO6 1NS

Owner: The National Trust   **Contact:** The Tenant

A merchant's house, dating from about 1500, with unusually rich panelling and wood carving. A display of lace, for which Coggeshall was famous, is on show. Delightful cottage garden leading down to small river.

Location: OS Ref. TL848 225. Signposted off A120.

Opening Times: 1 Apr - 14 Oct: Tues, Thurs, Suns & BH Mons, 2 - 5.30pm, last adm: 5pm.

Admission: £2.20, groups (10+) by prior arrangement, no reduction for groups. Joint ticket with Coggeshall Grange Barn £3.

♿ Access to ground floor and garden.   🅿️ NT's at the Coggeshall Grange Barn.

PRIORS HALL BARN ⌘

Tel: 01799 522842

Widdington, Newport, Essex
Owner/Contact: Audley End House

One of the finest surviving medieval barns in south-east England and representative of the group of aisled barns centred on north-west Essex.

Location: OS Ref. TL538 319. In Widdington, on unclassified road 2m SE of Newport, off B1383.

Opening Times: 1 Apr - 30 Sept: Sats & Suns, 10am - 6pm.

Admission: Telephone for further details.

RHS GARDEN HYDE HALL

RETTENDON, Nr CHELMSFORD, ESSEX CM3 8ET

Owner: The Royal Horticultural Society   *Contact: Pat Everitt*

Tel: 01245 400256 **Fax:** 01245 402100 **e-mail:** hydehall@rhs.org.uk

A charming hilltop garden. Highlights include the spring bulbs in profusion, an extensive colour themed herbaceous border, farmhouse garden and a large collection of roses of all kinds. Two ornamental ponds are home to a wide variety of bog plants and water lilies. Among a wide range of ornamental tree and shrub plantings is a National Collection of viburnums. New projects for 2001 include a rain-fed garden and an avenue of trees. Delightful hot and cold meals are available in the Essex thatched barn.

Location: OS Ref. TQ782 995. 2m E of Rettendon, 6m SE of Chelmsford. Signed off the A130.

Opening Times: 1 Apr - 28 Oct: daily, 11am - 6pm. Sept - Oct: 11am - 5pm. Last entry 1 hour before closing.

Admission: Adult £3, Child (under 6yrs) Free, Child (6 - 16yrs) £1. Pre-booked groups (10+), £2.50. Companion for wheelchair user or blind visitors Free.

⬚   ⚘   ▼Evenings only.   ♿   ⬛Licensed.   ⬛Licensed.
🏃By arrangement.   ▪   Ⓟ Limited for coaches.   🐕Guide dogs only.   ⓘ

SALING HALL GARDEN

Tel: 01371 850 243 **Fax:** 01371 850 274

Great Saling, Braintree, Essex CM7 5DT
Owner/Contact: Hugh Johnson Esq

Twelve acres including a walled garden dated 1698. Water gardens and landscaped arboretum.

Location: OS Ref. TL700 258. 6m NW of Braintree, 2m N of A120.

Opening Times: May, Jun & Jul: Weds, 2 - 5pm.

Admission: Standard £2.50, Child Free.

SHALOM HALL

Tel: 01206 330338

Layer Breton, Colchester, Essex CO2 0PT
Owner/Contact: Lady Hillingdon

19th century country house containing a collection of 17th and 18th century French furniture and portraits by famous English artists including Thomas Gainsborough and Sir Joshua Reynolds.

Location: OS Ref. TL960 160. 7m SW of Colchester, on the B1026 Colchester - Tolleshunt road.

Opening Times: Aug: Mon - Fri, 10am - 1pm & 2.30 - 5.30pm.

Admission: Free.

TILBURY FORT ⌘

Tel: 01375 858489

No. 2 Office Block, The Fort, Tilbury, Essex RM18 7NR
Owner: English Heritage   **Contact:** The Custodian

The best and largest example of 17th century military engineering in England, commanding the Thames. The fort shows the development of fortifications over the following 200 years. Exhibitions, the powder magazine and the bunker-like 'casemates' demonstrate how the fort protected London from seaborne attack. Elizabeth I gave a speech near here on the eve of the Spanish Armada.

Location: OS Ref. TQ651 754. $\frac{1}{2}$ m E of Tilbury off A126.

Opening Times: 1 Apr - 31 Oct: daily, 10am - 6pm (5pm in Oct). 1 Nov - 31 Mar: Wed - Sun, 10am - 4pm. Closed 24 - 26 Dec & 1 Jan.

Admission: Adult £2.75, Child £1.40, Conc. £2.10.

⬚   ❀   🛡 Tel. for details.

VALENCE HOUSE MUSEUM & ART GALLERY

Tel: 020 8227 5293

Becontree Avenue, Dagenham, Essex RM8 3HT
Owner: Barking & Dagenham Council   **Contact:** Ms Susan Curtis

The only remaining manor house in Dagenham, partially surrounded by a moat. Dates from 15th century. There is an attractive herb garden to the west of the house.

Location: OS Ref. TQ481 865. S side of Becontree Ave, $\frac{1}{2}$ m W of A1112 at Becontree Heath.

Opening Times: Tue - Fri, 9.30am - 1pm & 2 - 4.30pm. Sats, 10am - 4pm.

Admission: Free.

WALTHAM ABBEY GATEHOUSE & BRIDGE ⌘

Tel: 01992 702200

Waltham Abbey, Essex   **Contact:** The East of England Regional Office (01223 582700)
Owner: English Heritage

The late 14th century abbey gatehouse, part of the north range of the cloister and the medieval 'Harold's Bridge' of one of the great monastic foundations of the Middle Ages.

Location: OS Ref. TL381 008. In Waltham Abbey off A112. Just NE of the Abbey church.

Opening Times: Any reasonable time.

Admission: Free.

RHS Garden Hyde Hall, Essex.

Plant Sales Index ◀◀◀ page 47

Jerry Harpur.

HATFIELD HOUSE & GARDENS
Hatfield

This celebrated Jacobean house, which stands in its own great park, was built between 1607 and 1611 by Robert Cecil, 1st Earl of Salisbury and Chief Minister to King James I. It has been the family home of the Cecils ever since.

The main designer was Robert Lyminge helped, it is thought, by the young Inigo Jones. The interior decoration was the work of English, Flemish and French craftsmen, notably Maximilian Colt.

The State Rooms are rich in world-famous paintings including *The Rainbow Portrait of Queen Elizabeth I* and *The Ermine Portrait* by Nicholas Hilliard. Other paintings include works by Hoefnagel, Mytens, John de Critz the Elder and Sir Joshua Reynolds. Fine furniture from the 16th, 17th and 18th centuries, rare tapestries and historic armour can be found in the State Rooms.

Within the delightful gardens stands the surviving wing of The Royal Palace of Hatfield (1485) where Elizabeth I spent much of her girlhood and held her first Council of State in November 1558. Some of her possessions can be seen in the House.

GARDENS

John Tradescant the Elder, the celebrated plant hunter, was employed to plant and lay out the gardens after the completion of the house in 1611. During the 18th century, when landscape gardening became more fashionable, much of his work was neglected or swept away. The present Marchioness has continued with the work of restoration and redevelopment, started in the mid 19th century, so that the 42 acres of gardens now include formal, knot, scented and wilderness areas which reflects their Jacobean history. The gardens are managed entirely organically.

❖

Owner: The Marquess of Salisbury

CONTACT

The Curator
Hatfield House
Hatfield
Hertfordshire
AL9 5NQ

Tel: 01707 287010

Fax: 01707 275719

LOCATION

OS Ref. TL 237 084

21m N of London,
M25/J23 7m,
A1(M)/J4, 2m.

Bus: Local bus services from St Albans, Hertford.

Rail: From Kings Cross every 30 mins. Hatfield Station is immediately opposite entrance to Park.

Air: Luton (30 mins). Stanstead (45 mins).

Jerry Harpur.

ℹ️ No photography in house. National Collection of model soldiers, 5m of marked trails, children's play area.

🛍️ ❖

🍷 Wedding receptions, functions. Elizabethan Banquets held in Old Palace throughout year: 01707 262055.

♿ Visitors may alight at entrance. WCs & lift.

🍴🍴 Seats 120. Pre-booked lunch and tea for groups 10+. Tel: 01707 262030.

🚶 Tue - Thur, no extra charge. Available in French, German, Italian, Spanish or Japanese by prior arrangement. Garden tour £15.

🅿️ Ample. Hardstanding for coaches.

🏫 1:10 ratio. Teacher free. Guide provided. Model soldier collection, adventure playground and marked trails.

🐕 In grounds, on leads.

CONFERENCE/FUNCTION		
ROOM	SIZE	MAX CAPACITY
The Old Palace	112' x 33'	280

OPENING TIMES

24 March - 23 September (Closed Good Friday but open BH Mons).

House
Tue - Fri, guided tours only, 12 noon - 4pm.
Sat & Sun (no guided tours) 1 - 4.30pm.
BHs (no guided tours), 11am - 4.30pm.

Park
Daily: 10.30am - 8pm, on Fridays, 11am - 6pm.

Gardens
West: Tue - Sun.
East: Fridays only (Connoisseurs' Day), 11am - 6pm.

Restaurant: Tue - Sun, 10.30am - 5.30pm.

Shop: Tue - Sat, 11am - 5.30pm & Suns, 1 - 5.30pm.

ADMISSION

House, Park & West Garden
Adult £6.60
Child (5 - 15yrs)........£3.30
Groups (20+)*
Adult £5.60
Park only
Adult £2.00
Child (5 - 15yrs)........£1.00
Connoisseurs' Day (Fri)
House Tour, Park & Gardens £10.00

Park & Gardens £6.00

🛡️ SPECIAL EVENTS

- **MAY 10 - 13:**
Living Crafts.

- **JUN 23/24:**
Festival of Gardening.

- **AUG 3 - 5:**
Art in Clay.

- **SEPT 7 - 9:**
Country Homes & Garden Show.

Owner: The Hon Henry Lytton Cobbold

CONTACT

The Estate Office
Knebworth House
Knebworth
Hertfordshire
SG3 6PY

Tel: 01438 812661

Fax: 01438 811908

e-mail: info@ knebworthhouse.com

LOCATION

OS Ref. TL230 208

Direct access off the A1(M) J7 (Stevenage South A602). 28m N of London. 15m N of M25 J23.

Rail: Stevenage Station 2m (from Kings Cross).

Air: Luton Airport 15m Landing facilities.

Taxi: 01438 811122.

CONFERENCE/FUNCTION		
ROOM	SIZE	MAX CAPACITY
Banqueting Hall	26'x 41'	80
Dining Parlour	21'x 38'	50
Library	32'x 21'	40
Manor Barn	70'x 25'	250
Lodge Barn	75'x 30'	150

KNEBWORTH
Nr Stevenage

Home of the Lytton family since 1490, and still a lived-in family house. Transformed in early Victorian times by Edward Bulwer-Lytton, the author, poet, dramatist and statesman, into the unique high gothic fantasy house of today, complete with turrets, griffins and gargoyles.

Historically home to Constance Lytton, the Suffragette, and her father, Robert Lytton, the Viceroy of India who proclaimed Queen Victoria Empress of India at the Great Delhi Durbar of 1877. Visited by Queen Elizabeth I, Charles Dickens and Sir Winston Churchill.

The interior contains various styles including the magnificent Jacobean Banqueting Hall, a unique example of the 17th century change in fashion from traditional English to Italian Palladian. The high gothic State Drawing Room by John Crace contrasts with the Regency elegance of Mrs Bulwer-Lytton's bedroom and the 20th century designs of Sir Edwin Lutyens in the Entrance Hall, Dining Parlour and Library.

25 acres of beautiful gardens, simplified by Lutyens, including pollarded lime avenues, formal rose garden, maze and Gertrude Jekyll herb garden. 250 acres of gracious parkland, with herds of red and sika deer, includes children's giant adventure playground and miniature railway. World famous for its huge open-air rock concerts, and used as a film location for *Batman*, *The Shooting Party*, *Wilde*, *Jane Eyre* and *The Canterville Ghost*, amongst others.

The Jacobean Banqueting Hall.

Suitable for fashion shows, air displays, archery, shooting, equestrian events, cricket pitch, garden parties, shows, rallies, filming, helicopter landing. No pushchairs, photography, smoking or drinking in House.

Indian Raj Evenings and Elizabethan Banquets with jousting. Full catering service.

Visitors may alight at entrance. Ground floor accessible to wheelchairs.

Licensed tearoom. Special rates for advance bookings, menus on request.

Unlimited parking. Group visits must be booked in advance with Estate Office.

Daily at 30 min intervals or at booked times including evenings. Tour time 1hr. Shorter tours by arrangement. Room Wardens on duty on busy weekends. 'Gothick Visions' tour.

National Curriculum based worksheets & children's guide.

Guide dogs only in House. In Park, on leads.

OPENING TIMES

Park, Gardens, Fort Knebworth Adventure Playground & Miniature Railway
7 - 22 Apr; 26 May - 3 Jun; 7 Jul - 4 Sept: daily.

28 Apr - 20 May; 9 Jun - 1 Jul; 8 - 30 Sept: weekends & BHs.

Park, Gardens, Playground & Railway
11am - 5.30pm.

House & Exhibition:
12 noon - 5pm (last adm. 4.30pm)

Closed at other times, but pre-booked groups (20+) welcome all year (subject to special events).

ADMISSION

House, Gardens, Park, Playground & Railway

Adult £7.00
Child*/OAP £6.50
Family (2+2) £23.50

Groups (20+)
Adult £6.00
Child*/OAP £5.50
(subject to special events)

Gardens, Park, Playground & Railway

All persons..............£5.50
Family (2+2) £19.00

Groups (20+)
All persons..............£4.75
(subject to special events)

* Age 4 - 16yrs. Under 4s Free. Season Tickets available.

Eastern Region
England

ASHRIDGE

RINGSHALL, BERKHAMSTED, HERTFORDSHIRE HP4 1LT

Owner: The National Trust   *Contact: The Property Manager*

Tel: 01442 851227   **Fax:** 01442 842062   **e-mail:** tasgsc@smtp.ntrust.org.uk

The Ashridge Estate comprises over 1800ha of woodlands, commons and downland. At the northerly end of the Estate the Ivinghoe Hills are an outstanding area of chalk downland which supports a rich variety of plants and insects. The Ivinghoe Beacon itself offers splendid views. This area may be reached from a car park at Steps Hill. The rest of Ashridge is an almost level plateau with many fine walks through woods and open commons.

Location: OS Ref. SP970 131. Between Northchurch & Ringshall, just off B4506.

Opening Times: Visitor Centre, Shop & Tearoom: Apr - Oct: daily except Fris (open Good Fri). Mon - Thur, 2 - 5pm, Sats, Suns, BHs, 12 noon - 5pm. Monument: Sats & Suns, 12 noon - 5pm, Mon - Thur, by arrangement. Please telephone for details on winter openings.

Admission: Monument: £1, Child 50p.

ℹ️ Visitor Centre.   📷   ♿ Vehicles available.   🏫 ❄️ 💟 Tel. for details.

BERKHAMSTED CASTLE

Tel: 01442 871737

Berkhamsted, St Albans, Hertfordshire

Owner: English Heritage   **Contact:** Mr Stevens - The Key Keeper

The extensive remains of a large 11th century motte and bailey castle which held a strategic position on the road to London.

Location: OS165 Ref. SP996 083. Adjacent to Berkhamsted rail station.

Opening Times: All year: daily, 10am - 4pm.

Admission: Free.

CATHEDRAL & ABBEY CHURCH OF ST ALBAN

St Albans, Hertfordshire AL1 1BY   **Tel:** 01727 860780   **Fax:** 01727 850944

e-mail: mail@stalbanscathedral.org.uk   **Contact:** Deputy Administrator

Abbey church of Benedictine Monastery founded 793AD commemorating Britain's first martyr.

Location: OS Ref. TL145 071. Centre of St Albans.

Opening Times: All year: 9am - 5.45pm. Tel for details of services, concerts and special events Mon - Sat, 11am - 4pm.

Admission: Free of charge. (AV show, Adult £1.50, Child £1).

CROMER WINDMILL

Tel: 01279 843301

Ardeley, Stevenage, Hertfordshire SG2 7QA

Owner: Hertfordshire Building Preservation Trust   **Contact:** Cristina Harrison

17th century Post Windmill restored to working order.

Location: OS165, Ref. TL305 286. 4m NE of Stevenage on B1037. 1m SW of Cottered.

Opening Times: Mid-May - mid-Sept: Sun, 2nd & 4th Sat & BHs, 2.30 - 5pm.

Admission: Adult £1.50, Child 25p. Groups by arrangement.

FORGE MUSEUM & VICTORIAN COTTAGE GARDEN   **Tel/Fax:** 01279 843301

High Street, Much Hadham, Hertfordshire SG10 6BS

Owner: The Hertfordshire Building Preservation Trust   **Contact:** The Curator

The garden reflects plants that would have been grown in 19th century, also houses an unusual 19th century bee shelter.

Location: OS Ref. TL428 195. Village centre.

Opening Times: Fri, Sat, Sun & BHs, 11am - 5pm (dusk in winter).

Admission: Adult £1, Child/Conc. 50p.

BENINGTON LORDSHIP GARDENS

STEVENAGE, HERTFORDSHIRE SG2 7BS

Owner: Mr C H A Bott   *Contact: Mr or Mrs C H A Bott*

Tel: 01438 869668   **Fax:** 01438 869622   **e-mail:** rhbott@beningtonlordship.co.uk

A hilltop garden which appeals to everyone with its intimate atmosphere, ruins, Queen Anne Manor, herbaceous borders, old roses, lakes, vegetable garden, nursery and verandah teas. For films, fashion shoots etc. the gardens and estate offer excellent facilities. Mediaeval barns, cottages and other unique countryside features.

Location: OS Ref. TL296 236. In village of Benington next to the church. 4m E of Stevenage.

Opening times: Gardens only: Apr - Aug, Wed & BH Mons, 12 noon - 5pm, Sun 2 - 5pm. Sept: Weds only. Groups any time by arrangement.

Admission: Adult £3, Child Free.

ℹ️ Air-strip. Suitable for filming & fashion shoots.   ♿ Unsuitable.

📷 🐾 ❄️ 🅥🅦

THE GARDENS OF THE ROSE

CHISWELL GREEN, ST ALBANS, HERTFORDSHIRE AL2 3NR

Owner: The Royal National Rose Society   *Contact: Lt Col K J Grapes*

Tel: 01727 850461   **Fax:** 01727 850360   **e-mail:** mail@rnrs.org.uk

The Royal National Rose Society Gardens provide a wonderful display of one of the best and most important collections of roses in the world. There are some 30,000 roses in 1800 different varieties. The Society has introduced many companion plants which harmonise well with roses including over 100 varieties of clematis. The garden, named for the Society's Patron Her Majesty The Queen Mother, contains a fascinating collection of old garden roses. Various cultivation trials show just how easy roses are to grow and new varieties can be seen in the International Trial Ground. There are excellent facilities for films and fashion photography.

Location: OS Ref. TL124 045. 2m S of St Albans, M1/J6, M25/J21A. ½m W of B4630.

Opening times: 2 Jun - 30 Sept: Mon - Sat, 9am - 5pm, Sun & Aug BHs: 10am - 6pm.

Admission: Adult £4, Child (5-15) £1.50, OAP £3.50. Pre-arranged groups (min 20, max 100): Adult £3.50.

📷 🚻 🍴 ♿ 💟 Licensed.   🐕 In grounds, on leads.   🅦

GORHAMBURY

Tel: 01727 854051 **Fax:** 01727 843675

St Albans, Hertfordshire AL3 6AH

Owner: The Earl Of Verulam   **Contact:** The Administrator

Late 18th century house by Sir Robert Taylor. Family portraits from 15th - 20th centuries.

Location: OS Ref. TL114 078. 2m W of St Albans. Accessible via private drive from A4147 at St Albans.

Opening Times: May - Sept: Thur, 2 - 5pm.

Admission: House & Gardens: Adult £6, Child £3, OAP £4. Guided tour only. Groups by arrangement: Thursdays £5, other days £6.

HATFIELD HOUSE

See page 266 for full page entry.

HERTFORD MUSEUM

Tel: 01992 582686 **Fax:** 01992 534797

18 Bull Plain, Hertford

Owner: Hertford Museums Trust   **Contact:** Andrea George

Local museum in 17th century house, altered by 18th century façade, with recreated Jacobean knot garden.

Location: OS Ref. TL326 126. Town centre.

Opening Times: Tue - Sat, 10am - 5pm.

Admission: Free.

HITCHIN BRITISH SCHOOLS

Tel/Fax: 01462 420144
e-mail: brsch@britishschools.freeserve.co.uk

41 - 42 Queen Street, Hitchin, Hertfordshire SG4 9TS

Owner: Hitchin British Schools Trust   **Contact:** Mrs Judy Lee

Unique complex of school buildings dating from 1837 to 1905. Incorporates 1837 Lancasterian Schoolroom, believed to be the only surviving example, a now rare 1853 galleried classroom (both Grade II*), Girls and Infants School from 1857 as well as two Edwardian classrooms. Related displays and small museum.

Location: OS Ref. TL186 289. Hitchin town centre.

Opening Times: Feb - Nov: Tue, 10am - 4pm. Apr - Oct: Sun, 2.30 - 5pm. Feb - Nov: School visits, Wed & Thur, 9.45am - 12.45pm.

Admission: Adult £2, Child £1. Education programme with teaching session £2.75 plus VAT per child.

▢   ♿ Partially suitable. WC.   ▭   ⬛ Obligatory.   **P**   ▮   🐕 Guide dogs only.
❄

KNEBWORTH

See page 267 for full page entry.

OLD GORHAMBURY HOUSE

Tel: 01223 582700 (Regional Office)

St Albans, Hertfordshire

Owner: English Heritage   **Contact:** The East of England Regional Office

The remains of this Elizabethan mansion, particularly the porch of the Great Hall, illustrate the impact of the Renaissance on English architecture.

Location: OS166, Ref. TL110 077. ¼ m W of Gorhambury House and accessible only through private drive from A4147 at St Albans (2m). Call 01727 843675 for more information.

Opening Times: Any reasonable time.

Admission: Free.

ST PAULS WALDEN BURY

Tel/Fax: 01438 871218/871229

Hitchin, Hertfordshire SG4 8BP

Owner: S Bowes Lyon   **Contact:** S or C Bowes Lyon

A formal landscape garden, laid out in 1730, covering 40 acres. The childhood home of Queen Elizabeth, The Queen Mother.

Location: OS Ref. TL186 216. 5m S of Hitchin on B651.

Opening Times: By appointment.

Admission: Adult £2.50, Child 50p. Other times £5. (2000 prices.)

SCOTT'S GROTTO

Tel: 01920 464131

Ware, Hertfordshire

Owner: East Hertfordshire District Council   **Contact:** J Watson

One of the finest grottos in England built in the 1760s by Quaker Poet John Scott.

Location: OS Ref. TL355 137. In Scotts Rd, S of the A119 Hertford Road.

Opening Times: 1 Apr - 30 Sept: Sat & BH Mon, 2 - 4.30pm. Also by appointment.

Admission: Suggested donation of £1 for adults. Children Free. Please bring a torch.

THE WALTER ROTHSCHILD ZOOLOGICAL MUSEUM

Tel: 020 7942 6171

Akeman Street, Tring, Hertfordshire HP23 6AP   **Fax:** 020 7942 6150

Owner: The Natural History Museum   **Contact:** Anne Chapman

The museum was opened to the public by Lord Rothschild in 1892. It houses his private natural history collection. More than 4,000 species of animal in a unique Victorian setting.

Location: OS Ref. SP924 111. S end of Akeman Street, ¼ m S of High Street.

Opening Times: Mon - Sat, 10am - 5pm, Suns, 2 - 5pm.

Admission: Adult £3.50, Child (0-16yrs) Free, Conc. £2, Over 60s Free, School groups Free.

SHAW'S CORNER

NT Photographic Library/Matthew Antrobus.

AYOT ST LAWRENCE, WELWYN, HERTFORDSHIRE AL6 9BX

Owner: The National Trust   *Contact:* The Custodian

Tel/Fax: 01438 820307   **email:** tscgen@smtp.ntrust.org.uk

The fascinating home of playwright George Bernard Shaw until his death in 1950. The modest Edwardian villa contains many literary and personal relics, and the interior is still set out as it was in Shaw's lifetime. The garden, with its richly planted borders and views over the Hertfordshire countryside, contains the revolving summerhouse where Shaw retreated to write.

NT Photographic Library/Matthew Antrobus.

Location: OS Ref. TL194 167. At SW end of village, 2m NE of Wheathampstead, approximately 2m N from B653. A1(M)/J4, M1/J10.

Opening times: 31 Mar - 4 Nov: Wed - Sun & BH Mons, 1 - 5pm (closed Good Fri). Parties by written appointment, Mar - Nov. Last admission 4.30pm. On busy days admission by timed ticket. On event days closes at 3.30pm. No large hand luggage inside property.

Admission: Adult £3.50, Family £8.75.

♿ House & garden but some steps.   🚗 Car park only.   ▭ Tel. for details.

Owner:
The Earl of Leicester

CONTACT

The Administrator
Holkham Hall
Estate Office
Wells-next-the-Sea
Norfolk
NR23 1AB

Tel: 01328 710227

Fax: 01328 711707

e-mail: m.monk@
holkham.co.uk

LOCATION

OS Ref. TF885 428

From London 120m
Norwich 35m
King's Lynn 30m.

Rail: Norwich Station 35m
King's Lynn Station 30m.

Air: Norwich Airport 32m.

HOLKHAM HALL
Wells-next-the-Sea

HOLKHAM HALL has been the home of the Coke family and the Earls of Leicester for almost 250 years. Built between 1734 and 1764 by Thomas Coke, 1st Earl of Leicester and based on a design by William Kent, this fine example of 18th century Palladian style mansion reflects Thomas Coke's natural appreciation of classical art developed during the Grand Tour. It is constructed mainly of local yellow brick with a magnificent Entrance Hall of English alabaster.

The State Rooms occupy the first floor and contain Greek and Roman statuary, paintings by Rubens, Van Dyck, Claude, Poussin and Gainsborough and original furniture.

On leaving the House visitors pass Holkham Pottery and its adjacent shop, both under the

supervision of the Countess of Leicester. Fine examples of local craftsmanship are for sale including the famous Holkham Florist Ware.

Beyond are the 19th century stables now housing the Holkham Bygones Collection; some 4,000 items range from working steam engines, vintage cars and tractors to craft tools and kitchenware. A History of Farming exhibition is in the former Porter's Lodge.

The House is set in a 3,000-acre park with 600 head of fallow deer. On the lake, 1 mile long, are many species of wildfowl. Two walks encircle either the lake or agricultural buildings.

Holkham Nursery Gardens occupy the 18th century walled Kitchen Garden and a large range of stock is on sale to the public.

Grounds for shows, rallies and filming. No smoking or flash photography in the Hall.

Visitors may alight at entrance, stairs in Hall. WC.

Menus for pre-booked groups on request.

Guides are posted in each room. Audio tour £2, other times guided tours by arrangement.

Unlimited for cars, 20+ coaches. Parking, admission, refreshments free to coach drivers, coach drivers' rest room.

Welcome. Areas of interest: Bygones Collection, History of Farming, two nature walks, deer park, lake and wildfowl.

No dogs in Hall, on leads in grounds.

OPENING TIMES

SUMMER
27 May - 30 September
Sun - Thur (inclusive)
1 - 5pm.
Easter, May, Spring &
Summer BHs: Suns & Mons
11.30am - 5pm.
Last admission 4.45pm.
Restaurant, shop and
Holkham Nursery Gardens
from 10am.
21 & 22 July: Hall &
Museum closed for
Holkham Country Fair.

WINTER
October - May
By appointment for groups.

ADMISSION

SUMMER
Hall
  Adult £5.00
  Child (5-15yrs) £2.50
Bygones
  Adult £5.00
  Child (5-15yrs) £2.50
Combined Ticket
  Adult £8.00
  Child (5-15yrs) £4.00
GROUPS (min. 20)
Hall
  Adult £4.50
  Child (5-15yrs) £2.25
Bygones
  Adult £4.50
  Child (5-15yrs) £2.25
Combined Ticket
  Adult £7.20
  Child (5-15yrs) £3.60
Private guided tours by arrangement. Rates on application.

WINTER
By arrangement.
Visitors may walk in the Park without charge every day of the year.

SPECIAL EVENTS

• JUL 21/22
  Holkham Country Fair.

SANDRINGHAM
Norfolk

SANDRINGHAM is the charming country retreat of Her Majesty The Queen, hidden in the heart of 60 acres of beautiful wooded grounds. Still maintained in the style of Edward and Alexandra, Prince and Princess of Wales (later King Edward VII and Queen Alexandra), all the main ground floor rooms used by The Royal Family, full of their treasured ornaments, portraits and furniture, are open to the public. A display of paintings will be on show in the ballroom.

More family possessions are displayed in the Museum housed in the old stable and coach houses including vehicles ranging in date from the first car owned by a British monarch, a 1900 Daimler, to a half-scale Aston Martin used by Princes William and Harry. A new display tells the mysterious tale of the Sandringham Company who fought and died at Gallipolli in 1915, recently made into a TV film 'All the King's Men'.

In the Gardens informal glades, dells, lakes and lawns are surrounded by magnificent trees and bordered by colourful shrubs and flowers. A free Land Train from within the entrance will carry passengers less able to walk through the grounds to the House and back.

Owner: H M The Queen

CONTACT

Mrs Gill Pattinson
The Estate Office
Sandringham
Norfolk
PE35 6EN

Tel: 01553 772675

Fax: 01485 541571

LOCATION

OS Ref. TF695 287

8m NE of King's Lynn on B1440 off A148.

Rail: King's Lynn.

Air: Norwich.

OPENING TIMES

House, Museum & Gardens

14 April - 17 July
1 August - 28 October
Daily, 11am - 4.45pm.

ADMISSION

House, Museum and Gardens

Adult £6.00
Child (5-15yrs)..........£3.50
Conc......................£4.50

Groups (20+)
10% discount for payment one month in advance.

Brian Chapple.

 No photography in house.

 Plant centre.

Visitor Centre only.

Suitable.

Licensed.

Licensed.

By arrangement. Private evening tours.

P Ample.

 Guide dogs only.

CONFERENCE/FUNCTION		
ROOM	SIZE	MAX CAPACITY
Restaurant		200
Tearoom		60

BERNEY ARMS WINDMILL ⚎

Tel: 01493 700605

c/o 8 Manor Road, Southtown, Gt Yarmouth NR31 0QA

Owner: English Heritage　　　　　　**Contact:** The Custodian

A wonderfully situated marsh mill, one of the best and largest remaining in Norfolk, with seven floors, making it a landmark for miles around. It was in use until 1951.

Location: OS134 Ref. TG465 051. $3^1/_2$ m NE of Reedham on N bank of River Yare, 5m from Gt. Yarmouth. Accessible by boat or by footpath, from Halvergate ($3^1/_2$ m).

Opening Times: 1 Apr - 31 Oct: daily, 9am - 5pm (closed 1 - 2pm).

Admission: Adult £1.60, Child 80p, Conc. £1.20.

BINHAM PRIORY ⚎

Tel: 01223 582700 (Regional Office)

Binham-on-Wells, Norfolk

Owner: English Heritage　　　　　　**Contact:** The East of England Regional Office

Extensive remains of a Benedictine priory, of which the original nave of the church is still in use as the parish church.

Location: OS132 Ref. TF982 399. $^1/_4$ m NW of village of Binham-on-Wells, on road off B1388.

Opening Times: Any reasonable time.

Admission: Free.

BIRCHAM WINDMILL

Tel: 01485 578393

Snettisham Road, Great Bircham, Norfolk PE31 6SJ

Owner/Contact: Miss E Wagg/Mr S Chalmers

One of the last remaining complete windmills.

Location: OS Ref. TF760 326. $^1/_2$ m W of Bircham. N of the road to Snettisham.

Opening Times: Please contact for details.

Admission: Adult £2.50, Child £1, Retired £2.25. (2000 prices).

BLICKLING HALL 🌿

BLICKLING, NORWICH, NORFOLK NR11 6NF

Owner: The National Trust　*Contact: The Property Manager*

Tel: 01263 738030 **Fax:** 01263 731660

Built in the early 17th century and one of England's great Jacobean houses. Blickling is famed for its spectacular long gallery, superb library and fine collections of furniture, pictures and tapestries.

Location: OS133 Ref. TG178 286. $1^1/_2$ m NW of Aylsham on B1354. Signposted off A140 Norwich (15m) to Cromer.

Opening Times: House: 7 Apr - 28 Oct: Wed - Sun (open BH Mons), Apr - Sept: 1 - 4.30pm (last admission, house closes at 5pm). Oct: 1 - 3.30pm (last admission, house closes at 4pm). Garden: As house, also Tues in Aug. 1 Nov - 23 Dec: Thur - Sun. 5 Jan - end Mar 2002: Sats & Suns, 7 Apr - 28 Oct: 10.15am - 5.15pm. Nov - Mar 2002: 11am - 4pm. Park & Woods: daily, dawn - dusk.

Admission: Hall & Gardens: £6.70. Garden only: £3.80. Family & groups discounts. Groups must book.

🏛 Open as garden. ⎔ ⍝ ⟁ Partially suitable. ▣ �㈼ Licensed.
⚘ By arrangement. ⌸ 🅿 ♿ In park, on leads. ▣ ❋ ⌷ Tel for details.

NT Photographic Library; Nick Meers.

BURGH CASTLE ⚎

Tel: 01223 582700 (Regional Office)

Breydon Water, Great Yarmouth, Norfolk

Owner: English Heritage　　　　**Contact:** The East of England Regional Office

Impressive walls, with projecting bastions, of a Roman fort built in the late 3rd century as one of a chain to defend the coast against Saxon raiders.

Location: OS134 Ref. TG475 046. At far W end of Breydon Water, on unclassified road 3m W of Great Yarmouth. SW of the church.

Opening Times: Any reasonable time.

Admission: Free.

CASTLE ACRE PRIORY ⚎

Tel: 01760 755394

Stocks Green, Castle Acre, King's Lynn, Norfolk PE32 2XD

Owner: English Heritage　　　　**Contact:** The Custodian

The great west front of the 12th century church of this Cluniac priory still rises to its full height and is elaborately decorated. Other substantial remains include the splendid prior's lodgings and chapel and the delightful modern herb garden should not be missed.

Location: OS Ref. TF814 148. $^1/_4$ m W of village of Castle Acre, 5m N of Swaffham.

Opening Times: 1 Apr - 31 Oct: daily, 10am - 6pm (5pm in Oct). 1 Nov - 31 Mar: Wed - Sun, 10am - 4pm. Closed 24 - 26 Dec & 1 Jan.

Admission: Adult £3.50, Child £1.80, Conc. £2.60, Family £8.80.

🏛 ♿ Ground floor & grounds. 🅿 ❋ ⌷ Tel. for details.

CASTLE RISING CASTLE

Tel: 01553 631330 **Fax:** 01553 631724

Castle Rising, King's Lynn, Norfolk PE31 6AH

Owner: Greville Howard　　　　**Contact:** The Custodian

Possibly the finest mid-12th century Keep left in England: it was built as a grand and elaborate palace. It was home to Queen Isabella, grandmother of the Black Prince. Still in surprisingly good condition, the Keep is surrounded by massive ramparts up to 120 feet high. Picnic area adjacent to tearoom.

Opening Times: 1 Apr - 31 Oct: daily, 10am - 6pm, (5pm in Oct). 1 Nov - 31 Mar: Wed - Sun, 10am - 4pm. Closed 24 - 26 Dec & 1 Jan.

Admission: Adult £3.25, Child £1.50, Conc. £2.50. 15% discount for groups (11+). Prices include VAT.

ℹ Picnic area. ♿ Grounds suitable. WC. ⌷ ❋

DRAGON HALL

Tel: 01603 663922

115 - 123 King Street, Norwich, Norfolk NR1 1QE

Owner: Norfolk & Norwich Heritage Trust Ltd　　**Contact:** Mr Neil Sigsworth

Magnificent medieval merchants' hall described as "one of the most exciting 15th century buildings in England". A wealth of outstanding features include living hall, screens passage, vaulted undercroft, superb timber-framed Great Hall, crown-post roof and intricately carved and painted dragon. Built by Robert Toppes, a wealthy and influential merchant. Dragon Hall is a unique legacy of medieval life, craftsmanship and trade.

Location: OS Ref. TG235 084. SE of Norwich city centre.

Opening Times: Apr - Oct: Mon - Sat, 10am - 4pm. Nov - Mar: Mon - Fri, 10am - 4pm. Closed 23 Dec - 2 Jan & BHs.

Admission: Adult £2, Child 50p, Conc. £1.50.

🏛 ♿ House suitable. ⚘ Obligatory. 🐕 Guide dogs only. ❋

FAIRHAVEN WOODLAND & WATER GARDEN

Tel: 01603 270449

2 The Woodlands, Wymers Lane, South Walsham NR13 6EA

Owner: The Fairhaven Garden Trust　　**Contact:** George Debbage, Manager

180 acre woodland & water garden with private broad in the beautiful Norfolk Broads.

Location: OS Ref. TG368 134. 9m NE of Norwich just N of the B1140 at South Walsham.

Opening Times: Daily (except 25 Dec), 10am - 5pm, also May - Aug: Wed & Thurs evenings until 9pm.

Admission: Adult £3, Child £1 (under 5yrs Free), OAP £2.70. Group reductions.

FELBRIGG HALL

NT Photographic Library: Rupert Truman.

FELBRIGG, NORWICH, NORFOLK NR11 8PR

Owner: The National Trust *Contact:* The Property Manager

Tel: 01263 837444 **Fax:** 01263 837032

One of the finest 17th century houses in East Anglia, the hall contains its original 18th century furniture and Grand Tour paintings, as well as an outstanding library. The walled garden has been restored and features a dovecote and small orchard.

Location: OS133 Ref. TG193 394. Nr Felbrigg village, 2m SW of Cromer, entrance off B1436, signposted from A148 and A140.

Opening Times: House: 31 Mar - 4 Nov: daily except Thurs & Fris, 1 - 5pm; BH Suns & Mons, 11am - 5pm. House will close at 4pm on and after 29 Oct. Garden: As house, 11am - 5.30pm.

Admission: House & Garden: Adult £5.80, Child £2.90, Family £14.50. Garden only: £2.20. Groups: (except BHs), £4.80. Groups please book with SAE to the Property Manager.

Tel: 01263 837040. 01263 838237. Licensed. Licensed. Partially suitable. By arrangement. In park, on leads. Park. Tel. 01263 838297 for details.

GRIME'S GRAVES

Tel: 01842 810656

Lynford, Thetford, Norfolk IP26 5DE

Owner: English Heritage **Contact:** The Custodian

These remarkable Neolithic flint mines, unique in England, comprise over 300 pits and shafts. The visitor can descend some 30 feet by ladder into one excavated shaft, and look along the radiating galleries, from where the flint used for making axes and knives was extracted. Special flint-knapping days are advertised throughout the year.

Location: OS144 Ref. TL818 898. 7m NW of Thetford off A134.

Opening Times: 1 Apr - 31 Oct, daily, 10am - 6pm, (5pm in Oct). 1 Nov - 31 Mar: Wed - Sun, 10am - 4pm (closed 1 - 2pm) Closed 24 - 26 Dec & 1 Jan. Last visit to pit 20 mins before close. NB: Visits to pit for children under 5yrs at the discretion of the custodian.

Admission: Adult £2.10, Child £1.10, Conc. £1.60.

P ❄ ☗ Tel. for details.

HOLKHAM HALL

See page 270 for full page entry.

Wild Flowers at Houghton Hall, Norfolk.

HOUGHTON HALL

HOUGHTON, KING'S LYNN, NORFOLK PE31 6UE

Owner: The Marquess of Cholmondeley *Contact:* Susan Cleaver

Tel: 01485 528569 **Fax:** 01485 528167 **e-mail:** enquiries@houghtonhall.com

Houghton Hall was built in the 18th century by Sir Robert Walpole. Original designs were by Colen Campbell and revised by Thomas Ripley with interior decoration by William Kent. It is regarded as one of the finest examples of Palladian architecture in England. Houghton was later inherited by the 1st Marquess of Cholmondeley through his grandmother, Sir Robert's daughter. Situated in beautiful parkland, the house contains magnificent furniture, pictures and china. A private collection of 20,000 model soldiers and militaria. 5-acre walled garden.

Location: OS Ref. TF792 287. 13m E of King's Lynn, 10m W of Fakenham 1¹/₂ m N of A148.

Opening Times: 15 Apr - 30 Sept: Suns, Thurs & BH Mons, 1 - 5.30pm. House: 2 - 5.30pm. Last admission 5pm.

Admission: Adult £6, Child (5-16) £3, Groups (20+): Adult £5.50, Child £2.50. Excluding house: Adult £3.50, Child £2, Groups (20+) Adult £3, Child £1.50.

HOVETON HALL GARDENS

Tel: 01603 782798 **Fax:** 01603 784564

Wroxham, Norwich, Norfolk NR12 8RJ

Owner: Mr & Mrs Andrew Buxton   **Contact:** Mrs Buxton

10 acres of rhododendrons, azaleas, woodland and lakeside walks, walled herbaceous and vegetable gardens. Traditional tearooms and plant sales. The Hall (which is not open to the public) was built 1809 - 1812. Designs attributed to Humphry Repton.

Location: OS Ref. TG314 202. 8m N of Norwich. 1½ m NNE of Wroxham on A1151. Follow brown tourist signs.

Opening Times: Easter Sun - mid-Sept: Weds, Fris, Suns & BH Mons, 11am - 5.30pm. Also open Thurs in May.

Admission: Adult £3.50, Child £1, Wheelchairs users £2, Family £20, Season ticket £9.50. Groups: £3 (if booked in advance).

LETHERINGSETT WATERMILL

Tel: 01263 713153 **e-mail:** watermill@ic24.net

Riverside Road, Letheringsett, Holt, Norfolk NR25 7YD

Owner/Contact: M D Thurlow

Water-powered mill producing wholewheat flour from locally grown wheat. Built in 1802.

Location: OS Ref. TG062 387. Riverside Road, Letheringsett, Holt, Norfolk.

Opening Times: Whitsun - Oct: Mon - Fri, 10am - 5pm, Sat 9am - 1pm. Working demonstration, every afternoon, 2 - 4.30pm. Viewing may take place at any other time. Oct - Whitsun: Mon - Fri, 9am - 4pm. Sat, 9am - 1pm. Working demonstration, Tue - Fri, 1.30 3.30pm. BH Suns & Mons, 2 - 5pm.

Admission: Adult £2, Child £1.50. When demonstrating: Adult £3, Child £2, OAP £2.50, Family (2+2) £9.

MANNINGTON GARDENS & COUNTRYSIDE

Tel: 01263 584175

Mannington Hall, Norwich NR11 7BB   **Fax:** 01263 761214

Owner: The Lord & Lady Walpole   **Contact:** Lady Walpole

Gardens with lake, moat and woodland. Outstanding rose collection, heritage rose gardens.

Location: OS Ref. TG144 320. Signposted from Saxthorpe crossroads on the Norwich - Holt road B1149. 1½ m W of Wolterton Hall.

Opening Times: Gardens: May - Sept: Suns 12 - 5pm. Jun - Aug: Wed - Fri, 11am - 5pm. Walks: daily from 9am. Medieval Hall open by appointment.

Admission: Adult £3, Child (under 16yrs) Free, Conc. £2.50. Groups by arrangement.

No photography. | Grounds suitable. WCs. | Licensed. | By arrangement. | P | Guide dogs only.

THE MANOR HOUSE

Great Cressingham, Thetford, Norfolk IP25 6NJ

Owner/Contact: Mrs L R Chapman

Small Tudor manor house famous for its terracotta façade.

Location: OS Ref. TF852 020. 6m S of Swaffham. 1½ m E of A1065.

Opening Times: By written appointment only.

Admission: Prices on application.

NORWICH CASTLE MUSEUM

Tel: 01603 493625 **Fax:** 01603 493623

Norwich, Norfolk NR1 3JU   **e-mail:** museums@norfolk.gov.uk

Norman Castle Keep, housing displays of art, archaeology and natural history.

Location: OS Ref. TG233 085. City centre.

Opening Times: Norwich Castle Museum is closed until Spring 2001 due to extensive refurbishment of the historic Norman Keep and redisplay of the Museum's galleries.

Castle Rising Castle, King's Lynn, Norfolk.

OXBURGH HALL, GDNS & ESTATE

OXBOROUGH, KING'S LYNN, NORFOLK PE33 9PS

Owner: *The National Trust* **Contact:** *The Property Manager*

Tel: 01366 328258 **Fax:** 01366 328066

A moated manor house built in 1482 by the Bedingfeld family, who still live here. The rooms show the development from medieval austerity to Victorian comfort and include an outstanding display of embroidery done by Mary Queen of Scots. The attractive gardens include a French parterre, kitchen garden and orchard.

Location: OS143 Ref. TF742 012. At Oxborough, 7m SW of Swaffham on S side of Stoke Ferry road.

Opening Times: 31 Mar - 4 Nov: Sat - Wed, 1 - 5pm, BH Mons, 11am - 5pm. Last admission 4.30pm. Garden: 3 - 25 Mar: Sats & Suns, 11am - 4pm. 31 Mar - 4 Nov: Sat - Wed, also daily in Aug: 11am - 5.30pm.

Admission: Adult £5.30, Family discounts. Garden & Estate only: Adult £2.60. Groups: £4.20. Groups must book with SAE to the Property Manager.

Licensed. | Partially suitable. | By arrangement. | P | In grounds, on leads. | Send SAE for details.

PLANTATION GARDEN

Tel: 01603 621868 **Fax:** 0870 1692343

4 Earlham Road, Norwich   **e-mail:** chair@plantationgarden.co.uk

Owner: Plantation Garden Preservation Trust   **Contact:** Chairperson
(Reg. Charity No. 801095)

The Plantation Garden is a Grade II English Heritage registered garden established 143 years ago in an abondoned chalk quarry some 600 yards from the city centre. It comprises nearly 3 acres in all, and includes a huge gothic fountain, flower beds, lawns, Italianate terrace, 'medieval' terrace wall, woodland walkways and rustic bridge.

Location: OS Ref. TG223 085. Leave inner ring road on B1108 Earlham Road, on left immediatly after St John's Roman Catholic Cathedral (entry shared with Beeches hotel driveway).

Opening Times: Apr - mid-October: daily, 9am - 6pm and other times 10am - 4pm.

Admission: Normally £1.50 (honesty box if garden unattended). Child Free.

On Suns, pm only. | Partially suitable. | On Suns, pm only. | By arrangement. | P 300 metres. | By arrangement. | Tel. for details.

RAVENINGHAM HALL GARDENS

Tel: 01508 548480 **Fax:** 01508 548958

Raveningham, Norwich, Norfolk NR14 6NS   **e-mail:** raveningham@freenet.co.uk

Owner: Sir Nicholas Bacon Bt   **Contact:** Mrs J Woodard

Gardens laid out approximately 100 years ago around a red brick Georgian house which is not open to the public.

Location: OS Ref. TM399 965. Between Beccles and Loddon off B1136/B1140.

Opening Times: 1 Apr - 30 Sept: Suns, Weds & BH Mons, 2 - 5.30pm.

Admission: Adult £2.50, Child (under 16yrs) Free, OAP £2. Groups by prior arrangement.

ROW 111 HOUSE, OLD MERCHANT'S HOUSE, & GREYFRIARS' CLOISTERS

South Quay, Great Yarmouth, Norfolk NR30 2RQ   **Tel:** 01493 857900

Owner: English Heritage   **Contact:** The Custodian

Two 17th century Row Houses, rows 111 and 113, a type of building unique to Great Yarmouth, containing original fixtures and displays of local architectural fittings and early wall paintings.

Location: OS134 Ref. TG525 072. In Great Yarmouth, make for South Quay, by riverside and dock, ½ m inland from beach. Follow signs to dock and south quay.

Opening Times: 1 Apr - 31 Oct: daily, 10am - 5pm. Closed 1 - 2pm. Guided tours depart from Row 111 house at 10, 11am, 12 noon, 2, 3 & 4pm.

Admission: Adult £2.40. Child £1.20, Conc. £1.80. 15% discount for groups of 11+.

ST GEORGE'S GUILDHALL

Tel: 01553 765565

27-29 Kings Street, Kings Lynn, Norfolk PE30 1HA

Owner: The National Trust   **Contact:** The Administrator

The largest surviving English medieval guildhall, with adjoining medieval warehouse, now in use as an Arts Centre.

Location: OS132 Ref. TF616 202. On W side of King Street close to the Tuesday Market Place.

Opening Times: All year: Mon - Fri (closed Good Fri, BHs & 24 Dec - 1st Mon in Jan), 10am - 2pm. Times may vary in Jul & Aug. The Guildhall is not usually open on days when there are performances in the theatre, tel. box office 01553 764864 for details.

Admission: Free.

Access to galleries.   Licensed.

SANDRINGHAM

See page 271 for full page entry.

WALSINGHAM ABBEY GROUNDS & SHIREHALL MUSEUM

Little Walsingham, Norfolk NR22 6BP   **Tel:** 01328 820259 **Fax:** 01328 820098

Owner: Walsingham Estate Company   **Contact:** The Agent

Set in Walsingham, a picturesque medieval village, the grounds contain the remains of an Augustinian Priory founded in 1153.

Location: OS Ref. TF934 367. B1105 N from Fakenham - 5m.

Opening Times: Please contact for details.

Admission: Please telephone for details.

WOLTERTON PARK

Tel: 01263 584175 **Fax:** 01263 761214

Norwich, Norfolk NR11 7BB

Owner: The Lord and Lady Walpole   **Contact:** The Lady Walpole

18th century Hall. Historic park with lake.

Location: OS Ref. TG164 317. Situated near Erpingham village, signposted from Norwich - Cromer Rd A140.

Opening Times: Park: daily from 9am. Hall: Fridays Spring - Autumn, 2 - 5pm and by appointment.

Admission: £2 car park fee only. Groups by application. Hall tours: See local press, from £4 groups, £5 individuals.

Partially suitable. WC.   Obligatory for Hall.   P
In grounds, on leads.

Holkham Hall, Norfolk.

Owner:
Patrick Phillips Esq

CONTACT

Mrs J G Phillips
Kentwell Hall
Long Melford
Suffolk
CO10 9BA

Tel: 01787 310207

Fax: 01787 379318

LOCATION

OS Ref. TL864 479

Off the A134.
4m N of Sudbury, 14m S of
Bury St. Edmunds
1m NNW of
Long Melford off A134.

Rail: Sudbury Station 4m
Colchester Station 20m.

Air: Stansted 30m.
Airstrip at Kentwell
suitable for light aircraft
and microlites.

Taxi: Sudbury Town Taxis
01787 377366.

CONFERENCE/FUNCTION		
ROOM	SIZE	MAX CAPACITY
Great Hall	40' x 24'	120
Main Dining Room	24' x 24'	75
Drawing Rm	35' x 24'	75
Library	36' x 20'	20
Overcroft	120' x 22'	300

KENTWELL HALL
Long Melford

KENTWELL HALL is a beautiful redbrick Tudor Manor House surrounded by a broad moat.

Built by the Clopton Family, from wealth made in the wool trade, Kentwell has an air of timeless tranquillity. The exterior is little altered in 450 years. The interior was remodelled by Hopper in 1825 and his work has been embellished and enhanced in restoration by the present owners. Hopper's interiors, notably the Great Hall and Dining Room, emphasise their Tudor provenance, but the Drawing Room and Library are simply and restrainedly classical; all are eminently habitable.

Kentwell, as well as being a family home, conveys a deep feeling of the Tudor period with the service areas: great kitchen, bakery, dairy and forge always fully equipped in 16th century style. Kentwell's unique 16th century atmosphere and large collection of 16th century artefacts make it an ideal location for films and videos.

The gardens are part of Kentwell's delight. Intimate yet spacious, you are seldom far from a moat, clipped yews (some 30ft high) or mellow brick wall. There is a fine walled garden with original 17th century layout and a well established large Herb Garden and Potager.

The farm is run organically and is set around timber-framed buildings and stocked with rare breed farm animals.

Home to the award winning **'Re-creations of Tudor Domestic Life'** when visitors meet numerous 'Tudors' with dress, speech, activities and locations appropriate for the 16th century. These take place on selected weekends between April and September.

❖

Corporate events include conferences and 'company days', specially devised one-day programme of fun, stimulation and challenges. A wide range of Tudor activities can be arranged for visitors, including longbow shooting, working bakery, dairy and still-room, spinning, etc. or even clay pigeon shooting in the Park. No photography in house.

Genuine Tudor-style banquets, wedding receptions, formal but friendly luncheons and dinners.

Visitors may alight at house, with prior notice. WC.

Home-made food. The Undercroft comfortably seats 96. Overcroft can accommodate up to 300.

Ample.

There is a highly developed schools programme dealing with 700 parties per year. Schools can visit a re-creation of Tudor life, re-create Tudor life themselves for the day or take one of the tours conducted by experienced guides on the House, Garden, Farm or aspects of each.

No dogs.

OPENING TIMES

House, Gardens & Farm

• 22 April - 10 June: Suns only except:
  17 - 20 April: daily and Half-term: 29 May - 1 June.
  12 noon - 5pm.
• 11 July - 21 September daily 12 noon - 5pm.
• 30 Sept - 28 Oct Suns only, 12 noon - 5pm
• 21 - 26 Oct daily: 12 noon - 5pm.

Gardens & Farm only

• 4 March - 8 April: Suns only, 10am - 5pm.

The Great Annual Re-creation

• 17 June - 8 July: Sats & Suns only & Fri, 6 July, 11am - 5pm.

Other Re-creations

• 13 - 16 Apr: Easter
• 5 - 6 May: May Day
• 19 - 20 May: Land Girls
• 26 - 28 May: Whitsun
• 4 - 5 Aug: World War II
• 24 - 27 Aug: High Summer
• 22 - 23 Sept: Michaelmas
• 13 - 14 Oct: World War II
All 11am - 6pm, sometimes 5pm.
Special Prices apply.

ADMISSION

House, Gardens & Farm
Adult £5.70
Child (5-15yrs) £3.40
OAP.........................£4.90
Gardens & Farm only
Adult £3.60
Child (5-15yrs) £2.30
OAP.........................£3.20
Great Annual Re-creation
Adult £12.00
Child (5-15yrs) £9.00
OAP......................£10.50

THE ANCIENT HOUSE

Tel: 01628 825920 or 825925 (bookings)

Clare, Suffolk CO10 8NY

Owner: Leased to the Landmark Trust by Clare Parish Council

Contact: The Landmark Trust

A 14th century house extended in the 15th and 17th centuries, decorated with high relief pargetting. Half of the building is managed by the Landmark Trust, which lets buildings for self-catering holidays. The other half of the house is run as a museum. Full details of The Ancient House and 170 other historic buildings available for holidays are featured in The Landmark Handbook (price £9.50 refundable against booking), from The Landmark Trust, Shottesbrooke, Maidenhead, Berkshire SL6 3SW.

Location: OS Ref. TL769 454. Village centre, on A1092 8m WNW of Sudbury.

Opening Times: By appointment only and for Clare Arts Festival, week commencing 16 Jun.

Admission: Museum: Contact 01787 277662 for details.

BELCHAMP HALL

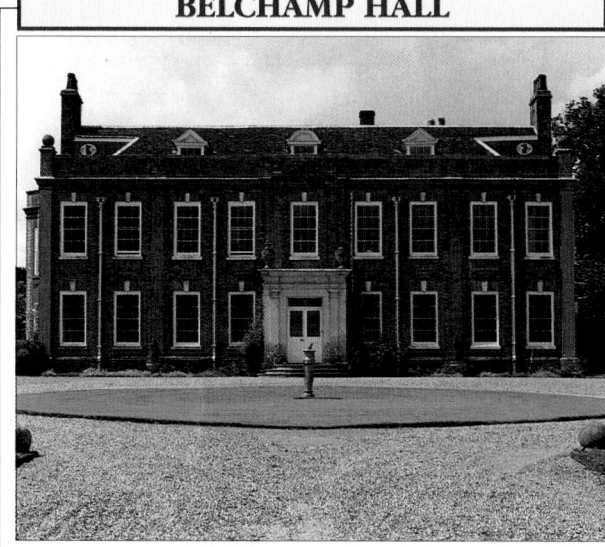

BELCHAMP WALTER, SUDBURY, SUFFOLK CO10 7AT
Owner/Contact: Mr C F V Raymond

Tel: 01787 881961 **Fax:** 01787 880729

Superb Queen Anne house on a site belonging to the Raymond family since 1611. Historic portraits and period furniture. Suitable for receptions and an ideal film location, often seen as Lady Jane's house in *Lovejoy*. Gardens including a cherry avenue, follies, a sunken garden, walled garden and lake. Medieval church with 15th century wall paintings.

Location: OS Ref. TL827 407. 5m SW of Sudbury, opposite Belchamp Walter Church.

Opening Times: By appointment only: May - Sept: Tues, Thurs & BHs, 2.30 - 6pm.

Admission: Adult £4, Child £1.75. No reduction for groups.

[i] No photography in house. [T] [By arrangement]. [Obligatory]. [P] Guide dogs only.

CHRISTCHURCH MANSION

Tel: 01473 253246 **Fax:** 01473 281274

Christchurch Park, Ipswich, Suffolk IP4 2BD

Owner/Contact: Ipswich Borough Council

A fine Tudor house set in beautiful parkland.

Location: OS Ref. TM165 450. Christchurch Park, near centre of Ipswich.

Opening Times: All year: Tue - Sat, 10am - 5pm (dusk in winter). Suns, 2.30 - 4.30pm (dusk in winter). Also open BH Mons. Closed 24 - 26 Dec, 1/2 Jan and Good Fri.

Admission: Free.

EAST BERGHOLT PLACE GARDEN

Tel/Fax: 01206 299224

East Bergholt, Suffolk CO7 6UP

Owner: Mr & Mrs R L C Eley **Contact:** Sara Eley

Fifteen acres of garden and arboretum originally laid out at the beginning of the century by the present owner's great-grandfather. A wonderful collection of fine trees and shrubs, many of which are rarely seen growing in East Anglia and originate from the famous plant hunter George Forrest. Particularly beautiful in the spring when the rhododendrons, magnolias and camellias are in flower. There is a specialist plant centre in the Victorian walled garden.

Location: OS Ref. TM084 343. 2m E of A12 on B1070, Manningtree Rd, on the edge of East Bergholt.

Opening Times: Mar - Sept: daily, 10am - 5pm. Closed Easter Sun.

Admission: Adult £2.50, Child Free. (Proceeds to garden up-keep).

[By arrangement].

EUSTON HALL

Tel: 01842 766366 **Fax:** 01842 766764

Estate Office, Euston, Thetford, Norfolk IP24 2QP

Owner: The Duke of Grafton **Contact:** Mrs L Campbell

18th century house contains a famous collection of paintings including works by Stubbs, Van Dyck, Lely and Kneller. The Pleasure Grounds were were laid out by John Evelyn and William Kent. 17th century parish church in Wren style. River walk, watermill and picnic area.

Location: OS Ref. TL897 786. 12m N of Bury St Edmunds, on A1088. 2m E of A134.

Opening Times: 7 Jun - 27 Sept: Thurs 2.30 - 5pm. Also Suns 24 Jun & 2 Sept: 2.30 - 5pm.

Admission: Adult £3, Child 50p, OAP £2.50. Groups (12+): £2.50pp.

Grounds suitable.

FLATFORD BRIDGE COTTAGE

Tel: 01206 298260 **Fax:** 01206 299193

Flatford, East Bergholt, Colchester, Essex CO7 6OL

Owner: The National Trust **Contact:** The Property Manager

Just upstream from Flatford Mill, the restored thatched cottage houses a display about John Constable, several of whose paintings depict this property. Facilities include a tea garden, shop, boat hire, an Information Centre and countryside walks.

Location: OS Ref. TM077 332. On N bank of Stour, 1m S of East Bergholt B1070.

Opening Times: Mar & Apr: Wed - Sun, 11am - 5.30pm. May - end Sept: daily, 10am - 5.30pm. Oct: daily, 11am - 5.30pm. Nov & Dec: Wed - Sun, 11am - 3.30pm. Jan & Feb 2002: Sats & Suns only, 11am - 3.30pm. Closed Christmas & New Year.

Admission: Guided walks £1.90, accompanied child Free.

Tea garden & shop accessible. WC. Charge applies. Guide dogs only.

FRAMLINGHAM CASTLE

FRAMLINGHAM, SUFFOLK IP8 9BT
Owner: English Heritage Contact: The Custodian

Tel: 01728 724189

A superb 12th century castle which, from the outside, looks almost the same as when it was built. From the continuous curtain wall linking 13 towers, there are excellent views of Framlingham and the charming reed-fringed mere. At different times the castle has been a fortress, an Elizabethan prison, a poor house and a school. The many alterations over the years have led to a pleasing mixture of historic styles.

Location: OS Ref. TM287 637. In Framlingham on B1116. NE of town centre.

Opening Times: 1 Apr - 31 Oct: daily 10am - 6pm (5pm in Oct). 1 Nov - 31 Mar: daily 10am - 4pm. Closed 24 - 26 Dec & 1 Jan.

Admission: Adult £3.50, Child £1.80, Conc. £2.60, Family £8.80. 15% discount for groups (11+).

Ground floor & grounds suitable. WCs. [P] Tel. for details.

GAINSBOROUGH'S HOUSE

46 GAINSBOROUGH ST, SUDBURY, SUFFOLK CO10 2EU

Owner: Gainsborough's House Society   *Contact:* Rosemary Woodward

Tel: 01787 372958   **Fax:** 01787 376991   **e-mail:** mail@gainsborough.org

Birthplace of Thomas Gainsborough RA (1727-88). Georgian-fronted town house, with attractive walled garden, displays more of the artist's work than any other gallery. The collection is shown together with 18th century furniture and memorabilia. Varied programme of contemporary exhibitions organised throughout the year includes: fine art, craft, photography, printmaking, sculpture and highlights the work of East Anglian artists.

Location: OS Ref. TL872 413. 46 Gainsborough Street, Sudbury town centre.

Opening Times: All year: Tue - Sat, 10am - 5pm, Suns & BH Mons, 2 - 5pm. Closes at 4pm Nov - Mar. Closed: Mons, Good Fri and Christmas to New Year.

Admission: Adult £3, Child/Student £1.50, OAP £2.50.

ℹ No photography. ⬛ ♿ Ground floor suitable. WCs.
🅿 No parking. ▥ ❄ Ⓦ

HADLEIGH GUILDHALL   **Tel:** 01473 827752

Hadleigh, Suffolk IP7 5DT

Owner: Hadleigh Market Feoffment Charity   **Contact:** Jane Haylock

Fine timber framed guildhall, one of the least known medieval buildings in Suffolk.

Location: OS Ref. TM025 425. S side of churchyard.

Opening Times: Jun - end Sept: Building: Thurs & Suns; Garden: daily (except Sats), 2 - 5pm

Admission: £1.50, Conc. £1. Garden only: Free.

HAUGHLEY PARK 🏛   **Tel:** 01359 240701

Stowmarket, Suffolk IP14 3JY

Owner/Contact: R J Williams Esq

Jacobean manor house, garden and woodland walks.

Location: OS Ref. TM005 618. 4m W of Stowmarket signed off A14.

Opening Times: Garden only: May - Sept: Tues & last Sun in Apr & 1st Sun in May, 2 - 5.30pm. House open by prior appointment on above Tues only (tel: 01359 240701).

Admission: Adult £2, Child £1.

Website Index page 39 ◄◄◄

HELMINGHAM HALL GARDENS 🏛

STOWMARKET, SUFFOLK IP14 6EF

Owner: The Lord & Lady Tollemache   *Contact:* Ms Jane Tresidder

Tel: 01473 890363   **Fax:** 01473 890776

The Tudor Hall surrounded by its wide moat is set in a 400 acre deer park. Two superb gardens, one surrounded by its own moat and walls extends to several acres and has wide herbaceous borders and an immaculate kitchen garden. The second enclosed within yew hedges, has a special rose garden with a herb and knot garden containing plants grown in England before 1750.

Location: OS Ref. TM190 578. B1077, 9m N of Ipswich, 5m S of Debenham.

Opening Times: Gardens only: 29 Apr - 9 Sept: Suns, 2 - 6pm. Groups: by appointment only on Weds, 2 - 5pm. (We can also accept individual bookings on a Wed if a group is booked.)

Admission: Adult £3.75, Child (5-15yrs) £2. Groups (30+) £3.25. Weds: £3.75pp.

⬛ 🍴 ♿ Grounds suitable. WCs. 🐾 Ⓚ By arrangement. 🅿
🐕 In grounds, on leads. Ⓦ

HENGRAVE HALL CENTRE

BURY ST EDMUNDS, SUFFOLK IP28 6LZ

Owner: Religious of the Assumption   *Contact:* Mr J H Crowe

Tel: 01284 701561   **Fax:** 01284 702950

e-mail: co-ordinator@hengravehallcentre.org.uk

Hengrave Hall is a unique Tudor house of stone and brick, built between 1525 and 1538 by Sir Thomas Kytson, Warden of the Mercers' Company. Former home to the Kytson and Gage families, it was visited by Elizabeth I on her Suffolk Progress in 1578. Set in 45 acres of cultivated grounds, the Hall is now run as a Conference and Retreat Centre by the Hengrave Community of Reconciliation. The Hall has many important and distinctive features, including beautiful stained glass and the magnificent Oriel Window and Frieze incorporating the Garter Arms and other Coats of Arms which were comprehensively restored in summer 2000. The ancient church with Saxon tower adjoins the Hall and continues to be used for daily prayer.

Location: OS Ref. TL824 686. 3¹/₂ m NW of Bury St Edmunds on the A1101.

Opening Times: Please telephone the Warden for conference facilities (day and residential); tours (by appointment); retreats; programme of events; schools' programme. Special group rates.

ℹ Children's playground. ⬛ 🍴 🚼 ♿ 🐾 Ⓚ By arrangement.
🎭 ❄ 🐕 Tel. for details. Ⓦ

ICKWORTH HOUSE & PARK

NT Photographic Library: Rupert Truman

THE ROTUNDA, HORRINGER, BURY ST EDMUNDS IP29 5QE

Owner: The National Trust   *Contact:* The Property Manager

Tel: 01284 735270 **Fax:** 01284 735175 **e-mail:** arorec@smtp.ntrust.org.uk

One of the most unusual houses in East Anglia. The huge Rotunda of this 18th century Italianate house dominates the landscape. Inside are collections of Georgian silver, Regency furniture, Old Master paintings and family portraits.

Location: OS155 Ref. TL816 611. In Horringer, 3m SW of Bury St Edmunds on W side of A143.

Opening Times: House: 24 Mar - 28 Oct: daily except Mons & Thurs (open BH Mons), 1 - 5pm, last admission 4.30pm (closes 4.30pm in Oct). Garden: 24 Mar - 28 Oct: daily; 29 Oct - end Mar 2002: Mon - Fri, 10am - 5pm, last admission 4.30pm. 1 Nov - end Mar 2002: 10am - 4pm. Park: daily, 7am - 7pm. Note: Garden & Park closed 25 Dec.

Admission: Adult £5.70, Child £2.50. Family discounts. Park & Garden only (includes access to shop & restaurant): Adult £2.50, Child 80p. Groups (must book): Adult £4.70, Child £2. No group discounts on Suns & BH Mons.

⬚ ♿Partially suitable. �'¶'Licensed. ☕ ✗By arrangement. ⬛ 🐕In park, on leads. ♨ Tel. for details.

KENTWELL HALL 🏛

See page 276 for full page entry.

LANDGUARD FORT ⊞   **Tel:** 01394 277767

Felixstowe, Suffolk

Owner: English Heritage   **Contact:** The Custodian

Impressive 18th century fort with later additions built on a site originally fortified by Henry VIII and in use until after World War II. There is also a museum (not EH).

Location: OS Ref. TM284 318. 1m S of Felixstowe at extreme S end of dock area.

Opening Times: 23 Apr - 29 Oct: Suns & BHs, 10.30am - 5pm. 6 Jun - 16 Sept: Tues, Weds & Sats, 1 - 5pm (2000/2001 openings). Please telephone for 2001 - 2002 details.

Admission: Adult £2, Child £1, Conc. £1.50.

LAVENHAM: THE GUILDHALL OF CORPUS CHRISTI 🌿 **Tel:** 01787 247646

The Market Place, Lavenham, Sudbury CO10 9QZ   **e-mail:** almjtg@smtp.ntrust.org.uk

Owner: The National Trust   **Contact:** The Property Manager

This splendid 16th century timber-framed building dominates the Market Place of the picturesque town of Lavenham with its many historic houses and wonderful church. Inside are exhibitions on local history, farming and industry, as well as the story of the medieval woollen cloth trade. There is also a walled garden with dye plants.

Location: OS155 Ref. TL915 942. 6m NNE of Sudbury. Village centre. A1141 and B1071.

Opening Times: Mar & Nov: Sats & Suns, 11am - 4pm. Apr - end Oct: daily, 11am - 5pm (closed Good Fri). The building or parts of it, may be closed occasionally for community use.

Admission: Adult £3, accompanied child Free. Groups: £2.50. School parties (by arrangement) 60p per child.

⬚ ♿Shop & tearoom suitable. ☕

LEISTON ABBEY ⊞   **Tel:** 01223 582700 (Regional Office)

Leiston, Suffolk

Owner: English Heritage   **Contact:** The East of England Regional Office

The remains of this abbey for Premonstratensian canons, including a restored chapel, are amongst the most extensive in Suffolk.

Location: OS Ref. TM445 642. 1m N of Leiston off B1069.

Opening Times: Any reasonable time.

Admission: Free.

LITTLE HALL   **Tel:** 01787 247179 **Fax:** 01787 248341

Market Place, Lavenham, Suffolk CO10 9QZ

Owner: Suffolk Building Preservation Trust   **Contact:** R Attew

Little Hall, a Grade II Listed Building with a Crown Post roof, reveals five centuries of change. Its history mirrors the rise and fall of Lavenham's cloth trade. Restored by the Gayer-Anderson twins in the 1930s.

Location: OS Ref. TL917 494. Market Place, Lavenham. 50yds E of Guildhall.

Opening Times: 1 Apr - end Oct: Weds, Thurs, Sats, Suns, 2 - 5pm. BHs: 11am - 5.30pm.

Admission: Adult £1.50, Child Free.

MANOR HOUSE MUSEUM

HONEY HILL, BURY ST EDMUNDS, SUFFOLK IP33 IHF

Owner: St Edmundsbury Borough Council   *Contact:* The Manager

Tel: 01284 757076 **Fax:** 01284 757079

A Georgian town house, built by the Earl of Bristol for his wife Elizabeth between 1736 and 1737 as her town house in which she would entertain her friends during the day and into the evening, before returning to Ickworth House, the family seat. Extensively restored in the '80s it now houses a collection of clocks, watches and wooden time pieces, a collection of costume, local and international artists. Also a friendly ghost.

Location: OS Ref. TL858 640. Bury town centre off A14. Just S of Abbey grounds.

Opening Times: Please telephone for details.

Admission: Please telephone for details.

⬚ 🔔 ✻ ♨ Tel. for details.

MELFORD HALL 🌿   **Tel:** 01787 880286

Long Melford, Sudbury, Suffolk CO10 9AA

Owner: The National Trust   **Contact:** The Administrator

A turreted brick Tudor mansion, little changed since 1578 with the original panelled banqueting hall, an 18th century drawing room, a Regency library and Victorian bedrooms, showing fine furniture and Chinese porcelain.

Location: OS Ref. TL867 462. In Long Melford off A134, 14m S of Bury St Edmunds, 3m N of Sudbury.

Opening Times: Apr & Oct: Sat, Sun & BH Mon, 2 - 5.30pm. May - Sept: Wed - Sun & BH Mon, 2 - 5.30pm. Last admission 5pm.

Admission: £4.40. Groups (pre-arranged) £3.30. Wed - Sat only, write with SAE to Senior Visitor Reception Assistant.

♿ Stairlift to 1st floor. WC. 🐕 In car park & park walk only, on leads.

MOYSES HALL MUSEUM   **Tel:** 01284 757069

e-mail: maggie.goodger@stedsbc.gov.uk

Cornhill, Bury St Edmunds, Suffolk IP33 1DX

Owner: St Edmundsbury Borough Council   **Contact:** The Gallery Supervisor

Very early 12th century flint house, now a museum of local history.

Location: OS Ref. TL853 644. Town centre off A14. 300 yds NW of Abbey grounds.

Opening Times: Museum will be closed for much of 2001 for redevelopment work. Please telephone or e-mail for details of re-opening.

Admission: Please telephone or e-mail for details.

ORFORD CASTLE

© English Heritage Photo Library. ©Skyscan Balloon Photography.

ORFORD, WOODBRIDGE, SUFFOLK IP12 2ND

Owner: English Heritage   *Contact:* The Custodian

Tel: 01394 450472

A royal castle built by Henry II for coastal defence in the 12th century. A magnificent keep survives almost intact with three immense towers reaching to 30m (90ft). Fine views over Orford and the surrounding countryside.

Location: OS169 Ref. TM419 499. In Orford on B1084, 20m NE of Ipswich.

Opening Times: 1 Apr - 31 Oct: daily 10am - 6pm (5pm in Oct). 1 Nov - 31 Mar: Wed - Sun, 10am - 4pm. Closed 1 - 2pm. Closed 24 - 26 Dec & 1 Jan.

Admission: Adult £3.10, Child £1.60, Conc. £2.30. 15% discount for groups (11+).

Tel. for details.

OTLEY HALL

OTLEY, IPSWICH, SUFFOLK IP6 9PA

Owner: Mr Nicholas & Mrs Ann Hagger   *Contact:* Mrs Chris Buckle (Administrator)

Tel: 01473 890264   **Fax:** 01473 890803

A stunning 15th century Moated Hall (Grade I), set in gardens and grounds of 10 acres, frequently described as "one of England's loveliest houses". Rich in history and architectural detail. Features of particular note are richly carved beams, superb linenfold, c1559 wall paintings, herringbone brickwork and vine-leaf pargetting. From around 1401 Otley Hall was the home of the Gosnold family for some 300 years. Bartholomew Gosnold voyaged to the New World in 1602 and named Cape Cod and Martha's Vineyard. He returned in 1607 to found the Jamestown settlement, the first English-speaking settlement in the US, 13 years before the Mayflower landed. The account of the 1602 voyage is thought to have provided the geography for Shakespeare's *Tempest*. The gardens are formal and informal, with canal, mount, nutteries, rose garden, woodland, and historically accurate Tudor features including a knot and herb garden, designed by Sylvia Landsberg (author of *The Medieval Garden*). The new Millennium Garden is a gravel garden with a Mediterranean theme.

Location: OS Ref. TM207 563. 7m N of Ipswich, off the B1079.

Opening Times: Every BH Sun & Mon, 12.30 - 6pm. Gardens: Mons & Weds only from 16 Apr - 24 Sept, 2 - 5pm.

Admission: Adult £4.50, Child £2.50. Garden days: Adult £3, Child £1, OAP £2.60. Coach parties welcome all year by appointment for private guided tours.

Partially suitable. By arrangement.

PAKENHAM WATERMILL   **Tel:** 01359 270570

Mill Road, Pakenham, Bury St Edmunds, Suffolk

Owner: Suffolk Building Preservation Trust   **Contact:** Roger Gillingham

Fine 18th century working watermill.

Location: OS Ref. TL937 694. Signposted from A143 Ixworth bypass.

Opening Times: 1 Apr - 30 Sept: Weds, Sats, Suns & BHs, 2 - 5.30pm.

Admission: Adult £2, Child £1.20, OAP £1.75.

ST EDMUNDSBURY CATHEDRAL   **Tel:** 01284 754933 **Fax:** 01284 768655

Angel Hill, Bury St Edmunds, Suffolk IP33 1LS   **e-mail:** cathedral@btconnect.com

Owner: The Church of England   **Contact:** Sarah Friswell

At the heart of Christian worship since Saxon times, evidence of previous churches is visible. The elegant, English Perpendicular 16th century Nave of St James' survived its patron, the once great, now ruined Abbey of St Edmund, to become the Cathedral of Suffolk in 1914. It was skilfully extended with Quire and Crossing in the 1960s and a magnificent gothic-style lantern tower, Transept and Apostles' Chapel, will complete the Cathedral to mark the millennium. Dedicated to St James, Patron Saint of Pilgrims, is subtly reflected in architectural hints of Spain.

Location: OS Ref. TL857 642. Bury St Edmunds town centre.

Opening Times: All year: daily 8.30am - 6pm, Jun - Aug: 8.30am - 7pm.

Admission: Donation invited.

SAXTEAD GREEN POST MILL   **Tel:** 01728 685789

Post Mill Bungalow, Saxtead Green, Woodbridge, Suffolk IP13 9QQ

Owner: English Heritage   **Contact:** The Custodian

The finest example of a Suffolk Post Mill. Still in working order, you can climb the wooden stairs to the various floors, full of fascinating mill machinery. Ceased production in 1947.

Location: OS Ref. TM253 645. 2½ m NW of Framlingham on A1120.

Opening Times: 1 Apr - 31 Oct: Mon - Sat, 10am - 6pm (5pm in Oct). Closed 1 - 2pm.

Admission: Adult £2.20, Child £1.10, Conc. £1.70.

SHRUBLAND PARK GARDENS   **Tel:** 01473 830221 **Fax:** 01473 832202

Ipswich, Suffolk IP6 9QQ

Owner/Contact: Lord de Suamarez

One of the finest examples of an Italianate garden in England, designed by Sir Charles Barry.

Location: OS Ref. TM125 525. 6m N of Ipswich to the E of A14/A140.

Opening Times: 15 Apr - 23 Sept: Suns & BH Mons, 2 - 5pm.

Admission: Adult £3, Child/OAP £2.

SOMERLEYTON HALL & GARDENS

SOMERLEYTON, LOWESTOFT, SUFFOLK NR32 5QQ

Owner/Contact: The Rt Hon Lord Somerleyton GCVO

Tel: 01502 730224 office or 01502 732950 (Entrance Gate) **Fax:** 01502 732143

Splendid early Victorian mansion built in Anglo-Italian style by Sir Morton Peto, with lavish architectural features, magnificent carved stonework and fine state rooms. Paintings by Landseer, Wright of Derby and Stanfield, wood carvings by Willcox of Warwick and Grinling Gibbons. Somerleyton's 12-acre gardens are justly renowned with beautiful borders, specimen trees and the 1846 yew hedge maze which ranks amongst the finest in the country. Special features include glasshouses by Paxton, 300ft pergola, walled garden, Vulliamy tower clock, Victorian ornamentation.

Location: OS134 Ref. TM493 977. 5m NW of Lowestoft on B1074, 7m SW of Great Yarmouth off A143.

Opening Times: Easter Sun - Sept: Thurs, Suns, BHs. Jul & Aug: Tue - Thur, Suns & BHs. Gardens: 12.30 - 5.30pm. Hall: 1 - 5pm. Closed all other dates except by appointment. Private group tours by arrangement.

Admission: Adult £5.50, Child £2.60, OAP £5, Family (2+2) £14.80. Groups: Adult £4.80, Child/Student £2.40. Prices and opening times subject to review.

No photography in house. Receptions/functions/conferences. By arrangement.

SOUTH ELMHAM HALL

ST CROSS, HARLESTON, NORFOLK IP20 0PZ

Owner: *John Sanderson* ***Contact:*** *Jo & John Sanderson*

Tel: 01986 782526 **Fax:** 01986 782203 **e-mail:** john@southelmham.co.uk

A Grade I listed medieval manor house set inside moated enclosure. Originally built by the Bishop of Norwich around 1270. Much altered in the 16th century. Self guided trail through former deer park to South Elmham Minster, a ruined Norman chapel with Saxon origins.

Location: OS30 Ref. TM778 324. Between Harleston and Bungay from the A143 take the B1062.

Opening Times: Minster, Walks (free) & Café: Easter - 31 Oct: Suns, Thurs, Fris & BH Mons. 1 Nov - Easter: Suns only, 10.30am - 5pm. Hall: Thurs, some Suns & BH Mons. 1 May - 30 Sept: Guided tours only, 2pm.

Admission: House: Adult £6, Child £3. Groups (12 - 50): Adult £4, Child £2.50.

⬜ 🍴 ♿ WC. ♨ 🚶Obligatory. 🚌 🅿️ Limited for coaches.
🐕 In grounds, on leads. 🔔 Licence applied for. ❄ (tw)

THE TIDE MILL

Tel: 01473 626618

Woodbridge, Ipswich, Suffolk

Owner/Contact: Geoff Gostling

First recorded in 1170, now fully restored, machinery demonstrated at low tide. Ring for wheel turning times.

Location: OS Ref. TM275 487. By riverside 1/4 m SE of Woodbridge town centre. 1 1/4 m off A12.

Opening Times: Easter, then May - Sept: daily. Apr & Oct: Sats & Suns only, 11am - 5pm.

Admission: Adult £1.50, Child Free, Conc. £1.

Saxtead Green Post Mill, Suffolk.

Patrick Lane.

WINGFIELD OLD COLLEGE & GDNS 🏛

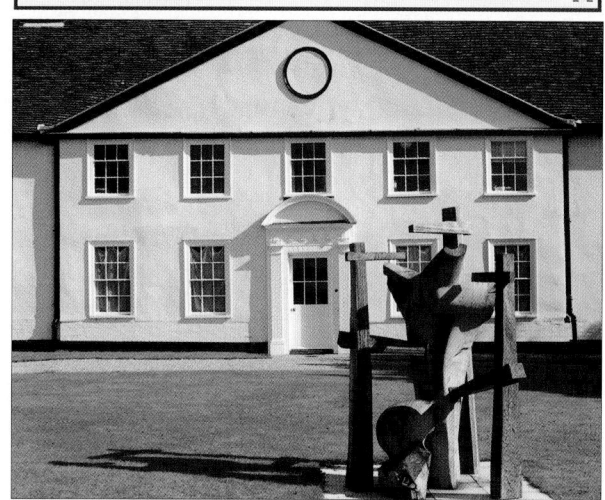

WINGFIELD, Nr STRADBROKE, SUFFOLK IP21 5RA

Owner: *Mr & Mrs Ian Chance* ***Contact:*** *Mrs H Chance*

Tel: 01379 384888 **Fax:** 01379 388082

Delightful family home with walled gardens. Lovely old Suffolk house with spectacular medieval great hall, contemporary art in the new College Yard Visual Arts Visitor Centre, garden sculpture, collections of ceramics and textiles, 4 acres of gardens with topiary, ponds and old roses, in unspoilt Suffolk countryside. Steeped in history, this "oasis of arts and heritage" offers an afternoon of discovery and relaxation. Children's play garden. Teas in College Yard. Open in 2001 – newly restored Walled Arts Garden.

Location: OS Ref. TM230 767. Signposted off B1118 (2m N of Stradbroke) and B1116 at Fressingfield.

Opening Times: 14 Apr - 30 Sept: Sats & Suns, 2 - 6pm.

Admission: Adult £3.60, Child/Student £1.50, OAP £3, Family £8.50 (2000 prices).

🎎 🍴 Wedding receptions. ♿ 💺 🚶 By arrangement for groups. 🅿️
🚾 🐕 Guide dogs only.

WYKEN HALL GARDENS

STANTON, BURY ST EDMUNDS, SUFFOLK IP31 2DW

Owner: *Sir Kenneth & Lady Carlisle* ***Contact:*** *Mrs Barbara Hurn*

Tel: 01359 250287 **Fax:** 01359 252256

The Elizabethan manor house is surrounded by a romantic, plant-lover's garden with maze, knot and herb garden and rose garden featuring old roses. A walk through ancient woodlands leads to Wyken Vineyards, winner of EVA Wine of the Year. In the 16th century barn, the Vineyard Restaurant serves our wines along with a varied menu from fresh local produce. It is a 'Bib Gourmand' in the Michelin Guide and features also in The Good Food Guide.

Location: OS Ref. TL963 717. 9m NE of Bury St. Edmunds 1m E of A143. Follow brown tourist signs to Wyken Vineyards from Ixworth.

Opening Times: 14 Jan - 24 Dec: Wed - Sun & BH Mons, 10am - 6pm. Also Fris & Sats dinner from 7pm. Garden closed on Sats. Gardens only: 1 Apr - 1 Oct.

Admission: Gardens: Adult £2.50, Child (under 12yrs) Free, Conc. £2. Groups by appointment.

⬜ ♿ Grounds suitable. WC. 🍴 Licensed. 🐕 In grounds, on leads. ❄

Cottesbrooke Hall & Gardens, Northamptonshire

East Midlands

Cottesbrooke Hall and Gardens

"My family and I consider that we are especially fortunate to live at Cottesbrooke, both in the house and for its surroundings."

Captain John Macdonald-Buchanan

Cottesbrooke Hall nestles in rolling open countryside in the northern corner of Northamptonshire, some 10 miles to the north of Northampton. This architecturally exquisite house, built in the reign of Queen Anne for Sir John Langham, 4th Baronet, happily remains delightfully untouched by the vagaries of future architectural styles.

It is thought that the original architect is most likely to have been Francis Smith of Warwick, but it remains a matter for speculation. Built of fine rose-pink brick enriched with pale Ketton stone, the plan of Cottesbrooke today includes a central block containing the principal rooms, with two wings or pavilions connected by blank quadrant walls, serving as arcades. The interior contains wonderful 18th century English and French furniture as well as fine English, Continental and Chinese porcelain. However, it is the 'Woolavington Collection', a collection of sporting and equestrian paintings, for which the house is renowned – considered the finest in Britain.

Regrettably, few records remain to tell the early history of the 18th century landscaping of the park vistas, lakes and garden at Cottesbrooke. However, a striking feature of the house is the way it is sited on an axis looking towards the Anglo-Saxon Brixworth Church, whose spire can be seen three miles away. It seems likely that the south side of the house was built to incorporate the spire as a focal point in the initial landscaping scheme for the Hall.

Today the true distinction of the garden at Cottesbrooke belongs almost entirely to the 20th century. A number of distinguished landscape designers have been involved. These include the Arts & Crafts architect Edward Weir Schultz, Sir Geoffrey Jellicoe before the Second World War, and Dame Sylvia Crowe afterwards.

Between 1911 and 1914 Schultz laid out a Rose Garden with an elaborate pergola south-west of the house. After World War I, the late Hon Lady Macdonald-Buchanan's time, many changes took place and it was she who gave the garden its present character. She removed the pergola in the present Pool Garden and commissioned an elegant pillared pavilion designed by Dame Sylvia Crowe.

There are several notable areas in the gardens. Firstly, the Forecourt – the formal garden to the south front and designed by Sir Geoffrey Jellicoe. It is from here the visitor can enjoy two of the magnificent vistas to the south and south-east of the Hall. To the west is the Statue Walk, more sombre in character – a wide grassy walk leads past a yew hedge, breaking out occasionally into buttresses dominated by its fine early 18th century statues by Peter Scheemakers and formerly at Stowe Park.

Altogether different in character is the Wild Garden leading away from the Hall which, with its acers and rhododendrons, becomes the highlight of the garden in the Spring and Autumn. As with every other aspect of Cottesbrooke, the visitor can wander at leisure through a tranquil scene, managed and maintained with the perfectionist standards of its loving owners.

For further details about *Cottesbrooke Hall and Gardens* see entry in East Midlands Region ➔ Northamptonshire.

Gary Rogers Hamburg.

Owner: Trustees of the Chatsworth Settlement. Home of the Duke & Duchess of Devonshire

CONTACT

Mr John Oliver
Chatsworth
Bakewell
Derbyshire
DE45 1PP

Tel: 01246 582204
01246 565300

Fax: 01246 583536

e-mail: visit@
chatsworth-house.co.uk

LOCATION

OS Ref. SK260 703

From London
3 hrs M1/J29,
signposted via
Chesterfield.

3m E of Bakewell,
off B6012,
10m W of Chesterfield.

Rail: Chesterfield
Station, 11m.

Bus: Chesterfield -
Baslow, 1¹/₂ m.

CONFERENCE/FUNCTION		
ROOM	SIZE	MAX CAPACITY
Hartington Rm.		70
Coffee Rm.		24

CHATSWORTH
Bakewell

The great Treasure House of Chatsworth was first built by Bess of Hardwick in 1552 and has been lived in by the Cavendish family, the Dukes of Devonshire, ever since. The House today owes its appearance to the 1st Duke who remodelled the building at the end of the 17th century, while the 6th Duke added a wing 130 years later. Visitors can see 26 rooms including the run of 5 virtually unaltered 17th century State Rooms and Chapel. There are painted ceilings by Verrio, Thornhill and Laguerre, furniture by William Kent and Boulle, tapestries from Mortlake and Brussels, a library of over 17,000 volumes, sculpture by Cibber and Canova, old master paintings by Rembrandt, Hals, Van Dyck, Tintoretto, Veronese, Landseer and Sargent; the collection of neo-classical sculpture, Oriental and European porcelain and the dazzling silver collection, including an early English silver chandelier. The present Duke has added to the collection. In 2001 the special exhibition in the House will be devoted to

20th century works of art collected by the present Duke and Duchess, including work by Epstein, Freud, Sickert and Gwen John. In 1996 and 1999 Chatsworth was voted the public's favourite house winning the NPI National Heritage Gold Award.

GARDEN

The 105 acre garden was created during three great eras in garden and landscape design. The 200 metre Cascade, the Willow Tree fountain and the Canal survive from the 1st Duke's formal garden. 'Capability' Brown landscaped the garden and park in the 1760s. The 6th Duke's gardener, Sir Joseph Paxton, built rockeries and designed a series of glasshouses. He also created the Emperor fountain, the tallest gravity-fed fountain in the world. More recent additions include the Rose, Cottage and Kitchen gardens, the Serpentine Hedge and the Maze. In 1999, a new water sculpture, Revelation, was unveiled.

ℹ️ 🛍️ Farmyard and Adventure Playground. Guide book translations and audio guides in French, German, Italian, Spanish and Japanese.

♿ No wheelchairs in house, but welcome in garden (3 electric, 7 standard available). WCs. Special leaflet.

🍵 New rooms available for conferences and private functions. Contact Head of Catering.

🍴 Restaurant (max 300); home-made food. Menus on request.

🚶 Private tours of house or Greenhouses and Behind the Scenes Days, by arrangement only (extra charges apply). Tape recorded tour may be hired at entrance. Groups please pre-book.

🅿️ Cars 100 yds, Coaches 25 yds from house.

📷 Guided tours, packs, trails and school room. Free preliminary visit recommended.

❄️

OPENING TIMES

SUMMER
21 March - 28 October.

Daily: 11am - 4.30pm.

WINTER
Closed.

The Park is open free throughout the year.

ADMISSION

House & Garden
Adult £7.00
Child £3.00
OAP/Student...........£5.75
Family £17.25
Pre-booked groups
Adult £6.25
School (no tour).......£3.00
School (w/tour).......£3.50
OAP/Student...........£5.00
Garden only
Adult £4.00
Child £1.75
OAP/Student...........£3.00
Family £9.50
Scots Suite
Adult £1.00
Child £0.50

Car Park £1.00

**Farmyard &
Adventure Playground**
All............................£3.50
Groups (5+)............£3.00
OAP/School £2.90

🛡️ SPECIAL EVENTS

• **MAY 12 - 13:**
International Horse Trials.

• **MAY 19 - 20:**
Angling Fair.

• **SEPT 1 - 2:**
Country Fair.

HADDON HALL
Bakewell

William the Conqueror's illegitimate son, Peverel, and his descendants held Haddon for a hundred years before it passed into the hands of the Vernons. Over the following four centuries, the existing medieval and Tudor manor house developed from its Norman origins. In the late 16th century, the estate passed through marriage to the Manners family, later to become Dukes of Rutland, in whose possession it has remained ever since.

Little has been added since the reign of Henry VIII, whose elder brother, Arthur, was a frequent guest of the Vernons. He would have been quite familiar with the house as it stands today – the Great Hall, kitchens and Chapel all dating from the 14th century. Incredibly, despite its time worn steps, no other medieval house has so triumphantly withstood the passage of time. *Jane Eyre* (1996), *The Prince and the Pauper* (1996) and *Elizabeth* (1997) were filmed at Haddon.

GARDENS

The award-winning terraced Rose Gardens are planned for year-round colour. Over 150 varieties of rose and clematis, many over 70 years old, provide colour and scent throughout the summer.

Owner:
Lord Edward Manners

CONTACT

Janet O'Sullivan
Estate Office
Haddon Hall
Bakewell
Derbyshire
DE45 1LA

Tel: 01629 812855

Fax: 01629 814379

e-mail: info@
haddonhall.co.uk

LOCATION

OS Ref. SK234 663

From London 3 hrs
Sheffield $1/2$ hr
Manchester 1 hr
Haddon is on the
E side of A6 $1^1/_2$ m
S of Bakewell.
M1/J30.

Rail: Chesterfield
Station, 12m.

Bus: Chesterfield
Bakewell.

OPENING TIMES

SUMMER

1 April - 30 September
(closed Sun 15 July).

Daily: 10.30am - 5.45pm
Last admission 5pm.

October: Mon - Thur
10.30am - 4.30pm
Last admission 4pm.

WINTER

November - 31 March
Closed.

ADMISSION

SUMMER

Adult	£5.90
Child (5 -15yrs)	£3.00
Conc.	£5.00
Family (2+3)	£15.00

Groups (20+)

Adult	£5.00
Child (5 -15yrs)	£2.75
Conc.	£4.25

SPECIAL EVENTS

Please telephone for details.

Recent productions testify to Haddon's suitability as a film location: *Jane Eyre* (1996) Rochester Films; *Prince and the Pauper* (1996) BBC; *Elizabeth I* (1997).

Not suitable, steep approach, varying levels of house.

Self-service restaurant (max 75). Home-made food.

Special tours £25 extra for groups of 15, 7 days' notice.

Ample, 450 yds from house. 50p per car.

Tours of the house bring alive Haddon Hall of old. Costume room also available, very popular!

Guide dogs only.

BAKEWELL OLD HOUSE MUSEUM

Tel: 01629 815294

Cunningham Place, Bakewell DE45 1DD

Owner: Bakewell District Historical Society

Contact: The Secretary

A rare and curious Peakland house built by Ralf Gell in 1534.

Location: OS Ref. SK215 685. 100 yds W of Bakewell Parish Church.

Opening Times: Please contact for details.

Admission: Adult £2.50, Child £1, Child under 5yrs free.

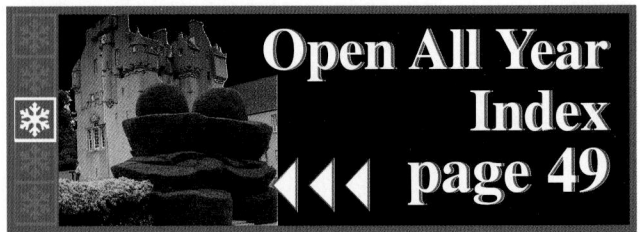

**Open All Year
Index
◀◀◀ page 49**

BOLSOVER CASTLE

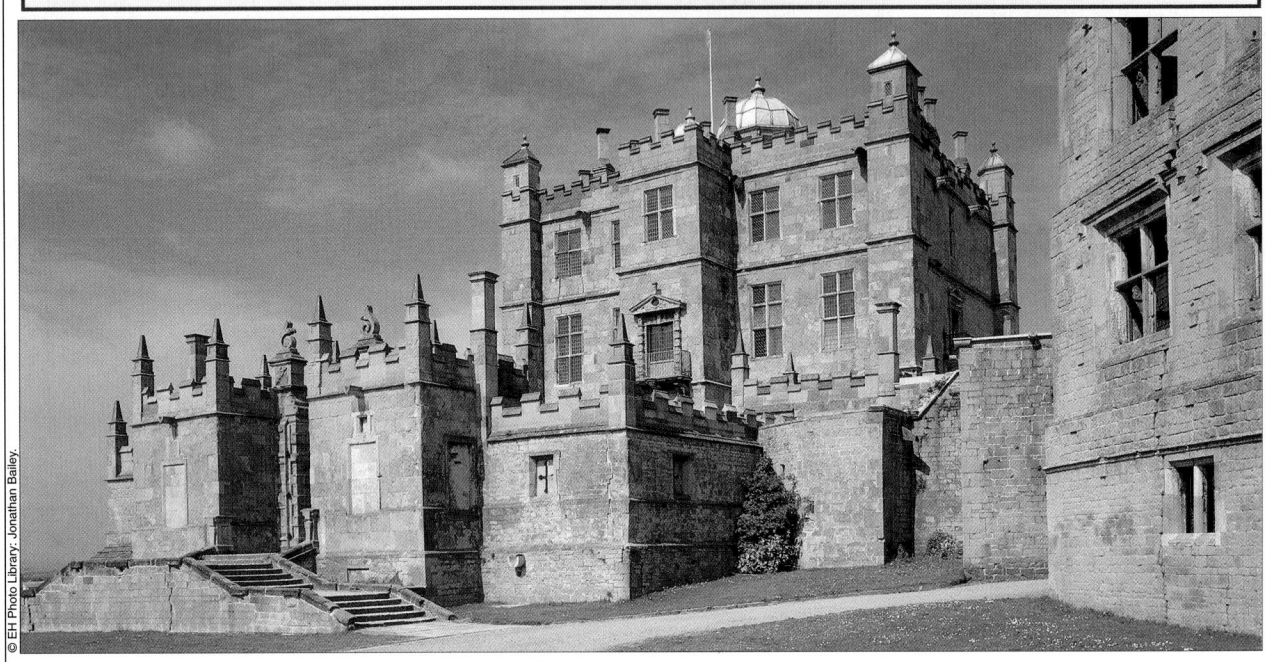

© EH Photo Library, Jonathan Bailey

CASTLE STREET, BOLSOVER, DERBYSHIRE S44 6PR

Owner: *English Heritage*   **Contact:** *The Custodian*

Tel: 01246 822844

An enchanting and romantic spectacle, situated high on a wooded hilltop dominating the surrounding landscape. Built on the site of a Norman castle, this is largely an early 17th century mansion. Most delightful is the 'Little Castle', a bewitching folly with intricate carvings, panelling and wall painting. See the restored interiors of the Little Castle and the working Venus Fountain and statuary. There is also an impressive 17th century indoor Riding House built by the Duke of Newcastle. Enjoy the Visitor and Discovery Centre. Bolsover is now available for civil weddings, receptions and corporate hospitality.

Location: OS120, Ref. SK471 707. Off M1/J29, 6m from Mansfield. In Bolsover 6m E of Chesterfield on A632.

Opening Times: 1 Apr - 31 Oct: daily, 10am - 6pm (5pm in Oct). 1 Nov - 31 Mar: Wed - Sun, 10am - 4pm. Closed 24 - 26 Dec & 1 Jan.

Admission: Adult £5, Child £2.50, Conc. £3.80, Family £12.50. 15% discount for groups (11+).

⊤ & Grounds suitable. WC. 🅿 🗡 🔔 ❄ 🛡 Tel. for details.

English Heritage Photo Library.

Bolsover Castle, Derbyshire.

CALKE ABBEY

NT Photographic Library: Rupert Truman.

NT Photographic Library: Andreas von Einsiedel.

TICKNALL, DERBYSHIRE DE73 1LE

Owner: The National Trust   *Contact: The Property Manager*

Tel: 01332 863822 **Fax:** 01332 865272

The house that time forgot, this baroque mansion, built 1701 - 3 for Sir John Harpur and set in a landscaped park. Little restored, Calke is preserved by a programme of conservation as a graphic illustration of the English country house in decline; it contains the family's collection of natural history, a magnificent 18th century state bed and interiors that are virtually unchanged since the 1880s. Walled garden, pleasure grounds and recently restored orangery. Early 19th century Church. Historic parkland with Portland sheep and deer. Staunton Harold Church is nearby.

Location: OS128 Ref. SK356 239. 10m S of Derby, on A514 at Ticknall between Swadlincote and Melbourne.

Opening Times: House, Garden & Church: 31 Mar - 4 Nov: Sat - Wed & BH Mons (closed Good Fri). House & Church: 1 - 5.30pm (last admission 5pm), Garden: 11am - 5.30pm (last adm. 5pm). Park: Most days until 9pm or dusk if earlier. Ticket office from 11am. Closed Sat 11 Aug for concert. Shop & Restaurant only: 10 Nov - 23 Dec & Jan - Mar 2002: Sats & Suns, 11am - 4pm.

Admission: All sites: Adult £5.20, Child £2.60, Family £13. Garden only: £2.50. Discount for pre-booked groups.

🖼 ♿House suitable. Braille guide. Wheelchairs. WCs. 🍴Licensed.
🚶By arrangement. 🐕In park, on leads only. ❋

CARNFIELD HALL

SOUTH NORMANTON, Nr ALFRETON, DERBYSHIRE DE55 2BE

Owner/Contact: J B Cartland

Tel: 01773 520084

Unspoilt Elizabethan 'Mansion House'. Panelled rooms, two 17th century staircases, great chamber. From 1502 the seat of the Revell, Wilmot and Cartland families. Atmospheric interior with three centuries of portraits, furniture, china, needlework, costumes, royal relics and manorial documents. Guided tours by the owner. Fine fan and costume collection, if booked for groups in advance, and candlelit evening visits in winter. Old walled garden

Location: OS Ref. SK425 561. 1 1/2 m W of M1/J28 on B6019. Alfreton Station 5 mins walk.

Opening Times: Spring & Summer BHs including Good Fri & Mon; Easter – 30 Sept: most weekends; 2 - 5 Jul & Aug: Most Tues & Thurs; 2 - 5pm. By appointment throughout the year (including evenings) for groups (4-22). Winter: Some weekends if fine, 2 - 4pm. NB. Times may vary. Please telephone to confirm dates and times.

Admission: Adult £4, Child (8-16yrs) £2, Conc. £3. Groups: Adult £3.50, Child (8-16yrs) £1.50, Conc. £2.50. Groups must book. No reduction for evening visits.

ℹ No photography in Hall. 🖼 👶 ♿Grounds suitable. WCs.
🍴Licensed. 🚶Obligatory. 🐕In grounds, on leads only. ❋

CATTON HALL

CATTON, WALTON-ON-TRENT, SOUTH DERBYSHIRE DE12 8LN

Owner/Contact: Robin & Katie Neilson

Tel: 01283 716311 **Fax:** 01283 712876 **e-mail:** kneilson@catton-hall.com

Catton, built in 1745, has been in the hands of the same family since 1405 and is still lived in by the Neilsons as their private home. This gives the house, with its original collection of 17th and 18th century portraits, pictures and antique furniture, a unique, relaxed and friendly atmosphere. Catton is available for corporate entertaining throughout the year. With its spacious reception rooms and luxury accommodation it is ideal for exclusive business meetings, lunches, dinners and for exhibitors and visitors to Birmingham. The 100 acres of parkland alongside the River Trent are ideal for all types of corporate and public events.

Location: OS Ref. SK206 154. 2m E of A38 at Alrewas between Lichfield & Burton-on-Trent (8m from each). Birmingham NEC 20m.

Opening Times: By arrangement only: Conferences/meetings, product launches, wedding receptions, team building, activity days, motorised sports, off road driving, shooting, falconry. Tours: Apr - Oct: Mons only, 1.30pm & 3pm. Groups by appointment only.

ℹConference facilities. 🍴By arrangement. ♿ 🚶By arrangement.
🛏 3 x four posters, 5 twin, all en-suite. ❋ 🛡 ♿

CHATSWORTH

See page 288 for full page entry.

CROMFORD MILL (SIR RICHARD ARKWRIGHT'S) Tel/Fax: 01629 823256

Cromford, Nr Matlock, Derbyshire DE4 3RQ   **Contact:** The Visitor Services Dept.

Built in 1771, Cromford Mill is the world's first successful water powered cotton spinning mill, set in the beautiful Derwent Valley surrounded by limestone tors and rolling hills. There is a wholefood restaurant on site with shops, free car parking and friendly staff. A tour guide will explain the story of this important historic site and describe the development plans for the future.

Location: OS Ref. SK296 569. 3m S of Matlock, 17m N of Derby just off A6.

Opening Times: All year except Christmas Day, 9am - 5pm.

Admission: Free entry. Guided tours: Adult £2, Conc. £1.50.

Partially suitable. WCs. In grounds, on leads.

ELVASTON CASTLE COUNTRY PARK   Tel: 01332 571342 Fax: 01332 758751

Borrowash Road, Elvaston, Derbyshire DE72 3EP

Owner: Derbyshire County Council   **Contact:** The Park Manager

200 acre park landscaped in 19th century. Walled garden. Estate museum with exhibitions of traditional crafts.

Location: OS Ref. SK407 330. 5m SE of Derby, 2m from A6 or A52.

Opening Times: Please contact park for details.

Admission: Museum: Adult £1.20, Child 60p, Family (2+2) £3. Park and Gardens free. Car park: Midweek 70p, weekends/BHs £1.30, Coaches £7.50.

Ground floor & grounds suitable. WCs. By arrangement. In grounds, on leads.

EYAM HALL

EYAM, HOPE VALLEY, DERBYSHIRE S32 5QW

Owner: Mr R H V Wright   *Contact: Mrs Nicola Wright*

Tel: 01433 631976 **Fax:** 01433 631603 **e-mail:** nicwri@globalnet.co.uk

This small but charming manor house in the famous plague village has been the home of the Wright family since 1671. The present family opened the house to the public in 1992, but it retains the intimate atmosphere of a much-loved private home. The Jacobean staircase, fine tapestries, family portraits and costumes and an impressive tester bed are among its interior treasures. Craft centre, buttery and shops in a historic farmyard, with crafts people at work and authentic local products for sale. Now licensed for Civil wedding ceremonies.

Location: OS119 Ref. SK216 765. Approx 10m from Sheffield, Chesterfield and Buxton. Eyam is off A623 between Stockport and Chesterfield. Eyam Hall is in the centre of the village, past the church.

Opening Times: Jun, Jul & Aug: Tue - Thur, Suns & BH Mons, 11am - 4pm. Victorian Christmas tours, school tours (booked groups only) please telephone for details.

Admission: Adult £4.25, Child £3.25, Conc. £3.75. Family (2+4) £13.50. Group rates available. Craft Centre & Buttery: All year: daily, except Mons, 10.30am - 5pm.

Craft centre. Partially suitable. WC. Licensed. Obligatory. In grounds, on leads. Guide dogs only in house. Tel. for details.

HADDON HALL

See page 289 for full page entry.

HARDSTOFT HERB GARDEN   Tel: 01246 854268

Hall View Cottage, Hardstoft, Chesterfield, Derbyshire S45 8AH

Owner: Mr Stephen Raynor/L M Raynor   **Contact:** Mr Stephen Raynor

Consists of four display gardens with information boards and well labelled plants.

Location: OS Ref. SK436 633. On B6039 between Holmewood & Tibshelf, 3m from J29 on M1.

Opening Times: 15 Mar - 15 Sept: daily (except Tues) 10am - 5pm. Closed Sunday follwng Aug BH weekend.

Admission: Adult £1, Child Free.

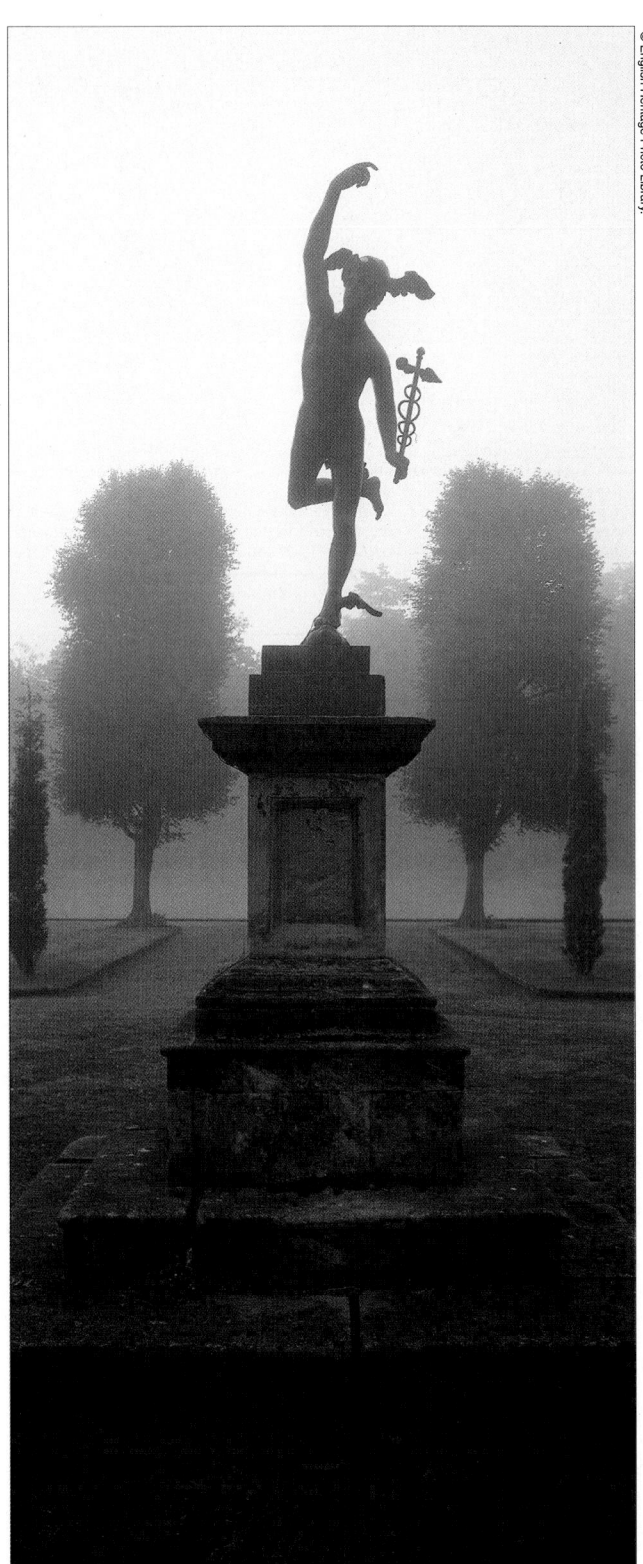

Melbourne Hall, Derbyshire.

HARDWICK HALL & STAINSBY MILL

DOE LEA, CHESTERFIELD, DERBYSHIRE S44 5QJ

Owner: The National Trust   *Contact:* The Property Manager

Tel: 01246 850430 **Fax:** 01246 854200 **Shop/Restaurant:** 01246 854088

Hardwick Hall: A late 16th century 'prodigy house' designed by Robert Smythson for Bess of Hardwick. The house contains outstanding contemporary furniture, tapestries and needlework including pieces identified in an inventory of 1601; a needlework exhibition is on permanent display. Walled courtyards enclose fine gardens, orchards and a herb garden. The country park contains Whiteface Woodland sheep and Longhorn cattle.

Location: OS120 Ref. SK456 651. 7¹/₂ m NW of Mansfield, 9¹/₂ m SE of Chesterfield: approach from M1/J29 via A6175.

Opening Times: Hall: 31 Mar - 28 Oct: Weds, Thurs, Sats, Suns & BH Mons, 12.30 - 5pm (closed Good Fri). Last adm. to Hall 4.30pm. Garden: 31 Mar - 28 Oct: daily 12 noon - 5.30pm. Restaurant: open as per Hall: 12 noon - 2pm lunches, 2 - 4.45pm teas.

Admission: Hall & Garden: Adult £6.20, Child £3.10, Family £15.50. Garden only:

Adult £3.30, Child £1.60, Family £8.20. Pre-booking for groups essential, discount for groups of 15+. Timed tickets on busy days, inc NT members. Joint ticket available (Old and New Hall).

Hardwick Estate - Stainsby Mill is an 18th century water-powered corn mill in working order.

Location: OS120 Ref. SK455 653. From M1/J29 take A6175, signposted to Clay Cross then first left and left again to Stainsby Mill.

Opening Times: 31 Mar - 31 May, 1 Oct - 4 Nov: Weds, Thurs, Sats, Suns & BH Mons; 1 Jun - 30 Sept: Wed - Sun & BH Mons, 11am - 4.30pm, last admission 4pm.

Admission: Adult £2, Child £1, Family £5. No discounts for groups. School Groups: Weds & Thurs (plus Fri: Jun - Sept), for information send SAE to Property Manager at Hardwick Hall.

📷 ♿Hall limited, garden suitable. 🍴Licensed. 🐕In park, on leads.

HARDWICK OLD HALL

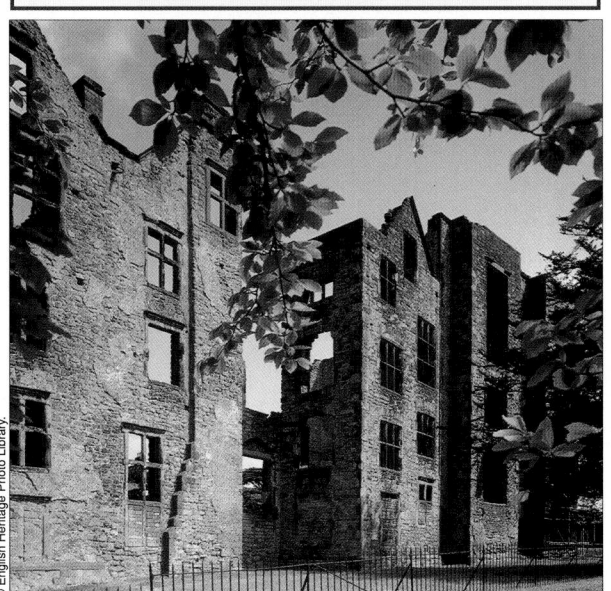

DOE LEA, Nr CHESTERFIELD, DERBYSHIRE S44 5QJ

Owner: National Trust, managed by English Heritage   *Contact:* The Custodian

Tel: 01246 850431

This large ruined house, finished in 1591, still displays Bess of Hardwick's innovative planning and interesting decorative plasterwork. The views from the top floor over the country park and 'New' Hall are spectacular.

Location: OS120 Ref. SK463 638. 7¹/₂ m NW of Mansfield, 9¹/₂ m SE of Chesterfield, off A6175, from M1\J29.

Opening Times: 1 Apr - 31 Oct: Wed - Sun, 10am - 6pm (5pm in Oct).

Admission: Adult £2.75, Child £1.40, Conc. £2.10. 15% discount for groups (11+).

🐕 On leads.

Hardwick Hall, Derbyshire.

KEDLESTON HALL

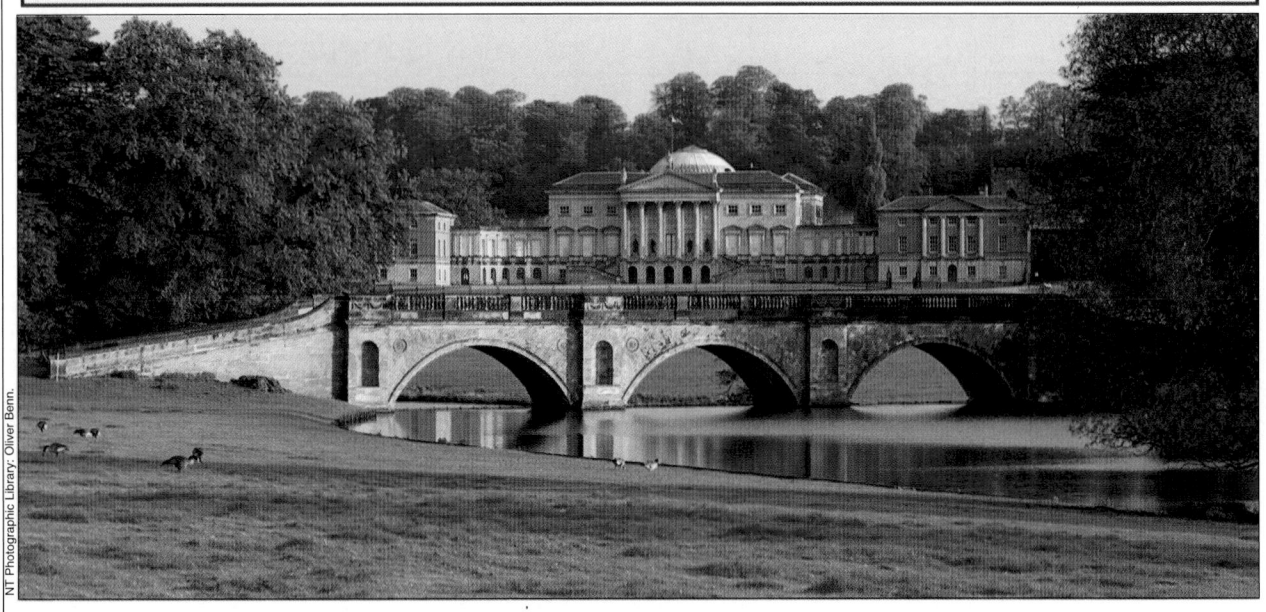

NT Photographic Library: Oliver Benn.

DERBY, DERBYSHIRE DE22 5JH

Owner: The National Trust   *Contact:* The Property Manager

Tel: 01332 842191 **Fax:** 01332 841972

Experience the age of elegance in this neo-classical house built between 1759 and 1765 for the Curzon family and little altered since. Set in 800 acres of parkland with an 18th century pleasure ground, garden and woodland walks – a day at Kedleston is truly an experience to remember. The influence of the architect Robert Adam is everywhere, from the Park buildings to the decoration of the magnificent state rooms. Groups are welcome and an introductory talk can be arranged.

Location: OS Ref. SK312 403. 5m NW of Derby, signposted from roundabout where A38 crosses A52 Derby ring road.

Opening Times: House: 31 Mar - 4 Nov: Sat - Wed, 12 - 4.30pm. Last adm. 4pm.

Park & Gardens: 11am - 6pm. Restaurant: 11am - 5pm. Shop: 11.30am - 5.30pm. Park only: Thur & Fri, 11am - 6pm, Vehicle charge. Park, Shop & Restaurant: Nov - 23 Dec: Sats & Suns, 12 noon - 4pm.

Admission: Adult £5.10, Child £2.50, Family £12.70. Garden & Park: Adult £2.30, Child £1. Discount for groups, please telephone.

⬜ ♿ Stairclimber & Batricar.   🍴 Licensed.   🐕 In grounds, on leads.
🔔 🎭 Tel. for details.

LEA GARDENS   **Tel:** 01629 534380/534260 **Fax:** 01629 534260

Lea, Matlock, Derbyshire DE4 5GH

Owner/Contact: Mr & Mrs J Tye

The gardens are sited on the remains of a medieval millstone quarry and cover 4 acres within a wooded hillside. A unique collection of rhododendrons, azaleas, kalmias.

Location: OS Ref. SK324 570. On W side of small lane 600yds SW of Lea village & ^{1}/$_2$ m N of Holloway. 1^1/$_2$ m NE of A6, 2^1/$_2$ m SE of Matlock.

Opening Times: 20 Mar - 30 Jun: 10am - 5.30pm.

Admission: Adult £3, Child 50p, Season ticket £5.

Peveril Castle, Derbyshire.

MELBOURNE HALL & GARDENS 🏛

© English Heritage Photo Library.

MELBOURNE, DERBYSHIRE DE73 1EN

Owner: Lord & Lady Ralph Kerr   *Contact:* Mrs Gill Weston

Tel: 01332 862502 **Fax:** 01332 862263

This beautiful house of history, in its picturesque poolside setting, was once the home of Victorian Prime Minister William Lamb. The fine gardens, in the French formal style, contain Robert Bakewell's intricate wrought iron arbour and a fascinating yew tunnel.

Location: OS Ref. SK389 249. 8m S of Derby. From London, exit M1/J24.

Opening Times: Hall: Aug only (not first 3 Mons) 2 - 5pm. Last admission 4.15pm. Gardens: 1 Apr - 30 Sept: Weds, Sats, Suns, BH Mons, 1.30 - 5.30pm.

Admission: Hall: Adult £3, Child £1.50, OAP £2.50. Gardens: Adult £3, Child/OAP £2. Hall & Gardens: Adult £5, Child £3, OAP £4.

ℹ Crafts. No photography in house.   ⬜ ♿ Partially suitable.   ▣
🚶 Obligatory.   🅿 Limited. No coach parking.   🐕 Guide dogs only.

PEVERIL CASTLE ⌗

Tel: 01433 620613

Market Place, Castleton, Hope Valley S33 8WQ

Owner: English Heritage   **Contact:** The Custodian

There are breathtaking views of the Peak District from this castle, perched high above the pretty village of Castleton. The great square tower stands almost to its original height. Formerly known as Peak Castle.

Location: OS110 Ref. SK150 827. S side of Castleton, 15m W of Sheffield on A6187.

Open: 1 Apr - 31 Oct: daily, 10am - 6pm (5pm in Oct). 1 Nov - 31 Mar, Wed - Sun, 10am - 4pm. Closed 24 - 26 Dec & 1 Jan.

Admission: Adult £2.30, Child £1.20, Conc. £1.70. 15% discount for groups (11+).

❄ 🛡 Tel: for details.

RENISHAW HALL 🏛

See opposite for quarter page entry.

REVOLUTION HOUSE

Tel: 01246 345727

High Street, Old Whittington, Chesterfield, Derbyshire S41 9LA

Contact: Ms A M Knowles

Originally the Cock and Pynot ale house, now furnished in 17th century style.

Location: OS Ref. SK384 749. 3m N of Chesterfield on B6052 off A61.

Opening Times: Good Fri - end Oct: daily, 10am - 4pm. Special opening over Christmas period.

Admission: Free.

Plant Sales Index ◀◀◀ page 47

RENISHAW HALL 🏛

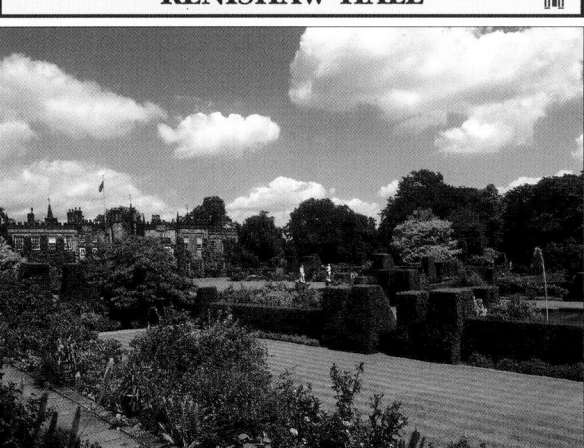

SHEFFIELD, DERBYSHIRE S31 9WB

Owner: Sir Reresby Sitwell Bt DL   **Contact:** The Administrator

Tel: 01246 432310   **Fax:** 01246 430760

e-mail: info@renishawhall.free-online.co.uk

Home of Sir Reresby and Lady Sitwell. Seven acres of Italian style formal gardens stand in 300 acres of mature parkland, encompassing statues, shaped yew hedges, a water garden and lakes. The Sitwell museum and art gallery (display of Fiori de Henriques sculptures) are located in the Georgian stables alongside craft workshops and café, furnished with contemporary art.

Location: OS Ref. SK435 786. 3m from M1/J30, equidistant from Sheffield & Chesterfield.

Opening Times: 6 Apr - 30 Sept: Fri - Sun & BHs, 10.30am - 4.30pm. Also Thurs in Jul & Aug.

Admission: House: by written application only. Garden only: Adult £3, Conc. £2.50. Museum & Art Exhib: Adult £3, Conc. £2.50. Garden, Museum & Art Exhibition: Adult £5, Conc. £3.50.

ℹ️ Conferences. 📷 🚻 🍽 ♿ 💷
🏃 By arrangement. 🅿 🐕 In grounds, on leads. 🔔 🐾

SUDBURY HALL & NATIONAL TRUST MUSEUM OF CHILDHOOD 🌼

ASHBOURNE, DERBYSHIRE DE6 5HT

Owner: The National Trust   **Contact:** The Property Manager

Tel: 01283 585305   **Fax:** 01283 585139

One of the most individual of late 17th century houses, begun by George Vernon c1660. The rich decoration includes wood carvings by Gibbons and Pierce, superb plasterwork, mythological decorative paintings by Laguerre. The great staircase is one of the finest of its kind in an English house. Also National Trust Museum of Childhood in 19th century service wing of the Hall. The museum contains fascinating and innovative displays about children from the 18th century onwards. There are chimney climbs for adventurous 'sweep-sized' youngsters, and Betty Cadbury's fine collection of toys and dolls is on show.

Location: OS128 Ref. SK160 323. 6m E of Uttoxeter at the junction of A50 Derby - Stoke & A515 Ashbourne.

Opening Times: 31 Mar - 4 Nov: Wed - Sun & BH Mons, 1 - 5.30pm. Last admission 30 mins before closing. Grounds: 12 noon - 6pm. Museum: As house.

Admission: Hall: Adult £3.80, Child £1.90, Family £9.50. Groups by prior arrangement. Museum: As house. Hall & Museum: Adult £6.10, Child £3, Family £15.20.

📷 ♿ Limited, braille guide. WC. 💷 Licensed. 🚗 Car park only.

SUTTON SCARSDALE HALL ⛫

Tel: 01604 735400 (Regional Office)

Chesterfield, Derbyshire

Owner: English Heritage   **Contact:** The East Midlands Regional Office

The dramatic hilltop shell of a great early 18th century baroque mansion.

Location: OS Ref. SK441 690. Between Chesterfield & Bolsover, 1¹/₂ m S of Arkwright Town.

Opening Times: 10am - 6pm (5pm Oct - Mar).

Admission: Free.

TISSINGTON HALL

ASHBOURNE, DERBYSHIRE DE6 1RA

Owner/Contact: Sir Richard FitzHerbert Bt

Tel: 01335 352200   **Fax:** 01335 352201   **e-mail:** tisshall@dircon.co.uk

Home of the FitzHerbert family for over 500 years. The Hall stands in a superbly maintained estate village, and contains wonderful panelling and fine old masters. A 10 acre garden and arboretum. Schools very welcome. Award-winning Old Coach House Tearoom, open daily 11am - 5pm for lunch and tea.

Location: OS Ref. SK175 524. 4m N of Ashbourne off A515 towards Buxton.

Opening Times: 10 Jul - 17 Aug: Tue - Fri, 1.30 - 4.30pm. 20 - 31 Aug: Mon - Fri, 1.30 - 4.30pm. Groups & societies welcome by appointment throughout the year. Corporate days and events also available, contact: The Estate Office on 01335 352200

Admission: Hall & Gardens: Adult £5.50, Child (10-16yrs) £2.50, Conc. £4.50, Gardens only: Adult £2, Child £1.

ⓘ No photography in house. ♿ Partially suitable. WCs at tearooms.

⛴ Tearoom adjacent to Hall. 🎫 Obligatory. 🅿 Limited. 🍴

🐕 Guide dogs only. ❄ ⓘⓦ

WINGFIELD MANOR ⛫

Tel: 01773 832060

Garner Lane, South Wingfield, Derbyshire DE5 7NH

Owner: Mr S Critchlow (managed by English Heritage)   **Contact:** The Custodian

Huge, ruined, country mansion built in the mid-15th century. Mary Queen of Scots was imprisoned here in 1569, 1584 and 1585.

Location: OS Ref. SK374 548. S side of B5035, ¹/₂ m S of South Wingfield village. Access by 600yd drive (**no vehicles**). From M1 J28, W on A38, A615 (Matlock road) at Alfreton and turn onto B5035 after 1¹/₂m.

Opening Times: 1 Apr - 30 Sept: Wed - Sun, 10am - 6pm. 1 - 31 Oct: Wed - Sun, 10am - 5pm. 1 Nov - 31 Mar: 10am - 4pm. Closed 24 - 26 Dec & 1 Jan. Closed 1 - 2pm in winter. The Manor incorporates a working farm. Visitors are requested to respect the privacy of the owners, to keep to visitor routes and refrain from visiting outside official opening times.

Admission: Adult £3, Child £1.50, Conc. £2.30.

Wingfield Manor, Derbyshire.

Chatsworth, Derbyshire.

BELVOIR CASTLE
Grantham

BELVOIR CASTLE, home of the Duke and Duchess of Rutland, commands a magnificent view over the Vale of Belvoir. The name Belvoir, meaning beautiful view, dates back to Norman times, when Robert de Todeni, Standard Bearer to William the Conqueror, built the first castle on this superb site. Destruction caused by two Civil Wars and by a catastrophic fire in 1816 have breached the continuity of Belvoir's history. The present building owes much to the inspiration and taste of Elizabeth, 5th Duchess of Rutland and was built after the fire.

Inside the Castle are notable art treasures including works by Poussin, Holbein, Rubens, and Reynolds, Gobelin and Mortlake tapestries, Chinese silks, furniture, fine porcelain and sculpture.

The Queen's Royal Lancers' Museum at Belvoir has a fascinating exhibition of the history of the Regiment, as well as a fine collection of weapons, uniforms and medals.

GARDENS

The Statue Gardens are built into the hillside below the castle and take their name from the collection of 17th century sculptures on view. The garden is planted so that there is nearly always something in flower.

The Duchess' private Spring Gardens are available for viewing throughout the year by pre-booked groups of 15 persons or more. Details from the Estate Office.

Owner: His Grace The Duke of Rutland

CONTACT

Andrew Norman
Castle Estate Office
Belvoir Castle
Grantham
Lincolnshire
NG32 1PD

Tel: 01476 870262
Fax: 01476 870443

e-mail: info@
belvoircastle.com

LOCATION

OS Ref. SK820 337

A1 from London 110m
York 100m
Grantham 7m.
A607 Grantham-Melton Mowbray.

Air: East Midlands International.

Rail: Grantham Station 7m

Bus: Melton Mowbray - Vale of Belvoir via Castle Car Park.

 Suitable for exhibitions, product launches, conferences, filming, photography welcomed (permit £2).

Banquets, private room available.

Ground floor and restaurant accessible. Please telephone for advice. WC.

Licensed restaurant. Groups catered for.

By prior arrangement Additional charge of £1pp. Tour time: 1¼ hrs.

Ample. Coaches can take passengers to entrance by arrangement but should report to the main car park and ticket office on arrival.

Guided tours. Teacher's pack. Education room. Picnic area and adventure playground.

Guide dogs only.

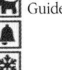

CONFERENCE/FUNCTION

ROOM	SIZE	MAX CAPACITY
State Dining Room	52' x 31'	130
Regents Gallery	131' x 16'	300
Old Kitchen	45' x 22'	100

OPENING TIMES

SUMMER
April: 13 - 17, 22, 29
May - Sept: Daily
October - Sundays only
11am - 5pm.

WINTER
Groups welcome by appointment.

ADMISSION

Adult £6.00
Child (5-16yrs)..........£3.50
OAP/Student £5.50
Family (2+2) £16.00

Groups (20-200)
Adult £5.50
Child (5-16yrs)..........£3.00
OAP/Student...........£5.00

Spring Garden Tours (15+)
Adult £5.00
OAP/Student...........£4.50

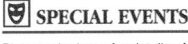 **SPECIAL EVENTS**

Please telephone for details of special events.

STANFORD HALL
Nr Rugby

STANFORD has been the home of the Cave family, ancestors of the present owner, Lady Braye, since 1430. In the 1690s, Sir Roger Cave commissioned the Smiths of Warwick to pull down the old Manor House and build the present Hall, which is an excellent example of their work and of the William and Mary period.

As well as over 5000 books, the handsome Library contains many interesting manuscripts, the oldest dating from 1150. The splendid pink and gold Ballroom has a fine coved ceiling with four *trompe l'oeil* shell corners. Throughout the house are portraits of the family and examples of furniture and objects which they collected over the centuries. There is also a collection of Royal Stuart portraits, previously belonging to the Cardinal Duke of York, the last of the male Royal Stuarts. An unusual collection of family costumes is displayed in the Old Dining Room, which also houses some early Tudor portraits and a fine Empire chandelier.

The Hall and Stables are set in an attractive Park on the banks of Shakespeare's Avon. There is a walled Rose Garden behind the Stables. An early ha-ha separates the North Lawn from the mile-long North Avenue.

Owner: The Lady Braye

CONTACT

Lt Col E H L Aubrey-
Fletcher
Stanford Hall
Lutterworth
Leicestershire
LE17 6DH

Tel: 01788 860250

Fax: 01788 860870

e-mail: stanford.hall
@virginnet.co.uk

LOCATION

OS Ref. SP587 793

M1/J18 6m,
M1/J19 (from/to
the N only) 2m,
M6 exit/access at
A14/M1(N)J 2m,
A14 2m.

Follow Historic
House signs.

Rail: Rugby Station
7$^{1}/_{2}$ m.

Air: Birmingham
Airport 27m.

Taxi: Fone-A-Car.
01788 543333.

CONFERENCE/FUNCTION

ROOM	SIZE	MAX CAPACITY
Ballroom	39' x 26'	100
Old Dining Rm	30' x 20'	70
Crocodile Room	39' x 20'	60

▣ ⓘ Craft centre (most Suns). No photography in house. Available for corporate days, clay pigeon shoots, filming, photography, small conferences and fashion shows. Parkland, helicopter landing area, lecture room, Blüthner piano.

🍽 Available for lunches, dinners and wedding receptions using outside caterers.

♿ Visitors may alight at the entrance. WC.

☕ Homemade teas, lunch, and supper. Groups (70 max.) must book.

🚶 Tour time: $^{3}/_{4}$ hr in groups of approx 25.

🅿 1,000 cars and 6 - 8 coaches. Free meals for coach drivers, coach parking on gravel in front of house.

🎒 £1.80 per child. Guide provided by prior arrangement, nature trail with guide book & map, motorcycle museum.

🐕 In park, on leads.

OPENING TIMES

SUMMER

7 April - 30 September:

Sats & BH Tues,
House: 1.30 - 5.30pm.
Museum closed.

Suns & BH Mons:
House & Museum:
1.30 - 5.30pm

Last admissions 5pm.

NB. On BH Mons & event days: grounds open at 12 noon.

House open any day or evening for pre-booked groups.

WINTER

October - Easter
Closed to public. Available during October for corporate events.

ADMISSION

House & Grounds
Adult £4.20
Child (4-15yrs) £2.00
Groups (20+)
Adult £3.90
Child (4-15yrs) £1.80

Grounds only
Adult £2.50
Child (4-15yrs) £1.00

Motorcycle Museum
Adult £1.00
Child (4-15yrs) £0.35
School Group
Adult ....FREE
Child (4-15yrs) £0.20

🎭 SPECIAL EVENTS

Please telephone for details of special events.

ABBEY PUMPING STATION

Tel: 0116 2995111 **Fax:** 0116 2995125

Corporation Road, Leicester LE4 5PX

Owner: Leicester City Council   **Contact:** Stuart Warburton

A Victorian sewage pumping station with four massive beam engines still working by steam. Exhibitions include: 'Flushed with Pride' which explores the history, science and technology of public health, 'Fun at the Flicks' and 'Transport of Delight'. Series of special events and steam rallies/days throughout the year.

Location: OS Ref. SK589 067. 2m N of city centre situated on River Soar riverside walk and 400m E of A6. 5 mins from Belgrave Hall.

Opening Times: Please contact Abbey Pumping Station for details.

Admission: Free except for special events.

⬚ �⏋ ♿ Partially suitable. 🍴 On event days. 🚶 By arrangement. 🅿 🏢
🐕 Guide dogs only. ✳ 🛡 Tel. for details.

ASHBY-DE-LA-ZOUCH CASTLE ⌗

Tel: 01530 413343

South Street, Ashby-de-la-Zouch, Leicestershire LE65 1BR

Owner: English Heritage   **Contact:** The Custodian

The impressive ruins of this late medieval castle are dominated by a magnificent tower, over 80 feet high, which was split in two during the Civil War. Panoramic views.

Location: OS Ref. SK363 167. In Ashby de la Zouch, 12m S of Derby on A511. SE of town centre.

Opening Times: 1 Apr - 31 Oct: daily, 10am - 6pm (5pm in Oct). 1 Nov - 31 Mar: Wed - Sun, 10am - 4pm. Closed 24 - 26 Dec & 1 Jan.

Admission: Adult £2.75, Child £1.40, Conc. £2.10.

♿ Grounds suitable. 🅿 🐕 On leads. ✳ 🛡 Tel. for details.

BELGRAVE HALL & GARDENS

Tel: 0116 2666590 **Fax:** 0116 2613063

Church Road, off Thurcaston Road, Leicester LE4 5PE

Owner: Leicester City Council   **Contact:** Emma Martin

Belgrave Hall and Gardens, famed for its ghost story, is a period house with period decoration ranging from 1750 - 1900. The three story house is open throughout, and a series of special events is organised throughout the year using themes and living interpretation. Includes period Victorian formal gardens. Displays include the Gimson Collection.

Location: OS Ref. SK593 072. 2m N of city centre, on riverside walk and off the A6/A46 Loughborough Road.

Opening Times: Please contact Belgrave Hall for details.

Admission: Free.

⬚ ⏋ ♿ Partially suitable. WC. Staff with sign language skills. 🚶 By arrangement.
🅿 Limited (on street). 🏢 🐕 Guide dogs only. ✳ 🛡 Tel. for details.

BELVOIR CASTLE 🏛

See page 297 for full page entry.

Oakham Castle, Leicestershire & Rutland.

BOSWORTH BATTLEFIELD

VISITOR CENTRE & COUNTRY PARK, SUTTON CHENEY, MARKET BOSWORTH CV13 0AD

Owner: *Leicestershire City Council*   **Contact:** *Ranger*

Tel: 01455 290429 **Fax:** 01455 292841 **e-mail:** countryparks@leics.gov.uk

Historic site of the Battle of Bosworth Field 1485, where King Richard III lost his crown and his life to the future Henry VII. Visitor Centre, film theatre, battle trail, picnic areas and car parks. Summer event programme: Medieval Spectacular 18th & 19th Aug 2001 (including battle re-enactment).

Location: OS Ref. SK404 001. Bounded by A5, A444, A447, B585. Clearly signposted from all these roads.

Opening Times: 1 Apr - 31 Oct: Mon - Sat, 11am - 5pm. Sun & BHs, 11am - 6pm. Nov & Dec: Suns, 11am - dusk. Mar: Sats & Suns, 11am - 5pm.

Admission: Adult £3, Child/Conc. £1.90, Family (2+3) £7.95. Groups (20+): Adult £2.30, Child/Conc. £1.60. (Opening times and charges subject to review.)

⬚ ⏋ ♿ Partially suitable. 🍴 Licensed. 🚶 By arrangement. 🅿 🏢
✳ 🛡 Ⓦ

BRADGATE PARK & SWITHLAND WOOD COUNTRY PARK

Bradgate Park, Newtown Linford, Leics   **Tel:** 0116 2362713

Owner: Bradgate Park Trust   **Contact:** M H Harrison

Includes the ruins of the brick medieval home of the Grey family and childhood home of Lady Jane Grey. Also has a medieval deer park.

Location: OS Ref. SK534 102. 7m NW of Leicester, via Anstey & Newtown Linford. Country Park gates in Newtown Linford. 1¼ m walk to the ruins.

Opening Times: All year during daylight hours.

Admission: No charge. Car parking charges.

DONINGTON-LE-HEATH MANOR HOUSE

Tel: 01530 831259

Manor Road, Donington-le-Heath, Leicestershire LE67 2FW

Owner/Contact: Leicestershire County Council

Medieval manor c1280 with 16th-17th century alterations.

Location: OS Ref. SK421 126. ½ m SSW of Coalville. 4½ m W of M1/J22, by A511.

Opening Times: Apr - Sept: daily, 11am - 5pm. Oct - Mar: daily 11am - 3pm.

Admission: Free.

THE GUILDHALL

Tel: 0116 2532569 **Fax:** 0116 2539626

Guildhall Lane, Leicester LE1 5FQ

Owner: Leicester City Council   **Contact:** Nicholas Ladlow

Magnificent timber-framed medieval building c1390. First used by the Corpus Christi Guild. Became town hall until 1876, includes 17th century town library and Victorian police cells. The great hall provides a unique setting for a varied programme of music, storytelling and theatre.

Location: OS Ref. SK584 044. Adjacent to High Street, Cathedral and St Nicholas Place.

Opening Times: Please contact The Guildhall for details.

Admission: Free.

⬚ ♿ Partially suitable. 🚶 Obligatory. 🅿 No parking. 🏢
🐕 Guide dogs only. ✳ 🛡 Tel. for details. Ⓦ

JEWRY WALL MUSEUM & SITE   **Tel:** 0116 2473021   **Fax:** 0116 2512257

St Nicholas Circle, Leicester LE1 4LB

Owner: Leicester City Council   **Contact:** John Lucas

Jewry Wall Museum focuses on the archaeology and history of Leicestershire from prehistoric times to 1485. Inside you can see the skeleton of the Saxon 'Glen Parva Lady' alongside fine mosaics, wall paintings and other legacies of the Roman settlement. The new 'Making of Leicester' exhibition uncovers the secrets of Leicester's past. After visiting the museum, explore the site of the Roman baths and wonder at the massive 2nd century Jewry Wall.

Location: OS Ref. SK581 044. On St Nicholas Circle, at W end of High Street, opposite the Holiday Inn, next to St Nicholas Church.

Opening Times: Please contact Jewry Wall Museum for details.

Admission: Free.

📷   ♿ Partially suitable. WC.   👤 By arrangement.   🅿 No parking.   🔲   🐕 Guide dogs only.   ❄

KIRBY MUXLOE CASTLE ⛨   **Tel:** 01162 386886

Kirby Muxloe, Leicestershire LE9 9MD

Owner: English Heritage   **Contact:** East Midlands Regional Office (01604 735400)

Picturesque, moated, brick built castle begun in 1480 by William Lord Hastings. It was left unfinished after Hastings was executed in 1483.

Location: OS Ref. SK524 046. 4m W of Leicester off B5380.

Opening Times: 1 Apr - 31 Oct: weekends & BH Mons only, 12 noon - 5pm.

Admission: Adult £2, Child £1, Conc. £1.50.

LYDDINGTON BEDE HOUSE ⛨   **Tel:** 01572 822438

Blue Coat Lane, Lyddington, Uppingham, Rutland LE15 9LZ

Owner: English Heritage   **Contact:** The Custodian

Set among golden-stone cottages, the Bede House was originally a medieval palace of the Bishops of Lincoln. It was later converted into an alms house.

Location: OS Ref. SP875 970. In Lyddington, 6m N of Corby, 1m E of A6003.

Opening Times: 1 Apr - 31 Oct: daily, 10am - 6pm (5pm in Oct).

Admission: Adult £2.75, Child £1.40, Conc. £2.10.

NEW WALK MUSEUM   **Tel:** 0116 2554100   **Fax:** 0116 2473005

New Walk, Leicester LE1 7EA

Owner: Leicester City Council   **Contact:** John Martin

Leicester's first public museum, opened in 1849, houses six permanent exhibitions: The Ancient Egypt Gallery, Natural History (including dinosaurs), German Expressionist, Victorian and European Art Galleries, Decorative Art Gallery and The Royal Leicestershire Regiment Gallery. The Discovery Room invites younger visitors to try on replica clothes, handle real objects and explore the natural world.

Location: OS Ref. SK591 039. Museum Sq, 150m W of Waterloo Way, 250m SW of station.

Opening Times: Please contact New Walk Museum for details.

Admission: Free.

📷   🍴   ♿   👤 By arrangement.   🅿 Limited.   🔲   🐕 Guide dogs only.   🔔   ❄

NEWARKE HOUSES MUSEUM   **Tel:** 0116 2473222   **Fax:** 0116 2470403

The Newarke, Leicester LE2 7BY

Owner: Leicester City Council   **Contact:** Philip French

Over 500 years of Leicester's social history can be traced through a visit to Newarke Houses. Everyday life at home and at work is represented in displays of domestic equipment, clocks, toys and furniture. Visit the 1940s village grocer's shop, the reconstructed Victorian street scene and workshops of various local trades. Items belonging to Daniel Lambert, Leicester's largest man, can be seen in the museum. Don't forget to visit the beautiful gardens to the rear of the museum.

Location: OS Ref. SK584 041. Just SW of city centre ring road.

Opening Times: Please contact Newarke Houses Museum for details.

Admission: Free.

ℹ Photography in house by permission only.   📷   ♿ Not suitable.   👤 By arrangement.   🅿 No parking.   🔲   🐕 Guide dogs only.   ❄

OAKHAM CASTLE   **Tel:** 01572 758440

Rutland County Museum, Catmos St, Oakham, Rutland LE15 6HW

Owner: Rutland County Council   **Contact:** Mr T Clough

Exceptionally fine Norman Great Hall of a late 12th century fortified manor house, with contemporary musician sculptures. Bailey earthworks and remains of earlier motte. The hall contains over 200 unique horseshoes forfeited by royalty and peers of the realm to the Lord of the Manor from Edward IV onwards.

Location: OS Ref. SK862 088. Near town centre, E of the church.

Opening Times: Late Mar - late Oct (BST): Mon - Sat, 10am - 1pm, 1.30 - 5pm. Sun, 1 - 5pm. Late Oct - Late Mar (GMT): As above, but closing at 4pm. Closed on Good Fri, on court Mons (normally once a month), and at Christmas.

Admission: Free.

📷   ♿ Great Hall suitable.   🅿 For disabled, on request.   🔔   ❄   🌐

PRESTWOLD HALL

LOUGHBOROUGH, LEICESTERSHIRE LE12 5SQ

Owner: E J Packe-Drury-Lowe   *Contact: Henry Weldon*

Tel: 01509 880236   **Fax:** 01509 889060   **e-mail:** henryweldon@hotmail.com

A magnificent private house, largely remodelled in 1843 by William Burn. For the past 350 years it has been the home of the Packe family and contains fine Italian plasterwork, 18th century English and European furniture and a collection of family portraits. The house is not open to the general public but offers excellent facilities as a conference centre, corporate entertainment and wedding venue. Up to 150 guests can be seated and the 20 acres of gardens provide a perfect setting for larger events using marquees. Excellent chefs provide a selection of varied menus complemented by a well stocked wine cellar. Activity days, clay pigeon shooting, motor sports and archery can also be organised on request.

Location: OS Ref. SK578 215. At the heart of the Midlands, 3m E of Loughborough on B675. 5m W of A46 via B676.

Admission: Corporate entertaining venue, conference centre and function venue by arrangement only.

ℹ Conferences.   🍴   ♿ Ground floor & grounds suitable. WC.   🔔   ❄

STANFORD HALL 🏛   See page 298 for full page entry.

STAUNTON HAROLD CHURCH 🌿   **Tel:** 01332 863822   **Fax:** 01332 865272

Staunton Harold Church, Ashby-de-la-Zouch, Leicestershire

One of the very few churches to be built during the Commonwealth, erected by Sir Robert Shirley, an ardent Royalist. The interior retains its original 17th century cushions and hangings, and includes fine panelling and painted ceilings.

Location: OS Ref. SK379 208. 5m NE of Ashby-de-la-Zouch, W of B587.

Opening Times: 31 Mar - 30 Sept: Wed - Sun & BH Mons (closed Good Fri), 1 - 5pm or sunset if earlier. Oct: Sats & Suns only, 1 - 5pm.

Admission: £1 donation.

♿ Partially suitable.   🅿 At hall.

WARTNABY GARDENS   **Tel:** 01664 822296   **Fax:** 01664 822231

Melton Mowbray, Leicestershire LE14 3HY

Owner: Lord and Lady King

This garden has delightful little gardens within it, including a white garden, a sunken garden and a purple border of shrubs and roses, and there are good herbaceous borders, climbers and old-fashioned roses. A large pool has an adjacent bog garden with primulas, ferns, astilbes and several varieties of willow. There is an arboretum with a good collection of trees and shrub roses, and alongside the drive is a beech hedge in a Grecian pattern. Greenhouses, a fruit and vegetable garden with rose arches and cordon fruit.

Location: OS Ref. SK709 228. 4m NW of Melton Mowbray. From A606 turn W in Ab Kettleby for Wartnaby.

Opening Times: Suns, 29 Apr, 20 May & 24 June: 11am - 4pm. Plant sales: 29 Apr & 20 May. Groups by appointment at other times (except Weds). Plant Fair: 24 June.

Admission: Adult £2.50, Child Free.

♿   🍴   👤 By arrangement.   🅿 Limited for coaches.   🐕 In grounds on leads.   ❄   🔲

BURGHLEY HOUSE
Stamford

BURGHLEY HOUSE, home of the Cecil family for over 400 years, was built as a country seat during the latter part of the 16th century by Sir William Cecil, later Lord Burghley, principal adviser and Lord Treasurer to Queen Elizabeth.

The House was completed in 1587 and there have been few alterations to the architecture since that date thus making Burghley one of the finest examples of late Elizabethan design in England. The interior was remodelled in the late 17th century by John, 5th Earl of Exeter who was a collector of fine art on a huge scale, establishing the immense collection of art treasures at Burghley. Burghley is truly a 'Treasure House', containing one of the largest private collections of Italian art, unique examples of Chinese and Japanese porcelain and superb items of 18th century furniture. The remodelling work of the 17th century means that examples of the work of the principal artists and craftsmen of the period are to be found at Burghley: Antonio Verrio, Grinling Gibbons and Louis Laguerre all made major contributions to the beautiful interiors.

PARK AND GARDENS

The house is set in a 300-acre deer park landscaped by 'Capability' Brown. A lake was created by him and delightful avenues of mature trees feature largely in his design. The park is home to a large herd of Fallow deer, established in the 16th century. The Sculpture Garden contains many specimen trees and shrubs and is a display area for a number of dramatic art works by contemporary sculptors. The sculptures are varied in style, but their placement is designed to provoke thought and accentuate the beauty of the surroundings. The private gardens around the house are open in April for the display of spring bulbs. Please telephone for details.

Owner:
Burghley House
Preservation Trust Ltd

CONTACT

David Parratt
Burghley House
Stamford
Lincolnshire
PE9 3JY

Tel: 01780 752451

Fax: 01780 480125

e-mail: burghley@
burghley.co.uk

LOCATION

OS Ref. TF048 062

Burghley House
is 1m SE of Stamford.
From London, A1 2hrs.

Visitors entrance
is on B1443.

Rail: Stamford Station
1^1/$_2$ m.

Taxi: Direct Line:
01780 481481.

OPENING TIMES

SUMMER

1 April - 7 October
(closed 1 September).
Daily: 11am - 4.30pm.

NB. The house is viewed by guided tour except on Sat and Sun afternoons when there are stewards throughout the house and visitors may wander.

WINTER

8 October - 1 April
closed to the
general public.

The Park and Sculpure Gardens are open all year and entry is free of charge.

ADMISSION

Adult	£6.80
Child*	£3.30
OAP	£6.30
Groups (20+)	
Adult	£5.90
School groups (up to 14 yrs)	£3.10

* (5 - 12 years) one child Free with every paying adult, otherwise £3.30.

 Suitable for a variety of events, large park, golf course, helicopter landing area, cricket pitch. No photography in house.

Visitors may alight at the entrance. WC. Chair lift to Orangery Coffee Shop, house tour involves two staircases one of which has a chairlift.

Restaurant/tea-room. Groups can book in advance.

Obligatory, except Sats & Suns after 1pm. Tour time: 1^1/$_2$ hrs at ^{1}/$_2$ hr intervals. Max. 25.

Ample. Free refreshments for coach drivers.

Welcome. Guide provided.

 No dogs in house.

CONFERENCE/FUNCTION		
ROOM	SIZE	MAX CAPACITY
Great Hall	70' x 30'	150
Orangery	100' x 20'	120

AUBOURN HALL

Tel: 01522 788270   **Fax:** 01522 788199

Lincoln LN5 9DZ

Owner/Contact: Lady Nevile

Late 16th century house with important staircase and panelled rooms. Garden.

Location: OS Ref. SK928 628. 6m SW of Lincoln. 2m SE of A46.

Opening Times: Aubourn Hall will not be opened on a regular basis during 2001. The garden will be opened on occasional Sundays.

Admission: Adult £3, OAP £2.50.

AYSCOUGHFEE HALL MUSEUM & GARDENS

CHURCHGATE, SPALDING, LINCOLNSHIRE PE11 2RA

Owner: South Holland District Council   *Contact: Mrs S Sladen*

Tel: 01775 725468   **Fax:** 01775 762715

A late Medieval wool merchant's house surrounded by five acres of walled gardens. The Hall contains the Museum of South Holland Life and has galleries on local villages, the history of Spalding, agriculture and horticulture. There is also a gallery dedicated to Matthew Flinders, the district's most famous son. Many specimens from the Ashley Maples bird collections are on display.

Location: OS Ref. TF240 230. E bank of the River Welland, 5 mins walk from Spalding town centre.

Opening Times: All year: Mon - Fri, 9am - 5pm, Sats, 10am - 5pm. Suns & BHs, 11am - 5pm. Closed weekends in Nov - Feb.

Admission: Free.

ℹ️ TIC located in Hall.   📷   ♿ Partially suitable.   💷   🧑‍🏫 By arrangement.
P Limited for coaches.   ▪️
🐕 In grounds, on leads. Guide dogs only in Hall   ❄️

BELTON HOUSE

GRANTHAM, LINCOLNSHIRE NG32 2LS

Owner: The National Trust   *Contact: The Property Manager*

Tel: 01476 566116 / 592900   **Fax:** 01476 579071

The crowning achievement of Restoration country house architecture, built 1685 - 88 for Sir John Brownlow, and altered by James Wyatt in the 1770s. Plasterwork ceilings by Edward Goudge and fine wood carvings of the Grinling Gibbons school. The rooms contain portraits, furniture, tapestries, oriental porcelain, silver and silver gilt. Gardens with orangery, landscaped park with lakeside walk, woodland adventure playground, and Bellmount Tower. Fine church with family monuments.

Location: OS Ref. SK929 395. 3m NE of Grantham on A607. Signed off the A1.

Opening Times: House: 31 Mar - 4 Nov: House: Wed - Sun & BH Mons (closed Good Fri), 1 - 5.30pm. Garden & Park: 11am - 5.30pm. Last admission to house, garden & park 5pm.

Admission: Adult £5.40, Child £2.70, Family £13.50. Groups (15+): Adult £4.40, Child £2.20.

📷   ♿ Partially suitable. Please telephone for arrangements.   🍴 Licensed.
P   ▪️   🔔

Belton House, Lincolnshire.

Burghley House, Lincolnshire.

BURGHLEY HOUSE 🏛️   **See page 301 for full page entry**

DODDINGTON HALL

LINCOLN LN6 4RU

Owner: Mr & Mrs A Jarvis **Contact:** *The House Manager*

Tel: 01522 694308 **Fax:** 01522 685259

e-mail: estateoffice@doddingtonhall.free-online.co.uk

Magnificent Smythson mansion was completed in 1600 and stands today with its contemporary walled gardens and gatehouse. The Hall is still very much the home of the Jarvis family and has an elegant Georgian interior with a fine collection of porcelain, furniture, paintings and textiles representing 400 years of unbroken family occupation. The beautiful gardens contain a superb layout of box-edged parterres, sumptuous borders that provide colour all seasons, and a wild garden with a marvellous succession of spring bulbs and flowering shrubs set among mature trees. Sandford Award winning schools project, and a nature trail into the nearby countryside.

Location: OS Ref. SK900 701. 5m W of Lincoln on the B1190, signposted off the A46 Lincoln bypass.

Opening Times: Gardens only: 4 Feb - 30 Apr: Suns, 2 - 6pm. House & Garden: May - Sept: Weds, Suns & BH Mons, 2 - 6pm.

Admission: House & Garden: Adult £4.50, Child £2.25, Family £12.50. 10% group discount on open days. Garden only half price.

i No photography. No stilettos. 📷 🍽 Occasional. ♿ Gardens. WC. 🍴
🏃 By arrangement. ▦ **P** 🐕 Guide dogs only. 🛏 Tel. for details. (IW)

GAINSBOROUGH OLD HALL ⌗

Tel: 01427 612669

Parnell Street, Gainsborough, Lincolnshire DN21 2NB

Owner: English Heritage **Contact:** The Custodian

A large medieval house with a magnificent Great Hall and suites of rooms. A collection of historic furniture and a re-created medieval kitchen are on display.

Location: OS Ref. SK815 895. In centre of Gainsborough, opposite library.

Opening Times: Easter Sun - 31 Oct: Mon - Sat, 10am - 5pm. Suns, 2 - 5.30pm. 1 Nov - Easter Sat: Mon - Sat, 10am - 5pm (closed Good Fri, 24 - 26 Dec & 1 Jan).

Admission: Adult £2.50, Child £1, Conc. £1.50 (2000/2001 prices).

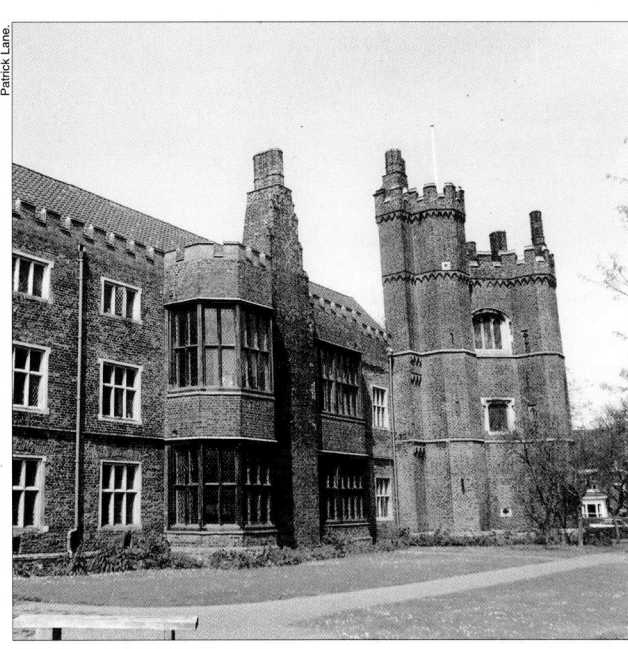

Patrick Lane.

Gainsborough Old Hall, Lincolnshire.

GRIMSTHORPE CASTLE, PARK & GARDENS

GRIMSTHORPE, BOURNE, LINCOLNSHIRE PE10 0NB

Owner: Grimsthorpe and Drummond Castle Trust Ltd **Contact:** *Ray Biggs*

Tel: 01778 591205 **Fax:** 01778 591259 **e-mail:** ray@grimsthorpe.co.uk

Home of the Willoughby de Eresby family since 1516. Examples of 13th century architecture, Tudor period and Sir John Vanbrugh's last major work. State Rooms and picture galleries contain magnificent contents and paintings. 3,000 acre landscaped park, with lakes, ancient woods, nature trail, woodland adventure playground, red deer herd, formal and woodland gardens, unusual ornamental vegetable garden, family cycle trail, events programme. Landrover tours with park ranger.

Location: OS Ref. TF040 230. 4m NW of Bourne on A151, 8m E of Colsterworth roundabout off A1.

Opening Times: 1 Apr - 30 Sept: Suns, Thurs & BHs. Aug: daily except Fris & Sats.

Park & Gardens: 11am - 6pm. Castle: 1 - 4.30pm (last admission). Tearoom: open from 11am (last orders 5.15pm).

Admission: Park & Garden: Adult £3, Child £1.50, Conc. £2, Family (2+2) £7.50. Castle, Park & Garden: Adult £6.50, Child £3.25, Conc. £4.75, Family (2+2) £16.25. Special charges may be made for special events. Group rates on application.

i No photography in house. 📷 🍴 Conferences (up to 70), inc catering
♿ Partially suitable. WC. 🍽 Licensed. 🏃 Obligatory except Suns.
P Limited for coaches. ▦ 🐕 In grounds, on leads. 🛏 Tel. for details. (IW)

Gunby Hall, Lincolnshire.

GUNBY HALL ❧

Tel: 01909 486411 **Fax:** 01909 486377

Gunby, Spilsby, Lincolnshire PE23 5SS

Owner: The National Trust **Contact:** Regional Office

A red brick house with stone dressings, built in 1700 and extended in 1870s. Within the house, there is good early 18th century wainscoting and a fine oak staircase, also English furniture and portraits by Reynolds. Also of interest is the contemporary stable block, a walled kitchen and flower garden, sweeping lawns and borders and an exhibition of Field Marshall Sir Archibald Montgomery-Massingberd's memorabilia. Gunby was reputedly Tennyson's 'haunt of ancient peace'.

Location: OS122 Ref. TF466 672. 2½ m NW of Burgh Le Marsh, 7m W of Skegness. On S side of A158 (access off roundabout).

Opening Times: Ground floor of house & garden: 4 Apr - end Sept: Weds, 2 - 6pm. Last admission 5.30pm. Closed BHs. Garden also open Thurs, 2 - 6pm. House & garden also open Tues, Thurs & Fris by written appointment to J D Wrisdale at above address.

Admission: House & Garden: Adult £3.60, Child £1.80, Family £9. Garden only: Adult £2.50, Child £1.20, Family £6.20. No reduction for groups. Access roads unsuitable for coaches which must park in layby at gates ½ m from Hall.

♿ Grounds suitable. 🐕 In grounds, on leads.

HARLAXTON MANOR

Tel: 01476 403000 **Fax:** 01476 403030

Harlaxton, Grantham, Lincolnshire NG32 1AG

Owner: University of Evansville **Contact:** Mrs F Watkins

Neo-Elizabethan house. Grandiose and imposing exterior by Anthony Salvin. Internally an architectural tour de force with various styles and an unparalleled Cedar Staircase.

Location: OS Ref. SK895 323. 3m W of Grantham (10 mins from A1) A607. SE of the village.

Opening Times: House: Sun 3 Jun & Sun 1 Jul: 11am - 5pm. House open at other times for group tours by appointment only.

Admission: House open days: Adult £4.50, Child £2, OAP £4.

HECKINGTON WINDMILL

Tel: 01529 461919

Heckington, Sleaford, Lincolnshire

Britain's last surviving eight sail windmill. **Location:** OS Ref. TF145 436. W side of B1394, S side of Heckington village.

Opening Times: Nov - Easter: Suns only, 2 - 5pm. Easter - 15 Jul: Thur - Sun & BH Mons, 12 noon - 5pm. 16 Jul - 2 Sept: daily, 12 noon - 5pm. 8 Sept - 28 Oct: Sats & Suns only, 2 - 5pm. Closed 23 & 30 Dec.

Admission: Ground floor: Free. Mill: Adult £1.50, Child 75p.

LEADENHAM HOUSE

Tel: 01400 273256 **Fax:** 01400 272237

Leadenham House, Lincolnshire LN5 0PU

Owner: Mr P Reeve **Contact:** Mr and Mrs P Reeve

Late eighteenth century house in park setting.

Location: OS Ref. SK949 518. Entrance on A17 Leadenham bypass (between Newark and Sleaford).

Opening Times: 8 - 12 May, 4 - 9, 11 - 16 & 18 - 21 Jun & 2 - 6 Jul. Also Spring & Aug BHs: 2 - 5pm.

Admission: £3. Groups by prior arrangement only.

ℹ️ No photography. ♿ ✖

LINCOLN CASTLE

Tel: 01522 511068

Castle Hill, Lincoln LN1 3AA

Contact: The Manager

Built by William the Conqueror in 1068. Informative exhibition of the 1215 Magna Carta.

Location: OS Ref. SK975 718. Opposite west front of Lincoln Cathedral.

Opening Times: BST: Sats, 9.30am - 5.30pm, Suns, 11am - 5.30pm. GMT: Mon - Sat: 9.30am - 4pm, Suns, 11am - 4pm. Closed Christmas Day, Boxing Day & New Year's Day.

Admission: Adult £2.50, Child £1, Family (2+3) £6.50.

LINCOLN CATHEDRAL

Tel: 01522 544544 **e-mail:** roybentham@aol.com

Lincoln LN2 1PZ

Contact: Communications Office

Medieval Gothic Cathedral of outstanding historical and architectural merit. Schools centre.

Location: OS Ref. SK978 718. At the centre of Uphill, Lincoln.

Opening Times: All year: May - Aug: 7.15am - 8pm, Suns, 7.15am - 6pm. Sept - May: 7.15am - 6pm, Suns, 7.15am - 5pm. Tours daily: Jan - Apr & Oct - Dec: 11am & 2pm. May - Sept: 11am, 1pm & 3pm. Roof tours available. Booked tours throughout the year.

Admission: £3.50, Child up to 14yrs Free, Conc. £3.

LINCOLN MEDIEVAL BISHOPS' PALACE ✠

Tel: 01522 527468

Minster Yard, Lincoln LN2 1PU

Owner: English Heritage **Contact:** The Custodian

In the shadow of Lincoln Cathedral are the remains of this medieval palace of the Bishops of Lincoln. Climb the stairs to the Alnwick Tower, explore the undercroft and see one of the most northerly vineyards in Europe.

Location: OS121 Ref. SK981 717. S side of Lincoln Cathedral, in Lincoln.

Opening Times: 1 Apr - 31 Oct: daily, 10am - 6pm (5pm in Oct). 1 Nov - 31 Mar: weekends only, 10am - 4pm. Closed 24 - 26 Dec & 1 Jan. Open daily for Lincoln Christmas Market.

Admission: Adult £2.50, Child £1.30, Conc. £1.90. 15% discount for groups (11+).

❄️ 🛡️ Tel. for details.

SIBSEY TRADER WINDMILL ✠

Tel: 01604 735400

Sibsey, Boston, Lincolnshire

Owner: English Heritage **Contact:** The East Midlands Regional Office

An impressive old mill built in 1877, with its machinery and six sails still intact. Flour milled on the spot can be bought here.

Location: OS Ref. TF345 511. ½ m W of village of Sibsey, off A16, 5m N of Boston.

Opening Times: Mill can be seen in action during the year, please telephone for details.

Admission: Adult £1.80, Child 90p, Conc. £1.40.

TATTERSHALL CASTLE ❧

Tel/Fax: 01526 342543

Tattershall, Lincoln, Lincolnshire LN4 4LR

Owner: The National Trust **Contact:** The Custodian

A vast fortified tower built c1440 for Ralph Cromwell, Lord Treasurer of England. The Castle is an important example of an early brick building, with a tower containing state apartments, rescued from dereliction and restored by Lord Curzon 1911-14. Four great chambers, with ancillary rooms, contain late gothic fireplaces and brick vaulting. There are tapestries and information displays in turret rooms.

Location: OS122 Ref. TF209 575. On S side of A153, 15m NE of Sleaford, 10m SW of Horncastle.

Opening Times: 1 Apr - 4 Nov: daily except Thurs & Fris, 10.30am - 5.30pm. 10 Nov - 16 Dec: Sats & Suns, 12 noon - 4pm.

Admission: Adult £3, Child £1.50, Family £7.50. Child Free Jul/Aug. Discount for groups.

♿ Ground floor. WC. 🐕 Car park only. 🅿️ Free. 🔔

WOOLSTHORPE MANOR ❧

Tel/Fax: 01476 860338

23 Newton Way, Woolsthorpe-by-Colsterworth, Grantham NG33 5NR

Owner: The National Trust **Contact:** The Custodian

This small 17th century farmhouse was the birthplace and family home of Sir Isaac Newton. Some of his major work was formulated here, during the Plague years (1665 - 67); an early edition of the *Principia* is on display. The orchard has a descendant of the famous apple tree. Science Discovery Centre and exhibition of Sir Isaac Newton's work.

Location: OS130 Ref. SK924 244. 7m S of Grantham, ½ m NW of Colsterworth, 1m W of A1.

Opening Times: House & Science Discovery Centre: 31 Mar - 4 Nov: Wed - Sun & BH Mons (closed Good Fri), 1 - 5.30pm. Last admission 5pm. Also Science Discovery Centre: 3/4, 10/11, 17/18 & 24/25 Mar (Sats & Suns) & 8/9 & 15/16 Dec: 1 - 5pm.

Admission: Adult £3.30, Child £1.60, Family £8.20, no reduction for groups which must book in advance. Science Discovery Centre on special opening days: Adult £2, Child £1, Family £5.

♿ Ground floor suitable. 🅿️ Limited. 🐕 Car park only.

Leadenham House, Lincolnshire.

East Midlands England

The Stable Block

Owner:
The Earl Spencer

CONTACT

Visitor Manager
Althorp
Northampton
NN7 4HQ

Tel: 01604 770107

Fax: 01604 770042

**Dedicated booking
line: 0870 1679000**

LOCATION

OS Ref. SP682 652

From the M1/J16, 7m
J18, 10m.
Situated on A428
Northampton - Rugby.
London on average 85
mins away.

Rail: 5m from
Northampton station.
14m from Rugby station.

ALTHORP
Northampton

The history of Althorp is the history of a family. The Spencers have lived and died here for nearly five centuries and twenty generations.

Since the death of Diana, Princess of Wales, Althorp has become known across the world, but before that tragic event, connoisseurs had heard of this most classic of English stately homes on account of the magnificence of its contents and the beauty of its setting.

Next to the mansion at Althorp lies the honey-coloured stable block, a truly breathtaking building which at one time accommodated up to 100 horses and 40 grooms. The stables are now the setting for the Exhibition celebrating the life of Diana, Princess of Wales and honouring her memory after her death. The freshness and modernity of the facilities are a unique tribute to a woman who captivated the world in her all-too-brief existence.

All visitors are invited to view the House, Exhibition and Grounds as well as the Island in the Round Oval where Diana, Princess of Wales is laid to rest.

Please contact the dedicated booking line (24 hour service) Tel: 0870 1679000 or www.althorp.com

The Picture Gallery

i Information leaflet issued to all ticket holders who book in advance. No indoor photography with still or video cameras.

Suitable. Visitor Centre and ground floor of house accessible. WCs.

Café.

P Limited for coaches.

Guide dogs only.

OPENING TIMES

SUMMER
1 July - 30 August
Daily, 9am - 5pm.

Last admission 4pm.

At the time of booking visitors will be asked to state a preference for a morning or an afternoon visit.

Pre-booking recommended.

WINTER
Closed.

ADMISSION

**House & Garden
(Pre-booked)**

Adult £10.00
Child* (5-17yrs) £5.00
OAP.........................£8.00

**(Paying at gate
subject to availability)**

Adult £11.00
Child* (5-17yrs) £5.00
OAP.........................£9.00

* under 5yrs Free.

There is a supplement to view the upstairs rooms of the House.

Group visits by arrangement only.

All the profits from visitor activity at Althorp are donated to the **Diana, Princess of Wales Memorial Fund**.

Numbers are limited each day. Advance booking is recommended.

East Midlands England

BOUGHTON HOUSE
Kettering

BOUGHTON HOUSE is the Northamptonshire home of the Duke of Buccleuch and Queensberry KT, and his Montagu ancestors since 1528. A 500 year old Tudor monastic building gradually enlarged around seven courtyards until the French style addition of 1695, which has lead to Boughton House being described as 'England's Versailles'.

The house contains an outstanding collection of 17th and 18th century French and English furniture, tapestries, 16th century carpets, porcelain, painted ceilings and notable works by El Greco, Murillo, Caracci and 40 Van Dyck sketches. There is an incomparable Armoury and Ceremonial Coach.

Beautiful parkland with historic avenues, lakes, picnic area, gift shop, adventure woodland play area, plant centre and tearoom. Boughton House is administered by The Living Landscape Trust, which was created by the present Duke of Buccleuch to show the relationship between the historic Boughton House and its surrounding, traditional, working estate.

For information on the groups visit programme and educational services, including fine arts courses run in conjunction with Sotheby's Institute, please contact The Living Landscape Trust. Our newly developed Internet website gives information on Boughton House and The Living Landscape Trust, including a 'virtual' tour, together with full details of our schools' educational facilities (Sandford Award winner 1988, 1993 and 1998).

Silver award winner of the 1st Historic House Awards, given by AA and NPI, in co-operation with the Historic Houses Association, for the privately-owned historic house open to the public which has best preserved its integrity, character of its architecture and furniture, while remaining a lived-in family home.

Owner:
His Grace The Duke of Buccleuch & Queensberry KT

CONTACT

Gareth Fitzpatrick
The Living Landscape Trust
Boughton House
Kettering
Northamptonshire
NN14 1BJ

Tel: 01536 515731

Fax: 01536 417255

e-mail:
llt@boughtonhouse.org.uk

LOCATION

OS Ref. SP900 815

3m N of Kettering on A43 - junction from A14.

Signposted through Geddington.

CONFERENCE/FUNCTION		
ROOM	SIZE	MAX CAPACITY
Lecture		100
Seminar Rm		25
Conference facilities available in stable block adjacent to House		

 Parkland available for film location and other events. Stable block contains 100 seats and lecture theatre. No inside photography. No unaccompanied children. Browse our web site for a 'virtual' tour of the house

Access and facilities, no charge for wheelchair visitors. WCs.

Tearoom seats 80, groups must book. Licensed.

By arrangement.

P

Heritage Education Trust Sandford Award winner 1988, 1993 & 1998. School groups free, teachers' pack.

No dogs in house and garden, welcome in Park on leads.

 By arrangement.

OPENING TIMES

SUMMER
House
1 August - 1 September
Daily, 2 - 4.30pm.

Grounds
1 May - 1 September
Daily:
(except Fris, May - July)
1 - 5pm.

During August opening staterooms on view strictly by prior appointment which can be made by telephone, fax or e-mail. For conservation reasons, numbers are restricted.

Opening of the Woodland Adventure Play Area is subject to weather conditions for reasons of health and safety.

WINTER
Daily by appointment throughout the year for educational groups - contact for details.

ADMISSION

SUMMER
House & Grounds
Adult £6.00
Child/Conc. £5.00

Grounds
Adult £1.50
Child/Conc. £1.00

Wheelchair visitors free. HHA Friends are admitted Free in August.

WINTER
Group rates available – contact for further details.

DEENE PARK
Corby

A very interesting house which developed over six centuries from a typical medieval manor around a courtyard into a Tudor and Georgian mansion. Many rooms of different periods are seen by visitors who enjoy the impressive yet intimate ambience of the family home of the Brudenells, seven of whom were Earls of Cardigan. The most flamboyant of them was the 7th Earl who led the Light Brigade charge at Balaklava and of whom there are some historic relics and pictures.

The present owner is Mr Edmund Brudenell

who has carefully restored the house from its dilapidated condition at the end of the last war and also added considerably to the furniture and picture collection.

The gardens have been made over the last thirty years, with long, mixed borders of shrubs, old fashioned roses and flowers, a recent parterre designed by David Hicks and long walks under fine old trees by the water.

The car park beside the big lake is a good place for picnics.

'Have you seen the new Millennium Column at Deene?'

❖

Owner:
E Brudenell Esq

CONTACT

The House Keeper
Deene Park
Corby
Northamptonshire
NN17 3EW

Tel: 01780 450278
or 01780 450223

Fax: 01780 450282

LOCATION

OS Ref. SP950 929

6m NE of
Corby off A43.
From London via M1/J15
then A43.
or via A1, A14,
A43 - 2 hrs.

From Birmingham
via M6, A14, A43, 90 mins.

Rail: Kettering Station
20 mins.

Suitable for indoor and outdoor events, filming, specialist lectures on house, its contents, gardens and history.
No photography in house.

Including buffets, lunches and dinners.

Partially suitable. Visitors may alight at the entrance, access to ground floor and garden. WC.

Special rates for groups, bookings can be made in advance, menus on request.

By arrangement.

Tours inclusive of admittance, tour time 90 mins. Owner will meet groups if requested.

Unlimited for cars, space for 3 coaches 10 yards from house.

In car park only.

Residential conference facilities by arrangement.

❄

CONFERENCE/FUNCTION		
ROOM	SIZE	MAX CAPACITY
Great Hall	–	150
Tapestry Rm	–	75
East Room	–	18

OPENING TIMES

SUMMER
June - August
Suns, 2 - 5pm

Open Suns & Mons for Easter, early and late Spring BHs & August BH 2 - 5pm.

Open at all other times by arrangement, including pre-booked parties.

WINTER
House and Gardens closed to casual visitors. Open at all other times by arrangement for groups.

ADMISSION

SUMMER
House & Gardens
Adult £5.00
Child (10-14yrs)........£2.50
Child (under 10).... Free*
Gardens only
Adult £3.00
Child (10-14yrs)........£1.50
Child (under 10).... Free*
Groups (20+)
Weekdays...............£4.00
(Min £80)
Weekends & BHs ...£5.00
(Min £100)

* Child up to 10yrs free with an accompanying adult.

WINTER
Groups visits only by prior arrangement.

 SPECIAL EVENTS

Telephone for details.

LAMPORT HALL & GARDENS
Northampton

Home of the Isham family from 1560 to 1976. The 17th and 18th century façade is by John Webb and the Smiths of Warwick and the North Wing of 1861 by William Burn.

The Hall contains a wealth of outstanding furniture, books and paintings including portraits by Van Dyck, Kneller, Lely and others. The fine rooms include the High Room of 1655 with magnificent plasterwork, the 18th century library with books from the 16th century, the early 19th century Cabinet Room containing rare Venetian cabinets with mythological paintings on glass and the Victorian Dining Room where refreshments are served.

The first floor has undergone lengthy restoration allowing further paintings and furniture to be displayed as well as a photographic record of Sir Gyles Isham, a Hollywood actor, who initiated the restoration.

The tranquil gardens were laid out in 1655 although they owe much to Sir Charles Isham, the eccentric 10th Baronet who, in the mid-19th century, created the Italian Garden and the Rockery where he introduced the first garden gnomes to England. There are also box bowers, a rose garden and lily pond and extensive walks, borders and lawns all surrounded by a spacious park.

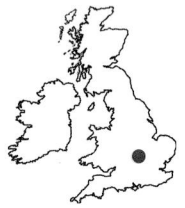

Owner:
Lamport Hall Trust

CONTACT

George Drye
Executive Director
Lamport Hall
Northampton
NN6 9HD

Tel: 01604 686272
Fax: 01604 686224

LOCATION

OS Ref. SP759 745

From London via M1/J15, 1¹/₄ hours. Entrance on A508, 8m N of Northampton at junction with B576. 3¹/₂ m S of A14 (A1/M1 link).

Rail: Kettering Station 9m. Northampton 8m.

Bus: From Northampton and Market Harborough.

Conferences, garden parties, activity days, clay pigeon shoots, equestrian events, fashion shows, air displays, archery, rallies, filming, parkland, grand piano, 2 exhibition rooms. Lectures on history of property and gardens. Lecture/meeting rooms. No unaccompanied children. No photography in house.

Special functions, buffets, lunches and dinners, wedding receptions.

Visitors may alight at the entrance, access to ground floor and gardens.

Dining/tearoom. Groups can book in advance. Licensed.

At no additional cost, by prior arrangement, max 70 people, tour time 1¹/₄ hours. On non-fair days.

100 cars & 3 coaches, 20 yds from property. Use main entrance only (on A508).

Work room, specialist advisory teacher study packs. Further information contact Education Officer or the Trust Office.

In grounds, on leads.

Tel. for details.

Tel. for further information.

OPENING TIMES

SUMMER
Easter - 7 October
Suns and BH Mons
2.15 - 5.15pm.
Last admission/tour 4pm.

August: Mon - Sat open for only one tour at 2.30pm.

20 & 21 October
2.15 - 5.15pm.

Tours on other days by prior arrangement.

WINTER
Group visits only by arrangement.

ADMISSION

SUMMER
House & Garden
Adult £4.00
Child (5-16yrs)..........£2.00
OAP.........................£3.50

Group*
Adult £4.00

* Min. payment £135.00 excluding refreshments

WINTER
Group visits only by prior arrangement.

CONFERENCE/FUNCTION		
ROOM	SIZE	MAX CAPACITY
Dining Rm	31' x 24' 6"	70

ROCKINGHAM CASTLE
Nr Corby

A Royal castle until 1530, since then home of the Watson family. Rockingham Castle was built by William the Conqueror on the site of an earlier fortification and was regularly used by the early Kings of England until the 16th century, when it was granted by Henry VIII to Edward Watson whose family still live there today.

The house itself is memorable not so much as representing any particular period, but rather a procession of periods. The dominant influence in the building is Tudor within the Norman walls, but practically every century since the 11th has left its mark in the form of architecture, furniture or works of art. The castle has a particularly fine collection of English 18th, 19th and 20th century paintings, and Charles Dickens, who was a frequent visitor, was so captivated by Rockingham that he used it as a model for Chesney Wold in *Bleak House*.

The castle stands in 12 acres of formal and wild garden and commands a splendid view of five counties. Particular features are the 400 year old elephant hedge and the rose garden marking the foundations of the old keep. See Special Exhibition: "450 years a royal castle, 450 years a family home".

Owner:
James Saunders Watson Esq

CONTACT

Administrator
Rockingham Castle
Market Harborough
Leicestershire
LE16 8TH

Tel: 01536 770240

Fax: 01536 771692

e-mail: rockinghamcastle@
lineone.net

LOCATION

OS Ref. SP867 913

2m N of Corby.
9m E of
Market Harborough.
14m SW of
Stamford on A427.
8m from
Kettering on A6003.

Vehicle entrance on A6003
just S of junction
with A6116.

CONFERENCE/FUNCTION		
ROOM	SIZE	MAX CAPACITY
Great Hall	37'6" x 22'	100
Panel Room	36' x 23'	100
Long Gallery	87' x 16'6"	100
Walkers House 1	31' x 17'6"	60
Walkers House 2	24' x 18'	50

Concerts, conferences, fashion shows, product launches, receptions, seminars, air displays, clay pigeon shoots, archery, equestrian events, fairs, garden parties, filming. Exhibition celebrating 900 years of life in the castle. Parkland and cricket pitch. Strip for light aircraft 4m. No photography in Castle.

Table licence.

Visitors may alight at entrance, ramps provided.

Home-made cream teas and light lunches.

All pre-booked parties have guided tour, except on open-days at no additional cost.

P Unlimited.

Winner of 3 Sandford Awards for Heritage Education, special pack designed with National Curriculum. Tours for schools. £1.80 per head (min. charge £40.00). 1 adult free/15 children.

OPENING TIMES

SUMMER
1 April - 30 September
Thurs, Suns, BH Mons &
Tues following and all
Tues in August: 1 - 5pm.
Grounds open 11.30am
on Suns & BHs. 1pm
on other open days.
Refreshments available on
open days.
Groups at any time by
appointment.

WINTER
By appointment for
booked parties and
schools.

ADMISSION

House & Garden
Adult £4.50
Child (up to 16 yrs) £3.00
Conc.......................£4.00
Family (2+2) £12.50

Groups (Min. charge £80.00)
Adult £4.00
Child (up to 16 yrs) ...£3.00

Grounds only
..............................£3.00

Schools (min. charge £40.00)
Each child £1.80
1 adult Free with every
15 children.

Groups and school parties
can be accommodated on
most days by arrangement.
Children qualify 5 - 16,
Under 5s Free.

Prices may vary for special
events held in grounds.

SPECIAL EVENTS
Please telephone for details.

ALTHORP   See page 305 for full page entry.

BOUGHTON HOUSE   See page 306 for full page entry.

CANONS ASHBY   **Tel:** 01327 860044 **Fax:** 01327 860168
           e-mail: ecaxxx@smtp.ntrust.org.uk

Canons Ashby, Daventry, Northamptonshire NN11 3SD
Owner: The National Trust   **Contact:** The Property Manager
Home of the Dryden family since the 16th century, this Elizabethan manor house was built c1550, added to in the 1590s, and altered in the 1630s and c1710; largely unaltered since. Within the house, Elizabethan wall paintings and outstanding Jacobean plasterwork are of particular interest. A formal garden includes terraces, walls and gate piers of 1710. There is also a medieval priory church and a 70 acre park.
Location: OS152 Ref. SP577 506. Access from M40/J11, or M1/J16. Signposted from A5 2m S of Weedon crossroads. Then 7m to SW.
Opening Times: House: 31 Mar - 4 Nov: Sat - Wed including BH Mons (closed Thurs & Fris) 1 - 5.30pm/dusk. Last admissions 5pm. Park, Gardens & Church open as house, 12 noon - 5.30pm; Oct - 4 Nov: 12 noon - 4.30pm, access through garden. Shop: 12.30 - 5pm; Tea Room 12 noon - 5pm.
Admission: Adult £5, Child £2.50, Family £12.50. Discount for booked groups, contact Property Manager.

   Suitable, some steps. WC.   In grounds, on leads.

Deene Park, Northamptonshire.

CASTLE ASHBY

CASTLE ASHBY HOUSE, CASTLE ASHBY, NORTHAMPTON NN7 1LQ
Owner: 7th Marquess of Northampton   *Contact:* Andrea Fowkes

Tel: 01604 696696 **Fax:** 01604 696516 **e-mail:** andreafowkes@castleashby.co.uk
Castle Ashby is the ancestral home of the 7th Marquess of Northampton, and was built in 1574 to entertain Queen Elizabeth. The castle itself has 26 exquisite bedrooms, including the State Suite, and is available on an exclusive basis for private events. The extensive gardens are open throughout the year and offer a combination of styles.
Location: OS Ref. SP862 582. 55m N of London, between Bedford and Northampton, off A428.
Opening Times: House not open to the public but available for private events. Gardens: All year, 10am - dusk.
Admission: Please telephone for details.

  Private & corporate events.

COTON MANOR GARDEN

GUILSBOROUGH, NORTHAMPTONSHIRE NN6 8RQ
Owner: Ian & Susie Pasley-Tyler   *Contact:* Sarah Ball

Tel: 01604 740219 **Fax:** 01604 740838
e-mail: pasleytyler@cotonmanor.fsnet.co.uk
Traditional English garden laid out on different levels surrounding a 17th century stone manor house. Many herbaceous borders, with extensive range of plants, old yew and holly hedges, rose garden, water garden and fine lawns set in 10 acres. Also wild flower meadow and bluebell wood.
Location: OS Ref. SP675 716. 9m NW of Northampton, between A5199 (formerly A50) and A428.
Opening Times: 1 Apr - 30 Sept: Wed - Sun & BHs, 12 noon - 5.30pm.
Admission: Adult £3.50, Child £2, Conc. £3. Groups: £3.

    Grounds suitable. WC.   By arrangement.   P

COTTESBROOKE HALL & GDNS

COTTESBROOKE, NORTHAMPTONSHIRE NN6 8PF

Owner: Capt & Mrs John Macdonald-Buchanan   *Contact:* The Administrator

Tel: 01604 505808 **Fax:** 01604 505619 **e-mail:** hall@cottesbrooke.co.uk

Architecturally magnificent house built in the reign of Queen Anne. The identity of the original architect remains a mystery but the house has stayed essentially the same since that time. Renowned picture collection, particularly of sporting and equestrian subjects. Fine English and Continental furniture and porcelain. House reputed to be the pattern for Jane Austen's *Mansfield Park.*

Celebrated gardens of great variety including herbaceous borders, water and wild gardens, fine old cedars and specimen trees. Magnolia, cherry and acer collections and several fine vistas across the Park. Notable planting of containers. A number of distinguished landscape designers have been involved including Rober Weir Schultz, the late Sir Geoffrey Jellicoe and the late Dame Sylvia Crowe.

Location: OS Ref. SP711 739. 10m N of Northampton near Creaton on A5199 (formerly A50), near Brixworth on A508 or Kelmarsh on A14.

Opening Times: House & Gardens: Easter - end Sept: Thurs & BH Suns & Mons & May - Sept: 1st Sun in each month, 2 - 5.30pm. Gardens only: 1 Jun - end Sept: Tue - Fri & BH Suns & Mons & May - Sept: 1st Sun in each month, 2 - 5.30pm.

Admission: House & Gardens: Adult £4.50. Gardens only: Adult £3, Child half price. RHS members Free. Private groups welcome (except weekends) by prior arrangement.

ℹ️ No photography in house. Craft Fairs & Open Air Concerts. Filming outside.

Unusual plants.

Banqueting facilities, corporate hospitality and catering for functions.

Gardens suitable. WC.   Obligatory.   **P**

DEENE PARK 🏛   See page 307 for full page entry.

EDGCOTE HOUSE

Edgcote, Banbury, Oxfordshire OX17 1AG
Owner/Contact: Christopher Courage
Early Georgian house with good rococo plasterwork.
Location: OS Ref. SP505 480. 6m NE of Banbury off A361.
Opening Times: By written appointment only.

ELEANOR CROSS ⚎   **Tel:** 01604 735400 (Regional Office)

Geddington, Kettering, Northamptonshire
Owner: English Heritage   **Contact:** The East Midlands Regional Office
One of a series of famous crosses, of elegant sculpted design, erected by Edward I to mark the resting places of the body of his wife, Eleanor, when brought for burial from Harby in Nottinghamshire to Westminster Abbey in 1290.
Location: OS Ref. SP896 830. In Geddington, off A43 between Kettering and Corby.
Opening Times: Any reasonable time.

HADDONSTONE SHOW GARDEN   **Tel:** 01604 770711 **Fax:** 01604 770027

The Forge House, East Haddon, Northampton NN6 8DB
e-mail: info@haddonstone.co.uk
Owner: Haddonstone Ltd   **Contact:** Marketing Director
See Haddonstone's classic garden ornaments in the beautiful setting of the walled manor gardens – including urns, troughs, fountains, statuary, bird baths, sundials and balustrading. The garden is on different levels with shrub roses, conifers, clematis and climbers. The newly opened Jubilee garden features a pavilion, temple and Gothic grotto.
Location: OS Ref. SP667 682. 7m NW of Northampton off A428. Signposted.
Opening Times: Mon - Fri, 9am - 5.30pm. Closed weekends, BHs & Christmas period.
Admission: Free. Groups by appointment only. Not suitable for coach groups.

  By arrangement. **P** Limited. Guide dogs only.

Cottesbrooke Gardens, Northamptonshire.

HOLDENBY HOUSE & GARDENS

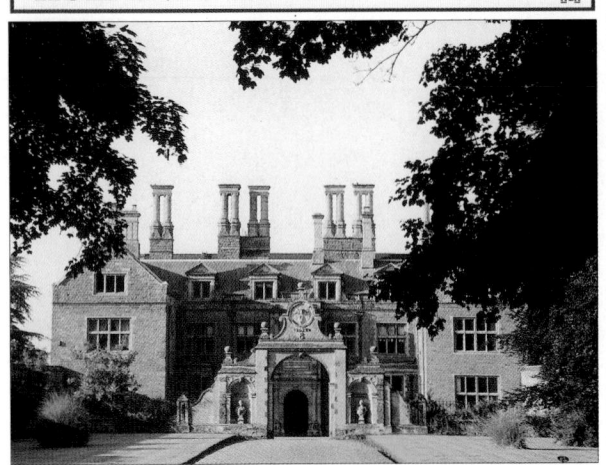

HOLDENBY, NORTHAMPTONSHIRE NN6 8DJ

Owner: James Lowther Esq   *Contact: Mrs Sarah Maughan*

Tel: 01604 770074 **Fax:** 01604 770962

On a hill across the fields from Althorp stands Holdenby. Once the largest house in England it was built to entertain Queen Elizabeth I and subsequently became the palace and prison of her successor Charles I. Now a family home, the house provides a splendid backdrop to the beautiful gardens re-created by Rosemary Verey and Rupert Golby, the rare breeds of farm animals, reconstructed 17th century farmstead and, overhead, our magnificent birds of prey soaring over the scene of so much history.

Location: OS Ref. SP693 681. M1/J15a. 7m NW of Northampton off A428 and A5199.

Opening times: Gardens & Falconry demonstrations: 1 Apr - end Sep: Suns, 1 - 5pm; Jul & Aug: daily (except Sats), 1 - 5pm. House: 16 Apr, 28 May, 27 Aug and by appointment. Events all BHs, 1 - 6pm.

Admission: Garden & Falconry: Adult £3, Child (3-15yrs) £1.75, OAP £2.50. House: Adult £5, Child £3, OAP £4.50. Events: Adult £4, Child £2, OAP £3.50.

[i] Children's play area. [ ] [ ] [T] [&] Partially suitable. WC.
[ ] Home-made teas. Groups must book. [K] By arrangement. [P]
[ ] Sandford Award-winner. [ ] In grounds, on leads. [ ] Tel. for details.

Kirby Hall, re-enactment, Northamptonshire.

Special Events Index ◀◀◀ page 33

KELMARSH HALL

Andrew Lawson.

KELMARSH, NORTHAMPTONSHIRE NN6 9LU

Owner: The Kelmarsh Trust   *Contact: General Manager*

Tel/Fax: 01604 686543

Built in 1732 to a James Gibbs design, Kelmarsh Hall is surrounded by its working estate, grazed parkland and beautiful gardens. In 1928 the Palladian house was occupied and decorated by Nancy Lancaster, and the Great Hall, Chinese Room and other rooms still bear her creative touch that has become known as the English Country House style. The gardens, with schemes and designs also by Geoffrey Jellicoe and Norah Lindsay, now have a unique place in garden history. Gifted to the Kelmarsh Trust by the Lancaster family the house, gardens and estate are now available for study, group and general visits.

Location: OS Ref. SP736 795. 500 metres N of A14 - A508 junction.

Opening Times: House: 15 Apr - 27 Aug: Suns & BH Mons, 2.30 - 5pm. Gardens: 15 Apr - 30 Aug: Tues, Thurs, Suns & BH Mons, 2.30 - 5pm. Sept: Tues & Thurs only.

Admission: House & Grounds: Adult £3.50, Child £2, Conc. £3. Garden only: £2. Group visits all year by arrangement.

[i] No photography in house. [&] Partially suitable. WC. [ ] On Suns only.
[K] Obligatory. [P] Limited for coaches. [ ] [ ] In grounds, on leads.

KIRBY HALL

Tel: 01536 203230

Deene, Corby, Northamptonshire NN17 5EN

Owner: English Heritage   **Contact:** The Custodian

Outstanding example of a large, stone-built Elizabethan mansion, begun in 1570 with 17th century alterations. There are fine gardens with topiary, home to peacocks. Jane Austen's *Mansfield Park* was filmed at Kirby Hall in 1998. Venue for *History in Action*, Europe's largest multi-period historical festival.

Location: OS141 Ref. SP926 927. On unclassified road off A43, Corby to Stamford road, 4m NE of Corby. 2m W of Deene Park.

Opening Times: 1 Apr - 31 Oct: daily 10am - 6pm (5pm in Oct). 1 Nov - 31 Mar: Sats & Suns, 10am - 4pm. Closed 24 - 26 Dec & 1 Jan.

Admission: Adult £3, Child £1.50, Conc. £2.30.

   Tel. for details.

LAMPORT HALL & GARDENS

See page 308 for full page entry.

LYVEDEN NEW BIELD

Tel: 01832 205358

Nr Oundle, Peterborough PE8 5AT

Owner: The National Trust   **Contact:** The Custodian

An incomplete Elizabethan garden house and moated garden. Begun in 1595 by Sir Thomas Tresham to symbolise his Catholic faith, Lyveden remains virtually unaltered since work stopped when Tresham died in 1605.

Location: OS141 Ref. SP983 853. 4m SW of Oundle via A427, 3m E of Brigstock, off Harley Way. Access by foot along a ½ m farm track.

Opening Times: All year: 9am - 5pm. Groups by arrangement with Custodian: Lyveden New Bield Cottage, Oundle, Peterborough PE8 5AT. Elizabethan water gardens and visitor information room open Apr - Nov: daily except Mons & Tues.

Admission: £2.

Limited.   On leads.

THE MENAGERIE

HORTON, NORTHAMPTON NN7 2BX

Owner: *Mr A Myers*   **Contact:** *Mr Neill Case (Head Gardener)*

Tel: 01604 870957

Folly built in the 1750s for the 2nd Earl of Halifax by the architect and astronomer Thomas Wright of Durham. The north front of the house has just been restored. The gardens, where Lord Halifax's animals were once kept, were created by the late Ian Kirby and include formal ponds, wetland and bog area, herbaceous border, two thatched arbours, one gothic and one circular and classical which is now a chapel. The whole grotto is covered in shells and minerals and devoted to Orpheus playing to the animals in the underworld.

Location: OS Ref. SP822 534. 5m SE of Northampton. Entry by field gate on E of A526.

Opening Times: Grotto & Gardens open to groups (20+) by arrangement £5. Gardens: Apr - Sept: Mons & Thurs, 2 - 5pm. Last Sun of each month 2 - 6pm.

Admission: Adult £3.50, Child £1.50.

   Grounds suitable.

NORTHAMPTON CATHEDRAL

Tel: 01604 714556   **Fax:** 01604 712066

Cathedral House, Kingsthorpe Road, Northampton NN2 6AG

Partly 19th century Pugin.   **Contact:** Cathedral Administrator, Canon D McSwenney

Location: OS Ref. SP753 617. ¾ m N of town centre.

Opening Times: Daily, 10am - 7pm. Sun Service: 7pm (Sat) 8.30am, 10.30am 5.15pm. Weekday services: 9.30am and 7pm.

Admission: Guided visit by prior application.

THE PREBENDAL MANOR HOUSE

NASSINGTON, PETERBOROUGH PE8 6QG

Owner/Contact: Mrs J Baile

Tel: 01780 782575   **e-mail:** info@prebendal-manor.demon.co.uk

Grade I listed and dating from the early 13th century, it is the oldest manor in Northamptonshire and one of the longest continually occupied houses in the country. The manor still retains many fine original medieval features and included in the visit are the 15th century dovecote, tithe barn museum and medieval fish ponds. Designed by Michael Brown and unique to the area and encompassing 5 acres are the 14th century re-created medieval gardens.

Location: OS Ref. TL063 962. 6m N of Oundle, 9m W of Peterborough, 7m S of Stamford.

Opening times: May, Jun & Sept: Suns, Weds & BH Mons. Jul/Aug: Suns, Weds & Thurs. 1 - 5.30pm. Closed Christmas.

Admission: Adult £4, Child £1.20. Groups (20 - 50) outside normal opening times by arrangement: Adult £3.50, Child £1.

No photography.   Partially suitable. Lunches & home-made teas.   Limited.   Free. Guide dogs only.

ROCKINGHAM CASTLE

See page 309 for full page entry.

RUSHTON TRIANGULAR LODGE

Tel: 01536 710761

Rushton, Kettering, Northamptonshire NN14 1RP

Owner: English Heritage   **Contact:** The Custodian

This extraordinary building, completed in 1597, symbolises the Holy Trinity. It has three sides, 33 ft wide, three floors, trefoil windows and three triangular gables on each side.

Location: OS Ref. SP830 831. 1m W of Rushton, on unclassified road 3m from Desborough on A6.

Opening Times: 1 Apr - 31 Oct: daily, 10am - 6pm (5pm in Oct).

Admission: Adult £1.75, Child 90p, Conc. £1.30.

SOUTHWICK HALL

Tel: 01832 274064

Nr Oundle, Peterborough PE8 5BL

Owner: Christopher Capron Esq   **Contact:** W J Richardson

A family home since 1300, retaining medieval building dating from 1300, with Tudor rebuilding and 18th century additions. Exhibitions: Victorian and Edwardian Life, collections of agricultural and carpentry tools and local archaeological finds.

Location: OS152 Ref. TL022 921. 3m N of Oundle, 4m E of Bulwick.

Opening Times: 15/16 Apr, 6/7 & 27/28 May, 26/27 Aug, also Weds May - Aug: 2 - 5pm (last admission 4.30pm).

Admission: Adult £3.50, Child £2, OAP £3.

Partially suitable. WC.   By arrangement.   In grounds on leads.

STOKE PARK PAVILIONS
Tel: 01604 862172

Stoke Bruerne, Towcester, Northamptonshire NN12 7RZ
Owner: A S Chancellor Esq   **Contact:** Mrs C Cook
The two Pavilions, dated c1630 and attributed to Inigo Jones, formed part of the first Palladian country house built in England by Sir Francis Crane. The central block, to which the Pavilions were linked by quadrant colonnades, was destroyed by fire in 1886. The grounds include extensive gardens and overlook the former park, now farmland.
Location: OS Ref. SP740 488. 7m S of Northampton.
Opening Times: Aug: daily, 3 - 6pm. Other times by appointment only.
Admission: Adult £3, Child £1.

Grounds suitable.   Limited.   In grounds, on leads.

WAKEFIELD LODGE
Tel: 01327 811493

Potterspury, Northamptonshire NN12 7QX
Owner/Contact: J H Richmond-Watson
Georgian Hunting Lodge with deer park.
Location: OS Ref. SP739 425. 4m S of Towcester on A5.
Opening Times: House: 30 Apr - 8 Jun: Mon - Fri (closed BHs).
Admission: £5.

No photography.   Not suitable.   Obligatory. Limited for coaches.   Guide dogs only.

SULGRAVE MANOR

Norman Hudson.

MANOR ROAD, SULGRAVE, BANBURY, OXON OX17 2SD
Owner: Sulgrave Manor Board   *Contact:* Martin Sirot-Smith

Tel: 01295 760205 **Fax:** 01295 768056 **e-mail:** sulgrave-manor@talk21.com
A delightful 16th century Manor House that was the home of George Washington's ancestors. Today it presents a typical wealthy man's home and gardens of Elizabethan times. Restored with scholarly care and attention to detail that makes a visit both a pleasure and an education. *'A perfect illustration of how a house should be shown to the public'* – Nigel Nicholson, *Great Houses of Britain*. New Courtyard development with fine visitor/education facilities.
Location: OS152 Ref. SP561 457. Off Banbury - Northampton road (B4525) 5m from M40/J11. 15m from M1/J15A.
Opening Times: 1 Apr - 31 Oct: daily except Weds. W/days 2 - 5.30pm. W/ends 10.30am - 1pm & 2 - 5.30pm. Nov, Dec & Mar: W/ends only, 10.30am - 1pm & 2 - 4.30pm. Also open 27 - 30 Dec. Closed 25 - 26 & 31 Dec & Jan. Open by appointment for groups and school groups out of normal hours.
Admission: Adult £4, Child £2, Conc. £4. Groups: Adult £3.50, Child £1.75, Conc. £3.50. Special Events: Adult £4.50, Child £2.25, Family £12. Groups: Adult £4, Child £2. Gardens only: £2. All visitors on non-event days are taken round the Manor House in regularly organized guided tours.

No photography in house.   Partially suitable. Obligatory.   In grounds, on leads. Tel. for details.

Hugh Palmer.

Cottesbrooke Gardens, Northamptonshire.

East Midlands
England

BREWHOUSE YARD MUSEUM
Tel: 0115 9153600 **Fax:** 0115 9153601

THE MUSEUM OF NOTTINGHAM LIFE

Castle Boulevard, Nottingham NG7 1FB

Owner/Contact:

Set in a group of 18th century cottages, the museum presents a realistic glimpse of life in Nottingham over the past 200 years.

Location: OS Ref. SK570 393. 500yds SW of City Centre.

Opening Times: Daily, 10am - 4.30pm (Nov - Feb: closed Fris).

Admission: Weekdays: Free. Weekends & BHs: Adult £1.50, Conc. 80p, Family £3.80.

CARLTON HALL
Tel: 01636 821421 **Fax:** 01636 821554

Carlton-on-Trent, Nottinghamshire NG23 6LP

Owner/Contact: Lt Col & Mrs Vere-Laurie

Mid 18th century house by Joseph Pocklington of Newark. Stables attributed to Carr of York. Family home occupied by the same family since 1832.

Location: OS Ref. SK799 640. 7m N of Newark off A1. Opposite the church.

Opening Times: By appointment only.

Admission: Hall and Garden £3.50. Minimum charge for a group £35.

Conferences. Not suitable. In grounds, on leads. Guide dogs in house.

CASTLE MUSEUM & ART GALLERY
Tel: 0115 9153700 **Fax:** 0115 9153653

Nottingham NG1 6EL
Contact: Janet Owen

17th century ducal mansion, home to a museum and art gallery.

Location: OS Ref. SK569 395. SW of the city centre on hilltop.

Opening Times: Daily (closed Fris from Nov-Feb): 10am - 5pm. Closed 24, 25 Dec & 1 Jan.

Admission: Weekdays Free. Weekends: Adult £2, Conc. £1 (2000 times & prices).

CLUMBER PARK
Tel: 01909 476592 **Fax:** 01909 500721

Clumber Park, Worksop, Nottinghamshire S80 3AZ

Owner: The National Trust **Contact:** Claire Herring, Property Manager

Historic parkland with peaceful woods, open heath and rolling farmland around a serpentine lake.

Location: OS120 Ref SK626 746. 4¹/₂m SE of Worksop, 6¹/₂m SW of Retford, just off A1/A57 via A614. 11m from M1/J30.

Opening Times: Park: All year during daylight hours, except 14 Jul & 18 Aug. Walled Kitchen Garden: Apr - end Sept: Weds & Thurs, 10.30am - 5.30pm, Sats, Suns & BH Mons, 10.30am - 6pm. Chapel: Apr - end Sept: Mon - Fri, 10.30am - 5.30pm, Sats & Suns, 10.30am - 6pm. Oct - 11 Jan 2001: daily, 10.30am - 4pm. Closed 12 Jan - end Mar for conservation cleaning.

Admission: Pedestrians: Free, NT Members: Free, Cars £3, Caravans/mini-coaches £4.30. Coaches Free weekday, £7 weekends & BH Mons. Walled kitchen garden 70p.

Partially suitable. Wheelchairs available.

In grounds on leads.

GREEN'S MILL
Tel: 0115 9156878

Windmill Lane, Sneinton, Nottingham NG2 4QB

Owner/Contact:

This fully operational windmill was once owned and operated by George Green, mathematician and physicist.

Location: OS Ref. SK585 398. ¹/₂ m due E of City Centre, between A612 and B686.

Opening Times: Wed - Sun & BH Mons, 10am - 4pm.

Admission: Free.

HODSOCK PRIORY GARDEN
Tel: 01909 591204 **Fax:** 01909 591578

Blyth, Nr Worksop, Nottinghamshire S81 0TY

Owner: Sir Andrew & Lady Buchanan **Contact:** Lady Buchanan

Sensational snowdrops, winter flowering plants and shrubs, woodland walk.

Location: OS Ref. SK612 853. W of B6045 Worksop/Blyth road, 1m SW of Blyth, less than 2m from A1.

Opening Times: Snowdrop period only: daily, 10am - 4pm. Please telephone for details.

Admission: Adult £3, accompanied Child (6-16yrs) 50p.

HOLME PIERREPONT HALL

HOLME PIERREPONT, Nr NOTTINGHAM NG12 2LD

Owner: Mr & Mrs Robin Brackenbury **Contact:** Robert Brackenbury

Tel: 0115 933 2371

This charming late medieval manor house is set in thirty acres of Park and Gardens with regional furniture and family portraits. The recently restored Ball Room, Dining Room and Long Gallery which seats 100 people are available, on an exclusive basis, for business events and wedding receptions. Filming welcome.

Location: OS Ref. SK628 392. 5m ESE of central Nottingham. Follow signs to the National Water Sports Centre and continue for 1¹/₂ m.

Opening Times: Easter, Spring & Summer BHs (Suns & Mons). Jun: Thurs, Jul: Weds & Thurs. Aug: Tue - Thurs, 2 - 5.30pm. Private functions at other times by arrangement.

Admission: Adult £3.50, Child £1.50. Gardens only £1.50.

Partially suitable. WC. Business & charity functions, wedding receptions.

In grounds on leads.

MUSEUM OF COSTUME & TEXTILES
Tel: 0115 9153500

Castle Gate, Nottingham NG1 6AF

Costume displays from 1790 to the mid-20th century are beautifully presented in period rooms.

Location: OS Ref. SK570 395. Just SW of City Centre.

Opening Times: Wed - Sun & BH Mons, 10am - 4pm.

Admission: Free.

NEWARK TOWN HALL
Tel: 01636 680333 **Fax:** 01636 680350

Market Place, Newark, Nottinghamshire NG24 1DU

Owner: Newark Town Council **Contact:** The Curator

A fine Georgian Grade I listed Town Hall containing a museum of the town's treasures. Disabled access – lift and WC.

Location: OS Ref. SK570 395. Close to A46 and A1.

Opening Times: Mon - Fri, 10.30am - 1pm & 2 - 4.30pm. Sats, 2 - 4.30pm (Apr - Oct). Closed BHs.

Admission: Free.

NEWSTEAD ABBEY
Tel: 01623 455900 **Fax:** 01623 455904

Newstead Abbey Park, Nottinghamshire NG15 8GE **Contact:** Julie DeLong

Historic home of the poet, Lord Byron, set in grounds of over 300 acres. Mementoes of Byron and period rooms from medieval to Victorian times.

Location: OS Ref. SK540 639. 12m N of Nottingham 1m W of the A60 Mansfield Rd.

Opening Times: 1 Apr - 30 Sept: 12 noon - 5pm, last adm. 4pm. Grounds: All year except last Fri in Nov. Apr - Sept: 9am - 7.30pm. Oct - Mar: 9am - 5pm.

Admission: House & Grounds: Adult £4, Child £1.50, Conc. £2. Grounds only: Adult £2, Conc. £1.50 (2000 prices).

Open All Year

Index ◀◀◀ **page 49**

NORWOOD PARK

SOUTHWELL, NOTTINGHAMSHIRE NG25 0PF

Owner: Sir John & Lady Starkey   *Contact: Sarah Dodd, Events Manager*

Tel: 01636 815649 **Fax:** 01636 815702 **e-mail:** events@norwoodpark.org.uk
Delightful Georgian country house and stables set in a medieval deer park, with ancient oaks, fishponds and eyecatcher Temple, overlooking apple orchards and cricket ground. Perfect venue for all manner of business or social occasion. Combination of reception/meeting/dining rooms available in the house for smaller groups. Unique Stables Gallery complex adjacent to the house, ideal for fairytale wedding receptions, corporate dances and promotions for larger groups. Idyllic and versatile grounds for activity days, promotional work and filming. USA designed 9-hole golf course and practice area in the magnificent parkland available for event days.
Location: OS Ref. SK688 545. ¾ m W of Southwell.
Opening Times: All year by appointment only.
Admission: Please telephone for information.

ⓘ Outdoor activity days. 🍽 Events/weddings. ♿ Partially suitable.
🖥 By arrangement. 🎟 By arrangement. 🅿 Limited for coaches.
🐾 In grounds, on leads. 🛏 Honeymoon suite only. 🔔 ❄ 🌐

PAPPLEWICK HALL 🏛   Tel: 0115 963 3491 Fax: 0115 964 2767

Papplewick, Nottinghamshire NG15 8FE
Owner: Dr R Godwin-Austen
A beautiful stone built classical house set in a park with woodland garden laid out in the 18th century. The house is notable for its very fine plasterwork and elegant staircase. Grade I listed.
Location: OS Ref. SK548 518. Halfway between Nottingham & Mansfield, 3m E of M1/J27 on B683.
Opening Times: By appointment and 1st, 3rd & 5th Wed in each month, 2-5pm.
Admission: Adult £5. Groups (10+): £4.

ⓘ No photography. 🎟 Obligatory. 🅿 Limited for coaches.
🐾 In grounds on leads. ❄

RUFFORD ABBEY ⌗   Tel: 01623 822944

Ollerton, Nottinghamshire NG22 9DF
Owner: English Heritage   **Contact:** Nottinghamshire County Council
The remains of a 17th century country house; displaying the ruins of a 12th century Cistercian Abbey. It is set in what is now Rufford Country Park.
Location: OS Ref. SK645 646. 2m S of Ollerton off A614.
Opening Times: 1 Apr - 31 Oct: Daily, 10am - 5pm. 1 Nov - 31 Mar: daily, 10am - 4pm. (Closed 24 - 26 Dec & 1 Jan).
Admission: Free - parking charge applies.

Website Index ◀◀ ◀ page 39

SUTTON BONINGTON HALL

Nr LOUGHBOROUGH, NOTTINGHAM LE12 5PF

Owner: Lady Anne Elton   Contact: Mr & Mrs Henry Weldon

Tel: 01509 672355 **Fax:** 01509 889060 **e-mail:** henryweldon@hotmail.com
Sutton Bonington Hall, home of the Paget family since 1750, is a magnificent example of Queen Anne architecture, with an early conservatory (1810), and fine Queen Anne furniture. Sutton Bonington is not open to the general public, but offers excellent facilities for small conferences, corporate dinners and weddings. Extensive formally laid-out gardens can accommodate marquees for larger events. Seven luxurious bedrooms (all en-suite) can accommodate up to 14 guests in style.
Location: SK505 255. 1m E of A6, 5m N of Loughborough. In the heart of the Midlands, a short distance from Nottingham, Derby, Leicester, M1 and East Midlands airport.
Opening Times: By arrangement.
Admission: Corporate/private entertainment and wedding venue by arrangement only. Residential rooms by prior reservation only.

🍽 ♿ Partially suitable. 🅿 Ample for cars. 🐾 In grounds, on leads.
🛏 7 doubles. 🔔 ❄

THRUMPTON HALL

THRUMPTON, NOTTINGHAM NG11 0AX

Owner/Contact: The Hon Mrs R Seymour

Tel: 01159 830333 **Fax:** 01159 831309
Fine Jacobean house, built in 1607 incorporating an earlier manor house. Priest's hiding hole, magnificent carved Charles II staircase, carved and panelled saloon. Other fine rooms containing beautiful 17th and 18th century furniture and many fine portraits. Large lawns separated from landscaped park by ha-ha and by lake in front of the house. The house is still lived in as a home and the owner will show parties around when possible. Dining room with capacity for 52 with silver service or buffet. Free access and meal for coach drivers.
Location: OS Ref. SK508 312. 7m S of Nottingham, 3m E M1/J24, 1m from A453.
Opening Times: By appointment. Parties of 20+ 10.30am - 7.30pm.
Admission: Adult £5, Child £2.50.

📷 🍽 Wedding receptions. ♿ Ground floor & grounds suitable. WC. 🍴
🐾 In grounds on leads. ❄

UPTON HALL

Tel: 01636 813795

Upton, Newark, Nottinghamshire NG23 5TE
Owner: British Horological Institute **Contact:** The Director
Location: OS Ref. SK735 544. A612 between Newark and Southwell.
Opening Times: Please telephone for details.
Admission: Adult £2.50, Child £1, (under 11yrs free), OAP £2.

WINKBURN HALL

Tel: 01636 636465 **Fax:** 01636 636717

Winkburn, Newark, Nottinghamshire NG22 8PQ **e-mail:** any@alderton.co.uk
Owner/Contact: Richard Craven-Smith-Milnes Esq
A fine William and Mary house.
Location: OS Ref. SK711 584. 8m W of Newark 1m N of A617.
Opening Times: Throughout the year by appointment only.
Admission: £4.50.

WOLLATON HALL NATURAL HISTORY MUSEUM

Tel: 0115 915 3900

Wollaton Park, Nottingham NG8 2AE
Owner: Nottingham City Council **Contact:** Phil Hackett
Tudor building set in 500 acres of parkland and home to the Natural History Museum.
Location: OS Ref. SK532 392. Wollaton Park, Nottingham. 3m W of city centre.
Opening Times: Summer: 11am - 5pm. Winter: 11am - 4pm. Closed Fridays from Nov - Mar.
Admission: Weekdays Free. Weekends & BHs Adult: £1.50, Child 80p. Joint ticket for Wollaton Hall & Industrial Museum. Grounds £1/car (free for orange badge holders). (2000 times and prices.)

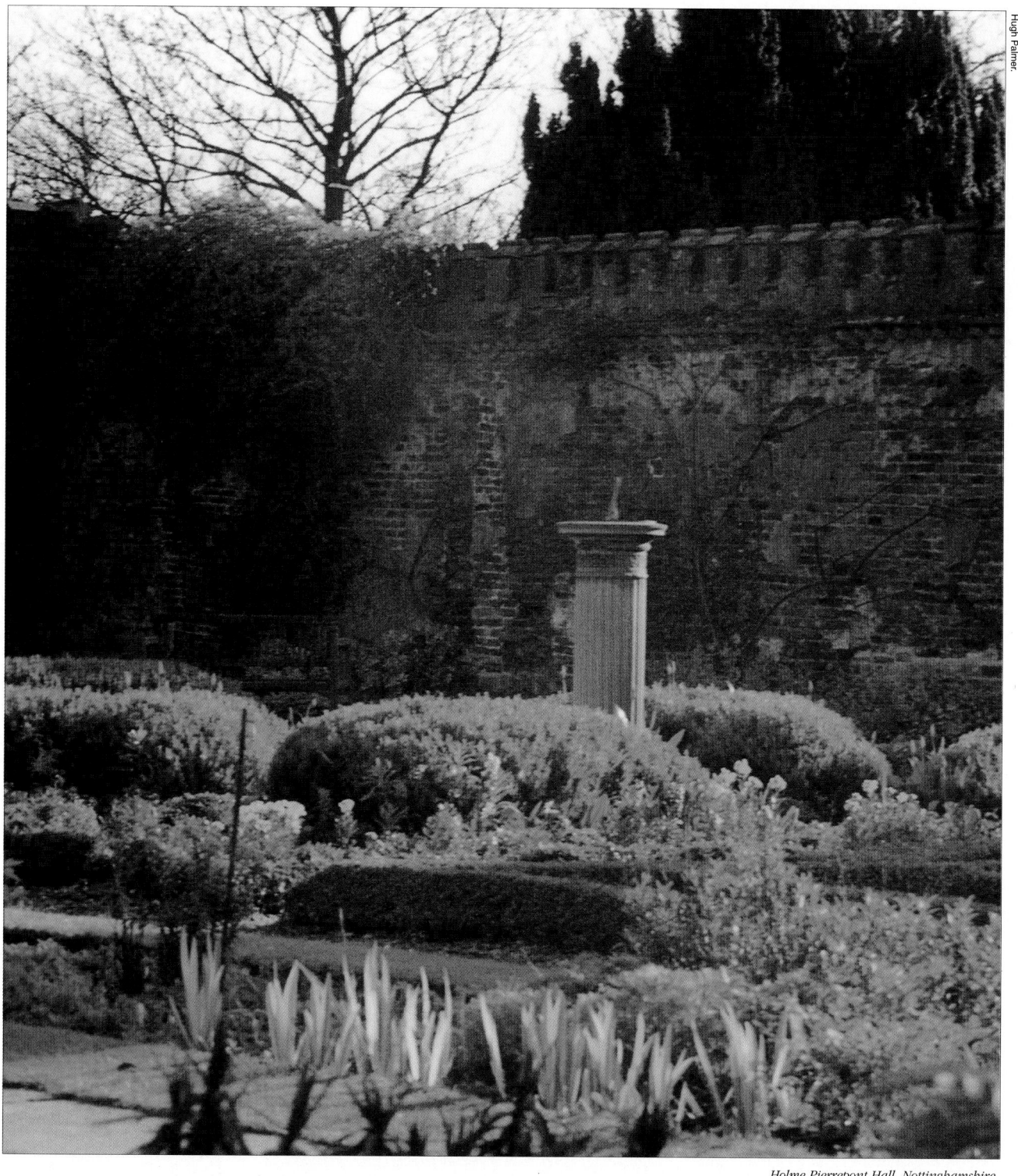

Holme Pierrepont Hall, Nottinghamshire.

Hugh Palmer.

Dorothy Clive Garden, Staffordshire

West Midlands

Dorothy Clive Garden

"A woodland garden, tranquil, silent; ever verdant, and in its seasonal splendour, elevating even the most grounded of human spirits."

The Dorothy Clive Garden at Willoughbridge near Market Drayton, is today owned by the Willoughbridge Garden Trust.

Set on the side of a hill, with some steep winding paths to tackle, this well stocked plantsman's garden is divided into two distinct parts. Above the house is the wonderfully naturally planted hillside garden, below it is more open and highly cultivated.

The garden was created by Col Harry Clive for his wife Dorothy in 1939. Col and Mrs Clive lived at Elds Gorse, the large house on the west side of the garden, visible from the road, and from the garden in winter when the trees have lost their leaves. During the last years of her life Dorothy, due to ill health, was restricted to monotonous daily circuits around the lawn. Col Clive therefore decided to transform a wooded and defunct quarry nearby into what is now a superb woodland garden.

Bowl-shaped, the woodland garden is filled with a mass of hybrid and unusual rhododendrons, and deciduous and evergreen azaleas. Sheltered from the wind, it is the ideal site for rhododendrons to grow. Weaving along paths in late spring, the top of this steep-sided dell is a riot of colour. Blood red *Rhododendron thomsonii*, pale yellow *R campyloarpum elatum* and groups of pink, orange and red Exbury and Knaphill azaleas flower magnificently.

The peak months for viewing this garden are May, June and the autumn. Native and specimen trees which have been planted in the hillside garden provide wonderful strong autumn colour. The clever tree planting also shelters the more tender and unusual shrubs – these in turn are underplanted with spring bulbs such as the cyclamen flowered daffodil and the *Narcissus cyclamineus* which has naturalised.

Following his wife's death in 1942 Col Clive built a bungalow below the dell and turned his energies to cultivating the field which sloped away below. He did not live to see this part of the garden completed, but the Willoughbridge Garden Trust was formed and the garden's future was secured.

This beautiful and thoughtfully planted garden is a wonderful lesson in how to lay out a rewarding but 'labour saving' garden and it is a delight to visit.

For further details about *Dorothy Clive Garden* see entry in West Midlands Region ➔ Staffordshire.

Hello Dolly

A reminiscence of the late Dorothy (Dolly) Clive 1883 - 1942
By her son Harry
Illustrations by her Grand Daughter Georgina

West Midlands England

NT Photographic Library.

Owner: The National Trust

CONTACT

The Property Manager
Berrington Hall
Nr Leominster
Herefordshire
HR6 0DW

Tel: 01568 615721

Fax: 01568 613263

Information Line:
01684 855367

Restaurant:
01568 610134

e-mail: berrington
@smtp.ntrust.org.uk

LOCATION

OS137 SP510 637

3m N of Leominster, 7m S
of Ludlow on
W side of A49.

Rail: Leominster 4m.

BERRINGTON HALL
Nr Leominster

BERRINGTON HALL is the creation of Thomas Harley, the 3rd Earl of Oxford's remarkable son, who made a fortune from supplying pay and clothing to the British Army in America and became Lord Mayor of London in 1767 at the age of thirty-seven. The architect was the fashionable Henry Holland. The house is beautifully set above the wide valley of a tributary of the River Lugg, with views west and south to the Black Mountains and Brecon Beacons. This was the site advised by 'Capability' Brown who created the lake with its artificial island. The rather plain neo-classical exterior with a central portico gives no clue to the lavishness of the interior. Plaster ceilings now decorated in muted pastel colours adorn the principal rooms. Holland's masterpiece is the staircase hall rising to a central dome. The rooms are set off with a collection of French furniture, including pieces which belonged to the Comte de Flahault, natural son of Talleyrand, and Napoleon's step-daughter Hortense.

In the dining room, vast panoramic paintings of battles at sea, three of them by Thomas Luny, are a tribute to the distinguished Admiral Rodney.

❖

NT Photographic Library.

OPENING TIMES

House

1 Apr - 31 Oct:
Daily except Thurs & Fris.
(open Good Fri)
1 - 5pm.
(4.30pm in Oct).

Garden

1 Apr - 31 Oct:
Daily except Thurs & Fris.
(open Good Fri)
12 noon - 5pm.
(4.30pm in Oct).

Park Walk

1 Jul - 31 Oct:
Daily except Thurs & Fris.
12 noon - 5pm
(4.30pm in Oct).

ADMISSION

Adult £4.30
Child (5-12yrs) £2.15
Family (2+3) £10.75

Groups (15-25)*
Reduced rate available.

Garden Ticket.........£2.15

Groups must pre-book. Two
groups can visit at a time.

 SPECIAL EVENTS

Please telephone for details of
special events.

No photography in the house. Groups by arrangement only.

Single seater batricar, stairclimber; pre-booking essential. Audio tours for the visually impaired

Licensed restaurant: open as house: 12.30 - 5.30pm (4.30pm in Oct).

By arrangement only. Tour time: 1 hr.

Ample for cars. Parking for coaches limited; instructions given when booking is made.

Children's quizzes. Play area in walled garden.

Guide dogs only.

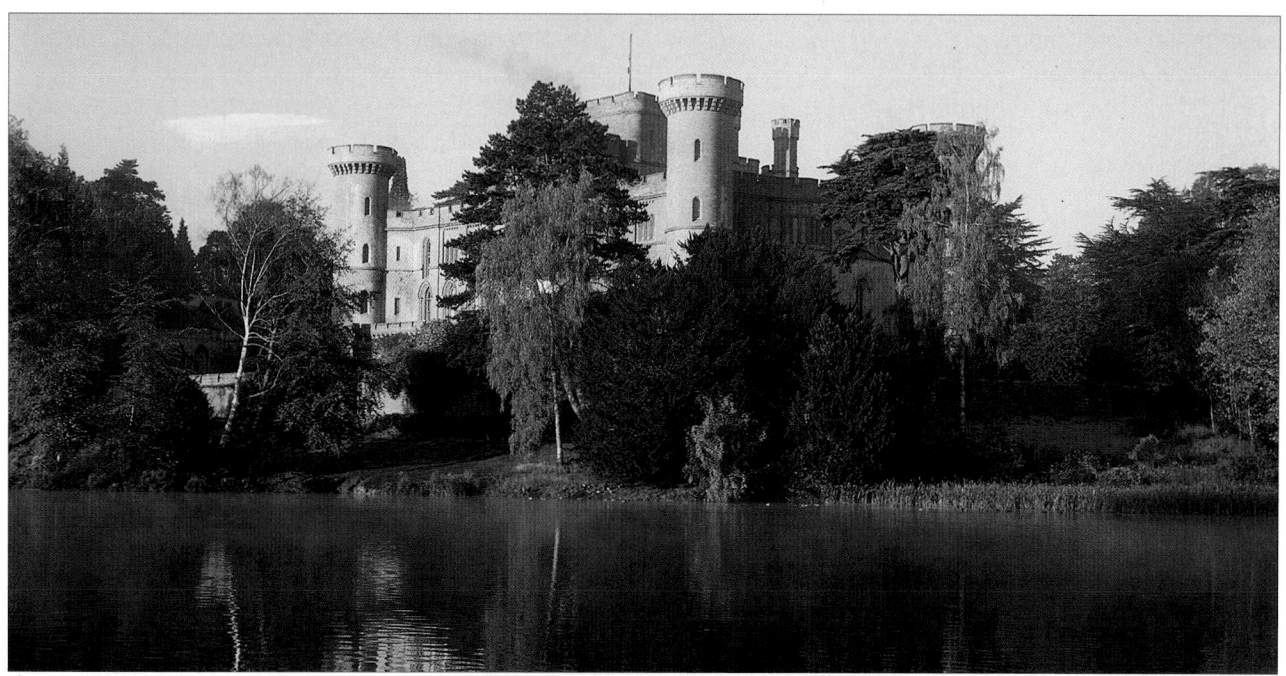

EASTNOR CASTLE
Ledbury

Encircled by the Malvern Hills and surrounded by a famous arboretum and lake, this fairytale castle looks as dramatic inside as it does outside.

The atmosphere Everyone is struck by it. The vitality of a young family brings the past to life and the sense of warmth and optimism is tangible. Eastnor, however grand, is a home.

'Sleeping' for the past fifty years, the Castle has undergone a triumphant renaissance – 'looking better than it probably ever has', *Country Life* 1993.

Hidden away in attics and cellars since 1939, many of the castle's treasures are now displayed for the first time – early Italian Fine Art, 17th century Venetian furniture and Flemish tapestries, mediaeval armour and paintings by Van Dyck, Romney, Wootton and Watts, photographs by Julia Margaret Cameron. Drawing Room by Pugin.

'The princely and imposing pile' as it was described in 1812 when it was being built to pitch the owner into the aristocracy, remains the home of his descendants. The castle contains letters diaries, clothes and furnishings belonging to friends and relations who include: Horace Walpole, Elizabeth Barrett Browning, Tennyson, Watts, Julia Margaret Cameron and Virginia Woolf.

Encircled by the Malvern Hills, the medieval beauty of the estate remains unchanged.

GARDENS

Castellated terraces descend to a 21 acre lake with a restored lakeside walk. The arboretum holds a famous collection of mature specimen trees. There are spectacular views of the Malvern hills across a 300 acre deer park, once part of a mediaeval chase and now designated a Site of Special Scientific Interest.

Owner:
Mr J & The Hon
Mrs Hervey-Bathurst

CONTACT

Simon Foster
Portcullis Office
Eastnor Castle
Nr Ledbury
Herefordshire HR8 1RL

Tel: 01531 633160

Fax: 01531 631776

e-mail: enquiries@
eastnorcastle.com

LOCATION

OS Ref. SO735 368

2m SE of Ledbury on the A438 Tewkesbury road. Alternatively M50/J2 & from Ledbury take the A449/A438.

Tewkesbury 20 mins, Malvern 20 mins, Gloucester 25 mins Hereford 25 mins, Worcester 30mins, Cheltenham 30 mins B'ham 1 hr, London 2¼ hrs.

Taxi: Meredith Taxis
01531 632852
Clive Fletcher 0589 299283

CONFERENCE/FUNCTION

ROOM	SIZE	MAX CAPACITY
Library	18 x 8m	120
Great Hall	16 x 8m	150
Dining Rm	11 x 7m	80
Gothic Rm	11 x 7m	80
Octagon Rm	9 x 9m	50

Plant Centre.

Maze, off-road driving, clay-pigeon shooting, quad bikes, archery and falconry. Survival training, team building activity days. Product launches, fashion shows, concerts, charity events, craft fairs, television and feature films. No photography in castle.

Wedding receptions. Catering for booked events.

Partially suitable. Visitors may alight at the castle. Priority parking.

Home-made food, menus on request, groups must book.

By arrangement.

Ample 10 - 200 yds from castle. Coaches phone in advance to arrange parking & catering. Free meal for drivers.

Welcome. Guides available if required. Children's fun worksheets.

On leads in Castle and grounds.

Luxury accommodation within castle for small groups. 1 single room and 10 double. Ensuite available.

SUMMER
15 April - 7 October:
Suns & BH Mons.
July - August: Sun - Fri
11am - 5pm.

NB. Groups by appointment at other times when the castle is closed to casual visitors.

ADMISSION

SUMMER
Castle & Grounds
Adult £5.00
Child (5-15yrs)..........£3.00
OAP......................£4.75
Family (2+2) £13.00
Groups* (with guide)
Adult £7.50
Groups* (without guide)
Adult £4.50
* Min. payment for 20 people.

Grounds only
Adult £3.00
Child (5-15yrs)..........£2.00
OAP......................£2.75

Season Ticket
Adult £15.00
Child (5-15yrs)..........£9.00
OAP......................£14.25
Family £39.00
Please telephone for admission prices for special events.

WINTER
By appointment.

SPECIAL EVENTS

- **MAY 6/7**
Spring Country Crafts Fair.

- **MAY 28**
Steam Fair & Country Show with Fred Dibnah.

- **JUL 1**
Wood Festival.

- **JUL 14/15**
Medieval Jousting and Hot Air Balloon Festival.

- **AUG 26/27**
Children's Fun Week

- **OCT 6/7**
Festival of Fine Food and Drink.

West Midlands England

ABBEYDORE COURT GARDENS
Tel/Fax: 01981 240419

Abbey Dore, Hereford HR2 0AD
Owner/Contact: Mrs C L Ward
6 acre rambling garden, intersected by the River Dore. Shrubs and herbaceous perennials, rock garden and ponds.
Location: OS Ref. SO387 309. 3 m W of A465 midway Hereford - Abergavenny.
Opening Times: Apr - Sept: daily except Weds & Fris, 11am - 6pm.
Admission: Adult £2.50, Child 50p.

BERRINGTON HALL
See page 324 for full page entry.

CONINGSBY HOSPITAL, MUSEUM & GARDENS
Tel: 01432 267821

Widemarsh Street, Hereford HR4 9HN
Contact: Mr D G Harding
Built in 1614 on the site of a Knights-Hospitallers Place.
Location: OS Ref. SO512 404. East side of Widemarsh Street. 500 yards N of City Centre.
Opening Times: Tue - Thur, weekends & BHs, 2 - 5pm.
Admission: Adult £2, Child/Conc. £1. Groups rates for educational visits.

BROCKHAMPTON ESTATE & LOWER BROCKHAMPTON

NT Severn Region: R Anderson.

BRINGSTY, WORCESTERSHIRE WR6 5UH
Owner: *The National Trust*   ***Contact:*** *The Administrator*

Tel: 01885 488099
A late 14th century moated manor house, with an attractive detached half-timbered 15th century gatehouse, a rare example of this type of structure. Also, the ruins of a 12th century chapel. Woodland walks including sculpture trail. Easy access for all, long and short waymarked walks.
Location: OS149, Ref. SO682 546. 2m E of Bromyard N side of A44, reached by narrow road through 1^1/$_2$ m of woods and farmland.
Opening Times: Medieval Hall, parlour, minstrel gallery, information room, gatehouse and chapel: 1 Apr - end Oct: Wed - Sun & BH Mons, 12.30 - 5pm. Weekends Jul & Aug: 10.30am - 5pm. Last admission ^{1}/$_2$ hr before closing. Estate: All year: daily during daylight hours.
Admission: Adult £2.70, Child £1.35, Family £6.75. Car park £1.50.

 Partially suitable.

CROFT CASTLE

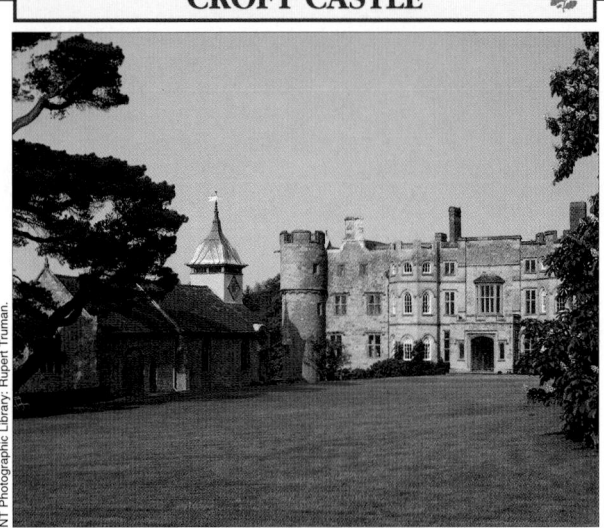

NT Photographic Library: Rupert Truman.

LEOMINSTER, HEREFORDSHIRE HR6 9PW
Owner: *The National Trust*   ***Contact:*** *The House Manager*

Tel: 01568 780246 **e-mail:** croft@smtp.ntrust.org.uk
Home of the Croft family since Domesday (with a break of 170 years from 1750). Walls and corner towers date from 14th and 15th centuries, interior mainly 18th century when fine Georgian-Gothic staircase and plasterwork ceilings were added; splendid avenue of 350 year old Spanish chestnuts. Iron Age Fort (Croft Ambrey) may be reached by footpath. The walk is uphill (approx. 40 mins).
Location: OS137 Ref. SO455 655. 5m NW of Leominster, 9m SW of Ludlow, approach from B4362.
Opening times: Castle: 31 Mar - 29 Apr: Sats & Suns, Good Fri & BH Mons; 2 May - 30 Sept: daily except Mons & Tues (open BH Mons); 6 Oct - 4 Nov: Sats & Suns. 1 - 5pm (closes 4.30pm in Oct & Nov). Park & Croft Ambrey: daily.
Admission: Adult £3.90, Child £1.95. Family £10. Grounds only: Car park £2 per car, £10 per coach.

EASTNOR CASTLE
See page 325 for full page entry.

GOODRICH CASTLE
Tel: 01600 890538

Ross-on-Wye, Herefordshire HR9 6HY
Owner: English Heritage   **Contact:** The Custodian
This magnificent red sandstone castle is remarkably complete with a 12th century keep and extensive remains from 13th & 14th centuries. From the battlements there are fine views over the Wye Valley to Symonds Yat. Marvel at the maze of small rooms and the 'murder holes'.
Location: OS162, Ref. SO579 199. 5m S of Ross-on-Wye, off A40.
Opening Times: 1 Apr - 31 Oct: daily, 10am - 6pm (5pm in Oct). 1 Nov - 31 Mar: daily, 10am - 4pm. Closed 1 - 2pm in winter. Closed 24 - 26 Dec & 1 Jan.
Admission: Adult £3.60, Child £1.80, Conc. £2.70. Family ticket £9. 15% discount for groups (11+).

   Tel. for details.

Open All Year Index page 49 ◀◀◀

HAMPTON COURT

HOPE UNDER DINMORE, LEOMINSTER, HEREFORDSHIRE HR6 0PN

Owner: Charity   *Contact: Ed Waghorn*

Tel: 01568 7977777 **Fax:** 01568 797472
e-mail: vankampengardens@hamptoncourt.org.uk

The Van Kampen Gardens at Hampton Court, Herefordshire are extensive new gardens in the historic grounds of a medieval fortified manor house. There is a walled organic garden, flower gardens, canals, pavilions, a maze and a secret tunnel, a hermit's grotto, waterfalls and a flooded sunken garden. There are beautiful parkland views and river walks. An organic teashop serves light lunches, tea and cake from a conservatory designed by Joseph Paxton.

Location: OS Ref. SO520 525. On the A417 near to the junction with the A49.

Opening times: 13 Apr - 28 Oct: Wed - Sun & BH Mons, 11am - 5pm. Groups by prior arrangement.

Admission: Adults £4, Child (6-13yrs) £2, OAP £3.50.

⬚ ✿ 🎪 ⬚ ⬚ 🔥By arrangement. **P** 🐕Guide dogs only.
🛡Tel. for details. ⓥ

HEREFORD CATHEDRAL   **Tel:** 01432 374202 **Fax:** 01432 374220
Hereford HR1 2NG   **e-mail:** visits@herefordcathedral.co.uk
                          Contact: Mr D Harding - The Visits Manager

Location: OS Ref. SO510 398. Hereford city centre on A49.

Opening Times: 7.30am - 5pm. Sun services: 8am, 10am, 11.30am & 3.30pm. Weekday services: 8am and 5.30pm.

Admission: Admission only for Mappa Mundi and Chained Library Exhibition: Adult £4, OAP/Student/Unemployed £3.50, Child under 5yrs Free. Family ticket (2+3) £10.00.

HERGEST COURT 🏛   **Tel/Fax:** 01544 230160

c/o Hergest Estate Office, Kington HR5 3EG

Owner/Contact: W L Banks

The ancient home of the Vaughans of Hergest, dating from the 13th century.

Location: OS Ref. SO283 554. 1m W of Kington on unclassified road to Brilley.

Opening Times: Strictly by appointment only through Estate Office.

Admission: Adult £4, Child £1.50. Groups: Adult £3.50, Child £1.

♿ Not suitable. **P** Limited. 🐕 Guide dogs only. ✳

HELLENS 🏛

MUCH MARCLE, LEDBURY, HEREFORDSHIRE HR8 2LY

Owner: Pennington-Mellor-Munthe Charity Trust **Contact:** *The Administrator*

Tel: 01531 660504

Built as a monastery and then a stone fortress in 1292 by Morhimes, Earl of March, with Tudor, Jacobean and Stuart additions and lived in ever since by descendants of the original builder. Visited by the Black Prince, Bloody Mary and the 'family ghost'. Family paintings, relics and heirlooms from the Civil War and possessions of the Audleys, Walwyns and Whartons as well as Anne Boleyn. Also beautiful 17th century woodwork carved by the 'King's Carpenter', John Abel. All those historical stories incorporated into guided tours, revealing the loves and lives of those who lived and died here. Goods and chattels virtually unchanged.

Location: OS149 Ref. SO661 332. Off A449 at Much Marcle. Ledbury 4m, Ross-on-Wye 4m.

Opening Times: Good Fri - 2 Oct: Weds, Sats, Suns & BH Mons. Guided tours only at 2pm, 3pm & 4pm. Other times only by arrangement with the Administrator.

Admission: Adult £3.50, Child £1.50.

ℹ️ No photography inside house. 🍴 ♿Partially suitable. 🔥Obligatory.
🍴 **P** 🐕In grounds, on leads. 🛡 Tel. for details.

West Midlands
England

HERGEST CROFT GARDENS

KINGTON, HEREFORDSHIRE HR5 3EG
Owner: W L Banks   *Contact:* Gill Wilson

Tel/Fax: 01544 230160 **e-mail:** banks@hergest.kc3.co.uk

From spring bulbs to autumn colour, this is a garden for all seasons. An old-fashioned kitchen garden has spring and summer borders and roses. Over 59 Champion trees and shrubs grow in one of the finest collections in the British Isles. Holds National Collection of birches, maples and zelkovas. Park Wood is a hidden valley with rhododendrons up to 30 ft tall.

Location: OS Ref. SO281 565. On W side of Kington. ½m off A44, left at Rhayader end of bypass. Turn right and gardens are ¼m on left. Signposted from bypass.

Opening Times: 1 Apr - 31 Oct: 1.30 - 6pm. Season tickets and groups by arrangement throughout the year. Winter by appointment.

Admission: Adult £4, Child (under 16yrs) Free. Groups (20+) £3.50. Guided groups (20+) £5.50 (must book). Season ticket £15.

Gift sales. Rare plants. In grounds, on leads. Tel. for details.

KINNERSLEY CASTLE

KINNERSLEY, HEREFORDSHIRE HR3 6QF
Contact: Caius Hawkins / Ekatherina Henning

Tel: 01544 327507 **Fax:** 01544 327663 **e-mail:** castle@kinnersley.com

Welsh border castle remodelled by Roger Vaughan in the 1580s. Still a family home, it has housed among others the de Kinnardsleys, the de la Beres and parliamentary general Sir Thomas Morgan. Shows some fine plasterwork and panelling. Gardens boast one of the largest ginkgo trees in the UK. Many yew hedges and a walled kitchen garden. Will be hosting open air theatrical events this summer.

Location: OS Ref. SO346 496. 4m W of Weobley on A4112, 15m W of Hereford.

Opening Times: Please contact the property or the local TIC.

Admission: Castle & Gardens: Adult £2.50, Child £1.50, Conc. £2. Groups: £2. Groups by arrangement throughout the year.

Teas by arrangement. Tel. for details.

HOW CAPLE COURT GARDENS   **Tel:** 01989 740626 **Fax:** 01989 740611

How Caple, Hereford HR1 4SX
Owner/Contact: Mr & Mrs Roger Lee
Exciting 11 acre garden overlooking River Wye.
Location: OS Ref. SO613 306. In NE end of How Caple. 1m W of the B4224 Ross-on-Wye/Fownhope Road.
Opening Times: Easter - end Sept: daily 10am - 5pm.
Admission: Adult £2.50.

Berrington Hall, Herefordshire.

LONGTOWN CASTLE   **Tel:** 0121 625 6820 (Regional Office)

Abbey Dore, Herefordshire
Owner: English Heritage   **Contact:** The West Midlands Regional Office
An unusual cylindrical keep built c1200 with walls 15ft thick. There are magnificent views of the nearby Black Mountains.
Location: OS Ref. SO321 291. 4m WSW of Abbey Dore.
Opening Times: Any reasonable time.
Admission: Free.

MOCCAS COURT   **Tel:** 01981 500381

Moccas, Herefordshire HR2 9LH
Owner: Trustees of the Baunton Trust   **Contact:** Ivor Saunders
18th century Adam interiors, 'Capability' Brown park.
Location: OS149 Ref. SO359 434. 1m N of B4352, 3½m SE of Bredwardine.
Opening Times: Apr - Sept: Thurs, 2 - 6pm.
Admission: £2.

OLD SUFTON   **Tel:** 01432 870268/850328 **Fax:** 01432 850381

Mordiford, Hereford HR1 4EJ
Owner: Trustees of Sufton Heritage Trust   **Contact:** Mr & Mrs J N Hereford
A 16th century manor house which was altered and remodelled in the 18th and 19th centuries and again in this century. The original home of the Hereford family (see Sufton Court) who have held the manor since the 12th century.
Location: OS Ref. SO575 384. Mordiford, off B4224 Mordiford - Dormington road.
Opening Times: By written appointment to Sufton Court or by fax.
Admission: Adult £2, Child 50p.

Partially suitable. Obligatory.

ROTHERWAS CHAPEL

Tel: 0121 625 6820 (Regional Office)

Hereford, Herefordshire

Owner: English Heritage   **Contact:** The West Midlands Regional Office

This Roman Catholic chapel, dating from the 14th and 16th centuries, is testament to the past grandeur of the Bodenham family and features an interesting mid-Victorian side chapel and High Altar.

Location: OS Ref. SO537 383. 1$^{1}/_{2}$ m SE of Hereford 500yds N of B4399.

Opening Times: Any reasonable time. Keykeeper at nearby filling station.

Admission: Free.

SUFTON COURT

Tel: 01432 870268/850328 **Fax:** 01432 850381

Mordiford, Hereford HR1 4LU

Owner: J N Hereford   **Contact:** Mr & Mrs J N Hereford

Sufton Court is a small Palladian mansion house. Built in 1788 by James Wyatt for James Hereford. The park was laid out by Humphrey Repton whose 'red book' still survives. The house stands above the rivers Wye and Lugg giving impressive views towards the mountains of Wales.

Location: OS Ref. SO574 379. Mordiford, off B4224 on Mordiford to Dormington road.

Opening Times: 15 - 28 May & 14 - 27 Aug: 2 - 5pm.

Admission: Adult £2, Child 50p.

🚻 Partially suitable. 🎦 Obligatory. 🅿 Only small coaches. 📷
🐕 In grounds, on leads.

THE WEIR

Tel: 01981 590509

Swainshill, Hereford, Herefordshire

Owner: The National Trust   **Contact:** Regional Office

Delightful riverside garden particularly spectacular in early spring, with fine view over the River Wye and Black Mountains.

Location: OS Ref. SO435 421. 5m W of Hereford on S side of A438.

Opening Times: 20 Jan - 11 Feb: Sats & Suns, 11am - 4pm. 14 Feb - 31 Oct: Wed - Sun, Good Fri & BH Mons, 11am - 6pm.

Admission: £2.50.

🚻 Not suitable. 🅿 No parking. 📷

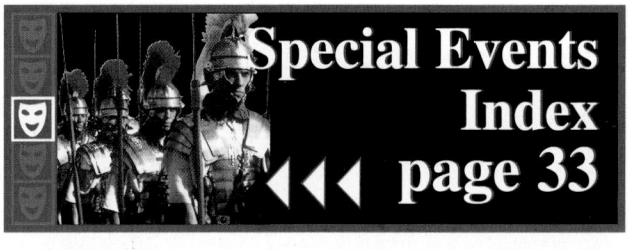

Special Events Index ◀◀◀ page 33

NT Photographic Library.

The Dining Room at Eastnor Castle, Herefordshire.

OAKLEY HALL
Market Drayton

OAKLEY HALL is situated in magnificent countryside on the boundary of Shropshire and Staffordshire. The present Hall is a fine example of a Queen Anne mansion house and was built on the site of an older dwelling mentioned in the Domesday Survey of 1085. Oakley Hall was the home of the Chetwode family until it was finally sold in 1919.

GARDENS
Set in 100 acres of rolling parkland, the Hall commands superb views over the surrounding countryside and the gardens include wild areas in addition to the more formal parts.

Oakley Hall is a privately owned family house and since it is not open to the general public it provides a perfect location for exclusive private or corporate functions. The main hall can accommodate 120 people comfortably and has excellent acoustics for concerts. The secluded location and unspoilt landscape make Oakley an ideal setting for filming and photography.

The surrounding countryside is rich in historical associations. St Mary's Church at Mucklestone, in which parish the Hall stands, was erected in the 13th century and it was from the tower of this Church that Queen Margaret of Anjou observed the Battle of Blore Heath in 1459. This was a brilliant victory for the Yorkist faction in the Wars of the Roses and the blacksmith at Mucklestone was reputed to have shod the Queen's horse back to front in order to disguise her escape.

Owner:
Mr & Mrs F Fisher

CONTACT

Mrs Ann E Fisher
Oakley Hall
Market Drayton
Shropshire
TF9 4AG

Tel: 01630 653472

Fax: 01630 653282

Wedding Enquiries:
Mrs D Hastie
Tel: 01244 572021

LOCATION

OS Ref. SJ701 367

From London 3hrs:
M1, M6/J14, then A5013 to Eccleshall, turn right at T-junction, 200 yards, then left onto B5026. Mucklestone is $1^3/_4$ m from Loggerheads on B5026. 3m NE of Market Drayton N of the A53, $1^1/_2$ m W of Mucklestone, off B5145.

CONFERENCE/FUNCTION		
ROOM	SIZE	MAX CAPACITY
Hall	50' x 30'	100
Dining Rm	40' x 27'	60
Ballroom	40' x 27'	60

WESTON PARK
Nr Shifnal

WESTON PARK is a magnificent Stately Home and Parkland situated on the Staffordshire/Shropshire border. The former home of the Earls of Bradford, the Park is now held in trust for the nation by The Weston Park Foundation.

Built in 1671 by Lady Elizabeth Wilbraham, this warm and welcoming house boasts a superb collection of paintings, including work by Van Dyck, Gainsborough and Stubbs, furniture and *objets d'art*, providing continued interest and enjoyment for all of its visitors.

Step outside to enjoy the 1,000 acres of glorious Parkland, designed by the legendary 'Capability' Brown - meander through the formal gardens,

take one of a variety of woodland walks and then relax in The Stables Restaurant. Take time to browse through the Gift Shop, completing your day with a delicious ice-cream from the Ice-Cream Parlour.

With the exciting Woodland Adventure Playground, Pets Corner and Deer Park, as well as the Miniature Railway, there is so much for children to do.

Weston Park has a long-standing reputation for staging outstanding events. The exciting and varied programme of entertainment includes Balloon Festivals, Music Festivals, Opera Evenings and Battle Re-enactments.

Owner:
The Weston Park Foundation

CONTACT

Alison Robbins
Weston Park
Weston-under-Lizard
Nr Shifnal
Shropshire
TF11 8LE

Tel: 01952 852100

Fax: 01952 850430

e-mail: enquiries@weston-park.com

LOCATION

OS Ref. SJ808 107

Birmingham 40 mins.
Manchester 1 hr.
Motorway access
M6/J12 or M54/J3.
House situated on A5 at
Weston-under-Lizard.

Rail: Nearest Railway Stations: Wolverhampton, Stafford or Telford.

Air: Birmingham, West Midlands, Manchester.

CONFERENCE/FUNCTION		
ROOM	SIZE	MAX CAPACITY
Dining Rm	52' x 23'	120
Orangery	51' x 20'	120
Music Rm	50' x 20'	80
The Old Stables	58' x 20'	60
Conference Room	40' x 7'6"	60

OPENING TIMES

Easter weekend:
14 - 16 April.

21 April - 30 June:
weekends.

1 July - 31 August:
Daily.

Every weekend in September until 16 September, then closed.

House: 1 - 5pm
Last admission 4.30pm.

Park: 11am - 7pm
Last admission 5pm.

NB. Visitors are advised to telephone first to check this information.

ADMISSION

Park & Gardens
Adult £2.50
Child (3 - 16yrs)........£2.00
OAP.......................£1.50

House
Adult £2.00
Child (3 - 16yrs)........£1.50
OAP.......................£1.00

ℹ️ House available on an exclusive use basis. Conferences, product launches, outdoor concerts and events, filming location. Helipad and airstrip. Sporting activities organised for private groups eg. clay pigeon shooting, archery, hovercrafts, rally driving. Interior photography by prior arrangement only.

🛍️ Gift Shop.

🍽️ Full event organisation service. Residential parties, special dinners, wedding receptions. Dine and stay arrangements in the house on selected dates.

♿ House and part of the grounds. WCs.

☕🍴 The Stables bar and restaurant provide meals and snacks. Licensed.

🅿️ Ample 100 yds away. Private booked groups may park vehicles at front door.

🏫 Tues, Weds and Thurs in the latter half of Jun and all Jul. Must book. Teachers' guidance notes and National Curriculum related workpacks available.

🛏️ Weston Park offers 28 delightful bedrooms with bathrooms, 20 doubles, 4 twins, 4 singles. On an exclusive only basis.

🐕 In grounds, on leads.

🎭 Telephone for details.

ACTON BURNELL CASTLE

Tel: 0121 625 6820 (Regional Office)

Acton Burnell, Shrewsbury, Shropshire
Owner: English Heritage   **Contact:** The West Midlands Regional Office
The warm red sandstone shell of a fortified 13th century manor house.
Location: OS Ref. SJ534 019. In Acton Burnell, on unclassified road 8m S of Shrewsbury.
Opening Times: Any reasonable time.
Admission: Free.

ADCOTE SCHOOL

Tel: 01939 260202 **Fax:** 01939 261300

Little Ness, Shrewsbury, Shropshire SY4 2JY
Owner: Adcote School Educational Trust Ltd   **Contact:** Mrs A Read
Adcote is a Grade I listed building designed by Norman Shaw, and built to a Tudor design in 1879. Its features include a Great Hall, Minstrels' Gallery, William De Morgan tiled fireplaces and stained glass windows. Landscaped gardens include many fine trees.
Location: OS Ref. SJ418 294. 7m NW of Shrewsbury. 2m NE of A5.
Opening Times: By appointment only.
Admission: Free, but the Governors reserve the right to make a charge.

ATTINGHAM PARK

SHREWSBURY, SHROPSHIRE SY4 4TP
Owner: The National Trust   *Contact:* The Property Manager
Infoline: 01743 708123   **Tel:** 01743 708162   **Fax:** 01743 708175
One of the great houses of the Midlands. An elegant late 18th century mansion by George Steuart, with a Picture Gallery by Nash. It has magnificent Regency interiors with exceptional collections of ambassadorial silver, Italian neo-classical furniture and Grand Tour paintings. The park was landscaped by Repton in 1797.
Location: OS127 Ref. SJ837 083. 4m SE of Shrewsbury on N side of B4380 in Atcham village.
Opening Times: 30 Mar - 28 Oct: daily (closed Wed & Thur), 1 - 4.30pm, last admission to house 4pm. Deer Park & Grounds: daily, closed 25 Dec. Mar - end Oct: 9am - 8pm. Nov - Feb 2001: 9am - 5pm. Introductory talks from 1pm.
Admission: House & Grounds: Adult £4.30, Child £2.15, Family £10.75. Park & Grounds only: Adult £2, Child £1. Booked groups (15+): Adult £3.90, Child £1.95.

[i] No photography in house. [ ] [ ] [ ] Licensed.
[ ] By arrangement. [P] [ ] [ ] In grounds on leads. [ ]

Ironbridge Gorge Museums, Shropshire.

BENTHALL HALL

Tel: 01952 882159

Benthall, Nr Broseley, Shropshire TF12 5RX
Owner: The National Trust   **Contact:** Mr R Benthall
A 16th century stone house with mullioned windows and moulded brick chimneys.
Location: OS Ref. SJ658 025. 1m NW of Broseley (B4375), 4m NE of Much Wenlock, 1m SW of Ironbridge.
Opening Times: 1 Apr - 30 Sept: Weds, Suns & BH Mons 1.30 - 5.30pm. Last adm. 5pm. Groups at other times by prior arrangement.
Admission: Adult: £3.50, Child: £1.75. Garden: £2.25. Reduced rates for groups.

[ ] Ground floor suitable. WC. [ ] By arrangement. [P] Limited.

BOSCOBEL HOUSE & THE ROYAL OAK

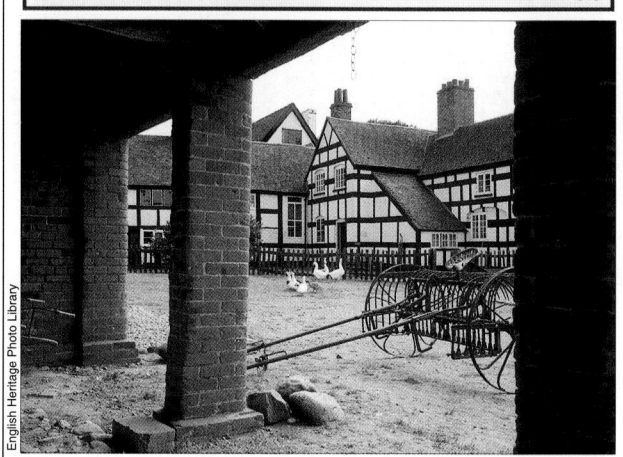

BREWOOD, BISHOP'S WOOD, SHROPSHIRE ST19 9AR
Owner: English Heritage   *Contact:* The Custodian
Tel: 01902 850244
This 17th century hunting lodge was destined to play a part in Charles II's escape from the Roundheads. A descendant of the Royal Oak, which sheltered the fugitive King from Cromwell's troops after the Battle of Worcester in 1651, still stands in the fields near Boscobel House. 2001 will be the 350th anniversary of this event. The timber-framed house where the King slept in a tiny 'sacred hole' has been fully restored and furnished in Victorian period and there are panelled rooms and secret hiding places. There is an exhibition in the house as well as the farmyard and smithy.
Location: OS127 Ref. SJ837 083. On unclassified road between A41 & A5. 8m NW of Wolverhampton.
Opening Times: 1 Apr - 30 Sept: daily: 10am - 6pm (5pm in Oct). 1 - 30 Nov: Wed - Sun, 10am - 4pm. 1 - 31 Dec: Sats & Suns, 10am - 4pm. Closed 1 Jan - 31 Mar. Last admission 45 mins before closing.
Admission: Adult £4.40, Child £2.20, Conc. £3.30, Family £11. 15% discount on groups (11+).

[ ] Grounds suitable. WC. [ ] [ ] Obligatory. [ ] [ ] [ ] Tel. for details.

BUILDWAS ABBEY

Tel: 01952 433274

Iron Bridge, Telford, Shropshire TF8 7BW
Owner: English Heritage   **Contact:** The Custodian
Extensive remains of a Cistercian abbey built in 1135, set beside the River Severn against a backdrop of wooded grounds. The remains include the church which is almost complete except for the roof.
Location: OS Ref. SJ642 044. On S bank of River Severn on A4169, 2m W of Ironbridge.
Opening Times: 1 Apr - 31 Oct: daily, 10am - 6pm (5pm in Oct).
Admission: Adult £2, Child £1, Conc. £1.50.

Civil Wedding Index ◀◀◀ page 29

BURFORD HOUSE GARDENS

TENBURY WELLS, WORCESTERSHIRE WR15 8HQ

Owner: *Treasures of Tenbury Ltd*   **Contact:** *Charles Chesshire*

Tel: 01584 810777 **Fax:** 01584 810673

Seven acre garden in beautiful riverside setting, home to the national clematis collection, with over 300 varieties, and 2,000 varieties of other plants. New designs include a wildflower garden, bamboo and grass garden. Also visit Treasures Garden Centre, Burford House Gallery, Home & Garden shop, café-bar, Mulu Exotic Plants and Jungle Giants Bamboos.

Location: OS Ref. SO585 680. 1m W of Tenbury Wells on the A456, 8m from Ludlow.

Opening Times: All year: daily, 10am - 5pm.

Admission: Adult £3.50, Child £1. Groups (10+): £3.

Licensed. By arrangement. P Guide dogs only.

DAVENPORT HOUSE

WORFIELD, Nr BRIDGNORTH, SHROPSHIRE WV15 5LE

Owner/Contact: *Roger Murphy*

Tel: 01746 716221 / 716345 **Fax:** 01746 716021

A Grade I listed country house of 1726 by the architect Francis Smith of Warwick. The house sits within an extensive estate and is a popular regional venue for wedding receptions, civil marriage ceremonies and corporate and social group entertainment. Open to the public as a restaurant Wednesday evenings, advance booking only.

Location: OS Ref. SO756 955. Worfield village, drive entrance by war memorial.

Opening Times: Available for weddings and other functions throughout the year.

Admission: Please telephone for details.

Partially suitable. Licensed. P

CLUN CASTLE

Tel: 0121 625 6820 (Regional Office)

Clun, Ludlow, Shropshire

Owner: English Heritage   **Contact:** The West Midlands Regional Office

Remains of a four-storey keep and other buildings of this border castle are set in outstanding countryside. Built in the 11th century.

Location: OS Ref. SO299 809. In Clun, off A488, 18m W of Ludlow. 9m W of Craven Arms.

Opening Times: Any reasonable time.

Admission: Free.

COLEHAM PUMPING STATION

Tel: 01743 362947 **Fax:** 01743 358411

Longden Coleham, Shrewsbury, Shropshire SY3 7DN

Owner: Shrewsbury & Atcham Borough Council   **Contact:** Mary White

Two Renshaw beam engines of 1901 are being restored to steam by members of Shrewsbury Steam Trust. 2001 is the centenary year of Coleham Pumping Station.

Location: OS Ref. SJ497 122. Shrewsbury town centre, near the River Severn.

Opening Times: 28 & 29 Apr: special centenary celebrations. Also Apr - Sept: 4th Sun in each month, 10am - 4pm. Plus occasional other days. Details: 01743 361196.

Admission: Adult £1, Child 50p, Student £1.

Partially suitable. By arrangement. P No parking. Guide dogs only.

COMBERMERE ABBEY

Tel: 01948 662880 **Fax:** 01948 660940

Whitchurch, Shropshire SY13 4AJ   **e-mail:** cottages@combermereabbey.co.uk

Owner: Mrs S Callander Beckett   **Contact:** Mrs Carol Sheard

Combermere Abbey, originally a Cistercian Monastery, and remodelled as a Gothic house in 1820 sits in a magnificent 1000 acre private parkland setting. Host to many remarkable historical personalities, the splendid 17th century Library and elegant Porter's Hall are licensed for weddings, receptions, concerts and lectures. Excellent accommodation is available on the Estate.

Location: OS Ref. SJ590 440. 5m E of Whitchurch, off A530.

Opening Times: By arrangement for groups.

Admission: Groups: £7 per person inclusive of refreshments.

No photography. Not suitable. By arrangement. By arrangement. P Limited.

DUDMASTON

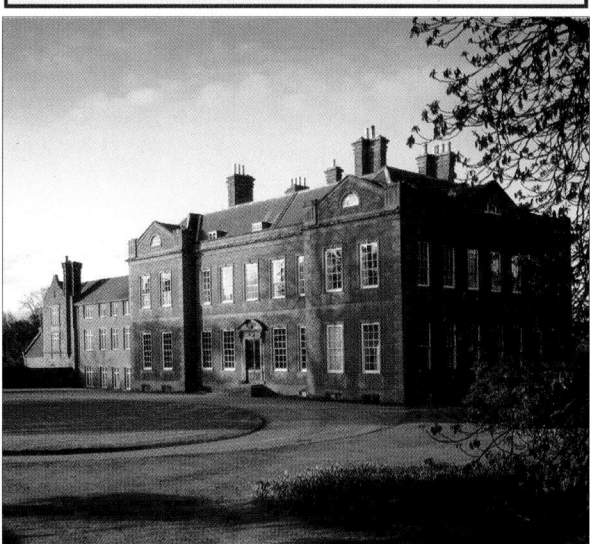

Michael Caldwell.

QUATT, BRIDGNORTH, SHROPSHIRE WV15 6QN

Owner: *The National Trust*   **Contact:** *The Administrator*

Tel: 01746 780866 **Fax:** 01746 780744 **e-mail:** mduefe@smtp.ntrust.org.uk

Late 17th century manor house. Contains furniture and china, Dutch flower paintings, watercolours, botanical art and modern pictures and sculpture, family and natural history. 9 acres of lakeside gardens and Dingle walk. Two estate walks 5^1/$_2$ m and 3^1/$_2$ m starting from Hampton Loade car park.

Location: OS Ref. SO748 888. 4m SE of Bridgnorth on A442.

Opening Times: 1 Apr - 30 Sept: House; Tues, Weds, Suns & BH Mons, 2 - 5.30pm. Mons booked groups by arrangement. Garden; Mon - Wed & Suns, 12 noon - 6pm. Tearoom: 11.30am - 5.30pm. Last admission to house 5pm.

Admission: House & Garden: Adult £3.85, Child £2.30, Family £9. Groups £3. Garden only: £2.80.

Countryside walks.   In grounds, on leads.

HAUGHMOND ABBEY

Tel: 01743 709661

Upton Magna, Uffington, Shrewsbury, Shropshire SY4 4RW

Owner: English Heritage   **Contact:** The Custodian

Extensive remains of a 12th century Augustinian abbey, including the Chapter House which retains its late medieval timber ceiling, and including some fine medieval sculpture.

Location: OS Ref. SJ542 152. 3m NE of Shrewsbury off B5062.

Opening Times: 1 Apr - 31 Oct: daily, 10am - 6pm (5pm in Oct).

Admission: Adult £2, Child £1, Conc. £1.50.

Tel. for details.

HAWKSTONE HALL & GARDENS

Tel: 01630 685242 **Fax:** 01630 685565

Marchamley, Shrewsbury SY4 5LG

Owner: The Redemptorists   **Contact:** Guest Mistress

Grade I Georgian mansion and restored gardens set in spacious parkland.

Location: OS Ref. SJ581 299. Entrance 1m N of Hodnet on A442.

Opening Times: 5 - 31 Aug, daily, 2 - 5pm.

Admission: Adult £3.50, Child £1.

HODNET HALL GARDENS

HODNET, MARKET DRAYTON, SHROPSHIRE TF9 3NN

Owner: Mr and the Hon Mrs A Heber-Percy   *Contact: Mrs M A Taylor*

Tel: 01630 685202 **Fax:** 01630 685853

Beautiful woodland walks through trees and shrubs in 60 acres of flowering lakeside gardens. Tearooms serve light lunches and afternoon teas. Gift shop.

Location: OS Ref. SJ613 286. 12m NE of Shrewsbury on A53; M6/J15, M54/J3.

Opening Times: 1 Apr - 30 Sept: Tue - Sun & BH Mons, 12 noon - 5pm.

Admission: Adult £3.25, Child £1.20, OAP £2.75. Reduced rates for groups.

Kitchen garden sales. For groups. On leads.

IRON BRIDGE

Tel: 0121 625 6820 (Regional Office)

Ironbridge, Shropshire

Owner: English Heritage   **Contact:** The West Midlands Regional Office

The world's first iron bridge and Britain's best known industrial monument. Cast in Coalbrookdale by local ironmaster, Abraham Darby, it was erected across the River Severn in 1779. Iron Bridge is a World Heritage Site.

Location: OS Ref. SJ672 034. In Ironbridge, adjacent to A4169.

Opening Times: Any reasonable time.

Admission: Free crossing.

IRONBRIDGE GORGE MUSEUMS

IRONBRIDGE, TELFORD, SHROPSHIRE TF8 7AW

Owner: Independent Museum   *Contact: Visitor Information*

Tel: 01952 432166 (7 day line) or 433522 **Fax:** 01952 432204

Freephone: 0800 590258 for a **free** colour guide.

Scene of pioneering events which led to the Industrial Revolution. The Ironbridge Gorge is home to nine unique museums set in six square miles of stunning scenery. These include Jackfield Tile Museum, Coalport China Museum and a recreated Victorian Town where you can chat to locals as they go about their daily business. You'll need two days here.

Location: OS Ref. SJ666 037. Telford, Shropshire via M6/M54.

Open: All year: daily from 10am - 5pm (closed 24/25 Dec & 1 Jan). Please telephone for winter details before visit.

Admission: Passport ticket which allows admission to all museums; Adult £10, Child/Student £6, OAP £9, Family £30. Prices valid until 31 March 2001. Group discounts available.

Licensed. Guide dogs only.

LANGLEY CHAPEL

Tel: 0121 625 6820 (Regional Office)

Acton Burnell, Shrewsbury, Shropshire

Owner: English Heritage   **Contact:** The West Midlands Regional Office

A delightful medieval chapel, standing alone in a field, with a complete set of early 17th century wooden fittings and furniture.

Location: OS Ref. SJ538 001. 1$^{1}/_{2}$ m S of Acton Burnell, on unclassified road 4m E of the A49, 9$^{1}/_{2}$ m S of Shrewsbury.

Opening Times: Open any reasonable time. Closed 24- 26 Dec & 1 Jan.

Admission: Free.

LILLESHALL ABBEY

Tel: 0121 625 6820 (Regional Office)

Oakengates, Shropshire

Owner: English Heritage   **Contact:** The West Midlands Regional Office

Extensive ruins of an abbey of Augustinian canons including remains of the 12th and 13th century church and the cloister buildings. Surrounded by green lawns and ancient yew trees.

Location: OS Ref. SJ738 142. On unclassified road off the A518, 4m N of Oakengates.

Opening Times: Any reasonable time.

Admission: Free.

LONGNER HALL

Tel: 01743 709215

Uffington, Shrewsbury, Shropshire SY4 4TG

Owner: Mr R L Burton   **Contact:** Mrs R L Burton

Designed by John Nash in 1803, Longner Hall is a Tudor Gothic style house set in a park landscaped by Humphry Repton. The home of one family for over 700 years. Longner's principal rooms are adorned with plaster fan vaulting and stained glass.

Location: OS Ref. SJ529 110. 4m SE of Shrewsbury on Uffington road, $^{1}/_{4}$ m off B4380, Atcham.

Opening Times: Apr - Oct: Tues & BH Mons, 2 - 5pm. Tours at 2pm & 3.30pm. Groups at any time by arrangement.

Admission: Adult £5, Child/OAP £3.

 No photography in house. Partially suitable. By arrangement for groups. Obligatory. Limited for coaches. By arrangement. Guide dogs only.

LUDLOW CASTLE

CASTLE SQUARE, LUDLOW, SHROPSHIRE SY8 1AY

Owner: The Earl of Powis & The Trustees of the Powis Estate   *Contact:* Helen J Duce

Tel: 01584 873355

900 year old castle of the Marches, dates from 1086 and greatly extended over the centuries to a fortified Royal Palace. Ludlow Castle became a seat of government with the establishment of the Council for Wales and the Marches. Privately owned by the Earls of Powis since 1811. A magnificent ruin set in the heart of Ludlow and surrounding countryside.

Location: OS Ref. SO509 745. Shrewsbury 28m, Hereford 26m. A49 centre of Ludlow.

Opening Times: Jan: weekends only, 10am - 4pm, Feb - Mar & Oct - Dec: 10am - 4pm. Apr - Jul & Sept: 10am - 5pm. Aug: 10am - 7pm. Last adm. 30mins before closing. Closed 25 Dec.

Admission: Adult £3, Child £1.50, Conc. £2.50, Family £8.50. 10% reduction for groups (10+).

Partially suitable. WC. Not available. No parking. In grounds on leads.

SPECIAL EVENTS

APR 16: Easter Egg Hunt
MAY 13: Vintage Vehicle Display
MAY 26 - 28: Festival of Crafts
JUN 23 - JUL 8: Ludlow Festival
SEPT 7 - 9: Food & Drink Fair
NOV 24 - 25: Medieval Christmas Fayre
Weds during summer school holidays: Birds of Prey & costumed tour guide.

MAWLEY HALL

CLEOBURY MORTIMER, DY14 8PN

Owner: R Galliers-Pratt Esq *Contact:* Mrs R Sharp

Tel: 01299 270869 **Fax:** 01299 270022 **e-mail:** administration@mawley.com

Built in 1730 and attributed to Francis Smith of Warwick, Mawley is set in 18th century landscaped parkland with extensive gardens and walks down to the River Rea. Magnificent plasterwork and a fine collection of English and Continental furniture and porcelain.

Location: OS137 Ref. SO688 753. 1m N of Cleobury Mortimer on the A4117 and 7m W of Bewdley.

Opening Times: 12 Apr - 15 Jul: Mons & Thurs, 3 - 5pm and throughout the year by appointment.

Admission: Adult £5, Child/OAP £3.

Lunches, dinners & functions in association with Sean Hill of the Michelin starred restaurant, The Merchant House, in Ludlow.

By arrangement. In grounds, on leads.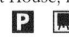

MORETON CORBET CASTLE

Tel: 0121 625 6820 (Regional Office)

Moreton Corbet, Shrewsbury, Shropshire

Owner: English Heritage   **Contact:** The West Midlands Regional Office

A ruined medieval castle with the substantial remains of a splendid Elizabethan mansion, captured in 1644 from Charles I's supporters by Parliamentary forces.

Location: OS Ref. SJ562 232. In Moreton Corbet off B5063, 7m NE of Shrewsbury.

Opening Times: Any reasonable time.

Admission: Free.

MORVILLE HALL

Tel: 01743 708100

Bridgnorth, Shropshire WV16 5NB

Owner: The National Trust   **Contact:** Dr & Mrs C Douglas

An Elizabethan house of mellow stone, converted in the 18th century and set in attractive gardens.

Location: OS Ref. SO668 940. Morville, on A458 3m W of Bridgnorth.

Opening Times: By written appointment only with the tenants.

Obligatory.

OAKLEY HALL

See page 330 for full page entry.

PREEN MANOR GARDENS

Tel: 01694 771207

Church Preen, Church Stretton, Shropshire SY6 7LQ

Owner: Mr & Mrs P Trevor-Jones   **Contact:** Mrs P Trevor-Jones

Six acre garden on site of Cluniac monastery, with walled, terraced, wild, water, kitchen and chess gardens. 12th century monastic church with a yew tree reputedly the oldest in Europe.

Location: OS Ref. SO544 981. 10m SSE of Shrewsbury. 7m NE of Church Stretton, 6m SW of Much Wenlock.

Opening Times: Refer National Gardens Scheme Yellow Book. Coach parties Jun & Jul by appointment only.

Admission: Adult £3, Child 50p.

ROWLEY'S HOUSE MUSEUM

Tel: 01743 361196 **Fax:** 01743 358411
e-mail: museums@shrewsbury-atcham.gov.uk

Barker Street, Shrewsbury, Shropshire SY1 1QH

Owner: Shrewsbury and Atcham Borough Council   **Contact:** Mrs M White

Impressive timber-framed building and attached 17th century brick mansion with costume, archaeology and natural history, geology, local history and temporary exhibitions.

Location: OS Ref. SJ490 126. Barker Street.

Opening Times: 9 Jan - Easter: Tue - Sat, 10am - 4pm. Easter - end Sept: Tue - Sat, 10am - 5pm. Also Suns, BHs & summer Mons, 10am - 4pm. Oct - Easter 2002: Tue - Sat, 10am - 4pm. Closed Christmas & New Year period.

Admission: Free.

ⓘ No photography.   📷   ♿ Not suitable.   Ⓟ No parking.   ▥
🐕 Guide dogs only.   ❄

SHIPTON HALL 🏛

Tel: 01746 785225 **Fax:** 01746 785125

Much Wenlock, Shropshire TF13 6JZ

Owner: Mr J N R Bishop   **Contact:** Mrs M J Bishop

Built around 1587 by Richard Lutwyche who gave the house to his daughter Elizabeth on her marriage to Thomas Mytton. Shipton remained in the Mytton family for the next 300 years. The house has been described as 'an exquisite specimen of Elizabethan architecture set in a quaint old fashioned garden, the whole forming a picture which as regards both form and colour, satisfies the artistic sense of even the most fastidious'. The Georgian additions by Thomas F Pritchard include some elegant rococo interior decorations and some noteworthy Tudor and Jacobean panelling. Family home. In addition to the house visitors are welcome to explore the gardens, the dovecote and the parish church which dates back to Saxon times.

Location: OS Ref. SO563 918. 7m SW of Much Wenlock on B4378. 10m W of Bridgnorth.

Opening Times: Easter - end Sept: Thurs, 2.30 - 5.30pm. Also Suns and Mons of BH, 2.30 - 5.30pm. Groups of 20+ at any time of day or year by prior arrangement.

Admission: Adult £4, Child £2. Discount of 10% for groups (20+).

♿ Not suitable.   🍴 By arrangement for groups (20+).   📷 Obligatory.
🐕 Guide dogs only.   ❄

SHREWSBURY ABBEY

Tel: 01743 232723 **Fax:** 01743 240172

Shrewsbury, Shropshire SY2 6BS   **Contact:** Mr Terence Hyde

Benedictine Abbey founded in 1083, tomb of Roger de Montgomerie and remains of tomb of St Winefride, 7th century Welsh saint. The Abbey was part of the monastery and has also been a parish church since the 12th century. Now made popular by Ellis Peters author of 'Brother Cadfael' novels. Historical exhibition from Saxon times to present.

Location: OS Ref. SJ499 125. Signposted from Shrewsbury bypass (A5 and A49). 500yds E of town centre, across English Bridge.

Opening Times: 25 Mar - 27 Oct: 9.30am - 5.30pm. 28 Oct - 23 Mar: 10.30am - 3pm.

Admission: Donation. Guided tours £10 per pre-arranged group.

SHREWSBURY CASTLE & SHROPSHIRE REGIMENTAL MUSEUM

Castle Street, Shrewsbury SY1 2AT   **Tel:** 01743 358516 **Fax:** 01743 358411
e-mail: museums@shrewsbury-atcham.gov.uk

Owner: Shrewsbury & Atcham Borough Council   **Contact:** Steve Martin

Norman Castle with 18th century work by Thomas Telford. Free admission to attractive floral grounds. The main hall houses the Shropshire Regimental Museum and displays on the history of the castle.

Location: OS Ref. SJ495 128. Town centre, adjacent BR and bus stations.

Opening Times: Main building & Museum: 7 Feb - Easter: Wed - Sat, 10am - 4pm. Easter - end Sept: Tue - Sat, 10am - 5pm. Also Suns & BHs, 10am - 4pm. Details of winter openings on request. Grounds: daily.

Admission: Museum: Adult £2, OAP £1, Shrewsbury residents, under 18s, Students & members of the regiments Free. Grounds: Mon - Sat, Free, Suns, charged as above.

ⓘ No photography.   📷   ♿   Ⓟ No parking.   ▥   🐕 Guide dogs only.   🔔

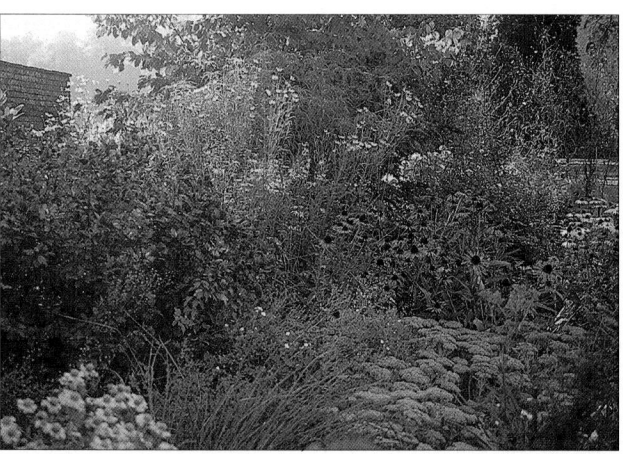

Burford House Gardens, Shropshire.

STOKESAY CASTLE

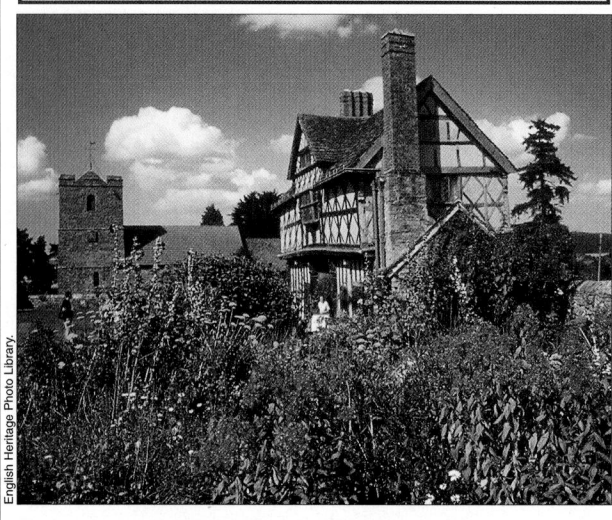

English Heritage Photo Library.

Nr CRAVEN ARMS, SHROPSHIRE SY7 9AH

Owner: *English Heritage*   **Contact:** *The Custodian*

Tel: 01588 672544

This perfectly preserved example of a 13th century fortified manor house gives us a glimpse of the life and ambitions of a rich medieval merchant. Lawrence of Ludlow built this country house to impress the landed gentry. Lawrence built a magnificent Great Hall where servants and guests gathered on feast days, but the family's private quarters were in the bright, comfortable solar on the first floor. From the outside the castle forms a picturesque grouping of castle, parish church and timber-framed Jacobean gatehouse set in the rolling Shropshire countryside.

Location: OS137 Ref. SO436 817. 7m NW of Ludlow off A49. 1m S of Craven Arms off A49.

Opening Times: 1 Apr - 31 Oct: daily, 10am - 6pm (5pm in Oct). 1 Nov - 31 Mar: Wed - Sun, 10am - 4pm. Closed 1 - 2pm in Winter. Closed 24 - 26 Dec & 1 Jan.

Admission: Adult £4, Child £2, Conc. £3, Family £10. Groups of 11+ 15% discount.

♿ Great Hall & gardens only. WC.   🍴   Ⓟ   ❄   ☎ Tel. for details.

WALCOT HALL

LYDBURY NORTH, Nr BISHOP'S CASTLE, SHROPSHIRE SY7 8AZ

Owner: *C R W Parish*   **Contact:** *Lesley Higgs, Marketing Manager*

Tel: 01584 874520 **Fax:** 01584 872679 **e-mail:** enquiries@walcothall.com

Georgian home of Lord Clive of India who commissioned Sir William Chambers to re-design it and the stable block, in 1763. His son added the free-standing Ballroom and developed 30 acres of arboretum and pools to the rear, with mile-long lakes in the front. Suitable for film locations, balls, corporate events, receptions, parties and shows.

Location: OS Ref. SO348 850. On the edge of the Clun Forest. 3m SE of Bishop's Castle on B4385; 1/2 m outside Lydbury North. The drive is adjacent to the Powis Arms Pub.

Opening Times: House & Garden: BHs, Suns & Mons (except Christmas and New Year), 2.15 - 4.30pm. All other times by appointment.

Admission: Adult £3, Child (under 15yrs) Free: Teas by arrangement.

♿ House suitable. WC.   🍴 By arrangement.   🐕 On leads.
▥ Holiday apartments, sleeping 2 - 32 people.   ❄

WENLOCK GUILDHALL

Tel: 01952 727509

Much Wenlock, Shropshire TF13 6AE

Owner/Contact: Much Wenlock Town Council

16th century half-timbered building has an open-arcade market area.

Location: OS127 Ref. SJ624 000. In centre of Much Wenlock, next to the church.

Opening Times: 1 Apr - 30 Sept: Mon - Sat, 10.30am - 1pm & 2 - 4pm. Suns: 2 - 4pm.

Admission: Adult 50p, Child Free.

WENLOCK PRIORY

Tel: 01952 727466

Much Wenlock, Shropshire TF13 6HS

Owner: English Heritage   **Contact:** The Custodian

A prosperous, powerful priory at its peak in the Middle Ages. A great deal of the structure still survives in the form of high, romantic ruined walls and it is the resting place of St Milburga the first Abbess. A monastery was first founded at Wenlock in the 7th century, and little more is known of the site until the time of the Norman Conquest when it became a Cluniac monastery. These majestic ruins of the priory church are set in green lawns and topiary, and there are substantial remains of the early 13th century church and Norman Chapter House.

Location: OS127 Ref. SJ625 001. In Much Wenlock.

Opening Times: 1 Apr - 31 Oct: daily: 10am - 6pm (5pm in Oct). 1 Nov - 31 Mar: Wed - Sun, 10am - 4pm (closed 1 - 2pm in winter). Closed 24 - 26 Dec & 1 Jan.

Admission: Adult £2.85, Child £1.40, Conc. £2.10. 15% discount for groups (11+).

  Tel. for details.

WESTON PARK

See page 331 for full page entry.

WILDERHOPE MANOR

Tel: 01694 771363

Longville, Much Wenlock, Shropshire TF13 6EG

Owner: The National Trust   **Contact:** The Warden

This limestone house stands on southern slope of Wenlock Edge in remote country with views down to Corvedale. Dating from 1586, it is unaltered but unfurnished. Features include remarkable wooden spiral stairs, unique bow rack and fine plaster ceilings.

Location: OS Ref. SO545 929. 7m SW of Much Wenlock. 7m E of Church Stretton, $^1/_2$ m S of B4371.

Opening Times: Apr - Sept: Weds & Sats, 2 - 4.30pm. Oct - Mar: Sats only, 2 - 4.30pm.

Admission: £1. No reduction for groups. Steep access to house.

WOLLERTON OLD HALL GARDEN

Tel: 01630 685760 **Fax:** 01630 685583

Wollerton, Market Drayton, Shropshire TF9 3NA

Owner: Mr & Mrs J D Jenkins   **Contact:** Mrs Di Oakes

Three acre plantsman's garden created around a 16th century house (not open).

Location: OS Ref. SJ623 296. 14m NE of Shrewsbury off A53 between Hodnet and Market Drayton.

Opening Times: 13 Apr - 28 Sept: Fris, Suns & BHs (Fris only in Sept), 12 noon - 5pm. Groups (25+) by appointment at other times.

Admission: Adult £3.50, Child £1.

WROXETER ROMAN CITY

Tel: 01743 761330

Wroxeter, Shrewsbury, Shropshire SY5 6PH

Owner: English Heritage   **Contact:** The Custodian

The part-excavated centre of the fourth largest city in Roman Britain, originally home to some 6,000 men and several hundred houses. Impressive remains of the 2nd century municipal baths. There is a site museum in which many finds are displayed, including those from recent work by Birmingham Field Archaeological Unit.

Location: OS Ref. SJ568 088. At Wroxeter, 5m E of Shrewsbury, on B4380.

Opening Times: 1 Apr - 31 Oct: daily 10am - 6pm (5pm in Oct). 1 Nov - 31 Mar: Wed - Sun, 10am - 4pm (closed for lunch 1 - 2pm in winter). Closed 24 - 26 Dec & 1 Jan.

Admission: Adult £3.50, Child £1.80, Conc. £2.60, Family £8.80.

  Tel. for details.

Wollerton Old Hall Garden, Shropshire.

West Midlands England

British Tourist Authority.

SHUGBOROUGH
Stafford

SHUGBOROUGH is the magnificent 900-acre ancestral home of the 5th Earl of Lichfield, who is known world-wide as Patrick Lichfield the leading photographer.

The 18th century mansion house contains a fine collection of ceramics, silver, paintings and French furniture. Part of the house is still lived in by the Earl and his family.

Visitors can enjoy the splendid 18-acre Grade I Historic Garden with its Edwardian Rose Garden and terraces. A unique collection of neo-classical monuments by James Stuart can be found in the parkland which also includes walks and trails.

Other attractions include the County Museum which is housed in the original servants' quarters. The working laundry, kitchens and

brewhouse have all been lovingly restored and are staffed by costumed guides who show how the servants lived and worked over 100 years ago.

Shugborough Park Farm is a Georgian working farm which features an agricultural museum, restored working corn mill and is also a rare breeds centre. In the farmhouse kitchen visitors can see bread baked in brick ovens and in the dairy, cheese and butter being made.

Throughout the year a lively collection of themed tours are in operation for the coach market and an award-winning educational programme for schools. From April to December an exciting events programme is in operation.

Shugborough is an ideal venue for weddings, conferences, corporate activity days and product launches.

Owner:
The National Trust

CONTACT

Sales and
Marketing Office
Shugborough
Milford
Stafford
ST17 0XB

Tel: 01889 881388

Fax: 01889 881323

e-mail: shugborough.
promotions@staffordshire.
gov.uk

LOCATION

OS Ref. SJ992 225

10mins from M6/J13 on
A513 Stafford/
Lichfield Road.

Rail: Stafford 6m.

Taxi: Anthony's
01785 252255

CONFERENCE/FUNCTION		
ROOM	SIZE	MAX CAPACITY
Banqueting Hall	15 x 6.5m	65
Saloon	15 x 6m	80
Conference Suite	6 x 6m	35
Granary	5.5 x 9.5m	60
Blue Drawing Rm	6.5 x 8m	20
Tower of the Winds	6.5 x 6.5m	20

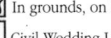 Private and corporate entertainment, conferences, product launches and dinner parties. Filming and event location. Over 900 acres of parkland and gardens available for hire. Themed activities. No photography in house.

Catering for special functions/conferences.

Visitors may alight at entrance before parking. WCs. Stairclimber to house. Batricars available. Disabled-friendly picnic tables available. Taped tours.

Licensed tearoom/café seating 95, also tearoom at Farm seats 30. Prior notice for large groups.

Tour time 1hr. Themed tours as required. Groups of 15+. Please telephone for details.

 Ample car and coach parking. Discounted vouchers for coach drivers' meals available.

Award-winning educational packages. Curriculum-related. Contact Sales & Development Officer.

In grounds, on leads.

Civil Wedding Licence.

OPENING TIMES

31 March - 30 September
Daily: 11am - 5pm except
Mondays (open holiday
Mondays).

Pre-booked parties
throughout the year.

ADMISSION

Each attraction
Adults......................£4.50
Conc* £3.00

**Voyager Tickets
(all 3 sites)**
Adult £9.00
Conc* £6.00
Family £22.00

Gardens and Parkland
Cars £2.00
Coaches ....Free

* Concessions for children
(under 5yrs Free), OAPs,
Students, registered
unemployed & groups.

** NT Members free admission
to Mansion House,
Museum and Farm.

SPECIAL EVENTS

• **APR 21/22:**
Gamekeepers' Fair.

• **MAY 26/27/28:**
Spring Craft Fair.

• **JUNE 30, JULY 1:**
Gardeners' Weekend.

• **AUGUST 5:**
Victorian Street Market.

• **AUGUST 25/26/27:**
Summer Craft Fair.

• **SEPTEMBER 9:**
Heavy Horse and Harvest.

• **DEC 4 - 7: (2001)**
Shugborough Victorian
Christmas Evening.

THE ANCIENT HIGH HOUSE

GREENGATE STREET, STAFFORD ST16 2JA

Owner: *Stafford Borough Council*   **Contact:** *K Stringer*

Tel: 01785 619131   **Fax:** 01785 619132   **e-mail:** ahh@staffordbc.gov.uk

This building is the largest timber-framed town house in England. Built in 1595 by the Dorrington family, this house is still very impressive on Stafford's skyline. It was lived in by Richard Sneyd, a member of one of Staffordshire's greatest families when King Charles I stayed here in 1642. It is now a registered museum with displays set out as period room settings which present aspects of the house's history. The Staffordshire Yeomanry Museum is on the top floor.

Location: OS Ref. SJ922 232. Town centre.

Opening Times: All year: Mon - Sat, 10am - 5pm. Check BHs.

Admission: Please telephone for details.

  Not suitable. Guide dogs only. Tel. for details.

BIDDULPH GRANGE GARDEN

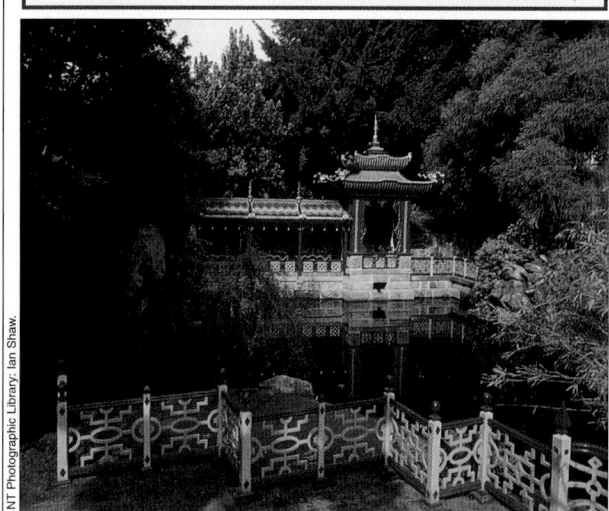

NT Photographic Library, Ian Shaw.

GRANGE ROAD, BIDDULPH, STOKE-ON-TRENT ST8 7SD

Owner: *The National Trust*   **Contact:** *The Garden Office*

Tel: 01782 517999   **Fax:** 01782 510624

A rare and exciting survival of a High Victorian garden, restored by the National Trust. The garden is divided into a series of themed gardens within a garden, with a Chinese temple, Egyptian court, pinetum, dahlia walk, glen and many other settings. Difficult uneven levels, unsuitable for wheelchairs.

Location: OS Ref. SJ891 592. E of A527, 3$\frac{1}{2}$ m SE of Congleton, 8m N of Stoke-on-Trent.

Opening Times: 28 Mar - 4 Nov: Wed - Fri, 12 noon - 6pm. Sats, Suns & BH Mons, 11am - 6pm. Closed Good Fri. 10 Nov - 17 Dec: Sats & Suns, 12 noon- 4pm or dusk if earlier.

Admission: Adult £4.40, Child £2.30, Family (2+2) £11. Nov and Dec: Adult £2, Child £1, Family £5. Joint ticket with Little Moreton Hall: Adult £6.75, Child £3.30, Family £16.50.

 Unsuitable for wheelchairs. In car park, on leads.

BARLASTON HALL

Tel: 01782 372749   **Fax:** 01782 372391

Barlaston, Staffordshire ST12 9AT

Owner/Contact: Mr & Mrs James Hall

Barlaston Hall is a mid-18th century Palladian villa, attributed to Sir Robert Taylor. Extensively restored during the 1990s with the help of English Heritage. The four public rooms open to visitors contain some fine examples of 18th century plasterwork.

Location: OS Ref. SJ895 391. $\frac{1}{2}$ m E of A34 between Stoke and Stafford.

Opening Times: By appointment to groups of 10-30. Admission includes refreshments. Please write to the above address or fax giving details of numbers, possible dates and a contact telephone number. Recorded message with other opening times on above number.

Admission: Pre-arranged groups: £3.50.

 No photography. Not suitable. Limited.

CHILLINGTON HALL

Tel: 01902 850236   **Fax:** 01902 850768

Codsall Wood, Wolverhampton, Staffordshire WV8 1RE

Owner/Contact: Mr & Mrs J W Giffard   **e-mail:** mrsplod@globalnet.co.uk

Georgian red brick house with fine saloon by Soane set in 'Capability' Brown park having one of the largest lakes created by Brown. Extensive woodland walks.

Location: OS Ref. SJ864 067. 2m S of Brewood off A449. 4m NW of M54/J2.

Opening Times: Easter Sun; Suns prior to both May BHs; Jul: Thurs; Aug: Thurs, Fris & Suns, 2 - 5pm.

Admission: Adult £3, Child £1.50. Grounds only: half price.

 Partially suitable. Obligatory. In grounds, on leads.

Patrick Lane.

Biddulph Grange Garden, Staffordshire.

THE DOROTHY CLIVE GARDEN

WILLOUGHBRIDGE, MARKET DRAYTON, SHROPSHIRE TF9 4EU
Owner: Willoughbridge Garden Trust *Contact: Mrs M Grime*

Tel: 01630 647237 **Fax:** 01630 647902

The Dorothy Clive Garden accommodates a wide range of choice and unusual plants providing year round interest. Features include a quarry with spectacular waterfall, flower borders, a scree and water garden. Tearoom serving home-baked hot and cold snacks throughout the day.

Location: OS Ref. SJ753 400. A51, 2m S of Woore, 3m from Bridgemere.

Opening Times: 1 Apr - 31 Oct: daily, 10am - 5.30pm.

Admission: Adult £3.20, Child (11-16yrs) £1, (under 11yrs Free), OAP £2.70. Groups (20+) £2.70.

 In grounds on leads.

FORD GREEN HALL
Tel: 01782 233195 **Fax:** 01782 233194
e-mail: ford-green-hall@stoke.gov.uk

Ford Green Road, Smallthorne, Stoke-on-Trent ST6 1NG
Owner: Stoke-on-Trent City Council   **Contact:** Angela Graham

A 17th century house, home to the Ford family for two centuries. The hall has been designated a museum with an outstanding collection of original and reproduction period furniture, ceramics and textiles. There is a Tudor-style garden. The museum has an award-winning education service and regular events.

Location: OS Ref. SJ887 508. NE of Stoke-on-Trent on B551, signposted from A500.

Opening Times: All year: (closed 25 Dec - 1 Jan), Sun - Thurs, 1 - 5pm.

Admission: Adult £1.50, Conc. £1. Special group packages (must book, min 10).

 Partially suitable. WC. In grounds, on leads. Telephone for details

SAMUEL JOHNSON BIRTHPLACE MUSEUM
Tel: 01543 264972

Breadmarket Street, Lichfield, Staffordshire WS13 6LG   **Fax:** 01543 414779
Owner: Lichfield City Council   **Contact:** Annette French

The house where Samuel's father had a bookshop is now a museum with many of Johnson's personal belongings.

Location: OS Ref. SK115 094. Breadmarket Street, Lichfield.

Opening Times: Daily: 10.30am - 4.30pm. Closed Suns, Nov - Jan.

Admission: Adult £2, Child/Conc. £1.10, Family £5.40. Groups: £1.10. (2000 prices).

LICHFIELD CATHEDRAL
Tel: 01543 306240 **Fax:** 01543 306109

Lichfield, Staffordshire WS13 7LD   **e-mail:** enquiries@lichfield-cathedral.org
Contact: Canon A Barnard

The only medieval cathedral with three spires, in the heart of an historic city. Meet a living Christian community, 1300 years old. See the 8th century illuminated 'Lichfield Gospels' manuscript; superb 16th century Flemish glass; sculpture by Chantrey & Epstein, modern silver collection and half-timbered buildings of Vicars' Close.

Location: OS Ref. SK115 097. Approach from A38 and A51, N from M42 and M6. N of city centre.

Opening Times: All year: daily.

Admission: Suggested donation, £3 per adult.

MOSELEY OLD HALL

FORDHOUSES, WOLVERHAMPTON WV10 7HY
Owner: The National Trust   *Contact: The Property Manager*

Tel/Fax: 01902 782808

An Elizabethan house with later alterations. Charles II hid here after the Battle of Worcester. The bed in which he slept is on view as well as the hiding place he used. An exhibition retells the story of the King's dramatic escape from Cromwell's troops, and there are optional, free guided tours. The garden has been reconstructed in 17th century style with formal box parterre, only 17th century plants are grown. The property is a Sandford Education Award Winner.

Location: OS Ref. SJ932 044. 4m N of Wolverhampton between A449 and A460.

Opening Times: 24 Mar - 4 Nov: Sats, Suns, Weds, BH Mons & following Tues. 11 Nov - 16 Dec: Suns (guided tour only). Times: Mar - end Oct: 1.30 - 5.30pm (garden & tearoom from 1pm). BH Mons: 11am - 5pm. Nov & Dec: 1.30 - 4pm. 4 Mar: special opening. Pre-booked groups at other times including evening tours.

Admission: Adult £4.10, Child £2.05, Family £10.25.

Ground floor & grounds suitable. WC. Tearoom in 18th century barn. Guide dogs only.

SANDON HALL

SANDON, STAFFORDSHIRE ST18 0BZ

Owner: The Earl of Harrowby   *Contact:* Michael Bosson

Tel/Fax: 01889 508004 **e-mail:** info@sandonhall.co.uk

Ancestral seat of the Earls of Harrowby, conveniently located in the heart of Staffordshire. The imposing neo-Jacobean house was rebuilt by William Burn in 1854. Set amidst 400 acres of glorious parkland, Sandon, for all its grandeur and elegance, is first and foremost a home. The family museum which opened in 1994 has received considerable acclaim, and incorporates several of the State Rooms. The 50 acre landscaped gardens feature magnificent trees and are especially beautiful in May and autumn.

Location: OS Ref. SJ957 287. 5m NE of Stafford on the A51, between Stone and Lichfield, easy access from M6/J14.

Opening Times: All year: for events, functions and for pre-booked visits to the museum and gardens. Evening tours by special arrangement. Closed Christmas Day, Boxing Day and New Year's Day.

Admission: Museum: Adult £4, Child £3, OAP £3.50. Gardens: Adult £1.50, Child £1, OAP £1. NB. Max group size 22 or 45 if combined Museum and Gardens.

♿ Grounds suitable. ♿ By arrangement. ♿ In grounds, on leads. ❊
▲ ♿

STAFFORD CASTLE & VISITOR CENTRE

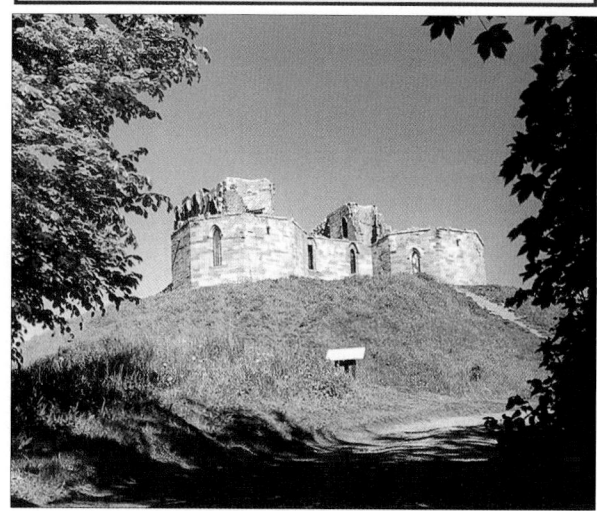

NEWPORT ROAD, STAFFORD ST16 1DJ

Owner: Stafford Borough Council   *Contact:* N Thomas

Tel/Fax: 01785 257698

This impressive site was once a Norman motte and bailey castle. Earl Ralph, a founder member of the Order of the Garter, spent part of his fortune building a stone keep in 1348. During the Civil War, the castle was successfully defended, but eventually demolished. The current building was erected in the early 19th century and fell into ruin through this century. The Visitor Centre displays artefacts found during recent excavations. An imaginative audio-visual presentation describes the castle's mixed fortunes.

Location: OS Ref. SJ904 220. On N side of A518, 1^1/$_2$ m WSW of town centre.

Opening Times: Apr - Oct: Tue - Sun, 10am - 5pm. Nov - Mar: Tue - Sun, 10am - 4pm.

Admission: Please telephone for details.

♿ ♿ Grounds suitable. WC. ♿ ♿ In grounds, on leads.
❊ ♿ Tel. for details.

SHUGBOROUGH   See page 338 for full page entry.

TAMWORTH CASTLE   **Tel:** 01827 709626 **Fax:** 01827 709630

The Holloway, Tamworth, Staffordshire B79 7LR

Owner: Tamworth Borough Council   **Contact:** Mrs Esme Ballard

Dramatic Norman castle with 15 rooms open to the public, spanning 800 years of history. Attractive town centre park with floral terraces.

Location: OS Ref. SK206 038. Town centre off A51.

Opening Times: All year: Mon - Sat, 10am - 5.30pm. Suns, 2 - 5.30pm. Last adm. 4.30pm. Please check opening times after 1 Nov. (2000 dates.)

Admission: Please telephone for 2001 prices.

TUTBURY CASTLE   **Tel:** 01283 812129

Tutbury, Staffordshire

Owner: The Duchy of Lancaster   **Contact:** Lesley Smith

Remains of a large motte and bailey castle overlooking the Dove Valley. Also recreated Tudor Garden/Herbery. Now possible to go into castle. Often costumed guides.

Location: OS Ref. SK210 291. W side of Tutbury off A50 Tutbury - Barton road.

Opening Times: Apr - Oct: Wed - Suns, 11am - 5pm.

Admission: Adult £3, Child/OAP £1.50.

WALL ROMAN SITE (Letocetum) ♿ ♿   **Tel:** 01543 480768

Watling Street, Nr Lichfield, Staffordshire WS14 0AW

Owner: English Heritage   **Contact:** The Custodian

The remains of a staging post alongside Watling Street. Foundations of an Inn and a Bath House can be seen and there is a display of finds in the site museum.

Location: OS139 Ref. SK099 067. Off A5 at Wall, nr Lichfield.

Opening Times: 1 Apr - 31 Oct: daily, 10am - 6pm (5pm in Oct).

Admission: Adult £2.40, Child £1.20, Conc. £1.80. 15% discount for groups (11+). (2000 prices.)

♿ Tel. for details.

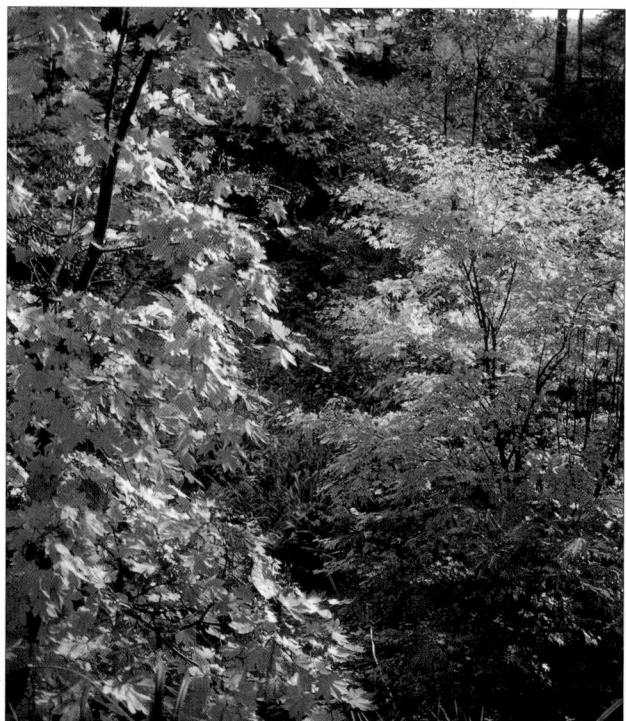

Dorothy Clive Garden, Staffordshire.

IZAAK WALTON'S COTTAGE

WORSTON LANE, SHALLOWFORD, Nr STAFFORD ST15 0PA

Owner: Stafford Borough Council　　　*Contact: S Bailey*

Tel/Fax: 01785 760278

Thatched, timber-framed cottage in the heart of the Staffordshire countryside. Bequeathed by Izaak Walton, author of the *Compleat Angler,* it has displays on the history of angling. Ground floor rooms are set out in 17th century style.

Location: OS Ref. SJ876 293. Shallowford, nr Great Bridgeford, 6m N of Stafford.

Opening Times: Apr - Oct: Wed - Sun & BHs, 1 - 5pm.

Admission: Please telephone for details.

⬜ ♿ 👤 By arrangement. 🅿 🐕 Guide dogs only.

🛡 **SPECIAL EVENTS:**
Events programme during the summer. Please telephone for details.

WHITMORE HALL

WHITMORE, NEWCASTLE-UNDER-LYME ST5 5HW

Owner: Mr Guy Cavenagh-Mainwaring　　*Contact: Mr Michael Cavenagh-Thornhill*

Tel: 01782 680478 **Fax:** 01782 680906

Whitmore Hall is a Grade I listed building, designated as a house of outstanding architectural and historical interest, and is a fine example of a small Carolinian manor house, although parts of the hall date back to a much earlier period. The hall has beautifully proportioned light rooms, curving staircase and landing. There are some good family portraits to be seen with a continuous line, from 1624 to the present day. It has been the family seat, for over 900 years, of the Cavenagh-Mainwarings who are direct descendants of the original Norman owners. The interior of the hall has recently been refurbished and is in fine condition. The grounds include a beautiful home park with a lime avenue leading to the house, as well as landscaped gardens encompassing an early Victorian summer house. One of the outstanding features of Whitmore is the extremely rare example of a late Elizabethan stable block, the ground floor is part cobbled and has nine oak-carved stalls.

Location: OS Ref. SJ811 413. On A53 Newcastle - Market Drayton Road, 3m from M6/J15.

Opening Times: 1 May - 31 Aug: Tues, Weds, 2 - 5pm. Groups of 15+ by arrangement outside normal opening days. (between 1 Apr - 31 Aug). Teas arranged for groups over 15.

Admission: Adult £3, Child 50p.

♿ Ground floor & grounds suitable. 🅿 🐕

Shugborough, Staffordshire.

Owner:
The Viscount Daventry

CONTACT

Colonel CMG Hendy OBE
Arbury Hall
Nuneaton
Warwickshire CV10 7PT

Tel: 024 7638 2804

Fax: 024 7664 1147

LOCATION

OS Ref. SP335 893

London, M1, M6/J3
(A444 to Nuneaton),
2m SW of Nuneaton.
1m W of A444.

Chester A51, A34, M6
(from J14 to J3), 2¹/₂ hrs.
Nuneaton 10 mins.

London 2 hrs, Birmingham
¹/₂ hr, Coventry 20 mins.

Bus: Nuneaton 3m.

Rail: Nuneaton Station 3m.

Air: Birmingham
International 17m.

ROOM	SIZE	MAX CAPACITY
CONFERENCE/FUNCTION		
Dining Room	35' x 28'	120
Saloon	35' x 30'	70
Long Gallery	48' x 11'	40
Stables Tearooms	31' x 18'	80

ARBURY HALL
Nuneaton

ARBURY HALL has been the seat of the Newdegate family for over 400 years and is the ancestral home of Viscount Daventry. This Tudor/Elizabethan House was gothicised by Sir Roger Newdegate in the 18th century and is regarded as the 'Gothic Gem' of the Midlands. The Hall contains a fine collection of both oriental and Chelsea porcelain, portraits by Lely, Reynolds, Devis and Romney and furniture by Chippendale and Hepplewhite. The principal rooms, with their soaring fan vaulted ceilings and plunging pendants and filigree tracery, stand as a most breathtaking and complete example of early Gothic Revival architecture and provide a unique and fascinating venue for corporate entertaining, product launches, receptions, fashion shoots and activity days. Exclusive use of this historic Hall, its gardens and parkland is offered to clients. The Hall stands in the middle of beautiful parkland with landscaped gardens of rolling lawns, lakes and winding wooded walks. Spring flowers are profuse and in June rhododendrons, azaleas and giant wisteria provide a beautiful environment for the visitor.

George Eliot, the novelist, was born on the estate and Arbury Hall and Sir Roger Newdegate were immortalised in her book '*Scenes of Clerical Life*'.

❖

Corporate hospitality, film location, small conferences, product launches and promotions, marquee functions, clay pigeon shooting, archery and other sporting activities, grand piano in Saloon, helicopter landing site. No cameras or video recorders.

Exclusive lunches and dinners for corporate parties in dining room, max. 50, buffets 120.

Visitors may alight at the Hall's main entrance. Parking in allocated areas. Ramp access to main hall.

By arrangement for groups.

Obligatory. Tour time: 1hr.

200 cars and 3 coaches 250 yards from house. Follow tourist signs. Approach map available for coach drivers.

Welcome, must book. School room available.

In gardens on leads. Guide dogs only in house.

OPENING TIMES

ALL YEAR

Open all year on Tues, Weds & Thurs only, for corporate events.

Pre-booked visits to the Hall and Gardens for groups of 25+ on Tues, Weds & Thurs (until 4pm) from Easter to the end of September.

Hall & Gardens open 2 - 5pm on BH weekends only (Suns & Mons) Easter - September.

ADMISSION

SUMMER

Hall & Gardens
Adult £5.00
Child (up to 14 yrs.)..£3.00
Family (2+2) £12.00

Gardens Only
Adult £4.00
Child (up to 14 yrs.)..£3.00

Groups (25+)
Adult £4.50

Special rates for
pre-booked groups of 25+.

 SPECIAL EVENTS

Please telephone for details.

NT Photographic Library.

Owner: The National
Trust

CONTACT

Linda Griffin
Charlecote Park
Warwick
CV35 9ER

Tel: 01789 470277

Fax: 01789 470544

e-mail: charlecote@
smtp.ntrust.org.uk

LOCATION

OS151 Ref. SP263 564

1m W of
Wellesbourne, 5m E of
Stratford-upon-Avon.

Rail: Stratford & Warwick.

Air: Birmingham.

CHARLECOTE PARK
Wellesbourne

Owned by the Lucy family since 1247, Sir Thomas Lucy built the house in 1558. Now, much altered, it is shown as it would have been a century ago, complete with Victorian kitchen, brewhouse and family carriages in the coach house and (new in 2000) two bedrooms, a dressing room and the main staircase. A video of Victorian life can be viewed. The formal gardens and informal parkland lie to the north and west of the house, Red Fallow Deer can be seen in the parkland also Jacob Sheep which were brought to Charlecote in 1756 by Sir Thomas Lucy. It is reputed that William Shakespeare was apprehended for poaching c1583 and Sir Thomas Lucy is said to be the basis of Justice Shallow in Shakespeare's '*Merry Wives of Windsor*'.

NT Severn SWT / D Sellman.

OPENING TIMES

House & Grounds

24 Mar - 4 Nov: daily except
Weds & Thurs.
Open Good Fri.
Jul & Aug: daily except
Thurs.
House: 12 noon - 5pm.
Grounds: 11am - 6pm.

Grounds only

3 Feb - 18 Mar: Sats & Suns,
1 - 4.30pm including
Brewhouse, Victorian
Kitchens & Carriage
Collection.

Park, Shop & Tearoom

3 Feb - 18 Mar: Sats & Suns,
1 - 4.30pm.

ADMISSION

Adult £5.60
Child (5-16).............£2.80
Family £14.00
Groups
Adult £4.60
Under 5s Free.
Grounds only.............£3.00

ℹ️ Children's play area.

🛍️

🍷

♿ Wheelchairs, braille guide.

☕ Licensed.

 Licensed. Open as grounds: 11am - 5.30pm.

🚶 Evening guided tours for booked groups May - Sept:
Tues, 7.30 - 9.30pm (£6.50 including NT members).
Minimum charge £150.

🅿️ Limited for coaches.

📖 By arrangement. Resource book.

🐕 On leads, in car park only.

Tel. for details.

COUGHTON COURT
Alcester

COUGHTON COURT has been the home of the Thockmortons since the 15th century and the family still live here today. The magnificent Tudor gatehouse was built around 1530 with the north and south wings completed 10 or 20 years later. The gables and the first storey of these wings are of typical mid-16th century half-timbered work.

Of particular interest to visitors is the Thockmorton family history from Tudor times to the present generation. On view are family portraits through the centuries with other family memorabilia and recent photographs. Also furniture, tapestries and porcelain.

A long-standing Roman Catholic theme runs through the family history as the Thockmortons have maintained their Catholic religion until the present day. The house has a strong connection with the Gunpowder Plot and also suffered damage during the Civil War. Exhibitions on the Gunpowder Plot as well as Children's Clothes (included in price).

Gardens

The house stands in 25 acres of gardens and grounds along with two churches and a lake. A formal garden was constructed in 1992 with designs based on an Elizabethan knot garden in the courtyard. A new $1^{1}/_{2}$ acre garden in the old walled garden opened in 1996. Visitors can also enjoy a specially created walk beside the River Arrow and a new bog garden opened in 1997.

Owner:
Mrs C Throckmorton

CONTACT

Mr A McLaren
Coughton Court
Alcester
Warwickshire
B49 5JA

Tel: 01789 400777

Fax: 01789 765544

Visitor Information:
01789 762435

e-mail: carol@throckmortons.co.uk

LOCATION

OS Ref. SP080 604

Located on A435, 2m N of Alcester, 8m NW of Stratford-on-Avon. 18m from Birmingham City Centre.

Rail: Birmingham International

Air: Birmingham International

CONFERENCE/FUNCTION		
ROOM	SIZE	MAX CAPACITY
Dining Rm	45' x 27'	60
Saloon	60' x 36'	100

The Saloon, which has particularly good acoustics, is often used for music recording.

Receptions, special dinners, filming, buffets, business meetings, fairs and garden parties. The excellent acoustics of the Saloon make it ideal for concerts, especially chamber music.Marquees can be erected on the large lawn area, grand piano. No photography or stiletto heels in house.

Buffet or sit-down meals can be provided by arrangement, in the Dining Room and Saloon. In-house catering can be arranged for other events. Wedding receptions welcome.

Ground floor of house and gardens. WC.

Licensed restaurant, 11am - 5.30pm. Capacity 100 inside and 60 outside.

By arrangement.

Unlimited for cars plus 4 coaches.

 Car park only.

OPENING TIMES

House
17 - 31 March: Sats & Suns
Apr - Sept: Wed - Sun
11.30am - 5pm
(BH Mons open 11am).

Also open BH Mon & Tue plus Tues in Aug (Closed Good Fri & Sat 23 Jun).

October: Sats & Suns (closes 28 Oct for winter).

Gardens, Restaurant, Gift Shop & Plant Centre: 11am - 5.30 on house open days.

Last admission to House and Gardens including Walled Garden, 4.30pm.

Grounds
As house: 11am - 5.30pm.

ADMISSION

House & Gardens
Adult £6.95
Child* (5-15yrs) £3.45
Family (2+4)...........£21.50
Booked Groups (15+)
Adult £5.60
Child £2.80

Gardens only
Adult £5.10
Child* (5-15yrs) £2.55
Family (2+4)...........£15.75
Groups (15+)
per person £4.10

*under 5yrs Free.
NT members Free admission to house, £2.50 charge to walled garden.

West Midlands England

RAGLEY HALL
Alcester

RAGLEY HALL, home of the Marquess and Marchioness of Hertford and their family, was designed by Robert Hooke in 1680 and is one of the earliest and loveliest of England's great Palladian houses. The perfect symmetry of its architecture remains unchanged except for the massive portico added by Wyatt in 1780.

In 1750, when Francis Seymour owned Ragley, James Gibbs designed the magnificent baroque plasterwork of the Great Hall. On completion, Francis filled the Hall with French and English furniture and porcelain and had portraits of himself and his sons painted by Sir Joshua Reynolds. Notable also is the mural, by Graham Rust, in the south Staircase Hall which was completed in 1983.

PARK, GARDENS & GROUNDS

Ragley is a working estate with more than 6000 acres of land, the house is situated in 27 acres of gardens that were designed by 'Capability' Brown, and include the beautiful Rose Garden. Near to the hall are the working stables, housing a carriage collection dating back to 1760 and a display of assorted historical equestrian equipment. For children there is the adventure playground and maze situated by the lake.

Owner:
The Marquess of Hertford

CONTACT

Mrs Julie Timms
Ragley Hall
Alcester
Warwickshire
B49 5NJ

Tel: 01789 762090

Fax: 01789 764791

e-mail:
ragley.hall@virginnet.co.uk

LOCATION

OS Ref. SP073 555

Off A46/A435 1m SW of Alcester.
From London 100m, M40 via Oxford and Stratford-on-Avon.

Rail: Evesham Station 9m.

Air: Birmingham International 20m.

Taxi: 007 Taxi 01789 414007

OPENING TIMES

9 April - 30 September (House, Park & Gardens are closed Good Friday).

House
Thurs, Fris & Suns,
12.30 - 5pm
(last adm. 4.30pm),
Sats, 11am - 3.30pm
(last adm. 3.00pm).
BH Mons, 11am - 5pm
(last adm. 4.30pm).

Park & Gardens
Thur - Sun & BH Mons
10am - 6pm
(last adm. 4.45pm).
Also open daily
9 - 22 Apr
24 May - 3 Jun
19 Jul - 2 Sept.

ADMISSION

House Park & Garden
Adult	£5.50
Child (5-16yrs)	£4.00
OAP	£5.00
Disabled Badge Holders	£5.00

Groups* (20-100)
Adult	£4.50
Schools	£2.50
OAP	£4.50

Park & Garden
Adult	£4.50
Child (5-16yrs)	£3.50
OAP	£4.00
Disabled Badge Holders	£4.00

Groups* (20-100)
Adult	£3.50
Schools	£2.50
OAP	£3.50

* Groups of 20+ must book and confirm in writing prior to visit.

Season tickets available.

SPECIAL EVENTS

See Special Events Index.

CONFERENCE/FUNCTION		
ROOM	SIZE	MAX CAPACITY
Great Hall	70' x 40'	150
Red Saloon	30' x 40'	40
Green Drawing Rm	20' x 30'	30
Hertford	45' x 22'	60
Seymour	25' x 23'	30

Product launches, dinners and activity days, film and photographic location, park, lake and picnic area, marquee. No photography or camcorders in the house.

Private and corporate entertainment, wedding receptions, conferences, seminars. Telephone for details.

Visitors may alight at entrance. Parking in allocated areas. WCs. Lifts.

Licensed tearooms 11am - 5pm. Groups must book.

Licensed.

By arrangement.

Coach drivers admitted free and receive info pack and luncheon voucher. Please advise of group visits.

Welcome, £2.50 per head. Teachers' packs and work modules on request. Adventure Wood and Woodland Walk.

In grounds, on leads.

Shakespeare's Birthplace

Anne Hathaway's Cottage.

THE SHAKESPEARE HOUSES
Stratford-upon-Avon

Step back in time to enjoy these beautifully preserved Tudor homes connected with William Shakespeare and his family; the architectural character, period furniture, special collections, attractive gardens, grounds and walks and craft displays.

In Town: Shakespeare's Birthplace: Step into the house where William Shakespeare was born in 1564 and re-enter the Tudor World. Newly refurbished, the house now offers visitors a fascinating insight into life as it was when Shakespeare was a child. See the Shakespeare Exhibition which provides an introduction to his life and background and the traditional English garden.

Nash's House and New Place: The site and grounds of Shakespeare's home from 1597 until his death, with its Elizabethan-style garden, is approached through Nash's House adjoining, which contains exceptional furnishings and displays of the history of Stratford.

Hall's Croft: A delightful Elizabethan town house, once the home of Dr Hall, Shakespeare's physician son-in-law. Exceptional furniture and paintings and exhibition on Tudor medicine. Fine walled garden. Meals and refreshments available which can also be served in the beautiful garden.

Out of Town: Anne Hathaway's Cottage: This famous, picturesque thatched cottage was Anne's home before her marriage to Shakespeare. Cottage garden and Shakespeare Tree Garden as well as a garden shop and attractive Shottery Brook and Jubilee Walks. Summer tea garden.

Mary Arden's House and The Shakespeare Countryside Museum: Tudor farmstead, home of Shakespeare's mother, with out-buildings and nearby Glebe Farm containing exhibits illustrating country life over 400 years. Gypsy caravans, dovecote, duck pond, rare breeds, field walk, and falconry displays. Refreshments and picnic area.

Owner:
The Shakespeare
Birthplace Trust

CONTACT

Tracey Powell
Marketing &
Publicity Manager
The Shakespeare
Birthplace Trust
Henley Street
Stratford-upon-Avon
CV37 6QW

Tel: 01789 204016
(General enquiries)

Tel: 01789 201806
(Group Visits)

Fax: 01789 296083

e-mail: info@
shakespeare.org.uk

LOCATION

OS Refs:
Birthplace - **SP201 552**
New Place - **SP201 548**
Hall's Croft - **SP200 546**
Hathaway's - **SP185 547**
Arden's - **SP166 582**

Direct rail services from
London (Paddington)

2 hrs from London
45 mins from
Birmingham by car.

4m from M40/J15
and well signed from
all approaches.

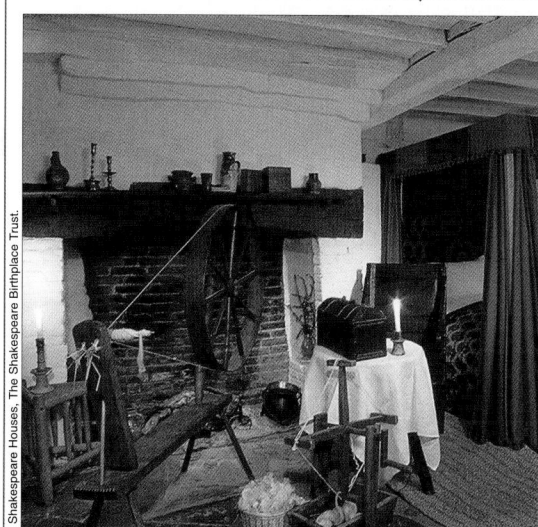

© Shakespeare Houses, The Shakespeare Birthplace Trust.

ℹ️ Regular Guide Friday, guided bus tour service connecting the town houses with Anne Hathaway's Cottage and Mary Arden's House, does not include admission to houses. No photography inside properties.

🛍️ Shops at Shakespeare's Birthplace, Hall's Croft, Anne Hathaway's Cottage and Mary Arden's House.

🍴 Available, details upon request.

♿ WCs. Naturally difficult levels but much for disabled to enjoy at Mary Arden's House, ground floor & gardens accessible.

🍽️ Available on site or close by.

🚶 By special arrangement.

🅿️ The Trust provides a free coach terminal for delivery and pick-up of groups, maximum stay 30 mins at Shakespeare's Birthplace. Parking at Anne Hathaway's Cottage and Mary Arden's House.

🏠 Available for all houses. For information 01789 201804.

 Guide dogs only. ❄️

OPENING TIMES

SUMMER
20 March - 19 October

**Birthplace & Anne
Hathaway's**
Mon - Sat: 9am - 5pm.
Suns: 9.30am - 5pm

**Nash's House/New Place,
Hall's Croft &
Mary Arden's House**
Mon - Sat: 9.30am - 5pm.
Suns: 10am - 5pm

WINTER
20 October - 19 March

**Birthplace & Anne
Hathaway's**
Mon - Sat: 9.30am - 4pm.
Suns: 10am - 4pm

**Nash's House/New Place,
Hall's Croft &
Mary Arden's House**
Mon - Sat: 10am - 4pm.
Suns: 10.30am - 4pm

Closed 23 - 26 December. Open evenings out of hours by special arrangement.

ADMISSION

Shakespeare's Birthplace
Adult............................£5.50
Child.............................£2.50
Conc. £5.00
Family (2+3)................£14.00

**New Place/Nash's
House or Hall's Croft**
Adult............................£3.50
Child.............................£1.70
Conc. £3.00
Family (2+3)..................£8.50

Anne Hathaway's Cottage
Adult............................£4.20
Child.............................£1.70
Conc. £3.70
Family (2+3)................£10.00

Mary Arden's House
Adult............................£5.00
Child.............................£2.50
Conc. £4.50
Family (2+3)................£12.50

3 in-town houses
Adult............................£8.50
Child.............................£4.20
Conc. £7.50
Family (2+3)................£20.00

All five houses
Adult..........................£12.00
Child.............................£6.00
Conc. £11.00
Family.........................£29.00

Accompanied groups
20+, 10% discount.

STONELEIGH ABBEY
Kenilworth

Owner:
Stoneleigh Abbey Ltd

CONTACT

Shahab Seyfollahi
The Estate Office
Stoneleigh Abbey
Kenilworth
Warwickshire
CV8 2LF

Tel: 01926 858585

Fax: 01926 850724

e-mail: enquiries
\@stoneleighabbey.org

Stoneleigh Abbey has been the subject of a major restoration programme funded by the Heritage Lottery Fund, English Heritage and the European Regional Development Fund.

The Abbey was founded in the reign of Henry II and after the Dissolution was granted to the Duke of Suffolk. The estate then passed into the ownership of the Leigh family who remained for 400 years. The estate is now managed on behalf of the nation by a charitable trust.

Visitors will experience a wealth of architectural styles spanning more than 600 years: the magnificent state rooms and chapel of the 18th century Baroque West Wing; a medieval Gatehouse, the Gothic Revival style Regency Stables, the first two bays of which have been fully restored using the same methods and materials employed in their original construction.

The River Avon flows through the estate's 690 acres of grounds and parkland which displays the influences of Humphry Repton and other major landscape architects. Repton designed an expanse of the river to form a lake in which the beauty of the Abbey was reflected. After World War II the lake was used as landfill. The Trust is extremely pleased to have been able to restore the lake and is indebted to Case United Kingdom for generously providing the resources and manpower to achieve this important goal.

LOCATION

OS Ref. SP318 712

Off A46/B4115, 2m W of Kenilworth. From London 100m, M40 to Warwick.

Rail: Coventry station 5m, Leamington Spa station 5m.

Air: Birmingham International 20m.

OPENING TIMES

From 1 April 2000
Tue - Thur & Suns
Please telephone for times.

ADMISSION

Please telephone for details.

 Production launches, dinners, weddings, corporate entertaining, film and photographic locations.

 Suitable.

By arrangement.

 In grounds, on leads.

 Parkland only.

Tel. for details.

© NT Severn/R Charlton

UPTON HOUSE
Banbury

Owner:
The National Trust

CONTACT

The Property Manager
Upton House
Banbury
Oxfordshire
OX15 6HT

Tel: 01295 670266

Infoline: 01684 855365

e-mail: upton_house
@smtp.ntrust.org.uk

LOCATION

OS151 Ref. SP371 461

On A422, 7m NW
of Banbury. 12m SE of
Stratford-upon-Avon

Rail: Banbury
Station, 7m.

UPTON HOUSE stands less than a mile to the south of the battlefield of Edgehill and there has been a house on this site since the Middle Ages. The present house was built at the end of the 17th century and remodelled 1927 - 29 for the 2nd Viscount Bearsted.

He was a great collector of paintings, china and many other valuable works of art, and adapted the building to display them. The paintings include works by El Greco, Bruegel, Bosch, Memling, Guardi, Hogarth and Stubbs. The rooms provide an admirable setting for the china collection which includes Chelsea figures and superb examples of beautifully decorated Sèvres porcelain. The set of 17th century Brussels tapestries depict the Holy Roman Emperor Maximilian I's boar and stag hunts.

Artists and Shell Exhibition of Paintings and Posters commissioned by Shell for use in its publicity 1921 - 1949, while the 2nd Viscount Bearsted was chairman of the company, founded by his father.

GARDEN

The outstanding garden is of interest throughout the season with terraces descending into a deep valley from the main lawn. There are herbaceous borders, the national collection of asters, over an acre of kitchen garden, a water garden laid out in the 1930s and pools stocked with ornamental fish.

Over a mile from the house, but just visible from the west end of the terrace on the garden front, is the lower lake which was formed in the mid-18th century after the fashion of 'Capability' Brown. A small temple with Doric columns and pediment sits in the centre of the one straight edge.

© NT Severn/R Charlton

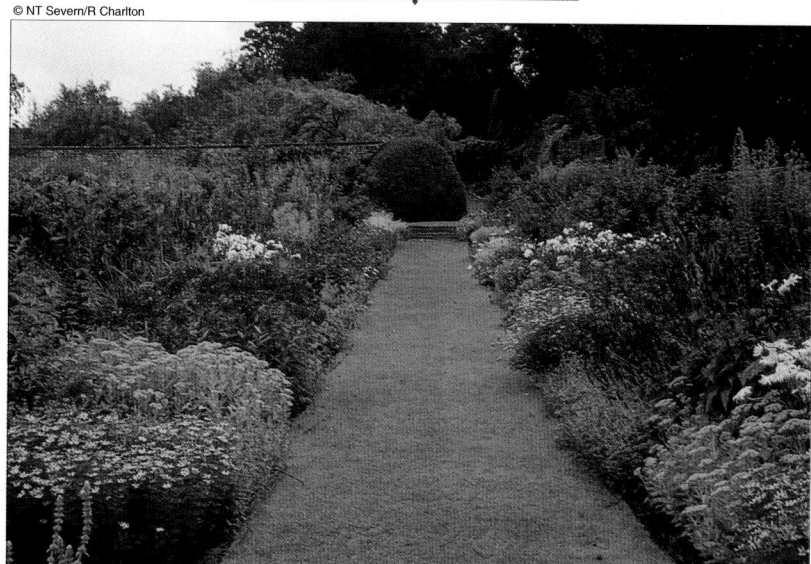

OPENING TIMES

SUMMER
31 March - 31 October
Sat - Wed including
BH Mons & Good Fri,
1 - 5pm. Last admission
4.30pm.

Closed Thurs & Fris

ADMISSION

Adult £5.50
Child £2.75
Family £13.75

Garden
Adult £2.70

Parent & baby room. No indoor photography.

Wheelchair available. Access to all ground floor rooms. WC. Motorised buggy to /from lower garden.

Tour time $1^1/_2$ - 2hrs. Groups (15+) must pre-book. Evening tours by written appointment (no reduction).

Coaches park in the main car park.

SPECIAL EVENTS

- **ALL YEAR:**
  Fine arts study tours, jazz concerts and other events, please send SAE or telephone for details

WARWICK CASTLE
Warwick

CONTACT

Sales Office
Warwick Castle
Warwick
CV34 4QU

Tel: 01926 495421 (Admin)
01926 406600 (Info)

Fax: 01926 401692

LOCATION

OS Ref. SP284 648

2m from M40/J15.
Birmingham 35 mins.
Leeds 2 hrs 5 mins
London, 1 hr 30 mins
Vehicle entrance from A429
1/2 m SW of town centre.

Rail: Intercity from London
Euston to Coventry.
Direct service Chiltern Line
from Marylebone &
Paddington to Warwick.

Over a thousand years of secrets hide in the shadows of Warwick Castle. Murder, mystery, intrigue and scandal: the Castle has witnessed it all, and now reveals the secret life of England as you have never seen it before.

From the days of William the Conqueror to the reign of Queen Victoria, the Castle has provided a backdrop for many turbulent times.

Here you can join a mediaeval household in our Kingmaker attraction, watching them prepare for the final battle of the Earl of Warwick. Enter the eerie Ghost Tower, where it is said that the unquiet spirit of Sir Fulke Greville, murdered most foully by a manservant, still roams.

Descend into the gloomy depths of the Dungeon and Torture Chamber, then step forward in time and marvel at the grandeur of the Great Hall and in 'Death or Glory', our

Armoury attraction, you can feel the weight of a sword and try on a helmet. The 14th century Great Hall lies at the heart of the Castle and here you can see the death mask of Oliver Cromwell and Bonnie Prince Charlie's shield.

Witness the perfect manners and hidden indiscretions of Daisy, Countess of Warwick and her friends at the Royal Weekend Party 1898 or stroll through the 60 acres of grounds and gardens, landscaped by 'Capability' Brown, which surround the Castle today.

Besides the secrets, there are a host of special events to enjoy throughout the year, with a unique opportunity to witness mediaeval life at the Mediaeval Festival (12 May to 9 September).

Warwick Castle really is one of the best days out in history.

OPENING TIMES

SUMMER
April - October
10am - 6pm
Last admission 5.30pm.

WINTER
November - March
10am - 5pm
Last admission 4.30pm.

ADMISSION

11 Sept 2000 - 28 Feb 2001

Adult £9.75
Child (4 - 16yrs) £5.95
Student.................. £7.45
OAP £7.00
Family (2+2) £28.00

Groups (20+)
Adult £7.95
Child(4 - 16yrs)........ £5.20
Student.................. £6.95
OAP £6.40

**Call the Warwick Castle
Information Line on:
01926 406600
for the latest
admission prices.**

 Corporate events, receptions, Kingmaker's Feasts and Highwayman's Supper. Guide books available in French, German, Japanese, Spanish and Italian.

Four shops.

Parking spaces in Stables Car Park, free admission for registered blind and visitors in wheelchairs.

Available, ranging from cream teas to three-course hot meals. During the summer there is an open air barbecue and refreshment pavilion in the grounds (weather permitting).

For groups (must be pre-booked). Guides in every room.

Limited free car parking in main car park. Free coach parking, free admission and refreshment voucher for coach driver.

Ideal location, being a superb example of military architecture dating back to the Norman Conquest and with elegant interiors up to Victorian times. Group rates apply. To qualify for group rates, groups must book in advance. Education packs available.

Registered assistance dogs only.

Tel. for details.

CONFERENCE/FUNCTION		
ROOM	SIZE	MAX CAPACITY
Great Hall	61' x 34'	130
State Dining Room	40' x 25'	32
Undercroft	46' x 26'	120
Coach House	44' x 19'	70
Marquees		2000

ARBURY HALL   See page 343 for full page entry.

CHARLECOTE PARK   See page 344 for full page entry.

COUGHTON COURT   See page 345 for full page entry.

BADDESLEY CLINTON

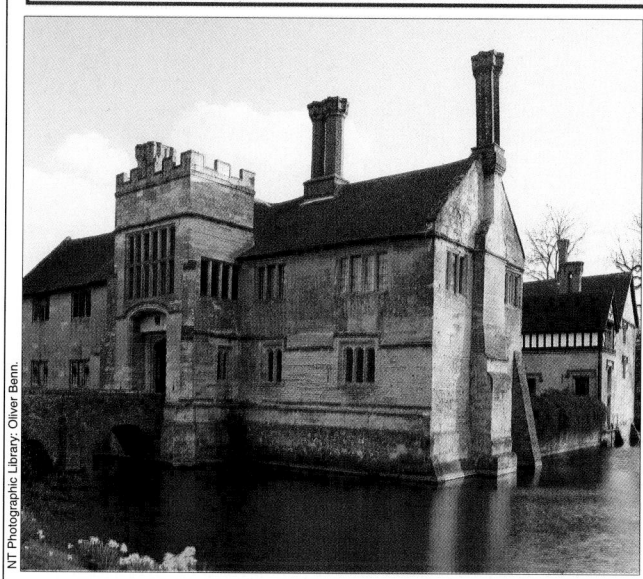

NT Photographic Library: Oliver Benn.

NT Photographic Library: Andreas von Einsiedel.

RISING LANE, BADDESLEY CLINTON, KNOWLE, SOLIHULL B93 0DQ

Owner: The National Trust   *Contact:* The Property Manager

Tel: 01564 783294   **Fax:** 01564 782706   **e-mail:** baddesley@smtp.ntrust.org.uk

A romantically sited medieval moated manor house, dating from 14th century; little changed since 1634; family portraits, priest holes; garden; ponds and lake walk. Make a day of it! Revised opening times and substantial discounts on joint ticket prices make a combined visit to Baddesley Clinton and Packwood House even more attractive, especially since both properties are only two miles apart.

Location: OS139, Ref. SP199 715. 3/4 m W of A4141 Warwick/Birmingham road at Chadwick End.

Opening Times: House: 28 Feb - 28 Oct: Wed - Sun & BH Mons (closed Good Fri). Feb - Apr & Oct: 1.30 - 5pm; May - end Sept: 1.30 - 5.30pm.

Grounds: 28 Feb - 16 Dec: Wed - Sun, Good Fri & BH Mons. Feb - Apr & Oct: 12 noon - 5pm; May - end Sept: 12 noon - 5.30pm; Nov - 16 Dec: 12 noon - 4.30pm.

Admission: Adult £5.60, Child £2.80, Family £14. Garden only: Adult £2.80, Child £1.40. Groups: £4.50. Guided tours (out of hours) £9.

Combined ticket with Packwood House: Adult £8, Child £4, Family £20. Garden only: Adult £4, Child £2. Groups £8.

Partially suitable. WC.   Licensed.   By arrangement. Guide dogs only. Tel. for details.

Honington Hall, Warwickshire.

FARNBOROUGH HALL

BANBURY, OXFORDSHIRE OX17 1DU

Owner: The National Trust   *Contact:* Mr G Holbech

Tel: 01295 690002

A classical mid-18th century stone house, home of the Holbech family for 300 years; notable plasterwork, the entrance hall, staircase and 2 principal rooms are shown; the grounds contain charming 18th century temples, a $^2/_3$ mile terrace walk and an obelisk.

Location: OS151, Ref. SP430 490. 6m N of Banbury, $^1/_2$ m W of A423.

Opening Times: House, grounds and terrace walk: Apr - end Sept: Weds & Sats also 6/7 May, 2 - 6pm. Terrace walk only, Thurs & Fris, 2 - 6pm, closed Good Fri. Last admission to house 5.30pm.

Admission: House, grounds & terrace walk: Adult £3.40. Garden & terrace walk: £1.70. Terrace walk only (Thurs & Fris) £1.

House & grounds, but steep terrace walk.   In grounds, on leads.

THE HILLER GARDEN

Tel: 01789 490991   **Fax:** 01789 490439

Dunnington Heath Farm, Alcester, Warwickshire B49 5PD

Owner: Mr & Mrs R Beach   **Contact:** Mr David Carvill

2 acre garden of unusual herbaceous plants and over 200 rose varieties.

Location: OS Ref. SP066 539. 1$^1/_2$ m S of Ragley Hall on B4088 (formerly A435).

Opening Times: All year: daily 10am - 5pm.

Admission: Free.

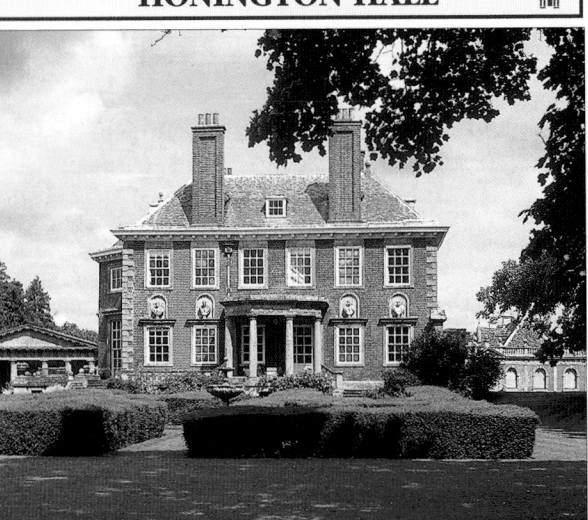

SHIPSTON-ON-STOUR, WARWICKSHIRE CV36 5AA

Owner/Contact: Benjamin Wiggin Esq

Tel: 01608 661434   **Fax:** 01608 663717

This fine Caroline manor house was built in the early 1680s for Henry Parker in mellow brickwork, stone quoins and window dressings. Modified in 1751 when an octagonal saloon was inserted. The interior was also lavishly restored around this time and contains exceptional mid-Georgian plasterwork. Set in 15 acres of grounds.

Location: OS Ref. SP261 427. 10m S of Stratford-upon-Avon. 1$^1/_2$ m N of Shipston-on-Stour. Take A3400 towards Stratford, then signed right to Honington.

Opening Times: Jun - Aug: Weds only. BH Mon, 2.30 - 5pm. Groups at other times by appointment.

Admission: Adult £3.50, Child £1.75.

Not suitable.   Obligatory.

HONINGTON HALL

KENILWORTH CASTLE

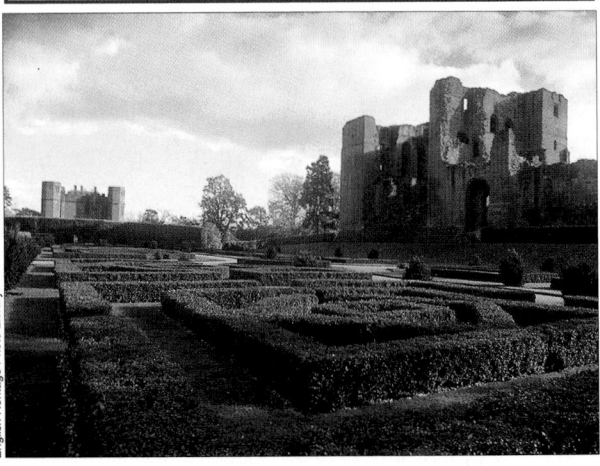

KENILWORTH, WARWICKSHIRE CV8 1NE

Owner: English Heritage   *Contact:* The Custodian

Tel: 01926 852078

Kenilworth is the largest castle ruin in England, the former stronghold of great Lords and Kings. Its massive walls of warm red stone tower over the peaceful Warwickshire landscape. The Earl of Leicester entertained Queen Elizabeth I with 'Princely Pleasures' during her 19 day visit. He built a new wing for the Queen to lodge in and organised all manner of lavish and costly festivities. The Great Hall, where Gloriana dined with her courtiers, still stands and John of Gaunt's Hall is second only in width and grandeur to Westminster Hall. Climb to the top of the tower beside the hall and you will be rewarded by fine views over the rolling wooded countryside. New exhibition, interactive castle model and café in Leicester's Barn.

Location: OS140 Ref. SP278 723. In Kenilworth, off A452, W end of town.

Opening Times: 1 Apr - 31 Oct: daily, 10am - 6pm (5pm in Oct). 1 Nov - 31 Mar: daily 10am - 4pm. Closed 24 - 26 Dec & 1 Jan.

Admission: Adult £4, Child £2, Conc. £3, Family £10. 15% discount for groups (11+).

   P Tel. for details.

The Obelisk, Farnborough Hall, Warwickshire.

LORD LEYCESTER HOSPITAL

HIGH STREET, WARWICK · CV34 4BH

Owner: The Governors   *Contact: The Master*

Tel/Fax: 01926 491422

This magnificent range of 14th century half-timbered buildings was adapted into almshouses by Robert Dudley, Earl of Leycester, in 1571. The Hospital still provides homes for ex-servicemen and their wives. The Guildhall, Great Hall, Chapel, Brethren's Kitchen and galleried Courtyard are still in everyday use. The Queen's Own Hussars regimental museum is here. The historic Master's Garden, featured in BBC TV's Gardener's World, has been restored and a new Knot Garden created for the Millennium.

Location: OS Ref. 280 648. 1m N of M40/J15 on the A429 in town centre.

Opening Times: All year: Tue - Sun & BHs, 10am - 5pm (4pm in winter). Garden: Apr - Sept: 10am - 4pm.

Admission: Adult £3, Child £2, Conc. £2.50. 5% discount for adult groups (20+).

Partially suitable. By arrangement. Limited. Guide dogs only.

MIDDLETON HALL   **Tel:** 01827 283095 **Fax:** 01827 285717

Middleton, Tamworth, Staffordshire B78 2AE

Owner: Middleton Hall Trust   **Contact:** Mrs B Ellerslie

Hall (1285 - 1824). Former home of Hugh Willoughby (Tudor explorer), Francis Willughby and John Ray (17th century naturalists).

Location: OS Ref. SP193 982. A4091, S of Tamworth.

Opening Times: Easter - 30 Sept: Suns, 2 - 5pm, BH Mons, 11am - 5pm.

Admission: Adult £2, OAP £1.

RAGLEY HALL   See page 346 for full page entry.

THE SHAKESPEARE HOUSES   See page 347 for full page entry.

STONELEIGH ABBEY   See page 348 for full page entry.

UPTON HOUSE   See page 349 for full page entry.

WARWICK CASTLE   See page 350 for full page entry.

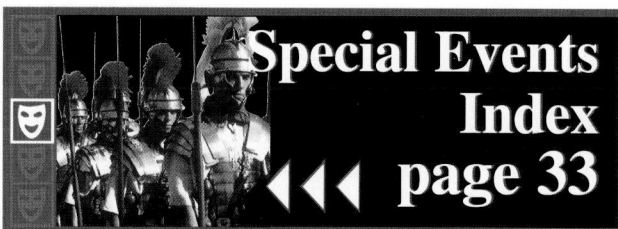

Special Events Index ◀◀◀ **page 33**

PACKWOOD HOUSE

© SWT / D Sellman.

LAPWORTH, SOLIHULL B94 6AT

Owner: The National Trust   *Contact: The Property Manager*

Tel: 01564 783294 **Fax:** 01564 782706 **e-mail:** baddesley@smtp.ntrust.org.uk

Originally a 16th century house, Packwood has been much altered over the years and today is the vision of Graham Baron Ash who recreated a Jacobean house in the 1920s and '30s. A fine collection of 16th century textiles and furniture. Important gardens with renowned herbaceous border and famous yew garden based on the Sermon on the Mount. Make a day of it! Revised opening times and substantial discounts on joint ticket prices make a combined visit to Baddesley Clinton and Packwood House even more attractive, especially since both properties are only two miles apart.

Location: OS139, Ref. 174 722. 2m E of Hockley Heath (on A3400), 11m SE of central Birmingham.

Opening Times: House: 28 Mar 28 Oct: Wed - Sun, Good Fri & BH Mons, 12 noon - 4.30pm. NB: on busy days entry may be by timed ticket. Garden: 3 - 25 Mar: Sats & Suns. 28 Mar - 28 Oct: Wed - Sun, Good Fri & BH Mons. Mar, Apr & Oct: 11am - 4.30pm; May - end Sept: 11am - 5.30pm. Park & Woodland Walks: All year: daily.

Admission: Adult £5, Child £2.50, Family £12.50, Garden only: Adult £2.50, Child £1.25. Groups £4. Guided tours (out of hours) £8.

Combined ticket with Baddesley Clinton: Adult £8, Child £4, Family £20. Garden only: Adult £4, Child £2. Groups £8.

Partially suitable. WC. By arrangement. Guide dogs only. Tel. for details.

CJB Photography.

Owner: Viscount Cobham

CONTACT

Mrs Lesley Haynes
Hagley Hall
Hagley
Worcestershire
DY9 9LG

Tel: 01562 882408

Fax: 01562 882632

LOCATION

OS Ref. SO920 807

Easily accessible from all
areas of the country.
1/4 m S of A456 at Hagley.

Close to the M42, M40, M6
and only 5m from
M5/J3/J4.

Birmingham City
Centre 12m.

Rail: Railway Station and
the NEC 25 mins.

Air: Birmingham
International Airport
25 mins.

CONFERENCE/FUNCTION		
ROOM	SIZE	MAX CAPACITY
Gallery	85' x 17'	130
Crimson Rm	23' x 31'	40
The Saloon	34' x 27'	70
Westcote	31' x 20'	60

HAGLEY HALL
Stourbridge

HAGLEY HALL is set in a 350-acre landscaped park yet is only 25 minutes from Birmingham city centre, the NEC and ICC and close to the motorway network of M5, M6, M40 and M42.

The house is available throughout the year on an exclusive basis for conferences, product launches, presentations, lunches, dinners, country sporting days, team building activities, themed evenings, murder mysteries, concerts, filming and wedding receptions.

Hagley's high standards of catering are now available at other venues as well as at Hagley Hall.

The elegant Palladian house, completed in 1760, contains some of the finest examples of Italian plasterwork. Hagley's rich rococo decoration is a remarkable tribute to the artistic achievement of great 18th century amateurs and is the much loved home of the 11th Viscount Cobham.

❖

ℹ️ Available on an exclusive basis for conferences, presentations, lunches, dinners, product launches, themed evenings, murder mysteries, concerts, wedding receptions. Extensive parkland for country sporting days, team-building activities, off-road driving and filming.

🍸 As well as in-house catering, Hagley also offers a unique catering service at the venue of your choice.

♿ Visitors may alight at the entrance. No WC.

☕ Teas available during opening times.

👤 Obligatory. Please book parties in advance, guided tour time of house 1 hr. Colour guide - book.

🅿️ Unlimited for coaches and cars.

👥 By arrangement.

🐕 Guide dogs only.

🔔

❄️

House

3 January - 25 January
29 January - 2 February
5 - 16 February
19 - 25 February
27 May - 1 June
26 - 31 August
Daily except Saturdays.

13 - 20 April
Daily, 2 - 5pm.

Please telephone prior
to visit to ensure the house
is open.

ADMISSION

House

Adult	£3.50
Child (under 14 yrs)	£1.50
OAP	£2.50
Student	£2.50

ASTON HALL

TRINITY ROAD, BIRMINGHAM, WEST MIDLANDS B6 6JD

Owner: Birmingham City Council   *Contact: Curator/Manager*

Tel: 0121 327 0062   **Fax:** 0121 327 7162

A large Jacobean mansion built 1618 - 1635 from plans by John Thorpe. The Hall is brick-built with a fairytale skyline of gables and turrets. The interior has period rooms from the 17th, 18th and 19th centuries and a splendid long gallery measuring 136ft. A large kitchen and servants' rooms are also on display.

Location: OS139, Ref. SP080 899. 3m NE of Birmingham, 1/4 m from A38(M).

Opening times: 13 Apr - 28 Oct: daily 2 - 5pm. Parkland open all year round.

Admission: Free.

Ground floor & grounds suitable.   Guide dogs only.

THE BIRMINGHAM BOTANICAL GARDENS AND GLASSHOUSES

WESTBOURNE ROAD, EDGBASTON, BIRMINGHAM B15 3TR

Owner: Birmingham Botanical & Horticultural Society   *Contact: Mrs H Champion*

Tel: 0121 454 1860   **Fax:** 0121 454 7835

e-mail: admin@bham-bot-gdns.demon.co.uk

Tropical, Mediterranean and Desert Glasshouses contain a wide range of exotic and economic flora. 15 acres of beautiful gardens with the finest collection of plants in the Midlands. Home of the National Bonsai Collection. Children's adventure playground, aviaries and gallery.

Location: OS Ref. SP048 855. 2m W of city centre. Follow signs to Edgbaston then brown tourist signs.

Opening times: Daily: 9am - Dusk (7pm latest except pre-booked groups). Suns opening time 10am.

Admission: Adult £4.80 (£5.20 on summer Suns & BHs), Child (under 5yrs) Free, Conc. £2.60, Family £12.50 (£13.50, Suns & BHs). Reduced rates for groups of 10+ (prices from April 2001).

 Licensed. Guide dogs only.
Tel. for details.

BLAKESLEY HALL   **Tel:** 0121 803 1675

Blakesley Road, Yardley, Birmingham B25 8RN

Owner: Birmingham City Council   **Contact:** Curator/Manager

Blakesley Hall has been awarded a grant by the Heritage Lottery Fund and will be closed during 2001 for development. For further details telephone 0121 303 1675.

Location: OS139, Ref. SP130 862. 6m E of Birmingham city centre off A4040 from A45.

Opening times: Closed for 2001.

CASTLE BROMWICH HALL GARDENS   **Tel/Fax:** 0121 749 4100

e-mail: enq@cbhgt.swinternet.co.uk

Chester Road, Castle Bromwich, Birmingham B36 9BT

Owner: Castle Bromwich Hall Gardens Trust   **Contact:** The Secretary

A unique example of 17th and 18th century formal garden design within a 10 acre walled area, comprising historic plants, vegetables, herbs and fruit, with a 19th century holly maze. Classical patterned parterres can be seen at the end of the holly walk, together with restored green house and summer house.

Location: OS Ref. SP142 898. Off B4114, 4m E of Birmingham city centre, 1m from M6/J5 (exit northbound only). Southbound M6/J6 and follow A38 & A452.

Opening Times: Apr - end Oct: Tue - Thur, 1.30 - 4.30pm. Sats, Suns & BHs 2 - 6pm. Closed Mons & Fris including Good Fri.

Admission: Adult £3, Child £1, OAP £2.

Daily. Limited for coaches.
In grounds, on leads. Tel. for details.

COVENTRY CATHEDRAL   **Tel:** 02476 227597   **Fax:** 02476 631448

7 Priory Row, Coventry CV1 5ES   **e-mail:** information@coventrycathedral.org

Owner: Provost & Canons of Coventry Cathedral   **Contact:** The Visits Secretary

The remains of the medieval Cathedral, bombed in 1940, stand beside the new Cathedral by Basil Spence, consecrated in 1962. Modern works of art include a huge tapestry by Graham Sutherland, a stained glass window by John Piper and a bronze sculpture by Epstein. '*Reconciliation*' statue by Josefina de Vasconcellos.

Location: OS Ref. SP336 790. City centre.

Opening Times: Cathedral: Easter - Oct: from 8.30am - 6pm. Nov - Easter: 9.30am - 5pm. Visitors Centre: Easter - Oct: Mon - Sat, 10am - 4pm. Nov - Easter: Mon - Sat, 11am - 3pm.

Admission: Cathedral: £2 donation. Visitor Centre: Adult £2, Child/Conc. £1. Groups (10+): Adult £1.50, Child/Conc. £1. Groups must book in advance.

Photo permit required Partially suitable. WC. By arrangement.
No parking. By arrangement. Guide dogs only.

HAGLEY HALL   See page 354 for full page entry.

HALESOWEN ABBEY   **Tel:** 0121 625 6820 (Regional Office)

Halesowen, Birmingham, West Midlands

Owner: English Heritage   **Contact:** The West Midlands Regional Office

Remains of an abbey founded by King John in the 13th century, now incorporated into a 19th century farm. Parts of the church and the monks' infirmary can still be made out.

Location: OS Ref. SO975 828. Off A456 Kidderminster road, 1/2m W of M5/J3, 6m W of Birmingham city centre.

Opening Times: 21/22 Jul only: 10am - 6pm.

Admission: Adult £2, Child £1.50, Conc. £1.

Blakesley Hall, West Midlands.

MUSEUM OF THE JEWELLERY QUARTER

75 - 79 VYSE STREET, HOCKLEY, BIRMINGHAM B18 6HA

Owner: Birmingham City Council　　**Contact:** *The Curator*

Tel: 0121 554 3598 **Fax:** 0121 554 9700

Built around the preserved workshops and offices of Smith and Pepper, a Birmingham jewellery firm. This lively working Museum offers a fascinating insight into the city's historic jewellery trade. Enjoy a tour of the factory with one of our knowledgeable guides and meet skilled jewellers at work. You can also explore the displays which tell the story of the Quarter and the jeweller's craft, practiced in this distinctive part of Birmingham for over 200 years. The museum is available for private evening bookings with catering provision if required.

Location: OS Ref. SP060 880. 3/4 m NW of city centre, just within A4540 (ring road).

Opening Times: Mon - Fri, 10am - 4pm. Sats, 11am - 5pm. Closed Suns.

Admission: Adult £2.50, Conc. £2, Family (2+3) £6.50. 10% discount for booked groups (10+).

i Temporary exhibitions.   🔲   ♿   🖥   🍴   P On street parking only. 🏛 🐕 Guide dogs only. ❄ 🛡 Tel. for details.

RYTON ORGANIC GARDENS　　　**Tel:** 024 7630 3517 **Fax:** 024 7663 9229

Ryton-on-Dunsmore, Coventry, West Midlands CV8 3LG

Owner: HDRA - The Organic Organisation　　**Contact:** Sally Furness

Beautiful and informative gardens including herbs, shrubs, flowers, rare and unusual vegetables, all organically grown.

Location: OS Ref. SP400 745. 5m SE of Coventry off A45 on the road to Wolston.

Opening Times: Daily (closed Christmas week): 9am - 5pm.

Admission: Adult £3 (no concessions), accompanied child free. Groups (14+) £2.50 plus 50p for garden tour.

SELLY MANOR　　　**Tel:** 0121 472 0199 **Fax:** 0121 471 4101

Maple Road, Bournville, West Midlands B30 1UB　　**e-mail:** gillianellis@bvt.org.uk

Owner: Bournville Village Trust　　**Contact:** Gillian Ellis

A beautiful half-timbered manor house in the heart of the famous Bournville village. The house has been lived in since the 14th century and was rescued from demolition by George Cadbury. It houses furniture dating back several centuries and is surrounded by a delightful typical Tudor garden.

Location: OS Ref. SP045 814. N side of Sycamore Road, just E of Linden Road (A4040). 4m SSW of City Centre.

Opening Times: All year: Tue - Fri, 10am - 5pm. Apr - Sept: Sats, Suns & BHs, 2 - 5pm. Closed Mons.

Admission: Adult £2, Child 50p, Conc. £1.50, Family £4.50.

🔲 ♿ Partially suitable. WC. 🍴 By arrangement. P Limited. 🏛 🐕 Guide dogs only. 🔔 ❄

SOHO HOUSE

SOHO AVENUE, HANDSWORTH, BIRMINGHAM B18 5LB

Owner: Birmingham City Council　　**Contact:** *Reception*

Tel: 0121 554 9122 **Fax:** 0121 554 5929

The elegant home of the industrial pioneer Matthew Boulton from 1766 to 1809, Soho House has been carefully restored. Special features include an early 19th century hot air heating system. Period rooms and displays on Boulton's businesses, family and associates as well as the architectural development of the house.

Location: OS Ref. SP054 893. S side of Soho Avenue, just SW of Soho Hill/Soho Road (A41). 2m NW of city centre. Follow signs for Handsworth then brown tourist signs.

Opening Times: Tue - Sat, 10am - 5pm. Suns, 12 noon - 5pm. Closed Mons except BHs.

Admission: Adult £2.50, Conc. £2, Family £6.50. 10% discount for booked groups.

i Meeting room.   🔲   ♿   🖥   🍴 By arrangement.   P Limited for cars. 🏛 🐕 Guide dogs only. ❄

WIGHTWICK MANOR　

WIGHTWICK BANK, WOLVERHAMPTON, WEST MIDLANDS WV6 8EE

Owner: The National Trust　　**Contact:** *The Property Manager*

Tel: 01902 761108 **Fax:** 01902 764663

Begun in 1887, the house is a notable example of the influence of William Morris, with many original Morris wallpapers and fabrics. Also of interest are pre-Raphaelite pictures, Kempe glass and De Morgan ware. The 17 acre Victorian/Edwardian garden designed by Thomas Mawson has formal beds, pergola, yew hedges, topiary and terraces, woodland and two pools.

Location: OS Ref. SO869 985. 3m W of Wolverhampton, up Wightwick Bank (A454), beside the Mermaid Inn.

Opening Times: 1 Mar - 31 Dec: Thurs & Sats, 1.30 - 5pm (last entry 4.30pm). Admission by timed ticket. Guided groups through ground floor, freeflow upstairs. Min. tour time approx. 1 hr 30 mins. Also open BH Sats, Suns & Mons, 1.30 - 5pm (last entry 4.30pm) - ground floor only, no guided tours. booked groups Weds & Thurs. Garden: Weds & Thurs, 11am - 6pm; Sats, BH Mons, 11am - 6pm.

Admission: Adult £5.50, Child £2.75. Garden only: £2.40, Child Free.

🔲 ♿ Ground floor & grounds suitable.   🖥   🐕 In grounds, on leads.

AVONCROFT MUSEUM OF HISTORIC BUILDINGS

Tel: 01527 831886
Fax: 01527 876934

Stoke Heath, Bromsgrove, Worcestershire **B60 4JR**

Owner: Council of Management   **Contact:** Dr Simon Penn

Historic buildings rescued and restored in 15 acres of Worcestershire countryside.

Location: OS Ref. SO954 684. 2m S of Bromsgrove just SE of A38 by-pass.

Opening Times: Mar & Nov: Tue - Thur, Sats & Suns 10.30am - 4pm. Apr - Jun & Sept - Oct: daily except Mons, 10.30am - 4.30pm. Jul & Aug: daily 10.30am - 5pm. (5.30pm Sat & Suns).

Admission: Adult £5, Child £2.50, OAP £4, Family (2+3) £13.50. Booked groups at reduced rates.

BROADWAY TOWER COUNTRY PARK

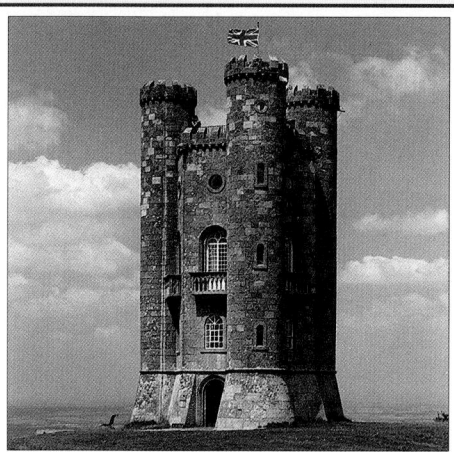

BROADWAY, WORCESTERSHIRE WR12 7LB

Owner: *Broadway Tower Country Park Ltd*   **Contact:** *Annette Gorton*

Tel: 01386 852390   **Fax:** 01386 858038   **e-mail:** broadway-tower@clara.net

Broadway Tower is a unique historic building on top of the Cotswold ridge, having been built by the 6th Earl of Coventry in the late 1790s. Its architecture, the fascinating views as well as its exhibitions on famous owners and occupants (including William Morris) make the Tower a "must" for all visitors to the Cotswolds. The Tower is surrounded by 35 acres of parkland with animal enclosures, picnic/BBQ facilities and adventure playground. A complete family day out.

Location: OS Ref. SP115 362. ¹/₂ m SW of the A44 Evesham to Oxford Rd. 1¹/₂ m E of Broadway.

Opening Times: 27 Mar – 31 Oct: daily, 10.30am - 5pm. Nov - Mar: Sats & Suns (weather permitting), 11am - 3pm.

Admission: Adult £4, Child £2.30, Conc. £3, Family (2+3) £11.50. Group rate on request. Passport Ticket: (free adm. for 1 yr) Adult £12, Child/Conc. £9, Family £34.50. Tower: Adult £3, Child £1.50.

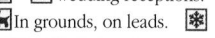 Wedding receptions. WC. P Licensed. In grounds, on leads.

Hartlebury Castle, Worcestershire.

THE COMMANDERY

SIDBURY, WORCESTER WR1 2HU

Owner: *Worcester City Council*   **Contact:** *Amanda Lunt*

Tel: 01905 361821   **Fax:** 01905 361822

A complex of mainly timber-framed buildings, the Commandery was originally founded as a monastic institution and served as the Royalist headquarters at the Battle of Worcester in 1651. Today it houses fascinating exhibitions including 'Civil War', 'The Commandery Chronicle' and plays host to a varied events programme.

Location: OS Ref. SO853 544. Worcester city centre. 350 yds SE of cathedral.

Opening Times: All year: Mon - Sat, 10am - 5pm; Suns, 1.30 - 5pm.

Admission: Adult £3.70, Child/Conc. £2.60, Family £9.90. Groups (20-100): Adult £2.70, Child/Conc. £2.10.

Partially suitable. By arrangement. P Limited. Guide dogs only.

CROOME PARK

SEVERN STOKE, WORCESTERSHIRE WR8 9JS

Owner: *The National Trust*   **Contact:** *The Property Manager*

Tel: 01905 371006   **Fax:** 01905 371090   **e-mail:** croome@smtp.ntrust.org.uk

Croome was 'Capability' Brown's first complete landscape, making his reputation and establishing a new parkland aesthetic which became universally adopted over the next fifty years. The elegant park buildings and other structures are mostly by Robert Adam and James Wyatt. The Trust acquired most of the park in 1996 with substantial grant aid from the Heritage Lottery Fund. The Trust has embarked on a ten year restoration plan, including dredging the water features, clearance and replanting of the gardens and parkland. Royal & Sun Alliance is making a major financial contribution towards the cost of this restoration.

Location: OS150 Ref. SO887 452. 8m S of Worcester and E of A38 and M5, 6m W of Pershore and A44.

Opening Times: 31 Mar - 29 Apr: Sats, Suns, Good Fri & BH Mon, 11am - 5pm. 1 May - 30 Sept: Fri - Mon, 11am - 5pm. 1 Oct - 4 Nov: Sat - Sun, 11am - 5pm. Church: as gardens. Open in association with the Churches Conservation Trust, who own the church. Last admission 4.30pm.

Admission: Adult £3, Child £1.50, Family £7.50.

THE ELGAR BIRTHPLACE MUSEUM

Tel/Fax: 01905 333224

Crown East Lane, Lower Broadheath, Worcester WR2 6RH

Owner: The Elgar Foundation   **Contact:** The Museum Services Manager

A fascinating insight into Elgar's life and music, family and friends. Photographs and memorabilia are displayed in the country cottage where the composer was born. Letters, manuscripts, concert programmes and other treasures from this unique collection feature in the new Elgar Centre's major exhibition, exploring his musical development and inspirations.

Location: OS Ref. SO807 556. 3m W of Worcester, signposted from A44 Worcester/Leominster road.

Opening Times: Daily, 11am - 5pm (last admission 4.15pm). Closed for four weeks in winter (telephone for details).

Admission: Adult £3.50, Child £1.50, OAP £2.60, Student. £1.75, Family £8.50. Booked groups (10+): Adult £3, Child £1, OAP £2, Student £1.25.

No inside photography. Partially suitable. WC. Limited for coaches. In grounds, on leads. Tel. for details.

THE GREYFRIARS

Tel: 01905 23571 **e-mail:** greyfriars@smtp.ntrust.org.uk

Worcester WR1 2LZ

Owner: The National Trust   **Contact:** The Custodian

Built in 1480, with early 17th and late 18th century additions, this timber-framed house was rescued from demolition at the time of the Second World War and has been restored and refurbished; interesting textiles and furnishings add character to the panelled rooms; an archway leads through to a delightful garden.

Location: OS150, Ref. SO852 546. Friar Street, in centre of Worcester.

Opening Times: 16 Apr - 25 Oct: Weds, Thurs & BH Mons, 2 - 5pm. Also open: 29/30 Nov & 1 Dec: Street Fayre.

Admission: Adult £2.80, Child £1.40, Family £7.

HARTLEBURY CASTLE

HARTLEBURY, NR KIDDERMINSTER DY11 7XZ

Owner: The Church Commissioners   Contact: The County Museum

Tel: 01299 250416 **Fax:** 01299 251890 **e-mail:** museum@worcestershire.gov.uk

Hartlebury Castle has been home to the Bishops of Worcester for over a thousand years. The three principal State Rooms – the medieval Great Hall, the Saloon and the unique Hurd Library – contain period furniture, fine plasterwork and episcopal portraits. In the former servants' quarters in the Castle's North Wing, the County Museum brings to life the past inhabitants of the county, from Roman times to the twentieth century. A wide range of temporary exhibitions and events are held each year, and detailed listings are available from the Museum.

Location: OS Ref. SO389 710. N side of B4193, 2m E of Stourport, 4m S of Kidderminster.

Opening Times: 1 Feb - 30 Nov. County Museum: Mon - Thur, 10am - 5pm. Fris & Suns, 2 - 5pm. Closed Good Fri and Sats. Staterooms: Tue - Thur, 10am - 5pm.

Admission: Combined ticket (Museum & State rooms): Adult £2.20, Child/OAP £1.10. Family (2+3) £6 (2000 prices).

Ground floor & grounds. WC. By arrangement for groups. Guide dogs only.

HANBURY HALL

DROITWICH, WORCESTERSHIRE WR9 7EA

Owner: The National Trust   Contact: The Property Manager

Tel: 01527 821214 **Fax:** 01527 821251 **e-mail:** hanbury@smtp.ntrust.org.uk

Set in 400 acres of parkland and gardens, this delightful William and Mary house was home to the Vernon family for three centuries. The permanent home of the Watney collection of fine porcelain and Dutch flower paintings, Hanbury Hall also boasts magnificent staircase and ceiling paintings by Sir James Thornhill. Restored 18th century garden, orangery and ice house.

Location: OS150, Ref. SO943 637. 4½ m E of Droitwich, 4m SE M5/J5.

Opening Times: 1 Apr - 31 Oct: Sun - Wed, 1.30- 5.30pm (open Good Fri). Last adm. 5.30pm or dusk if earlier. Gardens, shop & tearoom open at 12 noon.

Admission: House & Garden: Adult £3, Child £1.50, Family £7.50. Special rates for groups by prior arrangement. New for 2001: Reduced admission rate to celebrate Hanbury's tercentenary.

Ground floor & grounds suitable. WC. For pre-booked groups. Guide dogs only.

HARVINGTON HALL

HARVINGTON, KIDDERMINSTER, WORCESTERSHIRE DY104LR

Owner: Roman Catholic Archdiocese of Birmingham   Contact: The Administrator

Tel: 01562 777846 **Fax:** 01562 777190 **e-mail:** thehall@harvington.fsbusiness.co.uk

Harvington Hall is a moated, medieval and Elizabethan manor house. Many of the rooms still have their original Elizabethan wall paintings and the Hall contains the finest series of priest-holes in the country. A full programme of events throughout the year including outdoor plays, craft fairs, living history weekends and a pilgrimage is available.

Location: OS Ref. SO839 710. On minor road, ½ m NE of A450/A448 crossroads at Mustow Green. 3m SE of Kidderminster.

Opening Times: Mar & Oct: Sats & Suns; Apr - Sept: Wed - Sun & BH Mons (closed Good Fri), 11.30am - 5pm. Open throughout the year for pre-booked groups and schools. Occasionally the Hall may be closed for a private function.

Admission: Adult £3.80, Child £2.50, OAP £3, Family £10.50. Garden: £1.

Partially suitable. Licensed. Limited for coaches. Guide dogs only. Tel. for details.

HAWFORD DOVECOTE

Tel: 01684 855300

Hawford, Worcestershire
Owner: The National Trust   **Contact:** Regional Office
A 16th century half-timbered dovecote.
Location: OS Ref. SO846 607. 3m N of Worcester, 1/2 m E of A449.
Opening Times: Apr - 31 Oct: daily 9am - 6pm or sunset if earlier. Closed Good Fri, other times by prior appointment.
Admission: 60p.

LEIGH COURT BARN

Tel: 0121 625 6820 - Regional Office

Worcester
Owner: English Heritage   **Contact:** The West Midlands Regional Office
Magnificent 14th century timber-framed barn built for the monks of Pershore Abbey. It is the largest of its kind in Britain.
Location: OS Ref. SO784 534. 5m W of Worcester on unclassified road off A4103.
Opening Times: 1 Apr - 30 Sept: Thur - Sun, 10am - 6pm.
Admission: Free.

LITTLE MALVERN COURT

Tel: 01684 892988   **Fax:** 01684 893057

Nr Malvern, Worcestershire WR14 4JN
Owner: Trustees of the late T M Berington   **Contact:** Mrs T M Berington
Prior's Hall, associated rooms and cells, c1480, of former Benedictine Monastery. Formerly attached to, and forming part of the Little Malvern Priory Church which may also be visited. It has an oak-framed roof, 5-bay double-collared roof, with two tiers of cusped windbraces. Library. Collections of religious vestments, embroideries and paintings. Gardens: 10 acres of former monastic grounds with spring bulbs, blossom, old fashioned roses and shrubs.
Location: OS130, Ref. SO769 403. 3m S of Great Malvern on Upton-on-Severn Rd (A4104).
Opening Times: 18 Apr - 19 Jul: Weds & Thurs, 2.15 - 5pm. Last admission 4.30pm.
Admission: House & Garden: Adult £4.60, Child £2.50, Garden only: Adult £3.60, Child £1.50.

  Garden partially suitable.

Jerry Harpur.

Little Malvern Court, Worcestershire.

MADRESFIELD COURT

Tel: 01684 573614   **Fax:** 01684 569197

Madresfield, Malvern WR13 5AU   **e-mail:** madresfield@clara.co.uk
Owner: The Trustees of Madresfield Estate   **Contact:** Mr Peter Hughes
Elizabethan and Victorian house with medieval origins. Fine contents. Extensive gardens and arboretum.
Location: OS Ref. SO809 474. 6m SW of Worcester. 1 1/2 m SE of A449. 2m NE of Malvern.
Opening Times: Guided tours between mid-Apr and Jul on specified dates which are available from the Estate Office, Madresfield, Malvern, Worcs WR13 5AH, tel: 01684 573614. All visitors must join a guided tour and pre-booking is advisable to avoid disappointment.
Admission: £6.

  Not suitable.   Obligatory.

SPETCHLEY PARK GARDEN

SPETCHLEY, WORCESTER WR5 1RS
Owner: *Spetchley Garden Charitable Trust*   **Contact:** *Mr R J Berkeley*
Tel: 01905 345213/345224   **Fax:** 01453 511915
This lovely 30 acre private garden contains a large collection of trees, shrubs and plants, many rare or unusual. A garden full of secrets, every corner reveals some new vista, some treasure of the plant world. The exuberant planting and the peaceful walks make this an oasis of beauty, peace and quiet. Deer Park close by.
Location: OS Ref. SO895 540. 2m E of Worcester on A422. Leave M5/J6 or J7.
Opening Times: 1 Apr - 30 Sept: Tue - Fri & BH Mons, 11am - 5pm. Suns, 2 - 5pm. Closed all Sats and all other Mons.
Admission: Adult £3.40, Child £1.70. Groups: Adult £3.20, Child £1.60.

  Grounds suitable.

THE TUDOR HOUSE

Tel: 01684 592447/594522

16 Church Street, Upton-on-Severn, Worcestershire WR8 0HT
Owner: Mrs Lavender Beard   **Contact:** Mrs Wilkinson
Upton past and present, exhibits of local history.
Location: OS Ref. SO852 406. Centre of Upton-on-Severn, 7m SE of Malvern by B4211.
Opening Times: Apr - Oct: daily, 2 - 5pm (Suns until 4pm). Winter Suns only, 2 - 4pm.
Admission: Adult £1, Conc. 50p, Family £2.

WICHENFORD DOVECOTE

Tel: 01684 855300

Wichenford, Worcestershire
Owner: The National Trust   **Contact:** Regional Office
A 17th century half-timbered dovecote.
Location: OS Ref. SO788 598. 5 1/2 m NW of Worcester, N of B4204. Behind the barns.
Opening Times: Apr - 31 Oct: daily, 9am - 6pm or sunset if earlier. Closed Good Fri, other times by appointment.
Admission: 60p.

West Midlands
England

WITLEY COURT

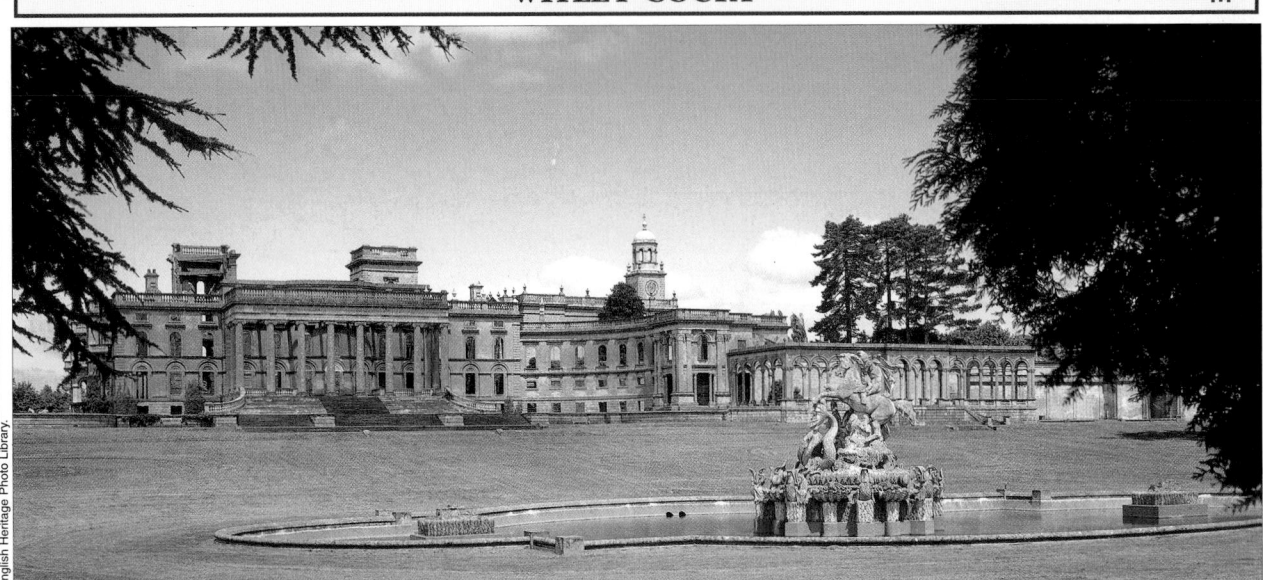

© English Heritage Photo Library.

GREAT WITLEY, WORCESTER WR6 6JT

Owner: English Heritage   *Contact:* The Custodian

Tel: 01299 896636

The spectacular ruins of a once great house. An earlier Jacobean manor house, converted in the 19th century into an Italianate mansion, with porticoes by John Nash. The adjoining church, by James Gibbs, has a remarkable 18th century baroque interior. The gardens, William Nesfield's 'Monster Work' were equally elaborate and contained immense fountains, which survive today. The largest is the Perseus and Andromeda Fountain, which will be fired on Easter Sun & Mon; early May BH, Sun & Mon and late May BH, Sun & Mon. The landscaped grounds, fountains and woodlands are being restored to their former glory. The historic parkland will contain the Jerwood Foundation Sculpture Park, eventually consisting of 40 modern British sculptures.

Location: OS150, Ref. SO769 649. 10m NW of Worcester on A443.

Opening Times: 1 Apr - 31 Oct: daily, 10am - 6pm (5pm in Oct). 1 Nov - 31 Mar: Wed - Sun, 10am - 4pm. Closed 24 - 26 Dec & 1 Jan.

Admission: Adult £3.80, Child £1.90, Conc. £2.90, Family £9.50. 15% discount for groups of 11+.

i Visitor welcome point.   📷   ♿ Grounds suitable. WC.   🍴   **P**   ❄   ♨ Tel. for details.

National Trust Photographic Library.

Hanbury Hall, Worcestershire.

Croome Landscape Park, Worcestershire.

Beningbrough Hall, Yorkshire
362

Yorkshire and the Humber

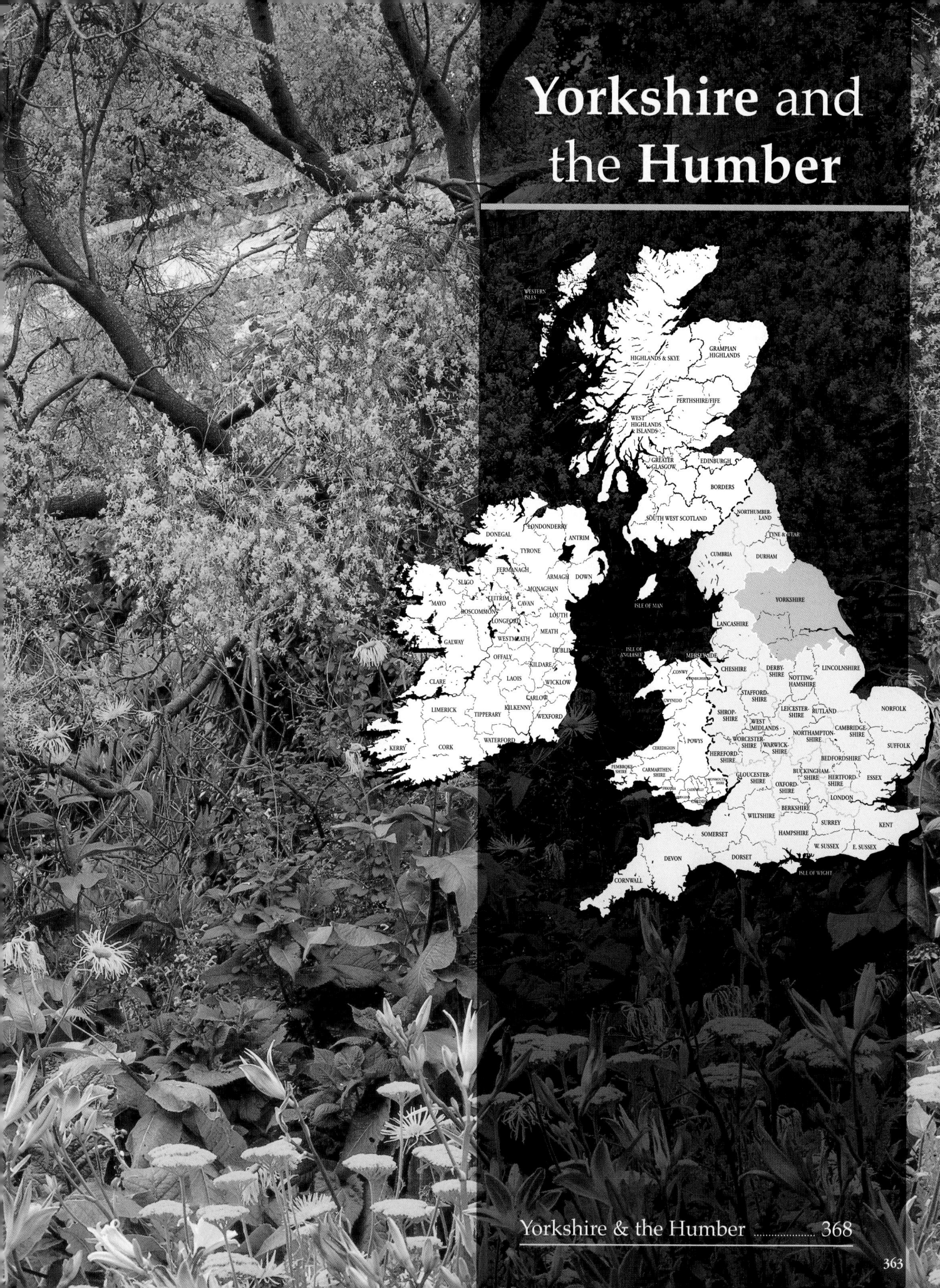

WESTERN ISLES

HIGHLANDS & SKYE

GRAMPIAN HIGHLANDS

PERTHSHIRE/FIFE

WEST HIGHLANDS & ISLANDS

GREATER GLASGOW

EDINBURGH

BORDERS

SOUTH WEST SCOTLAND

NORTHUMBER-LAND

TYNE & WEAR

CUMBRIA

DURHAM

YORKSHIRE

LANCASHIRE

ISLE OF MAN

LONDONDERRY

DONEGAL

ANTRIM

TYRONE

FERMANAGH

ARMAGH

DOWN

SLIGO

MONAGHAN

MAYO

LEITRIM

CAVAN

ROSCOMMON

LONGFORD

LOUTH

MEATH

GALWAY

WESTMEATH

DUBLIN

OFFALY

KILDARE

MERSEYSIDE

CHESHIRE

DERBY-SHIRE

NOTTING-HAMSHIRE

LINCOLNSHIRE

ISLE OF ANGLESEY

CONWY

DENBIGHSHIRE

CLARE

LAOIS

WICKLOW

CARLOW

STAFFORD-SHIRE

LEICESTER-SHIRE

RUTLAND

NORFOLK

LIMERICK

TIPPERARY

KILKENNY

WEXFORD

SHROP-SHIRE

GWYNEDD

WEST MIDLANDS

NORTHAMPTON-SHIRE

CAMBRIDGE-SHIRE

POWYS

WORCESTER-SHIRE

WARWICK-SHIRE

SUFFOLK

KERRY

CORK

WATERFORD

PEMBROKE-SHIRE

CARMARTHEN-SHIRE

CEREDIGION

HEREFORD-SHIRE

BEDFORDSHIRE

BUCKINGHAM-SHIRE

HERTFORD-SHIRE

ESSEX

SWANSEA

MONMOUTH-SHIRE

GLOUCESTER-SHIRE

OXFORD-SHIRE

LONDON

CARDIFF

BERKSHIRE

SURREY

KENT

WILTSHIRE

HAMPSHIRE

W. SUSSEX

E. SUSSEX

SOMERSET

DORSET

ISLE OF WIGHT

DEVON

CORNWALL

Beningbrough Hall

"Walked in the gardens which are very pretty with water and the river below. Fine bowling green, beautiful menagerie with pheasants, fine lawn and bosquets of foreign trees, heated glasshouses for pineapples. Magnificent outbuildings, beautiful stables, beautiful allée of oaks... English greenery which no other country can match."

A French visitor, June 1768

Beningbrough Hall, elegant and graceful, stands at the far end of an avenue of limes. Built of small, locally made, bright red bricks, and flanked by pavilions with cupola roofs, with interiors richly carved and finished, this handsome baroque house has changed little since it was built in the early 18th century. Set among water meadows, bordering the River Ouse, in the Vale of York – the scene is truly idyllic.

Yet although Beningbrough is one of the most remarkable baroque houses in England, it is also an enigma. Almost nothing is known of its building history, and all estate records have been lost.

What the visitor today sees at Beningbrough is therefore very much an attempt by the National Trust to recreate the spirit of a house and garden, rather than a restoration of its precise appearance at the time it was built. The result is a masterpiece.

The National Trust acquired Beningbrough in June 1958 on the death of the last private owner, Lady Chesterfield. However, the Trust's early years at Beningbrough were not easy. The second of six major houses accepted by them between 1957 and 1977 without any endowment to cover running costs – Beningbrough was very soon in dire financial straits. By the mid-1970s its future had become critical. With no money and few visitors, something radical had to be done.

In 1977 the Trust embarked upon a major restoration programme. Rooms were taken back to the soft whites and pale greys typical of early 18th century interiors and furnished with fine walnut pieces and porcelain, as a result of bequests and gifts to the Trust. Walls have been hung with over 100 portraits from the National Portrait Gallery.

By 1997 the gardens, too, were decaying quietly. Today the seven acres of gardens stretching from the south front of the house contain a mix of period and other features. The walled garden, which must have been a model kitchen garden in the 19th century, is now planted for a more labour-saving treatment, but the walls continue to shelter a range of apples, figs and pears, and the original pear arch has been retained as a centrepiece. To the west of the Walled Garden are more intricate planting schemes, with huge double borders having been redesigned to reflect the Edwardian theme of cool midsummer tints.

In capturing the 'spirit' of the place, the Trust has recreated a house and garden of great charm and tranquility, and a wonderful spot to visit.

For further details about *Beningbrough Hall* see entry in Yorkshire and Humber Region.

Yorkshire
England

© English Heritage Photo Library: John Critchley.

Owner: English Heritage

CONTACT

The Custodian
Brodsworth Hall
Brodsworth
Nr Doncaster
Yorkshire
DN5 7XJ

Tel: 01302 722598

Fax: 01302 337165

LOCATION

OS Ref. SE505 070

In Brodsworth, 5m NW of
Doncaster off A635. Use
A1(M)/J37.

Rail: Doncaster.

BRODSWORTH HALL & GDNS ⌗
Nr Doncaster

BRODSWORTH HALL is a rare example of a Victorian country house that has survived largely unaltered with much of its original furnishings and decorations intact. Designed and built in the 1860s it remains an extraordinary time capsule. The now faded grandeur of the reception rooms speaks of an opulent past whilst the cluttered servants wing, with its great kitchen from the age of Mrs Beeton, recalls a vanished way of life. Careful conservation by English Heritage has preserved the patina of time throughout the house to produce an interior that is both fascinating and evocative. The Hall is set within beautifully restored Victorian gardens rich in features which are a delight in any season.

❖

© English Heritage Photo Library.

OPENING TIMES

SUMMER

31 March - 4 November
Tue - Sun, & BHs.

House: 1 - 6pm
(last admission 1 hour
before closing).

Gardens: 12 noon - 6pm.

WINTER

**Gardens, Shop &
Tearoom only**
10 November - 26 March
Sats & Suns: 11am - 4pm.

ADMISSION

SUMMER

House
  Adult £5.00
  Child* (5-15yrs) £2.50
  Conc.....................£3.80

Groups (11+) 15% discount

Free admission for tour
leaders and coach drivers.

Gardens
  Adult £2.60
  Child* (5-15yrs) £1.30
  Conc.....................£2.00

WINTER
  Adult £1.60
  Child* (5-15yrs) £0.80
  Conc.....................£1.20

* Under 5yrs Free

🛍 ℹ Exhibitions about the family and their love of yachting, the servants and the gardens.

♿ Most of house is accessible. WCs.

☕ Seating for 70.

🚶 Groups must book. Booked coach parties: 10am - 1pm.

🅿 220 cars and 3 coaches. Free.

🎓 Education Centre. Free if booked in advance.

🐕 No dogs in gardens.

❄

 SPECIAL EVENTS

Please telephone for details.

CONFERENCE/FUNCTION		
ROOM	SIZE	MAX CAPACITY
Long Gallery	197' x 24'	280
Grecian Hall	40' x 40'	160

Owner:
The Hon Simon Howard

CONTACT

Mrs M E Carmichael
Castle Howard
York, North Yorks,
YO60 7DA

Tel: 01653 648444
Fax: 01653 648501

e-mail:
house@castlehoward.co.uk

LOCATION

OS Ref. SE716 701

Approaching from S, A64 to
Malton, on entering Malton,
take Castle Howard road
via Coneysthorpe village.
Or from A64 following
signs to Castle Howard via
the Carrmire Gate 9' wide
by 10' high.

York 15m (20 mins), A64.
From London: M1/J32,
M18 to A1(M) to A64,
York/Scarborough Road,
3$^{1}/_{2}$ hrs.

Train: London Kings
Cross to York 1hr. 50
mins. York to Malton
Station 30 mins.

Bus: Service and tour
buses from York Station.

CASTLE HOWARD
York

In a dramatic setting between two lakes with extensive gardens and impressive fountains, this 18th century Palace was designed by Sir John Vanbrugh in 1699. Undoubtedly the finest private residence in Yorkshire it was built for Charles Howard, 3rd Earl of Carlisle, whose descendants still live here.

With its painted and gilded dome reaching 80ft into the Yorkshire sky, this impressive house has collections of antique furniture, porcelain and sculpture, while its fabulous collection of paintings is dominated by the famous Holbein portraits of Henry VIII and the Duke of Norfolk.

GARDENS

Designed on a heroic scale covering 1,000 acres. The gardens include memorable sights like the Temple of the Four Winds and the Mausoleum, the New River Bridge and the recently restored waterworks of the South Lake, Cascade, Waterfall and Prince of Wales Fountain. The walled garden has collections of old and modern roses.

Ray Wood, acknowledged by the Royal Botanic Collection, Kew, 'as a "rare botanical jewel" has a unique collection of rare trees, shrubs, rhododendrons, magnolias and azaleas.

Suitable for concerts, craft fairs, fashion shows, clay pigeon shooting, equestrian events, garden parties, filming, product launches. Helicopter landing. Firework displays.

Booked private parties and receptions, min. 25.

Transport equipped for wheelchairs. Chairlift in house to main floor. WCs.

Two cafeterias.

Guides posted throughout house. Private garden tours and lectures by arrangement covering house, history, contents and garden.

400 cars, 20 coaches.

1:10 teacher/pupil ratio required. Special interest: 18th century architecture, art, history, wildlife, horticulture.

OPENING TIMES

SUMMER
16 March - 4 November
Daily, 11am - 4.30pm.

Last admission 4.30pm.

NB. Grounds, Rose
Gardens, Plant Centre
and Stable Courtyard
Complex open 10am.

WINTER
November - mid March

Grounds open most days
November, December and
January - telephone
for confirmation.

ADMISSION

SUMMER

House & Garden
Adult £7.50
Child (4-16yrs)..........£4.50
OAP........................£6.75

Groups (12+)
Adult £6.50
Child (4-16yrs)..........£4.00
OAP........................£6.00

Garden only
Adult £4.50
Child*.....................£2.50

WINTER
Grounds only.

FAIRFAX HOUSE
York

FAIRFAX HOUSE was acquired and fully restored by the York Civic Trust in 1983/84. The house, described as a classic architectural masterpiece of its age and certainly one of the finest townhouses in England, was saved from near collapse after considerable abuse and misuse this century, having been converted into a cinema and dance hall.

The richly decorated interior with its plaster-work, wood and wrought-iron, is now the home for a unique collection of Georgian furniture, clocks, paintings and porcelain.

The Noel Terry Collection, gift of a former treasurer of the York Civic Trust, has been described by Christie's as one of the finest private collections formed this century. It enhances and complements the house and helps to create that special 'lived-in' feeling, providing the basis for a series of set-piece period exhibitions which bring the house to life in a very tangible way.

Owner:
York Civic Trust

CONTACT

Mr Peter Brown
Fairfax House
Castlegate
York
YO1 9RN

Tel: 01904 655543

Fax: 01904 652262

LOCATION

OS Ref. SE605 515

In centre of York between Castle Museum and Jorvik Centre.

London 4 hrs by car,
2 hrs by train.

Rail: York Station,
10 mins walk.

Taxi: Station Taxis
01904 623332.

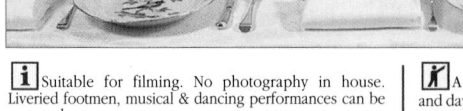

OPENING TIMES

SUMMER
17 February - 6 January
Mon - Thur: 11am - 5pm.
Fris: Guided tours only at 11am and 2pm.
Sats: 11am - 5pm.
Suns: 1.30 - 5pm.
Last admission 4.30pm.

WINTER
Closed
7 January - 16 February
& 24 - 26/31 December.

ADMISSION

Adult	£4.00
Child (5 -16yrs)	£1.50
Conc.	£3.50
Groups*	
Adult	£3.00
Child (5 -16yrs)	£1.00
Conc.	£3.00

* Min payment 15 persons.

SPECIAL EVENTS

- **MAR 1 - JUN 1:**
'Obsession' - The Collector and their Collections.

- **SEPT 1 - NOV 20:**
'Cutting Edge' - Evolution of of Cutlery and Place Settings.

- **DEC 3 - JAN 6:**
Annual exhibition on the 'Keeping of Christmas'. Information extracted from the family papers helps re-create, in a very tangible way, the ritual and decoration of Christmas celebrations in Fairfax House from 1760 -1840. Booked parties can be given mulled wine and mince pies at end of the tour.

ℹ️ Suitable for filming. No photography in house. Liveried footmen, musical & dancing performances can be arranged.

🛍️

🍷 Max. 28 seated. Groups up to 50: buffet can be provided.

♿ Visitors may alight at entrance prior to parking. No WCs except for functions.

🚶 A guided tour can be arranged at a cost of £5. Evening and daytime guided tours, telephone for details. Available in French and German. Tour time: 1½ hrs.

🅿️ 300 cars, 50 yds from house. Coach park is ½m away, parties are dropped off; drivers please telephone for details showing the nearest coach park and approach to the house.

Mike Williams.

Owner:
The National Trust

CONTACT

The National Trust
Fountains Abbey
and Studley Royal
Ripon
North Yorkshire
HG4 3DY

Tel: 01765 608888

Fax: 01765 608889

LOCATION

OS Ref. SE275 700

Abbey entrance;
4m W of Ripon off B6265.
8m W of A1.

FOUNTAINS ABBEY & STUDLEY ROYAL
Ripon

One of the most remarkable sites in Europe, sheltered in a secluded valley, Fountains Abbey and Studley Royal, a World Heritage Site, encompasses the spectacular remains of a 12th century Cistercian abbey, an Elizabethan mansion, and one of the best surviving examples of a Georgian green water garden. Elegant ornamental lakes, avenues, temples and cascades provide a succession of unforgettable eye-catching vistas in an atmosphere of peace and tranquillity. St Mary's Church, built by William Burges in the 19th century, provides a dramatic focal point to the medieval deer park with over 500 deer.

Fountains Mill opens Summer 2001. Over eight centuries of various industrial activity will be revealed. Considered to be one of the finest surviving examples of a monastic water mill in Britain.

The Abbey is maintained by English Heritage. St Mary's Church is owned by English Heritage and managed by the National Trust.

OPENING TIMES

April - September
Daily: 10am - 7pm.

January - March &
October - December
Daily: 10am - 5pm.

Last admission 1 hr
before closing.

Closes at 4pm on
6/7 July.

Closed 24/25 December,
and Fris in November -
January.

ADMISSION

Adult £4.50
Child (5-16yrs)..........£2.30
Family £11.00

Groups (15-30)
Adult £3.90
Child (5-16yrs)..........£2.10

Groups (31+)
Adult £3.50
Child (5-16yrs)..........£1.90

Under 5s Free.

Group discount
applicable only with
prior booking.

Group visits and disabled
visitors, please telephone
in advance, 01765 601005.

[i] Events held throughout the year. Exhibitions. Seminar facilities. Outdoor concerts, meetings, activity days, walks.

Two shops.

Dinners and dances.

Free batricars & wheelchairs, please book, tel. 01765 601005. 3-wheel Batricars not permitted due to terrain. Tours for visually impaired, please book. WC.

Groups please book, discounted rates. Licensed.

Licensed.

Free, but seasonal. Groups, please use Visitor Centre entrance.

[P] Drivers must book groups. Limited for coaches.

In grounds, on leads.

Tel. for details.

Harewood House.

HAREWOOD HOUSE
Leeds

Owner: The Earl of Harewood

CONTACT

Mary Stuart
Moor House
Harewood Estate
Harewood
Leeds
West Yorkshire
LS17 9LQ

Tel: 0113 2181010
Fax: 0113 2181002
e-mail: business@
harewood.org

LOCATION

OS Ref. SE311 446

A1 N or S to Wetherby.

A659 via Collingham, Harewood is on A61 between Harrogate and Leeds. Easily reached from A1, M1, M62 and M18. Half an hour from York, 15 mins from centre of Leeds or Harrogate.

Rail: Leeds Station 7m.

Bus: No. 36 from Leeds or Harrogate.

CONFERENCE/FUNCTION

ROOM	SIZE	MAX CAPACITY
State Dining Rm.		32
Gallery		96
Courtyard Suite		120
Courtyard Marquee	20' x 24'	400

Designed in 1759 by John Carr, Harewood House is the Yorkshire home of the Queen's cousin, the Earl of Harewood. His mother, HRH Princess Mary, Princess Royal - daughter of King George V - lived at Harewood for 35 years and much of her fascinating Royal memorabilia is still displayed throughout her former rooms.

The House, renowned for its stunning architecture and exquisite Adam interiors, contains a rich collection of Chippendale furniture, fine porcelain and outstanding art collections from Italian Renaissance masterpieces and Turner watercolours to 18th century and 20th century works. Also now on permanent display, is the opulent Chippendale State Bed - newly restored to its former glory and unseen for 150 years.

In the 1000 acres of parkland, landscaped by 'Capability' Brown are lakeside and woodland walks, magnificent collections of Rhododendron (April - June) and Sir Charles Barry's parterre Terrace which offers excellent views of the surrounding countryside beyond.

The hugely popular Bird Garden is home to around 100 rare and endangered species from Africa, America and Australia, as well as popular favourites - penguins, flamingos and owls.

Throughout the season are a host of special events including open-air concerts, theatre performances, craft festivals, car rallies and much more. During 2001, the dedicated Watercolour Rooms and Terrace Gallery will feature a changing programme of exhibitions from works by JMW Turner to historical and contemporary portraiture.

Marquees can be accommodated, concerts and product launches. No photography in the house.

Ideal for corporate entertaining including drinks receptions, buffets and wedding receptions. Specific rooms available for corporate entertaining plus Courtyard Suite for conferences/product launches.

Visitors may alight at entrance. Parking in allocated areas. Most facilities accessible. Wheelchair available at House and Bird Garden. WC. Special concessions apply to disabled groups. Some steep inclines.

Licensed.   Licensed.

Cars 400 yds from house. 50+ coaches 500 yds from house. Drivers to verify in advance.

By arrangement. Audio tour of house £1.50. Lectures by arrangement.

Dogs on leads in grounds, guide dogs only in house.

Civil Wedding Licence.

Harewood House.

OPENING TIMES

SUMMER

14 Mar - 4 Nov 2001
closed 8 June

House
Daily from 11am - 4.30pm.

Bird Garden & Grounds
Daily from 10am.

Café
10.30am - 4.30pm.

WINTER

House closed: Nov - Mar.
Grounds & Gardens:
Nov/Dec, open weekends
(ring to confirm times).

ADMISSION

All attractions

Adult £7.50
Child (4-15yrs) £5.00
Student.......................£5.00
OAP........................£6.75
Family (2+3) £26.00
Groups (15+)
Adult £6.25
OAP........................£5.75

Bird Garden & Grounds

Adult £6.25
Child (4-15yrs)...........£3.50
Student....................£3.50
OAP........................£5.25
Family (2+3) £19.00

SPECIAL EVENTS

- **MAY 26 - 28:**
  Live Crafts.

- **JUN 17:**
  Vintage & Classic Car Rally.

- **JUL 13 - 15**
  Food Lovers Fair.

- **JUL 28 - 30**
  Leeds Championship Dog Show.

Owner:
Mr Richard Compton

CONTACT

The Opening Administrator
Newby Hall
Ripon
North Yorkshire
HG4 5AE

Tel: 01423 322583

Fax: 01423 324452

e-mail:
info@newbyhall.com

NEWBY HALL & GARDENS
Ripon

NEWBY HALL, the Yorkshire home of the Compton family, is a late 17th century house built in the style of Sir Christopher Wren. William Weddell, an ancestor of Mr Compton, made the Grand Tour in the 1760s, and amongst the treasures he acquired were magnificent classical statuary and a superb set of Gobelin Tapestries. To house these treasures, Weddell commissioned Robert Adam to create the splendid domed Sculpture Gallery and Tapestry Room that we see today. The Regency dining room and billiard room were added later. There is much fine Chippendale furniture and in recent years Mrs Robin Compton restored the decoration of the house, painstakingly researching colour and decor of the Adam period.

GARDENS

25 acres of glorious gardens contain rare and beautiful shrubs and plants. Newby's famous double herbaceous borders, flanked by great bastions of yew hedges, sweep down to the River Ure. Formal gardens such as the Autumn and Rose Gardens – each with splashing fountains – a Victorian rock garden, the tranquillity of Sylvia's Garden, pergolas and even a tropical garden, make Newby a 'Garden for all Seasons'. Newby holds the National Collection of the Genus Cornus and in 1987 won the Christie's/ HHA Garden of the Year Award. The gardens also incorporate an exciting children's adventure garden and miniature railway.

LOCATION

OS Ref. SE348 675

Midway between London and Edinburgh, 4m W of A1, towards Ripon. S of Skelton 2m NW of (A1) Boroughbridge. 4m SE of Ripon.

Taxi: Ripon Taxi Rank 01765 601283.

Bus: On Ripon - York route.

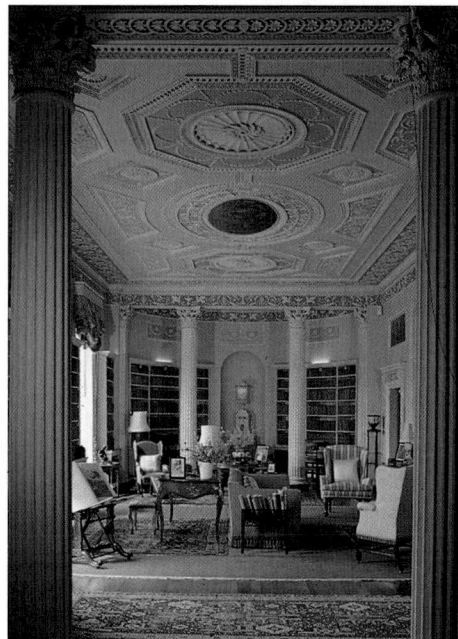

Suitable for filming and for special events, craft and country fairs, vehicle rallies etc, promotions and lectures. No indoor photography. Allow a full day for viewing house and gardens.

Wedding receptions & special functions.

5 wheelchairs available. Access to ground floor of house and key areas in gardens. WC.

Garden restaurant, teas, hot and cold meals. Booked groups in Grantham Room. Menus/rates on request.

Ample. Hard standing for coaches.

Welcome. Rates on request. Grantham Room for use as wet weather base subject to availability. Woodland discovery walk, adventure gardens and train rides on 10¼" gauge railway.

Guide dogs only.

SPECIAL EVENTS

- **MAY 13:**
  Spring Plant Fair.

- **JUN 8 - 10 & AUG 24 - 27:**
  Rainbow Craft Fair.

- **JUL 15:**
  Historic Vehicle Rally.

See Special Events Index for full details

OPENING TIMES

SUMMER

House
1 April - end September
Daily except Mons but
open BH Mons,
12 noon - 5pm
Last admission 4.30pm.

Garden
1 April - end September
Daily except Mons but
open BH Mons.
11am - 5.30pm
Last admission 5pm.

WINTER
October - end March
Closed.

ADMISSION

House & Garden

Adult	£6.80
Child (4-16yrs)	£4.00
OAP	£5.80
Disabled	£4.00

Group (15+)

Adult	£5.50
Child (4-16yrs)	£3.70

Garden only

Adult	£5.00
Child (4-16yrs)	£3.50
OAP	£4.00
Disabled	£3.50

Group (15+)

Adult	£4.00
Child (4-16yrs)	£3.00

Additional charge for train.

CONFERENCE/FUNCTION

ROOM	SIZE	MAX CAPACITY
Grantham Room	90' x 20'	200

RIPLEY CASTLE
Harrogate

RIPLEY CASTLE has been the home of the Ingilby family for twenty-six generations and Sir Thomas and Lady Ingilby together with their five children continue the tradition. The guided tours are amusing and informative, following the lives and loves of one family for over 670 years and how they have been affected by events in English history. The Old Tower dates from 1555 and houses splendid armour, books, panelling and a Priest's Secret Hiding Place, together with fine paintings, china, furnishings and chandeliers collected by the family over the centuries. The extensive Victorian Walled Gardens have been transformed and are a colourful delight through every season. In the Spring you can appreciate 150,000 flowering bulbs which create a blaze of colour through the woodland walks, and also the National Hyacinth Collection whose scent is breathtaking. The restored Hot Houses have an extensive tropical plant collection, and in the Kitchen Gardens you can see an extensive collection of rare vegetables from the Henry Doubleday Research Association.

Ripley village on the Castle's doorstep is a model estate village with individual charming shops, an art gallery, delicatessen and Farmyard Museum.

Owner:
Sir Thomas Ingilby Bt

CONTACT

Tours: Wendy McNae
Meetings/Dinners:
Chloë Drummond
Ripley Castle
Ripley
Harrogate
North Yorkshire
HG3 3AY

Tel: 01423 770152

Fax: 01423 771745

e-mail: enquiries@
ripleycastle.co.uk

LOCATION

OS Ref. SE283 605

W edge of village. Just off A61, 3$\frac{1}{2}$ m N of Harrogate, 8m S of Ripon. M1 18m S, M62 20m S.

Rail: London - Leeds/York 2hrs. Leeds/York - Harrogate 30mins.

Taxi: Blueline taxis Harrogate (01423) 503037.

CONFERENCE/FUNCTION		
ROOM	SIZE	MAX CAPACITY
Morning Rm	27' x 22'	80
Large Drawing Rm	30 'x 22'	80
Library	31 x 19'	75
Tower Rm	33' x 21'	75
Map Rm	19' x 14'	20
Dining Rm	23' x 19'	30

No photography inside castle unless by prior written consent. Parkland for outdoor activities & concerts. Murder mystery weekends.

VIP lunches & dinners (max. 66): unlimited in marquees. Full catering service, wedding receptions, banquets and medieval banquets.

5/7 rooms accessible. Gardens accessible (not Tropical Collection). WCs. Parking 50 yds.

The Castle Tearooms (seats 56) in Castle courtyard. Licensed. Pub lunches or dinner at hotel (100 yds). Groups must book.

Obligatory. Tour time 75 mins.

290 cars - 300 yds from castle entrance. Coach park 50 yds. Free.

Welcome by arrangement, between 10.30am - 7.30pm. Educational Fact Pack.

Guide dogs only.

Boar's Head Hotel (RAC***) 100 yds. Owned and managed by the estate.

Civil Wedding Licence.

Open all year.

OPENING TIMES

SUMMER
Castle & Gardens
January - May,
September - December:
Tues, Thurs, Sats & Suns:
10.30am - 3pm.

June - August:
Daily: 10.30am - 3pm.

Gardens
Daily, 10am - 5pm.

WINTER
December - May &
September - December:
Tues, Thurs, Sats & Suns.
10.30am - last guided tour 3pm.

ADMISSION

ALL YEAR
Castle & Gardens

Adult	£5.50
Child (5-16yrs)	£3.00
OAP	£4.50
Groups (15+)	
Adult	£4.50
Child (5-16yrs)	£2.50

Gardens only

Adult	£3.00
Child (5-16yrs)	£1.50
OAP	£2.50
Groups (15+)	
Adult	£2.50

SPECIAL EVENTS

- **APR 5 - 8:**
  Galloway Antiques Fair
- **JUNE 7 - 10:**
  Grand Summer Sale
- **JULY 12 - 15:**
  Galloway Antiques Fair

SKIPTON CASTLE
Skipton

Guardian of the gateway to the Yorkshire Dales for over 900 years, this is one of the most complete and well-preserved medieval castles in England. From 1310 stronghold of the Cliffords, two Lords of Skipton went out from here to die on Roses battlefields. In the Civil War this was the last Royalist bastion in the North, falling after a three year siege.

Every phase of this turbulent history has left its mark, from the Norman entrance arch and gateway towers to the beautiful early Tudor courtyard built in the heart of the castle by 'The Shepherd Lord'; it was there in 1659, that Lady Anne Clifford planted a yew tree (in whose shade you can sit today) to mark the completion of her repairs after the Civil War. Thanks to her, and to Cromwell, who permitted them on condition that the roofs should not be able to support cannon – the castle is still fully roofed,

making a visit well worthwhile at any time of year. A delightful picnic area has been created on the Chapel Terrace with views over the town and woods.

The gatehouse of the castle contains the Shell Room, decorated in 1620 with shells and Jamaican coral said to have been brought home by Lady Anne's father, George Clifford, 3rd Earl of Cumberland, Champion to Queen Elizabeth and one of her Admirals against the Armada; he lies beneath a splendid tomb in Skipton's parish church, a few yards from the castle gates.

On leaving the castle, the visitor is at once in the town's bustling High Street, with its four market days every week (and lots of other good shopping) and a great variety of pubs and restaurants. Close by, the Leeds and Liverpool canal presents a lively scene.

<hr>

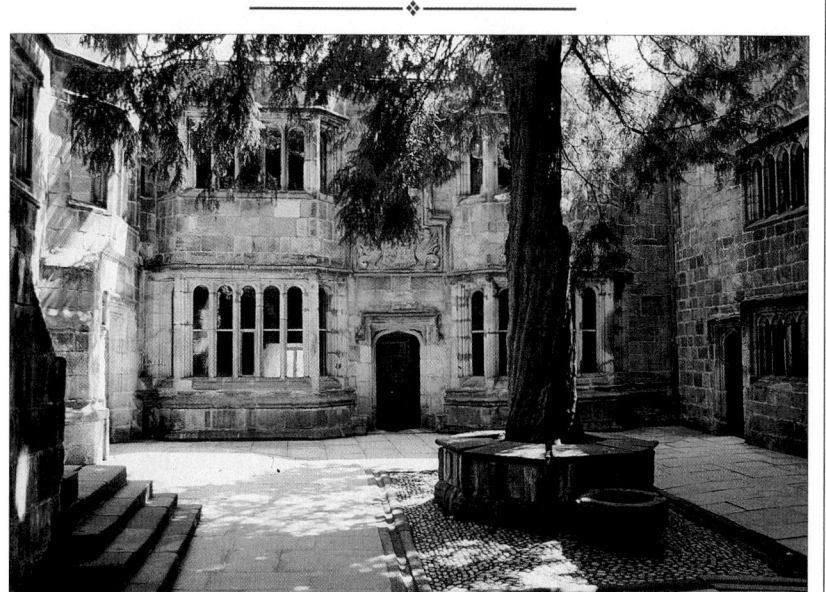

CONTACT

Judith Parker
Skipton Castle
Skipton
North Yorkshire
BD23 1AQ

Tel: 01756 792442

Fax: 01756 796100

e-mail: info@
skiptoncastle.co.uk

LOCATION

OS Ref. SD992 520

In the centre of Skipton, at the N end of High Street.

Skipton is 20m W of Harrogate on the A59 and 26m NW of Leeds on A65.

Rail: Regular services from Leeds & Bradford.

OPENING TIMES

ALL YEAR
(closed 25 December)

Mon - Sat: 10am - 6pm
Suns: 12 noon - 6pm
(October - February 4pm).

ADMISSION

Adult £4.40
Child (0 - 4yrs) ....Free
Child (5-17yrs)..........£2.20
OAP £3.80
Student (with ID)......£3.80
Family (2+3) £11.90
Groups (15+)
Adult £3.60
Child (0-17yrs).........£2.20

Includes illustrated tour sheet in a choice of eight languages, plus free badge for children.

Groups welcome:
Guides available for booked groups at no extra charge.

Not suitable.

Tearoom. Indoor and outdoor picnic areas.

By arrangement.

Large public coach and car park off nearby High Street. Coach drivers' rest room at Castle.

Welcome. Guides available. Teachers free.

In grounds on leads.

 SPECIAL EVENTS

Please telephone for details.

WHITE SCAR CAVE
Ingleton

Owner: White Scar
Caves Ltd

CONTACT

John Connaughton
White Scar Cave
Ingleton
North Yorkshire
LA6 3AW

Tel: 01524 241244

Fax: 01524 241700

e-mail: wsb@
oyez.freeserve.co.uk

WHITE SCAR CAVE is the longest show cave in Britain. The guided tour covers one mile, and takes about 80 minutes. The highlight of the tour is the impressive 200,000 year old Battlefield Cavern. Over 330 feet long, with its roof soaring in places to 100 feet, this is one of the largest caverns in Britain. It contains thousands of delicate stalactites, which hang from the roof in great clusters.

The tour begins near the original entrance found by Christopher Long, the student who discovered the cave in 1923. The path winds its way past cascading waterfalls, between massive banks of flowstone, and through galleries decorated with cream- and carrot-coloured stalactites and stalagmites. Under the steel-grid walkways you can see the stream rushing and foaming on its way. Your guide will show you curious cave formations, including the Devil's Tongue, the Arum Lily and the remarkably lifelike Judge's Head.

There is electric lighting throughout, and the principal features are floodlit. White Scar Cave is part of a Site of Special Scientific Interest. It enjoys a spectacular location in the Yorkshire Dales National Park on the slopes of Ingleborough Hill (2372 ft).

OPENING TIMES

ALL YEAR
Daily: 10am
Last tour at 5.30pm.
Closed 25 December.

ADMISSION

Adult £6.25
Child........................£3.45
Family £17.50

Groups (12+)
  Adult £5.00
  Child £2.70

LOCATION

OS Ref. SD713 745

1¹/₂ m from Ingleton on
B6255 road to Hawes.

Member of the International Show Caves Association.

Partially suitable.

Obligatory.

Fact sheets.

In grounds on leads.

ALDBOROUGH ROMAN TOWN

Tel: 01423 322768

High Street, Boroughbridge, North Yorkshire YO5 9ES

Owner: English Heritage   **Contact:** The Custodian

The principal town of the largest Roman tribe in Britain. The delightfully located remains include Roman defences and two mosaic pavements, a small museum displays finds.

Location: OS99 Ref. SE405 661. Close to Boroughbridge off A1.

Opening Times: 1 Apr - 30 Sept: daily, 10am - 6pm. 1 - 31 Oct: daily, 10am - 5pm. Closed 1 - 2pm.

Admission: Adult £1.80, Child 90p, Conc. £1.40. 15% discount for groups (11+).

ARCHAEOLOGICAL RESOURCE CENTRE

Tel: 01904 643211   **Fax:** 01904 627097   **e-mail:** arc@jvcyork.demon.co.uk

St Saviour's Church, St Saviourgate, York YO1 8NN

Owner: York Archaeological Trust   **Contact:** Nicola Bexon

Housed in the restored medieval church of St Saviour, the ARC offers a glimpse behind the scenes of a leading archaeological unit. Led by experienced archaeologists, visitors take part in hands-on activities with real finds, investigating a section of a layer from an archaeological dig and even examining Viking-Age artefacts.

Location: OS99 Ref. SE606 519. Central York, close to the Shambles.

Opening Times: School holidays: Mon - Sat, 11am - 3.30pm. Term time (pre-booked groups only): Mon - Fri, 10am - 3.30pm. Closed last two weeks of Dec & first week of Jan.

Admission: £3.60. Pre-booked groups (15+) £3.20. (valid to 30/4/01)

 Partially suitable. Obligatory. None. Guide dogs only.

ASKE HALL

See right.

BAGSHAW MUSEUM

Tel: 01924 326155   **Fax:** 01924 326164

Wilton Park, Batley, Yorkshire WF17 0AS

Owner: Kirklees Cultural Services   **Contact:** Melanie Brook

Travel through Asia, Africa and the Americas.

Location: OS Ref. SE235 257. From M62/J27 follow A62 to Huddersfield. At Birstall, follow tourist signs. Bagshaw Museum is approached through a small housing estate.

Opening Times: Mon - Fri, 11am - 5pm. Sats & Suns, 12 noon - 5pm. Pre-booked groups and school parties welcome.

Admission: Free.

BAYSGARTH HOUSE MUSEUM

Tel: 01652 632318

Caistor Road, Barton-on-Humber, North Lincolnshire DN18 6AH

Owner: North Lincolnshire Council   **Contact:** Mr D J Williams

18th century town house and park. Displays of porcelain and local history.

Location: OS Ref. TA035 215. Caistor Road, Barton-on-Humber.

Opening Times: Please contact for details.

Admission: Please contact for details.

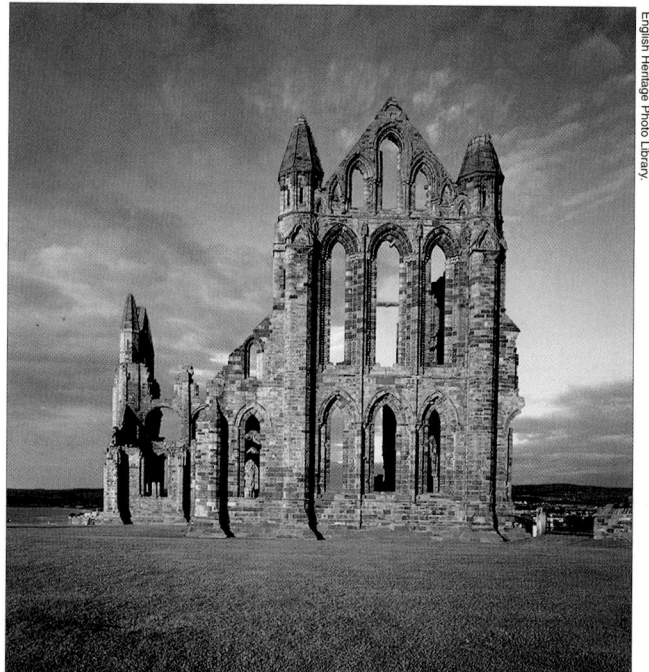

Whitby Abbey, Yorkshire.

English Heritage Photo Library

ASKE HALL

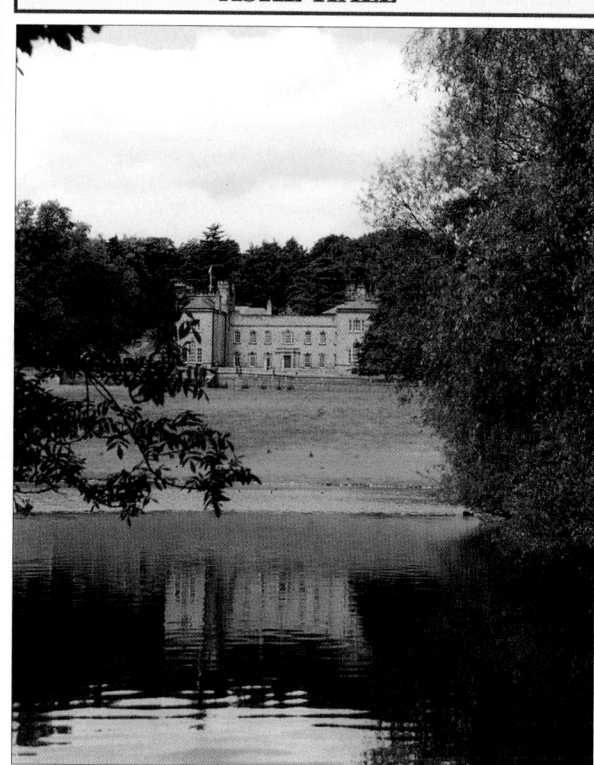

RICHMOND, NORTH YORKSHIRE DL10 5HJ

Owner: *The Marquess of Zetland*   **Contact:** *Mhairi Mercer*

Tel: 01748 850391   **Fax:** 01748 823252

Nestling in 'Capability' Brown landscaped parkland, Aske has been the family seat of the Dundas family since 1763. This Georgian treasure house boasts exquisite 18th century furniture, paintings and porcelain, including work by Robert Adam, Chippendale, Gainsborough, Raeburn and Meissen.

Aske is an architectural kaleidoscope. There is the original 13th century pele tower and remodelled Jacobean tower. John Carr's stable block, built in 1765, was later converted into a chapel with Italianate interior. A coach house with clock tower houses the family's carriage. There are follies and a lake as well as the new three tier terraced garden.

Location: OS Ref. NZ179 035. 2m SW of A1 at Scotch Corner, 1m from the A66, on the Gilling West road (B6274).

Opening Times: All year: for groups (15+) by appointment only.

Admission: House & grounds: Adult £6.50, Child £4.

Conferences. No photography in house. Partially suitable. By arrangement. In grounds on leads. Telephone for programme of special events.

BENINGBROUGH HALL & GARDENS

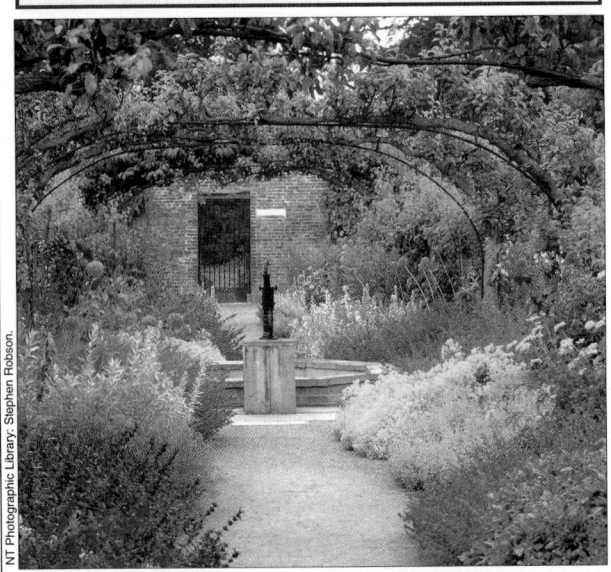

BENINGBROUGH, NORTH YORKSHIRE YO30 1DD

Owner: *The National Trust*   *Contact:* *The Visitor Services Manager*

Tel: 01904 470666 **Fax:** 01904 470002

Imposing 18th century house with over 100 portraits from the National Portrait Gallery. Walled garden, children's playground, Victorian laundry. Herbaceous borders and parkland.

Location: OS Ref. SE516 586. 8m NW of York, 3m W of Shipton, 2m SE of Linton-on-Ouse, follow signposted route.

Opening Times: 31 Mar - 31 Oct: Sat - Wed & Good Fri also Fris in Jul & Aug. House: 12 noon - 5pm. Last admission 4.30pm. Grounds: 11am - 5.30pm.

Admission: House & Garden: Adult £5.20, Child £2.60, Family £13. Garden: Adult £3.60, Child £1.80, Family £9.

◻ ♿ Partially suitable. WC. ♨ ✳ 🔔

BISHOPS' HOUSE
Tel: 0114 278 2600

Meersbrook Park, Norton Lees Lane, Sheffield, Yorkshire S8 9BE

Owner: Sheffield Galleries & Museums Trust   **Contact:** Ms K Streets

A beautiful 16th century timber-framed house, the oldest surviving building of its type in Sheffield.

Location: OS Ref. SK348 843. A61, 2m S of city centre E of the Chesterfield Road.

Opening Times: Sat, 10am - 4.30pm. Sun, 11am - 4.30pm. Mon - Fri: 10am - 3pm for pre-booked groups only.

Admission: Free.

BOLLING HALL MUSEUM
Tel: 01274 723057

Bowling Hall Road, Bradford, Yorkshire BD4 7LP

Owner: City of Bradford Metropolitan District Council   **Contact:** Jane Whittaker

Medieval tower with 17th century additions.

Location: OS Ref. SE174 315. 1¹/₂ m SE of Bradford centre, ¹/₄ m SE of A650.

Opening Times: Please telephone for details.

Admission: Free.

Bolling Hall Museum, Yorkshire.

BOLTON ABBEY

SKIPTON, NORTH YORKSHIRE BD23 6EX

Owner: *Trustees of the Chatsworth Settlement*   *Contact:* *Tourism Manager*

Tel: 01756 710533 **Fax:** 01756 710535

Wordsworth, Turner and Landseer were inspired by this romantic and varied landscape. The Estate, centred around Bolton Priory (founded 1154), is the Yorkshire home of the Duke and Duchess of Devonshire and provides 80 miles of footpaths to enjoy some of the most spectacular landscape in England.

Location: OS Ref. SE074 542. On B6160, N from the junction with A59 Skipton - Harrogate road, 23m from Leeds.

Opening Times: All year.

Admission: £3.50 per car, £2 for disabled (car park charge only).

◻ ⵀ ♿ ▣ Licensed. ♨ Licensed. Ⓟ ▥ ✖ In grounds, on leads.
🔔 ▤ Devonshire Arms Country House Hotel & Devonshire Fell Hotel nearby.
✳ Ⓦ

BOLTON CASTLE

LEYBURN, NORTH YORKSHIRE DL8 4ET

Owner/Contact: *Hon Mr & Mrs Harry Orde-Powlett*

Tel: 01969 623981 **Fax:** 01969 623332 **e-mail:** harry@boltoncastle.co.uk

A fine medieval castle that overlooks beautiful Wensleydale. Bolton Castle celebrated its 600th anniversary in 1999. Set your imagination free as you wander round this fascinating castle, which once held Mary Queen of Scots prisoner for 6 months and succumbed to a bitter Civil War siege. Don't miss the beautiful medieval garden and vineyard.

Location: OS Ref. SE034 918. Approx 6m from Leyburn. 1m NW of Redmire.

Opening Times: All year: daily, 10am - 5pm or dusk. Please telephone to confirm times from 14 Dec - 14 Feb.

Admission: Adult £4, Conc. £3. Groups: Adult £3, Conc. £2.

◻ ⵀ Wedding receptions. ♿ Partially suitable. ▣ Ⓟ ▥
✖ In grounds, on leads. 🔔 ✳ Ⓦ

BRAMHAM PARK

WETHERBY, WEST YORKSHIRE LS23 6ND

Owner: *George Lane Fox*   **Contact:** *Estate Office*

Tel: 01937 846005 **Fax:** 01937 846006

This Queen Anne house is 5 miles south of Wetherby on the A1, 10 miles from Leeds and 15 miles from York. The grand design of the gardens (66 acres) and pleasure grounds (100) are the only example of a formal, early 18th century landscape in the British Isles. Unexpected views and grand vistas, framed by monumental hedges and trees, delight the visitor, while temples, ornamental ponds and cascades focus the attention. The profusion of spring and summer wild flowers give a constant variety of colour and include many rare species.

Location: OS Ref. SE410 416. Half way from London to Edinburgh, 1m W of A1,

5m S of Wetherby, 10m NE of Leeds, 15m SW of York.

Opening Times: Gardens: 1 Apr - 30 Sept: daily, 10.30am - 5.30pm. Closed 7 - 10 Jun. House: by appointment for groups (6+).

Admission: Garden only: Adult £4, Child under 5yrs Free, Child (under 16yrs)/ OAP £2.

Grounds suitable. WC.   In grounds, on leads.

SPECIAL EVENTS

JUN 7 - 10: Bramham International Horse Trials & Yorkshire Country Fair.

BROCKFIELD HALL

Tel: 01904 489298

Warthill, York YO19 5XJ

Owner/Contact: Lord Martin Fitzalan Howard

Late Georgian house.

Location: OS Ref. SE664 550. 5m E of York off A166 or A64.

Opening Times: Aug: daily except Mons, 1 - 4pm. Tours by arrangement.

Admission: Adult £3.50, Child £1.

BRODSWORTH HALL & GARDENS   See page 368 for full page entry.

BRONTË PARSONAGE MUSEUM

Tel: 01535 642323 **Fax:** 01535 647131

e-mail: bronte@bronte.prestel.co.uk

Church St, Haworth, Keighley, West Yorkshire BD22 8DR

Owner: The Brontë Society   **Contact:** The Administrator

Georgian Parsonage, former home of the Brontë family, now a museum with rooms furnished as in the sisters' day and displays of their personal treasures.

Location: OS Ref. SE029 373. 8m W of Bradford, 3m S of Keighley.

Opening Times: Apr - Sept: 10am - 5.30pm, Oct - Mar: 11am - 5pm. Daily except 24 - 27 Dec & 8 Jan - 2 Feb 2001. Last admission ½ hour before closing.

Admission: Adult £4.50, Child £1.40, Conc. £3.30, Family £10. Discounts for booked groups.

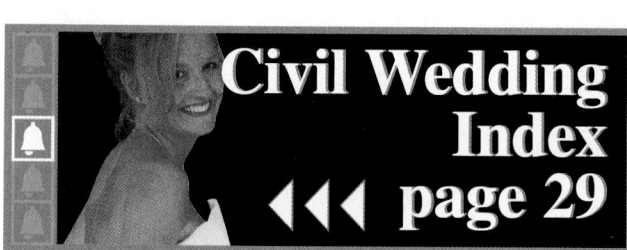

Civil Wedding Index ◀◀◀ page 29

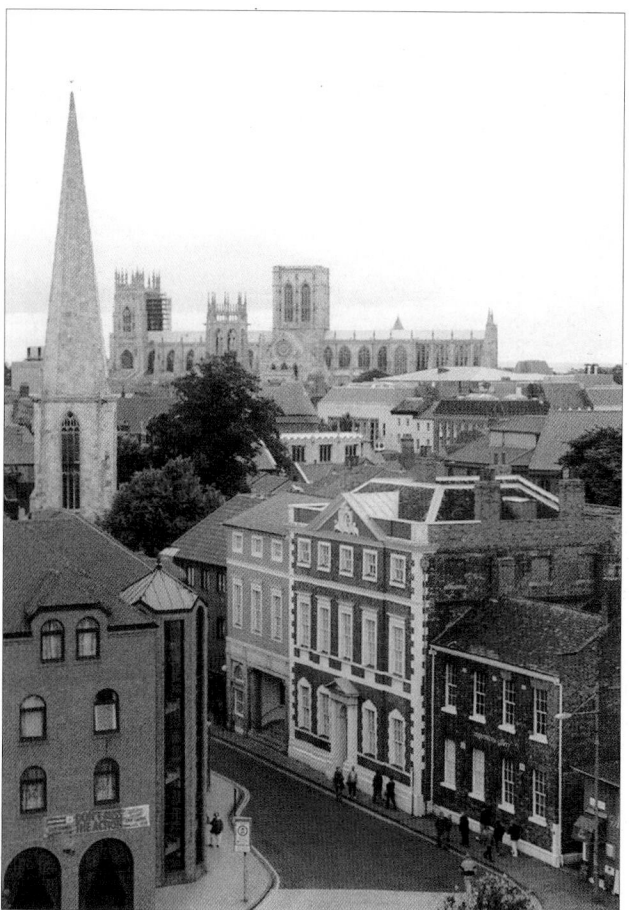

Patrick Lane.

View of York Minster (showing Fairfax House in the foreground), Yorkshire.

BROUGHTON HALL

SKIPTON, YORKSHIRE BD23 3AE

Tel: 01756 799608 **Fax:** 01756 700357
e-mail: tempest@broughtonhall.co.uk   **e-mail:** infor@ruralsolutions.co.uk

Owner: *The Tempest Family*   **Contact:** *The Estate Office*

The Hall was built in 1597 by the Tempest family and it continues to be their private home which provides it with a very special atmosphere. The building is Grade I listed and set in 3000 acres of parkland and rolling countryside. It is available to groups for tours by prior arrangement throughout the year and also as a prestigious venue for business promotions and functions. The grounds were designed by Nesfield in 1855 including fine Italianate gardens, gazebo, fountains and balustrades. The magnificent conservatory is a particular feature. Filming often takes place at Broughton with its wide diversity of settings and locations and the owners appreciate and understand production requirements.

Separate from the Hall is the Broughton Hall Business Park formed from listed Estate buildings housing 40 companies employing 500 people in quality office accommodation.

Location: OS Ref. SD943 507. On A59, 3m W of Skipton midway between the Yorkshire and Lancashire centres. Good air and rail links.

Open: Year round tours for groups by arrangement.

Admission: £5.

 By arrangement.

BURTON AGNES HALL

DRIFFIELD, YORKSHIRE YO25 0ND

Owner: *Burton Agnes Hall Preservation Trust Ltd*   **Contact:** *Mrs Susan Cunliffe-Lister*

Tel: 01262 490324 **Fax:** 01262 490513

A lovely Elizabethan Hall containing treasures collected by the family over four centuries from the original carving and plasterwork to modern and Impressionist paintings. The Hall is surrounded by lawns and topiary yew. The old walled garden contains a maze, potager, jungle garden, campanula collection and colour gardens incorporating giant game boards. Children's corner.

Location: OS Ref. TA103 633. Off A166 between Driffield and Bridlington.

Opening Times: 1 Apr - 31 Oct: daily, 11am - 5pm.

Admission: House & Gardens: Adult £4.80, Child £2.40, OAP £4.30. Gardens only: Adult £2.40, Child £1, OAP £2.20. 10% reduction for groups of 30+.

 Ground floor & grounds. Café. Ice-cream parlour.

Registered Charity No. 272796.

BURTON AGNES MANOR HOUSE   **Tel:** 01904 601901

Burton Agnes, Bridlington, Humberside

Owner: English Heritage   **Contact:** The North Regional Office

A rare example of a Norman house, altered and encased in brick in the 17th & 18th centuries.

Location: OS Ref. TA103 633. Burton Agnes village, 5m SW of Bridlington on A166.

Opening Times: Please telephone for details.

Admission: Free.

Burton Agnes Manor House, Yorkshire.

BURTON CONSTABLE HALL

SKIRLAUGH, EAST YORKSHIRE HU11 4LN

Owner: *Burton Constable Foundation*   **Contact:** *Mrs P Connelly*

Tel: 01964 562400 **Fax:** 01964 563229 **e-mail:** enquiries@burtonconstable.com

Built in the 16th century and set in 300 acres of parkland landscaped by 'Capability' Brown, Burton Constable Hall is the magnificent ancestral home of the Constable family. Superb interiors containing paintings, prints and fine English furniture. 30 rooms open to view including a unique 'Cabinet of Curiosities', a fascinating Lamp Room and servants' corridors.

Location: OS Ref. TA193 369. 14m E of Beverley via A165 Bridlington Road, follow Historic House signs. 7m NE of Hull via B1238 to Sproatley then follow Historic House signs.

Opening Times: Easter Sun - 31 Oct: Sat - Thur. Grounds & tearoom open 12 noon. Hall: 1 - 5pm.

Admission: Hall & Grounds: Adult £4, Child £1.50, OAP £3.70, Family £9. Grounds only: Adult £1, Child 50p. Groups (30+): special rates available.

ℹ️ No photography in house. 📷 ♿ 🖥️ 🎦 By arrangement. P 🏛️
🐕 In grounds on leads. ♿

Registered Charity No. 1010121

BYLAND ABBEY ⌗

Tel: 01347 868614

Coxwold, Helmsley, North Yorkshire YO6 4BD

Owner: English Heritage   **Contact:** The Custodian

Hauntingly beautiful ruin, set in peaceful meadows in the shadow of the Hambleton Hills. It illustrates later development of Cistercian churches, including a beautiful floor of mosaic tiles.

Location: OS100 Ref. SE549 789. 2m S of A170 between Thirsk and Helmsley, NE of Coxwold village.

Opening Times: 1 Apr - 30 Sept: daily 10am - 6pm. 1 - 31 Oct: daily, 10am - 5pm. Closed 1 - 2pm.

Admission: Adult £1.70, Child 90p, Conc. £1.30. 15% discount for groups (11+).

♿ P Limited. 🏛️ 🐕 On leads. ♿ Tel. for details.

CANNON HALL MUSEUM, PARK & GARDENS

Tel: 01226 790270

Cawthorne, Barnsley, South Yorkshire S75 4AT   **Fax:** 01226 792117
e-mail: cannonhall@barnsley.gov.uk

Owner: Barnsley Metropolitan Borough Council   **Contact:** The Keeper

Late 17th century house, remodelled in the 1760s by John Carr. Contains decorative arts collections including fine furniture and paintings. Moorcroft pottery and Glass galleries. Also the Regimental Museum of the 13th/18th Hussars. Surrounding 18th century park landscaped by Richard Woods, with Walled Garden. Events and education programme.

Location: OS Ref. SE272 084. 6m NW of Barnsley of A635.

Opening Times: 1 Nov - 31 Mar: Sats, 10.30am - 5pm. Suns, 12 noon - 5pm. 1 Apr - 31 Oct: Tue - Sat, 10.30am - 5pm. Suns, 12 noon - 5pm. Last admission 4.15pm. Closed Christmas and New Year's Day. Open BH Mons.

Admission: Adults £1, Child/Conc. 50p, (2000 prices, subject to change.). Group discount (10+).

📷 🍴 ♿ Partially suitable. WC. 🎦 Seasonal. P 🏛️
🐕 In grounds, on leads. ❄ ♿ Please telephone for details.

CASTLE HOWARD 🏛️   **See page 369 for full page entry.**

CAWTHORNE VICTORIA JUBILEE MUSEUM   **Tel:** 01226 790545/790246

Taylor Hill, Cawthorne, Barnsley, Yorkshire S75 4HQ

Owner: Cawthorne Village   **Contact:** Mrs Mary Herbert

A quaint and eccentric collection with something for everyone in a half-timbered building. Museum has a ramp and toilet for disabled visitors. School visits welcome.

Location: OS Ref. SE285 080. 4m W of Barnsley, just off the A635.

Opening Times: Palm Sun - end Oct: Sats, Suns & BH Mons, 2 - 5pm. Groups by appointment throughout the year.

Admission: Adult 50p, Child 20p.

CLIFFE CASTLE   **Tel:** 01535 618231

Keighley, West Yorkshire BD20 6LH

Owner: City of Bradford Metropolitan District Council   **Contact:** Jane Whittaker

Typical Victorian manufacturer's mansion of 1878 with tall tower and garden. Now a museum.

Location: OS Ref. SE057 422. ³⁄₄ m NW of Keighley off the A629.

Opening Times: Please telephone for details.

Admission: Free.

CLIFFORD'S TOWER ⌗   **Tel:** 01904 646940

Clifford Street, York, Yorkshire YO1 1SA

Owner: English Heritage   **Contact:** The Custodian

A 13th century tower on one of two mottes thrown up by William the Conqueror to hold York. There are panoramic views of the city from the top of the tower.

Location: OS105 Ref. SE 605 515. York city centre.

Opening Times: 1 Apr - 30 Sept: daily, 10am - 6pm (Aug: 9.30am - 7pm). 1 - 31 Oct: daily, 10am - 5pm. 1 Nov - 31 Mar: daily, 10am - 4pm. Closed 24/25 Dec.

Admission: Adult £2, Child £1, Conc. £1.50. Family ticket £5. 15% discount available for groups (11+).

📷 ♿ Not suitable. 🏛️ 🐕 In grounds, on leads. ❄

CLIFTON PARK MUSEUM   **Tel:** 01709 823635

Clifton Park, Rotherham, Yorkshire S65 2AA

Owner: Rotherham Metropolitan Borough Council.   **Contact:** Guy Kilminster

Furnished period rooms and one of the best collections of Rockingham porcelain in the country in an 18th century house set within a delightful park.

Location: OS Ref. SK435 926.

Opening Times: Mon - Thur & Sats, 10am - 5pm. Suns, 1.30 - 5pm (Apr - Sept) & 1.30 - 4.30pm (Oct - Mar).

Admission: Free.

❄ 🅦

CONISBROUGH CASTLE ⌗   **Tel:** 01709 863329

Conisbrough, Yorkshire

Owner: English Heritage   **Contact:** The Administrator

The oldest circular keep in England and one of the finest medieval buildings.

Location: OS111 Ref. SK515 989. 4¹⁄₂ m SW of Doncaster.

Opening Times: 1 Apr - 30 Sept: daily 10am - 5pm (6pm at weekends & BHs). 10 Oct - 31 Mar: daily, 10am - 4pm.

Admission: Adults £2.80, Child £1, Conc. £1.80, Family £6.75.

Shibden Hall, Yorkshire.

Patrick Lane.

CONSTABLE BURTON HALL GARDENS 🏛

LEYBURN, NORTH YORKSHIRE DL8 5LJ

Owner/Contact: *M C A Wyvill Esq*

Tel: 01677 450428   **Fax:** 01677.450622

A delightful terraced woodland garden of lilies, ferns, hardy shrubs, roses and wild flowers, attached to a beautiful Palladian house designed by John Carr (not open). Garden trails, rockery with an interesting collection of alpines. Stream garden with large architectural plants and reflection ponds. Impressive spring display of daffodils, aconites and snowdrops.

Location: OS Ref. SE164 913. 3m E of Leyburn off the A684.

Opening Times: Garden only: 24 Mar - 14 Oct: daily, 9am - 6pm.

Admission: Adult £2.50, Child (under 16yrs) 50p, OAP £2.

🛡 Tel. for details.

DUNCOMBE PARK 🏛

HELMSLEY, YORK YO62 5EB

Owner/Contact: *Lord & Lady Feversham*

Tel: 01439 770213   **Fax:** 01439 771114   **e-mail:** sally@duncombepark.com

Lord and Lady Feversham's restored family home in the North York Moors National Park. Built on a virgin plateau overlooking Norman Castle and river valley, it is surrounded by 35 acres of beautiful 18th century landscaped gardens and 400 acres of parkland with national nature reserve and veteran trees.

Location: OS SE604 830. Entrance just off Helmsley Market Square, signed off A170 Thirsk - Scarborough road.

Opening Times: 13 Apr - 28 Oct: Sun - Thur. House & Gardens: 10.30am - 6pm (last admission 4pm). Parkland, tearoom, shop & walks: 10.30am - 5.30pm (last orders in tearoom 5.15pm).

Admission: House & Gardens: Adult £6, Child £3, Conc. £5, Family (2+2) £13.50 Groups (15+) £4.50. Gardens & Parkland: Adult £4, Child (10-16yrs) £2. Parkland: Adult £2, Child (10-16yrs) £1. Season ticket (2+2) £20.

ℹ Country walks, nature reserve, orienteering, conferences.

📷 ♿ 🍽 Banqueting facilities. ♿ Partially suitable. 🅿 Licensed. 🚶 Obligatory. 🅿 🔔 🐕 In park on leads. 🔔 🛡 Tel. for details. 🅾

CRAKEHALL WATERMILL   **Tel:** 01677 423240

Little Crakehall, Nr Bedale, North Yorkshire DL8 1HU

Owner/Contact: Mrs Gill

Site of a mill since 1086, still milling stone-ground wholemeal flour.

Location: OS Ref. SE244 902. ½ m from village centre.

Opening Times: Easter - End September: Closed Mons & Tues. Please telephone for details.

Admission: Adult £1, Child/OAP 60p (2000 prices).

DANBY WATERMILL   **Tel:** 01287 660330

Danby, Whitby, Yorkshire YO21 2JL

Owner/Contact: Frank & Brenda Palmer

350 year old watermill restored to working order.

Location: OS Ref. NZ708 082. ½ m S of village.

Opening Times: Please contact for details.

Admission: Adult £1.50, Child/OAP 75p (2000 prices).

Duncombe Park, Yorkshire.

EASBY ABBEY ⛬   **Tel:** 01904 601901

Nr Richmond, North Yorkshire

Owner: English Heritage   **Contact:** The Custodian

Substantial remains of the medieval abbey buildings stand by the River Swale near Richmond.

Location: OS92 Ref. NZ185 003. 1m SE of Richmond off B6271.

Opening Times: Any reasonable time.

Admission: Free.

EAST RIDDLESDEN HALL   **Tel:** 01535 607075   **Fax:** 01535 691462

Bradford Road, Keighley, West Yorkshire BD20 5EL

Owner: The National Trust   **Contact:** Assistant Property Manager

Homely 17th century merchant's house with beautiful embroideries and textiles, Yorkshire carved oak furniture and fine ceilings. Delightful garden with lavender and herbs. Also wild garden with old varieties of apple trees. Magnificent Great Barn with timber structure. Handling collection Events.

Location: OS104 SE079 421. 1m NE of Keighley on S side of B6265 in Riddlesden. 50yds from Leeds/Liverpool Canal. Bus: Frequent services from Skipton, Bradford and Leeds. Railway station at Keighley 2m.

Opening Times: 31 Mar - 4 Nov: daily except Mons, Thurs & Fris (open Good Fri, BH Mons & Mons in Jul & Aug), 12 noon - 5pm, Sats, 1 - 5pm.

Admission: Adult £3.50, Child £1.80, Family £8.80.

📷 🍽 ♿ Partially suitable. WC. 🅿 🚶 🐕 🅿 Limited for coaches, please book. ✖ 🔔 🛡 Tel. for details.

ELSHAM HALL COUNTRY & WILDLIFE PARK & BARN THEATRE

Elsham, Brigg, Lincolnshire DN20 0QZ   **Tel:** 01652 688698   **Fax:** 01652 688240

Owner: Elwes Trust   **Contact:** Robert Elwes

Winner of Ten Awards for Tourism. Attractions include Falconry Centre, the Mini Zoo, Georgian Courtyard, Craft Workshops, Arboretum, Theatre and Conference Centre, Clocktower Museum, Garden Centre and beautiful lakeside gardens with Carp and Trout Lakes.

Location: OS Ref. TA030 120. 10 mins from M180/J5, Humber Bridge turn-off.

Opening Times: Easter - mid Sept: daily, closed Mons (except on Bank holidays and during Spring/Summer Holidays) 11am - 5pm. Theatre & Craft Centre open separately.

Admission: Adult £3.95, Child £2.50 (3+), OAP £3.75. Group rates for groups (20+).

📷 🍽 🍽 Medieval banquets. 🍽 Licensed. 🚶 By arrangement. 🐕 Guide dogs only. 🔔 🅾

EPWORTH OLD RECTORY

Tel: 01427 872268

1 Rectory Street, Epworth, Doncaster, South Yorkshire DN9 1HX

e-mail: epworth@oldrectory63.freeserve.co.uk

Owner: World Methodist Council   **Contact:** A Milson (Curator/Warden)

1709 Queen Anne period house, John and Charles Wesley's boyhood home. Portraits, period furniture, Methodist memorabilia. Garden, picnic facilities, cinematic presentation.

Location: OS Ref. SE785 036. Epworth lies on A161, 3m S M180/J2. 10m N of Gainsborough. When in Epworth follow the Wesley Trail information boards.

Opening Times: 1 Mar - 31 Oct. Mar, Apr & Oct: Mon - Sat, 10am - 12 noon & 2 - 4pm, Suns, 2 - 4pm. May - Sept: Mon - Sat, 10am - 4.30pm, Suns, 2 - 4.30pm.

Admission: Adult £2.50, Children in full-time education £1, OAP £2, Family £6. (2000 prices)

🗖 &Ground floor & grounds suitable. 🖝By arrangement. 🎬Obligatory. 🅿Limited. 🔲 🐕Guide dogs only. 🛏2 twins.

FAIRFAX HOUSE 🏛

See page 370 for full page entry.

FOUNTAINS ABBEY & STUDLEY ROYAL 🌿

See page 371 for entry.

HANDS ON HISTORY

Tel: 01482 613902 **Fax:** 01482 613710

Market Place, Hull HU1 1EP

Owner: Hull City Council   **Contact:** S R Green

Housed in the Old Grammar School this history resource centre offers hands on activities for the public and schools alike.

Location: OS Ref. TA099 285. 50 yds SW of the Church at centre of the Old Town.

Opening Times: School holidays and weekends open to the public. Please phone for details.

Admission: Free.

HAREWOOD HOUSE

See page 372 for full page entry.

HARLOW CARR BOTANICAL GARDENS Tel: 01423 565418 **Fax:** 01423 530663

Crag Lane, Harrogate, North Yorkshire HG3 1QB

e-mail: admin@harlowcarr.fsnet.co.uk

Owner: Northern Horticultural Society   **Contact:** Admin Manager

68 acre headquarters of the Northern Horticultural Society. Vegetable, fruit and flower trials; rock, foliage, winter and heather gardens; alpines and herbaceous beds.

Location: OS Ref. SE285 543. Off Otley Rd (B6162). 1¹/₂ m W from town centre.

Opening Times: Daily from 9.30am. Last admission 6pm or dusk if earlier.

Admission: Adult £4.50, Child (11-16yrs) £1, Child (under 11yrs) Free, OAPs/Groups (20+): £3.50.

HELMSLEY CASTLE ⚏

Tel: 014397 70442

Helmsley, North Yorkshire YO6 5AB

Owner: English Heritage   **Contact:** The Custodian

Close to the market square, with a view of the town, is this 12th century castle. Spectacular earthworks surround a great ruined Norman keep. Exhibition and tableau on the castle's history.

Location: OS100 SE611 836. In Helmsley town.

Opening Times: 1 Apr - 30 Sept: daily, 10am - 6pm. 1 - 31 Oct, daily, 10am - 5pm. 1 Nov - 31 Mar: Wed - Sun, 10am - 4pm (closed 1 - 2pm). Closed 24 - 26 Dec.

Admission: Adult £2.40, Child £1.20, Conc £1.80. 15% discount for groups (11+).

🗖 ❄ 🖾 Tel. for details.

HELMSLEY WALLED GARDEN

Tel/Fax: 01439 771427

Cleveland Way, Helmsley, North Yorkshire YO6 5AH

Owner: Helmsley Walled Garden Ltd   **Contact:** Paul Radcliffe/Lindsay Tait

A 5 acre walled garden under restoration. Orchid house being re-built. Plant sales area and café conservatory.

Location: OS100 SE611 836. 25m N of York, 15m from Thirsk. In Helmsley follow signs to Cleveland Way.

Open: 1 Apr - 31 Oct: daily, 10.30am - 5pm. Nov - Mar: Sats/Suns, 12 noon - 4pm.

Admission: Adult £2.50, Child Free, Conc. £1.50.

HOVINGHAM HALL

Tel: 01653 628206 **Fax:** 01653 628668

York, North Yorkshire YO62 4LU

Owner: Sir Marcus Worsley   **Contact:** Mrs Lamprey

Palladian house built c1760 by Thomas Worsley to his own design. Unique entry by huge riding school. Visitors see family portraits and rooms in everyday use; also extensive gardens with magnificent yew hedges, dovecot and private cricket ground, said to be the oldest in England.

Location: OS Ref. SE666 756. 18m N of York on Malton/Helmsley Road (B1257).

Opening Times: Apr - 30 Sept: 11am - 7pm by appointment only.

Admission: Adult £4. Groups(15+): £60 min. charge.

ℹNo photography in house. 🗖 🎦 & Partially suitable. 🖝 🎬Obligatory. 🅿 🐕Guide dogs only.

JERVAULX ABBEY

Tel: 01677 460391

Ripon, Yorkshire HG4 4PH

Owner/Contact: Mr I S Burdon

Extensive ruins of a former Cistercian abbey.

Location: OS100 Ref. SE169 858. Beside the A6108 Ripon - Leyburn road, 5m SE of Leyburn and 5m NW of Masham.

Opening Times: Daily during daylight hours. Visitor centre: Mar - end Nov: daily, 10am - 5pm.

Admission: Adult £2, Child £1.50.

KIPLIN HALL 🏛

KIPLIN, Nr SCORTON, RICHMOND, NORTH YORKSHIRE DL10 6AT

Owner: Kiplin Hall Trustees   *Contact: The Administrator*

Tel/Fax: 01748 818178

A Grade I Jacobean House built in 1620 by George Calvert, First Lord Baltimore, founder of the State of Maryland, USA, it contains a fascinating collection of paintings and furniture collected by different families over four centuries. Some rooms are undergoing major refurbishment and visitors should contact the Administrator for details of what can be viewed.

Location: OS Ref. SE274 976. Signposted from Scorton - Northallerton road (B6271).

Opening Times: 1 Jul - 2 Sept: daily except Mons, 2 - 5pm. Open at other times of the year by appointment with the Administrator.

Admission: Adult £3.50, Child £1.75, Conc. £2. Groups by arrangement.

Hovingham Hall, Yorkshire.

KIRKHAM PRIORY

Tel: 01653 618768

Kirkham, Whitwell-on-the-Hill, Yorkshire YO6 7JS

Owner: English Heritage   **Contact:** The Custodian

The ruins of this Augustinian priory include a magnificent carved gatehouse.

Location: OS100 Ref. SE735 657. 5m SW of Malton on minor road off A64.

Opening Times: 1 Apr - 30 Sept: daily, 10am - 6pm. 1 - 31 Oct: daily, 10am - 5pm.

Admission: Adult £1.70, Child 90p, Conc. £1.30. 15% discount for groups (11+).

🖭   🚻   **P**Limited.   🚌   🐕On leads.

KNARESBOROUGH CASTLE

Tel: 01423 556188   **Fax:** 01423 556130

Knaresborough, North Yorkshire HG5 8AS   **e-mail:** lg12@harrogate.gov.uk

Owner: Duchy of Lancaster   **Contact:** Ms Vanessa Hirst

Ruins of 14th century castle standing high above the town. Local history museum housed in Tudor Courthouse. Gallery devoted to the Civil War.

Location: OS Ref. SE349 569. 5m E of Harrogate, off A59.

Opening Times: Easter BH - 30 Sept: daily, 10.30am - 5pm.

Admission: Adult £2, Child/OAP £1.50, Family £5.50, Groups (10+) £1.50.

LEDSTON HALL

Tel: 01423 523423   **Fax:** 01423 521373

Hall Lane, Ledston, Castleford, West Yorkshire WF10 2BB

Owner/Contact: James Hare

17th century mansion with some earlier work.

Location: OS Ref. SE437 289. 2m N of Castleford, off A656.

Opening Times: Exterior only: May - Aug, Mon - Fri, 9am - 4pm. Other days by appointment.

Admission: Free.

LING BEECHES GARDEN

Tel: 0113 2892450

Ling Lane, Scarcroft, Leeds, Yorkshire LS14 3HX

Owner/Contact: Mrs A Rakusen

A 2 acre woodland garden designed by the owner.

Location: OS Ref. SE354 413. Off A58 midway between Leeds & Wetherby. At Scarcroft turn into Ling Lane, signed to Wike on brow of hill.

Opening Times: Twice a year for Northern Horticultural Society (telephone for details). Also by appointment.

Admission: Adult £2.50, Child Free.

LONGLEY OLD HALL

Tel: 01484 430852   **e-mail:** robingallagher@debrett.net

Longley, Huddersfield HD5 8LB

Owner: Christine & Robin Gallagher   **Contact:** Christine Gallagher

This timber framed Grade II* manor house dates from the 15th century and was owned by the Rambden family, the Lords of the Manors of Huddersfield and Almondbury, for 400 years. 2001 will see the end of the main restoration work and the start of the Elizabethan Garden.

Location: OS Ref. SE157 117. 1½ m SE of Huddersfield centre towards Castle Hill.

Opening Times: By appointment.

Admission: Please contact for details.

🍽   🚻Not suitable.   🚶Obligatory. By arrangement.   **P**Limited for coaches.   ❋

LOTHERTON HALL

Tel: 0113 2813259   **Fax:** 0113 2812100

Aberford, West Yorkshire LS25 3EB

Owner: Leeds City Council   **Contact:** Adam White

Late Victorian and Edwardian country house of great charm and character.

Location: OS92 Ref. SE450 360. 2½ m E of M1 J47 on B2177 the Towton Road.

Opening Times: 1 Apr - 31 Oct: Tue - Sat, 10am - 5pm, Suns, 1 - 5pm. 1 Nov - 31 Dec & Mar: Tue - Sat, 10am - 4pm, Suns, 12 noon - 4pm. Closed Jan & Feb.

Admission: Adult £2, Child 50p, Conc. £1. Groups: £1. Parking: £5 includes 1 yrs free admission to house. Day ticket: £2.

MARKENFIELD HALL

Tel: 01609 780306   **Fax:** 01609 777510

Nr Ripon, North Yorkshire HG4 3AD

Owner: The Lady Grantley   **Contact:** Strutt & Parker

Fine example of a moated English Manor House (14th and 15th century).

Location: OS Ref. SE294 672. Local access from gate on W side A61, 3m S of Ripon.

Opening Times: Groups by appointment only.

Admission: Please contact for details.

MERCHANT ADVENTURERS' HALL

FOSSGATE, YORK YO1 9XD

Owner: The Company of Merchant Adventurers   *Contact:* The Clerk

Tel/Fax: 01904 654818   **e-mail:** The.Clerk@mahall-york.demon.co.uk

The finest medieval guild hall in Europe, built in 1357/62 and substantially unaltered. In it the Merchants transacted their business, as their successors still do today. On the ground floor was their hospice, where they cared for the poor, and their private chapel, a unique survival in England. There are good collections of early portraits, furniture, silver and other objects used by the Merchants over the centuries, when their wealth and influence helped to make York the second city in England after London.

Location: OS Ref. SE606 518. Main entrance in Piccadilly, other entrance in Fossgate.

Opening Times: 2 Jan - 8 Apr, 6 Oct - 30 Mar: Mon - Sat, 9am - 3.30pm (closed Suns). 9 Apr - 5 Oct: Mon - Sat, 9am - 5pm, Suns, 12 noon - 4pm. Closed 24 Dec - 1 Jan 01.

Admission: Adult £2, Child (7-17yrs) 70p, Child under 7 Free, Conc. £1.70. Group rates available by prior arrangement.

🍽Wedding receptions.   🚻Ground floor & grounds suitable. WCs.   🚶By arrangement.   🚌   🐕In grounds, on leads.   🔔   ❋   ⓌⒾ

MIDDLEHAM CASTLE

Tel: 01969 623899

Middleham, Leyburn, Yorkshire DL8 4RJ

Owner: English Heritage   **Contact:** The Custodian

This childhood home of Richard III stands controlling the river that winds through Wensleydale. There is a massive 12th century keep with splendid views of the surrounding countryside from the battlements.

Location: OS99 Ref. SE128 875. At Middleham, 2m S of Leyburn of A6108.

Opening Times: 1 Apr - 30 Sept: daily, 10am - 6pm. 1 - 31 Oct, daily, 10am - 5pm. 1 Nov - 31 Mar: Wed - Sun, 10am - 4pm (closed 1 - 2pm). Closed 24 - 26 Dec.

Admission: Adult £2.40, Child £1.20, Conc. £1.80. 15% discount for groups (11+).

ⓘExhibition.   🖭   🚻Grounds suitable.   🚌   🐕In grounds, on leads.   ❋   🎫 Tel. for details.

MOTHER SHIPTON'S CAVE & PETRIFYING WELL

Tel: 01423 864600

Prophecy House, Knaresborough, North Yorkshire HG5 8DD

         Contact: Mr McBratney, General Manager

The cave and well lie at the heart of the Mother Shipton Estate - a relic of the ancient forest of Knaresborough.

Location: OS Ref. SE346 565. Access from A59 at S end of bridge then by riverside footpath.

Opening Times: 12 Feb - Sunday 2 Dec: daily 9.30am - 5pm. Also open weekends from 3 Dec - 11 Feb (2002).

Admission: Adult £4.95, Child £3.95 (under 5yrs Free), OAP £4.45, Family (2+2) £13.85. (2000 prices.)

MOUNT GRACE PRIORY

SADDLE BRIDGE, NORTH YORKSHIRE DL6 3JG

Owner: *National Trust*   **Managed by:** *English Heritage*   **Contact:** *The Custodian*

Tel: 01609 883494

Hidden in tranquil wooded countryside at the foot of the Cleveland Hills, one of the loveliest settings of any English priory, and the best preserved Carthusian monastery in England. Monks lived as hermits in their cells and one cell, recently restored, is furnished to give a clear picture of their austere routine of work and prayer. Visitors enter through the manor built by Thomas Lascelles in 1654 on the site of the monastery guest house. It was rebuilt at the turn of the century using traditional techniques, typical of the Arts and Crafts movement.

Location: OS Ref. SE449 985. 12m N of Thirsk, 7m NE of Northallerton on A19.

Opening Times: 1 Apr - 30 Sept: daily, 10am - 6pm. 1 - 31 Oct: daily, 10am - 5pm. 1 Nov - 31 Mar: Wed - Sun, 10am - 4pm (closed 1 - 2pm). Closed 24 - 26 Dec.

Admission: Adult £2.90, Child £1.50, Conc. £2.20. 15% discount for groups (11+).

Ground floor & grounds suitable. Tel. for details.

THE MUSEUM OF SOUTH YORKSHIRE LIFE
Tel: 01302 782342

Cusworth Hall, Cusworth Lane, Doncaster, South Yorkshire DN5 7TU

Owner: Doncaster Metropolitan Borough Council   **Contact:** Mr F Carpenter, Curator

A magnificent Grade I country house set in a landscaped parkland and built in 1740, with a chapel and other rooms designed by James Paine, the house is now the home of a museum showing the changing home, work and social conditions of the region over the last 250 years. Regular events and activities.

Location: OS Ref. SE547 039. A1(M)/J37, then A635 and right into Cusworth Lane.

Opening Times: Mon - Fri, 10am - 5pm. Sats, 11am - 5pm, Suns, 1 - 5pm. Closes at 4pm Dec & Jan.

Admission: Free.

NEWBURGH PRIORY
Tel: 01347 868435

Coxwold, York YO61 4AS

Owner/Contact: Sir George Wombwell Bt

Augustinian priory founded in 1145 converted into Tudor mansion, and again later in 18th century. Beautiful water garden.

Location: OS Ref. SE541 764. 7m SE Thirsk. ½ m SE of Coxwold.

Opening Times: Apr - end Jun: Weds & Suns: House: 2.30 - 4.45pm, Garden: 2 - 6pm. Guided tours approx 60 mins.

Admission: Gardens only: £2, Child Free. House & Grounds: £4. Child £1.

NEWBY HALL & GARDENS
See page 373 for full page entry.

NORMANBY HALL
See opposite for half page entry.

NORMANBY HALL

NORMANBY, SCUNTHORPE, NORTH LINCOLNSHIRE DN15 9HU

Owner: *North Lincolnshire Council*   **Contact:** *Park Manager*

Tel: 01724 720588 **Fax:** 01724 721248

The restored working Victorian Walled Kitchen Garden is growing produce for the 'big house' as it would have done 100 years ago. Victorian varieties of fruit and vegetables are grown using organic and Victorian techniques. Set in 300 acres of Park, visitors may also see the Regency Mansion, designed by Sir Robert Smirke, which the Garden was built to serve.

The ground floor rooms of the Hall are displayed in Regency style, while those upstairs reflect the changing styles of the Victorian and Edwardian eras. Costume from the Museum Service's collections is also exhibited.

Location: OS Ref. SE886 166. 4m N of Scunthorpe off B1430. Follow signs for M181 & Humber Bridge. Tours by arrangement.

Opening Times: Hall & Farming Museum: 26 Mar - 30 Sept: 1 - 5pm. Park: daily, 9am - dusk. Walled Garden: daily, 10.30am - 5pm (4pm in winter). Last admission at all venues ½ hour before closing.

Admission: Summer Season: Adult £2.90, Conc. £1.90, Family (2+3) £8. Discounts for North Lincolnshire residents. Winter Season: £2.20 per car. (2000 rates).

All details correct at time of going to press. For up to date information, please contact Normanby Hall Country Park.

Wedding receptions. Ground floor & grounds. WC. By arrangement. In grounds, on leads. Tel. for details.

NORTON CONYERS

Tel/Fax: 01765 640333

Nr Ripon, North Yorkshire HG4 5EQ
e-mail: norton.conyers@ripon.org
Owner: Sir James and Lady Graham
Contact: Lady Graham

Visited by Charlotte Brontë in 1839, Norton Conyers is an original of the 'Thornfield Hall' in *Jane Eyre* and a family legend was an inspiration for the mad Mrs Rochester. Building is late medieval with Stuart and Georgian additions. Friendly atmosphere, resulting from 377 years of occupation by the same family. 18th century walled garden near house, with orangery and herbaceous borders. Small plant sales area specialising in unusual hardy plants. Pick your own fruit in season.

Location: OS Ref. SF319 763. 4m N of Ripon. 3^1/$_2$m from the A1.

Opening Times: House & Garden: Easter Sun & Mon. BH Suns & Mons. Suns 13 May - 9 Sept. Daily 9 - 14 Jul. House: 2 - 5pm. Garden 11.30am - 5pm.

Admission: House: Adult £4, Child (10-16yrs)/Conc. £3. Reduced rate for two or more children. Garden: Free (donations welcome), but charges are made at charity openings.

ⓘ No photography. No stilettos in house. Partially suitable. WC. By arrangement. P In grounds, on leads.

NOSTELL PRIORY

DONCASTER ROAD, WAKEFIELD, WEST YORKSHIRE WF4 1QE

Owner: The National Trust *Contact:* The Property Manager

Tel: 01924 863892 **Fax:** 01924 865282

After a closed period of 18 months during which Nostell Priory, one of Yorkshire's finest jewels, benefited from substantial building works, redecoration and upgrading. The present house is an 18th century architectural masterpiece by James Paine built on the site of a medieval priory for Sir Rowland Winn, 4th Baronet, in 1733. Later, Robert Adam was commissioned to complete the State Rooms which are amongst the finest examples of his interiors. The Priory houses one of England's finest collections of Chippendale furniture, designed specially for the house by the great cabinet maker who was once apprentice on the estate. Nostell Priory's other treasures include an outstanding art collection with works by Pieter Breughel the younger and Angelica Kaufmann and the remarkable 18th century dolls house, complete with its original fittings and Chippendale furniture. In the grounds are delightful lakeside walks with a stunning collection of rhododendrons and azaleas in late spring. New attractions for this year include a new shop and guidebook, restoration of the Adam library and opening of the domestic areas of the house which include the Servant's Hall and unrestored Great Kitchen which houses an exhibition of recent works.

Location: OS Ref. SE403 175. 6m SE of Wakefield, off A638.

Opening Times: House: 31 Mar - 4 Nov: Wed - Sun & BH Mons, 1 - 5.30pm. 10 Nov - 9 Dec: Sats & Suns, 12 noon - 4.30pm. Grounds: as house, 11am - 6pm.

Admission: House & Gardens: Adult £4.50, Child £2.20, Family £11. Grounds only: Adult £2.50, Child £1.20. Guided tours for booked groups only, outside normal opening times: £250 min charge. Shop: Wed - Sun: 11am - 6pm.

ⓘ Baby facilities. Partially suitable. WC. By arrangement. P In grounds, on leads. Send SAE for details.

Scarborough Castle, Yorkshire.

NUNNINGTON HALL

NUNNINGTON, NORTH YORKSHIRE YO62 5UY

Owner: The National Trust *Contact:* The Visitor Manager

Tel: 01439 748283 **Fax:** 01439 748284

The sheltered walled garden on the bank of the River Rye with its delightful mixed borders, orchards of traditional Ryedale fruit varieties and spring flowering meadows, complements this mellow 17th century manor house. From the magnificent oak-panelled hall, follow three staircases to discover family rooms, the nursery, the haunted room and the attics, with their fascinating Carlisle collection of miniature rooms fully furnished to reflect different periods.

Location: OS Ref. SE670 795. In Ryedale, 4^1/$_2$ m SE of Helmsley, 1^1/$_2$ m N of B1257.

Opening Times: 31 Mar - 4 Nov: Wed - Sun & BH Mons. 1 Jun - 31 Aug: daily except Mons (open BH Mons). Apr - Oct: 1.30 - 4.30pm. 1 May - end Sept: 1.30 - 5pm.

Admission: House and Garden: Adult £4.50, Child £2. Family (2+3) £11. Garden only: Adult £2, Child Free. Groups (15+): £4.

Ground floor & grounds suitable. WC. 12.30 - 5pm. Guide dogs only.

OAKWELL HALL COUNTRY PARK

Tel: 01924 326240 **Fax:** 01924 326249

Nutter Lane, Birstall, Batley, West Yorkshire WF17 9LG

Owner: Kirklees Cultural Services

Location: OS99 Ref. SE217 271. On A652 in Birstall. Take J27/A62 towards Huddersfield to Birstall.

Opening Times: All year: Mon - Fri, 11am - 5pm. Sats & Suns, 12 noon - 5pm.

Admission: Adult £1.20, Child 50p, Family £2.50. Discounts available for booked groups. Admission charge seasonal - 2000 prices.

OLD SLENINGFORD HALL

Tel: 01765 635229 **Fax:** 01765 635485

Ripon, North Yorkshire HG4 3JD
e-mail: oldslen@fsnet.co.uk

Contact: Mrs Ramsden

Unusual garden with extensive lawns, interesting trees, lake and islands watermill in walled kitchen garden and Victorian fernery.

Location: OS99 Ref. SE265 768. From Ripon on A6108. After North Stainley take 2nd left, follow signs to Mickley for 1m from main road.

Opening Times: Spring BH Sun & Mon, Whit BH Sun & Mon. Also all year by appointment.

Admission: Adult £2.50, Child 50p.

ORMESBY HALL

The National Trust.

CHURCH LANE, ORMESBY, MIDDLESBROUGH TS7 9AS

Owner: *The National Trust*   **Contact:** *The House Manager*

Tel: 01642 324188   **Fax:** 01642 300937   **e-mail:** yorkor@smtp.ntrust.org.uk

A mid 18th century house with opulent decoration inside, including fine plaster-work by contemporary craftsmen. A Jacobean doorway with a carved family crest survives from the earlier house on the site. The stable block, attributed to Carr of York, is a particularly fine mid 18th century building with an attractive courtyard leased to the Mounted Police; also an attractive garden with holly walk.

Location: OS Ref. NZ530 167. 3m SE of Middlesbrough.

Opening Times: 1 Apr - 4 Nov: daily except Mons, Fris & Sats (open Good Fri & BH Mons), 2 - 5pm. Garden tours, last Thur of each month (please enquire for further details).

Admission: House, garden, railway and exhibitions: Adult £3.50, Child £1.70, Family £8.50. Garden, railway and exhibitions: Adult £2.20, Child £1.

⬛ ♿Ground floor & grounds suitable. WC. 🐕

PARCEVALL HALL GARDENS   **Tel:** 01756 720311

Skyreholme, Skipton, Yorkshire BD23 6DE   **Contact:** Jo Makin (Administrator)

Owner: Walsingham College (Yorkshire Properties) Ltd.

Location: OS Ref. SE068 613. E side of Upper Wharfedale, 1¹⁄₂ m NE of Appletreewick. 12m NNW of Ilkley by B6160 and via Burnsall.

Opening Times: 1 Apr - 31 Oct: 10am - 6pm.

Admission: £3, Child 50p. (Prices subject to increase in 2001.)

PICKERING CASTLE ⬛   **Tel:** 01751 474989

Pickering, Yorkshire YO18 7AX

Owner: English Heritage   **Contact:** The Custodian

A splendid motte and bailey castle, once a royal ranch. It is well preserved, with much of the original walls, towers and keep, and there are spectacular views over the surrounding countryside. There is an exhibition on the castle's history.

Location: OS100 Ref. SE800 845. In Pickering, 15m SW of Scarborough.

Opening Times: 1 Apr - 30 Sept: daily, 10am - 6pm. 1 - 31 Oct: daily, 10am - 5pm. 1 Nov - 31 Mar: Wed - Sun, 10am - 4pm (closed 1 - 2pm). Closed 24 - 26 Dec.

Admission: Adult £2.40, Child £1.20, Conc. £1.80. 15% discount for groups (11+).

⬛ ♿Partially suitable. 🅿Limited. 🖼 🐕In grounds, on leads. ✳

PLUMPTON ROCKS   **Tel:** 01423 863950

Plumpton, Knaresborough, North Yorkshire HG5 8NA

Owner: Edward de Plumpton Hunter   **Contact:** Robert de Plumpton Hunter

Grade II* listed garden extending to over 30 acres including an idyllic lake, dramatic millstone grit rock formation, romantic woodland walks winding through bluebells and rhododendrons. Declared by English Heritage to be of outstanding interest. Painted by Turner. Described by Queen Mary as 'Heaven on earth'.

Location: OS Ref. SE355 535. Midway between Harrogate and Wetherby on the A661, 1m SE of A661 junction with the Harrogate southern bypass.

Opening Times: Mar - Oct: Sat, Sun & BHs, 11am - 6pm.

Admission: Adult £1.50, Child/OAP £1, Student £1.50.

♿Not suitable. 👣By arrangement. 🅿Limited for coaches. 🖼 🐕In grounds, on leads.

RED HOUSE MUSEUM   **Tel:** 01274 335100   **Tel:** 01274 335105

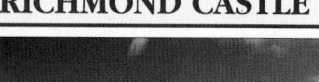

Oxford Road, Gomersal, Cleckheaton BD19 4JP

Owner: Kirklees Cultural Services

Location: OS Ref. SE210 260. On A651 in Gomersal. M62/J27, follow A62 towards Huddersfield to Birstall, follow brown tourist signs.

Opening Times: All year: Mon - Fri, 11am - 5pm. Sats & Suns, 12 noon - 5pm.

Admission: Free.

RICHMOND CASTLE ⬛

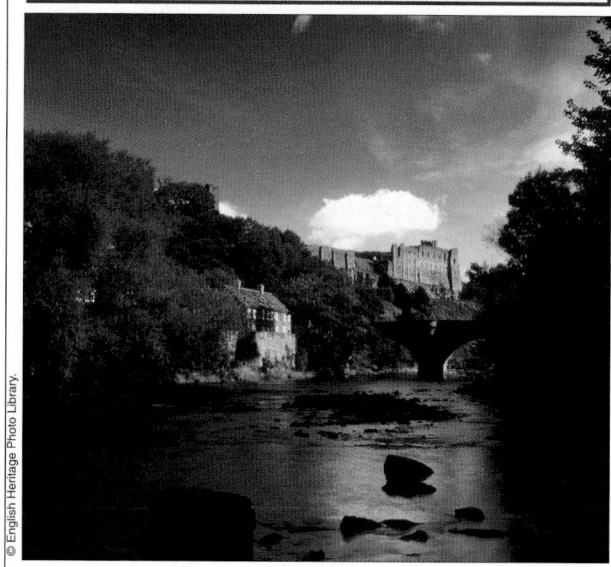

© English Heritage Photo Library.

RICHMOND, NORTH YORKSHIRE DL10 4QW

Owner: *English Heritage*   **Contact:** *The Custodian*

Tel: 01748 822493

A splendid medieval fortress, with a fine 12th century keep and 11th century remains of the curtain wall and domestic buildings. There are magnificent views from the 100 feet high keep. Exciting new interactive exhibition brings the history of the site alive.

Location: OS92 Ref. NZ174 006. In Richmond.

Opening Times: 1 Apr - 30 Sept: daily, 10am - 6pm. 1 - 31 Oct: daily, 10am - 5pm. 1 Nov - 31 Mar: daily, 10am - 4pm (closed 1 - 2pm). Closed 24- 26 Dec.

Admission: Adult £2.70, Child £1.40, Conc. £2. 15% discount for groups (11+).

ℹ New interactive exhibition. ⬛ ♿Partially suitable. 🖼 🐕In grounds, on leads. ✳ 🐕Tel. for details.

Ripley Castle, Yorkshire.

Yorkshire
England

RIEVAULX ABBEY

© English Heritage Photo Library.

RIEVAULX, Nr HELMSLEY, NORTH YORKSHIRE YO6 5LB

Owner: English Heritage   *Contact:* The Custodian

Tel: 01439 798228

In a deeply wooded valley by the River Rye you can see some of the most spectacular monastic ruins in England, dating from the 12th century. The church has the earliest large Cistercian nave in Britain. A fascinating exhibition shows how successfully the Cistercians at Rievaulx ran their many businesses and explains the part played by Abbot Ailred, who ruled for twenty years. New interactive museum, exhibition and interactive display.

Location: OS100 Ref. SE577 849. 2^1/$_4$ m W of Helmsley on minor road off B1257.
Opening Times: 1 Apr - 30 Sept: daily, 10am - 6pm (Aug: 9.30am - 7pm). 1 - 31 Oct: daily, 10am - 5pm. 1 Nov - 31 Mar: daily, 10am - 4pm. Closed 24- 26 Dec.
Admission: Adult £3.50, Child £1.80, Conc. £2.60. 15% discount for groups (11+).

Partially suitable.   P   On leads.   Tel. for details.

RIEVAULX TERRACE & TEMPLES

The National Trust.

RIEVAULX, HELMSLEY, NORTH YORKSHIRE YO62 5LJ

Owner: The National Trust   *Contact:* The Visitor Manager

Tel: 01439 748283   **Fax:** 01439 748284

A ^{1}/$_2$ m long grass-covered terrace and adjoining woodlands with vistas over Rievaulx Abbey (English Heritage) and Rye valley to Ryedale and the Hambleton Hills. There are two mid-18th century temples: the Ionic Temple has elaborate ceiling paintings and fine 18th century furniture. Note: no access to property Nov - end Mar.

Location: OS Ref. SE579 848. 2^1/$_2$ m NW of Helmsley on B1257. E of the Abbey.
Opening Times: 31 Mar - 4 Nov. Oct & Nov: daily, 10.30am - 4pm. Mar - Sept: daily, 10.30am - 5pm. Open Good Fri & BH Mons.
Admission: Adult £3.30, Child £1.50, Family (2+3) £8. Groups (15+): £2.80.

 Grounds suitable.   In grounds, on leads.

RIPLEY CASTLE   **See page 374 for full page entry.**

RIPON CATHEDRAL   Tel: 01765 604108 (information on tours etc.)

Ripon, Yorkshire HG4 1QR
Contact: Canon Keith Punshon
One of the oldest crypts in Europe (672). Marvellous choir stalls and misericords (500 years old). Almost every type of architecture. Treasury.
Location: OS Ref. SE314 711. 5m W signposted off A1, 12m N of Harrogate.
Opening Times: All year: 8am - 6pm.
Admission: Donations. £2 per head pre-booked guided tours.

RIPON WORKHOUSE   Tel: 01765 690799

Allhallowgate, Ripon, Yorkshire
Contact: Mr D Gowling
The workhouse shows restored vagrants' wards and the treatment of paupers.
Location: OS Ref. SE312 712 Close to Market Square.
Opening Times: 7 Apr - 28 Oct: daily, 11am - 4pm.
Admission: Adult £1.25, Child (6 - 16yrs) 75p, Child under 6yrs Free, Conc./Student £1.

ROCHE ABBEY   Tel: 01709 812739

Maltby, Rotherham, South Yorkshire S66 8NW
Owner: English Heritage   **Contact:** The Custodian
This Cistercian monastery, founded in 1147, lies in a secluded landscaped valley sheltered by limestone cliffs and trees. Some of the walls still stand to their full height and excavation has revealed the complete layout of the abbey.
Location: OS111 Ref. SK544 898. 1m S of Maltby off A634.
Opening Times: 1 Apr - 30 Sept: daily, 10am - 6pm. 1 - 31 Oct: daily, 10am - 5pm.
Admission: Adult £1.70, Child 90p, Conc. £1.30. 15% discount for groups (11+).

Partially suitable.   P Limited.   In grounds, on leads.   Tel. for details.

RYDALE FOLK MUSEUM

Tel: 01751 417367

Hutton Le Hole, York, North Yorkshire YO6 6UA

Owner: The Crosland Foundation **Contact:** Martin Watts

13 historic buildings showing the lives of ordinary folk from earliest times to the present day.

Location: OS Ref. SE705 902. Follow signs from Hutton Le Hole. 3m N of Kirby Moorside.

Opening Times: 11 Mar - 4 Nov: 10am - 5.30pm last admission 4.30pm.

Admission: Adult £3.25, Child £1.75, Conc. £2.75 (2000 prices).

ST WILLIAM'S COLLEGE

Tel: 01904 557233 **Fax:** 01904 557234

5 College Street, York, Yorkshire YO1 2JF

Owner: The Dean and Chapter of York **Contact:** Sandie Clarke

15th century medieval home of Minster Chantry Priests. Three large medieval halls, available for functions, conferences, weddings, medieval banquets, etc. Halls open to view when not in use. Information Centre.

Location: OS Ref. SE605 522. College Street, York. Adjoining E end of York Minster.

Opening Times: 10am - 5pm.

Admission: Adult 60p, Child 30p. For further details please telephone.

SCAMPSTON HALL

Tel: 01944 758224 **Fax:** 01944 758700

Scampston, Malton, North Yorkshire YO17 8NG **e-mail:** info@scampston.co.uk

Owner/Contact: Sir Charles Legard Bt

Opened for the first time in 1997, this country house has remained in the same family since it was built towards the end of the 17th century. The house was extensively remodelled in 1801 by the architect Thomas Leverton and has fine Regency interiors. It houses an important collection of works of art including pictures by Gainsborough, Marlow, Scott and Wilson. The park was laid out under the guidance of 'Capability' Brown and includes 10 acres of lakes and a Palladian bridge. The garden features a recently restored 19th century walk in rock and water garden with a collection of alpines, some of which are available for sale.

Location: OS100 Ref. SE865 755. 5m E of Malton, off A64.

Opening Times: 27 May - 10 Jun & 22 Jul - 5 Aug (closed Sats), 1.30 - 5pm. Last admission 4.30pm.

Admission: House & Garden: £5, Garden £2, no concessions. Groups and coaches by appointment only. Prices for groups by arrangement. Friends of the HHA admitted free.

SCARBOROUGH CASTLE

Tel: 01723 372451

Castle Road, Scarborough, North Yorkshire YO11 1HY

Owner: English Heritage **Contact:** The Custodian

Spectacular coastal views from the walls of this enormous 12th century castle. The buttressed castle walls stretch out along the cliff edge and remains of the great rectangular stone keep still stand to over three storeys high. There is also the site of a 4th century Roman signal station. The castle was frequently attacked, but despite being blasted by cannons of the Civil War and bombarded from the sea during World War I, it is still a spectacular place to visit.

Location: OS101, Ref. TA050 893. Castle Road, E of town centre.

Opening Times: 1 Apr - 30 Sept: daily, 10am - 6pm (7pm in Aug). 1 - 31 Oct: daily, 10am - 5pm. 1 Nov - 31 Mar: Wed - Sun, 10am - 4pm (closed 1 -2 pm). Closed 24 - 26 Dec.

Admission: Adult £2.40, Child £1.20, Conc. £1.80. 15% discount for groups (11+).

SEWERBY HALL & GARDENS

Tel: 01262 673769 **Fax:** 01262 673090

e-mail: museum@pop3.poptel.org.uk

Church Lane, Sewerby, Bridlington, East Yorkshire YO15 1EA

Owner: East Riding of Yorkshire Council **Contact:** Customer Service Officer

Sewerby Hall and Gardens, set in 50 acres of parkland, dates back to 1715. The Georgian house contains: 19th century orangery; history/archaeology displays; art galleries and an Amy Johnson Room. The Grounds include: walled gardens, woodland, children's zoo and play area, golf and putting.

Location: OS Ref. TA203 690. 2m N of Bridlington in Sewerby village.

Opening Times: Hall: 17 Feb - 27 Mar, Sat - Tues, 11am - 4pm; 31 Mar - 28 Oct, Daily 10am - 6pm; 29 Oct - 23 Dec, Sat - Tues, 11am - 4pm. Gardens only: daily, dawn - dusk.

Admission: Please telephone for admission prices.

SHANDY HALL

Tel/Fax: 01347 868465

Coxwold, York YO61 4AD

Owner: The Laurence Sterne Trust **Contact:** Mrs J Monkman

Built as a timber-framed hall in the 15th century.

Location: OS Ref. SE531 773. W end of Coxwold village, 4m E of A19 & 20m N of York, via Easingwold.

Opening Times: 1 May - 30 Sept: Weds, 2 - 4.30pm. Suns, 2.30 - 4.30pm. Other times by appointment. Garden: 1 May - 30 Sept: Sun - Fri, 11am - 4.30pm.

Admission: Hall & Garden: Adult £3.50, Child £1.50. Garden only: Adult £2.50, Child £1.

SHIBDEN HALL

Tel: 01422 352246 **Fax:** 01422 348440

Lister's Road, Halifax, West Yorkshire HX3 6XG

Owner: Calderdale MBC **Contact:** Valerie Stansfield

A half-timbered manor house, the home of Anne Lister set in a landscaped park. Oak furniture, carriages and an array of objects make Shibden an intriguing place to visit.

Location: OS Ref. SE106 257. 1½ m E of Halifax off A58.

Opening Times: 1 Mar - 30 Nov: Mon - Sat, 10am - 5pm. Suns, 12 noon - 5pm. Last admission 4.30pm. Dec - Feb: Mon - Sat, 10am - 4pm. Suns, 12 noon - 4pm.

Admission: Adult £2.50, Child/Conc. £1.50, Family £6.

Ground floor & grounds suitable. P Guide dogs only. ❄

SION HILL HALL

Tel: 01845 587206 **Fax:** 01845 587486

e-mail: enquiries.sionhall@virgin.net

Kirby Wiske, Thirsk, North Yorkshire YO7 4EU

Owner: H W Mawer Trust **Contact:** R M Mallaby

Falconry Centre: 01845 587522 **Fax:** 01845 523735

Antique Centre/Tearoom: 01845 587071

Sion Hill Hall was designed in 1912 by the renowned York Architect Walter H Brierley, 'the Lutyens of the North'. With its fine lines, unique character and superb layout, the Hall was designated by the Royal Institute of British Architects as being of Outstanding Architectural Merit. Sion Hill contains the H W Mawer collection of fine furniture, porcelain, paintings and clocks in superb room settings. Additionally the Edwardian kitchen has been recently restored to its former splendour. Member of the Herriot Country Attractions Group.

Location: OS Ref. SE373 844. 6m S of Northallerton off A167, 4m W of Thirsk, 6m E of A1 via A61.

Opening Times: Hall: 13 (Good Fri), 15, 16, 22 & 29 Apr. Also May - end Sept: Weds, Thurs, Suns & BH Mons, 1 - 5pm, last entry 4pm. Groups welcome by prior arrangement at other times.

Admission: Non-guided tours: Adult £4.50, Child under 12yrs Free (if accompanied by an adult), Conc. £4. Guided tours: £5.75 per person.

Partially suitable. WC. P In grounds, on leads.

SKIPTON CASTLE

See page 375 for full page entry.

SLEDMERE HOUSE

SLEDMERE, DRIFFIELD, EAST YORKSHIRE YO25 3XG

Owner: Sir Tatton Sykes Bt *Contact: Mrs Anne Hines*

Tel: 01377 236637 **Fax:** 01377 236500

Sledmere House is the home of Sir Tatton Sykes, 8th Baronet. There has been a manor house at Sledmere since medieval times. The present house was designed and built by Sir Christopher Sykes, 2nd Baronet, a diary date states "*June 17th, 1751 laid the first stone of the new house at Sledmere.*" Sir Christopher employed a fellow Yorkshireman, Joseph Rose, the most famous English plasterer of his day, to execute the decoration of Sledmere. Rose's magnificent work at Sledmere was unique in his career. A great feature at Sledmere is the 'Capability' Brown parkland and the beautiful 18th century walled rose gardens. Also worthy of note is the recently laid out knot-garden, all accessible by wheelchair.

Location: OS Ref. SE931 648. Off the A166 between York & Bridlington. ½ hr drive from York, Bridlington & Scarborough.

Opening Times: 13 - 17 Apr & 6 May - 30 Sept: closed Mons & Sats but open BHs: 11.30am - 4.30pm. Famous pipe organ played Weds, Fris & Suns.

Admission: House & Gardens: Adult £4.50, Child £2, OAP £4. Gardens & Park: Adult £2, Child £1.

No photography in house. Licensed. By arrangement. P In grounds on leads. Guide dogs in house.

SPOFFORTH CASTLE ⌗

Tel: 01904 601901

Harrogate, Yorkshire

Owner: English Heritage   **Contact:** The Northern Regional Office

This manor house has some fascinating features including an undercroft built into the rock. It was once owned by the Percy family.

Location: OS Ref. SE360 511. 3$^1/_2$ m SE of Harrogate on minor road off A661 at Spofforth.

Opening Times: 1 Apr - 30 Sept: daily, 10am - 6pm. 1 - 31 Oct: daily, 10am - 6pm or dusk if earlier. 1 Nov - 31 Mar: 10am - 4pm.

Admission: Free.

STOCKELD PARK

WETHERBY, YORKSHIRE LS22 4AH

Owner: Mr and Mrs P G F Grant   *Contact: Mrs L A Saunders*

Tel: 01937 586101 **Fax:** 01937 580084

Stockeld is a beautifully proportioned Palladian villa designed by James Paine in 1763, featuring a magnificent cantilevered staircase in the central oval hall. Stockeld is still very much a family home, with a fine collection of 18th and 19th century furniture and paintings. The house is surrounded by lovely gardens of lawns, large herbaceous and shrub borders, fringed by woodland, and set in 100 acres of fine parkland in the midst of an extensive farming estate.

Location: OS Ref. SE376 497. York 12m, Harrogate 5m, Leeds 12m.

Opening Times: 19 Apr - 11 Oct: Thurs only, 2 - 5pm. Groups please book.

Admission: Adult £4.50. Group prices on application.

🚫House only. ⒦Obligatory. ✕

STUDLEY ROYAL: ST MARY'S CHURCH ⌗

Tel: 01765 608888

Ripon, Yorkshire

Owner: English Heritage   **Contact:** The Custodian

A magnificent Victorian church, designed by William Burges in the 1870s, with a highly decorated interior. Coloured marble, stained glass, gilded and painted figures and a splendid organ.

Location: OS Ref. SE278 703. 2$^1/_2$ m W of Ripon off B6265, in grounds of Studley Royal estate.

Opening Times: 1 Apr - 30 Sept: daily, 1 - 5pm.

Admission: Free.

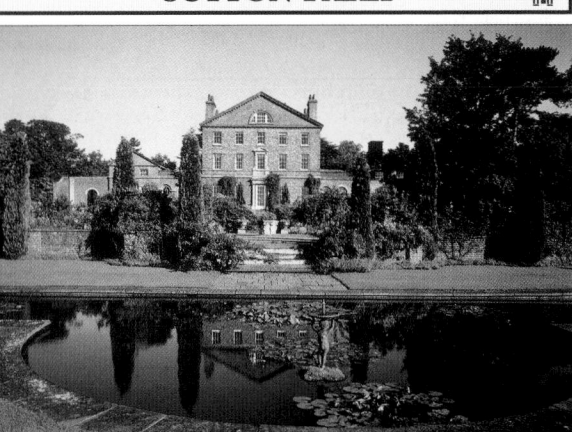

SUTTON PARK 🏛

SUTTON-ON-THE-FOREST, NORTH YORKSHIRE YO61 1DP

Owner: Sir Reginald & Lady Sheffield   *Contact: Mrs A Wilkinson*

Tel: 01347 810249/811239 **Fax:** 01347 811251 **e-mail:** suttonpark@fsbdial.co.uk

The Yorkshire home of Sir Reginald and Lady Sheffield. Charming example of early Georgian architecture. Magnificent plasterwork by Cortese. Rich collection of 18th century furniture, paintings, porcelain, needlework, beadwork. All put together with great style to make a most inviting house. Award winning gardens attract enthusiasts from home and abroad.

Location: OS Ref. SE583 646. 8m N of York on B1363 York - Helmsley Road.

Opening Times: House: 1 Apr - 30 Sept: Suns & Weds, also Good Fri - Easter Mon & BH Mons, 1.30 - 5pm. Tearoom: as house, 12 noon - 5pm. Private Groups: Any other day of the week by appointment. House open Oct - Mar for private groups only. Gardens: 1 Apr - 30 Sept, daily, 11am - 5pm.

Admission: House & Garden: Adult £5, Child £2.50, Conc. £4. Gardens only: Adult £2.50, Child 50p, Conc. £1.50. Coach parties: £4.50. Gardens only £2. Private Groups (15+): £5.50. Caravans: £4.50 per night.

ⓘNo photography. ⒯Hosted lunches & dinners. ⒢Partially suitable. ▦
ⓚObligatory. ⓟLimited for coaches. ✕
⒝3 double with ensuite bathrooms. ✳ ⒱ Tel. for details. 🌐

TEMPLE NEWSAM HOUSE

Tel: 0113 2647321 **Fax:** 0113 2602285

Leeds LS15 0AE

Owner: Leeds City Council   **Contact:** Denise Lawson

A Tudor-Jacobean mansion with over thirty rooms open to the public.

Location: OS Ref. SE358 321. 5m E of city centre, off A63 Selby Road. M1/J46.

Opening Times: 1 Apr - 31 Oct: Tue - Sat, 10am - 5pm. Suns, 1 - 5pm. 1 Nov - 31 Dec & Mar: Tue - Sat, 10am - 4pm, Suns, 12 noon - 4pm. Last admission ¾ hr before closing time. Closed Jan & Feb.

Admission: Adult £2, Child 50p, Conc. £1. Groups (10+): Adult £1, Child 50p.

THORNTON ABBEY ⌗

Tel: 01904 601901

Scunthorpe, Humberside

Owner: English Heritage   **Contact:** The Yorkshire Regional Office

The magnificent brick gatehouse of this ruined Augustine priory stands three storeys high.

Location: OS Ref. TA115 190. 18m NE of Scunthorpe on minor road N of A180.

Opening Times: 1 Apr - 30 Sept: 1st & 3rd Suns, 12 - 6pm. 1 Oct - 31 Mar: 3rd Suns, 12 - 4pm.

Admission: Free.

THORP PERROW ARBORETUM &
THE FALCONS OF THORP PERROW 🏛

Tel/Fax: 01677 425323

Bedale, North Yorkshire DL8 2PR   **e-mail:** louise@thorpperrow.freeserve.co.uk

Owner: Sir John Ropner Bt   **Contact:** Louise McNeill

85 acres of woodland walks. One of the largest collections of trees and shrubs in the north of England, including a 16th century medieval spring wood and 19th century pinetum. The Falcons of Thorp Perrow, an additional attraction which opened spring 2000. Various trails available, playground with mini beast station, tearoom and plant centre.

Location: OS Ref. SE258 851. Bedale - Ripon road, S of Bedale, 4m from Leeming Bar on A1.

Opening Times: All year: dawn - dusk.

Admission: Arboretum: Adult £3.50, Child £2, OAP £2.50, Family (2+2) £10, (2+4) £14. Arboretum & Falcons: Adult £7, Child £4, OAP £5, Family (2+2) £20, (2+4) £28.

ⓘPicnic area. Children's playground. ◻ ⒯ ⒯ ⒢ ▦
ⓚBy arrangement. ⓟLimited for coaches. ▣ ✕In grounds, on leads. ✳
⒱Tel. for details. 🌐

TREASURER'S HOUSE

MINSTER YARD, YORK, NORTH YORKSHIRE YO1 7JH

Owner: The National Trust   *Contact:* The Property Manager

Tel: 01904 624247 **Fax:** 01904 647372 **e-mail:** yorkth@smtp.ntrust.org.uk

An elegant townhouse situated in the tranquil surroundings of the Minster Close. A series of period rooms is the setting for a fine collection of furniture and paintings given to the National Trust by Yorkshire industrialist Frank Green, who lived here from 1897 to 1930. Introductory video and exhibition.

Location: OS Ref. SE604 523. The N side of York Minster. Entrance on Chapter House St.

Opening Times: 31 Mar - 31 Oct: daily except Fris, 11am - 5pm. Last adm. 4.30pm.

Admission: Adult £3.70, Child £2. Family £9.50. Booked groups (15+): Adult £3, Child £1.50.

⊤   ♿Partially suitable. WC.   ◻Licensed.   ⑪Licensed.   ⓅNone.   ▥
🐕In grounds, on leads.   🔔

WHITBY ABBEY

© English Heritage Photo Library.

WHITBY, NORTH YORKSHIRE YO22 4JT

Owner: English Heritage   *Contact:* The Custodian

Tel: 01947 603568

An ancient holy place, once a burial place of kings and an inspiration for saints. A religious community was first established at Whitby in 657 by Abbess Hilda and was the home of Caedmon, the first English poet. The remains we can see today are of a Benedictine church built in the 13th and 14th centuries, and include a magnificent three-tiered choir and north transept. It is perched high above the picturesque harbour town of Whitby.

Location: OS94, Ref. NZ904 115. On cliff top E of Whitby.

Opening Times: 1 Apr - 30 Sept: daily 10am - 6pm. 1 - 31 Oct: daily, 10am - 5pm. 1 Nov - 31 Mar: daily, 10am - 4pm. Closed 24 - 26 Dec.

Admission: Adult £1.80, Child 90p, Conc. £1.40. 15% discounts for groups (11+).

◻   ♿Ground floor suitable.   ▥   🐕In grounds, on leads.   ❄
⛉Tel. for details.

WAKEFIELD CATHEDRAL   **Tel:** 01924 373923 **Fax:** 01924 215054

Northgate, Wakefield, West Yorkshire WF1 1HG

Owner: Church of England   **Contact:** Mr F Arnold, Head Verger

Built on the site of a previous Saxon church, this 14th century Parish Church became a cathedral in 1888 and was extended by Pearson and completed by his son. It also boasts, at 247ft, the highest spire in Yorkshire.

Location: OS Ref. SE333 208. Wakefield city centre. M1/ J39-41, M62/J29W, J30 E.

Opening Times: Mon - Sat: 8am - 5pm. Suns: between services only. Sunday Services: Holy Communion: 8am. Parish Eucharist: 9.15am. Solemn Eucharist: 11am. Choral Evensong (Winter): 4pm. Choral Evensong (Summer): 6.30pm. Daily Services: Holy Communion: Daily, 8am plus 10.30am on Weds & Sats and 12.30pm on Fris. Choral Evensong: Thurs, 6.30pm. Said Evensong: Mons, Tues, Fris & Sats, 5pm. Weds (girls' choir) Choral Evensong 6pm.

Admission: Free admission. Donations welcome.

WENTWORTH CASTLE GARDENS   **Tel:** 01226 731269

Lowe Lane, Stainborough, Barnsley, Yorkshire S75 3ET

Owner: Barnsley MBC   **Contact:** Chris Margrave

300 years old, these gardens are the only Grade I listed gardens in South Yorkshire, 28 listed buildings and monuments and the National Collections of rhododendrons, magnolias and williamsii camellias.

Location: OS Ref. SE320 034. 5km W of Barnsley, M1/J36 via Birdwell & Rockley Lane then Lowe Lane.

Opening Times: Mid April - end June, mainly by guided tours. Please telephone 01226 731269 for a recorded message.

Admission: £2.50, Conc. £1.50.

WHITE SCAR CAVE   See page 376 for full page entry.

WILBERFORCE HOUSE   **Tel:** 01482 613902 **Fax:** 01482 613710

High Street, Hull, Yorkshire HU1 1NQ

Owner: Hull City Council   **Contact:** S R Green

Built c1660 the house is a museum to the memory of William Wilberforce.

Location: OS Ref. TA102 286. High Street, Hull.

Opening Times: Mon - Sat, 10am - 5pm. Suns, 1.30 - 4.30pm. Closed Good Fri & Christmas Day.

Admission: Free.

WORTLEY HALL   **Tel:** 0114 2882100 **Fax:** 0114 2830695

Wortley, Sheffield, Yorkshire S35 7DB

Owner: Labour, Co-operative & Trade Union Movement   **Contact:** John Howard

15 acres of formal Italianate gardens surrounded by 11 acres of informal pleasure grounds.

Location: OS Ref. SK313 995. 10kms S of Barnsley in Wortley on A629.

Opening Times: Gardens: All year except 7 - 14 Aug & 6 - 13 Nov.

Admission: Free. Groups must book for gardeners' tour, £1.50.

YORK MINSTER   **Tel:** 01904 557216 **Fax:** 01904 557218

Deangate, York YO1 7HH

Owner: Dean and Chapter of York   **Contact:** Dorothy Lee, Visitors' Officer

Large gothic church housing the largest collection of medieval stained glass in England.

Location: OS Ref. SE603 522. Centre of York.

Opening Times: Nov - Mar: 7am - 6pm, Apr: 7am - 6.30pm, May: 7am - 7.30pm, Jun - Aug: 7am - 8.30pm, Sept: 7am - 8pm, Oct: 7am - 7pm, daily.

Admission: By donation. Tour companies £3 per person, Child (6-16yrs) £1.

Special Events Index ◀◀◀ page 33

Holker Hall, Cumbria

The North West

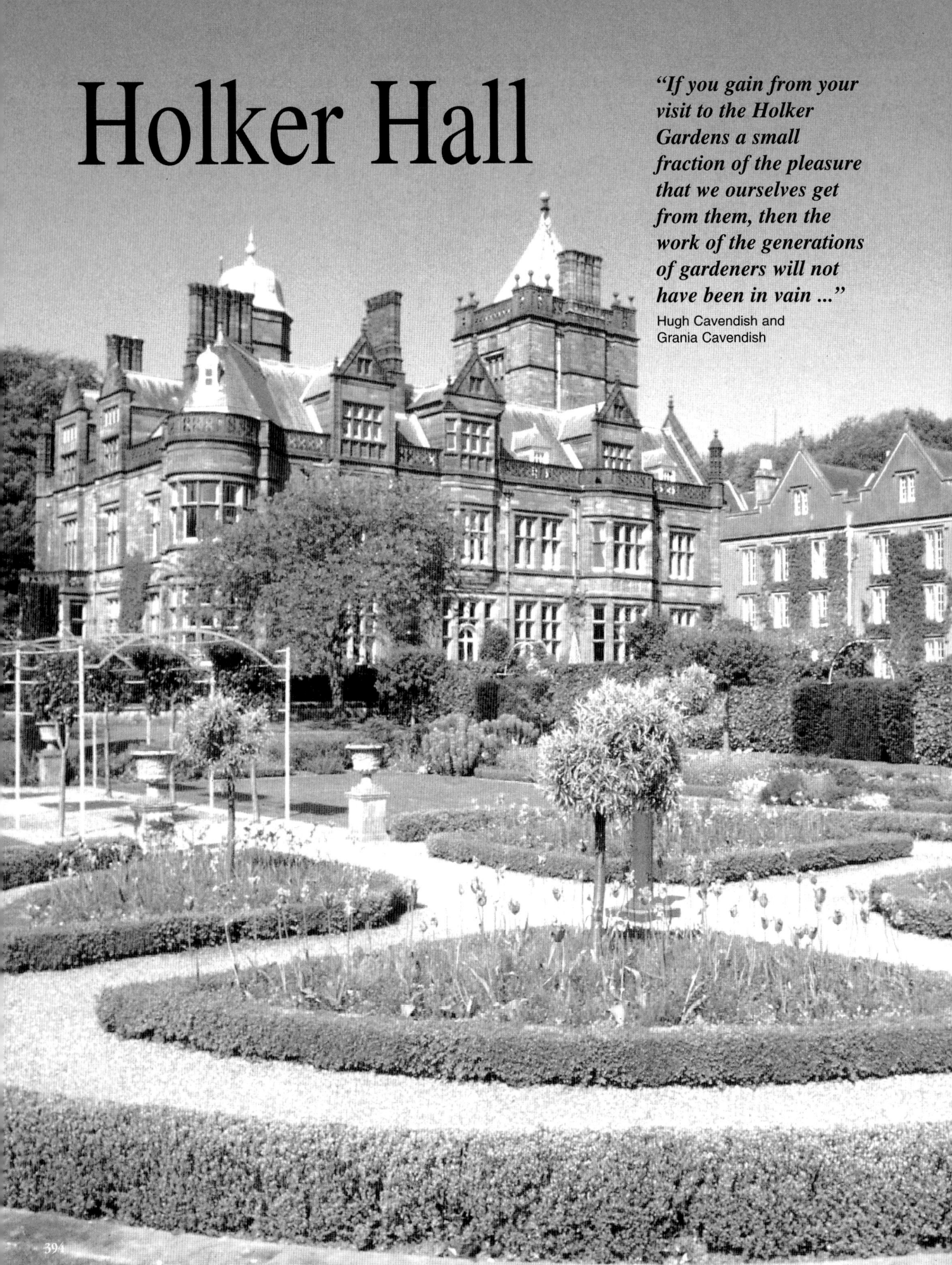

Holker Hall

"If you gain from your visit to the Holker Gardens a small fraction of the pleasure that we ourselves get from them, then the work of the generations of gardeners will not have been in vain ..."

Hugh Cavendish and
Grania Cavendish

Only a short distance from the sea, Holker Hall is magnificently situated on the wooded slopes of the Cartmel peninsula which juts out from the north into Morecombe Bay. Despite its grand scale, this handsome rose coloured neo-Elizabethan mansion and its gardens provide a soft and gentle contrast to the ruggedness of the Lakeland countryside to the north.

The earliest records of a house on the present site date back to the beginning of the 16th century. From then until the present day it has been home to three families: the Prestons, the Lowthers and Cavendishes. The estate has never been bought or sold, but has passed by inheritance through the family line, with each generation leaving its impressions, either by planning and altering the landscape or by changing the house by adding, refacing, embellishing or even rebuilding – as was necessary after the disastrous fire of 1871.

The present appearance of Holker, and the New Wing built by the 7th Duke of Devonshire, is chiefly the work in the 1870s of the Lancashire architects Paley and Austin. Through their work, Holker Hall exhibits all the grandeur, confidence, spaciousness and prosperity of the late Victorian age. Yet despite its sheer scale, Holker is still very much the family home and one which Lord and Lady Cavendish are delighted to share with thousands of visitors each year.

The immaculately kept gardens (25 acres in all) are part woodland, part formal and essentially Victorian in character, though never heavy or oppressive. The 200 acre 'natural' parkland is in fact the result of the late 18th century planting of Lord George Cavendish. In the early 19th century several new features were added: an arboretum, a conservatory, balustraded terraces by the house, and a large walled kitchen garden.

However, Lord and Lady Cavendish have sought not only to conserve the historic. Changes and additions are still being made to the gardens, with great liveliness and confidence: the shelter belt of trees, planted in the last 20 years, gives protection between park and garden; and the old croquet lawn planted as a garden 'room' is one of the formal highlights of a visit.

The Cascade, inspired by an ancient water garden in Rajasthan, creates movement among the spectacular Rhud as water flows over a zig-zag pattern picked out in slate. In the year 2000 a new Sunken Garden was completed where the former Rose Garden was situated, which has been redesigned and replanted.

In the Woodland Garden you will find recently planted specimen trees and shrubs mixed with ancient conifers, dogwoods and magnolias, all of which love the acid soil and high rainfall. This has made it one of the most interesting and worthwhile gardens to visit in the north of England. ⁕

For further details about *Holker Hall* see entry in North West Region → Cumbria.

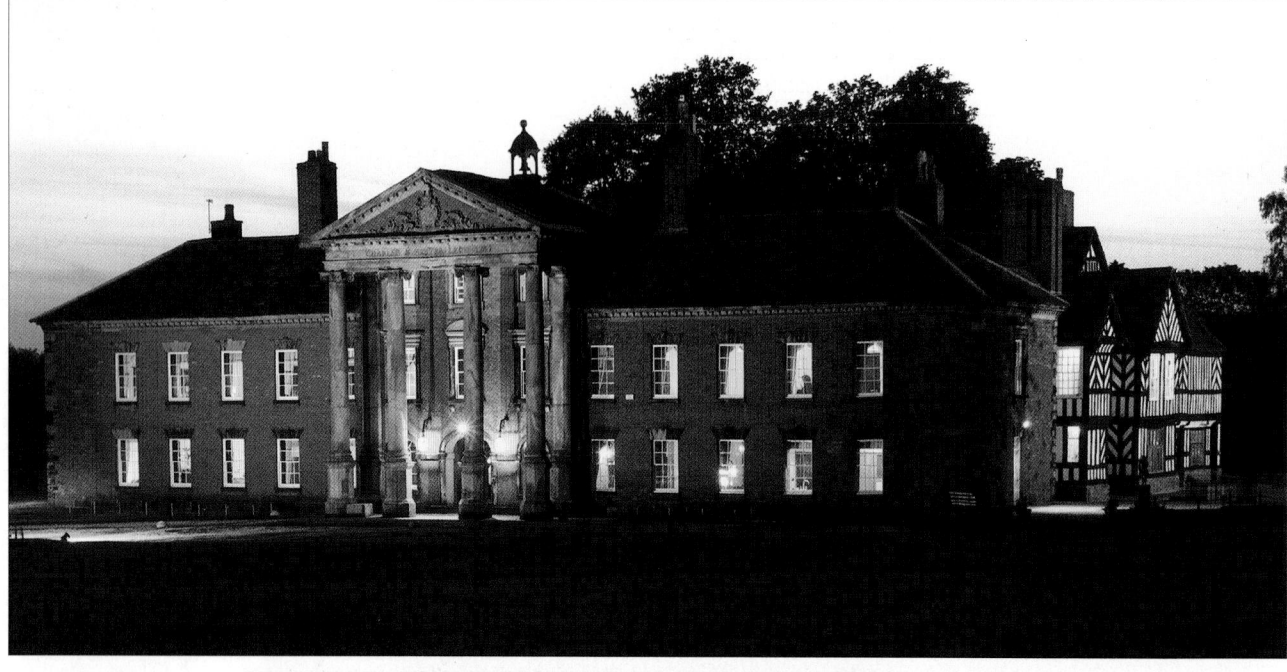

ADLINGTON HALL
Macclesfield

ADLINGTON HALL, the home of the Leghs of Adlington from 1315 to the present day, was built on the site of a Hunting Lodge which stood in the Forest of Macclesfield in 1040. Two oaks, part of the original building, remain with their roots in the ground and support the east end of the Great Hall, which was built between 1480 and 1505.

The Hall is a manor house, quadrangular in shape, and was once surrounded by a moat. Two sides of the Courtyard and the east wing were built in the typical 'Black and White' Cheshire style in 1581. The south front and west wing (containing the Drawing Room and Dining Room) were added between 1749 and 1757 and are built of red brick with a handsome stone portico with four Ionic columns on octagonal pedestals. Between the trees in the Great Hall stands an organ built by 'Father' Bernard Smith (c1670-80). Handel subsequently played on this instrument, and now fully restored, it is the largest 17th century organ in the country.

GARDENS
The gardens were landscaped in the style of 'Capability' Brown in the middle of the 18th century. Visitors may walk round the 'wilderness' area, among the follies to be seen are 'Temple to Diana', a 'Shell Cottage', Chinese bridge and T'ing house. There is a fine yew walk and a lime avenue planted in 1688. Old fashioned rose garden and yew maze recently planted. New for 2000 is a herbaceous border and woodlands area to enhance the North Lodge entrance.

Owner:
Mrs C J C Legh

CONTACT

Corporate Enquiries:
Julian Langlands-Perry
or Tessa Quayle
The Estate Office
Adlington Hall
Macclesfield
Cheshire
SK10 4LF

Tel: 01625 829206

Fax: 01625 828756

e-mail: enquiries@
adlingtonhall.com

Hall Tours:
Gwyn & Barbara Martin

Tel: 01625 820875

LOCATION

OS Ref. SJ905 804

5m N of
Macclesfield, A523,
13m S of Manchester.
London 178m.

Rail: Macclesfield
& Wilmslow stations 5m.

Air: Manchester
Airport 8m.

CONFERENCE/FUNCTION		
ROOM	SIZE	MAX CAPACITY
Great Hall	11 x 8m	120
Dining Rm	10.75 x 7m	90
Courtyard	27 x 17m	300

Open to the public in
June & July:
Mon & Wed, 2 - 5pm.

Also by prior arrangement
for groups throughout the
year. Please contact for
details.

ADMISSION

Hall & Gardens
Adult £4.50
Child £1.75
Student....................£1.75
Groups of 20+ £4.00

 Suitable for corporate events, product launches, business meetings, conferences, concerts, fashion shows, garden parties, rallies, clay-pigeon shooting and filming.

The Great Hall and Dining Room are available for corporate entertaining. Catering can be arranged.

Visitors may alight at entrance to Hall. WCs.

By arrangement.

 For 100 cars and 4 coaches, 100 yds from Hall.

Schools welcome. Guide can be provided.

No dogs.

CAPESTHORNE HALL
Macclesfield

Owner:
Mr & Mrs Bromley-Davenport

CONTACT

Gwyneth Jones,
Hall Manager
Capesthorne Hall
Siddington
Macclesfield
Cheshire
SK11 9JY

Tel: 01625 861221

Fax: 01625 861619

LOCATION

OS Ref. SJ840 727

5m W of Macclesfield.

30 mins S of Manchester
on A34.

Near M6, M63 and M62.

Airport: Manchester
International 20 mins.

Rail: Macclesfield 5m
(2 hrs from London).

Taxi: 01625 533464.

CONFERENCE/FUNCTION

ROOM	SIZE	MAX CAPACITY
Theatre	45' x 19'	155
Garden Room	52' x 20'	80
Saloon	40' x 25'	80
Queen Anne Room	34' x 25'	80
Board Room		10

CAPESTHORNE HALL, set in 100 acres of picturesque Cheshire parkland, has been touched by nearly 1,000 years of English history - Roman legions passed across it, titled Norman families hunted on it and, during the Civil War, a Royalist ancestress helped Charles II to escape after the Battle of Worcester. The Jacobean-style Hall has a fascinating collection of fine art, marble sculptures, furniture and tapestries. Originally designed by the Smiths of Warwick it was built between 1719 and 1732. It was altered by Blore in 1837 and partially rebuilt by Salvin in 1861 following a disastrous fire.

The present Squire is William Bromley-Davenport, Lord Lieutenant of Cheshire, whose ancestors have owned the estate since Domesday times when they were appointed custodians of the Royal Forest of Macclesfield.

In the grounds near the family Chapel the 18th century Italian *Milanese Gates* open onto the herbaceous borders and maples which line the beautiful lakeside gardens. But amid the natural spectacle and woodland walks, Capesthorne still offers glimpses of its man-made past... the remains of the Ice House, the Old Boat House and the curious Swallow Hole.

Facilities at the Hall can be hired for corporate occasions and family celebrations including Civil wedding ceremonies.

❖

[i] Available for corporate functions, meetings, product launches, promotions, exhibitions, presentations, seminars, activity days, Civil weddings and receptions, family celebrations, still photography, fishing, clay shooting, car rallies, garden parties, barbecues, firework displays, concerts, antique, craft, country and game fairs. No photography in Hall.

[Y] Catering can be provided for groups (full menus on request). Function rooms available for wedding receptions, corporate hospitality, meetings and other special events. 'The Butler's Pantry' serves tea, coffee and ices.

[♿] Compacted paths, ramps. WCs.

[🚶] For up to 50. Tours are by staff members or Hall Manager. Tour time 1 hr.

[P] 100 cars/20 coaches on hard-standing and unlimited in park, 50 yds from house. Rest room and free refreshment for coach drivers.

[🐕] Guide dogs in Hall. Under control in Park.

[🔔] Civil Wedding Licence. [❄]

OPENING TIMES

SUMMER
April - October
BHs, Weds & Suns.

House, Gardens & Chapel
Open at 1.30pm
Last admission 3.30pm.

Gardens & Chapel
12 noon - 6pm.

Groups welcome by appointment.

Caravan Park also open
Easter - end September.

Corporate enquiries:
March - December.

ADMISSION

Hall & Gardens
Adult £6.50
Child (5-18yrs) £3.00
OAP.........................£5.50
Family £12.00

Gardens & Chapel
Adult £4.00
Child (5-18yrs) £2.00
OAP.........................£3.00

Transfers to Hall
Adult/OAP £3.50
Child (5-18yrs) £1.50

Groups (25+) please
telephone for details.

Caravans
Up to 2 people £11.50 pn
Over 2 people £13.50 pn

 SPECIAL EVENTS

• APR 7 - 8 & SEPT 15 - 16:
Rainbow Craft Fair

See the Special Events Section
or telephone for more details
and other special events.

The National Trust Photographic Library.

Owner:
The National Trust

CONTACT

Conferences, exhibitions, social occasions
Sheila Hetherington
Sales & Booking Officer
01625 534406

Party Visits
Janet Gidman
Tatton Park
Knutsford
Cheshire WA16 6QN

Tel: 01625 534400/534428

Fax: 01625 534403

LOCATION

OS Ref. SJ745 815

From M56/J7 follow signs.
From M6/J19, signed on
A56 & A50.

Rail: Knutsford or
Altrincham Station,
then taxi.

Air: Manchester Airport 6m.

TATTON PARK
Knutsford

TATTON is one of the most splendid historic estates in the United Kingdom. The 1000 acres of parkland are home to herds of red and fallow deer and provide the setting for a Georgian Mansion, over 50 acres of Gardens, Tudor Old Hall and a working Farm. These attractions, plus private functions and a superb events programme attract over 700,000 visits each year.

Archaeologists have found evidence of occupation at Tatton since 8000 BC with the discovery of flints in the park. There is also proof of people living here in the Iron Age, Roman times, Anglo-saxon and medieval periods.

The neo-Classical Mansion by Wyatt is the jewel in Tatton's crown and was built in stages from 1780 - 1813. The Egerton family collection of Gillow furniture, Baccarat glass, porcelain and paintings by Italian and Dutch masters is found in the splendid setting of the magnificent staterooms. In stark contrast, the Victorian kitchens and cellars provide fascinating insight into life as it would have been 'downstairs'.

The Gardens extend over 50 acres and feature rare species of plants, shrubs and trees, and in fact are considered to be one of the most important gardens within the National Trust. Features include: a conservatory by Wyatt, Fernery by Paxton, plus the Japanese and Italian terraced gardens. The rare collection of plants including rhododendrons, tree ferns, bamboo and pines are the result of 200 years of collecting by the Egerton family.

The Home Farm has traditional breeds of animal including rare sheep and cattle, pigs and horses plus estate workshops. The Tudor Old Hall shows visitors how life would have been at Tatton Park over centuries past for the estate workers. Tours start in the smoky 16th century great hall lit by flickering candles and end in the 1950s home of an estate employee.

SUMMER
31 March - 30 September

Park: All year, daily 10am - 7pm, last entry 6pm

Gardens: All year: Tue - Sun (open BH Mons), 10.30am - 6pm, last entry 5pm

Mansion: Apr - Oct: Tue - Sun 1 - 5pm. (12 noon - 12.30pm guided tours by timed ticket limited number per tour)

Tudor Old Hall: Apr - Oct: Guided tours: Tue - Fri, 3pm & 4pm. Sats & Suns, hourly, 12 noon - 4pm.

Restaurant: Daily, 10.30am - 5pm.

Gift, Garden & Housekeeper's Store: Apr - Oct: Tue - Sun, 11.30am - 5pm.

Farm: Apr - Sept: Tue - Sun.

WINTER
Special openings in Oct & Dec: Mansion & Farm.
1 Oct - 31 Mar 2002

Park: Tue - Sun, 11.30am - 5pm, last entry 4pm.

Farm: Suns only, 11.30am - 4pm, last admission 3pm.

Gardens: Tue - Sun, 11am - 5pm, last entry 4pm.

ADMISSION

Any two attractions

	Single	Group*
Adult	£4.60	£3.70
Child**	£2.60	£2.10

Mansion, Gardens, Tudor Old Hall, Farm

	Single	Group*
Adult	£3.00	£2.40
Child**	£2.00	£1.60
Family	£8.00	

(50% reduction for NT members to Tudor Old Hall & Farm.)

Parking

Per car	£3.50
Coaches	Free

*Min. 12   ** Aged 4 - 15yrs.
OAP rate as Adult
Tours available outside normal openings phone for details.

CONFERENCE/FUNCTION

ROOM	SIZE	MAX CAPACITY
Tenants' Hall	125' x 45'	330 - 400
Foyer	23' x 20'	50 - 100

Tenants' Hall Event Wing – total of 8,000 sq.ft. available

Lord Egerton's Apartment	20' x 16'	16 - 40
	24' x 18'	19 - 40
Stable Block	31' x 20'	80

Conferences, trade exhibitions, presentations, product launches, concerts and fashion shows. Special family days. Spotlights, stages, dance floor, PA system. The Tenants' Hall seats up to 400 for presentations.

Telephone for details. Dinners, dances, weddings.

Upstairs in Mansion, Old Hall & areas of farm not accessible. Wheelchairs & electric vehicles available. WCs.

Self-service. Tuck shop.

By arrangement.

200-300 yds away. Meal vouchers for coach drivers.

Award-winning educational programmes, please book. Environmental days, Orienteering, adventure playground.

In grounds, on leads.

Civil Wedding Licence.

Please telephone for details.

ADLINGTON HALL See page 398 for full page entry.

ARLEY HALL & GARDENS

ARLEY, Nr NORTHWICH, CHESHIRE CW9 6NA

Owner: *Viscount Ashbrook*   **Contact:** *Estate Secretary*

Tel: 01565 777353 / 777284 **Fax:** 01565 777465
e-mail: enquiries@arleyestate.zuunet.co.uk

Set amongst beautiful parkland, Arley Hall, home to Viscount and Viscountess Ashbrook, offers visitors a delightful family hall and glorious gardens. The Hall can be used for all types of corporate entertaining and events and is licensed for weddings. The gardens, a plantsman's paradise, rank amongst the finest in England with many features. Special events throughout the year.

Location: OS Ref. SJ675 809. Knutsford 5m, NW Northwich 5m, N M6/J19 & 20 5m M56/J9 & 10, 5m.

Opening Times: 13 Apr - 30 Sept: Tue - Sun & BH Mons, 11am - 5pm. Hall: please telephone for open days, 12 noon - 5pm.

Admission: Gardens, Grounds & Chapel: Adult £4.40, Child £2.20, OAP £3.80, Family £11. Groups: Adult £3.75, Child £2, OAP £3.25. Season ticket £19.50, Family season ticket £50 (2+2). Hall & Gardens: Adult £6.90, Child £3.70, OAP £5.80, Family £17.50. Hall: Disabled Adult £1.50, Disabled Child £75p. Groups: Adult £6, Child £3.25, OAP £5.

 Photography in gardens only. Licensed. By arrangement. In grounds, on leads.

BEESTON CASTLE

Tel: 01829 260464

Beeston, Tarporley, Cheshire CW6 9TX

Owner: English Heritage   **Contact:** The Custodian

Standing majestically on sheer, rocky crags which fall sharply away from the castle walls, Beeston has possibly the best views of the surrounding countryside of any castle in England.

Location: OS117, Ref. SJ537 593. 11m SE of Chester on minor road off A49, or A41. 2m SW of Tarporley.

Opening Times: 1 Apr - 30 Sept: 10am - 6pm. 1 - 31 Oct: daily, 10am - 5pm. 1 Nov - 31 Mar: daily, 10am - 4pm. Closed 24 & 25 Dec.

Admission: Adult £2.90, Child £1.50, Conc. £2.20. 15% discount for groups (11+).

Exhibition. Not suitable. In grounds on leads. Tel. for details.

Beeston Castle, Cheshire.

BRAMALL HALL

BRAMHALL PARK, BRAMHALL, STOCKPORT SK7 3NX

Owner: *Stockport MBC*   **Contact:** *Ruth Maddocks*

Tel: 0161 485 3708 **Fax:** 0161 486 6959

Surrounded by 70 acres of beautiful parkland, Bramall Hall is a superb example of a Cheshire black and white timber-framed manor house, dating from the 14th century. The house has beautiful Tudor rooms with splendid Victorian additions. Extensive events programme and ideal for weddings.

Location: OS117, Ref. SJ886 863. 4m S of Stockport, off A5102.

Opening Times: Good Fri - 30 Sept: Mon - Sat, 1 - 5pm, Suns & BHs, 11am - 5pm. 1 Oct - 1 Jan: Tue - Sat, 1 - 4pm, Suns & BHs, 11am - 4pm. Closed 25/26 Dec. 2 Jan - 4 Apr: Sats & Suns, 12 noon - 4pm.

Admission: Adult £3.50, Child/Conc. £2. Group prices on request.

Partially suitable. By arrangement. Limited for coaches. In grounds on leads. Tel for details.

CAPESTHORNE HALL See page 399 for full page entry.

CHESTER CATHEDRAL

Tel: 01244 324756 **Fax:** 01244 341110

12 Abbey Square, Chester, Cheshire CH1 2HU   **Contact:** Mr N Fry

Founded in 1092 as a Benedictine monastery, it became an Anglican cathedral in 1541. All styles of architecture are represented as well as spectacular medieval woodwork.

Location: OS Ref. SJ406 665. Chester city centre.

Opening Times: 7.30am - 6.30pm, daily.

Admission: Donation.

CHESTER ROMAN AMPHITHEATRE

Tel: 0161 242 1400

Vicars Lane, Chester, Cheshire

Owner: English Heritage   **Contact:** The North Regional Office

The largest Roman amphitheatre in Britain, partially excavated. Used for entertainment and military training by the 20th Legion, based at the fortress of Deva.

Location: OS Ref. SJ404 660. On Vicars Lane beyond Newgate, Chester.

Opening Times: Any reasonable time.

Admission: Free.

CHOLMONDELEY CASTLE GARDEN

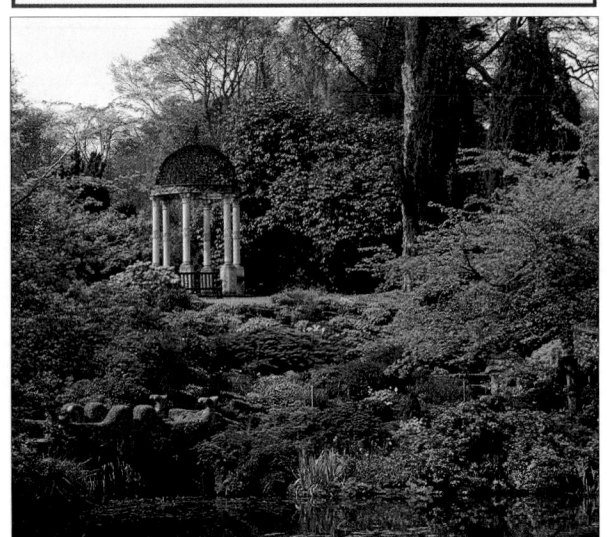

MALPAS, CHESHIRE SY14 8AH

Owner: The Marchioness of Cholmondeley   *Contact:* The Secretary

Tel/Fax: 01829 720383

Extensive ornamental gardens dominated by romantic Gothic Castle built in 1801 of local sandstone. Beautiful temple water garden, rose garden and many mixed borders. Lakeside picnic area, children's play areas, rare breeds of farm animals, including Llamas. Ancient private chapel in the park.

Location: OS Ref. SJ540 515. Off A41 Chester/Whitchurch Rd. & A49 Whitchurch/Tarporley Road. 7m N of Whitchurch.

Opening Times: 1 Apr - 30 Sept: Weds, Thurs, Suns & BH Mons, 11.30am - 5.30pm, last entry 5pm. Closed Good Fri. Groups (25+): other days by prior arrangement at reduced rates.

Admission: Adult £3, Child £1.50.

Limited suitability. WCs. In grounds on leads only.

DUNHAM MASSEY

Patrick Lane

ALTRINCHAM, CHESHIRE WA14 4SJ

Owner: The National Trust   *Contact:* The Property Manager

Tel: 0161 941 1025 **Fax:** 0161 929 7508

Originally an early Georgian house, Dunham Massey has sumptuous interiors, with collections of walnut furniture, paintings and magnificent Huguenot silver. The richly planted garden contains waterside plantings, late flowering azaleas, an orangery and Elizabethan mount. The surrounding deer park escaped the attentions of 18th century landscape gardeners and contains some notable specimen trees.

Location: OS Ref. SJ735 874. 3m SW of Altrincham off A56. M56/J7.

Opening Times: House: 31 Mar - 4 Nov: Sat - Wed, 12 noon - 5pm (11am - 5pm BH Sun & Mon; Oct & Nov: 12 noon - 4pm). Garden: 31 Mar - 4 Nov: daily, 11am - 5.30pm (4.30pm in Oct & Nov). Last admission normally $1/2$ hr before closing. Park open daily throughout the year.

Admission: House & Garden: Adult £5, Child £2.50, Family £12.50 (2 adults + children). House or Garden only: Adult £3.20, Child £1.60. Car entry: £3 per car. Coach /minibus entry: £5 (free to booked parties). Motorcycle: £1. Booked Groups: £4 for 15 or more paying adults, not available Suns & BHs.

No photography in house. Partially suitable. WC. Batricars. Licensed. Optional. No extra charge. In grounds, on leads.

DORFOLD HALL

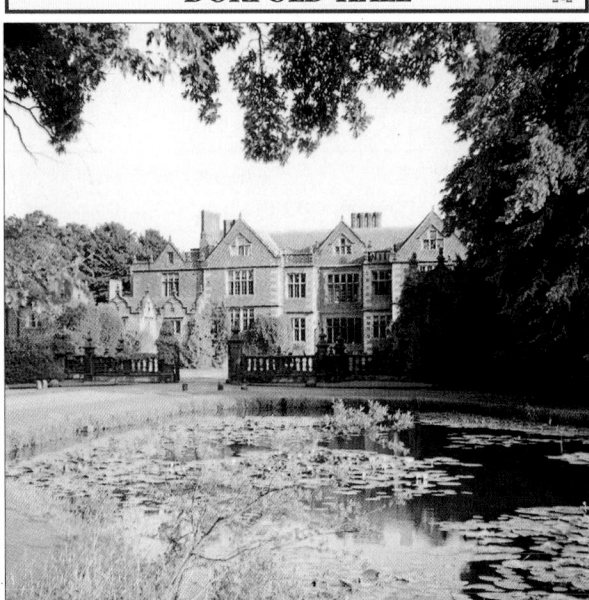

ACTON, Nr NANTWICH, CHESHIRE CW5 8LD

Owner/Contact: Richard Roundell

Tel: 01270 625245 **Fax:** 01270 628723

Jacobean country house built in 1616 for Ralph Wilbraham. Family home of Mr & Mrs Richard Roundell. Beautiful plaster ceilings and oak panelling. Attractive woodland gardens and summer herbaceous borders.

Location: OS Ref. SJ634 525. 1m W of Nantwich on the A534 Nantwich - Wrexham road.

Opening Times: Apr - Oct: Tues only and BH Mons, 2 - 5pm.

Admission: Adult £4.50, Child £3.

Obligatory. Limited. Narrow gates with low arch prevent coaches. In grounds on leads.

GAWSWORTH HALL

MACCLESFIELD, CHESHIRE SK11 9RN

Owner: Mr and Mrs T Richards   *Contact:* Mr T Richards

Tel: 01260 223456 **Fax:** 01260 223469 **e-mail:** gawsworth@lineone.net

Fully lived-in Tudor half-timbered manor house with Tilting Ground. Former home of Mary Fitton, Maid of Honour at the Court of Queen Elizabeth I, and the supposed 'Dark Lady' of Shakespeare's sonnets. Pictures, sculpture and furniture. Open air theatre with covered grandstand - June, July and August, please telephone for details. Situated halfway between Macclesfield and Congleton in an idyllic setting close to the lovely medieval church.

Location: OS Ref. SJ892 697. 3m S of Macclesfield on the A536 Congleton to Macclesfield road.

Opening Times: Easter - 7 Oct: Apr, May & Sept: Sun - Wed, 2 - 5pm plus special events & BH weekends. Jun, Jul & Aug: daily, 2 - 5pm.

Admission: Adult £4.50, Child £2.25.

  Guide dogs in garden only. Tel. for details.

HARE HILL

Over Alderley, Macclesfield, Cheshire SK10 4QB

Owner: The National Trust   **Contact:** The Head Gardener

A woodland garden surrounding a walled garden with pergola, rhododendrons and azaleas; parkland: link path to Alderley Edge (2m).

Location: OS Ref. SJ875 765. Between Alderley Edge and Prestbury, turn N at B5087, Greyhound Road.

Opening Times: 1 Apr - 30 Oct: Weds, Thurs, Sats, Suns & BH Mons, 10am - 5.30pm. Special opening to see rhododendrons & azaleas: 10 - 30 May: daily, 10am - 5.30pm. Closed Nov - Mar.

Admission: £2.50. Entrance per car £1.50 refundable on entry to garden. Groups by written appointment c/o Garden Lodge at address above.

Gravel paths - strong companion advisable.   Not in garden, elsewhere on leads.

LITTLE MORETON HALL

National Trust Photographic Library.

CONGLETON, CHESHIRE CW12 4SD

Owner: The National Trust   *Contact:* The Property Manager

Tel: 01260 272018   **Fax:** 01260 292802

Begun in 1450 and completed 130 years later, Little Moreton Hall is regarded as the finest example of a timber-framed moated manor house in the country. The drunkenly reeling South Front topped by its Elizabethan Long Gallery opens onto a cobbled courtyard and the main body of the Hall. The Chapel, Great Hall, wall paintings and Knot Garden are of particular interest.

Location: OS Ref. SJ833 589. 4m SW of Congleton on E side of A34.

Opening Times: 31 Mar - 4 Nov: daily (includes BH Mons & Good Fri), 11.30am - 5pm. 10 Nov - 22 Dec: weekends only, 11.30am - 4pm.

Admission: Adult £4.40, Child £2.20, Family £11. Groups: £3.50 (must book). Joint ticket with Biddulph Grange Garden £6.75, Child £3.30, Family £16.50.

Braille guide, wheelchair & electric vehicle. WCs.   Car park only.

Peover Hall, Cheshire.

LYME PARK

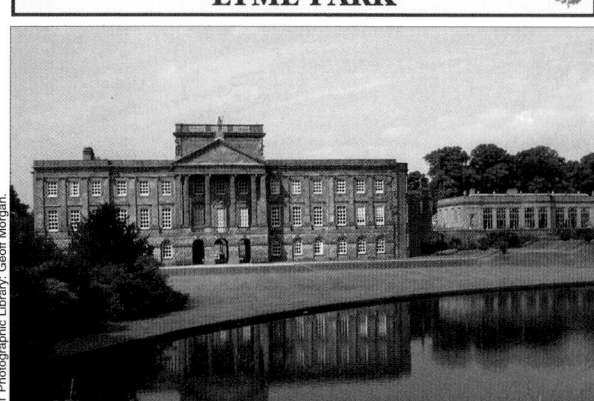

NT Photographic Library: Geoff Morgan.

DISLEY, STOCKPORT, CHESHIRE SK12 2NX

Owner: The National Trust   *Contact:* The Property Manager

Tel: 01663 762023   **Fax:** 01663 765035   **e-mail:** mlyrec@smtp.ntrust.org.uk

Legh family home for 600 years. Part of the original Elizabethan house survives with 18th and 19th century additions by Giacomo Leoni and Lewis Wyatt. Four centuries of period interiors – Mortlake tapestries, Grinling Gibbons carvings, unique collection of English clocks. Historic gardens with conservatory by Wyatt, a lake and a 'Dutch' garden. A 1,400 acre medieval deer park, home to red and fallow deer. Exterior featured as 'Pemberley' in BBC's *Pride and Prejudice*.

Location: OS Ref. SJ966 843. Off the A6 at Disley. 6^1/$_2$ m SE of Stockport.

Opening Times: Park: Apr - Oct: daily, 8am - 8.30pm; Nov - Mar 8am - 6pm. Gardens: 30 Mar - 30 Oct: Fri - Tue, 11am - 5pm, Wed & Thur 1 - 5pm. Nov - 18 Dec: Sats & Suns, 12 noon - 3pm. House: 30 Mar - 30 Oct: Fri - Tue, 1 - 5pm (last admission 4.30pm) (BH Mons, 11am - 5pm). Shop & Tearoom: 30 Mar - 30 Oct: daily, 11am - 5pm. Nov - Mar: Sats & Suns, 12 noon - 4pm.

Admission: House & Garden: £5, House only: £4, Garden only: £2.50, Park only: £3.50 per car. Combined Family Ticket: £15. NT members Free.

No photography in house.   Partially suitable. WC.   Licensed.   By arrangement.   In park, close control. Guide dogs only in house & garden.

MACCLESFIELD MUSEUMS

Tel: 01625 613210   **Fax:** 01625 617880

Roe Street, Macclesfield SK11 6UT   **e-mail:** postmaster@silk-macc.u-net.com

Owner: Macclesfield Museums Trust   **Contact:** Louanne Collins

Silk museum housed in Georgian Sunday School. Development of the silk industry is told through an award-winning audio-visual programme, exhibitions, models and costume. Nearby Paradise Mill houses 26 hand jacquard silk looms. Tours with knowledgeable guides, demonstrations of weaving, shows life in the 1930s.

Location: OS Ref. SJ917 733. Centre of Macclesfield.

Opening Times: Silk Museum: Mon - Sat, 11am - 5pm, BHs & Suns, 1 - 5pm (closed Good Fri, 25, 26 Dec, 1 Jan & Suns Jan - Mar). Paradise Mill: Tue - Sun, 1 - 5pm, Nov - Mar, 1 - 4pm (closed 23 Dec - 2 Jan 2001 & Suns Nov - Mar).

Admission: Adult £2.85, Child/Conc. £2, Family £7.60. Joint ticket: Adult £5, Conc. £2.90, Family £10.90. Special evening rates (2000 prices).

Licensed.   By arrangement.   Guide dogs only.

NESS BOTANIC GARDENS

Tel: 01513 530123   **Fax:** 01513 531004

Ness, Neston, Cheshire CH64 4AY   **e-mail:** ejs@liv.ac.uk

Owner: University of Liverpool   **Contact:** Dr E J Sharples

Location: OS Ref. SJ302 760 (village centre). Off A540. 10m NW of Chester. 1^1/$_2$ m S of Neston.

Opening Times: 1 Mar - 31 Oct: 9.30am - 5pm (last entry). Nov - Feb: 9.30am - 4pm.

Admission: Charge for Adults & Conc. Accompanied child (under 18yrs) Free. 10% discount for groups. Please telephone for details.

NETHER ALDERLEY MILL

Tel: 01625 523012   **Fax:** 01625 527139

Congleton Road, Nether Alderley, Macclesfield, Cheshire SK10 4TW

Owner/Contact: The National Trust

A fascinating overshot tandem wheel watermill, dating from the 15th century, with a stone-tiled low pitched roof. The machinery is in full working order, and grinds flour occasionally for demonstrations.

Location: OS Ref. SJ844 763. 1^1/$_2$ m S of Alderley Edge, on E side of A34.

Opening Times: Apr, May & Oct: Weds, Suns & BH Mons, 1 - 4.30pm. Jun - Sept: daily (except Mons but open BH Mons), 1 - 5pm.

Admission: Adult £2, Child £1. Groups by prior arrangement (max. 20).

Not suitable.   By arrangement.

NORTON PRIORY WALLED GARDEN & MUSEUM   **Tel:** 01928 569895

Tudor Road, Manor Park, Runcorn, Cheshire WA7 1SX
Owner/Contact: The Norton Priory Museum Trust
Site of medieval priory set in beautiful woodland gardens.
Location: OS Ref. SJ545 835. 3m from M56/J11. 2m E of Runcorn.
Opening Times: Garden: 1 Mar - 31 Oct, every afternoon. Museum: all year.
Admission: Adult £3.75, Child/Conc. £2.50. Family £9.80, Groups £2.20.

W/chairs, braille guide, audio tapes & WC.   By arrangement.
In grounds, on leads.   Telephone for details.

PECKFORTON CASTLE   **Tel:** 01829 260930 **Fax:** 01829 261230

Stonehouse Lane, Nr Tarporley CW6 9TN
Owner/Contact: Mrs Graybill
The only intact medieval style castle in Britain. Built mid-1800s, designed by Anthony Salvin.
Location: OS Ref. SJ533 581. Access by gateway on W side of minor road 3/4 m S of Beeston village, 3/4 m N of Peckforton village. 12m E of Chester.
Opening Times: Private functions and weddings only. No public access.

PEOVER HALL

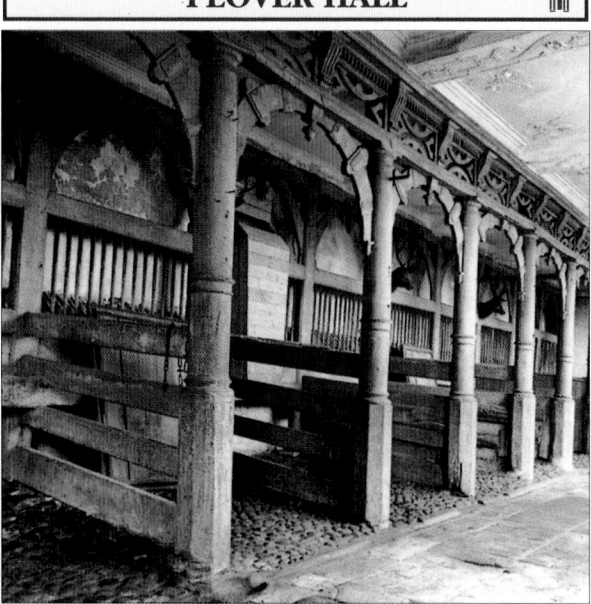

OVER PEOVER, KNUTSFORD WA16 9HN
Owner: Randle Brooks   Contact: I Shepherd

Tel: 01565 632358
An Elizabethan house dating from 1585. Fine Carolean stables. Mainwaring Chapel, 18th century landscaped park. Large garden with topiary work, also walled and herb gardens.
Location: OS Ref. SJ772 734. 4m S of Knutsford off A50 at Whipping Stocks Inn.
Opening Times: Apr - Oct: House, Stables & Gardens: Mons except BHs, 2 - 5pm. Tours of the House at 2.30 & 3.30pm. Stables & Gardens only: Thurs, 2 - 5pm.
Admission: House, Stables & Gardens: Adult £3, Child £2. Stables & Gardens only: £2.

Mondays only.   Obligatory.

QUARRY BANK MILL & STYAL COUNTRY PARK

Styal, Wilmslow, Cheshire SK9 4LA
Owner: The National Trust   **Tel:** 01625 527468 **Fax:** 01625 539267
Contact: The Property Manager
Location: OS Ref. SJ835 830. 1 1/2 m N of Wilmslow off B5166. 2 1/2 m from M56/J5.
Opening Times: Mill: Apr - end Sept: daily, 11am - 6pm, last admission 4.30pm. Oct - Mar: daily except Mons, 11am - 5pm, last admission 3.30pm. Apprentice House & garden: daily except Mons (but open BH Mons),Tue - Fri, 2 - 4.30pm, Sats, Suns & Aug: 11am - 6pm.
Admission: Adult £6, Child/Conc. £3.70, Family £16. Mill only: Adult £4.80, Child/ Conc. £3.40, Family £14.00. Apprentice House & Garden: Adult £3.80, Child/Conc. £2.70, Family £12. Advance bookings essential for groups (10+).

RODE HALL

CHURCH LANE, SCHOLAR GREEN, CHESHIRE ST7 3QP
Owner/Contact: Sir Richard Baker Wilbraham Bt

Tel: 01270 873237 **Fax:** 01270 882962
The Wilbraham family have lived at Rode since 1669; the present house was constructed in two stages, the earlier two storey wing and stable block around 1705 and the main building was completed in 1752. Later alterations by Lewis Wyatt and Darcy Braddell were undertaken in 1812 and 1927 respectively. The house stands in a Repton landscape and the extensive gardens include a woodland garden, with a terraced rock garden and grotto, which has many species of rhododendrons, azaleas, hellebores and climbing roses following snowdrops and daffodils in the early spring. The formal rose garden was designed by W Nesfield in 1860 and there is a large walled kitchen garden which is at its best from the middle of June. The icehouse in the park has recently been restored.
Location: OS Ref. SJ819 573. 5m SW of Congleton between the A34 and A50. Kidsgrove railway station 2m NW of Kidsgrove.
Opening Times: 4 Apr - 26 Sept: Weds & BHs (closed Good Fri) and by appointment. Garden only: Tues & Thurs, 2 - 5pm. Snowdrop Walk: 4 - 18 Feb: 12 noon - 4pm.
Admission: House, Garden & Kitchen Garden: Adult £4, OAP £2.50. Garden & Kitchen Garden: Adult £2.50, OAP £1.50. Snowdrop Walk: £2.50.

Home-made teas.   On leads.

TABLEY HOUSE

KNUTSFORD, CHESHIRE WA16 0HB
Owner: Victoria University of Manchester   Contact: The Administrator

Tel: 01565 750151 **Fax:** 01565 653230
The finest Palladian mansion in the North West of England, Grade I, by John Carr of York completed 1767 for the Leicester family who lived at Tabley for over 700 years. The first collection of English paintings ever made, furniture and memorabilia, can be seen in the State Rooms. Private chapel 1678 re-erected due to brine pumping.
Location: OS Ref. SJ725 777. M6/J19, A556 S on to A5033. 2m W of Knutsford.
Opening Times: Apr - end Oct inclusive: Thurs, Fris, Sats, Suns & BHs, 2 - 5pm.
Admission: Adult £4. Child £1.50. Groups by arrangement.

       Registered Charity 1047299.

TATTON PARK 🌱   See page 400 for full page entry.

Special Events
Index
◀◀◀ page 33

WOODHEY CHAPEL   **Tel:** 01270 524215

Faddiley, Nr Nantwich, Cheshire CW5 8JH   **Contact:** Mr Robinson, The Curator

Owner: The Trustees of Woodhey Chapel

Small private chapel that has been recently restored.

Location: OS Ref. SJ573 528. Proceeding W from Nantwich on A534, turn left 1m W of the Faddiley - Brindley villages onto narrow lane, keep ahead at next turn, at road end obtain key from farmhouse.

Opening Times: Apr - Oct: Sats & BHs, 2 - 5pm, or apply for key at Woodhey Hall.

Admission: £1.

Arley Hall, Cheshire.

ABBOT HALL ART GALLERY
Kendal

Abbot Hall is a jewel of a building in a beautiful setting on the banks of the River Kent, surrounded by a park and overlooked by the ruins of Kendal Castle. This is one of Britain's finest small art galleries and a wonderful place in which to see and enjoy changing exhibitions in the elegantly proportioned rooms of a Grade I Listed Georgian building. The collection includes works by Romney, Ruskin, Turner and Freud. The adjacent Museum of Lakeland Life is a popular family attraction with a Victorian street scene, farmhouse rooms, Arthur Ransome room and displays of Arts and Crafts Movement furniture and fabrics.

❖

Owner: Lake District Art Gallery & Museum Trust

CONTACT

Sandy Kitching
Abbot Hall Art Gallery
Kendal
Cumbria
LA9 5AL

Tel: 01539 722464

Fax: 01539 722494

e-mail: info@ abbothall.org.uk

LOCATION

OS Ref. SD516 922

10mins from M6/J36. Follow brown museum signs to South Kendal.

Rail: Oxenholme.

Air: Manchester.

OPENING TIMES

8 February - 21 December: Daily, 10.30am - 5pm, reduced hours in winter.

ADMISSION

Adult	£3.00
Child	£1.50
Student	£1.50
OAP	£2.80
Family	£7.50
Groups	£2.50

Friends of the Trust membership available.

All ages welcome.

ℹ No photography. No mobile phones.

♿ Chairlifts in split level galleries. WCs.

☕ Licensed.

🍴 By arrangement.

🅿 Ample. Free.

🐕 Guide dogs only.

❄

SPECIAL EVENTS

- **FEB 8 - MAR 18:** Andy Goldsworth - Photographic Works.

- **MAR 27 - JUN 3:** Li Yuan-chia

- **JUN 12 - OCT 7:** Paula Rego

- **OCT 16 - DEC 21:** Hughie O'Donoghue Carborundum Prints: Process and Content.

BLACKWELL - THE ARTISTIC HOUSE
Bowness on Windermere

Owner: Lake District Art Gallery & Museum Trust

CONTACT

Sandy Kitching
Blackwell
The Artistic House
Bowness on Windermere
Cumbria
LA23 3JR

Tel: 01539 722464

Fax: 01539 722494

e-mail: info@ blackwell.org.uk

LOCATION

OS Ref. SD400 945

$1^1/2$ m S of Bowness just off the A5074 on the B5360.

Rail: Windermere.

Air: Manchester.

Blackwell is a superb example of an Arts and Crafts Movement house situated in the Lake District. Completed in 1900, it sits in an elevated position overlooking Lake Windermere. Blackwell is the most important, and the largest, surviving early example of work by the architect Mackay Hugh Baillie Scott. Changing exhibitions of the highest quality applied arts and crafts can be seen in the setting of the Arts and Crafts Movement architecture itself.

In this treasure trove of 1890s Arts and Crafts design are fine examples of the decorative arts, drawn from natural forms. Lakeland birds and local wild flowers, trees and berries can be seen in the many original stained glass windows, pristine oak panelling and plasterwork. These rooms were designed for relaxation and everywhere you turn you will find inglenooks and places to sit and enjoy the views and garden terraces.

❖

OPENING TIMES

New attraction
6 July - 21 December 2001:
Daily, 10am - 5pm,
reduced hours in winter.

ADMISSION

Please contact for details.

Note: Concessions and Friends of the Trust/ Friends of Blackwell membership available.

All ages welcome.

SPECIAL EVENTS

- **JUL 6 - SEPT 23:**
  Magdalene Odundo - Ceramic Vessels.
- **OCT 4 - DEC 21:**
  Kokten Korgei - Contemporary Crafts from Japan.

ⓘ No photography. No mobile phones.

♿ Partially suitable. WCs.

☕ Licensed.

🚶 By arrangement.

🅿 Limited for cars and coaches.

🐕 Guide dogs only.

North West England

DALEMAIN
Penrith

Owner:
Robert Hasell McCosh Esq

CONTACT

Bryan McDonald
Administrator
Dalemain Estate Office
Dalemain
Penrith
Cumbria
CA11 0HB

Tel: 017684 86450

Fax: 017684 86223

LOCATION

OS Ref. NY477 269

On A592 1m S of A66.
4m SW of Penrith.
From London, M1,
M6/J40: 4 hrs.

From Edinburgh,
A73, M74,
M6/J40: 2¹/₂ hrs.

Rail: Penrith 4m.

Taxi: Lakeland Taxis:
Penrith 01768 865722.

DALEMAIN is a fine mixture of mediaeval, Tudor and early Georgian architecture. The imposing Georgian façade strikes the visitor immediately but in the cobbled courtyard the atmosphere of the north country Tudor manor is secure. The present owner's family have lived at Dalemain since 1679 and have collected china, furniture and family portraits. Visitors can see the grand Drawing Rooms with 18th century Chinese wallpaper and fine oak panelling, also the Nursery and Housekeeper's Room. The Norman pele tower contains the regimental collection of the Westmorland and Cumberland Yeomanry. The house is full of the paraphernalia of a well established family house which is still very much lived in by the family.

The 16th century Great Barn holds a collection of agricultural bygones and a Fell Pony Museum. Do not miss Mrs Mouse's house on the back stairs or the Nursery with toys from all ages. Something of interest for all the family. Location for ITV's production of *Jane Eyre*.

GARDENS

The Gardens have a long history stretching back to a mediaeval herb garden. Today a knot garden remains, with a fine early Roman fountain and box hedges enclosing herb beds.

The imposing terrace wall supports a full and colourful herbaceous border during the summer months. Visitors can enjoy the fine views of the park and the woodland and riverside walks. The gardens have been featured on television's *Gardener's World* and also in *Country Life*. Deer Park.

Fashion shows, archery, clay pigeon shooting, garden parties, rallies, filming, caravan rallies, antique fairs and children's camps. Business meetings and conferences. Grand piano available. Deer Park. Lectures on the house, gardens and history by arrangement (max 50). No photography in house. Moorings available on Ullswater.

Corporate events: telephone for details.

Visitors may drive into the Courtyard and alight near the gift shop. Electric scooter for visiting the gardens. Admission free for visitors in wheelchairs. WCs.

Licensed (in Mediaeval Hall). Seats 50. Groups must book for lunches/high teas. Free admission.

1 hr tours. German and French translations in every room. Garden tour for groups extra.

50 yds from house. Free.

Welcome. Guides can be arranged. Interest includes Military, Country Life, Agricultural and Fell Pony Museums, also country walk past Dacre Castle to St Andrew's Church, Dacre where there is a fine Laurence Whistler window.

Guide dogs in house only. Strictly no dogs in garden but allowed in grounds.

OPENING TIMES

SUMMER
25 March - 7 October
Sunday - Thursday

House: 11am - 4pm.

Gardens, restaurant, tearoom, gift shop, plant sales & museums: 10.30am - 5pm.

NB. Groups (12+) please book.

WINTER
October - Easter open by special arrangement with the Administrator.

ADMISSION

House & Garden

Adult	£5.00
Child (6-16yrs)	£3.00
Family	£13.00

Gardens only

Adult	£3.00
Child (6-16yrs)	Free

Groups (12+)

Adult	£4.00
Child (6-16yrs)	£3.00

All prices include VAT.

SPECIAL EVENTS

- **JUL 21 - 22:**
  Dalemain Rainbow Craft Fair.

- **AUG:**
  Cumbrian Classic Car Show. Please telephone for further details.

CONFERENCE/FUNCTION

ROOM	SIZE	MAX CAPACITY
Dining Room		40
Old Hall		50

Jarrold Publishing

Owner: Lord Cavendish of Furness

CONTACT

Holker Hall & Gardens
Cark-in-Cartmel
Grange-over-Sands
Cumbria
LA11 7PL

Tel: 01539 558328

Fax: 01539 558838

e-mail: publicopening@
holker.co.uk

(NW)

LOCATION

OS Ref. SD359 773

Close to Morecambe Bay,
5m W of Grange-over-
Sands by B5277.
From Kendal, A6, A590,
B5277, B5278: 16m.

Motorway: M6/J36.

Bus: From Grange-
over-Sands.

Rail: Cark Station.

Taxi: Parkers Motors,
Grange-over-Sands.

Air: Blackpool/
Manchester.

CONFERENCE/FUNCTION		
ROOM	SIZE	MAX CAPACITY
Burlington	16 x 6m	100
Cavendish	14.5 x 7.5m	120

HOLKER HALL & GARDENS
Cark-in-Cartmel

HOLKER HALL, home of Lord and Lady Cavendish, shows the confidence, spaciousness and prosperity of Victorian style on its grandest scale. The New Wing, built by the 7th Duke of Devonshire (1871-4), replaced a previous wing totally destroyed by fire. Workmanship throughout is of the highest quality, particularly the detailed interior carving and linenfold panelling.

Despite this grand scale, Holker is very much a family home. Visitors can wander freely throughout the New Wing. Photographs, beautiful floral displays and bowls of scented pot pourri create the warm and friendly atmosphere so often remarked upon by visitors. Varying in period and style, Louis XV pieces happily mix with the Victorian. Pictures range from an early copy of the famous triple portrait of Charles I by Van Dyck to a modern painting by Douglas Anderson.

GARDENS

Christie's/HHA Garden of the Year (1991), includes formal and woodland areas covering 24 acres. Designated *"amongst the best in the world in terms of design and content"* by the *Good Gardens Guide.* This wonderful Italianate-cum-English garden includes a lime-stone cascade, a fountain, a sunken garden and many rare and beautiful plants and shrubs. The gardens featured in BBC 2's *Gardeners' World.* Holker is home to the Holker Garden Festival 1 - 3 June.

❖

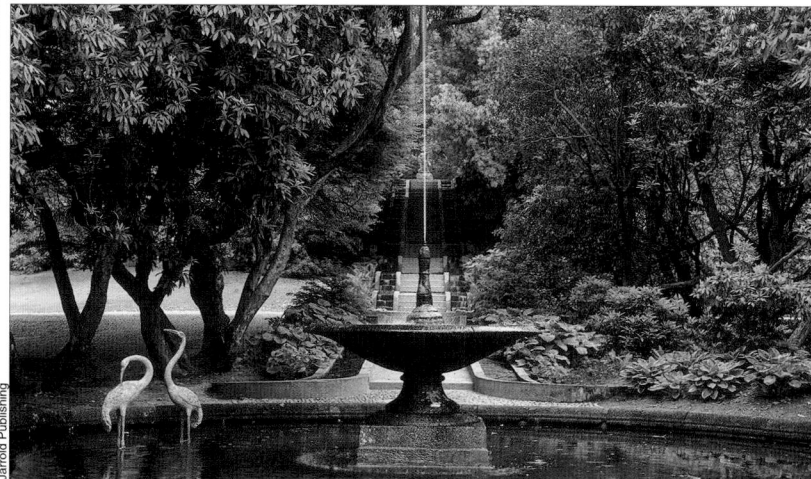

Jarrold Publishing

OPENING TIMES

SUMMER
1 April - 31 October
Daily except Sats
10am - 6pm.

Last admission 4.30pm.

WINTER
1 November - 31 March
Closed.

ADMISSION

SUMMER
House & Garden

Adult £6.50
Child* £3.95

Groups (20-100)
Adult £4.50
Child* £3.00
OAP........................£4.00

* Under 6yrs Free.

🎭 SPECIAL EVENTS

• **JUN 1 - 3:**
Holker Garden Festival. Magnificent horticultural displays & floral art combined with countryside displays and festival gardens. Family & children entertainment, craft demonstrations etc.
Tel: 01539 558838
Fax: 01539 558776

• **AUG:**
MG Rally. Post and Pre 1955 MGs in concours and driving trials. Discounted admission to MG drivers. Competition entries on the day.

Please telephone for further details.

ℹ️ Suitable for filming and photography. Deer Park. Lakeland Motor Museum, adventure playground and exhibitions. No photography in house. Guide book translations in French, Spanish, German, Dutch & Japanese.

⊤ Wedding receptions.

♿ Visitors alight at entrance. Ramps and unisex WCs.

☕ 🍴 The Courtyard Café (max 200).

👤 Pre-booked tours at additional cost from 50p each.

🅿️ 150 yds from Hall. Plus grass car parking.

📖 New programme of educational packages available in 2001 focusing on KS1 & 2 and tailor-made courses.

🐕 In grounds on leads. No dogs in the gardens.

North West England

Nicola Stocken-Jenkins

LEVENS HALL
Kendal

LEVENS HALL is an Elizabethan mansion built around a 13th century pele tower. The much loved home of the Bagot family, visitors comment on the warm and friendly atmosphere. Fine panelling and plasterwork, period furniture, Cordova leather wall coverings, paintings by Rubens, Lely and Cuyp, the earliest English patchwork and Wellingtoniana combine with other beautiful objects to form a fascinating collection.

The world famous Topiary Gardens were laid out by Monsieur Beaumont from 1694 and his design has remained largely unchanged to this day. Over ninety individual pieces of topiary, some over nine metres high, massive beech hedges and colourful seasonal bedding provide a magnificent visual impact. Past winner of the HHA/Christie's Garden of the Year Award. During 2001, the 'Year of the Artist', Julia Barton will be displaying a residency exhibition, adopting a contemporary approach to topiary and plant sculpture. Monty Don wrote in The Observer that the gardens at Levens are 'Considered to be in the top ten UK gardens'. Levens Hall provided the interior of Hamley Hall in the recent highly acclaimed BBC production of 'Wives and Daughters' by Elizabeth Gaskell.

On Sundays and Bank Holidays 'Bertha', a full size Showman's Engine, is in steam. Delicious home-made lunches and teas are available, together with the award winning Levens beer 'Morocco Ale', in the Bellingham Buttery.

Owner: C H Bagot

CONTACT

Peter Milner
Levens Hall
Kendal
Cumbria
LA8 0PD

Tel: 01539 560321

Fax: 01539 560669

e-mail: email@
levenshall.fsnet.co.uk

LOCATION

OS Ref. SD495 851

5m S of Kendal on the A6.
Exit M6/J36.

Rail: Oxenholme 5m.

Air: Manchester.

 No indoor photography.

 Partially suitable. WC.
Wheelchair loan - gardens
only suitable.

Licensed.

By arrangement.

 P

 Guide dogs only.

OPENING TIMES

SUMMER

1 April - 11 October
Sun - Thur
(closed Fris & Sats).

House: 12 noon - 5pm
Last admission 4.30pm.

Group tours of Hall
at 10am available by prior
arrangement.

Gardens, Plant Centre, Gift
Shop & Tearoom:
10am - 5pm.

WINTER

Closed.

ADMISSION

House & Gardens

Adult £6.00
Child £3.00
Groups (20+)
Adult £4.80
School £2.80
Family (2+3) £17.50

Gardens

Adult £4.50
Child £2.20
Groups (20+)
Adult £3.70
School £2.00
Family (2+3) £13.00

Evening Tours

House & Garden for
groups (20+)
by arrangement £7.00

Gardens only
groups (20+) by prior
arrangement £5.00

Morning Tours

House tours for groups
(20+/min charge £110.)
by arrangement £5.50

Season Tickets

Garden (single) £17.00

No admission charge for
gift shop, tearoom and
plant centre

MUNCASTER CASTLE
GARDENS & OWL CENTRE, Ravenglass

MUNCASTER CASTLE has been owned by the Pennington family since 1208. It has grown from the original pele tower built on Roman foundations to the impressive structure visible today. Outstanding features are the Great Hall and Salvin's Octagonal Library and the Drawing Room with its barrel ceiling.

The castle contains many treasures including beautiful furniture, exquisite needlework panels, tapestries and oriental rugs. The family silver is very fine and is accompanied in the Dining Room by the Ongley Service, the most ornamental set of porcelain ever created by the Derby factory, Florentine 16th century bronzes and an alabaster lady by Giambologna can be seen. The family are actively involved in entertaining their many visitors.

The woodland gardens cover 77 acres and command spectacular views of the Lakeland Fells, with many delightful walks. From mid-March to June the rhododendrons, azaleas, camellias and magnolias are at their best.

The Owl Centre boasts a fine collection of owls from all over the world. 'Meet the Birds' occurs daily at 2.30pm (11Mar to 4 Nov), when a talk is given on the work of the centre. Weather permitting, the birds fly free.

NEW – shrink to 2 inches tall and see if you can survive the dangers of meadowland by getting through the MeadowVole Maze without getting eaten. Great for kids of all ages!

Owner: Mrs Phyllida Gordon-Duff-Pennington

CONTACT

Peter Frost-Pennington
Muncaster Castle
Ravenglass
Cumbria
CA18 1RQ

Tel: 01229 717614
Fax: 01229 717010

e-mail: info@ muncastercastle.co.uk

LOCATION

OS Ref. SD103 965

On the A595 1m S of Ravenglass, 19m S of Whitehaven.

From London 6 hrs, Chester $2^1/_2$ hrs, Edinburgh $3^1/_2$ hrs, M6/J36, A590, A595 (from S). M6/J40, A66, A595(from E). Carlisle, A595 (from N).

Rail: Ravenglass (on Barrow-in-Furness-Carlisle Line) $1^1/_2$ m.

Air: Manchester $2^1/_2$ hrs.

CONFERENCE/FUNCTION		
ROOM	SIZE	MAX CAPACITY
Drawing Rm	–	120
Dining Rm	–	50
Family Dining Rm	–	60
Great Hall	–	110
Old Laundry	–	120
Library	–	40

Church. Suitable for fashion shoots, garden parties, film location, clay pigeon shooting. No photography inside the castle. Home of the World Owl Trust, run by TV naturalist Tony Warburton.

Wedding receptions. For catering and functions in the castle Tel: 01229 717614.

By prior arrangement visitors alight near Castle. Wheelchairs for loan. WCs. Special audio tour tapes for the partially sighted/those with learning difficulties. Allocated parking.

Creeping Kate's Kitchen (licensed) (max 80) – full menu. Groups can book: 01229 717432 to qualify for discounts.

Individual audio tour (40mins) included in price. Private tours with a personal guide (family member possible) can be arranged at additional fee. Lectures by arrangement.

P 500 cars 800 yds from House; coaches may park closer.

Guides available. Historical subjects, horticulture, conservation, owl tours.

In grounds, on leads.

OPENING TIMES

Castle
11 March - 4 November
Daily (closed Sat),
12 noon - 5pm.

Gardens & Owl Centre
All year: daily:
10.30am - 6pm or dusk
if earlier.

'Meet the Birds'
11 March - 4 November
Daily at 2.30pm.

'Heron Happy Hour'
Feeding of wild herons.
11 March - 4 November
Daily at 4.30pm.

Winter
Castle closed. Open by appointment for groups.

ADMISSION

Castle, Gardens & Owl Centre
Adult £6.50
Child (5-15yrs)..........£4.00
Under 5yrs...............Free
Family (2+2) £18.00
Groups
Adult £5.50
Child (5-15yrs)..........£3.00

Season Tickets
Adult £5.00
Family £32.50

Gardens & Owl Centre and MeadowVole Maze
Adult £5.00
Child (5-15yrs)..........£3.00
Under 5yrs...............Free
Family (2+2) £15.00
Groups
Adult £4.50
Child (5-15yrs)..........£2.00

North West England

ACORN BANK GDN & WATERMILL

TEMPLE SOWERBY, PENRITH, CUMBRIA CA10 1SP

Owner: The National Trust   *Contact:* The Custodian

Tel: 01768 361893   **e-mail:** racorn@smtp.ntrust.org.uk

A one hectare garden protected by fine oaks under which grow a vast display of daffodils. Inside the walls there are orchards containing a variety of fruit trees surrounded by mixed borders with shrubs, herbaceous plants and roses, while the impressive herb garden has the largest collection of culinary and medicinal plants in the north. A circular woodland walk runs beside the Crowdundle Beck to Acorn Bank Watermill, which although under restoration, is open to visitors. The house is open only during some events.

Location: Gate: OS Ref. NY612 281. Just N of Temple Sowerby, 6m E of Penrith on A66.

Opening Times: 31 Mar - 4 Nov: daily, 10am - 5pm. Last admission 4.30pm.

Admission: Adult £2.50, Child £1.20, Family £6.20. Pre-arranged groups £1.80.

[icons] Grounds only. WCs.

BROUGH CASTLE   **Tel:** 0161 242 1400

Brough, Cumbria

Owner: English Heritage   **Contact:** The North Regional Office

This ancient site dates back to Roman times. The 12th century keep replaced an earlier stronghold destroyed by the Scots in 1174.

Location: OS Ref. NY791 141. 8m SE of Appleby S of A66. South part of the village.

Opening Times: Any reasonable time.

Admission: Free.

BROUGHAM CASTLE   **Tel:** 01768 862488

Penrith, Cumbria CA10 2AA

Owner: English Heritage   **Contact:** The Custodian

These impressive ruins on the banks of the River Eamont include an early 13th century keep and later buildings. You can climb to the top of the keep and survey the domain of its eccentric one-time owner Lady Anne Clifford, who restored the castle in the 17th century. There is a small exhibition of Roman tombstones from the nearby fort.

Location: OS Ref. NY537 290. 1$^{1}/_{2}$ m SE of Penrith, between A66 & B6262.

Opening Times: 1 Apr - 30 Sept: daily, 10am - 6pm. 1 - 31 Oct: daily, 10am - 5pm.

Admission: Adult £2.10, Child £1.10, Conc. £1.60. 15% discount for groups (11+).

[icons] Grounds suitable.   P Limited.   [icon] In grounds, on leads.   [icon] Tel. for details.

BEATRIX POTTER GALLERY

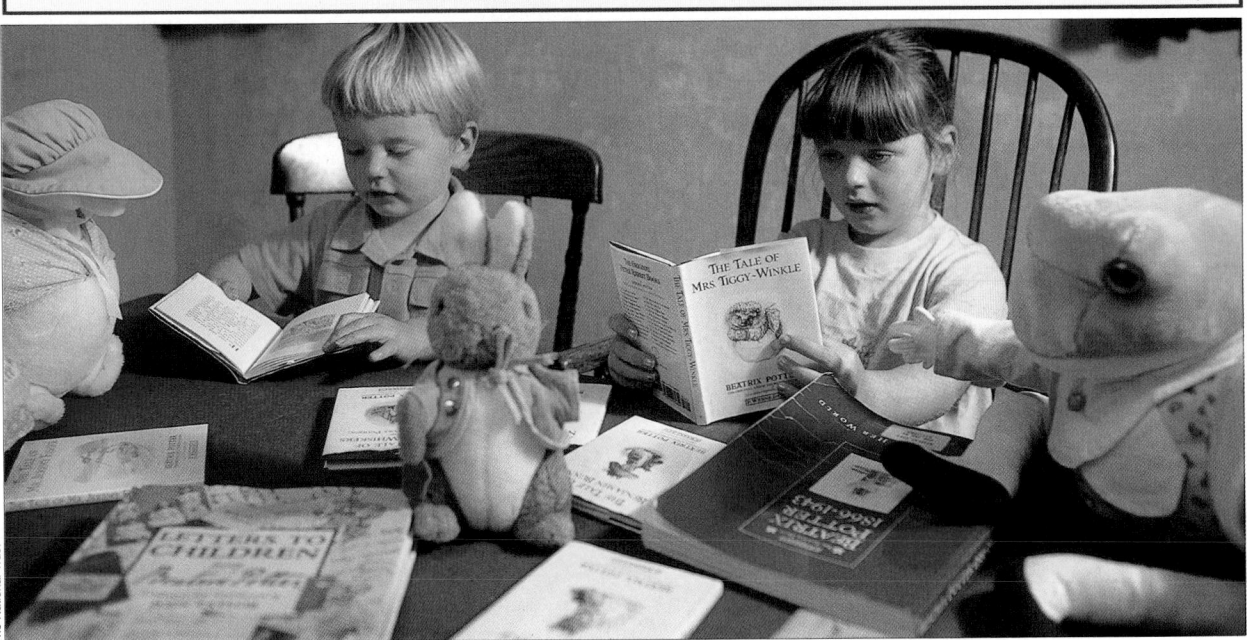

The National Trust

MAIN STREET, HAWKSHEAD, CUMBRIA LA22 0NS

Owner: The National Trust   *Contact:* The Custodian

Tel: 01539 436355

An annually changing exhibition of original sketches and watercolours painted by Beatrix Potter for her children's stories. Each year the new exhibition delights young and old as they discover the amazing delicacy and charm of her work. One of many historic buildings in this picturesque village, the gallery was once the office of Beatrix Potter's husband, William Heelis, and the interior remains substantially unaltered since his day. The gallery is ideally matched with a visit to Beatrix Potter's house, Hill Top, two miles away, where she wrote and illustrated many of her children's stories.

Location: OS Ref. SD352 982. 5m SSW of Ambleside. In the Square.

Opening Times: 1 Apr - 1 Nov: Sun - Thur (closed Fris & Sats except Good Fri) 10.30am - 4.30pm. Last admission 4pm. Admission is by timed ticket (incl. NT members).

Admission: Adult £3, Child £1.50. No reduction for groups.

[icons] 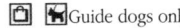 Guide dogs only.

CARLISLE CASTLE ⛉

© English Heritage Photo Library.

CARLISLE, CUMBRIA CA3 8UR

Owner: English Heritage   *Contact:* The Custodian

Tel: 01228 591922

This impressive medieval castle, where Mary Queen of Scots was once imprisoned, has a long and tortuous history of warfare and family feuds. A portcullis hangs menacingly over the gatehouse passage, there is a maze of passages and chambers, endless staircases to lofty towers and you can walk the high ramparts for stunning views. There is also a medieval manor house in miniature: a suite of medieval rooms furnished as they might have been when used by the castle's former constable. The castle is also the home of the Museum of the King's Own Border Regiment (included in the admission price).

Location: OS85 Ref. NY397 563. In Carlisle town, at N end of city centre.
Open: 1 Apr - 30 Sept: daily, 9.30am - 6pm. 1 - 31 Oct: daily, 10am - 5pm.
1 Nov - 31 Mar: daily, 10am - 4pm. Closed 24 - 26 Dec.
Admission: Adult £3.10, Child £1.60, Conc £2.30. 15% discount for groups (11+).

📷 ♿ Partially suitable, wheelchairs available. 🛈 By arrangement.
🅿 No parking. 🔇 🐕 Dogs on leads. ❊ 🎗 Tel. for details.

CARLISLE CATHEDRAL

Tel: 01228 548151 **Fax:** 01228 547049

Carlisle, Cumbria CA3 8TZ

e-mail: office@carlislecathedral.org.uk
Contact: Ms C Baines

Fine sandstone Cathedral, founded in 1122. Medieval stained glass. Gift shop. Restaurant.
Location: OS Ref. NY399 559. Carlisle city centre, 2m from M6/J43.
Opening Times: Mon - Sat: 7.45am - 6.15pm, Suns, 7.45 - 5pm. Closes 4pm between Christmas Day & New Year. Sun services: 8am, 10.30am & 3pm. Weekday services: 8am, 5.30pm & a 12.30 service on Weds, Fris and Saints' Days.
Admission: Donation.

CONISHEAD PRIORY & MANJUSHRI BUDDHIST TEMPLE

Ulverston, Cumbria LA12 9QQ   **Tel:** 01229 584029 **Fax:** 01229 580080
Owner: Manjushri Mahayana Buddhist Centre   **Contact:** Mr D Coote
A Georgian gothic mansion on site of a medieval Augustinian Priory.
Location: OS Ref. SD300 750. 2m S of Ulverston on Bardsea Coast Rd A5087.
Opening Times: Easter - Oct, w/e & BHs, 2 - 5pm. Closed 9 - 25 June & 21 July - 20 Aug.
Admission: Free. House tours and audio visual: Adult £2, Child 75p, OAP £1.

DALEMAIN 🏛

See page 408 for full page entry.

DOVE COTTAGE & WORDSWORTH MUSEUM

Tel: 01539 435544
Grasmere, Cumbria LA22 9SH
Fax: 01539 435748
See full page advertisement on page 24
e-mail: enquiries@wordsworth.org.uk
Owner: Wordsworth Trust
Contact: Enquiries

Wordsworth's home 1799 - 1808, Dove Cottage is beautifully preserved. Visitors are offered guided tours. The garden is open, weather permitting. The award-winning Wordsworth Museum displays a permanent exhibition and a programme of special exhibitions and events.

Location: OS Ref. NY342 070. Immediately S of Grasmere village on A591. Main car/coach park next to Dove Cottage Tea Rooms.
Opening Times: All year: daily, 9.30am - 5pm. Closed 10 Jan - 6 Feb (inc) & 24 - 26 Dec.
Admission: Adult £5, Child £2.50, Student £4.20, OAP £4.70 (2000 prices). Pre-arranged groups (15-60): Adult £4.40, Child £2.20. Reciprocal discount ticket with Rydal Mount and Wordsworth House, Cockermouth.

🛈 No photography. 📷 ♿ Partially suitable. WC. 🍴 🛈 Obligatory.
🅿 Limited. 🔇 🐕 Guide dogs only. ❊ 🎗 Please tel. for details. 📶

FELL FOOT PARK 🌿

Tel: 01539 531273 **Fax:** 01539 530049
Newby Bridge, Ulverston LA12 8NN
e-mail: rffoot@smtp.ntrust.org.uk
Owner: The National Trust
Contact: The Property Manager

This Victorian park, restored to its former glory, offers substantial access to the lakeshore of Windermere where there are leisure facilities in season. Fine picnic areas and boat hire make this property particularly rewarding for families.

Location: OS96, Ref. SD381 869. At the extreme S end of Lake Windermere on E shore, entrance from A592.
Opening Times: Daily, 9am - 7pm or dusk if earlier. Facilities & Shop: 25 Mar - 28 Oct: daily, 11am - 4.30pm.
Admission: Car park: £2 (up to 2hrs), £5 (all day).Coaches £10 by arrangement.

📷 ♿ Partially suitable. 🍴 🅿 Charge. 🐕 On leads. ❊ 🎗 Tel. for details.

FURNESS ABBEY ⛉

Tel: 01229 823420
Barrow-in-Furness, Cumbria LH13 0TJ
Owner: English Heritage   **Contact:** The Custodian

Hidden in a peaceful green valley are the beautiful red sandstone remains of the wealthy abbey founded in 1123 by Stephen, later King of England. This abbey first belonged to the Order of Savigny and later to the Cistercians. There is a museum and exhibition.

Location: OS96, Ref. SD218 717. 1½ m NE of Barrow-in-Furness.
Opening Times: 1 Apr - 30 Sept: daily, 10am - 6pm. 1 - 31 Oct:, daily, 10am - 5pm.
1 Nov - 31 Mar: Wed - Sun, 10am - 4pm. Closed 1 - 2pm in winter. Closed 24 - 26 Dec.
Admission: Adult £2.70, Child £1.40, Conc. £2. 15% discount for groups (11+).

📷 ♿ Grounds suitable. 🎧 Inclusive. 🅿 🔇 🐕 In grounds, on leads.
❊ 🎗 Tel. for details.

HARDKNOTT ROMAN FORT ⛉

Tel: 0161 242 1400
Ravenglass, Cumbria
Owner: English Heritage   **Contact:** The Regional Office
This fort, built between AD120 and 138, controlled the road from Ravenglass to Ambleside.
Location: OS Ref. NY218 015. At the head of Eskdale. 9m NE of Ravenglass, at W end of Hardknott Pass.
Opening Times: Any reasonable time. Access may be hazardous in winter.
Admission: Free.

HERON CORN MILL & MUSEUM OF PAPERMAKING   **Tel:** 015395 65027

Fax: 015395 65033 **e-mail:** ntstobbs@virgin.net
c/o Henry Cooke, Waterhouse Mills, Beetham, Milnthorpe LA7 7AR
Owner: Heron Corn Mill Beetham Trust   **Contact:** Mr Neil Stobbs
Location: OS Ref. SD497 800. At Beetham. 1m S of Milntorpe on the A6.
Opening Times: Easter: 1 Apr - 30 Sept: Tue - Sun & BH Mon, 11am - 5pm.
Admission: Adult £1.50, Child/OAP £1, Family (2+2) £4.50, Coach parties/groups 10% discount if pre-booked.

HILL TOP 🌿

Tel: 01539 436269 **e-mail:** rpmht@smtp.ntrust.org.uk
Near Sawrey, Ambleside, Cumbria LA22 0LF
Owner: The National Trust   **Contact:** The Property Manager
Beatrix Potter wrote many 'Peter Rabbit' books in this little 17th century house, which contains her furniture and china. There is a traditional cottage garden attached.
Location: OS Ref. SD370 955. 2m S of Hawkshead, in hamlet of Near Sawrey, behind the Tower Bank Arms.
Opening Times: Mar - May: 11am - 4.30pm. June - Aug, 10.30am - 5pm. Sept & Oct, 11am - 4.30pm. Last admission 30mins before closing. Booking prior to visit essential to guarantee entry.
Admission: Adult £4, Child £2, Family £9.75. No reduction for groups.

HOLEHIRD

Tel: 01539 446008   **e-mail:** george.feather@care4free.net

Patterdale Road, Windermere, Cumbria LA23 1NP

Owner: Lakeland Horticultural Society   **Contact:** The Hon Secretary

Over 4 acres of hillside gardens overlooking Troutbeck Valley, including a walled garden and national collection of astilbes, hydrangeas and polystichum ferns. All of the work in the gardens is done by volunteers.

Location: OS Ref. NY410 008. On A592, ³/₄ m N of junction with A591. ¹/₂ m N of Windermere. 1m from Townend.

Opening Times: All year: dawn to dusk.

Admission: Free. Donation appreciated (at least £2 suggested).

HOLKER HALL

See page 409 for full page entry.

LANERCOST PRIORY

Tel: 01697 73030

Brampton, Cumbria CA8 2HQ

Owner: English Heritage   **Contact:** The Custodian

This Augustinian priory was founded c1166. The nave of the church, which is intact and in use as the local parish church, contrasts with the ruined chancel, transepts and priory buildings.

Location: OS86, Ref. NY556 637. 2m NE of Brampton. 1m N of Naworth Castle.

Opening Times: 1 Apr - 30 Sept: daily, 10am - 6pm. 1 - 31 Oct: daily, 10am - 5pm.

Admission: Adult £2.10, Child £1.10, Conc. £1.60. Groups: 15% discount for groups (11+).

Ground floor suitable.   Inclusive.   Limited.   Tel. for details.

LEVENS HALL

See page 410 for full page entry.

HUTTON-IN-THE-FOREST

PENRITH, CUMBRIA CA11 9TH

Owner: *Lord Inglewood*   **Contact:** *Edward Thompson*

Tel: 01768 484449   **Fax:** 01768 484571   **e-mail:** hutton-in-the-forest@talk21.com

The home of Lord Inglewood's family since 1605. Built around a medieval pele tower with 17th, 18th and 19th century additions. Fine collections of furniture and paintings, ceramics and tapestries. Outstanding grounds with terraces, topiary, walled garden, dovecote and woodland walk through magnificent specimen trees.

Location: OS Ref. NY460 358. 6m NW of Penrith & 2 ¹/₂ m from M6/J41 on B5305.

Opening Times: 12 Apr - 30 Sept: Thur - Fri, Suns & BH Mons. 12.30 - 4pm (last entry).

Tearoom: As house: 11am - 4.30pm. Grounds: daily except Sats, 11am - 5pm.

Admission: House, Gardens & Grounds: Adult £4.50, Child £2.50, Family £12. Gardens & Grounds: Adult £2.50, Child Free.

Picnic area.   Gift stall.   By arrangement.   Partially suitable.

Obligatory (except Jul/Aug & BHs).

Acorn Bank Garden & Watermill, Cumbria

MIREHOUSE

KESWICK, CUMBRIA CA12 4QE

Owner: *James Fryer-Spedding*   **Contact:** *Clare Spedding*

Tel/Fax: 017687 72287   **e-mail:** info@mireho.freeserve.co.uk

'The Best Heritage Property for Families in the UK' 1999 NPI Award. Our visitors particularly appreciate the spectacular setting between mountain and lake, the extraordinary literary and artistic connections, varied gardens, walks, natural playgrounds, live classical music and the personal attention of members of the family. The tearoom is known for generous Cumbrian cooking.

Location: OS Ref. NY235 284. Beside A591, 3¹/₂ m N of Keswick. Good bus service.

Opening Times: 1 Apr - 31 Oct: Gardens & Tearoom: daily, 10am - 5.30pm. House: Suns & Weds (also Fris in Aug), 2 - 4.30pm (last entry). At other times for groups by appointment.

Admission: House & Garden: Adult £4, Child £2, Family £11.75. Gardens only: Adult £2, Child £1. 10% discount for groups (20+), booked in advance.

ℹ️ No photography in house. ⬛ ▣ 🎨 By arrangement. 🅿️ Limited. ⬛ 🐕 In grounds on leads. ❄️ Booked groups only.

MUNCASTER CASTLE

See page 411 for full page entry.

MUNCASTER WATER MILL

Tel: 01229 717232

Ravenglass, Cumbria CA18 1ST

Owner: Lake District Estates   **Contact:** E & P Priestly

Working old manorial mill with 13ft overshot wheel and all milling equipment.

Location: OS Ref. SD094 977. 1m N of Ravenglass on A595.

Opening Times: Easter - Oct: daily 10am - 5pm. Nov - Mar: weekends only, 11am - 4pm.

Admission: Adult £2, Child 50p, Family (2+3) £5. Groups by arrangement.

NAWORTH CASTLE

Tel: 01697 73229   **Fax:** 01697 73679

Brampton, Cumbria CA8 2HF

e-mail: philip@naworth.co.uk

Owner: Philip Howard   **Contact:** Colleen Hall

Cumbria's premier function venue for weddings and corporate events.

Location: OS Ref. NY560 626. ¹/₂ m off main A69 Carlisle - Newcastle road. 3m E of Brampton. Carlisle 12m, Newcastle 46m, M6 9m.

Opening Times: All year by appointment only.

🍽️ 🔔

PENRITH CASTLE

Tel: 0161 242 1400

Penrith, Cumbria

Owner: English Heritage   **Contact:** The North Regional Office

This 14th century castle, set in a park on the edge of the town, was built to defend Penrith against repeated attacks by Scottish raiders.

Location: OS Ref. NY513 299. Opposite Penrith railway station. W of the town centre. Fully visible from the street.

Opening Times: Park opening hours.

Admission: Free.

THE QUAKER TAPESTRY EXHIBITION CENTRE   **Tel/Fax:** 01539 722975

Friends Meeting House, Stramongate, Kendal, Cumbria LA9 4BH

e-mail: info@quaker-tapestry.co.uk

Owner: Trustees of the Quaker Tapestry   **Contact:** Bridget Guest

This unique exhibition of 77 panels of community embroidery delights visitors of all ages. Explore the Quaker journey from 17th century to the present day as you uncover over 300 years of social history, beautifully illustrated by 4000 men, women and children from 15 countries.

Location: OS Ref. SD517 927. Centre of Kendal, access from either Stramongate or New Road.

Opening Times: Apr - Oct: Mon - Sat, 10am - 5pm, last admission 4.15pm. Nov - Dec: Mon - Fri.

Admission: Adult £4, Child £1, Conc. £2.50.

ℹ️ No indoor photography. Demonstrations. ⬛ ♿ ▣ For group visits (20+). 🎨 By arrangement. 🎧 🅿️ Limited. ⬛ 🐕 Guide dogs only. Ⓦ

RYDAL MOUNT & GARDENS   **Tel:** 01539 433002   **Fax:** 01539 431738

Ambleside, Cumbria LA22 9LU

e-mail: Rydalmount.aol.com

Owner: Rydal Mount Trustees   **Contact:** Peter & Marian Elkington

See full page advertisement on page 24

The historic house of William Wordsworth from 1813 until his death in 1850, now the family home of his descendants. It contains family portraits and his personal possessions. The extensive garden, landscaped by the poet, includes terraces, rare shrubs, trees and the poet's summerhouse which overlooks beautiful Rydal Water.

Location: OS Ref. NY364 063. 1¹/₂ m N of Ambleside on A591 Grasmere Road.

Opening Times: Mar - Oct: Daily, 9.30am - 5pm. Nov - Feb: Daily except Tues, 10am - 4pm.

Admission: Adult £4, Child £1.25, Student £3, OAP £3.25. Pre-arranged groups £2.75. Garden only: £1.75. Free parking. Reciprocal discount ticket with Dove Cottage and Wordsworth House.

ℹ️ No inside photography. ⬛ ♿ Partially suitable. 🎨 By arrangement. 🅿️ Limited. ⬛ 🐕 In grounds, on leads. Guide dogs only in house. ❄️ Ⓦ

SIZERGH CASTLE & GARDEN

NT Photographic Library: Alasdair Ogilvie.

Nr KENDAL, CUMBRIA LA8 8AE

Owner: *The National Trust*   **Contact:** *The House Manager*

Tel: 01539 560070   **Fax:** 01539 561621

The Strickland family have lived here for more than 750 years. The impressive 14th century pele tower was extended in Tudor times, with some of the finest Elizabethan carved overmantels in the country. Contents include good English and French furniture and family portraits. A visit culminates in the important and impressive Inlaid Chamber. The castle is surrounded by gardens of beauty and interest, including the Trust's largest limestone rock garden; good autumn colour. Large estate; walks leaflet available in shop.

Location: OS Ref. SD498 878. 3¹/₂ m S of Kendal, NW of the A590/A591 interchange.

Opening Times: Castle: 1 Apr - 31 Oct: Sun - Thur, 1.30 - 5.30pm. Garden: As house: 12.30 - 5.30pm. Last admission 5pm.

Admission: Adult £4.80, Child £2.40, Family £12. Garden only: £2.40. Groups (15+): £3.80 by arrangement (not on BHs).

⬛ ♿ Partially suitable. ▣ 🦮

STAGSHAW GARDEN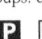

Tel / Fax: 015394 46027

Ambleside, Cumbria LA22 0HE

Owner: The National Trust   **Contact:** Windermere & Troutbeck Property Office

This woodland garden was created by the late Cubby Acland, Regional Agent for the National Trust. It contains a fine collection of azaleas and rhododendrons, planted to give good blends of colour under the thinned oaks on the hillside; also many trees and shrubs, including magnolias, camellias and embothriums.

Location: OS Ref 200. NY380 029. $^1/_2$ m S of Ambleside on A591.

Opening Times: 1 Apr - end Jun: daily, 10am - 6.30pm. Jul - end Oct: by appointment.

Admission: £1.50, no reduction for groups.

   Not suitable.   No parking.

STEAM YACHT GONDOLA

Tel/Fax: 015394 63856

(NT Gondola Bookings) National Trust Office, The Hollens, Grasmere, LA22 9QZ

Owner: The National Trust   **Contact:** The Manager

The Steam Yacht Gondola, first launched in 1859 and now completely renovated by the Trust, provides a steam-powered passenger service, carrying 86 passengers in opulently upholstered saloons. A superb way to see Coniston's scenery.

Location: OS Ref. SD305 975. Coniston ($^1/_2$ m to Coniston Pier).

Opening Times: Sails from Coniston Pier daily at 11am, 1 Apr - 31 Oct. The Trust reserves the right to cancel sailings in the event of high winds or lack of demand. Piers at Coniston and Brantwood (not NT). Open until 21 Dec for private bookings.

Admission: Ticket prices & timetable on application and published locally. Family ticket available. No reduction for NT members as Gondola is an enterprise and not held solely for preservation. Groups & private charters by prior arrangement.

   Not suitable.   Dogs on leads, outside saloons, 50p any journey.

STOTT PARK BOBBIN MILL

Tel: 01539 531087

Low Stott Park, Ulverston, Cumbria LA12 8AX

Owner: English Heritage   **Contact:** The Custodian

When this working mill was built in 1835 it was typical of the many mills in the Lake District which grew up to supply the spinning and weaving industry in Lancashire but have since disappeared. A remarkable opportunity to see a demonstration of the machinery and techniques of the Industrial Revolution. There is a working Static Steam Engine on Tuesdays to Thursdays.

Location: OS96 Ref. SD373 883. Near Newby Bridge on A590.

Opening Times: 1 Apr - 30 Sept: daily, 10am - 6pm. 1 - 31 Oct: daily, 10am - 5pm. Last admission 1hr before closing.

Admission: Adult £3.10, Child £1.60, Conc. £2.30. Groups: discount for groups (11+).

   Ground floor suitable. WC.   Inclusive.   P

HELENA THOMPSON MUSEUM

Tel: 01900 326255

Park End Road, Workington, Cumbria CA14 4DE

Owner: Allerdale Borough Council   **Contact:** Heritage & Arts Unit

The museum is housed in a fine listed mid-Georgian building. Displays include pottery, silver, glass, furniture and dress collection.

Location: OS Ref. NY007 286. Corner of A66, Ramsey Brow & Park End Road.

Opening Times: Apr - Sept: Mon - Sat, 10.30am - 4pm. Nov - Mar: Mon - Sat, 11am - 3pm.

Admission: Free.

Cumbria Tourist Board.

Lake Windermere, Cumbria.

TOWNEND

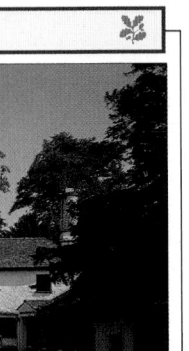

NT Photographic Library: Matthew Antrobus.

TROUTBECK, WINDERMERE, CUMBRIA LA23 1LB

Owner: The National Trust   *Contact: The Administrator*

Tel: 01539 432628

An exceptional relic of Lake District life during past centuries. Originally a 'statesman' (wealthy yeoman) farmer's house, built about 1626. Townend contains carved woodwork, books, papers, furniture and fascinating implements of the past which were accumulated by the Browne family who lived here from 1626 until 1943. Regular 'Living History' programme - Meet George Browne c1900.

Location: OS Ref. NY407 020. 3m SE of Ambleside at S end of Troutbeck village. 1m from Holehird, 3m N of Windermere.

Opening Times: 2 Apr - 31 Oct: Tue - Fri, Suns & BH Mons, 1 - 5pm or dusk if earlier. Last admission 4.30pm.

Admission: Adult £3, Child £1.50, Family £7.50. No reduction for groups which must be pre-booked. Townend and village unsuitable for coaches; 12 - 15 seater mini-buses are acceptable; permission to take coaches to Townend must be obtained from the Transportation and Highways Dept, Cumbria CC, Carlisle, Cumbria.

   Unsuitable for wheelchairs. Braille guide.

WORDSWORTH HOUSE

Tel: 01900 824805

Main Street, Cockermouth, Cumbria CA13 9RX   **e-mail:** rwordh@smtp.ntrust.org.uk

Owner: The National Trust   **Contact:** The Custodian

See full page advertisement on page 24   **e-mail:** wordh@smpt.ntrust.org.uk

A Georgian town house where William Wordsworth was born in 1770 in the ancient market town of Cockermouth. Several rooms contain some of the poet's personal effects. His childhood garden, with terraced walk attractively restored, with views over the River Derwent referred to in 'The Prelude'. Kitchen garden under restoration.

Location: OS Ref. NY118 307. Main Street, Cockermouth.

Opening Times: 2 Apr - 2 Nov: weekdays only, plus all BH Sats and Sats in Jun, Jul & Aug, 10.30am - 4.30pm. Last admission 4pm.

Admission: Adult £3, Child £1.50, Family £7.50. Pre-booked groups £2.20. Reciprocal discount ticket with Dove Cottage and Rydal Mount.

   By arrangement only.   P No parking.

WORKINGTON HALL

Tel: 01900 326408

Ramsey Brow, Workington, Cumbria

Owner: Allerdale Borough Council   **Contact:** Allerdale Borough Council Tourism Dept.

Refuge for Mary Queen of Scots during her last night of freedom in May 1568, this was one of the finest Manor houses in the region. Now a ruin.

Location: OS Ref. NY007 288. In public park on N side of A66

Opening Times: Easter - Oct: Tue - Fri & BHs, 10am - 1pm & 2 - 5pm, Sats & Suns 2 - 5pm.

Admission: Adult 85p, Conc. 55p, Family (2+2/1+3) £2.25.

Website Index   ◄◄◄ **page 39**

English Life Publication Ltd

Owner:
Richard Gillow
Reynolds Esq

CONTACT

Mrs C S Reynolds
Leighton Hall
Carnforth
Lancashire
LA5 9ST

Tel: 01524 734474

Fax: 01524 720357

e-mail: leightonhall@
yahoo.co.uk

LOCATION

OS Ref. SD494 744

9m N of Lancaster,
10m S of Kendal,
3m N of Carnforth.
1½ m W of A6.
3m from M6/A6/J35,
signed from J35A.

Rail: Lancaster
Station 9m.

Air: Manchester
Airport 65m.

Taxi: Carnforth Radio
Taxis, Carnforth 732763.

CONFERENCE/FUNCTION		
ROOM	SIZE	MAX CAPACITY
Music Room	24' x 21'6"	80
Dining Rm		30
Other		80

LEIGHTON HALL
Carnforth

LEIGHTON HALL is one of the most beautifully sited houses in the British Isles, situated in a bowl of parkland, with the whole panorama of the Lakeland Fells rising behind. The hall's neo-gothic façade was superimposed on an 18th century house, which, in turn, had been built on the ruins of the original medieval house. The present owner is descended from Adam d'Avranches who built the first house in 1246.

The whole house is lived in by the Reynolds family and emphasis is put on making visitors feel welcome in a family home.

Connoisseurs of furniture will be particularly interested in the 18th century pieces by Gillow of Lancaster. Mr Reynolds is directly descended from the founder of Gillow and Company, hence the strong Gillow connection with the house. Also on show are some fine pictures, clocks, silver and *objets d'art.*

GARDENS

The main garden has a continuous herbaceous border and rose covered walls, while the Walled Garden contains flowering shrubs, a herb garden, an ornamental vegetable garden and a maze. Beyond is the Woodland Walk, where wild flowers abound from early Spring.

A varied collection of Birds of Prey is on display in the Bird Garden, and flown each afternoon that the hall is open, weather permitting.

❖

Performing Arts

Product launches, seminars, filming, garden parties, conferences, rallies, overland driving, archery and clay pigeon shoots, grand piano. No photography in house. Large collection of birds of prey on display in the afternoon, some of which fly at 3.30pm, weather permitting.

Buffets, lunches, dinners and wedding receptions.

Partially suitable. WC. Visitors may alight at the entrance.

Groups must book, menus on request.

Obligatory. By prior arrangement owner may meet groups, tour time: 45 mins. House and flying display tour time: 2 hrs. Lectures on property, its contents, gardens and history.

Ample.

School programme 10am-2pm daily May-Sept except Mons & Sats. Birds of prey flown for schools at 12pm. Schools Visit Programme won the Sandford Award for Heritage Education in 1983 and in 1989.

In grounds, on leads.

❄

OPENING TIMES

SUMMER

1 May - 30 September
Daily except Mons & Sats
2 - 5pm. Open BH Mons.

August only:
12.30 - 5pm.
NB. Booked groups (25+)
at any time by
arrangement.

WINTER

1 October - 30 April
Open to booked
groups (25+).

ADMISSION

SUMMER

House, Garden & Birds
Adult £4.50
Child (5-12yrs)..........£3.00
OAP.......................£4.00
Groups (Min. payment £80)
Adult £3.50
Child (5-12yrs)..........£3.00
Family (2+3) £13.00
School £2.75

Children under 5yrs Free

Grounds only
(after 4.30pm)
Per person £1.50

WINTER

As above but groups by
appointment only.

SPECIAL EVENTS

- **JUL 6:**
  Concert & Fireworks:
  'Last Night of the Proms'.

- **JUL 22:**
  Classic Car Rally.

- **AUG 3 - 4:**
  Shakespeare in the Garden:
  'Henry V'.

- **SEPT 8 - 9:**
  Rainbow Craft Fair.

- **OCT 13:**
  Teddy Bear Fair.

- **OCT 14:**
  Dolls House & Miniaturist Fair.

North West England

ASTLEY HALL

ASTLEY PARK, OFF HALL GATE, CHORLEY PR7 1NP

Owner: Chorley Borough Council *Contact:* Dr Nigel Wright

Tel: 01257 515555 **Fax:** 01257 515556 **e-mail:** astleyhall@lineone.net

A charming house, dating back to 1580, with additions in the 1660s and 1820s. Interiors include sumptuous plaster ceilings, fine 17th century oak furniture and tapestries, plus displays of fine and decorative art. Set in parkland.

Location: OS Ref. SD574 183. 2m W of Chorley, off A581 Chorley - Southport road. 5 mins from M61/J8.

Opening Times: Easter - end Oct: Tue - Sun, 12 noon - 5pm. Plus BH Mons. Nov - Easter: weekends only, 12 noon - 4pm. Closed Christmas & New Year.

Admission: Adult £2.90, Child/Conc. £1.90. Groups: Adult £2.30, Child/Conc. £1.30.

ℹ️ No photography. 🏠 ☕ ♿ Partially suitable. Braille guide. 🍴
👔 By arrangement. 🎧 🎬 🅿️ 🐕 Guide dogs only. 🔔 ❄️ 🌐

BLACKBURN CATHEDRAL **Tel:** 01254 51491 **Fax:** 01254 689666

Cathedral Close, Blackburn, Lancashire BB1 5AA **Contact:** Mrs Alison Feeney

On an historic Saxon site in town centre. The 1826 Parish Church dedicated as the Cathedral in 1977 with new extensions to give a spacious and light interior. The distinctive 'crowning glory' Lantern Tower was rebuilt in 1998 with 56 panels of newly-designed symbolic stained glass to give a new and unique magnificence by day and night. Other features include a fine Walker organ, 12 peal bells and a 'corona' (crown of thorns) above the central altar.

Location: OS Ref. SD684 280. 9m E of M6/J31, via A59 and A677. City centre.

Opening Times: Daily, 9am - 5pm. Sun services: at 8am, 9.15am, 10.30am and 4pm.

Admission: Free. Donations invited.

♿ Wheelchair access. ☕ Wed & Fri, 10am - 2.30pm or Sats by arrangement.
👔 By arrangement. 🅿️ Nearby shopping centre. ❄️

BROWSHOLME HALL 🏛 **Tel:** 01254 826719 **Fax:** 01254 826739

Clitheroe, Lancashire BB7 3DE

Owner/Contact: Mr R R Parker

Built in 1507 and set in a landscaped park, the ancestral home of the Parker family.

Location: OS Ref. SD683 452. 5m NW of Clitheroe off B6243.

Opening Times: Spring Bank Hol. weekend. 1 - 14 July (except Mons). 14 Aug - Aug BH Mon (except other Mons), 2 - 4.30pm. Groups at other times by appointment.

Admission: Adult £4, Child £1. Pre-arranged groups: Adult £3.70, Child £2.

GAWTHORPE HALL   **Tel:** 01282 771004 **Fax:** 01282 770178

Padiham, Nr Burnley, Lancashire BB12 8UA

Owner: The National Trust **Contact:** The Property Manager

The house was built in 1600-05, and restored by Sir Charles Barry in the 1850s. Barry's designs have been re-created in the principal rooms. Gawthorpe was the home of the Shuttleworth family, and the Rachel Kay-Shuttleworth textile collections are on display in the house, private study by arrangement. Collection of portraits on loan from the National Portrait Gallery.

Location: OS Ref. SD806 340. M65/J8. On E outskirts of Padiham, 3/4 m to house on N of A671. Signed to Clitheroe, then signed from 2nd set of traffic lights.

Opening Times: Hall: 31 Mar - 31 Oct: daily except Mons & Fris, open Good Fri & BH Mons, 1 - 5pm. Last adm. 4.30pm. Garden: All year: daily, 10am - 6pm.

Admission: Hall: Adult £3, Child £1.30, Conc. £1.50, Family £8 (prices may change). Garden: Free. Groups must book.

♿ Prior warning of visit essential. 💻 🐕 In grounds on leads. ❄️

HALL I'TH'WOOD **Tel:** 01204 332370

off Green Way, Tonge Moor, Bolton BL1 8UA

Owner: Bolton Metropolitan Borough Council **Contact:** W H Farrell

Late medieval manor house with 17/18th century furniture, paintings and decorative art.

Location: OS Ref. SD724 116. 2m NNE of central Bolton. 1/4 m N of A58 ring road between A666 and A676 crossroads.

Opening Times: Please contact for details.

Admission: Adult £3, Conc. £1.50.

HOGHTON TOWER 🏛

HOGHTON, PRESTON, LANCASHIRE PR5 0SH

Owner: Sir Bernard de Hoghton Bt *Contact:* Office

Tel: 01254 852986 **Fax:** 01254 852109

Hoghton Tower, home of 14th Baronet, is one of the most dramatic looking houses in northern England. Three houses have occupied the hill site since 1100 with the present house re-built by Thomas Hoghton between 1560 - 1565. Rich and varied historical events including the Knighting of the Loin 'Sirloin' by James I in 1617.

Location: OS Ref. SD622 264. M65/J3. Midway between Preston & Blackburn on A675.

Opening Times: Jul, Aug & Sept: Mon - Thur, 11am - 4pm. Suns, 1 - 5pm. BH Suns & Mons excluding Christmas & New Year. Group visits by appointment all year.

Admission: House tours: Adult £3, Child/Conc. £2, Family £8. Gardens, Shop & Tearoom only: £2. Private tours by arrangement (25 min) £6, OAP £5.

🏠 ☕ Conferences, wedding receptions. ♿ Not suitable. 💻
👔 Obligatory. 🅿️ 🎬 ✖️ ❄️

LEIGHTON HALL

See page 417 for full page entry.

MANCHESTER CATHEDRAL

Tel: 0161 833 2220 **Fax:** 0161 839 6226

Manchester M3 1SX

In addition to regular worship and daily offices, there are frequent professional concerts, day schools, organ recitals, guided tours and brass-rubbing. The cathedral contains a wealth of beautiful carvings and has the widest medieval nave in Britain.

Location: OS Ref. SJ838 988. Manchester.

Opening Times: Daily.

Admission: Donations welcome.

MARTHOLME

Great Harwood, Blackburn, Lancashire BB6 7UJ

Owner: Mr & Mrs T H Codling   **Contact:** Miss P M Codling

Part of medieval manor house with 17th century additions and Elizabethan gatehouse.

Location: OS Ref. SD753 338. 2m NE of Great Harwood off A680 to Whalley.

Opening Times: Groups (8+) by written appointment only.

Admission: £3.50.

ROSSENDALE MUSEUM

Tel: 01706 217777 or 01706 226509

Whitaker Park, Rawtenstall, Rossendale, Lancashire BB4 6RE

Owner: Rossendale Borough Council   **Contact:** Mrs S Cruise

Former 19th century mill owner's house set in Whitaker Park. Displays include fine and decorative arts and furniture.

Location: OS Ref. SD805 226. Off A681, ¼ m from Rawtenstall Centre.

Opening Times: Apr - Oct: Mon - Fri, 1 - 5pm, Sats, 10am - 5pm, Suns, 12 noon - 5pm. Nov - Mar: Mon - Fri, 1 - 5pm, Sats, 10am - 4pm, Suns, 12 noon - 4pm. BHs, 1 - 5pm. Closed Christmas Day, Boxing Day and New Year's Day.

Admission: Free.

SAMLESBURY HALL

Tel: 01254 812010 **Fax:** 01254 812174

Preston New Road, Samlesbury, Preston PR5 0UP

Owner: Samlesbury Hall Trust   **Contact:** Mr David Hornby

Built in 1325, the hall is an attractive black and white timbered manor house set in extensive grounds.

Location: OS Ref. SD623 305. N side of A677, 4m WNW of Blackburn.

Opening Times: All year: daily except Mons: 11am - 4.30pm. Closed over Christmas and New Year.

Admission: Adult £2.50, Child £1.

SMITHILLS HALL MUSEUM

Tel: 01204 332377

Smithills Dean Road, Bolton BL1 7NP

Owner: Bolton Metropolitan Borough Council   **Contact:** Linda McKay

14th century fortified manor house with Tudor panelling. Stuart furniture. Stained glass.

Location: OS Ref. SD699 119. 2m NW of central Bolton, ½ m N of A58 ringroad.

Opening Times: Please contact for details.

Admission: Adult £3, Conc. £1.50.

STONYHURST COLLEGE

Tel: 01254 826345 **Fax:** 01254 826732

Stonyhurst, Clitheroe, Lancashire BB7 9PZ   **Contact:** Miss F Ahearne

The original house dates from the late 16th century. Set in extensive grounds.

Location: OS Ref. SD690 391. 4m SW of Clitheroe off B6243.

Opening Times: House: 16 Jul - 27 Aug: Sat - Thur (including Aug BH Mon), 1 - 5pm. Grounds & Gardens: 1 Jul - 27 Aug: Sat - Thur (including Aug BH Mon), 1 - 5pm.

Admission: House & Grounds: Adult £4.50, Child (4-14yrs)/OAP £3.50. Grounds only £1.

Website Index page 39

RUFFORD OLD HALL

RUFFORD, Nr ORMSKIRK, LANCASHIRE L40 1SG

Owner: *The National Trust*   **Contact:** *The Property Manager*

Tel: 01704 821254

There is a legend that William Shakespeare performed here for the owner Sir Thomas Hesketh in the Great Hall of this, one of the finest 16th century buildings in Lancashire. The playwright would have delighted in the magnificent hall with its intricately carved movable wooden screen. Built in 1530, it established the Hesketh family seat for the next 250 years. In the Carolean Wing, altered in 1821, there are fine collections of 16th and 17th century oak furniture, arms, armour and tapestries. An audio tour is available to guide visitors around the house. The attractive garden includes sculpture and topiary.

Location: OS Ref. SD463 160. 7m N of Ormskirk, in village of Rufford on E side of A59.

Opening Times: 31 Mar - 4 Nov: Sat - Wed, 1 - 5pm. Last admission 4.30pm. Garden: same days as house, 12 noon - 5.30pm.

Admission: House & Garden: Adult £3.80, Child £1.90, Family £9.50. Garden only: £2. Pre-booked groups £2.60 (no groups on Suns & BH Mons).

Partially suitable. In grounds, on leads.

TOWNELEY HALL ART GALLERY & MUSEUMS

Burnley BB11 3RQ   **Tel:** 01282 424213 **Fax:** 01282 436138
Owner: Burnley Borough Council   **Contact:** Miss Susan Bourne
House dates from the 14th century with 17th and 19th century modifications. Collections include oak furniture, 18th and 19th century paintings. There is a Museum of Local Crafts and Industries and a Natural History Centre with an aquarium in the grounds.
Location: OS Ref. SD854 309. 1/2 m SE of Burnley on E side of Todmorden Road (A671).
Opening Times: All year: Mon - Fri, 10am - 5pm. Suns, 12 noon - 5pm. Closed Sats. Closed Christmas - New Year.
Admission: Free. Guided tours: Tues, Weds & Thurs afternoons or as booked for parties.

🖻 ♿Ground floor & grounds suitable. WC. 💼 🏃 🛡 Tel. for details.
❄ 🅸🆆

TURTON TOWER

                                 Tel: 01204 852203 **Fax:** 01204 853759

Chapeltown Road, Turton BL7 0HG
Owner: Lancashire County Council   **Contact:** Martin Robinson-Dowland
Country house based on a medieval tower, extended in the 16th, 17th and 19th centuries.
Location: OS Ref. SD733 153. On B6391, 4m N of Bolton.
Opening Times: Feb & Nov: Suns, 1 - 4pm. Mar & Oct: Sat - Wed, 1 - 4pm. Apr: Sat - Wed, 2 - 5pm. May - Sept: Mon - Thur, 10am - 12 noon, 1 - 5pm. Sats & Suns 1 - 5pm.
Admission: Adult £3, Child/OAP £1.50, Family £8. Season ticket available.

WARTON OLD RECTORY 🏛

                                 Tel: 0161 242 1400

Warton, Carnforth, Lancashire
Owner: English Heritage   **Contact:** The Regional Office
A rare medieval stone house with remains of the hall, chambers and domestic offices.
Location: OS Ref. SD499 723. At Warton, 1m N of Carnforth on minor road off A6.
Opening Times: Any reasonable time.
Admission: Free.

Hoghton Tower, Lancashire.

Gawthorpe Hall, Lancashire.

BLUECOAT ARTS CENTRE

Tel: 0151 709 5297 **Fax:** 0151 707 0048
e-mail: admin@bluecoatartscentre.com

Bluecoat Chambers, School Lane, Liverpool L1 3BX

Owner: Bluecoat Arts Centre Ltd   **Contact:** Building Manager

Built in 1717, the Bluecoat is of outstanding historical and architectural interest, with Grade I listed building status, and is a popular tourist attraction in the heart of Liverpool. The oldest building in the city centre, and now, arguably the oldest arts centre in Britain, it is one of the most exciting arts venues in the region with an impressive Queen Anne style façade and walled garden. The unique mix of exhibitions and perfomances, café and shops, including local history, books and crafts and collectors' fairs offers visitors an alternative experience in the city.

Location: OS Ref. SJ346 902. $^1/_4$ m S of Lime Street station.

Opening Times: Mon - Sat, 9.30am - 6pm (unless there is an evening performance, outside hire or exhibition opening). Gallery closed Mons.

Admission: Free admission to Building and Gallery, with varying prices for the Performing Arts events.

Partially suitable. WC.

CROXTETH HALL & COUNTRY PARK **Tel:** 0151 228 5311 **Fax:** 0151 228 2817

Liverpool, Merseyside L12 0HB

Owner: Liverpool City Council   **Contact:** Mrs Irene Vickers

Ancestral home of the Molyneux family. 500 acres country park. Special events and attractions most weekends.

Location: OS Ref. SJ408 943. 5m NE of Liverpool city centre.

Opening Times: Parkland: daily throughout the year. Hall, Farm & Garden: daily, 11am - 5pm during main season. Telephone for exact dates.

Admission: Parkland: Free. Hall, Farm & Garden: prices on application.

LIVERPOOL CATHEDRAL

Tel: 0151 709 6271 **Fax:** 0151 709 1112

Liverpool, Merseyside L1 7AZ

Owner: The Dean and Chapter   **Contact:** Canon Noel Vincent

Sir Giles Gilbert Scott's greatest creation. Built this century from local sandstone with superb glass, stonework and major works of art, it is the largest cathedral in Britain and has a fine musical tradition, a tower offering panoramic views, and an award-winning refectory. There is a unique collection of church embroidery, and SPCK shop with a full range of souvenirs, cards and religious books.

Location: OS Ref. SJ354 893. Central Liverpool, $^1/_2$ m S of Lime Street Station.

Opening Times: 8am - 6pm. Sun services: 8am, 10.30am, 3pm, 4pm. Weekdays: 8am & 5.30pm. Sats: 8am & 3pm.

Admission: Donation. Lift to Tower and Embroidery Exhibition: £2.

 Grounds suitable. WC. Guide dogs only.

LIVERPOOL METROPOLITAN CATHEDRAL OF CHRIST THE KING

Liverpool, Merseyside L3 5TQ   **Tel:** 0151 709 9222 **Fax:** 0151 708 7274
e-mail: met.cathedral@cwcom.net

Owner: Roman Catholic Archdiocese of Liverpool   **Contact:** Rt Rev P Cookson

Modern circular cathedral with spectacular glass by John Piper and numerous modern works of art. Extensive earlier crypt by Lutyens. Grade II* listed.

Location: OS Ref. SJ356 903. Central Liverpool, $^1/_2$ m E of Lime Street Station.

Opening Times: 8am - 6pm (closes 5pm Suns in Winter). Sun services: 8.30am, 10am, 11am, 3pm & 7pm. Weekday services: 8am, 12.15pm, 5.15pm & 5.45pm. Sats, 9am & 6.30pm.

Admission: Donation.

Except crypt. WCs. By arrangement. Ample for cars. Guide dogs only.

MEOLS HALL

Tel: 01704 228326 **Fax:** 01704 507185

Churchtown, Southport, Merseyside PR9 7LZ

Owner: Robert Hesketh Esq   **Contact:** Pamela Whelan

17th century house with subsequent additions. Interesting collection of pictures and furniture.

Location: OS Ref. SD365 184. 3m NE of Southport town centre in Churchtown. SE of A565.

Opening Times: 14 Aug - 14 Sept: daily, 2 - 5pm.

Admission: Adult £3, Child £1. Groups £8.50 (inclusive of afternoon tea).

PORT SUNLIGHT VILLAGE & HERITAGE CENTRE

Tel: 0151 6446466 **Fax:** 0151 6458973

95 Greendale Road, Port Sunlight CH62 4XE   **Contact:** The Centre

Port Sunlight is a picturesque 19th century garden village on the Wirral.

Location: OS Ref. SJ340 845. Follow signs from M53/J4 or 5 or follow signs on A41.

Opening Times: All year, 10am - 4pm in summer; 11am - 4pm in winter.

Admission: Adult 60p, Child 30p, Conc. 50p. Group rates on application.

SPEKE HALL GARDEN & ESTATE **Tel:** 0151 427 7231 **Fax:** 0151 427 9860

The Walk, Liverpool L24 1XD   **Info Line:** 0345 585702 (local rate)

Owner: The National Trust   **Contact:** The Property Manager

One of the most famous half-timbered houses in the country.

Location: OS Ref. SJ419 825. North bank of the Mersey, 6m SE of city centre. Follow signs for Liverpool airport.

Opening Times: House: 28 Mar - 29 Oct: daily except Mons & Tues (open BH Mons), 1 - 5.30pm. 4 Nov - 10 Dec: Sats & Suns, 1 - 4.30pm. Woodland & Garden: 28 Mar - 29 Oct: Daily except Mons (open BH Mons) from 12 noon. Nov - Mar 2000: daily except Mons, 12 noon - 4pm. Closed Good Fri, 24/25/26/31 Dec & 1 Jan. Last admission 30 mins before close.

Admission: Estate: £2.50 per car (refunded when when garden or house ticket purchased). Garden: £2pp. House & Garden: £4.50. Family £12.

Speke Hall, Merseyside.

Patrick Lane.

Belsay Hall, Northumberland

North East

Belsay Hall

"At Belsay, a 12th century castle, 17th century manor house and an early 19th century hall, are surrounded by 30 acres of landscaped grounds. These contain a number of period garden features, one of them unique. The architectural style, period and surrounding terrain of a house inevitably influence the design of its garden. At Belsay, it was a by-product of the actual building of the house which triggered the creation of the extraordinary quarry garden that can be seen today.

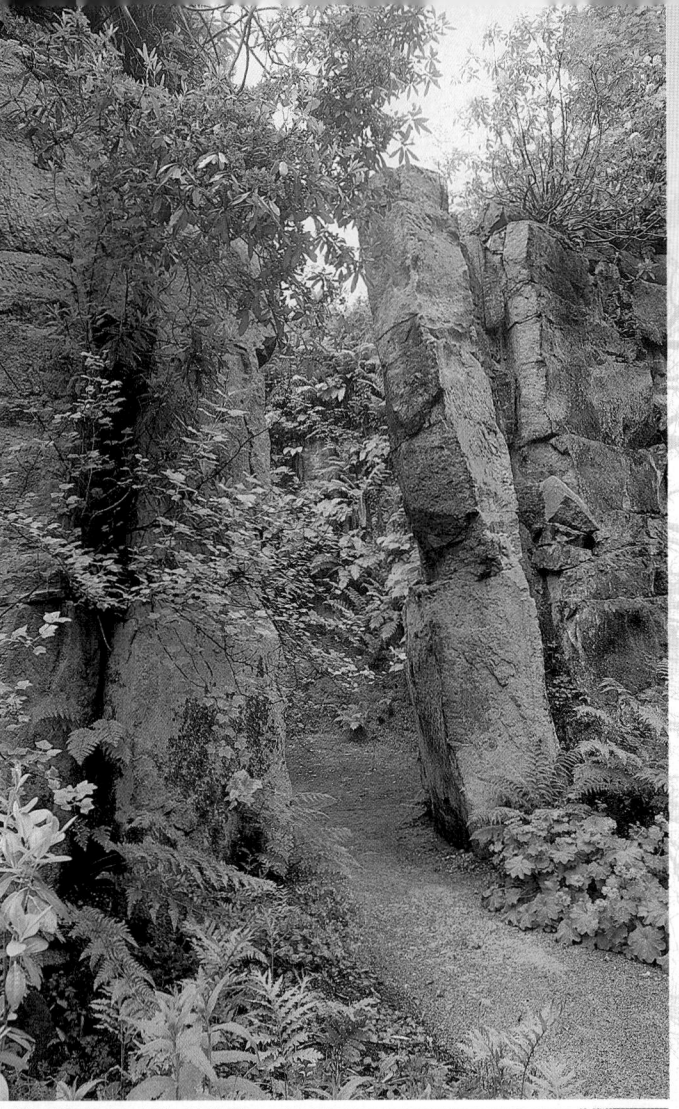

Belsay Hall is a Greek Revival mansion built, between 1810 and 1817, by its owner Sir Charles Monck, a keen classicist and talented draughtsman. Exactly 100' square, harsh and symmetrical in style, it was built of stone quarried from the grounds. The resulting ravine left by the quarrying was transformed by Sir Charles into a unique landscape inspired by the theories of the Picturesque.

The Picturesque was a reaction to the softness of the landscapes of 'Capability' Brown – it sought to be much rougher, exciting and dramatic. The quarry garden at Belsay is the prime example of this style. A man-made landscape, finished to look natural, then planted with exotic plants in such a way to make them seem natural too.

Other Picturesque scenes can be found, but it is the Quarry Garden's sheer scale and treatment which puts it in a class of its own, and it is this that enchants visitors to Belsay.

You are drawn into the Quarry Garden along a narrow, weaving path. This narrowing corridor is flanked on either side by sheer rock faces – sombre, raw and uncompromising. The ravine's height is exaggerated by the line of yews and Scots pines towering 70' above. The atmosphere is secluded and still. Glossy and feathery ferns grow out of rocky crevices at unusual angles. The two rock faces are finally linked by a great arch and beyond this the quarry opens out into a clearing, ringed by cliffs and rock pinnacles. In this sunnier more open space rhododendrons, up to 30'-40' high, flower in vivid and spectacular profusion in the early spring.

The path eventually emerges into pasture land, with the remains of the 12th century castle forming a wonderful eye-catcher. To emerge from the shade and damp of the ravine into the open meadows is an extraordinarily refreshing finale to this spectacular and captivating walk.

English Heritage have, at Belsay, buildings and gardens which are the very essence of the early 19th century Romantic taste for primitive style and wild nature – they provide a memorable and exhilarating visit and are deservedly listed Grade I in the Register of Gardens.

For further details about *Belsay Hall* see entry in North East Region ➔ Northumberland.

Lord Barnard

Owner: The Lord Barnard

CONTACT

Miss C Turnbull
Raby Estate Office
Staindrop
Darlington
Co. Durham
DL2 3NF

Tel: 01833 660207
01833 660202

Fax: 01833 660835

e-mail: rabyestate@
rabycastle.com

LOCATION

OS Ref. NZ129 218

On A688, 1m N of
Staindrop. 8m NE of
Barnard Castle, 12m WNW
of Darlington.

Rail: Darlington Station,
12m.

Air: Teesside Airport,
20m.

RABY CASTLE
Darlington

Raby is without doubt one of the most impressive lived in castles in England. Built mainly in the 14th century by the Nevill family on the site of an earlier manor house, it remained in their ownership until 1569. Since 1626 to the present day it has been the home of the Vane family. It was the childhood home of Cicely, Rose of Raby, mother of Kings Edward IV and Richard III, scene of the Plotting of the Rising of the North and a Parliamentary stronghold during the Civil War.

Despite its medieval exterior, Raby houses a fabulous art collection and sumptuous interiors. Treasures include one of the nation's most important collections of Meissen porcelain, tapestries, furniture, furnishings and paintings by De Hooch, Herring, Reynolds, Teniers, and Van Dyck.

Raby Castle is situated amidst a 200-acre Deer Park in the foothills of the North Pennines, where Red and Fallow Deer and Longhorn Cattle graze. Beautiful walled gardens with formal lawns, rose gardens and ornamental pond frame picturesque views of the Castle. The 18th century stable block contains a horse-drawn carriage collection and an Adventure Playground near the Stable Tearooms and Gift Shop means that Raby has something for everyone to enjoy.

❖

ⓘ Raby Castle beef, lamb, venison and game are available. Soft fruit available in season. No photography or video filming is permitted, slides are on sale.

⬛ ✳

♿ Partially suitable. WC.

☕ Licensed.

🚶 By arrangement. Tour time: 1½ hrs.

🅿

🎪 Suitable for up to 60 children.

🐕 Guide dogs welcome, others on leads in park & gardens only.

⬛ Tel. for details.

AUCKLAND CASTLE

BISHOP AUCKLAND, CO. DURHAM DL14 7NR

Owner: Church Commissioners   *Contact:* The Manager

Tel: 01388 601627   **Fax:** 01388 609323   **e-mail:** auckland.castle@zetnet.co.uk

Principal country residence of the Bishops of Durham since Norman times and now the official residence of the present day Bishops. The Chapel, reputedly the largest private chapel in Europe, was originally the 12th century banquet hall. Chapel and State Rooms including the Throne Room, Long Dining Room and King Charles Dining Room are open to the public. Exhibition in the medieval kitchens dedicated to the life of St Cuthbert and the history of the Durham diocese. Access to the adjacent Bishop's Park with its 18th century Deer House.

Location: OS Ref. NZ214 303. Bishop Auckland, N end of town centre.

Opening Times: 4 May - 15 Jul: Fris & Suns. 16 Jul - 31 Aug: daily except Sats. Sept: Fris & Suns. 2 - 5pm. Also open BH Mons & special event days.

Admission: Adult £3.50, Child/Conc. £2.50. Child (under 12yrs) Free. Special openings for groups (15+): £4.50pp.

Exhibitions. No indoor photography.   Wedding receptions, functions.
Guide dogs only.

AUCKLAND CASTLE DEER HOUSE   **Tel:** 0191 2691200

Bishop Auckland, Durham

Owner: English Heritage   **Contact:** The North Regional Office

A charming building erected in 1760 in the Park of the Bishops of Durham so that the deer could shelter and find food.

Location: OS Ref. NZ216 305. In Bishop Auckland Park, just N of town centre on A689. About 500 yds N of the castle.

Opening Times: Park opening times – see Auckland Castle.

Admission: Free.

BARNARD CASTLE   **Tel:** 01833 638212

Barnard Castle, Castle House, Durham DL12 9AT

Owner: English Heritage   **Contact:** The Custodian

The substantial remains of this large castle stand on a rugged escarpment overlooking the River Tees. Parts of the 14th century Great Hall and the cylindrical 12th century tower, built by the Baliol family can still be seen. New sensory garden.

Location: OS92 Ref. NZ049 165. In Barnard Castle.

Opening Times: 1 Apr - 30 Sept: daily, 10am - 6pm. 1 - 31 Oct: daily, 10am - 5pm. 1 Nov - 31 Mar: Wed - Sun, 10am - 4pm. Closed 24 - 26 Dec. Closed 1 - 2pm.

Admission: Adult £2.40, Child £1.20, Conc. £1.80. 15% discount for groups (11+).

Grounds suitable.   Inclusive.   No parking.
In grounds, on leads.   Tel. for details.

BINCHESTER ROMAN FORT   **Tel:** 0191 3834212

Bishop Auckland, Co. Durham   **e-mail:** archaeology@durham.gov.uk

Owner: Durham County Council   **Contact:** Niall Hammond

Once the largest Roman fort in Co Durham, the heart of the site has been excavated.

Location: OS92 Ref. NZ210 312. 1½ m N of Bishop Auckland, signposted from A690 Durham - Crook and from A688 Spennymoor - Bishop Auckland roads.

Opening Times: Easter weekend & 1 May - 30 Sept: daily, 11am - 5pm.

Admission: Please contact for details.

THE BOWES MUSEUM   **Tel:** 01833 690606

Barnard Castle, Durham DL12 8NP

Owner: The Bowes Museum Ltd

A stunning French-style château containing the largest collection of French paintings in the country.

Location: OS Ref. NZ055 164. ¼ m E of Market Place in Barnard Castle.

Opening Times: All year: Daily, 11am - 5pm.

Admission: Adult £3.90, Child/OAP £2.90, Family £12. Prices and opening times subject to review, please check with museum in advance.

CROOK HALL & GARDENS   **Tel:** 0191 3848028

Sidegate, Durham DH1 5SZ

Owner: Keith & Maggie Bell   **Contact:** Mrs Maggie Bell

Medieval manor house set in rural landscape on the edge of Durham city.

Location: OS Ref. NZ274 432. ½ m N of city centre.

Opening Times: Easter weekend, BHs & Suns in May; Jun, Jul & Aug: daily except Sats, 1 - 5pm.

Admission: Adult £3.75, Child/OAP £2.75, Family £9.

DERWENTCOTE STEEL FURNACE   **Tel:** 0191 2691200

Newcastle, Durham

Owner: English Heritage   **Contact:** The Custodian

Built in the 18th century it is the earliest and most complete authentic steel making furnace to have survived.

Location: OS Ref. NZ131 566. 10m SW of Newcastle N of the A694 between Rowland's Gill and Hamsterley.

Opening Times: 1 Apr - 30 Sept: 1 - 5pm, 1st & 3rd Sun of every month.

Admission: Free.

DURHAM CASTLE

Tel: 0191 3743863 **Fax:** 0191 3747470

Palace Green, Durham DH1 3RW   **Contact:** Mrs Julie Marshall
Durham Castle, founded in the 1070s, with the Cathedral is a World Heritage Site.
Location: OS Ref. NZ274 424. City centre, adjacent to cathedral.
Opening Times: Mar - Sept: 10am - 12 noon & 2 - 4.30pm. Oct - Mar: 2 - 4pm.
Admission: Adult £3, Child £2, Family £6.50. Guide book £2.50.

DURHAM CATHEDRAL

Tel: 0191 3864266 **Fax:** 0191 3864267

Durham DH1 3EH   **e-mail:** enquiries@durhamcathedral.co.uk
Contact: Miss A Heywood
A World Heritage Site. Norman architecture. Burial place of St Cuthbert and the Venerable
Bede.
Location: OS Ref. NZ274 422. Durham city centre.
Opening Times: Summer: 21 Jun - 21 Sept: 9.30am - 8pm. Open only for worship and
private prayer: All year: Mon - Sat, 7.30am - 9.30am and Suns, 7.45am - 12.30pm. The
Cathedral is closed to visitors during evening recitals and concerts.
Admission: Cathedral: £3 donation. Tower: Adult £2, Child (under 16) £1, Family £5. Monk's
Dormitory: Adult 80p, Child 20p, Family £1.50. AV: Adult 80p, Child 20p, Family £1.50.

EGGLESTONE ABBEY ⌗

Tel: 0191 2691200

Durham
Owner: English Heritage   **Contact:** The North Regional Office
Picturesque remains of a 12th century abbey, located in a bend of the River Tees.
Substantial parts of the church and abbey buildings remain.
Location: OS Ref. NZ062 151. 1¹/₂ m SE of Barnard Castle on minor road off B6277.
Opening Times: Any reasonable time.
Admission: Free.

ESCOMB CHURCH

Escomb, Bishop Auckland DL14 7ST   **Contact:** Mrs E Kitching (01388 662265)
Owner: Church of England   or The Vicar (01388 602861)
Saxon church dating from the 7th century built of stone from Binchester Roman Fort.
Location: OS Ref. NZ189 302. 3m W of Bishop Auckland.
Opening Times: Summer: 9am - 8pm. Winter: 9am - 4pm. Key available from 22 Saxon
Green, Escomb.
Admission: Free.

FINCHALE PRIORY ⌗

Tel: 0191 3863828

Finchdale Priory, Brasside, Newton Hall DH1 5SH
Owner: English Heritage   **Contact:** The Custodian
These beautiful 13th century priory remains are located beside the curving River Wear.
Location: OS85 Ref. NZ297 471. 4¹/₂ m NE of Durham.
Opening Times: 1 Apr - 30 Sept: daily, 10am - 6pm. 1 - 31 Oct: daily, 10am - 5pm.
Admission: Adult £1.40, Child 70p, Conc. £1.10. 15% discount for groups (11+).

PIERCEBRIDGE ROMAN FORT

Tel: 01325 460532

Piercebridge, Co. Durham
Owner: Darlington Borough Council   **Contact:** Heritage Manager
Visible Roman remains include the east gate and defences, courtyard building and Roman
road. Also remains of a bridge over the Tees.
Location: OS85 Ref. NZ211 157. Through narrow stile and short walk down lane opposite
car park off A67 NE of the village. Bridge via signposted footpath from George Hotel car park.
Opening Times: At all times.
Admission: Free.

RABY CASTLE 🏛

See page 428 for full page entry.

ROKEBY PARK 🏛

Tel: 01833 637334

Nr Barnard Castle, Co Durham DL12 9RZ
Owner: Trustees of Mortham Estate   **Contact:** Mrs P I Yeats (Curator)
Rokeby, a fine example of a 18th century Palladian-style country house.
Location: OS Ref. NZ082 142. Between A66 & Barnard Castle.
Opening Times: May BH Mon then each Mon & Tue from Spring BH until the first Tue in
Sept. Groups (25+) on other days by appointment.
Admission: Adult £5, Child £1.50, OAP £4.50. Group prices on request.

THE WEARDALE MUSEUM

Tel: 01388 517433

Ireshopeburn, Co. Durham DL13 1EY   **Contact:** D T Heatherington
Small folk museum in minister's house. Includes 1870 Weardale cottage room, Wesley room
and local history displays.
Location: OS Ref. NZ872 385. Adjacent to 18th century Methodist Chapel.
Opening Times: Easter & May - Sept: Wed - Sun & BH, 2 - 5pm. Aug: daily, 2 - 5pm.
Admission: Adult £1, Child 30p.

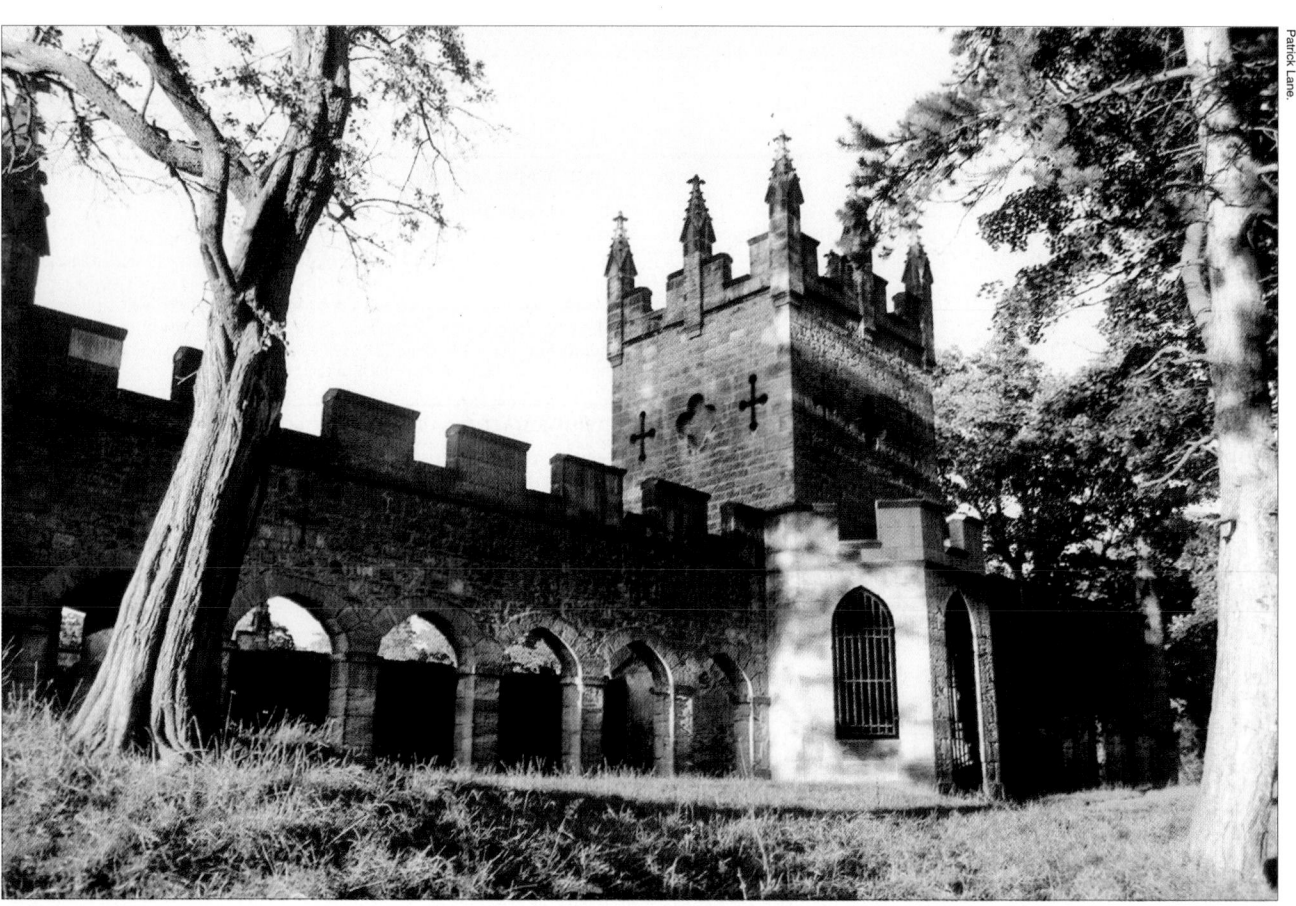

Auckland Castle Deer House, Co Durham.

Patrick Lane.

ALNWICK CASTLE
Alnwick

Described by the Victorians as the 'Windsor of the North', Alnwick Castle is the main seat of the Duke of Northumberland, whose family, the Percys, have lived here since 1309.

This Border stronghold has survived many battles, but now peacefully dominates the picturesque market town of Alnwick, overlooking landscape designed by 'Capability' Brown. The stern medieval exterior belies the treasure house within, furnished in palatial Renaissance style, with painting by Titian, Van Dyck and Canaletto, fine furniture and an exquisite collection of china.

The Regimental Museum of the Northumberland Fusiliers is housed in the Abbot's Tower of the Castle, while the Postern Tower contains an exhibition of the Duke's collection of archaeology. In the Constable's Tower is an exhibition of the Percy Tenantry Volunteers 1798 - 1814.

Other attractions include the Percy State Coach, dungeon, gun terrace and the grounds which offer peaceful walks and superb views over the surrounding countryside.

Alnwick Castle Guest Hall is one of the chief buildings of Anthony Salvin's 19th century restoration. Built as a magnificent coach house, it has throughout its history served as a venue for entertainment. This splendid Guest Hall is available for conferences, entertaining, wedding receptions, concerts, dinner dances and theatre productions. Please note that the Guest Hall is **not** open to Castle visitors.

Owner:
His Grace the Duke
of Northumberland

CONTACT

Alnwick Castle
Estate Office
Alnwick
Northumberland
NE66 1NQ

Tel: 01665 510777

Info: 01665 511100

Fax: 01665 510876

e-mail: enquiries@
alnwickcastle.com

LOCATION

OS Ref. NU187 135

In Alnwick 1^1/$_2$ m W of A1.

From London 6 hrs,
Edinburgh 2 hrs,
Chester 4 hrs,
Newcastle 40mins
North Sea ferry
terminal 30mins.

Bus: From bus station
in Alnwick.

Rail: Alnmouth Station 5m.
Kings Cross, London 3^1/$_2$hrs

Air: Newcastle 40mins.

OPENING TIMES

SUMMER
1 April - 26 October
Daily, 11am - 5pm,
last admission 4.15pm.

Private functions by
arrangement.

ADMISSION

SUMMER
House & Garden
Adult.......................£6.75
Child (5-16yrs) £3.50
Conc. £5.75
Family (2+2)........ £15.50

Pre-booked Groups (14+)
Adult.....................£5.75
Child (5-16yrs) £3.00
Conc. £5.50

CONFERENCE/FUNCTION		
ROOM	SIZE	MAX CAPACITY
The Guest Hall	100' x 30'	300

 Conference facilities. Fashion shows, fairs, filming, parkland for hire. No photography inside the castle. No un-accompanied children.

Wedding receptions.

Not suitable. By arrangement.

Coffee, light lunches and teas, seats 80.

70 cars and 4 coaches.

Guidebook and worksheet, special rates for children and teachers.

Guide dogs only.

Jarrold Colour Publications.

Owner:
Trustees Lord Armstrong
dec'd.

CONTACT

P Bolam
R G Bolam & Son
Townfoot
Rothbury
Northumberland
NE65 7SP

Tel: 01669 620314

Fax: 01669 621236

LOCATION

OS Ref. NU184 351

42m N of
Newcastle-upon-Tyne.
20m S of Berwick upon
Tweed. 6m E of Belford by
B1342 from A1 at Belford.

Bus: Bus service
200 yards.

Rail: Berwick-upon-
Tweed 20m.

Taxi: J Swanston
01289 306124.

Air: Newcastle-upon-
Tyne 45m.

BAMBURGH CASTLE
Bamburgh

BAMBURGH CASTLE is the home of the Armstrong family. The earliest reference to Bamburgh shows the craggy citadel to have been a royal centre by AD 547. Recent archaeological excavation has revealed that the site has been occupied since prehistoric times.

The Norman Keep has been the stronghold for nearly nine centuries, but the remainder has twice been extensively restored, initially by Lord Crewe in the 1750s and subsequently by the 2nd Lord Armstrong at the beginning of the 20th century. This Castle was the first to succumb to artillery fire – that of Edward IV.

The public rooms contain many exhibits, including the loan collections of armour from HM Tower of London, the John George Joicey Museum, Newcastle-upon-Tyne and other private sources, which complement the castle's armour. Porcelain, china, jade, furniture from many periods, oils, water-colours and a host of interesting items are all contained within one of the most important buildings of Britain's national heritage.

VIEWS

The views from the ramparts are unsurpassed and take in Holy Island, the Farne Islands, one of Northumberland's finest beaches and, landwards, the Cheviot Hills.

OPENING TIMES

April - October
Daily, 11am - 5pm.
Last entry 4.30pm.

Tours by arrangement
at any time.

ADMISSION

SUMMER

Adult	£4.50
Child (6 - 16yrs)	£1.50
OAP	£3.50
Groups *	
Adult	£3.00
Child (6 - 16yrs)	£1.00
OAP	£2.00

* Min payment £30

WINTER
Group rates only quoted.

 Filming. No photography in house.

Limited access. WC.

Tearooms for light refreshments. Groups can book.

By arrangement at any time, min charge out of hours £30.

100 cars, coaches park on tarmac drive at entrance.

Welcome. Guide provided if requested, educational pack.

Guide dogs only.

Owner:
Sir Humphrey Wakefield Bt

CONTACT

Anne Benson
Chillingham Castle
Northumberland
NE66 5NJ

Tel: 01668 215359

Fax: 01668 215463

e-mail: enquiries@
chillingham-castle.com

LOCATION

OS Ref. NU062 258

45m N of Newcastle
between A697 & A1.
2m S of B6348 at Chatton.
6m SE of Wooler.

Rail: Alnmouth or
Berwick.

CONFERENCE/FUNCTION

ROOM	SIZE	MAX CAPACITY
King James I Room		
Great Hall		100
Minstrels' Hall		60
2 x Drawing Room		
Museum		
Tea Room		35
Lower Gallery		
Upper Gallery		

CHILLINGHAM CASTLE
Nr Alnwick

This remarkable castle, the home of Sir Humphry Wakefield Bt, with its alarming dungeons has, since the 1200s, been continuously owned by the family of the Earls Grey and their relations. You will see active restoration of complex masonry, metalwork and ornamental plaster as the great halls and state rooms are gradually brought back to life with antique furniture, tapestries, arms and armour as of old and even a torture chamber.

At first a 12th century stronghold, Chillingham became a fully fortified castle in the 14th century. Wrapped in the nation's history it occupied a strategic position as a fortress during Northumberland's bloody border feuds, often besieged and at many times enjoying the patronage of royal visitors. In Tudor days there were additions but the underlying medieval character has always been retained. The 18th and 19th centuries saw decorative refinements and extravagances including the lake, garden and grounds laid out by Sir Jeffrey Wyatville, fresh from his triumphs at Windsor Castle.

GARDENS

With romantic grounds, the castle commands breathtaking views of the surrounding countryside. As you walk to the lake you will see, according to the season, drifts of snowdrops, daffodils or bluebells and an astonishing display of rhododendrons. This emphasises the restrained formality of the Elizabethan topiary garden, with its intricately clipped hedges of box and yew. Lawns, the formal gardens and woodland walks are all fully open to the public.

SUMMER
Easter
1 May - 30 September
Daily except Tues
12 noon - 5pm.

July - August,
Daily: 12 noon - 5pm.

WINTER
October - April: Groups any time by appointment. All function activities available.

ADMISSION

SUMMER

Adult	£4.50
OAP	£4.00
Child (3-13)	£0.50

Groups (10+)

Per person	£3.80
Tour	£25.00

 Corporate entertainment, lunches, drinks, dinners, wedding ceremonies and receptions.

Partially suitable.

Booked meals for up to 100 people.

By arrangement.

 Avoid Lilburn route, coach parties welcome by prior arrangement. Limited for coaches.

 Apartments.

Civil Wedding Licence.

ALNWICK CASTLE 🏛

See page 431 for full page entry.

AYDON CASTLE ⌗

Tel: 01434 632450

Corbridge, Northumberland NE45 5PJ

Owner: English Heritage   **Contact:** The Custodian

One of the finest fortified manor houses in England, dating from the late 13th century. Its survival, intact, can be attributed to its conversion to a farmhouse in the 17th century.

Location: OS87 Ref. NZ002 663. 2m NE of Corbridge, on minor road off B6321 or A68.

Opening Times: 1 Apr - 30 Sept: daily, 10am - 6pm. 1- 31 Oct: daily, 10am - 5pm.

Admission: Adult £2.10, Child £1.10, Conc. £1.60. 15% discount for groups (11+).

🛍 ♿Ground floor & grounds suitable.   🍴 🅿Limited. 🎦
🐕In grounds, on leads.   🛡Tel. for details.

BAMBURGH CASTLE 🏛

See page 432 for full page entry.

BELSAY HALL, CASTLE & GARDENS ⌗ See opposite for half page entry.

BERWICK BARRACKS ⌗

Tel: 01289 304493

The Parade, Berwick-upon-Tweed, Northumberland TD15 1DF

Owner: English Heritage   **Contact:** The Custodian

Among the earliest purpose built barracks, these have changed very little since 1717. They house an exhibition '*By Beat of Drum*', which recreates scenes such as the barrack room from the life of the British infantryman, the Museum of the King's Own Scottish Borderers and the Borough Museum with fine art, local history exhibition and other collections. Guided tours available.

Location: OS75 Ref. NT994 535. On the Parade, off Church Street, Berwick town centre.

Opening Times: 1 Apr - 30 Sept: daily, 10am - 6pm. 1 - 31 Oct: daily, 10am - 5pm. 1 Nov - 31 Mar: Wed - Sun, 10am - 4pm. Closed 24 - 26 Dec.

Admission: Adult £2.70, Child £1.40, Conc. £2. 15% discount for groups (11+).

🛍 ♿Ground floor & grounds suitable.   🍴 🅿Limited. 🎦
🐕In grounds, on leads.   ❄ 🛡Tel. for details.

BERWICK RAMPARTS ⌗

Tel: 0191 269 1200

Berwick-upon-Tweed, Northumberland

Owner: English Heritage   **Contact:** The Northern Regional Office

A remarkably complete system of town fortifications consisting of gateways, ramparts and projecting bastions built in the 16th century.

Location: OS Ref. NT994 535. Surrounding Berwick town centre on N bank of River Tweed.

Opening Times: Any reasonable time.

Admission: Free.

BRINKBURN PRIORY ⌗

Tel: 01665 570628

Long Framlington, Morpeth, Northumberland NE65 8AF

Owner: English Heritage   **Contact:** The Custodian

This late 12th century church is a fine example of early gothic architecture, almost perfectly preserved, and is set in a lovely spot beside the River Coquet.

Location: OS81, Ref. NZ116 984. 4¹/₂ m SE of Rothbury off B6344 5m W of A1.

Opening Times: 1 Apr - 30 Sept: daily, 10am - 6pm. 1 - 31 Oct, daily, 10am - 5pm.

Admission: Adult £1.70, Child 90p, Conc. £1.30. 15% discount for groups (11+).

♿Not suitable.   🅿Limited.   🎦   🐕On leads.   🛡Tel. for details.

CAPHEATON HALL

Tel: 01830 530253

Newcastle-upon-Tyne NE19 2AB

Owner/Contact: J Browne-Swinburne

Built for Sir John Swinburne in 1668 by Robert Trollope, an architect of great and original talent.

Location: OS Ref. NZ038 805. 17m NW of Newcastle off A696.

Opening Times: By written appointment only.

Admission: Adult £3.

❄

BELSAY HALL, CASTLE & GARDENS ⌗

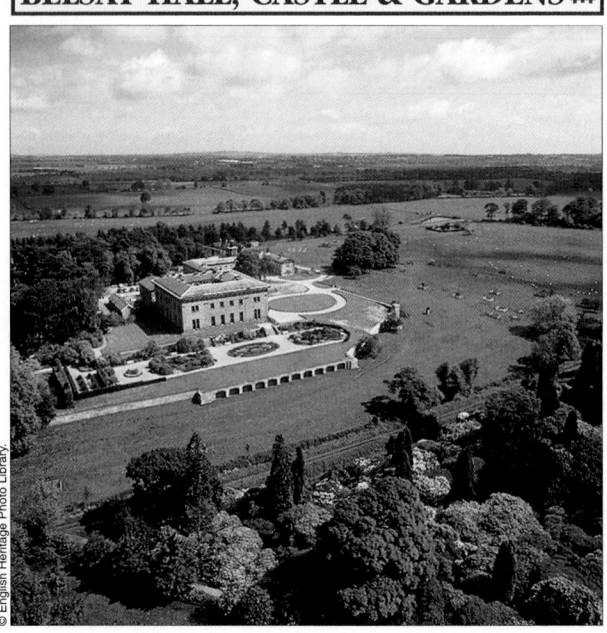

© English Heritage Photo Library.

BELSAY, Nr PONTELAND, NORTHUMBERLAND NE20 0DX

Owner: *English Heritage*   ***Contact:*** *The Custodian*

Tel: 01661 881636 **Fax:** 01661 881043

Belsay is one of the most remarkable estates in Northumberland's border country. The buildings, set amidst 30 acres of magnificent landscaped gardens, have been occupied by the same family for nearly 600 years. The gardens, created largely in the 19th century, are a fascinating mix of the formal and the informal with terraced gardens, a rhododendron garden, magnolia garden, mature woodland and even a winter garden. The buildings comprise a 14th century castle, a manor house and Belsay Hall, an internationally famous mansion designed by Sir Charles Monck in the 19th century in the style of classical buildings he had encountered during a tour of Greece.

© English Heritage Photo Library.

Location: OS87, Ref. NZ088 785. In Belsay 14m (22.4 km) NW of Newcastle on SW of A696. 7m NW of Ponteland. Nearest airport and station is Newcastle.

Opening Times: 1 Apr - 30 Sept: daily, 10am - 6pm. 1 - 31 Oct: daily, 10am - 5pm. 1 Nov - 31 Mar: daily, 10am - 4pm.

Admission: Adult £3.90, Child £2.90, Conc. £2. 15% discount for groups (11+).

🛍 🍴 ♿Partially suitable. WC.   🍴During summer & weekends Apr - Oct.
🅿 🎦 🐕In grounds, on leads.   🛡Tel. for details.

CHERRYBURN – THOMAS BEWICK BIRTHPLACE 🦋 Tel: 01661 843276

Station Bank, Mickley, Stocksfield, Northumberland NE43 7DD

Owner: The National Trust **Contact:** The Administrator

Birthplace of Northumbria's greatest artist, wood engraver and naturalist, Thomas Bewick, b.1753. The Museum explores his famous works and life with occasional demonstrations of wood block printing in the printing house. Farmyard animals, picnic area, garden.

Location: OS Ref. NZ075 627. 11m W of Newcastle on A695 (400yds signed from Mickley Square). 1¹/₂ m W of Prudhoe.

Opening Times: 1 Apr - 31 Oct: daily except Tues & Weds, 1 - 5.30pm. Last admission 5pm.

Admission: Adult £3. No group rate.

📷 ♿Some steps. WC. ☕Morning coffee for booked groups. 🎗Tel. for details.

CHESTERS ROMAN FORT & MUSEUM ⌗

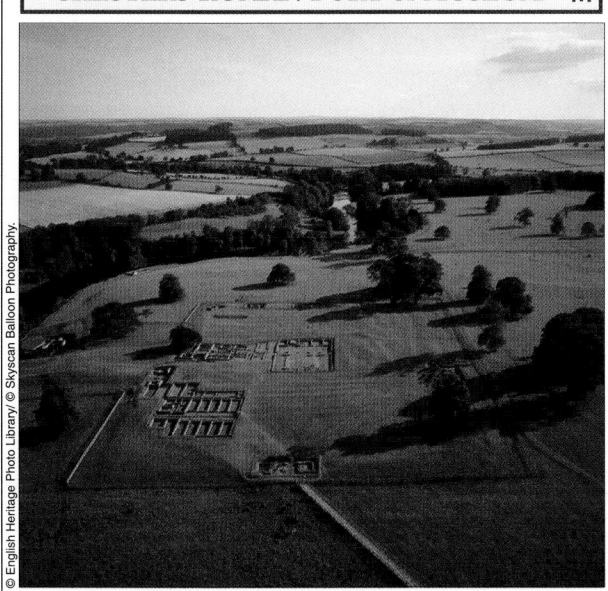

© English Heritage Photo Library/ © Skyscan Balloon Photography.

CHOLLERFORD, Nr HEXHAM, NORTHUMBERLAND NE46 4EP

Owner: English Heritage *Contact:* The Custodian

Tel: 01434 681379

The best preserved example of a Roman cavalry fort in Britain, including remains of the bath house on the banks of the River North Tyne. The museum houses a fascinating collection of Roman sculpture and inscriptions.

Location: OS87, Ref. NY913 701. 1¹/₂ m from Chollerford on B6318.

Opening Times: 1 Apr - 30 Sept: daily, 9.30am - 6pm. 1 - 31 Oct: daily, 10am - 5pm. 1 Nov - 31 Mar: daily, 10am - 4pm. Closed 24 - 26 Dec.

Admission: Adult £2.90, Child £1.50, Conc. £2.20. 15% discount for groups (11+).

📷 ♿Grounds suitable. WC. ☕Summer only. 🅿 🎟
🐕In grounds, on leads. ❄ 🎗Tel. for details.

CHILLINGHAM CASTLE 🏰 See page 433 for full page entry.

CHIPCHASE CASTLE 🏰 Tel: 01434 230203 Fax: 01434 230740

Wark, Hexham, Northumberland NE48 3NT

Owner/Contact: Mrs P J Torday

The castle overlooks the River North Tyne and is set in formal and informal gardens. One walled garden is used as a nursery specialising in unusual perennial plants.

Location: OS Ref. NY882 758. 10m NW of Hexham via A6079 to Chollerton. 2m SE of Wark.

Opening Times: Castle: 1 - 28 Jun: daily 2 - 5pm. Tours by arrangement at other times. Castle Gardens & Nursery: Easter - 31 Jul, Thur - Sun & BH Mons, 10am - 5pm.

Admission: Castle £4, Garden £1.50, concessions available. Nursery Free.

♿Not suitable. 🎟Obligatory. 🐕

CORBRIDGE ROMAN SITE ⌗ Tel: 01434 632349

Corbridge, Northumberland NE45 5NT

Owner: English Heritage **Contact:** The Custodian

A fascinating series of excavated remains, including foundations of granaries with a grain ventilation system. From artefacts found, which can be seen in the site museum, we know a large settlement developed around this supply depot.

Location: OS87 Ref. NY983 649. ¹/₂ m NW of Corbridge on minor road, signposted for Corbridge Roman Site.

Opening Times: 1 Apr - 30 Sept: daily, 10am - 6pm. 1 - 31 Oct: daily, 10am - 5pm. 1 Nov - 31 Mar: Wed - Sun, 10am - 4pm. Closed 1 - 2pm during winter & 24 - 26 Dec.

Admission: Adult £2.90, Child £1.50, Conc. £2.20. 15% discount for groups (11+).

📷 ♿Partially suitable. 🎧Inclusive. 🅿 Limited for coaches. 🎟
🐕In grounds, on leads. ❄ 🎗Tel. for details.

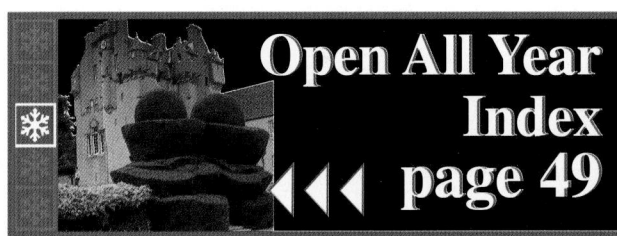

Open All Year
Index
◀◀◀ page 49

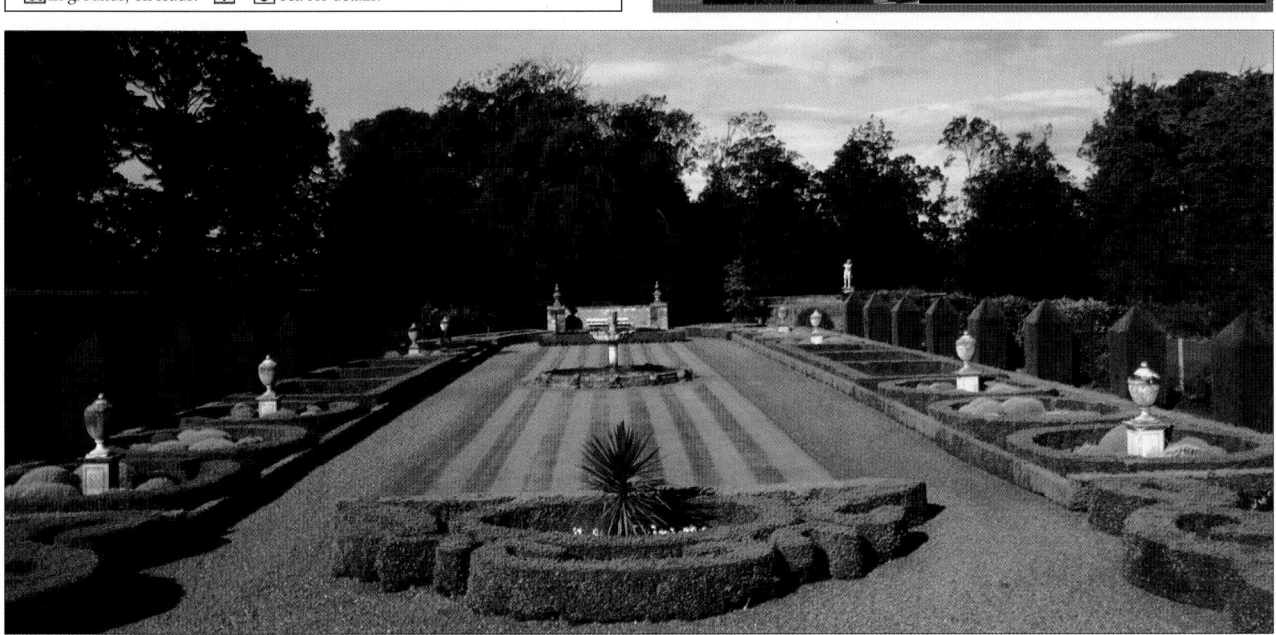

Seaton Delaval Hall, Northumberland.

CRAGSIDE

 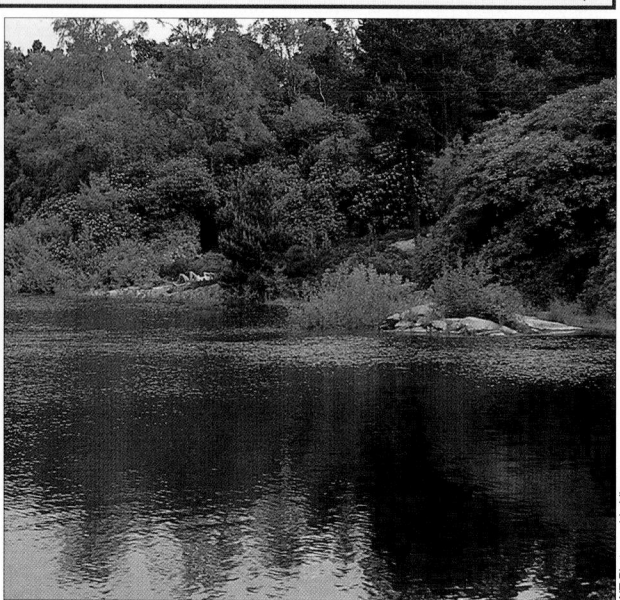

ROTHBURY, MORPETH, NORTHUMBERLAND NE65 7PX

Owner: *The National Trust*   **Contact:** *Property Manager*

Tel: 01669 620150   **Fax:** 01669 620066

Built for the 19th century's greatest gun-maker and innovator, 1st Lord Armstrong, Cragside became one of the most modern and surprising houses for its time in the country. In the 1880s, the house had hot and cold running water, central heating, telephones, a Turkish bath suite and a passenger lift but - most remarkable of all - it was the first house in the world to be lit by hydro-electricity. No wonder it was described as 'The Palace of a Modern Magician'. Children will love exploring the 1000-acre forest garden, which contains one of Europe's largest rock gardens, a formal garden, lakes and an exciting Adventure Play Area (new for 2001). Allow a whole day!

Location: OS Ref. NU073 022. $^1/_2$ m NE of Rothbury on B6341.

Opening Times: House: 31 Mar - 4 Nov: daily except Mons (open BH Mons), 1 - 5.30pm. Last admission 4.30pm. Estate & Formal Garden: 31 Mar - 4 Nov: daily except Mons (open BH Mons), 10.30am - 7pm. Last admission 5pm. 7 Nov - 16 Dec: Estate, Garden, Shop & Restaurant: Wed - Sun, 11am - 4pm (house closed).

Admission: House, Estate & Gardens: Adult £6.70, Child (5-17yrs) £3.40, Family (2+3) £16.80. Groups (15+) £5.70. Estate & Formal Garden: Adult £4.20, Child (5-17yrs) £2.10, Family (2+3) £10.50. Groups (15+) £3.50.

  Partially suitable.

DUNSTANBURGH CASTLE

Tel: 01665 576231

c/o 14 Queen Street, Alnwick, Northumberland NE66 1RD

Owner: The National Trust   **Guardian:** English Heritage   **Contact:** The Custodian

An easy, but bracing, coastal walk leads to the eerie skeleton of this wonderful 14th century castle sited on a basalt crag, rearing up more than 100 feet from the waves crashing on the rocks below. The surviving ruins include the large gatehouse, which later became the keep, and curtain walls.

Location: OS75 Ref. NU258 220. 8m NE of Alnwick.

Opening Times: 1 Apr - 30 Sept: daily, 10am - 6pm. 1 - 31 Oct, daily, 10am - 5pm. 1 Nov - 31 Mar: Wed - Sun, 10am - 4pm. Closed 24 - 26 Dec.

Admission: Adult £1.90, Child £1, Conc. £1.40. 15% discount for groups (11+).

Not suitable.   No parking.   In grounds, on leads.

EDLINGHAM CASTLE

Tel: 0191 269 1200

Edlingham, Alnwick, Northumberland

Owner: English Heritage   **Contact:** The Northern Regional Office

Set beside a splendid railway viaduct this complex ruin has defensive features spanning the 13th and 15th centuries.

Location: OS Ref. NU115 092. At E end of Edlingham village, on minor road off B6341 6m SW of Alnwick.

Opening Times: Any reasonable time.

Admission: Free.

ETAL CASTLE

Tel: 01890 820332

Cornhill-on-Tweed, Northumberland

Owner: English Heritage   **Contact:** The Custodian

A 14th century castle located in the picturesque village of Etal. Award-winning exhibition about the castle, Border warfare and the Battle of Flodden.

Location: OS75 Ref. NT925 394. In Etal village, 10m SW of Berwick.

Opening Times: 1 Apr - 30 Sept: daily, 10am - 6pm. 1 - 31 Oct: daily, 10am - 5pm.

Admission: Adult £2.90, Child £1.40, Conc. £2. 15% discount for groups (11+).

Partially suitable. WC.   Inclusive.   Limited.
In grounds, on leads.   Tel. for details.

HERTERTON HOUSE GARDENS

Tel: 01670 774278

Hartington, Cambo, Morpeth, Northumberland NE61 4BN

Owner/Contact: C J "Frank" Lawley

One acre of formal garden in stone walls around a 16th century farmhouse, including a small topiary garden, physic garden, flower garden, fancy garden and gazebo.

Location: OS Ref. NZ022 881. 2m N of Cambo, just off B6342.

Opening Times: 1 Apr - 30 Sept: Mons, Weds, Fri - Sun, 1.30 - 5.30pm.

Admission: Adult £2.40, Child (5-15yrs) £1. Groups by arrangement.

Not suitable.   By arrangement.   Limited for coaches.
Guided tours for adult students only.

HOUSESTEADS ROMAN FORT

Tel: 01434 344363

Nr Haydon Bridge, Northumberland NE47 6NN

Owner: The National Trust   **Guardian:** English Heritage   **Contact:** The Custodian

Perched high on a ridge overlooking open moorland, this is the best known part of the Wall. The fort covers five acres and there are remains of many buildings, such as granaries, barrack blocks and gateways. A small exhibition displays altars, inscriptions and models.

Location: OS87 Ref. NY790 687. 2m NE of Bardon Mill.

Opening Times: 1 Apr - 30 Sept: daily, 10am - 6pm. 1 - 31 Oct: daily, 10am - 5pm. 1 Nov - 31 Mar: daily, 10am - 4pm. Closed 24 - 26 Dec.

Admission: Adult £2.90, Child £1.50, Conc. £2.20. 15% discount for groups (11+).

Not suitable.   Charge.   In grounds, on leads.
Tel. for details.

HOWICK HALL GARDENS

Tel/Fax: 01665 577285

Howick, Alnwick, Northumberland NE66 3LB   **e-mail:** howickarb@compuserve.com

Owner: Howick Trustees Ltd   **Contact:** Lord Howick

Romantically landscaped grounds surrounding the house in a little valley, with rare rhododendrons and flowering shrubs and trees.

Location: OS Ref. NU249 175. 6m NE of Alnwick. 1m E of B1339.

Opening Times: Apr - Oct: daily 1 - 6pm.

Admission: Adult £2, Child/OAP £1, Student (up to 16yrs) £1. Season tickets available.

Grounds partly suitable. WC.   Limited.

KIRKLEY HALL GARDENS

Tel: 01661 860808 **Fax:** 01661 860047

Ponteland, Northumberland NE20 0AQ **Contact:** J Guy

Over 9 acres of beautiful gardens incorporating a Victorian walled garden, woodland walks, sunken garden and wildlife areas and ponds.

Location: OS Ref. NZ150 772. 10m from the centre of Newcastle upon Tyne. 2 1/2 m N of Ponteland on byroad to Morpeth.

Opening Times: 1 Apr - 30 Sept: daily, 10am - 5pm.

Admission: Free.

THE LADY WATERFORD HALL & MURALS

Ford, Berwick-upon-Tweed TD15 2QA **Tel:** 01890 820524 **Fax:** 01890 820384

Owner: Ford & Etal Estates **Contact:** The Caretaker

Commissioned in 1860 the walls of this beautiful building are decorated with beautiful murals depicting Bible stories.

Location: OS Ref. NT945 374. On the B6354, 9m from Berwick-upon-Tweed, midway between Newcastle-upon-Tyne and Edinburgh, close to the A697.

Opening Times: 1 Apr - 29 Oct: daily, 10.30am - 12.30pm & 1.30 - 5.30pm. By arrangement with the caretaker during winter months.

Admission: Adult £1.50, Child Free (over 12yrs 50p), Conc. £1. Groups by arrangement.

LINDISFARNE CASTLE

Tel: 01289 389244

Holy Island, Berwick-upon-Tweed, Northumberland TD15 2SH

Owner: The National Trust **Contact:** The Administrator

Built in 1550 to protect Holy Island harbour from attack, the castle was restored and converted into a private house for Edward Hudson by Sir Edwin Lutyens in 1903. Small walled garden was designed by Gertrude Jekyll. 19th century lime kilns in field by the castle.

Location: OS Ref. NU136 417. On Holy Island, 3/4 m E of village, 6m E of A1 across causeway. Usable at low tide.

Opening Times: 31 Mar - 31 Oct: daily except Fris (but open Good Fri), 12 noon - 3pm, but earlier or later as the tide allows. Last admission 1/2 before close. Admission to garden only when gardener in attendance. Holy Island is cut off by the tide from 2 hours before and 3 1/2 hours after high tide. Visitors are advised to check tide times before visiting.

Admission: £4, Family £10. No group rate. Groups (15+) must pre-book.

🏠 NT Shop (in Main St.) ♿ Not suitable. 🅿 No parking. 🐕 In grounds, on leads.

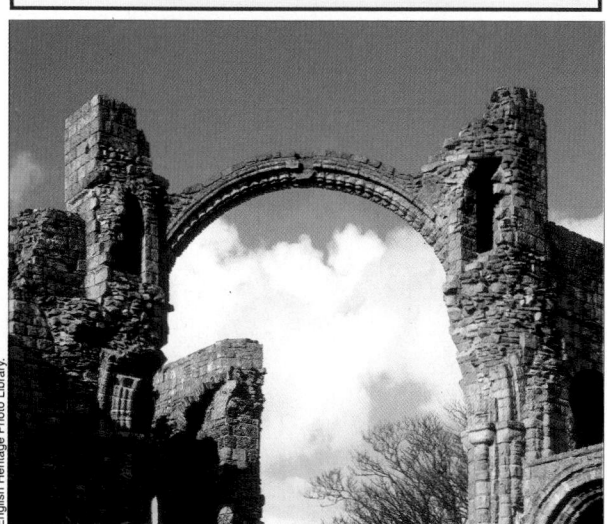

LINDISFARNE PRIORY

HOLY ISLAND, BERWICK-UPON-TWEED TD15 2RX

Owner: English Heritage *Contact: The Custodian*

Tel: 01289 389200

The site of one of the most important early centres of Christianity in Anglo-Saxon England. St Cuthbert converted pagan Northumbria, and miracles occurring at his shrine established this 11th century priory as a major pilgrimage centre. The evocative ruins, with the decorated 'rainbow' arch curving dramatically across the nave of the church, are still the destination of pilgrims today. The story of Lindisfarne is told in an exhibition which gives an impression of life for the monks, including a reconstruction of a monk's cell.

Location: OS75 Ref. NU126 418. On Holy Island, check tide times.

Opening Times: 1 Apr - 30 Sept: daily, 10am - 6pm. 1 - 31 Oct: daily, 10am - 5pm. 1 Nov - 31 Mar: daily, 10am - 4pm. Closed 24 - 26 Dec.

Admission: Adult £2.90, Child £1.50, Conc. £2.20. 15% discount for groups (11+).

🏠 ♿ Partially suitable. 🅿 Charge. 🐕 Restricted. ❄ ⛨ Tel. for details.

English Heritage Photo Library.

MELDON PARK

MORPETH, NORTHUMBERLAND NE61 3SW

Owner/Contact: M Cookson

Tel: 01670 772661

Isaac Cookson III purchased the Meldon land in 1832. John Dobson, the famous architect, was commissioned to build a house by Isaac Cookson and he recommended the present site. The entrance is through an Ionic porch having two rows of columns to the front door. Once inside you are in the main hall which has an enormous staircase lit by a large window to the north. Between the two World Wars Edwin Lutyens was employed to enrich the Hall, which included mahogany balustrades and 18th century decorations. The garden has a wonderful collection of rhododendrons best seen in early June, an old-fashioned kitchen garden and greenhouses.

Location: OS Ref. NZ105 856. 7m W of Morpeth on B6343. 5m N of Belsay. 7m W of Morpeth.

Opening Times: 26 May - 24 Jun, 2 - 5pm & Aug BH weekend, 2 - 5.30pm.

Admission: Adult £3, Child £1.50, OAP £2.

ℹ No photography. ♿ ☕ Sundays only. 🔑 By arrangement. 🅿 🐕 Guide dogs only.

NORHAM CASTLE

Tel: 01289 382329

Norham, Northumberland

Owner: English Heritage **Contact:** The Custodian

Set on a promontory in a curve of the River Tweed, this was one of the strongest of the Border castles, built c1160.

Location: OS75 Ref. NT907 476. 6m SW of Berwick.

Opening Times: 1 Apr - 30 Sept: daily, 10am - 6pm. 1 - 31 Oct: daily, 10am - 5pm.

Admission: Adult £1.90, Child £1, Conc. £1.40. 15% discount for groups (11+).

🏠 ♿ Partially suitable. 🎧 🅿 🍴 🐕 On leads. ⛨ Tel. for details.

PRESTON TOWER

Tel: 01665 589227

Chathill, Northumberland NE67 5DH

Owner/Contact: Major T Baker Cresswell

The Tower was built by Sir Robert Harbottle in 1392 and is one of the few survivors of 78 pele towers listed in 1415. The tunnel vaulted rooms remain unaltered and provide a realistic picture of the grim way of life under the constant threat of "Border Reivers". Two rooms are furnished in contemporary style and there are displays of historic and local information. Visitors are welcome to walk in the grounds which contain a number of interesting trees and shrubs. A woodland walk to the natural spring from which water is now pumped up to the Tower for the house and cottages.

Location: OS Ref. NU185 253. Follow Historic Property signs on A1 7m N of Alnwick.

Opening Times: Daylight hours all year.

Admission: Adult £1, Child/Conc./Groups 50p.

♿ Grounds suitable. ✿ ❄

PRUDHOE CASTLE

Tel: 01661 833459

Prudhoe, Northumberland NE42 6NA

Owner: English Heritage **Contact:** The Custodian

Set on a wooded hillside overlooking the River Tyne are the extensive remains of this 12th century castle including a gatehouse, curtain wall and keep. Small exhibition and video presentation.

Location: OS88 Ref. NZ092 634. In Prudhoe, on minor road N from A695.

Opening Times: 1 Apr - 30 Sept: daily, 10am - 6pm. 1 - 31 Oct: daily, 10am - 5pm.

Admission: Adult £1.90, Child £1, Conc. £1.40. 15% discount for groups (11+).

🏠 ♿ Partially suitable. ☕ 🅿 Limited. 🍴 🐕 In grounds, on leads. ⛨ Tel. for details.

SEATON DELAVAL HALL

SEATON SLUICE, WHITLEY BAY, NORTHUMBERLAND NE26 4QR

Owner: Lord Hastings   *Contact:* Mrs Mills

Tel: 0191 2371493/0191 2370786

The home of Lord and Lady Hastings, half a mile from Seaton Sluice, is the last and most sensational mansion designed by Sir John Vanbrugh, builder of Blenheim Palace and Castle Howard. It was erected 1718 - 1728 and comprises a high turreted block flanked by arcaded wings which form a vast forecourt. The centre block was gutted by fire in 1822, but was partially restored in 1862 and again in 1959 - 1962 and 1999 - 2000. The remarkable staircases are a visual delight, and the two surviving rooms are filled with family pictures and photographs and royal seals spanning three centuries as well as various archives. This building is used frequently for concerts and charitable functions. The East Wing contains immense stables in ashlar stone of breathtaking proportions. Nearby are the Coach House with farm and passenger vehicles, fully documented, and the restored ice house with explanatory sketch and description. There are beautiful gardens with herbaceous borders, rose garden, rhododendrons, azaleas, laburnum walk, statues, and a spectacular parterre by internationally famous Jim Russell, also a unique Norman Church.

Location: OS Ref. NZ322 766. 1/2 m from Seaton Sluice on A190, 3m from Whitley Bay.

Opening Times: May & Aug BH Mons; Jun - 30 Sept: Weds & Suns, 2 - 6pm.

Admission: Adult £3, Child £1, Conc. £2.50. Groups (20+): Adult £2.50, Child £1, Student £1.

⬚ ♿Partially suitable. WC. ▣ **P**Free. 🐕In grounds, on leads.

WALLINGTON 🌿

CAMBO, MORPETH, NORTHUMBERLAND NE61 4AP

Owner: The National Trust   *Contact:* The House Manager

Tel: 01670 774283 **Fax:** 01670 774420

A beautiful walled garden, Edwardian conservatory, woodland walks and ornamental ponds make a delightful setting for the Trevelyan's historic home. The house at Wallington dates from 1688 and boasts fine interiors, a superb collection of ceramics and William Bell-Scott's famous paintings of Northumbrian history but still retains the atmosphere of a much loved family home.

Location: OS Ref. NZ030 843. Near Cambo, 6m NW of Belsay (A696).

Opening Times: House: 31 Mar - 30 Sept: daily (except Tues), 1 - 5.30pm. 1 Oct - 4 Nov: daily (except Tues), 1 - 4.30pm. Gardens: daily, 10am - 7pm (summer). Grounds: all year.

Admission: House, Garden & Grounds: Adult £5.50, Child £2.75, Family £13.75, Group: £5. Garden & Grounds: Adult £4, Child £2, Groups £3.50.

ℹNo photography in house. ⬚ 🍴 🍵 ♿ ▣ 🎨By arrangement. **P** ▥ 🐕In grounds on leads. 🔔 ❄ ▣ Please telephone for details.

WARKWORTH CASTLE ⊞

WARKWORTH, MORPETH, NORTHUMBERLAND NE66 0UJ

Owner: English Heritage   *Contact:* The Custodian

Tel: 01665 711423

The great towering keep of this 15th century castle, once the home of the mighty Percy family, dominates the town and River Coquet. Warkworth is one of the most outstanding examples of an aristocratic fortified residence. Upstream by boat from the castle lies Warkworth Hermitage, cutting into the rock of the river cliff (separate charge applies).

Location: OS81 Ref. NU247 057. 7m S of Alnwick on A1068.

Opening Times: 1 Apr - 30 Sept: daily, 10am - 6pm. 1 - 31 Oct: daily, 10am - 5pm. 1 Nov - 31 Mar: daily, 10am - 4pm (closed 1 - 2pm). Closed 24 - 26 Dec.

Admission: Adult £2.50, Child £1.30, Conc. £1.90. 15% discount for groups (11+).

⬚ ♿Grounds suitable. 🎧 **P** ▥ 🐕On leads. ❄ ▣Tel. for details.

© Norman Hudson.

Seaton Delaval.

439

ARBEIA ROMAN FORT   Tel: 0191 456 1369 **Fax:** 0191 427 6862

Baring Street, South Shields, Tyne & Wear NE33 2BB
Owner: South Tyneside Metropolitan Borough Council   **Contact:** The Curator
Managed by: Tyne & Wear Museums
Extensive remains of 2nd century Roman fort, including fort defences, stone granaries, gateways and latrines. Full-scale reconstruction of Roman gateway and museum featuring finds including weapons, jewellery and tombstones. Watch excavations throughout the year.
Location: OS Ref. NZ365 679. Near town centre and Metro Station.
Opening Times: Easter - Oct: Mon - Sat: 10am - 5.30pm, Suns, 1 - 5pm. Open BH Mons. Winter: Mon - Sat, 10am - 4pm. Closed Christmas Day, Boxing Day, New Year's Day, Good Friday.
Admission: Free, except for Timequest Gallery: Adult £1.50, Conc. 80p.

BEDE'S WORLD MUSEUM   Tel: 0191 489 2106 **Fax:** 0191 428 2361

Church Bank, Jarrow, Tyne & Wear NE32 3DY
Managed by: Jarrow 700AD Ltd   **Contact:** Miss M Harte
A new museum telling the story of the Venerable Bede and Anglo-Saxon Northumbria.
Location: OS Ref. NZ339 652. Just off A19, S end of Tyne Tunnel.
Opening Times: Apr - Oct: Mon - Sat, 10am - 5.30pm, Suns, 12 noon - 5.30pm. Nov - Mar: Mon - Sat, 10am - 4.30pm, Suns, 12 noon - 4.30pm. Also open BH Mons.
Admission: Adult £4.50, Conc. £2.50, Family £9. Groups by arrangement.

BESSIE SURTEES HOUSE   Tel: 0191 269 1200

41 - 44 Sandhill, Newcastle, Tyne & Wear
Owner: English Heritage   **Contact:** The Custodian
Two 16th and 17th century merchants' houses stand on the quayside near the Tyne Bridge. One is a rare example of Jacobean domestic architecture. 3 rooms open.
Location: OS Ref. NZ252 639. 41- 44 Sandhill, Newcastle.
Opening Times: Weekdays only: 10am - 4pm. Closed BHs, 24 - 26 Dec and 1 Jan.
Admission: Free.

CATHEDRAL CHURCH OF ST NICHOLAS

Newcastle-upon-Tyne, Tyne & Wear NE1 1PF   **Tel:** 0191 232 1939 **Fax:** 0191 230 0735
e-mail: stnicholas@aol.com   **Contact:** Rev Canon Peter Strange
Mostly 14th century surmounted by 15th century lantern spire, one medieval window, two Renaissance memorials, one large 15th century Flemish brass.
Location: OS Ref. NZ250 640. City centre, $^1/_2$ m from A167 signposted from Swan House roundabout.
Opening Times: Suns: 7am - 12 noon, 4 - 7pm. Mon - Fri: 7am - 6pm. Sats: 8.30am - 4pm. BHs, 8am - 12 noon.

By arrangement. No parking. Guide dogs only.

GIBSIDE   Tel: 01207 542255

Nr Rowlands Gill, Burnopfield, Newcastle-upon-Tyne NE16 6BG
Owner: The National Trust   **Contact:** The Property Manager
Gibside is one of the finest 18th century designed landscapes in the north of England. The Chapel was built to James Paine's design soon after 1760. Outstanding example of Georgian architecture approached along a terrace with an oak avenue. Walk along the River Derwent through woodland.
Location: OS Ref. NZ172 583. 6m SW of Gateshead, 20m NW of Durham. Entrance on B6314 between Burnopfield and Rowlands Gill.
Opening Times: Grounds: 1 Apr - 31 Oct: daily except Mons (open BH Mons), 10am - 6pm. Last admission 4.30pm. 1 Nov - 31 Mar: 10am - sunset. Last admission 1 hour before sunset. Chapel: 1 Apr - 31 Oct: as grounds, otherwise by arrangement.
Admission: Chapel and Grounds: Adult £3, Child half price. Booked groups £2.60.

NEWCASTLE CASTLE GARTH   Tel: 0191 232 7938

Castle Keep, Castle Garth, Newcastle-upon-Tyne NE1 1RQ
Owner: Newcastle City Council   **Contact:** Paul MacDonald
The Keep originally dominated the castle bailey. The 'new' castle was founded in 1080.
Location: OS Ref. NZ251 638. City centre between St Nicholas church and the high level bridge.
Opening Times: All year: daily, 9.30am - 5pm.
Admission: Adult £1.50, Child/Conc. 50p.

ST PAUL'S MONASTERY   Tel: 0191 489 2106

Jarrow, Tyne & Wear
Owner: English Heritage   **Contact:** The Custodian
The home of the Venerable Bede in the 7th and 8th centuries, partly surviving as the chancel of the parish church. It has become one of the best understood Anglo-Saxon monastic sites.
Location: OS Ref. NZ339 652. In Jarrow, on minor road N of A185.
Opening Times: Any reasonable time.
Admission: Free.

SOUTER LIGHTHOUSE   Tel: 0191 529 3161

Coast Road, Whitburn, Tyne & Wear SR6 7NR
Owner: The National Trust   **Contact:** The Property Manager
Shore-based lighthouse and associated buildings, built in 1871, the first to be powered by an alternating electric current.
Location: OS Ref. NZ408 641. 2¹/₂ m S of South Shields on A183. 5m N of Sunderland.
Opening Times: 1 Apr - 31 Oct: daily except Fris (open Good Fri), 11am - 5pm. Last admission 4.30pm. Open after 31 Oct for events & activities – contact property for details.
Admission: Adult £2.80, Child half price. Booked Groups: £2.30. Family £7.

TYNEMOUTH PRIORY & CASTLE   Tel: 0191 257 1090

North Pier, Tynemouth, Tyne & Wear NE30 4BZ
Owner: English Heritage   **Contact:** The Custodian
The castle walls and gatehouse enclose the substantial remains of a Benedictine priory founded c1090 on a Saxon monastic site. Their strategic importance has made the castle and priory the target for attack for many centuries. In World War I, coastal batteries in the castle defended the mouth of the Tyne.
Location: OS88 Ref. NZ374 695. In Tynemouth.
Opening times: 1 Apr - 30 Sept: daily, 10am - 6pm. 1 - 31 Oct: daily, 10am - 5pm. 1 Nov - 31 Mar: Wed - Sun, 10am - 4pm (closed 1 - 2 pm).
Admission: Adult £1.90, Child £1, Conc. £1.40. 15% discount for groups (11+).

Grounds suitable.   By arrangement.   In grounds, on leads.   Tel. for details.

WASHINGTON OLD HALL   Tel: 0191 416 6879 **Fax:** 0191 419 2065

The Avenue, Washington Village, District 4, Washington, Tyne & Wear NE38 7LE
Owner: The National Trust   **Contact:** The Property Manager
Jacobean manor house incorporating portions of 12th century house of the Washington family. Displays of George Washington commemoratives. Small Jacobean knot garden.
Location: OS Ref. NZ312 566. In Washington on E side of The Avenue. 5m W of Sunderland (2m from A1), S of Tyne Tunnel, follow signs for Washington District 4 and then village.
Opening Times: 1 Apr - 31 Oct: Sun - Wed. Closed Thur - Sat (open Good Fri), 11am - 5pm. Last admission 4.30pm.
Admission: Adult £2.80, Child half-price, Family £7. Groups (15+) by arrangement only: £2.30.

Conferences.   Ground floor & grounds suitable.   By arrangement.   Limited.   In grounds, on leads.

Tynemouth Priory & Castle, Tyne & Wear.

THE REGIONS OF
SCOTLAND

S C O T L A N D

S C O T L A N D

Dirleton Castle & Gardens, Edinburgh
442

Scotland

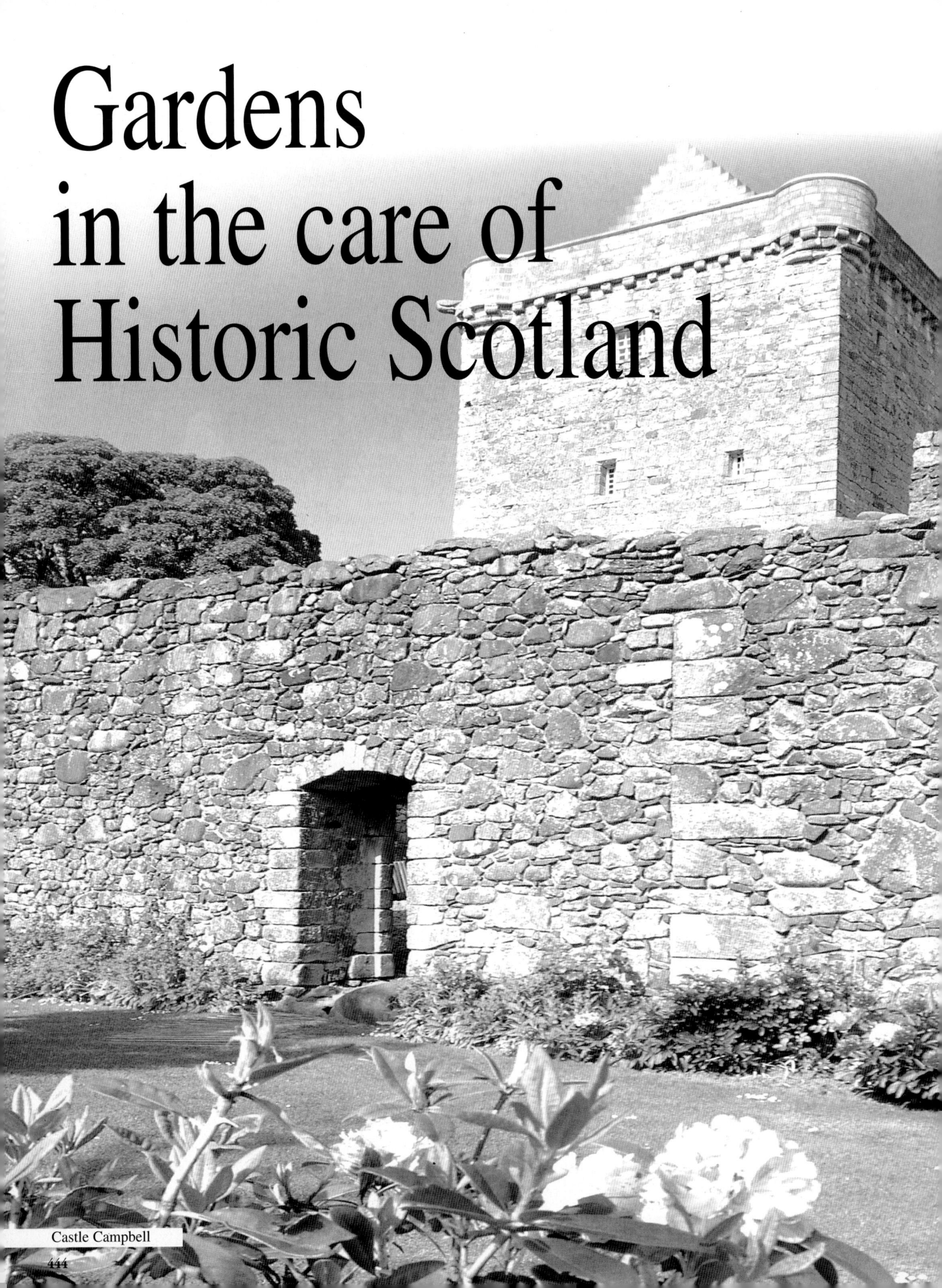

Gardens
in the care of
Historic Scotland

Castle Campbell

▲ Edzell Castle ~ Topiary Garden

▲ Stirling Castle

▲ Dirleton Castle ~ herbaceous border

Edzell Castle ~ Topiary Garden

445

▲ Dirleton   ▲ Stirling Castle ~ The King's Knot

▲ Dirleton ~ summer flower border

The gardens in the care of Historic Scotland vary in spirit, character and history – all have their own charm.

Edzell, Aberdour, Dirleton Castle and Stirling Castle, the nearby wild splendour of Castle Campbell, make an ideal itinerary for a garden lovers' tour.

Edzell

"... delicat gardine with walls sumptuously built of hewen stone polisht, with pictures and coats of armes in the walls."
Ouclerlony of Guinde, c1700

Built for Sir David Lindsay, Lord Edzell, about 1604 and recreated in the 1930s, the walled garden at Edzell features extraordinary carvings depicting the Planetary Deities, Liberal Arts and Cardinal Virtues. Visitors see decorative hedges shaped and trimmed into the Fleur de Lys, Scottish Thistle and English Rose. Sir David intended his garden to stimulate both mind and senses, and it does.

Dirleton Castle

"... some of the best examples of modern flower gardening, together with others of a style some two centuries old."
Journal account, 1865

The gardens at Dirleton emphasise the attractiveness of this castle. The castle's buildings divide into three distinct periods ranging from the 1200s to the 1500s, through the hands of three families: the de Vauxs, Halyburtons and Ruthvens. The terraced garden to the west of the castle was devised and laid out by William Ruthven, the Earl of Gowrie, in the late 1500s. A sunken bowling green probably started life as a formal parterre surrounded by yew hedges. Beyond lay lawns planted with specimen trees, leading to a well-preserved beehive doocot, which provided winter meat. Historic Scotland has also recreated the Victorian garden devised by the castle's owners in the 1860s. The castle is approached by passing along officially the world's longest herbaceous borders which are some of the most magnificent to be seen.

Aberdour

"I was lead in through the garden which was so fragrant and delightful that I thought I was still in England."
Anne Murray, 1650

Aberdour is a wonderful example of how a medieval castle could be extended and modified over several centuries. A castle stood on the site from as early as the 13th century but first known mention of a garden is not until 1540. The walled garden was converted into a bowling green by 1668, a use which continued at least until 1745, and the area still abounds with plants which, when in season, provide cuttings for sale.

Castle Campbell

Castle Campbell sits above the small village of Dollar. This spectacularly sited 15th century fortress was the lowland stronghold of the Campbells. Stunning views from the parapet walk look down on the rushing waters of the Burn of Care and Burn of Sorrow. Evidence of a formal garden remains at Castle Campbell and the entrance is dominated by the ancient 'Maiden Tree', but its wilderness setting close to Stirling makes it a particularly beautiful and accessible site.

Stirling Castle

In the 16th century Stirling Castle reflected Scotland's cultural ascendancy. Vast formal gardens were created by James IV and V, and these attracted lavish attention for many years after. Visitors in the Queen Anne rose garden can still look down and see the ghostly relief map beyond the castle walls, clearly showing the 1620s layout of what is known as the King's Knot.

Historic Scotland has 300 properties in its care, and its gardens are a rich jewel in its crown, offering hours of enjoyment.

Edzell Castle

'The Pink Boy' - Sir Joshua Reynolds.

BOWHILL HOUSE & COUNTRY PARK
Selkirk

Scottish Borders home of the Duke and Duchess of Buccleuch, dating mainly from 1812 and christened 'Sweet Bowhill' by Sir Walter Scott in his *Lay of the Last Minstrel.*

Many of the works of art were collected by earlier Montagus, Douglases and Scotts or given by Charles II to his natural son James, Duke of Monmouth and Buccleuch. Paintings include Canaletto's *Whitehall*, works by Guardi, Claude, Ruysdael, Gainsborough, Raeburn, Reynolds, Van Dyck and Wilkie. Superb French furniture, Meissen and Sèvres porcelain, silver and tapestries.

Historical relics include Monmouth's saddle and execution shirt, Sir Walter Scott's plaid and some proof editions, Queen Victoria's letters and gifts to successive Duchesses of Buccleuch, her Mistresses of the Robes.

There is also a completely restored Victorian Kitchen, 19th century horse-drawn fire engine, 'Bowhill Little Theatre', a lively centre for the performing arts and where, prior to touring the house, visitors can see 'The Quest for Bowhill', a 20 minute audio-visual presentation by Dr Colin Thompson.

Conference centre, arts courses, literary lunches, education service, visitor centre. Shop, tearoom, adventure playground, woodland walks, nature trails, picnic areas. Garden and landscape designed by John Gilpin.

Owner: His Grace the Duke of Buccleuch & Queensberry KT

CONTACT

Buccleuch Heritage Trust
Bowhill House &
Country Park
Bowhill
Selkirk
TD7 5ET

Tel/Fax: 01750 22204

e-mail:
bht@buccleuch.com

LOCATION

OS Ref. NT426 278

3m W of Selkirk off A708
Moffat Road,
A68 from Newcastle,
A7 from Carlisle
or Edinburgh.

Bus: 3m Selkirk.

Taxi: 01750 20354.

Fashion shows, air displays, archery, clay pigeon shooting, equestrian events, charity garden parties, shows, rallies, filming, lecture theatre. House is open by appointment outside public hours to groups led by officials of a recognised museum, gallery or educational establishment. No photography inside house.

Inside caterers normally used but outside caterers considered.

Visitors may alight at entrance. WC. Wheelchair visitors free.

Groups can book in advance (special rates), menus on request.

For groups. Tour time 1¼ hrs.

60 cars and 6 coaches within 50yds of house.

Welcome. Projects in Bowhill House and Victorian kitchen, Education Officers (service provided free of charge), schoolroom, ranger-led nature walks, adventure playground. Heritage Education Trust Sandford Award winner 1993 and 1998.

On leads.

'Winter' - Sir Joshua Reynolds.

CONFERENCE/FUNCTION

ROOM	SIZE	MAX CAPACITY
Bowhill Little Theatre		72

Skyscan Photo Library.

FLOORS CASTLE
Kelso

Owner: His Grace the
Duke of Roxburghe

CONTACT

Philip Massey
Director of Operations
Roxburghe Estates Office
Kelso
Roxburghshire
Scotland
TD5 7SF

Tel: 01573 223333

Fax: 01573 226056

FLOORS CASTLE, home of the Duke and Duchess of Roxburghe, is situated in the heart of the Scottish Border Country. It is reputedly the largest inhabited castle in Scotland. Designed by William Adam, who was both masterbuilder and architect, for the first Duke of Roxburghe, building started in 1721.

It was the present Duke's great-great-grandfather James, the 6th Duke, who embellished the plain Adam features of the building. In about 1849 Playfair, letting his imagination and talent run riot, transformed the castle, creating a multitude of spires and domes.

The apartments now display the outstanding collection of French 17th and 18th century furniture, magnificent tapestries, Chinese and European porcelain and many other fine works of art. Many of the treasures in the castle today were collected by Duchess May, American wife of the 8th Duke.

The castle has been seen on cinema screens worldwide in the film *Greystoke*, as the home of Tarzan, the Earl of Greystoke.

Gardens

The extensive parkland and gardens overlooking the Tweed provide a variety of wooded walks. The walled garden contains splendid herbaceous borders and in the outer walled garden a parterre to commemorate the Millennium can be seen. An excellent children's playground and picnic area are very close to the castle.

LOCATION

OS Ref. NT711 347

From South A68, A698.

From North A68, A697/9
In Kelso follow signs.

Bus: Kelso Bus Station 1m.

Rail: Berwick 20m.

OPENING TIMES

SUMMER

13 April - 28 October
Daily: 10am - 4.30pm.

Last admission 4pm.

WINTER

November - March
Closed to the general
public, available for events.

ADMISSION

SUMMER

Adult	£5.50
Child (5 - 15yrs)	£3.25
OAP/Student	£4.75
Family	£12.00

Groups (min 20)

Adult	£4.25
Child (5 - 15yrs)	£2.75
OAP/Student	£4.00

Grounds only

	£3.00
Groups	£2.50

Under 5yrs Free.

SPECIAL EVENTS

- **AUG 26:**
Family Day with Massed
Pipe Bands.

Gala dinners, conferences, product launches, 4 x 4 driving, incentive groups, highland games and other promotional events. Extensive park, helicopter pad, fishing, clay pigeon and pheasant shooting. No photography inside the castle.

Visitors may alight at the entrance. WC.

Self-service, licensed, seats 125 opens 10am.

By arrangement for up to 100. Tour time 1¼ hrs.

Unlimited for cars, 100 yds away, coach park 50 yds. Coaches can be driven to the entrance, waiting area close to restaurant exit. Lunch or tea for coach drivers.

Welcome, guide provided. Playground facilities.

Guide dogs only.

CONFERENCE/FUNCTION		
ROOM	SIZE	MAX CAPACITY
Dining Rm	18m x 7m	150
Ballroom	21m x 8m	150

Owner: The Lord Palmer

CONTACT

The Lord or Lady Palmer
Manderston
Duns
Berwickshire
Scotland
TD11 3PP

Tel: 01361 883450
Secretary: 01361 882636

Fax: 01361 882010

e-mail: palmer@
manderston.co.uk

LOCATION

OS Ref. NT810 544

From Edinburgh
47m, 1hr.
1¹/₂ m E of Duns on
A6105.

Bus: 400 yds.

Rail: Berwick Station 12m.

Taxi: Chirnside 818216.

Airport: Edinburgh or
Newcastle both
60m or 80 mins.

CONFERENCE/FUNCTION

ROOM	SIZE	MAX CAPACITY
Dining Rm	22'x 35'	100
Ballroom	34' x 21'	150
Hall	22' x 38'	130
Drawing Rm	35' x 21'	150

MANDERSTON
Duns

MANDERSTON, together with its magnificent stables, stunning marble dairy and 56 acres of immaculate gardens, forms an ensemble which must be unique in Britain today.

The house was completely rebuilt between 1903 and 1905, with no expense spared.

Visitors are able to see not only the sumptuous State Rooms and bedrooms, decorated in the Adam manner, but also all the original domestic offices, in a truly 'upstairs downstairs' atmosphere. Manderston boasts a unique and recently restored silver staircase.

There is a special museum with a nostalgic display of valuable tins made by Huntley and Palmer from 1868 to the present day. Winner of the AA/NPI Bronze Award UK 1994.

GARDENS

Outside, the magnificence continues and the combination of formal gardens and picturesque landscapes is a major attraction: unique amongst Scottish houses.

The stables, still in use, have been described by *Horse and Hound* as "probably the finest in all the wide world."

❖

Corporate & incentives venue. Ideal retreat: business groups, think-tank weekends. Fashion shows, air displays, archery, clay pigeon shooting, equestrian events, garden parties, shows, rallies, filming, product launches and marathons. Two airstrips for light aircraft, approx 5m, grand piano, billiard table, fox-hunting, pheasant shoots, sea angling, salmon fishing, stabling, cricket pitch, tennis court, lake. Nearby: 9-hole golf course, indoor swimming pool, squash court. No photography in house.

Available. Buffets, lunches and dinners. Wedding receptions.

Special parking available outside the House.

Tearoom (open as house) with waitress service. Can be booked in advance, menus on request.

Included. Available in French. Guides in rooms. If requested, the owner may meet groups. Tour time 1¹/₄ hrs.

400 cars 125yds from house, 30 coaches 5yds from house. Appreciated if group fees are paid by one person.

Welcome. Guide can be provided. Biscuit Tin Museum of particular interest.

Grounds only, on leads.

5 twin, 4 double and 1 single.

OPENING TIMES

SUMMER
Mid-May - end September
Thurs & Suns
2 - 5pm.

BH Mons, late May
& August
2 - 5pm.

Groups welcome all year
by appointment.

WINTER
September - May
Group visits welcome
by appointment.

ADMISSION

(2000 prices -
subject to alteration)

House & Grounds
Adult £6.00
Child £3.00
Groups (20+ on open days)
Per person £5.00

Grounds only
Including Stables &
Marble Dairy
Adult £3.50
Child £1.50

On days when the house is closed to the public, groups viewing by appointment will have personally conducted tours. The Gift Shop will be open. On these occasions reduced party rates (except for school children) will not apply. Group visits (20+) other than open days are £6 (minimum £120). Cream teas on open days only.

ABBOTSFORD HOUSE

Tel: 01896 752043 **Fax:** 01896 752916

Melrose, Roxburghshire TD6 9BQ

Sir Walter Scott purchased the Cartley Hall farmhouse on the banks of the Tweed in 1812. Together with his family and servants he moved into the farm which he renamed Abbotsford. Scott had the old house demolished in 1822 and replaced it with the main block of Abbotsford as it is today. Scott was a passionate collector of historic relics including an impressive collection of armour and weapons and over 9,000 rare volumes in his library.

Location: OS Ref. NT508 343. 35m S of Edinburgh. Melrose 3m, Galashiels 2m.

Opening Times: 18 Mar - 31 Oct: Mon - Sat, & Suns (Jun - Sept only) 10am - 5pm. Also Suns in Mar - May & Oct, 2 - 5pm. Other dates by arrangement.

Admission: Adult £4, Child £2. Groups: Adult £3, Child £1.50.

House suitable. WC. Guide dogs only.

AIKWOOD TOWER & JAMES HOGG EXHIBITION

Tel: 01750 52253 **Fax:** 01750 52261 **e-mail:** steel@aikwoodscottishborders.com

Ettrick Valley, Nr Selkirk TD7 5HJ

Owner: Lord & Lady Steel of Aikwood **Contact:** Judy Steel

A fine 16 century peel tower and exhibition of James Hogg.

Location: OS Ref. NT419 260. SE side of B7009, 4m SW of Selkirk.

Opening Times: May - Sept: Tues, Thurs & Suns, 2 - 5pm.

Admission: £2.

AYTON CASTLE

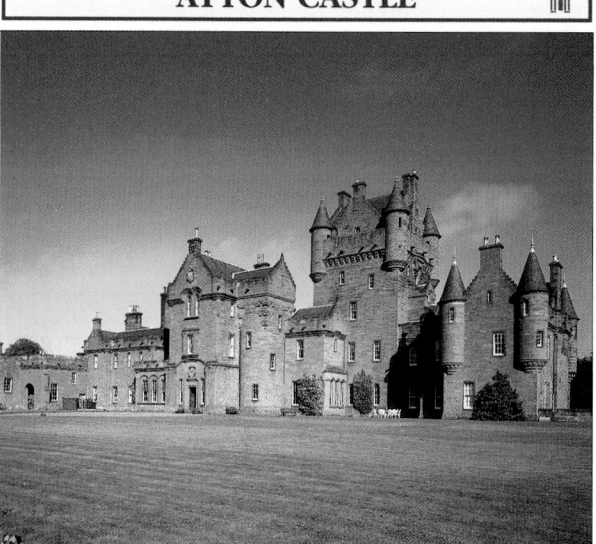

AYTON, EYEMOUTH, BERWICKSHIRE TD14 5RD

Owner: *D I Liddell-Grainger of Ayton* **Contact:** *The Curator*

Tel: 018907 81212 or 018907 81550

Built in 1846 by the Mitchell-Innes family and designed by the architect James Gillespie Graham. Over the last ten years it has been fully restored and is now a family home. It is a unique restoration project and the quality of the original and restored workmanship is outstanding. The castle stands on an escarpment surrounded by mature woodlands containing many interesting trees and has been a film-making venue due to this magnificent setting.

Location: OS Ref. NT920 610. 7m N of Berwick-on-Tweed on Route A1.

Opening Times: 6 May - 30 Sept: Suns, 2 - 5 pm or by appointment.

Admission: Adult £3, Child (under 15yrs) Free.

Obligatory. In grounds, on leads.

Corporate Hospitality Index ◄◄◄ page 30

BOWHILL HOUSE & COUNTRY PARK

See page 448 for full page entry.

BUGHTRIG GARDEN

Tel: 01890 840678 **Fax:** 01890 840509

Bughtrig, Coldstream, Berwickshire TD12 4JP

Owner: Major General C A & the Hon Mrs Ramsay **Contact:** The Secretary

Bughtrig is a classic Georgian family house c1785 with later additions. The formal garden is hedged and close to the house, surrounded by fine specimen trees which provide remarkable shelter. Its 2½ acres contain an interesting combination of herbaceous plants, roses, shrubs, annuals, fruit, vegetables and a tree nursery. Small picnic area.

Location: OS Ref. NT797 447. ¼ m E of Leitholm Village on B6461.

Opening Times: Garden: Jun - Sept: daily, 11am - 5pm. House: by appointment only.

Admission: Adult £2, Child (under 18yrs) £1. Rates for House or accommodation by arrangement.

Partially suitable. Limited. Guide dogs only. 4 twin bedrooms/3 bathrooms.

DAWYCK BOTANIC GARDEN

Tel: 01721 760254 **Fax:** 01721 760214

Stobo, Peeblesshire EH45 9JU **Contact:** The Curator

Renowned historic arboretum. Amongst mature specimen trees – some over 40 metres tall – are a variety of flowering trees, shrubs and herbaceous plants. Explore the world's first Cryptogamic Sanctuary and Reserve for 'non-flowering' plants.

Location: NT168 352. 8m SW of Peebles on B712.

Opening Times: 1 Mar - 31 Oct: daily, 9.30am - 6pm.

Admission: Adult £3, Child £1, Family £7, Conc. £2.50, Group discounts available.

DRUMLANRIG'S TOWER

Tel: 01450 373457 **Fax:** 01450 378506

Tower Knowe, Hawick TD9 9EN **e-mail:** hawickmuseum@hotmail.com

Owner: Scottish Borders Council **Contact:** The Curator

An 18th century town house containing the remains of a fortified tower of the 1550s.

Location: OS Ref. NT502 144. In Hawick town centre at W end of the High Street.

Opening Times: Please contact for details: open all year.

Admission: Adult £2, Conc. £1. 10% group discount. Free for local residents. Free for under 16s if accompanied.

DRYBURGH ABBEY

Tel: 01835 822381

St Boswells, Melrose

Owner: Historic Scotland **Contact:** The Steward

The ruins of Dryburgh Abbey are remarkably complete. The burial place of Sir Walter Scott and Field Marshal Earl Haig. Perhaps the most beautiful of all the Border abbeys.

Location: OS Ref. NT591 317. 5m SE of Melrose off B6356. 1½ m N of St Boswells.

Opening Times: 1 Apr - 30 Sept: daily, 9.30am - 6.30pm. Last ticket 6pm. 1 Oct - 31 Mar: Mon - Sat, 9.30am - 4.30pm, Suns, 2 - 4.30pm, last ticket 4pm.

Admission: Adult £2.80, Child £1, Conc. £2.

Bughtrig Garden, Borders.

DUNS CASTLE

DUNS, BERWICKSHIRE TD11 3NW

Owner: Alexander Hay of Duns   *Contact:* Mrs Aline Hay

Tel: 01361 883211 **Fax:** 01361 882015 **e-mail:** aline_hay@lineone.net

This historical 1320 pele tower has been home to the Hay family since 1696, and the current owners Alexander and Aline Hay offer it as a welcoming venue for individuals, groups and corporate guests to enjoy. They have renovated it to produce the highest standards of comfort while retaining all the character of its rich period interiors. Wonderful lakeside and parkland setting.

Location: OS Ref. NT777 544. 10m off A4. Rail: Berwick station 16m. Airports: Newcastle & Edinburgh, 1 hr.

Opening Times: Not open to the public except by arrangement and for individuals, groups and companies for day or residential stays. Available all year.

Admission: Rates for private and corporate visits, wedding receptions, filming by arrangement.

 4 x 4-poster, 3 x double, 3 x twin (all with bathrooms), 2 single.

FERNIEHIRST CASTLE

JEDBURGH, ROXBURGHSHIRE TD8 6NX

Owner: The Marquess of Lothian   *Contact:* Mrs J Fraser

Tel: 01835 862201 **Fax:** 01835 863992

Ferniehirst Castle – Scotland's Frontier Fortress. Ancestral home of the Kerr family. Restored (1984/1987) by the 12th Marquess of Lothian. Unrivalled 16th century Border architecture. Grand Apartment and Turret Library. A 16th century Chamber Oratory. The Kerr Chamber – Museum of Family History. A special tribute to Jedburgh's Protector to Mary Queen of Scots – Sir Thomas Kerr. Riverside walk by Jed Water. Archery Field opposite the Chapel where sheep of Viking origin still graze as they did four centuries ago.

Location: OS Ref. NT653 181. 2m S of Jedburgh on the A68.

Opening Times: Jul: Tue - Sun (closed Mons), 11am - 4pm.

Admission: Adult £3, Child £1.50. Groups (max. 50) by prior arrangement (01835 862201).

♿ Partially suitable. WCs.

Guided tours only, groups by arrangement.

P Ample for cars and coaches.

In grounds, on leads.

FLOORS CASTLE

See page 449 for full page entry.

HALLIWELL'S HOUSE MUSEUM

Tel: 01750 20096 **Fax:** 01750 23282

Halliwell's Close, Market Place, High Street, Selkirk

Owner: Scottish Borders Council   **Contact:** Ian Brown

Re-creation of buildings, formerly used as a house and ironmonger's shop.

Location: OS Ref. NT472 286. In Selkirk town centre.

Opening Times: Easter - 31 Oct: Mon - Sat, 10am - 5pm, Suns, 2 - 4pm. Jul & Aug: Mon - Sat, 9.30am - 5.30pm, Suns, 2 - 5pm.

Admission: Free.

HARMONY GARDEN

Tel: 01721 722502 **Fax:** 01721 724700

St Mary's Road, Melrose TD6 9LJ

Owner: The National Trust for Scotland   **Contact:** Head Gardener

A tranquil garden offering herbaceous and mixed borders, lawns, vegetable and fruit areas. Fine views of Melrose Abbey and the Eildon Hills. Garden set around 19th century house (not open to visitors).

Location: OS Ref. NT549 342. In Melrose, opposite the Abbey.

Opening Times: 1 Apr - 30 Sept: Mon - Sat, 10am - 5.30pm, Suns, 1.30 - 5.30pm.

Admission: £2 (honesty box).

P No parking. 🚫 (W)

HERMITAGE CASTLE 🏰

Tel: 01387 376222

Liddesdale, Newcastleton

Owner: In the care of Historic Scotland   **Contact:** The Steward

Eerie fortress at the heart of the bloodiest events in the history of the Borders. Mary Queen of Scots made her famous ride here to visit her future husband.

Location: OS Ref. NY497 961. In Liddesdale 5½ m NE of Newcastleton, B6399.

Opening Times: 1 Apr - 30 Sept: daily, 9.30am - 6.30pm, last ticket 6pm.

Admission: Adult £2, Child 75p, Conc. £1.50.

THE HIRSEL GARDENS, COUNTRY PARK & HOMESTEAD MUSEUM 🏛

Coldstream, Berwickshire TD12 4LP   **Tel/Fax:** 01890 882834

Owner: Lord Home of the Hirsel   **Contact:** Peter Goodall, Hirsel Estate Office

Wonderful spring flowers and rhododendrons. Homestead museum and crafts centre. Displays of estate life and adaption to modern farming.

Location: OS Ref. NT838 393. Immediately W of Coldstream off A697.

Opening Times: Please contact property for details.

Admission: Please contact property for details.

JEDBURGH ABBEY 🏰

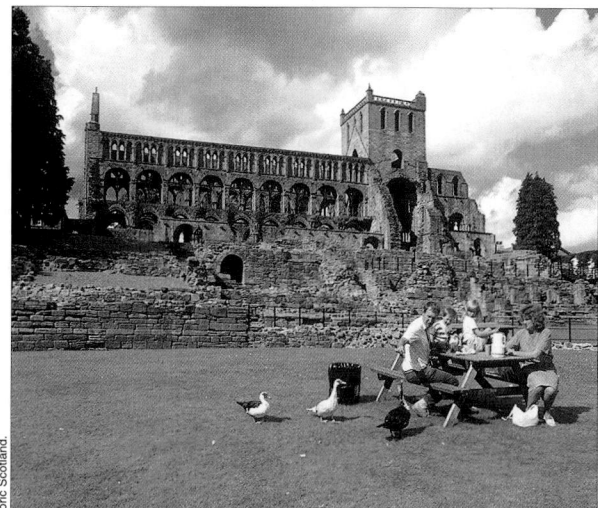

Historic Scotland.

4/5 ABBEY BRIDGEND, JEDBURGH TD8 6JQ

Owner: In the care of Historic Scotland   *Contact: The Steward*

Tel: 01835 863925

Founded by David I c1138 for Augustinian Canons. The church is mostly in the Romanesque and early Gothic styles and is remarkably complete. The award-winning visitor centre contains the priceless 12th century 'Jedburgh Comb' and other artefacts found during archaeological excavations.

Location: OS Ref. NT650 205. In Jedburgh on the A68.

Opening Times: Apr - Sept: daily, 9.30am - 6.30pm. Oct - Mar: Mon - Sat, 9.30am - 4.30pm, Suns, 2 - 4.30pm. Last ticket 30 mins before closing. 10% discount for groups (10+).

Admission: Adult £3.30, Child £1.20, Conc. £2.50.

ℹ️ Picnic area. 📷 ♿ Partially suitable. WC. P 🏠 Free when booked. 🐕 Guide dogs only. ❄️

Duns Castle, Borders.

MANDERSTON 🏛

See page 450 for full page entry.

MARY QUEEN OF SCOTS' HOUSE

Tel/Fax: 01835 863331

Jedburgh, Roxburghshire   **e-mail:** hawickmuseum@hotmail.com

Owner: Scottish Borders Council   **Contact:** The Curator

16th century fortified bastel house. Telling the story 'Scotland's tragic Queen'.

Location: OS Ref. NT652 206. In Queen Street between High Street and A68.

Opening Times: Mar - Nov: Mon - Sat, 10am - 4.30pm, Suns, 12 noon - 4.30pm. Jun - Aug: Suns, 10am - 4pm.

Admission: Adult £2, Accompanied child (under 16yrs) Free, Conc. £1. 10% group discount. Free for local residents.

Website Index page 39

Borders
Scotland

MELLERSTAIN HOUSE

MELLERSTAIN, GORDON, BERWICKSHIRE TD3 6LG

Owner: The Earl of Haddington   *Contact:* Mr A Ashby

Tel: 01573 410225   **Fax:** 01573 410636   **e-mail:** mellerstain.house@virgin.net

One of Scotland's great Georgian houses and a unique example of the work of the Adam family; the two wings built in 1725 by William Adam, the large central block by his son, Robert 1770-78. Rooms contain fine plasterwork, colourful ceilings and marble fireplaces. The library is considered to be Robert Adam's finest creation. Many fine paintings and period furniture.

Location: OS Ref. NT648 392. From Edinburgh A68 to Earlston, turn left 5m, signed.

Opening Times: Easter weekend (4 days), 1 May - 30 Sept: daily except Sats, 12.30 - 5pm. Groups at other times by appointment. Last admission 4.30pm. Tearoom & shops: daily, except Sats, 11.30am - 5.30pm.

Admission: Adult £5, Child £2, Conc. £4.50. Groups (20+) £4.50. Grounds only: £2.

[i] No photography or video cameras.   Partially suitable. Licensed. Licensed. By arrangement. In grounds, on leads, Guide dogs only in house. Tel. for details.

MELROSE ABBEY

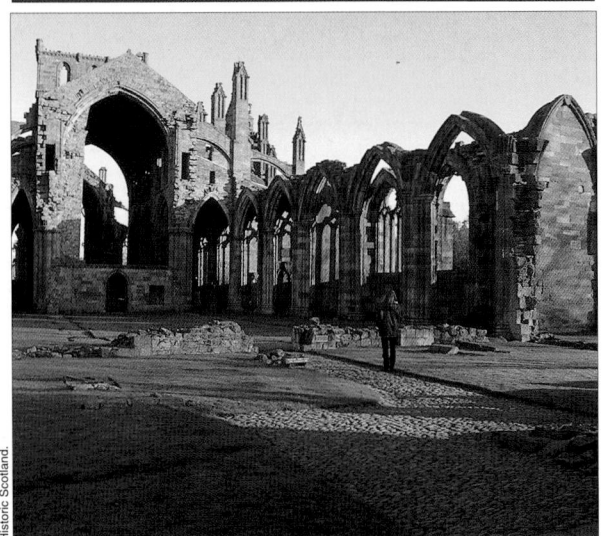

MELROSE, ROXBURGHSHIRE TD6 9LG

Owner: Historic Scotland   *Contact:* The Steward

Tel: 01896 822562

The Abbey was founded about 1136 by David I as a Cistercian Abbey and at one time was probably the richest in Scotland. Richard II's English army largely destroyed it in 1385 but it was rebuilt and the surviving remains are mostly 14th century. Burial place of Robert the Bruce's heart. Local history displays.

Location: OS Ref. NT549 342. In the centre of Melrose off the A68 or A7.

Opening Times: Apr - Sept: daily, 9.30am - 6.30pm. Oct - Mar: Mon - Sat, 9.30am - 4.30pm, Suns, 2 - 4.30pm. Last ticket 30 mins before closing.

Admission: Adult £3.30, Child £1.20, Conc. £2.50. 10% discount for groups (10+).

[i] Picnic area. Tape for visitors with learning difficulties. Pre-booked visits free. Guide dogs only.

MERTOUN GARDENS   **Tel:** 01835 823236   **Fax:** 01835 822474

St Boswells, Melrose, Roxburghshire TD6 0EA

Owner: His Grace the Duke of Sutherland   **Contact:** Mrs Barnsley

26 acres of beautiful grounds. Walled garden and well-preserved circular dovecote.

Location: OS Ref. NT617 318. Entrance off B6404 2m NE of St Boswells.

Opening Times: Apr - Sept: weekends & Public Holiday Mons only, 2 - 6pm. Last admission 5.30pm.

Admission: Adult £2, Child 50p, OAP £1.50. Groups by arrangement: 10% reduction.

By arrangement.   P

MONTEVIOT HOUSE GARDEN   **Tel:** 01835 830380 (mornings only)

Jedburgh, Roxburghshire TD8 6UQ

     Fax: 01835 830288

     Contact: The Administrator

The river garden planted with herbaceous shrub borders, has a beautiful view of the River Teviot. A semi-enclosed rose garden with a collection of hybrid teas, floribunda and shrub roses. The pinetum is full of unusual trees and nearby a water garden of islands is linked by bridges.

Location: OS Ref. NT648 247. 3m N of Jedburgh. S side of B6400 (to Nisbet). 1m E of A68.

Opening Times: Apr - Oct: daily, 12 noon - 5pm. Coach parties by prior arrangement.

Admission: Adult £2, Child (under 14yrs) Free.

Partially suitable. Parking & WCs. By arrangement.   P In grounds, on leads.

NEIDPATH CASTLE   **Tel/Fax:** 01721 720333

Peebles, Scottish Borders EH45 8NW

Owner: Wemyss and March Estates   **Contact:** The Custodian

Authentic 14th century castle converted to tower house (17th century) home of Fraser, Hay and Douglas families. Pit prison, Laigh Hall with displays, Great Hall with 'Life of Mary Stuart - Queen of Scots' in Batik wall hangings. Wonderful setting in wooded gorge of River Tweed. Popular film location (7 to date).

Location: OS Ref. NT237 405. In Tweeddale 1m W of Peebles on A72.

Opening Times: Easter week. Both May BHs: Fri - Mon. 29 Jun - 9 Sept: Mon - Sat, 11am - 6pm, Suns, 1 - 5pm. Group bookings available outside listed opening hours.

Admission: Adult £3, Child £1, Conc. £2.50, Family (2+3) £7.50. 10% discount for groups in season (20+). School rate available, 1 teacher free for every 10 children.

Ground floor & grounds suitable.   P In grounds, on leads.

OLD GALA HOUSE   **Tel:** 01750 20096

Scot Crescent, Galashiels TD1 3JS

Owner: Scottish Borders Council

Dating from 1583, the former house of the Lairds of Gala. Particularly memorable is the painted ceiling dated 1635.

Location: OS Ref. NT492 357. S of town centre, signed from A7.

Opening Times: Apr - Sept: Tue - Sat, 10am - 4pm. Jul & Aug: Mon - Sat, 10am - 4pm, Suns, 2 - 4pm. Oct: Tue - Sat, 1 - 4pm.

Melrose Abbey, Borders.

PAXTON HOUSE & COUNTRY PARK

BERWICK-UPON-TWEED TD15 1SZ

Owner: The Paxton Trust   *Contact:* Jacky Miller

Tel: 01289 386291 **Fax:** 01289 386660 **e-mail:** info@paxtonhouse.com

Highly Commended by the Scottish Tourist Board 1999

Award-winning country house and country park built from 1758-62 to the design of John and James Adam for Patrick Home, Laird of Wedderburn. The house boasts the pre-eminent collection of Chippendale furniture in Scotland, the largest picture gallery in a Scottish country house built by Robert Reid in 1814, now acting as the first outstation of the National Galleries of Scotland, and a fine collection of regency furniture by William Trotter of Edinburgh. The estate has woodland trails, riverside walks, gardens, park land, red squirrel hide, highland cattle and croquet. There are shops, a stables tearoom, a function suite and a temporary exhibition programme.

Location: OS Ref. NT931 520. 3m off the A1 Berwick-upon-Tweed on B6461.

Opening Times: 1 Apr - 31 Oct: Grounds: 10am - sunset. House: 11am - 5pm. Last house tour 4.15pm. Open to groups/schools all year by appointment.

Admission: Adult £5, Child £2.50, OAP £4.75, Student £4. Groups (pre-arranged, 12+). Adult £4, Child £1.50, OAP £4. Grounds only: Adult £2.25, Child £1.

No photography. Conferences, wedding receptions. Partially suitable. Licensed. Obligatory. In grounds, on leads. Tel for details.

PRIORWOOD GARDEN & DRIED FLOWER SHOP

Melrose TD6 9PX   **Tel:** 01896 822493

Owner: The National Trust for Scotland   **Contact:** Mrs Cathy Ross

Overlooked by the Abbey's 15th century ruins is this unique garden, where most of the plants are suitable for drying. With the aid of volunteers, Priorwood Garden markets a wide variety of dried flower arrangements through its own dried flower shop.

Location: OS Ref. NT549 341. In the Border town of Melrose, beside the Abbey.

Opening Times: 1 Apr - 30 Sept: Mon - Sat, 10am - 5.30pm, Suns, 1.30 - 5.30pm. 1 Oct - 24 Dec: Mon - Sat, 10am - 4pm, Suns, 1.30 - 4pm.

Admission: Honesty box £2.

Grounds suitable. WC. No parking. Guide dogs only.

ROBERT SMAIL'S PRINTING WORKS

High Street, Innerleithen, Perthshire EH44 6HA   **Tel:** 01896 830206

Owner: The National Trust for Scotland   **Contact:** Edward Nicol

A printing time-capsule featuring a completely restored Victorian printing works. Visitors can experience the almost forgotten craft of hand typesetting. They will discover the secrets of the printing works from the archive-based posters and see the fully restored machines in action. The buildings also contain the Victorian office with its acid-etched windows, reconstructed waterwheel and many historic items which provide an insight into the history of the Border town of Innerleithen.

Location: OS Ref. NT333 366. In High Street, Innerleithen, 30m S of Edinburgh.

Opening Times: 13 - 16 Apr; 1 May - 30 Sept: Mon - Sat, 10am - 1pm & 2 - 5pm, Suns, 2 - 5pm. W/ends in Oct: Sats: 10am - 1pm & 2 - 5pm, Suns, 2 - 5pm. Last admission 45 mins before closing morning or afternoon.

Admission: Adult £2.50, Conc. £1.70, Family £7. Groups: Adult £2, Child/School £1.

Ground floor suitable. No parking.

SMAILHOLM TOWER

Smailholm, Kelso   **Tel:** 01573 460365

Owner: In the care of Historic Scotland   **Contact:** The Steward

Set on a high rocky knoll this well preserved 16th century tower houses an exhibition of tapestries and costume dolls depicting characters from Sir Walter Scott's *Minstrelsy of the Scottish Borders.*

Location: OS Ref. NT638 347. Nr Smailholm Village, 6m W of Kelso on B6937.

Opening Times: 1 Apr - 30 Sept: daily, 9.30am - 6.30pm. Last tickets ½ hour before closing.

Admission: Adult £2, Child 75p, Conc. £1.50.

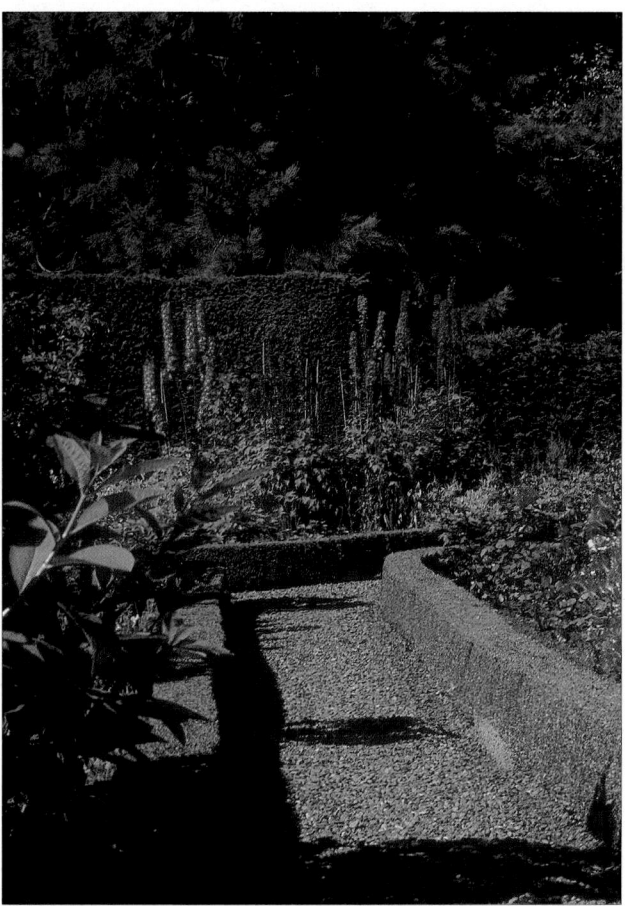

Bughtrig Garden, Borders.

THIRLESTANE CASTLE

LAUDER, BERWICKSHIRE TD2 6RU

Owner: Thirlestane Castle Trust   *Contact:* Peter Jarvis

Tel: 01578 722430   **Fax:** 01578 722761
e-mail: admin@thirlestanecastle.co.uk

One of the seven 'Great Houses of Scotland', Thirlestane Castle was the ancient seat of the Earls and Duke of Lauderdale and is still home to the Maitlands. Standing in beautiful Border countryside, Thirlestane has exquisite 17th century plasterwork ceilings, a fine portrait collection, historic toys, kitchens and country life exhibitions. Facilities include free parking, audio visual display, gift shop, café, adventure playground and woodland picnic tables. Four star STB award; Registered Museum. The state rooms are available for banquets, dinners and receptions. Non-destructive events can be held in the grounds which overlook the Leader Valley and Lammermuir Hills.

Location: OS Ref. NT540 473. Off A68 at Lauder, 28m S of Edinburgh.

Opening Times: 1 Apr - 31 Oct: daily except Sats, 10.30am - 4.15pm (last admission).

Admission: Adult £5.20, Child £3, Family £13. Groups (30+): Adult £4.50, Child £3.

🖼 🍴 ♿Not suitable. 🎧 🦌By arrangement. 🅿 🏚
🐕In grounds, on leads. ⓦ

TRAQUAIR

INNERLEITHEN, PEEBLESSHIRE EH44 6PW

Contact: Ms C Maxwell Stuart

Tel: 01896 830323   **Fax:** 01896 830639
e-mail: enquiries@traquair.co.uk

Traquair, situated amidst beautiful scenery and close by the River Tweed, is the oldest inhabited house in Scotland - visited by twenty-seven kings. Originally a Royal hunting lodge, it was owned by the Scottish Crown until 1478 when it passed to a branch of the Royal Stuart family whose descendants still live in the house today. Nearly ten centuries of Scottish political and domestic life can be traced from the collection of treasures in the house. It is particularly rich in associations with the Catholic Church in Scotland, Mary Queen of Scots and the Jacobite Risings.

There is an 18th century working brewery in one of the wings of the house where the famous Traquair House Ales are produced. Maze, Craft Workshops, Children's Adventure Playground.

Location: OS Ref. NY330 354. On B709 near junction with A72. Edinburgh 1hr, Glasgow 1½ hrs, Carlisle 1½ hrs, Newcastle 1½ hrs.

Opening Times: 14 Apr - 31 Oct: daily, 12.30 - 5.30pm. Jun, Jul & Aug: 10.30am - 5.30pm. Last admission 5pm. Restaurant: open from 11am. Jun, Jul & Aug open from 10.30am.

Admission: House & Garden: Adult £5.30, Child (under 15yrs) £2.80. Groups: Adult £4.80, Child (under 15yrs) £2. Garden only: Adult £2, Child (under 15yrs) £1. Winter: Groups: £7, includes glass of wine/whisky/Traquair Ale and shortbread (min charge £116).

🖼 ℹNo photography in house. 🍴 ♿ 🍷Licensed, self-service.
🦌Outside opening hours. 🅿Coaches please book. 🐕In grounds on leads.
🛏2 four-poster suites, B&B. ⓦ

🎪 **SPECIAL EVENTS**
• **APR 15:** Easter Egg Extravaganza.   • **MAY 26/27:** Scottish Beer Festival.
• **AUG 4/5:** Traquair Fair.

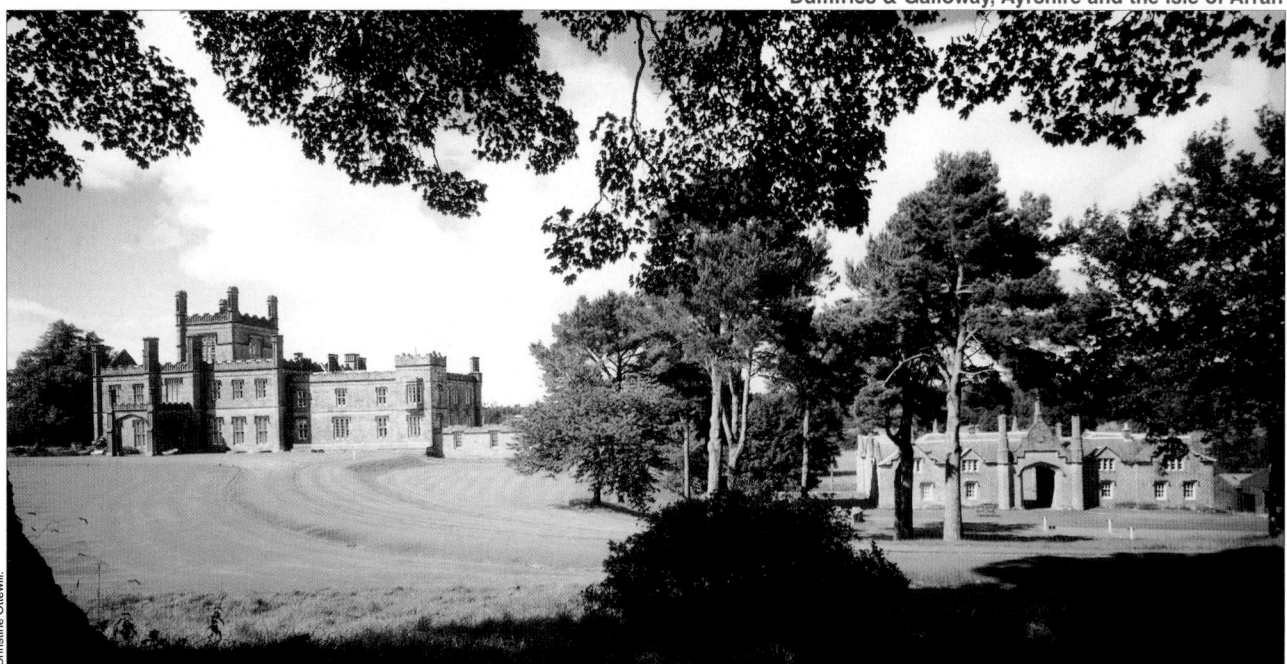

Christine Ottewill.

BLAIRQUHAN CASTLE
Maybole

Owner: James Hunter Blair

CONTACT

James Hunter Blair
Blairquhan Castle
Maybole
Ayrshire
KA19 7LZ

Tel: 01655 770239

Fax: 01655 770278

e-mail: enquiries@
blairquhan.co.uk

LOCATION

OS Ref. NS366 055

From London M6 to
Carlisle, A75 to
Crocketford, A712 to
A713 nr New Galloway,
B741 to Straiton, B7045 to
Ayr. Turn left $^1/_4$ m beyond
village. 6m SE of Maybole
off B7045.

Rail: Maybole 7m.

Air: Prestwick Airport,
15m. Direct flights to
London, Belfast & Dublin.
Executive Travel: contact
01655 882666.

BLAIRQUHAN is the home of James Hunter Blair, the great-great-grandson of Sir David Hunter Blair, 3rd Baronet for whom it was designed by William Burn and built in 1821-24.

All the Regency furniture bought for the house remains, and the house has not been altered except discreetly to bring it up-to-date. There are ten double bedrooms including four four-poster beds, with en-suite bathrooms, five singles, and many public rooms which can be used for conferences and every sort of occasion.

The castle is approached by a 3 mile private drive along the River Girvan and is situated in one of the most charming parts of south west Scotland. There is a well-known collection of pictures. It is particularly suitable for conferences because the house is entirely at your disposal.

A five minute walk from the Castle are the walled gardens, laid out around the 1800s and recently replanned and replanted.

Blairquhan is only 50 miles from Glasgow. It is within about half an hour's drive of the world-famous golf courses of Prestwick, Troon and Turnberry, the last two of which are venues for the British Open Golf Championships.

Christine Ottewill.

  Tree trail, fashion shows, shooting, equestrian events, garden parties, shows, rallies, filming, grand piano, snooker, fishing. Slide projector, overhead projector, screen, and secretarial assistance for meetings. No photography in castle.

Wedding receptions.

Two main floors suitable. WC.

Teas, lunches, buffets and dinners. Groups can book in advance, special rates for groups.

By arrangement. Also available in French.

Unlimited.

Guide and schoolroom provided, cost negotiable.

10 doubles (4 4-posters) with bathrooms en-suite, 5 singles. The Dower House at Milton has 10 doubles, 1 single, 6 bathrooms. 7 holiday cottages on the Estate.

In grounds on leads.

SUMMER
14 July - 12 August
Daily (except Mons)
1.30 - 4.15pm
(Last admission).

Open at all other times
by appointment.

WINTER
Open by appointment.

ADMISSION

House & Garden
Adult £5.00
Child (6-16yrs)..........£3.00
Conc.......................£4.00

Groups*
Negotiable

* Minimum payment £20.

SPECIAL EVENTS

- **EVENTS EVERY WEEKEND INCLUDING:**
  Model aeroplane flying
  Battle re-enactments
  Kite-flying
  Highland Dancing
  Music

CONFERENCE/FUNCTION		
ROOM	SIZE	MAX CAPACITY
Drawing Rms	1200 sq ft	100
Dining Rm	750 sq ft	100
Library	400 sq ft	25
Saloon	600 sq ft	100
Meeting Rm	255 sq ft	50

NTS Photo Library.

Owner: The National
Trust for Scotland

CONTACT

Jonathan Cardale
Culzean Castle &
Country Park
Maybole
KA19 8LE

Tel: 01655 884455

Fax: 01655 884503

e-mail: culzean@
nts.org.uk

LOCATION

OS Ref. NS240 100

12m SW of Ayr, on A719,
4m W of Maybole.

CULZEAN CASTLE & COUNTRY PARK
Maybole

One of Scotland's major attractions – a perfect day out for all the family. Robert Adam's romantic 18th century masterpiece – a real 'castle in the air' – is perched on a cliff high above the the Firth of Clyde. The interior, with its spectacular oval staircase and circular saloon, has been restored to the original elegant colour scheme. Gifted to the Trust by the 5th Marquess of Ailsa and the Kennedy family in 1945, the top floor was given to General Eisenhower as a Scottish holiday home. Today the Eisenhower Apartments offer country house style accommodation for that special occasion.

Culzean was Scotland's first country park and has been described as 'the most magnificent in Britain'. The 560 acres include 5km of coastline, woodland walks, ponds, a deer park, gardens, picnic areas and a new children's playground. Fascinating restored buildings include the Gas House, Ruined Arch and Viaduct, Ice House, Camellia House and unique Pagoda. The Victorian Vinery has recently been rebuilt in the Walled Garden. A new exhibition in the Visitor Centre tells the history of the castle and estate and 50 years of the Trust's conservation work. Three exciting shops offer an exclusive range of gifts and souvenirs and the self-service restaurant provides snacks and full meals.

NTS Photo Library/ Douglas MacGregor.

Suitable.

Licensed.

By arrangement.

In grounds on leads.

Contact for details.

Tel. for details.

DRUMLANRIG CASTLE
Thornhill

DRUMLANRIG CASTLE, Gardens and Country Park, the home of the Duke of Buccleuch and Queensberry KT was built between 1679 and 1691 by William Douglas, 1st Duke of Queensberry. Drumlanrig is rightly recognised as one of the first and most important buildings in the grand manner in Scottish domestic architecture. James Smith, who made the conversion from a 15th century castle, made a comparable transformation at Dalkeith a decade later.

The castle, of local pink sandstone, offers superb views across Nithsdale. It houses a renowned art collection, including work by Leonardo, Holbein, and Rembrandt, as well as cabinets made for Louis XIV's Versailles, relics of Bonnie Prince Charlie and a 300 year old silver chandelier.

The story of Sir James Douglas, killed in Spain while carrying out the last wish of Robert Bruce, pervades the castle in the emblem of a winged heart. Douglas family historical exhibition. Working forge. The gardens, now being restored to the plan of 1738, add to the overall effect. The fascination of Drumlanrig as a centre of art, beauty and history is complemented by its role in the Queensberry Estate, a model of dynamic and enlightened land management.

Owner: His Grace the Duke of Buccleuch & Queensberry KT

CONTACT

Claire Fisher
Drumlanrig Castle
Thornhill
Dumfriesshire
DG3 4AQ

Tel: 01848 330248

Fax: 01848 331682

Countryside Service:
01848 331555

e-mail: bre@
drumlanrigcastle.org.uk

LOCATION

OS Ref. NX851 992

18m N of Dumfries,
3m NW of Thornhill
off A76.
16m from M74 at
Elvanfoot.
Approx. 1$\frac{1}{2}$ hrs
by road from Edinburgh,
Glasgow and Carlisle.

📷 ℹ️ No photography inside the castle.

♿ Suitable. WC. Please enquire about facilities before visit.

🍷 Licensed.

🍴 Snacks, lunches and teas during opening hours.

🅿️ Adjacent to the castle.

Children's quiz and worksheets. Ranger-led activities, including woodlands and forestry. Adventure playground. School groups welcome throughout the year by arrangement.

🐕 In grounds on leads.

❄️

OPENING TIMES

SUMMER

Castle
14 - 16 April
28 April - 12 August
25 - 31 August:
Weekdays: 11am - 4pm,
Suns, 12 noon - 4pm.

1 - 30 September groups
by appointment only.

**Country Park, Gardens
& Adventure Woodland**
14 April - 30 September:
daily, 11am - 5pm.

WINTER
By appointment only.

ADMISSION

Castle and Country Park

Adult £6.00
Child £2.00
OAP/Student...........£4.00
Family (2+4) £14.00
Disabled in
wheelchairs ....Free

Pre-booked groups (20+)
Adult £4.00
Child £2.00
Outside normal opening
times...........................£8.00

Country Park only
Adult £3.00
Child £2.00

CONFERENCE/FUNCTION

ROOM	SIZE	MAX CAPACITY
Visitors' Centre	6m x 13m	50

South West Scotland

ARDWELL GARDENS
Tel: 01776 860227

Ardwell, Nr Stranraer, Dumfries and Galloway DG9 9LY
Owner: Mr Francis Brewis   **Contact:** Mrs Terry Brewis
The gardens include a formal garden, wild garden and woodland.
Location: OS Ref. NX102 455. A716 10m S of Stranraer.
Opening Times: 1 Apr - 30 Sept: daily, 10am - 5pm.
Admission: Adult £2, Child/Conc. £1.

BACHELORS' CLUB
Tel: 01292 541940

Sandgate Street, Tarbolton KA5 5RB
Owner: The National Trust for Scotland   **Contact:** The Manager
17th century thatched house in which poet Robert Burns and friends formed a debating society in 1780. Burns' mementos and relics, period furnishings.
Location: OS Ref. NS430 270. In Tarbolton, B744, 7¹/₂ m NE of Ayr, off B743.
Opening Times: 1 Apr - 30 Sept: daily, 1.30 - 5.30pm. Weekends in Oct: 1.30 - 5.30pm. Last admission 5pm.
Admission: Adult £2.50, Conc. £1.70, Family £7. Groups: Adult £2, School £1.

Ground floor suitable.

BARGANY GARDENS
Tel: 01465 871249   **Fax:** 01465 871282

Girvan, Ayrshire KA26 9QL
Owner/Contact: Mr John Dalrymple Hamilton
Lily pond, rock garden and a fine collection of hard and softwood trees.
Location: OS Ref. NS250 001. 4m ENE of Girvan by B734. After 2¹/₂ m keep ahead on to minor road to Old Dailly.
Opening Times: Weekends & Mons in May only, 10am - 6pm.
Admission: £2 per head, Child Free. Buses by arrangement.

BLAIRQUHAN CASTLE
See page 457 for full page entry.

BRODICK CASTLE & COUNTRY PARK

Harvey Wood

ISLE OF ARRAN KA27 8HY
Owner: *The National Trust for Scotland*   **Contact:** *Administrator*
Tel: 01770 302202   **Fax:** 01770 302312
This is a castle you will never forget! The tall, stately building beckons you with the glow of its warm red sandstone. The setting is staggering, fronted by the sea, bedecked with gardens and overlooked by the majestic mountain of Goatfell. The castle was built on the site of a Viking fortress and dates from the 13th century. The contents are magnificent and include superb silver, porcelain, paintings and sporting trophies. The woodland garden ranks as one of Europe's finest.
Location: OS Ref. NS010 360. Isle of Arran. Ferries from Ardrossan & Claonaig and Kintyre. Ferry enquiries: 01475 650100.
Opening Times: Castle: 1 Apr - 30 Jun & 1 Sept - 31 Oct: daily, 11am - 4.30pm, (last admission 4pm). 1 Jul - 31 Aug: daily, 11am - 5pm (last admission 4.30pm). Reception Centre and shop: (dates as castle) 10am - 5pm; restaurant: 11am - 5pm. Shop & Restaurant: weekends in Nov & Dec: 11am - 3pm. Walled Garden: All year: daily, 9.30am - 5pm. Country Park: All year, daily 9.30am - sunset. Goatfell open all year.
Admission: Castle & Garden: Adult £6, Conc. £4.50, Family £16.50. Groups: Adult £4.80, Child/ School £1. Garden & Country Park: Adult £2.50, Conc. £1.70. Groups: Adult £2, Child/School £1. Garden only: Family £7.

Suitable. WC. Licensed. In grounds, on leads.

BROUGHTON HOUSE & GARDEN
Tel/Fax: 01557 330437

High Street, Kirkcudbright DG6 4JX
Owner: The National Trust for Scotland   **Contact:** Frances Scott
This fascinating 18th century house in the pleasant coastal town of Kirkcudbright was the home and studio from 1901 - 1933 of the artist E A Hornel, one of the 'Glasgow Boys'. It contains many of his works, along with paintings by other contemporary artists, and an extensive collection of rare Scottish books, including valuable editions of Burns' works.
Location: OS Ref. NX684 509. Off A711 / A755, in Kirkcudbright, at 12 High St.
Opening Times: House & Garden: 1 - 12 Apr; 17 Apr - 30 Jun & 1 Sept - 31 Oct: daily, 1 - 5.30pm. 13 - 16 Apr & 1 Jul - 31 Aug: daily, 11am - 5.30pm (last entry 4.45pm). Garden only: 24/25 Feb & 1 - 30 Nov: Mon - Fri, 11am - 4pm.
Admission: Adult £3.50, Conc. £2.50, Family £9.50. Groups: Adult £3, Child/School £1.

Not suitable. By arrangement. Limited.

BURNS' COTTAGE
Tel: 01292 441215

Alloway, Ayrshire KA7 4PY
Contact: J Manson
Thatched cottage, birthplace of Robert Burns in 1759, with adjacent museum.
Location: OS Ref. NS335 190. 2m SW of Ayr.
Opening Times: Apr - Oct: daily, 9am - 6pm. Nov - Mar: daily, 10am - 4pm (Suns, 12 noon - 4pm).
Admission: Adult £2.80, Child/OAP £1.40, Family £8. Admission charge includes entry to Burns' Monument and Gardens.

CAERLAVEROCK CASTLE

Historic Scotland.

GLENCAPLE, DUMFRIES DG1 4RU
Owner: *In the care of Historic Scotland*   **Contact:** *The Steward*
Tel: 01387 770244
One of the finest castles in Scotland on a triangular site surrounded by moats. Its most remarkable features are the twin-towered gatehouse and the Renaissance Nithsdale lodging. The site of two famous sieges. Children's park, replica siege engines and nature trail to site of earlier castle.
Location: OS84 NY025 656. 8m S of Dumfries on the B725.
Opening Times: Apr - Sept: daily, 9.30am - 6.30pm. Oct - Mar: Mon - Sat, 9.30am - 4.30pm, Suns, 2 - 4.30pm. Last ticket sold 30 mins before closing.
Admission: Adult £2.80, Child £1, Conc. £2. 10% discount for groups (10+).

Partially suitable. WCs. Limited for coaches. Free if pre-booked. In grounds, on leads.

CARDONESS CASTLE
Tel: 01557 814427

Gatehouse of Fleet
Owner: In the care of Historic Scotland   **Contact:** The Steward
Well preserved ruin of a four storey tower house of 15th century standing on a rocky platform above the Water of Fleet. Ancient home of the McCullochs. Very fine fireplaces.
Location: OS Ref. NX591 553. 1m SW of Gatehouse of Fleet, beside the A75.
Opening Times: 1 Apr - 30 Sept: daily, 9.30am - 6.30pm. Last ticket 6pm. 1 Oct - 31 Mar: Sats, 9.30am - 4.30pm, Suns, 2 - 4.30pm. Last ticket 4pm.
Admission: Adult £2, Child 75p, Conc. £1.50.

THOMAS CARLYLE'S BIRTHPLACE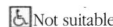

Tel: 01576 300666

Ecclefechan, Dumfriesshire DG11 3DG

Owner: The National Trust for Scotland   **Contact:** The Manager

Thomas Carlyle was born here in The Arched House in 1795, the year before Burns died. Carlyle was a brilliant essayist, historian, social reformer, visionary and literary giant. When he was 14 he walked the 84 miles to Edinburgh University - taking three days. Upstairs is the bedroom in which Carlyle was born. There is also a little museum with a notable collection of photographs, manuscripts and other documents.

Location: OS Ref. NY193 745. Off M74, 6m SE of Lockerbie. In Ecclefechan village.

Opening Times: 1 Apr - 30 Sept: Fri - Mon, 1.30 - 5.30pm. Last admission 5pm.

Admission: Adult £2.50, Conc. £1.70, Family £7. Groups: Adult £2, Child/School £1.

 Not suitable. By arrangement. Limited. 🖾 🕅

CASTLE KENNEDY GARDENS

Tel: 01776 702024   **Fax:** 01776 706248

Stair Estates, Rephad, Stranraer, Dumfries and Galloway DG9 8BX

Owner: The Earl & Countess of Stair   **Contact:** The Earl of Stair

75 acres of gardens, originally laid out in 1730, includes rhododendrons, pinetum, walled garden and circular lily pond.

Location: OS Ref. NX109 610. 3m E of Stranraer on A75.

Opening Times: Apr - Sept: daily.

Admission: Adult £3, Child £1, OAP £2 (2000 prices).

CRAIGDARROCH HOUSE

Tel: 01848 200592

Moniaive, Dumfriesshire DG3 4JB

Owner/Contact: Mr Alexander Sykes

Location: OS Ref. NX741 909. S side of B729, 2m W of Moniaive, 19m WNW of Dumfries.

Opening Times: Jul: daily, 2 - 4pm.

Admission: £2.

CRAIGIEBURN GARDEN

Tel: 01683 221250

Craigieburn House, Nr Moffat, Dumfriesshire DG10 9LF   **e-mail:** ajmw1@aol.com

Owner/Contact: Janet Wheatcroft

A plantsman's garden with a huge range of rare and unusual plants surrounded by natural woodland.

Location: OS Ref. NT117 053. NW side of A708 to Yarrow & Selkirk, 2$^{1}/_{2}$ m E of Moffat.

Opening Times: Easter - Sept: Sats & Suns (open for charity).

Admission: Adult £2, Child Free.

CROSSRAGUEL ABBEY 🏛

Tel: 01655 883113

Maybole, Strathclyde

Owner: In the care of Historic Scotland   **Contact:** The Steward

Founded in the early 13th century by the Earl of Carrick. Remarkably complete remains include church, cloister, chapter house and much of the domestic premises.

Location: OS Ref. NS275 083. 2m S of Maybole on the A77.

Opening Times: 1 Apr - 30 Sept: daily, 9.30am - 6.30m. Last ticket 6pm.

Admission: Adult £2, Child 75p, Conc. £1.50.

CULZEAN CASTLE & COUNTRY PARK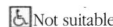

See page 458 for full page entry.

DALGARVEN MILL MUSEUM

Tel: 01294 552448

Dalry Road, Kilwinning, Ayrshire K13 6PL

Owner: Dalgarven Mill Trust   **Contact:** The Administrator

Water-driven flour mill and Ayrshire country life & costume museum.

Location: OS Ref. NS295 460. On A737 2m from Kilwinning.

Opening Times: All year: Summer: Easter - end Oct: Tue - Sat, 10am - 5pm. Suns, 11am - 5pm. Winter: Tue - Sat, 10am - 4pm. Suns, 11am - 5pm. Closed Mons.

Admission: Charges.

DEAN CASTLE COUNTRY PARK

Tel: 01563 574916

Dean Road, Kilmarnock, East Ayrshire KA3 1XB

Owner: East Ayrshire Council   **Contact:** Andrew Scott-Martin

Set in 200 acres of Country Park. Visits to castle by guided tour only.

Location: OS Ref. NS437 395. Off A77. 1$^{1}/_{4}$ m NNE of town centre.

Opening Times: Country Park & Visitor Centre: All year. Castle: Easter - end Oct: daily, 12 noon - 5pm (last tour 4.15pm). Oct - Easter: weekends only, 12 noon - 4pm (last tour 3.15pm).

Admission: Free (group charge on application).

DRUMLANRIG CASTLE 🏛

See page 459 for full page entry.

DUNDRENNAN ABBEY 🏛

Tel: 01557 500262

Kirkcudbright

Owner: Historic Scotland   **Contact:** The Steward

Mary Queen of Scots spent her last night on Scottish soil in this 12th century Cistercian Abbey founded by David I. The Abbey stands in a small and secluded valley.

Location: OS Ref. NX749 475. 6$^{1}/_{2}$ m SE of Kirkcudbright on the A711.

Opening Times: 1 Apr - 30 Sept: daily, 9.30am - 6.30pm. Last ticket 6pm. 1 Oct - 31 Mar: Sats, 9.30am - 4.30pm, Suns, 2 - 4.30pm.

Admission: Adult £1.80, Child 75p, Conc. £1.30.

GALLOWAY HOUSE GARDENS

Tel: 01988 600680

Garlieston, Newton Stewart, Wigtownshire DG8 8HF

Owner: Galloway House Gardens Trust   **Contact:** D Marshall

Created in 1740 by Lord Garlies, currently under restoration.

Location: OS Ref. NX478 453. 15m S of Newton Stewart on B7004.

Opening Times: 1 Mar - 31 Oct: 9am - 5pm.

Admission: £1 per person.

GILNOCKIE'S TOWER

Tel: 01387 371876

Hollows, Canonbie, Dumfriesshire

Owner/Contact: Edward Armstrong

16th century tower house, occupied by the Clan Armstrong Centre.

Location: OS Ref. NY383 787. 2m N of Canonbie on minor road E of A7 just N of Hollows.

Opening Times: Summer months by guided tours: 10am & 2.30pm (closed 11.45am - 2pm). Winter months open by appointment.

Admission: Adult £3, Child (under 14yrs) £1.50.

GLENLUCE ABBEY 🏛

Tel: 01581 300541

Glenluce

Owner/Contact: In the care of Historic Scotland

A Cistercian Abbey founded in 1190. Remains include a 16th century Chapter House.

Location: OS Ref. NX185 587. 2m NW of Glenluce village off the A75.

Opening Times: 1 Apr - 30 Sept: daily 9.30am - 6.30pm. Last ticket 6pm. 1 Oct - 31 Mar: Sats, 9.30am - 4.30pm, Suns, 2 - 4.30pm. Last ticket 4pm.

Admission: Adult £1.80, Child 75p, Conc. £1.30.

GLENWHAN GARDENS

Tel: 01581 400222   **Fax:** 01581 400295

Dunragit, Stranraer, Wigtownshire DG9 8PH

Contact: Tessa Knott

Beautiful 12 acre garden overlooking Luce Bay and the Mull of Galloway.

Location: OS Ref. NX150 580. N side of A75, 6m E of Stranraer.

Opening Times: 1 Apr - 30 Sept: daily, 10am - 5pm or by appointment at other times.

Admission: Adult £3, Child £1, Conc. £2.50.

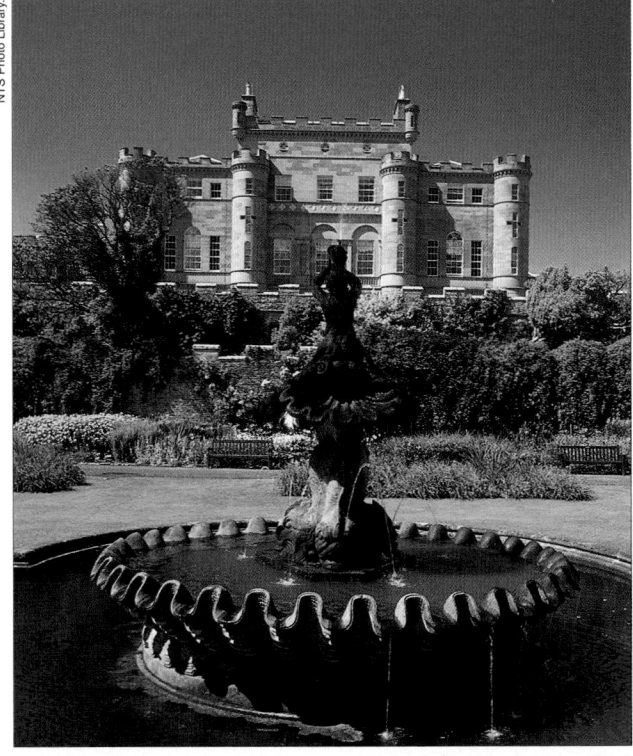

NTS Photo Library.

Culzean Castle, South West Scotland.

LOGAN BOTANIC GARDEN
Tel: 01776 860231 **Fax:** 01776 860333

Port Logan, Stranraer, Wigtownshire DG9 9ND

Owner: Royal Botanic Garden Edinburgh   **Contact:** The Curator

Scotland's most exotic garden. Take a trip to the south west of Scotland and experience the southern hemisphere!

Location: OS Ref. NX097 430. 14m S of Stranraer on B7065.

Opening Times: 1 Mar - 31 Oct: daily, 9.30am - 6pm.

Admission: Adult £3, Child £1, Conc. £2.50, Family £7. Group discount available.

MACLELLAN'S CASTLE
Tel: 01557 331856

Kirkcudbright

Owner: In the care of Historic Scotland   **Contact:** The Steward

Castellated mansion, built in 1577 using stone from an adjoining ruined monastery by the then Provost. Elaborately planned with fine architectural details, it has been a ruin since 1752.

Location: OS Ref. NX683 511. Centre of Kirkcudbright on the A711.

Opening Times: 1 Apr - 30 Sept: daily, 9.30am - 6.30pm. Last ticket 6pm.

Admission: Adult £1.80, Child 75p, Conc. £1.30.

NEW ABBEY CORN MILL
Tel: 01387 850260

New Abbey Village

Owner: Historic Scotland   **Contact:** The Custodian

This carefully renovated 18th century water-powered oatmeal mill is in full working order and regular demonstrations are given for visitors in the summer.

Location: OS Ref. NX962 663. 8m S of Dumfries on the A710. Close to Sweetheart Abbey.

Opening Times: 1 Apr - 30 Sept: daily, 9.30am - 6.30pm. Last ticket 6pm. 1 Oct - 31 Mar: Mon - Wed & Sat, 9.30am - 4.30pm, Thurs, 9.30am - 12 noon, Fris closed, Suns, 2 - 4.30pm. Last ticket 4pm.

Admission: Adult £2.50, Child £1, Conc. £1.90. Joint entry ticket with Sweetheart Abbey: Adult £3, Child £1.20, Conc. £2.25.

RAMMERSCALES
Tel: 01387 810229/810361 **Fax:** 01387 810940

Lockerbie, Dumfriesshire DG11 1LD

Owner/Contact: Mr M A Bell Macdonald

Georgian house.

Location: OS Ref. NY080 780. W side of B7020, 3m S of Lochmoben.

Opening Times: Last week in Jul, 1st three weeks in Aug: daily (excluding Sats), 2 - 5pm.

Admission: £5.

SHAMBELLIE HOUSE MUSEUM OF COSTUME

New Abbey, Dumfries DG2 8HQ   **Tel:** 01387 850375 **Fax:** 01387 850461

Owner: National Museums of Scotland   **Contact:** Sheila Watt

Shambellie House is a modest country house designed by David Bryce in 1856 for William Stewart, It is set in woodland just outside the village of New Abbey. Shambellie offers visitors the chance to see period clothes in appropriate room settings, with accessories, furniture and decorative art.

Location: OS Ref. NX960 665. On A710, 7m outside Dumfries on Solway coast road.

Opening Times: 1 Apr - 31 Oct: daily, 11am - 5pm.

Admission: Adult £2.50, Child Free, Conc. £1.50. Season ticket for all National Museums of Scotland sites: Adult £8, Conc. £5, Family £15.

⬛ ℹ️ No photography in house. 🍽️ ♿ Not suitable. 📷
🏃 By arrangement. 🅿️ Limited. ▦ 🐕 In grounds, on leads.

SORN CASTLE
Tel: 01290 551555

Ayrshire KA5 6HR

Owner/Contact: Mrs R G McIntyre

14th century castle. Enlarged several times, most recently in 1908.

Location: OS Ref. NS555 265. 4m E of Mauchline on B743.

Opening Times: 14 Jul - 11 Aug: daily, 2 - 4pm.

Admission: Adult £3.50.

SOUTER JOHNNIE'S COTTAGE
Tel: 01655 760603

Main Road, Kirkoswald KA19 8HY

Owner: The National Trust for Scotland   **Contact:** Ms Jan Gibson

The home of John Davidson, original 'Souter' (cobbler) of Robert Burns' famous narrative poem *Tam O' Shanter*. Burns mementos and restored cobbler's workshop. Life-sized stone figures in adjacent 'ale-house'.

Location: OS Ref. NS240 070. On A77, in Kirkoswald village, 4m SW of Maybole.

Opening Times: 1 Apr - 30 Sept: daily, 11.30am - 5pm. Weekends in Oct: 11.30am - 5pm (last admission 4.30pm).

Admission: Adult £2.50, Conc. £1.70, Family £7. Groups: Adult £2, Child/School £1.

♿ House suitable. 🅿️ Limited. ▦

Culzean Castle, South West Scotland.

STRANRAER CASTLE
Tel: 01776 705088 **Fax:** 01776 705835

Stranraer, Galloway

Owner: Dumfries & Galloway Council   **Contact:** John Pickin

Much altered 16th century L-plan tower house, now a museum telling the history of the castle.

Location: OS Ref. NX061 608. In Stranraer, short distance SW of junction between A77 & B737, ¼ m short of the harbour.

Opening Times: Easter - mid-Sept: Mon - Sat, 10am - 1pm & 2 - 5pm.

Admission: Adult £1.20, Conc. 60p, Family £3.

SWEETHEART ABBEY
Tel: 01387 850397

New Abbey Village

Owner: In the care of Historic Scotland   **Contact:** The Steward

Cistercian abbey founded in 1273 by Devorgilla, in memory of her husband John Balliol. A principal feature is the well-preserved precinct wall enclosing 30 acres.

Location: OS Ref. NX965 663. In New Abbey Village, on A710 8m S of Dumfries.

Opening Times: 1 Apr - 30 Sept: daily, 9.30am - 6.30pm. Last ticket 6pm. 1 Oct - 31 Mar: Mon - Wed & Sat, 9.30am - 4.30pm, Thurs, 9.30am - 12 noon, Fris closed, Suns, 2 - 4.30pm. Last ticket 4pm.

Admission: Adult £1.50, Child 50p, Conc. £1.10. Joint entry ticket with New Abbey Corn Mill: Adult £3, Child £1.20, Conc. £2.25.

THREAVE CASTLE
Tel: 01831 168512

Castle Douglas

Owner: The National Trust for Scotland   **Contact:** Historic Scotland

Built by Archibald the Grim in the late 14th century, early stronghold of the Black Douglases. Around its base is an artillery fortification built before 1455 when the castle was besieged by James II. Ring the bell and the custodian will come to ferry you over. Long walk to property. Owned by The National Trust for Scotland but under the guardianship of Historic Scotland.

Location: OS Ref. NX739 623. 2m W of Castle Douglas on the A75.

Opening Times: 1 Apr - 30 Sept: daily, 9.30am - 6.30pm. Last ticket 6pm.

Admission: Adult £2, Child 75p, Conc. £1.50. Charges include ferry trip.

THREAVE GARDEN & ESTATE
Tel: 01556 502575 **Tel:** 01556 502683

Castle Douglas DG7 1RX

Owner: The National Trust for Scotland   **Contact:** Trevor Jones

The garden has a wide range of features and a good collection of plants. There are peat and woodland garden plants and a colourful rock garden. Summer months bring a superb show from the herbaceous beds and borders. The heather gardens give a splash of colour, along with bright berries in the autumn. Truly a garden for all seasons.

Location: OS Ref. NX752 605. Off A75, 1m SW of Castle Douglas.

Opening Times: Estate & garden: All year: daily, 9.30am - sunset. Walled garden & glasshouses: all year: daily, 9.30am - 5pm. Visitor Centre, Exhibition, Countryside Centre, Shop & Restaurant: 1 - 31 Mar & 1 Nov - 23 Dec: Wed - Sun, 10am - 4pm. 1 Apr - 31 Oct: daily, 9.30am - 5.30pm.

Admission: Adult £4.50, Conc. £3.50, Family £12.50. Groups: Adult £3.60.

⬛ ♿ Grounds suitable. WC. 🍽️ ❄️

WHITHORN PRIORY
Tel: 01988 500700

Whithorn

Owner: In the care of Historic Scotland   **Contact:** The Project Manager

The site of the first Christian church in Scotland. Founded as 'Candida Casa' by St Ninian in the early 5th century it later became the cathedral church of Galloway.

Location: OS Ref. NX445 403. At Whithorn on the A746.

Opening Times: Please telephone for details.

Admission: Joint ticket gives entry to Priory, Priory Museum and archaeological dig.

Owner: The Earl of Rosebery

CONTACT

The Administrator
Dalmeny House
South Queensferry
Edinburgh
EH30 9TQ

Tel: 0131 331 1888

Fax: 0131 331 1788

e-mail: events@
dalmeny.co.uk

LOCATION

OS Ref. NT167 779

From Edinburgh A90,
B924, 7m N, A90 ½ m.

On south shore
of Firth of Forth.

Bus: From St Andrew
Square to Chapel Gate
1m from House.

Rail: Dalmeny railway
station 3m.

Taxi: Queensferry Fare
Radio Cabs 0131 331 1041.

DALMENY HOUSE
South Queensferry

DALMENY HOUSE rejoices in one of the most beautiful and unspoilt settings in Great Britain, yet it is only seven miles from Scotland's capital, Edinburgh, fifteen minutes from Edinburgh airport and less than an hour's drive from Glasgow. It is an eminently suitable venue for group visits, business functions, meetings and special events, including product launches. Outdoor activities such as off-road driving, also feature strongly.

Dalmeny Estate, the family home of the Earls of Rosebery for over 300 years, boasts superb collections of porcelain and tapestries, fine paintings by Gainsborough, Raeburn, Reynolds and Lawrence, together with the exquisite Mentmore Rothschild collection of 18th century French furniture. There is also the Napoleonic collection, assembled by the 5th Earl of Rosebery, Prime Minister, historian and owner of three Derby winners.

The Hall, Library and Dining Room will lend a memorable sense of occasion to corporate receptions, luncheons and dinners. A wide range of entertainment can also be provided, from piano recitals to a floodlit pipe band Beating the Retreat.

OPENING TIMES

SUMMER

July and August
Sun - Tue, 2 - 5.30pm.
Last admission 4.30pm.

WINTER

Open at other times by appointment only.

ADMISSION

SUMMER

Adult £4.00
Child (10-16yrs)......£2.00
OAP........................£3.50
Student...................£3.00
Groups (20+)..........£3.00

Edinburgh Scotland

Owner: Humphrey & Rozi Spurway

CONTACT

Rozi Spurway
Harburn House
Harburn
West Calder
West Lothian
EH55 8RN

Tel: 01506 461818

Fax: 01506 416591

e-mail: information@
harburnhouse.com

LOCATION

OS Ref. NT045 608

Off B7008, 2^1/$_2$ m S of A71. 2m N of A70. 20m SW of Edinburgh. Almost equidistant between Glasgow and Edinburgh, within 1hr of Perth, Stirling, Dundee and the Border country.

HARBURN HOUSE
Nr Livingston

HARBURN HOUSE offers its guests the perfect alternative to a first class hotel. This privately owned Georgian mansion, surrounded by its own 3000 acre sporting and leisure estate, is ideally situated offering unparalleled accessibility.

Harburn is essentially small and very personal. It is therefore frequently taken over exclusively for conferences, incentive travel, training seminars and product launches, etc. In this way guests may enjoy the luxury of a five star hotel, combined with the comfort and privacy of their own home.

The policies and lawns of Harburn are ideal for larger events and these can be complemented by our own fully lined and floored marquee.

A stay at Harburn is a very relaxed and informal affair. The staff are first class and the atmosphere is one of a private house party.

The estate provides the full range of sporting and leisure activities including, golf, game shooting, fishing, clay pigeon shooting, tennis, riding and archery to name but a few.

The complete privacy and outstanding scenery, so accessible to the major cities and beauty spots, makes Harburn the ultimate choice for the discerning event or conference organiser.

❖

OPENING TIMES

All year by appointment for exclusive use of house and grounds.

ADMISSION

The exclusive use of House and Grounds for activity days (without accommodation).

Per day from £700.00

Accommodation Rates

On application

Day Delegate Rate

Per person..............£45.00

24 hour rate

Per person............£130.00

VAT is not included in the above rates.

CONFERENCE/FUNCTION		
ROOM	SIZE	MAX CAPACITY
Conference Room	30' x 18'	20
Drawing Rm	30' x 18'	40
Dining Rm	30' x 18'	40
Library	14' x 12'	15
Morning Rm	16' x 15'	20
Whole house		80
Marquee	120' x 40'	500

i Filming, conferences, activity days, product launches, golf, riding, fishing, archery, buggies, game shooting, falconry, etc. Golf and Country Club nearby.

High quality in-house catering by our own top chef and fully trained staff. Prices and menus on request. Wedding receptions.

Ground floor bedroom, dining room and drawing room.

P Parking for 300 cars and 10 coaches in summer, 100+/10 in winter. Follow one way system and 20 mph speed limit, vehicles should not park on grass verges.

On leads.

20 bedrooms, all with their own bathrooms, exclusive to one group at a time.

HOPETOUN HOUSE
Edinburgh

Owner: Hopetoun House
Preservation Trust

CONTACT

Lois Bayne Jardine
Hopetoun House
South Queensferry
Edinburgh
West Lothian
EH30 9SL

Tel: 0131 331 2451

Fax: 0131 319 1885

LOCATION

OS Ref. NT089 790

2¹/₂ m W of Forth Road
Bridge.

12m W of Edinburgh
(25 mins. drive).

34m E of Glasgow
(50 mins. drive).

HOPETOUN HOUSE is a unique gem of Europe's architectural heritage and undoubtedly 'Scotland's Finest Stately Home'. Situated on the shores of the Firth of Forth, it is one of the most splendid examples of the work of Scottish architects Sir William Bruce and William Adam. The interior of the house, with opulent gilding and classical motifs, reflects the aristocratic grandeur of the early 18th century, whilst its magnificent parkland has fine views across the Forth to the hills of Fife. The house is approached from the Royal Drive, used only by members of the Royal Family, notably King George IV in 1822 and Her Majesty Queen Elizabeth II in 1988.

Hopetoun is really two houses in one, the oldest part of the house was designed by Sir William Bruce and built between 1699 and 1707. It shows some of the finest examples in Scotland of carving, wainscotting and ceiling painting. In 1721 William Adam started enlarging the house by adding the magnificent façade, colonnades and grand State apartments which were the focus for social life and entertainment in the 18th century.

The house is set in 100 acres of rolling parkland including fine woodland walks, the red deer park, the spring garden with a profusion of wild flowers, and numerous picturesque picnic spots.

Hopetoun has been home of the Earls of Hopetoun, later created Marquesses of Linlithgow, since it was built in 1699 and in 1974 a charitable trust was created to preserve the house with its historic contents and surrounding landscape for the benefit of the public for all time.

OPENING TIMES

SUMMER

1 April - 30 September:
daily, 10am - 5.30pm
Last admission 4.30pm.

WINTER

By appointment only
for groups of 15+.

ADMISSION

Adult £5.30
Child (5-16yrs)........£2.70
Conc.......................£4.70
Groups
Adult £4.70
Child (5-16yrs)........£2.20

Under 5yrs Free.

Winter prices on request.

Admission to Shop & Adam Stables Restaurant Free.

SPECIAL EVENTS

- **MAR 9 - 11**
Antiques Fair.

- **APR 7 - 12**
Sotheby's Spring Sale.

- **JUN 1 - 2**
Hopetoun Carriage
Driving Event.

- **JUN 3**
Dolls House & Miniatures Fair.

- **OCT 12 - 14**
Antiques Fair.

- **NOV 23 - 25**
Hopetoun's Present Event
Shopping Fair.

CONFERENCE/FUNCTION		
ROOM	SIZE	MAX CAPACITY
Ballroom	92' x 35'	300
Tapestry Rm	37' x 24'	100
Red Drawing Rm	44' x 24'	100
State Dining Rm	39' x 23'	20

Private functions, special events, antiques fairs, concerts, Scottish gala evenings, conferences, grand piano, boules (petanque) piste, croquet lawn, helicopter landing. No smoking or flash photography in house.

Receptions, gala dinners.

Restaurant and exhibitions on ground floor. WC.

Licensed. Groups (up to 250) can book in advance, menus on request tel: 0131 331 4305.

By arrangement. Foreign language guides are usually available.

Close to the house for cars and coaches. Book if possible, allow 1-2hrs for visit (min).

Holders of 2 Sandford Awards for Heritage Education. Special tours of house and/or grounds for different age/interest groups. Teachers' information pack.

No dogs in house, (on leads) in grounds.

AMISFIELD MAINS
Tel: 01875 870201 **Fax:** 01875 870620

Nr Haddington, East Lothian EH41 3SA
Owner: Wemyss and March Estates Management Co Ltd   **Contact:** M Andrews
Georgian farmhouse with gothick barn and cottage.
Location: OS Ref. NT526 755. Between Haddington and East Linton on A1 Edinburgh-Dunbar Road.
Opening Times: Exterior only: By appointment, Wemyss and March Estates Office, Longniddry, East Lothian EH32 0PY.
Admission: Please contact for details.

ARNISTON HOUSE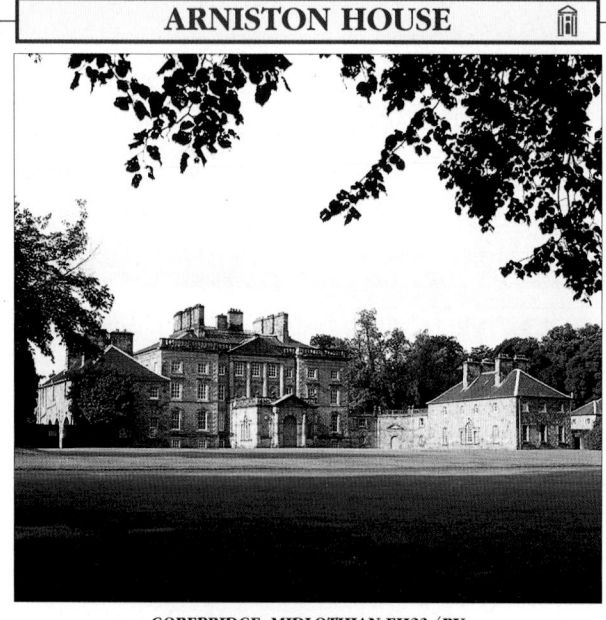

GOREBRIDGE, MIDLOTHIAN EH23 4RY

Owner: Mrs A Dundas-Bekker   Contact: Miss H Dundas-Bekker

Tel/Fax: 01875 830515

Magnificent William Adam mansion started in 1726. Fine plasterwork, Scottish portraiture, period furniture and other fascinating contents. Beautiful country setting beloved by Sir Walter Scott.

Location: OS Ref. NT326 595. Off B6372, 1m from A7, Temple direction.

Opening Times: Apr, May & Jun: Tues. Guided tours at 2pm & 3.30pm. 1 Jul - 13 Sept: Sun, Tue & Thur, 2 - 5pm. Guided tours at ½ hourly intervals. Pre-arranged groups (10-50) accepted throughout the rest of the year.

Admission: Adult £4, Child £1.50 (under school age Free).

 Obligatory.   In grounds, on leads.

BEANSTON
Tel: 01875 870201 **Fax:** 01875 870620

Nr Haddington, East Lothian EH41 3SB
Owner: Wemyss and March Estates Management Co Ltd   **Contact:** M Andrews
Georgian farmhouse with Georgian orangery.
Location: OS Ref. NT546 763. Between Haddington and East Linton on A1 Edinburgh-Dunbar Road.
Opening Times: Exterior only: By appointment, Wemyss and March Estates Office, Longniddry, East Lothian EH32 0PY.
Admission: Please contact for details.

BIEL
Tel: 01620 860355

Dunbar, East Lothian EH42 1SY
Owner/Contact: C G Spence
Originally a fortified tower, considerably added to over time.
Location: OS Ref. NT635 759. 5m from Dunbar on the A1 towards Edinburgh.
Opening Times: By appointment.
Admission: Contribution to charity.

BLACKNESS CASTLE
Tel: 01506 834807

Blackness
Owner: In the care of Historic Scotland   **Contact:** The Steward
One of Scotland's most important strongholds. Built in the 14th century and massively strengthened in the 16th century as an artillery fortress, it has been a Royal castle and a prison armaments depot and film location for *Hamlet*. It was restored by the Office of Works in the 1920s. It stands on a promontory in the Firth of Forth.
Location: OS Ref. NT055 803. 4m NE of Linlithgow on the Firth of Forth, off the A904.
Opening Times: 1 Apr - 30 Sept: daily, 9.30am - 6.30pm, last ticket 6pm. 1 Oct - 31 Mar: Mon - Sat, 9.30am - 4.30pm, last ticket 4pm. Closed Thur pm, Fri & Sun in winter.
Admission: Adult £2, Child 75p, Conc. £1.50.

CRAIGMILLAR CASTLE
Tel: 0131 661 4445

Edinburgh
Owner: In the care of Historic Scotland   **Contact:** The Steward
Mary Queen of Scots fled to Craigmillar after the murder of Rizzio and it was here that the plot was hatched for the murder of her husband Lord Darnley. This handsome structure with courtyard and gardens covers an area of one and a quarter acres. Built around an L-plan tower house of the early 15th century including a range of private rooms linked to the hall of the old tower.
Location: OS Ref. NT285 710. 2½ m SE of Edinburgh off the A68.
Opening Times: 1 Apr - 30 Sept: daily, 9.30am - 6.30pm, last ticket 6pm. 1 Oct - 31 Mar: Mon - Sat, 9.30am - 4.30pm, Suns, 2 - 4.30pm, last ticket 4pm. Closed Thur pm & Fri in winter.
Admission: Adult £2, Child 75p, Conc. £1.50.

CRICHTON CASTLE
Tel: 01875 320017

Pathhead
Owner: In the care of Historic Scotland   **Contact:** The Steward
A large and sophisticated castle with a spectacular façade of faceted stonework in an Italian style added by the Earl of Bothwell between 1581 and 1591 following a visit to Italy. Mary Queen of Scots attended a wedding here.
Location: OS Ref. NT380 612. 2½ m SSW of Pathhead off the A68.
Opening Times: 1 Apr - 30 Sept: daily, 9.30am - 6.30pm, last ticket 6pm.
Admission: Adult £2, Child 75p, Conc. £1.50.

DALKEITH COUNTRY PARK
Tel: 0131 663 5684

Dalkeith, Midlothian EH22 2NJ   **e-mail:** cameron@dalkeith.freeserve.co.uk
Contact: J C Manson
Extensive grounds of Dalkeith Palace. 18th century bridge and orangery. Interpretation area.
Location: OS Ref. NT333 679. 7m SE of Edinburgh.
Opening Times: Mar - Oct: 10am - 6pm.
Admission: Adult/Child £2, Family £7, Groups £1.50.

DALMENY HOUSE
See page 463 for full page entry.

Historic Scotland.

Crichton Castle, Edinburgh.

DIRLETON CASTLE & GARDEN

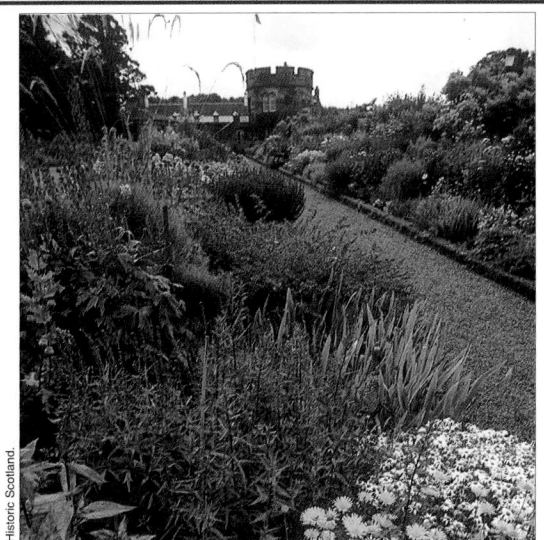

Historic Scotland.

DIRLETON, EAST LOTHIAN EH39 5ER
Owner: In the care of Historic Scotland   **Contact:** The Steward

Tel: 01620 850330

The oldest part of this romantic castle dates from the 13th century, when it was built by the De Vaux family. The renowned gardens, first laid out in the 16th century, now include a magnificent Arts and Crafts herbaceous border (the longest in the world) and a re-created Victorian Garden. In the picturesque village of Dirleton.

Location: OS Ref. NT516 839. In Dirleton, 7m W of North Berwick on the A198.

Opening Times: Apr - Sept: daily, 9.30am - 6.30pm. Oct - Mar: Mon - Sat, 9.30am - 4.30pm, Suns, 2 - 4.30pm. Last ticket 30 mins before closing.

Admission: Adult £2.80, Child £1, Conc. £2. 10% discount for groups (10+).

 Partially suitable. **P** ⬛ Free if booked. 🐕 Guide dogs only. ❄

DUNGLASS COLLEGIATE CHURCH   **Tel:** 0131 668 8800

Cockburnspath

Owner: In the care of Historic Scotland

Founded in 1450 for a college of canons by Sir Alexander Hume. A handsome cross-shaped building with vaulted nave, choir and transepts.

Location: OS Ref. 67 NT766 718. 1m NW of Cockburnspath. SW of A1.

Opening Times: All year.

Admission: Free.

Historic Scotland.

Crichton Castle, Edinburgh.

EDINBURGH CASTLE

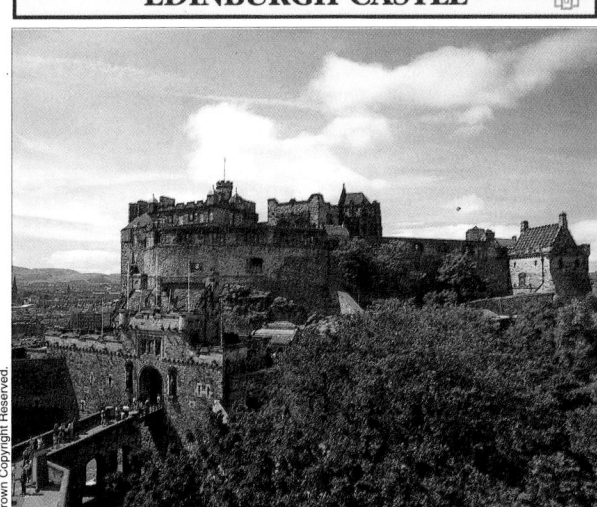

Crown Copyright Reserved.

CASTLEHILL, EDINBURGH EH1 2NG
Owner: Historic Scotland   **Contact:** Barbara Smith

Tel: 0131 225 9846   **Fax:** 0131 220 4733

Scotland's most famous castle, dominating the capital's skyline and giving stunning views of the city and countryside. Home to the Scottish crown jewels, the Stone of Destiny and Mons Meg. Other highlights include St Margaret's Chapel, the Great Hall and the Scottish National War Memorial.

Location: OS Ref. NT252 736. At the top of the Royal Mile in Edinburgh.

Opening Times: Apr - Sept: daily, 9.30am - 6pm. Oct - Mar: daily, 9.30am - 5pm. Last ticket 45 mins before closing.

Admission: Adult £7.50, Child £2, Conc. £5.50. Pre-booked school visits available free, except May - Aug.

🖷 ⊤ Private evening hire.
♿ Partially suitable. WCs. Courtesy vehicle. 🍴 Licensed. ▣ 🍴
🎧 In 6 languages. **P** Ample (except Jun-Oct) ⬛ 🐕 Guide dogs. ❄

THE GEORGIAN HOUSE

Douglas MacGregor.

7 CHARLOTTE SQUARE, EDINBURGH EH2 4DR
Owner: The National Trust for Scotland   **Contact:** Jacqueline Wright

Tel/Fax: 0131 226 3318

The north side of Charlotte Square is Robert Adam's masterpiece of urban architecture - a splendid example of the neo-classical 'palace front'. The three floors of No.7, The Georgian House, are delightfully furnished as they would have been around 1796. There is a fascinating array of china and silver, pictures and furniture, gadgets and utensils from the decorative to the purely functional.

Location: OS Ref. NT247 740. In Edinburgh's city centre, NW of Princes St.

Opening Times: 1 Mar - 31 Oct: Mon - Sat, 10am - 5pm, Suns, 2 - 5pm (last admission 4.30pm); 1 Nov - 24 Dec: Mon - Sat, 11am - 4pm, Suns, 2 - 4pm (last entry 3.30pm). Shop: As house, but opens at 11am.

Admission: Adult £5, Conc. £4, Family £14. Groups: Adult £4.

🖷 🎧 Inclusive in price. **P** No parking.

GLADSTONE'S LAND

Tel: 0131 226 5856 **Fax:** 0131 226 4851

477b Lawnmarket, Royal Mile, Edinburgh EH1 2NT

Owner: The National Trust for Scotland   **Contact:** Pat Wigston

Gladstone's Land was the home of a prosperous Edinburgh merchant in the 17th century. On the Royal Mile, near the Castle, it is decorated and furnished with great authenticity to give visitors an impression of life in Edinburgh's Old Town some 300 years ago. Features of the 6-storey building are the painted ceilings and the reconstructed shop both complete with replicas of 17th century goods.

Location: OS Ref. NT255 736. In Edinburgh's Royal Mile, near the castle.

Opening Times: House & Shop: 1 Apr - 31 Oct: Mon - Sat, 10am - 5pm, Suns, 2 - 5pm, last admission 4.30pm.

Admission: Adult £3.50, Conc. £2.50, Family £9.50. Groups: Adult £3. Group visits must be booked.

Ground floor suitable. No parking.

GOSFORD HOUSE

LONGNIDDRY, EAST LOTHIAN EH32 0PX

Owner/Contact: The Earl of Wemyss

Tel: 01875 870201

Though the core of the house is Robert Adam, the family home is in the South Wing built by William Young in 1890. This contains the celebrated Marble Hall and a fine collection of paintings and works of art. The house is set in extensive policies with an 18th century Pleasure Garden and Ponds. Greylag geese and swans abound.

Location: OS Ref. NT453 786. Off A198 2m NE of Longniddry.

Opening Times: 4 Jul - 5 Aug (inclusive): Wed - Sun, 2 - 5pm.

Admission: Adult £5, Child £1.

In grounds, on leads.

Edinburgh Castle.

GREYWALLS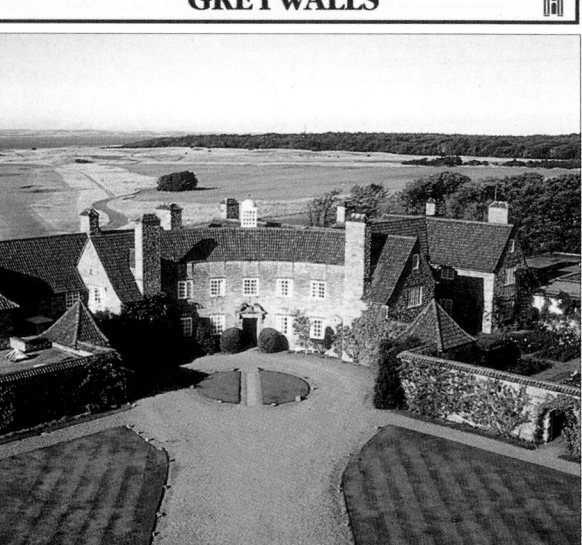

MUIRFIELD, GULLANE, EAST LOTHIAN EH31 2EG

Owner: Giles Weaver   Contact: Mrs Sue Prime

Tel: 01620 842144 **Fax:** 01620 842241 **e-mail:** hotel@greywalls.co.uk

Stunning Edwardian Country House Hotel only 30 minutes from the centre of Edinburgh. Close to wonderful golf courses and beaches. Designed by Sir Edwin Lutyens with secluded walled gardens attributed to Gertrude Jekyll. Greywalls offers the delights of an award-winning menu and an excellent wine list in this charming and relaxed environment. There is a welcome whether you stay or simply spend a peaceful few hours in this oasis of calm.

Location: OS Ref. NT490 835. Off A198, 5m W of North Berwick, 30 mins from Edinburgh.

Opening Times: Apr - Oct.

HAILES CASTLE   **Tel:** 0131 668 8800

East Linton

Owner: In the care of Historic Scotland

Beautifully-sited ruin incorporating a fortified manor of the 13th century. It was extended in the 14th and 15th centuries. There are two vaulted pit prisons.

Location: OS Ref. NT575 758. 1½ m SW of East Linton. 4m E of Haddington. S of A1.

Opening Times: All year.

Admission: Free.

HARBURN HOUSE   See page 464 for full page entry.

HARELAW FARMHOUSE   **Tel:** 01875 870201 **Fax:** 01875 870620

Nr Longniddry, East Lothian EH32 0PH

Owner: Wemyss and March Estates Management Co Ltd   **Contact:** M Andrews

Early 19th century 2-storey farmhouse built as an integral part of the steading. Dovecote over entrance arch.

Location: OS Ref. NT450 766. Between Longniddry and Drem on B1377.

Opening Times: Exteriors only: By appointment, Wemyss and March Estates Office, Longniddry, East Lothian EH32 0PY.

Admission: Please contact for details.

HOPETOUN HOUSE   See page 465 for full page entry

HOUSE OF THE BINNS

Tel: 01506 834255

Linlithgow, West Lothian EH49 7NA

Owner: The National Trust for Scotland   **Contact:** Tam & Kathleen Dalyell

A 17th century house, the home of the Dalyells, one of Scotland's great families, since 1612. Here in 1681, General Tam Dalyell raised the Royal Scots Greys Regiment, named after the colour of their uniforms. The house contains fine Italian-style plasterwork and an outstanding collection of family paintings.

Location: OS Ref. NT051 786. Off A904, 15m W of Edinburgh. 3m E of Linlithgow

Opening Times: House: 1 May - 30 Sept: daily except Fris, 1.30 - 5.30pm, last admission 5pm. Parkland: 1 Apr - 31 Oct: daily, 10am - 7pm. 1 Nov - 31 Mar: daily, 10am - 4pm, last admission 30mins before close.

Admission: House & Parkland: Adult £4, Conc. £3, Family £11. Groups: Adult £3.20, Child/School £1. Group visits must be booked. Members of the Royal Scots Dragoon Guards admitted Free.

Partially suitable. WCs.   Limited.   Obligatory.   Guide dogs only.

INVERESK LODGE GARDEN

Tel: 01721 722502 **Fax:** 01721 724700

24 Inveresk Village, Musselburgh, East Lothian EH21 7TE

Owner: The National Trust for Scotland   **Contact:** Head Gardener

Small garden in grounds of 17th century house, with large selection of plants. House closed.

Location: OS Ref. NT348 718. A6124, S of Musselburgh, 6m E of Edinburgh.

Opening Times: 1 Apr - 31 Oct: Mon - Fri, 10am - 6pm, Sats & Suns, 12 noon - 6pm; 1 Nov - 31 Mar: Mon - Fri, 10am - 4.30pm, Suns, 2 - 5pm.

Admission: £2 (honesty box).

Grounds suitable.   Limited.   No dogs in the garden.   Cars to be parked by garden wall only.

LAURISTON CASTLE

Tel: 0131 336 2060 **Fax:** 0131 312 7165

Cramond Road South, Edinburgh EH4 5QD

Owner: City of Edinburgh Council   **Contact:** Robin Barnes

A beautiful house overlooking the Firth of Forth. The oldest part is a 16th century tower house.

Location: OS Ref. NT203 761. Between Davidsons Mains and Cramond, NW Edinburgh.

Opening Times: 1 Apr - 31 Oct: daily except Fris, 11.20am, 12.20pm, 2.20pm, 3.20pm, 4.20pm. 1 Nov - 31 Mar: Sats & Suns, 2 - 4pm. Admission by guided tour only. Booking only required for groups of 10+.

Admission: Adult £4.50, Conc. £3.

LENNOXLOVE HOUSE

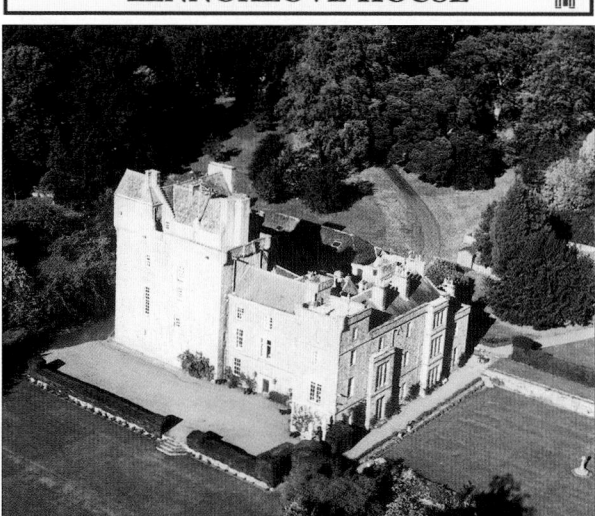

HADDINGTON, EAST LOTHIAN EH41 4NZ

Owner: Lennoxlove House Ltd   *Contact:* House Administrator

Tel: 01620 823720   **Fax:** 01620 825112   **e-mail:** lennoxlove@compuserve.com

Home of the Duke of Hamilton. The 14th century keep houses a death mask said to be that of Mary Queen of Scots, a silver casket which once contained incriminating letters that helped send Mary to her death, and a sapphire ring given to her by Lord John Hamilton. The 17th century part of the house contains the Hamilton Palace collection of pictures, furniture and porcelain arranged in classic stately home style.

Location: OS Ref. NT515 721. 20m SE of Edinburgh, near Haddington.

Opening Times: Easter - end Oct: Wed, Thur, Sat & Sun, 2 - 4.30pm. Guided tours. Please check if house is open on a Sat before arriving.

Admission: Adult £4, Child £2. Group charges on application.

No photography in house.   Weddings, gala dinners.   Obligatory.

LIBERTON HOUSE

Tel: 0131 467 7777 **Fax:** 0131 467 7774

e-mail: mail@nicholas-groves-raines-architects.co.uk

73 Liberton Drive, Edinburgh EH16 6NP

Owner/Contact: Nicholas Groves-Raines

Built around 1600 for the Littles of Liberton, this harled L-plan house has been carefully restored by the current architect owner using original detailing and extensive restoration of the principal structure. Public access restricted to the Great Hall and Old Kitchen. The restored garden layout suggests the original and there is a late 17th century lectern doocot by the entrance drive.

Location: OS Ref. NT267 694. 73 Liberton Drive, Edinburgh.

Opening Times: 1 Mar - 31 Oct: 10am - 4.30pm, by prior appointment only.

Admission: Free.

Not suitable.   Limited.

LINLITHGOW PALACE

LINLITHGOW, WEST LOTHIAN EH49 7AL

Owner: Historic Scotland   *Contact:* The Steward

Tel: 01506 842896

The magnificent remains of a great royal palace set in its own park and beside Linlithgow Loch. A favoured residence of the Stewart monarchs, James V and his daughter Mary Queen of Scots were born here. Bonnie Prince Charlie stayed here during his bid to regain the British crown.

Location: OS Ref. NT003 774. In the centre of Linlithgow off the M9.

Opening Times: Apr - Sept: daily, 9.30am - 6.30pm. Oct - Mar: Mon - Sat, 9.30am - 4.30pm, Suns, 2 - 4.30pm. Last ticket 30 mins before closing.

Admission: Adult £2.80, Child £1, Conc. £2. 10% discount for groups (10+).

Picnic area.   Private evening hire.   Partially suitable.   By arrangement.   Cars only.   Free if booked.   In grounds, off leads.

NEWLISTON

Tel: 0131 333 3231 **Fax:** 0131 335 3596

Kirkliston, West Lothian EH29 9EB

Owner/Contact: Mrs Caroline Maclachlan

Late Robert Adam house. Costumes on display. 18th century designed landscape, rhododendrons, azaleas and water features. On Sundays tea is in the Edinburgh Cookery School in the William Adam Coach House. Also on Sundays there is a ride-on steam model railway from 2 - 5pm. An inventory of chattels not on public display can be inspected and such chattels can be viewed by request when the house is open to the public.

Location: OS Ref. NT110 735. 8m W of Edinburgh, 3m S of Forth Road Bridge, off B800.

Opening Times: 2 May - 3 Jun: Wed - Sun, 2 - 6pm. Also by appointment.

Admission: Adult £1.50, Child/OAP 50p, Student £1.

Grounds suitable.   In grounds, on leads.

THE PALACE OF HOLYROODHOUSE

Andrew Holt.

© HM Queen Elizabeth II.

EDINBURGH EH8 8DX

Owner: *HM The Queen*   ***Contact:*** *The Superintendent*

Tel: 0131 556 1096 **Fax:** 0131 557 5256

The Palace of Holyroodhouse, Buckingham Palace and Windsor Castle are the Official residences of the Sovereign and are used by The Queen as both a home and office. The Queen's personal standard flies when Her Majesty is in residence. Furnished with works of art from the Royal Collection, these buildings are used extensively by The Queen for State ceremonies and Official entertaining. They are opened to the public as much as the commitments allow. At the end of the Royal Mile stands the Palace of Holyroodhouse. Set against the spectacular backdrop of Arthur's Seat, Holyroodhouse has evolved from a medieval fortress into a baroque residence. The Royal Apartments, an extensive suite of rooms, epitomise the elegance and grandeur of this ancient and noble house, and contrast with the historic tower apartments of Mary, Queen of Scots', which are steeped in intrigue and sorrow. These intimate rooms where she lived on her return from France in 1561, witnessed the murder of David Rizzio, her favourite secretary, by her jealous husband, Lord Darnley and his accomplices.

Location: OS Ref. NT269 739. Central Edinburgh, E end of Royal Mile.

Opening Times: Apr - Oct: daily, 9.30am - 5.15pm. Nov - Mar: daily, 9.30am - 3.45pm. 25 - 26 Dec & 13 Apr and during Royal visits. Opening arrangements may change at short notice.

Admission: Adult £6.50, Child (up to 17yrs) £3.30, Over 60yrs £5, Family (2+2) £16.30.

 Suitable. P Guide dogs only.

PARLIAMENT HOUSE

Tel: 0131 225 2595

Parliament Square, Royal Mile, Edinburgh   **Contact:** Reception Desk at Door 11

Supreme Court for Scotland, adjacent exhibition detailing the history of Parliament House and its important features.

Location: OS Ref. NT258 736. In the centre of Edinburgh's Royal Mile.

Opening Times: All year: Mon - Fri, 9am - 5pm.

Admission: Free.

PRESTON MILL

Tel: 01620 860426

East Linton, East Lothian EH40 3DS

Owner: The National Trust for Scotland   **Contact:** Property Manager

For centuries there has been a mill on this site and the present one operated commercially until 1957. While the interior of the mill is exciting, the exterior is extremely evocative and much favoured by artists who come from near and far to paint the attractive old buildings, with their red pantile roofs, fringed by the tranquillity of the mill pond with its ever present ducks.

Location: OS Ref. NT590 770. Off the A1, in East Linton, 23m E of Edinburgh.

Opening Times: 13 Apr - 30 Sept: Mon - Sat, 11am - 1pm and 2 - 5pm, Suns, 1.30 - 5pm. Weekends in Oct: 1.30 - 4pm (last admission 20mins before closing, morning and afternoon).

Admission: Adult £2.50, Conc. £1.70, Family £7. Group: Adult £2, Child/School £1. Group visits must book.

 Grounds suitable. WC. P Limited. Guide dogs only.

ROSSLYN CHAPEL

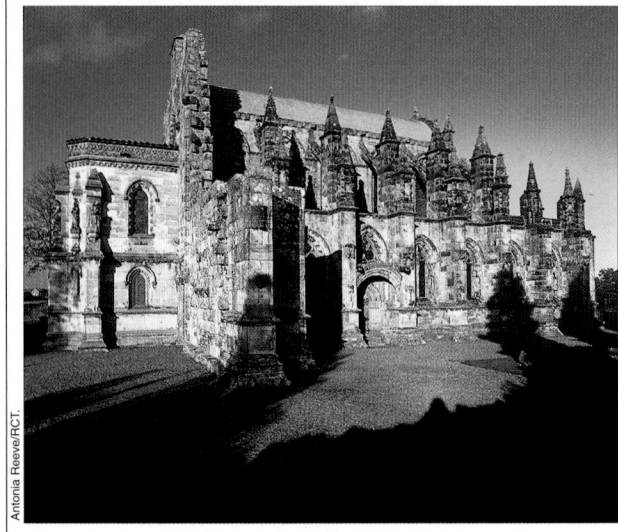

Antonia Reeve/RCT.

ROSLIN, MIDLOTHIAN EH25 9PU

Owner: *The Earl of Rosslyn*   ***Contact:*** *Stuart Beattie*

Tel: 0131 440 2159 **Fax:** 0131 440 1979 **e-mail:** rosslynch@aol.com

This most remarkable of churches was founded in 1446 by William St Clair, Prince of Orkney. Set in the woods of Roslin Glen and overlooking the River Esk, the Chapel is renowned for its richly carved interior and world famous apprentice pillar. Visitors to the chapel can enjoy a walk in some of Scotland's most romantic scenery. As Sir Walter Scott wrote,'*A morning of leisure can scarcely be anywhere more delightfully spent than in the woods of Rosslyn*'. The chapel is available for weddings throughout the year.

Location: OS Ref. NT275 630. 6m S of Edinburgh off A701. Follow B7006.

Opening Times: All year: Mon - Sat, 10am - 5pm, Suns, 12 noon - 4.45pm.

Admission: Adult £4, Child £1, Conc. £3.50. 10% discount for groups (20-40).

 Chapel. Grounds suitable. WC. P Limited for coaches.

Website Index page 39

ROYAL BOTANIC GARDEN EDINBURGH

Tel: 0131 552 7171
Fax: 0131 248 2901
Contact: Press Office

20A Inverleith Row, Edinburgh EH3 5LR

Scotland's premier garden. Discover the wonders of the plant kingdom in over 70 acres of beautifully landscaped grounds.

Location: OS Ref. NT249 751. Off A902, 1m N of city centre.

Opening Times: Daily (except 25 Dec & 1 Jan): open from 9.30am. Closing: Feb 5pm; Mar 6pm; Apr - Aug 7pm; Sept 6pm; Oct 5pm; Nov - Jan 4pm.

Admission: Free. Donations welcome.

ST GILES' CATHEDRAL

Tel: 0131 225 9442 **Fax:** 0131 220 4763

Royal Mile, Edinburgh EH1 1RE

Owner: St Giles' Cathedral
Contact: Jan-Andrew Henderson

St Giles' Cathedral dates from the 12th century and is central to Scotland's turbulent history. This beautiful building was the church of John Knox during the Reformation.

Location: OS Ref. NT258 736. In the centre of Edinburgh's Royal Mile.

Opening Times: Easter - Mid Sept: Mon - Fri, 9am -7pm, Sats, 9am - 5pm, Suns, 1 - 5pm. Mid Sept - Easter: Mon - Sat, 9am - 5pm, Suns, 1 - 5pm.

Admission: Admission free - donation of £1 per head suggested.

ST MARY'S CATHEDRAL

Tel: 0131 225 6293 **Fax:** 0131 225 3181
e-mail: office@cathedral.net
Contact: Cathedral Secretary

Palmerston Place, Edinburgh EH12 5AW

Neo-gothic grandeur in the classical new town.

Location: OS Ref. NT241 735. $^1/_2$ m W of west end of Princes Street.

Opening Times: 7.30am - 6pm. Sun services: 8am, 10.30am and 3.30pm. Weekday services: 7.30am, 1.05pm and 5.30pm. Sat service: 7.30am.

Admission: Free.

SCOTTISH NATIONAL PORTRAIT GALLERY

Tel: 0131 624 6200

1 Queen Street, Edinburgh EH2 1JD
Contact: Catriona Black

Unique visual history of Scotland.

Location: OS Ref. NT256 742. At E end of Queen Street, 300yds N of Princes Street.

Opening Times: All year: Mon - Fri, 10am - 5pm. Suns, 12 noon - 5pm. Closed 25 & 26 Dec.

Admission: Free

Winton House, Edinburgh.

TANTALLON CASTLE

Crown Copyright.

BY NORTH BERWICK, EAST LOTHIAN EH39 5PN

Owner: In the care of Historic Scotland   *Contact: The Steward*

Tel: 01620 892727

Set on the edge of the cliffs, looking out to the Bass Rock, this formidable castle was a stronghold of the powerful Douglas family. The castle has earthwork defences and a massive 80-foot high 14th century curtain wall. Interpretive displays include a replica gun.

Location: OS67 Ref. NT595 850. 3m E of North Berwick off the A198.

Opening Times: Apr - Sept: daily, 9.30am - 6.30pm. Oct - Mar: Mon - Sat, 9.30am - 6.30pm (but closed Thur pm & all day Fri), Suns, 2 - 4.30pm.

Admission: Adult £2.80, Child £1, Conc. £2. 10% discount for groups (10+).

ℹ️ Picnic area. 📷 ♿ Partially suitable. 🅿️ 🏫 Booked school visits free. 🐴 In grounds, on leads. ❄️

WINTON HOUSE

PENCAITLAND, TRANENT, EAST LOTHIAN EH34 5AT

Owner: The Winton Trust   *Contact: Barbara Smith*

Tel: 01620 824986 **Fax:** 01620 823961 **e-mail:** enquiries@wintonhouse.co.uk

A masterpiece of the Scottish Renaissance with famous stone twisted chimneys and magnificent plaster ceilings. A family home, still after 500 years with many treasures inside, including paintings by some of Scotland's most notable artists, and fine furniture. New Loch. Specimen trees and terraced gardens.

Location: OS Ref. NT439 695. 14m SE of Edinburgh off the A1 at Tranent. Lodge gates S of New Winton (B6355) and in Pencaitland (A6093).

Opening Times: 2/3 Jun; 7/8 Jul; 4/5 Aug: 12.30 - 4.30pm. Other times by prior arrangement.

Admission: Adult £4.50, Child £2, Conc. £3.80, Family £11.50 Groups should pre-book (10+).

ℹ️ Filming, product launches. Pottery. 🍽️ ♿ Suitable. WCs. 🍴 🎫 Obligatory. 🅿️ 🐴 In grounds, on leads. 🏠 ❄️ 📶 Tel. for details. ♿

BOTANIC GARDENS
Tel: 0141 334 2422 **Fax:** 0141 339 6964

730 Great Western Road, Glasgow G12 0UE
Owner: Glasgow City Council   **Contact:** The General Manager
Location: OS Ref. NS568 674.
Opening Times: All year: 7am - dusk. Glasshouse: Daily, 10am - 4.15pm (Winter), 10am - 4.45pm (Summer).
Admission: Free.

BOTHWELL CASTLE
Tel: 01698 816894

Uddingston, Strathclyde
Owner: In the care of Historic Scotland   **Contact:** The Steward
The largest and finest 13th century stone castle in Scotland, much fought over during the Wars of Independence. Part of the original circular keep survives, but most of the castle dates from the 14th and 15th centuries. In a beautiful setting overlooking the Clyde.
Location: OS Ref. NS688 593. 1m NW of Bothwell. At Uddingston off the B7071.
Opening Times: 1 Apr - 30 Sept: daily, 9.30am - 6.30pm, last ticket 6pm. 1 Oct - 31 Mar: Mon - Sat, 9.30am - 4.30pm, Suns, 2 - 4.30pm, last ticket 4pm. Closed Thur pm & Fri & Sun mornings in winter.
Admission: Adult £2, Child 75p, Conc £1.50.

BURRELL COLLECTION
Tel: 0141 287 2550

Pollok Country Park, 2060 Pollokshaws Road, Glasgow G2 3EH
Owner: Glasgow Museums   **Contact:** Mr Mark McTee
An internationally renowned, outstanding collection of art.
Location: OS Ref. NS560 615.
Opening Times: All year: Mon - Thur & Sats, 10am - 5pm. Fri & Sun, 11am - 5pm. Closed Christmas Day, Boxing Day & 1 & 2 Jan.
Admission: Free.

CHATELHERAULT HUNTING LODGE
Tel: 01698 426213 **Fax:** 01698 421532

Ferniegair, Hamilton ML3 7UE
Owner: South Lanarkshire Council   **Contact:** Alison Reid
Built for James, 5th Duke of Hamilton, designed by William Adam, completed around 1744. Set in 500 acre country park.
Location: OS Ref. NS737 540. W side of A72, 1¹/₂ m SE of Hamilton.
Opening Times: Mon - Sat, 10am - 5pm. Suns, 12 noon - 5pm (Easter Sun - end Sept, 5pm). Closed Christmas and New Year.
Admission: Free.

COLZIUM HOUSE & WALLED GARDEN
Tel/Fax: 01236 828156

Colzium-Lennox Estate, off Stirling Road, Kilsyth G65 0RZ
Owner: North Lanarkshire Council   **Contact:** Charlie Whyte
A walled garden with an extensive collection of conifers, rare shrubs and trees. Kilsyth Heritage Museum, curling pond, picnic tables, woodland walks.
Location: OS Ref. NS762 786. Off A803 Banknock to Kirkintilloch Road. ¹/₂ m E of Kilsyth.
Opening Times: House: All year, daily, 9am - 4pm (closed 25 Dec & 1 Jan). Walled garden: Apr - Sept: daily, 12 noon - 7pm; Oct - Mar: Sats & Suns, 12 noon - 4pm.
Admission: Free.

COREHOUSE
Tel: 01555 663126 or 0131 667 1514

Lanark ML11 9TQ
Owner: The Trustees of the late Lt Col A J E Cranstoun MC   **Contact:** Estate Office
Designed by Sir Edward Blore and built in the 1820s, Corehouse is a pioneering example of the Tudor Architectural Revival in Scotland.
Location: OS Ref. NS882 416. On S bank of the Clyde above the village of Kirkfieldbank.
Opening Times: 1 Aug - 2 Sept: Wed - Sun; Guided tours. Weekdays: 1 & 2pm, Weekends: 12 noon & 4pm. Closed Mons & Tues.
Admission: Adult £4, Child (under 14yrs) £2, OAP £2.

CRAIGNETHAN CASTLE
Tel: 01555 860364

Lanark, Strathclyde
Owner: Historic Scotland   **Contact:** The Steward
In a picturesque setting overlooking the River Nethan and defended by a wide and deep ditch with an unusual caponier, a stone vaulted artillery chamber, unique in Britain.
Location: OS Ref. NS815 463. 5¹/₂ m WNW of Lanark off the A72. ¹/₂ m footpath to W.
Opening Times: 1 Apr - 30 Nov: daily, 9.30am - 6.30pm.
Admission: Adult £2, Child 75p, Conc. £1.50.

GLASGOW CATHEDRAL
Tel: 0141 552 6891

Glasgow
Owner: Historic Scotland   **Contact:** The Steward
The only Scottish mainland medieval cathedral to have survived the Reformation complete. Built over the tomb of St Kentigern. Notable features in this splendid building are the elaborately vaulted crypt, the stone screen of the early 15th century and the unfinished Blackadder Aisle.
Location: OS Ref. NS603 656. E end of city centre. In central Glasgow.
Admission: Free.

GREENBANK GARDEN

Tel: 0141 639 3281

Clarkston, Glasgow G76 8RB
Owner: The National Trust for Scotland   **Contact:** Mr Jim May
Be allured by the beautiful bronze water nymph 'Foam' whose exquisite form complements the circular pool and surrounding greenery. There are several small gardens including a parterre layout illustrating different aspects of gardening. The larger borders contain a wide range of shrub roses and perennial and annual flowers.
Location: OS Ref. NS563 566. Flenders Road, off Mearns Road, Clarkston. Off M77 and A726, 6m S of Glasgow city centre.
Opening Times: Garden & Grounds: All year: daily, 9.30am - sunset. Shop & tearoom: 1 Apr - 31 Oct: daily, 11am - 5pm. 1 Nov - 31 Mar: Sats & Suns, 2 - 4pm. House: 1 Apr - 31 Oct: Suns only & during special events (subject to functions in progress).
Admission: Adult £3.50, Conc. £2.50, Family £9.50. Groups: Adult £3.

Grounds suitable. WC. In grounds, on leads. No dogs in garden.

Greenbank Garden, Glasgow.

HOLMWOOD HOUSE

61 NETHERLEE ROAD, CATHCART, GLASGOW G44 3YG

Owner: The National Trust for Scotland   *Contact: The Property Manager*

Tel: 0141 637 2129

This unique villa has been described as Alexander 'Greek' Thomson's finest domestic design. It was built in 1857-8 for James Couper who owned Millholm Paper Mills. The architectural style of the house is classical Greek and many rooms are richly ornamented in wood, plaster and marble. Conservation work continuing to reveal this decoration.

Location: OS Ref. NS580 593. Netherlee Road, off Clarkston road (off A77 and B767).

Opening Times: 1 Apr - 31 Oct: daily, 1.30 - 5.30pm. Access may be restricted at peak times and at the discretion of the property. Groups must book.

Admission: Adult £3.50, Conc. £2.50, Family £9.50. Groups: Adult £3, Child/School £1.

No photography in house. **P** Limited for coaches.

HUTCHESONS' HALL

    Tel: 0141 552 8391   **Fax:** 0141 552 7031

158 Ingram Street, Glasgow G1 1EJ

Owner: The National Trust for Scotland   **Contact:** Carla Sparrow

Described as one of Glasgow city centre's most elegant buildings, the Hall by David Hamilton, replaced the earlier 1641 hospice founded by George and Thomas Hutcheson. Reconstructed in 1876, the building is now 'A-Listed' as being of national importance. New 'Glasgow Style' exhibition & shop now open.

Location: OS Ref NS594 652. Glasgow city centre, near SE corner of George Square.

Opening Times: Gallery, Shop & Hall: All year, Mon - Sat (except Public Holidays & 24 Dec - 8 Jan): 10am - 5pm. (Hall on view subject to functions in progress).

Admission: Free.

Conferences. Up to 120. Stairlift. WC. By arrangement.

KELBURN

    Tel: 01475 568685/568204

Fairlie, Nr Largs, Ayrshire KA29 0BE

Owner/Contact: The Earl of Glasgow

The home of the Boyle family, later the Earls of Glasgow since the 13th century.

Location: OS Ref NS210 580. A78 to Largs, 2m S of Largs.

Opening Times: Castle: Jul & Aug and first week in Sept.

Admission: Castle: Adult £1.50, Student £1.20. Country Centre: Adult £4.50, Child £3, Groups (12+): Adult £3, Child/OAPs £2, Family (2+3) £13.00.

Open All Year
Index
page 49

DAVID LIVINGSTONE CENTRE

    Tel: 01698 823140

165 Station Road, Blantyre, Glasgow G72 9BT

Owner: The National Trust for Scotland   **Contact:** Karen Carruthers

Scotland's most famous explorer and missionary was born here in 1813 and today the Centre commemorates his life and work. Livingstone's childhood home - consisting of just one room - remains much as it would have done in his day and gives a fascinating insight into the living conditions endured by industrial workers in the 19th century. The museum contains a wide range of his personal belongings and travel aids.

Location: OS Ref NS690 575. In Blantyre town centre.

Opening Times: Museum & Shop: 8 Jan - 31 Mar & 1 Nov - 23 Dec: Mon - Sat, 10.30am - 4.30pm, Suns, 12.30 - 4.30pm. 1 Apr - 31 Oct: Mon - Sat, 10am - 5.30pm, Suns, 12.30 - 5.30pm.

Admission: Adult £3, Conc. £2, Family £8. Group: Adult £2.50.

MOTHERWELL HERITAGE CENTRE

    Tel: 01698 251000

High Road, Motherwell ML1 3HU

Owner: North Lanarkshire Council   **Contact:** The Manager

Multimedia exhibition and other displays of local history. STB Commended attraction.

Location: OS Ref. NS750 570.

Opening Times: All year: Wed - Sat, 10am - 5pm. Suns, 12 noon - 5pm. (closed 25/26 Dec & 1 Jan).

Admission: Free.

NEW LANARK

NEW LANARK MILLS, LANARK, S. LANARKSHIRE ML11 9DB

Owner: New Lanark Conservation Trust   *Contact: Richard Evans*

Tel: 01555 661345   **Fax:** 01555 665738   **e-mail:** visit@newlanark.org

Surrounded by native woodlands and close to the famous Falls of Clyde, this cotton mill village was founded in 1785 and became famous as the site of Robert Owen's radical reforms. Now beautifully restored as both a living community and attraction, the fascinating history of the village is interpreted in an award-winning Visitor Centre. Accommodation is available in the New Lanark Mill Hotel and Waterhouses, a stunning conversion from an original 18th century mill. New Lanark is now a nominated World Heritage Site.

Location: OS Ref. NS880 426. 1m S of Lanark.

Opening Times: All year: daily, 11am - 5pm (closed 25 Dec & 1/2 Jan).

Admission: Visitor Centre: Adult £3.95, Child/OAP £2.95. Groups: 1 free/10 booked.

 Conference facilities. Partially suitable. WC. Visitor Centre is wheelchair friendly. By arrangement. **P** 5 min walk. In grounds, on leads.

NEWARK CASTLE

    Tel: 01475 741858

Port Glasgow, Strathclyde

Owner: In the care of Historic Scotland   **Contact:** The Steward

The oldest part of the castle is a tower built soon after 1478 with a detached gatehouse, by George Maxwell. The main part was added in 1597 - 99 in a most elegant style. Enlarged in the 16th century by his descendent, the wicked Patrick Maxwell who murdered two of his neighbours.

Location: OS Ref. NS329 744. In Port Glasgow on the A8.

Opening Times: 1 Apr - 30 Sept: daily, 9.30am - 6.30pm. Last ticket 6pm.

Admission: Adult £2, Child 75p, Conc. £1.50.

POLLOK HOUSE

POLLOK COUNTRY PARK, POLLOKSHAWS ROAD, GLASGOW G43 1AT

Owner: Glasgow City Council (Managed by The National Trust for Scotland)
Contact: The Property Manager

Tel: 0141 616 6410

The Maxwell family have lived at Pollok since the 13th century. Three earlier castles here were replaced by the present house (c1740) after consultation with William Adam. The house now contains an internationally famed collection of paintings as well as porcelain and furnishings appropriate to an Edwardian house.

Location: OS Ref. NS550 616. In Pollok Country Park, off M77/J1, follow signs for Burrell Collection.

Opening Times: House, Shop & Restaurant: 1 Apr - 31 Oct: daily, 10am - 5pm. 1 Nov - 31 Mar: daily, 11am - 4pm. Closed 25, 26 Dec & 1, 2 Jan.

Admission: Adult £4, Conc. £3, Family £11. Groups: Adult £3.20, Child/School £1. 1 Nov - 31 Mar: Free.

ℹ️ No photography in house.   Partially suitable. 🍴 🅿️

THE TENEMENT HOUSE   **Tel:** 0141 333 0183

145 Buccleuch Street, Glasgow G3 6QN

Owner: The National Trust for Scotland   **Contact:** Miss Lorna Hepburn

A typical Victorian tenement flat of 1892, and fascinating time capsule of the first half of the 20th century. It was the home of an ordinary Glasgow shorthand typist, who lived up this 'wally close' for more than 50 years. It is exceptional as the gaslit flat retains many of its original fittings and items such as her mother's sewing machine.

Location: OS Ref. NS583 662. Garnethill (three streets N of Sauchiehall Street, near Charing Cross), Glasgow.

Opening Times: 1 Mar - 31 Oct; daily, 2 - 5pm, last admission 4.30pm. Weekday morning visits by educational and other groups (max 15) by advance booking only.

Admission: Adult £3.50, Conc. £2.50, Family £9.50. Groups: Adult £3, Child/School £1.

 Not suitable. 🅿️ Very restricted.

THE TOWER OF HALLBAR   **Tel:** 020 7930 8030 **Fax:** 020 7930 2295

Braidwood Road, Braidwood, Lanarkshire   **e-mail:** aniela@vivat.demon.co.uk

Owner: The Vivat Trust   **Contact:** Miss Aniela Waitt

A 16th century defensive tower and Bothy set in ancient orchards and meadowland. Converted into self-catering holiday accommodation and furnished and decorated in keeping with its history, by The Vivat Trust. Hallbar sleeps up to seven people, including facilities for a disabled person and their carer.

Location: OS Ref. NS834 471. 45mins outsite Glasgow, on B7056 in Braidwood.

Opening Times: All year: Sats afternoon only, 2 - 3pm, by appointment. Also four open days a year.

Admission: Free.

♿ Partially suitable. 🔓 By arrangement. 🅿️ Limited. 🐕 In grounds, on leads. 🛏️ 3 single, 1 twin & 1 double.

WEAVER'S COTTAGE   **Tel:** 01505 705588

Shuttle Street, Kilbarchan, Renfrew PA10 2JG

Owner: The National Trust for Scotland   **Contact:** Grace Murray

Typical cottage of an 18th century handloom weaver contains looms, weaving equipment and domestic utensils. Attractive cottage garden. Regular weaving demonstrations.

Location: OS Ref. NS402 633. Off A740 (off M8) and A737, at The Cross, Kilbarchan, (nr Johnstone, Paisley) 12m SW of Glasgow.

Opening Times: 1 Apr - 30 Sept: daily, 1.30 - 5.30pm. Weekends in Oct: 1.30 - 5.30pm. (last admission 5pm).

Admission: Adult £2.50, Conc. £1.70, Family £7. Groups: Adult £2, Child/School £1.

ST MARY'S EPISCOPAL CATHEDRAL   **Tel:** 0141 339 6691   **Fax:** 0141 334 5669

e-mail: cathedral@glasgow.anglican.org

300 Great Western Road, Glasgow G4 9JB   **Contact:** Rev Griff Dines

Fine Gothic Revival church by Sir George Gilbert Scott, with outstanding contemporary murals by Gwyneth Leech. Regular concerts and exhibitions.

Location: OS Ref. NS578 669. ¼m after the Dumbarton A82 exit from M8 motorway.

Opening Times: Mon - Fri, 9.30am - 5pm, Sat, 9.30am - 12 noon. Sun services: 8.30am, 10am, 12 noon & 6.30pm. Weekday services: please telephone. The Cathedral will be closed for restoration from Nov 2000 - Nov 2001. Please call for details of services.

SUMMERLEE HERITAGE PARK   **Tel:** 01236 431261

Heritage Way, Coatbridge, North Lanarkshire ML5 1QD

Owner: North Lanarkshire Council   **Contact:** The Manager

STB 'Commended' attraction. 22 acres of industrial heritage including Scotland's only remaining electric tramway; a re-created addit mine and mine workers' cottages.

Location: OS Ref. NS730 650.

Opening Times: All year. Summer, 10am - 5pm. Winter: 10am - 4pm (closed 25/26 Dec & 1/2 Jan).

Admission: Free. Tram ride: Adult 70p, Child 35p.

Website Index page 39 ◀◀◀

The Tenement House, Glasgow.

Owner: Blair Castle
Charitable Trust

CONTACT

Geoff G Crerar
Tourism Administrator
Blair Castle
Blair Atholl
Pitlochry
Perthshire
PH18 5TL

Tel: 01796 481207

Fax: 01796 481487

e-mail: office@
blair-castle.co.uk

LOCATION

OS Ref. NN880 660

From Edinburgh 80m,
M90 to Perth, A9, follow
signs for Blair Castle,
1½ hrs.
Trunk Road A9 2m.

Bus: Bus stop 1m
in Blair Atholl.

Train: 1m, Blair Atholl
Euston-Inverness line.

BLAIR CASTLE
Pitlochry

BLAIR CASTLE has been the ancient home and fortress of the Earls and Dukes of Atholl for over 725 years. Its central location makes it easily accessible from all major Scottish centres in less than two hours.

The castle has known the splendour of Royal visitations, submitted to occupation by opposing forces on no less than four occasions, suffered siege and changed its architectural appearance to suit the taste of successive generations.

Today 32 rooms of infinite variety display beautiful furniture, fine collections of paintings, arms, armour, china, costumes, lace and embroidery, Jacobite relics and other unique treasures giving a stirring picture of Scottish life

from the 16th to 20th centuries.

The Duke of Atholl has the unique distinction of having the only remaining private army in Europe - The Atholl Highlanders.

GARDENS

Blair Castle is set in extensive parklands. Near the car and coach parks, there is a picnic area, a deer park and a unique two acre plantation of large trees known as 'Diana's Grove.' It has been said that "it is unlikely that any other two acres in the world contain such a number of different conifers of such heights and of such small age." A restored 18th century garden re-opened to visitors in 1996.

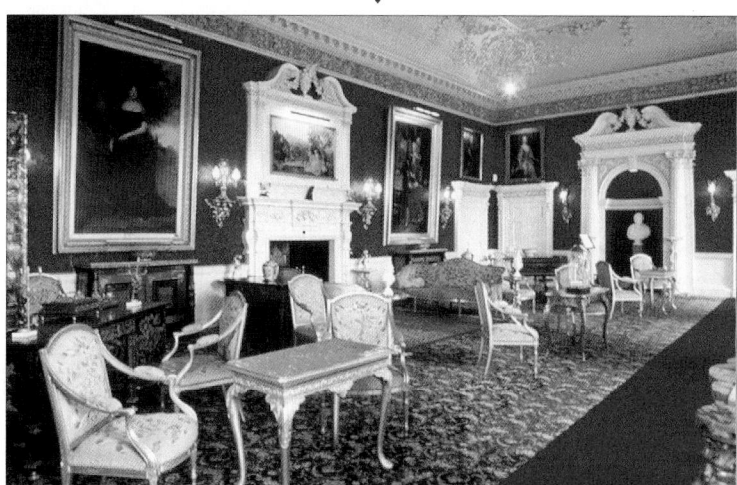

OPENING TIMES

SUMMER

1 April - 26 October
Daily, 10am - 6pm
Last admission 5pm.
(Jul & Aug: opens 9.30am).
At other times by special arrangement.

WINTER

Access by arrangement.

ADMISSION

House & Grounds

Adult	£6.25
Child (5-16yrs)	£4.00
OAP/Student	£5.25
Family	£18.00
Disabled	£2.00

Groups (12-40) (Please book)

Adult	£5.00
Child (5-16yrs)	£4.00
Primary School	£3.00
OAP	£4.50
Student	£4.00
Disabled	£2.00

Grounds only

Adult	£2.00
Child	£1.00
OAP/Student	£2.00
Family	£5.00
Disabled	Free

SPECIAL EVENTS

- **APR 20 - 22:**
  Needlework & Lace Exhibition.

- **MAY 26:**
  Atholl Highlanders' Parade.

- **MAY 27:**
  Atholl Gathering & Highland Games.

- **JUL 5:**
  Charity Day in Aid of McMillan Cancer Research.

- **JUL 16 - 22:**
  Contemporary Textile Art Exhibition by Northern Fringes.

- **AUG 23 - 26:**
  Bowmore Blair Castle Int'l Horse Trials & Country Fair.

- **OCT 27:**
  Glenfiddich Piping Championships.

FUNCTION

ROOM	SIZE	MAX CAPACITY
Ballroom	89' x 35'	400
State Dining Rm	36' x 25'	200
Exhibition Hall	55' x 27'	90

ℹ️ Fashion shows, garden parties, equestrian events, shows, rallies, filming, highland and charity balls, piping championships, grand piano, helicopter pad, cannon firing by Atholl Highlanders, resident piper, needlework displays. No smoking.

🍽️ Buffets, dinners, wedding receptions and banquets.

♿ Visitors may alight at the entrance. WC & wheelchair.

🍴 Non-smoking. Seats up to 125.

🎧 In English, German and French at no extra cost. Max group size 25, tour time 1½ hrs (max).

🅿️ 200 cars, 20 coaches. Coach drivers/couriers free, plus free meal and shop voucher, information pack.

🐾 Nature walks, deer park, children's games & pony trekking.

🐕 Grounds only.

❄️

GLAMIS CASTLE
by Forfar

GLAMIS CASTLE is the family home of the Earls of Strathmore and Kinghorne and has been a royal residence since 1372. It is the childhood home of Her Majesty Queen Elizabeth The Queen Mother, the birthplace of Her Royal Highness The Princess Margaret and the legendary setting of Shakespeare's play *Macbeth*. Although the castle is open to visitors it remains a family home lived in and loved by the Strathmore family.

The castle, a five-storey 'L' shaped tower block, was originally a royal hunting lodge. It was remodelled in the 17th century and is built of pink sandstone. It contains the Great Hall, with its magnificent plasterwork ceiling dated 1621, a beautiful family Chapel constructed inside the Castle in 1688, an 18th century billiard room housing what is left of the extensive library once at Glamis, a 19th century dining room containing family portraits and the Royal Apartments which have been used by Her Majesty Queen Elizabeth The Queen Mother.

The castle stands in an extensive park, landscaped towards the end of the 18th century, and contains the beautiful Italian Garden and the Pinetum which reflect the peace and serenity of the castle and grounds.

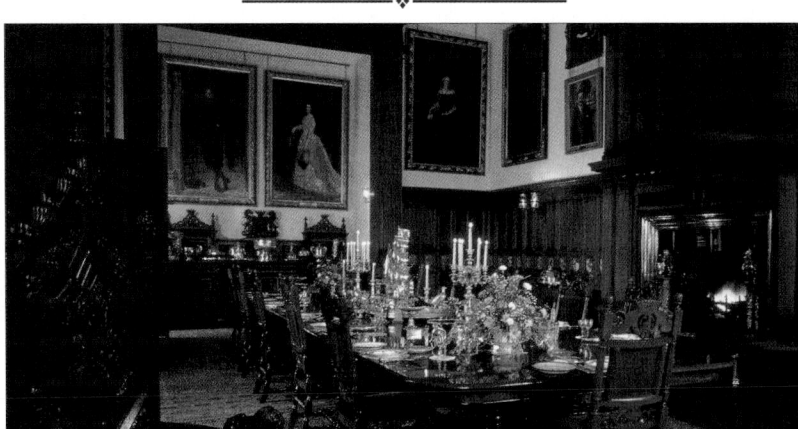

Owner: The Earl of Strathmore & Kinghorne

CONTACT

Lt Col P J Cardwell Moore
(The Administrator)
Estates Office
Glamis Castle
Glamis
by Forfar
Angus
DD8 1RJ

Tel: 01307 840393

Fax: 01307 840733

e-mail: glamis@great-houses-scotland.co.uk

LOCATION

OS Ref. NO386 480

From Edinburgh M90,
A94, 81m.
From Forfar A94, 6m.
From Glasgow 93m.

Motorway: M90.

Rail: Dundee Station 12m.

Air: Dundee Airport 12m.

Taxi: K Cabs
01575 573744.

CONFERENCE/FUNCTION

ROOM	SIZE	MAX CAPACITY
Dining Rm	84 sq.m.	120
Restaurant	140 sq.m.	100
16th century Kitchens		50

Fashion shoots, archery, clay pigeon shooting, equestrian events, shows, rallies, filming, product launches, highland games, new cricket pavilion, grand piano. No photography in the castle.

Shopping complex.

The State Rooms are available for grand dinners, lunches and wedding receptions.

Disabled visitors may alight at entrance. Those in wheelchairs will be unable to tour the castle but may visit the two exhibitions. WC.

Morning coffees, light lunches, afternoon teas. Self-service, licensed restaurant.

All visits are guided, tour time 50 - 60 mins. Tours leave every 10 - 15 mins. Tours in French, German, Italian and Spanish by appointment at no additional cost. Three exhibitions.

500 cars and 20 coaches 200 yds from castle. Coach drivers and couriers admitted free. Beware narrow gates; they are wide enough to take buses (10ft wide).

One teacher free for every 10 children. Nature trail, family exhibition rooms, dolls' house, play park. Glamis Heritage Education Centre in Glamis village. Education pack. Winner of Sandford Award in 1997.

In grounds, on leads.

OPENING TIMES

31 March - 28 October
Daily, 10.30am - 5.30pm.

(July - August
opens 10am).

Last admission 4.45pm.

Groups welcome by appointment at other times.

WINTER

By arrangement.

ADMISSION

SUMMER
House & Grounds

Adult	£6.20
Child (5-16yrs)*	£3.10
OAP/Student	£4.70
Family	£16.50

Groups (20+)

Adult	£5.20
Child (5-16yrs)*	£2.60
OAP/Student	£4.20

Grounds only

Adult	£3.10
Child (5 - 16yrs)*	£1.60
OAP/Student	£1.60
Disabled	Free

Under 5yrs Free

SPECIAL EVENTS

Please telephone for details.

SCONE PALACE & GROUNDS
Perth

Owner: The Earl of Mansfield

CONTACT

The Administrator
Scone Palace
Perth
PH2 6BD

Tel: 01738 552300

Fax: 01738 552588

e-mail: visits@
scone-palace.co.uk

LOCATION

OS Ref. NO114 266

From Edinburgh Forth
Bridge M90,
A93 1 hr.

Bus: Regular buses
from Perth
(including
open-top tours).

Rail: Perth Station 3m.

Motorway: M90 from
Edinburgh.

Taxi: 01738 636777.

SCONE PALACE, on the outskirts of Perth, sits on one of Scotland's most historic sites. The crowning place of Scottish kings including Macbeth and Robert the Bruce, and until its infamous removal by Edward I, home of the Stone of Destiny on the Moot Hill.

The Palace was built on the ruins of the old Abbey and Bishop's Palace which were destroyed in the Reformation. After a brief spell under the Gowrie family, in 1600 Scone passed to the Murray family who continue to own and live in it. Extensively rebuilt by the 3rd Earl around 1804, Scone now houses unique collections of Vernis Martin, French furniture, clocks, 16th century needlework (including pieces by Mary Queen

of Scots), ivories, *objets d'art* and one of the country's finest porcelain collections.

Winner of a 2000 Sandford Award from the Heritage Education Trust for education services.

GARDENS
The grounds of the Palace house magnificent collections of shrubs, with woodland walks through the pinetum containing David Douglas' original fir and are home to the Murray Star Maze. There are Highland cattle and peacocks to admire and an adventure play area for children. Like the Palace, the grounds and wooded parklands that stretch down to the River Tay are available for a variety of events, including corporate and private entertaining.

OPENING TIMES

SUMMER
1 April - 31 October
Daily: 9.30am - 5.15pm.

Last admission 4.45pm.

Evening tours by appointment.

WINTER
By appointment only.

ADMISSION

SUMMER
Palace & Garden
Adult £5.90
Child (5-16)............. £3.40
Conc........................ £5.10
Family £17.00
Groups (20+)
Adult £5.10
Child (5-16)............. £2.80
Conc........................ £4.40

Grounds only
Adult £2.90
Child (5-16)............. £1.50
Conc........................ £2.50

Under 5s Free
Private Tour £30
supplement.

WINTER
On application.

 SPECIAL EVENTS

- **MAY - SEPT (Monthly):**
  Horse Trials.

- **APR - SEPT:**
  Perth Races (01738 551597).

- **JUL 7/8:**
  Game Conservancy
  Scottish Fair.

- **AUG 3/4** (to be confirmed)
  Perth Agricultural Show.

CONFERENCE/FUNCTION		
ROOM	**SIZE**	**MAX CAPACITY**
Long Gallery	140' x 20'	200
Queen Victoria's Rm	20' x 20'	20
Drawing Rm	48' x 25'	80

Receptions, fashion shows, war games, archery, clay pigeon shooting, equestrian events, garden parties, shows, rallies, filming, shooting, fishing, floodlit tattoos, product launches, highland games, parkland, cricket pitch, helicopter landing, croquet, racecourse, polo field, firework displays, adventure playground.

Grand dinners in state rooms, buffets, receptions, wedding receptions, cocktail parties.

Ramp at front door. All state rooms on one level, wheelchair access to restaurants. Visitors may alight at entrance. WC.

Licensed. Teas, lunches & dinners, can be booked, menus upon request, special rates for groups.

By arrangement. Guides in rooms, tour time 45 mins. French and German guides available by appointment.

Welcome.

300 cars and 15 coaches, groups please book, couriers and coach drivers free meal and admittance.

In grounds on leads.

477

ABERDOUR CASTLE

Tel: 01383 860519

Aberdour, Fife

Owner: In the care of Historic Scotland   **Contact:** The Steward

A 14th century castle built by the Douglas family. The gallery on the first floor gives an idea of how it was furnished at the time. The castle has a 14th century tower extended in the 16th and 17th centuries, a delightful walled garden and a circular dovecote.

Location: OS Ref. NT193 854. In Aberdour 5m E of the Forth Bridge on the A921.

Opening Times: 1 Apr - 30 Sept: daily, 9.30am - 6.30pm, last ticket 6pm. 1 Oct - 31 Mar: Mon - Sat, 9.30am - 4.30pm, Suns, 2 - 4.30pm, last ticket 4pm. Closed Thur pm & Fris in winter.

Admission: Adult £2, Child 75p, Conc. £1.50.

ALLOA TOWER

Tel: 01259 211701

Alloa Park, Alloa, Clackmannanshire FK10 1PP

Owner: The National Trust for Scotland   **Contact:** The Manager

Alloa Tower is a beautifully restored and furnished 14th century Tower House with an unusual 18th century interior. It contains several rare medieval features including the original oak-beamed roof, groin vaulting and interior well. Alloa Tower was the ancestral home of the Erskines, Earls of Mar, and contains a superb collection of family portraits, including works on loan from the present Earl.

Location: OS Ref. NS886 925. On A907, in Alloa.

Opening Times: 1 Apr - 30 Sept: daily, 1.30 - 5.30pm. Weekends in Oct, 1.30 - 5.30pm, last admission 5pm.

Admission: Adult £3, Conc. £2, Family £8. Groups: Adult £2.50, Child/ School £1. 25% discount to Clackmannanshire residents.

Partially suitable. WC.

ANGUS FOLK MUSEUM

Tel: 01307 840288

Fax: 01307 840233

Kirkwynd, Glamis, Forfar, Angus DD8 1RT

Owner: The National Trust for Scotland   **Contact:** Kathleen Ager

Where will you find cruisie lamps, pirn winders, cloutie rugs, bannock spades and a thrawcrook? All these fascinating items, and many more, are to be found in the Angus Folk Museum, one of Scotland's finest. The domestic section is housed in six charming 18th century cottages in Kirkwynd, and the agricultural collection is in the farmsteading opposite. The displays inside the building explain and illustrate changes in the Angus countryside in the last 200 years.

Location: OS Ref. NO385 467. Off A94, in Glamis, 5m SW of Forfar.

Opening Times: 1 Apr - 30 Jun & 1 - 30 Sept: daily, 11am - 5pm. 1 Jul - 31 Aug: daily, 10am - 5pm. Weekends in Oct: 11am - 5pm (last admission 4.30pm).

Admission: Adult £3, Conc. £2, Family £8. Groups: Adult £2.50, Child/School £1.

 Partially suitable. WC. Limited.

ARBROATH ABBEY

Tel: 01241 878756

Arbroath, Tayside

Owner: In the care of Historic Scotland   **Contact:** The Steward

The substantial ruins of a Tironensian monastery, notably the gate house range and the abbot's house. Arbroath Abbey holds a very special place in Scottish history. Scotland's nobles swore their independence from England in the famous 'Declaration of Arbroath' in 1320. New visitor centre opening in 2001.

Location: OS Ref. NO644 414. In Arbroath town centre on the A92.

Opening Times: 1 Apr - 30 Sept: daily 9.30am - 6.30pm, last ticket 6pm. 1 Oct - 31 Mar: Mon - Sat, 9.30am - 4.30 pm, Suns, 2 - 4.30pm, last ticket 4pm.

Admission: Adult £2, Child 75p, Conc. £1.50. Prices will change when visitor centre opens.

BALGONIE CASTLE

Tel: 01592 750119 **Fax:** 01592 753103

Markinch, Fife KY7 6HQ

Owner/Contact: The Laird of Balgonie

14th century tower, additions to the building up to 1702. Still lived in by the family. 14th century chapel for weddings.

Location: OS Ref. NO313 006. 1/2 m S of A911 Glenrothes - Leven road at Milton of Balgonie on to B921.

Opening Times: All year: daily, 10am - 5pm.

Admission: Adult £3, Child £1.50, OAP £2.

BALHOUSIE CASTLE (BLACK WATCH MUSEUM)

Tel: 0131 310 8530

Hay Street, North Inch Park, Perth PH1 5HR

Owner: MOD   **Contact:** Major Proctor

Regimental museum housed in the castle.

Location: OS Ref. NO115 244. 1/2 m N of town centre, E of A9 road to Dunkeld.

Opening Times: May - Sept: Mon - Sat, 10am - 4.30pm. Oct - Apr: Mon - Fri, 10am - 3.30pm. Closed 23 Dec - 5 Jan & last Sat in Jun.

Admission: Free.

J M BARRIE'S BIRTHPLACE

Tel: 01575 572646

9 Brechin Road, Kirriemuir, Angus DD8 4BX

Owner: The National Trust for Scotland   **Contact:** Karen Gilmour or Mrs Sheila Philip

'Do you believe in fairies?' The creator of the eternal magic of *Peter Pan*, J M Barrie, was born here in 1860. He was the ninth of ten children born to David Barrie, a handloom weaver and his wife Margaret Ogilvy. See the imaginative exhibition about this famous novelist and dramatist with life-size figures, miniature stage sets, dioramas, theatre posters and stage costumes, while a darting light, 'Tinkerbell', moves around the room!

Location: OS Ref. NO388 542. On A926/B957, in Kirriemuir, 6m NW of Forfar.

Opening Times: 1 Apr - 30 Sept: Mon - Sat, 11am - 5.30pm, Suns, 1.30 - 5.30pm. Weekends in Oct: Sats, 11am - 5.30pm, Suns, 1.30pm - 5.30pm, last adm. 5pm.

Admission: Adult £3, Conc. £2, Family £8. Groups: Adult £2.50, Child/School £1.

Stairlift. No parking.

BARRY MILL

Tel: 01241 856761

Barry, Carnoustie, Angus DD7 7RJ

Owner: The National Trust for Scotland   **Contact:** Peter Ellis

19th century meal mill. Demonstrations and displays. Waymarked walks. Picnic area.

Location: OS Ref. NO533 349. N of village between A92 & A930, 2m W of Carnoustie.

Opening Times: 1 Apr - 30 Sept: daily, 11am - 5pm. Weekends in Oct: 11am - 5pm.

Admission: Adult £3, Conc £2, Family £8. Groups: Adult £2.50, Child/School £1.

BLAIR CASTLE

See page 475 for full page entry.

BOLFRACKS GARDEN

Tel: 01887 820207

Aberfeldy, Perthshire PH15 2EX

Owner/Contact: Mr J D Hutchison

A garden of approximately 4 acres with splendid views over the River Tay to the hills beyond. A walled garden contains a wide collection of trees, shrubs and perennials. Also a burn garden with rhododendrons, azaleas, meconopsis, primulas etc. with peat wall arrangements. Lots of bulbs and good autumn colour.

Location: OS Ref. NN822 481. 2m W of Aberfeldy on A827 towards Kenmore.

Opening Times: 1 Apr - 31 Oct: daily, 10am - 6pm.

Admission: Adult £2.50, Child (under 16 yrs) Free.

BRANKLYN GARDEN

Tel: 01738 625535

Dundee Road, Perth PH2 7BB

Owner: The National Trust for Scotland   **Contact:** Steve McNamara

Small but magnificent garden with an impressive collection of rare and unusual plants. Among the most breathtaking is the Himalayan blue poppy, *Meconopsis x sheldonii*. There is a rock garden with purple maple and the rare golden *Cedrus*. Seasonal highlights in May and June are the alpines and rhododendrons and in autumn the fiery red *Acer palmatum*.

Location: OS Ref. NO125 225. On A85 at 116 Dundee Road, Perth.

Opening Times: 1 Mar - 31 Oct; daily, 9.30am - sunset.

Admission: Adult £3, Conc. £2, Family £8. Groups: Adult £2.50, Child/School £1.

 Grounds suitable, but limited access.

CAMBO GARDENS

Tel: 01333 450054 **Fax:** 01333 450987

Cambo Estate, Kingsbarns, St Andrews, Fife KY16 8QD

Owner: Mr & Mrs T P N Erskine   **Contact:** Catherine Erskine

Enchanting Victorian walled garden designed around the Cambo Burn. Snowdrops, lilac and roses are specialities. Ornamental potager, autumn borders. Garden supplies mansion house (not open) with fruit, vegetables and flowers. Woodland walks to sandy beach.

Location: OS Ref. NO603 114. 3m N of Crail. 7m SE of St Andrews on A917.

Opening Times: All year: daily except Christmas and New Year, 10am - dusk.

Admission: Adult £2.50, Child Free.

Conferences. Mail order snowdrops in the green. Limited for coaches. In grounds, on leads. 2 doubles & self-catering apartments/cottages.

CASTLE MENZIES

Tel: 01887 820982

Weem, Aberfeldy, Perth PH15 2JD

Owner: Menzies Charitable Trust   **Contact:** The Administrator

Magnificent example of a 16th century 'Z' plan fortified tower house, seat of the Chiefs of Clan Menzies for over 400 years. 'Bonnie Prince Charlie' was given hospitality here in 1746. Visitors can explore the whole building, together with part of 19th century addition. Small clan museum and gift shop.

Location: OS Ref. NN838 497. 1 1/2 m from Aberfeldy on B846.

Opening Times: 31 Mar - 13 Oct: Mon - Sat, 10.30am - 5pm, Suns, 2 - 5pm, last entry 4.30pm.

Admission: Adult £3.50, Child £2, Conc. £3, Groups (20+): Adult £3.

  Ground floor suitable. WC. Guide dogs only.

CHARLETON HOUSE

Tel: 01333 340249 **Fax:** 01333 340583

Colinsburgh, Leven, Fife KY9 1HG

Location: OS Ref. NO464 036. Off A917. 1m NW of Colinsburgh. 3m NW of Elie.

Opening Times: Sept: 12 noon - 3pm. Admission every ½ hr with guided tours only.

Admission: £6.

 Obligatory.

CULROSS PALACE

Tel: 01383 880359 **Fax:** 01383 882675

Culross, Fife KY12 8JH

Owner: The National Trust for Scotland   **Contact:** Property Manager

Relive the domestic life of the 16th and 17th centuries at this Royal Burgh fringed by the River Forth. Here the old buildings and cobbled streets create a time warp for visitors as they explore the old town. Enjoy too the Palace, dating from 1597 and the medieval garden.

Location: OS Ref. NS985 860. Off A985. 12m W of Forth Road Bridge and 4m E of Kincardine Bridge, Fife.

Opening Times: Palace, Study & Town House: 1 - 12 Apr, 17 Apr - 31 May & 1 - 30 Sept: daily, 12.30 - 4.30pm; 13 - 16 Apr & 1 Jun - 31 Aug: daily, 10am - 5pm; weekends in Oct: 12.30 - 4.30pm. (last admission to Palace 1 hour before closing, to Town House & Study 15mins before closing). Groups at other times by appointment.

Admission: Combined ticket: Adult £5, Conc. £4, Family £14. Groups: Adult £4, Child/School £1.

WC.   By arrangement.   P ⚔ ❄ ⓘⓦ

DRUMMOND CASTLE GARDENS

See below.

DUNFERMLINE ABBEY & PALACE

Tel: 01383 739026

Dunfermline, Fife

Owner: In the care of Historic Scotland   **Contact:** The Steward

The remains of the Benedictine abbey founded by Queen Margaret in the 11th century. The foundations of her church are under the 12th century Romanesque-style nave. Robert the Bruce was buried in the choir. Substantial parts of the Abbey buildings remain, including the vast refectory.

Location: OS Ref. NY090 873. In Dunfermline off the M90.

Opening Times: 1 Apr - 30 Sept: daily, 9.30am - 6.30pm, last ticket 6pm. 1 Oct - 31 Mar: Mon - Sat, 9.30am - 4.30pm, Suns, 2 - 4.30pm, last ticket 4pm. Closed Thur pm and Fris in winter.

Admission: Adult £2, Child 75p, Conc. £1.50.

DUNNINALD

Tel: 01674 674842 **Fax:** 01674 674860

Montrose, Angus DD10 9TD

Owner/Contact: J Stansfeld

This house, the third Dunninald built on the estate, was designed by James Gillespie Graham in the gothic Revival style, and was completed for Peter Arkley in 1824. It has a superb walled garden and is set in a planned landscape dating from 1740. It is a family home.

Location: OS Ref. NO705 543 2m S of Montrose, between A92 and the sea.

Opening Times: 30 Jun - 29 Jul: Tue - Sun, 1 - 5pm. Garden: from 12 noon.

Admission: Adult £4, Child £2.50, Conc. £2.50. Garden only: £2.

ⓘ No photography in house. 📷 ⚌ ♿ Not suitable. 🍴   Obligatory. P
⬛ 🐕 In grounds, on leads.

EDZELL CASTLE AND GARDEN

Tel: 01356 648631

Edzell, Angus

Owner: In the care of Historic Scotland   **Contact:** The Steward

The beautiful walled garden at Edzell is one of Scotland's unique sights, created by Sir David Lindsay in 1604. The 'Pleasance' is a delightful formal garden with walls decorated with sculptured stone panels, flower boxes and niches for nesting birds. The fine tower house, now ruined, dates from the last years of the 15th century. Mary Queen of Scots held a council meeting in the castle in 1562 on her way north as her army marched against the Gordons.

Location: OS Ref. NO585 691. At Edzell, 6m N of Brechin on B966. 1m W of village.

Opening Times: 1 Apr - 30 Sept: daily, 9.30am - 6.30pm, last ticket 6pm. 1 Oct - 31 Mar: Mon - Sat, 9.30am - 4.30pm, Suns, 2 - 4.30pm, last ticket 4pm. Closed Thur pm and Fris in winter.

Admission: Adult £2.80, Child £1, Conc. £2.

ELCHO CASTLE

Tel: 01738 639998

Perth

Owner: In the care of Historic Scotland

This handsome and complete fortified mansion of 16th century date has four projecting towers. The original wrought-iron grilles to protect the windows are still in place.

Location: OS Ref. NO164 211. On the Tay, 3m SE of Perth.

Opening Times: 1 Apr - 30 Sept: daily, 9.30am - 6.30pm, last ticket 6pm.

Admission: Adult £2, Child 75p, Conc. £1.50.

DRUMMOND CASTLE GARDENS

Kathy Collins.

MUTHILL, CRIEFF, PERTHSHIRE PH5 2AA

Owner: Grimsthorpe & Drummond Castle Trust   **Contact:** *Pat Keith*

Tel: 01764 681257 **Fax:** 01764 681550 **Weekends:** 01764 681433

e-mail: the gardens@drummondcastle.sol.co.uk

Scotland's most important formal gardens, among the finest in Europe. A mile of beech-lined avenue leads to a formidable ridge top tower house. Enter through the woven iron yett to the terraces and suddenly revealed is a magnificent Italianate parterre, celebrating the saltire and family heraldry, surrounding the famous multiplex sundial by John Milne, master mason to Charles I. First laid out in the early 17th century by John Drummond, the 2nd Earl of Perth and renewed in the early 1950s by Phyllis Astor, Countess of Ancaster.

Location: OS Ref. NN844 181. 2m S of Crieff off the A822.

Opening Times: Easter weekend, then 1 May - 31 Oct: 2 - 6pm, last entry 5pm.

Admission: Adult £3, Child £1.50, OAP £2.

♿ Partially suitable. WC. By arrangement.   P   🐕 In grounds, on leads.

📋 **SPECIAL EVENTS**

AUG 5: Open Day, entertainments, teas, raffle.

FALKLAND PALACE

FALKLAND KY15 7BU

Owner: The National Trust for Scotland   *Contact:* Mrs Margaret Marshall

Tel: 01337 857397 **Fax:** 01337 857980

The Royal Palace of Falkland, set in the heart of a unique medieval village, was the country residence and hunting lodge of eight Stuart monarchs, including Mary Queen of Scots. Built between 1502 and 1541, the Palace is an extremely fine example of Renaissance architecture. It includes the exceptionally beautiful Chapel Royal, and is surrounded by internationally known gardens, laid out in the 1950s. The Royal Tennis Court, reputedly the world's oldest, is still used today.

Location: OS Ref. NO253 075. A912, 11m N of Kirkcaldy.

Opening Times: Palace & Garden: 1 Apr - 31 May & 1 Sept - 31 Oct: Mon - Sat, 11am - 5.30pm, Suns, 1.30 - 5.30pm. 1 Jun - 31 Aug: Mon - Sat, 10am - 5.30pm, Suns, 1.30 - 5.30. Last admission to Palace 4.30pm, to Garden 5pm. Groups at other times by appointment. Town Hall: as Palace.

Admission: Palace & Garden: Adult £5, Conc. £4, Family £14. Groups: Adult £4, Child/School £1. Garden only: Adult £2.50, Conc. £1.70, Family £7. Groups: Adult £2, Child/School £1. Members of Scots Guards' Association admitted Free.

  Grounds suitable.

HOUSE OF DUN

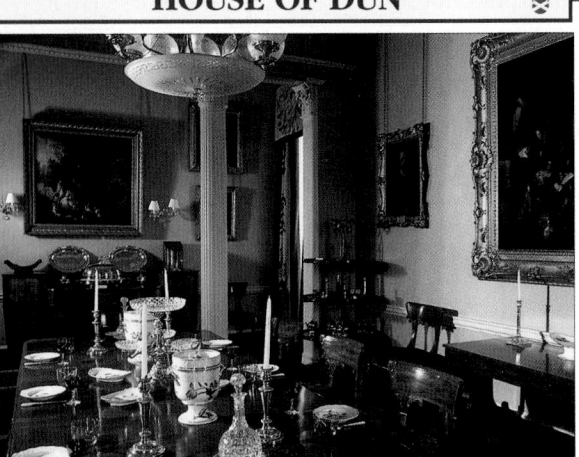

MONTROSE, ANGUS DD10 9LQ

Owner: The National Trust for Scotland   *Contact:* The Manager

Tel: 01674 810264 **Fax:** 01674 810722

This beautiful Georgian house, overlooking the Montrose Basin, was designed by William Adam and built in 1730 for David Erskine, Lord Dun. Lady Augusta Kennedy-Erskine was the natural daughter of William IV and Mrs Jordan and House of Dun contains many royal mementos. The house features superb plasterwork by Joseph Enzer.

Location: OS Ref. NO670 599. 3m W Montrose on A935.

Opening Times: House & shop: 13 - 16 Apr; 1 May - 30 Jun & 1 -30 Sept: daily, 1.30 - 5.30pm; 1 Jul - 31 Aug: daily, 11am - 5.30pm; weekends in Oct, 1.30 - 5.30pm (last admission 5pm). Restaurant opens at 11am. Gardens & Grounds: All year, daily, 9.30am - sunset.

Admission: House & Gardens: Adult £6, Conc. £4.50, Family £16.50. Groups: Adult £4.80, Child/ School £1. Gardens only: £1.

 Conferences.   Ground floor & basement suitable. WC. In grounds, on leads. Special dog walk.

GLAMIS CASTLE   See page 476 for full page entry.

GLENEAGLES   **Tel:** 01764 682388

Auchterarder, Perthshire PH3 1PJ
Owner: Gleneagles 1996 Trust   **Contact:** J Martin Haldane of Gleneagles
Gleneagles has been the home of the Haldane family since the 12th century. The 18th century pavilion is open to the public by written appointment.
Location: OS Ref. NS931 088. Auchterarder.
Opening Times: By written appointment only.

HILL OF TARVIT MANSIONHOUSE   **Tel/Fax:** 01334 653127

Cupar, Fife KY15 5PB
Owner: The National Trust for Scotland   **Contact:** The Manager
This fine house was rebuilt in 1906 by Sir Robert Lorimer, the renowned Scottish architect, for a Dundee industrialist, Mr F B Sharp. The house still presents a perfect setting for Mr Sharp's notable collection of superb French, Chippendale and vernacular furniture. Fine paintings by Raeburn and Ramsay and a number of eminent Dutch artists are on view together with Chinese porcelain and bronzes. Don't miss the restored Edwardian laundry behind the house which is set in the midst of a delightful garden.
Location: OS Ref. NO379 118. Off A916, 2^1/$_2$ m S of Cupar, Fife.
Opening Times: House: 13 - 16 Apr; 1 May - 30 Jun & 1 - 30 Sept: daily, 1.30 - 5.30pm; 1 Jul - 31 Aug: daily, 11am - 5.30pm; weekends in Oct, 1.30 - 5.30pm (last admission 4.45pm). Tearoom opens at 12.30pm when house opens at 1.30pm. Garden & Grounds: All year: daily, 9.30am - sunset.
Admission: House & Garden: Adult £5, Conc. £4, Family £14. Groups: Adult £4, Child/School £1. Garden only: £2, Conc. £1 (honesty box).

 Ground floor & grounds suitable. WC. By arrangement. P

HUNTINGTOWER CASTLE   **Tel:** 01738 627231

Perth
Owner: In the care of Historic Scotland   **Contact:** The Steward
The splendid painted ceilings are especially noteworthy in this castle, once owned by the Ruthven family. Scene of a famous leap between two towers by a daughter of the house who was nearly caught in her lover's room. The two towers are still complete, one of 15th - 16th century date, the other of 16th century origin. Now linked by a 17th century range.
Location: OS Ref. NO084 252. 3m NW of Perth off the A85.
Opening Times: 1 Apr - 30 Sept: daily, 9.30am - 6.30pm, last ticket 6pm. 1 Oct - 31 Mar: Mon - Sat, 9.30am - 4.30pm, Suns, 2 - 4.30pm, last ticket 4pm. Closed Thur pm & Fris in winter.
Admission: Adult £2, Child 75p, Conc. £1.50.

INCHCOLM ABBEY   **Tel:** 01383 823332

Inchcolm, Fife
Owner: In the care of Historic Scotland   **Contact:** The Steward
Known as the 'Iona of the East'. This is the best preserved group of monastic buildings in Scotland, founded in 1123. Includes a 13th century octagonal chapter house.
Location: OS Ref. NT190 826. On Inchcolm in the Firth of Forth. Reached by ferry from South Queensferry (30 mins). Tel 01383 823332 for times.
Opening Times: 1 Apr - 30 Sept: daily, 9.30am - 6.30pm, last ticket 6pm.
Admission: Adult £2.80, Child £1, Conc. £2. Additional charge for ferries.

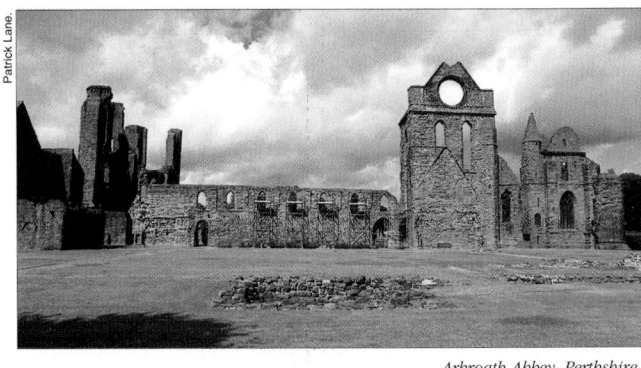

Arbroath Abbey, Perthshire.

KELLIE CASTLE & GARDEN

PITTENWEEM, FIFE KY10 2RF

Owner: *The National Trust for Scotland*   **Contact:** *The Property Manager*

Tel: 01333 720271   **Fax:** 01333 720326

This very fine example of domestic architecture in Lowland Scotland dates from the 14th century and was sympathetically restored by the Lorimer family in the late 19th century. The castle contains magnificent plaster ceilings and painted panelling as well as fine furniture designed by Sir Robert Lorimer. Of particular interest are the Victorian nursery and the old kitchen. The late Victorian garden features a fine collection of old-fashioned roses and herbaceous plants which are cultivated organically.

Location: OS Ref. NO519 051. On B9171, 3m NW of Pittenweem, Fife.

Opening Times: Castle: 13 Apr - 30 Sept: daily, 1.30 - 5.30pm, weekends in Oct, 1.30 - 5.30pm (last admission 4.45pm). Garden: All year, daily, 9.30am - sunset.

Admission: House & Garden: Adult £5, Conc. £4, Family £14. Groups: Adult £4, Child/ School £1. Garden only: £2, Conc. £1 (honesty box).

Ground floor & grounds suitable.

LOCH LEVEN CASTLE   Tel: 0388 040483

Loch Leven, Kinross

Owner: In the care of Historic Scotland   **Contact:** The Steward

Mary Queen of Scots endured nearly a year of imprisonment in this 14th century tower before her dramatic escape in May 1568. During the First War of Independence it was held by the English, stormed by Wallace and visited by Bruce.

Location: OS Ref. NO138 018. On island in Loch Leven reached by ferry from Kinross off the M90.

Opening Times: 1 Apr - 30 Sept: daily, 9.30am - 6.30pm, last ticket 6pm.

Admission: Adult £3.30, Child £1.20, Conc. £2.50. Prices include ferry trip.

MEGGINCH CASTLE GARDENS   Tel: 01821 642222   Fax: 01821 642708

Errol, Perthshire PH2 7SW

Owner: Captain Drummond of Megginch and Lady Strange

15th century castle, 1,000 year old yews, flowered parterre, double walled kitchen garden, topiary, astrological garden, pagoda dovecote in courtyard. Part used as a location for the film *Rob Roy*.

Location: OS Ref. NO241 245. 8m E of Perth on A90.

Opening Times: Apr - Oct: Weds. Aug: daily, 2.30 - 6pm. (2000 details.)

Admission: Adult £2.50, Child £1. (2000 details.)

Partially suitable.   By arrangement.   Limited for coaches.
In grounds, on leads.

MEIGLE SCULPTURED STONE MUSEUM   Tel: 01828 640612

Meigle

Owner: In the care of Historic Scotland

A remarkable collection of 25 sculptured monuments of the Celtic Christian period. This is one of the finest collections of Dark Age sculpture in Western Europe.

Location: OS Ref. NO287 446. In Meigle on the A94.

Opening Times: 1 Apr - 30 Sept: daily, 9.30am - 6.30pm, last ticket 6pm.

Admission: Adult £2, Child 75p, Conc. £1.50.

MONZIE CASTLE   Tel: 01764 653110

Crieff, Perthshire PH7 4HD

Owner/Contact: Mrs C M M Crichton

Built in 1791. Destroyed by fire in 1908 and rebuilt and furnished by Sir Robert Lorimer.

Location: OS Ref. NN873 244. 2m NE of Crieff.

Opening Times: 12 May - 10 Jun: daily, 2 - 5pm. By appointment at other times.

Admission: Adult £3, Child £1. Groups: Adult £2.50.

PITTENCRIEFF HOUSE MUSEUM   Tel: 01383 313838

Dunfermline, Fife

Owner: Fife Council   **Contact:** Ms Lin Collis

A temporary exhibition programme.

Location: OS Ref. NN087 873. In Dunfermline, S of A994 in Pittencrieff Park.

Opening Times: All year. May - Sept: 11am - 5pm. Oct - Apr: 11am - 4pm.

Admission: Free.

ST ANDREWS CASTLE

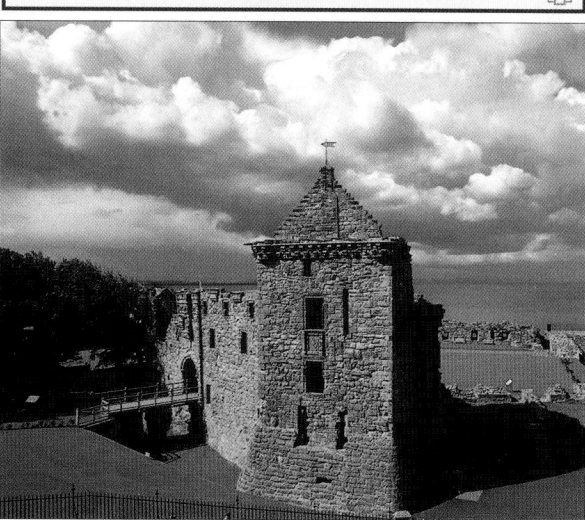

THE SCORES, ST ANDREWS, KY16 9AR

Owner: *Historic Scotland*   **Contact:** *The Steward*

Tel: 01334 477196

This was the castle of the Bishops of St Andrews and has a fascinating mine and counter-mine, rare examples of medieval siege techniques. There is also a bottle dungeon hollowed out of solid rock. Cardinal Beaton was murdered here and John Knox was sent to the galleys when the ensuing siege was lifted.

Location: OS Ref. NO513 169. In St Andrews on the A91.

Opening Times: Apr - Sept: daily, 9.30am - 6.30pm. Oct - Mar: Mon - Sat, 9.30am - 4.30pm; Suns, 2 - 4.30pm. Last ticket 30 mins before closing. Joint ticket with St Andrews Cathedral available.

Admission: Adult £2.80, Child £1, Conc. £2. 10% discount for groups (10+). Free pre-booked school visits.

Visitor centre.   Private evening hire.   Partially suitable. WCs.
By arrangement.   On street.   Free if booked.   Guide dogs.

SCONE PALACE GROUNDS   See page 477 for full page entry.

STOBHALL GARDENS & CHAPEL   Tel: 01821 640332

Stobhall, Guildtown, Perthshire PH2 6DR

Owner: The Earl of Perth   **Contact:** J Stormonth-Darling

Dramatic shrub gardens surround this unusual and charming cluster of historic buildings in a magnificent situation overlooking the River Tay. Access to 14th century chapel with its unique painted ceiling (1630).

Location: OS Ref. NO132 343. 8m N of Perth on A93.

Opening Times: 26 May - 24 Jun: 1 - 5pm. Also 21 & 28 Oct: 2 - 5pm.

Admission: Adult £2, Child £1.

Partially suitable. WC.   Limited.
Schools welcome if suitably accompanied. No education programme.
Guide dogs only.

Historic Scotland.

Owner: Historic Scotland

CONTACT

Neil Young
Argyll's Lodging
Castle Wynd
Stirling
FK8 1EJ

Tel: 01786 431319

Fax: 01786 448194

LOCATION

OS Ref. NS793 938

At the top and on
E side of Castle
Wynd in Stirling.

Train: Stirling.

Air: Edinburgh or
Glasgow.

ARGYLL'S LODGING
Stirling

ARGYLL'S LODGING, the residence of the Earls of Argyll in Stirling, is the finest and most complete surviving example in Scotland of a 17th century town residence. Set back behind a screen wall on the upper approaches to Stirling Castle, its fine architecture marks it out as a town house intended for the household of a great nobleman serving the Royal Stewart Court within the Castle. The principal rooms within the lodging – including the Laigh Hall, Dining Room, Drawing Room and Bedchamber – have recently been restored and furnished as they would have been when the 9th Earl of Argyll lived there in 1680. The Earl was executed for treason in 1685.

OPENING TIMES

April - September:
Daily: 9.30am - 6pm.

October - March:
Daily: 9.30am - 5pm.

ADMISSION

Adult £3.00
Child* £1.20
Conc........................£2.25

*up to 16 years

FUNCTION

ROOM	SIZE	MAX CAPACITY
Laigh Hall	11 x 6m	60 for reception
High Dining Room	11 x 6m	26 for dinner
Both rooms: 120 for receptions		

Interpretation scheme includes computer animations; joint ticket with Stirling Castle available.

Evening receptions/dinners.

Partially suitable. No wheelchair access to upper floor.

Ample parking for coaches and cars on Stirling Castle Esplanade.

Free pre-booked school visits scheme.

Guide dogs only.

INVERARAY CASTLE
Inveraray

The Duke of Argyll's family have lived in Inveraray since the early 15th century. The present Castle was built between 1745 and 1790.

The ancient Royal Burgh of Inveraray lies about 60 miles north west of Glasgow by Loch Fyne in an area of spectacular natural beauty combining the ruggedness of highland scenery with the sheltered tidal loch 90 miles from the open sea.

The Castle is the home of the Duke and Duchess of Argyll. Its fairytale exterior belies the grandeur of its gracious interior. The building was designed by Roger Morris and decorated by Robert Mylne, the clerk of works being William Adam, father of Robert and John, who did much of the laying out of the present Royal Burgh, an unrivalled example of an early planned town.

Visitors may see the famous Armoury Hall containing some 1300 pieces, French tapestries made especially for the Castle, fine examples of Scottish, English and French furniture together with a wealth of other works of art including china, silver and family artifacts, all of which form a unique collection spanning the generations which are identified by a magnificent genealogical display in the Clan Room.

Owner: Trustees of the 10th Duke of Argyll

CONTACT

The Factor
Dept HHD
Argyll Estates Office
Cherry Park
Inveraray
Argyll
PA32 8XE

Tel: 01499 302203

Fax: 01499 302421

e-mail: enquiries@ inveraray-castle.com

LOCATION

OS Ref. NN100 090

From Edinburgh 2¹/₂ - 3 hrs via Glasgow.

Just NE of Inveraray on A83. W shore of Loch Fyne.

Bus: Bus route stopping point within ¹/₂ m.

OPENING TIMES

7 April - 14 October

April, May, June, September & October:
Mon -Thur & Sats:
10am - 1pm & 2 - 5.45pm
Fris: Closed
Suns: 1 - 5.45pm.

July & August
Daily: 10am - 5.45pm
(including Friday)
Suns: 1 - 5.45pm.

Last admissions
12.30 & 5pm.

WINTER
Closed.

ADMISSION

House only

Adult £5.50
Child (under 16yrs) ...£3.50
OAP/Student...........£4.50
Family (2+2)...........£14.00
Groups (20+)
.... 20% discount

No photography. Guide books in French, Italian, Japanese and German translations.

Visitors may alight at the entrance. 2 wheelchair ramps to castle. All main public rooms suitable but two long flights of stairs to the smaller rooms upstairs. WCs.

Seats up to 50. Licensed. Menus available on request. Groups book in advance. Tel: 01786 813317.

Available for up to 100 people at no additional cost. Groups please book. Tour time: 1 hr.

100 cars. Separate coach park close to Castle

£1.50 per child. A guide can be provided. Areas of interest include a nature walk.

In grounds, on leads. Guide dogs only inside Castle.

ACHAMORE GARDENS

Tel: 01583 505254/505267

Isle of Gigha, Argyll PA41 7AD
Owner: Mr and Mrs Derek Holt   **Contact:** Mr William Howden
Gardens only open. Sub-tropical gardens created by Sir James Horlick who bought Gigha in 1944.
Location: OS Ref. NR650 500. Off the Mull of Kintyre. Ferry from Tayinloan.
Opening Times: Dawn until dusk every day.
Admission: Adult £2, Child £1.

ANGUS'S GARDEN

Tel: 01866 822375 **Fax:** 01866 822652

Barguillean, Taynuilt, Argyll, West Highlands PA35 1HY
Owner: Mr Sam MacDonald   **Contact:** Mr Sam MacDonald
Memorial garden of peace, tranquillity and reconciliation.
Location: OS Ref. NM999 298.
Opening Times: All year: daily, 9am - 5pm.
Admission: £2.

ARDENCRAIG GARDENS

Tel: 01700 504225 **Fax:** 01700 504225

Ardencraig, Rothesay, Isle of Bute, West Highlands PA20 9BP
Owner: Argyll and Bute Council   **Contact:** Allan Macdonald
Walled garden, greenhouses, aviaries.
Location: OS Ref. NS105 645. 2m from Rothesay.
Opening Times: May - Sept: Mon - Fri, 10am - 4.30pm, Sats & Suns, 1 - 4.30pm.

ARDKINGLAS ESTATE

Tel: 01499 600261 **Fax:** 01499 600241
e-mail: ardkinglas@btinternet.com

Cairndow, Argyll PA26 8BH
Owner: S J Noble   **Contact:** The Estate Manager
Location: OS Ref. NN179 106. Head of Loch Fyne, just off the A83 at Cairndow, 10m W of Arrochar. About 1hr from Glasgow.
Opening Times: Woodland Garden & woodland trails: All year: dawn - dusk. Tree Shop: All year: daily.
Admission: Garden: Adult £2.

ARDUAINE GARDEN

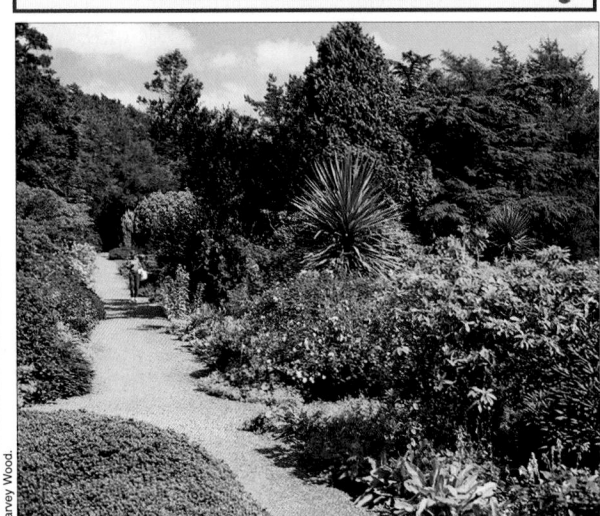

Harvey Wood.

ARDUAINE, BY OBAN, ARGYLL PA34 4XQ
Owner: *The National Trust for Scotland*   **Contact:** *Maurice Wilkins*

Tel/Fax: 01852 200366
A haven of tranquillity nestling on the west coast, Arduaine Garden is most spectacular in the late spring and early summer when the rhododendrons and azaleas are at their glorious best. With informal perennial borders giving a delightful display of colour throughout the season, the garden offers pleasant surroundings for a relaxing walk through the woodland garden to the coastal viewpoint, or simply an opportunity to sit and enjoy the peaceful atmosphere of the water garden.
Location: OS Ref. NM798 105. On A816, 20m S of Oban and 17m N of Lochgilphead.
Opening Times: All year: daily, 9.30am - sunset.
Admission: Adult £3, Conc. £2, Family £8. Groups: Adult £2.50. Child/School £1.

 By arrangement.   **P**   Guide dogs only.

ARGYLL'S LODGING

See page 482 for full page entry.

AUCHINDRAIN TOWNSHIP

Tel: 01499 500235

Auchindrain, Inveraray, Argyll PA32 8XN
Owner: Auchindrain Trust   **Contact:** Peter Fairweather
Open-air museum of an original West Highland township.
Location: OS Ref. NN050 050. On A83, 6m SW of Inveraray.
Opening Times: Please contact for details.
Admission: Please contact for details.

BALLOCH CASTLE COUNTRY PARK

Tel: 01389 758216 **Fax:** 01389 720922

Balloch, Dunbartonshire G83 8LX
Contact: Loch Lomond Park Authority Ranger Service
A 200 acre country park on the banks of Loch Lomond.
Location: OS Ref. NS390 830. SE shore of Loch Lomond, off A82 for Balloch or A811 for Stirling.
Opening Times: Visitor Centre: Easter - Oct: daily, 10am - 5.30pm. Country Park: All year: dawn - dusk.
Admission: Free for both Visitor Centre and Country Park.

BANNOCKBURN HERITAGE CENTRE

Tel: 01786 812664
Fax: 01786 810892

Glasgow Road, Stirling FK7 0LJ
Owner: The National Trust for Scotland   **Contact:** Judith Fairley
In 1314 from this battlefield the Scots 'sent them homeward to think again', when Edward II's English army was soundly defeated by King Robert the Bruce. Inside the Heritage Centre there is a life-size statue of William Wallace, Bruce on his throne, a display enriched with replicas, vignettes of Scottish life and a panorama of historical characters.
Location: OS Ref. NS810 910. Off M80 & M9/J9, 2m S of Stirling.
Opening Times: Site: All year: daily. Heritage Centre shop & café: 1 - 31 Mar and 1 Nov - 23 Dec: daily, 10.30am - 4pm. 1 Apr - 31 Oct: daily, 10am - 5.30pm (last audio-visual show 1/2 hr before closing).
Admission: Adult £2.50, Conc. £1.70, Family £7. Groups: Adult £2, Child/School £1.

In grounds, on leads.

BONAWE IRON FURNACE

Tel: 01866 822432

Taynuilt, Argyll
Owner: In the care of Historic Scotland   **Contact:** The Steward
Founded in 1753 by Cumbrian iron masters this is the most complete remaining charcoal fuelled ironworks in Britain. Displays show how iron was once made here.
Location: OS Ref. NN005 310. By the village of Taynuilt off the A85.
Opening Times: 1 Apr - 30 Sept: daily, 9.30am - 6.30pm, last ticket 6pm.
Admission: Adult £2.50, Child £1, Conc. £1.90.

CASTLE CAMPBELL

Tel: 01259 742408

Dollar Glen, Central District
Owner: The National Trust for Scotland   **Contact:** Historic Scotland
Known as 'Castle Gloom' this spectacularly sited 15th century fortress was the lowland stronghold of the Campbells. Stunning views from the parapet walk.
Location: OS Ref. NS961 993. At head of Dollar Glen, 10m E of Stirling on the A91.
Opening Times: 1 Apr - 30 Sept: daily, 9.30am - 6.30pm, last ticket 6pm. 1 Oct - 31 Mar: Mon - Sat, 9.30am - 4.30pm (closed Thurs pm & Fris all day) Suns, 2 - 4.30pm, last ticket 4pm.
Admission: Adult £2.80, Child £1, Conc. £2.

CASTLE STALKER

Tel: 01883 622768 **Fax:** 01883 626238

Portnacroish, Appin, Argyll PA38 4BA
Owner: Mrs M Allward   **Contact:** Messrs R & A Allward
Early 15th century tower house and ancient seat of the Stewarts of Appin. Picturesquely set on a rocky islet approx 400 yds off the mainland on the shore of Loch Linnhe. Reputed to have been used by James IV as a hunting lodge. Garrisoned by Government troops during the 1745 rising. Restored from a ruin by the late Lt Col Stewart Allward following acquisition in 1965 and now retained by his family.
Location: OS Ref. NM930 480. Approx. 20m N of Oban on the A828. On islet 1/4 m off-shore.
Opening Times: Apr - Sept for 25 days. Telephone for details. Times variable depending on tides and weather.
Admission: Adult £6, Child £3.

i Not suitable for coach parties.   Not suitable.

DOUNE CASTLE

Tel: 01786 841742

Doune

Owner: Earl of Moray (leased to Historic Scotland)   **Contact:** The Steward

A formidable 14th century courtyard castle, built for the Regent Albany. The striking keep-gatehouse combines domestic quarters including the splendid Lord's Hall with its carved oak screen, musicians' gallery and double fireplace.

Location: OS Ref. NN720 020. In Doune, 8m S of Callendar on the A84.

Opening Times: 1 Apr - 30 Sept: daily, 9.30am - 6.30pm. 1 Oct - 31 Mar: Mon - Wed & Sats, 9.30am - 4.30pm, Thurs, 9.30am - 12 noon, Fris, closed, Suns, 2 - 4.30pm, last admission 1/2 hr before closing.

Admission: Adult £2.50, Child £1, Conc. £1.90.

DUART CASTLE

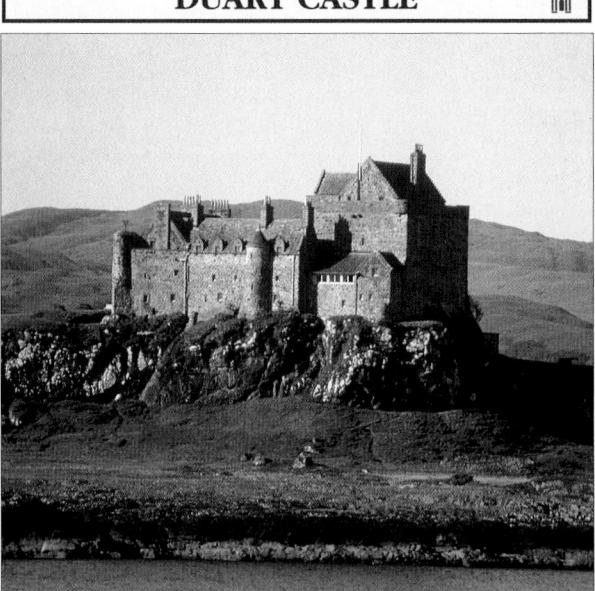

ISLE OF MULL, ARGYLL PA64 6AP
Owner/Contact: Sir Lachlan Maclean Bt

Tel: 01680 812309 or 01577 830311 **e-mail:** duartguide@isle-of-mull.demon.co.uk
Duart Castle has been a Maclean stronghold since the 12th century. The keep was built by Lachlan Lubanach, 5th Chief, in 1360. Burnt by the English in 1758, the castle was restored in 1912 and today is still the home of the Chief of the Clan Maclean. It has a spectacular position overlooking the Sound of Mull.

Location: OS Ref. NM750 350. Off A849 on the east point of the Isle of Mull.

Opening Times: 1 May - 14 Oct: 10.30am - 6pm.

Admission: Adult £3.80, Child £1.90, Conc. £3, Family £9.50.

Not suitable.   By arrangement.
In grounds, on leads.

DUMBARTON CASTLE

Tel: 01389 732167

Dumbarton, Strathclyde

Owner: Historic Scotland   **Contact:** The Steward

Location: OS Ref. NS401 744. In Dumbarton on the A82.

Opening Times: 1 Apr - 30 Sept: daily, 9.30am - 6.30pm, last ticket 6pm. 1 Oct - 31 Mar: Mon - Wed & Sats, 9.30am - 4.30pm, Thurs, 9.30am - 12 noon, Fris closed, Suns, 2 - 4.30pm, last ticket 4pm.

Admission: Adult £2, Child 75p, Conc £1.50.

DUNBLANE CATHEDRAL

Tel: 01786 823388

Dunblane

Owner: Historic Scotland   **Contact:** The Steward

One of Scotland's noblest medieval churches. The lower part of the tower is Romanesque but the larger part of the building is of the 13th century. It was restored in 1889 - 93 by Sir Rowand Anderson.

Location: OS Ref. NN782 015. In Dunblane.

Opening Times: All year.

Admission: Free.

DUNSTAFFNAGE CASTLE

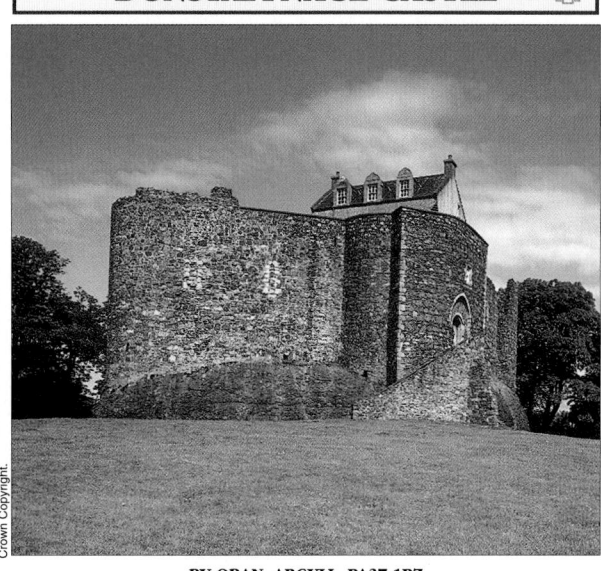

Crown Copyright.

BY OBAN, ARGYLL PA37 1PZ
Owner: In the care of Historic Scotland   *Contact:* The Steward

Tel: 01631 562465

A very fine 13th century castle built on a rock with a great curtain wall. The castle's colourful history stretches across the Wars of Independence to the 1745 rising. The castle was briefly the prison of Flora Macdonald. Marvellous views from the top of the curtain wall. Close by are the remains of a chapel with beautiful architectural detail.

Location: OS49 NM882 344. By Loch Etive, 3 1/2 m from Oban on the A85.

Opening Times: Apr - Sept: daily, 9.30am - 6.30pm, last ticket 1/2 hr before closing. Oct - Mar: Mon - Sat, 9.30am - 4.30pm; Suns, 2 - 4.30pm.

Admission: Adult £2, Child 75p, Conc. £1.50. 10% discount for groups (10+).

  Partially suitable.   By arrangement.   P
Free pre-booked school visits.   In grounds, on leads.

GLENCOE

Tel: 01855 811307/811729 (during closed season) **Fax:** 01855 811772

Ballachulish, Argyll PA39 4HX

Owner: The National Trust for Scotland   **Contact:** Derrick Warner

This is a breathtaking, dramatic glen with jagged peaks incised on either side by cascading water. In 1692 many of the MacDonald clan were massacred by soldiers of King William's army, to whom they had given hospitality. Wildlife abounds and herds of red deer, wildcat and golden eagle enjoy this wilderness area.

Location: OS Ref. NN100 590. Off A82, 17m S of Fort William.

Opening Times: Please contact property for details.

Admission: Please contact property for details.

Ground floor suitable. WC.   Guide dogs only.

THE HILL HOUSE

Tel: 01436 673900 **Fax:** 01436 674685

Upper Colquhoun Street, Helensburgh G84 9AJ

Owner: The National Trust for Scotland   **Contact:** Mrs Anne Ellis

Certainly the finest domestic creation of the famous Scottish architect and artist, Charles Rennie Mackintosh. He set this 20th century masterpiece high on a hillside overlooking the Firth of Clyde. Mackintosh also designed furniture, fittings and decorative schemes to complement the house, and suggested a layout for the garden which has been renovated by the Trust.

Location: OS Ref. NS300 820. Off B832, between A82 & A814, 23m NW of Glasgow.

Opening Times: 1 Apr - 31 Oct: daily, 1.30 - 5.30pm (last admission 5pm). Tearoom: 1.30 - 4.30pm. Access may be restricted at peak times and at the discretion of the Property Manager. Groups must pre-book.

Admission: Adult £6, Conc. £4.50, Family £16.50. Groups must book.

INCHMAHOME PRIORY

Tel: 01877 385294

Port of Menteith

Owner: In the care of Historic Scotland   **Contact:** The Steward

A beautifully situated Augustinian priory on an island in the Lake of Menteith founded in 1238 with much of the building surviving. The five year old Mary Queen of Scots was sent here for safety in 1547.

Location: OS Ref. NN574 005. On an island in Lake of Menteith. Reached by ferry from Port of Menteith, 4m E of Aberfoyle off A81.

Opening Times: 1 Apr - 30 Sept: daily, 9.30am - 6.30pm, last ticket 6pm.

Admission: Adult £3.30, Child £1.20, Conc. £2.50. Charge includes ferry trip.

INVERARAY CASTLE

See page 483 for full page entry.

INVERARAY JAIL

Tel: 01499 302381 **Fax:** 01499 302195

Church Square, Inveraray, Argyll PA32 8TX   **e-mail:** inverarayjail@btclick.com

Owner: Visitor Centres Ltd   **Contact:** J Linley

A living 19th century prison! Uniformed prisoners and warders, life-like figures, imaginative exhibitions, sounds, smells and trials in progress, bring the 1820 courtroom and former county prison back to life. See the 'In Prison Today' exhibition.

Location: OS Ref. NN100 090. Church Square, Inveraray, Argyll.

Opening Times: Apr - Oct: 9.30am - 6pm, last adm. 5pm. Nov - Mar: 10am - 5pm, last adm. 4pm.

Admission: Adult £4.90, Child £2.40, OAP £3.10, Family £13.40. Groups (10+): £3.90, OAP £2.60 (from 2 Apr 2001).

IONA ABBEY & NUNNERY

IONA, WEST HIGHLANDS

Owner: *In the care of Historic Scotland*   **Contact:** *Chris Calvert*

Tel/Fax: 01681 700512 **e-mail:** hs.ionaabbey@scotland.gov.uk

One of Scotland's most historic and venerated sites, Iona Abbey is a celebrated Christian centre and the burial place for many Scottish kings. The abbey and nunnery grounds house one of the most comprehensive collections of Christian carved stones in Scotland, dating from 600AD to the 1600s. Includes the Columbia Centre, Fionnphort exhibition and giftshop.

Location: OS Ref. NM270 240. Ferry service from Fionnphort, Mull.

Opening Times: All year, daily.

Admission: Adult £2.80, Child (under 16) £1.20, Conc. £2. Columba Centre, exhibition & giftshop: Free.

KILCHURN CASTLE

Tel: 01786 431323

Loch Awe, Dalmally, Argyll

Owner: In the care of Historic Scotland   **Contact:** The Steward

A square tower, built by Sir Colin Campbell of Glenorchy c1550, it was much enlarged in 1693 to give the building, now a ruin, its present picturesque outline. Spectacular views of Loch Awe.

Location: OS Ref. NN133 276. At the NE end of Loch Awe, 2¹⁄₂ m W of Dalmally.

Opening Times: Ferry service operates in the summer. Tel: 01838 200440 for times.

Admission: Adult £4, Child £2, Conc.£3, Family £10.

MOUNT STUART

ISLE OF BUTE PA20 9LR

Owner: *The Mount Stuart Trust*   **Contact:** *The Administrator*

Tel: 01700 503877 **Fax:** 01700 505313 **e-mail:** contactus@mountstuart.com

Spectacular High Victorian Gothic house, ancestral home of the Marquesses of Bute. Splendid interiors, art collection and architectural detail. Set in 300 acres of stunning woodlands, mature pinetum, arboretum and exotic gardens. Countryside Ranger Service. Scottish Tourism Oscar winner.

Location: OS Ref. NS100 600. 5m S of Rothesay Pierhead, local bus service to house. Frequent ferry service from Wemyss Bay, Renfrewshire & Colintraive, Argyll. 1 hr from Glasgow Airport.

Opening Times: May - Sept: daily (except Tues & Thurs). House: 11am - 5pm. Gardens: 10am - 6pm.

Admission: House & Garden: Adult £6, Child £2.50, Family £15, Season £15. Gardens: Adult £3.50, Child £2, Family £9. Conc. & group rates given. Pre-booked guided tours available. (2000 prices.)

Picnic area.   By arrangement.

ROTHESAY CASTLE

Tel: 01700 502691

Rothesay, Isle of Bute

Owner: In the care of Historic Scotland   **Contact:** The Steward

A favourite residence of the Stuart Kings, this is a wonderful example of a 13th century circular castle of enclosure with 16th century forework containing the Great Hall. Attacked by Vikings in its earlier days.

Location: OS Ref. NS088 646. In Rothesay, Isle of Bute. Ferry from Wemyss Bay on the A78.

Opening Times: 1 Apr - 30 Sept: daily, 9.30am - 6.30pm, last ticket 6pm. 1 Oct - 31 Mar: Mon - Wed & Sats, 9.30am - 4.30pm, Thurs 9.30am - 12 noon, Fris closed, Suns, 2 - 4.30pm, last ticket 4pm.

Admission: Adult £2, Child 75p, Conc. £1.50.

ST BLANE'S CHURCH

Tel: 0131 668 8800

Kingarth, Isle of Bute

Owner: In the care of Historic Scotland

This 12th century Romanesque chapel stands on the site of a 12th century Celtic monastery.

Location: OS Ref. NS090 570. At the S end of the Isle of Bute.

Opening Times: All year: daily.

Admission: Free.

STIRLING CASTLE

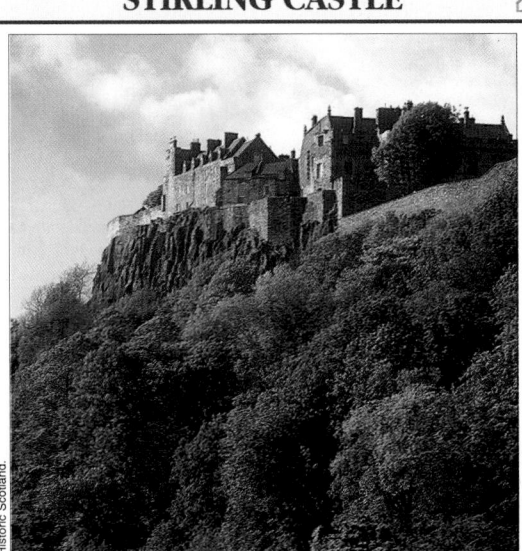

Historic Scotland.

CASTLE WYND, STIRLING FK8 1EJ
Owner: Historic Scotland Contact: Neil Young

Tel: 01786 450000 **Fax:** 01786 464678

Stirling Castle has played a key role in Scottish history, dominating the North–South and East–West routes through Scotland. The battles of Stirling Bridge and Bannockburn were fought in its shadow and Mary Queen of Scots lived here as a child. Marvellous Renaissance architecture and restored Great Hall.

Location: OS Ref. NS790 941. At the top of Castle Wynd in Stirling.

Opening Times: Apr - Sept: 9.30am - 6pm. Oct - Mar: 9.30am - 5pm, last ticket 45 mins before closing.

Admission: Adult £6.50, Child £2, Conc. £5. 10% discount for groups (10+). Free booked school visits, except May - August.

ℹ️ Picnic area. Joint ticket with Argyll's Lodging. 📷 ⏳Private hire. ♿Partially suitable. WC. ☕Licensed. 🍴 P 🚻 🐕Guide dogs. ✳️

Website Index page 39 ◀◀◀

TOROSAY CASTLE & GARDENS 🏛

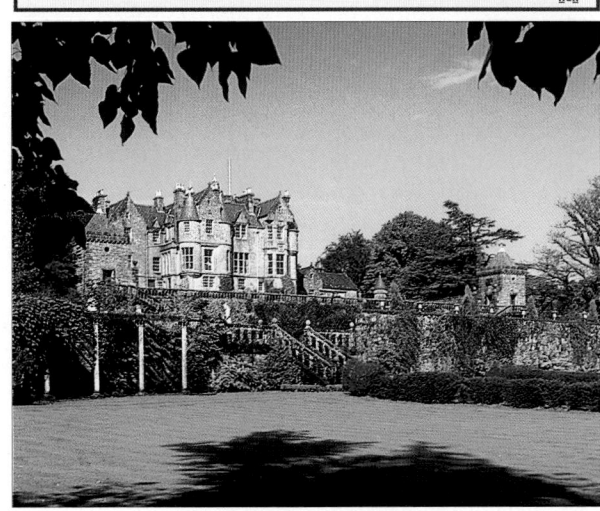

CRAIGNURE, ISLE OF MULL PA65 6AY
Owner/Contact: Mr Chris James

Tel: 01680 812421 **Fax:** 01680 812470 **e-mail:** torosay@aol.com

Torosay Castle and Gardens set on the magnificent Island of Mull, was completed in 1858 by the eminent architect David Bryce in the Scottish baronial style, and is surrounded by 12 acres of spectacular gardens which offer an exciting contrast between formal terraces, impressive statue walk and informal woodland, also rhododendron collection, alpine, walled, bog and oriental gardens. The house offers family history, portraits, scrapbooks and antiques in an informal and relaxed atmosphere.

Location: OS Ref. NM730 350. $1^1/2$ m SE of Craignure by A849.

Opening Times: House: Easter - mid-Oct: daily, 10.30am - 5.30pm, last admission 5pm. Gardens: All year: daily, 9am - 7pm or daylight hours in winter.

Admission: Adult £4.50, Child £1.50, Conc. £3.50. Groups: Adult £3.50, Child £1, Conc. £3.50.

📷 ♿Grounds suitable. WC. ☕ 🐕In grounds, on leads. ✳️ 🅦

YOUNGER BOTANIC GARDEN BENMORE

Tel: 01369 706261
Fax: 01369 706369

Dunoon, Argyll PA23 8QU

Contact: The Curator

A botanical paradise. Enter the magnificent avenue of giant redwoods and follow trails through the Formal Garden and hillside woodlands with its spectacular outlook over the Holy Loch and the Eachaig Valley.

Location: OS Ref. NS150 850. 7m N of Dunoon on A815.

Opening Times: 1 Mar - 31 Oct: daily, 9.30am - 6pm.

Admission: Adult £3, Child £1, Conc. £2.50, Family £7. Group discounts available.

Mount Stuart, West Highlands.

NTS Photo Library/ Richard Schofield.

CRATHES CASTLE & GDN
Banchory

Part of Aberdeenshire's Castle Trail: fairytale-like turrets, gargoyles of fantastic design, superb painted ceilings and the ancient Horn of Leys given in 1323 to Alexander Burnett by King Robert the Bruce, are just a few of the exciting features at this most picturesque castle. The building of the castle began in 1553 and took 40 years to complete. Just over 300 years later, Sir James and Lady Burnett began developing the walled garden and created not just one but eight superb gardens which now provide a riot of colour throughout the summer.

Owner: The National Trust for Scotland

CONTACT

The Property
Administrator
Crathes Castle
Banchory
AB31 3QJ

Tel: 01330 844525

Fax: 01330 844797

e-mail: crathes@nts.org.uk

LOCATION

OS Ref. NO733 969

On A93, 3m E of Banchory and 15m W of Aberdeen.

NTS Photo Library.

🛍   🍴 Licensed.

✿   🅿

⊤   ▣

♿ Partially suitable.   ❄

☕   🎭 Tel. for details.

OPENING TIMES

Castle, Visitor Centre & Shop

1 Apr - 30 Sept: daily,
10.30am - 5.30pm.

1 - 31 Oct: daily,
10.30am - 4.30pm
(last admission to Castle
45mins before closing).

Other times by
appointment.

Plant sales: same dates,
except weekends only
in October.

Licensed Restaurant:
10 Jan - 31 Mar & 1 Nov -
23 Dec: Wed - Sun,
10.30am - 4pm;
1 Apr - 31 Oct: daily,
10.30am - 5.30pm.

To help you to enjoy your
visit, admission to the
Castle is by timed ticket
and entry may be delayed.

Garden & Grounds

All year: daily,
9am - sunset.
Grounds may be closed at
short notice on very busy
days due to the limited
capacity for car parking.

ADMISSION

Castle & Garden

Adult	£7.00
Conc.	£5.00
Family	£19.00

Groups

Adult	£5.20
Child/School	£1.00
Car Park	£1.00

Castle or Walled Garden only

Adult	£4.50
Conc.	£3.00

ARBUTHNOTT HOUSE

Tel: 01561 361226 **Fax:** 01561 320476

Arbuthnott, Laurencekirk AB30 1PA
e-mail: keith@arbuthnott.co.uk
Owner: The Viscount of Arbuthnott   **Contact:** The Master of Arbuthnott

Arbuthnott family home for 800 years with formal 17th century walled garden on unusually steep south facing slope. Well maintained grass terraces, herbaceous borders, shrubs and greenhouses.

Location: OS Ref. NO796 751. Off B967 between A90 and A92, 25m S of Aberdeen.
Opening Times: House: 15/16 Apr, 27/28 May, 10/11 Jun, 5/6 & 26/27 Aug. Guided tours: 2 - 5pm. Garden: All year: 9am - 5pm.
Admission: House: £3. Garden: £2.

Ground floor suitable. Obligatory. P

BALFLUIG CASTLE

Tel: 020 7624 3200

Alford, Aberdeenshire AB33 8EJ
Owner/Contact: Mark Tennant of Balfluig

Small 16th century tower house in farmland, restored in 1967.

Location: OS Ref. NJ586 151. Alford, Aberdeenshire.
Opening Times: Please write to M I Tennant Esq, 30 Abbey Gardens, London NW8 9AT. Occasionally let by the week for holidays. Scottish Tourist Board ***.

Not suitable.   1 single, 4 double.

BALMORAL CASTLE (GROUNDS & EXHIBITIONS)

Tel: 013397 42334/42335
Fax: 013397 42034

Balmoral, Ballater, Aberdeenshire AB35 5TB
e-mail: info@balmoralcastle.com
Owner: Her Majesty The Queen   **Contact:** Captain Roger Wilson

Holiday home of The Royal Family, bought by Prince Albert in 1852. Grounds, gardens and exhibition of paintings and works of art in the Ballroom. Exhibition of royal heraldry, commemorative china and a display of native wildlife in their natural habitat in the Carriage Hall. Display of carriages and Upper Deeside Art Society exhibition on view in the Stables.

Location: OS Ref. NO256 951. Off A93 between Ballater and Braemar. 50m W of Aberdeen.
Opening Times: 12 Apr - 31 Jul: daily, 10am - 5pm (last recommended admission 4pm).
Admission: Adult £4.50, Child (5-16yrs) £1, OAP £3.50.

BALVENIE CASTLE

Tel: 01340 820121

Dufftown
Owner: In the care of Historic Scotland   **Contact:** The Steward

Picturesque ruins of 13th century moated stronghold originally owned by the Comyns. Visited by Edward I in 1304 and by Mary Queen of Scots in 1562. Occupied by Cumberland in 1746.

Location: OS Ref. NJ326 408. At Dufftown on A941.
Opening Times: 1 Apr - 30 Sept: daily, 9.30am - 6.30pm, last ticket 6pm.
Admission: Adult £1.50, Child 50p, Conc. £1.10.

Historic Scotland.

Huntly Castle, Grampian Highlands.

BRAEMAR CASTLE

BRAEMAR, ABERDEENSHIRE AB35 5XR

Owner: Capt A A C Farquharson of Invercauld   *Contact:* Bruce & Carrol McCudden

Tel/Fax: 013397 41219 **e-mail:** invercauld@freenet.com

Braemar Castle has been the ancestral home of the Clan Farquharson for over 200 years. The 'Black' Colonel of Inverey, the enemy clan leader, attacked and burned the castle in 1689 and after being rebuilt was garrisoned by Hanoverian troops for some 60 years after the 1745 Jacobite rebellion. In some of the rooms you can see the 'graffiti' of the English soldiers. Nowadays, the castle is peaceful, and this family home attracts thousands of visitors each year to see the impressive selection of furnished rooms covering decades of the Farquharson history. A massive iron yett leads you to the pit dungeon, which was a gruesome place in years gone by.

Location: OS Ref. NO156 924. ¹/₂ m NE of Braemar on A93.
Opening Times: 1 Apr - 31 Oct: Sat - Thur (plus Fris during Jul & Aug), 10am - 6pm (last entry 5.30pm).
Admission: Adult £3, Child £1, Conc. £2.50.

Picnic area. Not suitable. By arrangement. P
In grounds on leads.

BRODIE CASTLE

FORRES, MORAY IV36 0TE

Owner: The National Trust for Scotland   *Contact:* Dr Stephanie Blackden

Tel: 01309 641371 **Fax:** 01309 641600

This imposing Castle stands in rich Morayshire parkland. The lime harled building is a typical 'Z' plan tower house with ornate corbelled battlements and bartizans, with 17th & 19th century additions. The interior has unusual plaster ceilings, a major art collection, porcelain and fine furniture. There is a woodland walk by a large pond with access to wildlife observation hides. In springtime the grounds are carpeted with many varieties of daffodils for which Brodie Castle is rightly famous.

Location: OS Ref. NH980 577. Off A96 4¹/₂ m W of Forres and 24m E of Inverness.
Opening Times: Castle & Shop: 1 Apr - 30 Sept: Mon - Sat, 11am - 5.30pm, Suns, 1.30 - 5.30pm; weekends in Oct, Sats, 11am - 5.30pm, Suns, 1.30 - 5.30pm (last admission 4.30pm). Tearoom closes at 4.30pm. Other times by appointment. Grounds: All year: daily, 9.30am - sunset.
Admission: Adult £6, Conc. £4.50, Family £16.50. Groups: Adult £4.80, Child/Schools £1. Grounds only: £1 honesty box.

   In grounds, on leads.

CANDACRAIG GARDEN & GALLERY
Tel: 01975 651226 **Fax:** 01975 651391

Candacraig Gardens, Strathdon AB36 8XT

Owner/Contact: Harry Young

1820s B listed walled display garden, art gallery and specialist plant nursery. Wedding ceremonies conducted in beautiful Victorian Gothic marriage room.

Location: OS Ref. NJ339 110. On A944 1½ m SW of Strathdon, 20m from Alford.

Opening Times: 1 May - 30 Sept: daily, 10am - 6pm.

Admission: Donation box. Pre-arranged groups: Adult £1, Child Free.

CASTLE FRASER & GARDEN

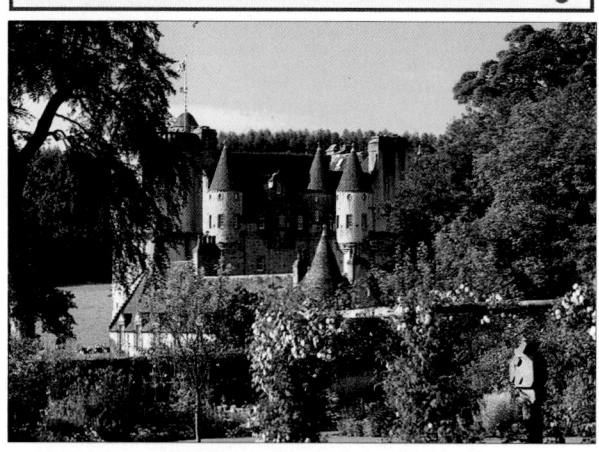

SAUCHEN, INVERURIE AB51 7LD

Owner: The National Trust for Scotland   *Contact: Eric Wilkinson*

Tel: 01330 833463

Over 400 years of history could be told if the stout walls of Castle Fraser could speak. Begun in 1575 by the 6th Laird, Michael Fraser, the two low wings contribute to the scale and magnificence of the towers rising above them, combining to make this the largest and most elaborate of the Scottish castles built on the 'Z' plan. The stunning simplicity of the Great Hall, which occupies the entire first floor of the main block, with its striking fireplace, almost 3 metres wide, immediately creates for the visitor the atmosphere of past centuries.

Location: OS Ref. NJ723 125. Off A944, 4m N of Dunecht & 16m W of Aberdeen.

Opening Times: Castle: 13 Apr - 31 May & 1 - 30 Sept: daily, 1.30 - 5.30pm. 1 Jun - 31 Aug: daily, 11am - 5.30pm; weekends in Oct, 1.30 - 5.30pm (last admission 4.45pm). Shop & Café: open at 12.30pm when Castle opens at 1.30pm. Garden: All year: daily, 9.30am - 6pm. Grounds: All year: daily, 9.30am - sunset.

Admission: Castle & Garden: Adult £6, Conc. £4.50, Family £16.50. Groups: Adult £4.80, Child/School £1. Garden & grounds only: Adult £2, Conc. £1.30, Family £6. Groups: Adult £1.60, Child/School £1. Car Park: All year: £1.

CORGARFF CASTLE
Tel: 013398 83635

Strathdon

Owner: In the care of Historic Scotland   **Contact:** The Steward

A 16th century tower house converted into a barracks for Hanoverian troops in 1748. Its last military use was to control the smuggling of illicit whisky between 1827 and 1831. Still complete and with star-shaped fortification.

Location: OS Ref. NJ255 086. 8m W of Strathdon on A939. 14m NW of Ballater.

Opening Times: 1 Apr - 30 Sept: daily, 9.30am - 6.30pm. 1 Oct - 31 Mar: Sats, 9.30am - 4.30pm. Suns, 2 - 4.30pm, last admission ½ hr before closing.

Admission: Adult £2.80, Child £1, Conc. £2.

CRATHES CASTLE & GARDEN
See page 488 for full page entry.

CRAIGSTON CASTLE
Tel: 01888 551228/551640

Turriff, Aberdeenshire AB53 5PX

Owner: William Pratesi Urquhart   **Contact:** Mrs Fiona Morrison

Built in 1607 to John Urquhart Tutor of Cromarty's individualistic plan. An arch and ornate sculptured balcony joins two towers, one noticeably wider than the other, to accommodate the Laird's private apartments. The largely unchanged interior, still lived in by the Urquhart family, includes carved portraits of the Scottish Kings.

Location: OS Ref. NJ762 550. On B9105, 4½ m NE of Turriff.

Opening Times: 22 Jul - 5 Aug: daily (closed Mons & Tues), 10am - 4pm. 25 Aug - 9 Sept: daily (closed Mons & Tues), 10am - 4pm. Groups throughout the year by appointment. (2000 details.)

Admission: Adult £3.50, Child £1, OAP £3, Student £1.50. (2000 details.)

Not suitable.   Obligatory.   P   In grounds on leads.

CRUICKSHANK BOTANIC GARDEN
Tel: 01224 272704 **Fax:** 01224 272703

St Machar Drive, Aberdeen AB24 3UU

Owner: University of Aberdeen   **Contact:** R B Rutherford

Extensive collection of shrubs, herbaceous and alpine plants and trees. Rock and water gardens.

Location: OS Ref. NJ938 084. In old Aberdeen.

Opening Times: All year: Mon - Fri, 9am - 4.30pm. May - Sept: Sats & Suns, 2 - 5pm.

Admission: Free.

DALLAS DHU DISTILLERY
Tel: 01309 676548

Forres

Owner: In the care of Historic Scotland   **Contact:** The Steward

A completely preserved time capsule of the distiller's craft. Wander at will through this fine old Victorian distillery then enjoy a dram. Visitor centre, shop and audio-visual theatre.

Location: OS Ref. NJ035 566. 1m S of Forres off the A940.

Opening Times: 1 Apr - 30 Sept: daily, 9.30am - 6.30pm, last ticket 6pm. 1 Oct - 31 Mar: Mon - Sat, 9.30am - 4.30pm, Suns, 2 - 4.30pm, last ticket 4pm. Closed Thurs pm and Fris in winter.

Admission: Adult £3, Child £1, Conc. £2.30.

DELGATIE CASTLE

TURRIFF, ABERDEENSHIRE AB53 5TD

Owner: Delgatie Castle Trust   *Contact: Mrs Joan Johnson*

Tel/Fax: 01888 563479 **e-mail:** jjohnson@delgatie-castle.freeserve.co.uk

11th century castle which has largely remained in the Hay family for the last 650 years and is now officially the Clan Hay centre. Mary Queen of Scots stayed here in 1562. Her bed-chamber is on view. Painted ceilings dated 1592 and 1597. Widest turnpike stair of its kind in Scotland. Lake and woodland walks.

Location: OS Ref. NJ754 506. Off A947 Aberdeen to Banff Road.

Opening Times: 2 Apr - 25 Oct: 10am - 5pm.

Admission: Adult £3, Child/OAP £2.

 Ground floor suitable. WC.   Home-baking.   By arrangement.   Guide dogs only.

National Trust for Scotland

Drum Castle, Grampian Highlands.

DRUM CASTLE

Tel: 01330 811204

Drumoak, by Banchory AB31 3EY

Owner: The National Trust for Scotland   **Contact:** The Property Manager

The combination over the years of a 13th century square tower, a very fine Jacobean mansion house and the additions of the Victorian lairds make Drum Castle unique among Scottish castles. Owned for 653 years by one family, the Irvines, every stone and every room is steeped in history. Superb furniture and paintings provide a visual feast for visitors. In the 16th century chapel, the stained glass windows, the font copied from the Saxon one in Winchester Cathedral and the Augsburg silver Madonna, all add immense interest for visitors.

Location: OS Ref. NJ796 004. Off A93, 3m W of Peterculter and 10m W of Aberdeen.

Opening Times: Castle: 13 Apr - 31 May & 1 - 30 Sept: daily, 1.30 - 5.30pm. 1 Jun - 31 Aug: daily, 11am - 5.30pm; weekends in Oct: 1.30 - 5.30pm (last admission 4.45pm). Garden: same dates, daily, 10am - 6pm. Grounds: All year, daily, 9.30am - sunset.

Admission: Castle & Garden: Adult £6, Conc. £4.50, Family £16.50. Groups: Adult £4.80, Child/ School £1. Garden & Grounds only: £1.

DRUMMUIR CASTLE

Tel: 01542 810332 **Fax:** 01542 810302

Drummuir, by Keith, Banffshire AB55 5JE

Owner: The Gordon-Duff Family   **Contact:** Liz Robson

Castellated Victorian Gothic-style castle built in 1847 by Admiral Duff. 60ft high lantern tower with fine plasterwork. Family portraits, interesting artefacts and other paintings. Organic walled garden and plant sales.

Location: OS Ref. NO881 839. Midway between Keith (5m) and Dufftown, off the B9014.

Opening Times: 25/26 Aug, 1/2 & 5 - 26 Sept: Tours at 2pm & 3pm.

Admission: Adult £2, Child £1.50. Pre-arranged groups: Adult £2, Child £1.50.

Obligatory. P In grounds on leads.

DUFF HOUSE

Tel: 01261 818181 **Fax:** 01261 818900

Banff, AB45 3SX

Contact: The Chamberlain

One of the most imposing and palatial houses in Scotland.

Location: OS Ref. NJ691 634. Banff. 47m NW of Aberdeen on A947.

Opening Times: 1 Apr - 31 Oct: daily, 11am - 5pm. 1 Nov - 31 Mar: Thur - Sun, 11am - 4pm.

Admission: Adult £3.50, Conc. £2.50, Family £8.50. Groups (10+): £2.50.

DUNNOTTAR CASTLE

Tel: 01569 762173

The Lodge, Stonehaven AB39 2TL   **Contact:** P McKenzie

Spectacular ruin. Impregnable fortress to the Earls Marischals of Scotland.

Location: OS Ref. NO881 839. Just off A92. 1¹/₂ m SE of Stonehaven.

Opening Times: Easter weekend - 11 Oct: Mon - Sat, 9am - 6pm. Suns, 2 - 5pm. 1 Nov - Easter weekend: Mon - Fri, 9am - sunset (closed weekends). Last admission: 30 mins before closing.

Admission: Adult £3.50, Child £1.

DUTHIE PARK & WINTER GARDENS

Tel: 01224 585310 **Fax:** 01224 210532

Polmuir Road, Aberdeen, Grampian Highlands AB11 7TH

Owner: Aberdeen City Council   **Contact:** Alan Findlay

45 acres of parkland and gardens. Glasshouses.

Location: OS Ref. NJ97 044. Just N of River Dee, 1m S of city centre.

Opening Times: All year: daily from 9.30pm.

Admission: Free.

ELGIN CATHEDRAL

Tel: 01343 547171

Elgin

Owner: Historic Scotland   **Contact:** The Steward

When entire this was perhaps the most beautiful of Scottish cathedrals, known as the Lantern of the North. 13th century, much modified after almost being destroyed in 1390 by Alexander Stewart, the infamous 'Wolf of Badenoch'. The octagonal chapterhouse is the finest in Scotland. You can see the Bishop's home at Spynie Palace, 2m north of the town.

Location: OS Ref. NJ223 630. In Elgin on the A96.

Opening Times: 1 Apr - 30 Sept: daily, 9.30am - 6.30pm, last ticket 6pm. 1 Oct - 31 Mar: Mon - Sat, 9.30am - 4.30pm, Suns, 2 - 4.30pm, last ticket 4pm. Closed Thurs pm & Fris in winter.

Admission: Adult £2.80, Child £1, Conc. £2. Joint entry ticket with Spynie Palace: Adult £3.30, Child £1.20, Conc. £2.80.

Website Index page 39

FASQUE

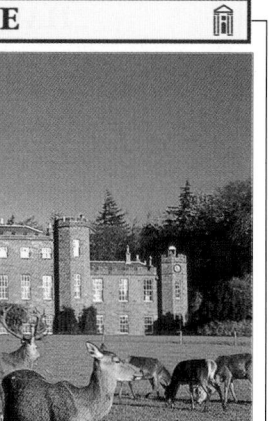

FETTERCAIRN, LAURENCEKIRK, KINCARDINESHIRE AB30 1DN

Owner: Charles Gladstone   *Contact:* Scott Traynor

Tel/Fax: 01561 340569

Fasque is a spectacular example of a Victorian 'Upstairs-Downstairs' stately home. Bought by Sir John Gladstone in 1829, it was home to William Gladstone, four times Prime Minister, for much of his life. In front of the house red deer roam in the park, and behind the hills rise dramatically towards the Highlands. Inside very little has changed since Sir John's days. Fasque is not a museum, but rather an unspoilt old family home.

Location: OS Ref. NO648 755. On the B974, 1m N of Fettercairn, 4m from A90. Aberdeen/ Dundee 35m.

Opening Times: 1 May - 30 Sept: daily, 11am - 5.30pm. Groups by arrangement any time.

Admission: Adult £4, Child £1.50, OAP £3.

By arrangement. P Tel. for details.

FYVIE CASTLE

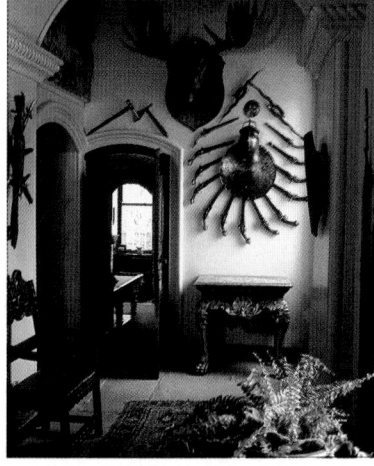

TURRIFF, ABERDEENSHIRE AB53 8JS

Owner: The National Trust for Scotland   *Contact:* The Property Manager

Tel: 01651 891266 **Fax:** 01651 891107

The south front of this magnificent building employs a plethora of crow-stepped gables, turrets, sculpted dormers and finials in the form of musicians, to create a marvellous façade. The five towers of the castle bear witness to the five families who have owned it. Fyvie Castle boasts the finest wheel stair in Scotland and there is a superb collection of arms and armour and paintings, including works by Batoni, Raeburn, Romney, Gainsborough, Opie and Hoppner.

Location: OS Ref. NJ763 393. Off A947, 8m SE of Turriff, and 25m N of Aberdeen.

Opening Times: Castle: 13 Apr - 31 May and 1 - 30 Sept: daily, 1.30 - 5.30pm; 1 Jun - 31 Aug: daily, 11am - 5.30pm; weekends in Oct: 1.30 - 5.30pm (last admission 4.45pm). Tearoom & Shop: open at 12.30pm when Castle opens at 1.30pm. Grounds: All year, daily, 9.30am - sunset.

Admission: Adult £6, Conc. £4.50, Family £16.50. Groups: Adult £4.80, Child/ School £1.

HADDO HOUSE

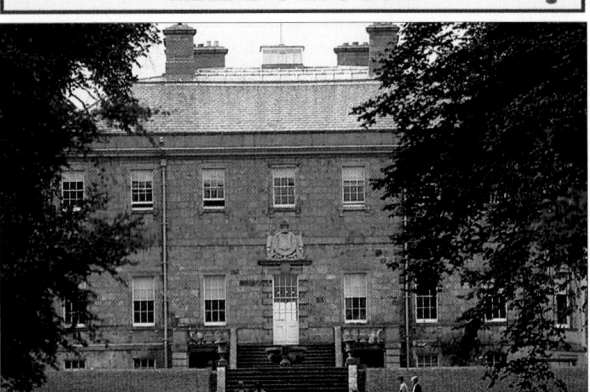

TARVES, ELLON, ABERDEENSHIRE AB41 0ER

Owner: The National Trust for Scotland *Contact:* Craig Ferguson

Tel: 01651 851440 **Fax:** 01651 851888

This appealing house was designed by William Adam in 1731 for William, 2nd Earl of Aberdeen. Much of the splendid interior is 'Adam Revival' carried out about 1880 for John, 7th Earl and 1st Marquess of Aberdeen and his Countess, Ishbel. It is arguably the most elegant house in the north east, a classic English-style stately home transplanted to Scotland. Features of the house include the Italianate sweeping twin staircases at the front of the house, the atmospheric library and the subtlety of the great curving corridor.

Location: OS Ref. NJ868 348. Off B999, 4m N of Pitmedden, 10m NW of Ellon.

Opening Times: House: 13 - 16 Apr & 1 May - 30 Sept: daily, 1.30 - 5.30pm; weekends in Oct: 1.30 - 5.30pm (last admission 4.45pm). Shop & Tearoom: same dates, 11am - 5.30pm. Shop also open weekends in Mar. & Apr, 11am - 5.30pm. Tearoom: open weekends in Mar & daily in Apr, 11am - 5.30pm. Garden: 1 Apr - 31 Oct: daily, 9.30am - 6pm; 1 Nov - 31 Mar: daily, 9.30am - 4pm. Country Park: All year, daily, 9.30am - sunset.

Admission: Adult £6, Conc. £4.50, Family £16.50. Groups: Adult £4.80, Child/School £1.

HUNTLY CASTLE

Tel: 01466 793191

Huntly

Owner: In the care of Historic Scotland **Contact:** The Steward

Known also as Strathbogie Castle, this glorious ruin stands in a beautiful setting on the banks of the River Deveron. Famed for its fine heraldic sculpture and inscribed stone friezes.

Location: OS Ref. NJ532 407. In Huntly on the A96. N side of the town.

Opening Times: 1 Apr - 30 Sept: daily, 9.30am - 6.30pm, last ticket 6pm. 1 Oct - 31 Mar: Mon - Sat, 9.30am - 4.30pm, Suns, 2 - 4.30pm, last ticket 4pm. Closed Thur pm & Fris in winter.

Admission: Adult £2.80, Child £1, Conc £2.

KILDRUMMY CASTLE

Tel: 01975 571331

Alford, Aberdeenshire

Owner: In the care of Historic Scotland **Contact:** The Steward

Though ruined, the best example in Scotland of a 13th century castle with a curtain wall, four round towers, hall and chapel of that date. The seat of the Earls of Mar, it was dismantled after the first Jacobite rising in 1715.

Location: OS Ref. NJ455 164. 10m W of Alford on the A97. 16m SSW of Huntley.

Opening Times: 1 Apr - 30 Sept: daily, 9.30am - 6.30pm, last ticket 6pm.

Admission: Adult £2, Child 75p, Conc. £1.50.

KILDRUMMY CASTLE GARDEN

Tel: 01975 571203 / 571277

Kildrummy, Aberdeenshire **Contact:** Alastair J Laing

Ancient quarry, shrub and alpine gardens renowned for their interest and variety. Water gardens below ruined castle.

Location: OS Ref. NJ455 164. On A97 off A944 10m SW of Alford. 16m SSW of Huntley.

Opening Times: Apr - Oct: daily, 10am - 5pm.

Admission: Adult £2, Child free.

LEITH HALL

Tel: 01464 831216 **Fax:** 01464 831594

Huntly, Aberdeenshire AB54 4NQ

Owner: The National Trust for Scotland **Contact:** The Property Manager

This mansion house is built around a courtyard and was the home of the Leith family for almost 400 years. With an enviable family record of military service over the centuries, the house contains a unique collection of military memorabilia displayed in an exhibition *'For Crown and Country'.* The graciously furnished rooms are a delight to wander through and present a fine impression of the lifestyle of the Leith family.

Location: OS Ref. NJ541 298. B9002, 1m W of Kennethmont, 7m S of Huntley.

Opening Times: House & tearoom: 13 - 16 Apr & 1 May - 30 Sept: daily, 1.30 - 5.30pm; weekends in Oct: 1.30 - 5.30pm (last admission 4.45pm). Garden & Grounds: All year, daily, 9.30am - sunset.

Admission: Adult £6, Conc. £4.50, Family £16.50. Groups: Adult £4.80, Child/School £1. Gardens & grounds only: Adult £2, Conc. £1.30, Family £6. Groups: Adult £1.60, Child/School £1.

Partially suitable. WC.

MONYMUSK WALLED GARDEN

Tel: 01467 651543

Home Farm, Monymusk, Aberdeen AB51 7HL

Owner/Contact: Mrs E Whyte

Mainly herbaceous plants in walled garden setting.

Location: OS Ref. NJ692 152. N side of B993, 1/2 m E of Monymusk village.

Opening Times: Nov - Mar: Mons, Weds, Fris & Sats, 10am - 3pm, Suns, 12 noon - 3pm. Apr - Oct: Mon - Sat, 10am - 5pm, Suns, 12 noon - 5pm.

Admission: Donations welcome.

PITMEDDEN GARDEN

Doug Westland.

ELLON, ABERDEENSHIRE AB41 0PD

Owner: The National Trust for Scotland *Contact:* The Property Manager

Tel: 01651 842352 **Fax:** 01651 843188

The centrepiece of this property is the Great Garden which was originally laid out in 1675 by Sir Alexander Seton, 1st Baronet of Pitmedden. The elaborate designs, inspired by the garden at the Palace of Holyroodhouse in Edinburgh, have been painstakingly recreated for the enjoyment of visitors. The 100 acre estate contains the very fine Museum of Farming Life, which presents a vivid picture of the lives and times of bygone days when the horse was the power in front of the plough and farm machinery was less complicated than it is today.

Location: OS Ref. NJ885 280. On A920 1m W of Pitmedden village and 14m N of Aberdeen.

Opening Times: Garden, Visitor Centre, museum & tearoom: 1 May - 30 Sept: daily, 10am - 5.30pm (last admission 5pm). Grounds: All year, daily.

Admission: Adult: £5, Conc. £4, Family £14. Groups: Adult £4, Child/School £1.

PLUSCARDEN ABBEY

Tel: 01343 890257 **Fax:** 01343 890258 **e-mail:** monks@pluscardenabbey.org

Nr Elgin, Moray IV30 8UA **Contact:** Father Giles

Valliscaulian, founded 1230.

Location: OS Ref. NJ142 576. On a minor road 6m SW of Elgin. Follow B9010 for first mile.

Opening Times: All year: 4.45am - 8.30pm. Shop open 8.30am - 5pm.

Admission: Free.

PROVOST SKENE'S HOUSE

45 GUEST ROW, OFF BROAD STREET, ABERDEEN AB10 1AS

Owner: *Aberdeen City Council*   **Contact:** *Christine Rew*

Tel: 01224 641086 **Fax:** 01224 632133

Built in the 16th century, Provost Skene's House is one of Aberdeen's few remaining examples of early burgh architecture. Splendid room settings include a suite of Georgian rooms, an Edwardian nursery, magnificent 17th century plaster ceilings and wood panelling. Costume gallery features changing displays of historic dress. The painted gallery houses the most important cycle of religious painting in North East Scotland.

Location: OS Ref. NJ943 064. Aberdeen city centre, off Broad Street.

Opening Times: All year: Mon - Sat, 10am - 5pm, Suns, 1 - 4pm (closed 25/26/31 Dec & 1/2 Jan).

Admission: Free.

ℹ️ No photography in house. 📷 🍵 Small functions. ♿ Not suitable. 🍽️
🎭 By arrangement. 🅿️ Nearby. Ⓜ️ 🐕 Guide dogs only. ❄️ (W)

ST MACHAR'S CATHEDRAL TRANSEPTS   **Tel:** 0131 668 8800

Old Aberdeen

Owner: In the care of Historic Scotland

The nave and towers of the Cathedral remain in use as a church, and the ruined transepts are in care. In the south transept is the fine altar tomb of Bishop Dunbar (1514 - 32).

Location: OS Ref. NJ939 088. In old Aberdeen. ½ m N of King's College.

Admission: Free.

SPYNIE PALACE   **Tel:** 01343 546358

Elgin

Owner: In the care of Historic Scotland   **Contact:** The Steward

Spynie Palace was the residence of the Bishops of Moray from the 14th century to 1686. The site is dominated by the massive tower built by Bishop David Stewart (1461-77) and affords spectacular views across Spynie Loch.

Location: OS Ref. NJ231 659. 2m N of Elgin off the A941.

Opening Times: 1 Apr - 30 Sept: daily, 9.30am - 6.30pm. 1 Oct - 31 Mar: Sats, 9.30am - 4.30pm, Suns, 2 - 4.30pm. Last ticket 30 mins before closing.

Admission: Adult £2, Child 75p, Conc. £1.50. Joint entry ticket with Elgin Cathedral: Adult £3.30, Child £1.20, Conc. £2.50.

TOLQUHON CASTLE   **Tel:** 01651 851286

Aberdeenshire

Owner: In the care of Historic Scotland   **Contact:** The Steward

Tolquhon was built for the Forbes family. The early 15th century tower was enlarged between 1584 and 1589 with a large mansion around the courtyard. Noted for its highly ornamented gatehouse and pleasance.

Location: OS Ref. NJ874 286. 15m N of Aberdeen on the A920. 6m N of Ellon.

Opening Times: 1 Apr - 30 Sept: daily, 9.30am - 6.30pm. 1 Oct - 31 Mar: Sats, 9.30am - 4.30pm, Suns, 2 - 4.30pm. Last ticket 30 mins before closing.

Admission: Adult £2, Child 75p, Conc. £1.50.

National Trust for Scotland.

Brodie Castle, Grampian Highlands.

Cawdor Castle

"This castle hath a pleasant seat; the air nimbly and sweetly recommends itself unto our gentle senses."

William Shakespeare

Cawdor Castle means so many different things to so many different people. For some it epitomises the world of the great 19th century writer Sir Walter Scott – a wonderfully romantic 14th century private fortress protecting its inhabitants from vengeful hostile neighbours and the unforgiving climate of the rugged Scottish Highlands. For others, Cawdor will for ever be linked with Shakespeare's *Macbeth*.

Above all, Cawdor Castle is an exciting and unusual building to visit – built on superstition, its massive, severe exterior belies an intimate interior that gives the visitor to Cawdor a welcoming and surprisingly personal and friendly tour of the Cawdor family home.

Calder and Cawdor are different spellings of the same name which means, roughly, the woodland stream. The foundations of the present castle are thought to date from around 1370, when the choice of site was decided through a mixture of tradition and superstition. A donkey is said to have led the way to a high, rocky position with water nearby. The fortified tower was then built around a living holly tree, a symbol of life and luck and, as some people believed, a protection against fiends, lightning and fairies. Whatever the reasons, the tree soon died on being deprived of light, but it remains standing in the vaulted ground floor Guard Room.

The family history of the Thanes of Cawdor over the last 600 years is, as one would imagine, a bloody and colourful story. A story of kidnappings, successful marriage alliances, courage and valour – something which has passed down to this century. Discounting minor honours, foreign and civil decorations, 12 men of the clan won a total of 24 awards for valour: six Military Crosses, 15 Distinguished Service Orders and three Victoria Crosses. The late Lord Cawdor (who died in 1993) was, like many of his ancestors, cast in the same mould – a rainbow of knowledge, anger, wit, courage and silence.

The interior of Cawdor has well-proportioned rooms, stunning stone fireplaces and striking décor. Much of this style is owed to the occupation by the 1st and 2nd Earls Cawdor of the castle in the 19th century. Following a devastating fire, the interior was redecorated and made more comfortable for modern living. Good furniture, family portraits and pictures abound at Cawdor and are cleverly mixed with modern works of art bought by the family. There is also a fine display of tapestries in the Tapestry Room and the Tower Sitting Room.

The gardens at Cawdor also have a family feel to them, where plants are chosen out of affection rather than affectation. The Flower Garden is a particularly lovely spot to visit between Spring and Summer. The Walled Garden has been restored with a Holly Maze and there is also a Paradise Garden, Knot Garden and Thistle Garden.

Cawdor will provide a wonderfully memorable highlight to a visit to the Scottish Highlands – and one to which the visitor is sure to want to return.

For further details about *Cawdor Castle* see entry in Scotland ➔ Highlands & Skye..

CAWDOR CASTLE
Nairn

This splendid romantic castle dating from the late 14th century was built as a private fortress by the Thanes of Cawdor, and remains the home of the Cawdor family to this day. The ancient medieval tower was built around the legendary holly tree.

Although the house has evolved over 600 years, later additions mainly of the 17th century were all built in the Scottish vernacular style with slated roofs over walls and crow-stepped gables of mellow local stone. This style gives Cawdor a strong sense of unity, and the massive, severe exterior belies an intimate interior that gives the place a surprisingly personal, friendly atmosphere.

Good furniture, fine portraits and pictures, interesting objects and outstanding tapestries are arranged to please the family rather than to echo fashion or impress. Memories of Shakespeare's *Macbeth* give Cawdor an elusive, evocative quality that delights visitors.

GARDENS
The flower garden also has a family feel to it, where plants are chosen out of affection rather than affectation. This is a lovely spot between spring and late summer. The walled garden has been restored with a holly maze, paradise garden, knot garden and thistle garden. The wild garden beside its stream leads into beautiful trails through a spectacular mature mixed woodland, through which paths are helpfully marked and colour-coded.

❖

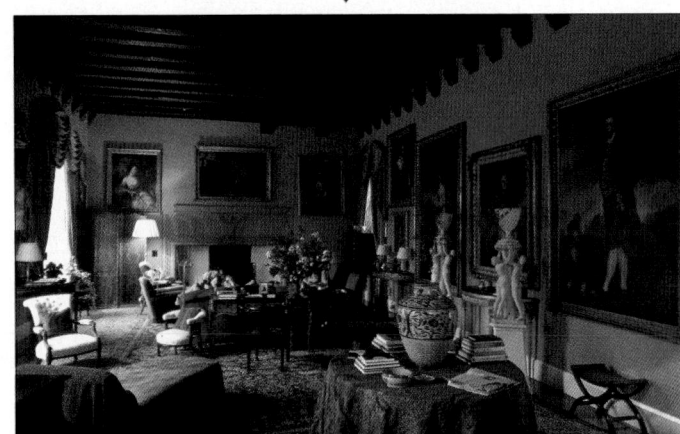

Owner: The Dowager Countess Cawdor

CONTACT

The Secretary
Cawdor Castle
Nairn
Scotland
IV12 5RD

Tel: 01667 404615

Fax: 01667 404674

e-mail: info@
cawdorcastle.com

LOCATION

OS Ref. NH850 500

From Edinburgh
A9, 3¹/₂ hrs,
Inverness 20 mins,
Nairn 10 mins.
Main road: A9, 14m.

Rail: Nairn Station
5m.

Bus: Inverness to Nairn
bus route 200 yds.

Taxi: Cawdor Taxis
01667 404315.

Air: Inverness Airport 5m.

CONFERENCE/FUNCTION		
ROOM	SIZE	MAX CAPACITY
Cawdor Hall		40

OPENING TIMES

SUMMER

1 May - 14 October
Daily: 10am - 5.30pm.

Last admission 5pm.

WINTER

15 October - 30 April
Closed.

ADMISSION

SUMMER
House & Garden
Adult £5.90
Child (5-15yrs)..........£3.00
OAP/Student...........£4.90
Family (2+5)...........£17.00

Groups (20+)
Adult £5.10
Child (5-15yrs)..........£2.60
OAP/Student...........£4.90

Garden only
Per person £3.00

SPECIAL EVENTS

• **JUN 2 - 3:**
Special Gardens Weekend:
Guided tours of gardens and
Cawdor Big Wood.

ℹ️ 9 hole golf course, putting green, golf clubs for hire, Conferences, whisky tasting, musical entertainments, specialised garden visits. No photography, video taping or tripods inside.

🏪 Gift, book and wool shops.

🍽 Lunches, sherry or champagne receptions.

♿ Visitors may alight at the entrance. WC. Only ground floor accessible.

☕ Licensed buttery, May-Oct, groups should book.

🅿 250 cars and 25 coaches. Two weeks' notice for group catering, coach drivers/couriers free.

£2.60 per child. Room notes, quiz and answer sheet can be provided. Ranger service and nature trails.

🐕 Guide dogs only.

DUNVEGAN CASTLE
Isle of Skye

Owner: John Macleod of
Macleod

CONTACT

The Administrator
Dunvegan Castle
Isle of Skye
Scotland
IV55 8WF

Tel: 01470 521206

Fax: 01470 521205

Seal Tel: 01470 521500

e-mail: info@
dunvegancastle.com

LOCATION

OS Ref. NG250 480

1m N of village. NW
corner of Skye.

From Inverness A82 to
Invermoriston, A887 to
Kyle of Lochalsh 82m.
From Fort William A82 to
Invergarry, A87 to Kyle of
Lochalsh 76m.

Kyle of Lochalsh to
Dunvegan 45m via
Skye Bridge (toll).

Ferry: To the Isle of Skye,
'roll-on, roll-off',
30 minute crossing.

Rail: Inverness to Kyle of
Lochalsh 3 - 4 trains per
day - '45m.

Bus: Portree 25m,
Kyle of Lochalsh 45m.

DUNVEGAN is unique. It is the only Great House in the Western Isles of Scotland to have retained its family and its roof. It is the oldest home in the whole of Scotland continuously inhabited by the same family – the Chiefs of the Clan Macleod. A Castle placed on a rock by the sea - the curtain wall is dated before 1200 AD – its superb location recalls the Norse Empire of the Vikings, the ancestors of the Chiefs.

Dunvegan's continuing importance as a custodian of the Clan spirit is epitomised by the famous Fairy Flag, whose origins are shrouded in mystery but whose ability to protect both Chief and Clan is unquestioned. To enter Dunvegan is to arrive at a place whose history combines with legend to make a living reality.

GARDENS

The gardens and grounds extend over some ten acres of woodland walks, peaceful formal lawns and a water garden dominated by two spectacular natural waterfalls. The temperate climate aids in producing a fine show of rhododendrons and azaleas, the chief glory of the garden in spring. One is always aware of the proximity of the sea and many garden walks finish at the Castle Jetty, from where traditional boats make regular trips to view the delightful Seal Colony.

❖

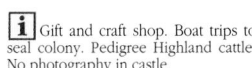 Gift and craft shop. Boat trips to seal colony. Pedigree Highland cattle. No photography in castle.

Visitors may alight at entrance. WC.

Licensed restaurant, (cap. 70) special rates for groups, menus upon request. Tel: 01470 521310. Open late peak season for evening meals.

By appointment in English or Gaelic at no extra charge. If requested owner may meet groups, tour time 45mins.

P 120 cars and 10 coaches. Do not attempt to take passengers to Castle Jetty (long walk). If possible please book. Seal boat trip dependent upon weather.

Welcome by arrangement. Guide available on request.

In grounds only, on lead.

4 self-catering units, 3 of which sleep 6 and 1 of which sleeps 7.

OPENING TIMES

SUMMER

20 March - 31 October
Daily: 10am - 5.30pm.
Last admission 5pm.

WINTER

November - March
Daily: 11am - 4pm.
Last admission 3.30pm.

Closed Christmas Day,
Boxing Day, New Year's
Day and 2 January.

ADMISSION

2000 prices

SUMMER

Castle & Gardens
Adult £5.50
Child* (5 -15yrs) £3.00
Conc.........................£4.80
Family (2+3) £15.00

Groups (10+)
...............................£5.00

Gardens only
Adult £3.80
Child* (5 -15yrs) £2.00

Seal Boats
Adult £4.00
Child* (5 -15yrs) £2.50

*Child under 5yrs Free.

WINTER

11am - 4pm.
No boat trips.

Highlands & Skye
Scotland

ATTADALE GARDENS

Tel: 01520 722217 **Fax:** 01520 722546

By Strathcarron, Ross-shire IV54 8YX   **e-mail:** cottages@attadale.com

Owner/Contact: Mr & Mrs Ewen Macpherson

The garden and woodland walks were planted by the Schroder family from 1890 onwards with species rhododendrons, azaleas and southern hemisphere plants made possible by the warm gulf stream. Outstanding water garden.

Location: OS Ref. NG920 400. On A890 between Strathcarron and South Strome. 12m N of A87.

Opening Times: 1 Apr - 31 Oct: Mon - Sat, 10am - 5.30pm.

Admission: Adult £2, Child £1. Coaches/guided tours by prior arrangement.

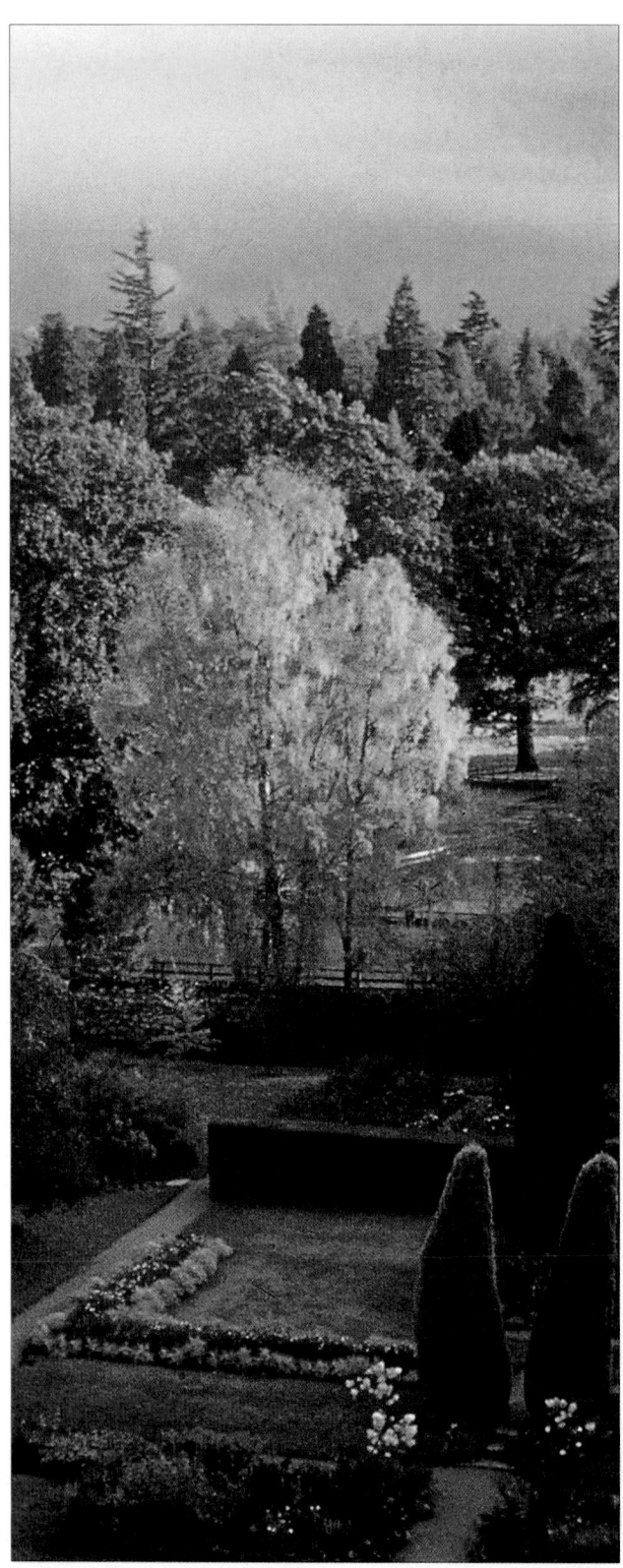

Cawdor Castle, Highlands & Skye.

ARMADALE CASTLE GARDENS & MUSEUM OF THE ISLES

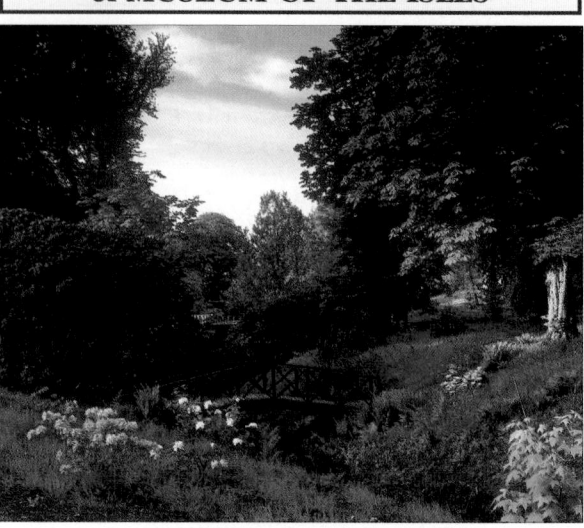

ARMADALE, SLEAT, ISLE OF SKYE IV45 8RS

Owner/Contact: Clan Donald Lands Trust

Tel: 01471 844305 **Fax:** 01471 844275

40 acre gardens with sea views to Knoydart across the Sound of Sleat. Sheltered and due to the warming effect of the gulf stream allowing exotic trees, shrubs and flowers to grow. Enjoy a complete experience to Armadale by visiting the Museum of the Isles within the gardens.

Location: OS Ref. NG630 020. 1m from Armadale - Mallaig ferry terminal and approximately 21m S of Skye Bridge.

Opening Times: Apr - Oct: 9.30am - 5.30pm.

Admission: Adult £3.90, Child/Conc. £2.85. Booked Groups (min 8): £2.50.

 ☐ ♦ T ♿ Licensed. ⚏Licensed. ☒By arrangement. **P**
☷ ⚐In grounds, on leads. ⊡Self-catering cottages. ⓦ

BALLINDALLOCH CASTLE ⛫

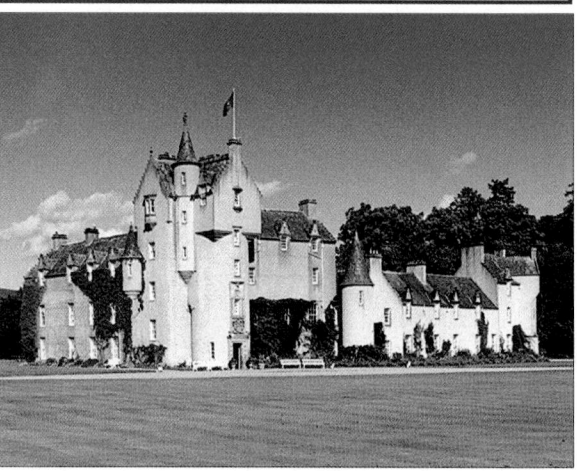

GRANTOWN-ON-SPEY, BANFFSHIRE AB37 9AX

Owner: Mr & Mrs Russell   *Contact: Mrs Clare Russell*

Tel: 01807 500206 **Fax:** 01807 500210 **e-mail:** enquiries@ballindallochcastle.co.uk

Ballindalloch is a much loved family home and one of the few castles lived in continuously by its original owners, the Macpherson-Grants, since 1546. Filled with family memorabilia and a magnificent collection of 17th century Spanish paintings, it is home to the famous breed of Aberdeen Angus cattle. Beautiful rock and rose garden, river walks.

Location: OS Ref. NJ178 366. 14m NE of Grantown-on-Spey on A95, 22m S of Elgin on A95.

Opening Times: 15 Apr - 30 Sept: 10.30am - 5.30pm. Coaches welcome all year by appointment.

Admission: House & Grounds: Adult £5.20, Child (5-16) £2.50, Conc. £4.50, Family (2+3) £13. Grounds only: Adult £2, Child £1. Groups: (20+) Adult £4.50, Child £2.

 ☐ ♿Ground floor & grounds. WC. ⊡ **P** ☊Audio-visual.
⚐In grounds, on leads in dog walking area. ⓦ

CAWDOR CASTLE

See page 498 for full page entry.

CROMARTY COURTHOUSE

Tel: 01381 600418 **Fax:** 01381 600408

Church Street, Cromarty IV11 8XA

Contact: David Alston

18th century town courthouse, visitor centre and museum.

Location: OS Ref. NH790 680. 25m N of Inverness.

Opening Times: Apr - Oct: 10am - 5pm. Nov, Dec & Mar: 12 noon - 4pm.

Admission: Adult £3, Conc. £2, Family (2+4) £8.

CULLODEN

Tel: 01463 790607 **Fax:** 01463 794294

Culloden Moor, Inverness IV1 2ED

Owner: The National Trust for Scotland

Contact: Ross Mackenzie

No name in Scottish history evokes more emotion than that of Culloden, the bleak moor which in 1746 saw the hopes of the young Prince Charles Edward Stuart crushed, and the end of the Jacobite Rising, the 'Forty-Five'. The Prince's forces, greatly outnumbered by those of the brutal Duke of Cumberland, nevertheless went into battle with a courage which has passed into legend.

Location: OS Ref. NH745 450. On B9006, 5m E of Inverness.

Opening Times: Site: All year: daily. Visitor Centre & Shop: 15 Jan - 31 Mar & 1 Nov - 31 Dec (closed 24 - 26 Dec): daily, 10am - 4pm. 1 Apr - 31 Oct: daily, 9am - 6pm (last admission 30 mins before closing). Restaurant & audio-visual show close 30 mins earlier.

Admission: Visitor Centre & Old Leanach Cottage: Adult £4, Conc. £3, Family £11. Groups: Adult £3.20, Child/School £1.

i Visitor centre.   🍴   ⏏ Audio-visual.   In dog walking area only. ❄ W

DOCHFOUR GARDENS

Tel: 01463 861218 **Fax:** 01463 861366

Dochgarroch, Inverness IV3 6JY

Owner: Dochfour Estate

Contact: Miss J Taylor

Victorian terraced garden near Inverness with panoramic views over Loch Dochfour. Magnificent specimen trees, naturalised daffodils, rhododendrons, water garden, yew topiary.

Location: OS Ref. NH620 610. 6m SW of Inverness on A82 to Fort William.

Opening Times: Gardens: Apr - Sept, Mon - Fri, 10am - 4pm. House not open.

Admission: Garden walk - £1.50.

THE DOUNE OF ROTHIEMURCHUS

Tel: 01479 812345

By Aviemore PH22 1QH

Owner: J P Grant of Rothiemurchus

Contact: Rothiemurchus Visitor Centre

The family home of the Grants of Rothiemurchus was nearly lost as a ruin and has been under an ambitious repair programme since 1975. This exciting project may be visited on selected Mondays throughout the year. Book with the Visitor Centre for a longer 2hr 'Highland Lady' tour which explores the haunts of Elizabeth Grant of Rothiemurchus, born 1797, author of *Memoirs of a Highland Lady*, who vividly described the Doune and its surroundings from the memories of her childhood.

Location: OS Ref. NH900 100. 2m S of Aviemore on E bank of Spey river.

Opening Times: House: selected Mons. Grounds: May - Aug: Mon, 10am - 12.30pm & 2 - 4.30pm, also 1st Mon in the month during winter.

Admission: House £5. Grounds only: £1. Booking essential.

i Visitor Centre.   🔘   ⫟ Obligatory.   P Limited.   In grounds, on leads.

DUNROBIN CASTLE

See below.

DUNVEGAN CASTLE

See page 499 for full page entry.

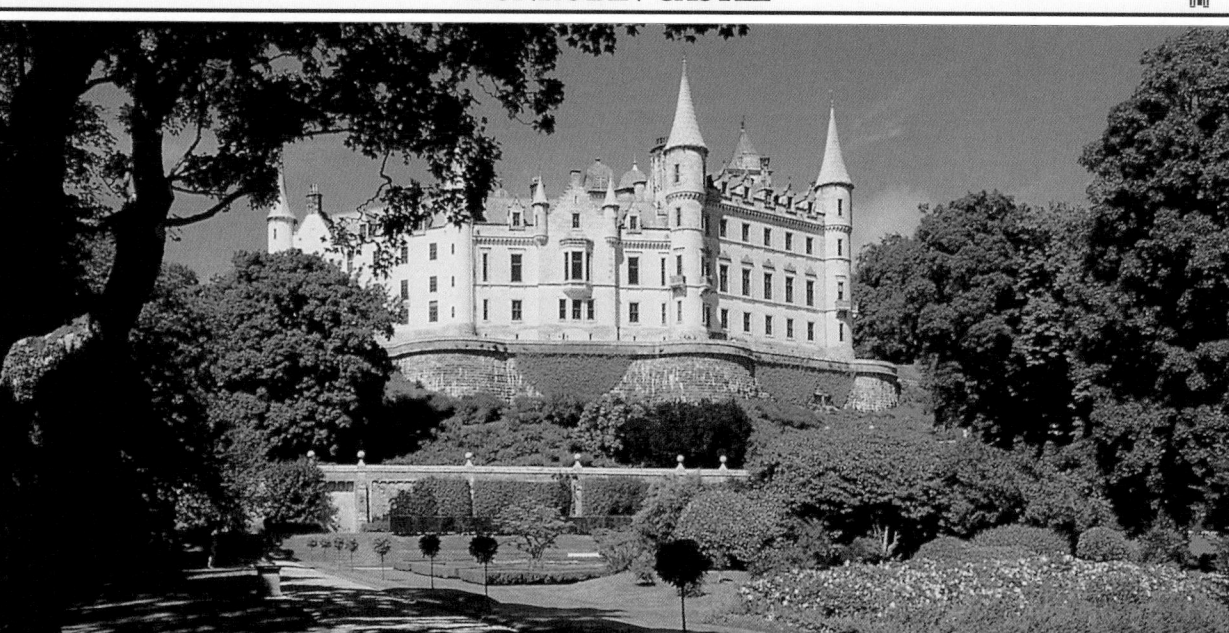

DUNROBIN CASTLE

GOLSPIE, SUTHERLAND KW10 6SF

Owner: *The Sutherland Trust*   **Contact:** *Keith Jones, Curator*

Tel: 01408 633177 **Fax:** 01408 634081 **e-mail:** dunrobin.est@btinternet.com

Dates from the 13th century with additions in the 17th, 18th and 19th centuries. Wonderful furniture, paintings, library, ceremonial robes and memorabilia. Victorian museum in grounds with a fascinating collection including Pictish stones. Set in fine woodlands overlooking the sea. Magnificent formal gardens, one of few remaining French/Scottish formal parterres. Falconry display.

Location: OS Ref. NC850 010. 50m N of Inverness on A9. 1m NE of Golspie.

Opening Times: 1 Apr - 31 May & 1 - 15 Oct: Mon - Sat, 10.30am - 4.30pm. Suns, 12 noon - 4.30pm. 1 Jun - 30 Sept: Mon - Sat, 10.30am - 5.30pm. Suns, 12 noon - 5.30pm (Jul & Aug: Suns, opens at 10.30am).

Admission: Adult £6, Child/Conc. £4.50. Groups: Adult £5.50, Child/Conc £4.50. Family (2+2) £17.

🔘   🍴 ⫟ By arrangement.

EILEAN DONAN CASTLE

Tel: 01599 555202   **Fax:** 01599 555262

Dornie, Kyle of Lochalsh, Wester IV40 8DX   **e-mail:** info@eileandonancastle.com

Contact: Rod Stenson – Castle Keeper

Location: OS Ref. NG880 260. On A87 8m E of Skye Bridge.

Opening Times: Mar & Nov: 10am - 3.30pm. Apr - Oct: 10am - 5.30pm.

Admission: Adult £3.95, Conc. £3.20.

FORT GEORGE

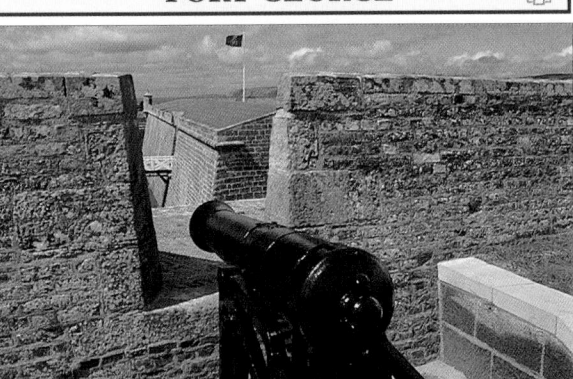

Historic Scotland.

ARDERSIER BY INVERNESS IV1 2TD

Owner: *In the care of Historic Scotland*   **Contact:** *Tommy Simpson*

Tel: 01667 462777   **Fax:** 01667 462698

Built following the Battle of Culloden to subdue the Highlands, Fort George never saw a shot fired in anger. One of the most outstanding artillery fortifications in Europe with reconstructed barrack room displays. The Queen's Own Highlanders' Museum.

Location: OS Ref. NH762 567. 11m NE of Inverness off the A96 by Ardersier.

Opening Times: Apr - Sept: daily, 9.30am - 6.30pm. Oct - Mar: Mon - Sat, 9.30am - 4.30pm; Suns, 2 - 4.30pm. Last ticket sold 45 mins before closing.

Admission: Adult £4.50, Child £1.50, Conc. £3.50. 10% discount for groups (10+).

[i] Picnic tables.   [📷]   [☎] Private evening hire.   [♿] Wheelchairs available. WCs.   [▣] In summer.   [P]   [▦] Free if pre-booked.   [🐕] In grounds, on leads.   [❄]

GLENFINNAN MONUMENT

Tel/Fax: 01397 722250

Inverness-shire PH37 4LT

Owner: The National Trust for Scotland   **Contact:** Mrs Lillias Grant

The monument, situated on the scenic road to the Isles, is set amid superb Highland scenery at the head of Loch Shiel. It was erected in 1815 in tribute to the clansmen who fought and died in the Jacobite cause. Prince Charles Edward Stuart's standard was raised near here in 1745. Despite its inspired beginnings, the campaign came to a grim conclusion on the Culloden battlefield in 1746.

Location: OS Ref. NM906 805. On A830, 18m W of Fort William, Lochaber.

Opening Times: Site: All year: daily. Monument & Visitor Centre: 1 Apr - 18 May & 1 Sept - 31 Oct: daily, 10am - 5pm. 19 May - 31 Aug: daily, 9.30am - 6pm. Glenfinnan Games: 18 August.

Admission: Adult £1.50, Conc. £1 (includes parking).

[i] Visitor centre.   [📷]   [♿] Grounds suitable. WC.   [▣]   [P]   [🐕] In grounds, on leads.   [❄]   [▣]   (WW)

HUGH MILLER'S COTTAGE

Tel: 01381 600245

Cromarty IV11 8XA

Owner: The National Trust for Scotland   **Contact:** Ms Frieda Gostwick

Furnished thatched cottage of c1698, birthplace of eminent geologist and writer Hugh Miller. Exhibition and video.

Location: OS Ref. NH790 680. Via Kessock Bridge & A832, in Cromarty, 22m NE of Inverness.

Opening Times: 1 May - 30 Sept: Mon - Sat, 11am - 1pm & 2 - 5pm. Suns, 2 - 5pm. Last entry 4.30pm.

Admission: Adult £2.50, Conc. £1.70, Family £7. Groups: Adult £2, Child/School £1.

[♿] Not suitable.   [P] Public parking at shore.   [🐕] Guide dogs only.   (WW)

INVEREWE GARDEN

POOLEWE, ROSS & CROMARTY IV22 2LQ

Owner: *The National Trust for Scotland*   **Contact:** *Keith Gordon*

Tel: 01445 781200   **Fax:** 01445 781497

Where in Scotland will you see the tallest Australian gum trees in Britain, sweetly scented Chinese rhododendrons, exotic trees from Chile and Blue Nile lilies from South Africa, all growing on a latitude more northerly than Moscow? The answer is Inverewe: you are in Wester Ross, you are also in a sheltered garden, blessed by the North Atlantic Drift. In a spectacular lochside setting among pinewoods, Osgood Mackenzie's Victorian dreams have produced a glorious 50 acre mecca for garden lovers.

Location: OS Ref. NG860 820. On A832, by Poolewe, 6m NE of Gairloch, Highland.

Opening Times: Garden: 15 Mar - 31 Oct: daily, 9.30am - 9pm. 1 Nov - 14 Mar: daily, 9.30am - 5pm. Visitor Centre & shop: 15 Mar - 31 Oct: daily, 9.30am - 5.30pm. Restaurant: 10am - 5pm. Guided garden walks: 15 Apr - 15 Sept: Mon - Fri at 1.30pm.

Admission: Adult £5, Conc. £4, Family £14. Groups: Adult £4, Child/School £1.

[i] Visitor centre.   [📷]   [♿] Grounds suitable. WC.   [🍴] Licensed.   [P] No shade for dogs.   [🐕] Guide dogs only.   [❄]   (WW)

URQUHART CASTLE

Tel: 01456 450551

Drumnadrochit, Loch Ness

Owner: In the care of Historic Scotland   **Contact:** The Steward

The remains of one of the largest castles in Scotland dominate a rocky promontory on Loch Ness. Most of the existing buildings date from the 16th century. New visitor centre opening autumn 2001.

Location: OS Ref. NH531 286. On Loch Ness, 1$\frac{1}{2}$ m S of Drumnadrochit on A82.

Opening Times: 1 Apr - 30 Sept: daily, 9.30am - 6.30pm, last ticket 5.45pm. 1 Oct - 31 Mar: daily, 9.30am - 4.30pm, last ticket 3.45pm.

Admission: Adult £3.80, Child £1.20, Conc. £2.80.

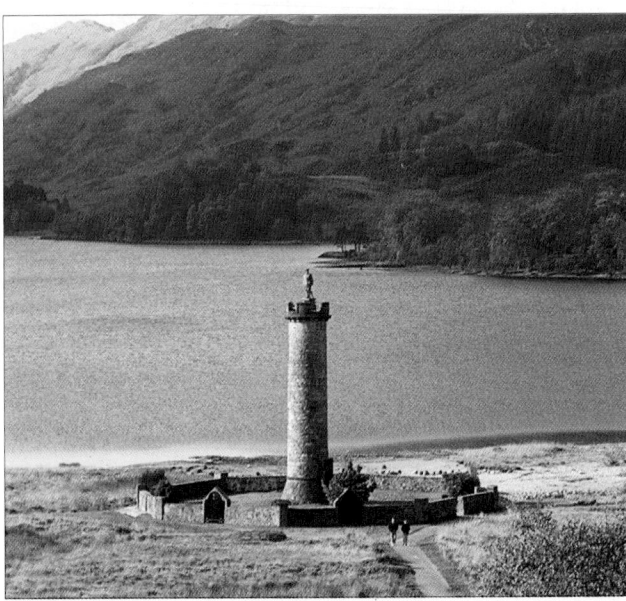

Glenfinnan Monument, Highlands & Skye.

Dunvegan Castle, Highlands & Skye.

BALFOUR CASTLE

Tel: 01856 711282 **Fax:** 01856 711283
e-mail: balfourcastle@btinternet.com

Shapinsay, Orkney Islands KW17 2DY

Owner/Contact: Mrs Lidderdale

Built in 1848.

Location: OS Ref. HY475 164 on Shapinsay Island, 3¹/₂ m NNE of Kirkwall.

Opening Times: Mid-May – mid-Sept: Weds, 2.30 - 5.30pm.

Admission: £15 including boat fare, guided tour, gardens & afternoon tea. Child £7.50.

BISHOP'S & EARL'S PALACES

Tel: 01856 875461

Kirkwall, Orkney

Owner: In the care of Historic Scotland   **Contact:** The Steward

The Bishop's Palace is a 12th century hall-house with a round tower built by Bishop Reid in 1541-48. The adjacent Earl's Palace built in 1607 has been described as the most mature and accomplished piece of Renaissance architecture left in Scotland.

Location: Bishop's Palace: OS Ref. HY447 108. Earl's Palace: OS Ref. HY448 108. In Kirkwall on A960.

Opening Times: 1 Apr - 30 Sept: daily, 9.30am - 6.30pm, last ticket 6pm.

Admission: Adult £2, Child 75p, Conc. £1.50. Joint entry ticket available for all the Orkney monuments: Adult £11, Child £3.50, Conc. £8.

BLACK HOUSE

Tel: 01851 710395

Arnol, Isle of Lewis

Owner: In the care of Historic Scotland   **Contact:** The Steward

A traditional Lewis thatched house, fully furnished, complete with attached barn, byre and stock-yard. A peat fire burns in the open hearth. New visitor centre open and restored 1920s croft house.

Location: OS Ref. NB320 500. In Arnol village, 11m NW of Stornoway on A858.

Opening Times: 1 Apr - 30 Sept: Mon - Sat, 9.30am - 6.30pm, last ticket 6pm. 1 Oct - 31 Mar: Mon - Thur & Sat, 9.30am - 4.30pm, last ticket 4pm.

Admission: Adult £2.80, Child £1, Conc. £2.

BROCH OF GURNESS

Tel: 01831 579478

Aikerness, Orkney

Owner: In the care of Historic Scotland   **Contact:** The Steward

Protected by three lines of ditch and rampart, the base of the broch is surrounded by a warren of Iron Age buildings.

Location: OS Ref. HY383 268. At Aikerness, about 14m NW of Kirkwall on A966.

Opening Times: 1 Apr - 30 Sept: daily, 9.30am - 6.30pm, last ticket 6pm.

Admission: Adult £2.80, Child £1, Conc. £2. Joint entry ticket available for all Orkney monuments: Adult £11, Child £3.50, Conc. £8.

CALANAIS STANDING STONES

Tel: 01851 621422

Calanais, Stornoway, Lewis, Outer Islands

Owner: In the care of Historic Scotland

A cross-shaped setting of standing stones, unique in Scotland.

Location: OS Ref. NB213 330. 12m W of Stornaway off A859.

Opening Times: Visitor Centre: please telephone for opening times and admission costs.

CARRICK HOUSE

Tel: 01857 622260

Carrick, Eday, Orkney KW17 2AB

Owner: Mr & Mrs Joy   **Contact:** Mrs Rosemary Joy

17th century house of 3 storeys, built by John Stewart, Lord Kinclaven Earl of Carrick younger brother of Patrick, 2nd Earl of Orkney in 1633.

Location: OS Ref. NT227 773. N of island of Eday on minor roads W of B9063 just W of the shore of Calf Sound. Regular ferry service.

Opening Times: Mid-Jun - mid-Sept: Sun afternoons, also guided tours of the house, 2pm onwards. Other times by arrangement.

Admission: Adult £2, Child £1.

JARLSHOF PREHISTORIC & NORSE SETTLEMENT

Tel: 01950 460112

Shetland

Owner: In the care of Historic Scotland   **Contact:** The Steward

Over 3 acres of remains spanning 3,000 years from the Stone Age. Oval-shaped Bronze Age houses, Iron Age broch and wheel houses. Viking long houses, medieval farmstead and 16th century laird's house.

Location: OS Ref. HY401 096. At Sumburgh Head, 22m S of Lerwick on the A970.

Opening Times: 1 Apr - 30 Sept: daily, 9.30am - 6.30pm. Last adm. ¹/₂ hr before closing.

Admission: Adult £2.80, Child £1, Conc. £2.

KIESSIMUL CASTLE

Tel: 01871 810449

Castlebray, Isle of Barra, Western Isles HF9 5XD

Owner/Contact: Ian Allen MacNeil of Barra

Home of the Chief of the MacNeil clan. Dating from the 13th century, the castle has been restored to its 17th century condition.

Location: OS Ref. NL670 990. Just S of Castlebay on Barra, by boat S of A888 in Castlebay.

Opening Times: Apr - Sept: Mon Wed & Sat, 2 - 5pm wind and tide permitting. Please telephone to check.

Admission: Boat and entrance to castle: Adult £3, Child 50p.

MAES HOWE

Tel: 01856 761606

Orkney

Owner: In the care of Historic Scotland   **Contact:** The Steward

This world-famous tomb was built in Neolithic times, before 2700 BC. The large mound covers a stone-built passage and a burial chamber with cells in the walls. Runic inscriptions tell of how it was plundered of its treasures by Vikings.

Location: OS Ref. NY318 128. 9m W of Kirkwall on the A965.

Opening Times: 1 Apr - 30 Sept: daily, 9.30am - 6.30pm. 1 Oct - 31 Mar: daily, 9.30am - 5pm except Thurs pm, Fris and Suns am.

Admission: Adult £2.80, Child £1, Conc. £2. Joint entry ticket available for all Orkney monuments: Adult £11, Child £3.50, Conc. £8. Admission, shop and refreshments at nearby Tormiston Mill.

RING OF BRODGAR STONE CIRCLE & HENGE

Tel: 0131 668 8800

Stromness, Orkney

Owner/Contact: In the care of Historic Scotland

A magnificent circle of upright stones with an enclosing ditch spanned by causeways. Of late Neolithic date.

Location: OS Ref. HY294 134. 5m NE of Stromness.

Opening Times: Any reasonable time.

Admission: Free.

ST MAGNUS CATHEDRAL

Tel: 01856 874894

Broad Street, Kirkwall, Orkney

Owner: Orkney Islands Council   **Contact:** Mr J Rousay

Location: OS Ref. HY449 108. Centre of Kirkwall.

Opening Times: 1 Apr - end Sept: Mon - Sat, 9am - 6pm, Suns, 2 - 6pm. 1 Oct - end Mar: Mon - Sat, 9am - 1pm & 2 - 5pm.

Admission: Free.

SKARA BRAE & SKAILL HOUSE

Historic Scotland.

SANDWICK, ORKNEY

Owner: Historic Scotland/Major M R S Macrae   *Contact:* The Steward

Tel: 01856 841815

Skara Brae is one of the best preserved groups of Stone Age houses in Western Europe. Built before the Pyramids, the houses contain stone furniture, hearths and drains. New visitor centre and replica house with joint admission with Skaill House – 17th century home of the Laird who excavated Skara Brae.

Location: OS6 HY231 188. 19m NW of Kirkwall on the B9056.

Opening Times: Apr - Sept: daily, 9.30am - 6.30pm. Oct - Mar: Mon - Sat, 9.30am - 4.30pm, Suns, 2 - 4.30pm.

Admission: Apr - Sept: Adult £4.50, Child £1.30, Conc. £3.30. Oct - Mar: Adult £3.50, Child £1.20, Conc. £2.60. 10% discount for groups (10+). Joint ticket with other Orkney sites available.

ℹ Visitor centre. 🖻 ♿Partially suitable. WCs. 🍴Licensed. 🅿
▦Free school visits when booked. 🦮Guide dogs only. ❄

TANKERNESS HOUSE

Tel: 01856 873191 **Fax:** 01856 871560

Broad Street, Kirkwall, Orkney

Owner: Orkney Islands Council   **Contact:** Bryce S Wilson

A fine vernacular 16th century town house contains Museum of Orkney.

Location: OS Ref. HY446 109. In Kirkwall opposite W end of cathedral.

Opening Times: Oct - Apr: Mon - Sat, 10.30am - 12.30pm & 1.30 - 5pm. May - Sept: Mon - Sat, 10.30am - 5pm, Suns, 2 - 5pm. Gardens always open.

Admission: Free.

WALES

W A L E S

W A L E S

Castell Coch, Wales

Wales

Castell Coch

"A castle of dreams and romance."

With the sharp conical roofs of its towers rising theatrically from the beech woods of Fforest Fawr, Castell Coch – the Red Castle – is an irresistibly striking landmark to those who chance to travel along one of the major roads north of Cardiff.

*C*astell Coch stands proudly on the hillside, a dazzling architectural tour de force of the High Victorian era, a fairytale, romanticised and dream-like castle with sumptuous Gothic fantasy interiors.

However the extravagant building we see today would not have been created had it not been for a highly successful Victorian partnership. The patron – the eccentric academic John Patrick Crichton Stuart (1847 – 1900) 3rd Marquis of Bute, the richest industrialist in the British Isles, and the 'pre-Raphaelite' architect – William Burges (1827 – 81). These men could hardly have been more different: Bute serious and reclusive; Burges raffish and clubbable, but since both were instinctive antiquarians, learned travellers and erudite aesthetes, their relationship blossomed.

Both men were deeply intoxicated with the spirit of Romanticism and fantasists of Victorian medievalism. Together, Bute and Burges were to produce two of the most remarkable expressions of this form to be seen anywhere in the British Isles – here at Castell Coch and at Cardiff Castle.

Viewing the extravagant Victorian mantle of Castell Coch today, it is easy to forget that it is built on the remains of a medieval castle. In Burges's report to Lord Bute of 1872, he wrote:

"There are two courses open with regard to the ruins; – one is to leave them as they are and the other to restore them so as to make a Country residence for your occasional occupation in the Summer."

Bute chose to rebuild and the work of construction at Castell Coch began in earnest in the summer of 1875, though regrettably Burges died in 1881 before the project was fully completed. It would, in fact, take a further 10 years before the assembled team of craftsmen were able to realise the dreams of Lord Bute. Working from detailed interior drawings prepared by Burges before his death, as well as a domed model of the decorative scheme in Lady Bute's bedroom, little of the intensity of Burges's plans have been lost. The interiors dazzle with rich ruby reds, blues and gold; the exterior has an almost Wagnerian splendour about it.

Today this fabulous masterpiece of Victorian medieval escapism is cared for on behalf of the State by Cadw: Welsh Historic Monuments. It is a beguiling jewel, and very much worth a visit.

For further details about *Castell Coch* see entry in South Wales Region.

510

North Wales

ABERCONWY HOUSE
Tel: 01492 592246 **Fax:** 01492 585153

Castle Street, Conwy LL32 8AY

Owner: The National Trust   **Contact:** The Custodian

Dating from the 14th century, this is the only medieval merchant's house in Conwy to have survived the turbulent history of this walled town for nearly six centuries. Furnished rooms and an audio-visual presentation show daily life from different periods in its history.

Location: OS Ref. SH781 775. At junction of Castle Street and High Street.

Opening Times: 31 Mar - 4 Nov: daily except Tues, 11am - 5pm. Last adm. 30mins before close.

Admission: Adult £2, Child £1, Family (2+2) £5. Pre-booked groups (15+) £1.80. National Trust members Free.

[i] No indoor photography.   [📷] Open all year.   [🎦] By arrangement.   [🎧]
[P] In town car parks only.   [🍴]   [♿] Guide dogs only.

BEAUMARIS CASTLE

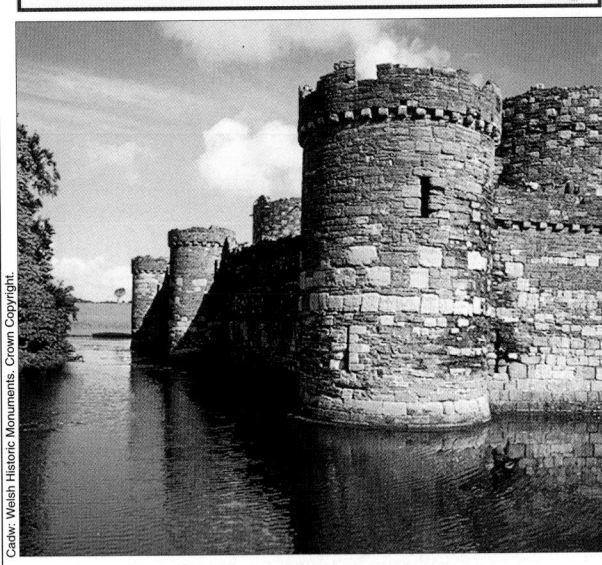

Cadw: Welsh Historic Monuments. Crown Copyright.

BEAUMARIS, ANGLESEY LL58 8AP
Owner: In the care of Cadw   *Contact: The Custodian*

Tel: 01248 810361

The most technically perfect medieval castle in Britain, standing midway between Caernarfon and Conwy, commanding the old ferry crossing to Anglesey. A World Heritage Listed Site.

Location: OS Ref. SH608 762. 5m NE of Menai Bridge (A5) by A545. 7m from Bangor.

Opening Times: 27 Mar - 26 May: 9.30am - 5pm. 27 May - 1 Oct: 9.30am - 6pm. 2 - 29 Oct: 9.30am - 5pm. 30 Oct - 31 Mar: Mon - Sat, 9.30am - 4pm, Suns, 11am - 4pm. Closed 24 - 26 Dec & 1 Jan.

Admission: Adult £2.20, Child/Conc. £1.70, Family £6.10.

    Guide dogs only.

Criccieth Castle, North Wales.

BODELWYDDAN CASTLE

BODELWYDDAN, DENBIGHSHIRE LL18 5YA
Owner: Denbighshire County Council   *Contact: Piers Norbury*

Tel: 01745 584060 **Fax:** 01745 584563

This magnificently restored Victorian mansion set in rolling parkland, displays extensive collections from the National Portrait Gallery, furniture from the Victoria and Albert Museum and John Gibson sculpture from the Royal Academy. There are exhibitions of Victorian Amusements and Inventions and a programme of temporary exhibitions takes place throughout the year.

Location: OS Ref. SH999 749. Follow signs off A55 expressway. 2m W of St Asaph, opposite Marble Church.

Opening Times: Apr - Oct: daily except Fri, 11am - 5pm. Nov - Mar: daily except Mon & Fri, 11am - 3.30pm. Last admission to site 1hr before closing. Note: minimum opening times - please telephone for further details.

Admission: Adult £4, Child (under 16yrs) £2.50 (under 5yrs Free), Conc. £3.50, Family (2+2) £10. Group: Adult £3.50, Child (under 16yrs) £2.15, Conc. £3. Season Ticket: Adult £12.60, Child/Student/Disabled £8.40, OAP/UB40 £10.50, Family (2+2) £27.30.

[📷] [🍴] [♿] Partially suitable. WCs. [🚻] [🎦] By arrangement. [P] [🍴]
 Guide dogs only. [❄]

BODNANT GARDEN

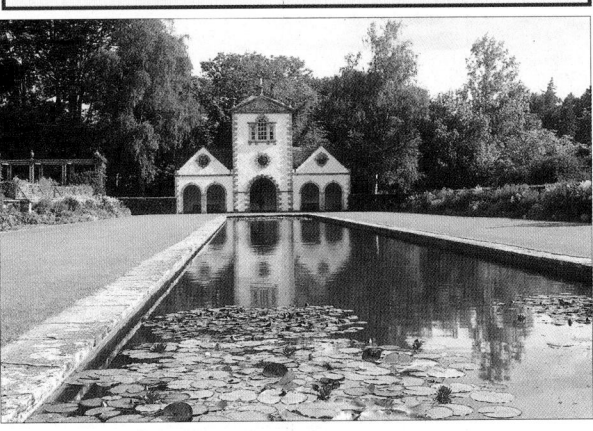

TAL-Y-CAFN, COLWYN BAY LL28 5RE
Owner: The National Trust   *Contact: General Manager & Head Gardener*

Tel: 01492 650460 **Fax:** 01492 650448

Bodnant Garden is one of the finest gardens in the country not only for its magnificent collections of rhododendrons, camellias and magnolias but also for its idyllic setting with extensive views of the River Conwy and the Snowdonia range. Visit in early Spring and be rewarded by the sight of masses of golden daffodils and other spring bulbs, as well as the beautiful blooms of the magnolias, camellias and flowering cherries. The spectacular rhododendrons and azaleas will delight from mid-April until late May, whilst the famous original Laburnum Arch is an overwhelming mass of yellow bloom from mid-May to mid-June. The herbaceous borders, roses, hydrangeas, clematis and water lilies flower from the middle of June until September. This 32-ha garden has many interesting features including the Lily Terrace, pergola, Canal Terrace, Pin Mill and the Dell Garden.

Location: OS Ref. SH801 723. 8 miles S of Llandudno and Colwyn Bay, off A470. Signposted from A55.

Opening Times: 17 Mar - 31 Oct: daily, 10am - 5pm.

Admission: Adult £5, Child £2.50. Groups (20+) £4.50. Refreshment Pavilion: Daily from 11am (Entrance fee does not have to be paid for the Pavilion).

  Partially suitable. WCs. [P] Guide dogs only.

BODRHYDDAN

RHUDDLAN, CLWYD LL18 5SB

Owner/Contact: Colonel The Lord Langford OBE DL

Tel: 01745 590414

The home of Lord Langford and his family, Bodrhyddan is basically a 17th century house with 19th century additions by the famous architect, William Eden Nesfield, although traces of an earlier building exist. The house has been in the hands of the same family since it was built over 500 years ago. There are notable pieces of armour, pictures, period furniture, a 3,000 year old mummy, a formal parterre, a woodland garden and attractive picnic areas. Bodrhyddan is a Grade I listing, making it one of few in Wales to remain in private hands.

Location: OS Ref. SJ045 788. On the A5151 midway between Dyserth and Rhuddlan, 4m SE of Rhyl.

Opening Times: Jun - Sept inclusive: Tues & Thurs, 2 - 5.30pm.

Admission: House & Gardens: Adult £4, Child £2. Gardens only: Adult £2, Child £1.

Receptions by special arrangement. Partially suitable. Obligatory.

BRYN BRAS CASTLE   **Tel/Fax:** 01286 870210

Llanrug, Caernarfon, Gwynedd LL55 4RE

Owner: Mr & Mrs N E Gray-Parry   **Contact:** Marita Gray-Parry

Built in the Neo-Romanesque style in 1830, on an earlier structure and probably designed by Thomas Hopper. Elegantly romantic family home with fine stained-glass, panelling, interesting ceilings and richly carved furniture. The castle stands in the beautiful Snowdonian range and the extensive gardens include herbaceous borders, walled knot garden, woodland walks, stream and pools, 1/4 m mountain walk with superb views of Snowdon, Anglesey and the sea. Picnic area.

Location: OS Ref. SH543 625. 1/2 m off A4086 at Llanrug, 4 1/2 m E of Caernarfon.

Opening Times: Only for groups by prior appointment.

Admission: By arrangement. No young children please.

Self-catering apartments for twos within castle.

CAERNARFON CASTLE

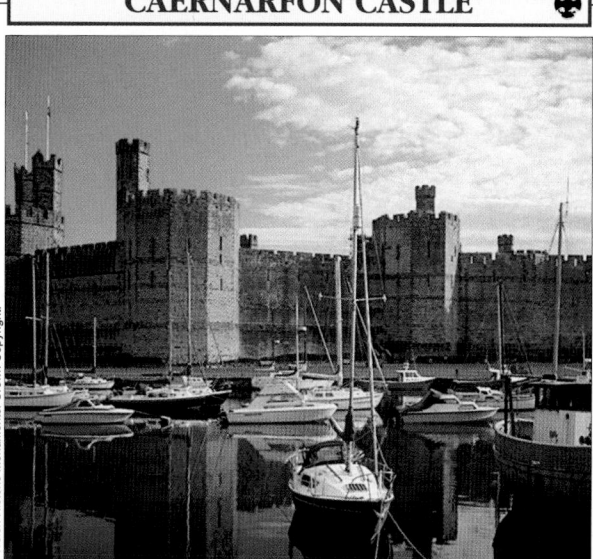

Cadw: Welsh Historic Monuments. Crown Copyright.

CASTLE DITCH, CAERNARFON LL55 2AY

Owner: In the care of Cadw   Contact: The Custodian

Tel: 01286 677617

The most famous, and perhaps the most impressive castle in Wales. Taking nearly 50 years to build, it proved the costliest of Edward I's castles. A World Heritage Listed Site.

Location: OS Ref. SH477 626. In Caernarfon, just W of town centre.

Opening Times: 27 Mar - 26 May: 9.30am - 5pm. 27 May - 1 Oct: 9.30am - 6pm. 2 - 29 Oct: 9.30am - 5pm. 30 Oct - 31 Mar: Mon - Sat, 9.30am - 4pm, Suns, 11am - 4pm. Closed 24 - 26 Dec & 1 Jan.

Admission: Adult £4.20, Child/Conc. £3.20, Family £11.60.

  Guide dogs only.

CHIRK CASTLE

National Trust Photographic Library; Matthew Antrobus.

CHIRK LL14 5AF

Owner: The National Trust   Contact: The Property Manager

Tel: 01691 777701   **Fax:** 01691 774706

700 year old Chirk Castle, a magnificent marcher fortress, commands fine views over the surrounding countryside. Rectangular with a massive drum tower at each corner, the castle has beautiful formal gardens with clipped yews, roses and a variety of flowering shrubs. Voted best National Trust garden in 1999. The dramatic dungeon is a reminder of the castle's turbulent history, whilst later occupants have left elegant state rooms, furniture, tapestries and portraits. The castle was sold for five thousand pounds to Sir Thomas Myddelton in 1595, and his descendants continue to live in part of the castle today.

Location: OS Ref. SJ269 380. 8m S of Wrexham off A483, 2m from Chirk village.

Opening Times: 28 Mar - 28 Oct: daily (except Mons & Tues) & BH Mons. Castle: Mar - Sept: 12 noon - 5pm. Oct: 12 noon - 4pm. Last admission 1/2 hr before close. Garden: Mar - Sept: 11am - 6pm. Oct: 11am - 5pm. Last admission 1hr before closing.

Admission: Adult £5, Child £2.50, Family (2+3) £12.50. Pre-booked groups (15+) £4. Garden only: Adults £2.80, Child £1.40.

No indoor photography. Licensed. By arrangement. Guide dogs only.

North Wales

COCHWILLAN OLD HALL
Tel: 01248 355853

Talybont, Bangor, Gwynedd LL57 3AZ

Owner: R C H Douglas Pennant   **Contact:** Mrs G Lloyd

A fine example of medieval architecture with the present house dating from about 1450. It was probably built by William Gryffydd who fought for Henry VII at Bosworth. Once owned in the 17th century by John Williams who became Archbishop of York. The house was restored from a barn in 1971.

Location: OS Ref. SH606 695. 3¹/₂ m SE of Bangor. 1m SE of Talybont off A55.

Opening Times: By appointment.

Admission: Please telephone for details.

CONWY CASTLE

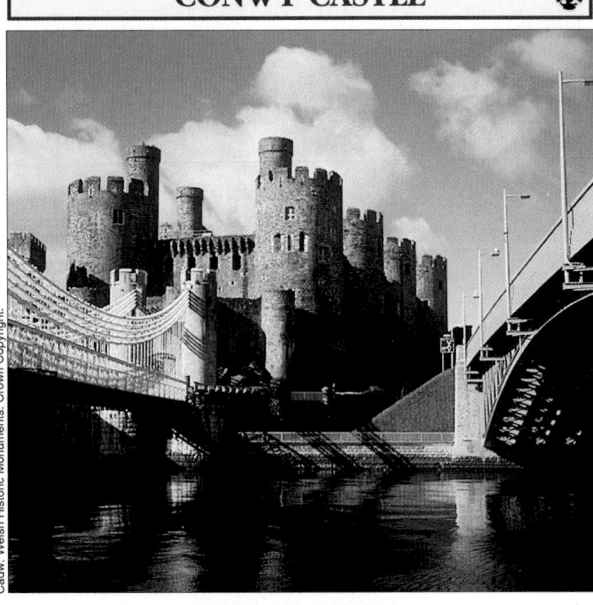

CONWY LL32 8AY
Owner: In the care of Cadw   Contact: The Custodian

Tel: 01492 592358

Taken together the castle and town walls are the most impressive of the fortresses built by Edward I, and remain the finest and most impressive in Britain. A World Heritage Listed Site.

Location: OS Ref. SH783 774. Conwy by A55 or B5106.

Opening Times: 27 Mar - 26 May: 9.30am - 5pm. 27 May - 1 Oct: 9.30am - 6pm. 2 - 29 Oct: 9.30am - 5pm. 30 Oct - 31 Mar: Mon - Sat, 9.30am - 4pm, Suns, 11am - 4pm. Closed 24 - 26 Dec & 1 Jan.

Admission: Adult £3.50, Child/OAP £2.50, Family £9.50.

 By arrangement. P Guide dogs only.

CRICCIETH CASTLE
Tel: 01766 522227

Castle Street, Criccieth, Gwynedd LL52 0DP

Owner: In the care of Cadw   **Contact:** The Custodian

Overlooking Cardigan Bay, Criccieth Castle is the most striking of the fortresses built by the native Welsh Princes. Its inner defences dominated by a powerful twin-towered gatehouse.

Location: OS Ref. SH500 378. A497 to Criccieth from Porthmadog or Pwllheli.

Opening Times: 1 Apr - 26 May: 9.30am - 5pm. 27 May - 24 Sept: 9.30am - 6pm.

Admission: Adult £2.20, Child/Conc. £1.70, Family £6.10.

P Guide dogs only.

CYMER ABBEY
Tel: 01341 422854

Dolgellau, Gwynedd

Owner: In the care of Cadw   **Contact:** The Custodian

The modest little Abbey at Cymer, with its simple church, stands amid remote and beautiful countryside. Situated near the head of the Mawddach estuary.

Location: OS Ref. SH722 195. 2m NW of Dolgellau on A470.

Opening Times: Early Apr - end Oct: 9.30am - 6.30pm. End Oct - end Mar: 9.30am - 4pm. Closed 24 - 26 Dec & 1 Jan.

Admission: Adult £1.20, Conc. 70p, Family £3.10.

 Limited. Guide dogs only.

DENBIGH CASTLE
Tel: 01745 813385

Denbigh, Clwyd

Owner: In the care of Cadw   **Contact:** The Custodian

Crowning the summit of a prominent outcrop dominating the Vale of Clwyd, the principal feature of this spectacular site is the great gatehouse dating back to the 11th century. Some of the walls can still be walked by visitors.

Location: OS Ref. SJ052 658. Denbigh via A525 or B5382.

Opening Times: Early Apr - late Oct: Mon - Fri, 10am - 5.30pm. Sats & Suns, 9.30am - 5.30pm. Winter: open site.

Admission: Castle: Adult £2, Child/Conc. £1.50, Family £5.50.

P Guide dogs only.

DOLWYDDELAN CASTLE
Tel: 01690 750366

Blaenau Ffestiniog, Gwynedd

Owner: In the care of Cadw   **Contact:** The Custodian

Standing proudly on a ridge, this stern building remains remarkably intact and visitors cannot fail to be impressed with the great solitary square tower, built by Llewelyn the Great in the early 13th century.

Location: OS Ref. SH722 522. A470(T) Blaenau Ffestiniog to Betws-y-Coed, 1m W of Dolwyddelan.

Opening Times: Early Apr - late Oct: daily, 9.30am - 6.30pm. Late Oct - late Mar: Mon - Sat, 9.30am - 4pm, Suns, 11am - 4pm. Closed 24 - 26 Dec & 1 Jan.

Admission: Adult £2, Child/Conc. £1.50, Family £5.50.

P Guide dogs only.

ERDDIG

Nr WREXHAM LL13 0YT
Owner: The National Trust   Contact: Sally Smith

Tel: 01978 355314 **Fax:** 01978 313333 **Info Line:** 01978 315151

One of the most fascinating houses in Britain, not least because of the unusually close relationship that existed between the family of the house and their servants. The beautiful and evocative range of outbuildings includes kitchen, laundry, bakehouse, stables, sawmill, smithy and joiner's shop, while the stunning state rooms display most of their original 18th & 19th century furniture and furnishings, including some exquisite Chinese wallpaper. The large walled garden has been restored to its 18th century format design with Victorian parterre and yew walk, and also contains the National Ivy Collection. There is an extensive park with woodland walks.

Location: OS Ref. SJ326 482. 2m S of Wrexham.

Opening Times: 31 Mar - 4 Nov: daily except Thurs & Fris, open Good Fri. House: 12 noon - 5pm. Garden: 11am - 6pm (10am - 6pm during Jul & Aug). From 1 Oct: House: 12 noon - 4pm, Garden: 11am - 5pm. Last admission 1 hr before closing.

Admission: All-inclusive ticket: Adult £6, Child £3, Family (2+3) £15. Pre-booked group (15+) £5. Below stairs (including outbuildings & Garden): Adult £4, Child £2, Family (2+3) £10, Pre-booked groups (15+) £3.20. NT members Free.

Partially suitable. WCs. Licensed. AV presentation. P Guide dogs only.

FFERM

Tel/Fax: 01352 770217

Pontblyddyn, Mold, Flintshire

Owner/Contact: Dr M Jones-Mortimer

17th century farmhouse. Viewing is limited to 7 persons at any one time. Prior booking is recommended. No toilets or refreshments.

Location: OS Ref. SJ279 603. Access from A541 in Pontblyddyn, 3^1/$_2$ m SE of Mold.

Opening Times: 2nd Wed in every month, 2 - 5pm. Pre-booking is recommended.

Admission: £4.

GLANSEVERN HALL GARDENS

Tel: 01686 640200 **Fax:** 01686 640829

Berriew, Welshpool, Powys SY21 8AH

Owner: Mr G and Miss M Thomas   **Contact:** Mr & Mrs R N Thomas

A classic Greek revival house romantically positioned on banks of River Severn. Over 18 acres of mature gardens notable for variety of unusual tree species. Also much new planting. Lakeside and woodland walks, water and rock gardens, grotto, walled rose garden.

Location: OS Ref. SJ195 001. On A483, 5m S of Welshpool, 1m SE of Berriew.

Opening Times: May - Sept: Fris, Sats and BH Mons, 12 noon - 6pm. Groups by appointment on other days.

Admission: Adult £3, Child (under 16) Free.

  Grounds suitable. **P** In grounds, on leads.

GWYDIR CASTLE

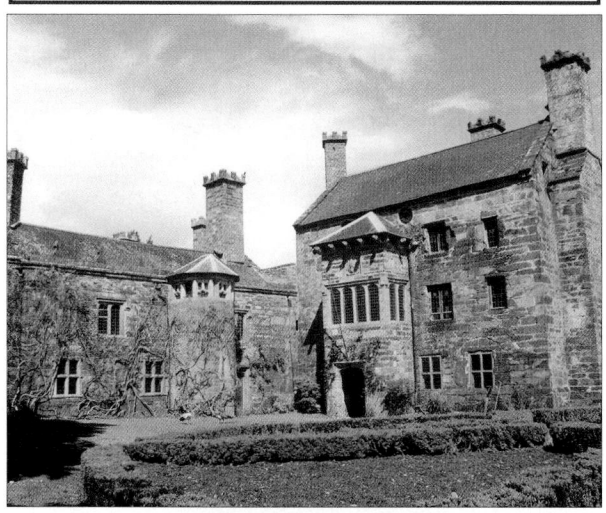

LLANRWST, GWYNEDD LL26 0PN

Owner/Contact: Mr & Mrs Welford

Tel/Fax: 01492 641687

Gwydir Castle is situated in the beautiful Conwy Valley and is set within a Grade I listed, 10 acre garden. Built by the illustrious Wynn family c1500, Gwydir is a fine example of a Tudor courtyard house, incorporating re-used medieval material from the dissolved Abbey of Maenan. Further additions date from c1600 and c1826. The important 1640s panelled Dining Room has now been reinstated, following its repatriation from the New York Metropolitan Museum.

Location: OS Ref. SH795 610. ^{1}/$_2$ m W of Llanrwst on A5106.

Opening Times: 1 Mar - 31 Oct: daily, 10am - 5pm. Limited openings at other times. Occasional weddings on Sats.

Admission: Adult £3, Child £1.50. Group discount 10%.

Partially suitable. By arrangement. By arrangement. **P** 2 doubles.

HARLECH CASTLE

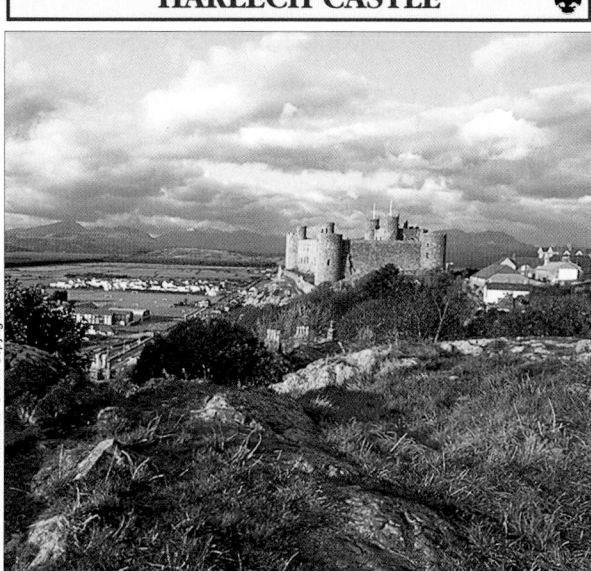

HARLECH LL46 2YH

Owner: In the care of Cadw   *Contact:* The Custodian

Tel: 01766 780552

Set on a towering rock above Tremadog Bay, this seemingly impregnable fortress is the most dramatically sited of all the castles of Edward I. A World Heritage Listed Site.

Location: OS Ref. SH581 312. Harlech, Gwynedd on A496 coast road.

Opening Times: 27 Mar - 26 May: 9.30 - 5pm. 27 May - 1 Oct: 9.30am - 6pm. 2 - 29 Oct: 9.30am - 5pm. 30 Oct - 31 Mar: Mon - Sat, 9.30am - 4pm, Suns, 11am - 4pm. Closed 24 - 26 Dec & 1 Jan.

Admission: Adult £3, Child/OAP £2, Family £8.

P Guide dogs only.

Cadw: Welsh Historic Monuments. Crown Copyright.

HARTSHEATH

Tel/Fax: 01352 770217

Pontblyddyn, Mold, Flintshire

Owner/Contact: Dr M Jones-Mortimer

18th and 19th century house set in parkland. Viewing is limited to 7 persons at any one time. Prior booking is recommended. No toilets or refreshments.

Location: OS Ref. SJ287 602. Access from A5104, 3^1/$_2$ m SE of Mold between Pontblyddyn and Penyffordd.

Opening Times: 1st, 3rd & 5th Wed in every month, 2 - 5pm.

Admission: £4.

ISCOYD PARK

Nr Whitchurch, Shropshire SY13 3AT

Owner/Contact: Mr P C Godsal

18th century Grade II* listed redbrick house in park.

Location: OS Ref. SJ504 421. 2m W of Whitchurch on A525.

Opening Times: By written appointment only.

GYRN CASTLE

Tel/Fax: 01745 853500

Llanasa, Holywell, Flintshire CH8 9BG

Owner/Contact: Sir Geoffrey Bates BT

Dating, in part, from 1700, castellated 1820. Large picture gallery, panelled entrance hall. Pleasant woodland walks and fantastic views to the River Mersey and the Lake District.

Location: OS Ref. SJ111 815. 26m W of Chester, off A55, 4^1/$_2$ m SE of Prestatyn.

Opening Times: All year by appointment.

Admission: £4. Discount for groups.

Grounds suitable. By arrangement. Obligatory. **P** Limited for coaches. On leads.

North Wales

PENRHYN CASTLE

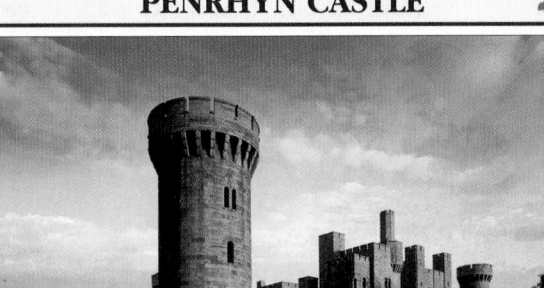

BANGOR LL57 4HN

Owner: *The National Trust*   **Contact:** *The Property Manager*

Tel: 01248 353084

This dramatic neo-Norman fantasy castle sits between Snowdonia and the Menai Strait. Built by Thomas Hopper between 1820 and 1845 for the wealthy Pennant family, who made their fortune from Jamaican sugar and Welsh slate. The castle is crammed with fascinating things such as a 1-ton slate bed made for Queen Victoria, elaborate carvings, mock-Norman furniture and an outstanding collection of paintings. With a countryside exhibition, industrial railway and railway model museums and a superb doll museum. Its grounds include parkland, an extensive exotic tree and shrub collection and a Victorian walled garden. New in 2001: Victorian kitchens fully restored and open to the public for the first time.

Location: OS Ref. SH602 720. 1m E of Bangor, at Llandygai on A5122.

Opening Times: 28 Mar - 2 Nov: daily except Tues. Castle: 12 noon - 5pm (Jul & Aug: 11am - 5pm). Grounds: 11am - 5pm (Jul & Aug: 10am - 5.30pm). Last audio tour 4pm. Last admission 4.30pm.

Admission: All inclusive ticket: Adult £6, Child £3, Family (2+2) £15. Pre-booked groups (15+) £5. Garden & Stableblock Exhibitions only: Adult £4, Child £2. Audio tour: 50p (including NT members). NT members Free.

Licensed.

PLAS MAWR

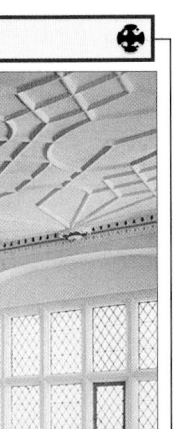

HIGH STREET, CONWY LL32 8EF

Owner: *In the care of Cadw*   **Contact:** *The Custodian*

Tel: 01492 580167

The best preserved Elizabethan town house in Britain, the house reflects the status of its builder Robert Wynn. A fascinating and unique place allowing visitors to sample the lives of the Tudor gentry and their servants, Plas Mawr is famous for the quality and quantity of its decorative plasterwork.

Location: OS Ref. SH779 777. Conwy by A55 or B5106.

Opening Times: 1 Apr - 26 May: 9.30am - 5pm. 27 May - 3 Sept: 9.30am - 6pm. 4 Sept - 1 Oct: 9.30am - 5pm. 2 - 29 Oct: 9.30am - 4pm. Closed on Mons except BHs.

Admission: Adult £4, Child/OAP £3, Family £11.

Limited.   Guide dogs only.

PLAS BRONDANW GARDENS

Tel: 01766 770228

Plas Brondanw, Llanfrothen, Gwynedd LL48 6SW

Italianate gardens with topiary.

Owner: Trustees of the Second Portmeirion Foundation

Location: OS Ref. SH618 423. 3m N of Penrhyndeudraeth off A4085, on Croesor Road.

Opening Times: All year: daily 9am - 5pm.

Admission: Adult £1.50, Child 25p, Group £1 (if pre-booked).

PLAS NEWYDD

LLANFAIRPWLL, ANGLESEY LL61 6DQ

Owner: *The National Trust*   **Contact:** *The Property Manager*

Tel: 01248 714795   **Fax:** 01248 713673   **e-mail:** ppnmsn@smtp.ntrust.org.uk

Set amidst breathtaking beautiful scenery and with spectacular views of Snowdonia. Fine spring garden and Australasian arboretum with an understorey of shrubs and wildflowers. Summer terrace, and , later, massed hydrangeas and Autumn colour. A woodland walk gives access to a marine walk on the Menai Strait. Rhododendron garden open April - early June only. Elegant 18th century house by James Wyatt, famous for its association with Rex Whistler whose largest painting is here. Military museum contains relics of 1st Marquess of Anglesey and Battle of Waterloo. A historic cruise, a boat trip on the Menai Strait operates from the property weather and tides permitting (additional charge). New for 2001 – 5 seater buggy to rhododendron garden and woodland walk.

Location: OS Ref. SH521 696. 2m S of Llanfairpwll and A5.

Opening Times: 31 Mar - 31 Oct: Sat - Wed. House: 12 noon - 5pm. Garden: 11am - 5.30pm. Last admission ½ hr before closing.

Admission: House & Garden: Adult £4.50, Child £2.25 (under 5s Free), Family (2+3) £11. Groups (15+) £3.70. Garden only: Adult £2.50, Child £1.25.

No indoor photography.

Partially suitable. WCs. Minibus from car park to house.

Licensed. Award winning.   By arrangement.   P

Tel for details.

Plas Mawr, North Wales.

PLAS YN RHIW

Tel/Fax: 01758 780219

Rhiw, Pwllheli LL53 8AB

Owner: The National Trust　　　　　　**Contact:** The Custodian

A small manor house, with garden and woodlands, overlooking the west shore of Porth Neigwl (Hell's Mouth Bay) on the Llyn Peninsula. The house is part medieval, with Tudor and Georgian additions, and the ornamental gardens have flowering trees and shrubs, divided by box hedges and grass paths, rising behind to the snowdrop wood.

Location: OS Ref. SH237 282. 12m SW of Pwllheli, 3m S of the B4413 to Aberdaron. No access for coaches.

Opening Times: 31 Mar - 14 May: daily except Tues & Weds. 16 May - 30 Sept: daily except Tues. 1 - 31 Oct: Sats & Suns only, 12 noon - 5pm.

Admission: Adult £3.20, Child £1.60, Family (2+3) £8. Guided tour for pre-booked groups additional £1.40 (including NT members). Gardens only: Adult £2, Child £1, Family (2+3) £5.

Partially suitable. WCs. By arrangement. Limited. Guide dogs only.

PORTMEIRION

Tel: 01766 770000　**Fax:** 01766 771331

Portmeirion, Gwynedd LL48 6ET

e-mail: info@portmeirion-village.com

Owner: The Portmeirion Foundation　　　　**Contact:** Mr R Llywelyn

Portmeirion was built by Clough Williams-Ellis as an 'unashamedly romantic' village resort. All the houses form part of the hotel with rooms and suites within comfortable walking distance from the main building on the quayside. The curvilinear dining room overlooking the estuary serves fresh local produce in elegant surroundings.

Location: OS Ref. SH590 371. Off A487 at Minffordd between Penrhyndeudraeth and Porthmadog.

Opening Times: All year (except Christmas Day): daily, 9.30am - 5.30pm.

Admission: Adult £5, Child £2.50, OAP £4, Family (2+2) £12.50.

Conference facilities. Partially suitable. Licensed. 40 double. Ensuite.

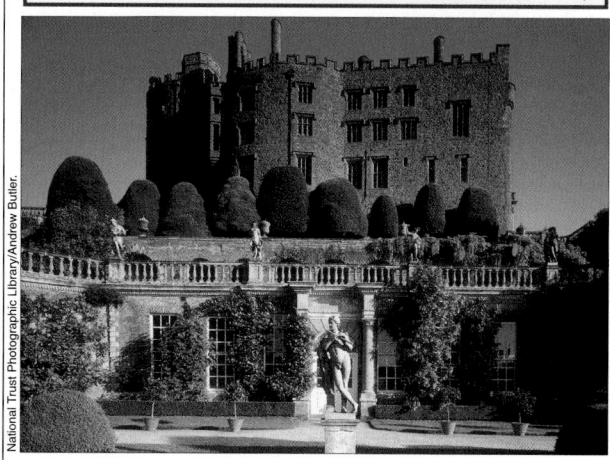
Nr WELSHPOOL SY21 8RF

Owner: The National Trust　*Contact: Amanda Whitmore*

Tel: 01938 554338/551920　**Fax:** 01938 554336　**e-mail:** gpcajw@smtp.ntrust.org.uk

The world-famous garden, overhung with enormous clipped yew trees, shelters rare and tender plants in colourful herbaceous borders. Laid out under the influence of Italian and French styles, the garden retains its original lead statues and, an orangery on the terraces. Perched on a rock above the garden terraces, the medieval castle contains one of the finest collections of paintings and furniture in Wales.

Location: OS Ref. SJ195 001. 1m W of Welshpool, 1m SE of Berriew, car access on A483.

Opening Times: Castle & Museum: 31 Mar - 4 Nov: daily except Mons & Tues (Jul & Aug: daily except Mons), but open BH Mons, 1 - 5pm. Garden: as Castle, 11am - 6pm. Shop & Tearoom: Also open 9 Nov - 16 Dec, Fri - Sun, 11am - 4pm.

Admission: All inclusive: Adult £7.50, Child £3.75, Family £18.75. Groups: (15+ booked): £6.50. Garden only: Adult £5, Child £2.50, Family £12.50. Groups (15+ booked): £4. No groups rates on Suns or BH Mons. NT members & under 5s Free.

No indoor photography. Partially suitable. Licensed. By arrangement. Limited for coaches. Guide dogs only.

RHUDDLAN CASTLE

Tel: 01745 590777

Castle Gate, Castle Street, Rhuddlan LL18 5AD

Owner: In the care of Cadw　　　　　　**Contact:** The Custodian

Guarding the ancient ford of the River Clwyd, Rhuddlan was the strongest of Edward I's castles in North-East Wales. Linked to the sea by an astonishing deep water channel nearly 3 miles long, it still proclaims the innovative genius of its architect.

Location: OS Ref. SJ025 779. SW end of Rhuddlan via A525 or A547.

Opening Times: Apr - Sept: daily, 10am - 5pm.

Admission: Adult £2, Child/OAP £1.50, Family £5.50.

Guide dogs only.

RUG CHAPEL & LLANGAR CHURCH

Tel: 01490 412025

c/o Coronation Cottage, Rug, Corwen LL21 9BT

Owner: In the care of Cadw　　　　　　**Contact:** The Custodian

Prettily set in a wooded landscape, Rug Chapel's exterior gives little hint of the wonders within. Nearby the attractive medieval Llangar Church still retains its charming early Georgian furnishings.

Location: Rug Chapel: OS Ref. SJ065 439. Off A494, 1m N of Corwen. Llangar Church: OS Ref. SJ064 423. Off B4401, 1m S of Corwen (obtain key at Rug).

Opening Times: Rug Chapel: 21 Apr - 24 Sept:10am - 2pm & 3 - 5pm. Closed Mons & Tues except BHs. Llangar Church: Interior access between 2 - 3pm, Apr - Sept through the Custodian at Rug Chapel. Both sites closed in winter.

Admission: Adult £2, Child/Conc. £1.50, Family £5.50.

By arrangement. Guide dogs only.

Wales Tourist Board.

Rhuddlan Castle, North Wales.

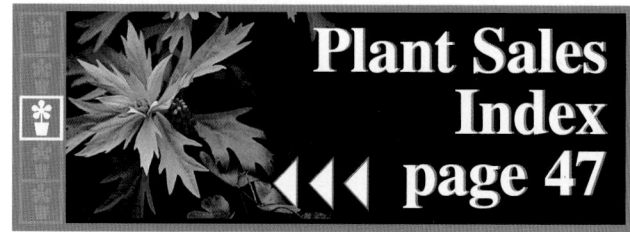

ST ASAPH CATHEDRAL
Tel: 01745 583597

St Asaph, Denbighshire LL17 0RL

Contact: The Dean

Britain's smallest ancient cathedral founded in 560AD by Kentigern, a religious community enclosed in a 'llan', hence Llanelwy. Present building dates from 13th century. Post reformation period, close association with the translators of the Welsh Prayer Book and Bible. A copy of the William Morgan Bible of 1588 can be seen. The Translators' Memorial, erected in 1888, stands outside. Within, a 17th century Spanish Madonna in ivory, stained glass, an exhibit of literary treasures, the only recumbent effigy, from 1268 - 93, an iron chest (1738) and four painted angels in the choir roof are just some of the things of interest. Housing an original Hill organ and home to the International North Wales Music Festival yearly, in September.

Location: OS Ref. SJ039 743. In St Asaph, S of A55.

Opening Times: Summer: 7.30am - 6pm. Winter: 7.30am - dusk.
Sun services: 8am, 11am, 3.30pm.

  Ground floor suitable. Guide dogs only.

TOWER
Tel: 01352 700220

Nercwys, Mold, Flintshire CH7 4EN

Owner/Contact: Wendy Wynne-Eyton

This Grade I listed building is steeped in Welsh history and bears witness to the continuous warfare of the time. A fascinating place to visit or for overnight stays.

Location: OS Ref. SJ240 620. 1m S of Mold.

Opening Times: Summer: BHs plus most of May. Please telephone for exact dates and times. Groups welcome at other times by appointment.

Admission: Adult £3, Child £2.

TREWERN HALL
Tel: 01938 570657

Trewern, Welshpool, Powys SY21 8DT

Owner: Chapman Family   **Contact:** Mr John Chapman/Mrs Edna Chapman

Trewern Hall is a Grade II* listed building standing in the Severn Valley. It has been described as 'one of the most handsome timber-framed houses surviving in the area'. The porch contains a beam inscribed RF1610, though it seems likely that parts of the house are earlier. The property has been in the ownership of the Chapman family since 1918.

Location: OS Ref. SJ269 113. Off A458 Welshpool - Shrewsbury Road, 4m from Welshpool.

Opening Times: Last week in Apr. May: Mon - Fri, 2 - 5pm.

Admission: Adult £2, Child/Conc. £1. (2000 prices).

Not suitable. No parking.

VALLE CRUCIS ABBEY
Tel: 01978 860326

Llangollen, Clwyd

Owner: In the care of Cadw

Contact: The Custodian

Set in a beautiful valley location, Valle Crucis Abbey is the best preserved medieval monastery in North Wales, enhanced by the only surviving monastic fish pond in Wales.

Location: OS Ref. SJ205 442. B5103 from A5, 2m NW of Llangollen, or A542 from Ruthin.

Opening Times: 21 Apr - 24 Sept: 10am - 5pm. Winter: open site.

Admission: Adult £2, Child/Conc. £1.50. Family £5.50.

  Guide dogs only.

WERN ISAF
Tel: 01248 680437

Penmaen Park, Llanfairfechan LL33 0RN

Owner/Contact: Mrs P J Phillips

This Arts and Crafts house was built in 1900 by the architect H L North as his family home and it contains much of the original furniture and William Morris fabrics. It is situated in a woodland garden and is at its best in the Spring. It has extensive views over the Menai Straits and Conwy Bay. One of the most exceptional houses of its date and style in Wales.

Location: OS Ref. SH685 752.

Opening Times: 3 - 30 Mar: daily except Mons, 12 noon - 4pm. Please telephone for details.

Admission: £1

Website Index page 39

Powis Castle & Garden, North Wales.

South Wales

ABERDULAIS FALLS

Tel: 01639 636674

Aberdulais, Vale of Neath SA10 8EU

Owner: The National Trust **Contact:** The Property Warden

For over 300 years this famous waterfall has provided the energy to drive the wheels of industry, from the first manufacture of copper in 1584 to present day remains of the tinplate works. It has also been visited by famous artists such as J M W Turner in 1796. The site today houses a unique hydro-electrical scheme which has been developed to harness the waters of the Dulais river.

Location: OS Ref. SS772 995. On A4109, 3m NE of Neath. 4m from M4/J43, then A465.

Opening Times: Mar: Sats & Suns only, 11am - 4pm. 1 Apr - 28 Oct: Mon - Fri, 10am - 5pm, Sats, Suns & BHs 11am - 6pm. Shop: as property. 2 Nov - 23 Dec: Fri - Sun, 11am - 4pm (closed 2pm on 23 Dec).

Admission: Adult £3, Child £1.50, Family £7.40. Groups (15+): Adult £2.40, Child £1.20. National Trust members Free.

🔲 🖝Light refreshments (summer only) 🅿Limited. 🔳

ABERGLASNEY GARDENS

Tel/Fax: 01558 668998

Llangathen, Carmarthenshire SA32 8QH **e-mail:** info@aberglasney.org.uk

Contact: Booking Department

In a sheltered glade of the beautiful Towy Valley stands Aberglasney and its gardens. What sets this property apart from others are the extraordinary, enigmatic structures within the gardens. The restoration project has already restored the structures and will bring both the house and gardens back to their former glory.

Location: OS Ref. SN581 221. 4m W of Llandeilo, 10m E of Carmarthen.

Opening Times: 1 Apr - 31 Oct: daily, 10am - 6pm. 1 Nov - 31 Mar: please telephone for opening times.

Admission: Adult £3.95, Child £1.95, OAP £3.45. Booked groups (10+): Adult £3.45, Child £1.45, OAP £2.95.

🔲 🚻 ♿Partially suitable. WC. 🖝Licensed. 🎟By arrangement. 🅿Limited for coaches. 🔳 🐕Guide dogs only. ❄ Ⓦ

BLAENAVON IRONWORKS

Tel: 01495 792615

Winter Bookings: 01633 648082

Nr Brecon Beacons National Park, Blaenavon, Gwent

Owner: In the care of Cadw **Contact:** The Custodian

The famous ironworks at Blaenavon were a milestone in the history of the Industrial Revolution. Visitors can view much of the ongoing conservation work as well as 'Stack Square' - a rare survival of housing built for pioneer ironworkers.

Location: OS Ref. SO248 092. Via A4043 follow signs to Big Pit Mining Museum and Blaenavon Ironworks. Abergavenny 8m. Pontypool 8m. From carpark, cross road, then path to entrance gate.

Opening Times: Easter - end Oct: 9.30am - 4.30pm. For opening times outside this period call the above number or 029 2050 0200.

Admission: Adult £1.50, Child/Conc. £1, Family £4.

♿Partially suitable. 🎟By arrangement. 🅿 🐕Guide dogs only. Ⓦ

CAE HIR GARDENS

Tel: 01570 470839

Cae Hir, Cribyn, Lampeter, Cardiganshire SA48 7NG

Owner/Contact: Mr W Akkermans

This transformed 19th century smallholding offers a succession of pleasant surprises and shows a quite different approach to gardening.

Location: OS Ref. SN521 520. W on A482 from Lampeter, after 5m turn S on B4337. Cae Hir is 2m on left.

Opening Times: Daily, excluding Mons (open BH Mons), 1 - 6pm.

Admission: Adult £2.50, Child 50p, OAP £2. Groups: (20+) £2.

CAERLEON ROMAN BATHS & AMPHITHEATRE

Tel: 01633 422518

High Street, Caerleon NP6 1AE

Owner: In the care of Cadw **Contact:** The Custodian

Caerleon is the most varied and fascinating Roman site in Britain – incorporating fortress and baths, well-preserved amphitheatre and a row of barrack blocks, the only examples currently visible in Europe.

Location: OS Ref. ST340 905. 4m ENE of Newport by B4596 to Caerleon, M4/J25.

Opening Times: 27 Mar - 29 Oct: 9.30am - 5pm. 30 Oct - 31 Mar: Mon - Sat, 9.30am - 5pm, Suns, 1 - 5pm. Closed 24 - 26 Dec & 1 Jan.

Admission: Adult £2, Child/Conc. £1.50, Family £5.50.

♿ 🅿 🐕Guide dogs only. ❄ Ⓦ

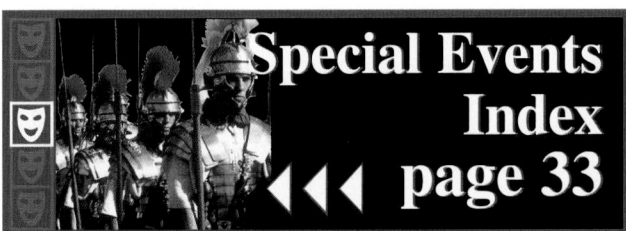

Special Events Index ◀◀◀ page 33

CAERPHILLY CASTLE

Cadw: Welsh Historic Monuments. Crown Copyright.

CAERPHILLY CF8 1JL

Owner: *In the care of Cadw* **Contact:** *The Custodian*

Tel: 029 2088 3143

Often threatened, never taken, this vastly impressive castle is much the biggest in Wales. 'Red Gilbert' de Clare, Anglo-Norman Lord of Glamorgan, flooded a valley to create the 30 acre lake, setting his fortress on 3 artificial islands. Famous for its leaning tower, its fortifications are scarcely rivalled in Europe.

Location: OS Ref. ST156 871. Centre of Caerphilly, A468 from Newport, A470, A469 from Cardiff.

Opening Times: 27 Mar - 26 May: 9.30am - 5pm. 27 May - 1 Oct: 9.30am - 6pm. 2 - 29 Oct: 9.30am - 5pm. 30 Oct - 31 Mar: Mon - Sat, 9.30am - 4pm, Suns, 11am - 4pm. Closed 24 - 26 Dec & 1 Jan.

Admission: Adult £2.50, Child/Conc. £2, Family £7.

🔲 🎧 🅿Limited. 🐕Guide dogs only. 🔔 ❄ Ⓦ

CARDIFF CASTLE

Tel: 029 2087 8100 **Fax:** 029 2023 1417

Castle Street, Cardiff CF10 3RB

Owner: City and County of Cardiff **Contact:** Mrs Jean Brown

2000 years of history, including Roman Walls, Norman Keep and Victorian interiors.

Location: OS Ref. ST181 765. Cardiff city centre, signposted from M4.

Opening Times: 1 Mar - 30 Oct: daily, 9.30am - 6pm, last entry 5pm. Nov - Feb: daily, 9.30am - 4.30pm, last entry 3.15pm. Closed Christmas and New Year.

Admission: Adult £5, Child/OAP £3 (2000 prices).

CAREW CASTLE & TIDAL MILL

Tel/Fax: 01646 651782

Tenby, Pembrokeshire SA70 8SL

Owner: Pembrokeshire Coast National Park **Contact:** Mr G M Candler

A magnificent Norman castle which later became an Elizabethan country house. Royal links with Henry Tudor and the setting for the Great Tournament of 1507. The Mill is one of only four restored tidal mills in Britain. Introductory slide programme, automatic 'talking points' and special exhibition on *The Story of Milling*.

Location: OS Ref. SN046 037. ¹/₂ m N of A477, 5m E of Pembroke.

Opening Times: Easter - end Oct: daily, 10am - 5pm.

Admission: Adult £2.75, Child/OAP £1.80, Family £7.30 (prices under review).

🔲 ♿Partially suitable. WC. 🎟By arrangement. 🅿 🐕In grounds on leads.

CARREG CENNEN CASTLE

Tel: 01558 822291

Tir-y-Castell Farm, Llandeilo

Owner: In the care of Cadw **Contact:** The Custodian

Spectacularly crowning a remote crag 300 feet above the River Cennen, the castle is unmatched as a wildly romantic fortress sought out by artists and visitors alike. The climb from Rare Breeds Farm is rewarded by breathtaking views and the chance to explore intriguing caves beneath.

Location: OS Ref. SN668 190. Minor roads from A483(T) to Trapp village. 5m SE of A40 at Llandeilo.

Opening Times: early Apr - late Oct: 9.30am - 7.30pm. Late Oct - late Mar: 9.30am - dusk. Closed 25 Dec.

Admission: Adult £2.50, Child/Conc. £2, Family £7.

🎧 🅿 🐕Guide dogs only. ❄ Ⓦ

CASTELL COCH

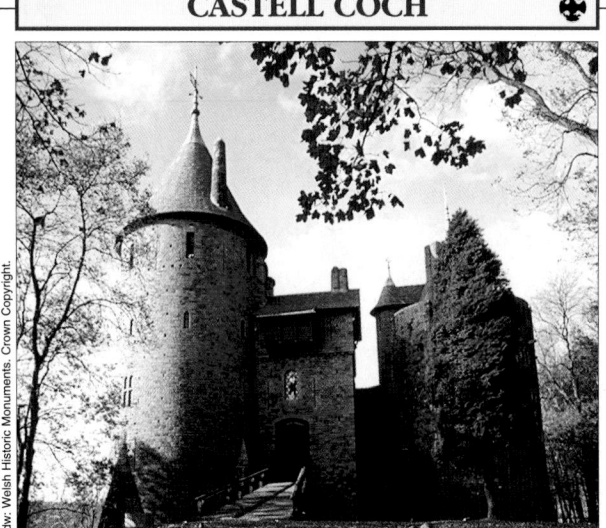

Cadw: Welsh Historic Monuments. Crown Copyright.

TONGWYNLAIS, CARDIFF CF4 7JS

Owner: In the care of Cadw　　*Contact: The Custodian*

Tel: 029 2081 0101

A fairytale castle in the woods, Castell Coch embodies a glorious Victorian dream of the Middle Ages. Designed by William Burges as a country retreat for the 3rd Lord Bute, every room and furnishing is brilliantly eccentric, including paintings of Aesop's fables on the drawing room walls.

Location: OS Ref. ST131 826. M4/J32, A470 then signposted. 5m NW of Cardiff city centre.

Opening Times: 27 Mar - 26 May: 9.30am - 5pm. 27 May - 1 Oct: 9.30am - 6pm. 2 - 29 Oct: 9.30am - 5pm. 30 Oct - 31 Mar: Mon - Sat, 9.30am - 4pm, Suns, 11am - 4pm. Closed 24 - 26 Dec & 1 Jan. Teashop: Summer: daily. Winter: weekends.

Admission: Adult £2.50, Child/Conc. £2, Family £7.

 Guide dogs only.

CHEPSTOW CASTLE

Tel: 01291 624065

Chepstow, Gwent

Owner: In the care of Cadw　　　　**Contact:** The Custodian

This mighty fortress has guarded the route from England to South Wales for more than nine centuries. So powerful was this castle that it continued in use until 1690, being finally adapted for cannon and musket after an epic civil war siege. This huge, complex, grandiosely sited castle deserves a lengthy visit.

Location: OS Ref. ST533 941. Chepstow via A465, B4235 or A48. 1¹/₂ m N of M4/J22.

Opening Times: 27 Mar - 26 May: 9.30am - 5pm. 27 May - 1 Oct: 9.30am - 6pm. 2 - 29 Oct: 9.30am - 5pm. 30 Oct - 31 Mar: Mon - Sat: 9.30am - 4pm, Suns, 11am - 4pm. Closed 24 - 26 Dec & 1 Jan.

Admission: Adult £3, Child/OAP £2, Family £8.

 Partially suitable. Guide dogs only.

CILGERRAN CASTLE

Tel: 01239 615007

Cardigan, Dyfed

Owner: In the care of Cadw　　　　**Contact:** The Custodian

Perched high up on a rugged spur above the River Teifi, Cilgerran Castle is one of the most spectacularly sited fortresses in Wales. It dates from the 11th - 13th centuries.

Location: OS Ref. SN195 431. Main roads to Cilgerran from A478 and A484. 3¹/₂ m SSE of Cardigan.

Opening Times: Late Mar - late Oct: 9.30am - 6.30pm. Late Oct - late Mar: 9.30am - 4pm. Closed 24 - 26 Dec & 1 Jan.

Admission: Adult £2, Child/OAP £1.50, Family £5.50.

Guide dogs only.

Accommodation Index ◀◀◀ page 27

CLYNE GARDENS

Tel: 01792 401737

Mill Lane, Blackpill, Swansea SA3 5BD

Owner: City and County of Swansea　　**Contact:** Steve Hopkins

50 acre spring garden, large rhododendron collection, 4 national collections, extensive bog garden, native woodland.

Location: OS Ref. SS614 906. S side of Mill Lane, 500yds W of A4067 Mumbles Road, 3m SW of Swansea.

Opening Times: All year: daily.

Admission: Free.

COLBY WOODLAND GARDEN

Tel: 01834 811885/01492 860123

Amroth, Narbeth, Pembrokeshire SA67 8PP

Owner: The National Trust　　　**Contact:** The Centre Manager

An attractive woodland garden. There are walks through secluded valleys along open woodland pathways. Nearby is the coastal resort of Amroth.

Location: OS Ref. SN155 080. ¹/₂ m inland from Amroth beside Carmarthen Bay. Signs from A477.

Opening Times: 1 Apr - 4 Nov: daily, 10am - 5pm. Walled Garden: 1 Apr - 31 Oct: 11am - 5pm.

Admission: Adult £2.80, Child £1.40, Family £7. Groups: by arrangement (15+): Adult £2.30, Child £1.15. National Trust members Free.

ⓘ Gallery events.

CRESSELLY

Fax: 01646 687045

Kilgetty, Pembrokeshire SA68 0SP

Owner/Contact: H D R Harrison-Allen Esq MFH

Home of the Allen family for 250 years. The house is of 1770 with matching wings of 1869 and contains good plasterwork and fittings of both periods. The Allens are of particular interest for their close association with the Wedgwood family of Etruria and a long tradition of foxhunting.

Location: OS Ref. SN065 065. In the Pembrokeshire National Park, W of the A4075 between Canaston Bridge and Carew in Cresselly village.

Opening Times: 30 days between May & Sept. Please write or fax for details.

Admission: Adult £3.50, no children under 12.

Ground floor only. Obligatory. Coaches by arrangement.

CYFARTHFA CASTLE MUSEUM

Tel/Fax: 01685 723112

Brecon Road, Merthyr Tydfil, Mid Glamorgan CF47 8RE

Owner: Merthyr Tydfil County Borough Council　　**Contact:** Mrs Claire Dovey-Evans

Castle originates from 1824/1825, now a museum and school.

Location: OS Ref. S0041 074. NE side of A470 to Brecon, ¹/₂ m NW of town centre.

Opening Times: 1 Apr - 1 Oct: Mon - Sun, 10am - 5.30pm. Winter: Tue - Fri, 10am - 4pm, Sat & Sun, 12 noon - 4pm.

Admission: Adult £2, Conc. £1.

ⓘ Conference facilities. By appointment.
Guide dogs only.

DINEFWR

Tel: 01558 823902　**Fax:** 01558 822036

Llandeilo SA19 6RT　　　　**e-mail:** gdroff@smtp.ntrust.org.uk

Owner: The National Trust　　　**Contact:** The House Manager

A deeply historic site with particular connections to the medieval Princes of Wales. An 18th century part 'naturalistic', part designed landscape parkland, with deer herd and White Park cattle, surrounds a 17th century mansion. Access to Dinefwr Castle (Cadw).

Location: OS Ref. SN615 225. On outskirts of Llandeilo. M4 from Swansea to Pont Abraham. A48 to Cross Hands and A476 to Llandeilo. Entrance by police station (A40).

Opening Times: House, Garden, Deer Park: 31 Mar - 4 Nov: daily except Tues & Weds, 11am - 5pm. Parkland: All year: 11am - 5pm (Nov - Mar: daily during daylight hours).

Admission: House & Park: Adult £3, Child £1.50, Family £7.50. Groups: (pre-booked 15+) £2.40. Park only (charges apply between 1 Apr - 29 Oct): Adult £2, Child £1, Family £5. National Trust members Free.

By arrangement. Limited for coaches.
In grounds on leads.

THE DINGLE

Tel: 01437 764370　**Fax:** 01437 768844

Dingle Lane, Crundale, Haverfordwest, Pembrokeshire SA62 4DJ

Owner/Contact: Andrew Barton

18th century country gentleman's home, surrounded by gardens. Gardens only open.

Location: OS Ref. SM973 175. 2m NE of Haverfordwest 600yds SE of B4329.

Opening Times: 10am - 6pm.

Admission: Gardens: Adult £2, Child £1. Nursery & tearooms Free.

DYFFRYN GARDENS

Tel: 029 2059 3328 **Fax:** 029 2059 1966

St Nicholas, Cardiff CF5 6SU

Owner: The Vale of Glamorgan Council   **Contact:** Miss G Donovan

Grade I listed Edwardian garden. 55 acres of landscaped gardens, beautiful at all times of year. Numerous small theme gardens, arboretum and extensive lawns.

Location: OS Ref. ST095 723. 3m NW of Barry, J33/M4. 1¹/₂ m S of St Nicholas on A48.

Opening Times: Summer: daily, 10am - 8pm. Winter: daily, 10am - 5pm.

Admission: Adult £3. Please telephone for details of concessions and tours.

FONMON CASTLE

RHOOSE, BARRY, SOUTH GLAMORGAN CF62 3ZN

Owner: Sir Brooke Boothby Bt   *Contact: Sophie Katzi*

Tel: 01446 710206 **Fax:** 01446 711687 **e-mail:** fonmon_castle@msn.com

Occupied as a home since the 13th century, this medieval castle has the most stunning Georgian interiors and is surrounded by extensive gardens. Available for weddings, concerts, corporate entertainment and multi-activity days.

Location: OS Ref. ST047 681. 15m W of Cardiff, 1m W of Cardiff airport.

Opening Times: 1 Apr - 30 Sept: Tues & Weds, 2 - 5pm (last tour 4pm). Other times by appointment. Groups: by appointment.

Admission: Adult £4, Child Free.

ⓘ Conferences. ⊤ By arrangement (up to 120). ♿ Partially suitable. WC. Ⓟ 🦮 Guide dogs only. 🔔 ❄

The Judge's Lodging, South Wales.

THE JUDGE'S LODGING

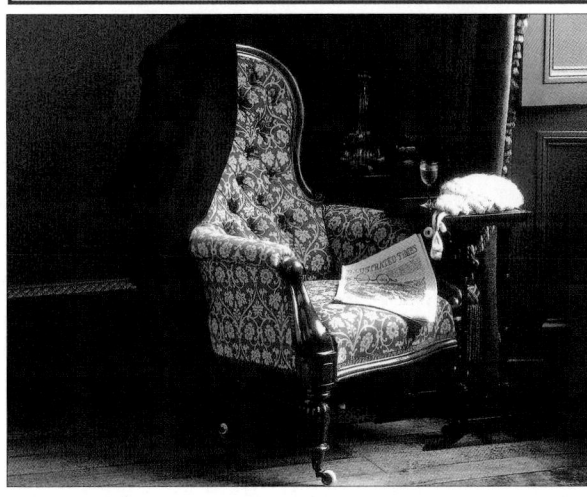

BROAD STREET, PRESTEIGNE, POWYS LD8 2AD

Owner: Powys County Council   *Contact: Gabrielle Rivers*

Tel: 01544 260650 **Fax:** 01544 260652 **e-mail:** gaby@lodging.fsnet.co.uk

This stunningly restored Judge's Lodging captures the 'upstairs, downstairs' heyday of a most unusual Victorian household - by gaslight, lamp and candle. An 'eavesdropping' audio tour features actor Robert Hardy - A Victorian Revelation. Interpret Britain Award winner 1998 and Britain's 'Local Museum of the Year', *The Good Guide to Britain 1999.*

Location: OS Ref. SO314 644. In town centre, off A44 and A4113. Easy reach from Herefordshire and mid-Wales.

Opening Times: 1 Mar - 31 Oct: daily, 10am - 6pm. 1 Nov - 22 Dec: Wed - Sun, 10am - 4pm. Bookings by arrangement accepted all year.

Admission: Adult £3.75, Child/Conc. £2.75. Groups (10-80): Adult £3,Child/Conc. £2.25, Family £11.

📷 ⊤ ♿ Partially suitable (access via lift). 🎧 Ⓟ In town. 🏛 🦮 Guide dogs only. ❄ 🆆

KIDWELLY CASTLE ✠

Tel: 01554 890104

Kidwelly, West Glamorgan SA17 5BG

Owner: In the care of Cadw   **Contact:** The Custodian

A chronicle in stone of medieval fortress technology this strong and splendid castle developed during more than three centuries of Anglo-Welsh warfare. The half-moon shape stems from the original 12th century stockaded fortress, defended by the River Gwendraeth on one side and a deep crescent-shaped ditch on the other.

Location: OS Ref. SN409 070. Kidwelly via A484. Kidwelly Rail Station 1m.

Opening Times: 27 Mar - 26 May: 9.30am - 5pm. 27 May - 1 Oct: 9.30am - 6pm. 2 - 29 Oct: 9.30am - 5pm. 30 Oct - 31 Mar: Mon - Sat, 9.30am - 4pm, Suns, 11am - 4pm. Closed 24 - 26 Dec & 1 Jan.

Admission: Adult £2.20, Child/OAP £1.70, Family £6.10.

♿ 🦮 By arrangement. 🎧 Ⓟ 🦮 Guide dogs only. ❄ 🆆

LAMPHEY BISHOP'S PALACE ✠

Tel: 01646 672224

Lamphey, Dyfed

Owner: In the care of Cadw   **Contact:** The Custodian

Lamphey marks the place of the spectacular Bishop's Palace but it reached its height of greatness under Bishop Henry de Gower who raised the new Great Hall. Today the ruins of this comfortable retreat reflect the power enjoyed by the medieval bishops.

Location: OS Ref. SN018 009. A4139 from Pembroke or Tenby. N of village (A4139).

Opening Times: Daily, 10am - 5pm. Closed 25 Dec.

Admission: Adult £2, Child/Conc. £1.50, Family £5.50.

🎧 Ⓟ 🦮 Guide dogs only. ❄ 🆆

LAUGHARNE CASTLE ✠

Tel: 01994 427906

King Street, Laugharne SA33 4SA

Owner: In the care of Cadw   **Contact:** The Custodian

Picturesque Laugharne Castle stands on a low ridge overlooking the wide Taf estuary, one of a string of fortresses controlling the ancient route along the South Wales coast.

Location: OS Ref. SN303 107. 4m S of A48 at St Clears via A4066.

Opening Times: Apr - Sept: daily, 10am - 5pm.

Admission: Adult £2, Child/Conc. £1.50, Family £5.50.

🦮 Guide dogs only. 🆆

LLANCAIACH FAWR MANOR

Tel: 01443 412248 **Fax:** 01443 412688

Nelson, Treharris CF46 6ER

Owner: Caerphilly County Borough Council   **Contact:** The Administrator

Tudor fortified manor dating from 1530 with Stuart additions.

Location: OS Ref. ST114 967. S side of B4254, 1m N of A472 at Nelson.

Opening Times: All year: weekdays, 10am - 5pm. weekends, 10am - 6pm. Last admission 1¹/₂ hours before closing. Nov - Feb: closed Mons. Closed Christmas week.

Admission: Adult £4.50, Child/Conc. £3, Family £12.

LLANDAFF CATHEDRAL

Tel: 029 2056 4554

Llandaff, Cardiff, Glamorgan CF5 2YF

Contact: The Cathedral Office

Oldest cathedral in the British Isles. Epstein's *'Christ in Majesty'* and Rosetti's *'Seed of David'*.

Location: OS Ref. ST155 781. 2¹/₂ m NW of city centre, ¹/₄ m W of A48 ring road.

Opening Times: Daily: 7am - 7pm. Sun services: 8am, 9am, 11am, 12.15pm (Holy Eucharist), 3.30pm Choral Evensong and 6.30pm Parish Evensong. Weekday evening service: 6pm, (Wed 5.30pm).

Admission: Donation.

MARGAM PARK

Tel: 01639 881635 **Fax:** 01639 895897

Port Talbot, Glamorgan SA13 2TJ

Owner: Neathport Talbot County Borough Council   **Contact:** Mr Ray Butt

Margam Orangery is the largest of its kind in Britain. Castle and Abbey ruins, 850 acres of parkland and forest, with waymarked signs.

Location: OS Ref. SS804 865. NE side of A48, 1m SE of M4/J38, 4m SE of Port Talbot.

Opening Times: Summer: daily, 10am - 5pm, last entry 4pm. Winter: Wed - Sun, 10am - 5pm, last entry 3pm.

Admission: Adult £3.85, Child £2.85, Family (2+4) £11.85.

MUSEUM OF WELSH LIFE

Tel: 029 2057 3500 **Fax:** 029 2057 3490

St Fagans, Cardiff CF5 6XB

St Fagans Castle, a 16th century building built within the walls of a 13th century castle.

Location: OS Ref. ST118 772. 4m W of city centre, 1¹/₂m N of A48, 2m S of M4/J33 off A4232.

Opening Times: All year: daily, 10am - 5pm.

Admission: Summer: Adult £5.50, Child (under 18) Free, Over 60s & unemployed Free, Conc. £3.90. Winter: Adult £4.50 Child (under 18) Free, Over 60s & unemployed Free, Conc. £2.65.

THE NATIONAL BOTANIC GARDEN OF WALES

Tel: 01558 668768

Port Talbot, Glamorgan SA13 2TJ   **Tel:** 01558 667134 **Fax:** 01558 667138

Owner: The National Botanic Garden of Wales   **Contact:** Ian Ball

The first national botanic garden to be created in the United Kingdom for more than two hundred years.

Location: OS159 Ref. SN518 175. ¹/₂ m off A48 (M4), 4¹/₂ m NW Cross Hands.

Opening Times: Please contact property for details.

Admission: Please contact property for details.

OXWICH CASTLE

Tel: 01792 390359

c/o Oxwich Castle Farm, Oxwich SA3 1NG

Owner: In the care of Cadw   **Contact:** The Custodian

Beautifully sited in the lovely Gower peninsula, Oxwich Castle is a striking testament to the pride and ambitions of the Mansel dynasty of Welsh gentry.

Location: OS159 Ref. SS497 864. A4118, 11m SW of Swansea, in Oxwich village.

Opening Times: Apr - Sept: daily, 10am - 5pm.

Admission: Adult £2, Child/OAP £1.50, Family £5.50.

  Guide dogs only.

PEMBROKE CASTLE

Tel: 01646 681510 **Fax:** 01646 622260

Pembroke, Dyfed SA71 4LA

Owner: Trustees of Pembroke Castle   **Contact:** I B Ramsden

Early 13th century Norman castle. Birthplace of Henry VII the first Tudor monarch. Exhibitions and video. Brass Rubbing Centre. Stroll around its idyllic millpond and town walls to complete the day.

Location: OS Ref. SM983 016. W end of the main street in Pembroke.

Opening Times: 1 Apr - 30 Sept: daily, 9.30am - 6pm. Mar & Oct: daily, 10am - 5pm. Nov - Feb: daily, 10am - 4pm. Closed Christmas Day, Boxing Day and New Year's Day.

Admission: Adult £3, Child/Conc. £2. Groups (20+): Adult £2.60, OAP £1.70.

Summer only. By arrangement. In grounds on leads.

PENHOW CASTLE

Nr NEWPORT, GWENT NP6 3AD

Owner: *Stephen Weeks Esq*   **Contact:** *The Administrator*

Tel: 01633 400800 **Fax:** 01633 400990 **e-mail:** admin@penhowcastle.com

Wales' oldest lived-in Castle, the first home in Britain of the Seymour family. Now lovingly restored by the present owner, visitors explore the varied period rooms from battlements to kitchens. Discover the Norman bedchamber, 15th century Great Hall with minstrels' gallery, elegant panelled Carolean dining room, guided by the acclaimed 'Time Machine' audio tours included in the admission; also in French and German. Penhow holds 8 awards for careful restoration and imaginative interpretation. Exciting children's tours and school visits.

Location: OS Ref. ST423 908. Midway between Chepstow and Newport on the A48. Use M4/J24.

Opening Times: Summer: Good Fri - 30 Sept: Wed - Sun & BHs. Aug: daily, 10am - 5.15pm (last adm.) Winter: Weds, 10am - 4pm. Selected Suns, 1 - 4pm. Evening Candlelit Tours all year by arrangement. Christmas Tours: 15 Nov - 5 Jan.

Admission: Adult £3.80, Child £2.60, Family (2+2) £10.20. Groups: by arrangement all year, 10% discount for 20+.

Not suitable. By arrangement. Limited. Guide dogs only. 1 double.

PENPERGWM LODGE

Tel/Fax: 01873 840208

Abergavenny, Gwent   **e-mail:** penpergwmplants@dial.pipex.com

Owner/Contact: Mrs Catriona Boyle

3 acre terraced garden including rose and vine walks.

Location: OS Ref. SO335 104. ¹/₄ m N of B4598 to Usk, 3m SE of Abergavenny.

Opening Times: Mar - Oct: Thur - Sun, 2 - 6pm.

Admission: Adult £2, Child Free.

St Davids Bishop's Palace, South Wales.

PICTON CASTLE

HAVERFORDWEST, PEMBROKESHIRE SA62 4AS

Owner: *Picton Castle Trust*   **Contact:** *D Pryse Lloyd*

Tel/Fax: 01437 751326 **e-mail:** pct@pictoncastle.freeserve.co.uk

Built in the 13th century by Sir John Wogan, his direct descendants still use the castle as their family home, carrying the family name of Philipps. Retaining its external appearance, the castle was remodelled inside, above the undercroft in the 1750s and extended around 1800. The woodland and walled gardens cover 40 acres and are part of The Royal Horticultural Society access scheme for beautiful gardens. There is a unique collection of rhododendrons and azaleas, mature trees, unusual shrubs, wild flowers and a large collection of herbs as featured on television. The Picton Gallery is used for nationally acclaimed exhibitions. Events include spring and autumn plant sales.

Location: OS Ref. SN011 135. 4m E of Haverfordwest, 2m S of A40.

Opening Times: Castle: Apr - Sept. Closed Mon & Sat except BHs, open all other afternoons for guided tours. Garden & Gallery: Apr - Oct: Tue - Sun, 10.30am - 5pm.

Admission: Castle, Garden & Gallery: Adult £4.95, Child £1.95, OAP £4.75. Garden & Gallery: Adult £3.95, Child £1.95, OAP £3.75. Groups (20+): reduced prices by prior arrangement.

ⓘNo indoor photography. 🏛 ♣ 🍽 ♿ 🍴Licensed. 📷Obligatory. 🅿 🐕In grounds, on leads. 🔔 🛡 (WT)

RAGLAN CASTLE

Tel: 01291 690228

Raglan NP5 2BT

Owner: In the care of Cadw   **Contact:** The Custodian

Undoubtedly the finest late medieval fortress-palace in Britain, it was begun in the 1430s by Sir William ap Thomas who built the mighty 'Yellow Tower'. His son William Lord Herbert added a palatial mansion defended by a gatehouse and many towered walls. The high quality is still obvious today.

Location: OS Ref. SO415 084. Raglan, NE of Raglan village off A40 (eastbound) and signposted.

Opening Times: 27 Mar - 26 May: 9.30am - 5pm. 27 May - 1 Oct: 9.30am - 6pm. 2 - 29 Oct: 9.30am - 5pm. 30 Oct - 31 Mar: Mon - Sat, 9.30am - 4pm, Suns, 11am - 4pm. Closed 24 - 26 Dec & 1 Jan.

Admission: Adult £2.40, Child/Conc. £1.90, Family £6.70.

🏛 ♿ 🅿 🐕Guide dogs only. ❄ (WT)

ST DAVIDS BISHOP'S PALACE ✠

Tel: 01437 720517

St Davids, SA62 6PE

Owner: In the care of Cadw   **Contact:** The Custodian

The city of St Davids boasts not only one of Britain's finest cathedrals but also the most impressive medieval palace in Wales. Built in the elaborate 'decorated' style of gothic architecture, the palace is lavishly encrusted with fine carving.

Location: OS Ref. SM750 254. A487 to St Davids, minor road past the Cathedral.

Opening Times: 27 Mar - 26 May: 9.30am - 5pm. 27 May - 1 Oct: 9.30am - 6pm. 2 - 29 Oct: 9.30am - 5pm. 30 Oct - 31 Mar, Mon - Sat, 9.30am - 4pm, Suns, 12 noon - 2pm. Closed 24 - 26 Dec & 1 Jan.

Admission: Adult £2, Child/Conc. £1.50, Family £5.50.

♿ 🅿 🐕Guide dogs only. ❄ (WT)

ST DAVIDS CATHEDRAL

Tel: 01437 720691 **Fax:** 01437 721885

St Davids, Dyfed SA62 6QW   **Contact:** Mr R G Tarr

St Davids is Britain's smallest city by Royal Charter, March 1994. Premier cathedral of church in Wales. Over eight centuries old. Many unique and 'odd' features.

Location: OS Ref. SM751 254. 5-10 mins walk from car/coach parks: signs for pedestrians.

Opening Times: Daily: 7.30am - 6.30pm. Suns: 12.30 - 5.30pm, may be closed for services in progress. Sun services: 8am, 9.30am, 11.15am & 6pm. Weekday services: 8am & 6pm. Weds extra service: 10am.

Admission: Donations. Guided tours (Adult £3, Child £1.20) must be booked in advance.

STRATA FLORIDA ABBEY ✠

Tel: 01974 831261

Ystrad Meurig, Pontrhydfendigaid SY25 6BT

Owner: In the care of Cadw   **Contact:** The Custodian

Remotely set in the green, kite-haunted Teifi Valley with the lonely Cambrian mountains as a backdrop, the ruined abbey has a wonderful doorway with Celtic spiral motifs and preserves a wealth of beautiful medieval tiles.

Location: OS Ref. SN746 658. Minor road from Pontrhydfendigaid 14m SE of Aberystwyth by the B4340.

Opening Times: 21 Apr - 24 Sept: daily, 10am - 5pm. Winter: open site.

Admission: Adult £2, Child/Conc. £1.50, Family £5.50.

♿ 🅿 🐕Guide dogs only. ❄ (WT)

TINTERN ABBEY ✠

Tel: 01291 689251

Tintern NP6 6SE

Owner: In the care of Cadw   **Contact:** The Custodian

Tintern is the best preserved abbey in Wales and ranks among Britain's most beautiful historic sites. Elaborately decorated in 'gothic' architecture style this church stands almost complete to roof level. Turner sketched and painted here, while Wordsworth drew inspiration from the surroundings.

Location: OS Ref. SO533 000. Tintern via A466, from M4/J22. Chepstow 6m.

Opening Times: 27 Mar - 26 May: 9.30am - 5pm. 27 May - 1 Oct: 9.30am - 6pm. 2 - 29 Oct 9.30am - 5pm. 30 Oct - 31 Mar: Mon - Sat, 9.30am - 4pm, Suns, 11am - 4pm. Closed 24 - 26 Dec & 1 Jan.

Admission: Adult £2.40, Child/Conc. £1.90, Family £6.70.

🏛 ♿ 🎧 🅿 🐕Guide dogs only. ❄ (WT)

TREDEGAR HOUSE & PARK

NEWPORT, SOUTH WALES NP1 9YW

Owner: *Newport County Borough Council*   **Contact:** *The Manager*

Tel: 01633 815880 **Fax:** 01633 815895 **e-mail:** tredegar.house@newport.gov.uk

South Wales' finest country house, ancestral home of the Morgan family. Parts of a medieval house remain, but Tredegar owes its reputation to lavish rebuilding in the 17th century. Visitors have a lively and entertaining tour through 30 rooms, including glittering State Rooms and 'below stairs'. Set in 90 acres of parkland with formal gardens. Winner of Best Public Park and Garden in Great Britain 1997. Craft workshops.

Location: OS Ref. ST290 852. M4/J28 signposted. From London 2½ hrs, from Cardiff 20 mins. 2m SW of Newport town centre.

Opening Times: Easter - Sept: Wed - Sun & BHs, 11.30am - 4pm. Evening tours & groups by appointment. Nov - Mar: Groups only by appointment.

Admission: Adult £4.75, Child £2.25, Conc. £3.65, Family £12.95. Special discounts for Newport residents (2000 prices).

ⓘConferences. No photography in house. 🏛 🍽 ♿Partially suitable. WC. 🍷 📷Obligatory. 🅿 🍴 🐕In grounds, on leads. 🔔 🛡Tel. for details.

TREOWEN

Tel/Fax: 01600 712031

Wonastow, Nr Monmouth NP5 4DL   **e-mail:** john.wheelock@virgin.net

Owner: R A & J P Wheelock   **Contact:** John Wheelock

Early 17th century mansion built to double pile plan with magnificent well-stair to four storeys.

Location: OS Ref. SO461 111. 3m WSW of Monmouth.

Opening Times: May, Jun, Aug & Sept: Fris. Also Sat & Sun on 12/13 & 19/20 May and 15/16, 22/23 & 29/30 Sept: 10am - 4pm.

Admission: £4. £2.50 if appointment made. Groups by appointment only.

🍽 🏠Entire house let, self-catering. Sleeps 24+. 🔔 (WT)

TRETOWER COURT & CASTLE

Tel: 01874 730279

Tretower, Crickhowell NP8 2RF

Owner: In the care of Cadw   **Contact:** The Custodian

A fine fortress and an outstanding medieval manor house, Tretower Court and Castle range around a galleried courtyard, now further enhanced by a beautiful recreated medieval garden.

Location: OS Ref. SO187 212. Signposted in Tretower Village, off A479, 3m NW of Crickhowell.

Opening Times: 1 - 26 Mar: 10am - 4pm. 27 Mar - 26 May: 10am - 5pm. 27 May - 3 Sept: 10am - 6pm. 4 Sept - 29 Oct: 10am - 5pm.

Admission: Adult £2.20, Child/Conc. £1.70, Family £6.10.

🕭 🎧 🅿 🐕 Guide dogs only. 🚻

TUDOR MERCHANT'S HOUSE 🦋

Tel: 01834 842279

Quay Hill, Tenby SA70 7BX

Owner: The National Trust   **Contact:** The Custodian

A late 15th century town house, characteristic of the building tradition of south west Wales. The ground-floor chimney at the rear of the house is a fine vernacular example, and the original scarfed roof-trusses survive. The remains of early frescoes can be seen on three interior walls. Access to small herb garden, weather permitting. Furniture and fittings re-create the atmosphere from the time when a Tudor family was in residence.

Location: OS Ref. SN135 004. Tenby. W of alley from NE corner of town centre square.

Opening Times: 1 Apr - 30 Sept: daily except Weds, 10am - 5pm; Suns, 1 - 5pm. 1 Oct - 4 Nov: daily except Weds & Sats, 10am - 3pm; Suns, 12 noon - 3pm.

Admission: Adult £1.80, Child 90p. Groups: Adult £1.40, Child 70p. NT members Free.

ℹ No indoor photography. 🅿 No parking. ▦ 🐕 Guide dogs only.

USK CASTLE

Tel: 01291 672563

Usk, Monmouthshire NP15 1SD

Owner/Contact: J H L Humphreys

Romantic, ruined castle overlooking the picturesque town of Usk. Inner and outer baileys, towers and earthwork defences. Surrounded by enchanting gardens (open under NGS) incorporating The Castle House, the former medieval gatehouse lived in by owner.

Location: OS Ref. SO376 011. Off Monmouth Road in Usk, opposite fire station.

Opening Times: Castle ruins: daily, 11am - 5pm. Groups by appointment. Gardens & Castle House: Jun & BHs: 2 - 5pm, prior arrangement advised.

Admission: Castle ruins: Adult £2, Child Free. Gardens & Castle House: Adult £5, Child £2.

🍸 🕭 Partially suitable. 🔧 By arrangement. 🅿 Limited. 🐕 In grounds, on leads. ❄ 🚻

WEOBLEY CASTLE

Tel: 01792 390012

Weobley Castle Farm, Llanrhidian SA3 1HB

Owner: In the care of Cadw   **Contact:** The Custodian

Perched above the wild northern coast of the beautiful Gower peninsula, Weobley Castle was the home of the Knightly de Bere family. Its rooms include a fine hall and private chamber as well as numerous 'garderobes' or toilets and an early Tudor porch block.

Location: OS Ref. SN477 928. B4271 or B4295 to Llanrhidian Village, then minor road for 1¹/₂ m.

Opening Times: Apr - early Oct: 9.30am - 6pm. 2 - 29 Oct: 9.30am - 5pm. Late Oct - late Mar: 9.30am - 4pm. Closed 24 - 26 Dec & 1 Jan.

Admission: Adult £2, Child/Conc. £1.50, Family £5.50.

🅿 🐕 Guide dogs only. ❄ 🚻

WHITE CASTLE

Tel: 01600 780380

Llantillio Crossenny, Gwent

Owner: In the care of Cadw   **Contact:** The Custodian

With its high walls and round towers reflected in the still waters of its moat, White Castle is the ideal medieval fortress. It was rebuilt in the mid-13th century by the future King Edward I to counter a threat from Prince Llywelyn the Last.

Location: OS Ref. SO380 167. By minor road 2m NW from B4233 at A7 Llantilio Crossenny. 8m ENE of Abergavenny.

Opening Times: 21 Apr - 24 Sept: 10am - 5pm. Winter: Open site.

Admission: Adult £2, Conc. £1.50, Family £5.50.

🅿 🐕 Guide dogs only. ❄ 🚻

Colby Woodland Garden, South Wales

NT Photographic Library: Andrew Butler.

South Wales

IRELAND

I R E L A N D

I R E L A N D

Rowallane Garden, Ireland

Ireland

Rowallane Garden

"As with the first act of any good play, you soon become enthralled, as each turn reveals a different scene."

a visitor to Rowallane

Rowallane is a garden for all seasons and for all people, with appeal both for the connoisseur of rare plants and for those who just like to wander through a beautiful landscape. Eleven miles south of Belfast and one mile south of Saintfield, it nestles in the rolling hills of Co Down.

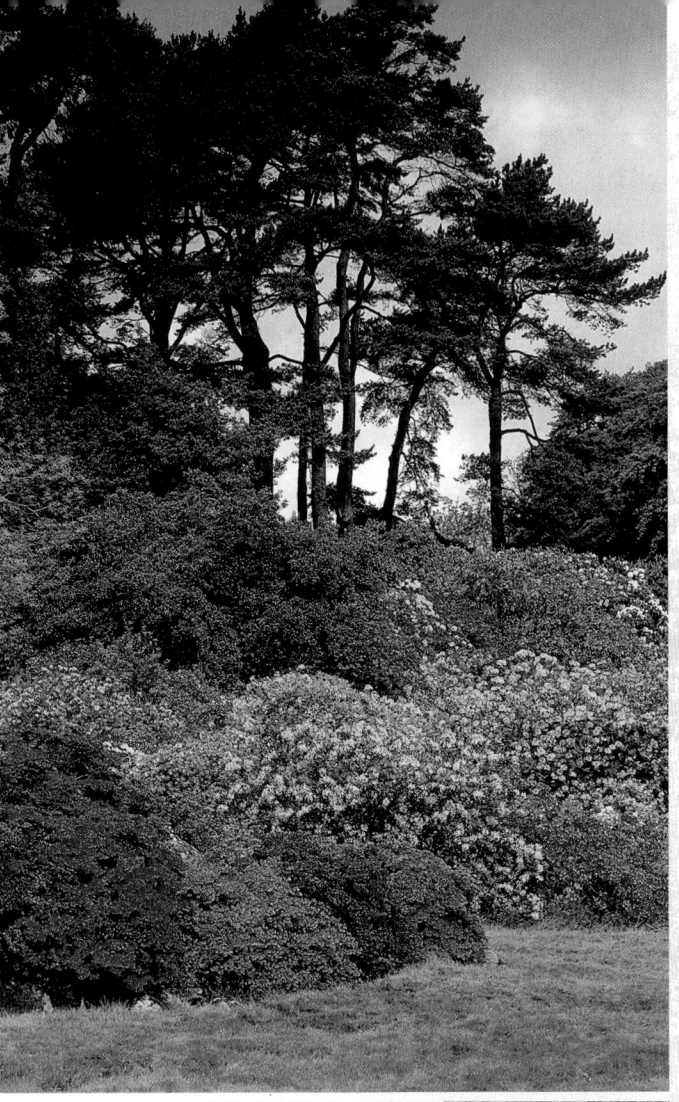

Formerly the farm belonging to the Reverend John Moore who acquired it in the 1860s, Rowallane has become one of the foremost gardens in the British Isles in this century – and a rare jewel in the National Trust's collections of gardens. Unlike gardens such as Mount Stewart it was never 'landscaped' but dropped in around natural outcrops of whinstone rock and dry stone walled fields.

The 52 acres of gardens that can be visited today are the work of the Reverend Hugh Moore, who began the task some 130 years ago, and his nephew Hugh Armytage Moore, who continued the work. In the past 20 years, the gardens have been cared for and maintained by Mike Snowden, the National Trust's Head Gardener.

Although late spring may find Rowallane at its most spectacular, it is an enthralling place to visit in high summer, when part of its attraction is the fine herbaceous display in the Walled Garden. Sheltered by high walls, the visitor can enjoy wonderfully lush plantings. Great drifts of Himalayan Poppies, in particular the scintillating turquoise blue Meconopsis x grandis. Also to be found is a National Collection of penstemons, alongside phlox and the soft yellow Japanese Kirengeshoma palmata which provide colour in the late summer.

Autumn is also a magnificent time for the garden – rich reds, russets, golds and browns form banks or single flames of colour, whilst a heavy frost or a fall of crisp snow still highlight the fine evergreens and the colourful bark and fruit of deciduous trees planted for winter interest as well as their summer colour. However, the garden is perhaps best loved for its spectacular arrangement and variety of rhododendrons and azaleas. These thrive on the high rainfall and acid thin soil of the region. Some of these plants are well over 60 years old; they have been planted with the expert eye of shade, colour and form, sometimes in groups of over 50 or more – this is no timid planting scheme.

The trees at Rowallane are superb – quietly setting the mood and structure of this plantsman's garden. Monterey, Scots, Bishop and Umbrella Pines, redwood, Wellingtonia, cypresses, multi-stemmed Western Red Cedar, and Douglas Fir are just some of the species.

The joy of Rowallane is not only its trees and its rainbow rhododendrons. Like any great garden, it is a continuing story and a gardener's garden. Through the efforts of Mike Snowden visitors can enjoy walking through meadows of pig-nut, wild orchids and meadow buttercup, or wooded areas with bluebells, cuckoo-pint and wood anemones.

For any keen plantsman a first visit to Rowallane would be a revelation – take a notebook and take time to stroll through this wonderfully captivating garden in Northern Ireland – you will not be disappointed.

For further details about *Rowallane Garden* see entry in Ireland.

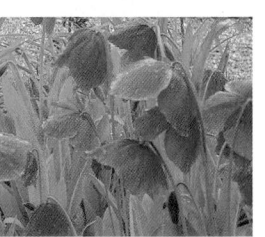

ANNES GROVE GARDENS
Tel: +353 22 26145

Castletownroche, Co Cork
Owner/Contact: Mr P Annesley
The gardens around the 18th century house contain magnolias, eucryphias and hoherias of unusual size. Winding paths and riverside walks.
Location: 1.6 km N of Castletownroche.
Opening Times: 17 Mar - 30 Sept: Mon - Sat, 10am - 5pm; Suns, 1 - 6pm. Other times by arrangement.
Admission: Adult £3, Child £1.50, Conc. £2.

ANTRIM CASTLE GARDENS
Tel: 028 9442 8000 **Fax:** 028 9446 0360

Randalstown Road, Antrim BT41 4LH
e-mail: clotworthy@antrim.gov.uk
Owner: Antrim Borough Council **Contact:** Kate Wimpress
Situated adjacent to Antrim Town, the Sixmilewater River and Lough Neagh's shore, these recently restored, 17th century Anglo-Dutch water gardens are maintained in a manner authentic to the period. The gardens comprise of ornamental canals, round pond, ancient motte and a parterre garden planted with 17th century plants - many with culinary or medicinal uses. An interpretative display introducing the history of the gardens and the process of their restoration, along with a scale model of former Antrim Castle is located in the reception of Clotworthy Arts Centre.
Location: Outside Antrim town centre off A26 on A6.
Opening Times: All year: Mon - Fri, 9.30am - 9.30pm (dusk if earlier). Sats, 10am - 5pm. July & Aug: also open Suns, 2 - 5pm.
Admission: Free. Charge for guided group tours (by arrangement only).

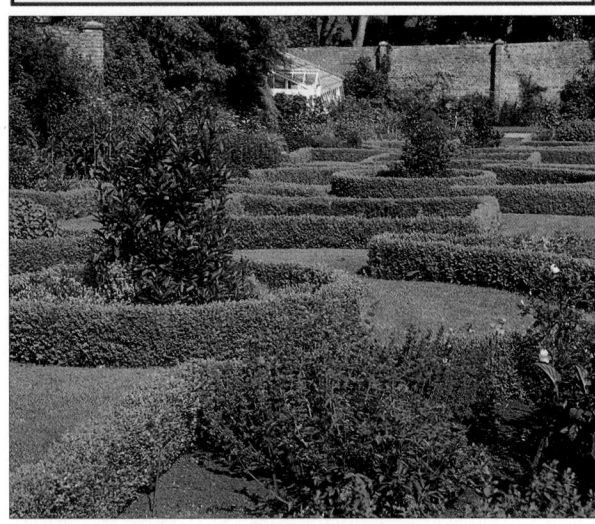

ARDGILLAN CASTLE GARDEN

BALBRIGGAN, Co DUBLIN
Owner: Fingal County Council **Contact:** *Brenda Kenny*

Tel: +353 1 849 2212 **Fax:** +353 1 849 2786
"Flúirse talamh is mara" – Rich in land and sea – part of the Fingal Region of North County Dublin crest and nowhere more true than in Ardgillan Demesne. 194 acres of parkland and gardens surround this early 18th century house.
Location: 30km N of Dublin, off the N1.
Opening Times: All year: Jul & Aug: daily. 1 Apr - end May & Sept: Tue - Sun & Public Hols, 11am - 6pm. 1 Oct - 31 Mar: Tue - Sun & Public Hols, 11am - 4.30pm. Closed 23 Dec - 1 Jan.
Admission: Castle by guided tour only: Adult £3, Conc. £2, Family £6.50. Groups: (10+) £2.
ⓘNo photography.
Castle: Obligatory. Gardens: Thurs in Jun/Jul/Aug at 3pm.
In grounds, on leads.

Website Index page 39

ARDRESS
Tel/Fax: 028 3885 1236 **e-mail:** uagest@smtp.ntrust.org.uk

64 Ardress Road, Portadown, Co Armagh BT62 1SQ
Owner: The National Trust **Contact:** The Custodian
A 17th century farmhouse with elegant 18th century additions by owner-architect George Ensor. Includes a farmyard, popular with children, with rare breeds and traditional farm implements. House tours include the Adam-style drawing room, fine furniture and pictures. Also an attractive garden with woodland and riverside walks amid apple orchards.
Location: On B28, 5m from Moy, 5m from Portadown, 3m from M1/J13.
Opening Times: 13 - 17 Apr: daily, 2 - 6pm. Apr, May & Sept: Weekends & BHs, 2 - 6pm. Jun & Aug: daily except Tue, 2 - 6pm.
Admission: House tour & Farmyard: Adult £2.70, Child £1.35, Family £6.75. Groups £2.20. Farmyard only: Adult £2.40, Child £1.20, Family £6.
Ground floor suitable. WC. Obligatory. P

THE ARGORY
Tel: 028 8778 4753 **Fax:** 028 8778 9598

Moy, Dungannon, Co Tyrone BT71 6NA
e-mail: uagest@smtp.ntrust.org.uk
Owner: The National Trust **Contact:** The Property Manager
The Argory is a handsome 19th century Victorian house furnished as it was in 1900, providing an excellent illustration of Victorian/Edwardian interior taste and interests. Includes the 1824 Bishop's barrel organ, still in working order. Imposing stableyard with horse carriages, harness room, acetylene gas plant, laundry and children's playground. It is set in 130 hectares of wooded countryside overlooking the River Blackwater. Variety of garden, woodland or riverside walks suitable for all ages. Note: In Autumn 2001 a major restoration will start, house tours may not be on offer during September.
Location: On Derrycaw road, 4m from Moy, 3m from M1/J13 or J14 (coaches J13).
Opening Times: 13 - 17 Apr: daily, 2 - 6pm. Apr, May & Sept: Weekends & BHs, 2 - 6pm (BHs, 1 - 6pm). Jun & Aug: daily except Tues, 2 - 6pm. Grounds only: 4 & 11 Feb; Mar: Suns, 2 - 5pm.
Admission: House: Adult £3, Child £1.50, Family £7.50. Groups £2.55. Groups outside normal hours £2.55. Car park: £1.50.
Ground floor suitable. WC. Obligatory. P £1.50.

BALLINDOOLIN HOUSE & GARDEN
Tel: +353 405 31430 **Fax:** +353 405 32377

Carbery, Co Kildare
e-mail: sundial@iol.ie
Owner: R Molony **Contact:** Esther Molony
Large Georgian country house and farmyards surrounded by extensive gardens and ancient woods.
Location: 5.6km N of Edenderry on the R401 to Kinnegad.
Opening Times: 1 May - 30 Sept: Tue - Sun, 12 noon - 6pm.
Tyrrells Restaurant: All year, tel. +353 405 32400.
Admission: House: £2.50. Garden: Adult £4, Child £2. Under 5s Free. Booked groups (20+): House: £2. Garden: Adult £3, Child £1.50. Under 5s Free.
ⓘNo photography in house. Partially suitable. WC. Obligatory for house. P Guide dogs only. Restaurant only.

BALLINLOUGH CASTLE GARDENS
Tel: +353 46 33135 **Fax:** +353 46 33331

Ballinlough Castle, Clonmellon, Co Westmeath
Owner: Sir John & Lady Nugent **Contact:** Sir John Nugent
Set in the lakeland county of Westmeath the gardens comprise of herbaceous borders, roses, fruit and much more.
Location: On N52 half-way between Clonmellon and Delvin. Signed from Athboy.
Opening Times: 1 May - 30 Sept: Tue - Sat, 11am - 6pm. Suns & BHs, 2 - 6pm. Gardens: closed 1st two weeks in Aug.
Admission: Adult £4, Child £1, Conc. £3. Groups (10+): £3.

BALLYWALTER PARK
Tel: 028 4275 8264 **Fax:** 028 4275 8818

Nr Newtownards, Co Down BT22 2PP
e-mail: enquiries@dunleath-estates.co.uk
Owner: Lord & Lady Dunleath **Contact:** The Secretary, The Estate Office
Victorian mansion, situated in 40 acres of landscaped grounds, built in the mid-19th century by Charles Lanyon, with Edwardian additions by W J Fennell. Currently undergoing major restoration works. Self-catered (4 star) listed gatelodge overlooking beach available for holiday lets (sleeps four).
Location: 1km S of Ballywalter village.
Opening Times: Please telephone for access, due to major restoration work.
Admission: House or Gardens: Adult £4, Child/Conc. £3. House and gardens: Adult £7, Conc. £5.50. Groups (Max. 50): Adult £4, Child/Conc. £2.
ⓘNo photography indoors. Pick-your-own, Jun - Aug. Obligatory. P

BANTRY HOUSE & GARDENS

BANTRY, Co CORK

Owner/Contact: Mr & Mrs Egerton Shelswell-White

Tel: +353 27 50047 **Fax:** +353 27 50795 **e-mail:** bantryhouse@eircom.net

Overlooking Bantry Bay, with views to the Cork-Kerry mountains, the house and gardens enjoy one of the most spectacular views in Ireland. Bantry House, home to the White family since 1739, is one of the finest stately homes in Ireland, containing a unique collection of tapestries, furniture, carpets and art treasures, collected mainly by the 2nd Earl in the 19th century. The magnificent gardens and grounds (under restoration) are home to many sub-tropical plants and shrubs – reflecting the best European design and style. Other features within the 45 acre grounds include the renowned 100-stepped 'Stairway to the Sky', the Italian Garden and the largest wisteria circle in the country. Bantry House and Gardens is a member of the Houses, Castles and Gardens of Ireland Scheme.

Location: E outskirts of Bantry town on the main Cork - Killarney coast road (N71).

Opening Times: 1 Mar - end Oct: daily, 9am - 5pm (last admission).

Admission: House & Gardens: Adult £6, Child Free, OAP £4.50, Student £4. Groups (min 20): £4, Child Free. Gardens only: Adult £2, Child Free, Conc. £2.

Partially suitable. In grounds, on leads. 8 doubles.

BARONS COURT

Tel: 028 8166 1683 **Fax:** 028 8166 2059

Newtownstewart, Omagh, Co Tyrone BT78 4EZ

Owner: Mount Castle Trust **Contact:** The Agent

The home of the Duke and Duchess of Abercorn, Barons Court was built in the late 18th century and subsequently extensively remodelled by William and Richard Morrison (1819 - 1841), Sir Albert Richardson (1947-49) and David Hicks (1975-76).

Location: 5km SW of Newtownstewart.

Opening Times: By appointment only.

Admission: Adult £4.50, Conc. £3. Groups max. 50.

Partially suitable. WCs. By arrangement.

BENVARDEN GARDEN

Tel: 028 2074 1331 **Fax:** 028 2074 1955

Dervock, Ballymoney, Co Antrim

Owner/Contact: Mr H J Montgomery

Beautiful walled gardens with woodland walks on the banks of the River Bush.

Location: 10km from Giants' Causeway on B67 Coleraine - Ballycastle road, then follow brown tourist signs.

Opening Times: 1 Jun - 31 Aug: daily (except Mons), 1.30 - 5pm. Other times by arrangement.

Admission: Adult £2.50, Child £1. Group rates on request.

Small museum. By arrangement.

Open All Year
Index
◀◀◀ page 49

BIRR CASTLE DEMESNE

Tel: +353 509 20336 **Fax:** +353 509 21583

Birr, Co Offaly **e-mail:** info@birrcastle.com

Contact: A Parsons

Discover the largest telescope for over 70 years; constructed here at Birr Castle in the 1840s by the 3rd Earl of Rosse. The telescope looks and moves just as it did over 150 years ago. Magnificent award-winning gardens which feature collections of rare trees, imaginative planting, the tallest box hedges in the world, beautiful landscapes with lake, rivers and waterfalls. At the science centre discover many pioneering achievements of the Parsons family and of other great Irish scientists in the fields of astronomy, photography, engineering, botany and horticulture.

Location: In town of Birr. 130km from Dublin; 90km from Shannon via Limerick.

Opening Times: All year: 9am - 6pm or dusk if earlier. Science Centre: As gardens.

Admission: Adult £5, Child £2.50, Conc. £3.50, Family (2+2) £12. Groups (20+): Adult £4, Child £2.50, Conc. £3.

Partially suitable. WC. By arrangement. Limited for coaches. In grounds, on leads.

BLARNEY CASTLE & ROCK CLOSE

Tel: +353 21 385252 **Fax:** +353 21 381215

Co Cork **e-mail:** info@blarneyc.iol.ie

Owner: Sir Richard La T Colthurst Bart **Contact:** Mervyn Johnston Esq

Site of the Blarney Stone.

Location: 5m from Cork city, off N20.

Opening Times: May & Sept: Mon - Sat, 9am - 6pm; Suns, 9.30am - 5.30pm. Jun - Aug: Mon - Sat, 9am - 7pm; Suns, 9.30am - 5.30pm, Oct - Apr: Mon - Sat, 9am - 5pm or sundown; Suns, 9.30am - sundown. Closed 24 & 25 Dec.

Admission: Adult £3.50, Child £1, Student/OAP £2.50.

CARRIGGLAS MANOR

Tel: +353 43 45165 **Fax:** +353 43 41026

Longford

Owner: Mr J G Lefroy **Contact:** Mrs J G Lefroy or Miss Flynn

A romantic Tudor Gothic house. Family occupied. Robinsonia garden.

Location: 4.8km from Longford town on T15/R194.

Opening Times: Please telephone for details.

Admission: Teashop & Shop: Free. Gardens & museum: Adult £2.50, Child (under 7yrs) Free, Conc. £2.

House: £3 extra. Pre-booked groups welcome (10+), Apr - Oct. (2000 prices)

CASTLE COOLE

NT Photographic Library: Matthew Antrobus.

ENNISKILLEN, Co FERMANAGH BT74 6JY

Owner: The National Trust Contact: The Property Manager

Tel: 028 6632 2690 **Fax:** 028 6632 5665 **e-mail:** ucasco@smtp.ntrust.org.uk

Castle Coole is one of the finest neo-classical houses in Ireland, built by James Wyatt in the late 18th century, and sited in a rolling landscape park right on the edge of Enniskillen. Features opulent Regency interior decoration, furnishings and furniture. Guided tour includes ornate state bedroom prepared for George IV in 1821. Also includes stables, Belmore private coach, servants' tunnel, laundry house, dairy and icehouse. The surrounding parkland is ideal for long walks and picnics and includes a children's play area. Tea-room in Tallow House for light refreshments.

Location: On A4, 1m from Enniskillen on A4, Belfast - Enniskillen road.

Opening Times: 13 - 17 Apr: daily. Apr, May & Sept: Sats, Suns & BHs. Jun - Aug: daily (except Thurs), 1 - 6pm. Park: all year, dawn - dusk.

Admission: House tour: Adult £3, Child £1.50, Family £8. Groups: £2.50. Groups after hours £3.50. Park Free.

Partially suitable. WC. In grounds, on leads.

Ireland

CASTLE LESLIE
Tel: +353 47 88109 Fax: +353 47 88256

Glaslough, Co Monaghan
e-mail: ultan@castle-leslie.ie
Owner/Contact: Samantha Leslie
The present castle was built in 1878. Contains Italian and Spanish furniture, tapestries and carpets. The family home of the Leslies.
Location: 6 km N of Monaghan at Glaslough village.
Opening Times: Open for accommodation and dining throughout the year.

CASTLE WARD

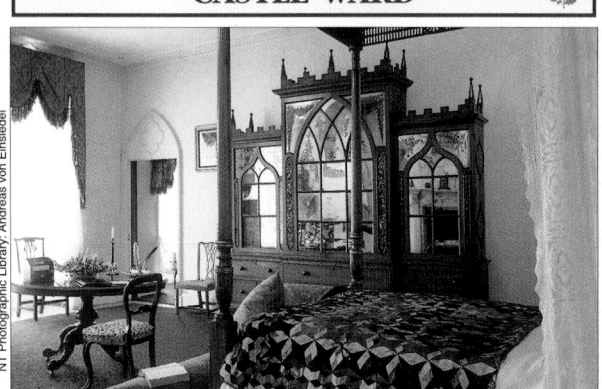

STRANGFORD, DOWNPATRICK, Co DOWN BT30 7LS
Owner: The National Trust *Contact: The Property Manager*
Tel: 028 4488 1204 **Fax:** 028 4488 1729 **e-mail:** ucwest@smtp.ntrust.org.uk
Castle Ward is a beautiful 750 acre walled estate in a stunning location overlooking Strangford Lough. The mid-Georgian mansion is one of the architectural curios of its time, built inside and out in two distinct architectural styles. Due to a difference of opinion between its 18th century owners, Bernard and Anne Ward, the house features Classical styling on one side and Gothic on the other. The picturesque estate also includes a Victorian laundry and children's playroom, water-driven cornmill demonstrations, a disused leadmine and sawmill, which provide a fascinating insight into how the house and estate worked. Paths and horse trails wind their way throughout the estate. Also formal gardens, the Old Castle Ward tower house from 1610, the Temple Water (a man-made lake) and the Strangford Lough Wildlife Centre. Stableyard includes tearoom and a large Trust shop.
Location: On A25, 7m from Downpatrick and 1½ m from Strangford.
Opening Times: House: 13 - 22, 28 & 29 Apr: daily; May, Sept & Oct: Sats, Suns & BHs. Jun - Aug: daily (except Thurs), 1 - 6pm. Estate: All year: dawn - dusk.
Admission: House tour: Adult £3, Child £1.50, Family £7.50. Groups: £2.50 (after hours £3.50). Grounds: £3 per car. £1 if facilities closed, Coach £15 (free if booked for house tour), Horse box £5.

Ground floor & grounds suitable. Obligatory. P £3. In grounds, on leads. Caravan park, holiday cottages, basecamp.

CLONALIS HOUSE
Tel: +353 907 20014

Castlerea, Co Rosscommon
Owner: P O'Conor Nash Esq
Ancestral home of the O'Conors of Connaught, descendants of the last High Kings of Ireland.
Location: W of Castlerea town on N60.
Opening Times: 1 Jun - 15 Sept: daily (except Suns), 11am - 5pm. Open all year to groups by arrangement.
Admission: Adult £3.75, Child £1.50, Conc. £2.50.

CRATLOE WOODS HOUSE
Tel: +353 61 327028 Fax: +353 61 327031

Cratloe, Co Clare
Owner/Contact: Mr & Mrs G Brickenden
House dates from the 17th century and is the only example of the Irish longhouse which is still a home.
Location: 8 km from Limerick and 16 km from Shannon airport on N7 westbound carriageway. Enter at Red Gate Lodge.
Opening Times: 1 Jun - mid Sept: Mon - Sat, 2 - 6pm. Open other times by arrangement.
Admission: Adult £3, Child £1.50, Conc. £2.50. Special rate for guided tour in morning with lunch, for groups of 20 - 40.

CREAGH GARDENS
Tel/Fax: +353 28 22121

Skibbereen, Co Cork
Owner: Creagh Gardens Trust
Contact: Martin Sherry
Woodland glades with varied wild-life. Walled orchard garden with rare breed fowl.
Location: 6 km from Skibbereen on Baltimore Road.
Opening Times: 1 Mar - 31 Oct: daily, 10am - 6pm.
Admission: Adult £3, Child £2.

CROM ESTATE
Tel/Fax: 028 6773 8118 (Visitor Centre)
028 6773 8174 (Estate)
Newtownbutler, Co Fermanagh BT92 8AP e-mail: ucrvfm@smtp.ntrust.org.uk
Owner: The National Trust **Contact:** The Visitor Facilities Manager
Crom is one of Ireland's most important nature conservation areas. It is set in 770 hectares of romantic and tranquil islands, woodland and ruins on the shores of Upper Lough Erne. Things to look out for include the spotted flycatcher, curlew, purple hairstreak butterfly, pine marten and fallow deer. Lots of well-maintained nature trails take in the Old Castle, boathouse and summer house. Wildlife exhibition, information point and tearoom for light snacks in visitor centre. Further facilities include jetty for boats, boat hire, award-winning holiday cottages, coarse angling, pike fishing, overnight woodland hide, lecture and conference facilities. The 19th century castle within the estate is private.
Location: 3m from A34, well signposted from Newtownbutler. Jetty at Visitor Centre.
Opening Times: 17 Mar - end Sept: daily, 10am - 6pm; Suns, 12 noon - 6pm.
Admission: £3 per car or boat. Minibus £10, Coach £20.

Holiday cottages.

CURRAGHMORE
Tel: +353 51 387 101 Fax: +353 51 387 481

Portlaw, Co Waterford
Owner/Contact: Lord Waterford
Magnificent home of the Marquis of Waterford and his ancestors since 1170.
Location: 14m from Waterford. 8m from Kilmacthomas.
Opening Times: Jan: Mon - Fri, 9am - 1pm. May - Jun & 1 - 15 Jul: Mon - Sat, 9am - 1pm.
Admission: House £4. Grounds & Shell House: £3

DERRYMORE HOUSE
Tel: 028 3083 8361

Bessbrook, Newry, Co Armagh BT35 7EF
Owner: The National Trust
An elegant late 18th century thatched cottage, built by Isaac Corry, who represented Newry in the Irish House of Commons. Good walks in picturesque park laid out in the style of 'Capability' Brown. Good attraction to break journey between Belfast and Dublin.
Location: On A25, 2m from Newry on road to Camlough.
Opening Times: 14, 16 & 17 Apr: daily; May - Aug: Thur, - Sat, 2 - 5.30pm.
Admission: House tour: Adult £2, Child £1, Family £4.50. Groups: £1.30.

P On leads.

DRIMNAGH CASTLE
Tel: +353 450 2530

Longmile Road, Drimnagh, Dublin 12
Medieval castle with a flooded moat and boasts a barrel-vaulted undercroft.
Location: 5 km SW of Dublin. Buses: 18, 56, 77.
Opening Times: 1 Apr - 1 Oct: Wed, Sat & Sun, 12 noon - 5pm. 1 Oct - 31 Mar: Suns only, 2 - 5pm. Last tour 4.15pm.
Admission: Adult £2.50, Student/OAP £2, Child £1.

DUBLIN WRITERS MUSEUM
Tel: +353 1 8722077 Fax: +353 1 8722231

18 Parnell Square, Dublin 1
Owner: Dublin Tourism Enterprises **Contact:** Eilish Rafferty
The museum features the lives and works of Dublin's literary celebrities over the past 300 years.
Location: City Centre, N of O'Connell Street.
Opening Times: Jan - Dec: Mon - Sat, 10am - 5pm. Suns & BHs, 11am - 5pm. Jun - Aug: late opening Mon - Fri, 10am - 6pm.
Admission: Adult £4, Child (3-11yrs) £2, Conc. £3, Family £11.

DUNKATHEL
Tel: +353 21 821014 Fax: +353 21 821023

Glanmire, Co Cork
Owner: The Russell Family **Contact:** Mr John Russell
House dates from c1790. Contains splendid bifurcated staircase of Bath stone.
Location: 5 km from Cork off N25.
Opening Times: 1 May - mid Oct: Wed - Sun, 2 - 6pm.
Admission: Adult £2, Child £1, Conc. £1.50. Special group rate.

DUNLOE CASTLE HOTEL GARDENS **Tel:** +353 64 44111 **Fax:** +353 64 44583

Beaufort, Killarney, Co Kerry
Owner: The Liebherr Family   **Contact:** Mary Rose Hickey
Collection of trees, shrubs and plants from around the world.
Location: 13 km from Killarney.
Opening Times: May - Oct: Groups and tours by appointment.
Admission: Free. Catalogue £1.

FERNHILL **Tel:** +353 1 295 6000

Sandyford, Co. Dublin
Owner/Contact: Mrs Sally Walker
200 year old garden for all seasons. Fine trees, rare shrubs and Victorian kitchen garden.
Location: On the NE slope of the Three Rock mountain, 11 km S of the city centre on the Enniskerry Road. 6 km inland from Dun Laoghaire.
Opening Times: 1 Mar - 30 Sept: Tue - Sat & BH Mons, 11am - 5pm; Suns, 2 - 6pm.
Admission: Adult £3, Child £1, Conc. £2. Groups: £2.50.

FLORENCE COURT

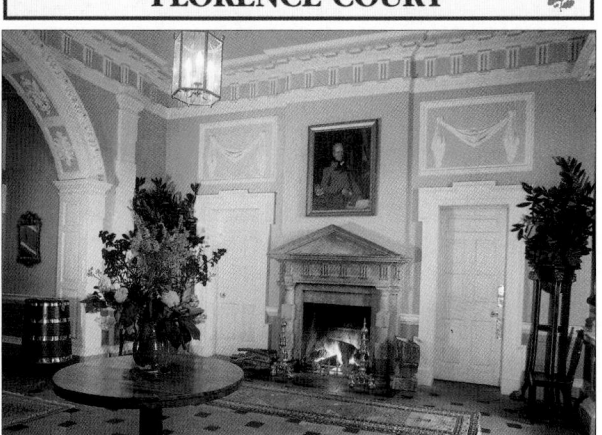

NT Photographic Library: Patrick Prendergast.

ENNISKILLEN, Co FERMANAGH BT92 1DB

Owner: The National Trust   *Contact:* The Property Manager

Tel: 028 6634 8249 **Fax:** 028 6634 8873 **e-mail:** ufcest@smtp.ntrust.org.uk

Florence Court is a fine mid-18th century house and estate set against the stunning backdrop of the Cuilcagh Mountains. It was the home of the Earls of Enniskillen and is one of the most important houses in Ulster. It is now a popular attraction for all the family. Exquisite rococo ceilings and panels, fine Irish furniture. Original paintings, furniture and artefacts returned in 1998 and 1999. House tour includes service quarters popular with all ages. Water-powered sawmill; ice-house; summer house; beautiful walled garden and lots of walks in grounds. Morning coffee, lunches and afternoon teas in Stables Restaurant, gift shop. Also children's playground and holiday cottage.
Location: 8m SW of Enniskillen via A4 and then A32 to Swanlinbar.
Opening Times: House: Easter (13 - 17 Apr): daily, 1 - 6pm. Apr, May & Sept: Sats, Suns & BHs. Jun - Aug: daily (except Tues), 1 - 6pm. Estate: Apr - Sept: daily, 10am - 7pm, Oct - Mar: daily, 10am - 4pm. Closed 25 Dec.
Admission: House tour: Adult £3, Child £1.50, Family £8. Groups: £2.50. Groups outside opening hours £3.50. Estate: £2 per car.

[icons] Ground floor suitable. WC. Obligatory. P In grounds, on leads. Holiday cottage.

THE FRY MODEL RAILWAY **Tel:** +353 1 846 3779 **Fax:** +353 1 846 3723

Malahide Castle Demesne, Malahide, Co Dublin
Owner: Dublin Tourism Enterprises   **Contact:** John Dunne
The Fry Model Railway is a unique collection of handmade models of Irish trains from the beginning of travel to modern times.
Location: 10m N of Dublin.
Opening Times: Apr - Oct: Mon - Sat, 10am - 5pm, Suns & BHs 2 - 6pm. Nov - Mar: Sat, Sun & BHs, 2 - 5pm. Closed 1 - 2pm daily all year.
Admission: Adult £4, Child (3-11yrs) £2, Conc. £3, Family (2+4) £11.

GLIN CASTLE **Tel:** +353 68 34173 **Fax:** +353 68 34364

Glin, Co Limerick   **e-mail:** knight@iol.ie
Owner: The Knight of Glin   **Contact:** Bob Duff
Glin Castle, one of Ireland's most historic properties and home to the FitzGerald family, hereditary Knights of Glin. The castle, with its superb interiors, decorative plasterwork and collections of Irish furniture and paintings stands on the banks of the River Shannon.
Location: Co Limerick.
Opening Times: Tours by appointment only.
Admission: Adult £3.

GRAY'S PRINTING PRESS **Tel:** 028 7188 4094

49 Main Street, Strabane, Co Tyrone BT82 8AU
Owner: The National Trust   **Contact:** The Administrator
Historic printworks, featuring 18th century printing press and 19th century hand-printing machines. John Dunlap, printer of the American Declaration of Independence, and James Wilson, grandfather of President Woodrow Wilson, are said to have learned their trade here. Tour includes audio-visual presentation, check in advance for compositor demonstrations. Strabane District Council local history museum in the same building.
Location: In the centre of Strabane.
Opening Times: Apr - Sept: Tue - Sat, 2 - 5pm.
Admission: Tour price: Adult £2, Child £1, Family £4.50. Group £1.30.

[icons]

HAMWOOD HOUSE **Tel:** +353 44 8255210

Dunboyne, Co Meath
Owner: Major and Mrs Hamilton   **Contact:** Mrs Hamilton
Palladian-style house, built in 1779, contains a fine collection of 18th century furniture.
Location: 2m from Dunboyne on Maynooth Rd.
Opening Times: 1 Feb - 31 Mar: Mon - Fri, 10am - 2pm. 1 Apr - 31 Aug: Mon - Fri. 2 - 6pm. 3rd Sun of each month, 2 - 6pm.
Admission: House: Adult £3. Garden: Adult £3. Groups by arrangement.

HEZLETT HOUSE **Tel/Fax:** 028 7084 8567 **e-mail:** undpmx@smtp.ntrust.org.uk

107 Sea Road, Castlerock, Coleraine, Co Londonderry BT51 4TW
Owner: The National Trust   **Contact:** The Custodian
Charming 17th century thatched house with 19th century furnishings. Interesting cruck-truss roof construction viewed from specially exposed attic. One of only a few pre-18th century Irish buildings still surviving. Excellent attraction for visitors en-route from Causeway to Londonderry.
Location: 5m W of Coleraine on Coleraine - Downhill coast road, A2.
Opening Times: Easter (13 - 17 Apr): daily. Apr, May & Sept: Sats, Suns & BHs only. Jun - Aug: daily except Tues, 12 noon - 5pm.
Admission: Adult £2, Child £1, Family £5. Groups £1.50 (outside hours £2.50).

[icon] Ground floor suitable. [icon] Obligatory. P [icon] In grounds, on leads.

HILTON PARK **Tel:** +353 47 56007 **Fax:** +353 47 56033

Hilton Park, Clones, Co Monaghan
Owner/Contact: Mr John Madden
Lakeside pleasure grounds, herb garden, parterre and herbaceous border in rolling parkland.
Location: 3m due S of Clones on L46, Ballyhaise Rd.
Opening Times: By appointment.
Admission: Adult £3.

NT Photographic Library: Matthew Antrobus.

Castle Coole, Ireland.

THE IRISH MUSEUM OF MODERN ART

Tel: + 353 1 612 9900

Fax: +353 1 612 9999

Royal Hospital, Military Rd, Kilmainham, Dublin 8

e-mail: info@modernart.ie

Owner: Irish Museum of Modern Art

Contact: Monica Cullinane

The Irish Museum of Modern Art opened in 1991 in the magnificently restored Royal Hospital building and grounds, which include a formal garden, meadow and medieval burial grounds as well as a series of other historic buildings. A series of new galleries, housing exhibitions from important collections worldwide opened in March 2000 and are located in the Deputy Master's House. The museum presents, through its permanent collection and temporary exhibitions, an exciting and innovative range of Irish and international art of the 20th century, alongside strong education and community, national and artists' residency programmes.

Location: Near Heuston Station, 2km from city centre. Buses: 69, 78A, 79, 90.

Opening Times: Tue - Sat, 10am - 5.30pm. Suns, 12 noon - 5.30pm. Guided tours: Weds & Fris at 2.30pm, Suns at 12.15pm. Closed Mons. Other times by appointment.

Admission: Free.

ℹ️ No inside photography.
🐕 On leads in grounds. ❄️ (Ⓦ)

JAMES JOYCE MUSEUM

Tel/Fax: +353 1 280 9265

Joyce Tower, Sandycove, Co Dublin

Owner: Dublin Tourism Enterprises

Contact: Robert Nicholson

A martello tower containing a museum devoted to the life and works of James Joyce.

Location: Dun Laoghaire, 8m S of Dublin.

Opening Times: Apr - Oct: Mon - Sat, 10am - 5pm. Closed 1 - 2pm. Suns & BHs, 2 - 6pm.

Admission: Adult £4, Child (3 - 11yrs) £2, Conc. £3, Family £11. Group rates on request.

JAPANESE GARDENS & ST FIACHRA GARDEN

Tel: +353 45 521617

Fax: +353 45 522964 **e-mail:** stud@irish-national-stud.ie

Tully, Kildare Town, Co Kildare

Owner: Irish National Stud

Contact: Freda O'Connell

Created 1906 - 1910. St Fiachra's Garden created 1999.

Location: 1m from Kildare Town. 30m from Dublin off M/N7.

Opening Times: 12 Feb - 12 Nov: daily 9.30am - 6pm.

Admission: Adult £6, Child (under 12yrs) £3, Conc. £4.50, Family (2+4) £14. One ticket includes National Stud and Japanese Garden & St Fiachra's Garden.

KILLYLEAGH CASTLE

Tel/Fax: 028 4482 8261

e-mail: rowanhamilton.killyleaghcastle@virgin.net

Killyleagh, Downpatrick, Co Down BT30 9QA

Owner/Contact: Lt Col D Rowan-Hamilton

Oldest occupied castle in Ireland. Self-catering towers available to sleep 4-15. Swimming pool and tennis court available. Access to garden.

Location: At the end of the High Street.

Opening Times: By arrangement. Groups (30-50): by appointment.

Admission: Adult £3.50, Child £2. Groups: Adult £2.50, Child £1.50.

ℹ️ No photography in house. 🍷 Wedding receptions. ♿ Not suitable. 🎫 Obligatory.
🅿️ 🖼️ 🔔 ❄️

Rowallane, Ireland.

KING HOUSE

Tel: +353 79 63242 **Fax:** +353 79 63243

Boyle, Co Roscommon

e-mail: kinghouse-boyle@hotmail.com

Owner: Roscommon County Council

Contact: The Administrator

Four-storey Georgian mansion dating from the early 18th century.

Location: In the centre of Boyle.

Opening Times: Apr - Oct: daily. Late October: weekends, 10am - 6pm. Last admission 5pm.

Admission: Adult £3, Child £2, Conc. £2.50, Family (2+4) £8. Group rates on request.

KYLEMORE ABBEY & GARDEN

CONNEMARA, CO GALWAY

Owner: Benedictine Nuns   *Contact:* Sister Magdalena OSB

Tel: +353 95 41146 **Fax:** +353 95 41145 **e-mail:** info@kylemoreabbey.ie

Set in the heart of the Connemara mountains. Kylemore is a premier tourist attraction, international girls' boarding school, a magnificent gothic church, superb restaurant and one of the finest craft shops in Ireland. Victorian Walled Garden, currently undergoing restoration. The walls stretch for up to half a mile to enclose: the kitchen garden, flower or pleasure garden, gardener's cottage, bothy and the glass (hot) house complex. The Benedictine Nuns at Kylemore continue to restore the estate and open it to the education and enjoyment of all who visit.

Location: Between Reccess & Letterfrack, West of Ireland.

Opening Times: Abbey, exhibition, church, lake walk & video: All year (closed Good Fri & Christmas week), 9am - 5.30pm. Garden, Dawros walk, museum, tearoom, shop & exhibition: Easter - Oct:10.30am - 4.30pm.

Admission: Abbey: Adult £3.30, Conc. £2.30, Family £7. Groups (10+): Adult £2.30. Gardens: Adult £4, Conc. £2.75, Family £8.50. Groups (10+): Adult £2.75. Joint ticket: Adult £6.50, Conc. £4.50, Family £14. Groups (10+): £4.50.

📷 ♿ Ground floor & grounds suitable. WC. ❄️ (Ⓦ)

LISNAVAGH GARDENS

Tel: +353 503 61104 **Fax:** +353 503 61148

Lisnavagh, Rathvilly, Co Carlow, Ireland

Owner/Contact: Lord and Lady Rathdonnell

Ten acres of outstanding trees and shrubs, mixed borders, rock garden and cruciform yew walk, with panoramic views of the Wicklow Hills and Mount Leinster.

Location: Situated 2m S of Rathvilly. Signposted.

Opening Times: May - July: Suns, 2 - 6pm. Other times by appointment.

Admission: Adult £3, Child £1.50.

LISSADELL HOUSE

Tel: +353 71 63150 **Fax:** +353 71 66906

Ballinfull, Co Sligo

House built in the 1830s by Sir Robert Gore-Booth, and still the family home.

Location: 13km NW of Sligo.

Opening Times: 1 Jun - mid Sept: (except Suns), 10.30am - 11pm & 2 - 5pm. Last admission 12.30pm & 4.30pm. Guided tours.

Admission: Adult £3, Child £1.50. Group: (20+) £2.50.

LODGE PARK WALLED GARDENS & STEAM MUSEUM

STRAFFAN, CO KILDARE

Owner: Mr R Guinness

Tel: +353 1 6273155 **Fax:** +353 1 6273477 **e-mail:** garden@steam-museum.ie

Lodge Park Walled Garden with brick lined north wall of 18th century origin is a plantsman's delight. From the axis of the long walk it features garden rooms extending to a long rosarie. The Steam Museum building incorporates the roof, windows and other architectural features taken from the c1865 Great Southern & Western Railway Church of St Jude (attributed to the architect Sancton Wood) Inchicore, Dublin. Taken down in 1988 it was rebuilt here, under the consultant architect Mr Percy Le Clerc, and opened by the President of Ireland in 1992 as the Steam Museum. The Richard Guinness model hall displays his collection of historic prototype locomotive models. The Power Hall displays restored stationary engines working in steam. Interactive area for educational use. Memorabilia gallery.

Location: 16m from Dublin, signposted off the N7 road at Kill junction traffic lights.

Opening Times: Easter Sun - May: Suns & BHs, 2.30 - 5.15pm. Jun - Aug: Tue - Sun & BHs, 2 - 5.45pm. Sept: Suns & BHs 2.30 - 5.15pm.

Admission: Adult £3, Conc. £2. Groups (10+) less 10%. Garden only: £2. Tech Student + card Free.

    By arrangement.

MOUNT STEWART

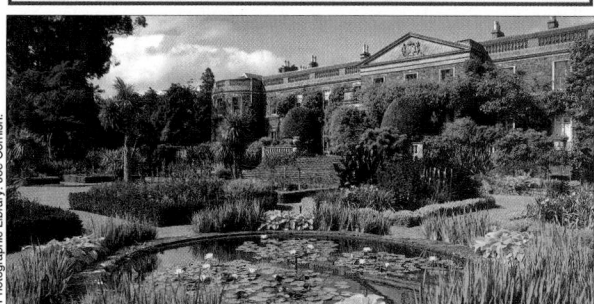

NEWTOWNARDS, Co DOWN BT22 2AD

Owner: The National Trust **Contact:** *The Property Manager*

Tel: 028 4278 8387 **Fax:** 028 4278 8569 **e-mail:** umsest@smtp.ntrust.org.uk

Home of the Londonderry family since the early 18th century, Mount Stewart was Lord Castlereagh's house and played host to many prominent political figures. The magnificent gardens planted in the 1920s have made Mount Stewart famous and earned it a World Heritage Site nomination. They feature a series of formal outdoor 'rooms', vibrant parterres, and formal and informal vistas, some with Strangford Lough views. Many rare and unusual plants thrive in the mild climate of the Ards, including eucalyptus, beschorneria, mimosa, and cordyline. The garden is also home to national collections of phormium and libertia. The house includes 'Hambletonian' (*The Independent* rated it in the top 100 British paintings of all time), as well as the full set of chairs used at Congress of Vienna. The Temple of the Winds, a 1785 banqueting hall, is in the grounds. Due to a building programme the shop and tearoom may not be available during 2001.

Location: On A20, 5m from Newtownards on the Portaferry road.

Opening Times: House: 13 - 22 Apr: daily; Apr & Oct: Sats, Suns & BHs; May - Sept: daily, except Tues; 1 - 6pm. Garden: Mar: Suns, 2 - 5pm. 17, 19 Mar: 11am - 6pm. Apr - Sept: daily, 11am - 6pm. Oct: weekends, 11am - 6pm. Nov & 1, 2, 8, 9 Dec: weekends, 2 - 5pm (lake only). Temple of the Winds: Apr - Oct: weekends, 2 - 5pm.

Admission: House tour, Gardens & Temple: Adult £3.50, Child £1.75, Family £8.75. Group £3 (outside normal hours £6). Garden & Temple only: Adult £3, Child £1.50, Family £7.50. Group £2.50. Temple of the Winds only: Adult £1, Child 50p.

  Obligatory. In grounds, on leads.

MALAHIDE CASTLE

Tel: +353 1 846 2184 **Fax:** +353 1 846 2537

Malahide, Co Dublin

Owner: Fingal County Council **Contact:** Maria Morgan

The castle has changed very little in 800 years, surrounded by parklands.

Location: 10m N of Dublin city.

Opening Times: Apr - Oct: Mon - Sat, 10am - 5pm. Suns & BHs 11am - 6pm. . Nov - Mar: Mon - Fri, 10am - 5pm. Sat, Sun & BH, 2 - 5pm. Closed 12.45 - 2pm daily. Closed for tours 12.45 - 2pm daily.

Admission: Adult £3.15, Child £1.75, Conc. £2.65, Family £8.75 (2000 prices).

> **Admission prices for properties in Northern Ireland are given in £ Sterling.**
> **Admission prices for properties in the Republic of Ireland are given in Irish Punt.**

Crom Boathouse, Ireland.

MUSSENDEN TEMPLE

Tel/Fax: 028 7084 8728

Castlerock, Co. Londonderry   **e-mail:** undpmx@smtp.ntrust.org.uk

Owner: The National Trust

The Temple is part of the landscaped Downhill Estate laid out in the 18th century. Woodland glen and cliff top walks.

Location: 1m W of Castlerock.

Opening Times: Downhill Estate: All year: dawn - dusk. Mussenden Temple: Apr - Jun & Sept: weekends & BHs, 12 noon - 6pm. Jul & Aug: daily.

Admission: Grounds open free.

P | On leads. |

THE NATIONAL BOTANIC GARDENS

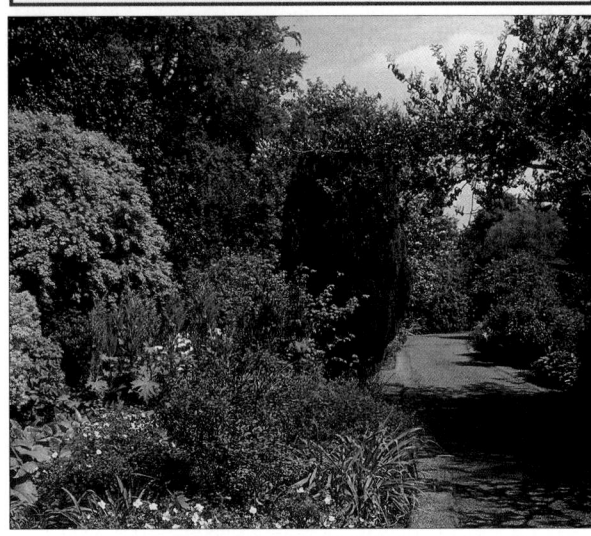

MALAHIDE DEMESNE, MALAHIDE, CO DUBLIN

Owner: Fingal County Council

Tel: +353 1 872 7777   **Fax:** +353 1 8727530

Botanical garden containing over 4,000 species of non-ericaceous plants with a comprehensive collection of southern hemisphere plants, many rare and unusual. The gardens now extend to 9ha including a Walled Garden of 1.6ha, which includes many tender shrub borders, alpine yard, pond and 7 glasshouses.

Location: 13km NE of Dublin City.

Opening Times: Summer: Mon - Sat, 9am - 6pm, Suns, 11am - 6pm. Winter: Mon - Sat, 10am - 4.30pm, Suns, 11am - 4.30pm.

Admission: Adult £2, Child/OAP Free. Groups (10+) £1.50. Guided tours of walled garden £2 (2000 prices).

[icons] Partially suitable. | Licensed. | By arrangement. | P | In grounds on leads.

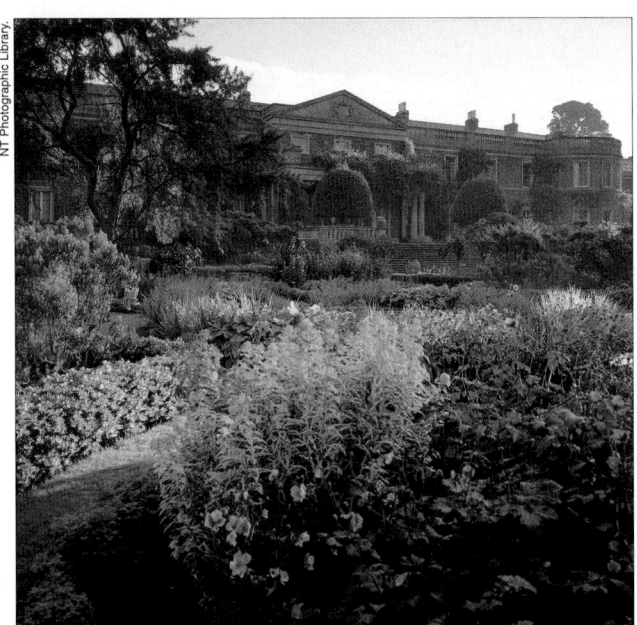

Mount Stewart, Ireland.

NT Photographic Library

NEWBRIDGE HOUSE

DONABATE, Co DUBLIN

Owner: Fingal County Council   *Contact: Brigid Dunne*

Tel: +353 1 843 6534   **Fax:** +353 1 846 2537

This delightful 18th century manor is set in 350 acres of parkland 12 miles north of Dublin City. It boasts one of the finest Georgian interiors in Ireland. Each room open to the public has its own style of antique and original furniture – indeed the house appears much as it did 150 years ago.

Location: 12m N of Dublin City.

Opening Times: Apr - Sept: Tue - Sat, 10am - 5pm, Suns & BHs, 2 - 6pm (closed Mons). Closed 1 - 2pm daily. Oct - Mar: Sat, Sun & BHs, 2 - 5pm.

Admission: Adult £4, Child £2, Conc. £3, Family £11.

 [icons]

NEWMAN HOUSE

Tel: +353 1 706 7422   **Fax:** +353 1 706 7211

85/86 St Stephen's Green, Dublin

Owner: University College, Dublin   **Contact:** Ruth Ferguson, Curator

Two Georgian houses containing examples of Dublin's finest 18th century plasterwork.

Location: Central Dublin.

Opening Times: Jun, Jul & Aug only. Tue - Fri, 12 noon - 5pm. Sats, 2 - 5pm. Suns, 11am - 2pm.

Admission: Adult £3, Conc. £2.

NUMBER TWENTY-NINE

Tel: +353 1 702 6165   **Fax:** +353 1 702 7796

Lower Fitzwilliam Street, Dublin 2

Owner: Electricity Supply Board & National Museum of Ireland   **Contact:** K Burns

Restored middle-class house of the late 18th century.

Location: Lower Fitzwilliam Street, adjacent Merrion Square.

Opening Times: Tue - Sat, 10am - 5pm. Suns, 2 - 5pm. Closed Mons & 2 weeks before Xmas.

Admission: Adult £2.50, Conc. £1.

PALM HOUSE BOTANIC GARDENS

Tel: 028 9032 4902

Belfast City

Owner: Belfast City Council   **Contact:** Mr Reg Maxwell

Built by Richard Turner who later built the Great Palm House at Kew.

Location: Between Botanic Avenue & Stranmillis Road, South Belfast.

Opening Times: Palm House & Tropical Ravine: Apr - Sept: Mon - Fri, 10am - 12 noon & 1 - 5pm; Sats & Suns, 1 - 5pm. Oct - Mar: Mon - Fri, 10am - 12 noon & 1 - 4pm; Sats & Suns, 1 - 4pm. BHs as Sats & Suns. Park: 8am - sunset.

Admission: Free.

PATTERSON'S SPADE MILL

Tel/Fax: 028 9443 3619

Templepatrick, Co Antrim BT39 0AP

Owner: The National Trust

Founded in 1919, this is the last surviving water-driven spade mill in Ireland. The original equipment is working for visitors to see, complete with hammers, a turbine and a press. An authentic workshop setting, complete with the smell of oil, metal and wood shavings. Guided tour includes traditional spade-making demonstration, and the history and culture of the humble turf and garden spade. Excellent exhibition in the reception. Good outing from Belfast, or as a stop-off from the M2. Garden spades made in the mill are for sale and make a popular gift. Spades are available by mail order.

Location: On A6 (between Sandyknowes roundabout and Templepatrick roundabout), M2/J4. 1st left at Templepatrick roundabout after exiting motorway.

Opening Times: Easter (13 - 17 Apr): daily; Apr, May - Sept: Sats, Suns & BH Mons; Jun & Aug: daily (except Tues), 2 - 6pm.

Admission: Adult £3, Child £1.25, Family £7.25, Groups £1.75 (outside normal hours £3.50).

POWERSCOURT ESTATE

ENNISKERRY, Co WICKLOW

Owner: *The Slazenger Family*   ***Contact:*** *The Estate office*

Tel: +353 1 204 6000 **Fax:** +353 1 204 6900 **e-mail:** gardens@powerscourt.ie

One of the world's great gardens, situated in the foothills of the Wicklow Mountains. It is a sublime blend of formal gardens, sweeping terraces, statuary and ornamental lakes together with secret hollows, rambling walks, walled gardens and over 200 varieties of trees and shrubs. Powerscourt House incorporates an exhibition on the history of the estate, a terrace café overlooking the gardens and speciality shops, including Interiors Gallery and Garden Pavilion. 5km from the gardens is Powerscourt Waterfall, the highest in Ireland.

Location: 12m S of Dublin City centre, off N11 adjacent to Enniskerry village.

Opening Times: 1 Mar - 31 Oct: daily, 9.30am - 5.30pm. 1 Nov - 28 Feb: daily, 9.30am - dusk. Closed 25/26 Dec.

Admission: House Exhibition & Gardens: Adult £6, Child £3, Conc. £5. Groups: Adult £5, Child £2.80, Conc. £4.30. Special prices for groups (20+).

POWERSCOURT TOWN HOUSE

Tel: +353 1 679 4144 **Fax:** +353 1 671 7505

South William St, Dublin 2

Owner: Clarendon Properties

Built for the 4th Viscount Powerscourt between 1771 and 1774.

Location: Central Dublin.

Opening Times: All year: Mon - Sat, 10am - 6pm. Suns, 12 noon - 6pm.

Admission: Free.

Accommodation Index ◀◀◀ page 27

RAM HOUSE GARDEN

Tel/Fax: +353 402 37238

Ram House, Coolgreany, Gorey, Co Wexford

Owner: Godfrey & Lolo Stevens   **Contact:** Mrs Lolo Stevens

A two acre romantic scented garden. Twice shown on TV and judged 'Best in Co Wexford' in the 2000 Shamrock National Gardens Competition. There are gravel and woodland areas, terraces, pergola, gazebo, mixed borders in soft colours, ponds, lavish planting around a little stream and over 70 varieties of clematis.

Location: In Coolgreany village, 3km off N11 between Arklow and Gorey.

Opening Times: May - Aug: Fri - Sun & BHs, 2.30 - 6pm. Other times and groups by appointment.

Admission: Adult £3, Child £2.

ℹ️ Garden plan & plant list. ♿ Not suitable. 💷 🅿️ Limited. 🐕 Guide dogs only. ❄️

RIVERSTOWN HOUSE

Tel: +353 21 4821205

Glanmire, Co Cork

Owner: Mr & Mrs D Dooley   **Contact:** Mrs D Dooley

Georgian House. Plasterwork by Lafrancini Bros.

Location: 1m from Glanmire Village, turn right at Riverstown Cross.

Opening Times: May - mid Sept: Wed - Sat, 2 - 6pm. Other times by appointment.

Admission: £3.

ROTHE HOUSE

Tel/Fax: +353 56 22893

Parliament St, Kilkenny

Owner: Kilkenny Archaeological Society   **Contact:** Mary Flood

Built 1594. Various exhibitions. Also houses the County Genealogical Research Service.

Location: Parliament Street, in Kilkenny City.

Opening Times: All year: Mon - Sat, 10.30am - 5pm. Suns, 3 - 5pm.

Admission: Adult £2, Child £1, Conc. £1.50. Groups (20+): Adult £1.50.

ROWALLANE GARDEN

Tel: 028 9751 0131 **Fax:** 028 9751 1242

Saintfield, Ballynahinch, Co Down BT24 7LH   **e-mail:** uroest@smtp.ntrust.org.uk

Owner: The National Trust   **Contact:** The Property Manager

Rowallane is a natural landscape of some 21 hectares, planted with an outstanding collection of trees, shrubs and other plants from many parts of the world, creating a beautiful display of form and colour throughout the year. The garden was established in the 1860s by the Rev John Moore, and carried on by his plant-collecting nephew in the early 1900s. Planting and collecting continue today. In spring the garden features a magnificent display of rhododendrons, azaleas, bulbs, flowering trees and shrubs. Summer brings hypericum, viburnum, shrub roses and fuschias in the walled garden; primulas and heathers in the rock garden and wild flower meadows rich with orchids. The scarlet and gold foliage of autumn gives way to winter, when Rowallane's plentiful supplies of fruit and berries attracts an array of interesting birds.

Location: On A7, 1m from Saintfield on road to Downpatrick.

Opening Times: 17 Mar - end Oct: Mon - Fri, 10.30am - 6pm, Sats & Suns, 12 noon - 6pm. Nov - 16 Mar: Mon - Fri, 10.30am - 5pm. Closed 24 & 25 Dec & 1 Jan.

Admission: Apr - Oct: Adult £3, Child £1.25, Family £6.25. Groups £1.75. Nov - Mar: Adult £1.40, Child 70p. Groups 80p.

♿ Grounds suitable. WC. 💷 Apr - Aug. 🐕 In grounds, on leads. ❄️

RUSSBOROUGH

Tel: + 353 45 865239 **Fax:** +353 45 865054

Blessington, Co Wicklow   **Contact:** The Administrator

A beautifully maintained 18th century house housing the Beit collection, fine furniture, tapestries, carpets, porcelain, silver and bronzes.

Location: 30km from Dublin on N81. 3km S of Blessington.

Opening Times: From Easter Sun, Apr & Oct: Sun & BHs, 10.30am - 5.30pm. May - Sept: daily, 10.30am - 5.30pm.

Admission: Main rooms: Adult £4, Conc. £3, Child £2. Upstairs: £2.50

SEAFORDE GARDENS

Tel: 028 44811 225 **Fax:** 028 44811 370

Seaforde, Co Down BT30 8PG

Owner/Contact: Patrick Forde

18th century walled garden and adjoining pleasure grounds, containing many rare and beautiful trees and shrubs; many of them tender. There are huge rhododendrons and the National Collection of Eucryphias. The oldest maze in Ireland is in the centre of the walled garden, which can be viewed from the Mogul Tower. The tropical butterfly house contains hundreds of beautiful highly coloured butterflies; also a collection of parrots, insects and reptiles. The nursery garden contains many interesting plants for sale.

Location: 20m S of Belfast on the main road to Newcastle.

Opening Times: Easter - end Sept: Mon - Sat, 10am - 5pm; Suns, 1 - 6pm. Oct - Mar: Mon - Fri, 10am - 5pm.

SHAW BIRTHPLACE
Tel: + 353 1 4750854 **Fax:** +353 1 8722231

33 Synge Street, Dublin 8

Owner: Dublin Tourism Enterprises   **Contact:** Eilish Rafferty

The first home of the Shaw family and the renowned playwright, George Bernard Shaw.

Location: 10 mins from City centre.

Opening Times: May - Oct: Mon - Sat, 10am - 5pm, Suns & BHs 11am - 5pm. Closed 1 - 2pm.

Admission: Adult £4, Child £2, Conc. £3, Family £11.

SPRINGHILL ❧
Tel/Fax: 028 8674 8210 **e-mail:** uspest@smtp.ntrust.org.uk

20 Springhill Road, Moneymore, Co Londonderry BT45 7NQ

Owner: The National Trust   **Contact:** The Property Manager

A charming and atmospheric 17th century 'plantation' house, said by many to be one of the prettiest houses in Ulster. It was home to ten generations of the Conyngham family, originally from Ayr. 50 minutes drive from Belfast or Londonderry, 35 minutes from Coleraine. House tour takes in exceptional library, gun room, nursery, and includes the story of resident ghost. Colourful costume collection, with some Irish 17th century pieces. Beautiful walks in walled gardens and way-marked paths in estate. Excellent tearoom, small shop and children's play area.

Location: 1m from Moneymore on B18 to Coagh, 5m from Cookstown.

Opening Times: Easter (13 - 17 Apr): daily; Apr - Jun & Sept: Sats, Suns and BHs; Jul - Aug: daily except Thurs; 2 - 6pm.

Admission: Adult £3, Child £1.50, Family £6.50, Group £2.50 (outside hours £3.50).

📷   ♿ Partially suitable. WC.   🎧   🅿   🐕In grounds, on leads.

STROKESTOWN PARK HOUSE
Tel: +353 78 33013 **Fax:** +353 78 33712

Strokestown, Co Roscommon

Owner: Westward Group   **Contact:** Declan Jones

The Palladian-style house is complete with its original contents. Houses the National Famine Museum. Recently restored Georgian fruit and vegetable garden.

Location: 114 km from Dublin on N5.

Opening Times: 1 Apr - 31 Oct: daily, 11am - 5.30pm. Tours, other times by appointment.

Admission: £3.50 for one attraction. £6.50 for 2 attractions. £9 for 3 attractions.

TULLYNALLY CASTLE & GARDENS
Tel: +353 44 61159 **Fax:** +353 44 61856

Castlepollard, Co. Westmeath   **e-mail:** tpakenham@tinet.ie

Owner: Thomas & Valerie Pakenham   **Contact:** Valerie Pakenham

Romantic woodland and walled gardens laid out in the early 19th century, with follies, grotto and ornamental lakes. The present owners have added a Chinese garden complete with pagoda and a Tibetan garden of waterfalls and streams, and a local sculptor has carved fantastic shapes from existing trees. The Gothick Revival castle forms a splendid backdrop.

Location: 1m from Castlepollard on Granard Road off N52, or N4 via Mullingar.

Opening Times: Gardens: 1 May - 31 Aug: 2 - 6pm. Castle: 15 Jun - 30 Jul:, 2 - 6pm. Open to groups at other times by appointment. Tearoom: daily, 2 - 6pm.

Admission: Castle & Gardens: Adult £5, Child £2.50. Groups: Adult £4. Gardens only: Adult £3, Child £1.

♿   🎧   📷Obligatory.   🐕In grounds, on leads.   ❄

WELLBROOK BEETLING MILL ❧
Tel: 028 8674 8210/8675 1735
e-mail: uspest@smtp.ntrust.org.uk

20 Wellbrook Road, Corkhill, Co. Tyrone BT80 9RY

Owner: The National Trust   **Contact:** The Custodian

Wellbrook is an 18th century water-powered beetling mill with the only working beetling engines on show in Northern Ireland. Costumed guides lead visitors through hands-on demonstration of the linen process, from the flax growing next to the car park to watching the beetles pound rolls of linen. Includes new exhibition on the history of linen and its importance to Ireland. Set in picturesque wooded glen with good paths.

Location: 4m from Cookstown, following signs from A505 Cookstown - Omagh road.

Opening Times: Easter (13 - 17 Apr): daily; Apr, Jun & Sept: Sats, Suns & BHs only; Jul & Aug: daily except Tues; 2 - 6pm.

Admission: Adult £2.50, Child £1.25, Family £5. Group: £2 (outside hours £3).

📷   🅿

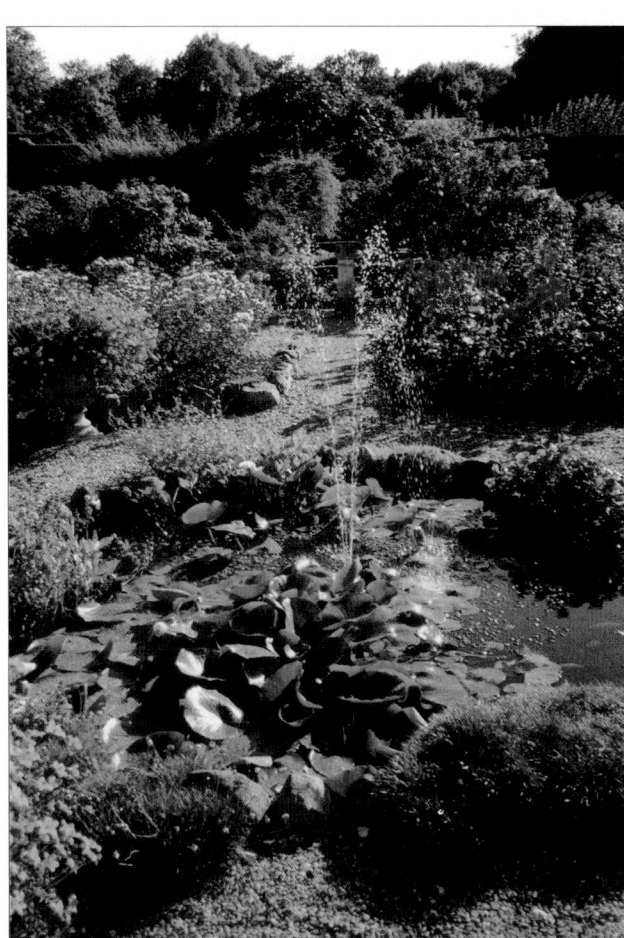

Benvarden Garden, Ireland.

Dúchas – The Heritage Service

- Ardfert Cathedral
- Athenry Castle
- Aughnanure Castle
- Ballyhack Castle
- Barryscourt Castle
- Boyle Abbey
- Brú na Boinne Visitor Centre
- Cahir Castle
- The Casino
- Castletown House
- Charles Fort
- Clonmacnoise
- Derrynane House
- Desmond Castle (French Prison)
- Desmond Hall
- Donegal Castle
- Dunguaire Castle
- Dún Aonghusa
- Dwyer McAllister Cottage
- Emo Court
- Ennis Friary
- Fota Arboretum & Gardens
- Glebe House & Gallery
- Glendalough Visitor Centre
- Glenveagh Castle & Gardens
- Heywood Gardens
- Ilnacullin, Garinish Island
- JFK Arboretum
- Jerpoint Abbey
- Kilkenny Castle
- Kilmacurragh
- Kilmainham Gaol
- Lusk Heritage Centre
- Muckross House & Garden
- National Botanic Gardens
- Newmills Corn & Flax Mills
- Old Mellifont Abbey
- Ormond Castle
- Parke's Castle
- Pearse's Cottage
- Portumna Castle & Gardens
- Rathfarnham Castle
- Rock of Cashel
- Roscrea Heritage (Castle & Damer House)
- Ross Castle
- St Audeon's Church
- St Mary's Church
- Scattery Island Centre
- Sligo Abbey
- Swiss Cottage
- Tintern Abbey

For information on sites under the care of Dúchas please contact:

The Education and Visitor Service,
51 St Stephen's Green, Dublin 2, Ireland.
TEL: +353 1 661 3111   **FAX:** +353 1 661 6764
E-MAIL: info@heritageireland.ie
WEBSITE: www.heritageireland.ie

Opening Arrangements at Properties grant-aided by English Heritage

ENGLISH HERITAGE

ENGLISH HERITAGE

23 Savile Row, London W1S 2ET

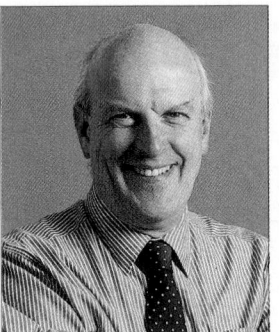

Last year for the first time we published a list of opening arrangements at properties grant-aided by English Heritage. I am pleased to introduce this year's list which has been expanded to make it even more useful to potential visitors and to include National Trust properties which have received grant-aid from English Heritage. Over half the properties are open free but we give details of admission charges where appropriate, as well as a brief description of each property and information on disabled access and parking.

The extent of public access varies from one property to another. The building's size, nature and function are all taken into account. Some buildings, such as town halls, museums or railway stations are regularly open to all by virtue of their use. For other properties, especially those which are family homes or work places, access may need to be arranged in a way which also recognises the vulnerability of the building or the needs of those who live or work in it. Usually this will mean opening 'by appointment' or on an agreed number of days each year. This is made clear by each entry.

Some properties are open 'by written appointment' only. In most cases you should still be able to make initial contact by telephone, but you will be asked to confirm your visit in writing. This is to confirm the seriousness of the visitor's intention as you would for example with a hotel booking. It also provides a form of identification, enabling owners to feel more secure about inviting strangers into their house.

It has always been a condition of grant-aid from English Heritage that the public should have a right to see the buildings to whose repair they have contributed. We therefore welcome feedback from visitors on the quality of their visit to grant-aided properties. In particular, please let us know if you are unable to gain access to any of the buildings on the list on the days or at the times specified, or if you have difficulty in making an appointment to visit and do not receive a satisfactory explanation from the owner. Please contact English Heritage Customer Services at PO Box 569, Swindon SN2 2YR (telephone: 01793 414910; e-mail: customers@english-heritage.org.uk).

Information about public access is also included on our website (www.english-heritage.org.uk). The website is regularly updated to include new properties, any subsequent changes which have been notified to us or any corrections. We suggest that you consult our website for up to date information before visiting. If long journeys or special requirements are involved, we recommend that you telephone the properties in advance, even if no appointment is required.

I hope that you enjoy discovering some of the lesser-known treasures as well as the more well-known buildings we have supported.

Neil Cossons.

Sir Neil Cossons
Chairman

542

Opening arrangements at properties grant-aided by English Heritage ⊞

BERKSHIRE

Basildon Park

Lower Basildon, Reading, Berkshire RG8 9NR
Designed in the 18th century by Carr of York and set in parkland in the Thames Valley. Rich interiors with fine plasterwork. Small flower garden, pleasure ground and woodland walks.
Website Address: www.nationaltrust.org.uk
Grant Recipient/Owner: The National Trust
Access contact: Property Manager
Tel: 0118 9 843040   **Fax:** 0118 9 841267
Opening Arrangements: House: 31 March to 4 November: daily except Mondays and Tuesdays (but open pm Bank Holiday Mondays and Good Friday) 1 - 5.30pm. Park, garden and woodland walks: as house 12 - 5.30pm. Property closes at 5pm on 17/18 August for concerts. Wheelchair access to ground floor, stairlift to first floor, and garden. Car park 400 metres from property.
Heritage Open Days: No
P Yes. Spaces: 80
♿ Partial. Disabled WC: Yes. Guide Dogs: Yes
£ Yes
Adult: £4.30 (house & gardens). £1.80 (park & gardens).
Child: £2.15 (house & gardens). £0.90 (park & gardens).
Other: £10.50 (family: house & gardens). £4.50 (family: park & gardens). £3.00 (per head for groups of 15+, on application).

Highclere Castle & Park

Highclere, Newbury, Berkshire RG20 9RN
Early Victorian mansion rebuilt by Sir Charles Barry in 1842, surrounded by 'Capability' Brown parkland with numerous listed follies. Family home of the 7th Earl and Countess of Carnarvon.
Website Address: www.highclerecastle.co.uk
Grant Recipient/Owner:
Earl of Carnarvon and Lord Porchester
Access contact: H W Dean & Son
Tel: 01223 351421   **Fax:** 01223 324554
Email Address: agent@hwdean.co.uk
Opening Arrangements: 1 July - 2 September: daily. Wheelchair access to ground floor only. Access enquiries may be made direct to the Castle (01635 253210). Unlimited parking.
Heritage Open Days: No
P See above
♿ Partial. Disabled WC: Yes   Guide Dogs: Yes
£ Yes
Adult: £6.50
Child: £3.00
Other: £5.00 (senior citizens and students)

Welford Park

Welford, Newbury, Berkshire RG20 8HU
Red brick country house c1652 and remodelled in 1702, when a third storey was added and the front façade was decorated with Ionic columns. Other alterations were made in the Victorian period.
Grant Recipient/Owner: Mr J H L Puxley
Access contact: Mr J H L Puxley
Tel: 01488 608203
Opening Arrangements: 28 May, 1 - 26 June inclusive and 27 August, 11am - 5pm. Interior of house (4 principal rooms) by prior arrangement for interior of house only.
Heritage Open Days: No
P Yes. Spaces: 40
♿ Yes. Disabled WC: No. Guide Dogs: Yes
£ Yes
Adult: £3.50
Child: £2.00
Other: £2.00

BUCKINGHAMSHIRE

Abbey Farmhouse

Church Street, Great Missenden, Buckinghamshire HP16 0AZ
Thought to have been the gatehouse to Missenden Abbey. The major part was built in the early 15th century and was converted to a farmhouse probably in the mid 16th century with further 19th century alterations.
Grant Recipient/Owner: Mr N F Pearce
Access contact: Mr N F Pearce
Tel: 01494 862767
Opening Arrangements: By prior arrangement (written appointments preferred). A few days notice will usually be sufficient. Access for wheelchair users to ground floor only.
Heritage Open Days: Yes
P Yes. Spaces: 2
♿ Partial. Disabled WC: No. Guide Dogs: Yes
£ No

Chicheley Hall

Newport Pagnell, Buckinghamshire MK16 9JJ
Built by Sir John Chester between 1719 and 1724 and

containing ornate plasterwork, panelling and furniture which was specially made for the house. Home of the 2nd Earl Beatty after the Second World War.
Website Address: www.chicheleyhall.co.uk
Grant Recipient/Owner: Trustees of Mrs Nutting
Access contact: Mrs Valerie Child
Tel: 01234 391252   **Fax:** 01234 391388
Email Address: enquiries@chicheleyhall.co.uk
Opening Arrangements: By prior written arrangement. Wheelchair access to ground floor only.
Heritage Open Days: No
P Yes. Spaces: 60
♿ Partial. Disabled WC: No. Guide Dogs: Yes
£ Yes
Adult: £6.00
Child: £1.50

Chilton House

Chilton, Aylesbury, Buckinghamshire HP18 9LR
Country house, built in the 16th century and remodelled c1740 for Chief Justice Carter based on William Winde's Buckingham House of c1705 in London.
Website Address: www.chiltonhouse.co.uk
Grant Recipient/Owner: Chilton House Ltd
Access contact: Lady Aubrey-Fletcher
Tel: 01844 265200   **Fax:** 01844 265202
Email Address: chiltonhouse@farming.co.uk
Opening Arrangements: By prior arrangement any day 11am - 5pm.
Heritage Open Days: Yes
P Yes. Spaces: 50
♿ Yes. Disabled WC: Yes. Guide Dogs: Yes
£ No

Claydon House

Middle Claydon, nr. Buckingham, Buckinghamshire MK18 2EY
18th century house with fine rococo decoration. A series of great rooms have wood carvings in chinese and gothic styles, and tall windows overlook parkland and a lake. In continuous occupation by the Verney family for over 350 years.
Website Address: www.nationaltrust.org.uk
Grant Recipient/Owner: The National Trust
Access contact: The Custodian
Tel: 01296 730349   **Fax:** 01296 738511
Opening Arrangements: 31 March to 4 November: 1 - 5pm (closed 10 July and Thursdays and Fridays). House closes at 4pm on event days. Wheelchair access to ground floor and all of garden.
Heritage Open Days: Yes
P Yes. Spaces: 300
♿ Partial. Disabled WC: Yes. Guide Dogs: Yes
£ Yes
Adult: £4.30
Child: £2.15
Other: £10.50 (family). £3.60 (groups 15+ Saturdays, Mondays to Wednesdays).

Cliveden Mansion & Clock Tower

Cliveden, Taplow, Maidenhead, Buckinghamshire SL6 0JA
Built by Charles Barry in 1851, once inhabited by Lady Astor now let as a hotel. Series of gardens, each with its own character, featuring roses, topiary, water gardens, a formal parterre, informal vistas, woodland and riverside walks.
Website Address: www.nationaltrust.org.uk
Grant Recipient/Owner: The National Trust
Access contact: Property Manager
Tel: 01628 605069   **Fax:** 01628 66461
Opening Arrangements: House (three rooms) and Octagon Room: April to October Thursdays and Sundays 3 - 5.30pm. Estate and garden: 14 March to 31 December daily 11am - 6pm (closed 10 July and closes at 4pm from 4 November). Woodland car park: open all year daily 11am - 5.30pm (closes at 4pm November to March). Wheelchair access to house (some steps in house) and much of garden.
Heritage Open Days: No
P Yes. Spaces: 300
♿ Partial. Disabled WC: Yes. Guide Dogs: Yes
£ Yes
Adult: £1.00 (house). £5.00 (grounds). £3.00 (car park).
Child: £0.50 (house). £2.50 (grounds). £1.50 (car park).
Other: £12.00 (family: grounds). £7.50 (family: car park).

Freeman Mausoleum

St Mary's Churchyard, Fawley, Buckinghamshire
Built in 1752 for the Freeman family who owned the Fawley Estate. Design by John Freeman based on the mausoleum of Cecilia Metella on the Appian Way in Rome, which he visited while on his Grand Tour. It contains 30 coffin slots with 12 being filled by the Freemans before they sold the Estate in 1850.
Grant Recipient/Owner:
St Mary's Parochial Church Council
Access contact: Mr J B Stuart
Tel: 01491 638782
Opening Arrangements: Mausoleum visible externally

at any time, inside can be seen through entrance archway. For full access contact Mr J B Stuart, St Mary's Parochial Church Council, Fawley, Buckinghamshire (tel.01491 638782) for key. Parking on road adjacent to church.
Heritage Open Days: Yes
P Yes. Spaces: 10
♿ Yes. Disabled WC: No. Guide Dogs: Yes
£ No

Hughenden Manor Disraeli Monument

High Wycombe, Buckinghamshire
The home of Prime Minster Benjamin Disraeli from 1848-1881. Hughenden has a red brick 'gothic' exterior. Much of his furniture, books and paintings remain. The garden has been recreated in the spirit of his wife, Mary Anne colourful designs. Park and woodland walks.
Website Address: www.nationaltrust.org.uk
Grant Recipient/Owner: The National Trust
Access contact: Property Manager
Tel: 01494 755575
Opening Arrangements: House: 3 to 31 March: Saturdays and Sundays 1 - 5pm. 1 April to 4 November: Tuesdays to Sundays (open Bank Holiday Mondays, closed Good Friday) 1 - 5pm. Gardens: as house 12 - 5pm. Park and woodlands all year. Wheelchair access to ground floor of house, and terrace.
Heritage Open Days: No
P Yes. Spaces: 100
♿ Partial. Disabled WC: Yes. Guide Dogs: Yes
£ Yes
Adult: £4.30. £1.50 (garden only).
Child: £2.15. £0.75 (garden only).
Other: £10.50 (family). Park & woods free.

Princes Risborough Market House

Market Square, Princes Risborough, Buckinghamshire HA27 0AS
17th/18th century brick building, with slate roof, built on wooden stilts. Originally used to store grain, straw and hay. The market was held under the store room. Now used as a meeting room by town council.
Grant Recipient/Owner:
Princes Risborough Town Council
Access contact: Mr D J Phillips
Tel: 01844 273934
Email Address: dennisphillips@tinyworld.co.uk
Opening Arrangements: Weekdays by prior telephone or written arrangement to Mr D J Phillips, Town Clerk, Princes Risborough Town Council, 3 Barn Road, Longwick, Princes Risborough, Buckinghamshire HP27 9RW (tel. 01844 273934). Short term parking (10 spaces) in High Street, public car park within 100 yards (next to parish church).
Heritage Open Days: Yes
P Yes. Spaces: 10
♿ No
£ No

Stowe House, Buckingham

Buckinghamshire MK18 5EH
Mansion built 1680 and greatly altered and enlarged in the 18th century, surrounded by important 18th century gardens. House and gardens variously worked on by Vanbrugh, Gibbs, Kent and Leoni. Many of the greatest alterations carried out for Viscount Cobham, one of Marlborough's Generals, between 1715 and 1749. Gardens cover 325 acres and contain 6 lakes and 32 garden temples. Kent designed the Elysian Fields in the 1730s, one of the first experiments in 'natural' landscaping, and 'Capability' Brown worked here for 10 years as head gardener and was married in the church in the grounds in 1744. The House is now a public school, the Gardens are owned by the National Trust.
Website Address: www.stowe.co.uk
Grant Recipient/Owner:
The Commercial Director, Stowe School
Access contact: Mr Bob Sharp
Tel: 01280 818282   **Fax:** 01280 818186
Email Address: sses@stowe.co.uk
Opening Arrangements: 24 March - 16 April: Wednesday - Friday 2 - 5pm, Saturday and Sunday 10am - 1pm; 8 July - 31 August: Wednesday and Thursday 2 - 5pm, Friday - Sunday 10am - 1pm; 14-23 December: Friday and Saturday 10am - 1pm; 16 April: Bank Holiday Monday 2 - 5pm.
Heritage Open Days: Yes
P Yes. Spaces: 30
♿ Yes. Disabled WC: Yes. Guide Dogs: Yes
£ Yes
Adult: £3.00
Child: £1.50 (under 16)
Other: £3.00

CAMBRIDGESHIRE

The Black Hostelry

The College, Ely, Cambridgeshire
Built c1291-2 of Carr stone rubble with Barnack, or similar,

stone dressings, upper storey is timber-framed and plastered on the south and east sides with stone on the west side. Has early 13th century undercroft with ribbed vaults, 13-14th century King Post roof, and 15th century red brick chimney and doorway. Constructed to accommodate visiting monks from other Benedictine monasteries.
Grant Recipient/Owner: The Dean & Chapter of Ely Cathedral
Access contact: The Dean & Chapter of Ely Cathedral
Tel: 01353 667735
Opening Arrangements: By prior written arrangement with the Dean & Chapter of Ely Cathedral, Chapter House, The College, Ely, Cambridgeshire CB7 4DL. Wheelchair access to ground floor only, disabled parking in Cathedral car park by prior arrangement. Parking in town car parks.
Heritage Open Days: No
P See above
♿ Partial. Disabled WC: No. Guide Dogs: Yes
£ No

Buckden Towers

High Street, Buckden, Cambridgeshire PE18 9TA
Victorian house set in 15 acres of gardens and grounds, which include a gatehouse built in 1480.
Grant Recipient/Owner: Claretian Missionaries
Access contact: Mr D J Riddell
Tel: 01480 810344
Opening Arrangements: By prior arrangement. Tea shop open on Saturday and Sunday afternoons in summer.
Heritage Open Days: No
P Yes. Spaces: 50
♿ Yes. Disabled WC: Yes. Guide Dogs: Yes
£ No

Canonry House

The College, Ely, Cambridgeshire
Probably originally 11th/12th century, the ground floor has massive walls and a Norman barrel vault. Much of the original building was demolished in 1770 when current dwelling was built on the south side. Contains part of the 12th century Infirmary.
Grant Recipient/Owner:
The Dean & Chapter of Ely Cathedral
Access contact:
The Dean & Chapter of Ely Cathedral
Tel: 01353 667735
Opening Arrangements: By prior written arrangement with the Dean & Chapter of Ely Cathedral, Chapter House, The College, Ely, Cambridgeshire CB7 4DL. Wheelchair access to ground floor only, disabled parking in Cathedral car park by prior arrangement. Parking in town car parks.
Heritage Open Days: No
P See above
♿ Partial. Disabled WC: No. Guide Dogs: Yes
£ No

The Chapter House

The College, Ely, Cambridgeshire CB7 4DN
Originally the chapel of the Infirmary, now the remains of this house the Deanery. Contains part of the arch, ribbed vaulting and arcade of the 12th century chancel.
Grant Recipient/Owner:
The Dean & Chapter of Ely Cathedral
Access contact: The Dean & Chapter of Ely Cathedral
Tel: 01353 667735
Opening Arrangements: By prior written arrangement with the Dean & Chapter of Ely Cathedral, Chapter House, The College, Ely, Cambridgeshire CB7 4DL. Wheelchair access to ground floor only, disabled parking in Cathedral car park by prior arrangement. Parking in town car parks.
Heritage Open Days: No
P See above
♿ Partial. Disabled WC: No. Guide Dogs: Yes
£ No

Elton Hall

Elton, nr. Peterborough, Cambridgeshire PE8 6SH
Grade I historic building and country house. Late 15th century gatehouse built by Sapcote family. Main entrance façade built by Sir Thomas Proby in the 16th century and remodelled by Henry Ashton for 1st Earl of Carysfort in the 19th century. South Garden façade built between 1789 and 1812 in Gothic style.
Grant Recipient/Owner: Mr William Proby
Access contact: Mr W H Proby
Tel: 01832 280468   **Fax:** 01832 280584
Email Address: whp@eltonhall.com
Opening Arrangements: 27/28 May; Wednesdays in June; Wednesdays, Thursdays and Sundays in July and August, plus August Bank Holiday Monday 2 - 5pm. Private groups by arrangement on weekdays April - September. Wheelchair and guide dog access to gardens only.

Heritage Open Days: No
P Yes. Spaces: 500
♿ See above. Disabled WC: No. Guide Dogs: No
£ Yes
Adult: £5. £2.50 (garden only)
Child: Free, if accompanied.

Madingley Post Mill

Mill Farm, Madingley Road, Coton, Cambridgeshire CB3 7PH
Historic post mill with machinery intact.
Grant Recipient/Owner: Mr Matthew Mortlock
Access contact: Mr Matthew Mortlock
Tel: 01954 211047   **Fax:** 01954 210752
Opening Arrangements: Open weekdays and Saturdays between 11am and 4pm by prior telephone arrangement. Parking available in car park of American Cemetery (next door). Wheelchair access only around base of windmill.
Heritage Open Days: No
P See above
♿ Partial. Disabled WC: No. Guide Dogs: Yes
£ No

The Manor

Hemingford Grey, Huntingdon, Cambridgeshire PE18 9BN
Built c1130 and reputedly the oldest continuously inhabited house in Britain, much of the Norman house remains. The house of 'Green Knowe' in the writing of Lucy Boston was based on the Manor.
Grant Recipient/Owner: Mrs Diana Boston
Access contact: Mrs Diana Boston
Tel: 01480 463134   **Fax:** 01480 465026
Email Address: diana_boston@hotmail.com
Opening Arrangements: House: by guided tours at 10am, 12, 2 & 4pm during August (booking advisable), rest of year by prior arrangement. Garden: daily 10am - 6pm (dusk in winter). Parking for disabled visitors at house, otherwise parking in High Street. Wheelchair access to dining room only.
Heritage Open Days: No
P See above
♿ Partial. Disabled WC: No. Guide Dogs: Yes
£ Yes
Adult: £4.00
Child: £1.50
Other: £3.50

The Old Palace

Sue Ryder Care, Ely, Cambridgeshire CB7 4EW
Grade I listed building formerly a bishops palace opposite cathedral, with an Elizabethan promenading gallery, bishops chapel and monks room. 2 acre garden contains the oldest plane tree in Europe.
Grant Recipient/Owner: The Sue Ryder Foundation
Access contact: Mrs Mavis Garner
Tel: 01353 667686   **Fax:** 01353 669425
Email Address: suerely@dialstart.net
Opening Arrangements: Opening arrangements to be confirmed at time of going to print, please check the English Heritage website for current information.
Heritage Open Days: No
P No
♿ Partial. Disabled WC: Yes. Guide Dogs: Yes
£ No

Peckover House

North Brink, Wisbech, Cambridgeshire PE13 1JR
Town house built c1722. Plaster and wood Rococo decoration. Victorian garden includes an orangery, summer houses, fernery and croquet lawn.
Website Address: www.nationaltrust.org.uk
Grant Recipient/Owner: The National Trust
Access contact: Property Manager
Tel: 01945 583463   **Fax:** 01945 583463
Email Address: aprigx@smtp.ntrust.org.uk
Opening Arrangements: House: 31 March to 30 September: Wednesdays, Saturdays, Sundays and Bank Holiday Mondays 12.30 - 5.30pm; 3 October to 4 November 12.30 - 4.00pm. Garden: 31 March to 4 November daily except Fridays 12.30 - 5.30pm. Wheelchair access to garden and reed barn. Self-drive vehicle (telephone to check availability). Parking in courtyard by arrangement. Car park 300 metres from property.
Heritage Open Days: No
P Yes. Spaces: 100
♿ Partial. Disabled WC: No. Guide Dogs: Yes
£ Yes
Adult: £3.80. £2.50 (on garden only days).
Other: £3.00 (groups). Family discount.

Prior Crauden's Chapel

The College, Ely, Cambridgeshire
Private chapel built by Prior Crauden in 1524-5 of Barnack stone ashlar with clunch carved interior, over a 13th century vaulted undercroft. Has windows in the "Decorated" style, octagonal entrance and tower with spiral staircase; richly carved interior and a 14th century mosaic tile floor.

Grant Recipient/Owner:
The Dean & Chapter of Ely Cathedral
Access contact: The Dean & Chapter of Ely Cathedral
Tel: 01353 667735
Opening Arrangements: By prior written arrangement with the Dean & Chapter of Ely Cathedral, Chapter House, The College, Ely, Cambridgeshire CB7 4DL. Wheelchair access to the undercroft only, disabled parking in Cathedral car park by prior arrangement. Parking in town car parks.
Heritage Open Days: No
P See above
♿ Partial. Disabled WC: No Guide Dogs: Yes
£ No

Priory House

Ely, Cambridgeshire
Rebuilt early 14th century by Prior Crauden (1321-1341) of mainly Carr stone rubble with Barnack stone dressings and a considerable amount of brick. Has 12th century undercroft with groined vaults and transverse arches, 14th century pointed arched windows with "Decorated" tracery and early 14th century fireplace.
Grant Recipient/Owner:
The Dean & Chapter of Ely Cathedral
Access contact: The Dean & Chapter of Ely Cathedral
Tel: 01353 667735
Opening Arrangements: By prior written arrangement with the Dean & Chapter of Ely Cathedral, Chapter House, The College, Ely, Cambridgeshire CB7 4DL. Wheelchair access to ground floor only, disabled parking in Cathedral car park by prior arrangement. Parking in town car parks.
Heritage Open Days: No
P See above
♿ Partial. Disabled WC: No. Guide Dogs: Yes
£ No

Queen's Hall

The Gallery, Ely, Cambridgeshire
Built by Prior Crauden c1330 of Carr stone rubble with Barnack, or similar, stone dressings and much brick patching. Has original undercroft with ribbed vaulting, 14th century pointed arched windows with curvilinear tracery and corbels carved in the shape of crouching figures. Reputedly constructed for entertaining Queen Philippa, wife of Edward III.
Grant Recipient/Owner:
The Dean & Chapter of Ely Cathedral
Access contact: The Dean & Chapter of Ely Cathedral
Tel: 01353 667735
Opening Arrangements: By prior written arrangement with the Dean & Chapter of Ely Cathedral, Chapter House, The College, Ely, Cambridgeshire CB7 4DL. Wheelchair access to ground floor only, disabled parking in Cathedral car park by prior arrangement. Parking in town car parks.
Heritage Open Days: No
P See above
♿ Partial. Disabled WC: No. Guide Dogs: Yes
£ No

Sacrewell Watermill

Sacrewell Farm & Country Centre, Sacrewell, Thornhaugh, Peterborough, Cambridgeshire PE8 6HJ
18th century pitch back wheel watermill and millers house, with range of 18th century buildings housing various bygones (domestic, farming and country life).
Website Address: www.peterborough.net/sacrewell
Grant Recipient/Owner: William Scott Abbott Trust
Access contact: Mr M Armitage
Tel: 01780 782254   **Fax:** 01780 782254
Email Address: wsatrust@supanet.com
Opening Arrangements: Daily (except Christmas Day, Boxing Day and New Year's Day) 9.30am - 4pm (winter), 9.30am - 5pm (summer). Wheelchair access to ground floor only. Refreshments available.
Heritage Open Days: No
P Yes. Spaces: 300
♿ Partial. Disabled WC: Yes. Guide Dogs: Yes
£ Yes
Adult: £3.00
Child: £1.50
Other: £2.00 (senior citizens)

Sir John Jacob's Almshouses' Chapel

Church Street, Gamlingay, Cambridgeshire SG19 3JH
Built 1745 of Flemish bond red brick with plain tiled roof, in keeping with adjoining terrace of 10 almshouses constructed 80 years before. Now used as parish council offices.
Grant Recipient/Owner:
The Trustees of Sir John Jacob's Almshouses
Access contact: Mrs I. Mayne
Tel: 01767 650310   **Fax:** 01767 650310
Opening Arrangements: Monday and Friday mornings and Wednesday afternoons. Parking in street.

Heritage Open Days: Yes
P See above
♿ Yes. Disabled WC: Yes. Guide Dogs: Yes
£ No

Thomas à Becket Chapel

The Song School, Minster Precincts, Peterborough, Cambridge PE1 1XX

The Chapel was originally built by Abbot Benedict, circa 1180, along with the Norman Arch which gives access to the Cathedral precincts from Cathedral Square. The Chapel and School are now a restaurant called Becket's.

Grant Recipient/Owner:
The Dean & Chapter of Peterborough Cathedral
Access contact:
The Dean & Chapter of Peterborough Cathedral
Tel: 01733 343342   **Fax:** 01733 552465
Opening Arrangements: Open Monday to Saturday from 9.30am - 5pm all the year round.
Heritage Open Days: Yes
P No
♿ Partial. Disabled WC: Yes. Guide Dogs: No
£ No

Thorpe Hall

Sue Ryder Care Centre, Longthorpe, Peterborough, Cambridgeshire PE3 6LW

Built in the 1650s by Peter Mills for Oliver St John, Oliver Cromwell's Lord Chief Justice. Ground floor retains many original features.

Grant Recipient/Owner: Sue Ryder Foundation
Access contact: Mrs P Bartlett
Tel: 01733 330060   **Fax:** 01733 269078
Opening Arrangements: Opening arrangements to be confirmed at time of going to print, please check the English Heritage website for current information.
Heritage Open Days: No
P Yes. Spaces: 30
♿ Yes. Disabled WC: Yes. Guide Dogs: Yes
£ No

The Verger's House & The Old Sacristy

High Street, Ely, Cambridgeshire

The Sacristy is part of a long range of buildings which back onto the High Street on the north side. Originally built by Alan of Walsingham soon after he became sacrist in 1322, but mainly rebuilt in the 19th century.

Grant Recipient/Owner:
The Dean & Chapter of Ely Cathedral
Access contact: The Dean & Chapter of Ely Cathedral
Tel: 01353 667735
Opening Arrangements: By prior written arrangement with the Dean & Chapter of Ely Cathedral, Chapter House, The College, Ely, Cambridgeshire CB7 4DL. Wheelchair access to ground floor only, disabled parking in Cathedral car park by prior arrangement. Parking in town car parks.
Heritage Open Days: No
P See above
♿ Partial. Disabled WC: No. Guide Dogs: Yes
£ No

Wimpole Hall

Arrington, Royston, Cambridgeshire SG8 0BW

18th century house set in extensive wooded park. Interior features work by Gibbs and Soane. The park was landscaped by Bridgeman, Brown and Repton.

Website Address: www.nationaltrust.org.uk
Grant Recipient/Owner: The National Trust
Access contact: Property Manager
Tel: 01223 207257   **Fax:** 01223 207838
Email Address: aweusr@smtp.ntrust.org.uk
Opening Arrangements: Hall: 31 March to 30 July and 2 September to 4 November: daily except Mondays and Fridays (but open Good Friday and Bank Holiday Mondays); August: daily except Mondays (but open Bank Holiday Monday); 11, 18 and 25 November: Sundays only. Times: 1- 5pm (Bank Holiday Mondays 11am -5pm, closes 4pm after 28 October). Garden: 17 March to 2 July, 1 September to 4 November: daily except Mondays and Fridays (but open Good Friday and Bank Holiday Mondays); July and August: daily except Mondays (but open Bank Holiday Mondays); November to March 2002 Saturday and Sunday (open February Half term week). Times: 17 March to 4 November 10.30am to 5pm; 1 November to March 2002 11am to 4pm. Wheelchair access to garden (gravel paths) and restaurant. Disabled visitors may be set down near Hall. Telephone in advance for details.
Heritage Open Days: No
P Yes. Spaces: 500
♿ No. Disabled WC: Yes. Guide Dogs: Yes
£ Yes
Adult: £5.90. £2.50 (garden only).
Child: £2.70
Other: £8.50 (joint ticket with Wimpole Home Farm, adult). £4.90 (group rate). (No group rates on Sundays and Bank Holidays).

CHESHIRE

Bramall Hall

Bramhall Park, Stockport, Cheshire SK7 3NX

Black and white timber-framed manor house dating back to the 14th century, with subsequently several renovations (many during the Victorian period). Contains 14th century wallpaintings, an Elizabethan plaster ceiling and Victorian kitchen and servants quarters.

Grant Recipient/Owner:
Stockport Metropolitan Borough Council
Access contact: Ms Caroline Egan
Tel: 0161 485 3708   **Fax:** 0161 486 6959
Email Address: charlotte.bertin@stockport.gov.uk
Opening Arrangements: Good Friday - end of September: Monday - Saturday 1 - 5pm, Sundays and Bank Holidays 11am - 5pm; October - 1 January: Tuesday - Saturday 1 - 4pm, Sundays and Bank Holidays 11am - 4pm; 2 January - Easter: weekends only 1 - 4pm. Wheelchair access to ground floor only.
Heritage Open Days: No
P Yes. Spaces: 60
♿ Partial. Disabled WC: Yes. Guide Dogs: Yes
£ Yes
Adult: £3.80
Child: £2.00
Other: £2.00

Capesthorne Hall

Macclesfield, Cheshire SK11 9JY

Jacobean style hall with a collection of fine art, sculpture, furniture, tapestry and antiques from Europe, America and the Far East. The Hall dates from 1719 when it was originally designed by the Smith's of Warwick. Altered in 1837 by Blore and rebuilt by Salvin in 1861 following a disastrous fire.

Grant Recipient/Owner:
Mr William Arthur Bromley-Davenport
Access contact: Mrs Gwyneth Jones
Tel: 01625 861221   **Fax:** 01625 861619
Opening Arrangements: April - October: Sundays, Wednesdays and Bank Holidays (except Christmas and New Year). Gardens and Chapel from 12 noon to 5.30pm, Hall from 1.30pm (last admission 3.30pm). Parties on other days by arrangement. Access for wheelchair users to ground floor of Hall, Butler's Pantry and Gardens (compacted paths with some gravel).
Heritage Open Days: No
P Yes. Spaces: 2000
♿ Partial. Disabled WC: Yes. Guide Dogs: Yes
£ Yes
Adult: £6.50
Child: £3.50
Other: £5.50 (senior citizen)

Chester Town Hall

Northgate Street, Chester, Cheshire CH1 2HS

Victorian town hall situated in centre of city, home to the Chester Tapestry, portraits of the Grosvenor family, and World War I memorial dedicated to Chester citizens. There is also a memorial to the Polish air force. One of many stained glass windows, shows the Common Seal of the city.

Grant Recipient/Owner: Chester City Council
Access contact: Ms Rebecca Pinfold
Tel: 01244 402320   **Fax:** 01244 341965
Email Address: r.pinfold@chestercc.gov.uk
Opening Arrangements: Monday to Friday from 8.30am to 7pm. Saturdays by prior arrangement. Please telephone for details of annual open day. Parking in Princess Street.
Heritage Open Days: No
P See above
♿ Yes. Disabled WC: Yes. Guide Dogs: Yes
£ No

Gawsworth Hall

Gawsworth, Cheshire SK11 9RN

Fully lived-in Tudor half-timbered manor house with Tiliting Ground. Former home of Mary Fitton, Maid of Honour at the Court of Queen Elizabeth I, and the supposed 'Dark Lady' of Shakespeare's sonnets. Pictures, sculpture and furniture. Open air theatre with covered grandstand.

Website Address: www.gawsworthhall.com
Grant Recipient/Owner: Mr T Richards
Access contact: Mr T Richards
Tel: 01260 223456   **Fax:** 01260 223469
Email Address: gawsworth@lineone.net
Opening Arrangements: Easter to late September 12 - 5.30pm. Closed Saturdays in April, May, June and September. For confirmation see details on internet/website. Wheelchair and guide dog access to garden only. Disabled parking near house.
Heritage Open Days: No
P Yes. Spaces: 600
♿ See above. Disabled WC: Yes. Guide Dogs: See above
£ Yes
Adult: £4.20
Child: £2.10
Other: £3.00 (for groups of 20+)

Highfields

Audlem, nr. Crewe, Cheshire CW3 0DT

Small half-timbered manor house dating back to c1600.
Grant Recipient/Owner: Mr J B Baker
Access contact: Mrs Susan Baker
Tel: 01630 655479
Opening Arrangements: By prior written arrangement. Wheelchair access to ground floor only, disabled toilet with assistance (down 2 steps).
Heritage Open Days: No
P Yes. Spaces: 20
♿ Partial. Disabled WC: Yes. Guide Dogs: Yes
£ Yes
Adult: £4.00
Child: £2.00
Other: £4.00

Lightshaw Hall Farm

Lightshaw Lane, Golborne, Warrington, Cheshire WA3 3UJ

16th century timber-framed farmhouse largely rebuilt in the 18th and 19th centuries. Historical evidence suggests there was an estate and probably a house on the site by the end of the 13th century if not before. The west range is supposed to represent the solar apartments of an early post-medieval house. External walls were replaced by bricks in the 18th and 19th centuries. Timber trusses and main roof timbers survive.

Grant Recipient/Owner: Mrs J Hewitt
Access contact: Mrs J Hewitt
Tel: 01942 717429
Opening Arrangements: All year by prior telephone arrangement. Access for wheelchair users to the ground floor only. Video and photographs available for those unable to climb stairs.
Heritage Open Days: No
P Yes. Spaces: 20
♿ Partial. Disabled WC: No. Guide Dogs: Yes
£ No

Little Moreton Hall

Congleton, Cheshire CW12 4SD

Begun in 1450 and completed 130 years later, Little Moreton Hall is regarded as one of the most outstanding timber-framed manor houses in the County. The south range, topped by a spectacular long gallery, opens onto a cobbled courtyard. The Chapel, wall paintings and knot garden are of particular interest.

Website Address: www.nationaltrust.org.uk
Grant Recipient/Owner: The National Trust
Access contact: Dean Thomas
Tel: 01260 272018   **Fax:** 01260 292802
Email Address: mlmsca@smtp.ntrust.org.uk
Opening Arrangements: March 31 - 4 November: open Wednesday to Sunday (including Good Friday and Bank Holiday Mondays) 11.30am - 5pm. 10 November to 22 December weekends only 11.30am to 4pm. Wheelchair access to ground floor only.
Heritage Open Days: No
P Yes. Spaces: 90
♿ Partial. Disabled WC: Yes. Guide Dogs: Yes
£ Yes
Adult: £4.40
Child: £2.20
Other: Family tickets.

Lyme Park

Disley, Stockport, Cheshire SK12 2NX

Home to the Legh family for 600 years, Lyme Park comprises a 1400 acre medieval deer park, a 17 acre Victorian garden and a Tudor hall which was transformed into an Italianate palace in the 18th century. Location for 'Pemberley' in the BBC TV's production of Pride and Prejudice.

Grant Recipient/Owner:
Stockport Metropolitan Borough Council
Access contact: Mr Kevin Reid
Tel: 01663 762023   **Fax:** 01663 765035
Email Address: mlyrec@smtp.ntrust.org.uk
Opening Arrangements: Hall: 30 March - 30 October, daily except Wednesdays and Thursdays 1 - 5pm. Garden: 30 March - 30 October, Friday - Tuesday 11am - 5pm, Wednesday and Thursday 1 - 5pm; November - 18 December, weekends 12 - 3pm. Park: April - October, daily 8am - 8.30pm; November - March, daily 8am - 6pm. Wheelchair access to garden, first floor of house, parts of park, shop and restaurant.
Heritage Open Days: No
P Yes. Spaces: 1500
♿ Partial. Disabled WC: Yes. Guide Dogs: Yes
£ Yes
Adult: £5.00
Child: £2.50
Other: National Trust members free

Quarry Bank Mill

Styal, Cheshire SK9 4LA

Georgian cotton mill, now a museum and the only water

powered cotton mill in the world. Working demonstrations of cotton processing, a giant iron water wheel and two mill engines steaming daily. Restored Apprentice House once housed child workers.
Website Address: www.quarrybankmill.org.uk
Grant Recipient/Owner: The Quarry Bank Mill Trust
Access contact: Mr Josselin Hill
Tel: 01625 527468   **Fax:** 01625 539267
Email Address: enquiries@quarrybankmill.org.uk
Opening Arrangements: Mill: April - September daily 11am - 6pm (last admission 4.30pm), October - March (closed Mondays) 11am - 5pm (last admission 3.30pm); Apprentice House and Garden: Easter daily during August as Mill, weekends throughout the year as Mill and Tuesdays - Fridays all year 2pm - Mill closing (Mondays closed). Wheelchair access to ground and lower ground floors only.
Heritage Open Days: No
P Yes. Spaces: 350
Partial. Disabled WC: Yes. Guide Dogs: Yes
£ Yes
Adult: £6.00
Child: £3.70
Other: £3.70

Rode Hall
Church Lane, Scholar Green, Cheshire ST7 3QP
Country house built early - mid 18th century, with later alterations. Set in a parkland designed by Repton. Home to the Wilbraham family since 1669.
Grant Recipient/Owner: Sir Richard Baker Wilbraham Bt
Access contact: Sir Richard Baker Wilbraham Bt
Tel: 01270 873237   **Fax:** 01270 882962
Opening Arrangements: Hall and Gardens: 4 April - 26 September, Wednesdays and Bank Holidays (closed Good Friday) 2 - 5pm; Gardens only: Tuesdays and Thursdays 2 - 5pm. Wheelchair access with assistance to ground floor, disabled parking available adjacent to entrance by arrangement.
Heritage Open Days: No
P Yes. Spaces: 200
Partial. Disabled WC: No. Guide Dogs: Yes
£ Yes
Adult: £4.00 House & Garden, £2.50 Garden only.
Other: £2.50 House & Garden (senior citizens), £1.50 Garden only.

St Chad's Church Tower
Wybunbury, Nantwich, Cheshire
Grade II* listed 15th or 16th century church tower, rest of Church demolished in 1977. 96ft high and containing six restored bells, spiral staircase, charity boards and monuments.
Grant Recipient/Owner: Mrs D Lockhart
Access contact: Mrs D Lockhart
Tel: 01270 841481   **Fax:** 01270 842659
Opening Arrangements: Saturday 26 May 2 - 5pm and Heritage Open Days 11am - 4pm. At other times by prior arrangement with Mrs D Lockhart, Wybunbury Tower Preservation Trust, Hawthorn House, 1 Main Road, Wybunbury, Nantwich, Cheshire CW5 7NA (tel.01270 841481) or Mr Sam Wood (tel.01270 841188). Wheelchair access to ground floor only.
Heritage Open Days: Yes
P Yes. Spaces: 20
Partial. Disabled WC: No. Guide Dogs: Yes
£ Yes
Adult: £1.00
Child: 50p

Tatton Park Fernery
Knutsford, Cheshire WA16 6QN
Designed by Joseph Paxton in the 1850s to house the Egerton family's collection of New Zealand ferns and is situated adjacent to a conservatory by Lewis Wyatt.
Website Address: www.tattonpark.org.uk
Grant Recipient/Owner:
Cheshire County Council/ National Trust
Access contact: Mr A J Pellatt
Tel: 01625 534400   **Fax:** 01625 534403
Email Address: tattonpark@cheshire.gov.uk
Opening Arrangements: Fernery open every day except Monday and Christmas Day (open Bank Holidays), 10.30am - 4pm in summer, 11am - 3pm in winter.
Heritage Open Days: No
P Yes. Spaces: 1000
Yes. Disabled WC: Yes. Guide Dogs: Yes
£ Yes
Adult: £3.00
Child: £2.00
Other: £3.50 (car entry)

Watergate House
85 Watergate Street, Chester, Cheshire CH1 2LF
Town house, then headquarters of North Western Command, now offices. Built in 1820 by Thomas Harrison for Henry Potts, Clerk of the Peace.
Grant Recipient/Owner: Ferry Homes Ltd
Access contact: Mrs Hayley Cain

Tel: 01352 713353   **Fax:** 01352 713838
Opening Arrangements: By prior telephone arrangement from 9am - 11am, and 3pm - 6pm.
Heritage Open Days: Yes
P No
No. Disabled WC: No. Guide Dogs: Yes
£ No

CO DURHAM

9 & 10 The College
Durham, DH1 3EH
Independent preparatory school housed in part of the Cathedral Close at Durham. 18th and 19th century buildings, mainly local sandstone with some brickwork. Medieval basement rooms.
Grant Recipient/Owner:
The Dean & Chapter of Durham Cathedral
Access contact: Mr C S S Drew
Tel: 0191 3842935   **Fax:** 0191 3839261
Email Address: head@choristers.durham.sch.uk
Opening Arrangements: During September for 28 days by prior arrangement only.
Heritage Open Days: No
P No
No.
£ No

Croxdale Hall
Durham, County Durham DH6 5JP
18th century re-casing of an earlier Tudor building, containing comfortably furnished mid-Georgian rooms with Rococo ceilings. There is also a private chapel in the north elevation, walled gardens, a quarter-of-a-mile long terrace, an orangery and lakes which date from the mid-18th century.
Grant Recipient/Owner:
Trustees of the Low Butterby Settlement
Access contact: Mrs Caroline Broadfoot
Tel: 0191 3780911   **Fax:** 0191 3783854
Email Address: broadfoot@croxdale99.freeserve.co.uk
Opening Arrangements: By prior arrangement on Tuesdays and Wednesdays from the first Tuesday in May to the second Wednesday in July, 11am - 1pm.
Heritage Open Days: No
P Yes. Spaces: 20
Yes. Disabled WC: Yes. Guide Dogs: Yes
£ Yes
Adult: £5.00
Child: £5.00
Other: £5.00

Durham Castle
Palace Green, Durham, County Durham DH1 3RW
Dating from 1072, the castle was the seat of the Prince Bishops until 1832. Together with the Cathedral, the castle is a World Heritage site. It now houses University College, the Foundation College of Durham University, and is a conference, banqueting and holiday centre in vacations.
Grant Recipient/Owner: University of Durham
Access contact: Bursar
Tel: 0191 374 3800   **Fax:** 0191 374 7470
Email Address: e.a.gibson@dur.ac.uk
Opening Arrangements: Easter - end of September: guided tours daily from 10am - 4pm; 1 October - Easter Monday: Wednesdays, Fridays, Saturdays and Sundays (afternoons only). Access for wheelchair users to courtyard only. Parking in city car parks.
Heritage Open Days: No
P See above
See above. Disabled WC: No. Guide Dogs: Yes
£ Yes
Adult: £3.00
Child: £2.00
Other: £6.50 (family)

Former Stockton & Darlington Railway
Booking Office
48 Bridge Road, Stockton-on-Tees,
Co. Durham TS18 3AX
Original booking office of the Stockton and Darlington Railway. Cottage of plain brick with slate roof facing railway line. A bronze tablet on the gable ends "Martin 1825 the Stockton and Darlington Company booked first passenger, thus marking an epoch in the history of mankind". The first rail of the Railway was laid outside the building. Now used as an administration office and accommodation for single homeless men.
Grant Recipient/Owner: Stockton Church Mission
Access contact: Mr Tom Lane
Tel: 01642 800311   **Fax:** 01642 800322
Opening Arrangements: Monday - Friday 9am - 3pm.
Heritage Open Days: No
P No
No
£ No

Low Butterby Farmhouse
Croxdale & Hett, Co. Durham DH6 5JN
Stone built farmhouse constructed on medieval site incorporating elements of 17th, 18th and 19th century phases of development.
Grant Recipient/Owner: Mr W H T Salvin
Access contact: Mr W H T Salvin
Tel: 01833 690100   **Fax:** 01833 637004
Email Address: williamsalvin@compuserve.com
Opening Arrangements: By prior written or telephone arrangement with Mr W H T Salvin, The Estate Office, Egglestone Abbey, Barnard Castle, Co. Durham DL12 9TN (tel.01833 690100).
Heritage Open Days: No
P Yes. Spaces: 2
Partial. Disabled WC: No. Guide Dogs: No
£ No

Lumley Castle
Chester-le-Street, Co. Durham DH3 4NX
Large 14th century castle, now a hotel, altered c1570-80 and in 1721 by Sir John Vanbrugh.
Grant Recipient/Owner: Mr H B Morris
Access contact: Mr H B Morris
Tel: 0191 389 1111   **Fax:** 0191 389 1881
Opening Arrangements: Hotel open to the public seven days a week.
Heritage Open Days: No
P Yes. Spaces: 100
No. Disabled WC: No. Guide Dogs: Yes
£ No

The Priest's House
Croxdale Hall, Croxdale, Co. Durham DH6 5JP
18th century stone built cottage with 19th century extension adjacent to and ancillary to the Old Church and Croxdale Hall.
Grant Recipient/Owner: Mr W H T Salvin
Access contact: Mr W H T Salvin
Tel: 01833 690100   **Fax:** 01833 637004
Email Address: williamsalvin@compuserve.com
Opening Arrangements: By prior written or telephone arrangement with Mr W H T Salvin, The Estate Office, Egglestone Abbey, Barnard Castle, Co. Durham DL12 9TN (tel.01833 690100). Wheelchair access only to ground floor.
Heritage Open Days: No
P Yes. Spaces: 2
Partial. Disabled WC: No. Guide Dogs: Yes
£ No

Raby Castle
PO Box 50, Staindrop, Darlington,
County Durham DL2 3AY
Medieval castle, once the seat of the Nevills, has been home to Lord Barnard's family since 1626. Contains a collection of art and highly decorated interiors. Surrounded by a 200-acre Deer Park and walled gardens.
Website Address: www.rabycastle.com
Grant Recipient/Owner: Lord Barnard TD
Access contact: Miss Catherine Turnbull
Tel: 01833 660207   **Fax:** 01833 660835
Email Address: rabyestate@rabycastle.com
Opening Arrangements: Easter and Bank Holiday weekends: Saturday to Wednesday. May and September: Wednesdays and Sundays only. June, July and August: daily except Saturday. Castle open from 1pm-5pm. Garden and Park from 11am to 5.30pm. Partially suitable for wheelchair users. Guided tours available weekday mornings from Easter to the end of September.
Heritage Open Days: No
P Yes. Spaces: 500
Partial. Disabled WC: Yes. Guide Dogs: Yes
£ Yes
Adult: £5.00 Castle, Park & Gardens; £3.00
Child: £2.00 Castle, Park & Gardens; £2.00
Other: £4.00 Castle, Park & Gardens; £2.00 Park & Gardens; £12.00 (family), £7.50 (guided tour), £12.00 & £10.00 (season ticket).

Rokeby Hall
Barnard Castle, County Durham DL12 9RZ
Early 18th century Palladian country house with fine needlework pictures.
Grant Recipient/Owner: Trustees of Mortham Estates
Access contact: Mr W H T Salvin
Tel: 01833 690100   **Fax:** 01833 637004
Email Address: williamsalvin@compuserve.com
Opening Arrangements: May Bank Holiday Monday and Spring Bank Holiday Monday and Tuesday, then Mondays and Tuesdays until the second Tuesday in September 2 - 5pm (last admission 4.30pm). Wheelchair access to ground floor only.
Heritage Open Days: No
P Yes. Spaces: 15
Partial. Disabled WC: No. Guide Dogs: No
£ Yes
Adult: £5.00

CORNWALL

Antony

Torpoint, Plymouth, Cornwall PL11 2QA
Early 18th century mansion. The main block is faced in lustrous silver-grey stone, flanked by mellow brick pavilions. The ancestral home of the Carew family for nearly 600 years. Set within grounds landscaped by Repton, 'Antony' houses the national collection of day lilies.
Website Address: www.nationaltrust.org.uk
Grant Recipient/Owner: The National Trust
Access contact: Peter Morgan
Tel: 01752 812191 **Fax:** 01752 812191
Opening Arrangements: Antony House and garden: 3 April - 31 May, 4 September - 1 November Tuesday, Wednesdays, Thursdays and Bank Holiday Mondays, also Sundays in June, July and August: 1.30 - 5.30pm. Last admission 4.45pm. Woodland garden (not National Trust): 1 March - 31 October: daily except Mondays and Fridays (but open Bank Holidays) 11am - 5.30pm. No wheelchair access to House. Wheelchair access to: garden: largely accessible, shop, tea room and family history exhibition. Parking available for 2 coaches.
Heritage Open Days: No
P Yes. Spaces: 60
Partial. Disabled WC: Yes. Guide Dogs: Yes
£ Yes
Adult: £4.20 (house & garden). £2.00 (Antony garden only). £3.00 (Woodland garden). £3.60 (combined gardens only).
Child: £2.10 (house & garden). £1.00 (Antony garden only). £1.50 (Woodland garden). £1.80 (combined gardens only).
Other: £10.50 (family). £3.50 (pre-booked group: house & garden). £3.00 (pre-booked groups: combined gardens).

Caerhays Castle & Gardens

Gorran, St Austell, Cornwall PL26 6LY
Built by John Nash in 1808. Set in 60 acres of informal woodland gardens created by J C Williams, who sponsored plant hunting expeditions to China at the turn of the 19th century.
Website Address: www.caerhays.co.uk
Grant Recipient/Owner: Mr F J Williams
Access contact: Miss A B Mayes
Tel: 01872 501144 **Fax:** 01872 501870
Email Address: estateoffice@caerhays.co.uk
Opening Arrangements: House: 19 March - 27 April, Mondays - Fridays 2 - 4pm; Gardens: 12 March - 18 May, Mondays - Fridays 10am - 4pm. Charity openings (Gardens only): Sunday 25 March, Sunday 15 April and Monday 7 May, 10am - 4pm.
Heritage Open Days: No
P Yes. Spaces: 500
Partial. Disabled WC: No. Guide Dogs: Yes
£ Yes
Adult: £3.50 House, £3.50 Gardens, £6.00 combined
Child: £3.50 House, £3.50 Gardens, £6.00 combined.
Other: £4.50 Group guided tour of Gardens.

Cotehele

St Dominick, Saltash, Cornwall PL12 6TA
Cotehele, situated on the west bank of the River Tamar, was built mainly between 1485-1627. Home of the Edgcumbe family for centuries. Its granite and slatestone walls contain intimate chambers adorned with tapestries, original furniture and armour.
Website Address: www.nationaltrust.org.uk
Grant Recipient/Owner: The National Trust
Access contact: Lewis Enyon
Tel: 01579 351346 **Fax:** 01579 351222
Email Address: cctlco@smtp.ntrust.org.uk
Opening Arrangements: House and restaurant: 31 March to 4 November daily except Fridays (but open Good Friday) 11am - 5pm; October and November 11am - 4.30pm. Mill: 31 March to 30 June and 1 September to 4 November daily except Fridays (but open Good Friday), July and August daily; March, June and September: 1 - 5.30pm, July and August: 1- 6pm, October and November: 1 - 4.30pm. Garden: all year round daily 10.30am until dusk. Gallery and tea-room on quay: 31 March to 4 November daily 11am - 5pm; gallery 12 - 5pm or dusk; November and December Christmas opening telephone 01579 351494. Wheelchair access to: House: hall and kitchen; garden: area around house; restaurant and shop: ramps available; woodland walks: some paths accessible. Parking space available for coaches.
Heritage Open Days: No
P Yes. Spaces: 100
Partial. Disabled WC: Yes. Guide Dogs: Yes
£ Yes
Adult: £6.20 (house, garden & mill). £3.40 (garden & mill).
Child: £3.10 (house, garden & mill). £1.70 (garden & mill).
Other: £15.50 (family: house, garden & mill). £5.20 (pre-booked groups). £8.50 (family: garden & mill).

Cullacott Farmhouse

Werrington, Launceston, Cornwall PL15 8NH
Grade I listed medieval hall house, built in the 1480s as a long house, and extended 1579. Contains wall paintings of fictive tapestry, Tudor arms, St James of Compostella and remains of representation of St George and the Dragon. Extensively restored 1995-7 but still retains many original features. Now used as holiday accommodation.
Grant Recipient/Owner: Mrs Cole
Access contact: Mrs Cole
Tel: 01566 772631
Opening Arrangements: By prior arrangement.
Heritage Open Days: No
P Yes. Spaces: 20
Partial. Disabled WC: Yes. Guide Dogs: Yes
£ Yes
Adult: £2.00
Child: Free

Godolphin House

Godolphin Cross, Helston, Cornwall, TR13 9RE
Tudor-Stuart mansion of granite round a courtyard. For many generations seat of the Godolphin family who were courtiers from the 16th to the 18th century, the 1st Earl (who was born here) rose to be Queen Anne's Lord Treasurer. Has late Elizabethan stables with wagon collection and a large medieval and other gardens.
Grant Recipient/Owner: Mrs S E Schofield
Access contact: Mrs Joanne Schofield
Tel: 01736 763194 **Fax:** 01736 763194
Email Address: godo@euphony.net
Opening Arrangements: May - June: Thursdays and Sundays 2 - 5pm; July - September: Thursdays, Fridays and Sundays 2 - 5pm; Bank Holiday Mondays (except Christmas) 2 - 5pm. Groups all year by prior arrangement. Wheelchair access to all of the house except one room, but no access to the stables and gardens may be difficult. Parking for 3 coaches.
Heritage Open Days: No
P Yes. Spaces: 100
Partial. Disabled WC: Yes. Guide Dogs: Yes
£ Yes
Adult: £3.00
Child: £1.00

Mount Edgcumbe House & Country Park

Cremyll, Torpoint, Cornwall PL10 1HZ
Grade II former home of the Earls of Mount Edgcumbe in Grade I registered landscape park of 850 acres. Includes 52 listed buildings and 16 acres of formal gardens. 16th - 18th centuries. Spectacular setting above River Tamar and Plymouth Sound. Landscape noted by Horace Walpole and Alexander Pope in 18th century. Used as starting point for D-Day landings by American troops in 1944.
Grant Recipient/Owner:
Mount Edgcumbe Country Park Joint Committee
Access contact: The Manager
Tel: 01752 822236 **Fax:** 01752 822199
Opening Arrangements: Country Park (with listed structures): all year from dawn to dusk. Mount Edgcumbe House and Earls Garden: 4 April - 30 September; Wednesday - Sunday and Bank Holidays 11am - 4.30pm. Wheelchair access to flat areas of garden and most of house.
Heritage Open Days: No
P Yes. Spaces: 120
Partial. Disabled WC: Yes. Guide Dogs: Yes
£ Yes
Adult: £4.50 (house only)
Child: £2.25
Other: £3.50 (concessions & groups)

Prideaux Place

Padstow, Cornwall PL28 8RP
Elizabethan mansion, with various subsequent alterations and additions, built by and still lived in by the Prideaux family. Remodelled in Gothic style in late 18th or early 19th century. Has formal garden, Temple, Gothic dairy and exhibition areas in the stables.
Grant Recipient/Owner: Mr Peter Prideaux-Brune
Access contact: Mr Peter Prideaux-Brune
Tel: 01841 532411 **Fax:** 01841 532945
Opening Arrangements: Easter Sunday - 26 April, 27 May - 4 October: Sunday - Thursday 1.30 - 5pm. Coach parties all year by prior arrangement. Wheelchair access to ground floor, tea-room and grounds.
Heritage Open Days: No
P Yes. Spaces: 40
Partial. Disabled WC: No. Guide Dogs: Yes
£ Yes
Adult: £4.50
Child: £2.00
Other: £4.00 (groups, £4.50 Friday and Saturday).

Southgate Arch

Southgate Street, Launceston, Cornwall PL15 7AR
Only remaining gateway of the three original entrances to the old walled town. Main arch part of original 12th century town wall. Used as a jail for many years, now houses art gallery.
Grant Recipient/Owner: Launceston Town Council
Access contact: Mr P J Freestone

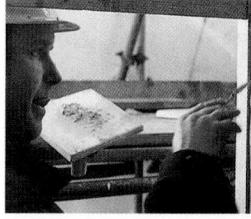

Tel: 01566 773693 **Fax:** 01566 773693
Email Address: ltc@talk21.com
Opening Arrangements: 1 April - 25 December: Mondays, Tuesdays, Wednesdays, Fridays and Saturdays 10am - 4.30pm.
Heritage Open Days: Yes
P No
No. Disabled WC: No. Guide Dogs: Yes
£ No

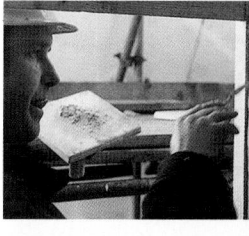

Tintagel Old Post Office

Tintagel, Cornwall PL34 0DB
Small 14th century manor house is furnished with local oak pieces. One room used in the 19th century as the letter-receiving office for the district is now restored to that period and function.
Website Address: www.nationaltrust.org.uk
Grant Recipient/Owner: The National Trust
Access contact: Sandy Chadwick
Tel: 01840 770024
Opening Arrangements: 31 March to 4 November: daily 11am - 5.30pm; October - 4 November 11am - 4pm. Wheelchair access to: House: ground floor only, garden accessible with help (no ramps) staff will assist. Private car park directly opposite (with lavatories including lavatory for disabled people). National Trust car park 1/4 mile from house.
Heritage Open Days: No
P See above
Partial. Disabled WC: See above. Guide Dogs: Yes
£ Yes
Adult: £2.30
Child: £1.15
Other: £5.70 (family). £1.80 (pre-booked groups).

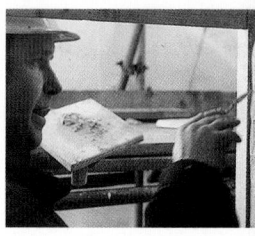

Tregithew

Manaccan, Helston, Cornwall TR12 6HX
18th century farmhouse, barn and buildings, and horse engine house. Some parts of the property may date back to the 16th century. Panelled parlour, original windows and fireplaces, barrel ceiling in one bedroom and 3 leaded windows.
Grant Recipient/Owner: Mrs B Faull
Access contact: Mrs B Faull
Tel: 01326 231382
Opening Arrangements: By prior written arrangement between June and September.
Heritage Open Days: No
P Yes. Spaces: 2
No.
£ No

CUMBRIA

Brantwood

Coniston, Cumbria LA21 8AD
Brantwood, situated on Coniston Water, was the former home of Victorian writer and artist, John Ruskin, from 1872 to 1900. Displays a collection of paintings by Ruskin and his circle, his furniture, books and personal items. Video, bookshop, craft gallery and restaurant on site. Gardens include the Harbour Walk and Professor's Garden where Ruskin experimented with native flowers and fruit.
Website Address: www.brantwood.org.uk
Grant Recipient/Owner: Brantwood Education Trust Ltd
Access contact: Mr Howard Hull
Tel: 015394 41396 **Fax:** 015394 41263
Email Address: enquiries@brantwood.org.uk
Opening Arrangements: All year: 15 March - 15 November, everyday 11am - 5.30pm; 16 November - 14 March, Wednesday - Sunday 11am - 4.30pm. Open daily during school holidays (except Christmas Day and Boxing Day). Wheelchair access to house, toilets and restaurant only.
Heritage Open Days: No
P Yes. Spaces: 50
Partial. Disabled WC: Yes. Guide Dogs: Yes
£ Yes
Adult: £4.50
Child: £1.00
Other: £3.00 (student)

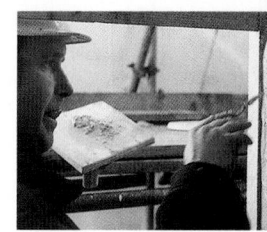

Coop House

Netherby, nr. Carlisle, Cumbria CA6 5PX
Stands on the bank of the River Esk where 'coops' or traps were set to catch salmon. This summerhouse was built c1765 by Dr Robert Graham as an ornament in the landscape around Netherby Hall and as a place to enjoy the river. By 1980 it was completely derelict.
Website Address: www.landmarktrust.co.uk
Grant Recipient/Owner: The Landmark Trust
Access contact: Ms Victoria Piggott
Tel: 01628 825920 **Fax:** 01628 825417
Email Address: vpiggott@landmarktrust.co.uk
Opening Arrangements: The Landmark Trust is an independent charity, which rescues small buildings of historic or architectural importance from decay or

unsympathetic improvement. Landmark's aim is to promote the enjoyment of these historic buildings by making them available to stay in for holidays. Coop House can be rented by anyone, at all times of the year, for periods ranging from a weekend to three weeks. Bookings can be made by telephoning the Booking Office on 01628 825925. As the building is in full-time use for holiday accommodation, it is not normally open to the public. However the public can view the building by prior arrangement by telephoning the access contact (Victoria Piggott on 01628 825920) to make an appointment. Potential visitors will be asked to write to confirm the details

Heritage Open Days: No
P No
♿ No. Disabled WC: No. Guide Dogs: Yes
£ No

Crown & Nisi Prius Court

The Courts, English Street, Carlisle, Cumbria CA3 8NA
Former Crown Court in Carlisle situated at southern entrance to the city. One of a pair of sandstone towers built in the early 19th century as replicas of the medieval bastion. The towers were built to house the civil and criminal courts, used until the 1980s.
Grant Recipient/Owner: Cumbria Crown Court
Access contact: Mr Mike Telfer
Tel: 01228 606116
Opening Arrangements: 16 July - 14 September: Monday - Friday, two tours daily at 11am and 1pm. At other times by prior arrangement with Mr Mike Telfer, Office Superintendent, The Courts, English Street, Carlisle, Cumbria CA3 8NA (tel.01228 606116).
Heritage Open Days: Yes
P No
♿ No. Disabled WC: Yes. Guide Dogs: Yes
£ Yes
Adult: £3.00
Child: £2.00
Other: £2.00

Dalton Castle

Dalton-in-Furness, Cumbria LA22 0EJ
14th century tower in the main street of Dalton-in-Furness, with a local exhibition by the Friends of Dalton Castle and a display about the painter George Romney, a native of Dalton.
Website Address: www.nationaltrust.org.uk
Access contact: Property Manager
Tel: 01524 7011778   **Fax:** 01524 7011778
Email Address: raaspm@smtp.ntrust.org.uk
Opening Arrangements: Easter to the end of September Saturdays 2 - 5pm. On street parking.
Heritage Open Days: No
P See above
♿ No. Disabled WC: No. Guide Dogs: Yes
£ No

Kirkby Hall Wallpaintings

Kirkby-in-Furness, Cumbria LA17 7UX
Chapel in west wing, accessible only from trap door in dairy passage. Wallpaintings in red ochre and black consisting of panels with stylised trees, animals and birds with texts above of the Lord's Prayer, Creed, Ten Commandments and Galations 5, 16-21 from the Great Bible of 1541.
Grant Recipient/Owner: Holker Estates Company Ltd
Access contact: Mr D P R Knight
Tel: 015395 58313   **Fax:** 015395 58966
Email Address: estateoffice@holker.co.uk
Opening Arrangements: By prior written arrangement with the Holker Estate Office, Cark-in-Cartmel, Grange-over-Sands, Cumbria LA11 7PH (tel.015395 58313).
Heritage Open Days: No
P Yes. Spaces: 3
♿ No. Disabled WC: No. Guide Dogs: No
£ No

Muncaster Castle

Ravenglass, Cumbria CA18 1RQ
Large house incorporating medieval fortified tower, remodelled by Anthony Salvin for the 4th Lord Muncaster in 1862-66. Ancestral home of the Pennington family for 800 years containing a panelled Hall and octagonal library. Headquarters of the World Owl Trust.
Website Address: www.muncastercastle.co.uk
Grant Recipient/Owner:
Mrs P R Gordon-Duff-Pennington
Access contact: Mr Peter Frost-Pennington
Tel: 01229 717614   **Fax:** 01229 717010
Email Address: info@muncastercastle.co.uk
Opening Arrangements: 11 March - 4 November: Castle open daily Sunday - Friday (closed Saturdays) 12 noon - 5pm; Gardens, Owl Centre and Maze 10.30am - 6pm. Wheelchair access to ground floor of Castle only but other attractions and facilities are accessible. The hilly nature of the site can create access difficulties so please ask for further information on arrival. Refreshments available.
Heritage Open Days: No

P Yes. Spaces: 150
♿ Partial. Disabled WC: Yes. Guide Dogs: Yes
£ Yes
Adult: £6.50 Castle, Gardens, Owls & Maze; £5.00 Gardens, Owls & Maze only.
Child: £4.00 Castle, Gardens, Owls & Maze; £3.00 Gardens, Owls & Maze.
Other: £18.00 Castle, Gardens, Owls & Maze (family); £15.00 Gardens, Owls & Maze (family).

Orthwaite Hall Barn

Uldale, Wigton, Cumbria CA7 1HL
Grade II* listed agricultural barn. Former house adjoining later Hall, probably late 16th or early 17th century, now used for storage and housing animals.
Grant Recipient/Owner: Mrs S Hope
Access contact: Mr Jonathan Hope
Tel: 016973 71344
Opening Arrangements: By prior telephone arrangement.
Heritage Open Days: No
P Yes. Spaces: 3
♿ No. Disabled WC: No. Guide Dogs: Yes
£ No

Prior Slee Gatehouse

Carlisle Cathedral, Carlisle, Cumbria CA3 8TZ
Dated 1528, the Gatehouse would have replaced an earlier one. It has a large chamber over the gate, with two Tudor fireplaces. Graffiti carved in the stonework is believed to include merchants' marks. One of two integral lodges survives on the north-east side of the building. Now used as residential accommodation.
Grant Recipient/Owner:
The Dean & Chapter of Carlisle Cathedral
Access contact: Mr E T Amos
Tel: 01228 548151   **Fax:** 01228 547049
Email Address: office@carlislecathedral.org.uk
Opening Arrangements: By prior arrangement with Mr E T Amos, The Dean & Chapter of Carlisle Cathedral, 7 The Abbey, Carlisle, Cumbria CA3 8TZ (tel.01228 548151). Parking in nearby City centre car parks. Disabled WC in Cathedral grounds.
Heritage Open Days: No
P See above
♿ No. Disabled WC: No. Guide Dogs: Yes
£ No

Sizergh Castle

nr. Kendal, Cumbria LA8 8AE
Sizergh Castle has been the home of the Strickland family for over 760 years. Its core is the 14th century pele tower, later extended and containing some fine Elizabethan carved wooden chimney-pieces and inlaid chamber. The Castle is surrounded by gardens, including a rock garden.
Website Address: www.nationaltrust.org.uk
Grant Recipient/Owner: The National Trust
Access contact: Property Manager
Tel: 015395 60951   **Fax:** 015395 60951
Email Address: rsizpm@smtp.ntrust.org.uk
Opening Arrangements: Castle: 1 April to 31 October: daily except Fridays and Saturdays 1.30pm - 5.30pm. Garden: 1 April to 31 October: daily except Fridays and Saturdays 12.30 - 5.30pm. Wheelchair access to garden only. Parking for disabled visitors available near the house.
Heritage Open Days: No
P Yes. Spaces: 250
♿ See above. Disabled WC: Yes. Guide Dogs: Yes
£ Yes
Adult: £4.80. £2.40 (garden only).
Child: £2.40
Other: £12.00 (family).

Strickland Hall

Little Strickland, Penrith, Cumbria CA10 3EG
Elizabethan farmhouse, with 17th century alterations. Most notable feature is the Elizabethan plasterwork ceiling in the Lord's Parlour.
Grant Recipient/Owner: W H O'Connor
Access contact: W H O'Connor
Tel: 01931 716 780
Opening Arrangements: By prior written arrangement. Also various open evenings.
Heritage Open Days: No
P Yes. Spaces: 3
♿ Yes. Disabled WC: No. Guide Dogs: Yes
£ No

Wray Castle

Low Wray, Ambleside, Cumbria
A large Gothic mock castle and arboretum. Built in the 1840s over looking the western shore of Lake Windermere.
Website Address: www.nationaltrust.org.uk
Grant Recipient/Owner: The National Trust
Access contact: Property Manager
Tel: 015394 47997   **Fax:** 015394 47997
Opening Arrangements: Castle: July & August, weekdays, entrance hall only 2 - 4pm. Gardens and

grounds all year. Telephone the Property Manager for further details.
Heritage Open Days: No
P Yes. Spaces: 20
♿ No
£ No

DERBYSHIRE

Barlborough Hall

Barlborough, Chesterfield, Derbyshire S43 4TL
Built by Sir Francis Rhodes in the 1580s, the Hall is square in plan and stands on a high basement with a small internal courtyard to provide light. Contains Great Chamber, now a chapel, bearing a date of 1584 on the overmantel whilst the porch is dated 1583. Now a private school.
Grant Recipient/Owner:
The Governors of Barlborough Hall School
Access contact: C F A Bogie
Tel: 01246 435138   **Fax:** 01246 435090
Opening Arrangements: Opening arrangements under review at time of going to print, please check the English Heritage website for current information.
Heritage Open Days: No
P Yes. Spaces: 50
♿ No. Disabled WC: No. Guide Dogs: Yes
£ No

Calke Abbey

Ticknall, Derbyshire DE73 1LE
Baroque mansion, built 1701-3 for Sir John Harpur and set in a landscaped park. Little restored, Calke is preserved by a programme of conservation as a graphic illustration of the English house in decline. It contains the natural history collection of the Harpur Crewe family, an 18th century state bed and interiors that are essentially unchanged since the 1880s.
Website Address: www.nationaltrust.org.uk
Grant Recipient/Owner: The National Trust
Access contact: Property Manager
Tel: 01332 863822   **Fax:** 01332 865272
Email Address: eckxxx@smtp.ntrust.org.uk
Opening Arrangements: House, garden and Church: 31 March to 4 November: daily except Thursdays and Fridays. House and Church: 1- 5.30pm (ticket office opens at 11am). Garden: 11am - 5.30pm. Park: most days until 9pm or dusk if earlier. Timed ticket system is in operation. All visitors (including NT members) require a ticket from the ticket office. Wheelchair access to ground floor of house, stables, shop and restaurant.
Heritage Open Days: No
P Yes. Spaces: 75
♿ Partial. Disabled WC: Yes. Guide Dogs: Yes
£ Yes
Adult: £5.20
Child: £2.60
Other: £13.00 (family). £2.50 (garden only).

Caudwell's Mill

Rowsley, Matlock, Derbyshire DE4 2EB
Victorian (1874) Grade II*, complete, 'automatic', water-turbine powered roller flour mill and provender mill. Four floors with a collection of early original milling machinery illustrating the changes over the years in the milling process. Exhibitions, displays and 'hands-on' models. Craftspeople around Stable Courtyard.
Grant Recipient/Owner: The Manager
Access contact: The Manager
Tel: 01629 734374   **Fax:** 01629 734374
Email Address: raymarjoram@compuserve.com
Opening Arrangements: Mill building: 1 March - 31 October daily 10am - 6pm; rest of year weekends 10am - 4.30pm, closed Christmas. Rest of site and shops: daily except 24-26 December and weekdays in January. Introductory film to mill available. Some wheelchair access. Special parking for disabled drivers in the mill yard.
Heritage Open Days: Yes
P Yes. Spaces: 50
♿ Partial. Disabled WC: Yes. Guide Dogs: Yes
£ Yes
Adult: £3.00
Child: £1.00
Other: £2.00 (senior citizens)

Hardwick Hall

Doe Lea, Chesterfield, Derbyshire S44 5QJ
A late 16th century 'prodigy house' designed by Robert Smythson for Bess of Hardwick. Contains an outstanding collection of 16th century furniture, tapestries and needlework. Walled courtyards enclose gardens, orchards and herb garden.
Website Address: www.nationaltrust.org.uk
Grant Recipient/Owner: The National Trust
Access contact: Property Manager
Tel: 01246 850430   **Fax:** 01246 854200
Email Address: ehwxxx@smtp.ntrust.org.uk
Opening Arrangements: 31 March to 28 October: daily except Mondays, Tuesdays and Fridays (but open Bank

Holiday Mondays) 12.30 - 5pm. Garden: daily 12 - 5.30pm. Parkland: daily. Wheelchair access to ground floor of house, Great Kitchen, shop and garden.
Heritage Open Days: No
P Yes. Spaces: 200
Partial. Disabled WC: Yes. Guide Dogs: Yes
£ Yes
Adult: £6.20
Child: £3.10
Other: £15.50 (family). £3.30 (garden only). £8.30 joint ticket with Hardwick Old Hall (EH property).

Kedleston Hall
Derby, Derbyshire DE22 5JH
A classical Palladian mansion built 1759-65 for the Curzon family and little altered since. Robert Adam interior with state rooms retaining their collection of paintings and original furniture. The Eastern museum houses a range of objects collected by Lord Curzon when Viceroy of India (1899-1905). Set in 800 acres of parkland and 18th century pleasure ground, garden and woodland walks.
Website Address: www.nationaltrust.org.uk
Grant Recipient/Owner: The National Trust
Access contact: Property Manager
Tel: 01332 842191   **Fax:** 01332 841972
Email Address: ekdxxx@smtp.ntrust.org.uk
Opening Arrangements: House: 31 March to 4 November: daily except Thursdays and Fridays 12 - 4.30pm. Garden: as house 11am - 6pm. Park: 31 March to 4 November: daily 11am - 6pm; November to 23 December Saturdays and Sundays 12 - 4pm. Wheelchair access to ground floor of house, garden, restaurant and shop.
Heritage Open Days: No
P Yes. Spaces: 60
Partial. Disabled WC: Yes. Guide Dogs: Yes
£ Yes
Adult: £5.10
Child: £2.50
Other: £12.70 (family). £2.30 (park and garden only). £2.00 (car park charge on Thursdays and Fridays).

Masson Mills
Derby Road, Matlock Bath, Derbyshire DE4 3PY
Built in 1783 as the showpiece mills of Sir Richard Arkwright, they are the oldest continuously occupied mills in the world. Now a working textile museum producing cloth on old looms. Originally water-powered by the River Derwent the water turbines are still in use.
Website Address: www.massonmills.co.uk
Grant Recipient/Owner: Mara Securities Ltd
Access contact: The Co-ordinator
Tel: 01629 581001   **Fax:** 01629 582403
Opening Arrangements: Open all year except Christmas Day and Easter Day: Monday - Friday 10am - 4pm, Saturday 11am - 5pm and Sunday 11am - 4pm.
Heritage Open Days: No
P Yes. Spaces: 200
Partial. Disabled WC: Yes. Guide Dogs: No
£ Yes
Adult: £2.50
Child: £1.50
Other: £2.00

Melbourne Hall & Gardens
Church Square, Melbourne, Derbyshire DE73 1EN
Historic house and formal 18th century garden with yew tunnel and wrought iron arbour by Bakewell. House once home of Victorian Prime Minister William Lamb, who as Viscount Melbourne named the Australian city. A family home since 1628, the hall is lived in by Lord Ralph Kerr (a descendant of the original owner Sir John Coke) and his family.
Grant Recipient/Owner:
Trustees of the Melbourne Garden Charity
Access contact: Mrs Gill Weston
Tel: 01332 862502   **Fax:** 01332 862263
Email Address: melbhall@globalnet.co.uk
Opening Arrangements: Hall: daily during August (except first three Mondays) 2 - 5pm. Gardens: April - September, Wednesdays, Saturdays, Sundays and Bank Holiday Mondays 1.30 - 5.30pm. No specially designed lavatory for disabled people but one cubicle slightly larger than others with handrail.
Heritage Open Days: Yes
P Yes. Spaces: 6
Yes. Disabled WC: See above. Guide Dogs: Yes
£ Yes
Adult: £3.00 Hall, £3.00 Gardens, £5.00 combined.
Child: £1.50 Hall, £2.00 Gardens, £3.00 combined.
Other: £2.50 Hall, £2.00 Gardens, £4.00 combined.

Sudbury Hall
Sudbury, Ashbourne, Derbyshire DE6 5HT
17th century house with rich interior decoration including wood carvings by Laguerre. The Great Staircase (c1676) with white-painted balustrade with luxuriantly carved foliage by Edward Pierce, is one of the finest staircases of its date in an English house. 19th century service wing houses the National Trust Museum of Childhood.

Website Address: www.nationaltrust.org.uk
Grant Recipient/Owner: The National Trust
Access contact: Property Manager
Tel: 01283 585305   **Fax:** 01283 585139
Email Address: esuxxx@smtp.ntrust.org.uk
Opening Arrangements: Hall: 31 March to 4 November: daily except Mondays and Tuesdays (but open Bank Holiday Mondays and closed Good Fridays) 1 - 5.30pm. Grounds: as Hall 12 - 6pm. Wheelchair access to museum, shop and restaurant. Car park is a short distance from the Hall; six-seater volunteer driven buggy available.
Heritage Open Days: No
P Yes. Spaces: 100
Partial. Disabled WC: Yes. Guide Dogs: Yes
£ Yes
Adult: £3.80, £6.10 (Hall & Museum).
Child: £1.90, £3.00 (Hall & Museum).
Other: £9.50 (family). £15.20 (Hall & Museum).

DEVON

Broomham Farm
King's Nympton, Devon EX37 9TS
Late medieval Grade II* listed Devon long-house of stone and cob construction with thatched roof. Contains a smoking room. Currently undergoing renovation.
Grant Recipient/Owner: Mr Clements
Access contact: Miss J Clements
Tel: 01769 572322
Opening Arrangements: By prior telephone arrangement.
Heritage Open Days: No
P Yes. Spaces: 3
No
£ No

Canonsleigh Abbey Gatehouse
Burlescombe, Devon EX16 7JF
15th century Augustinian priory gatehouse. Large double gateway with chamber over. Much contemporary decoration.
Grant Recipient/Owner: Mr Burroughs
Access contact: Mr Burroughs
Opening Arrangements: By prior written arrangement any day from 1 April - 1 October, at least 10 days notice is required. Wheelchair access to ground floor only.
Heritage Open Days: Yes
P Yes. Spaces: 5
Partial. Disabled WC: No. Guide Dogs: Yes
£ No

Castle Drogo
Drewsteignton, Devon EX6 6PB
A granite castle built between 1910 and 1930 for Julius Drewe by Sir Edwin Lutyens. The interior has an interesting kitchen and scullery. Terraced formal gardens.
Website Address: www.nationaltrust.org.uk
Grant Recipient/Owner: The National Trust
Access contact: Alex Raeder
Tel: 01392 881691   **Fax:** 01392 881954
Email Address: dlaarx@smtp.ntrust.org.uk
Opening Arrangements: March: daily except Mondays and Tuesdays, pre-season guided tours only. 31 March to 4 November: daily except Friday (but open Good Friday) 11am - 5.30pm. Special guided tours on Friday 20 July and 31 August 11am, 1pm and 3pm. Garden open all year, daily 10.30 am to dusk. Wheelchair access to: Hall, Library, Chapel and Gun Room, restaurant, shop and garden. Lift with seat (too small for most wheelchairs) to lower ground floor of Castle via 2 steps, to dining and kitchen area. Wheelchairs and buggy service available.
Heritage Open Days: No
P Yes. Spaces: 250
Partial. Disabled WC: Yes. Guide Dogs: Yes
£ Yes
Adult: £5.60 (castle & gardens). £2.80 (garden and grounds).
Child: Free for under 5s. Half adult price for 5-16.
Other: £14.00 (family). £4.70 (booked parties).

Colleton Manor Chapel
Chulmleigh, Devon EX18 7JS
Small chapel over gatehouse, possibly one mentioned in licence of 1381. Stone walls, slate roof, west wall recently rebuilt in stone and cob. Plain interior with Edwardian matchboard panelling and exposed timbers. Still used as a chapel.
Grant Recipient/Owner: Mr Phillips
Access contact: Mr Phillips
Tel: 01769 580240
Opening Arrangements: By prior telephone arrangement. Voluntary donation.
Heritage Open Days: No
P Yes. Spaces: 3
No. Disabled WC: No. Guide Dogs: No
£ See above

The Devon & Exeter Institution Library & Reading Rooms
7 Cathedral Close, Exeter, Devon EX1 1EZ
Building housing the Library and Reading Rooms of the Devon and Exeter Institution since 1813 but was formerly the town house of the Courtenay family and one time home of the Parliamentary General, Sir William Waller. Part of the Tudor house remains at the rear and also the gatehouse range which fronts The Close. In the early 19th century the two lofty libraries were built on the site of the old hall and kitchen.
Grant Recipient/Owner:
Devon & Exeter Institution Library & Reading Rooms
Access contact: Mrs M M Rowe
Tel: 01392 274727
Opening Arrangements: Open Monday - Friday 9am - 5pm. Closed for a week at Easter and Christmas.
Heritage Open Days: No
P No
Yes. Disabled WC: Yes. Guide Dogs: Yes
£ No

Dunkeswell Abbey
nr. Honiton, Devon EX14 ORP
Ruins of Cistercian abbey.
Grant Recipient/Owner:
Dunkeswell Abbey Preservation Fund
Access contact: Reverend N J Wall
Tel: 01404 891243
Opening Arrangements: Always open. Roadside parking.
Heritage Open Days: No
P See above
Yes. Disabled WC: No. Guide Dogs: Yes
£ No

Eastleigh Manor
Eastleigh, Bideford, Devon EX39 4PA
Late 15th or early 16th century manor house, remodelled in late 16th or early 17th century and again c1800. Contains interesting features from each stage of its building history, including a medieval ceiling in one room.
Grant Recipient/Owner: Mr D Grigg
Access contact: Mr D Grigg
Tel: 01271 860418
Opening Arrangements: By prior written arrangement between October and March.
Heritage Open Days: No
P Yes. Spaces: 5
No
£ No

Endsleigh House
Milton Abbot, Tavistock, Devon PL19 0PQ
Built 1811-14 by the 6th Duke of Bedford to the designs of Sir Jeffry Wyatville, the grounds were laid out by Humphry Repton.
Grant Recipient/Owner: Endsleigh Fishing Club Ltd
Access contact: Mr D Bradbury
Tel: 01822 870248   **Fax:** 01822 870502
Opening Arrangements: April - September: Friday - Tuesday 11am - 5pm, plus Wednesdays and Thursdays by prior arrangement.
Heritage Open Days: No
P Yes. Spaces: 20
Yes. Disabled WC: Yes. Guide Dogs: Yes
£ Yes
Adult: £3.00

Finch Foundry
Sticklepath, Okehampton, Devon EX20 2NW
19th century water-powered forge, which produced agricultural and mining hand tools. Still in working order with regular demonstrations. The foundry has three water-wheels driving the huge tilt hammer and grindstone.
Website Address: www.nationaltrust.org.uk
Grant Recipient/Owner: The National Trust
Access contact: Alex Raeder
Tel: 01392 881691   **Fax:** 01392 881954
Email Address: dlaarx@smtp.ntrust.org.uk
Opening Arrangements: 31 March to 4 November daily except Tuesdays 11am to 5.30pm. Access to car park is narrow and unsuitable for coaches and wide vehicles. Partial wheelchair access: foundry can be viewed through shop windows; access to workshop and museum is difficult; shop is accessible.
Heritage Open Days: No
P Yes. Spaces: 50
Partial. Disabled WC: No. Guide Dogs: Yes
£ Yes
Adult: £2.90
Child: Free for under 5s. Half adult price for 5-16.

Gittisham Town House
Gittisham, Honiton, Devon EX14 3AJ
Grade II* late 16th century cross passage farmhouse with 17th and 18th century additions. The south side of the

house is bounded by a walled garden.
Grant Recipient/Owner: Mr R J T Marker
Access contact: Andrew Hill
Tel: 01404 851 041   **Fax:** 01404 851 289
Opening Arrangements: By prior written arrangement. Closed Easter and Christmas.
Heritage Open Days: No
Ⓟ Yes. Spaces: 4
♿ No. Disabled WC: No. Guide Dogs: Yes
💷 No

Higher Thornham

Romansleigh, South Molton, Devon EX36 4JS
16th century through passage house, remodelled in the 17th century. Built of stone and cob, with a thatched roof. Beamed ceilings on ground floor and one moulded door frame. Recently renovated using traditional materials.
Grant Recipient/Owner: Mr S W Chudley
Access contact: Mr S W Chudley
Opening Arrangements: By prior written arrangement 1 May - end of September: Monday or Friday 2 - 4.30pm. Dogs not allowed and children must be accompanied by an adult. No photography. Guide dog access to ground floor only.
Heritage Open Days: No
Ⓟ Yes. Spaces: 2
♿ No. Disabled WC: No. Guide Dogs: Yes
💷 Yes
Adult: £4.00
Child: £1.50

Killerton House Chapel

Broadclyst, nr. Exeter, Devon EX5 3LE
The Chapel of the Holy Evangelists was built in 1841 for Sir Thomas Acland. The architect was C R Cockerell RA, better known for designing in the classical tradition than in the Victorian - Neo-Norman style of Killerton Chapel. It is an approximate copy of the Chapel of St Joseph at Glastonbury Abbey.
Website Address: www.nationaltrust.org.uk
Grant Recipient/Owner: The National Trust
Access contact: Alex Raeder
Tel: 01392 881691   **Fax:** 01392 881954
Email Address: dlaarx@smtp.ntrust.org.uk
Opening Arrangements: 10 March to 4 November: daily except Tuesdays 11am to 5.30pm. (Closed Mondays in March and October). Access to the Chapel is free. There is an admission charge to Killerton House and remainder of the grounds. Approach to Chapel is difficult for wheelchairs. Lavatory for disabled people available at Killerton House and car park at entrance to Killerton House.
Heritage Open Days: No
Ⓟ Yes. Spaces: 20
♿ Partial. Disabled WC: Yes. Guide Dogs: Yes
💷 No

Lawrence Castle Haldon Belvedere

Higher Ashton, nr. Dunchideock, Exeter, Devon EX6 7QY
Grade II* listed building built in 1788 as the centrepiece to a 11,600 acre estate. Stands 800ft above sea level overlooking the cathedral city of Exeter, the Exe estuary and the surrounding countryside. Contains a spiral staircase and miniature ballroom.
Website Address: www.haldonbelvedere.co.uk
Grant Recipient/Owner: Mr Ian Turner
Access contact: Mr Ian Turner
Tel: 01392 833668   **Fax:** 01392 833668
Email Address: turner@haldonbelvedere.co.uk
Opening Arrangements: March - October: Sundays and Bank Holidays 2 - 5pm. At other times by prior arrangement. Wheelchair access to ground floor only, disabled parking adjacent to building.
Heritage Open Days: No
Ⓟ Yes. Spaces: 15
♿ Partial. Disabled WC: No. Guide Dogs: Yes
💷 Yes
Adult: £1.50
Child: 75p

Saltram House

Plympton, Plymouth, Devon PL7 1UH
A remarkable survival of a George II mansion, complete with its original contents and set in landscaped park. Robert Adam worked here on two occasions to create the state rooms. Three rooms are decorated with the original Chinese wallpaper. 18th century gardens.
Website Address: www.nationaltrust.org.uk
Grant Recipient/Owner: The National Trust
Access contact: Alex Raeder
Tel: 01392 881691   **Fax:** 01392 881954
Email Address: dlaarx@smtp.ntrust.org.uk
Opening Arrangements: 1 April to 4 November: daily except Friday and Saturday (but open Good Friday) at the following times: 1 April to 30 September 12 - 5pm, last admission 4.15pm; 1 October - 4 November 12 - 4pm, last admission 3.15pm (due to poor light). Garden: 1 February to 31 March: Saturday and Sunday only, 11am - 4pm; 1

April to 4 November as for house 10.30am - 5.30pm. Wheelchair access to: first floor via lift (66cm wide by 86.5cm deep); restaurant, tea room, ticket office over cobbles. Wheelchairs available at house. Parking is 500 metres from house. 30 marked car parking spaces on tarmac, remainder on grass.
Heritage Open Days: No
Ⓟ Yes. Spaces: 250
♿ Yes. Disabled WC: Yes. Guide Dogs: Yes
💷 Yes
Adult: £6.00 (house & garden). £3.00 (garden only).
Child: Free for under 5s. Half adult price for 5-16.
Other: Discount for booked parties. Rates on application.

Tawstock Court Elizabethan Gatehouse

Tawstock, Barnstaple, Devon EX31 3HY
Elizabethan gatehouse at entrance to Tawstock Court, taking the form of two towers joined by a pitched roof covering a small cobbled area. Open on one side, oak doors on the other.
Grant Recipient/Owner:
Governors of St Michael's School
Access contact: Mrs S M Bennett
Tel: 01271 343242   **Fax:** 01271 346771
Opening Arrangements: Easter - August during daylight hours.
Heritage Open Days: No
Ⓟ Yes. Spaces: 2
♿ No. Disabled WC: No. Guide Dogs: Yes
💷 No

Ugbrooke Park

Chudleigh, Devon TQ13 0AD
House and Chapel built c1200 and redesigned by Robert Adam in the 1760s for the 4th Lord Clifford. Chapel and library wing in Adam's characteristic castle style. Set in 'Capability' Brown landscaped park with lakes and 18th century Orangery. Home of the Lords Clifford of Chudleigh for 300 years.
Website Address: www.historichouses.co.uk
Grant Recipient/Owner: Clifford Estate Company Ltd
Access contact: Mrs Lee Martin
Tel: 01626 852179   **Fax:** 01626 853322
Email Address: leececo@netscape.co.uk
Opening Arrangements: 8 July - 6 September: Tuesdays, Wednesdays, Thursdays, Sundays and August Bank Holiday Monday 1.30 - 5.30pm. Group tours and private functions by prior arrangement.
Heritage Open Days: No
Ⓟ Yes. Spaces: 200
♿ Yes. Disabled WC: Yes. Guide Dogs: Yes
💷 Yes
Adult: £4.80
Child: £2.00
Other: £4.50 (senior citizens and groups)

DORSET

Bindon Abbey House

Wool, Dorset
House and chapel built c1794 in gothic style re-using materials from the ruins of Bindon Abbey, with 19th century rear extension. Chapel situated in front part of house on the first floor. Good example of early Gothic Revival.
Grant Recipient/Owner: Mr P Gready
Access contact: Mr S Down
Tel: 01929 400352   **Fax:** 01929 400563
Email Address: wd@lulworth.com
Opening Arrangements: By prior arrangement with Mr Simon Down at the Lulworth Estate Office, Lulworth Castle, Wareham, Dorset BH20 5QS (tel.01929 400352). Wheelchair access to ground floor only.
Heritage Open Days: No
Ⓟ Yes. Spaces: 5
♿ Partial. Disabled WC: No. Guide Dogs: Yes
💷 No

Highcliffe Castle

Rothesay Drive, Highcliffe-on-Sea, Christchurch, Dorset BH23 4LE
Cliff-top mansion built in the 1830s by Charles Stuart. Constructed in the romantic, picturesque style, much of its stonework is medieval coming from France. Exterior has been restored, interior houses changing exhibitions and the 16th century stained glass Jesse window.
Website Address: www.highcliffecastle.co.uk
Grant Recipient/Owner: Mr B J Kees
Access contact: Mr Mike Allen
Tel: 01425 278807   **Fax:** 01425 280423
Email Address: m.allen@christchurch.gov.uk
Opening Arrangements: Daily 5 May - 28 October, 1 - 5pm (except special events, please phone for details). Although there is currently no wheelchair access to the building, there are toilet facilities for the disabled at the site.
Heritage Open Days: Yes
Ⓟ Yes. Spaces: 108

♿ No. Disabled WC: Yes. Guide Dogs: Yes
💷 Yes
Adult: £1.50

Parnham House & Gardens

Beaminster, Dorset DT8 3NA
Elizabethan manor house built in 1540 and enlarged by John Nash in 1810, situated in 14 acres of formal and informal gardens.
Grant Recipient/Owner: Mr John Makepeace
Access contact: Mr John Makepeace
Tel: 01308 862204   **Fax:** 01308 863806
Opening Arrangements: 1 April - 31 October: Wednesdays only 1pm - 5pm. Wheelchair access to ground floor and gardens only.
Heritage Open Days: No
Ⓟ Yes. Spaces: 200
♿ Partial. Disabled WC: Yes. Guide Dogs: Yes
💷 Yes
Adult: £5.50 (including senior citizens)
Child: £2.50 (5-16)
Other: £2.50 (students)

Woodsford Castle

nr. Dorchester, Dorset
What remains is one side of a quadrangular castle completed in 1370. The grand apartment and lodgings that make up the existing building were the work of Sir Guy de Bryan, a close friend of Edward III. The castle eventually became a farmhouse with an enormous thatched roof replacing the original turrets and crenellations. The castle has a steep staircase inside and outside, steps without railings.
Website Address: www.landmarktrust.co.uk
Grant Recipient/Owner: The Landmark Trust
Access contact: Ms Victoria Piggott
Tel: 01628 825920   **Fax:** 01628 825417
Email Address: vpiggott@landmarktrust.co.uk
Opening Arrangements: The Landmark Trust is an independent charity, which rescues small buildings of historic or architectural importance from decay or unsympathetic improvement. Landmark's aim is to promote the enjoyment of these historic buildings by making them available to stay in for holidays. Woodsford Castle can be rented by anyone, at all times of the year, for periods ranging from a weekend to three weeks. Bookings can be made by telephoning the Booking Office on 01628 825925. As the building is in full-time use for holiday accommodation, it is not normally open to the public. However the public can view the building by prior arrangement by telephoning the access contact (Victoria Piggott on 01628 825920) to make an appointment. Potential visitors will be asked to write to confirm the details of their visit.
Heritage Open Days: No
Ⓟ Yes. Spaces: 3
♿ No. Disabled WC: No. Guide Dogs: Yes
💷 No

EAST RIDING OF YORKSHIRE

Church of Our Lady & St Everilda

Everingham, East Riding of Yorkshire YO42 4JA
Roman Catholic parish church for Everingham, built between 1836 and 1839 to the designs of Agostino Giorgiola. Interior has columned walls and a barrelled ceiling with a semi-dome above the high altar. Also of note are the altar, font and statues and the 1839 organ by William Allen.
Grant Recipient/Owner: Mr N J M Turton
Access contact: Mr N J M Turton
Tel: 01904 627436   **Fax:** 01904 610869
Opening Arrangements: Key available during reasonable hours by telephoning: 01430 861443 or 01759 302226.
Heritage Open Days: No
Ⓟ Yes. Spaces: 12
♿ No. Disabled WC: No. Guide Dogs: Yes
💷 No

Maister House

160 High Street, Kingston-upon-Hull, East Riding of Yorkshire HU1 1NL
Rebuilt in 1743 during Hull's heyday as an affluent trading centre, this house is a typical but rare survivor of a contemporary merchant's residence. The restrained exterior belies the spectacular plasterwork staircase inside. The house is now let as offices.
Website Address: www.nationaltrust.org.uk
Grant Recipient/Owner: The National Trust
Access contact: Gelder & Kitchen Architects
Tel: 01482 324114   **Fax:** 01482 227003
Opening Arrangements: Daily except Saturdays and Sundays (closed Good Friday and all Bank Holidays) 10am - 4pm. Public access is to staircase and entrance hall only. Unsuitable for groups. No WC.
Heritage Open Days: No
Ⓟ No

No. Disabled WC: No. Guide Dogs: Yes
£ Yes
Adult: 80p
Child: 80p
Other: Admission charge includes guidebook.

Old Hall

2-4 Fletchergate, Hedon,
East Riding of Yorkshire HU12 8ER
Grade II* listed building built in 1620 by Sir John Waterland. Contains two panelled rooms and a staircase which have been recently restored. One of the doors in the ground floor room possesses a fine case with a plain frieze and pilasters of the Doric style. Renovation is still ongoing.
Grant Recipient/Owner: Mr George Head
Access contact: Mr George Head
Tel: 01482 899472 **Fax:** 01482 899472
Opening Arrangements: By prior telephone or fax arrangement. Wheelchair access to ground floor only.
Heritage Open Days: Yes
P Yes. Spaces: 50
Partial. Disabled WC: No. Guide Dogs: Yes
£ No

EAST SUSSEX

Brickwall House

Northiam, Rye, East Sussex TN31 6NL
Jacobean manor house containing a front hall, drawing room and chamber room with leather panels. Previously home of the Frewen family, now a school for dyslexic boys aged 9-17.
Grant Recipient/Owner: Frewen Educational Trust
Access contact: Mr Peter Mold
Tel: 01797 253388 **Fax:** 01797 252567
Email Address: post@frewcoll.demon.co.uk
Opening Arrangements: April 3,4,10,11,13,16,17 & 18; May 7,28 & 30; July 10,11,17,18,24,25 & 31; August 1,7,8,14,15,21,22,27,28 & 29; 1 - 5pm.
Heritage Open Days: No
P Yes. Spaces: 40
Yes. Disabled WC: Yes. Guide Dogs: Yes
£ Yes
Adult: £3.50

The Flushing Inn

4 Market Street, Rye, East Sussex TN31 7LA
15th century timber-framed building with large recently restored 16th century wallpainting, now a restaurant.
Grant Recipient/Owner: Mr Flynn
Access contact: Mr Flynn
Tel: 01797 223292
Opening Arrangements: Restaurant open Wednesday - Sunday for Lunches and Dinners, Mondays Lunch only and Tuesdays closed. Closed first two weeks in January and October. Unless dining, visiting to view the Fresco is restricted to 10.30 - Noon. Wheelchair access to Fresco with assistance (entrance steps to be negotiated). Parking on street but restricted to 1hr, otherwise public parking elsewhere in Rye.
Heritage Open Days: No
P See above
Partial. Disabled WC: No. Guide Dogs: Yes
£ No

Glynde Place

Glynde, nr. Lewes, East Sussex BN8 6SX
Elizabethan manor house built in 1589 from local flint and stone from Normandy, then extensively added on to in the 18th century. Contains a collection of Old Masters, family portraits, furniture, embroidery and silver belonging to the family who have lived there for over 400 years.
Grant Recipient/Owner: Viscount Hampden
Access contact: Viscount Hampden
Tel: 01273 858224 **Fax:** 01273 858224
Email Address: info@glyndeplace.co.uk
Opening Arrangements: Sundays and Bank Holidays in May; Sundays and Wednesdays in June and September; Sundays, Wednesdays, Thursdays and Bank Holidays in July and August 2 - 5pm (last admission 4.45pm). House open at other times by prior arrangement. Admission prices for groups if booked in advance. Refreshments available.
Heritage Open Days: No
P Yes. Spaces: 150
No. Disabled WC: No, Guide Dogs: No
£ Yes
Adult: £4.00
Child: £2.00
Other: £2.50 (groups of 25+ on open days), £5.00 (groups of 25+ at other times).

Great Dixter House & Gardens

Northiam, nr. Rye, East Sussex TN31 6PH
Original medieval hall house built c1450 comprising three rooms, the Great Hall, Parlour and Solar. Bought by Nathanial Lloyd in 1910 who employed Lutyens to restore and extend the property. A Yeoman's hall, originally located in Benenden, was dismantled and re-erected at Great Dixter.
Grant Recipient/Owner: Mr Christopher Lloyd
Access contact: Ms Elaine Francis
Tel: 01797 252878 **Fax:** 01797 252878
Email Address: greatdixter@compuserve.com
Opening Arrangements: 1 April - 28 October: Tuesday - Sunday (and Bank Holiday Mondays) 2 - 5.30pm (last admission 5pm). Wheelchair access to Great Hall and Parlour only.
Heritage Open Days: No
P Yes. Spaces: 100
Partial. Disabled WC: Yes. Guide Dogs: Yes
£ Yes
Adult: £6.00 House & Garden, £4.50 Garden only.
Child: £1.50 House & Garden, £1.00 Garden only.
Other: Half price for disabled visitors.

Lamb House
(Coromandel Lacquer Panels)

3 Chapel Hill, Lewes, East Sussex, BN7 2BB
The incised lacquer panels in the study of Lamb House are a unique surviving example of imported late 17th century Chinese lacquer work that remains as decorative wall panelling. Recently restored.
Grant Recipient/Owner: Prof. Paul Benjamin
Access contact: Prof. Paul Benjamin
Tel: 01273 475657
Opening Arrangements: Weekends only by prior telephone arrangement. Street parking.
Heritage Open Days: No
P See above
Partial. Disabled WC: No. Guide Dogs: No
£ No

The Royal Pavilion

Brighton, East Sussex BN1 1EE
Former seaside residence of George IV in Indian style with Chinese-inspired interiors. Originally a neo-classical villa by Henry Holland was built on the site in 1787, but this was subsequently replaced by the current John Nash building constructed between 1815-23.
Website Address: www.royalpavilion.brighton.co.uk
Grant Recipient/Owner: Brighton & Hove Council
Access contact: Ms Cara Bowen
Tel: 01273 292810 **Fax:** 01273 292871
Email Address: cara.bowen@brighton-hove.gov.uk
Opening Arrangements: 1 October - 31 May: daily 10am - 5pm (closed Christmas Day and Boxing Day); 1 June - 30 September: daily 10am - 6pm. Admission charges are valid until 31 March 2001, for rates after that date please check with the Royal Pavilion. There is no admission charge for wheelchair users as access is to the ground floor only. Disabled parking is available in the grounds of the Pavilion by prior arrangement.
Heritage Open Days: No
P See above
Partial. Disabled WC: Yes. Guide Dogs: Yes
Adult: £4.90 (see above), £2.00 (local residents).
Child: £3.00 under 16 (free local residents).
Other: £3.55 (seniors/students/unemployed). £12.80 (family of 2 adults, 4 children), £7.90 (1 adult, 4 children).

ESSEX

Alderford Mill

Alderford Street, Sible Hedingham, Halstead, Essex CO9 3HX
18th century weatherboarded watermill on the River Colne. Internal waterwheel drove two pairs of French Burr millstones. Also contains remains of two pairs of stones which were steam driven, although the engine, boiler and drive mechanism now no longer exist.
Grant Recipient/Owner: Essex County Council
Access contact: Mr M N Hoyle
Tel: 01621 828162 **Fax:** 01621 828764
Opening Arrangements: By prior arrangement with Mr M N Hoyle of Essex County Council Planning Department, County Hall, Chelmsford, Essex CM1 1QH (te.01621 828162). There is limited access to the Mill this year due to on-going restoration work.
Heritage Open Days: No
P No
No. Disabled WC: No. Guide Dogs: No
£ No

Grange Farm Barns

Little Dunmow, Essex CM6 3HY
Wooden barns, probably 15th century or earlier.
Grant Recipient/Owner: Mr John Kirby
Access contact: Mr John Kirby
Tel: 01371 820205
Opening Arrangements: By prior telephone arrangement.
Heritage Open Days: No

P Yes. Spaces: 6
No. Disabled WC: No. Guide Dogs: Yes
£ No

Harwich Redoubt Fort

behind 29 Main Road, Harwich, Essex CO12 3LT
180ft diameter circular fort commanding the harbour entrance built in 1808 to defend the port against a Napoleonic invasion. Surrounded by a dry moat, there are 11 guns on the battlements. 18 casements which originally sheltered 300 troops in siege conditions now house a series of small museums.
Website Address: www.harwich-society.com
Grant Recipient/Owner: Harwich Society
Access contact: Mr A Rutter
Tel: 01255 503429 **Fax:** 01255 503429
Email Address: theharwichsociety@quista.net
Opening Arrangements: 1 May - 31 August: daily 10am - 5pm. Rest of year: Sundays only from 10am - 4pm.
Heritage Open Days: Yes
P No
No. Disabled WC: No. Guide Dogs: Yes
£ Yes
Adult: £1.00
Child: Accompanied children free.
Other: £1.00

Hylands House

Hylands Park, London Road, Widford, Chelmsford, Essex CM2 8WQ
Grade II* listed building, surrounded by 600 acres of landscaped parkland, partly designed by Humphrey Repton. Built c1730, the original house was a red brick Queen Anne style mansion, subsequent owners set about enlarging the property, which produced a neo-classical style house. Internal inspection of the house reveals its Georgian and Victorian features.
Grant Recipient/Owner: Chelmsford Borough Council
Access contact: Ms Linda Pittom
Tel: 01245 606396 **Fax:** 01245 250783
Opening Arrangements: Sundays, Mondays and Bank Holidays (except Christmas Day) throughout the year 11am - 6pm. Group visits by prior arrangement with Ms Linda Pittom, Hylands House Manager, Leisure Services, Chelmsford Borough Council, Civic Centre, Duke Street, Chelmsford, Essex CM1 1JE (tel.01245 606396). Events programme. 4 disabled parking spaces.
Heritage Open Days: Yes
P Yes. Spaces: 54
Yes. Disabled WC: Yes. Guide Dogs: Yes
£ Yes
Adult: £3.00
Child: Free (under 12)
Other: £2.00

John Webb's Windmill

Fishmarket Street, Thaxted, Essex
Brick tower mill built in 1804 consisting of five floors. Has been fully restored as a working mill. On two floors there is a museum of rural and domestic bygones. There is also a small picture gallery of early photographs of the mill and the surrounding countryside.
Grant Recipient/Owner: Thaxted Parish Council
Access contact: Mr L A Farren
Tel: 01371 830285 **Fax:** 01371 830285
Opening Arrangements: May - September: Saturdays, Sundays and Bank Holidays 2 - 6pm. Conducted parties at other times by prior arrangement with Mr L A Farren, Borough Hill, Bolford Street, Thaxted, Essex CM6 2PY (tel.01371 830285). Wheelchair access to ground floor only. Parking in Thaxted.
Heritage Open Days: Yes
P No
Partial. Disabled WC: No. Guide Dogs: Yes
£ Yes
Adult: 50p
Child: 25p

Maldon Moot Hall

Maldon, Essex
15th century listed building which once housed a police station and still has the exercise yard, a brickbuilt spiral staircase with brick handrail, courtroom and council chamber. Access to the roof gives good views of the Blackwater estuary and surrounding district.
Grant Recipient/Owner: The Town Clerk
Access contact: The Town Clerk
Tel: 01621 857373 **Fax:** 01621 850793
Email Address: maldontowncouncil@u.genie.co.uk
Opening Arrangements: By prior telephone arrangement with the Town Clerk of Maldon Town Council on 01621 857373. Otherwise open August - end of October Saturday afternoons for visits at 2 and 3.30pm. (This may be extended). Wheelchair access to ground floor only.
Heritage Open Days: Yes
P No
Partial. Disabled WC: No. Guide Dogs: Yes
£ Yes

Adult: £1.00
Child: 50p
Other: 50p (senior citizens)

Old Friends Meeting House

High Street, Stebbing, Essex

The Stebbing Meeting House is the earliest Quaker meeting House in Essex. Built circa 1674 it is a particularly fine and complete example and its historical importance is recognised by its Grade II* listing.
Grant Recipient/Owner:
The Trustees of the Old Friends Meeting House
Access contact: Mr J B Newbrook
Tel: 01371 856464   **Fax:** 01371 856464
Email Address: jimnewbrook@aol.com
Opening Arrangements: By prior telephone arrangement.
Heritage Open Days: Yes
P Yes. Spaces: 10
⬙ Yes. Disabled WC: Yes. Guide Dogs: Yes
£ No

Rainham Hall

The Broadway, Rainham, Essex RM13 9YN

Georgian house built in 1729 to a symmetrical plan and with fine wrought iron gates, carved porch and interior panelling plasterwork.
Website Address: www.nationaltrust.org.uk
Grant Recipient/Owner: The National Trust
Access contact: Thames & Chilterns Regional Office
Tel: 01494 528051   **Fax:** 01494 463310
Opening Arrangements: April to end October: Wednesdays and Bank Holiday Mondays 2 - 6pm. Saturdays by written arrangement (Thames & Chilterns Regional Office, Hughenden Manor, High Wycombe, Buckinghamshire, HP14 4LA). Wheelchair access to ground floor. Guide dogs by prior arrangement. Parking on street (pay and display).
Heritage Open Days: No
P See above
⬙ Partial. Disabled WC: Yes. Guide Dogs: See above
£ Yes
Adult: £2.10
Other: No group reductions.

St Mary

Mundon, Essex

Listed Grade I church, now redundant and owned by the Friends of Friendless Churches since 1975. Two-tier timber-framed weatherboarded tower of the 16th century and roughly contemporary north porch. The nave is partly 14th century and retains a complete set of 18th century box pews. The chancel is also Georgian but with simple 19th century fittings. There is a naïve Baroque trompe l'oeil painting of murals on the east wall.
Grant Recipient/Owner:
Friends of Friendless Churches
Access contact: Mr Matthew Saunders
Tel: 020 7236 3934   **Fax:** 020 7329 3677
Email Address: ancientmonuments@talk21.com
Opening Arrangements: Open at all reasonable times.
Heritage Open Days: Yes
P No
⬙ Partial. Disabled WC: No. Guide Dogs: Yes
£ No

Stansted Windmill

Millside, Stansted Mountfitchet, Essex CM24 8BL

Brick tower mill, built 1787 and a scheduled ancient monument. Ceased working in 1910 but most of the original machinery remains in situ. Given in trust to the village by Lord Blyth in 1935.
Grant Recipient/Owner: Stansted Mountfitchet Council
Access contact: Mrs D P Honour
Tel: 01279 647213   **Fax:** 01279 813160
Opening Arrangements: April - October: first Sunday of each month 2 - 6pm; plus Bank Holiday Sundays and Mondays and every Sunday in August. Parties by prior arrangement with Mrs D P Honour, 59 Blythwood Gardens, Stansted, Essex CM24 8HH (tel.01279 647213). For school groups contact Mrs Minshull (01279 812230). Children must be accompanied. Small souvenir shop.
Heritage Open Days: No
P No
⬙ No. Disabled WC: No. Guide Dogs: No
£ Yes
Adult: 50p
Child: 25p
Other: £20.00 (for group guided tour)

Steeple Bumpstead Moot Hall

Steeple Bumpstead, nr. Haverhill, Essex CB9 7DQ

Elizabethan two-storey timber-framed building with jettied upper hall, hipped tiled roof supported by crown post and surmounted by mutilated stone lion at the apex. Originally considered to have been a guildhall but subsequently housed a school founded in 1592. Currently used for meetings and public library.

Grant Recipient/Owner:
The Moot Hall (Old School) Trustees
Access contact: Mr P E Bruty
Tel: 01440 730558
Opening Arrangements: Thursdays 2 - 4pm, at other times by prior written arrangement with Mr P E Bruty of the Moot Hall (Old School) Trustees, 5 Blois Road, Steeple Bumpstead, nr. Haverhill, Essex CB9 7BN (tel.01440 730558). Wheelchair and guide dog access to ground floor only. Parking on street.
Heritage Open Days: No
P See above
⬙ Partial. Disabled WC: No. Guide Dogs: Yes
£ No

Stock Windmill

Mill Lane, Stock, Ingatestone, Essex

Early 19th century tower mill, modernised in the late 1890s. Five floors, all of which may be visited. The mill has patent sails driving 3 pairs of French Burr millstones. The mill is in working order and occasionally grinds flour.
Grant Recipient/Owner: Essex County Council
Access contact: Mr M Hoyle
Tel: 01621 828162   **Fax:** 01621 828764
Opening Arrangements: April - September: second Sunday of each month 2 - 5pm, plus any reasonable time by prior arrangement for guided visits. Admission charge for guided group visit only.
Heritage Open Days: No
P Yes. Spaces: 6
⬙ No. Disabled WC: No. Guide Dogs: Yes
£ Yes
Adult: £2.00 (guided)
Child: £1.50 (guided)
Other: £2.00 (guided)

Thorrington Tide Mill

Brightlingsea Road, Thorrington, Colchester, Essex

Weatherboarded watermill built in 1831 on a creek off the River Colne. The breastshot water wheel is external and drives two pairs of French Burr millstones, a sack hoist and a reel separator. There is provision for a drive from an external portable engine. The mill has been restored and is in working order.
Grant Recipient/Owner: Essex County Council
Access contact: Mr M Hoyle
Tel: 01621 828162   **Fax:** 01621 828764
Opening Arrangements: March - September: last Sunday of each month and Bank Holiday Mondays 2 - 5pm, plus guided group visits at other times by prior arrangement. Admission charge for group guided visits only. Wheelchair access to ground floor with assistance, there is always someone available to help when mill is open. Disabled people may be dropped off at mill door.
Heritage Open Days: No
P Yes. Spaces: 8
⬙ Partial. Disabled WC: No. Guide Dogs: Yes
£ Yes
Adult: £2.00 (guided)
Child: £1.50 (guided)
Other: £2.00 (guided)

GLOUCESTERSHIRE

Abbey Gatehouse

Tewkesbury, Gloucestershire

The gatehouse dates from 1500 and was restored in 1849. It has only one very fine room on the first floor. Steep staircase.
Website Address: www.landmarktrust.co.uk
Grant Recipient/Owner: The Landmark Trust
Access contact: Ms Victoria Piggott
Tel: 01628 825920   **Fax:** 01628 825417
Email Address: vpiggott@landmarktrust.co.uk
Opening Arrangements: The Landmark Trust is an independent charity, which rescues small buildings of historic or architectural importance from decay or unsympathetic improvement. Landmark's aim is to promote the enjoyment of these historic buildings by making them available to stay in for holidays. Abbey Gatehouse can be rented by anyone, at all times of the year, for periods ranging from a weekend to three weeks. Bookings can be made by telephoning the Booking Office on 01628 825925. As the building is in full-time use for holiday accommodation, it is not normally open to the public. However the public can view the building by prior arrangement by telephoning the access contact (Victoria Piggott on 01628 825920) to make an appointment. Potential visitors will be asked to write to confirm the details of their visit.
Heritage Open Days: No
P Yes. Spaces: 1
⬙ No. Disabled WC: No. Guide Dogs: No
£ No

Acton Court

Latteridge Road, Iron Acton, Gloucestershire BS17 1TJ

Seat of the Poyntzes, an influential courtier family who died out in the 17th century. Their moated medieval manor house has gone, but a Tudor wing survives. This was constructed in 1534 to accommodate King Henry VIII, Queen Anne Boleyn and part of their retinue. The state rooms are unfurnished, but contain important traces of original decoration.
Grant Recipient/Owner: Rosehill Corporation
Access contact: Ms Clare Standen
Tel: 01454 228224
Opening Arrangements: Guided tours by prior arrangement June to mid-September. Please contact Clare Standen for further details. Acton Court will also be open for five weekends in the period June to October. Further details from Clare Standen and on the English Heritage website in the Spring.
Heritage Open Days: No
P Yes. Spaces: 30
⬙ No. Disabled WC: No. Guide Dogs: Yes
£ Yes
Adult: £4.00
Child: £3.00

Beach Hall Gazebo

Witcombe Park, Great Witcombe, Gloucestershire

Summerhouse, dated 1697, interior altered in the 19th century. Formerly stood at corner of walled garden.
Grant Recipient/Owner: Mrs Diana Hicks-Beach
Access contact: Mrs M Hicks-Beach
Tel: 01452 863591
Opening Arrangements: By prior arrangement with Mrs M Hicks-Beach, Witcombe Farm, Great Witcombe, Gloucestershire (tel.01452 863591). Donation requested for St. Mary's Church.
Heritage Open Days: No
P Yes. Spaces: 20
⬙ Partial. Disabled WC: No. Guide Dogs: Yes
£ No

Berkeley Castle

Berkeley, Gloucestershire GL13 9BQ

Begun in 1117 and in the same family for nearly 850 years. Scene of the murder of Edward II and beseiged by Oliver Cromwell. The State Apartments contain collections of furniture, tapestries, and rare paintings by English and Dutch masters. Part of the Berkeley silver is on display in the Dining Room.
Grant Recipient/Owner: Mr R J Berkeley
Access contact: Mr D Attwood
Tel: 01453 810332
Opening Arrangements: April - May: Tuesday - Sunday 2 - 5pm; June and September: Tuesday - Saturday 11am - 5pm and Sundays 2 - 5pm; July and August: Monday - Saturday 11am - 5pm and Sundays 2 - 5pm; October: Sundays 2 - 4.30pm; Bank Holiday Mondays 11am - 5pm. Last admission half an hour before closing time. Grounds open until 6pm (5.30pm in October).
Heritage Open Days: No
P Yes. Spaces: 150
⬙ No. Disabled WC: No. Guide Dogs: Yes
£ Yes
Adult: £5.50
Child: £3.00
Other: £4.50

Chastleton House

Chastleton, Moreton-in-Marsh, Gloucestershire GL56 0SU

Jacobean house filled with a mixture of rare and everyday objects, furniture and textiles collected since 1612. Continually occupied for 400 years by the same family. Emphasis here lies on conservation rather than restoration.
Website Address: www.nationaltrust.org.uk
Grant Recipient/Owner: The National Trust
Access contact: The Custodian
Tel: 01608 674355   **Fax:** 01608 674355
Opening Arrangements: 4 April to 3 November: Wednesdays to Saturdays. Times: April to September 1 - 5pm (last admission 4pm); October and November 1 - 4pm (last admission 3pm). Booking is essential at all times (tel. 01494 755585 between 1.30 - 4.30pm Tuesday to Friday). Wheelchair access to ground floor and parts of garden.
Heritage Open Days: No
P Yes. Spaces: 50
⬙ Partial. Disabled WC: Yes. Guide Dogs: Yes
£ Yes
Adult: £5.20
Child: £2.60
Other: £13.00 (family). Groups by written arrangement only.

Chavenage

Tetbury, Gloucestershire GL8 8XP

Elizabethan Manor House (c1576), contains tapestry rooms, furniture and relics from the Cromwellian Period. Has been the home of only two families since the time of Elizabeth I.

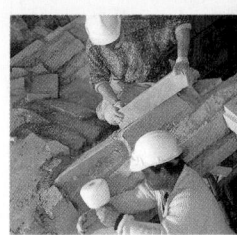

Website Address: www.chavenage.com
Grant Recipient/Owner:
Trustees of the Chavenage Settlement
Access contact: Miss Caroline Lowsley-Williams
Tel: 01666 502329   **Fax:** 01453 836778
Email Address: caroline@chavenage.com
Opening Arrangements: May - September: Thursdays, Sundays and Bank Holidays 2 - 5pm; plus Easter Sunday and Monday. Groups at other times by prior arrangement. Limited access for wheelchair users (ground floor only).
Heritage Open Days: No
P Yes. Spaces: 40
Partial. Disabled WC: Yes. Guide Dogs: Yes
£ Yes
Adult: £4.00
Child: £2.00

Court Farm Dovecote

Quenington, Cirencester, Gloucestershire GL7 5BN
Reputed to be dovecote mentioned in 1338, belonging to the Knights Hospitallers, but possibly 17th century. Small round structure of rubble stone with conical stone slate roof with retractable lantern "lid". Contains 600 dove holes stacked at an angle one above another inside wall, above rat rail around which moves revolving ladder on central wooden pin.
Grant Recipient/Owner: Mrs B Gollins
Access contact: Mrs B Gollins
Tel: 01285 750371   **Fax:** 01285 750322
Opening Arrangements: By prior arrangement.
Heritage Open Days: No
P Yes. Spaces: 5
Yes. Disabled WC: No. Guide Dogs: Yes
£ No

East Banqueting House

Calf Lane, Chipping Campden, Gloucestershire
The East Banqueting House stands opposite the West Banqueting House across a broad terrace that ran in front of Sir Baptist Hick's mansion, which was deliberately destroyed by the Royalists in 1645 only 30 years after it had been built. It is elaborately decorated with spiral chimney stacks, finials and ebullient strapwork parapets. Steep staircases.
Website Address: www.landmarktrust.co.uk
Grant Recipient/Owner: The Landmark Trust
Access contact: Ms Victoria Piggott
Tel: 01628 825920   **Fax:** 01628 825417
Email Address: vpiggott@landmarktrust.co.uk
Opening Arrangements: The Landmark Trust is an independent charity, which rescues small buildings of historic or architectural importance from decay or unsympathetic improvement. Landmark's aim is to promote the enjoyment of these historic buildings by making them available to stay in for holidays. East Banqueting House can be rented by anyone, at all times of the year, for periods ranging from a weekend to three weeks. Bookings can be made by telephoning the Booking Office on 01628 825925. As the building is in full-time use for holiday accommodation, it is not normally open to the public. However the public can view the building by prior arrangement by telephoning the access contact (Victoria Piggott on 01628 825920) to make an appointment. Potential visitors will be asked to write to confirm the details of their visit. Parking available in town only.
Heritage Open Days: No
P No
No.
£ No

Ebley Mill

Westward Road, Stroud, Gloucestershire GL5 4UB
19th century riverside textile mill, now restored and converted into offices occupied by Stroud District Council. Has Gothic-style clock tower and block designed by George Bodley.
Website Address: www.stroud.gov.uk
Grant Recipient/Owner: Stroud District Council
Access contact: Mr D Marshall
Tel: 01453 754646   **Fax:** 01453 754934
Email Address: information@stroud.gov.uk
Opening Arrangements: Monday - Thursday 8.45am - 5pm, Fridays 8.45am - 4.30pm (closed Bank Holidays). Tours by prior arrangement.
Heritage Open Days: No
P Yes. Spaces: 30
Yes. Disabled WC: Yes. Guide Dogs: Yes
£ No

Great House Farm

Hasfield, Gloucestershire GL19 4LQ
16th, 17th and 19th century former manor house of stone, timber-frame and brick construction.
Grant Recipient/Owner: Hasfield Estate Trust
Access contact: Mr D Banwell
Tel: 01452 780206
Opening Arrangements: By prior arrangement between 1 April and the end of September.

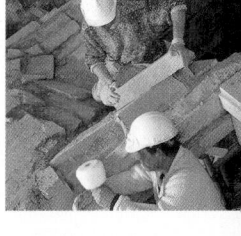

Heritage Open Days: No
P Yes. Spaces: 6
Yes. Disabled WC: Yes. Guide Dogs: Yes
£ No

Newark Park

Ozleworth, nr. Wotton-under-Edge, Gloucestershire GL12 7PZ
Tudor hunting lodge converted into a castellated county house by James Wyatt.
Website Address: www.ntrustsevern.org.uk
Grant Recipient/Owner: The National Trust
Access contact: South Gloucestershire Office
Tel: 01452 814213
Opening Arrangements: Provisional: April to September Wednesday and Thursdays 2 - 5pm. Viewing arrangements are under review for 2001. Contact South Gloucestershire Office (01452 814213) for confirmation.
Heritage Open Days: No
P Yes. Spaces: 10
No. Disabled WC: No. Guide Dogs: No
£ Yes
Adult: £2.50

Painswick Rococo Garden

Painswick, Gloucestershire GL6 6TH
18th century garden with contemporary buildings situated in a Cotswold combe. Winding woodland walks, formal vistas and early spring show of snowdrops.
Website Address: www.rococogarden.co.uk
Grant Recipient/Owner: Lord Dickinson
Access contact: Mr P R Moir
Tel: 01452 813204   **Fax:** 01452 813204
Email Address: paulmoir@rococogarden.co.uk
Opening Arrangements: Second Wednesday in January - 30 November: Wednesday - Sunday and Bank Holidays 11am - 5pm, plus daily May - September 11am - 5pm. Groups by prior arrangement. Access is possible for wheelchair users but not easy.
Heritage Open Days: No
P Yes. Spaces: 80
Partial. Disabled WC: Yes. Guide Dogs: Yes
£ Yes
Adult: £3.30
Child: £1.75
Other: £3.00 (senior citizens)

St Mary Magdalene Chapel

Hillfield Gardens, London Road, Gloucester, Gloucestershire
Chancel of former church serving the inmates of St Mary Magdalene Hospital, originally a leper hospital, then later almshouses. Medieval graffiti visible on exterior, perhaps mementos of visiting pilgrims. Interior contains south and west doorways rebuilt after the church was demolished in 1861 and tomb of 13th century lady, removed from St Kyneburgh's Chapel near the South Gate in 1550.
Grant Recipient/Owner:
Gloucester Historic Buildings Trust Ltd
Access contact: Mr Malcolm J Watkins
Tel: 01452 396620   **Fax:** 01452 396622
Email Address: culture@gloucester.gov.uk
Opening Arrangements: By prior arrangement with Mr Malcolm J Watkins, Heritage Manager, Cultural Services, Gloucester City Council, Herbert Warehouse, The Docks, Gloucestershire GL1 2EQ (tel.01452 396620), plus part of the Heritage Open Days weekend. Exterior accessible at all reasonable times in public park. Wheelchair access to interior with assistance (entrance steps to be negotiated).
Heritage Open Days: Yes
P No
Partial. Disabled WC: No. Guide Dogs: Yes
£ No

Stancombe Park Temple

Dursley, Gloucestershire GL11 6AU
One in a series of buildings built in the folly gardens at Stancombe Park, in the form of a Greek temple.
Grant Recipient/Owner: Mr N D Barlow
Access contact: Mrs G T Barlow
Tel: 01453 542815
Opening Arrangements: All year by prior telephone arrangement.
Heritage Open Days: No
P Yes. Spaces: 50
No. Disabled WC: No. Guide Dogs: Yes
£ No

Stanley Mill

Kings Stanley, Stonehouse, Gloucestershire GL10 3HQ
Built 1813, with large addition c1825, of Flemish bond red brick with ashlar dressings and Welsh slate roof. Early example of fireproof construction (which survived a major fire in 1884).
Grant Recipient/Owner: Mr Peter Griffiths
Access contact: Mr Mark Griffiths
Tel: 01453 824444

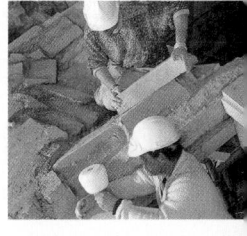

Opening Arrangements: By prior written arrangement. Parking available by prior arrangement.
Heritage Open Days: No
P See above
No. Disabled WC: No. Guide Dogs: No
£ No

Stanway House (Kitchen Court)

Stanway, Gloucestershire
Exterior of Kitchen Court. Courtyard surrounded by domestic buildings including 18th century brewhouse and servants quarters, and 19th century kitchen range. Adjoins Jacobean manor house.
Grant Recipient/Owner:
The Trustees of the Lord Wemyss Trust
Access contact: Lord Neidpath
Tel: 01386 584469   **Fax:** 01386 584688
Email Address: neidpath@btinternet.com
Opening Arrangements: Exterior only. 25 March, 20 May, 30 June, 7 July, and 13 July - 28 September: Mondays - Fridays.
Heritage Open Days: No
P Yes. Spaces: 10
No. Disabled WC: No. Guide Dogs: Yes
£ Yes
Adult: £1.00
Child: Free
Other: £1.00

Sudeley Castle

Winchcombe, nr. Cheltenham, Gloucestershire GL54 5JD
Historic house containing elements from the Tudor, Stuart and Victorian periods. Former home of Queen Katherine Parr and Headquarters of Prince Rupert during the Civil War. Visitors have included Henry VIII, Anne Boleyn, Elizabeth I, Charles I and George III. St Mary's Church, restored by Sir George Gilbert Scott, contains the tomb of Katherine Parr.
Website Address: www.stratford.co.uk/sudeley
Grant Recipient/Owner: The Trustees of Sudeley Castle
Access contact: Mr Timothy Baylis
Tel: 01242 602308   **Fax:** 01242 602959
Email Address: tim.baylis@sudeley.org.uk
Opening Arrangements: Gardens, grounds, shop, exhibition and plant centre: daily 3 March - 28 October 10.30am - 5.30pm; Castle apartments and St Mary's Church: daily 31 March - 28 October 11am - 5pm, restaurant open 10.30am - 5.30pm. Wheelchair access to gardens, shop and restaurant only.
Heritage Open Days: No
P Yes. Spaces: 700
See above. Disabled WC: No. Guide Dogs: Yes
£ Yes
Adult: £6.20 (Castle & Gardens), £4.70 (Gardens & Exhibition).
Child: £3.20 (Castle & Gardens), £2.50 (Gardens & Exhibition).
Other: £5.20 (Castle & Gardens), £3.70 (Gardens & Exhibition).

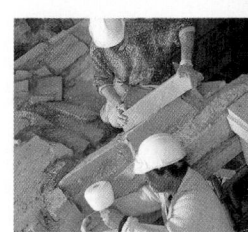

Wick Court

Overton Lane, Arlingham, Gloucestershire GL2 7JJ
Medieval, 16th and 17th century Grade II* listed manor house with a range of farm buildings enclosed by a moat. The house is now a Farms for City Children centre.
Grant Recipient/Owner: Farms for City Children
Access contact: Ms Heather Tarplee
Tel: 01452 741023   **Fax:** 01452 741023
Opening Arrangements: By prior arrangement.
Heritage Open Days: No
P Yes. Spaces: 20
Partial. Disabled WC: Yes. Guide Dogs: Yes
£ Yes
Adult: £2.50 (guided tour)

GREATER MANCHESTER

1830 Warehouse

Museum of Science & Industry in Manchester, Liverpool Road, Castlefield, Manchester, Greater Manchester M3 4FP
Former railway warehouse, c1830, originally part of the Liverpool Road Railway Station (the oldest surviving passenger railway station in the world) which was the terminus of the Liverpool and Manchester Railway built by George Stephenson and his son Robert. Now part of the Manchester Museum of Science and Industry.
Grant Recipient/Owner:
Museum of Science & Industry in Manchester
Access contact: Ms Kathryn Morgan
Tel: 0161 832 2244   **Fax:** 0161 833 1471
Email Address: marketing@msim.org.uk
Opening Arrangements: Daily (except 24/25/26 December) 10am - 5pm.
Heritage Open Days: No
P Yes. Spaces: 50
Yes. Disabled WC: Yes. Guide Dogs: Yes

£ Yes
Adult: £6.50
Child: £2.00 for special exhibitions, free to permanent collections.
Other: £3.50 concessions. Group rates also available.

Albion Warehouse

Penny Meadow, Ashton-under-Lyne, Greater Manchester
School, now warehouse. Built 1861-2 by Paull and Ayliffe in Italianate style.
Grant Recipient/Owner: G A Armstrong Ltd
Access contact: G A Armstrong Ltd
Tel: 061 339 5353 **Fax:** 061 339 5353
Opening Arrangements: All year except Christmas Day and New Year's Day.
Heritage Open Days: No
P Yes. Spaces: 80
♿ No. Disabled WC: No. Guide Dogs: Yes
£ No

Alkrington Hall

Middleton, Manchester, Greater Manchester M24 1WD
Grade II* listed building, built 1735, by Giacomo Leoni for Darcy Lever in Classical style. Sub-divided into four dwellings in 1995 but much of the original interior detail survives.
Grant Recipient/Owner: Mr James Pickup
Access contact: Mr James Pickup
Tel: 0161 643 7713
Opening Arrangements: By prior written arrangement with Mr James Pickup, Alkrington Hall East, Middleton, Manchester M24 1WD.
Heritage Open Days: Yes
P Yes. Spaces: 4
♿ Partial. Disabled WC: No. Guide Dogs: No
£ No

Heaton Hall

Heaton Park, Prestwich, Greater Manchester M25 2SW
18th century country house designed by James Wyatt in 1772, containing scrolling plasterwork, wall and ceiling paintings, furniture and paintings. Set in 650 acres of parkland.
Grant Recipient/Owner: Manchester City Council
Access contact: Ms Ruth Shrigley
Tel: 0161 234 1456 **Fax:** 0161 236 2880
Opening Arrangements: Easter - end of October: Wednesday - Sunday 10am - 5.30pm (opening arrangements correct at time of going to print but may change, please contact Manchester City Art Galleries, Room 1025, Lloyd Street, Manchester M60 2LA (tel.0161 234 1456) for current details. Wheelchair access to ground floor only.
Heritage Open Days: No
P Yes. Spaces: 200
♿ Partial. Disabled WC: No. Guide Dogs: Yes
£ No

Manchester Jewish Museum

190 Cheetham Hill Road, Manchester M8 8LW
Grade II* listed building located in the premises of the former Spanish and Portuguese Synagogue, completed in 1874 in Moorish style containing stained-glass windows and distinctive cast-iron fitments.
Website Address: www.manchesterjewishmuseum.com
Grant Recipient/Owner:
Trustees of the Manchester Jewish Museum
Access contact: Mr Don Rainger
Tel: 0161 834 98798 **Fax:** 0161 834 9801
Email Address: info@manchesterjewishmuseum.com
Opening Arrangements: Monday - Thursday 10.30am - 4pm, Sundays 10.30am - 5pm and Fridays by prior arrangement. Closed 1 January; 8, 9 & 15 April; 28 & 29 May; 18, 19 & 27 September; 2, 3, 9 & 10 October; 24-26 December. Early closing (1pm) 17 & 26 September; 1 & 8 October. May participate in the Heritage Open Days weekend on the Sunday, please contact Museum for current information. Groups only by prior arrangement. Wheelchair access to ground floor only. Street parking immediately outside museum.
Heritage Open Days: Yes
P See above
♿ Partial. Disabled WC: No. Guide Dogs: Yes
£ Yes
Adult: £3.50
Child: £2.60
Other: £8.50 (family)

Manchester Law Library

14 Kennedy Street, Manchester M2 4BY
Built in Venetian Gothic style in 1885 to a design by Manchester architect, Thomas Hartas. Has stained glass windows by Evans of Birmingham.
Website Address: www.manchester-law-library.co.uk
Grant Recipient/Owner:
Manchester Incorporated Law Library Society

Access contact: Mrs Julia Bragg
Tel: 0161 236 63128 **Fax:** 0161 236 6119
Email Address: librarian@manchester-law-library.co.uk
Opening Arrangements: By prior telephone or written arrangement.
Heritage Open Days: Yes
P No
♿ No. Disabled WC: No. Guide Dogs: Yes
£ No

Portico Library

57 Mosley Street, Manchester, Greater Manchester M2 3HY
19th century subscription library with Reading Room and Gallery, situated in Manchester city centre. 25,000 volumes, mainly 19th century. Particularly valuable for Victorian studies. Gallery shows mainly art exhibitions of new and established artists' work - local, national and international. Occasionally literary/local history exhibitions also shown.
Grant Recipient/Owner:
The Trustees of the Portico Library
Access contact: Emma Marigliano
Tel: 0161 236 6785 **Fax:** 0161 236 6803
Opening Arrangements: Monday - Friday 9.30am - 4.30pm, except Christmas period - usually 22 December - 2 January. Trial period of Sunday openings currently in operation and for 3rd Sunday of each month. Closed Bank Holidays.
Heritage Open Days: Yes
P No
♿ No. Disabled WC: No. Guide Dogs: Yes
£ No

Smithills Hall

Smithills Dean Road, Bolton, Greater Manchester BL1 7NP
Hall, some parts of which date back to the medieval period. The early East Wing contains collection of mainly 17th century oak furniture. The largely Victorian West Wing has been recently conserved and includes Victorian period rooms, a shop, toilets and refreshments.
Grant Recipient/Owner:
Bolton Metropolitan Borough Council
Access contact: Ms Angela Thomas
Tel: 01204 332212
Opening Arrangements: Easter - end of September: Tuesday - Saturday 11am - 5pm, plus Sundays 2 - 5pm. Groups at other times of the year by prior arrangement with Ms Angela Thomas, Senior Keeper, Bolton Central Museum and Art Gallery, Le Mans Crescent, Bolton, Greater Manchester, BL1 (tel.01204 332212). Access for wheelchair users to lower floor only.
Heritage Open Days: Yes
P Yes. Spaces: 40
♿ Partial. Disabled WC: Yes. Guide Dogs: Yes
£ Yes
Adult: £3.00
Child: £1.50
Other: £1.50 (concessions)

Tonge Hall

Middleton, Manchester, Greater Manchester M24 2JT
Grade II* listed timber-framed hall c1580s with 18th and 19th century alterations. The Hall is a good example of 16th century carpentry and has a distinctive display of quatrefoil panels to front and left elevations.
Grant Recipient/Owner: Mr Norman Wolstonecroft
Access contact: Mr Norman Wolstonecroft
Tel: 0161 643 2995 or 01224 867893
Opening Arrangements: By prior arrangement. Wheelchair access to ground floor only, disabled parking at front door.
Heritage Open Days: Yes
P Yes. Spaces: 100
♿ Partial. Disabled WC: No. Guide Dogs: Yes
£ No

Victoria Baths

Hathersage Road, Manchester, Greater Manchester M13 0FE
Swimming pool complex built 1906, with 2 pools, Turkish and Russian Bath suite, Aerotone and extensive stained glass and tilework. Currently closed awaiting restoration.
Grant Recipient/Owner:
The Manchester Victoria Baths Trust
Access contact: Miss Gill Wright
Tel: 0161 224 2020/8437 **Fax:** 0161 224 0707
Opening Arrangements: Afternoons of Heritage Open Days and at other times by prior arrangement with Miss Gill Wright of the Manchester Victoria Baths Trust, 3 Birch Polygon, Rusholme, Manchester M14 5HX (tel.0161 224 2020/8437). On street parking during the week and use of large adjacent car park at weekends by arrangement. Wheelchair access to ground floor with assistance.
Heritage Open Days: Yes
P Yes. Spaces: 5°
♿ Partial. Disabled WC: No. Guide Dogs: Yes
£ No

HAMPSHIRE

Avington Park

Winchester, Hampshire SO21 1DB
Palladian mansion dating back to the 11th century, enlarged in 1670 by the addition of two wings and a classical Portico surmounted by three statues. Visited by Charles II and George IV. Has highly decorated State rooms and a Georgian church in the grounds.
Website Address: www.avingtonpark.co.uk
Grant Recipient/Owner: Mrs Sarah Bullen
Access contact: Mrs Sarah Bullen
Tel: 01962 7792608 **Fax:** 01962 779864
Email Address: sarah@avingtonpark.co.uk
Opening Arrangements: May - September: Sundays and Bank Holidays 2.30 - 5.30pm. At other times by prior arrangement.
Heritage Open Days: Yes
P Yes. Spaces: 150
♿ Yes. Disabled WC: Yes. Guide Dogs: Yes
£ Yes
Adult: £3.50
Child: £1.75

Breach Farm Barn

Sherfield-on-Loddon, Hampshire
15th century barn. Timber frame of 5 bays on a masonry base, with central entrances (projecting slightly on the east side). Cruck construction. Weather-boarded walls. Listed Grade II*.
Grant Recipient/Owner: Mr D Mitchell
Access contact: Mr D Mitchell
Tel: 01962 734275
Opening Arrangements: By prior telephone arrangement at any reasonable time.
Heritage Open Days: No
P Yes. Spaces: 20
♿ Partial. Disabled WC: No. Guide Dogs: Yes
£ No

Breamore Home Farm Tithe Barn

Breamore, nr. Fordingbridge, Hampshire SP6 2DD
Late 16th century tithe barn with dwarf walls supporting a timber-frame and external cladding under a tiled roof with massive timber aisle posts, double doors in the centre of each side and an area of threshing boards.
Grant Recipient/Owner:
Breamore Ancient Buildings Conservation Trust
Access contact: Mr Michael Hulse
Tel: 01725 5128588 **Fax:** 01725 512858
Opening Arrangements: Weekdays by prior arrangement with Mr Michael Hulse of Breamore House.
Heritage Open Days: Yes
P Yes. Spaces: 10
♿ Yes. Disabled WC: No. Guide Dogs: Yes
£ No

The Deanery

The Close, Winchester, Hampshire SO23 9LS
Earliest remains are late 12th or early 13th century, fragments visible in a stairwell cupboard of the Prior's Hall. The hall itself is probably 13th century in origin. Until 1539 the Prior's House, now home of the Dean of Winchester.
Grant Recipient/Owner:
Dean & Chapter of Winchester Cathedral
Access contact: Mrs Judy George
Tel: 01962 857225 **Fax:** 01962 857201
Email Address:
cathedral.office@winchester-cathedral.org.uk
Opening Arrangements: By prior written arrangement with the Cathedral Office, 1 The Close, Winchester, Hampshire SO23 9LS. Open Heritage Open Days 2 - 4pm.
Heritage Open Days: Yes
P No
♿ No. Disabled WC: No. Guide Dogs: No
£ Yes
Adult: £2.50
Child: £1.00
Other: £2.00 (per head for prebooked groups).

Manor Farmhouse

Hambledon, Hampshire PO7 4RW
12th century stone built house with later medieval wing. 17th and 18th century re-fronting of part and minor renovation.
Grant Recipient/Owner: Mr Stuart Mason
Access contact: Mr Stuart Mason
Tel: 023 92632433
Opening Arrangements: By prior arrangement only.
Heritage Open Days: No
P Yes. Spaces: 2
♿ Yes. Disabled WC: No. Guide Dogs: Yes
£ No

St Agatha

Market Way, Portsmouth, Hampshire
Italianate basilica of 1894 built for the Anglo Catholic priest, Fr R Dolling. Highly decorated interior of marble, alabaster, polished granite, carved stone and coloured glass. The apse has a sgraffito mural c1901 by Heywood Summer.
Grant Recipient/Owner: St Agatha's Trust
Access contact: J D Maunder
Tel: 01329 230330   **Fax:** 01329 230330
Opening Arrangements: October - May: Saturdays and Sundays 10am - 2pm; June - September: Saturdays, Sundays and Wednesdays 10am - 3pm. At other times by prior written arrangement with St Agatha's Trust, 9 East Street, Fareham, Hampshire PO16 0BW (tel.01329 230330).
Heritage Open Days: Yes
P Yes. Spaces: 50
Partial. Disabled WC: No. Guide Dogs: Yes
£ No

The Vyne

Sherborne St John, Basingstoke, Hampshire RG24 9HL
Built in the early 16th century for Henry VIII's Lord Chamberlain. The house acquired a classical portico mid 17th century (the first of its kind in England). Tudor chapel with Renaissance glass, Palladian staircase, old panelling and fine furniture. Grounds, containing wild garden, lakes and woodland walks.
Website Address: www.nationaltrust.org.uk
Grant Recipient/Owner: The National Trust
Access contact: Mr Jonathan Ingram
Tel: 01256 881337   **Fax:** 01256 881720
Email Address: svygen@smtp.ntrust.org.uk
Opening Arrangements: House: 31 March to 4 November: daily except Thursdays and Fridays (but open Good Friday 1 - 5pm (last entry 4.30pm). Grounds: weekends in February and March 11am - 4.30pm; 31 March to 4 November: daily except Thursdays and Fridays (but open Good Friday) 11am - 6pm. Wheelchair access to ground floor. Car park is 140 metres from house. New car park to open late summer (with capacity for 140 cars and 3 coaches) will be located 450 metres from house (buggy service available). Disabled drivers will be able to park by house.
Heritage Open Days: No
P Yes. Spaces: 70
Partial. Disabled WC: Yes. Guide Dogs: Yes
£ Yes
Adult: £5.50
Child: £2.75
Other: £13.75 (family). £4.50 (group rate per head Mondays, Tuesdays and Wednesdays only).

Whitchurch Silk Mill

28 Winchester Street, Whitchurch, Hampshire RG28 7AL
Grade II* watermill built c1800 and has been in continuous use as a silk weaving mill since the 1820s. Now a working museum, the winding, warping and weaving machinery installed between 1890 and 1927 produces traditional silks for theatrical costume, historic houses, fashion and artworks.
Grant Recipient/Owner:
Hampshire Building Preservation Trust Ltd
Access contact: Mill Manager
Tel: 01256 892065   **Fax:** 01256 893882
Opening Arrangements: Mill and shop: Tuesday - Sunday 10.30am - 5pm (last admission 4.15pm). Mill and shop closed Mondays (except Bank Holidays) and between Christmas and New Year. Access for wheelchair users to ground floor of Mill, shop and gardens. Free parking next to Mill, 2 disabled spaces next to shop.
Heritage Open Days: No
P Yes. Spaces: 20
Partial. Disabled WC: Yes. Guide Dogs: Yes
£ Yes
Adult: £3.00
Child: £1.50
Other: £2.50

Woodgreen Village Hall

Hale Road, Woodgreen, Fordingbridge, Hampshire SP6 2BQ
Village hall built in 1930 with murals depicting life in the village covering every wall.
Grant Recipient/Owner:
Woodgreen Village Hall Committee
Access contact: Mrs Angela Sales
Tel: 01725 512288
Opening Arrangements: Any time but advisable to book first (contact Mrs Sales, or Mrs Windel on 01725 512529).
Heritage Open Days: No
P Yes. Spaces: 20
Yes. Disabled WC: Yes. Guide Dogs: Yes
£ Yes

Adult: 50p
Child: 50p
Other: 50p

HEREFORDSHIRE

Chandos Manor

Rushall, Ledbury, Herefordshire HR8 2PA
Farmhouse, probably late C16 with C18 extensions. Timber-frame, partly rendered.
Website Address:
Grant Recipient/Owner: Mr Richard White
Access contact: Mr Richard White
Tel: 01531 660208
Opening Arrangements:
Easter - September: Sundays by prior arrangement.
Heritage Open Days: No
P Yes. Spaces: 12
No. Disabled WC: No. Guide Dogs: Yes
£ No
Adult: Donations to charity.

Chapel Farm

Wigmore, nr. Leominster, Herefordshire HR6 9UQ
Timber-framed farmhouse c1400 of rectangular plan, originally a hall-house with first floor inserted in the 16th century. Contains an open roof with foliate carved windbraces, ornate post-heads and late Elizabethan wall painting. Associated with the Lollards around 1400.
Grant Recipient/Owner: Mr M Pollitt
Access contact: Mr M Pollitt
Opening Arrangements: By prior written arrangement Mondays (except Bank Holidays) May - September 2 - 4.30pm. Maximum 2 persons per visit. No children under 16 and no animals.
Heritage Open Days: No
P Yes. Spaces: 1
No. Disabled WC: No. Guide Dogs: No
£ No

College of the Vicars Choral

Cathedral Close, Hereford, Herefordshire HR1 2NG
College, c1473, of coursed sandstone rubble with a Welsh slate roof and 7 stepped buttress stacks with ashlar chimneys.
Grant Recipient/Owner:
Dean & Chapter of Hereford Cathedral
Access contact: Andrew Eames
Tel: 01432 374200   **Fax:** 01432 374220
Email Address: office@herefordcathedral.co.uk
Opening Arrangements: Sundays (except Palm Sunday, Easter Day and Christmas Day) 11am - 12.30pm and on other days by prior arrangement with the Chapter Clerk, Cathedral Office, 5 College Cloisters, Cathedral Close, Hereford HR1 2NG (tel.01432 374200).
Heritage Open Days: No
P No
Yes. Disabled WC: Yes. Guide Dogs: Yes
£ No

Croft Castle

nr. Leominster, Herefordshire HR6 9PW
Home of the Croft family since Domesday (with a break of 170 years from 1750). Walls and corner towers date from 14th and 15th centuries interior mainly 18th century. The park contains an avenue of 350 year old Spanish chestnuts. The walled garden is independently maintained by the Croft Trust and contains various historic fruit trees and plants.
Website Address: www.ntrustsevern.org.uk
Grant Recipient/Owner: The National Trust
Access contact: Mr David Atkins
Tel: 01568 780246   **Fax:** 01568 780462
Email Address: croft@smtp.ntrust.org.uk
Opening Arrangements: Castle: 31 March to 29 April: Saturday and Sunday, Good Friday and Bank Holiday Monday. 2 May to 30 September: daily except Mondays and Tuesdays (but open Bank Holiday Mondays). 6 October to 4 November: Saturday and Sundays. Times: 1- 5pm (closes 4.30pm in Ocotber and November). Park and Croft Ambrey: daily.
Heritage Open Days: No
P Yes. Spaces: 300
Yes. Disabled WC: Yes. Guide Dogs: No
£ Yes
Adult: £3.90
Child: £1.95
Other: £10.00 (family). £2.00 (parking).

Eastnor Castle

nr. Ledbury, Herefordshire HR8 1RL
Norman-style castellated mansion set in the western slopes of the Malvern Hills. Constructed 1812 - 1820 and designed by Sir Robert Smirke, the castle has 15 state and other rooms fully-furnished and open to visitors. The decoration includes tapestries, paintings, armour and a

drawing room by Augustus Pugin.
Website Address: www.eastnorcastle.com
Grant Recipient/Owner: Mr J Hervey-Bathurst
Access contact: Mr S Foster
Tel: 01531 633160   **Fax:** 01531 631776
Email Address: enquiries@eastnorcastle.com
Opening Arrangements: Easter - end of September: Sundays and Bank Holiday Mondays, plus every day in July and August except Saturdays, 11am - 5pm. Wheelchair access to grounds, tea room and ground floor with assistance (always available).
Heritage Open Days: No
P Yes. Spaces: 150
Partial. Disabled WC: Yes. Guide Dogs: Yes
£ Yes
Adult: £5.00
Child: £3.00
Other: £2.75 (senior citizens)

Hergest Court

Kington, Herefordshire
House dates back to 1267 and was the ancestral home of the Clanvowe and Vaughan families. It is an unusual example of a fortified manor in the Welsh Marches. It has literary associations with Sir John Clanvowe and Lewis Glyn Cothi.
Grant Recipient/Owner: Mr W L Banks
Access contact: Mr W L Banks
Tel: 01544 230160   **Fax:** 01544 230160
Email Address: banks@hergest.kc3.co.uk
Opening Arrangements:
By prior arrangement with the Hergest Estate Office, Kington, Herefordshire HR5 3EG (telephone and fax: 01544 230160). Bookings by phone or fax with five days notice. Wheelchair access to ground floor only.
Heritage Open Days: No
P Yes. Spaces: 5
Partial. Disabled WC: No. Guide Dogs: Yes
£ Yes
Adult: £5.00

Lower Brockhampton

Brockhampton-by-Bromyard, Herefordshire WR6 5UH
A late 14th century moated manor house with a detached half-timbered 15th century gatehouse. Also, the ruins of a 12th century chapel. Woodland walks.
Website Address: www.ntrustsevern.org.uk
Grant Recipient/Owner: The National Trust
Access contact: Mr Les Rogers
Tel: 01885 488099
Email Address: brockhampton@smtp.ntrust.org.uk
Opening Arrangements:
House: 1 April to 31 October: daily except Mondays and Tuesdays (but open Bank Holiday Mondays). Times: April to October 12.30 - 5pm (closes at 4pm in October). Weekends in July and August 10.30am to 5pm. Wheelchair access to ground floor of house, chapel and estate. Two car parks, 1 1/2 miles and 200 yards from house. Parking for disabled near house.
Heritage Open Days: No
P Yes. Spaces: 60
Partial. Disabled WC: No. Guide Dogs: Yes
£ Yes
Adult: £2.70
Other: £6.75 (family). £1.50 (car park). Estate free to pedestrians.

The Painted Room

Town Council Offices, Church Street, Ledbury, Herefordshire HR8 1DH
The wall paintings, discovered here in 1989, are a unique example of domestic wall painting dating from the Tudor period. They are clearly the work of a commoner, created to imitate the rich tapestries or hangings that would have been found in the homes of the gentry.
Grant Recipient/Owner: Ledbury Town Council
Access contact: Mrs J McQuaid
Tel: 01531 632306   **Fax:** 01531 631193
Email Address: ledburytowncouncil@ledbury.org.uk
Opening Arrangements: Easter - end of September: guided tours Monday - Friday 11.30am - 3pm. Rest of year: Mondays, Tuesdays, Wednesdays and Fridays, if member of staff available. Town centre car parks nearby.
Heritage Open Days: Yes
P See above
No. Disabled WC: No. Guide Dogs: Yes
£ No

St Katharine's Hall and Chapel

High Street, Ledbury, Herefordshire
Part of Hospital founded in 1232 by Bishop Hugh Foliot, the Hall and Chapel were built c1330-40 of local stone rubble with a tiled gabled roof.
Grant Recipient/Owner:
The Trustees of St Katharine's Hospital Charity
Access contact:
Clerk to the Trustees of St Katharine's Hospital Charity
Tel: 01432 374200   **Fax:** 01432 374220

Email Address: office@herefordcathedral.co.uk
Opening Arrangements:
The Hall is normally open during the week. Access to the Chapel is by prior arrangement with the Clerk to the Trustees of St Katharine's Hospital Charity, Cathedral Office, 5 College Cloisters, Hereford HR1 2NG (tel.01432 374200).
Heritage Open Days: No
P No
♿ No. Disabled WC: No. Guide Dogs: No
£ No

HERTFORDSHIRE

Bishop Seth Ward's Almshouse

Market Hill, High Street, Buntingford, Hertfordshire
Almshouses c1684 (possibly by Robert Hooke) for Seth Ward, Bishop of Exeter and Salisbury, mathematician and astronomer and friend of Wren.
Grant Recipient/Owner: Mr R C Woods
Access contact: Mr R C Woods
Tel: 01763 271974   **Fax:** 01763 271974
Opening Arrangements: The exterior and gardens by prior arrangement with Mr R C Woods, Chairman of the Trustees, Bishop Seth Ward's Almshouse Trust, 58 Hare Street Road, Buntingford, Hertfordshire SG9 9HN (tel.01763 271974).
Heritage Open Days: No
P No
♿ No. Disabled WC: No. Guide Dogs: No
£ No

Bridgewater Monument

Aldbury, Hertfordshire
The monument was erected in 1832 to commemorate the Duke of Bridgewater. It is the focal point of Ashridge Estate which runs across the borders of Hertfordshire and Buckinghamshire along the main ridge of the Chilterns.
Website Address: www.nationaltrust.org.uk
Grant Recipient/Owner: The National Trust
Access contact: Property Manager
Tel: 01442 851227   **Fax:** 01442 842062
Opening Arrangements: 1 April to 29 October: Mondays to Thursdays 2 - 5pm, Saturdays, Sundays and Bank Holiday Mondays 2 - 5.30pm, (closed Fridays, but open Good Friday). Full wheelchair access, although some routes difficult in bad weather.
Heritage Open Days: No
P Yes. Spaces: 100
♿ Yes. Disabled WC: Yes. Guide Dogs: Yes
£ Yes
Adult: £1.00
Child: £0.50

Cromer Windmill

Ardeley, Stevenage, Hertfordshire SG2 7QA
Grade II* postmill dated 1674, last surviving postmill in Hertfordshire. Restored to working order (but not actually working).
Website Address: www.hertsmuseums.org.uk
Grant Recipient/Owner: Ms Cristina Harrison
Access contact: Ms Cristina Harrison
Tel: 01279 843301
Email Address: cristinaharrison@hotmail.com
Opening Arrangements: Open Saturday before National Mill Day, ie. second Sunday in May. Thereafter every Sunday and Bank Holidays, and second and fourth Saturdays until Heritage Open Days 2.30 - 5pm. Wheelchair access to ground floor only but video of upper floors showing all the time. 30 minute video available for schools and other groups. Guided tours. Special parties by prior arrangement with Ms Cristina Harrison, The Forge Museum, High Street, Much Hadham, Hertfordshire SG10 6BS (tel.01279 843301). Refreshments available.
Heritage Open Days: Yes
P Yes. Spaces: 20
♿ Partial. Disabled WC: No. Guide Dogs: Yes
£ Yes
Adult: £1.50
Child: 25p

Ducklake House Wallpainting

Springhead, Ashwell, Baldock, Hertfordshire SG7 5LL
16th century wall painting, located on the ground floor, containing classical grotesques holding cartouches.
Grant Recipient/Owner: Mr P W H Saxton
Access contact: Mr P W H Saxton
Opening Arrangements: By prior written arrangement to view the wall painting only. Parking available.
Heritage Open Days: No
P Yes. Spaces: 1
♿ No. Disabled WC: No. Guide Dogs: No
£ No

Knebworth House

Knebworth, nr. Stevenage, Hertfordshire SG3 6PY
Originally a Tudor manor house, rebuilt in gothic style in 1843. Contains rooms in various styles, which include a Jacobean banqueting hall. Set in 250 acres of parkland with 25 acres of formal gardens. Home of the Lytton family since 1490.
Website Address: www.knebworthhouse.com
Grant Recipient/Owner:
Knebworth House Education & Preservation Trust
Access contact: Miss Jacky Wilson
Tel: 01438 812661   **Fax:** 01438 811908
Email Address: info@knebworthhouse.com
Opening Arrangements: 7-22 April, 26 May - 3 June, 7 July - 4 September: daily; 28 April - 20 May, 9 June - 1 July, 8-30 September: weekends and Bank Holidays. Gardens, Park and playground 11am - 5.30pm, House 12 noon - 5pm (last admission 4.30pm). Groups (20+) all year by prior arrangement. Wheelchair access to ground floor only, disabled parking available at front of house on request. Unlimited parking.
Heritage Open Days: No
P See above
♿ Partial. Disabled WC: Yes. Guide Dogs: Yes
£ Yes
Adult: £7.00 (£6.00 group)
Child: £6.50 (£5.50 group)
Other: £6.50 (senior citizens, £5.50 group).

Old Palace

23 Kneeworth Street, Royston, Hertfordshire SG8 5AB
Built 1610 by James I, much altered (half of original building has subsequently been demolished). Has Georgian façade to the rear, the street frontage is in fact the dividing wall of the original building which has been left exposed following demolition of part of the building.
Grant Recipient/Owner: Mr Peter Franks
Access contact: Mr Peter Franks
Opening Arrangements: By prior written arrangement.
Heritage Open Days: No
P Yes. Spaces: 1
♿ No. Disabled WC: No. Guide Dogs: Yes
£ No

Redbournbury Mill

Redbournbury Lane, Redbourn Road, St Albans, Hertfordshire AL3 6RS
18th century watermill in full working order after 10 year restoration programme following 1987 fire. Supplementary power from Crossley oil engine.
Grant Recipient/Owner: Mr J T James
Access contact: Mrs A L James
Tel: 01582 792874
Email Address: redbrymill@aol.com
Opening Arrangements: 21 March - 3 October: Sundays 2.30 - 5pm, plus Easter, late May and August Bank Holidays. National Mills Weekend, Heritage Open Days and New Year's Day open all day. Special events throughout the year. Private parties by prior arrangement. Wheelchair access to ground floor only. Refreshments available. Milling demonstrations. Organic flour and bread for sale.
Heritage Open Days: Yes
P Yes. Spaces: 30
♿ Partial. Disabled WC: No. Guide Dogs: No
£ Yes
Adult: £1.50
Child: 80p
Other: 80p

Torilla

11 Wilkins Green Lane, Nast Hyde, Hatfield, Hertfordshire AL10 9RT
'Torilla' (house at Nast Hyde) was built by F R S Yorke in 1935 in the international style and features a flat roof, 2 balconies and a large double height living room. Constructed of concrete with large steel framed windows. F R S Yorke was a key figure in the evolution of modern architecture in Britain.
Grant Recipient/Owner: Mr Alan Charlton
Access contact: Mr Alan Charlton
Tel: 01707 259582   **Fax:** 01707 259583
Opening Arrangements: Sunday 20th May and Sunday 19th August, 11am - 5pm. At other times by prior written arrangement.
Heritage Open Days: No
P Yes. Spaces: 5
♿ Partial. Disabled WC: No. Guide Dogs: Yes
£ No

Woodhall Park

Watton-at-Stone, Hertfordshire
Country house, now school. Designed and built by Thomas Leverton in 1785 in neo-Classical style. Normally associated with London houses, this is one of his few country houses. Highly decorated interiors which include the Print Room with walls covered in engraved paper, reproductions of paintings with frames, ribbons, chains, busts, candelabra and piers with vases.
Grant Recipient/Owner:
Trustees of R M Abel Smith 1991 Settlement
Access contact:
The Trustees of R M Abel Smith 1991 Settlement
Tel: 01920 830286   **Fax:** 01920 830162
Email Address: woodhallest@dial.pipex.com
Opening Arrangements: At all reasonable times, preferably school holidays, by prior arrangement with the Trustees of R M Abel Smith 1991 Settlement, Estate Office, Woodhall Park, Watton-at-Stone, Hertfordshire SG14 3NF (tel.01920 830286). Wheelchair access to ground floor only. During school holidays there is parking for up to 50 cars, but during school terms this is limited to about 10.
Heritage Open Days: No
P Yes. Spaces: 50
♿ Partial. Disabled WC: No. Guide Dogs: Yes
£ No

KENT

Chiddingstone Castle

Chiddingstone, nr. Edenbridge, Kent TN8 7AD
Tudor mansion subsequently twice remodelled by the Streatfeilds whose seat it was. William Atkinson "Master of the picturesque" is responsible for the romantic design, c1805, of the building as it is today. Rescued from dereliction by Denys Bower in the 20th century, now managed by a charitable trust.
Grant Recipient/Owner:
Trustees of the Denys Eyre Bower Bequest
Access contact: Miss M R Eldridge
Tel: 01892 870347
Opening Arrangements: Easter and Spring Bank Holidays, June - September: Wednesday, Thursdays, Fridays and Sundays; 2 - 5.30pm weekdays, Sundays and Bank Holidays 11.30am - 5.30pm (last admission 5pm). Groups (minimum 20) during winter by prior arrangement. Also school groups when Castle is normally closed by prior arrangement. Wheelchair access to ground floor only but this includes everything except the Egyptian collection.
Heritage Open Days: No
P Yes. Spaces: 50
♿ Partial. Disabled WC: Yes. Guide Dogs: Yes
£ Yes
Adult: £4.00
Child: £2.00 (5-15, under 5 free but must be accompanied by an adult).

Church House

72 High Street, Edenbridge, Kent TN8 5AR
Late 14th century timber-framed farmhouse, now houses the Eden Valley Museum.
Grant Recipient/Owner: Mr M Downing
Access contact: Ms Elisabeth Wright
Tel: 01732 868102   **Fax:** 01732 867866
Email Address: eden_tc@thebarn72.freeserve.co.uk
Opening Arrangements: November - March: Tuesdays - Fridays 2 - 4.30pm; April - October: Tuesdays - Fridays and Sundays 2 - 4.30pm, Saturdays 10am - 4.30pm. Private/educational groups by prior arrangement. Wheelchair access to ground floor only (computer link to provide vision of upstairs under development). Free parking in town centre car park 200yds from House.
Heritage Open Days: Yes
P Yes. Spaces: 150
♿ Partial. Disabled WC: Yes. Guide Dogs: Yes
£ Yes
Adult: £1.50
Child: 75p
Other: 75p

Cobham Hall Dairy

Cobham, Kent DA12 3BL
Gothic-style dairy in grounds of Cobham Hall, built by James Wyatt c1790.
Grant Recipient/Owner: Cobham Hall Heritage Trust
Access contact: Mr N G Powell
Tel: 01474 823371   **Fax:** 01474 825904
Opening Arrangements: Easter - end of August: Hall open Wednesdays and Sundays 2 - 5pm (last tour 4.30pm). Please telephone to confirm opening times. At other times (and coach parties) by prior arrangement. Wheelchair access to ground floor only. Self-guided tour of Gardens and Parkland (historical/conservation tour by prior arrangement). Special events.
Heritage Open Days: No
P Yes. Spaces: 100
♿ Partial. Disabled WC: Yes. Guide Dogs: Yes
£ Yes
Adult: £3.50
Child: £2.50
Other: £2.50 (seniors & groups)

Foord Almshouses

Priestfields, Rochester, Kent ME1 3AF
Main Hall of almshouses built in 1932 of English bond red brick with stone dressings and old tile roof in neo-vernacular style of the 17th century with Baroque reference.
Grant Recipient/Owner:
Trustees of the Foord Almshouses
Access contact: Mr David Hubbard
Tel: 01634 844138
Opening Arrangements: By prior arrangement.
Heritage Open Days: No
P Yes. Spaces: 10
Yes. Disabled WC: Yes. Guide Dogs: Yes
£ No

Gad's Hill Place

Higham-by-Rochester, Kent ME3 7PA
Former home of Charles Dickens, who lived here from 1856 until his death in 1870 whilst writing The Mystery of Edwin Drood. Built c1780 with Dickensian additions, it is now an Independent School and stands in 11 acres of meadowland and gardens.
Grant Recipient/Owner: Gad's Hill School
Access contact: Miss Anne Carter
Tel: 01474 822366   **Fax:** 01474 822977
Opening Arrangements: Easter - October: first Sunday of each month plus Bank Holiday Sundays 2 - 5pm (last admission 4pm). Summer and Christmas Dickens Festivals 11am - 4.30pm. Guided tours at other times by prior arrangement. Access for only certain types of wheelchair, please check with Place for details. Admission charges are provisional at time of going to print, again please check with Place for clarification. Refreshments available.
Heritage Open Days: Yes
P Yes. Spaces: 40
Partial. Disabled WC: Yes. Guide Dogs: Yes
£ Yes
Adult: £2.50 (see above)
Child: £1.50

Herne Windmill

Mill Lane, Herne Bay, Kent CT6 7DR
Kentish smock mill built 1789, worked by wind until 1952 and then by electricity until 1980. Bought by Kent County Council in 1985, which carried out some restoration. Now managed by Friends of Herne Mill on behalf of the County Council. Much of the original machinery is in place, some is run for demonstration and the sails used when the wind conditions permit.
Website Address: www.kentwindmills.co.uk
Grant Recipient/Owner: Kent County Council
Access contact: Mr Ken Cole
Tel: 01227 361326
Opening Arrangements: Easter - end of September: Sundays and Bank Holidays, plus Thursdays in July and August, 2 - 5pm. National Mills Day 11am - 5pm. Wheelchair and guide dog access to ground floor of Mill and meeting room.
Heritage Open Days: No
P Yes. Spaces: 12
Partial. Disabled WC: Yes. Guide Dogs: Yes
£ Yes
Adult: £1.00
Child: 25p (accompanied by adult)

The Hospital of St Thomas the Martyr

Eastbridge, 25 High Street, Canterbury, Kent CT1 2BD
12th century building providing hospitality for pilgrims visiting the shrine of St Thomas Becket at Canterbury Cathedral. Contains two chapels, an undercroft and refectory. Of particular interest is a 12th century fresco of "Our Lord in Glory". Private areas of the Hospital are almshouses for eight people.
Grant Recipient/Owner: Hospital of St Thomas the Martyr, Eastbridge
Access contact: Miss Louise Fittall
Tel: 01227 471688
Opening Arrangements: Monday - Saturday 10am - 4.45pm (except Good Friday, Christmas Day and other occasional Church Festival Days).
Heritage Open Days: No
P No
No. Disabled WC: No. Guide Dogs: Yes
£ Yes
Adult: £1.00
Child: 50p (5-16), under 5s free.
Other: 75p (seniors/students/groups).

Ightham Mote

Ivy Hatch, Sevenoaks, Kent TN15 0NT
Moated manor house covering 650 years of history from medieval times to 1960s. Extended visitor route now includes the newly refurbished north-west quarter with Tudor Chapel, Billiards Room and Drawing Room. Interpretation displays and special exhibition featuring conservation in action.

Website Address: www.nationaltrust.org.uk/regions/kentessex
Grant Recipient/Owner: The National Trust
Access contact: The Property Manager
Tel: 01732 810378   **Fax:** 01732 811029
Email Address: kimxxxx@smtp.ntrust.org.uk
Opening Arrangements: 1 April - 4 November: daily except Tuesday and Saturday 11am - 5.30pm. Last admission 4.30pm.
Heritage Open Days: No
P Yes. Spaces: 350
Partial. Disabled WC: Yes. Guide Dogs: Yes
£ Yes
Adult: £5.00
Child: £2.50
Other: £12.50 (family), £4.25 (groups). NT members free

Knole

Sevenoaks, Kent TN15 0RP
The largest private house in England, Knole is a fine example of late medieval architecture. It has been the home of the Sackville family since 1603, including four Dukes of Dorset. Knole houses an extensive collection of furnishing and paintings, many in the house since the 17th century, and the prototype of the 'Knole' settee.
Website Address: www.nationaltrust.org.uk/regions/kentessex
Grant Recipient/Owner: The National Trust
Access contact: The Property Manager
Tel: 01732 462100   **Fax:** 01732 465528
Email Address: kknxxxx@smtp.ntrust.org.uk
Opening Arrangements: 31 March - 4 November: Wednesday - Saturday 12 - 4pm (last admission 3.30pm), Sunday, Bank Holiday Monday and Good Friday 11am - 5pm (last admission 4pm). Garden: May - September: first Wednesday of each month only 12 - 4pm.
Heritage Open Days: No
P Yes. Spaces: 500
Partial. Disabled WC: Yes. Guide Dogs: Yes
£ Yes
Adult: £5.00
Child: £2.50
Other: £12.50 (family), £4.25 (groups). Garden only £1.00, Parking £2.50. NT members free.

Littlebourne Tithe Barn

Church Road, Littlebourne, nr. Canterbury, Kent CT3 1TU
Early 14th century timber-framed aisled barn of 7 and a half bays. Aisled on all four sides with crown-post roof construction, has oak-riven boarding to walls and now thatched in water reed (formerly long straw). The two hipped roof entrances date from 1961.
Grant Recipient/Owner: Canterbury City Council
Access contact: Secretary, Conservation Section
Tel: 01227 862190   **Fax:** 01227 862020
Email Address: conservation@canterbury.gov.uk
Opening Arrangements: Open for events during the year, otherwise at other times by prior arrangement. For details and access, please contact the Conservation Section at Canterbury City Council, Military Road, Canterbury, Kent CT1 1TW (tel.01227 862190).
Heritage Open Days: Yes
P Yes. Spaces: 15
Yes. Disabled WC: Yes. Guide Dogs: Yes
£ No

Nurstead Court

Nurstead Church Lane, Meopham, nr. Gravesend, Kent DA13 9AD
Grade I listed medieval aisled timber-framed hall built 1320, containing massive oak pillars with craved capitals supporting a frame-work of arched braces and tie beams with central crown-post supporting the clay-peg tiled roof. The walls are of knapped flint. Probably built by the Bishop of London, Stephen de Gravesend.
Grant Recipient/Owner: Mrs S M H Edmeades-Stearns
Access contact: Mrs S M H Edmeades-Stearns
Tel: 01474 812121   **Fax:** 01474 815133
Opening Arrangements: Every Wednesday and Thursday in September, plus 3 & 4 October, 2 - 5pm. At other times by prior arrangement.
Heritage Open Days: No
P Yes. Spaces: 30
Yes. Disabled WC: No. Guide Dogs: Yes
£ Yes
Adult: £4.00
Child: £3.00
Other: £3.00 (senior citizens)

Prospect Tower

Belmont Park, Faversham, Kent
This small flint tower stands on the edge of Belmont Park. It was built in 1808 for Lord Harris of Seringapatam as his 'whim', prize money won in India. The 4th Lord Harris's enthusiasm was cricket. He commandeered the tower as a changing room. Narrow spiral staircase.
Website Address: www.landmarktrust.co.uk
Grant Recipient/Owner: The Landmark Trust

Access contact: Ms Victoria Piggott
Tel: 01628 825920   **Fax:** 01628 825417
Email Address: vpiggott@landmarktrust.co.uk
Opening Arrangements: The Landmark Trust is an independent charity, which rescues small buildings of historic or architectural importance from decay or unsympathetic improvement. Landmark's aim is to promote the enjoyment of these historic buildings by making them available to stay in for holidays. Prospect Tower can be rented by anyone, at all times of the year, for periods ranging from a weekend to three weeks. Bookings can be made by telephoning the Booking Office on 01628 825925. As the building is in full-time use for holiday accommodation, it is not normally open to the public. However the public can view the building by prior arrangement by telephoning the access contact (Victoria Piggott on 01628 825920) to make an appointment. Potential visitors will be asked to write to confirm the details of their visit.
Heritage Open Days: No
P Yes. Spaces: 1
No. Disabled WC: No. Guide Dogs: No
£ No

Roper Gateway

adjacent to 33 St Dunstan's Street, Canterbury, Kent
16th century red brick gateway which originally led to Place House (house of Margaret Roper, daughter of Sir Thomas More). Has a crow stopped gable and a large 4-centred arch with a pair of wooden doors (dating from the 18-19th centuries). Nothing now remains of Place House and the gate now leads to former 19th century brewery buildings. The gateway is clearly visible from St Dunstan's Street.
Grant Recipient/Owner: Canterbury City Council
Access contact: The Secretary Conservation Section
Tel: 01227 862190   **Fax:** 01227 862020
Opening Arrangements: The gateway building can be inspected from St Dunstan's Street and Roper Close. Contact the Conservation Section of Canterbury City Council, Military Road, Canterbury, Kent CT1 1YW (tel.01227 862190) for further information. Parking at West Station.
Heritage Open Days: No
P Yes. Spaces: 100
Yes. Disabled WC: No. Guide Dogs: Yes
£ No

Sissinghurst Tower

Sissinghurst, Cranbrook, Kent TN17 2AB
Red-brick prospect tower and walls - surviving part of an Elizabethan mansion. Surrounded by a world-famous garden. The study where Vita Sackville-West worked and Long Library are open to the public.
Website Address: www.nationaltrust.org.uk/regions/kentessex
Grant Recipient/Owner: The National Trust
Access contact: Ms Sarah Cook
Tel: 01580 710700   **Fax:** 01580 710702
Email Address: ksisdc@smtp.ntrust.org.uk
Opening Arrangements: 31 March - 14 October: Tuesday - Friday 1pm - 6.30pm, Saturday, Sunday and Good Friday 10am - 5.30pm. Last admission 30 minutes before close.
Heritage Open Days: No
P Yes. Spaces: 500
Partial. Disabled WC: Yes. Guide Dogs: Yes
£ Yes
Adult: £6.50
Child: £3.00
Other: £16.00 (family)

Somerhill

Tonbridge, Kent TN11 0NJ
Grade I Jacobean mansion with Victorian addition set in 150 acres of parkland. Now used as a school, but original ceilings, panelling and stables have been retained.
Grant Recipient/Owner:
Somerhill Charitable Trust Ltd
Access contact: Diane M Huntingford
Tel: 01732 352121   **Fax:** 01732 363381
Opening Arrangements:
By prior written or telephone arrangement plus the Sunday of the Heritage Open Days weekend. Wheelchair access to ground floor only.
Heritage Open Days: Yes
P Yes. Spaces: 170
Partial. Disabled WC: No. Guide Dogs: Yes
£ No

Willesborough Windmill

Willesborough, Ashford, Kent, TN24 0GQ
Grade II* listed windmill built in 1869 and coaching barn. A 1911 Hornsby 14HP gas oil engine now installed to give auxiliary power. The barn is now enclosed and houses a heritage museum.
Grant Recipient/Owner: Ashford Borough Council
Access contact: Willesborough Windmill Trust

Tel: 01233 661866
Opening Arrangements: April to end September: Saturdays, Sundays and Bank Holiday Mondays 2 -5pm. Wheelchair access to ground floor of mill, all of barn.
Heritage Open Days: Yes
P Yes. Spaces: 30
⚅ Partial. Disabled WC: Yes. Guide Dogs: Yes
£ Yes
Adult: £1.00
Child: £0.50
Other: £0.50 (seniors)

LANCASHIRE

Gawthorpe Hall

Padiham, nr. Burnley, Lancashire BB12 8UA
An Elizabethan property in the heart of industrial Lancashire. Restored and refurbished in the mid 19th century by Sir Charles Barry. There are many notable paintings on display loaned to the National Trust by the National Portrait Gallery, and a collection of needlework, assembled by the last family member to live there, Rachel Kay-Shuttleworth.
Website Address: www.nationaltrust.org.uk
Grant Recipient/Owner: The National Trust
Access contact: Property Manager
Tel: 01282 770353   **Fax:** 01282 770353
Email Address: rpmgaw@smtp.ntrust.org.uk
Opening Arrangements: Hall: 1 April to 31 October daily except Mondays and Fridays (but open Good Friday and Bank Holiday Mondays) 1 - 5pm. Garden: all year 10am - 6pm. Wheelchair access to garden only.
Heritage Open Days: No
P Yes. Spaces: 50
⚅ See above. Disabled WC: Yes. Guide Dogs: Yes
£ Yes
Adult: £3.00
Child: £1.30
Other: £8.00 (family). Garden free.

Hoghton Tower

Hoghton, Preston, Lancashire PR5 0SH
16th century fortified manor house, ancestral home of the de Hoghton family since William the Conqueror. Associated with many kings and queens (the Banqueting Hall is where James I knighted the Loin of Beef 'Sirloin') and William Shakespeare. Various staterooms open to the public, as well as a Tudor horse-drawn well, dungeons and underground passages.
Grant Recipient/Owner: Hoghton Tower Preservation Trust
Access contact: Mr John Graver
Tel: 01254 852986   **Fax:** 01254 852109
Opening Arrangements: Guided tours of the house: Bank Holiday Sundays/Mondays (excluding Christmas and New Year); July - September: Monday - Thursday, 11am - 4pm (Sundays 1 - 5pm). Private tours throughout the year by prior arrangement.
Heritage Open Days: No
P Yes. Spaces: 250
⚅ No. Disabled WC: No. Guide Dogs: Yes
£ Yes
Adult: £3.00
Child: £2.00
Other: £2.00 (senior citizens & students), £8 (family)

Leighton Hall

Carnforth, Lancashire LA5 9ST
Country House, 1765, probably by J Hird, with earlier remains. Gothic south-east front early 19th century, possibly by Thomas Harrison. Tower at west end of the façade 1870 by Paley and Austin. Ancestral home of the Gillow family with fine furniture, paintings and objets d'art.
Website Address: www.leightonhall.co.uk
Grant Recipient/Owner: Mr Richard Reynolds
Access contact: Mr Richard Reynolds
Tel: 01524 734474   **Fax:** 01524 720357
Email Address: leightonhall@yahoo.co.uk
Opening Arrangements: Daily 1 May - end of September (except Saturdays and non-Bank Holiday Mondays) 2 - 5pm (11.30am - 5pm in August). Groups all year by prior arrangement. The owner reserves the right to close or restrict access to the Hall and grounds for special events (dates to be confirmed). Refreshments available.
Heritage Open Days: No
P Yes. Spaces: 100
⚅ Yes. Disabled WC: Yes. Guide Dogs: Yes
£ Yes
Adult: £4.50
Child: £3.00
Other: £4.00 (senior citizen)

Rufford Old Hall

Rufford, nr. Ormskirk, Lancashire L40 1SG
Fine 16th century building with intricately carved movable wooded screen and hammerbeam roof. Owned by the Hesketh family for 250 years, the house contains

collections of 16th and 17th century oak furniture, arms, armour and tapestries.
Website Address: www.nationaltrust.org.uk
Grant Recipient/Owner: The National Trust
Access contact: Property Manager
Tel: 01704 821254   **Fax:** 01704 821254
Email Address: rrufoh@smtp.ntrust.org.uk
Opening Arrangements: House: 1 April to 31 October: daily except Thursdays and Fridays (but open Good Friday) 1- 5pm. Garden: as house 12.30pm - 5.30pm. Wheelchair access to garden, tea room and shop.
Heritage Open Days: No
P Yes. Spaces: 130
⚅ Partial. Disabled WC: Yes. Guide Dogs: Yes
£ Yes
Adult: £3.80
Child: £1.90
Other: £9.50 (family). £2.00 (garden only).

Stonyhurst College

Stonyhurst, Clitheroe, Lancashire BB7 9PZ
16th century manor house, now home to a Catholic independent boarding and day school. Contains dormitories, library, chapels, school-rooms and historical apartments.
Website Address: www.stonyhurst.ac.uk
Grant Recipient/Owner: Stonyhurst College
Access contact: Miss Frances Ahearne
Tel: 01254 826345   **Fax:** 01254 826732
Opening Arrangements: House: 16 July - 27 August daily (except Friday), plus August Bank Holiday Monday, 1 - 5pm; Gardens: 1 July - 27 August daily (except Friday), plus August Bank Holiday Monday, 1 - 5pm. Limited wheelchair access but assistance is available by prior arrangement. Coach parties by prior arrangement.
Heritage Open Days: No
P Yes. Spaces: 20
⚅ Partial. Disabled WC: Yes. Guide Dogs: Yes
£ Yes
Adult: £4.50
Child: £3.50
Other: £3.50

Towneley Hall Art Gallery & Museum

Todmorden Road, Burnley, Lancashire BB11 3RQ
Former home of the Towneley family on outskirts of Burnley, Towneley Hall has been the town's. art gallery and museum since 1903. The earliest part of the building dates from c1450. There is a 16th century chapel and Long Gallery, Baroque entrance hall and two reception rooms by Jeffrey Wyat c1820.
Website Address: www.towneleyhall.com
Grant Recipient/Owner: Burnley Borough Council
Access contact: Jackie Sims
Tel: 01282 424213   **Fax:** 01282 436138
Opening Arrangements: Monday - Friday 10am - 5pm, Sunday 12 - 5pm (Saturday closed). Also open Bank Holidays but closed for approximately one week over Christmas and New Year. No parking at site this year due to building works, some rooms may also be closed. Wheelchair access to ground floor only. Refreshments available.
Heritage Open Days: No
P No
⚅ Partial. Disabled WC: Yes. Guide Dogs: Yes
£ No

Turton Tower

Chapeltown Road, Turton, nr. Bolton, Lancashire BL7 0HG
Late medieval stone tower house with mainly late 16th and early 19th century alterations and timber-framed additions. Contains period rooms depicting domestic styles in such a building in the 16th, 17th, 19th and early 20th centuries.
Grant Recipient/Owner: Lancashire County Museums Service
Access contact: Mr Martin Robinson-Dowland
Tel: 01204 8522038   **Fax:** 01204 853759
Email Address: museum@lancashire.co.uk
Opening Arrangements:
February: Sundays 1 - 4pm; March: Saturday - Wednesday 1 - 4pm; April: Saturday - Wednesday 2 - 5pm; May - September: Saturday and Sunday 1 - 5pm, Monday - Thursday 10am - 12 noon and 1 - 5pm; October: Saturday - Wednesday 1 - 4pm; November: Sunday 1 - 4pm. Wheelchair access to ground floor, tea-room and shop. Additional parking for 2 coaches.
Heritage Open Days: No
P Yes. Spaces: 55
⚅ Yes. Disabled WC: Yes. Guide Dogs: Yes
£ Yes
Adult: £3.00
Child: £1.50
Other: £1.50

Whalley Abbey

Whalley, Clitheroe, Lancashire BB7 9SS
14th century Cistercian abbey ruins. Exhibition centre on site.

Grant Recipient/Owner:
Blackburn Diocesan Board of Finance
Access contact: Mr John Wilson
Tel: 01254 828400   **Fax:** 01254 828401
Opening Arrangements: Ruins and Gardens: daily Easter - October 11am - 5pm, November - Easter 11am - 4pm. 17th century Retreat House: Open Days and by prior arrangement. Refreshments available. Wheelchair access to most of ruins, coffee shop and exhibition centre.
Heritage Open Days: Yes
P Yes. Spaces: 25
⚅ Partial. Disabled WC: Yes. Guide Dogs: Yes
£ Yes
Adult: £2.00
Child: 50p
Other: £1.25 (seniors/students), £4.50 (family), £1.00 (coach 40+).

LEICESTERSHIRE

The Old Rectory

Cossington, Leicestershire LE7 4UU
16th century Closet with plank and muntin walls and oak coffered ceiling with paintings of flowers.
Grant Recipient/Owner: Mrs V H Jones
Access contact: Mrs V H Jones
Tel: 01509 812623   **Fax:** 01509 812110
Opening Arrangements: By prior written arrangement.
Heritage Open Days: No
P Yes. Spaces: 6
⚅ No. Disabled WC: No. Guide Dogs: Yes
£ No

Rockingham Castle

Market Harborough, Leicestershire LE16 8TH
Royal castle from William the Conqueror to Henry VIII, since then the home of the Watson family. Castle has remains from practically every century since the 11th. Fine collection of English 18th, 19th and 20th century paintings. Charles Dickens, who was a frequent visitor, used the castle as a model for Chesney Wold in Bleak House.
Website Address: www.rockinghamcastle.com
Grant Recipient/Owner: Commander L M M Saunders Watson
Access contact: The Administrator
Tel: 01536 770240   **Fax:** 01536 771692
Email Address: rockinghamcastle@liveone.net
Opening Arrangements: 1 April - 30 September: Sundays, Thursdays, Bank Holidays, Tuesdays after Bank Holidays and Tuesdays in August, 1 - 5pm (last admission 4.30pm); grounds open 11.30am Sundays and Bank Holidays, 1pm on other open days. Refreshments available. Wheelchair access to ground floor only.
Heritage Open Days: No
P Yes. Spaces: 500
⚅ Partial. Disabled WC: No. Guide Dogs: Yes
£ Yes
Adult: £4.50
Child: £3.00
Other: £4.00, £12.50 (family), also party & school rates.

Stanford Hall

Lutterworth, Leicestershire LE17 6DH
William and Mary house, built by the Smiths of Warwick (begun 1697), for Sir Roger Cave, ancestor of present owner whose family home it is. Visitors see every room on the ground floor (except modern kitchen), the "flying staircase" and two bedrooms. Contents include collection of Royal Stuart paintings.
Grant Recipient/Owner: Lady Braye
Access contact: E H Aubrey-Fletcher
Tel: 01788 860250   **Fax:** 01788 860870
Email Address: stanford.hall@virginnet.co.uk
Opening Arrangements: 7 April - 30 September: Saturdays, Sundays, Bank Holiday Mondays and following Tuesdays, 1.30 - 5.30pm (last admission 5pm). Also groups by prior arrangement any day or evening during this period. Special events. On Bank Holiday Mondays and Event days grounds open 12 noon. Closed October - Easter except for corporate events in October. Wheelchair access to the Park, the Gardens, the Motorcycle Museum, the 1898 Flying Machine, and the ground floor of the Hall if entrance steps can be negotiated.
Heritage Open Days: No
P Yes. Spaces: 1500
⚅ Partial. Disabled WC: Yes. Guide Dogs: Yes
£ Yes
Adult: £4.20 House & Grounds, £2.50 Grounds only.
Child: £2.00 House & Grounds, £1.50 Grounds only.
Other: £3.90 Adult, £1.80 Child (groups 20+).

LINCOLNSHIRE

12 Eastgate

Lincoln, Lincolnshire LN2 1QG
Georgian house, located on the north side of the cathedral, based on earlier medieval foundations. Now

occupied by the Dean of Lincoln.
Grant Recipient/Owner:
Dean of Lincoln Cathedral
Access contact: Mr William Roberts
Tel: 01522 527637
Opening Arrangements: By prior written arrangement with the Clerk of Works, Lincoln Cathedral, 28 Eastgate, Lincoln LN2 4AA.
Heritage Open Days: No
Ⓟ No
♿ No. Disabled WC: No. Guide Dogs: Yes
💷 No

12 Minster Yard

Lincoln, Lincolnshire LN2 1PJ
House of early 14th, late 17th and 19th centuries.
Grant Recipient/Owner:
Dean & Chapter of Lincoln Cathedral
Access contact: Mr William Roberts
Tel: 01522 527637
Opening Arrangements: By prior written arrangement with the Clerk of Works, Lincoln Cathedral, 28 Eastgate, Lincoln LN2 4AA.
Heritage Open Days: No
Ⓟ No
♿ No. Disabled WC: No. Guide Dogs: Yes
💷 No

13/13a Minster Yard

Lincoln, Lincolnshire LN2 1PW
Houses, mid-18th century, with late 18th and 19th century alterations.
Grant Recipient/Owner:
Dean & Chapter of Lincoln Cathedral
Access contact: Mr William Roberts
Tel: 01522 527637
Opening Arrangements: By prior written arrangement with the Clerk of Works, Lincoln Cathedral, 28 Eastgate, Lincoln LN2 4AA.
Heritage Open Days: No
Ⓟ No
♿ No. Disabled WC: No. Guide Dogs: Yes
💷 No

17 Minster Yard

Lincoln, Lincolnshire LN2 1PX
13th and 14th century building with 15th century additions. Sacked in 1644 and restored 1671-94 and 1704-32 with internal alterations, c1813, by William Fowler. Further additions to the building were made in the late 19th century.
Grant Recipient/Owner:
Dean & Chapter of Lincoln Cathedral
Access contact: Mr William Roberts
Tel: 01522 527637
Opening Arrangements: By prior written arrangement with the Clerk of Works, Lincoln Cathedral, 28 Eastgate, Lincoln LN2 4AA.
Heritage Open Days: No
Ⓟ No
♿ No. Disabled WC: No. Guide Dogs: Yes
💷 No

18/18a Minster Yard

Lincoln, Lincolnshire LN2 1PX
13th and 14th century building with 17th century additions. Remodelled and extended in 1827 and refronted 1873 by J L Pearson.
Grant Recipient/Owner:
Dean & Chapter of Lincoln Cathedral
Access contact: Mr William Roberts
Tel: 01522 527637
Opening Arrangements: By prior written arrangement with the Clerk of Works, Lincoln Cathedral, 28 Eastgate, Lincoln LN2 4AA.
Heritage Open Days: No
Ⓟ No
♿ No. Disabled WC: No. Guide Dogs: Yes
💷 No

2/2a Exchequergate

Lincoln, Lincolnshire LN2 1PZ
Late 15th century house, rebuilt 1834-48.
Grant Recipient/Owner:
Dean & Chapter of Lincoln Cathedral
Access contact: Mr William Roberts
Tel: 01522 527637
Opening Arrangements: By prior written arrangement with the Clerk of Works, Lincoln Cathedral, 28 Eastgate, Lincoln LN2 4AA.
Heritage Open Days: No
Ⓟ No
♿ No. Disabled WC: No. Guide Dogs: Yes
💷 No

22 Minster Yard, Lincoln

Lincoln LN2 1PX
Early 18th century house, altered early 19th and divided mid-19th century.
Grant Recipient/Owner:
Dean & Chapter of Lincoln Cathedral
Access contact: Mr William Roberts
Tel: 01522 527637
Opening Arrangements: By prior written arrangement with the Clerk of Works, Lincoln Cathedral, 28 Eastgate, Lincoln LN2 4AA.
Heritage Open Days: No
Ⓟ No
♿ No. Disabled WC: No. Guide Dogs: Yes
💷 No

3/3a Pottergate

Lincoln, Lincolnshire LN2 1PH
17th century house, now 2 houses, incorporating medieval walling. Remodelled in early 18th century with late 18th and 19th century alterations.
Grant Recipient/Owner:
Dean & Chapter of Lincoln Cathedral
Access contact: Mr William Roberts
Tel: 01522 527637
Opening Arrangements: By prior written arrangement with the Clerk of Works, Lincoln Cathedral, 28 Eastgate, Lincoln LN2 4AA.
Heritage Open Days: No
Ⓟ No
♿ No. Disabled WC: No. Guide Dogs: No
💷 No

3/3a Vicars Court

Lincoln, Lincolnshire LN2 1PT
Former priests' vicars lodgings, now 2 houses. Begun late 13th century by Bishop Sutton and completed c1309. Altered 15th century, reroofed and altered late 17th and further altered late 17th, 18th and 19th centuries.
Grant Recipient/Owner:
Dean & Chapter of Lincoln Cathedral
Access contact: Mr William Roberts
Tel: 01522 527637
Opening Arrangements: By prior written arrangement with the Clerk of Works, Lincoln Cathedral, 28 Eastgate, Lincoln LN2 4AA.
Heritage Open Days: No
Ⓟ No
♿ No. Disabled WC: No. Guide Dogs: Yes
💷 No

4 Pottergate

Lincoln, Lincolnshire LN2 1PH
14th and 15th century house, with mid-17th century additions. Altered c1760 and in the 19th century.
Grant Recipient/Owner:
Dean & Chapter of Lincoln Cathedral
Access contact: Mr William Roberts
Tel: 01522 527637
Opening Arrangements: By prior written arrangement with the Clerk of Works, Lincoln Cathedral, 28 Eastgate, Lincoln LN2 4AA.
Heritage Open Days: No
Ⓟ No
♿ No. Disabled WC: No. Guide Dogs: Yes
💷 No

Belton House & Bellmount Tower

Grantham, Lincolnshire NG32 2LS
Belton was built in 1685-88 and later altered by James Wyatt. The interiors contain fine plasterwork and wood-carving, plus important collections of paintings, furniture, tapestries and silverware. Also formal gardens, orangery and landscape park.
Website Address: www.nationaltrust.org.uk
Grant Recipient/Owner: The National Trust
Access contact: Property Manager
Tel: 01476 566116   **Fax:** 01476 579071
Email Address: ebedxb@smtp.ntrust.org.uk
Opening Arrangements: House: 31 March to 4 November: daily except Mondays and Tuesdays (but open Bank Holiday Mondays and closed Good Friday) 1 - 5.30pm. Garden & Park: as house 11am - 5.30pm (closes 4.30pm on 21 July). Park only: all year on foot only from Lion Lodge gates (no access from this entrance to house, garden or adventure playground). Bellmount Woods: daily access from separate car park. Wheelchair access to ground floor of house, garden, park, restaurant, shop and refreshment kiosk.
Heritage Open Days: No
Ⓟ Yes. Spaces: 50
♿ Partial. Disabled WC: Yes. Guide Dogs: Yes
💷 Yes
Adult: £5.40
Child: £2.70
Other: £13.50 (family)

Brocklesby Mausoleum

Brocklesby Park, N E Lincolnshire DN41 8PN
Family Mausoleum designed by James Wyatt and built between 1787 and 1794 by Charles Anderson Pelham, who subsequently became Lord Yarborough, as a memorial to his wife Sophia who died at the age of 33. The classical design is based on the Temples of Vesta at Rome and Tivoli.
Grant Recipient/Owner: The Earl of Yarborough
Access contact: Mr H A Rayment
Tel: 01469 560214
Opening Arrangements: Exterior viewable from permissive paths through Mausoleum Woods 1 April - 31 August at all reasonable times, interior (excluding private crypt) by prior arrangement with the Estate Office. Parking in village or walks car park about a quarter of a mile from Mausoleum.
Heritage Open Days: No
Ⓟ See above
♿ No. Disabled WC: No. Guide Dogs: Yes
💷 Yes
Adult: £2.00 (to view interior)

Burghley House

Stamford, Lincolnshire PE9 3JY
Large country house built by William Cecil, Lord High Treasurer of England, between 1565 and 1587, and still lived in by descendants of his family. Eighteen State Rooms, many decorated by Antonio Verrio in the 17th century, housing a collection of artworks including 17th Italian paintings, Japanese ceramics, European porcelain and wood carvings by Grinling Gibbons and his followers. There are also four State Beds, English and continental furniture, and tapestries and textiles. 'Capability' Brown parkland.
Grant Recipient/Owner:
Burghley House Preservation Trust
Access contact: Mr David Parratt
Tel: 01780 752451   **Fax:** 01780 480125
Email Address: burghley@burghley.co.uk
Opening Arrangements: 1 April - 7 October: daily (except 8 September) 11am - 4.30pm. By guided tour only apart from Saturday and Sunday afternoons when there are guides in each room. Partially accessible for wheelchair users, please telephone for information. Disabled parking available close to visitors' entrance.
Heritage Open Days: No
Ⓟ Yes. Spaces: 500
♿ Partial. Disabled WC: Yes. Guide Dogs: Yes
💷 Yes
Adult: £6.80
Child: £3.30
Other: £6.30 (senior)

Doddington Hall

Lincoln LN6 4RU
Late Elizabethan mansion with original garden walls, gatehouse and outbuildings. Contents, including furniture, textiles, porcelain and pictures, reflect 400 years of domestic use.
Website Address:
www.doddingtonhall.free-online.co.uk
Grant Recipient/Owner: Mr Antony Jarvis
Access contact: Mr Antony Jarvis
Tel: 01522 694308   **Fax:** 01522 685259
Email Address: estateoffice@doddingtonhall.free-online.co.uk
Opening Arrangements: House & Gardens: May - September, Wednesdays, Sundays and Bank Holiday Mondays 2 - 6pm; Gardens only: February - April, Sundays 2 - 6pm. Opening arrangements provisional at time of going to print, please check with Mr Antony Jarvis or Miss Fiona Cairns-Watson at the Hall for current details. Wheelchair access to Gardens and ground floor of Hall only.
Heritage Open Days: No
Ⓟ Yes. Spaces: 250
♿ Partial. Disabled WC: Yes. Guide Dogs: Yes
💷 Yes
Adult: £4.50 (£2.25 garden only)
Child: £2.25 (£1.50 garden only)
Other: £12.50 (family ticket)

Harding House

48-54 Steep Hill, Lincoln, Lincolnshire
Grade II listed house of the 16th century, remodelled in the 18th and restored in the 20th. Built of coursed rubble and brick with a pantile roof, now houses a craft studio.
Grant Recipient/Owner:
The Chief Executive, Lincoln City Council
Access contact: Mr Mark Wheater
Tel: 01522 873464
Opening Arrangements: Open during normal shop opening hours.
Heritage Open Days: No
Ⓟ No
♿ No. Disabled WC: No. Guide Dogs: Yes
💷 No

Heggy's Cottage

Hall Road, Haconby, nr. Bourne, Lincolnshire PE10 0UY
Built c1500 of mud and stud construction, a good example of early conversion to two storeys. Restored to its original state in 1995.
Grant Recipient/Owner: Mrs J F Atkinson
Access contact: Mrs J F Atkinson
Tel: 01778 570790
Opening Arrangements: By prior written arrangement with Mrs J F Atkinson, Haconby Hall, nr. Bourne, Lincolnshire PE10 0UY.
Heritage Open Days: No
P Yes. Spaces: 1
No. Disabled WC: No. Guide Dogs: No
£ No

Kyme Tower

Manor Farm, South Kyme, Lincoln, Lincolnshire LN4 4JN
23.5m high tower with four storeys and a stair turret. Remainder of a fortified medieval manor house, built on the site of an Augustinian priory, itself built on an Anglo-Saxon religious establishment. There are also visible earthworks of the former moat and fishponds on the site.
Grant Recipient/Owner: Kathy Hayward
Access contact: Mr W B Lamyman
Tel: 01526 860603
Opening Arrangements:
By prior telephone arrangement.
Heritage Open Days: No
P Yes. Spaces: 3
No. Disabled WC: No. Guide Dogs: No
£ No

Maud Foster Windmill

Boston, Lincolnshire PE21 9EG
Built 1819 and still working daily as a commercial flour mill. Access to all 7 floors, a tea-room and shop.
Grant Recipient/Owner: Mr T E Waterfield
Access contact: Mr James Waterfield
Tel: 01205 352188
Opening Arrangements: All year: Wednesdays and Saturdays 11am - 5pm, Sundays 1 - 5pm; July and August: Thursdays and Fridays 11am - 5pm; Bank Holidays 10am - 5pm. Closed Christmas and New Year.
Heritage Open Days: No
P Yes. Spaces: 16
No. Disabled WC: No. Guide Dogs: No
£ Yes
Adult: £2.50
Child: £1.50
Other: £2.00 (senior citizens)

Tattershall Castle

Tattershall, Lincoln, Lincolnshire LN4 4LR
A vast fortified and moated red-brick tower, built c1440 for Ralph Cromwell, treasurer of England. The building was rescued from becoming derelict by Lord Curzon 1911-14 and contains four great chambers with enormous Gothic fireplaces, tapestries and brick vaulting. Gatehouse with museum room.
Website Address: www.nationaltrust.org.uk
Grant Recipient/Owner: The National Trust
Access contact: The Custodian
Tel: 01526 342543   **Fax:** 01526 342543
Email Address: etcxxx@smtp.ntrust.org.uk
Opening Arrangements: 1 April to 4 November: daily except Thursdays and Fridays 10.30am - 5.30pm. 10 November to 16 December: Saturdays and Sundays 12 - 4pm. Ground floor of castle may occasionally be closed for functions or events. Wheelchair access to ground floor only via ramp.
Heritage Open Days: No
P No
Partial. Disabled WC: Yes. Guide Dogs: Yes
£ Yes
Adult: £3.00
Child: £1.50
Other: £7.50 (family). Accompanied children free July & August.

Uffington Manor Gatepiers

Main Street, Uffington, nr. Stamford, Lincolnshire
Pair of Grade II* listed gate piers, possibly by John Lumley c1700, surmounted by urns with wrought iron entrance gates with a coat of arms over of later 19th century date.
Grant Recipient/Owner: Mr David Pike
Access contact: Mr David Pike
Tel: 01780 751944   **Fax:** 01780 764256
Opening Arrangements: Can be viewed from public roadway, otherwise by prior written arrangement.
Heritage Open Days: No
P Yes. Spaces: 2
Yes. Disabled WC: No. Guide Dogs: Yes
£ No

Waltham Windmill

Brigsley Road, Waltham, Grimsby, Lincolnshire DN37 0JZ
Grade II listed six-sailed tower mill, one of only three in the country. Built in 1880 by John Sanderson of Louth, 90ft high with 6 publicly accessible floors. Museum of rural life at site.
Grant Recipient/Owner: Waltham Windmill Trust
Access contact: Mrs M A Stennett
Tel: 01472 822236
Opening Arrangements: Easter - September: Saturdays and Sundays 10am - 4pm and Bank Holiday Mondays. Group visits can be arranged by contacting Mrs Diana Le-Core (01472 752122 or fax 01472 316788). Wheelchair and guide dog access to ground floor only.
Heritage Open Days: Yes
P Yes. Spaces: 30
Partial. Disabled WC: No. Guide Dogs: Yes
£ Yes
Adult: £1.00
Child: 50p

LONDON

Bruce Castle

Lordship Lane, London N17 8NU
Originally built in the 16th century but altered extensively in the 17th, 18th and 19th centuries. Now a museum containing displays about the building and local district, and an archive.
Website Address: www.brucecastlemuseum.org.uk
Grant Recipient/Owner: London Borough of Haringey
Access contact: Ms Sian Harrington
Tel: 020 8808 8772   **Fax:** 020 8808 4118
Email Address: museum.services@haringey.gov.uk
Opening Arrangements: Wednesday - Sunday 1 - 5pm plus Easter Monday, May Day, late May Bank Hoilday and August Bank Holiday. Closed Good Friday, Christmas Day, Boxing Day and New Year's Day. Groups at other times by prior arrangement. Archive open by prior arrangement.
Heritage Open Days: Yes
P Yes. Spaces: 15
Yes. Disabled WC: Yes. Guide Dogs: Yes
£ No

College of Arms

Queen Victoria Street, London EC4V 4BT
Built in 1670s/1680s to the design of Francis Sandford and Morris Emmett to house the Heralds' offices, on the site of their earlier building, Derby Place, which was destroyed in the Great Fire of 1666. The principal room is Earl Marshal's Court which is two floors high with gallery, panelling and throne. New record room added 1842 and portico and terrace in 1867.
Website Address: www.college-of-arms.gov.uk
Grant Recipient/Owner: College of Arms
Access contact: Officer in Waiting
Tel: 020 7248 2762   **Fax:** 020 7248 6448
Email Address: enquiries@college-of-arms.gov.uk
Opening Arrangements: Earl Marshal's Court only: all year (except Public Holidays and State and Special Occasions), Monday - Friday 10am - 4pm. Group visits (up to 10) by prior arrangement with the Officer in Waiting. Group tours of Record Room (up to 20) also by prior arrangement.
Heritage Open Days: Yes
P No
No. Disabled WC: No. Guide Dogs: Yes
£ No

Dissenters' Chapel

Kensal Green Cemetery, London
Grade II* building within Grade II* cemetery. Cemetery dates from 1832 and is London's oldest. The Chapel was designed in Greek Revival style by John Griffith in 1834. It is now used by the Friends of Kensal Green Cemetery as a headquarters, exhibition space and art gallery.
Website Address: www.hct.org.uk
Grant Recipient/Owner: Historic Chapels Trust
Access contact: Mr Henry Vivian-Neal
Tel: 020 8960 1030
Opening Arrangements: Cemetery: daily; Dissenters' Chapel: weekends and at other times by prior arrangement. Guided tours of chapels and cemetery at weekends for modest charge. Parking in adjacent streets, disabled parking in cemetery.
Heritage Open Days: Yes
P See above
Yes. Disabled WC: Yes. Guide Dogs: Yes
£ See above

Garrick's Temple

Hampton Court Road, Richmond-upon-Thames, London TW12 2EJ
The actor-manager David Garrick built the Temple in 1756 to celebrate the genius of William Shakespeare. The Temple was restored between 1997-1999 and now houses an exhibition of Garrick's acting career and life at Hampton, while the grounds have been landscaped to echo their original 18th century layout.
Website Address: www.hampton.online.co.uk
Grant Recipient/Owner:
London Borough of Richmond-upon-Thames
Access contact: The Curator
Tel: 020 8892 0221   **Fax:** 020 8744 0501
Email Address: leisure@richmond.gov.uk
Opening Arrangements: Temple: Sundays: first Sunday in April to last Sunday in September 2 - 5pm. Bank Holiday Mondays 2 - 5pm. London Open House weekend Saturday and Sunday 10am - 5pm. Also pre-arranged visits for small groups throughout the year (tel: 020 8892 0221). Lawn: open all year 7.30am - dusk. Wheelchair access only to lawn gardens.
Heritage Open Days: No
P No
See above. Disabled WC: No. Guide Dogs: Yes
£ No

Great Stanmore Old Church

Church Road, Stanmore, London HA7 4AQ
Early all red brick church attributed to Nicholas Stone and consecrated in 1632 by William Laud, later Archbishop of Canterbury. Used until partial demolition in 1851. Contains the tombs of the 4th Earl of Aberdeen, Victorian Prime Minister, and the Marquess of Abercorn.
Grant Recipient/Owner: Dr Frederick Hicks
Access contact: Dr Frederick Hicks
Tel: 020 8954 1677
Opening Arrangements: April - September: Saturdays 2.30 - 4.30pm. At other times by prior arrangement with Dr Frederick Hicks, 30 Elm Park, Stanmore, London HA7 4BJ (tel.020 8954 1677). Wheelchair access may be difficult as there is some 50 metres of grass from car park to church.
Heritage Open Days: Yes
P Yes. Spaces: 10
See above. Disabled WC: No. Guide Dogs: Yes
£ No

Highgate Cemetery

Swain's Lane, London N6 6PJ
Western, older cemetery, opened in 1839, has good examples of Victorian funerary architecture. Eastern cemetery opened in 1854. Some 168,000 persons are buried in the cemetery including many notables.
Grant Recipient/Owner:
Friends of Highgate Cemetery Ltd
Access contact: Mrs J A Pateman
Tel: 020 8340 1834
Opening Arrangements: Western cemetery: March - November daily tours at 12, 2 & 4pm, weekends tours hourly 11am - 3pm (winter) and 11am - 4pm (summer); Eastern cemetery: daily (unescorted) weekdays 10am - 3.45pm (winter) and 10am - 4.45pm (summer), weekends always. Both cemeteries closed 25 & 26 December, plus during funerals. Wheelchair access to Eastern cemetery only. Some street parking.
Heritage Open Days: No
P See above
Partial. Disabled WC: No. Guide Dogs: Yes
£ Yes
Adult: £3.00 Tour of West (£1.00 small cameras only);
Child: £2.00 East (£1.00 small cameras only).
Other: £1.00 (9-15) West; East free, but donations welcome.

Highpoint

North Hill, Highgate, London N6
Two blocks of flats built in 1935 and 1938 by Lubetkin and Tecton. Constructed of reinforced concrete with decorative features.
Grant Recipient/Owner: Mr Gamble
Access contact: Mr Stephen Ellman
Tel: 020 7554 5800
Opening Arrangements: By prior arrangement with Mr Stephen Ellman of Gross Fine, 14/16 Stephenson Way, London NW1 2HD (tel.020 7554 5800).
Heritage Open Days: No
P No
No. Disabled WC: No. Guide Dogs: Yes
£ No

The House Mill

Three Mill Lane, Bromley-by-Bow, London E3 3DU
Industrial water mill, originally built 1776 as part of a distillery. Contains 4 floors with remains of unrestored machinery, 4 water wheels and gearing. Originally had 2 pairs of millstones and has unique survival of Fairbairn-style "silent millstone machinery".
Grant Recipient/Owner: River Lea Tidal Mill Trust
Access contact: Mr Brian Strong
Tel: 020 8440 3654
Email Address: brian.strong@tesco.net

Opening Arrangements: Sunday of National Mills Weekend, Heritage Open Days and the first Sunday of each month April - December 11am - 4pm. Groups by prior arrangement with Mr Brian Strong, 14 Eversleigh Road, New Barnet, Hertfordshire EN5 1NE (tel.020 8440 3654). For further information ring 020 8980 4626. Car park nearby.
Heritage Open Days: Yes
P See above
♿ Yes. Disabled WC: Yes. Guide Dogs: Yes
£ Yes
Adult: £3.00
Child: Free
Other: £1.00

Prendergast School Murals

Hilly Fields, Adelaide Avenue, London SE4 1LE
Painted in the school hall in the 1930s by students of the Royal College of Art, they depict classical tales and incorporate local features.
Grant Recipient/Owner:
Governors of Prendergast School
Access contact: Miss E Pienaar
Tel: 020 8690 3710   **Fax:** 020 8690 3155
Opening Arrangements: By prior written arrangement during school hours in term-time.
Heritage Open Days: Yes
P No
♿ Yes. Disabled WC: No. Guide Dogs: Yes
£ No

The Queen's Chapel of the Savoy

Savoy Hill, Strand, London WC2R 0DA
Originally part of a hospital founded in 1512 by Henry VII. Rebuilt by Robert Smirke after a fire in 1864, from which time dates the ceiling covered with heraldic emblems. Recently restored.
Grant Recipient/Owner: Duchy of Lancaster
Access contact: John Robson
Tel: 020 7836 7221   **Fax:** 020 7379 8088
Opening Arrangements:
All year except August and September: Tuesday - Friday 10.30am - 3.30pm; Sundays for Morning Service only. Closed the week after Christmas Day and the week after Easter Day. Parking on meters in adjoining streets.
Heritage Open Days: No
P See above
♿ No. Disabled WC: No. Guide Dogs: Yes
£ No

Royal Geographical Society

(with the Institute of British Geographers), Lowther Lodge, 1 Kensington Gore, London SW7 2AR
Norman Shaw building in the Queen Anne style, built in the 1870s as a private house with a two acre garden for the Lowthers. Owned by the Royal Geographic Society since 1912 and houses their large collection of geographical material, which comprises archives, books, maps and pictures, dating from the 15th century to the present day. The Lecture Theatre extension was built in 1930 in order to mark the Society's centenary.
Grant Recipient/Owner: Royal Geographical Society
Access contact: Ms Denise Prior
Tel: 020 7591 3090   **Fax:** 020 7591 3091
Email Address: d.prior@rgs.org
Opening Arrangements: Weekdays (except Bank Holidays) 9.30am - 5.30pm. Closed between Christmas and New Year. Use of collections, library, map room and picture library by prior arrangement only: Mondays - Fridays 11am - 5pm; archives on Thursdays and Fridays 11am - 5pm. Charges levied for use of collections. Parking by prior arrangement only. Wheelchair access to all areas except Council Room and Lecture Theatre balcony.
Heritage Open Days: No
P Yes. Spaces: 1
♿ Partial. Disabled WC: Yes Guide Dogs: Yes
£ No

The Royal Institution of Great Britain

21 Albemarle Street, London W1X 4BS
Houses the Michael Faraday Museum and a 200 year old lecture theatre. Regular public lectures on scientific themes.
Grant Recipient/Owner:
Royal Institution of Great Britain
Access contact: Mr Alan Winter
Tel: 020 7409 2992   **Fax:** 020 7670 2920
Address: alanw@ri.ac.uk
Opening Arrangements: Monday - Friday 9am - 5pm. Public lectures/events on various days of the week usually starting at 6.30pm or 7.30pm. Lecture lists published on RI website (www.ri.ac.uk). Entry charge for Faraday Museum only. Parking on meters in adjoining street.
Heritage Open Days: Yes
P See above
♿ Yes. Disabled WC: Yes. Guide Dogs: Yes
£ Yes

Adult: £1.00 (museum), £5.00 (lecture).
Child: £1.00 (museum), £3.00 (lecture).
Other: Schools free.

St Pancras Chambers

Euston Road, London NW1 2QR
Grade I listed Gothic-style building fronting St Pancras Station. Built as the Midland Grand Hotel between 1868 and 1876 to designs by Sir George Gilbert Scott.
Grant Recipient/Owner: British Railways Board/London & Continental Stations & Property Ltd
Access contact: Ms Lynda Nolan
Tel: 020 7304 3900   **Fax:** 020 7304 3901
Email Address: lnolan@lcsp.co.uk
Opening Arrangements: The front entrance and former ground floor coffee lounge are generally open each weekday 11.30am - 3.30pm without charge. For information on guided tours of the remainder of the building contact 020 7304 3900. Please note that tours involve climbing several flights of stairs and that there are no working lifts or other facilities for disabled visitors.
Heritage Open Days: Yes
P No
♿ No. Disabled WC: No. Guide Dogs: No
£ Yes
Adult: £7.50 for tour.

Sutton House

2-4 Homerton High Street, Hackney, London E9 6JQ
A unique survival in London's East End, Sutton House was built in 1535 by Ralph Sadleir, Principal Secretary of State for Henry VIII. Rare example of a Tudor red brick house with 18th century alterations and later additions. Features include original linenfold panelling and 17th century wall paintings.
Website Address: www.nationaltrust.org.uk
Grant Recipient/Owner: The National Trust
Access contact: The Property Manager
Tel: 020 8986 2264
Opening Arrangements: 7 February to 28 November: Wednesdays and Sundays only and Bank Holiday Mondays 11.30am - 5.30pm. Gallery, shop and café: 10 January to 21 December Wednesday to Sunday 11am - 5pm. Wheelchair access to ground floor. On street parking.
Heritage Open Days: No
P See above
♿ Partial. Disabled WC: Yes. Guide Dogs: Yes
£ Yes
Adult: £2.10
Child: £0.60
Other: £4.70 (family)

Walpole's House

St Mary's College, Strawberry Hill, Waldegrave Road, Twickenham, London TW1 4SX
Bought by Horace Walpole in 1749 and over the next half century converted into his own vision of a 'gothic' fantasy. Reputedly the first substantial building of the Gothic Revival.
Grant Recipient/Owner: St Mary's, Strawberry Hill
Access contact: Conference Officer
Tel: 020 8240 4114/4044   **Fax:** 020 8255 6174
Email Address: evansn@smuc.ac.uk
Opening Arrangements: Easter - mid-October: Sundays 2 - 3.30pm. Guided group tours (minimum 10 people) by prior arrangement on any day except Saturday. Wheelchair access to ground floor and grounds.
Heritage Open Days: Yes
P Yes. Spaces: 60
♿ Partial. Disabled WC: Yes. Guide Dogs: Yes
£ Yes
Adult: £5.00
Other: £4.25

MERSEYSIDE

Bluecoat Chambers

School Lane, Liverpool, Merseyside L1 3BX
Queen Anne building dated 1716 housing contemporary art gallery, café bar, crafts centre and shops. Reputedly the oldest arts centre in the country.
Grant Recipient/Owner: Bluecoat Arts Centre Ltd
Access contact: Mr A Hurley
Tel: 0151 709 5297   **Fax:** 0151 707 0048
Email Address: bluecoat@dircon.co.uk
Opening Arrangements: All year (except Sundays and Bank Holidays) Monday - Saturday 9am - 5.30pm. Wheelchair access to ground floor only.
Heritage Open Days: No
P No
♿ Partial. Disabled WC: Yes. Guide Dogs: Yes
£ No

Broughton Hall Conservatory

Convent of Mercy, Yew Tree Lane, West Derby, Liverpool, Merseyside L12 9HH
Victorian conservatory of rectangular shape with an entrance porch at one end and an access bay to main building, at the other. The cast iron structure is mounted on a stone plinth. The elevations are divided into a series of panels with decorated cast iron circular columns. From the capitols spring semi-circular arches. These form the bases of the frieze moulding which runs round the periphery of the building. The flooring is of quarry tiles.
Grant Recipient/Owner:
Institute of Our Lady of Mercy
Access contact: Sister Superior
Tel: 0151 228 9232
Opening Arrangements: By prior written arrangement only, Monday - Saturday 10am - 4pm. No access on Sundays, Religious Holidays and Bank Holidays. Wheelchair and guide dog access by prior arrangement.
Heritage Open Days: No
P Yes. Spaces: 4
♿ See above. Disabled WC: Yes. Guide Dogs: Yes
£ No

Liverpool Collegiate Apartments

Shaw Street, Liverpool, Merseyside L6
Grade II* former school built 1843 of red sandstone in Tudor Gothic style, gutted by fire and now converted into residential block.
Website Address: www.urbansplash.co.uk
Grant Recipient/Owner: Mr Bill Maynard
Access contact: Mr Bill Maynard
Tel: 0151 707 1493   **Fax:** 0151 708 0479
Email Address: design@urbansplash.co.uk
Opening Arrangements: Exterior only.
Heritage Open Days: No
P No
♿ No
£ No

Speke Hall

The Walk, Liverpool, Merseyside L24 1XD
One of the most important timber framed manor houses in the country, dating from 1490. The interior spans many periods: the Great Hall and priest holes evoke Tudor times, the Oak Parlour and smaller rooms, some with William Morris wallpapers, show the Victorian desire for privacy and comfort. There is some Jacobean plasterwork and intricately caved furniture. Restored garden and woodland walks.
Website Address: www.nationaltrust.org.uk
Grant Recipient/Owner: The National Trust
Access contact: Simon Osborne
Tel: 0151 427 7231   **Fax:** 0151 427 9860
Opening Arrangements: House: 28 March to end October, Wednesdays to Sundays (open Bank Holidays). November and December, Saturdays and Sundays only. Times: March to mid October 1 - 5.30pm, mid October to December 1 - 4.30pm. Woodland and garden: open daily throughout the year except Mondays (open Bank Holidays), closed 24-26 and 31 December, 1 January. Times: March to mid October 11am - 5.30pm., mid October - end March 2002 11am - 4pm. Wheelchair access to ground floor of house. Car park is 500 yards from the property. Courtsey shuttle service available.
Heritage Open Days: No
P Yes. Spaces: 400
♿ Partial. Disabled WC: Yes. Guide Dogs: Yes
£ Yes
Adult: £4.50
Child: £2.50

Turner Memorial Home of Rest

Dingle Lane, Liverpool, Merseyside L8 9RN
Grade II listed red sandstone ashlar building with tile roof, c1881-3, by Alfred Waterhouse. Used as a nursing home for elderly men. Contains a chapel.
Grant Recipient/Owner:
Trustees of the Turner Memorial Home of Rest
Access contact: Mrs Alison Charlesworth
Tel: 0151 727 4177   **Fax:** 0151 727 7788
Opening Arrangements: By prior arrangement.
Heritage Open Days: No
P Yes. Spaces: 10
♿ Yes. Disabled WC: Yes. Guide Dogs: Yes
£ No

NORFOLK

Billingford Cornmill

Scole, Norfolk
Built in 1860. One pair of stones have been repaired to full working order and are run occasionally.
Grant Recipient/Owner: Norfolk Windmills Trust
Access contact: Miss A L Jaques
Tel: 01603 222708   **Fax:** 01603 224413
Email Address: amanda.jaques.pt@norfolk.gov.uk

Opening Arrangements: For current opening arrangements please contact. Miss A L Jaques, Conservation Officer, Building Conservation Section, Department of Planning and Transportation, Norfolk County Council, County Hall, Martineau Lane, Norwich, Norfolk NR1 2SG (tel.01603 222708). Admission charges are also provisional at time of going to press, please check with Miss Jaques for up-to-date information.
Heritage Open Days: No
P Yes. Spaces: 2
No. Disabled WC: No. Guide Dogs: No
£ Yes
Adult: 70p (provisional)
Child: 30p (provisional)

Churchman House

71 Bethel Street, Norwich, Norfolk NR2 1NR
Georgian town house with Victorian additions, contains plastered and panelled rooms, and carved fireplaces.
Grant Recipient/Owner: Norwich City Council
Access contact: Superintendent Registrar
Tel: 01603 767600   **Fax:** 01603 632677
Opening Arrangements: By prior arrangement on Tuesday or Thursday afternoons. Wheelchair access to ground floor only. Parking for disabled only.
Heritage Open Days: No
P See above
Partial. Disabled WC: Yes. Guide Dogs: Yes
£ No

Denver Windmill

Sluice Road, Denver, Downham Market, Norfolk PE38 0EG
Working windmill on edge of the fens, built in 1835 and recently restored.
Website Address: www.denvermill.co.uk
Grant Recipient/Owner: The Norfolk Windmills Trust
Access contact: Mr Richard Townsley
Tel: 01366 384009
Opening Arrangements: 1 April - end of October: Monday - Saturday 10am - 5pm, Sunday 12 - 5pm; 1 November - end of March: Monday - Saturday 10am - 4pm, Sunday 12 - 4pm. Wheelchair access to ground floor of windmill only, there is a video shown of the mill in the new visitor facilities which are accessible to wheelchair users.
Heritage Open Days: No
P Yes. Spaces: 50
Partial. Disabled WC: Yes. Guide Dogs: Yes
£ Yes
Adult: £2.50
Child: £1.20
Other: £2.25

Dragon Hall

115-123 King Street, Norwich, Norfolk NR1 1QE
Medieval timber-framed merchant's hall. The 15th century great hall has a crown post roof with an intricately carved and painted dragon.
Website Address:
http://freespace.virgin.net/dragon.hall/index.htm
Grant Recipient/Owner:
Norfolk & Norwich Heritage Trust
Access contact: Mr Neil Sigsworth
Tel: 01603 663922   **Fax:** 01603 663922
Email Address: dragon.hall@virgin.net
Opening Arrangements: 1 November - 31 March: Mondays - Fridays 10am - 4pm; 1 April - 31 October: Mondays - Saturdays 10am - 4pm; closed Bank Holidays and 22 December - New Year's Day. Wheelchair access to ground floor only.
Heritage Open Days: Yes
P Yes. Spaces: 6
Partial. Disabled WC: No. Guide Dogs: Yes
£ Yes
Adult: £1.50
Child: 50p
Other: £1.00

Felbrigg Hall

Felbrigg, Norwich, Norfolk NR11 8PR
17th century house containing its original 18th century furniture and paintings. The walled garden has been restored and features a working dovecote and fine and aged trees.
Website Address: www.nationaltrust.org.uk
Grant Recipient/Owner: The National Trust
Access contact: Property Manager
Tel: 01263 837444   **Fax:** 01263 837032
Email Address: atgusr@smtp.ntrust.org.uk
Opening Arrangements: House: 31 March to 4 November: daily except Thursdays and Fridays. Times: 1 - 5pm, Bank Holiday Sundays and Bank Holiday Mondays 11am - 5pm. House will close at 4pm on and after 29 October. Garden: 31 March to 4 November: daily except Thursdays and Fridays. Times: 11am to 5.30pm. Estate walks: daily, dawn to dusk. Wheelchair access to ground floor, photograph album on first floor, garden, shop and bookshop (ramp), tea room and restaurant accessible.

Visitors with disabilities may be set down at Reception by arrangement.
Heritage Open Days: No
P Yes. Spaces: 200
Partial. Disabled WC: Yes. Guide Dogs: Yes
£ Yes
Adult: £5.80
Child: £2.90
Other: £14.50 (family). £2.20 (gardens only).

Gowthorpe Manor

Swardeston, Norwich, Norfolk NR14 8DS
Small family house, built in brick in 16th century by Augustine Steward, thrice Mayor of Norwich and MP. Some original features remain but has been altered over the years, especially in early 19th century.
Grant Recipient/Owner: Mrs D M Watkinson
Access contact: Mrs D M Watkinson
Tel: 01508 570216
Opening Arrangements: By prior arrangement on Mondays and occasionally at other times, such as groups in the evening.
Heritage Open Days: No
P Yes. Spaces: 15
No. Disabled WC: No. Guide Dogs: Yes
£ No

Hales Hall Barn

Loddon, Norfolk NR14 6QW
Late 15th century brick and thatch barn 180ft long, built by James Hobart, Henry VII's Attorney General. Queen post roof, and crown post roof to living accommodation, and richly patterned brickwork. The Barn and similar sized gatehouse, ranged around defended courtyards, are all that remain of the house that once stood on this site.
Grant Recipient/Owner: Mr Terence Read
Access contact: Mr Terence Read
Tel: 01508 548395   **Fax:** 01508 548040
Opening Arrangements: All year: Tuesday - Saturday 10am - 5pm (or dusk if earlier); plus Easter - October: Sunday afternoons and Bank Holiday Mondays 11am - 4pm. Closed 25 December - 5 January and Good Friday. Garden with yew and box topiary included in admission charge. Parties and guided tours by prior arrangement with Mr Terence Read, Hales Hall, Loddon, Norfolk NR14 6QW (tel.01508 548395).
Heritage Open Days: No
P Yes. Spaces: 40
Yes. Disabled WC: No. Guide Dogs: Yes
£ Yes
Adult: £1.50
Child: Free
Other: £1.50, £2.50 (guided tours).

King's Lynn Custom House

Purfleet Quay, King's Lynn, Norfolk PE30 1HP
Built 1683 as a merchants exchange, become official Custom House in 1703. Building purchased by the Crown in 1717 for £800 and was used by HM Customs until 1989. The Borough Council of King's Lynn and West Norfolk obtained a lease of the building in 1995 and restored it.
Grant Recipient/Owner:
King's Lynn & West Norfolk Council
Access contact: Mr Tim Hall
Tel: 01553 774297   **Fax:** 01553 772361
Email Address: gaolhouse@west-norfolk.gov.uk
Opening Arrangements: Easter - end of October: Monday - Saturday 9.15am - 5pm, Sunday 10am - 4pm; November - March: daily 10.30am - 4pm. Wheelchair access to ground floor only. Parking in public car parks.
Heritage Open Days: Yes
P See above
Partial. Disabled WC: No. Guide Dogs: Yes
£ No

Old Buckenham Cornmill

Green Lane, Old Buckenham, Norfolk
Mill with the largest diameter tower in England, which had five sets of stones when it was working. Once owned by the Colmans of Norwich and Prince Duleep Singh. Built by John Burlingham in 1818.
Grant Recipient/Owner: Norfolk Windmills Trust
Access contact: Miss A L Jaques
Tel: 01603 222708   **Fax:** 01603 224413
Email Address: amanda.jaques.pt@norfolk.gov.uk
Opening Arrangements: May - September: second Sunday of each month 2 - 5pm. Groups at other times by prior arrangement with Miss A L Jaques, Conservation Officer, Building Conservation Section, Department of Planning and Transportation, Norfolk County Council, County Hall, Martineau Lane, Norwich, Norfolk NR1 2SG (tel.01603 222708).
Heritage Open Days: No
P Yes. Spaces: 6
No. Disabled WC: No. Guide Dogs: No
£ Yes
Child: 70p
Adult: 30p

Old Hall

Norwich Rd, South Burlingham, Norfolk NR13 4EY
Small Elizabethan manor house with a painted stucco fireplace, painted stucco mermaids and scrollwork on the front porch, and a long gallery of hunting scenes in grisaille, c1600.
Grant Recipient/Owner: Mr P Scupham
Access contact: Mr P Scupham
Tel: 01493 750804   **Fax:** 01493 750804
Email Address: goodman@dircon.co.uk
Opening Arrangements: By prior telephone arrangement with Mr P Scupham or Ms M E Steward. No access for guide dogs to the Long Gallery.
Heritage Open Days: Yes
P Yes. Spaces: 8
No. Disabled WC: No. Guide Dogs: Yes, see above.
£ No

Old Meeting House/ Congregational Church

Colegate, Norwich, Norfolk NR3 1BW
Built 1693 in brick with classical dressings and black glazed pantile roof. Unusual sun dial with date of building on front elevation, which is a feature of Free Church buildings. Contains tiered pews to a gallery on three sides and an organ in working order dating from 1650. External paving mirrors the Dutch influence.
Grant Recipient/Owner: Norwich City Council
Access contact: Mr G F D Eve
Tel: 01603 212343   **Fax:** 01603 212345
Email Address: property@norwich.gov.uk
Opening Arrangements: April - September: Wednesdays 12.30 - 4pm. At other times by prior arrangement with Mr G F D Eve, Property Services, St Giles House, St Giles Street, Norwich NR2 1UZ (tel.01603 212343).
Heritage Open Days: Yes
P Yes. Spaces: 2
Partial. Disabled WC: Yes. Guide Dogs: Yes
£ No

Oxburgh Hall

Oxborough, King's Lynn, Norfolk PE33 9PS
Moated manor house with tudor gatehouse, was built in 1428 by the Bedingfeld family who still live there. The rooms show the development from medieval austerity to Victorian comfort, and include a display of embroidery done by Mary, Queen of Scots. Gardens include a French Parterre and woodland walks, as well as a Catholic chapel.
Website Address: www.nationaltrust.org.uk
Grant Recipient/Owner: The National Trust
Access contact: Property Manager
Tel: 01366 328258   **Fax:** 01366 328066
Email Address: aohusr@smtp.ntrust.org.uk
Opening Arrangements: House: 31 March to 4 November daily except Thursdays and Fridays. Times: 1-5pm, Bank Holidays 11am - 5pm. Last admission 4.30pm. Garden: 3 to 25 March Saturdays and Sundays; 31 March to 4 November: daily except Thursdays and Fridays; August: daily. Times: March 11am - 4pm, 31 March to 4 November 11am - 5.30pm. Wheelchair access to ground floor rooms (shallow ramp), difficult stairs to upper floors, garden largely accessible, tea room and shop accessible.
Heritage Open Days: No
P Yes. Spaces: 100
Partial. Disabled WC: Yes. Guide Dogs: Yes
£ Yes
Adult: £5.30
Other: Family discounts.

Ruined Church of St Mary the Virgin

Houghton-on-the-Hill, Norfolk
Ancient church at least 900 years old. Many original features remain including double splay windows, keyhole chancel, arch built with Roman brick, 12th century North door and early wall paintings.
Grant Recipient/Owner: Norfolk County Council
Access contact: Mr & Mrs R Davey
Tel: 01760 440470
Opening Arrangements: All year at any reasonable time.
Heritage Open Days: Yes
P Yes. Spaces: 40
Yes. Disabled WC: No. Guide Dogs: Yes
£ No

St Andrew's Hall

St Andrew's Street, Norwich, Norfolk
Remains of medieval friary, including the nave (St Andrew's Hall), choir (Blackfriars Hall), crypt, cloisters, private chapel (Beckets) and chapter house. Hammerbeam roof in nave, medieval bosses in choir and a 13th century 7 light East Window. A civic hall in use since 1540.
Grant Recipient/Owner: Norwich City Council
Access contact: Mr Tim Aldous
Tel: 01603 628477   **Fax:** 01603 762182

Email Address: taldous.ncc.sah@gtnet.gov.uk
Opening Arrangements: Monday - Saturday 9am - 5pm, subject to events. Wheelchair access to ground floor only. Parking in multi-storey car park in city centre. Green Badge on site, Orange Badge if space is available.
Heritage Open Days: No
P See above
♿ Partial. Disabled WC: Yes. Guide Dogs: Yes
£ No

St Benet's Level Mill
Ludham, Norfolk
Typical example of a Broadland drainage mill with tapering red brick tower, white boat shaped cap, sails and fantail. Built in 18th century and altered over the years, it became redundant in the 1940s. Ground and first floors accessible. Information boards on site.
Grant Recipient/Owner: Crown Estates Commissioners
Access contact: Mr D L Ritchie
Tel: 01692 678232   **Fax:** 01692 678055
Email Address: d.l.ritchie@farmline.com
Opening Arrangements: Open days: second Sunday in May and first Sunday in August. At other times by prior arrangement with Mr D L Ritchie at Hall Farm, Ludham, Great Yarmouth, Norfolk NR29 5NU (tel.01692 678232) or Miss Jenny Henderson, Carter Jonas, 6-8 Hills Road, Cambridge CB2 1NH (tel.01223 368771). Guide dog access to ground floor only.
Heritage Open Days: No
P No
♿ No. Disabled WC: No. Guide Dogs: Yes, see above.
£ No

St Mary's Abbey
West Dereham, Norfolk
The present six bay house is the remains of the service block of Sir Thomas Dereham's renaissance style mansion, which he built after 1689 incorporating the surviving parts of a Premonstratensian Abbey founded in 1188 by Hubert Walter. Had become a ruin and was only recently restored, with the building re-roofed, re-fenestrated and a first floor and stair tower added. The house is now a private residence.
Grant Recipient/Owner: Mr G Shropshire
Access contact: Miss Sue Watkins
Tel: 01353 727200
Opening Arrangements: By prior arrangement with Miss Sue Watkins, G's Marketing Ltd, Barway, Ely, Cambridgeshire CB7 5TZ (tel.01353 727200). Toilet facilities for the disabled are available on request, although they are not specifically designed.
Heritage Open Days: No
P Yes. Spaces: 20
♿ Yes. Disabled WC: Yes. Guide Dogs: Yes
£ No

St Peter
Dunton, Norfolk
Grade II* redundant medieval church constructed of flint with stone dressings. Has Victorian stained glass, rebuilt porch of 1896, 15th century tower, 14th century nave and remains of previous building. Occasionally used for services.
Grant Recipient/Owner: Norfolk Churches Trust
Access contact: Mr Malcolm Fisher
Tel: 01603 767576
Opening Arrangements: At any reasonable time.
Heritage Open Days: Yes
P Yes. Spaces: 3
♿ Yes. Disabled WC: No. Guide Dogs: Yes
£ No

Shotesham Park Dairy Farm Barn
Newton Flotman, Norfolk
Built c1500 with later additions, part weather-boarded and part-rendered 5-bay timber framed barn with double queen post thatched roof.
Grant Recipient/Owner: Norfolk Historic Buildings Trust/ Mr Christopher Bailey
Access contact: Mr John Nott
Tel: 01508 470113
Opening Arrangements: All year by prior arrangement with either Mr John Nott (tel.01508 470113) or Mr Christopher Bailey (tel.01508 499285). The Barn is in a busy farmyard but parking can usually be found (apart from at harvest time) for at least two cars by prior arrangement.
Heritage Open Days: No
P Yes. Spaces: 2
♿ No. Disabled WC: Yes. Guide Dogs: No
£ No

Thornage Hall Dovecote
Thornage, Holt, Norfolk NR25 7QH
Square dovecote, dated 1728, built of red brick in English bond with hipped roof in red black and black glazed pantiles terminating in square wooden glover. Contains 20

---

tiers of holes on all 4 sides and on brick spokes projecting from each corner toward the centre.
Grant Recipient/Owner: Norfolk Dovecote Trust/ Camphill Communities East Anglia
Access contact: Ms A Gimelli
Tel: 01263 860305
Opening Arrangements: Open for village fete in July, plus first Sunday in September, 2 - 5pm. At other times by prior written arrangement with Ms A Gimelli at Thornage Hall.
Heritage Open Days: No
P Yes. Spaces: 50
♿ No. Disabled WC: No. Guide Dogs: Yes
£ No

NORTH YORKSHIRE

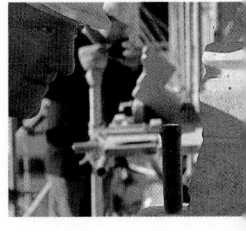

Beningbrough Hall
Shipton-by-Beningbrough,
North Yorkshire YO30 1DD
Country house, 1716, contains an impressive baroque interior. A very high standard of craftmanship is displayed throughout, most of the original work surviving with extremely fine woodcarvings and unusual central corridor running the full length of the house. Over 100 pictures on loan from the National Portrait Gallery are on display. There is a fully equipped Victorian laundry and walled garden.
Website Address: www.nationaltrust.org.uk
Grant Recipient/Owner: The National Trust
Access contact: Property Manager
Tel: 01904 470666   **Fax:** 01904 470002
Email Address: ybbrgb@smtp.ntrust.org.uk
Opening Arrangements: House: 31 March to 30 June, 1 September to 31 October daily except Thursdays and Fridays (but open Good Friday); July and August daily except Thursdays. Times: House: 12 noon - 5pm last admission 4.30pm, grounds 11am - 5.30pm. Wheelchair access (ramped) to ground floor only.
Heritage Open Days: No
P Yes. Spaces: 250
♿ Partial. Disabled WC: Yes. Guide Dogs: Yes
£ Yes
Adult: £5.20 (house). £3.60 (garden & exhibition).
Child: £2.60 (house). £1.80 (garden & exhibition).
Other: £13.00 (family: house). £9.00 (family: garden & exhibition). Discount for cyclists.

Braithwaite Hall
East Witton, Leyburn, North Yorkshire DL8 4SY
17th century stone farmhouse with fine original features including fireplaces, panelling and oak staircase.
Website Address: www.nationaltrust.org.uk
Grant Recipient/Owner: The National Trust
Access contact: Mrs David Duffus
Tel: 01969 640287
Opening Arrangements: By arrangement with the tenant Mrs David Duffus. No access for coaches. No WC.
Heritage Open Days: No
P Yes. Spaces: 10
♿ No. Disabled WC: No. Guide Dogs: Yes
£ Yes
Adult: £1.00 (including leaflet)
Child: £1.00 (including leaflet)

Castle Howard
York, North Yorkshire YO60 7DA
Large stately home dating from the beginning of the 18th century and designed by Sir John Vanbrugh. Situated in 1000 acres of landscaped grounds which include numerous monuments.
Website Address: www.castlehoward.co.uk
Grant Recipient/Owner: The Hon. Simon Howard
Access contact: Mr D N Peake
Tel: 01653 648444   **Fax:** 01653 648529
Email Address: estatemanager@castlehoward.co.uk
Opening Arrangements: 16 March - 4 November: daily 11am - 4.30pm (Grounds only from 10am); November - mid-March: grounds open most days but please telephone for confirmation in November, December and January. Wheelchair access to all but chapel and first floor of exhibition wing.
Heritage Open Days: No
P Yes. Spaces: 300
♿ Partial. Disabled WC: Yes. Guide Dogs: Yes
£ Yes
Adult: £7.50
Child: £4.50
Other: £6.75

Cawood Castle
nr. Selby, North Yorkshire
This decorated gatehouse, and wing to one side, is all that remains of the castle, once a stronghold of the Archbishops of York. Visitors have included Thomas Wolsey, Henry III, Edward I, and Henry VIII. In the 16th century it was used as a courtroom eventually ending up in domestic use. Extremely steep spiral staircase.

Website Address: www.landmarktrust.co.uk
Grant Recipient/Owner: The Landmark Trust
Access contact: Ms Victoria Piggott
Tel: 01628 825920   **Fax:** 01628 825417
Email Address: vpiggott@landmarktrust.co.uk
Opening Arrangements: The Landmark Trust is an independent charity, which rescues small buildings of historic or architectural importance from decay or unsympathetic improvement. Landmark's aim is to promote the enjoyment of these historic buildings by making them available to stay in for holidays. Cawood Castle can be rented by anyone, at all times of the year, for periods ranging from a weekend to three weeks. Bookings can be made by telephoning the Booking Office on 01628 825925. As the building is in full-time use for holiday accommodation, it is not normally open to the public. However the public can view the building by prior arrangement by telephoning the access contact (Victoria Piggott on 01628 825920) to make an appointment. Potential visitors will be asked to write to confirm the details of their visit.
Heritage Open Days: No
P Yes. Spaces: 1
♿ No. Disabled WC: No. Guide Dogs: No
£ No

Church Cottage
Studley Royal, Ripon, North Yorkshire
Situated adjacent to St Mary's Church, Church Cottage is the original Rectory, designed by Burges to complement the high Victorian Gothic church. It has a muscular, ornate style with intricate heraldic carving above the main entrance. The house sits by the main vista of the Deer Park which visually links St Mary's Church with Ripon Cathedral.
Website Address: www.fountainsabbey.org.uk
Grant Recipient/Owner: The National Trust
Access contact: Sarah Kay
Tel: 01765 608888   **Fax:** 01765 608889
Email Address: yfnsak@smtp.ntrust.org.uk
Opening Arrangements: Viewing on request Monday to Friday 10am - 4pm.
Heritage Open Days: No
P Yes. Spaces: 100
♿ No. Disabled WC: No. Guide Dogs: Yes
£ No

Duncombe Park
Helmsley, York, North Yorkshire YO62 5EB
Recently restored family home of Lord and Lady Feversham. Originally built in 1713 and then rebuilt after a fire in 1879 largely to the original design. Early 18th century gardens.
Website Address: www.duncombepark.com
Grant Recipient/Owner: Lord Feversham
Access contact: The Agent
Tel: 01439 770213   **Fax:** 01439 771114
Email Address: sally@duncombepark.com
Opening Arrangements: House and Gardens: Friday 13 April - 28 October, Sundays - Thursdays 10.30am - 6pm (hourly tours 11am - 4pm). Free flow visits (visitors do not need to join a guided tour) Sundays and Bank Holidays. For group and school visits contact the Estate Office. Special events. Wheelchair access to ground floor only.
Heritage Open Days: No
P Yes. Spaces: 200
♿ Partial. Disabled WC: Yes. Guide Dogs: Yes
£ Yes
Adult: £6.00
Child: £3.00 (10-16)
Other: £5.00

Farnley Hall
Farnley, Otley, North Yorkshire LS21 2QF
Grade I listed building, older part of the house (generally referred to as the Manor House) dates from the mid-17th century. It was Jacobeanized in the 1840s and in recent years has been renovated and modernised and is now let as a separate assured shorthold. The chief visitor interest lies in the Reception Wing added in 1785, designed and built by John Carr of York. The Carr Wing houses a collection of gouache drawings by J M W Turner depicting the Hall itself and the surrounding countryside. Also collections of 18th and early 19th century furniture.
Grant Recipient/Owner: Mr G N Le G Horton-Fawkes
Access contact: Mr G N Le G Horton-Fawkes
Tel: 01943 467905   **Fax:** 01943 463031
Email Address: farnley.hall@farming.co.uk
Opening Arrangements: May - August by prior written arrangement. Some assistance may be required for wheelchair users at certain points, please check with the Farnley Hall Estate.
Heritage Open Days: No
P Yes. Spaces: 20
♿ Partial. Disabled WC: Yes. Guide Dogs: Yes
£ Yes
Adult: £5.00

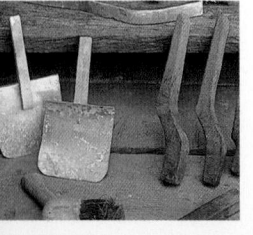

Fountains Hall

Studley Royal, Ripon, North Yorkshire HG4 3DY
Elizabethan mansion, built between 1589 and 1604 for Stephen Proctor. Two rooms; the Stone Hall and the Arkell Room, both unfurnished, are open to the public. During summer 2001 a third room, the Great Chamber, will be opened to guided tours. This upper room features an ornate chimney piece depicting the Biblical story of the Judgement of Solomon.
Website Address: www.fountainsabbey.org.uk
Grant Recipient/Owner: The National Trust
Access contact: Sarah Kay
Tel: 01765 608888   **Fax:** 01765 608889
Email Address: yfnsak@smtp.ntrust.org.uk
Opening Arrangements: Open as part of the Fountain's Abbey and Studley Royal estate. January to March: 10am - 4pm; April to September 10am - 6pm; October to December 10am - 4pm. Estate closed 24, 25 December and Fridays in January, November and December.
Heritage Open Days: No
P Yes. Spaces: 500
Yes. Disabled WC: Yes. Guide Dogs: Yes
£ Yes
Adult: £4.30
Child: £2.10
Child: £10.30 (family).

Giggleswick School Chapel

Giggleswick, Settle, North Yorkshire BD24 0DE
Built 1897-1901 by T G Jackson for Walter Morrison as a gift to the school to commemorate the Diamond Jubilee of Queen Victoria. Constructed of Gothic Banded rockfaced millstone grit sandstone and limestone, with copper hipped roof to nave and copper covered terracotta dome to chancel. Contains Italian sgraffito work throughout.
Website Address:
www.giggleswick.n-yorks.sch.uk/chapel
Grant Recipient/Owner:
The Governors of Giggleswick School
Access contact: The Bursar and Clerk to the Governors
Tel: 01729 893000/893012   **Fax:** 01729 893150
Email Address: bursar@giggleswick.n.yorks.sch.uk
Opening Arrangements: By prior arrangement, apart from July to September when restoration works are due to be undertaken.
Heritage Open Days: No
P Yes. Spaces: 25
Partial. Disabled WC: No. Guide Dogs: Yes
£ No

Grand Assembly Rooms

Blake Street, York, North Yorkshire
Important surviving early Palladian style building (exact model of his Egyptian Hall, based on Vitruvius) designed by Lord Burlington and built by public subscription between 1732 and 1736. Originally used for balls and assemblies, after World War II and in the last 10 years the Rooms have been fully restored and now house a restaurant.
Grant Recipient/Owner: Director of Environment & Development Services, City of York
Access contact: Shona Davies
Tel: 01904 637254
Opening Arrangements: Daily 12 noon - 12 midnight. Closed Christmas Day only. Parking at Marygate car park 5 minutes away, disabled parking adjacent in Blake Street.
Heritage Open Days: No
P See above
Yes. Disabled WC: Yes. Guide Dogs: Yes
£ No

Jervaulx Abbey

East Witton Without, York, North Yorkshire
Ruins of Cistercian Abbey moved to this site in 1156, built of sandstone ashlar in Early English style. Remains of nave, transepts and choir, with a cloister on the south side of the nave, flanked by a chapter house to the east and a kitchen and dorter to the south.
Grant Recipient/Owner: Mr Burdon
Access contact: Mr Ian Burdon
Tel: 01677 460391
Opening Arrangements: At any reasonable time. Wheelchair access is limited by uneven terrain and steps to various parts of the site.
Heritage Open Days: Yes
P Yes. Spaces: 55
Partial. Disabled WC: Yes. Guide Dogs: Yes
£ Yes
Adult: £2.00 (honesty box)
Child: £1.50 (honesty box)

Merchant Taylors Hall

Aldwark, York, North Yorkshire YO1 2BX
Guildhall of the Merchant Taylors' Company, c1400 with late 15th century wing. Mainly timber-framed and refaced in brick with tile roofs and brick chimney stacks. Refenestrated early 17th century and extended, refaced and porch added 1714-15, entrance front and wing

refaced c1730. Restored with some rebuilding and further extensions in 20th century. Contains painted glass, c1700, by Henry Gyles.
Grant Recipient/Owner:
Company of Merchant Taylors
Access contact: Mrs Audrey Lambert
Tel: 01904 624889
Opening Arrangements: May - September: Tuesdays 10am - 4pm. At other times by prior arrangement. For Hall bookings (apart from visits) contact 01904 624889.
Heritage Open Days: No
P No
Yes. Disabled WC: Yes. Guide Dogs: Yes
£ No

The Mount School - Lindley Murray Summerhouse

Dalton Terrace, York, North Yorkshire YO24 4DD
Grade II* listed summerhouse built c1774, formerly situated in the grounds of Holgate House, York. Octagonal timber structure on raised stepped circular base with lead ogee roof and decorated with Doric columns. Restored in 1997.
Website Address: www.mount.n-yorks.sch.uk
Grant Recipient/Owner: The Mount School
Access contact: Ms Anne Bolton
Tel: 01904 667506   **Fax:** 01904 667524
Email Address: abolton.mount@talk21.com
Opening Arrangements: By prior arrangement Monday - Friday all year (except Bank Holidays) 9am - 4.30pm.
Heritage Open Days: No
P Yes. Spaces: 3
Yes. Disabled WC: Yes. Guide Dogs: Yes
£ No
Donations welcome.

Newburgh Priory

Coxwold, York, North Yorkshire YO6 4AS
Priory originally built in 1145 with alterations in Tudor, Jacobean and Georgian periods. Tomb of Oliver Cromwell in the House, extensive grounds, walled garden and walks with views across the lake to the White Horse. Tea rooms.
Access contact: Sir George Wombwell Bt
Tel: 01347 868372
Opening Arrangements: April, May and June; Wednesdays and Sundays, Easter Sunday and Bank Holiday Monday and May Bank Holiday Mondays. Guided tours every 30 minutes starting at 2.30pm. Last tour 4.30pm. Grounds open 2 - 6pm. Coach parties and groups by arrangement. Wheelchair access to ground floor of house, parts of garden.
Heritage Open Days: No
P No
Partial. Disabled WC: Yes. Guide Dogs: No
£ Yes
Adult: £2.00 (house). £2.00 (grounds).
Child: £1.00 (house). Free (grounds).

Norton Conyers Hall

nr. Ripon, North Yorkshire HG4 5EQ
Medieval house with Stuart and Georgian additions. 18th century walled garden nearby. Family pictures, furniture and costumes. Visited by Charlotte Bronte in 1839, a family legend of a mad woman confined in an attic room inspired the mad Mrs Rochester in 'Jane Eyre' and the Hall was the model for 'Thornfield Hall'.
Grant Recipient/Owner: Sir James Graham Bt
Access contact: Sir James Graham Bt
Tel: 01765 640333   **Fax:** 01765 640333
Email Address: norton.conyers@ripon.org
Opening Arrangements: House and Garden: 13 May - 9 September Sundays, 9 - 14 July daily, Easter Sunday and Monday, Bank Holiday Sundays and Mondays. House 2 - 5pm, Garden (no admission charge but donations welcome) 11.30am - 5pm. Wheelchair access to ground floor only.
Heritage Open Days: No
P Yes. Spaces: 60
Partial. Disabled WC: Yes. Guide Dogs: Yes
£ Yes
Adult: £4.00
Child: £3.00 (10-16)
Other: £3.00 (senior citizens)

Ormesby Hall

Church Lane, Ormesby, Middlesbrough TS7 9AS
A mid-18th century Palladian mansion, notable for its fine plasterwork and carved wood decoration. The Victorian laundry and kitchen with scullery and game larder are interesting. 18th century stable block, attributed to Carr of York, is leased to the Cleveland Mounted Police. Large model railway and garden with holly walk.
Website Address: www.nationaltrust.org.uk
Grant Recipient/Owner: The National Trust
Access contact: Property Manager
Tel: 01642 324188   **Fax:** 01642 300937
Email Address: yorkor@smtp.ntrust.org.uk

Opening Arrangements: 1 April to 4 November daily except Mondays, Fridays and Saturdays (but open Good Friday and Bank Holiday Mondays) 2 - 5pm. Wheelchair access to: ground floor of house (shallow step at entrance), shop, tea room and garden. Car park is approximately 100 metres from house.
Heritage Open Days: No
P Yes. Spaces: 100
Partial. Disabled WC: Yes. Guide Dogs: Yes
£ Yes
Adult: £3.50. £2.20 (garden, railway and exhibition only).
Child: £1.70. £1.00 (garden, railway and exhibition only).
Other: £8.50 (family).

The Pigsty

Fyling Hall, Fylingthorpe, North Yorkshire
Two pigs were the excuse for this exercise in primitive classicism, inspired by buildings seen by Squire Barry of Fyling Hall on his travels around the Mediterranean in the 1880s. Uneven steps from parking place.
Website Address: www.landmarktrust.co.uk
Grant Recipient/Owner: The Landmark Trust
Access contact: Ms Victoria Piggott
Tel: 01628 825920   **Fax:** 01628 825417
Email Address: vpiggott@landmarktrust.co.uk
Opening Arrangements: The Landmark Trust is an independent charity, which rescues small buildings of historic or architectural importance from decay or unsympathetic improvement. Landmark's aim is to promote the enjoyment of these historic buildings by making them available to stay in for holidays. The Pigsty can be rented by anyone, at all times of the year, for periods ranging from a weekend to three weeks. Bookings can be made by telephoning the Booking Office on 01628 825925. As the building is in full-time use for holiday accommodation, it is not normally open to the public. However the public can view the building by prior arrangement by telephoning the access contact (Victoria Piggott on 01628 825920) to make an appointment. Potential visitors will be asked to write to confirm the details of their visit.
Heritage Open Days: No
P Yes. Spaces: 1
No. Disabled WC: No. Guide Dogs: No
£ No

St Paulinus

Brough Park, Richmond, North Yorkshire DL10 7PJ
Catholic neo-Gothic chapel designed by Bonomi with priest's accommodation and school room in undercroft.
Grant Recipient/Owner: Mr Greville Worthington
Access contact: Mr Greville Worthington
Tel: 01748 812127
Email Address: tote@grev.demon.co.uk
Opening Arrangements: By prior arrangement.
Heritage Open Days: No
P Yes. Spaces: 2
No. Disabled WC: No. Guide Dogs: Yes
£ No

St Saviour's Church

(Archaeological Resource Centre)
St Saviourgate, York, North Yorkshire YO1 8NN
Church on site by late 11th century, present building dates from the 15th and extensively remodelled in 1845. Now houses the Archaeological Resource Centre which contains an archaeological collection excavated by the York Archaeological Trust and promotes access to archaeological material through hands-on displays.
Grant Recipient/Owner: Dr R A Hall
Access contact: Miss Christine McDonnell
Tel: 01904 643211   **Fax:** 01904 627097
Email Address: cmcdonnell@yorkarchaeology.co.uk
Opening Arrangements: School holidays: Monday - Friday 11am - 15.30pm; groups by prior arrangement only during school term. For further details please check with Miss Christine McDonnell, York Archaeological Trust, Cromwell House, 13 Ogleforth, York, North Yorkshire YO1 7FG (tel.01904 643211). Visitors who simply want to view the building may look round free of charge, otherwise admission charged for entrance to Archaeological Resource Centre, £3.60 for adults and children (carers/enablers free when helping disabled person). Disabled parking just outside entrance, otherwise public car parks close by. Sensory garden on architectural theme.
Heritage Open Days: No
P See above
Yes. Disabled WC: Yes. Guide Dogs: Yes
£ No

Scampston Hall

Scampston, Malton, North Yorkshire, YO17 8NG
Late 17th century country house, extensively remodelled in 1801 by Thomas Leverton. Contains Regency interiors and an art collection. Set in a parkland designed by

'Capability' Brown with 10 acres of lakes and a Palladian bridge.
Website Address: www.scampston.co.uk
Grant Recipient/Owner: Sir Charles Legard Bt
Access contact: Sir Charles Legard Bt
Tel: 01944 758224   **Fax:** 01944 758700
Email Address: legard@scampton.co.uk
Opening Arrangements: 27 May - 10 June and 22 July - 5 August (closed Saturdays), 1.30 - 5pm. Groups at other times by prior arrangement. Wheelchair access to ground floor only.
Heritage Open Days: No
P Yes. Spaces: 50
Partial. Disabled WC: Yes. Guide Dogs: Yes
Yes
Adult: £5.00 House, Garden & Park.

Temple of Victory

Allerton Park, nr. Knaresborough, North Yorkshire HG5 0SE
Attributed to Henry Holland, architect for the Duke of York, but possibly by James Payne. Late 18th century octagon tower in the Grecian style. The entrance is by a double flight of steps secured by iron palisades.
Grant Recipient/Owner: The Gerald Arthur Rolph Foundation for Historic Preservation & Education
Access contact: The Gerald Arthur Rolph Foundation for Historic Preservation & Education
Tel: 01423 330927
Opening Arrangements: Easter Sunday - end of September: Sundays and Bank Holiday Mondays 1 - 5pm. Parking half a mile away.
Heritage Open Days: No
P Yes. Spaces: 30
No. Disabled WC: No. Guide Dogs: No
No

Thompson Mausoleum

Little Ouseburn Churchyard, Little Ouseburn, North Yorkshire YO26 9TS
18th century Mausoleum in magnesian limestone. It is a rotunda encircled by 13 Tuscan columns, above which a frieze and cornice support a plain drum and ribbed domed roof. Listed Grade II*.
Grant Recipient/Owner: Mr H Hibbs
Access contact: Mr H Hibbs
Tel: 01423 330414
Email Address: helier@clara.net
Opening Arrangements: Always available to view from the outside but no access to interior at present as it is awaiting repair.
Heritage Open Days: No
P Yes. Spaces: 4
Partial. Disabled WC: No. Guide Dogs: Yes
No

NORTHAMPTONSHIRE

Hall Farmhouse

Hall Yard, Kings Cliffe, Peterborough, Northamptonshire PE8 6XQ
Former medieval open hall. Music room, c1795, with coved and ornamented ceiling. Home of William Law 1740-61.
Grant Recipient/Owner: Mr J A R Grove
Access contact: Mr J A R Grove
Tel: 01780 470748
Opening Arrangements: By prior arrangement.
Heritage Open Days: No
P Yes. Spaces: 3
No. Disabled WC: No. Guide Dogs: Yes
No

Laxton Hall

Corby, Northamptonshire NN17 3AU
Built in 18th century. Formerly a boys school, now a Polish residential care home.
Grant Recipient/Owner:
Polish Benevolent Housing Association Ltd
Access contact: Mr J Palmi
Tel: 01780 444292   **Fax:** 01780 444574
Opening Arrangements: By prior written arrangement with Mr J Palmi, PBF Housing Association, 2 Devonia Road, London N1 8JJ, in the early afternoon of the first Monday of each month (except during Religious Festivals).
Heritage Open Days: No
P Yes. Spaces: 10
No. Disabled WC: No. Guide Dogs: No
No

The Manor House

Hardwick, Wellingborough, Northamptonshire PE8 5HZ
Manor house dating back to the 12th century. The exterior of the building has been restored including a fine example of a Collyweston roof. Now part of a modern working farm.

Grant Recipient/Owner: Mr Siddons
Access contact: Mr Siddons
Tel: 01933 678785   **Fax:** 01933 678166
Email Address: siddons@siddons.fsbusiness.co.uk
Opening Arrangements: Exterior only. Opening arrangements under review at time of going to print, please check English Heritage website for current information.
Heritage Open Days: No
P Yes. Spaces: 4
No. Disabled WC: No. Guide Dogs: No
No

Nunnery Cottages

1/2 The Maltings, Desborough Road, Rothwell, Northamptonshire NN14 6JZ
Farmhouse, now two houses, built 1660 (part may be earlier, mid-16th century) of ironstone with limestone and brick dressings, plain tile and thatched roofs.
Grant Recipient/Owner: Rothwell Preservation Trust
Access contact: Mrs C E Mackay
Tel: 01536 713252/711086 **Fax:** 01536 713252
Opening Arrangements: By prior written arrangement with Mrs C E Mackay, Secretary of the Rothwell Preservation Trust, 23 High Street, Rothwell, Northamptonshire NN14 6AD.
Heritage Open Days: No
P No
No
No

The Prebendal Manor House

Nassington, nr. Peterborough, Northamptonshire PE8 6QG
Reputedly the oldest manor house in Northamptonshire, dating from the early 13th century and on the site of a Saxon hall. The House has been much altered over the centuries. The Prebend of Nassington was established in Lincoln Cathedral in the 12th century and the House was occupied by the Prebendary and his tenants until 1836 when the Prebend was dissolved. Also on site is a tithe barn museum, 15th century dovecote, fish ponds and a recreated medieval garden.
Website Address: www.prebendal-manor.demon.co.uk
Grant Recipient/Owner: Mrs Jane Baile
Access contact: Mrs Jane Baile
Tel: 01780 782575
Email Address: info@prebendal-manor.demon.co.uk
Opening Arrangements: May, June and September: Wednesdays and Sundays 1 - 5.30pm; July and August: Wednesdays, Thursdays and Sundays 1 - 5.30pm; Bank Holiday Mondays 1 - 5.30pm. Closed Christmas. Groups by prior arrangement. Free audio tours.
Heritage Open Days: No
P Yes. Spaces: 14
Partial. Disabled WC: No. Guide Dogs: Yes
Yes
Adult: £4.00
Child: £1.20
Other: £3.50 (groups 20+), free (National Archaeology Days).

NORTHUMBERLAND

Bamburgh Castle

Bamburgh, Northumberland, NE69 7DF
Rocky fortress with Norman keep, Kings Hall, Cross Hall, bakehouse, Victorian scullery, armoury and dungeon containing a collection of fine china, porcelain, glassware, paintings, furniture, tapestries, arms and armour. Home of the Armstrong family.
Website Address: www.bamburghcastle.com
Grant Recipient/Owner:
Trustees of Lord Armstrong Deceased/ Lady Armstrong
Access contact: Mr R Bewley
Tel: 01668 214515   **Fax:** 01668 214060
Email Address: bamburghcastle@aol.com
Opening Arrangements: 17 March - 31 October: daily 11am - 5pm (last admission 4.30pm). Wheelchair access to first 5 rooms only.
Heritage Open Days: No
P Yes. Spaces: 100
Partial. Disabled WC: Yes. Guide Dogs: Yes
Yes
Adult: £4.50
Child: £1.50
Other: £3.50 (senior citizens)

Belford Hall

Belford, Northumberland NE70 7EY
Country house, 1754-56 by James Paine, wings and rear entrance added 1818 by John Dobson. The property stood derelict for 40 years until it was restored by the North East Civic Trust and the Monument Trust between 1984-87.
Grant Recipient/Owner: North East Civic Trust
Access contact: Ms Sheila Fairbairn
Tel: 01668 213794
Opening Arrangements: Every day in the months of

May and September to include the spring and summer bank holidays from 12 noon to 6pm. Wheelchair access to ground floor with assistance (three steps to main entrance). No public toilets.
Heritage Open Days: No
P Yes. Spaces: 8
Partial. Disabled WC: No. Guide Dogs: Yes
No

Brinkburn Mill

Longframlington, Rothbury, Northumberland NE65 8AR
Brinkburn Priory was founded c1135 within a loop of the River Coquet. The Mill was built c1800 near the site of its medieval predecessor, but dressed up later to improve the view from the house. The wheel and grinding stones are still in place, although long unused.
Website Address: www.landmarktrust.co.uk
Grant Recipient/Owner: The Landmark Trust
Access contact: Ms Victoria Piggott
Tel: 01628 825920 **Fax:** 01628 825417
Email Address: vpiggott@landmarktrust.co.uk
Opening Arrangements: The Landmark Trust is an independent charity, which rescues small buildings of historic or architectural importance from decay or unsympathetic improvement. Landmark's aim is to promote the enjoyment of these historic buildings by making them available to stay in for holidays. Brinkburn Mill can be rented by anyone, at all times of the year, for periods ranging from a weekend to three weeks. Bookings can be made by telephoning the Booking Office on 01628 825925. As the building is in full-time use for holiday accommodation, it is not normally open to the public. However the public can view the building by prior arrangement by telephoning the access contact (Victoria Piggott on 01628 825920) to make an appointment. Potential visitors will be asked to write to confirm the details of their visit.
Heritage Open Days: No
P Yes. Spaces: 1
No. Disabled WC: No. Guide Dogs: Yes
No

Chillingham Castle

Chillingham, Northumberland NE66 5NJ
Medieval castle owned by the same family for 800 years, housing collection of antiques and artefacts from all over the world and a museum. Set in grounds designed by Sir Jeffrey Wyatville. Due to its strategic position close to the Scottish border the Castle was often besieged and was visited many times by royalty.
Website Address: www.chillingham-castle.com
Grant Recipient/Owner: Sir Humphry Wakefield Bt
Access contact: Mr A S de Courtenay-Wellum
Tel: 01668 215359   **Fax:** 01668 215463
Email Address: enquiries@chillingham-castle.com
Opening Arrangements: May - September: daily 12 noon - 5pm. Closed Tuesdays in May, June and September. Limited wheelchair access to parts of ground floor only due to varying floor levels, steep and spiral staircases.
Heritage Open Days: No
P Yes. Spaces: 50
Partial. Disabled WC: Yes. Guide Dogs: Yes
Yes
Adult: £4.50
Child: Free
Other: £4.00 (senior citizens), £3.80 (groups).

Cragside

Rothbury, Morpeth, Northumberland NE65 7PX
High Victorian mansion by Norman Shaw, with original furniture and fittings including William Morris's stained glass and earliest wallpapers. Built for the inventor-industrialist and armaments manufacturer, Lord Armstrong, who installed the world's first hydro-electric lighting. The mansion is set in a 1,000-acre wooded estate, with rock garden, formal garden, man-made lakes and hydro-electric machinery.
Website Address: www.nationaltrust.org.uk
Grant Recipient/Owner: The National Trust
Access contact: Mr John O'Brien
Tel: 01669 620333 ex 101   **Fax:** 01669 620066
Email Address: nrcjob@smtp.ntrust.org.uk
Opening Arrangements: 31 March to 4 November: Tuesday - Sunday (and Bank Holiday Mondays). Times: House 1- 5.30pm (last admission 4.30pm); estate and gardens 10.30am - 7pm (last admission 5pm). Winter opening (estate only) 7 November to 16 December: Wednesday - Sunday 11am - 4pm. Wheelchair access to ground floor of house and one landing area on first floor.
Heritage Open Days: No
P Yes. Spaces: 400
Partial. Disabled WC: Yes. Guide Dogs: Yes
Yes
Adult: £6.70 (house & estate). £4.20 (estate only).
Child: £3.40 (house & estate). £2.10 (estate only).
Other: £16.80 (family: house & estate). £10.50 (family: estate only). No admission charge to estate during winter opening.

⊞ Opening arrangements at properties grant-aided by English Heritage

Cruck Barn

Towhouse, Bardon Mill, Hexham, Northumberland NE47 7EQ
Grade II* 17th century heather-thatched cruck barn.
Grant Recipient/Owner: Mrs J G Hayward
Access contact: Mrs J G Hayward
Tel: 01434 344473   **Fax:** 01434 344473
Opening Arrangements: By prior arrangement.
Heritage Open Days: No
🅿 Yes. Spaces: 2
♿ Yes. Disabled WC: No. Guide Dogs: Yes
£ No

Hexham Moot Hall

Market Place, Hexham, Northumberland NE46 3NH
Built c1400 and used as a home, office and court for the Archbishop of York's bailiff who administered Hexhamshire from the Hall. The former stores on the ground floor are now an art gallery, the first floor courtroom houses the Border Library and the second floor hall is used for community activities.
Grant Recipient/Owner: Tynedale District Council
Access contact: Ms Janet Goodridge
Tel: 01434 652351   **Fax:** 01434 652425
Email Address: museum@tynedale.gov.uk
Opening Arrangements: Mondays, Tuesdays, Thursdays and Fridays 10am - 12.30pm and 1.30 - 3pm. Closed Christmas to New Year.
Heritage Open Days: No
🅿 No
♿ No. Disabled WC: No. Guide Dogs: Yes
£ No

High Meadows Cottage Barn

Whitshields, Bardon Mill, Northumberland NE47 7BN
18th century stone walled, cruck roofed heather thatched barn with flagged floor. Perhaps a unique survival of a once-common vernacular building type, remaining virtually unaltered.
Grant Recipient/Owner: Mr D W Collinson
Access contact: Dr M Crick
Tel: 0777 1996 838
Opening Arrangements: By prior telephone arrangement. Wheelchair access not without difficulty.
Heritage Open Days: No
🅿 Yes. Spaces: 4
♿ Partial. Disabled WC: No. Guide Dogs: Yes
£ No

High Staward Farm

Langley-on-Tyne, Hexham, Northumberland NE47 5NS
Georgian farmhouse standing inside a walled garden surrounded by the farm steading. Has a ging gang, threshing machine, pig stys with stone troughs and a blacksmiths shop. Most of the house and buildings are of dressed stone and the house has flagged floors, ceiling hooks, cheeseboard and rail, large pantry and servants staircase. Still a working hill farm.
Grant Recipient/Owner: Mr R J Coulson
Access contact: Mr R J Coulson
Tel: 01434 683619
Opening Arrangements: By prior arrangement.
Heritage Open Days: No
🅿 Yes. Spaces: 2
♿ No. Disabled WC: No. Guide Dogs: Yes
£ No

Lady's Well

Holystone, Harbottle, Northumberland
The Lady's Holy Well is considered to be of Roman origin and is located on a halting place along the Roman road. The main feature of the well today is a rectangular stone tank which is fed by a natural spring.
Website Address: www.nationaltrust.org.uk
Grant Recipient/Owner: The National Trust
Access contact: Mr John O'Brien
Tel: 01669 620333 ex 101   **Fax:** 01669 620066
Email Address: ncrjob@smtp.ntrust.org.uk
Opening Arrangements: Open all day throughout the year.
Heritage Open Days: No
🅿 No
♿ No. Disabled WC: No. Guide Dogs: Yes
£ No

Lambley Viaduct

Lambley, Tynedale, Northumberland
17 arch stone viaduct, 100ft high and 1650ft long, spanning the South Tyne river. Originally carried single track, now used as a footpath.
Grant Recipient/Owner: British Rail Property Board/ North Pennines Heritage Trust
Access contact: Mr David Flush
Tel: 01434 382045

Email Address: np.ht@virgin.net
Opening Arrangements: At all times as part of the South Tyne Trail between Featherstone Park and Alston. Wheelchair access from Coanwood End.
Heritage Open Days: No
🅿 Yes. Spaces: 30
♿ Yes. Disabled WC: No. Guide Dogs: Yes
£ No

Lindisfarne Castle

Holy Island, Berwick-upon-Tweed, Northumberland TD15 2SH
Built in 1550 to protect Holy Island harbour from attack, the castle was converted into a private house for Edward Hudson by Sir Edwin Luytens in 1903. Small walled garden was designed by Gertrude Jekyll. 19th century lime kilns in field by the castle.
Website Address: www.nationaltrust.org.uk
Grant Recipient/Owner:
Access contact: Property Manager
Tel: 01289 389244   **Fax:** 01289 389349
Opening Arrangements:
1 April to 31 October: daily except Fridays (but open Good Friday). Opening times 12 noon - 3pm, but sometimes earlier or later as the tide allows. Council car park one mile from site.
Heritage Open Days: No
🅿 See above
♿ No. Disabled WC: No. Guide Dogs: Yes
£ Yes
Adult: £4.20
Child: £2.10
Other: £10.50 (family). NT members free.

Little Harle Tower

Kirkwhelpington, Newcastle-upon-Tyne, Northumberland NE19 2PD
Medieval tower with 17th century range and a Victorian wing which contains a recently restored 1740s drawing room. It has been one family's home since 1830 though part is now let.
Grant Recipient/Owner: Mr J P Palmer Anderson
Access contact: Mr John Clark
Tel: 01434 320363   **Fax:** 01434 320675
Email Address: post.haltwhistle@csh.co.uk
Opening Arrangements: By prior arrangement (at least two weeks notice required) with Mr John Clark of Clark Scott Harden, Market Place, Haltwhistle, Northumberland NE49 0BP (tel.01434 320363).
Heritage Open Days: No
🅿 Yes. Spaces: 6
♿ Partial. Disabled WC: No. Guide Dogs: Yes
£ No
Donations to the church requested.

Mitford Hall Camellia House

Morpeth, Northumberland
East wing and conservatory of country house built c1820 by John Dobson, detached from main house by demolition of north-east wing in 20th century.
Grant Recipient/Owner: Shepherd Offshore plc
Access contact: Mr B Shepherd
Opening Arrangements: By prior written arrangement during the summer. Wheelchair access by prior arrangement. Ordinary toilet on site may be accessible for some disabled persons, please contact Hall for further information.
Heritage Open Days: No
🅿 Yes. Spaces: 3
♿ Yes. Disabled WC: Yes. Guide Dogs: Yes
£ No

St Cuthbert's Chapel

Farne Islands, Northumberland
St Cuthbert's Chapel was completed in 1370. By the early 19th century it was in a ruinous condition. Restored in 1840 by Archdeacon Thorp it includes some fine 17th century woodwork from Durham Cathedral and a memorial to Grace Darling. Remains of an original window.
Website Address: www.nationaltrust.org.uk
Grant Recipient/Owner: The National Trust
Access contact: Mr John Walton
Tel: 01665 720651   **Fax:** 01665 720651
Email Address: john.walton@ntrust.org.uk
Opening Arrangements: 1 to 30 April, 1 August to 30 September: daily, Inner Farne Island (St Cuthbert's Chapel) and Staple Island 10.30am - 6pm (Low Season). 1 May to 31 July: daily, Staple Island 10.30am - 1.30pm, Inner Farne Island 1.30pm - 5pm (High Season). Inner Farne Island is accessible for wheelchairs, Staple Island is not accessible. Lavatory for disabled on Inner Farne Island. Guide dogs are allowed on boat but not on islands. Parking in Seahouse (nearest mainland village).
Heritage Open Days: No
🅿 See above
♿ Partial. Disabled WC: Yes. Guide Dogs: See above
£ Yes

Adult: £3.00 (Low Season). £4.00 (High Season). Provisional.
Child: £1.50 (Low Season). £2.00 (High Season). Provisional.

The Tower

Elsdon, Northumberland NE19 1AA
14th century Tower House, residence of the Rector until 1961 and originally used as a refuge against Border raids.
Grant Recipient/Owner: J F Wollaston
Access contact: J F Wollaston
Fax: 01830 520904
Opening Arrangements: By previously arranged guided tour, weekends only, 1 April - 30 October. Parking in village.
Heritage Open Days: No
🅿 Yes. Spaces: 30
♿ No. Disabled WC: No. Guide Dogs: Yes
£ Yes
Adult: £3.00

Wallington Hall & Clock Tower

Cambo, Morpeth, Northumberland NE61 4AP
House was built in 1688 on site of a former pele tower for Sir Walter Blackett, a wealthy Newcastle upon Tyne merchant. It served as a shooting box until Sir Walter's grandson, Sir Walter Calverley Blackett decorated the interiors and erected the Clock Tower and stable buildings.
Website Address: www.nationaltrust.org.uk
Grant Recipient/Owner: The National Trust
Access contact: Property Manager
Tel: 01670 774283   **Fax:** 01670 774420
Email Address: nwabmp@smtp.ntrust.org.uk
Opening Arrangements: House: 31 March to 30 September: daily except Tuesdays 1 - 5.30pm (last entry 5.00pm). 1 to 28 October: daily except Tuesdays 1 - 4.30pm (last entry 4pm). The grounds are open 365 days a year. No wheelchair access to first floor of house.
Heritage Open Days: No
🅿 Yes. Spaces: 500
♿ Partial. Disabled WC: Yes. Guide Dogs: Yes
£ Yes
Adult: £5.50 (house, garden & grounds). £4.00 (garden & grounds only).
Child: £2.75 (house, garden & grounds). £2.00 (garden & grounds only).
Other: £13.75 (family).

NOTTINGHAMSHIRE

Kiln Warehouse

Castle Station, Newark, Nottinghamshire
Grade II* former warehouse. Early example of the use of massed concrete construction. Interior completely destroyed by fire in the early 1990s, the exterior walls have been restored and warehouse converted into offices.
Grant Recipient/Owner: The Regional Director
Access contact: Mr Edward Vanstone
Tel: 0115 950 7577   **Fax:** 0115 950 7688
Email Address: edwardv@fhp.co.uk
Opening Arrangements: The exterior walls for which the property is notable can be viewed without arrangement. Access to internal courtyard is by prior arrangement with Mr Edward Vanstone of Fisher Hargreaves Proctor, Chartered Surveyors, 10 Oxford Street, Nottingham NG1 5BG (tel.0115 950 7577). Parking available on adjacent land.
Heritage Open Days: No
🅿 See above
♿ Yes. Disabled WC: No. Guide Dogs: Yes
£ No

Newdigate House

Castle Gate, Nottingham, Nottinghamshire NG1 6AF
House, c1675, built for Thomas Newdigate. Stucco with ashlar dressings, hipped slate roof, sash windows, panelled rooms and Adam-style plasterwork. Crested wrought-iron railings, central gateway and overthrow, probably by Francis Foulgham, to the exterior. Marshal Tallard was held prisoner here after the battle of Blenheim. The ground floor is now a restaurant.
Grant Recipient/Owner: Mr Alan Trease
Access contact: Mr Ashley Walters
Tel: 0115 8475587
Opening Arrangements: Daily 11am - 11pm. Some assistance may be required for wheelchair access, please check with Mr Walters on 0115 8475587.
Heritage Open Days: No
🅿 No
♿ Partial. Disabled WC: No. Guide Dogs: Yes
£ No

OXFORDSHIRE

Blenheim Palace & Park

Woodstock, Oxfordshire OX20 1PX
Ancestral home of the Dukes of Marlborough and birthplace of Winston Churchill. Built between 1705-22 for John Churchill, the 1st Duke, in recognition of his victory at the Battle of Blenheim in 1704. Designed by Sir John Vanbrugh, the house contains in its many state rooms a collection of paintings, furniture, bronzes and the Marlborough Victories tapestries. A five-room Churchill Exhibition includes his birth room. 'Capability' Brown park and gardens.
Website Address: www.blenheimpalace.com
Grant Recipient/Owner: Duke of Marlborough
Access contact: Mr N Day
Tel: 01993 811325 **Fax:** -1993 813527
Email Address: nickday@blenheimpalace.com
Opening Arrangements: Palace: 12 March - end of October, daily 10.30am - 5.30pm (last admission 4.45pm). Park: daily (except Christmas Day) 9am - 6pm (last admission 4.45pm). High Lodge may be visited by prior written arrangement with the Estate Office.
Heritage Open Days: No
Ⓟ Yes. Spaces: 10000
♿ Yes. Disabled WC: Yes. Guide Dogs: Yes
£ Yes
Adult: £9.30
Child: £4.80
Other: £7.50 (senior citizens). £23.00 (family ticket)

Broughton Castle

Banbury, Oxfordshire OX15 5EB
Originally built c1300, the castle stands on an island site surrounded by a 3 acre moat. Greatly enlarged in 1550 and decorated with plaster ceilings, panelling and fireplaces. Ancestral home of the Lords Saye and Sele since 1450.
Website Address: www.broughtoncastle.demon.co.uk
Grant Recipient/Owner: Lord Saye & Sele
Access contact: Lord Saye & Sele
Tel: 01295 262624 **Fax:** 01295 276070
Opening Arrangements: 20 May - 12 September: Wednesdays and Sundays, plus Thursdays in July and August and Bank Holiday Mondays (including Easter) 2 - 5pm. Groups at any time throughout the year by prior arrangement. Wheelchair access to ground floor only.
Heritage Open Days: No
Ⓟ Yes. Spaces: 150
♿ Partial. Disabled WC: Yes. Guide Dogs: Yes
£ Yes
Adult: £4.50
Child: £2.00 (5-15)
Other: £4.00 (seniors/students)

Clattercote Priory Farm

Claydon, Banbury, Oxfordshire OX17 1QB
Founded c1150, the Priory is now a family house - part farmhouse, part tenanted. A rare example of a Gilbertine Priory with cellars and 'chapel', probably medieval.
Grant Recipient/Owner: Mr Adrian Taylor
Access contact: Mr Adrian Taylor
Tel: 01295 690476 **Fax:** 01295 690476
Email Address: clattercote1@aol.com
Opening Arrangements: By prior written arrangement. Donations requested, with proceeds to charity.
Heritage Open Days: No
Ⓟ Yes. Spaces: 4
♿ No. Disabled WC: No. Guide Dogs: Yes
£ No

The Cottage

Aston Street, Aston Tirrold, Oxfordshire OX11 9DQ
House dating back to 1286, with later 16th and 17th century alterations and additions. Timber-framed with water reed thatched roof. The 13th century west wing is one of very few known domestic timber-framed buildings of this date in which aisled construction is not used.
Grant Recipient/Owner: Mr B C Bateman
Access contact: Mr B C Bateman
Fax: 01235 850351
Email Address: bateman5@supanet.com
Opening Arrangements: By prior written arrangement.
Heritage Open Days: No
Ⓟ No
♿ No. Disabled WC: No. Guide Dogs: Yes
£ No

Farnborough Hall

Farnborough, Banbury, Oxfordshire OX17 1DU
Mid-18th century honey-coloured stone built home of the Holbech family for over 300 years, contains impressive plasterwork. Set in grounds with 18th century temples, a terrace walk and an obelisk.
Website Address: www.ntrustsevern.org.uk
Grant Recipient/Owner: The National Trust
Access contact: Mr & Mrs G Holbech

Tel: 01295 690002
Opening Arrangements: April - end of September. House and grounds: Wednesdays and Saturdays 2 - 6pm, also 6 & 7 May 2 - 6pm; Terrace walk: Thursdays and Fridays 2 - 6pm (closed Good Friday). Wheelchair access to ground floor of house, Terrace walk may be difficult as it is very steep.
Heritage Open Days: No
Ⓟ Yes. Spaces: 10
♿ Partial. Disabled WC: No. Guide Dogs: Yes
£ Yes
Adult: £3.40. £1.70 (Garden). £1.00 (Terrace walk only).
Child: £1.70. £1.35 (Garden).

Pope's Tower & Chapel

The Manor House, Stanton Harcourt, Witney, Oxfordshire OX8 1RJ
Over the Chapel, the Tower was used by Alexander Pope during the summers of 1717 and 1718, while he translated the 5th volume of Homer's Illiad and was the inspiration for other houses planned by Pope. The Chapel has a fan-vaulted Chancel roof and wooden moulded ceiling in the Nave. Still used by both Parish and Manor House.
Grant Recipient/Owner: The Hon. Mrs Gascoigne
Access contact: The Hon. Mrs Gascoigne
Tel: 01865 881928 **Fax:** 01865 880117
Opening Arrangements: Open 15, 26 & 29 April; 3, 6, 17, 20, 24 & 27 May; 14, 17 & 28 June; 1, 5, 8, 19 & 22 July; 2, 5, 16, 19, 23 & 26 August; 6, 9, 20 & 23 September; and Bank Holiday Mondays 2 - 6pm. Groups by prior arrangement with the Hon. Mrs Gascoigne at the Manor House.
Heritage Open Days: No
Ⓟ Yes. Spaces: 15
♿ Yes. Disabled WC: Yes. Guide Dogs: Yes
£ Yes
Adult: £5.00 House & Garden, £3.00 Garden only.
Child: Under 12 £3.00 House & Garden, £2.00 Garden only.
Other: £3.00 (senior) House & Garden , £2.00 Garden only.

Shotover Park

Wheatley, Oxfordshire OX33 1QS
Early 18th century garden follies. The Gothic Temple (designer unknown) lies east of the house at the end of a long canal vista. Has a battlemented gable with a central pinnacle and a rose-window, below which is an open loggia of three pointed arches. The other temple, west of the house, designed by William Kent, is of a domed octagonal construction.
Grant Recipient/Owner: Sir John Miller
Access contact: Sir John Miller
Tel: 01865 872450
Opening Arrangements: Access to Temples at all reasonable times (lie close to public rights of way). Parking for a few cars at the Gothic Temple, otherwise other arrangements can be made in advance with Sir John Miller on 01865 872450 or Mrs Price on 01865 874095. Wheelchair access to the Gothic Temple with assistance.
Heritage Open Days: Yes
Ⓟ Yes. Spaces: 50
♿ Partial. Disabled WC: No. Guide Dogs: Yes
£ No

Stonor Chapel

Stonor Park, Henley-on-Thames, Oxfordshire RG9 6HF
Medieval Catholic Chapel used throughout the years of Catholic repression.
Grant Recipient/Owner: Lord Camoys
Access contact: Ms Lisa Absalom
Tel: 01491 638587 **Fax:** 0870 128 6834
Email Address: lisa@stonorpark.demon.co.uk
Opening Arrangements: April - September: Sundays and Bank Holiday Mondays, plus Sundays and Wednesdays in July and August; also Saturdays 26 May and 25 August 2 - 5.30pm (last admission 5pm). Groups by prior arrangement Tuesday - Thursday. Open for Mass 10.30am on Sundays and Days of Holy Obligation. Admission charge to House, Chapel and Gardens (£4.50 for adults, children are free) but none to visit Chapel only. Wheelchair access to Chapel very limited and none to House.
Heritage Open Days: No
Ⓟ Yes. Spaces: 100
♿ Partial. Disabled WC: No. Guide Dogs: No
£ No

Swalcliffe Tithe Barn

Shipston Road, Swalcliffe, nr. Banbury, Oxfordshire
15th century barn built by New College, Oxford, for estates in north Oxfordshire. Built for the Rectorial Manor of Swalcliffe by New College, who owned the Manor. Constructed between 1400 and 1409, much of the medieval timber half-cruck roof remains intact.
Grant Recipient/Owner:
Oxfordshire Building Trust Ltd

Access contact: Mr Martyn Brown
Tel: 01993 814114 **Fax:** 01993 813239
Email Address: martyn.brown@oxfordshire.gov.uk
Opening Arrangements: Easter - end of October: Sundays and Bank Holidays 2 - 5pm. At other times by prior arrangement (contact Jeff Demmar 01295 788278).
Heritage Open Days: Yes
Ⓟ Yes. Spaces: 10
♿ Yes. Disabled WC: Yes. Guide Dogs: Yes
£ No

Tudor House

East Hagbourne, Oxfordshire OX11 9LR
Early 17th century barn with thatched roof and queen post construction. Three bays and an aisle on one side. Original wattle and daub infill at ends only.
Grant Recipient/Owner: Mr I C Barfoot
Access contact: Mr I C Barfoot
Tel: 01235 818968 **Fax:** 01235 818968
Opening Arrangements:
By prior arrangement. Parking on street.
Heritage Open Days: No
Ⓟ See above
♿ Partial. Disabled WC: No. Guide Dogs: Yes
£ No

Tusmore Park Old Granary & Dovecote

Tusmore, nr. Bicester, Oxfordshire OX27 7SP
Timber framed structure of a type peculiar to Oxfordshire. 16th century but may be earlier, the top storey was converted into a dovecote probably in the 18th century.
Grant Recipient/Owner: Tusmore Park Holdings SA
Access contact: A D T Barkas
Tel: 01869 346075 **Fax:** 01869 346003
Opening Arrangements: By prior arrangement in August.
Heritage Open Days: No
Ⓟ Yes. Spaces: 5
♿ Yes. Disabled WC: No. Guide Dogs: Yes
£ No

SHROPSHIRE

2/3 Milk Street

Shrewsbury, Shropshire
Timber-framed 2 and a half storey building dating from the 15th century with later alterations and additions. Medieval shop front to rear. Still a shop.
Grant Recipient/Owner: Mr M J Cockle
Access contact: Mr Peter Napier
Tel: 01743 236789
Opening Arrangements: Ground floor shop open 6 days a week all year, upper floor flats can be visited only by prior arrangement with Mr Peter Napier, Pooks, 26 Claremont Hill, Shrewsbury, Shropshire SY1 1RE (tel.01743 236789). Wheelchair access to ground floor only.
Heritage Open Days: No
Ⓟ No
♿ Partial. Disabled WC: No. Guide Dogs: No
£ No

Attingham Park

Atcham, Shrewsbury, Shropshire SY4 4TP
Built 1785 by George Steuart for the 1st Lord Berwick, with a picture gallery by John Nash. Contains Regency interiors, Italian neo-classical furniture and Grand Tour paintings. Park landscaped by Repton in 1797.
Grant Recipient/Owner: The National Trust
Access contact: The Property Manager
Tel: 01743 708162 **Fax:** 01743 708175
Email Address: matsec@smtp.ntrust.org.uk
Opening Arrangements: House: 30 March - 28 October; daily except Wednesdays and Thursdays 1 - 4.30pm (last admission 4pm). Park: all year, except Christmas Day; March - October 9am - 8pm, November - February 9am - 5pm.
Heritage Open Days: No
Ⓟ Yes. Spaces: 150
♿ Yes. Disabled WC: Yes. Guide Dogs: Yes
£ Yes
Adult: £4.30
Child: £2.15
Other: £10.75 (family)

Benthall Hall

Broseley, Shropshire TF12 5RX
16th century stone house situated on a plateau above the gorge of the River Severn, with mullioned and transomed windows, carved oak staircase, decorated plaster ceilings and oak panelling. Also has a restored plantsman's garden, old kitchen garden and a Restoration church.
Grant Recipient/Owner: The National Trust
Access contact: The Custodian
Tel: 01952 882159
Opening Arrangements: 1 April - 30 September: Wednesdays, Sundays and Bank Holiday Mondays 1.30 -

5.30pm. Groups by prior arrangement with the Custodian. Wheelchair access to ground floor of Hall and part of garden only.
Heritage Open Days: No
P Yes. Spaces: 50
⌂ Partial. Disabled WC: No. Guide Dogs:Yes
£ Yes
Adult: £3.50
Child: £1.75
Other: £2.25 (garden only)

Blodwell Summerhouse

Blodwell Hall, Llanyblodwell, Oswestry, Shropshire SY10 8LT
Square red brick summerhouse with ashlar dressings and slate roof, built 1718, at end of terrace in a restored formal garden.
Grant Recipient/Owner:
Trustees of the Bradford Estate
Access contact: Mr R J Taylor
Tel: 07977 239955
Opening Arrangements: By prior arrangement.
Heritage Open Days: No
P Yes. Spaces: 2
⌂ Yes. Disabled WC: No. Guide Dogs: Yes
£ No

Bromfield Priory Gatehouse

nr. Ludlow, Shropshire
The Benedictine monks of Bromfield Priory added a new stone gatehouse before 1400, and after the Dissolution a timber-framed upper storey was added to this. The main room over the arch was used for the manorial court; then as the village school, ending up as the parish recreational room.
Website Address: www.landmarktrust.co.uk
Grant Recipient/Owner: The Landmark Trust
Access contact: Ms Victoria Piggott
Tel: 01628 825920   **Fax:** 01628 825417
Email Address: vpiggott@landmarktrust.co.uk
Opening Arrangements: The Landmark Trust is an independent charity, which rescues small buildings of historic or architectural importance from decay or unsympathetic improvement. Landmark's aim is to promote the enjoyment of these historic buildings by making them available to stay in for holidays. Bromfield Priory Gatehouse can be rented by anyone, at all times of the year, for periods ranging from a weekend to three weeks. Bookings can be made by telephoning the Booking Office on 01628 825925. As the building is in full-time use for holiday accommodation, it is not normally open to the public. However the public can view the building by prior arrangement by telephoning the access contact (Victoria Piggott on 01628 825920) to make an appointment. Potential visitors will be asked to write to confirm the details of their visit.
Heritage Open Days: No
P Yes. Spaces: 1
⌂ No. Disabled WC: No. Guide Dogs: Yes
£ No

Dudmaston

Quatt, Bridgnorth, Shropshire WV15 6QN
Queen Anne mansion of red brick with stone dressings, situated in parkland overlooking the Severn. Contains furniture, Dutch flower paintings, contemporary paintings and sculpture.
Grant Recipient/Owner: The National Trust
Access contact: The Administrator
Tel: 01746 780866   **Fax:** 01746 780744
Email Address: mduefe@smtp.ntrust.org.uk
Opening Arrangements: 1 April - 30 September. House & Garden: Tuesdays, Wednesdays, Sundays and Bank Holiday Mondays 2 - 5.30pm; Garden: Mondays, Tuesdays, Wednesdays and Sundays 12 - 6pm. Groups by prior arrangement on Monday afternoons only. Tea Room open same days as garden, 11.30am - 5.30pm; Shop open same days as garden, 1.30 - 5.30pm. Wheelchair access to main and inner halls, Library, oak room, No 1 and Derby galleries, old kitchen, garden and grounds (some estate walks).
Heritage Open Days: No
P Yes. Spaces: 150
⌂ Partial. Disabled WC: Yes. Guide Dogs: Yes
£ Yes
Adult: £3.85
Child: £2.30
Other: £9.00 (family), £2.80 (garden only).

Hawkstone Hall

Marchamley, Shrewsbury, Shropshire SY4 5LG
Grade I Georgian mansion and restored gardens set in spacious parkland. Ancestral home of the Hill family from 1556-1906.
Grant Recipient/Owner: Rector & Trustees of Hawkstone Hall/ Redemptorists
Access contact: Guest Mistress
Tel: 01630 685242   **Fax:** 01630 685565
Opening Arrangements: 5 - 31 August 2 - 5pm, plus

Spring Bank Holiday Monday.
Heritage Open Days: No
P Yes. Spaces: 40
⌂ Yes. Disabled WC: No. Guide Dogs: Yes
£ Yes
Adult: £3.50
Child: £1.00

Hospital of the Undivided Trinity

Clun, Shropshire
Founded in 1607 by Henry Howard, Earl of Northampton and built in 1618 with alterations of 1857. Dwellings and other rooms arranged around a square courtyard. A well preserved example of a courtyard-plan almshouses.
Grant Recipient/Owner:
The Trustees of Trinity Hospital
Access contact: Mr B Corley
Tel: 01588 640830
Opening Arrangements: By prior arrangement with the Warden, Mr Corley. Gardens and chapel open each day apart from Christmas Day.
Heritage Open Days: No
P Yes. Spaces: 4
⌂ Yes. Disabled WC: No. Guide Dogs: Yes
£ No

Langley Gatehouse

Acton Burnell, Shropshire
This gatehouse has two quite different faces: one is of plain dressed stone; the other, which once looked inwards to long demolished Langley Hall, is timber-framed. It was probably used for the Steward or important guests. It was rescued from a point of near collapse and shows repair work of an exemplary quality.
Website Address: www.landmarktrust.co.uk
Grant Recipient/Owner: The Landmark Trust
Access contact: Ms Victoria Piggott
Tel: 01628 825920   **Fax:** 01628 825417
Email Address: vpiggott@landmarktrust.co.uk
Opening Arrangements: The Landmark Trust is an independent charity, which rescues small buildings of historic or architectural importance from decay or unsympathetic improvement. Landmark's aim is to promote the enjoyment of these historic buildings by making them available to stay in for holidays. Langley Gatehouse can be rented by anyone, at all times of the year, for periods ranging from a weekend to three weeks. Bookings can be made by telephoning the Booking Office on 01628 825925. As the building is in full-time use for holiday accommodation, it is not normally open to the public. However the public can view the building by prior arrangement by telephoning the access contact (Victoria Piggott on 01628 825920) to make an appointment. Potential visitors will be asked to write to confirm the details of their visit.
Heritage Open Days: No
P Yes. Spaces: 2
⌂ No. Disabled WC: No. Guide Dogs: Yes
£ No

Porch House

Bishop's Castle, Shropshire SY9 5BE
Originally built as 'L' shaped timber-framed building, probably house, 1565 and subsequently infilled and partly re-built. Now used as owner's house with shop and self-contained flats. Ground floor front wall recently completely re-built.
Grant Recipient/Owner: Mrs J McColl
Access contact: Mrs J McColl
Tel: 01588 638854   **Fax:** 01938 555851
Opening Arrangements: By prior written arrangement.
Heritage Open Days: No
P No
⌂ No. Disabled WC: No. Guide Dogs: Yes
£ No

St Winifred's Well

Woolston, nr. Oswestry, Shropshire
St Winifred was a 7th century Welsh princess who was brought back to life after being decapitated by an angry suitor. The well here has been venerated for centuries and the little building above was the well chapel, a miraculous survival preserved since the Reformation as a court house and then cottage. Approached by a public footpath.
Website Address: www.landmarktrust.co.uk
Grant Recipient/Owner: The Landmark Trust
Access contact: Ms Victoria Piggott
Tel: 01628 825920   **Fax:** 01628 825417
Email Address: vpiggott@landmarktrust.co.uk
Opening Arrangements: The Landmark Trust is an independent charity, which rescues small buildings of historic or architectural importance from decay or unsympathetic improvement. Landmark's aim is to promote the enjoyment of these historic buildings by making them available to stay in for holidays. St Winifred's Well can be rented by anyone, at all times of the year, for periods ranging from a weekend to three weeks. Bookings can be made by telephoning the Booking Office

on 01628 825925. As the building is in full-time use for holiday accommodation, it is not normally open to the public. However the public can view the building by prior arrangement by telephoning the access contact (Victoria Piggott on 01628 825920) to make an appointment. Potential visitors will be asked to write to confirm the details of their visit. Roadside parking only.
Heritage Open Days: No
P Yes. Spaces: 1
⌂ No. Disabled WC: No. Guide Dogs: Yes
£ No

Weston Park

Weston-under-Lizard, Shifnal, Shropshire TF11 8LE
Stately home, built 1671, designed by Lady Wibraham. Houses collection of paintings by Van Dyck, Gainsborough, Lely and Stubbs, and is surrounded by 1000 acres of 'Capability' Brown parkland and formal gardens. Formerly home to the Earls of Bradford, now held in trust for the nation by The Weston Park Foundation.
Website Address: www.weston-park.com
Grant Recipient/Owner: Weston Park Foundation
Access contact: Mr Colin Sweeney
Tel: 01952 852100   **Fax:** 01952 850430
Email Address: enquiries@weston-park.com
Opening Arrangements: Easter 14-16 April - 30 June: weekends only; 30 June - 31 August: daily; 31 August - 16 September: weekends only, 11am - 5pm. Wheelchair access to all areas except open parkland and some formal gardens.
Heritage Open Days: No
P Yes. Spaces: 300
⌂ Partial. Disabled WC: Yes. Guide Dogs: Yes
£ Yes
Adult: £2.50
Child: £1.50
Other: £2.00

SOMERSET

Bath Assembly Rooms

Bennett Street, Bath, Somerset BA1 2QH
Built in 1771 by John Wood the Younger, now owned by the National Trust and administered by Bath and North East Somerset District Council. Each of the rooms has a complete set of original chandeliers. The Museum of Costume is located on the lower ground floor.
Grant Recipient/Owner:
Bath City Council/National Trust
Access contact: Mrs P C Ruddock
Tel: 01225 477752   **Fax:** 01225 444793
Email Address: penny_ruddock@bathnes.gov.uk
Opening Arrangements: Daily 10am - 5pm when not in use for pre-booked functions. Telephone in advance (01225 477789) to check availability. There are no pre-booked functions during the day during August. Closed Christmas Day and Boxing Day. On-street car parking available with pre-paid voucher.
Heritage Open Days: No
P See above
⌂ Yes. Disabled WC: Yes. Guide Dogs: Yes
£ No

Dovecote

adjacent to Church Memorial Garden, Priory Green, Dunster, Somerset
Scheduled medieval circular tower dovecote 8.5 metres high with internal diameter of 4.5 metres. Probably 13-14th century part of the monastic estate of the Benedictine Priory of Dunster, a cell of Bath Priory, sent to build the church of St George in 1150. Contains over 500 nest sites lining the 4' thick round stone wall, which was served by a revolving ladder from a central vertical ash post with two alighting platforms for feeding the birds when enclosed.
Grant Recipient/Owner: Dunster Parish Council
Access contact: M P Grantham
Tel: 01643 821812
Opening Arrangements: Interior can be viewed all year from barred doorway, otherwise access by arrangement with the Reverend M P Grantham, The Rectory, St George's Street, Dunster TA24 6RS (tel.01643 821812) or the Churchwarden (tel.01643 708056).
Heritage Open Days: No
P No
⌂ No. Disabled WC: No. Guide Dogs: Yes
£ No

Dunster Castle

Dunster, nr. Minehead, Somerset TA24 6SL
Sited atop a wooded hill, there has been a castle on the site since Norman times. The 13th century gatehouse survives, but the present building was remodelled in 1862-72 by Antony Salvin for the Luttrell family.
Website Address: www.nationaltrust.org.uk

Grant Recipient/Owner: The National Trust
Access contact: The Property Manager
Tel: 01643 821314 **Fax:** 01643 823000
Opening Arrangements: Castle: 31 March to 4 November; daily (except Thursdays and Fridays) at the following times: 31 March to 26 September 11am - 5pm; 29 September to 4 November 11am - 4pm. Garden and park: daily (closed 25/26 December) at the following times: January to March, 29 September to 31 December 11am - 4pm; 31 March to 28 September 10am - 5pm. Castle is a ten-minute steep climb from car park. Multi-seater vehicle available for lifts if required. Castle is accessible to manual wheelchairs via stairclimber. Castle and garden on steep hill.
Heritage Open Days: No
P Yes. Spaces: 180
♿ Partial. Disabled WC: Yes. Guide Dogs: Yes
£ Yes
Adult: £6.00 (Castle, garden & park). £3.00 (garden & park).
Child: £3.00 (Castle, garden & park). £1.50 (garden & park).
Other: £15.00 (family; Castle, garden & park). £7.50 (family; garden & park). Separate rates for booked groups.

Empire & Commonwealth Museum

Clock Tower Yard, Temple Meads, Bristol BS1 6QH
Museum housed in world's earliest surviving railway terminus, which was completed in 1840 and was originally part of the Great Western Railway designed by I.K. Brunel. Over 220ft long with timber and iron roof spans of 72ft, this Grade I listed building has been nominated as a world heritage site. Contains the Passenger shed and the adjoining former Engine and Carriage shed, the latter currently holds the Museum's temporary exhibitions until a permanent gallery opens in 2002.
Website Address: www.empiremuseum.co.uk
Grant Recipient/Owner: Empire Museum Ltd
Access contact: Ms Holly Bown
Tel: 0117 925 4980 **Fax:** 0117 9254983
Email Address: staff@empiremuseum.co.uk
Opening Arrangements: Daily 10am - 6pm.
Heritage Open Days: Yes
P Yes. Spaces: 25
♿ Yes. Disabled WC: Yes. Guide Dogs: Yes
£ No

Englishcombe Tithe Barn

Rectory Farmhouse, Englishcombe, Bath, Somerset BA2 9DU
Early 14th century cruck framed tithe barn. Recently restored with new crucks, masonry and straw lining to the roof, and filigree windows unblocked. There are masons and other markings on the walls. Now used as a venue, principally for wedding receptions.
Website Address: www.barnhire.com
Grant Recipient/Owner: Mrs Jennie Walker
Access contact: Mrs Jennie Walker
Tel: 01225 425073
Email Address: tithebarn@ntlworld.com
Opening Arrangements: 15 - 20 April, 6 - 11 May, 27 May - 1 June, 25 - 29 June and 26 - 30 August, 3 - 6pm. At other times by prior arrangement.
Heritage Open Days: Yes
P Yes. Spaces: 34
♿ Yes. Disabled WC: Yes. Guide Dogs: Yes
£ No
£1 per person donation requested from groups.

Eyre Mortuary Chapel

Perrymead Cemetery, Bath, Somerset
Mid-19th century Gothic Revival Catholic building, built as a mortuary chapel for the Eyre family. Constructed of Bath stone from the designs of Charles Hanson. The interior has recessed arches supported on columns of Devonshire marble, a screen of hammered ironwork and an elaborate marble altar with a Minton tile floor.
Grant Recipient/Owner: Trustees of the Eyre Mortuary Chapel
Access contact: Mrs B Carruthers
Tel: 01684 292600 **Fax:** 01684 292042
Opening Arrangements: By prior arrangement with Mrs B Carruthers, Walton Cardiff Manor, nr. Tewkesbury, Gloucestershire GL20 7BL (tel.01684 292600). Donation requested.
Heritage Open Days: No
P Yes. Spaces: 4
♿ No. Disabled WC: No. Guide Dogs: Yes
£ No

Forde Abbey

Chard, Somerset TA20 4LU
Cistercian monastery founded in 1140 and dissolved in 1539 when the monks quarters were demolished. The monks quarters were converted in 1640 into an Italian style "palazzo" by Sir Edmund Prideaux. Interior has plaster

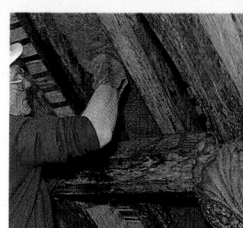

ceilings and Mortlake tapestries.
Website Address: www.fordeabbey.co.uk
Grant Recipient/Owner: Trustees of the Roper Settlement
Access contact: Mrs Clay
Tel: 01460 220231
Opening Arrangements: Gardens: daily 10am - 4.30pm. House: April - October; Tuesday - Thursday, Sunday and Bank Holidays 1 - 4.30pm. Access for wheelchairs and guide dogs to garden only.
Heritage Open Days: No
P Yes. Spaces: 500
♿ See above. Disabled WC: No. Guide Dogs: See above
£ Yes
Adult: £5.20 house & garden, £4.00 gardens (provisional).
Child: Free
Other: £5.00 (seniors) house and garden, £3.80 gardens only (provisional).

Gants Mill

Gants Mill Lane, Bruton, Somerset BA10 0DB
Working watermill with deeds dating back to owner John le Gaunt in 1290. The documents were saved for posterity by the model for "Tom Jones's" Sophia Weston. Corn grinding demonstrations, historical displays and timeline of a millennium of milling - corn, wool and silk.
Website Address: www.gantsmill.co.uk
Grant Recipient/Owner: Mr Brian Shingler
Access contact: Brian & Alison Shingler
Tel: 01749 812393
Email Address: shingler@gantsmill.co.uk
Opening Arrangements: Mill: Easter - end of May, Thursdays and Bank Holiday Mondays; Mill & Garden: June - end of September, Sundays, Thursdays and Bank Holiday Mondays 2 - 5pm. Groups by prior arrangement. Refreshments available.
Heritage Open Days: No
P Yes. Spaces: 20
♿ No. Disabled WC: No. Guide Dogs: Yes
£ Yes
Adult: £3.50
Child: £1.00
Other: Group reductions by arrangement.

Great House Farm

Theale, Wedmore, Somerset BS28 4SJ
17th century farmhouse with Welsh slate roof, oak doors and some original diamond paned windows. Inside is a carved well staircase with two murals on the walls. There are four servants rooms at the top, three of which are dark and occupied by Lesser Horseshoe bats.
Grant Recipient/Owner: Mr A R Millard
Access contact: Mr A R Millard
Tel: 01934 713133
Opening Arrangements: April - August: Tuesdays and Thursdays 2 - 6pm by prior telephone arrangement.
Heritage Open Days: No
P Yes. Spaces: 6
♿ No. Disabled WC: No. Guide Dogs: Yes
£ Yes
Adult: £2.00

Gurney Manor

Cannington, Somerset TA5 2MW
Late medieval house built around a courtyard. Used as a tenant farm before converted into flats in the 1940s, now restored to its original undivided state.
Website Address: www.landmarktrust.co.uk
Grant Recipient/Owner: The Landmark Trust
Access contact: Ms Victoria Piggott
Tel: 01628 825920 **Fax:** 01628 825417
Email Address: vpiggott@landmarktrust.co.uk
Opening Arrangements: The Landmark Trust is an independent charity, which rescues small buildings of historic or architectural importance from decay or unsympathetic improvement. Landmark's aim is to promote the enjoyment of these historic buildings by making them available to stay in for holidays. Gurney Manor can be rented by anyone, at all times of the year, for periods ranging from a weekend to three weeks. Bookings can be made by telephoning the Booking Office on 01628 825925. As the building is in full-time use for holiday accommodation, it is not normally open to the public. However the public can view the building by prior arrangement by telephoning the house (Victoria Piggott on 01628 825920) to make an appointment. Potential visitors will be asked to write to confirm the details of their visit.
Heritage Open Days: No
P Yes. Spaces: 3
♿ No. Disabled WC: No. Guide Dogs: Yes
£ No

Hall Farm High Barn

Stogumber, Taunton, Somerset TA4 3TQ
17th century Grade II* listed building with seven bays of red local sandstone rubble with jointed cruck roof. South wall supported by four buttresses but there are none on

the North wall. There are blocked windows on the South wall and two stub walls extend north. Lines of joist holes were provided for internal flooring and the two main entrances were to the north and south.
Grant Recipient/Owner: Mr G R Hayes
Access contact: Mr G R Hayes
Tel: 01984 656321
Opening Arrangements: By prior arrangement with Mr G R Hayes at Hall Farm.
Heritage Open Days: No
P Yes. Spaces: 4
♿ Yes. Disabled WC: No. Guide Dogs: Yes
£ No

Hestercombe

Cheddon Fitzpaine, Taunton, Somerset TA2 8LG
Formal gardens, featuring terraces, rills and an orangery, designed by Sir Edwin Lutyens and Gertrude Jekyll. The newly restored Landscape Garden was designed by Bampfylde in 1750 and comprises 40 acre pleasure grounds with classical temples and a Great Cascade.
Website Address: www.hestercombegardens.com
Grant Recipient/Owner: Somerset County Council
Access contact: Mrs J Manning
Tel: 01823 413923 **Fax:** 01823 413747
Email Address: info@hestercombegardens.com
Opening Arrangements: Every day of the year, including Christmas Day, 10am - 5pm (last admission). Limited wheelchair access.
Heritage Open Days: No
P Yes. Spaces: 100
♿ Partial. Disabled WC: Yes. Guide Dogs: Yes
£ Yes
Adult: £3.60
Child: £1.00 (5-15yrs)

Lancin Farmhouse

Wambrook, Chard, Somerset TA20 3EG
14th century farmhouse with old oak beams, fireplaces with the original smoking thatch, flagstone floors and breadoven.
Grant Recipient/Owner: Mr S J Smith
Access contact: Mrs R A Smith
Tel: 01460 62290
Opening Arrangements: June - October: Monday - Thursday 2 - 5pm by prior arrangement.
Heritage Open Days: No
P Yes. Spaces: 5
♿ No. Disabled WC: No. Guide Dogs: No
£ Yes
Adult: £3.00

Lytes Cary Manor

nr. Charlton Mackrell, Somerton, Somerset TA11 7HU
Manor house with a 14th century chapel and Tudor Great Hall, much added to in the 16th century and rescued from dereliction by Sir Walter Jenner in the 20th century. The interiors have been refurbished in period style.
Website Address: www.nationaltrust.org.uk
Grant Recipient/Owner: The National Trust
Access contact: Property Manger
Tel: 01985 843600 **Fax:** 01985 843624
Email Address: wlybxp@smtp.ntrust.org.uk
Opening Arrangements: 2 April to 31 October: Monday, Wednesday and Saturdays 2- 6pm or dusk if earlier; also Fridays in June, July and August 2 - 6pm. Wheelchair access to garden only.
Heritage Open Days: No
P Yes. Spaces: 50
♿ Partial. Disabled WC: Yes. Guide Dogs: Yes
£ Yes
Adult: £4.50
Child: £2.00

Merefield House Gazebo

East Street, Crewkerne, Somerset TA18 7AB
18th century garden house/gazebo, set in walled terraced town garden, approached by flight of steps. The stucco faced cube building has steep Dutch gable, supporting large lead eagle and sundial to the front. Virtually complete 18th century interior with hemispherical dome in the centre with vine leaves and grapes, set in a square moulded frame, with views over Crewkerne and the Dorset Hills.
Grant Recipient/Owner: Mr Roger Rousell
Access contact: Mr Roger Rousell
Tel: 01460 73222
Opening Arrangements: By prior arrangement with Mr Rousell at Merefield House.
Heritage Open Days: Yes
P No
♿ No. Disabled WC: No. Guide Dogs: Yes
£ No

The Old Manse

14 Bath Road, Beckington, Somerset BA3 6SW
Late 16th/early 17th century gabled stone built dwelling

with mullioned windows with transoms to front elevation and stone tiled roof. Contains 2 large Plantagenet/Tudor fireplaces, 16th century oak staircase, strapwork ceilings and transitional rococo fireplaces. Gallery of attic rooms reveal an unusual roof structure.
Grant Recipient/Owner: Mr J Evans
Access contact: Mr J Evans
Tel: 01373 831401   **Fax:** 01373 831401
Email Address: jennie@stackridge.com
Opening Arrangements: By prior arrangement. On street parking.
Heritage Open Days: Yes
P See above
No. Guide Dogs: Yes
£ No

Orchard Wyndham

Williton, Somerset TA4 4HH
Manor house, originally medieval but with many subsequent alterations and additions. Family home of the Wyndhams and their ancestors, the Orchards and Sydenhams, for 700 years.
Grant Recipient/Owner: Wyndham Estate
Access contact: Estate Office
Tel: 01984 632309   **Fax:** 01984 633526
Email Address: wyndhamest@talk21.com
Opening Arrangements: August: Thursdays and Fridays 2 - 5pm, Bank Holiday 11am - 5pm, by guided tour (groups of maximum 8 persons, last tour 4pm). At other times by prior arrangement (at least 2 weeks notice requested). Wheelchair access to ground floor and gardens only.
Heritage Open Days: No
P Yes. Spaces: 25
Partial. Disabled WC: No. Guide Dogs: Yes
£ Yes
Adult: £5.00
Child: £1.00 (under 12)

Penniless Porch

Market Place, Wells, Somerset BA5 2RB
Comprising the upper two floors of the mid-15th century gateway to the Close, together with the 17th/18th century eastward extension associated with it. The gatehouse belongs to the improvements to the Close and Market Place under Bishop Thomas Bekynton, c1451, the adjoining eastern extension may incorporate fifteenth and sixteenth century fabric, but is ostensibly of the following two centuries, containing a good 18th century stair to the rear.
Grant Recipient/Owner:
Dean & Chapter of Wells Cathedral
Access contact: Mr Peter Bird
Tel: 01749 677561   **Fax:** 01749 676207
Email Address: wells@caroe.co.uk
Opening Arrangements: By prior telephone arrangement.
Heritage Open Days: No
P No
No. Disabled WC: No. Guide Dogs: No
£ No

Priest's House

Muchelney, Langport, Somerset TA10 0DQ
A late medieval hall house, built by Muchelney Abbey in 1308 for the parish priest and little altered since the hall was divided in the early 17th century. Interesting features include the Gothic doorway, beautiful tracery windows and a massive 15th century stone fireplace. The house is occupied and furnished by tenants.
Website Address: www.nationaltrust.org.uk
Grant Recipient/Owner: The National Trust
Access contact: Sir Anthony Denny
Tel: 01458 252621
Opening Arrangements: 1 April to 30 September: Sunday and Mondays 2.30 - 5.30pm; last admission 5.15pm. Parking in nearby roads.
Heritage Open Days: No
P See above
No. Disabled WC: No. Guide Dogs: Yes
£ Yes
Adult: £2.00
Child: £2.00

Prior Park College Chapel

Mansion & Old Gymnasium, Ralph Allen Drive, Bath, Somerset BA2 5AH
Built for Ralph Allen in the mid-18th century as an early and successful demonstration of the quality of Bath stone. The Chapel and Old Gymnasium are part of the mid-19th century additions to adapt the property as a Catholic seminary for Bishop Baines. Now a boarding and day school.
Website Address: www.priorpark.co.uk
Grant Recipient/Owner:
Governors of Prior Park College
Access contact: C J Freeman
Tel: 01225 837491   **Fax:** 01225 835753
Email Address: bursar@priorpark.co.uk

Opening Arrangements: Chapel: Sundays throughout the year for public worship, plus 17 June (to be confirmed), 2 - 5pm, otherwise by prior arrangement. Mansion: certain Sundays March - July 11.30am - 6pm, please telephone or e-mail for details, plus 17 June (to be confirmed) 2 - 5pm; also limited number of group tours in July and August by prior arrangement. Old Gymnasium: 10 July - 18 August, Monday - Fridays 10am - 4pm but please telephone in advance. Limited wheelchair access.
Heritage Open Days: No
P Yes. Spaces: 50
Partial. Disabled WC: No. Guide Dogs: Yes
£ Yes
Adult: £2.50
Child: £2.50
Other: £2.50

Robin Hood's Hut

Halswell Park, Goathurst, nr. Bridgwater, Somerset TA5 2DH
Thatched banqueting house, built in the 1760s to designs probably by Henry Keene, Surveyor of the Fabric at Westminster Abbey. Designed to look like a hermit's hut from the South, its Northern Italianate loggia has views over the Bristol Channel.
Grant Recipient/Owner:
Somerset Building Preservation Trust Ltd
Access contact: Mr D R Miller
Tel: 01460 52604
Opening Arrangements: Access to the exterior of the building and umbrello at all times. Access to the interior by prior arrangement with Mr D R Miller of the Somerset Building Preservation Trust, Acacia House, 37 Station Road, Ilminster, Somerset TA19 9BG (tel.01460 52604) or The Landmark Trust, Shottesbrooke, Maidenhead, Berkshire SL6 3SW (tel.01628 825920). One mile country walk with stiles.
Heritage Open Days: Yes
P No
No. Disabled WC: No. Guide Dogs: Yes
£ No

Rowes Leadworks

('Wildscreen at Bristol' and Firehouse restaurant), Deanery Road, Harbourside, Bristol BS1 5DB
A former leadworks built in 19th century. One of a few surviving structures associated with the industrial character of this area with a goods station and nearby warehouses. Now transformed into a restaurant/bar, 'The Firehouse Rotisseries'. Attached to this is a modern canopied, large open structure, the entrance to 'Wildscreen at Bristol' which features imagery and interactive exhibits of the natural world. It includes an Imax cinema and living botanical house.
Website Address: www.at-bristol.org.uk
Grant Recipient/Owner: Bristol City Council
Access contact: Mr Gerwyn House
Tel: 0117 9092000   **Fax:** 0117 9157202
Email Address: gerwyn.house@at-bristol.org.uk
Opening Arrangements: All venues: 10am - 6pm. Possible late openings for August (ring for confirmation). Parking is operated by Bristol City Council and there is a charge.
Heritage Open Days: No
P Yes. Spaces: 500
Yes. Disabled WC: Yes. Guide Dogs: Yes
£ No. Charges for access to 'Wildscreen at Bristol'.

Rowlands Mill

Rowlands, Ilminster, Somerset TA19 9LE
Grade II* stone and brick 3-storey millhouse and machinery, c1620, with a mill pond, mill race, overshooting wheel and waterfall. The millhouse is now a holiday let but the machinery has separate access and is in working condition.
Grant Recipient/Owner: Mr P G H Speke
Access contact: Mr P G H Speke
Tel: 01460 52623   **Fax:** 01460 52623
Opening Arrangements: Millhouse Fridays and machinery Monday - Friday 10am - 4pm by prior written arrangement (at least 1 week's notice required). Heritage Open Days machinery only unless a Friday, then whole building.
Heritage Open Days: Yes
P Yes. Spaces: 7
No. Disabled WC: No. Guide Dogs: Yes
£ Yes
Adult: £3.00
Child: Free
Other: Free

Temple of Harmony

Halswell Park, Goathurst, nr. Bridgwater, Somerset TA5 2DH
18th century folly, a copy of the Temple of Verilis, forms part of the 18th century Pleasure Gardens at Halswell House. Restored in 1994.
Website Address: www.somersite.co.uk/temple.htm
Grant Recipient/Owner: Halswell Park Trust

Access contact: Mr H M Humphreys
Tel: 01823 443955
Email Address: mick@somersite.co.uk
Opening Arrangements: 1 June - end of September: Saturdays and Sundays 2 - 5pm, plus Easter Weekend and May Day Bank Holiday. Any other day by prior arrangement with Mr H M Humphreys, Honorary Secretary, The Halswell Park Trust, Creech Barn, Creech St Michael, Taunton, Somerset TA3 5PP (tel.01823 443955).
Heritage Open Days: Yes
P Yes. Spaces: 4
No. Disabled WC: No. Guide Dogs: Yes
£ Yes
Adult: £1.00
Child: 50p
Other: 50p (senior citizens)

Wells Old Almshouses

Chamberlain Street, Wells, Somerset
Comprises 4 unchanged almshouses, the oldest dating from 1435, with a Guild Room, chapel and gardens.
Grant Recipient/Owner: Wells Old Almshouses Trust
Access contact: Mr Adrian I'Anson
Tel: 01749 677499
Email Address: adrian.ianson@virginnet.co.uk
Opening Arrangements: Heritage Open Days, and at other times by prior arrangement with the Secretary, Wells Old Almshouses Trust, 66 Portway, Wells, Somerset BA5 2BP (tel.01749 677499).
Heritage Open Days: Yes
P No
Yes. Disabled WC: No. Guide Dogs: Yes
£ No

Westbury College

Westbury-on-Trym, Bristol, Somerset
The 15th century gatehouse of the College of Priests (founded in the 13th century), of which John Wycliff was prebend.
Website Address: www.nationaltrust.org.uk
Grant Recipient/Owner: The National Trust
Access contact: Rev G M Collins
Tel: 0117 926 1536
Opening Arrangements: Access by key only, to be collected by written or telephone appointment with Rev GM Collins, The Vicarage, 44 Eastfield Road, Westbury on Trym, Bristol, BS9 4AG (tel: 0117 926 1536, or the National Trust Wessex Regional Office: 01985 843600). Wheelchair access to ground floor only. Street parking only.
Heritage Open Days: No
P See above
Partial. Disabled WC: No. Guide Dogs: Yes
£ Yes
Adult: £1.10
Child: £0.50
Other: £0.50

SOUTH YORKSHIRE

Cusworth Hall

Museum of South Yorkshire Life, Cusworth Lane, Doncaster, South Yorkshire DN5 7TU
Grade I listed 18th century country house designed by George Platt with additions by James Paine, set in a landscaped park designed by Richard Woods. Home of the Battie-Wrightson family until 1952, now converted into a museum of South Yorkshire life.
Grant Recipient/Owner:
Doncaster Metropolitan Borough Council
Access contact: Mr F Carpenter
Tel: 01302 782342   **Fax:** 01302 782342
Email Address: museum@doncaster.gov.uk
Opening Arrangements: Monday - Friday 10am - 5pm, Saturdays 11am- 5pm, Sundays 1 - 5pm. Early closing at 4pm in December and January. Closed Christmas Day, Boxing Day and Good Friday. Wheelchair access to ground floor, tea room, shop and Great Kitchen. Refreshments available.
Heritage Open Days: No
P Yes. Spaces: 150
Partial. Disabled WC: Yes. Guide Dogs: Yes
£ No

The Mansion House

High Street, Doncaster, South Yorkshire DN1 1DG
One of only 3 Mansion Houses in the country, the others being in London and York. Originally built as a residence for the Mayor in the late 1740s, now used as a meeting place for the local authority. Contains ballroom with many paintings of local dignitaries, a banqueting room which is now used as the Council Chamber, the Peace Window at the top of the main staircase depicting local history and the coat of arms, and a kitchen with many original fittings.
Grant Recipient/Owner: The Chief Executive
Access contact: Mr Horace Shillito
Tel: 01302 734032   **Fax:** 01302 734040
Opening Arrangements: Monday - Friday 8.30am - 5pm and evenings by prior arrangement only with

Doncaster Metropolitan Borough Council, 2 Priory Place, Doncaster, South Yorkshire DN1 1BN (tel.01302 734032). Wheelchair access to upper floors restricted by small lift which will not accommodate large wheelchairs, for further information please check with council. Parking in town centre car parks during the day, street parking in evening. Disabled parking adjacent to property day and night.
Heritage Open Days: No
P See above
♿ Partial. Disabled WC: No. Guide Dogs: No
£ Yes
Adult: £2.00 (evenings only)

Moated Site & Chapel
Thorpe Lane, Thorpe-in-Balne, nr. Doncaster, South Yorkshire, DN6 0DY
Medieval chapel, moated site and fishponds. Built 12th century with 13th, 14th, 15th and 19th century alterations. Restored and reroofed in 1994/5. In 1452 the chapel was the scene of the forcible abduction of Joan, wife of Charles Nowel, by Edward Lancaster of Skipton in Craven, which resulted in the passing of an Act of Parliament for the redress of grievance and the better protection of females.
Grant Recipient/Owner: Mr Attey
Access contact: Mrs Attey
Tel: 01302 883160
Opening Arrangements: By prior arrangement with Mrs Attey at the Manor House.
Heritage Open Days: Yes
P Yes. Spaces: 10
♿ No. Disabled WC: No. Guide Dogs: Yes
£ No
Donation for charity welcomed.

STAFFORDSHIRE

10 The Close
Lichfield, Staffordshire WS13 7LD
Early 15th century timber-framed house, originally one-up one-down and part of a five-dwelling range in the Vicar's Close. Notable doors and solid tread staircase remains in attic. Currently residence of assistant cathedral organist.
Grant Recipient/Owner:
Dean & Chapter of Lichfield Cathedral
Access contact: Mr Robert Sharpe
Tel: 01543 306201
Opening Arrangements: By prior written arrangement.
Heritage Open Days: No
P No
♿ No. Disabled WC: No. Guide Dogs: Yes
£ No

2-6 The Close
Lichfield, Staffordshire WS13 7LD
External steps and handrails to (mainly) early 18th century houses in the Cathedral Close.
Grant Recipient/Owner:
The Dean & Chapter of Lichfield Cathedral
Access contact:
The Dean & Chapter of Lichfield Cathedral
Tel: 01543 306100   **Fax:** 01543 306109
Email Address: enquiries@lichfield-cathedral.org
Opening Arrangements: At all reasonable times (exterior only).
Heritage Open Days: No
P No
♿ Yes. Disabled WC: No. Guide Dogs: Yes
£ No

7 Vicar's Close
Cathedral Close, Lichfield, Staffordshire
Grade II* listed building forming part of the medieval complex constructed for the Lay Vicars' Choral of the Cathedral and arranged around two courtyards. Mostly 15th century timber-frame with brick stacks and brick rebuilding. Now a private residence.
Grant Recipient/Owner:
The Dean & Chapter of Lichfield Cathedral
Access contact:
The Dean & Chapter of Lichfield Cathedral
Tel: 01543 306100   **Fax:** 01543 306109
Email Address: enquiries@lichfield-cathedral.org
Opening Arrangements: By prior arrangement (21 days notice requested) with the Dean & Chapter of Lichfield Cathedral, 19a The Close, Lichfield, Staffordshire WS13 7LD (tel.01543 306100). Wheelchair access to ground floor only.
Heritage Open Days: No
P No
♿ Partial. Disabled WC: No. Guide Dogs: Yes
£ No

8/9 Vicar's Close
Lichfield, Staffordshire
Grade II* listed building forming part of the medieval complex constructed for the Lay Vicars' Choral of the Cathedral and arranged around two courtyards. Mostly 15th century timber-frame with brick stacks and brick rebuilding. Now a private residence.
Grant Recipient/Owner:
The Dean & Chapter of Lichfield Cathedral
Access contact:
The Dean & Chapter of Lichfield Cathedral
Tel: 01543 306100   **Fax:** 01543 306109
Email Address: enquiries@lichfield-cathedral.org
Opening Arrangements: By prior arrangement (21 days notice requested) with the Dean & Chapter of Lichfield Cathedral, 19a The Close, Lichfield, Staffordshire WS13 7LD (tel. 01543 306100). Wheelchair access to ground floor only.
Heritage Open Days: No
P No
♿ Partial. Disabled WC: No. Guide Dogs: Yes
£ No

Barlaston Hall
Barlaston, nr. Stoke-on-Trent, Staffordshire ST12 9AT
Mid-18th century Palladian villa attributed to Sir Robert Taylor, with public rooms containing some fine examples of 18th century plasterwork. Extensively restored during the 1990s.
Grant Recipient/Owner: Mr James Hall
Access contact: Mr James Hall
Fax: 01782 372391
Opening Arrangements: 6 March - 11 September: Tuesdays, entrance at 2,3,4 & 5pm.
Heritage Open Days: Yes
P Yes. Spaces: 6
♿ No. Disabled WC: No. Guide Dogs: No
£ Yes
Adult: £2.50
Child: £1.50
Other: No charge for Historic House Association members.

Biddulph Grange Garden
Biddulph, Stoke-on-Trent, Staffordshire ST8 7SD
Garden with series of connected apartments designed to display specimens from James Bateman's extensive and wide ranging plant collection. Visitors are taken on a miniature tour of the world featuring the Egyptian court, China, a Scottish glen, as well as a pineture and rock areas. West Wing also built by James Bateman houses the tea room, shop and toilets.
Website Address: www.nationaltrust.org.uk
Access contact: Christine Belford/Andrew Humphris
Tel: 01782 517999   **Fax:** 01782 510624
Email Address: mbgwxm@smtp.ntrust.org.uk
Opening Arrangements: 28 March to 4 November: Wednesdays to Fridays 12 noon - 6pm, Saturdays and Sundays 11am - 6pm (High Season). 10 November to 16 December: Saturdays and Sundays 12 noon to 4pm (Low Season). Wheelchair access to Lime Avenue, Lake, Pinetum, Cheshire Cottage, Egypt and East Terrace. West Wing open as for garden.
Heritage Open Days: No
P Yes. Spaces: 100
♿ Partial. Disabled WC: Yes. Guide Dogs: Yes
£ Yes
Adult: £4.40 (High Season). £2.00 (Low Season).
Child: £2.30 (High Season). £1.00 (Low Season).
Other: £11.00 (High Season). £5.00 (Low Season).

Claymills Pumping Engines
The Victorian Pumping Station, The Sewage Works, Meadow Lane, Stretton, Burton-on-Trent, Staffordshire DE13 0BA
Large Victorian steam-operated sewage pumping station built in 1885. Four beam engines housed in two Italianate engine houses, one operational on steaming weekends. Boiler house with range of five Lancashire boilers, large Victorian steam-operated workshop with blacksmith's forge, steam hammer, and steam driven machinery. 1930s dynamo house with very early D.C. generating equipment, earliest dynamo 1889 (all operational).
Grant Recipient/Owner: Severn Trent Water Ltd
Access contact: Mr Roy Barratt
Tel: 01283 534960
Email Address: roybarratt@yahoo.co.uk
Opening Arrangements: Steaming weekends: 31 December 2000 & 1 January, 15 - 16 April, 16 - 17 June, 26 - 27 August, 22 - 23 September, 20 - 21 October; otherwise open every Saturday throughout the year. Admission charged for steaming weekends, donations requested on other open days. Refreshments available. Wheelchair access to ground floor only (workshop, boiler house and engine house), shop and refreshment area. Parking for 6 coaches.
Heritage Open Days: Yes
P Yes. Spaces: 100

♿ Partial. Disabled WC: Yes. Guide Dogs: Yes
£ Yes
Adult: £2.00
Child: £1.00

Goat Maltings
Clarence Street Mill, Clarence Street, Burton-on-Trent, Staffordshire DE14 3LG
Grade II* listed maltings, built 1883 by Sir Peter Wacker. First octagonal malting to be built. Then owned by Yeomans, Cherry and Curtis and now partly used as an animal food manufacturing facility and storage depot. Weathervane in the shape of a goat on top of the octagonal malting kiln.
Grant Recipient/Owner: Mr Geo L White Ltd
Access contact: Mr George White
Tel: 01283 564641   **Fax:** 01283 511967
Email Address: gw-glw@freezone.co.uk
Opening Arrangements: All year 9am - 4.30pm (excluding weekends and Bank Holidays except by prior written arrangement). Guide dog access to ground floor only.
Heritage Open Days: No
P Yes. Spaces: 6
♿ No. Disabled WC: No. Guide Dogs: Yes
£ No

Ingestre Pavilion
Tixall, nr. Stafford, Staffordshire
The pavilion was built in 1752 as part of a formal garden layout subsequently altered by 'Capability' Brown. The façade is a powerful and distinguished one, although the architect is not known. The building behind it had been demolished by 1802 and so there are now new ones including an octagonal saloon.
Website Address: www.landmarktrust.co.uk
Grant Recipient/Owner: The Landmark Trust
Access contact: Ms Victoria Piggott
Tel: 01628 825920   **Fax:** 01628 825417
Email Address: vpiggott@landmarktrust.co.uk
Opening Arrangements: The Landmark Trust is an independent charity, which rescues small buildings of historic or architectural importance from decay or unsympathetic improvement. Landmark's aim is to promote the enjoyment of these historic buildings by making them available to stay in for holidays. Ingestre Pavilion can be rented by anyone, at all times of the year, for periods ranging from a weekend to three weeks. Bookings can be made by telephoning the Booking Office on 01628 825925. As the building is in full-time use for holiday accommodation, it is not normally open to the public. However the public can view the building by prior arrangement by telephoning the access contact (Victoria Piggott on 01628 825920) to make an appointment. Potential visitors will be asked to write to confirm the details of their visit.
Heritage Open Days: No
P Yes. Spaces: 2
♿ No. Disabled WC: No. Guide Dogs: Yes
£ No

Kinver Edge (Hill Fort)
nr. Stourbridge, Staffordshire
A sandstone ridge covered in woodland and heath with Iron Age hill fort with views across surrounding countryside.
Grant Recipient/Owner: The National Trust
Access contact: The Warden
Tel: 01384 872418
Opening Arrangements: Kinver Edge is open at all times.
Heritage Open Days: No
P Yes. Spaces: 100
♿ No. Disabled WC: No. Guide Dogs: Yes
£ No

Newton's College
The Close, Lichfield, Staffordshire WS13
Grade II* range of 10 almshouses built 1800 for widows and unmarried daughters of clergymen who had served the Cathedral. Faced in Hallington stone to a classical style, 2 storeys with central pedimented break. Now private residences.
Grant Recipient/Owner:
The Dean & Chapter of Lichfield Cathedral
Access contact:
The Dean & Chapter of Lichfield Cathedral
Tel: 01543 306100   **Fax:** 01543 306109
Email Address: enquiries@lichfield-cathedral.org
Opening Arrangements: By prior arrangement (21 days notice requested) with the Dean & Chapter of Lichfield Cathedral, 19a The Close, Lichfield, Staffordshire WS13 7LD (tel.01543 306100).
Heritage Open Days: No
P No
♿ No. Disabled WC: No. Guide Dogs: Yes
£ No

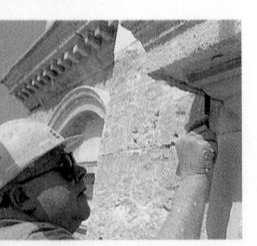

Shugborough

Milford, Stafford, Staffordshire ST17 0XB

The present house was begun circa 1695. Between 1760 and 1770 it was enlarged and again partly remodelled by Samuel Wyatt at end of 18th century. The interior is particularly notable for its plaster work and other decorations. Ancestral home of the Earls of Lichfield. Houses the Staffordshire County Museum, Georgian working farm and Rare Livestock Breed project.

Grant Recipient/Owner: The National Trust
Access contact: Staffordshire County Council
Tel: 01889 881388
Opening Arrangements: Saturday 31 March to Sunday 30 September 2001: Mansion House, County Museum, farm and gardens: open daily except Mondays (but open Bank Holiday Mondays) 11am - 5pm; October Sundays only. Open to booked parties only: Monday 1 October to Friday 29 March 2002: Mansion house, County Museum, farm and gardens Monday to Friday 10.30am - 4pm. Wheelchair access to ground floor of house, museum and farm.
Heritage Open Days: No
P Yes. Spaces: 600
Partial. Disabled WC: Yes. Guide Dogs: Yes
£ Yes
Adult: £4.50 (per site). £9.00 (to all sites).
Child: £3.00 (per site). £6.00 (to all sites).
Other: £12.00 (per site). £22.00 (to all sites).

Sinai Park

Branston, Shobnall, Staffordshire

Timber-framed E-shaped house, two-thirds derelict, on moated hill-top site, dating from the 13th century. House built variously during 15th, 16th and 17th centuries with later additions, including wall paintings and carpenters marks. 18th century bridge and plunge pool in the grounds.

Grant Recipient/Owner: Ms C A Newton
Access contact: Ms C A Newton
Tel: 01283 544161
Email Address: knewton@brookes-vernons.co.uk
Opening Arrangements: By prior arrangement only.
Heritage Open Days: No
P No
No. Disabled WC: No. Guide Dogs: Yes
£ No

SUFFOLK

Culford School Iron Bridge

Culford, Bury St Edmunds, Suffolk IP28 6TX

Constructed for the second Marquis Cornwallis in the late 1790s by Samuel Wyatt, brother of James, to a design patented by Wyatt. The bridge, in Culford Park, is one of the earliest surviving bridges with an unmodified cast iron structure, being the earliest known example with hollow ribs.

Grant Recipient/Owner: Mr J W Beaty
Access contact: Michael Woolley
Tel: 01284 729318   **Fax:** 01284 729077
Email Address: bursary@culfordschool.freeserve.co.uk
Opening Arrangements: Access to the iron bridge and Culford Park is available at any time throughout the year. Disabled access may be difficult as over grass and toilet facilities are limited, being only available when Culford Hall is open and the facility having low steps at the entrance to the Hall and the toilets. Temporary ramps will be provided at the entrance to the Hall on Heritage Open Days.
Heritage Open Days: Yes
P Yes. Spaces: 100
Yes. Disabled WC: Yes. Guide Dogs: Yes
£ No

Elms Farm Wallpaintings

Old Station Road, Mendlesham, Suffolk IP14 5RS

Wealden hall house dating from 1480, wallpaintings consist of 16th century floral design and Biblical texts in the upper hall and solar and 17th century armorial patterning in the parlour.

Grant Recipient/Owner: Mrs Pamela Gilmour
Access contact: Mrs Pamela Gilmour
Opening Arrangements: By prior written arrangement.
Heritage Open Days: No
P Yes. Spaces: 10
No. Disabled WC: No. Guide Dogs: No
£ No

Flatford Mill & Willy Lott's Cottage

Flatford, East Bergholt, Suffolk CO7 6OL

Flatford watermill, 1733 datestone, incorporating possibly earlier but altered former granary range to rear and further C19 range adjoining granary. Later alterations. The mill was in the possession of the Constable family from the mid C18. Willy Lott's farmhouse, late C16-C17. Grade I listing of both buildings reflects their significance in the life and work of John Constable. Both buildings are leased by the National Trust to the Field Studies Council. Flatford Bridge Cottage 16th century thatched cottage, upstream from Flatford Mill houses an exhibition on John Constable.

Website Address: www.nationaltrust.org.uk
Grant Recipient/Owner: The National Trust
Access contact: Property Manager
Tel: 01206 298260   **Fax:** 01206 299193
Email Address: atdcykx@smtp.ntrust.org.uk
Opening Arrangements: Public access to Flatford Mill and Willy Lott's Cottage is to the exterior and by virtue of their use as a course centre for the Field Studies Council (for information on courses tel: 01206 298283). The Field Studies Council will also arrange tours for groups. (Flatford Bridge Cottage is open March and April daily except Mondays and Tuesdays 11am - 5.30pm; May to end September daily 10am - 5.30pm; October daily 11am - 5.30pm; November and December daily except Mondays and Tuesdays 11am - 3.30pm. Closed Christmas. Car park 200 metres from cottage. Parking near cottage available for disabled visitors. Lavatory for disabled available in car park owned by Babergh DC, 25 yards from the cottage. For further information contact the Property Manager 01206 298260).
Heritage Open Days: No
P Yes. Spaces: 200
Partial. Disabled WC: Yes. Guide Dogs: Yes
£ No

Hadleigh Deanery

Hadleigh, Ipswich, Suffolk IP7 5DT

Built 1495 by the then Dean, William Pykenham. Ornate red brick building, originally constructed as a gateway but became a study/library (on first floor) for subsequent Deans. The present house was built onto it in 1831. Has a spiral staircase, dovecot, turrets, vaulted oratory and secret chamber.

Grant Recipient/Owner:
Diocese of St Edmundsbury and Ipswich
Access contact: Canon David Stranack
Tel: 01473 822218
Opening Arrangements: Sunday 16 September 2 - 5pm. Other opening arrangements under review at time of going to print, please check English Heritage website for current information. Also by prior arrangement. Parking in Magdalen Street.
Heritage Open Days: No
P See above
No.
£ No
Donations requested.

Hall Farm Barn

Withersfield, Suffolk

100ft long by 30ft wide thatched barn built c1400, with later alterations. Floor is split into 3 levels with the east wall having been bricked inbetween the timbers and the west wall still consisting of horsehair, lathe and plaster. Situated in working farmyard.

Grant Recipient/Owner: Mr C R W Bradford
Access contact: Mr T Mytton-Mills
Tel: 01440 702146   **Fax:** 01440 702552
Email Address: tom@hall-farm.fsnet.co.uk
Opening Arrangements: By prior telephone arrangement.
Heritage Open Days: No
P Yes. Spaces: 12
Yes. Disabled WC: Yes. Guide Dogs: Yes
£ No

Horseman's House

Boundary Farm, Framsden, Suffolk IP14 6LH

Mid 17th century brick stable. Gable ended with brick pinnacles along upper edge with panels of diaper work in dark headers below round vents/owl holes. Original three bay, two storey structure housed horseman above his charges in unusually ornate accommodation for all. Now horse and rider holiday accommodation.

Grant Recipient/Owner: Mr Bacon
Access contact: Mr Bacon
Tel: 01728 860370   **Fax:** 01728 860370
Email Address: info@boundaryfarm.co.uk
Opening Arrangements: By prior arrangement only. Wheelchair access to ground floor only.
Heritage Open Days: No
P Yes. Spaces: 4
Partial. Disabled WC: Yes. Guide Dogs: Yes
£ No

Ickworth House

Ickworth, Horringer, Bury St Edmunds, Suffolk IP29 5QE

The Earl of Bristol created this eccentric house, with its central rotunda and curved corridors, in 1795 to display his collections. These include paintings by Titian, Gainsborough and Velasquez and a Georgian silver collection. The house is surrounded by an Italianate garden set in a 'Capability' Brown park with woodland walks, deer enclosure, vineyard, Georgian summerhouse and lake.

Website Address: www.nationaltrust.org.uk
Grant Recipient/Owner: The National Trust
Access contact: Property Manager
Tel: 01284 735270   **Fax:** 01284 735175
Email Address: arore@smtp.ntrust.org.uk
Opening Arrangements: House: 24 to 28 October: daily except Mondays and Thursdays (but open Bank Holiday Mondays) 1 - 5 (last admission 4.30pm). Closes 4.30pm in October. Garden: 24 March to 28 October: daily; 29 October to end March 2002: daily except Saturdays and Sundays. Times: 10am - 5pm (last admission 4.30pm) 1 November to end March 2002; 10am to 4pm. Park daily. Wheelchair access to House: ramped access (restricted access in House for large powered vehicles/chairs); lift to first floor; stairlift to basement (shop and restaurant) suitable to wheelchair users able to transfer; wheelchair on each floor; garden largely accessible, some changes of level, gravel drive and paths.
Heritage Open Days: No
P Yes. Spaces: 2000
Partial. Disabled WC: Yes. Guide Dogs: Yes
£ Yes
Adult: £5.70. £2.50 (park & garden only).
Child: £2.50. £0.80 (park & garden only).
Other: £4.70 (group rate). No group rates Sundays & Bank Holiday Mondays. Family discounts.

Melford Hall

Long Melford, nr. Sudbury, Suffolk CO10 9AA

Elizabethan house, little changed externally since 1578 and with panelled banqueting hall. Regency library, Victorian bedrooms and collections of furniture and porcelain. Garden and parkland.

Website Address: www.nationaltrust.org.uk
Grant Recipient/Owner: The National Trust
Access contact: Property Manager
Tel: 01787 880286
Opening Arrangements: April and October: Saturdays, Sundays and Bank Holidays; May to end September: daily except Mondays and Tuesdays (but open Bank Holiday Mondays) 2 - 5.30pm. Wheelchair access to ground floor (ramps on request). Stairlift to first floor.
Heritage Open Days: No
P Yes. Spaces: 50
Partial. Disabled WC: Yes. Guide Dogs: Yes
£ Yes
Adult: £4.40
Other: £3.30 (per-booked groups daily except Sundays, Mondays & Tuesdays).

St Peter

College Street, Ipswich, Suffolk

Large medieval church near the docks, owned by Ipswich Borough Council and redundant since the 1970s. Noted for a Tournai font and adjacent to Thomas Wolsey's gateway.

Grant Recipient/Owner:
Ipswich Historic Churches Trust
Access contact: Mr J S Hall
Tel: 01473 232300   **Fax:** 01473 230524
Opening Arrangements: By prior arrangement with Mr J S Hall, Secretary, Ipswich Historic Churches Trust, 24-26 Museum Street, Ipswich, Suffolk IP1 1HZ (tel.01473 232300). Wheelchair access to all of the church apart from the vestry and parts of the chancel.
Heritage Open Days: Yes
P No
Partial. Disabled WC: No. Guide Dogs: Yes
£ No

Samson's Tower (Abbey Visitor Centre) and 1-3 West Front

Great Churchyard, Bury St Edmunds, Suffolk IP33 1RS

Ruined Grade I medieval west front of the Abbey of St Edmund, now converted into a visitor centre interpreting the life of Edmund and private residences.

Grant Recipient/Owner:
St Edmundsbury District Council
Access contact: Director of Leisure Services, St Edmundsbury Borough Council
Tel: 01284 764667   **Fax:** 01284 757084
Email Address: steve.palframan@stedmundsbury.gov.uk
Opening Arrangements: Abbey Visitor Centre (Samson's Tower): January - Easter, weekends 11am - 4pm; Easter - October, daily except Tuesdays and Thursdays 11am - 4pm; closed November and December. Opening arrangements for Visitor Centre may change, please check English Heritage website for up-to-date information. Opening arrangements for no.s 1,2 & 3 West Front under review at time of going to print, again please check English Heritage website for up-to-date information. Wheelchair access only to visitor centre. Disabled parking available within 10yds by prior arrangement and disabled toilets 150 metres away. Parking at pay and display car park on Angel Hill 150 metres away. Open Heritage Open Days at time of going to print but again this may change, please check English Heritage website for up-to-date information.

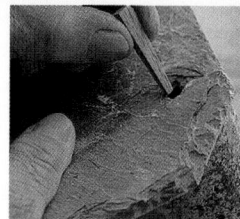

Heritage Open Days: Yes
P See above
Partial. Disabled WC: No. Guide Dogs: Yes
£ No

Somerleyton Hall & Gardens

Somerleyton, Lowestoft, Suffolk NR32 5QQ
Early Victorian stately home, built in Anglo-Italian style for Sir Morton Peto by John Thomas upon former Jacobean mansion. Contains carved stonework and state rooms. Has 12 acres of gardens with a yew hedge maze.
Website Address: www.somerleyton.co.uk
Grant Recipient/Owner:
The Rt Hon Lord Somerleyton GCVO
Access contact: Mr Ian Pollard
Tel: 01502 730224   **Fax:** 01502 732143
Email Address: enquiries@somerleyton.co.uk
Opening Arrangements: Easter Sunday - end of September: Thursdays, Sundays and Bank Holidays, plus Tuesdays and Wednesdays in July and August, 12.30 - 5.30pm. Admission charges are provisional at time of going to print, please check with Hall for current rates.
Heritage Open Days: No
P Yes. Spaces: 200
Yes. Disabled WC: Yes. Guide Dogs: Yes
£ Yes
Adult: £5.00 (see above)
Child: £2.50
Other: £4.80 (senior citizens), £14.20 (family).

Theatre Royal

Westgate Street, Bury St Edmunds,
Suffolk IP33 1QR
A rare example of a late Georgian playhouse. Built 1819, later used as a warehouse but restored and re-opened as a theatre in 1965. Constructed of white brick and stucco with a slate roof.
Website Address: www.theatreroyal.org
Grant Recipient/Owner: The National Trust
Access contact: The Administrator
Tel: 01284 755127   **Fax:** 01284 706035
Email Address: admin@theatreroyal.org
Opening Arrangements: By guided tour only by prior arrangement: Mondays and Wednesdays 11am - 1pm and 2 - 4pm, Saturdays 11am - 1pm. Limited wheelchair access, please ring 01284 769505 for details. Limited parking in Westgate Street.
Heritage Open Days: No
P See above
Partial. Disabled WC: No. Guide Dogs: No
£ Yes
Adult: £2.00
Child: £1.00

Woodbridge Lodge

Rendlesham, nr Woodbridge, Suffolk IP12 2RA
Late 18th century small gothic folly. Originally a gatehouse to Rendlesham Hall, now part of a dwelling house.
Grant Recipient/Owner: Dr C P Cooper
Access contact: Dr C P Cooper
Tel: 01394 460642
Opening Arrangements: Exterior only by prior arrangement..
Heritage Open Days: No
P Yes. Spaces: 3
No. Disabled WC: No. Guide Dogs: No
£ No

SURREY

Carshalton Water Tower

West Street, Carshalton, Surrey
18th century garden building with an Orangery, Saloon, plunge-bath lined with Delft tiles, part-restored water wheel and stone pump chamber. Built 1721 for Sir John Fellowes, sub-Governor of the South Sea Company.
Grant Recipient/Owner: Carshalton Water Tower Trust
Access contact: Mrs Julia Gertz
Tel: 020 8647 0984
Opening Arrangements: First Sunday in April - last Sunday in September 2.30 - 5pm, plus local and national Heritage Open Days. Private tours by prior arrangement with the Friends of Carshalton Water Tower, 136 West Street, Carshalton, Surrey SM5 2NR (tel.020 8647 0984). Parking available by arrangement.
Heritage Open Days: Yes
P See above
Yes. Disabled WC: Yes. Guide Dogs: Yes
£ Yes
Adult: 75p
Child: 25p

Clandon House

West Clandon, Guildford, Surrey, GU4 7RQ
Palladian mansion, built c1730 by Venetian architect Giacomo Leoni. Two-storeyed Marble Hall, collection of

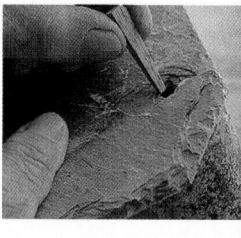

18th century furniture, porcelain, textiles, carpets, the Ivo Forde Meissen collection of Italian comedy figures and a series of Mortlake tapestries.
Grant Recipient/Owner: The National Trust
Access contact: Mr David Brock-Doyle
Tel: 01483 222482   **Fax:** 01483 223479
Email Address: sclsea@smtp.ntrust.org.uk
Opening Arrangements: House: 1 April - 4 November; daily except Monday, Friday and Saturday (but open Good Friday, Easter Saturday and Bank Holiday Mondays) 11am - 5pm (last admission 4.30pm). Museum: as for house 12 - 5pm. Garden: all year as for house 11am - 5pm. Wheelchair access to lower ground floor and five steps to ground floor.
Heritage Open Days: No
P Yes. Spaces: 200
Partial. Disabled WC: Yes. Guide Dogs: Yes
£ Yes
Adult: £5.00
Child: £2.50
Other: £12.50 (family), £4.00 (group rate, per head Tuesdays, Wednesdays & Thursdays only).

Claremont House

Claremont Drive, Esher, Surrey KT10 9LY
Built 1772 in Palladian style by 'Capability' Brown for Clive of India. Henry Holland and John Soane were responsible for the interior decoration. For over a century it was a royal residence, home to Charlotte, Princess of Wales, the young Queen Victoria, and the Duke and Duchess of Albany.
Website Address: www.claremont-school.co.uk
Grant Recipient/Owner:
Claremont Fan Court Foundation Ltd
Access contact: Mrs C Bradley
Tel: 01372 467841   **Fax:** 01372 471109
Email Address: library@intonet.co.uk
Opening Arrangements: Guided tours: 1 & 2 April, 6 & 7 May, 3 & 4 June, 2 July, 5 & 6 August, 2 & 3 September and 7 & 8 October, 2 - 5pm (last tour 4.30pm). Groups and individuals at other times by prior arrangement. Wheelchair access also by prior arrangement.
Heritage Open Days: No
P Yes. Spaces: 100
Partial. Disabled WC: No. Guide Dogs: Yes
£ Yes
Adult: £3.00
Child: £1.50
Other: £2.00

Great Hall

Virginia Park, Christchurch Road, Virginia Water, Surrey GU25 4BM
By W H Crossland for Charas Holloway and opened 1884. Built of red brick with Portland stone dressings and slate roofs in Franco-Flemish Gothic style. Formerly part of the Royal Holloway Sanatorium.
Grant Recipient/Owner: Octagon Virginia Ltd
Access contact: Mr John Ellams
Tel: 01344 845276   **Fax:** 01344 842428
Email Address: virginiapark@aol.com
Opening Arrangements: Entrance Hall, Staircase and Great Hall of former Sanatorium open on the following Wednesdays and Sundays 10am - 4pm: February 21 & 25, March 28, April 1, 18, 25 & 29, May 16, 23 & 27, June 20, 24 & 27, July 18, 25 & 29, August 15, 22 & 26, September 19, 26 & 30, October 17,24 & 28, November 21 & 25 and December 5 & 9. At other times by prior telephone arrangement with the Estate Office. Public car park nearby. No coach parties. Wheelchair access with assistance (steps from building to be negotiated).
Heritage Open Days: No
P See above
Partial. Disabled WC: Yes. Guide Dogs: Yes
£ Yes
Adult: £3.00

Hospital of the Blessed Trinity (Abbot's Hospital)

High Street, Guildford, Surrey GU1 3AJ
17th century almshouse with enclosed courtyard and turreted tower entrance. Rear gardens with other 17th century buildings and matching new development. Tour visitors may also view the panelled common rooms with interesting furniture and paintings and the Chapel, which has well-known painted-glass windows.
Grant Recipient/Owner:
Access contact: Mr John W Moss
Tel: 01483 562670
Opening Arrangements: 1 May to end September: Mondays and Wednesdays 2.30pm only guided walks of chapel courtyard and terrace. Special organised guided walks with the Master's permission Monday to Saturdays 10.30am to 5pm (contact the Master, John Moss, 01483 562670). Wheelchair access to lower rooms and gardens, please notify if intending to use a wheelchair.
Heritage Open Days: Yes
P No
Partial. Disabled WC: No. Guide Dogs: Yes
£ No

Kingston Grammar School – Lovekyn Chapel

70 London Road, Kingston-upon-Thames, Surrey KT2 6PY
Chapel of St Mary Magdalene, known as the Lovekyn Chantry Chapel, was consecrated in 1310 and is one of the oldest buildings in Kingston. Built by Edward Lovekyn in 1299 and restored and re-endowed in 1352 by his son John, twice Lord Mayor of London. In 1561 Queen Elizabeth established her grammar school in the Chapel. The school continues to use it for a wide variety of activities and public use.
Website Address: www.kingston-grammar.surrey.sch.uk
Grant Recipient/Owner:
Governors of Kingston Grammar School
Access contact: Mr A G Howard-Harwood
Tel: 020 8939 8825   **Fax:** 020 8974 5177
Email Address: bursar@kingston-grammar.surrey.sch.uk
Opening Arrangements: By prior written arrangement with Mr A G Howard-Harwood, Bursar & Clerk to the Governors at the school. Public car park nearby.
Heritage Open Days: Yes
P See above
Yes. Disabled WC: Yes. Guide Dogs: Yes
£ No

The Old Mill

Outwood Common, nr. Redhill, Surrey RH1 5PW
England's oldest working windmill, built in 1665. Houses museum of bygones.
Website Address: www.outwoodwindmill.co.uk
Grant Recipient/Owner: Mrs Sheila Thomas
Access contact: Mrs Sheila Thomas
Tel: 01342 843644   **Fax:** 01342 843458
Email Address: sheila@outwoodwindmill.co.uk
Opening Arrangements: Easter - October:Sundays and Bank Holidays 2 - 6pm, plus parties by prior arrangement. Wheelchair access to museum and ground floor of mill only.
Heritage Open Days: No
P Yes. Spaces: 2
Partial. Disabled WC: Yes. Guide Dogs: Yes
£ Yes
Adult: £2.00
Child: £1.00

The Old Palace School

Old Palace Road, Croydon, Surrey CRO 1AX
Residence of Archbishop's of Canterbury between 12th and 18th centuries. Contains 15th century banqueting hall, guard room and chapel, a Norman undercroft, a Tudor long gallery, Elizabeth I's bedroom and some of the earliest medieval brickwork in England. Currently home of the Old Palace School of John Whitgift.
Grant Recipient/Owner: Whitgift Foundation
Access contact: Dr Andrew Bradstock
Tel: 020 8688 2414
Opening Arrangements: By guided tour only: 17-21 April, 28 May - 1 June, 16-21 & 23-28 July. Doors open 1.45pm, last tour commences 2.15pm. Groups by prior arrangement on these dates, please contact Dr Andrew Bradstock on 020 8680 0467. Refreshments available.
Heritage Open Days: Yes
P No
No. Disabled WC: No. Guide Dogs: No
£ Yes
Adult: £4.00
Child: £3.00 (senior citizens)
Other: £10.00 (family ticket)

Oxenford Farm

Milford Road, Elstead, Godalming, Surrey GU8 6LA
1840 Gothic-style stone barn by Pugin with cowsheds and gatehouse.
Grant Recipient/Owner: Mr C F Baker
Access contact: Mr A C Baker
Tel: 01252 702109   **Fax:** 01252 702109
Opening Arrangements: 1 - 24 December: daily 9am - 5pm. At other times by prior written arrangement. Wheelchair access to barn and cowsheds.
Heritage Open Days: No
P Yes, Spaces: 10
Partial. Disabled WC: No. Guide Dogs: Yes
£ No

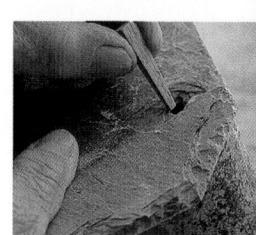

Painshill Park

Portsmouth Road, Cobham, Surrey KT11 1JE
Restored Grade I 18th century landscape garden of 150 acres, designed by Charles Hamilton between 1738 and 1773. Contains a Gothic temple, Chinese bridge, ruined abbey, Turkish tent, grotto and 14 acre serpentine lake fed by a waterwheel.
Website Address: www.brainsys.com/cobham/painshill
Grant Recipient/Owner: Painshill Park Trust Ltd
Access contact: Mrs Harriet Richards
Tel: 01932 868113   **Fax:** 01932 868001
Opening Arrangements: April - October: Tuesday -

Sunday and Bank Holidays 10.30am - 6pm (last admission 4.30pm); November - March (except Christmas Day and Boxing Day): Tuesday - Thursday, Saturdays, Sundays and Bank Holidays 11am - 4pm or dusk if earlier (last admission 3pm). Guided tours by prior arrangement. Wheelchair access to most of the site, apart from the grotto and Alpine Valley. Admission charges are provisional at time of going to print, please check with Park for current rates. Parking for 8 coaches.
Heritage Open Days: No
P Yes. Spaces: 400
♿ Partial. Disabled WC: Yes. Guide Dogs: Yes
£ Yes
Adult: £4.20 (see above)
Child: £1.70 (free under five)
Other: £3.65

Red House
Frith Hill Road, Godalming, Surrey GU7 2DZ
Built by Lutyens 1897-9 for Revd Evans. An irregular mass built into steep hill with Jekyll garden. Each façade contrasting: North, street entrance low Georgian; West, English vernacular; East, romantic; South, keep-like with two bays accentuating the elevation, similar to the later Castle Drogo. Wide top-lit ramp-like staircase with rooms off to each façade on three split levels. Drawing room and dining room fireplaces are also contrasting features, with the former baroque and the latter neo-Georgian.
Grant Recipient/Owner: Mr H A Laws
Access contact: Mrs Shula Laws
Tel: 01483 429284   **Fax:** 01483 429284
Opening Arrangements: By prior written arrangement (at least 4 weeks in advance) in April, May, June, July and September (excluding Wednesdays, Thursdays and Sundays). Additional street parking.
Heritage Open Days: Yes
P Yes. Spaces: 2
♿ No. Disabled WC: No. Guide Dogs: Yes
£ No

TYNE & WEAR

21-23 Leazes Terrace
Newcastle-upon-Tyne, Tyne & Wear NE1 4LY
Elongated square of houses built 1829-34 in classical style. Now owned by the University of Newcastle and used as halls of residence.
Grant Recipient/Owner: University of Newcastle
Access contact: Miss Helen Stonebank
Tel: 0191 222 7565
Opening Arrangements: Exterior accessible at all times, only one room of the interior can be viewed (Room 21F, which is in near original condition) by prior arrangement with Miss Helen Stonebank, Accommodation Manageress, 10 Leazes Terrace, Newcastle-upon-Tyne, Tyne & Wear (tel.0191 222 7565). Parking at off street car park (metered).
Heritage Open Days: No
P See above
♿ No. Disabled WC: No. Guide Dogs: No
£ No

Fulwell Mill
Newcastle Road, Sunderland, Tyne & Wear
Grade II* listed mill built in 1821 using local limestone, remaining in use until 1949. Restoration of Mill to full working order and to provide visitor facilities expected to be completed early this year.
Grant Recipient/Owner:
Tyne & Wear Industrial Monuments Trust
Access contact: Mr Les Milne
Tel: 0191 553 1279   **Fax:** 0191 553 1460
Email Address: les.milne@sunderland.gov.uk
Opening Arrangements: Mill expected to re-open after restoration at Easter and then be open weekends and Bank Holidays until end of September, Sundays rest of the year. Time 2pm - 4pm. Specialist groups/school parties by prior arrangement. Admission charges yet to be confirmed at time of going to print, please check with Mr Les Milne of the City of Sunderland Planning Implementation Section, PO Box 102, Civic Centre, Sunderland, Tyne & Wear SR2 7DN (tel.0191 553 1279). Wheelchair access to ground floor and visitor centre.
Heritage Open Days: No
P Yes. Spaces: 13
♿ Partial. Disabled WC: Yes. Guide Dogs: Yes
£ See above

Gibside Chapel & Column of Liberty
Gibside, nr. Rowlands Gill, Burnopfield, Tyne & Wear NE16 6BG
Palladian Chapel 1760-69; completed 1812 designed by James Paine for George Bowes, MP and coal owner, and Column of Liberty 1750-57 by Daniel Garrett until 1753; then James Paine, situated in extensive landscape. Much of the landscape is SSSI, and embracing many miles of riverside and forest walks. A forest garden is under restoration. The estate is the former home of the Queen

Mother's family, the Bowes-Lyons.
Website Address: www.nationaltrust.org.uk
Grant Recipient/Owner: Regional Director
Access contact: Visitor Services Manager
Tel: 01207 542255
Email Address: joan.gardner@ntrust.org.uk
Opening Arrangements: Chapel: 1 April to 31 October 11am - 4.30pm. Winter by appointment only. Grounds: open Tuesdays to Sundays and Bank Holiday Mondays 10am. Last admission 4.30pm summer and 3.30pm winter. Wheelchair access to tea room, shop, toilets and part of the grounds. Wheelchair access is difficult to Chapel and the Avenue. Staff very happy to assist. Telephone the Visitor Services Manager (01207 542255) in advance. Parking for disabled near the site.
Heritage Open Days: Yes
P Yes. Spaces: 1000
♿ Partial. Disabled WC: Yes. Guide Dogs: Yes
£ Yes
Adult: £3.00
Child: £1.50
Other: £8.00 (family (2+4)). £5.00 (family (1+3)).

Old Town Hall
Market Place, South Shields,Tyne & Wear
Built 1768 by the Dean and Chapter of Durham in the centre of the Market Place. Square two-storey building with an open arcaded ground floor and a central pillar on steps supporting what may have been a former market cross. Upper floor reached by a symmetrical, double branch stone staircase. Restored 1977.
Grant Recipient/Owner: The Chief Executive
Access contact: Director of Community Services
Tel: 0191 4271717   **Fax:** 0191 4270469
Opening Arrangements: Access to ground floor at all reasonable times, first floor by prior arrangement with the Director of Community Services, South Tyneside Metropolitan Borough Council, Central Library Building, Prince George Square, South Shields, Tyne & Wear NE33 2PE (tel.0191 4271717). Wheelchair and guide dog access to ground floor only. Paid parking locally, with disabled parking close to site.
Heritage Open Days: No
P Yes. Spaces: 450
♿ Partial. Disabled WC: No. Guide Dogs: Yes
£ No

Washington Old Hall
The Avenue, Washington Village, District 4, Washington, Tyne & Wear NE38 7LE
17th century manor house, incorporating the 12th century remains of the home of George Washington's ancestors. Recreated 17th century interiors and displays of 'Washingtonabilia' celebrating the close connection with the USA. Permanent exhibition on the recent tenement period of the property. Jacobean knot-garden.
Website Address: www.nationaltrust.org.uk
Grant Recipient/Owner: The National Trust
Access contact: Property Manager
Tel: 0191 4166879   **Fax:** 0191 4192065
Opening Arrangements: 1 April to 31 October: Sundays to Wednesdays (but open Good Friday) 11am to 5pm (last admission 4.30pm). Wheelchair access to ground floor of house and upper garden.
Heritage Open Days: No
P Yes. Spaces: 10
♿ Partial. Disabled WC: Yes. Guide Dogs: Yes
£ Yes
Adult: £2.80
Child: £1.40
Other: £7.00 (family).

WARWICKSHIRE

The Bath House
Walton, Stratford-upon-Avon, Warwickshire
Designed in 1748 by the architect Sanderson Miller. The upper room, where the bathers recovered, is decorated with dripping icicles and festoons of sea shells - the work of Mrs Delaney, better known for her flower pictures. Narrow steep staircases.
Website Address: www.landmarktrust.co.uk
Grant Recipient/Owner: The Landmark Trust
Access contact: Ms Victoria Piggott
Tel: 01628 825920   **Fax:** 01628 825417
Email Address: www.landmarktrust.co.uk
Opening Arrangements: The Landmark Trust is an independent charity, which rescues small buildings of historic or architectural importance from decay or unsympathetic improvement. Landmark's aim is to promote the enjoyment of these historic buildings by making them available to stay in for holidays. The Bath House can be rented by anyone, at all times of the year, for periods ranging from a weekend to three weeks. Bookings can be made by telephoning the Booking Office on 01628 825925. As the building is in full-time use for holiday accommodation, it is not normally open to the public. However the public can view the building by prior arrangement by telephoning the access contact (Victoria Piggott on 01628 825920) to make an appointment.

Potential visitors will be asked to write to confirm the details of their visit.
Heritage Open Days: No
P Yes. Spaces: 1
♿ No. Disabled WC: No. Guide Dogs: No
£ No

Charlecote Park
Wellesbourne, Warwick, Warwickshire CV35 9ER
Owned by the Lucy family since 1247, Sir Thomas built the house in 1558. Now, much altered, it is shown as it would have been a century ago. The balustraded formal garden gives onto a deer park landscaped by 'Capability' Brown.
Website Address: www.ntrustsevern.org.uk
Grant Recipient/Owner: The National Trust
Access contact: Property Manager
Tel: 01789 470277   **Fax:** 01789 470544
Email Address: charlecote@smtp.ntrust.org.uk
Opening Arrangements: House and Garden: 24 March to end June: daily except Wednesday and Thursday (open Good Friday). July and August: daily except Thursdays. September to 4 November: daily except Wednesdays and Thursdays. Grounds: 3 February to 18 March Saturdays and Sundays. Times: House 12 - 5pm; grounds 11am-6pm. Grounds only: November and December Saturdays and Sundays 11am to 4pm. Wheelchair access to ground floor of house, restaurant and shop. Parking for disabled near house.
Heritage Open Days: No
P Yes. Spaces: 200
♿ Partial. Disabled WC: Yes. Guide Dogs: Yes
£ Yes
Adult: £5.60 (house & grounds).
Child: £2.70 (house & grounds).
Other: £14.00 (family). £4.60 (group rate, max 40).

Lord Leycester Hospital
High Street, Warwick, Warwickshire CV34 4BH
14th century chantry chapel, Great Hall, galleried courtyard and Guildhall. Acquired by Robert Dudley, Earl of Leicester in 1571 as a home for his old soldiers. Still operating as a home for ex-servicemen.
Grant Recipient/Owner:
Patron & Governors of Lord Leycester Hospital
Access contact: D I Rhodes
Tel: 01926 491422   **Fax:** 01926 491422
Opening Arrangements: Tuesday - Sunday 10am - 4pm (winter), 10am - 5pm (summer) plus Bank Holiday Mondays. Closed Good Friday and Christmas Day. Wheelchair access to ground floor only.
Heritage Open Days: No
P Yes. Spaces: 15
♿ Partial. Disabled WC: No. Guide Dogs: Yes
£ Yes
Adult: £3.00
Child: £2.00
Other: £2.50

Nicholas Chamberlaine's Almshouses' Pump House
All Saints Square, Bedworth, Nuneaton, Warwickshire
Built 1840 of English bond brick with sandstone dressings and stone pyramid roof in Tudor Gothic style. Contains original cast iron pump. Stands in front of the almshouses and originally provided water for the residents, illuminated at night.
Grant Recipient/Owner:
Nicholas Chamberlaine's Hospital Charity
Access contact: Mr David Dumbleton
Tel: 024 76227331   **Fax:** 024 76221293
Opening Arrangements: Two sessions Saturday and Sunday of Heritage Open Days weekend and at other times by prior arrangement with Mr David Dumbleton, Clerk to the Governors, Nicholas Chamberlaine's Hospital Charity, Rotherhams and Co, 8/9 The Quadrant, Coventry, Warwickshire CV1 2EG (tel.024 76227331). Exterior visible from All Saints Square at all times. Parking at public car parks nearby.
Heritage Open Days: Yes
P See above
♿ Yes. Disabled WC: Yes. Guide Dogs: Yes
£ No

Packwood House
Lapworth, Solihull, Warwickshire B94 6AT
Originally a 16th century house, Packwood has been much altered over the years and today is a vision of Graham Baron Ash who recreated a Jacobean house in the 1920s and 30s. Collection of 16th century textiles and furniture. Yew garden based on Sermon on the Mount.
Website Address: www.ntrustsevern.org.uk
Grant Recipient/Owner: The National Trust
Access contact: Mr Alan Langstaff
Tel: 01564 783294   **Fax:** 01564 782706
Email Address: baddesley@smtp.ntrust.org.uk
Opening Arrangements: House: 28 March to 28 October: daily except Mondays and Tuesdays (but open Bank Holidays and Good Friday) 12 - 4.30pm. Gardens:

3 to 25 March Saturdays and Sundays. 28 March to 28 October: daily except Mondays and Tuesdays (but open Bank Holiday Mondays and Good Friday). Times: March, April and October 11am to 4.30pm; May to September 11am to 5.30pm.
Heritage Open Days: No
P Yes. Spaces: 140
Yes. Disabled WC: Yes. Guide Dogs: Yes
£ Yes
Adult: £5.00 (house & garden). £2.50 (grounds).
Child: £2.50 (house & garden). £1.25 (grounds).
Other: £12.50 (family). £4.00 (groups 15+). Discount for combined ticket to Packwood House & Baddesley Hall.

Polesworth Nunnery Gateway

22-24 High Street, Polesworth, nr. Tamworth, Warwickshire
Abbey gatehouse, late 14th century with later alterations. Upper floors now in residential use.
Grant Recipient/Owner: Mr W E Thompson
Access contact: Mr W E Thompson
Tel: 01827 706861
Opening Arrangements: Exterior at all reasonable times, ground floor interior by prior arrangement with Mr W E Thompson, 46 Kiln Way, Polesworth, nr. Tamworth, Warwickshire B78 1JE (tel. 01827 706861). Wheelchair access to ground floor only. Parking in Abbey driveway. For further information contact Mr Thompson.
Heritage Open Days: Yes
P See above
Partial. Disabled WC: No. Guide Dogs: Yes
£ No

Ragley Hall

Alcester, Warwickshire B49 5NJ
Family home of the Marquess and Marchioness of Hertford. Built in 1680 to a design by Robert Hooke in the Palladian style, with portico added by Wyatt in 1780. Contents include baroque plasterwork by James Gibb, family portraits by Sir Joshua Reynolds and a mural by Graham Rust completed in 1983. Surrounding gardens designed by 'Capability' Brown.
Grant Recipient/Owner: Marquess of Hertford & Earl of Yarmouth
Access contact: Mr G Timms
Tel: 01789 762090   **Fax:** 01789 764791
Email Address: ragley.hall@virginnet.co.uk
Opening Arrangements: 9 April - 30 September. House: Thursday - Sunday and Bank Holiday Monday; Thursday, Friday and Sunday 12.30 - 5pm, Saturday 11am - 3.30pm and Bank Holiday Monday 11am - 5pm. Park, Gardens and Adventure Wood: Thursday - Sunday and Bank Holiday Monday 10am - 6pm; also every day 9 April - 22 April, 24 May - 3 June and 19 July - 2 September.
Heritage Open Days: No
P Yes. Spaces: 4000
Yes. Disabled WC: Yes. Guide Dogs: Yes
£ Yes
Adult: £5.50 House & Garden, £4.50 Garden only.
Child: £4.00 House & Garden, £3.50 Garden only.
Other: £5.00 House & Garden, £4.00 Garden (seniors/Orange Badge); £20.00 (family) House & Garden, £15.00 (family) Garden only.

St Peter & St Paul

The Presbytery, Friars Lane, Lower Brailes, Warwickshire OX15 5HU
Roman Catholic chapel built in 1726 on first floor of old malthouse. Contains Victorian stained glass, an 18th century crucifixion painting over the altar and original altar rails and pews.
Grant Recipient/Owner: St Philip's Presbytery
Access contact: Anthony Sims
Tel: 01608 682241
Opening Arrangements: Chapel open daily 9am - 6pm.
Heritage Open Days: Yes
P Yes. Spaces: 30
No. Disabled WC: No. Guide Dogs: Yes
£ No

WEST MIDLANDS

Baddesley Clinton Hall,

Rising Lane, Baddesley Clinton, Knowle, Solihull, West Midlands B93 0DQ
A moated manor house, dated from the 15th century. The interiors reflect the house's heyday in the Elizabethan era, when it was a haven for persecuted Catholics. There are three priest-holes. Garden, lake walk and nature walk.
Website Address: www.ntrustsevern.org.uk
Grant Recipient/Owner: The National Trust
Access contact: Mr Alan Langstaff
Tel: 01564 783294   **Fax:** 01564 782706
Email Address: baddesley@smtp.ntrust.org.uk
Opening Arrangements: House: 28 February to 28 October: daily except Mondays and Tuesdays (open Bank Holiday Mondays but closed Good Friday). Times:

February, March, April and October 1.30 - 5pm; May to end September 1.30 - 5.30pm. Grounds: 28 February to 16 December: daily except Mondays and Tuesdays (open Bank Holidays and Good Friday). Times: February, March, April and October 12 - 5pm; May to end September 12 - 5.30pm; November to 16 December 12 - 4.30pm. Wheelchair access to ground floor of house and garden.
Heritage Open Days: No
P Yes. Spaces: 500
Partial. Disabled WC: Yes. Guide Dogs: Yes
£ Yes
Adult: £5.60
Child: £2.80
Other: £14.00 (family). £4.50 (groups 15+). Discount for combined ticket to Baddesley Hall & Packwood House.

Bratch Pumping Station

Bratch Lane, Wombourne, Wolverhampton, West Midlands
Built 1895 of red brick and hipped slate roof in a castellated style with elements of Venetian Gothic. Contains re-furbished steam engines and adjoining workshop with achival photographs, news items and artefacts.
Grant Recipient/Owner: Severn Trent Water Ltd
Access contact: Mr Carlos Abraham
Tel: 0121 722 4563   **Fax:** 0121 722 4800
Opening Arrangements: Arrangements to be confirmed on the establishment of a charitable trust to manage the building. Please contact Mr Carlos Abraham, Conservation, Access & Recreation Adviser, Severn Trent Water Ltd, 2297 Coventry Road, Birmingham, West Midlands B26 3PU (tel.0121 722 4563) for the latest information. Engine room not accessible to wheelchair users.
Heritage Open Days: Yes
P Yes. Spaces: 200
Partial. Disabled WC: Yes. Guide Dogs: Yes
£ Yes
Adult: £1.00
Child: 50p

St James

Great Packington, Meriden, nr. Coventry, West Midlands CV7 7HF
Red brick building with four domes topped by finules in neo-classical style. Built to celebrate the return to sanity of King George III. The organ was designed by Handel for his librettist, Charles Jennens, who was the cousin of the 4th Earl of Aylesford, who built the church.
Grant Recipient/Owner:
St James Great Packington Trust
Access contact: Packington Estate Office
Tel: 01676 522020   **Fax:** 01676 523399
Opening Arrangements: Monday - Friday 9am - 5pm, key can be obtained from the Estate Office at Packington Hall, preferably by phoning in advance on 01676 522020. At other times by prior arrangement with Lord Guernsey (tel. 01676 522274). Wheelchair access with assistance (entrance steps and heavy door to be negotiated).
Heritage Open Days: No
P Yes. Spaces: 10
Yes. Disabled WC: No. Guide Dogs: Yes
£ Donations towards restoration welcomed.

St Mary's Convent

Hunters Road, Handsworth, Birmingham, West Midlands
Highly original and carefully detailed Tudor-Gothic style building. 1840-41 by A W N Pugin. The cloister to the rear has simple exposed timber truss roof and tiled floors. The original chapel was destroyed in the war. The convent is contemporary with a group of Pugin's innovatory rationally designed religious houses.
Grant Recipient/Owner: Sr Evelyn Gallagher
Access contact: Kyran Rigney/Mary Leonard
Tel: 0121 554 3271
Opening Arrangements: By appointment only, written or telephone. Parking on road only.
Heritage Open Days: No
P No
No. Disabled WC: No. Guide Dogs: No
£ No

Wightwick Manor

Wightwick Bank, Tettenhall, Wolverhampton, West Midlands
Built 1887, the house is a notable surviving example of the Arts and Crafts Movement. Contains original William Morris wallpapers and fabrics, Pre-Raphaelite paintings, Kempe glass and de Morgan ware. Also has a 17 acre Victorian/Edwardian garden designed by Thomas Mawson.
Grant Recipient/Owner: The National Trust
Access contact: The Property Manager
Tel: 01902 761400   **Fax:** 01902 764663
Email Address: mwtman@smtp.ntrust.org.uk
Opening Arrangements: By guided tour only 1 March - 31 December: Thursdays and Saturdays (also Bank Holiday Sunday and Monday to ground floor only) 1.30 - 4.30pm. Also family open days Wednesdays in August

1.30 - 4.30pm. Admission by timed ticket issued from 1pm at front door. Garden: Wednesdays, Thursdays, Saturdays and Bank Holiday Sunday and Monday 11am - 6pm. Wheelchair access to ground floor only (up 2 steps).
Heritage Open Days: No
P Yes. Spaces: 50
Partial. Disabled WC: No. Guide Dogs: Yes
£ Yes
Adult: £5.50
Child: £2.75 (children and students)
Other: £13.00 (family)

WEST SUSSEX

Hammerwood Park

nr. East Grinstead, West Sussex RH19 3QE
Designed by Benjamin Latrobe in 1792 as a grand hunting lodge with porticos dedicated to Apollo. Latrobe's White House portico in Washington D C is based on those at Hammerwood. The 18th century parkland incorporates subsequent gardens around the house.
Website Address: www.name.is/hammerwood
Grant Recipient/Owner: Mr David Pinnegar
Access contact: Mr David Pinnegar
Tel: 01342 850594   **Fax:** 01342 850864
Email Address: latrobe@mistral.co.uk
Opening Arrangements: By guided tour Easter Bank Holiday Monday - end of September: Wednesdays, Saturdays and Bank Holidays (tours start at 2.05pm).
Heritage Open Days: No
P Yes. Spaces: 60
Yes. Disabled WC: Yes. Guide Dogs: Yes
£ Yes
Adult: £5.00
Child: £2.00
Other: £5.00

Hiorne Tower

Arundel Park, Arundel, West Sussex BN18 9AB
Constructed 1789 to design by Hiorne of Warwick, it was originally just a decorative landscape feature and lookout but was converted into a keeper's cottage in the mid 19th century when the boundary wall was built. Restored 1992.
Grant Recipient/Owner: Earl of Arundel & Surrey
Access contact: Mr M C G Baxter
Tel: 01903 883400   **Fax:** 01903 884482
Opening Arrangements:
Arundel Park is open to the public daily (except 24 March). Access to the interior of the Hiorne Tower by prior arrangement with the Duke of Norfolk's Estate Office, Arundel, West Sussex BN18 9AS (tel.01903 883400).
Heritage Open Days: No
P No
No. Disabled WC: No. Guide Dogs: Yes
£ No

Parham House

Parham Park, nr. Pulborough, West Sussex RH20 4HS
Granted to the Palmer family in 1540 by Henry VIII, the foundation stone of this grey-stone Elizabethan house was laid in 1577. From the panelled Great Hall to the Long Gallery running the length of the roof-space, the house contains a collection of paintings, furniture and needlework.
Website Address: www.parhaminsussex.co.uk
Grant Recipient/Owner: Parham Park Ltd
Access contact: Ms Patricia Kennedy
Tel: 01903 742021   **Fax:** 01903 746557
Email Address: parham@dial.pipex.co.uk
Opening Arrangements: 1 April - 31 October: Wednesdays, Thursdays, Sundays and Bank Holiday Mondays (also Saturdays 19 May, 14 July and 1 September). Gardens open at 12 noon, House at 2pm with last entry at 5pm. Wheelchair access to ground floor only by prior arrangement, there is a reduced admission charge for wheelchair users and free loan of recorded tour tape. Disabled parking close to house. Admission charges are provisional at time of going to print, please check with House for current rates.
Heritage Open Days: No
P Yes. Spaces: 300
Partial. Disabled WC: Yes. Guide Dogs: Yes
£ Yes
Adult: £5.25 (see above)
Child: £1.00 (5-15)
Other: £4.50 (senior citizens)

Petworth House

Petworth, West Sussex GU28 0AE
Late 17th century mansion in 'Capability' Brown parkland. The house contains the Trust's largest collection of pictures including Turners and Van Dycks. Sculptures, furniture and Grinling Gibbons carvings. Servants' quarters including interesting kitchens and other service

rooms. Extra rooms open at the weekend by kind permission of Lord and Lady Egremont.
Website Address: www.nationaltrust.org.uk
Grant Recipient/Owner: The National Trust
Access contact: Dr Diana Owen
Tel: 01798 342207   **Fax:** 01798 342963
Email Address: spegen@smtp.ntrust.org.uk
Opening Arrangements: House and Servants' Quarters: 31 March to 4 November: daily except Thursdays and Fridays (but open Good Friday and every Friday in July and August). Extra rooms shown weekdays (but not Bank Holiday Mondays) as follows: Mondays, White and Gold Room and Library; Tuesdays and Wednesdays, three bedrooms on first floor. Times: 1 - 5.30pm. Last admission to house 4.30pm; Servants' Quarters 5pm. Wheelchair access to ground floor of house, shop and tea room.
Heritage Open Days: No
P Yes. Spaces: 150
Partial. Disabled WC: Yes. Guide Dogs: Yes
Yes
Adult: £6.00
Child: £3.00
Other: £15.00 (family). £5.00 (booked groups of 15+, per head).

St Hugh's Charterhouse

Henfield Road, Partridge Green, nr. Horsham, West Sussex RH13 8EB
Large monastery covering 10 acres. One large cloister of over 100 sq yds comprising 34 four-room hermitages where the monks live. The fore part is a smaller cloister about 200ft square which contains the cells of the Brothers and their work places. There is also a large church, library, refectory, Brothers Chapel and other monastic buildings. The large quad encloses a cemetery. The spire is 203ft high and has a five-bell chime.
Grant Recipient/Owner: St Hugh's Charterhouse
Access contact: Fr Cyril Pierce
Tel: 01403 864231   **Fax:** 01403 864231
Opening Arrangements: By prior arrangement, with due respect for the rules of the Charterhouse monastery. For further details please contact the monastery.
Heritage Open Days: No
P Yes. Spaces: 20
No. Disabled WC: No. Guide Dogs: Yes
No

Sackville College

East Grinstead, West Sussex RH19 3AZ
Early Jacobean almshouse with original furniture, hall, chapel, common room, John Mason Neale study and library. Built with Sussex sandstone around a quadrangle. Founded in 1609 and still in use, providing 15 flats for elderly people together with the Warden's lodging.
Grant Recipient/Owner:
Warden & Trustees of Sackville College
Access contact: Mr David Russell
Tel: 01342 326561   **Fax:** 01342 326561
Opening Arrangements: June, July and August: Wednesday - Sunday 2 - 5pm. Groups by prior arrangement April - October.
Heritage Open Days: Yes
P Yes. Spaces: 8
Yes. Disabled WC: Yes. Guide Dogs: No
Yes
Adult: £2.50
Child: £1.00
Other: £2.50

The Shell House

Goodwood House, Chichester, West Sussex PO18 0PX
One room Shell House dating from 1740s. Walls and ceiling decorated with hundreds of thousands of shells in classical design, with coffering, niches and cornucopia. Floor with inset horses teeth.
Grant Recipient/Owner:
Goodwood Estate Company Ltd
Access contact: Mrs Rosemary Andreae
Tel: 01243 755018   **Fax:** 01243 755005
Email Address: ra@goodwood.co.uk
Opening Arrangements: By pior written arrangement, usually on set Connoisseurs' Days (15 May, 3 July, 25 September and 23 October) or on Sunday mornings April - September. Two weeks' notice preferred. Bookings can be made with Rosemary Andreae or Kathryn Bellamy (tel. 01243 755048, email: kathryn@goodwood.co.uk). Large car park 40 metres from house. Lavatory for disabled only available when Goodwood House is open to the public.
Heritage Open Days: No
P Yes. Spaces: 4
No. Disabled WC: Yes. Guide Dogs: No
Yes
Adult: £3 on Connoisseurs' Days as part of House visit, £5 on other days.
Child: Free for under 12s

Shipley Windmill

Shipley, nr. Horsham, West Sussex RH13 8PL
Grade II* listed Smock mill with five floors, built 1879 and restored in 1990 to full working order. Once owned by the Sussex writer and poet, Hilaire Belloc, who lived nearby. The milling process is demonstrated on open days for the benefit of visitors.
Grant Recipient/Owner:
Shipley Windmill Charitable Trust
Access contact: Ms Penny Murray
Tel: 01243 777642   **Fax:** 01243 777848
Email Address: penny.murray@westsussex.gov.uk
Opening Arrangements: April - October: first and third Sunday of each month, plus Bank Holiday Mondays. Also National Mills Day, Shipley Festival (May), Horsham and District Arts Fanfare (June) and the Sunday of the Heritage Open Days weekend. It is planned to open the windmill on more Sundays, please check current opening arrangements with Ms Penny Murray, Assistant Clerk to the Trustees, Shipley Windmill Charitable Trust, County Hall, Chichester, West Sussex PO19 1RQ (tel.01243 777642).
Heritage Open Days: Yes
P Yes. Spaces: 10
No. Disabled WC: No. Guide Dogs: No
Yes
Adult: £1.50
Child: 50p
Other: £1.00 (senior citizens)

WEST YORKSHIRE

Bankhouse

Bankhouse Lane, Halifax, West Yorkshire
16th century yeomans hall with cross wing and lower end cottages.
Grant Recipient/Owner: Mr H Haigh
Access contact: Mr H Haigh
Tel: 01422 354589
Opening Arrangements: By prior arrangement.
Heritage Open Days: No
P Yes. Spaces: 2
No. Disabled WC: No. Guide Dogs: Yes
No

Bramham Park Lead Lads Temple

Wetherby, West Yorkshire LS23 6ND
18th century open temple in the classical style in Bramham Park (about a mile from the house in woodland called Black Fen, close to a public footpath).
Grant Recipient/Owner: Mr G F Lane Fox
Access contact: Mr G F Lane Fox
Tel: 01937 846004   **Fax:** 01937 846001
Opening Arrangements: Accessible at all times, close to a public footpath.
Heritage Open Days: No
P No
No. Disabled WC: No. Guide Dogs: No
No

Crossley Pavilion

The People's Park, King Cross Road, Halifax, West Yorkshire
Grade II* listed building, designed by Sir Joseph Paxton and constructed in 1857. Contains seating and a statue of the park's benefactor, Sir Francis Crossley (1860), by Joseph Durham. Four gargoyle fountains supply pools flanking each side of the pavilion, set on formal terrace, balustrades and steps.
Grant Recipient/Owner:
Calderdale Metropolitan Borough Council
Access contact: Miss Deborah Comyn-Platt
Tel: 01422 359454   **Fax:** 01422 348301
Email Address: d.a.comyn-platt@calderdale.gov.uk
Opening Arrangements: By prior arrangement with Calderdale Metropolitan Borough Council Leisure Services, Wellesley Park, Halifax, West Yorkshire (tel.01422 359454). Exterior viewing all year during park opening hours 8am - dusk. Street parking available on Park Road. Information Centre and toilets, including disabled toilets, due to be completed by June.
Heritage Open Days: Yes
P See above
Yes. Disabled WC: Yes. Guide Dogs: Yes
No

Friends Meeting House

off Bolton Road, Addingham, nr. Ilkley, West Yorkshire LS29
Land for burial ground purchased in 1666, followed by construction of Meeting House in 1669. A simple single cell building with rubblestone walls, mullioned windows, stone-slated roof and stone-flagged floor. Contains loose benches and an oak minister's stand of an unusual panelled design with turned balusters.
Website Address: www.hct.org.uk
Grant Recipient/Owner: Historic Chapels Trust

Access contact: John Spencer
Tel: 01756 710225
Opening Arrangements: At all reasonable times by application to keyholders Mr & Mrs John Spencer, who live opposite the Meeting House at Cook's Cottage, 3 Farfield Cottages, Bolton Road, Addingham, nr. Ilkley, West Yorkshire LS29 0RQ (tel.01756 710225).
Heritage Open Days: Yes
P Yes. Spaces: 2
No. Disabled WC: No. Guide Dogs: Yes
No

Harewood House

Harewood, Leeds, West Yorkshire LS17 9LQ
Designed in neo-classical style by John Carr and completed in 1772. Contains Adam interiors, Chippendale furniture and art collection. Home of the Earl and Countess of Harewood.
Website Address: www.harewood.org
Grant Recipient/Owner:
The Trustees of Harewood House Ltd
Access contact: The Trustees of Harewood House Ltd
Tel: 0113 218 1010
Opening Arrangements: Daily 14 March - 4 November: Grounds & Bird Garden open 10am - 4.30pm (last admission 4pm); House and Terrace Gallery 11am - 4.30pm (last admission 4pm). Grounds close at 6pm. Grounds and Bird Garden also open weekends between 10 November and 17 December. Disabled visitors can alight at entrance. Wheelchair access to most facilities but with some steep inclines. Wheelchair available at house and Bird Garden. Special concessions for disabled groups. Guide dogs are not allowed in the Bird Garden but a free sound guide is available for the partially sighted visitor and a babysitter for the dog.
Heritage Open Days: No
P Yes. Spaces: 200
Yes. Disabled WC: Yes. Guide Dogs: See above
Yes
Adult: £7.50
Child: £5.00
Other: £6.75 (senior), £26.00 (family), (annual season tickets also available).

Holdsworth House Gazebo

Holdsworth, Halifax, West Yorkshire HX2 9TG
Probably built, c1633, at about the same time as the house at the corner of the sunken garden.
Grant Recipient/Owner: Cavalier Country Club
Access contact: Mr Peter Phillips
Tel: 01422 240024   **Fax:** 01422 245174
Email Address: info@holdsworthhouse.co.uk
Opening Arrangements: Hotel open throughout the year (except Christmas).
Heritage Open Days: No
P Yes. Spaces: 40
No. Disabled WC: No. Guide Dogs: Yes
No

Ledston Hall

Hall Lane, Ledston, Castleford, West Yorkshire WF10 2BB
17th century mansion with some earlier work.
Grant Recipient/Owner: Mr G H H Wheler
Access contact: Mr J F T Hare
Tel: 01423 523423   **Fax:** 01423 521373
Email Address: james.hare@carterjonas.co.uk
Opening Arrangements: May - August: Monday - Friday 9am - 4pm. At other times by prior arrangement with Mr J F T Hare, Carter Jonas, Regent House, 13/15 Albert St, Harrogate, West Yorkshire HG1 1JF (tel.01423 523423).
Heritage Open Days: Yes
P Yes. Spaces: 5
Yes. Disabled WC: No. Guide Dogs: Yes
No

Marlborough Hall

Crossley Street, Halifax, West Yorkshire HX1 1UG
Built in 1857 as a Mechanics Institute, which it remained until 1932. From 1917 to 1922 it doubled as the Gem Cinema, the first permanent cinema in Halifax. Contains four floors with many meeting rooms and an auditorium, the frontage hall and stairways have many original features.
Grant Recipient/Owner: Halifax & District YMCA
Access contact: Mr C F Love
Tel: 01422 353626
Email Address: admin@halifax.ymca.co.uk
Opening Arrangements: Daily 10am - 4pm (except Bank Holidays and weekends). Wheelchair access to ground floor and lower ground floor only.
Heritage Open Days: No
P No
Partial. Disabled WC: Yes. Guide Dogs: Yes
No

Marshall Mill

Marshall Street, Leeds, West Yorkshire LS11 9YJ
Textile mill built c1800 and now converted to offices containing lobby, external and common areas.
Grant Recipient/Owner: Marshall Mill Ltd
Access contact: Mr John Wright
Tel: 0113 245 3324   **Fax:** 0113 245 3317
Opening Arrangements: By prior arrangement.
Heritage Open Days: No
P No
Yes. Disabled WC: Yes. Guide Dogs: Yes
£ No

Nostell Priory

Doncaster Road, Nostell, Wakefield, West Yorkshire WF4 1QE
Country house, 1736-1750, by James Paine for Sir Rowland Winn 4th baronet. Later Robert Adam was commissioned to complete the State Rooms. On display is a collection of Chippendale furniture, designed especially for the house, an art collection with works by Pieter Breughel the Younger and Angelica Kauffmann, and an 18th century dolls house, complete with its original fittings and Chippendale furniture. Lakeside walks.
Website Address: www.nationaltrust.org.uk
Grant Recipient/Owner: The National Trust
Access contact: Property Manager
Tel: 01924 863892   **Fax:** 01924 865282
Email Address: yorknp@smtp.ntrust.org.uk
Opening Arrangements: House: 31 March to 4 November: daily except Mondays and Tuesdays (but open Bank Holiday Mondays) 1- 5.30pm; 10 November to 9 December: Saturdays and Sundays 12 - 4.30pm. Grounds: open same days as house 11am - 6pm. Wheelchair access to ground floor of house with lift to first floor, tea room, children's playground and shop.
Heritage Open Days: No
P Yes. Spaces: 120
Partial. Disabled WC: No. Guide Dogs: Yes
£ Yes
Adult: £4.50. £2.50 (grounds only).
Child: £2.20. £1.20 (grounds only).
Other: £11.00 (family). (No family ticket for grounds only).

The Roundhouse

Wellington Road, Leeds, West Yorkshire LS12 1DR
Grade II* railway roundhouse built in 1847 for the Leeds and Thirsk Railway by Thomas Granger. In full use by the North-Eastern Railway until 1904, now home to Leeds Commercial Van and Truck Hire.
Grant Recipient/Owner: Wellbridge Properties Ltd
Access contact: Mr J D Miller
Tel: 0113 2435964   **Fax:** 0113 246 1142
Email Address: sales@leedscommercial.co.uk
Opening Arrangements: By prior written arrangement with the occupiers, Leeds Commercial, who manage the property as a working garage.
Heritage Open Days: No
P Yes. Spaces: 30
Yes. Disabled WC: Yes. Guide Dogs: Yes
£ No

Todmorden Unitarian Church

Honey Hole Road, Todmorden, West Yorkshire OL14 6LE
Grade I church with a large wooded burial ground and ornamental gardens designed by John Gibson, 1865-69. Victorian Gothic style with tall tower and spire. Detached smaller burial ground nearby and listed lodge in churchyard.
Website Address: www.hct.org.uk
Grant Recipient/Owner: Historic Chapels Trust
Access contact: Mr Rob Goldthorpe
Tel: 01706 815648
Opening Arrangements: At all reasonable times by application to the keyholder, Mr Rob Goldthorpe, at 14 Honey Hole Close, Todmorden, West Yorkshire OL14 6LH (tel.01706 815648) or by calling at the caretaker's house, Todmorden Lodge, at the entrance to the churchyard.
Heritage Open Days: Yes
P Yes. Spaces: 50
Yes. Disabled WC: Yes. Guide Dogs: Yes
£ No

WILTSHIRE

Cherhill Monument

Cherhill Down, Wiltshire
Cherhill Monument (also known as Lansdowne Monument) is situated on the summit of the chalk ridge at Cherhill Down. Built in 1845 by the 3rd Marquis of Landsdowne in memory of the economist Sir William Petty.
Website Address: www.nationaltrust.org.uk
Grant Recipient/Owner: The National Trust
Access contact: The National Trust

Tel: 01985 843600   **Fax:** 01985 843624
Opening Arrangements: Open access via footpaths and bridleways across the Down. Parking available in laybys off the A4.
Heritage Open Days: No
P See above
No. Disabled WC: No. Guide Dogs: Yes
£ No

The Cloisters

Iford Manor, Bradford-on-Avon, Wiltshire BA15 2BA
Small stone-built cloister in gardens of Manor, completed 1914 by Harold Peto and based on 13th century Italian style. Interesting early contents.
Website Address: www.iford.manor@which.com
Grant Recipient/Owner: Mrs E Cartwright-Hignett
Access contact: Mrs E Cartwright-Hignett
Tel: 01225 863146   **Fax:** 01225 862364
Email Address: iford.manor@which.com
Opening Arrangements: Gardens only: April - October, Sundays and Easter Monday 2 - 5pm; May - September, daily (except Mondays and Fridays) 2 - 5pm. Children under 10 not admitted at weekends. Coaches and groups by prior arrangement only. Wheelchair access by prior arrangement to Cloisters and part of the gardens.
Heritage Open Days: No
P Yes. Spaces: 100
Partial. Disabled WC: No. Guide Dogs: Yes
£ Yes
Adult: £3.00
Child: £2.50 (10-16, under 10 free).
Other: £2.50 (seniors & students)

Dyrham Park

nr. Chippenham, Wiltshire SN14 8ER
17th century house set within an ancient deer park, woodlands and formal garden. The house was furnished in the Dutch style and still has many original contents including paintings, ceramics, furniture and 17th century tapestries. The Victorian domestic rooms include the kitchen, larder, bakehouse, dairy and tenants hall.
Grant Recipient/Owner: The National Trust
Access contact: The Property Manager
Tel: 01179 372501   **Fax:** 01179 372501
Email Address: wdymxa@smtp.ntrust.og.uk
Opening Arrangements: House: 31 March - 4 November: daily except Wednesday and Thursday 12- 5.30 (last admission to house 4.45pm). Garden: as for house 11am - 5.30pm or dusk if earlier. Park: daily (closed 25 December) 12 - 5.30pm or dusk if earlier (when gardens are open, the park opens at 11am). Winter opening for Domestic Rooms: 10 November - 16 December: Saturday and Sunday 12 - 4.00pm. Note: property is closed 6-9 July for concerts. Wheelchair access to all but four upstairs rooms. A photograph album of these rooms is available. A free bus takes visitors from the car park to the house.
Heritage Open Days: No
P Yes. Spaces: 250
Partial. Disabled WC: Yes. Guide Dogs: Yes
£ Yes
Adult: £7.80, £3.00 (grounds only), £1.90 (Park only when house & garden closed). £4.00 (Winter: Park & Domestic Rooms).
Child: £3.90, £1.50 (grounds only), 90p (Park only when house and garden closed), £2.00 (Winter: Park & Domestic Rooms).
Other: £19.00 (family).

Fonthill Underground Bath House

Fonthill Bishop, Salisbury, Wiltshire SP3 5SH
18th century boathouse or water temple of aisled 'basilica' plan with transepts and apsidal west end, the wet dock being the 'nave' and 'crossing' and the walkways the 'aisles'. Constructed of limestone ashlar with vaulted roof covered in earth.
Grant Recipient/Owner: Lord Margadale
Access contact: Resident Agent
Tel: 01747 820246
Opening Arrangements: 1 March - 31 July: by prior written arrangement with the Estate Office, Fonthill Bishop, Salisbury, Wiltshire SP3 5SH. Wellington boots will be required by visitors.
Heritage Open Days: No
P No
No. Disabled WC: No. Guide Dogs: No
£ Yes
Adult: £2.50
Child: Free
Other: Free

Lacock Abbey

Lacock, nr. Chippenham, Wiltshire SN15 2LG
Founded in 1232 and converted into a county house c1540, the fine medieval Cloisters, Sacristy, Chapter house and monastic rooms of the Abbey have survived largely intact. The 16th century stable courtyard has half timbered gables, a clock house, brewery and bakehouse. Victorian

garden, Former residents include William Fox Talbot 'the father of modern photography'.
Website Address: www.nationaltrust.org.uk
Grant Recipient/Owner: The National Trust
Access contact: Property Manager
Tel: 01249 730141   **Fax:** 01249 730501
Opening Arrangements: Abbey: 13 March to 4 November: daily 1 - 5.30pm (closed Tuesdays and Good Friday). Museum, cloisters and garden: 3 March to 4 November: daily 11am - 5.30pm (closed Good Friday). Museum also open winter weekends, but closed 22/23 December to 30 December, telephone the Property Manager for details. Wheelchair access to Abbey is difficult as four sets of stairs. Garden, cloisters and museum are accessible. Short walk from car park to Abbey. Limited parking in Abbey courtyard by arrangement.
Heritage Open Days: No
P Yes. Spaces: 300
Partial. Disabled WC: Yes. Guide Dogs: Yes
£ Yes
Adult: £6.00 (Abbey, museum, cloisters & garden). £4.80 (Abbey & garden). £3.80 (garden, cloisters & museum). **Child:** £3.30 (Abbey, museum, cloisters & garden). £2.70 (Abbey & garden). £2.30 (garden, cloisters & museum). **Other:** £16.30 (family: Abbey, museum, cloisters & garden). £12.30 (family: Abbey & garden). £10.90 (Abbey: garden, cloisters & museum). Group rates. Free NT members.

Lydiard Park

Lydiard Tregoze, Swindon, Wiltshire SN5 9PA
Ancestral home of the Bolingbrokes, the restored Palladian mansion contains family furnishings and portraits, plasterwork, rare 17th century painted window and room dedicated to 18th century society artist Lady Diana Spencer.
Grant Recipient/Owner: Swindon Borough Council
Access contact: Mrs Sarah Finch-Crisp
Tel: 01793 770401   **Fax:** 01793 877909
Opening Arrangements: House: Monday - Friday 10am - 1pm & 2 - 5pm, Saturdays and school summer holidays 10am - 5pm, Sundays 2 - 5pm. November - February early closing at 4pm. Grounds all day, closing at dusk. Admission prices may increase, please check with the Park.
Heritage Open Days: No
P Yes. Spaces: 400
Yes. Disabled WC: Yes. Guide Dogs: Yes
£ Yes
Adult: £1.20 (provisional)
Child: 60p (provisional)

Manor Farm

Coate, Wiltshire SN10 3LP
16-17th century thatched farmhouse.
Grant Recipient/Owner: Roy Stokes & Company
Access contact: Roy & Ann Stokes
Tel: 01380 860234   **Fax:** 01380 860234
Opening Arrangements: By prior arrangement from May to September. As the building is part of a working farm, visitors are requested not to bring their pets.
Heritage Open Days: No
P Yes. Spaces: 2
No. Disabled WC: No. Guide Dogs: No
£ Donation to a charity

Merchant's House

132 High Street, Marlborough, Wiltshire SN8 1HN
17th century town house built by the Bayly family, mercers between 1653 and c1700. Situated prominently in the High Street it contains a unique stripe-painted dining room c1665, painted balustrading to the oak staircase and a panelled chamber of the Commonwealth period.
Website Address: www.themerchantshouse.co.uk
Access contact: Mr Michael Gray
Tel: 01672 511491   **Fax:** 01672 511491
Email Address: manager@themerchantshouse.co.uk
Opening Arrangements: Saturdays all year 10am - 4pm. Public parking outside building in High Street.
Heritage Open Days: Yes
P See above
No. Disabled WC: No. Guide Dogs: Yes
£ No

Old Bishop's Palace

Salisbury Cathedral School, 1 The Close, Salisbury, Wiltshire SP1 2EQ
13th century building, much altered over the centuries, with 13th century undercroft, Georgian drawing room and a chapel.
Grant Recipient/Owner:
Salisbury Diocesan Board of Finance
Access contact: A J Craigie
Tel: 01722 555300   **Fax:** 01722 410910
Email Address: aspire@salisbury.enterprise-plc.com
Opening Arrangements: Opening arrangements under review at time of going to print, please check the English Heritage website or with Mr Craigie for current information.
Heritage Open Days: Yes

P No
& No. Disabled WC: No. Guide Dogs: No
£ Yes
Adult: £2.00

Sarum College

19 The Close, Salisbury, Wiltshire SP1 2EE
Grade I listed house, c1677, attributed to Sir Christopher Wren. In the 1870s collegiate buildings were added, designed by William Butterfield. The college is an ecumenical education, training and conference centre.
Website Address: www.sarum.ac.uk
Grant Recipient/Owner: Trustees of Salisbury & Wells Theological College/Sarum College
Access contact: Mrs Linda Cooper
Tel: 01722 424800   **Fax:** 01722 338508
Email Address: admin@sarum.ac.uk
Opening Arrangements: Daily during term-time, please check with College for details of term-times. Wheelchair access to ground floor only.
Heritage Open Days: No
P Yes. Spaces: 37
& Partial. Disabled WC: Yes. Guide Dogs: Yes
£ No

Stourhead

nr. Warminster, Wiltshire BA12 6QH
Country house, built 1721-24 for Henry Hoare by Colen Campbell. Following fire in 1902, central block was rebuilt between 1902-06. Set in landscaped parkland and with the fine Stourhead Gardens to the west. Landscape garden laid out between 1741 and 1780. Classical temples including the Pantheon and Temple of Apollo are set around the lake. King Alfred's tower is an intriguing red-brick folly. Woodlands with collection of exotic trees.
Website Address: www.nationaltrust.org.uk
Grant Recipient/Owner: The National Trust
Access contact: Property Manager
Tel: 01747 841152   **Fax:** 01747 841152
Email Address: wstest@smtp.ntrust.org.uk
Opening Arrangements: House: 31 March to 4 November: daily (except Thursdays and Fridays) 12 - 5.30pm. Garden: daily 9am - 7pm or sunset if earlier. King Alfred's Tower: 31 March to 4 November daily except Mondays (but open on Bank Holiday Mondays) at following times: Tuesdays to Fridays 2 - 5.30pm, Saturday, Sunday and Bank Holiday Mondays, 11.30am - 5.30pm or dusk if earlier. Wheelchair access to: house with use of stairclimber (must be booked in advance); 1 1/2 mile path around lake, but steep in places. Parking close to house for Orange Badge holders.
Heritage Open Days: No
P Yes. Spaces: 500
& Partial. Disabled WC: Yes. Guide Dogs: Yes
£ Yes
Adult: £8.50 (house & garden). £4.80 (house). £4.80-£3.70 (garden). £1.60 (King Alfred's Tower).
Adult: £4.00 (house & garden). £2.60 (house). £2.60-£1.80 (garden). £0.80 (King Alfred's Tower).
Adult: £20.00 (family: house & garden). £12.00 (family: house). £12.00-£9.00 (family: garden). £4.00 (family: King Alfred's Tower). Group rates. Free NT members.

Tottenham House

Savernake Forest, Marlborough, Wiltshire SN8 3HP
Great house built of Bath stone in 1820 by Thomas Cundy for the 1st Marquess of Ailesbury. Most of the house is unfurnished, and it is currently leased to the Amber Foundation, a charity for homeless/jobless young people.
Grant Recipient/Owner:
Trustees of the Savernake Estate
Access contact: Earl of Cardigan
Tel: 01672 512161   **Fax:** 01672 512105
Opening Arrangements: By prior arrangement with the Savernake Estate Office. Wheelchair access with assistance (entrance steps to be negotiated).
Heritage Open Days: No
P Yes. Spaces: 30
& Partial. Disabled WC: No. Guide Dogs: Yes
£ No

Wilton House

Wilton, Salisbury, Wiltshire SP2 0BJ
Ancestral home of the Earls of Pembroke for 450 years, rebuilt by Inigo Jones and John Webb in the Palladian style with further alterations by James Wyatt c1801. Contains 17th century state rooms and an art collection including works by Van Dyck, Rubens, Joshua Reynolds and Brueghel. Surrounded by landscaped parkland.
Website Address: www.wiltonhouse.com
Grant Recipient/Owner: Wilton House Charitable Trust
Access contact: Mr Ray Stedman
Tel: 01722 746720   **Fax:** 01722 744447
Email Address: tourism@wiltonhouse.com
Opening Arrangements: 4 April - 28 October 10.30am - 5.30pm (last admission 4.30pm).
Heritage Open Days: No
P Yes. Spaces: 200
& Yes. Disabled WC: Yes. Guide Dogs: Yes
£ Yes
Adult: £7.25
Child: £4.50
Other: £6.25 (senior citizens)

Wilton Windmill

East Grafton, Wiltshire, SN8 3SS
Built 1821. Only working windmill in Wiltshire, standing on a chalk ridge 550ft high.
Grant Recipient/Owner: Wiltshire County Council
Access contact: Mr John Talbot
Tel: 01672 870072
Email Address: jctalbot@waitrose.com
Opening Arrangements: Easter - end of September: guided tours on Sundays and Bank Holidays 2 - 5pm.
Heritage Open Days: No
P Yes. Spaces: 8
& No. Disabled WC: No. Guide Dogs: Yes
£ Yes
Adult: £2.00
Child: 50p
Other: £1.50 (senior), £4.00 (family).

WORCESTERSHIRE

Detton Hall

Neen Savage, Cleobury Mortimer, Kidderminster, Worcestershire DY14 8LW
Large farmhouse built between the late 16th and early 18th centuries. Part half-timbered, part local stone and with roofs of clay tiles. There are 4 tall Tudor star chimney stacks and the main stairs have fretted panels. Extensively restored between 1991 and 1996.
Grant Recipient/Owner: Mr E C Ratcliff
Access contact: Mr E C Ratcliff
Tel: 01299 270387   **Fax:** 01299 270387
Opening Arrangements: By guided tour only by prior telephone or written arrangement with Mr E C or Mr E B Ratcliff. Wheelchair access to ground floor only with assistance (a few steps). Admission charges include light refreshment if required. Please note that the property is in Shropshire.
Heritage Open Days: Yes
P Yes. Spaces: 10
& Partial. Disabled WC: No. Guide Dogs: Yes
£ Yes
Adult: £5.00
Child: £3.00

Edgar Tower

Worcester, Worcestershire
Gateway dates from mid-14th century and consists of a central block containing a larger arched opening for vehicular access to the precinct and a smaller pedestrian doorway. Blocks to north and south provided accommodation while the corner turrets contained stairs, garderobes, etc.
Grant Recipient/Owner:
Dean & Chapter of Worcester Cathedral
Access contact: Cathedral Steward
Tel: 01905 28854   **Fax:** 01905 611139
Email Address: worcestercathedral@compuserve.com

Opening Arrangements: The Tower is one of the entrances through which visitors pass when approaching the Cathedral from the south. Visits to the interior (King's Library) during school holidays by prior written arrangement to the Cathedral Steward, Chapter Office, 10a College Green, Worcester WR1 2LH. Please note that visits to the Tower can be physically demanding as the stairway is steep and narrow.
Heritage Open Days: Yes
P No
& No. Disabled WC: No. Guide Dogs: No
£ No

Hanbury Hall

Hanbury, Droitwich, Worcestershire WR9 7EA
Built in 1701, this William and Mary-style house contains painted ceilings and staircase. It has an orangery, ice house and Moorish gazebos. The re-created 18th century garden is surrounded by parkland and has a parterre, wilderness, fruit garden, open grove and bowling green pavilions.
Website Address: www.ntrustsevern.org.uk
Grant Recipient/Owner: The National Trust
Access contact: Mr Stewart Alcock
Tel: 01527 821214   **Fax:** 01527 821251
Email Address: hanbury@smtp.ntrust.org.uk
Opening Arrangements: 1 April to 31 October: Sunday to Wednesday 1.30 - 5.30pm (but open Good Friday) last admission 5pm or dusk if earlier. Garden opens at 12.00pm. Car parking 200 metres from house. Parking for disabled near house.
Heritage Open Days: No
P Yes. Spaces: 80
& Yes. Disabled WC: Yes. Guide Dogs: Yes
£ Yes
Adult: £3.00
Child: £1.60
Other: £7.50 (family).

Hopton Court Conservatory

Cleobury Mortimer, Kidderminster, Worcestershire DY14 0EF
Grade II* listed conservatory, c1830, of cast iron with a rounded archway leading to a rear room roofed with curved glass. Two rooms either side, one housing the boiler beneath to supply heat by way of cast iron grilles running around the floor of the interior.
Grant Recipient/Owner: Mr C R D Woodward
Access contact: Mr Christopher Woodward
Tel: 01299 270734   **Fax:** 01299 271132
Email Address: hoptoncourt@hotmail.com
Opening Arrangements: Weekend of 23/24 June and at other times by prior arrangement.
Heritage Open Days: No
P Yes. Spaces: 150
& Yes. Disabled WC: Yes. Guide Dogs: Yes
£ Yes
Adult: £3.50

Worcester Assembly Rooms

Shaw Street, Worcester, Worcestershire WR1 3QQ
Built c1740 for the Hoppole Hotel. Such rooms were fashionable throughout the 18th century, Worcester had 3 all of which remain. Constructed over stables with 1st floor access and tea rooms. Survives virtually unaltered with much of its fine interior decoration intact. Possibly among the best early 18th century inn assembly rooms remaining in England.
Grant Recipient/Owner: Mr J Rudge
Access contact: Mr J Rudge
Tel: 01886 821190
Opening Arrangements: By prior arrangement with Mr J Rudge, Pacemark Developments Ltd, The Old School, Knightwick, Worcester WR6 5PJ (tel.01886 821190).
Heritage Open Days: No
P No
& No
£ No

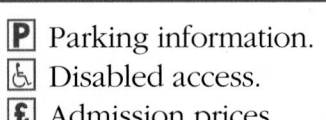

P Parking information.
& Disabled access.
£ Admission prices.

London Detail

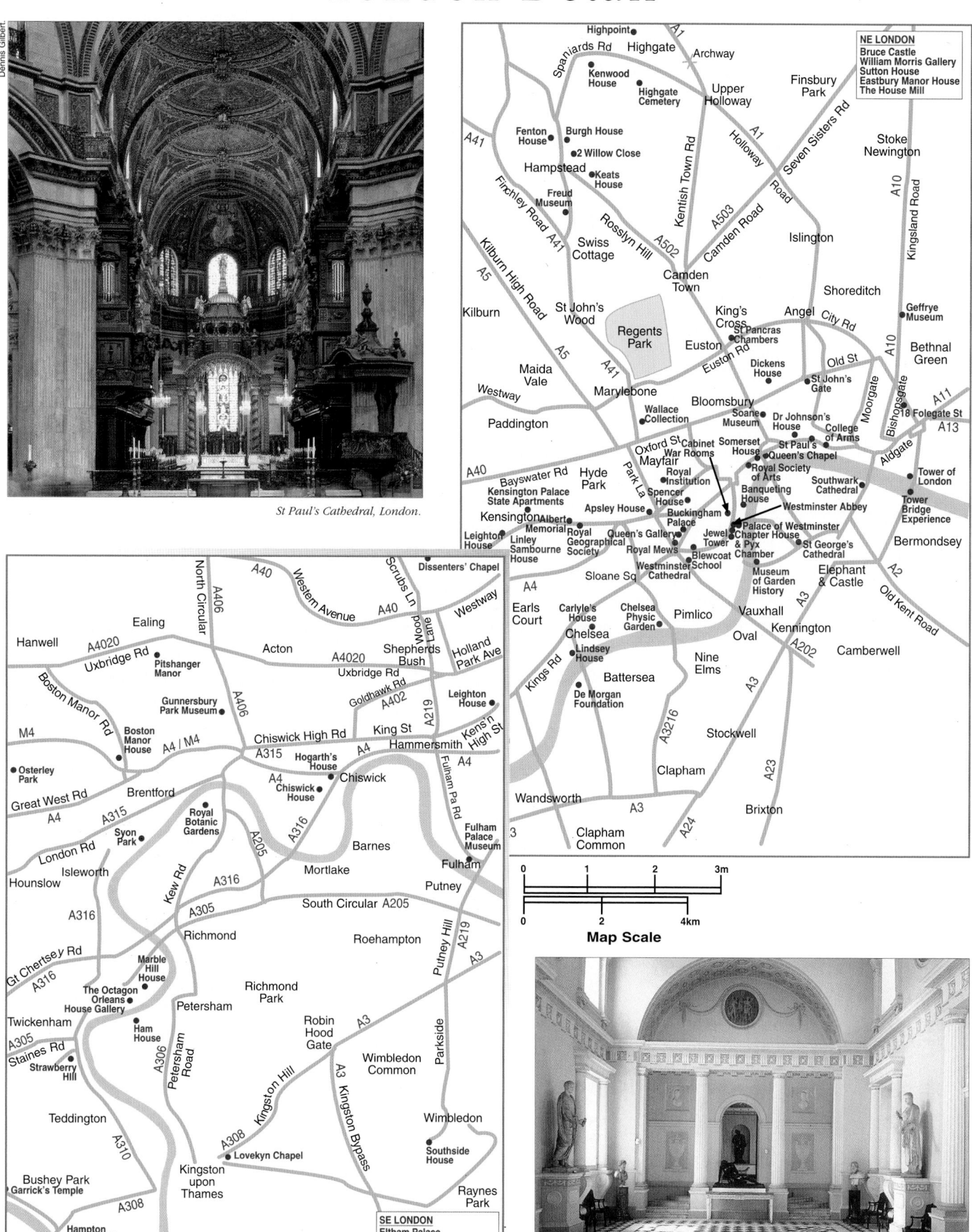

St Paul's Cathedral, London.

NE LONDON
Bruce Castle
William Morris Gallery
Sutton House
Eastbury Manor House
The House Mill

Highpoint
Highgate
Archway
Spaniards Rd
Kenwood House
Highgate Cemetery
Upper Holloway
Finsbury Park
Stoke Newington
Fenton House
Burgh House
2 Willow Close
Hampstead
Keats House
Holloway Road
Seven Sisters Rd
A1
A10 Kingsland Road
A41
Finchley Road A41
Freud Museum
Rosslyn Hill
Camden Road
Islington
Shoreditch
Geffrye Museum
Bethnal Green
Swiss Cottage
Kilburn High Road
Camden Town
King's Cross
Angel
City Rd
A10
Bishopsgate
A11
A13
Kilburn
St John's Wood
St Pancras Chambers
Euston
Euston Rd
Dickens House
Old St
St John's Gate
Moorgate
18 Folegate St
Maida Vale
Regents Park
Bloomsbury
Soane Museum
Dr Johnson's House
College of Arms
Aldgate
Westway
Marylebone
Wallace Collection
St Paul's
Queen's Chapel
Tower of London
Paddington
Oxford St
Cabinet War Rooms
Somerset House
Royal Society of Arts
Southwark Cathedral
Tower Bridge Experience
A40
Bayswater Rd
Hyde Park
Park La
Royal Institution
Banqueting House
Kensington Palace State Apartments
Spencer House
Buckingham Palace
Westminster Abbey
Bermondsey
Kensington
Albert Memorial
Apsley House
Queen's Gallery
Palace of Westminster
Chapter House & Pyx Chamber
A2
Leighton House
Linley Sambourne House
Royal Geographical Society
Royal Mews
Jewel Tower
Blewcoat School
St George's Cathedral
Old Kent Road
Sloane Sq
Westminster Cathedral
Museum of Garden History
Elephant & Castle
A4
Earls Court
Carlyle's House
Chelsea Physic Garden
Pimlico
Vauxhall
Kennington
Kings Rd
Lindsey House
Chelsea
Oval
A202
Camberwell
Battersea
Nine Elms
A3
De Morgan Foundation
A3216
Stockwell
A23
Wandsworth
A3
Clapham
Brixton
A24
Clapham Common

Map Scale

0   1   2   3m

0   2   4km

A40
Western Avenue
North Circular
A406
Scrubs Ln
Wood Lane
Dissenters' Chapel
A40
Westway
Ealing
Hanwell
A4020
Uxbridge Rd
Acton
A4020
Shepherds Bush
Holland Park Ave
Pitshanger Manor
Uxbridge Rd
Boston Manor Rd
Gunnersbury Park Museum
A406
Goldhawk Rd
A402
Leighton House
M4
Boston Manor House
A4 / M4
Chiswick High Rd
A315
Hogarth's House
A4
King St
Hammersmith
Kens'n High St
A4
Osterley Park
Great West Rd
A4
A315
Brentford
Royal Botanic Gardens
Chiswick House
Chiswick
Fulham Pa Rd
A4
London Rd
Syon Park
A316
Barnes
Fulham Palace Museum
Hounslow
Isleworth
Kew Rd
Mortlake
Fulham
A316
A305
South Circular A205
Putney
Gt Chertsey Rd
A316
Richmond
Roehampton
Putney Hill
A219
A3
Marble Hill House
Richmond Park
Parkside
The Octagon Orleans House Gallery
Petersham
Robin Hood Gate
Twickenham
Ham House
Kingston Hill
Wimbledon Common
A305
Petersham Road
A306
Staines Rd
Strawberry Hill
A3
Kingston Bypass
Wimbledon
Teddington
A310
A308
Lovekyn Chapel
Southside House
Bushey Park
Garrick's Temple
A308
Kingston upon Thames
Raynes Park
Hampton Court Palace
Hampton Court Park
Surbiton

SE LONDON
Eltham Palace,
The Royal Observatory
& Queens House,
Ranger's House,
Prendergast School Murals

Syon Park, London.

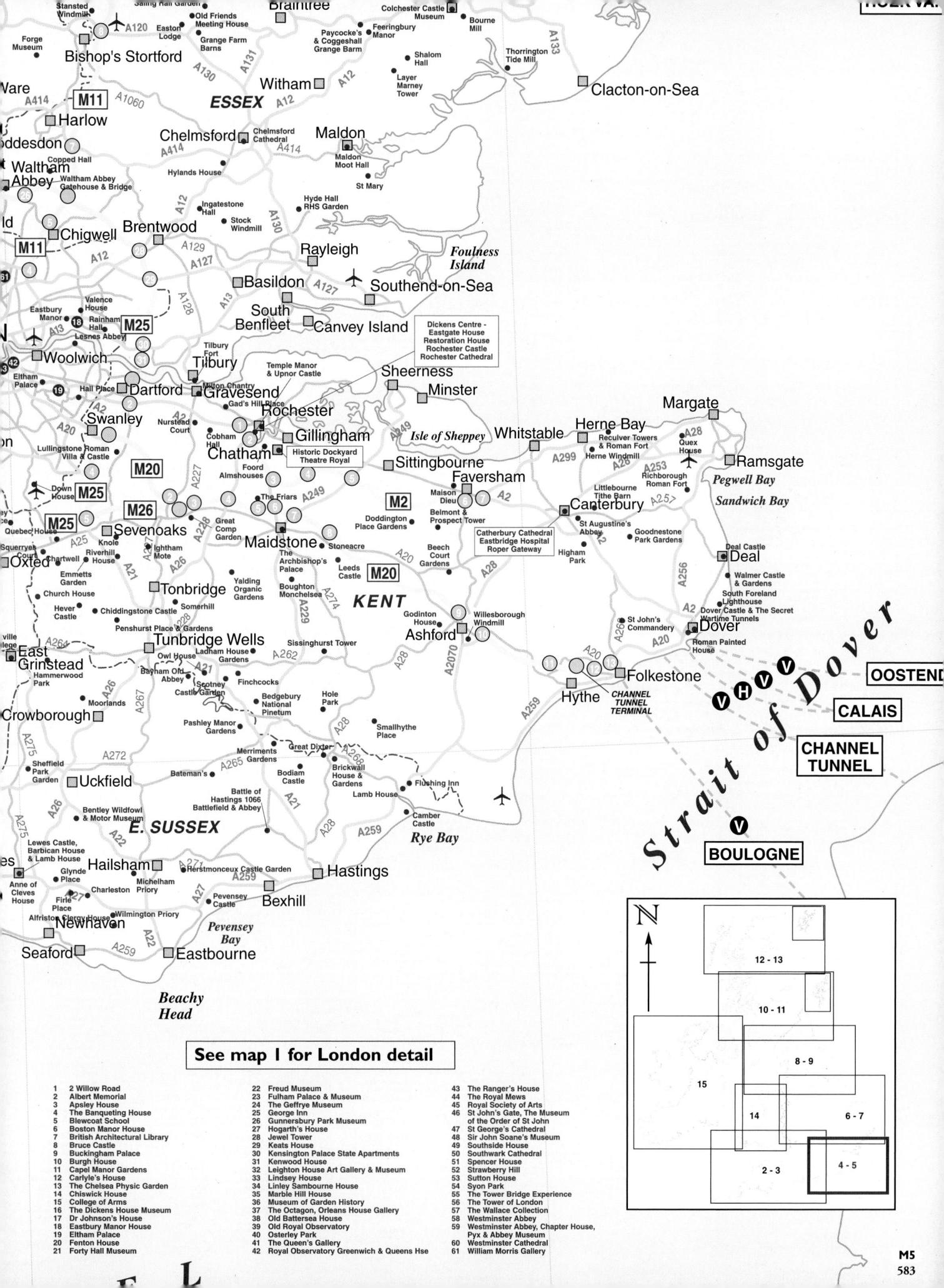

See map 1 for London detail

1 2 Willow Road	22 Freud Museum	43 The Ranger's House
2 Albert Memorial	23 Fulham Palace & Museum	44 The Royal Mews
3 Apsley House	24 The Geffrye Museum	45 Royal Society of Arts
4 The Banqueting House	25 George Inn	46 St John's Gate, The Museum of the Order of St John
5 Blewcoat School	26 Gunnersbury Park Museum	47 St George's Cathedral
6 Boston Manor House	27 Hogarth's House	48 Sir John Soane's Museum
7 British Architectural Library	28 Jewel Tower	49 Southside House
8 Bruce Castle	29 Keats House	50 Southwark Cathedral
9 Buckingham Palace	30 Kensington Palace State Apartments	51 Spencer House
10 Burgh House	31 Kenwood House	52 Strawberry Hill
11 Capel Manor Gardens	32 Leighton House Art Gallery & Museum	53 Sutton House
12 Carlyle's House	33 Lindsey House	54 Syon Park
13 The Chelsea Physic Garden	34 Linley Sambourne House	55 The Tower Bridge Experience
14 Chiswick House	35 Marble Hill House	56 The Tower of London
15 College of Arms	36 Museum of Garden History	57 The Wallace Collection
16 The Dickens House Museum	37 The Octagon, Orleans House Gallery	58 Westminster Abbey
17 Dr Johnson's House	38 Old Battersea House	59 Westminster Abbey, Chapter House, Pyx & Abbey Museum
18 Eastbury Manor House	39 Old Royal Observatory	60 Westminster Cathedral
19 Eltham Palace	40 Osterley Park	61 William Morris Gallery
20 Fenton House	41 The Queen's Gallery	
21 Forty Hall Museum	42 Royal Observatory Greenwich & Queens Hse	

Map Scale

| 0 | 10 | 20 | | 40m |
| 0 | 10 | 20 | 40 | 60km |

EAST AYRSHIRE

Ayr
Bachelor's Club
Burns Cottage
A70
A74(M)

BORDERS

Jedburgh Abbey & Mary Queen of Scots' House
Drumlanrig's Tower
Ferniehurst Castle
Edlingham Castle
Lady's Well
Cragside
Brinkburn Priory
The Tower
Herterton House
Wallington

NORTHUMBERLAND

Little Harle Tower
Capheaton Hall
Belsay Hall
Chipchase Castle
Chesters Roman Fort & Museum
Housesteads Roman Fort
Vindolanda
High Meadows Cottage Barn
Hexham Moot Hall
Aydon Castle
Cherryburn
Corbridge Roman Site
High Staward Farm

21-23 Leazes Terrace
Bessie Surtees House
Castle Garth
Cathedral Church of St Nicholas

Culzean Castle
Souter Johnnie's Cottage
Crossraguel Abbey
Blairquhan Castle

SOUTH AYRSHIRE

Bargany Gardens
Craigdarroch House

Drumlanrig Castle

Craigieburn Woodland Garden

Hermitage Castle

Gilnockie's Tower
Netherby Coop House
Lanercost Priory
Naworth Castle
Lambley Rail Viaduct
Cruck Barn Townhouse

DUMFRIES AND GALLOWAY

Dumfries
Rammerscales
Carlyle's Birthplace
A74(M)
Caerlaverock Castle
Sweetheart Abbey
Shambellie House
New Abbey Corn Mill

Threave Castle
Threave Garden
Cardoness Castle
MacLellan's Castle
Broughton House
Dundrennan Abbey

Castle Kennedy Gardens
Glenwhan
Stranraer
Castle
Glenluce Abbey

Ardwell Gardens
Logan Botanic Garden
Whithorn Priory

Luce Bay
Galloway House Gardens
Burrow Head

Carlisle
Carlisle Castle
Carlisle Cathedral
Prior Slee Gatehouse
Crown & Nisi Prius Court

Wetheral Priory Gatehouse

Workington Hall & Helena Thompson Museum
Workington
Whitehaven
St Bees Head

Orthwaite Hall Barn

Wordsworth House
Hutton-in-the-Forest
Mirehouse
Penrith
Penrith Castle
Acorn Bank
Dalemain
Brougham Castle
Strickland Hall
Brough Castle

CUMBRIA

Dove Cottage & Wordsworth Museum
Hardknott Roman Fort
Muncaster Water Mill
Wray Castle
Rydal Mount & Gardens
Stagshaw Garden
Townend
Holehird
Beatrix Potter Gallery
Steam Yacht Gondola
Brantwood
Hill Top
Blackwell
Kendal
Abbot Hall Art Gallery & Quaker Tapestry
Muncaster Castle
Stott Park Bobbin Mill
Sizergh Castle
Fellfoot Park
Levens Hall
Heron Cornmill
Kirkby Hall
Ulverston
Holker Hall
Leighton Hall
Warton Old Rectory
Furness Abbey
Dalton Castle
Conishead Priory
Barrow-in-Furness
Isle of Walney

Morecambe
Heysham
Lancaster

DURHAM

Weardale Museum
Bishop...
Raby Castle
Bowes Museum
Barnard Castle
Egglestone Abbey

Hawes
Bolton Castle
Braithwaite Hall
Middleh...
Jerva...
White Scar Cave
Giggleswick School Chapel
Parcevall Hall
Fountain's...
St Mary's C...
Knaresborough Castle & Mother Shipton's Cave
Skipton
Skipton Castle
Broughton Hall

Isle of Man

ISLE OF MAN

Douglas

Belfast - Liverpool

**1830 Warehouse
Cathedral
Heaton Hall
Jewish Museum
Law Library
Liverpool Rd Station
Portico Library
Victoria Baths**

Fleetwood

Blackpool

Lytham St Anne's

LANCASHIRE

Browsholme Hall
Clitheroe
Clitheroe Castle
Stonyhurst College
Whalley Abbey
Gawthorpe Hall
Marthome
Colne
Nelson
Burnley
Towneley Hall
Keighley
Parsonage Museum
BRADFO...

Preston
Samlesbury Hall
Hoghton Tower
Blackburn
Blackburn Cathedral
Accrington
Oswaldtwistle
Leyland
Darwen
Turton Tower
Rossendale Museum
Rawtenstall
Todmorden
Halifax
Unitarian Church
Brigho...

Dublin - Liverpool

**Bluecoat Chambers
Convent Conservatory
Croxteth Hall
Liverpool Cathedral
Liverpool Cathedral
Church of Christ the King
Liverpool Collegiate
Turner Home**

Meols Hall
Southport
Rufford Old Hall
Chorley
Astley Hall
Hall i'th' Wood
Smithills Hall
Rochdale
Shibden Hall
Marlborough Hall
Crossley Pavilion
Bankhouse Gazebo

Ormskirk
Standish
Bolton
Bury
Formby
Skelmersdale
Wigan
Middleton
Tonge
Oldham
Albion Warehouse
Lightshaw Hall Farm
GREATER MANCHESTER
Crosby
Kirkby
St Helens
Bootle
Wallasey
LIVERPOOL
Birkenhead
Bebington
Port Sunlight
MANCHESTER
Salford
Sale
Altrincham
Dunham Massey
Stockport
Bramhall
Glossop
Warrington
Runcorn
Cheadle Hall
Quarry Bank Mill
Lyme Park

Anglesey

Holyhead
Holy Island
Carmel Head
Great Ormes Head
Llandudno
Conwy
Aberconwy House
Conwy Castle
Plas Mawr
Prestatyn
Rhyl
Gwrych Castle
Colwyn Bay
Abergele
Rhuddlan Castle
Bodelwyddan Castle
Flint
Speke Hall
Ellesmere Port
Frodsham
Norton Priory
Arley
Tabley House
Nether Alderley Mill
Hare Hill
Adlington Hall
Museums
Macclesfield
Buxton

Caernarfon Bay

Beaumaris Castle
Wern Isaf
Plas Newydd
Bangor
Penrhyn Castle
Cochwillan Old Hall
Bryn Bras Castle
Caernarfon Castle
Dolwyddelan Castle
Gwydir Castle
Rug Chapel
Bodnant Garden
St Asaph Cathedral
Denbigh Castle
Tower
Fferm
Hartsheath
Chester Cath
Chester Roman Amphitheatre
Town Hall
Watergate Hs
Ch...
Widnes
Norton
Peover Hall
Capesthorne Hall
Gawsworth Hall
Rode Hall
Little Moreton Hall
Biddulph
Kidsgrove
Ford Green
Leek

Wrexham
Erddig
Valle Crucis Abbey
Chirk Castle
Peckforton Castle
Beeston Castle
Sandbach
CHESHIRE
Cholmondeley Castle
Dorfold Hall
Crewe
Nantwich
Woodhay Hall
St Chads
Newcastle-under-Lyme
Highfields
STOKE-ON-TRENT
Plas Brondanw

Shetland Islands

Unst

Yell

Mainland

Lerwick

Jarlshof Prehistoric & Norse Settlement

Map Scale

589

N

12 - 13

10 - 11

8 - 9

15

14   6 - 7

2 - 3   4 - 5

Isle of Lewis

Rudha Rhobhanais
(Butt of Lewis)

Cellar Head

Black House

Handa Island

Gt.
Bernera

Tolsta Head

Gallan
Head

W. LOCH
ROAG

Broad
Bay

Point of
Stoer

Calanais
Standing
Stones

Tiumpan Head

Chicken
Head

Rhu
Coigach

Mealasta I.

LOCH ERISORT

Stornaway - Ullapool

Scarp

LOCH
LANGAVAT

Kebock Head

Summer
Isles

Hushinish Point

L. CLAIN

LOCH
SHELL

Greenstone
Point

WESTERN
ISLES

Taransay

W. LOCH
TARBERT

LOCH
BROLLUM

Shiant
Islands

Rudha
Reidh

Inverewe
Garden

Sound of Taransay

Toe
Head

Harris

EAST
LOCH
TARBERT

Scalpay

Shillay

Renish
Point

Lochmaddy - Tarbert

Tarbert - Uig

Red
Point

Pabbay

Sound of Harris

Berneray

Boreray

Vallay

Lochmaddy - Uig

Rona

Uibhist a Tuath
(North Uist)

LOCH
SNIZORT

Attadale Gardens

Urquhart Castle

Heisker or
Monach Islands

Sound of Monach

Dunvegan
Head

Dunvegan
Castle

Sound of Raasay

Inner Sound

Ronay

Neist
Point

Raasay

Beinn na Faoghla
(Benbecula)

Wiay

Eilean Donan Castle

HI

Scalpay

Crowlin
Islands

Rudha
Hallagro

Pabay

Uibhist a Deas
(South Uist)

Isle of
Skye

Soay

Sound of Sleat

Canna

Sound of Canna

Cuillin Sound

Armadale
Castle Gardens

Sound of Barra

Eriskay

Greian
Head

Rum

Barraigh
(Barra)

Vatersay

Kiessimul
Castle

Lochboisdale -Oban

Sound of Rum

Eigg

Sandray

Rosinish

Castlebay-Oban

Muck

Sound of Arisaig

Glenfinnan
Monument

Mingulay

Fort William

Berneray

Barra
Head

Glencoe

Coll

Oransay

Loch Linnhe

Castle Stalker

Tiree

Ulva

Lismore

Dunstaffnage
Castle

Iona

Isle of
Mull

Torosay
Castle

Bonawe Iron
Furnace

Kilchurn Castle

Duart Castle

Kerrera

Angus's
Gardens

Iona
Abbey

Firth of Lorne

Garvellachs

Arduaine
Garden

Inveraray Castle

Luing

ARGYLL
AND BUTE

Inverarary Jail

Ardkinglas

Lunga

0   10   20   40m

0 10 20   40   60km

Map Scale

Orkney Islands

Carrick House

Broch of Gurness

Skaill House

Mainland

Skara Brae

Ring of Brodgar Stone Circles & Henge

Maes Howe

Balfour Castle

Kirkwall

Tankerness House
Bishop's Palace
Earl's Palace
St Magnus' Cathedral

Hoy

Scotland

Pentland Firth

Faraid Head

Whiten Head

Strathy Point

Dunnet Head

To Stromness - L

Island of Stroma

Duncansby Head

Noss Head

LOCH HOPE

LOCH AN DEERIE

LOCH LOYAL

LOCH CALDER

LOCH SHURRERY

LOCH TACK

LOCH MEADIE

LOCH NAN CLAR

LOCH RIMSDALE

LOCH MORE

LOCH MERKLAND

LOCH FIAG

LOCH NAVER

LOCH BADANLOCH

LOCH AN RUATHAIR

LOCH CHOIRE

LOCH SHIN

Dunrobin Castle

Dornoch Firth

LOCH MORIE

LOCH GLAS

Moray Firth

Cromarty Courthouse

Hugh Miller's Cottage

Fort George

Brodie Castle

Spynie Palace

Elgin

Elgin Cathedral

Pluscarden Abbey

Fraserburgh

Duff House

Craigston Castle

LOCH LUICHART

Dallas Dhu Distillery

Delgatie Castle

Inverness

Dochfour Gardens

Cawdor Castle

Culloden

MORAY

Drummuir Castle

Balvenie Castle

Huntly Castle

Fyvie Castle

Haddo House

Peterhead

Ballindalloch Castle

LOCH DUNTELCHAIG

Tolquhon Castle

LOCH NESS

LOCH MHOR

Urquhart Castle

HIGHLAND

Leith Hall

Pitmedden Garden

ABERDEENSHIRE

Doune of Rothiemurcus

Kildrummy Castle

Kildrummy Castle Garden

Monymusk Walled Garden

Candacraig Garden

Castle Fraser

ABERDEEN CITY

Corgarff Castle

Crathes Castle

Drum Castle

Aberdeen

Cruickshank Botanic Garden
Duthie Park
Provost Skene's House
St Machar's Cathedral Transepts

Braemar Castle

Balmoral Castle

LOCH LAGGAN

LOCH ERICHT

LOCH OSSIAN

Dunnottar Castle

Arbuthnott House

Fasque

Edzell Castle & Garden

ANGUS

House of Dun

Montrose

Blair Castle

LOCH RANNOCH

LOCH TUMMEL

Cluny House Gardens

Barrie's Birthplace

Dunninald

Lunan Bay

Castle Menzies

PERTH AND

Glamis Castle

Forfar

Angus Folk Museum

Arbroath Abbey

Arbroath

LOCH LYON

Bolfracks Garden

Meigle Sculptured Stone Museum

Stobhall

DUNDEE CITY

LOCH TAY

KINROSS

Barry Mill

Dundee

LOCH LEDNOCK

Monzie Castle

Huntingtower Castle

Scone Palace

Perth

Balhousie Castle

Megginch Castle

Firth of Tay

LOCH TURRET

LOCH VOILE

LOCH EARN

Branklyn Garden

Elcho Castle

St Andrews Bay

St Andrews Castle

St Andrews

Drummond Castle Gardens

M90

Hill of Tarvit Mansionhouse

Cambo Gardens

STIRLING

Dunblane Cathedral

Gleneagles

Falkland Palace

FIFE

Charleton House

Kellie Castle & Garden

LOCH KATRINE

Loch Leven Castle

BERG
SUMMER

TÓRSHA
SUMMER

LERWI
STROMN

Edinburgh & York Detail

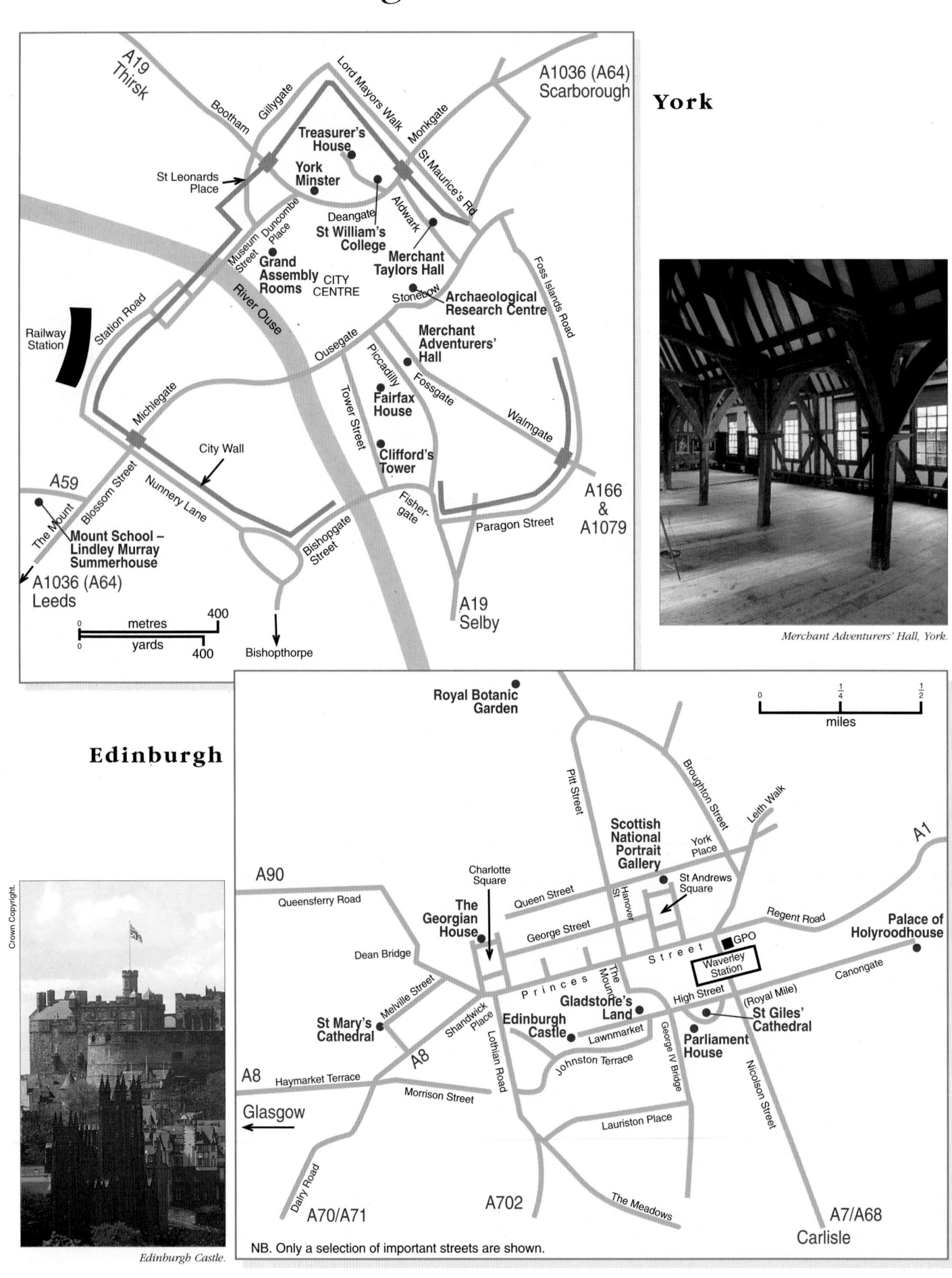

York

- **Treasurer's House**
- **York Minster**
- St Leonards Place
- Deangate
- **St William's College**
- **Grand Assembly Rooms**
- **Merchant Taylors Hall**
- Aldwark
- Museum Street
- Duncombe Place
- CITY CENTRE
- Stonebow
- **Archaeological Research Centre**
- **Merchant Adventurers' Hall**
- Piccadilly
- Fossgate
- **Fairfax House**
- **Clifford's Tower**
- River Ouse
- Ousegate
- Tower Street
- Walmgate
- Station Road
- Railway Station
- Michlegate
- City Wall
- Fishergate
- Paragon Street
- A59
- Blossom Street
- Nunnery Lane
- Bishopgate Street
- The Mount
- **Mount School – Lindley Murray Summerhouse**
- A1036 (A64) Leeds
- Bishopthorpe
- A19 Thirsk
- Bootham
- Gillygate
- Lord Mayors Walk
- Monkgate
- St Maurice's Rd
- A1036 (A64) Scarborough
- Foss Islands Road
- A166 & A1079
- A19 Selby

```
metres
0         400
yards
0              400
```

Merchant Adventurers' Hall, York.

Edinburgh

- **Royal Botanic Garden**
- **Scottish National Portrait Gallery**
- Pitt Street
- Broughton Street
- Leith Walk
- York Place
- Hanover St
- St Andrews Square
- Charlotte Square
- **The Georgian House**
- Queen Street
- George Street
- Regent Road
- **Palace of Holyroodhouse**
- A90
- Queensferry Road
- Dean Bridge
- Melville Street
- Shandwick Place
- P r i n c e s   S t r e e t
- The Mound
- GPO
- Waverley Station
- Canongate
- **St Mary's Cathedral**
- **Gladstone's Land**
- **Edinburgh Castle**
- Lawnmarket
- Johnston Terrace
- Lothian Road
- High Street
- (Royal Mile)
- **St Giles' Cathedral**
- **Parliament House**
- George IV Bridge
- A8
- Haymarket Terrace
- Morrison Street
- Lauriston Place
- Nicolson Street
- Glasgow
- Dairy Road
- A70/A71
- A702
- The Meadows
- A7/A68
- Carlisle
- A1

Crown Copyright.

Edinburgh Castle.

NB. Only a selection of important streets are shown.

Index of all Properties

Index of all Properties

Index of all Properties

Index of all Properties

Index of all Properties

Acknowledgments

The publishers are grateful to the following for permission to reproduce the photographs on the pages listed below.

Page No.	Position on page	Description/Property	Photographer/Owner/Organisation
Front cover		Charlecote Park, Warwickshire	NTPL/Matthew Antrobus
Frontispiece		Bourton House Garden, Gloucestershire	Mr & Mrs Richard Paice
6	Main image	Tintinhull House Garden, Somerset	NTPL/Nick Meers
7	Bottom left	Urn with cherubs, Lanhydrock, Devon	NTPL/Jerry Harpur
7	Main image	The Triton Fountain, Lytes Carey, Somerset	NTPL/Nick Meers
8	Top left	Blickling Hall, Norfolk	NTPL/Nick Meers
8	Top right	Wallington, Northumberland	NTPL/Marianne Majerus
8	Middle right	Colby Woodland Garden, Wales	NTPL/Andrew Butler
8	Lower right	Beningbrough Hall, Yorkshire	NTPL/Stephen Robson
8	Left central image	(detail) Anglesey Abbey, Cambridgeshire	NTPL/Nick Meers
8	Middle central image	(detail) Emmetts Garden, Kent	NTPL/Jerry Harpur
8	Right central image	(detail) Fenton House, London	NTPL/Jerry Harpur
8	Bottom main image	Prior Park Landscape Garden, Somerset	NTPL/David Norton
9	Top right	Ham House, London	NTPL/Stephen Robson
9	Bottom right	Dunham Massey, Cheshire	NTPL/Neil Campbell-Sharp
9	Main left	Powis Castle, Wales	NTPL/Andrew Butler
15	Main image	Maze at Chatsworth, Derbyshire	Chatsworth House Trust
16	Top centre	Maze at Leeds Castle, Kent	Leeds Castle Enterprises Limited
16	Bottom centre	Sun Maze & Lunar Labyrinth at Longleat, Wiltshire	City Photography
17	Top centre	Love Labyrinth at Longleat, Wiltshire	City Photography
17	Bottom left	Maze at Leeds Castle, Kent	City Photography
18	Main image	Tudor Rose Maze at Kentwell Hall, Suffolk	Kentwell Hall
19	Top centre	Maze at Chatsworth, Derbyshire	Chatsworth House Trust
19	Middle left	Maze at Leeds Castle, Kent	Leeds Castle Enterprises Limited
19	Bottom right	Archbishop's Maze at Greys Court, Oxfordshire	NTPL/Nick Meers
20 & 21	Top spread	Water Maze at Hever Castle, Kent	Hever Castle Limited
20	Middle right	Maze at Blenheim Palace, Oxfordshire	Chris Andrews
20	Bottom right	(detail) Hedge Maze at Longleat, Wiltshire	Longleat
21	Bottom centre	Hedge Maze at Longleat, Wiltshire	Longleat
22	Top centre	Veronica's Maze at Parham House & Gardens, Sussex	Walter Gardiner Photography
57	Main image	The Long Gallery, Parham House & Gardens, Sussex	Parham Park Trust
58 & 59	Main image	The Tower of London, London	Crown Copyright HRP
60	Main image	Raven Master & Raven, Tower of London, London	Crown Copyright HRP
61	Left	Sceptre with Cross, Tower of London, London	Crown Copyright HRP
61	Top right	Scaffold Site, Tower of London, London	Crown Copyright HRP
61	Middle	Imperial Crown of India, Tower of London, London	Crown Copyright HRP
61	Middle right	Orbs, Tower of London, London	Crown Copyright HRP
61	Bottom right	Gun Salutes, Tower of London, London	Crown Copyright HRP
62	Top left	Henry VII's Armour for Man & Horse, Tower of London, London	Crown Copyright HRP
62	Top centre	The White Tower, Tower of London, London	Crown Copyright HRP
62	Bottom left	Wakefield Tower, Tower of London, London	Crown Copyright HRP
62	Bottom right	Tower Menagerie, Tower of London, London	Crown Copyright HRP
63	Main image	Sir Thomas More's Cell, Tower of London, London	Crown Copyright HRP
88 & 89	Main image	Kingston Bagpuize, Oxfordshire	Mr & Mrs Francis Grant
90	Main image	Kingston Bagpuize, Oxfordshire	Mr & Mrs Francis Grant
91	Top left	(detail) Cantilevered Staircase, Kingston Bagpuize, Oxfordshire	Mr & Mrs Francis Grant
91	Top right	Kingston Bagpuize, Oxfordshire	Mr & Mrs Francis Grant
91	Middle right	The Dining Room, Kingston Bagpuize, Oxfordshire	Mr & Mrs Francis Grant
91	Bottom right	The Library, Kingston Bagpuize, Oxfordshire	Mr & Mrs Francis Grant
92	Top right	(detail) Magnolia *soulangeana*, Kingston Bagpuize, Oxfordshire	Mr & Mrs Francis Grant

Page No.	Position on page	Description/Property	Photographer/Owner/ Organisation
92	Top centre	The drive looking west from the house, Kingston Bagpuize	Mr & Mrs Francis Grant
92	Middle centre	(detail) Colchicum, Kingston Bagpuize, Oxfordshire	Mr & Mrs Francis Grant
92	Bottom right	View of the house in winter, Kingston Bagpuize, Oxfordshire	Mr & Mrs Francis Grant
93	Main image	The Drawing Room, Kingston Bagpuize, Oxfordshire	Mr & Mrs Francis Grant
184 & 185	Main image	View of bridge, and bank of bluebells, Minterne Gdns, Dorset	The Lord Digby
186	Main image	View of the house, Minterne Gardens, Dorset	The Lord Digby
187	Top right	(detail) Davidia Involcrata, Minterne Gardens, Dorset	The Lord Digby
187	Middle right	(detail) Pieris Forrestii, Minterne Gardens, Dorset	The Lord Digby
187	Bottom right	Acer brillantissimum, Minterne Gardens, Dorset	The Lord Digby
188	Top right	(detail) of page 184 & 185	
188	Top middle	Rhododendrons, Minterne Gardens, Dorset	The Lord Digby
188	Bottom right	Lake with maple trees in background, Minterne Gdns, Dorset	The Lord Digby
189	Main image	Stream with yellow bog irises, Minterne Gardens, Dorset	The Lord Digby
248 & 249	Main image	The annual border, Helmingham Hall, Suffolk	Jerry Harpur/Lord Tollemache
250	Main image	Helmingham Hall, Suffolk	Jerry Harpur/Lord Tollemache
251	Top left	(detail) Lupin 'Galaxy White' & daisies, Helmingham Hall, Suffolk	Jerry Harpur/Lord Tollemache
251	Top right	(detail) Irises & roses, Helmingham Hall, Suffolk	Jerry Harpur/Lord Tollemache
251	Middle right	The Knot Garden, Helmingham Hall, Suffolk	Jerry Harpur/Lord Tollemache
251	Bottom right	The Gourd Tunnel, Helmingham Hall, Suffolk	Jerry Harpur/Lord Tollemache
252	Top left	(detail) Poppies 'Patty's Plum', Helmingham Hall, Suffolk	Jerry Harpur/Lord Tollemache
252	Top right	(detail) Sweetpeas, Helmingham Hall, Suffolk	Jerry Harpur/Lord Tollemache
252	Bottom left	(detail) White Daisies, Helmingham Hall, Suffolk	Jerry Harpur/Lord Tollemache
253	Main image	The old bridge to the apple walk, Helmingham Hall, Suffolk	Jerry Harpur/Lord Tollemache
282	Main image	The Wild Garden, Cottesbrooke, Northamptonshire	Captain John Macdonald-Buchanan
284 & 285	Main image	Cottesbrooke Hall & Gardens, Northamptonshire	Hugh Palmer
285	Top right	Pine Court, Cottesbrooke Hall & Gardens, Northamptonshire	Captain John Macdonald-Buchanan
285	Top left	Back of house, Cottesbrooke Hall & Gardens, Northamptonshire	Captain John Macdonald-Buchanan
285	Middle left	Statue Walk, Cottesbrooke Hall & Garden, Northamptonshire	Captain John Macdonald-Buchanan
285	Bottom left	Rose Garden, Cottesbrooke Hall & Garden, Northamptonshire	Captain John Macdonald-Buchanan
286	Top right	(detail) Pine Court, Cottesbrooke Hall & Gardens	Captain John Macdonald-Buchanan
286	Top middle	View of Spouting Fountain, Cottesbrooke Hall & Gardens	Captain John Macdonald-Buchanan
286	Bottom centre	Bronze of Empress Elizabeth, Cottesbrooke Hall & Gardens	Captain John Macdonald-Buchanan
287	Main image	Steps with sphinx and agapanthus, Cottesbrooke Hall	Captain John Macdonald-Buchanan
318 & 319	Main image	Summer perennial border, Dorothy Clive Gardens, Staffordshire	Dorothy Clive Gardens
320	Main image	Sundial with flower border, Dorothy Clive Gardens, Staffordshire	Dorothy Clive Gardens
321	Top left	Statue with yellow laburnum, Dorothy Clive Gardens	Dorothy Clive Gardens
321	Top right	Waterfall in woodland glade, Dorothy Clive Gardens	Dorothy Clive Gardens
321	Bottom right	Heather Garden, Dorothy Clive Gardens, Staffordshire	Dorothy Clive Gardens
322	Top left	Child on a swing, Dorothy Clive Gardens, Staffordshire	Dorothy Clive Gardens
322	Top centre	Rhododendrons, Dorothy Clive Gardens, Staffordshire	Dorothy Clive Gardens
322	Bottom left	Lily Pond, Dorothy Clive Gardens, Staffordshire	Dorothy Clive Gardens
323	Bottom right	Photograph of Dorothy Clive, Dorothy Clive Gardens	Dorothy Clive Gardens
323	Main image	Autumn foliage, Dorothy Clive Gardens, Staffordshire	Dorothy Clive Gardens
362 & 363	Main image	Herbaceous border, Beningbrough Hall, Yorkshire	NTPL/Stephen Robson
364	Main image	Beningbrough Hall, Yorkshire	NTPL/Horst Kolo
365	Top left	(detail) Flowers in garden, Beningbrough Hall, Yorkshire	NTPL/Stephen Robson
365	Top right	Walled Kitchen Garden, Beningbrough Hall, Yorkshire	NTPL/Stephen Robson
365	Middle centre	Drawing Room, Beningbrough Hall, Yorkshire	NTPL/Andreas von Einsiedel
365	Middle right	The Countess of Chesterfield, Beningbrough Hall, Yorkshire	NTPL/Andreas von Einsiedel
365	Bottom right	Drawing Room, Beningbrough Hall, Yorkshire	NTPL/Andreas von Einsiedel
366	Top right	(detail) Flower Garden, Beningbrough Hall, Yorkshire	NTPL/Stephen Robson
366	Top centre	View of house flanked by formal borders, Beningbrough Hall	NTPL/Ian Shaw
366	Bottom left	The Saloon, Beningbrough Hall, Yorkshire	NTPL/Andreas von Einsiedel
367	Main image	Walled Garden, Beningbrough Hall, Yorkshire	NTPL/Stephen Robson
392 & 393	Main image	Shrub border, Holker Hall, Cumbria	Lord & Lady Cavendish
394	Main image	Holker Hall, Cumbria	Lord & Lady Cavendish
395	Top left	(detail) Summer Garden, Holker Hall, Cumbria	Lord & Lady Cavendish
395	Top right	(detail) North West view of Holker Hall, Cumbria	Lord & Lady Cavendish
395	Middle right	The Water Fountain, Holker Hall, Cumbria	Lord & Lady Cavendish
395	Bottom right	Laurel Arch, Holker Hall, Cumbria	Lord & Lady Cavendish
396	Top left	(detail) Water Fountain, Holker Hall, Cumbria	Lord & Lady Cavendish
396	Top right	Summer Garden, Holker Hall, Cumbria	Lord & Lady Cavendish
396	Bottom right	"Texture", Holker Hall, Cumbria	Lord & Lady Cavendish

Page No.	Position on page	Description/Property	Photographer/Owner/Organisation
397	Main image	Wild Flowers at Holker Hall, Cumbria	Lord & Lady Cavendish
422 & 423	Main image	The Quarry Garden, Belsay Hall, Northumberland	English Heritage Photo Library
424	Main image	East Front of Belsay Hall, Northumberland	English Heritage Photo Library
425	Top left	(detail) The Quarry Garden, Belsay Hall, Northumberland	English Heritage Photo Library
425	Top right	View of Belsay Castle, Belsay Hall, Northumberland	English Heritage Photo Library
425	Middle centre	The Archway in the Quarry Garden, Belsay Hall, Northumberland	English Heritage Photo Library
425	Bottom right	The Quarry Garden, Belsay Hall, Northumberland	English Heritage Photo Library
426	Top left	Pathway in Quarry Garden, Belsay Hall, Northumberland	English Heritage Photo Library
426	Top right	The Quarry Garden in summer, Belsay Hall, Northumberland	English Heritage Photo Library/Clay Perry
426	Bottom left	The Quarry Garden, Belsay Hall, Northumberland	English Heritage Photo Library
426	Bottom right	Face carving on latrine, Belsay Hall, Northumberland	English Heritage Photo Library
427	Main image	Pillar Hall, Belsay Hall, Northumberland	English Heritage Photo Library
441	Main image	The Drawing Room, Scone Palace, Perthshire	The Earl of Mansfield
442 & 443	Main image	Dirleton Castle Gardens, Edinburgh	Historic Scotland
444	Main image	Castle Campbell, West Highlands & Islands	Historic Scotland
445	Top left	(detail) Stirling Castle, West Highlands & Islands	Historic Scotland
445	Top right	The Topiary Garden, Edzell Castle, Perthshire, Dundee & Kingdom of Fife	Historic Scotland
445	Middle right	Herbaceous border, Dirleton Castle, Edinburgh	Historic Scotland
445	Bottom right	The Topiary Garden, Edzell Castle, Perthshire, Dundee & Kingdom of Fife	Historic Scotland
446	Top left	(detail) Formal planting, Dirleton Castle, Edinburgh	Crown Copyright reserved/Historic Scotland
446	Top right	The King's Knot, Stirling Castle, West Highlands & Islands	Historic Scotland
446	Bottom right	(detail) Summer border, Dirleton Castle, Edinburgh	Historic Scotland
447	Main image	Edzell Castle, Perthshire, Dundee & Kingdom of Fife	Historic Scotland
494	Main image	Aerial view of Cawdor Castle, Highlands & Skye	The Dowager Countess Cawdor
495	Top left	(detail) The Staircase, Cawdor Castle, Highlands & Skye	Christopher Sykes
495	Top right	Bedroom, Cawdor Castle, Highlands & Skye	Cawdor Castle (Tourism) Limited
495	Middle right	Snow covered scene of Cawdor Castle, Highlands & Skye	Cawdor Castle (Tourism) Limited
495	Bottom right	The Drawing Room, Cawdor Castle, Highlands & Skye	Christopher Sykes
496	Top left	(detail) Fireplace in the Drawing Room, Cawdor Castle	Christopher Sykes
496	Top right	Herbaceous border with Irish yews, Cawdor Castle	The Dowager Countess Cawdor
496	Bottom left	The Cawdor Tree, Cawdor Castle, Highlands & Skye	The Dowager Countess Cawdor
497	Main image	Cawdor Castle viewed through trees, Highlands & Skye	The Dowager Countess Cawdor
505	Main image	The Long Gallery, Powis Castle, North Wales	NTPL/Andreas von Einsiedel
506 & 507	Main image	The Drawing Room ceiling, Castell Coch, South Wales	CADW (Welsh Historic Monuments) Photo Library
508	Main image	Castell Coch, South Wales	CADW (Welsh Historic Monuments) Photo Library
509	Top left	(detail) The Banqueting House, Castell Coch, South Wales	CADW (Welsh Historic Monuments) Photo Library
509	Top right	The Entrance to Castell Coch, South Wales	CADW (Welsh Historic Monuments) Photo Library
509	Middle right	(detail) Dado panelling, Castell Coch, South Wales	CADW (Welsh Historic Monuments) Photo Library
509	Bottom right	(detail) The Three Fates, Castell Coch, South Wales	CADW (Welsh Historic Monuments) Photo Library
510	Top centre	The Drawing Room, Castell Coch, South Wales	CADW (Welsh Historic Monuments) Photo Library
510	Top left	(detail) Drawing room dado panelling, Castell Coch	CADW (Welsh Historic Monuments) Photo Library
510	Middle right	(detail) Zodiac tiles in Drawing Room fireplace, Castell Coch	CADW (Welsh Historic Monuments) Photo Library
510	Bottom left	The Lady's Bedroom, Castell Coch, South Wales	CADW (Welsh Historic Monuments) Photo Library
510	Bottom right	The Kitchen, Castell Coch, South Wales	CADW (Welsh Historic Monuments) Photo Library
511	Main image	(detail) Lord Bute's Bedroom, Castell Coch, South Wales	CADW (Welsh Historic Monuments) Photo Library
525	Main image	Staircase at The Argory, Ireland	NTPL/Andreas von Einsiedel
526 & 527	Main image	Rowallane Garden, Co Down, Ireland	NTPL/Stephen Robson
528	Main image	View of the Walled Garden, Rowallane Garden, Co Down	NTPL/Stephen Robson
529	Top left	(detail) Walled Garden, Rowallane Garden, Co Down, Ireland	NTPL/Jerry Harpur
529	Top right	Pump in Walled Garden, Rowallane Garden, Co Down	NTPL/Stephen Robson
529	Middle right	Gateway to the Old Wood, Rowallane Garden, Co Down	NTPL/Stephen Robson
529	Bottom right	Rock Garden, Rowallane Garden, Co Down	NTPL/Jerry Harpur
530	Top left	(detail) Walled Garden, Rowallane Garden, Co Down	NTPL/Jerry Harpur
530	Top right	Azaleas and rhododendrons, Rowallane Garden, Co Down	NTPL/Stephen Robson
530	Bottom left	Azaleas and rhododendrons, Rowallane Garden, Co Down	NTPL/Jerry Harpur
531	Main image	Blue *meconopsis betonicifolia* flowers at Rowallane Garden	NTPL/Jerry Harpur
IBC		View of the Saloon at Uppark, Sussex	NTPL/Nadia Mackenzie
Back cover	Left image	(detail) Agapanthus plant at Cottesbrooke Hall, Northants	Captain John Macdonald-Buchanan
Back cover	Middle image	Bride and Groom	Sarah Ward-Hendry Photography
Back cover	Right image	... Helmingham Hall, Suffolk	Jerry Harpur/Lord Tollemache